Pet Friendly
Places to Stay
2012

AA Lifestyle Guides

This 11th edition published 2011 © AA Media Limited 2011.
AA Media Limited retains the copyright in the current edition © 2011
and in all subsequent editions, reprints and amendments to editions.
The information contained in this directory is sourced entirely from the
AA's establishment database, AA Lifestyle Guides. The contents of this
publication are believed correct at the time of printing. Nevertheless,
the publishers cannot be held responsible for any errors or omissions or
for changes in the details given in this guide or for the consequences
of any reliance on the information provided by the same. This does not
affect your statutory rights. Assessments of AA inspected establishments
and campsites are based on the experience of the Hotel and Restaurant
Inspectors and Campsite Inspectors on the occasion(s) of their visit(s)
and therefore descriptions given in this guide necessarily contain an
element of subjective opinion which may not reflect or dictate a reader's
own opinion on another occasion.

The AA strives to ensure accuracy in this guide at the time of printing.
Due to the constantly evolving nature of the subject matter the
information is subject to change. The AA will gratefully receive any
advice from our readers of any necessary updated information.

Please contact Advertisement Sales: advertisingsales@theaa.com
Editorial Department: lifestyleguides@theaa.com
AA Hotel & Guest Accommodation enquiries: 01256 844455
AA Campsite enquiries: 01256 491577

Website addresses are included where they have been supplied and
specified by the respective establishment. Such websites are not under
the control of AA Media Limited and as such AA Media Limited has no
control over them and will not accept any responsibility or liability in
respect of any and all matters whatsoever relating to such websites
including access, content, material and functionality. By including the
addresses of third party websites the AA does not intend to solicit
business or offer any security to any person in any country, directly
or indirectly.

Every effort has been made to trace the copyright holders, and we
apologise in advance for any unintentional omissions or errors.
We would be pleased to apply any corrections in a following edition
of this publicaion.

Front cover: (t) Keith Davey; (bl) Julie Brody; (br) Haydn Tomlinson;
Back cover: (l) Sarah Montgomery; (c) Trudie Spires; (r) Caroline Walford

Typeset/Repro: Servis Filmsetting Ltd, Manchester
Printed in Italy by Printer Trento SRL, Trento.

Directory compiled by the AA Lifestyle Guides Department and managed
in the Librios Information Management System and generated from the
AA establishment database system.

Published by AA Publishing, a trading name of AA Media Limited,
whose registered office is Fanum House, Basing View, Basingstoke,
Hampshire RG21 4EA. Registered number 06112600

A CIP catalogue record for this book is available from the British Library

ISBN: 978-0-7495-7142-9

A04680

Maps prepared by the Mapping Services Department of AA Publishing.

Maps © AA Media Limited 2011.

Contains Ordnance Survey data
© Crown copyright and database right 2011.

Land &   This is based upon Crown Copyright and is
Property reproduced with the permission of Land & Property
Services. Services under delegated authority from the
Controller of Her Majesty's Stationery Office.
© Crown copyright and database rights 2011. Licence number 100,363.
Permit number 110025

Ordnance   Republic of Ireland mapping based on
OSi Survey   © Ordnance Survey Ireland/Government of Ireland.
Ireland   Copyright Permit number MP000611
Ireland's National Mapping Agency

Contents

Now in 3D

nintendögs™ +cats

Out now on **NINTENDO 3DS**

Take your best friend wherever you go

Whether you're off to the beach or on a break in the country, your favourite furry friend can come along too with nintendogs + cats™ for Nintendo 3DS™.
There are three different editions of nintendogs + cats available, each with nine types of puppies and three kittens to choose as your pet. Picking your new pal might be tricky, but becoming inseparable won't. Who will you bring with you?

Welcome to the Guide

This guide is perfect for pet owners who are reluctant to put their animals into kennels or catteries while they go on holiday. In these pages you can find not only places where dogs and cats are welcome, but also where horses can be stabled on site or very close by.

Hints on booking your stay

As this guide shows, there are a great many hotels, bed and breakfasts and campsites that offer a warm welcome and an extensive range of facilities to both pet lovers and their animal companions. Though all the establishments listed have told us they are happy to admit animals, some go out of their way to make you and your pet feel at home, offering animal welcome packs, comfortable dog baskets, water bowls, special blankets, home-made treats and comprehensive information on local country walks.

Do remember though, that even the pet-friendliest of proprietors appreciate advance warning if you intend to bring your animal with you. See pages 12-15 for helpful hints and tips on planning your trip. While summer is an obvious time to book a holiday, you might like to consider taking an off-peak break when animals – dogs in particular – are more likely to enjoy cooler temperatures and crowd-free destinations.

And just a friendly word of warning. On sending us information for this guide many establishments stated that they very much welcome pets but they must be accompanied by well behaved owners!

How to Use the Guide

① Locations The guide is divided into countries. Each country is listed in county order and then alphabetically in town/village order within a county.

② Map reference Each town/village is given a map reference for the atlas section at the back of the guide. For example:
Map 03 SY29
03 refers to the page number of the atlas section at the back of the guide
SY is the National Grid lettered square (represents 100,000sq metres) in which the location will be found
2 is the figure reading across the top or bottom of the map page
9 is the figure reading down each side of the map page
Campsites (and some B&Bs) include a 6-figure National Grid reference as many are located in remote areas.
A county map appears before the atlas section at the back of the guide.

③ Which pets are accepted Five symbols show at a glance what type of animal is welcome – dogs, cats, small caged animals, caged birds and horses. 🐾 indicates places that provide kennels.

④ Establishment name & rating For further information on AA ratings and awards see page 10. If the name of the establishment appears in italic type this indicates that not all the information has been confirmed for 2012.
Within each location hotels are listed first, in descending order of stars and % score, followed by B&Bs in descending orders of stars, then campsites in order of their pennant rating (see page 11).

⑤ Contact details

⑥ Directions Short details of how to find the establishment or campsite.

---

① | **AXMINSTER** | **Map 3 SY29** | **②**

③ 🐾 🐱 | | LOGO | **⑮**

④ ## Fairwater Head Hotel
★ ★ ★ 75% ⊛ HOTEL
Hawkchurch EX13 5TX
⑤ ☎ 01297 678349   📠 01297 678459
e-mail: stay@fairwaterheadhotel.co.uk
web: www.fairwaterheadhotel.co.uk
⑥ dir: *Off B3165 (Crewkerne to Lyme Regis road). Hotel signed to Hawkchurch*

⑦ PETS: **Bedrooms** (8 GF) unattended **Sep accom** cabin with pen **Public areas** except dining room on leads **Grounds** on leads disp bin **Exercise area** surrounding countryside **Facilities** food (pre-bookable) food bowl water bowl dog chews scoop/disp bags leads pet sitting washing facs cage storage walks info vet info **On Request** fridge access torch towels **Stables** 400mtrs **Other** charge for damage **Resident Pets:** Mocca
⑧ (Springer/Cocker Spaniel cross), Lollipop (Black Labrador)

This elegant Edwardian country house provides a perfect location for anyone looking for a peaceful break. Surrounded by extensive gardens and rolling countryside, the setting guarantees relaxation. Bedrooms are located both within the main house and the garden wing; all provide good levels of comfort. Public areas have much appeal and include lounge areas, a bar and an elegant restaurant. Food is a highlight with excellent local produce prepared with care and skill.

⑨ Rooms 16 (4 annexe) (8 GF) **S** £70-£125; **D** £85-£180 (incl. bkfst)* **Facilities** FTV Library Xmas New Year Wi-fi **Parking** 30 **Notes** LB Closed 1-30 Jan

⑫ **⑩** **⑪**

7 Pet facilities **(PETS:)**
Bedrooms GF Ground floor bedrooms; **unattended** indicates that the establishment allows a pet to be left unattended in the bedroom; **sign** indicates that a sign is provided to hang on the door stating an animal is in the room.

Sep accom (separate accommodation) some places have kennels or outbuildings available.

Public areas indicates that pets are allowed in public areas. Any exceptions are as stated. Most hotes and B&Bs in this guide request that dogs are kept on leads when passing through public areas to the bedrooms.

Charges £ (€ Republic of Ireland) The price shown is the charge per animal per night, per week or per stay. The charges shown for campsites are for touring pitches only.

Grounds Establishments that allow pets access to their gardens or grounds, or in the case of campsites there may be specified areas for exercise.

Exercise area The type of area available (ie fields, beach, coastal path etc) and the distance from the establishment (ie 100yds).

Facilities Information and specific facilities that guests who are staying with their pets might find useful. Campsites may sell certain pet related items in their on-site shop.

Other Additional information supplied by the establishment.

Restrictions Certain establishments have rules on the number of pets, or the size or the breed of dog allowed.* We strongly advise readers to check with the hotel, B&B or campsite at the time of booking that their pet will be permitted to accompany them during their stay.

*Some establishments have stated that they do not accept 'dangerous dogs'. The following breeds are covered under the Dangerous Dogs Act 1991 – Pit Bull Terrier, Japanese Tosa, Dogo Argentino and Fila Brazilierio.
For further details see:
www.defra.gov.uk/wildlife-pets/pets/dangerous/index.htm
For the Republic of Ireland see the Control of Dogs Act 1986 & 1992. www.environ.ie

8 Resident Pets Lists the names and breeds of the proprietors' own pets.

9 Rooms The number of bedrooms, and whether they are en suite, family or ground floor rooms. **Prices** These are per room per night. These are given by the proprietors in good faith, and are indications only, not firm quotations. (✱ indicates 2011 prices). At the time of going to press up-to-date prices for campsites were not available. Please check the AA website **theAA.com** for current information. Smoking is not permitted in the public areas of hotels and guest houses, but some bedrooms may be set aside for smokers. Please check with the establishment when you book your room. Please note that not all bedrooms in B&Bs have TVs.

10 Facilities **Leisure facilities** are as stated in the entries. **Child Facilities** (Ch fac), these vary from place to place so please check that the establishment can meet your requirements.

11 Parking Shows the numbers of spaces available for the use of guests. This may include covered parking. Please note that some establishments make a charge to use their car park.

12 Notes This section can include the following:
No Children followed by an age indicates that a minimum age is required (ie No children 4yrs)
RS (Restricted Service) Some establishments have a restricted service during quieter months and some of the listed facilities may not be available.
LB Some establishments offer leisure breaks.
Dinner (B&Bs only) indicates that an evening meal is available, although prior notice may be needed. **Licensed (B&Bs only)** indicates that the establishment is licensed to serve alcohol.
Payment The majority of establishments in this guide accept credit and debit cards.

13 Description This is written by the AA Inspector at the time of their visit.

14 Photograph Establishments do not pay for a text entry in the guide but may choose to enhance their entry with a photograph, for which there is a cost.

15 Hotel logo If a symbol appears in the entry it indicates that the hotel belongs to a group or consortium.

Symbols and Abbreviations

Key to symbols

🐕	Dogs	🚫	No credit cards
🐈	Cats	✳	2011 prices
🐇	Small caged animals e.g. rabbits, hamsters		Heated indoor swimming pool
🐦	Caged birds		Outdoor swimming pool
	Kennels available		Heated outdoor swimming pool
🐴	Horses (stables or paddock)		Tennis court/s
★	The best hotels (see page 10)		Croquet lawn
☆	The best B&Bs (see page 10)	⚑	Golf course
★	Hotel and B&B rating (see page 10)	♫	Entertainment
%	Merit score (see page 10)		
U	AA Rating not confirmed (see page 11)		
◎	AA Rosette Award for quality of food (see page 11)		
▶	Campsite rating (see page 11)		
	Holiday Centre (see page 11)		

Bed & Breakfast only

	A very special breakfast, with an emphasis on freshly prepared local ingredients
	A very special dinner, with an emphasis on freshly prepared local ingredients

Key to abbreviations

Air con	Air conditioning	RS/rs	Restricted services
BH/bank hols	Bank Holidays	S	Single bedroom
Ch fac	Special facilities for children	STV	Satellite television in bedrooms
D	Double bedroom	Spa	Establishment has own spa facilities
Etr	Easter	Whit	Whitsun Bank Holiday
Fmly	Family bedroom	Wi-fi	Wireless network access
Fr	From	wk	Week
FTV	Freeview television in bedrooms	wkend	Weekend
GF	Ground floor bedroom	Xmas	Special Christmas programme
hrs	Hours		
incl. bkfst	Including breakfast	**Bed & Breakfast only**	
LB	Special leisure breaks	Cen ht	Full central heating
m	Miles	Last d	Last time dinner can be ordered
mtrs	Metres	pri facs	Bedroom with separate, private facilities
mdnt	Midnight	rms	Bedrooms in main building
New Year	Special New Year programme	Tea/coffee	Tea & coffee making facilities
No Children	No children can be accommodated	TVL	Television lounge
rdbt	Roundabout		

AA Classifications and Awards

Hotel and Guest Accommodation Ratings

In collaboration with VisitBritain, VisitScotland and VisitWales, the AA uses Common Quality Standards for inspecting and rating accommodation. All Hotels and B&Bs in this guide have received an inspection under these standards.

Hotel Ratings

If you stay in a **one-star** hotel you should expect a relatively informal yet competent style of service and an adequate range of facilities. The majority of the bedrooms are en suite, with a bath or shower room always available. A **two-star** hotel is run by smartly and professionally presented management and offers at least one restaurant or dining room for breakfast and dinner, while a **three-star** hotel includes direct-dial telephones, a wide selection of drinks in the bar and last orders for dinner no later than 8pm. A **four-star** hotel is characterised by uniformed, well-trained staff, with additional services, a night porter and a serious approach to cuisine. A **five-star** hotel, offers many extra facilities, attentive staff, top quality rooms and a full concierge service.

The **Merit Score** (%) AA inspectors supplement their reports with an additional quality assessment of everything the hotel offers, including hospitality, based on their findings as a 'mystery guest'. This results in a overall Merit Score. Shown as a pecentage score beside the hotel name, you can see at a glance that a hotel with a percentage score of 69% offers a higher standard than one in the same star classification but with a percentage score of 59%. To gain AA recognition initially, a hotel must achieve a minimum quality score of 50%.

★ Red stars The very best hotels within each star category are indicated by red stars.

There are six descriptive designators for establishments in the Hotel Recognition scheme:

HOTEL Formal accommodation with full service. Minimum of six guest bedrooms but more likely to be in excess of 20.

TOWN HOUSE HOTEL A small, individual city or town centre property, which provides a high degree of personal service and privacy.
COUNTRY HOUSE HOTEL A rurally and quietly located establishment with ample grounds.
SMALL HOTEL Has less than 20 bedrooms and is personally run by the proprietor.
METRO HOTEL A hotel in an urban location that does not offer dinner.
BUDGET HOTEL Inexpensive group lodge accommodation, usually purpose built by main roads and motorways and in town or city centres.

Guest Accommodation Ratings

Stars in the AA Guest Accommodation scheme reflect five levels of quality, from one at the simplest level to five offering the highest quality. The criteria for eligibility is guest care plus the quality of the accommodation rather than the choice of extra facilities. Guests should receive a prompt, professional check in and check out, comfortable accommodation equipped to modern standards, regularly changed bedding and towels, a sufficient hot water supply at all times, well-prepared meals and a full continental breakfast.

★ Yellow stars The top 10% of three, four and five star establishments are indicated by yellow stars.

There are six descriptive designators for establishments in this scheme:
B&B A private house run by the owner with accommodation for no more than six paying guests.
GUEST HOUSE Run on a more commercial basis than a B&B, the accommodadtion provides for more than six paying guests and there are more services.
FARMHOUSE The B&B or guest house accommodation is part of a working farm or smallholding.
INN The accommodation is provided in a fully licensed establishment. The bar will be open to non-residents and provide food in the evenings.
RESTAURANT WITH ROOMS This is a destination restaurant offering overnight accommodation, with dining being the main business, and open to non-residents. The restaurant should offer a high

standard of food, and restaurant service at least five nights a week. A liquor licence and maximum of 12 bedrooms.

GUEST ACCOMMODATION Any establishment that meets the minimum entry requirements is eligible for this general category.

◉ AA Rosettes

The AA awards Rosettes for the quality of food. These range from one Rosette for food prepared with care, understanding and skill, up to five Rosettes for the very finest cooking that stands comparison with the best cuisine in the world.

AA AA Campsite Ratings

AA sites are classified from one to five pennants according to their style and the range of facilities they offer. **1 pennant** – these parks offer a fairly simple standard of facilities. **2 pennants** – offer an increased level of facilities, services, customer care, security and ground maintenance. **3 pennants** – have a wide range of facilities and are of a very good standard. **4 pennants** – these parks

achieve an excellent standard throughout that will include landscaped grounds, natural screening and immaculately maintained toilets. **5 pennant Premier Parks** – the very best parks with superb mature landscaping and all facilities, customer care and security will be of exceptional quality.

Campsites have shortened entries in this guide. For more detailed information visit our website **theAA.com** and follow the 'Places to Stay' link.

Holiday Centres

This category indicates parks which cater for all holiday needs including cooked meals and entertainment.

U A small number of establishments in the guide have this symbol because their star or pennant rating was not confirmed at the time of going to press. This may be because there has been a change of ownership, or because the establishment has only recently joined one of the AA rating schemes.

To find out more about AA ratings and awards please visit our website **theAA.com**

Useful Information

Britain

Fire Regulations

The Fire Precautions Act does not apply to the Channel Islands, Republic of Ireland, or the Isle of Man, which have their own rules. As far as we are aware, all establishments listed in Great Britain have applied for and not been refused a fire certificate.

Licensing laws

These laws differ in England, Wales, Scotland, Northern Ireland, the Republic of Ireland, the Isle of Man, the Isles of Scilly and the Channel Islands.

Public houses are generally open from mid morning to early afternoon, and from about 6 or 7pm until 11pm, although closing times may be earlier or later and some pubs are open all afternoon. Unless otherwise stated, hotels listed in this guide are licensed. (For guest accommodation, please refer to the individual gazetteer entry. Note that licensed premises are not obliged to remain open throughout the permitted hours.) Hotel residents can obtain alcoholic drinks at all times, if the licensee is prepared to serve them. Non-residents eating at the hotel restaurant can have drinks with meals. Children under 14 (or 18 in Scotland) may be excluded from bars where no food is served. Those under 18 may not purchase or consume alcoholic drinks. A club licence means that drinks are served to club members only. 48 hours must elapse between joining and ordering.

Prices

The AA encourages the use of the Hotel Industry Voluntary Code of Booking Practice, which aims to ensure that guests know how much they will have to pay and what services and facilities that includes, before entering a financially binding agreement. If the price has not previously been confirmed in writing, guests should be given a card stipulating the total obligatory charge when they register at reception.

Facilities for disabled guests

The Equality Act 2010 provides legal rights for disabled people including access to goods, services and facilities, and means that service providers may have

to consider making adjustments to their premises. For more information about the Act see:
www.equalities.gov.uk.
or **www.direct.gov.uk/en/DisabledPeople/ RightsAndObligations/DisabilityRights/ DG_4001068**

The establishments in this guide should be aware of their obligations under the Act. We recommend that you always telephone in advance to ensure that the establishment you have chosen has appropriate facilities.

Useful websites:
www.holidaycare.org.uk
www.dptac.independent.gov.uk/door-to-door

Northern Ireland and Republic of Ireland

Licensing Regulations

Northern Ireland:
Public houses open Mon-Sat 11.30-23.00. Sun 12.30-22.00. Hotels can serve residents without restriction. Non-residents can be served 12.30-22.00 on Christmas Day. Children under 18 are not allowed in the bar area and may neither buy nor consume liquor in hotels.

Republic of Ireland:
General licensing hours are Mon-Thu 10.30-23.30, Fri & Sat 10.30-00.30. Sun 12.30-23.00 (or 00.30 if the

following day is a Bank Holiday). There is no licensed service (except for hotel residents) on Christmas Day or Good Friday.

Fire Regulations

The Fire Services (NI) Order 1984. This covers establishments accommodating more than six people, which must have a certificate from the Northern Ireland Fire Authority. Places accommodating fewer than six people need adequate exits. AA inspectors check emergency notices, fire fighting equipment and fire exits here.

The Republic of Ireland safety regulations are a matter for local authority regulations. For your own and others' safety, read the emergency notices and be sure you understand them.

Telephone numbers

Area codes for numbers in the Republic of Ireland apply only within the Republic. If dialling from outside check the telephone directory (from the UK the international dialling code is 00 353). Area codes for numbers in Britain and Northern Ireland cannot be used directly from the Republic.

For the latest information on the Republic of Ireland visit the AA Ireland's website: **AAireland.ie**

Useful websites for pet owners:

www.thekennelclub.org.uk The Kennel Club provides lots of information on microchipping and runs a pet reunification scheme. The website also includes information on lost micro-chipped pets: The European Pet Network has access to several animal databases from various European countries.
If a lost micro-chipped and registered pet is found, the EPN aims to find the owner.
www.petsbureau.co.uk A national missing pets register.
www.defra.gov.uk/wildlife-pets/pets/travel/index.htm for details of the Pet Travel Scheme and for comprehensive information and advice on travelling with your pet.
www.rcvs.org.uk website of the Royal College of Veterinary Surgeons that will help you find a vet near your holiday destination.

Bank and Public Holidays 2012	
New Year's Day	1st January
New Year's Holiday	4th January (Scotland)
Good Friday	6th April
Easter Monday	9th April
Early May Bank Holiday	7th May
Spring Bank Holiday	4th June
Diamond Jubilee Holiday	5th June
August Holiday	2nd August (Scotland)
Summer Bank Holiday	27th August
St Andrew's Day (Scotland)	30th November
Christmas Day	25th December
Boxing Day	26th December

Away from home

At first, the prospect of taking your pet away with you may seem a little daunting. There is their welfare to think of and the responsibility of trying to ensure they fit comfortably into their new surroundings. Many proprietors have cats and dogs of their own and will quickly build up a good rapport with your pet. This can play a vital role in the success of your holiday, and if all goes well, owners who are genuine animal lovers will be welcoming you back year after year. On the whole, proprietors report favourably on their pet guests, often commenting that their behaviour is at least as good as their owners!

We all love our pets and want to give them the care they deserve, but holidays can mean a certain amount of stress for us and also for our pets. Changes in routine can upset an animal as much as its owner. So keep them to their regular mealtimes if possible, take plenty of water for them on your journey, especially in hot weather.

Planning ahead

Always remember to advise the proprietor when booking that you intend bringing your pet with you. This gives you both the opportunity to establish whether the accommodation really is suitable for your pet's needs. Some establishments impose restrictions on the type, size or number of animals permitted; for example, those that accept dogs may not accommodate the larger breeds. Many establishments can provide foods but is it advisable to take the food your pet is familiar with.

Not all rooms will necessarily be available to guests with animals and some rooms may be set aside for people with allergies.

When booking, you should also check the establishment's supervision policy. Some may require your pet to be caged when unattended, or may ask you not to leave your pet alone at all.

The gazetteer entry in this guide indicates whether you should expect to pay an additional charge or deposit for your pet, but we recommend that you confirm the amount when booking.

The countryside

For your family holiday to be a complete success, you'll need to do a little research and planning. As well as finding somewhere suitable to stay, you might like to contact the tourist board for leaflets and brochures on pet-friendly places of interest, or you might find the ideal place listed in the AA Days Out guide. Remember to 'Mind that Pet!' and keep your dog under tight control when visiting local attractions.

Time to adjust

Remember that an animal shut in a strange hotel room for long periods may become distressed. We have stories from our hotels and B&Bs of dogs chewing up furniture or howling mournfully while their owners are out and these are symptoms of boredom and separation anxiety, particularly if your pet is a rescue animal.

On arrival, give your pet time to adjust to the new surroundings and if you think he will be upset and bark or howl, don't leave him alone in your room.

Watching our pets let off steam in a different environment is one of the pleasures of a good holiday, but although they are cherished members of the family who provide many hours of fun and enjoyment, owners have a duty to ensure that their pet is kept under proper control at all times.

In the case of dogs, allowing them to socialise with people and other animals from an early age means that, under your supervision, they will be at ease with other residents and their pets during your stay. It's not uncommon to end up swapping dog stories with guests or even members of staff. Lasting friendships are sometimes formed this way!

House rules

Unless otherwise indicated by the management, please don't allow your pet on the furniture, or in the bed. If he or she likes to sleep on the bed, remember to take a sheet, a blanket or a bedspread of your own, unless the proprietor provides one. Remember also to take an old towel to dry your pet after a walk in the rain and don't use the bath or shower for washing your animal.

Clean up after your pet immediately – inside the room and out – and leave no trace of them on departure. Take a supply of supermarket carrier bags with you and poop scoop anywhere in the hotel or grounds. Management will advise on disposal of the bags – some hotels/B&Bs have an animal toilet area and provide bags. If something has been damaged by your pet, notify the management immediately. It's really a case of simple common sense.

If the hotel/B&B allows you to take animals into public areas, be sure that you keep your pet under control at all times. Keep dogs on leads, especially when around small children. Your dog may be easily distracted by the sights and smells of unfamiliar surroundings, and may not respond to your commands as well as at home.

Bear in mind that dogs need to be exercised regularly – even on holiday – and time should be set aside for this as often as possible, especially if they have been travelling with you in the car for most of the day. Most country hotels and B&Bs will have plenty of good walks on the doorstep, which makes the chore of exercising your dog that much more enjoyable.

A lot of the establishments listed in this guide are surrounded by farmland so please remember to keep your dog under strict control near livestock – even letting your dog walk in the same field as farm animals may be considered as "worrying". (Remember a farmer is entitled to kill your dog if it is worrying livestock.)

Just in case

One final tip is to check your insurance for the level of cover it offers before taking your pet away. Pet insurance may not cover personal liability but your house insurance might. Should your pet chew the furniture or take a nip at a passing ankle, you would be well advised to have covered this eventuality by having the appropriate, up-to-date insurance policy.

The AA offers Pet Insurance.
Please visit **theAA.com** or call **0800 294 2713** for further information.

Why not spend less and relax more on UK breaks?

Make AA Travel your first destination and you and your pets are on the way to a more relaxing short break or holiday.

AA Members and customers can get great deals on accommodation, from B&Bs to farmhouses, inns and hotels.

You can also save up to 10% at cottages4you, enjoy a 5% discount with Hoseasons, and up to 60% off the very best West End shows.

Thinking of going further afield?

Check out our attractive discounts on car hire, airport parking, ferry bookings, travel insurance and much more.

Then simply relax.

These are just some of our well-known partners:

Visit theAA.com/travel

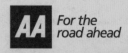

Microchipping your pet

Reliable identification

Microchipping was introduced more than 20 years ago, and adopted worldwide as a reliable method of pet identification because collars can be lost and tattoos may fade or be altered.

For your much loved dog or cat this is definitely a worthwhile procedure, for as much as every responsible owner endeavours to know the whereabouts of their pet every hour of the day, there could be a moment when they make a dash for freedom. For cats, certainly known to be independently-minded in their daily habits, being microchipped is an obvious choice for the owner. But it has to be remembered that many thousands of dogs also go missing each year, and it is estimated that less than half will be reunited with their owners.

The Control of Dogs Order 1992 states that all dogs (with a few specified exceptions), when in a public place or on a highway, must wear a collar showing the owner's name and address on a plate or disk attached to it; ideally it should also include their telephone number. Any dog seen without a collar in public place may be seized by the local authority and treated as a stray*. The owner may be prosecuted and fined.

How microchipping works

Microchipping can be undertaken at most veterinary practices in the UK, through some local authorities and also by animal welfare organisations. For any pet other than a dog or cat a veterinary surgeon should be consulted as the correct positioning of the chip is vitally important.

In a quick procedure, where an anaesthetic is not normally required, the chip is implanted under the skin, usually between the shoulder blades; the discomfort to the animal is no worse than a vaccination injection. The microchip will last for the pet's lifetime.

The microchip is a small electronic device, only the size of a grain of rice, which has a unique number that can be read by a scanner. The scanner's low frequency radio waves activate the chip so that the unique number can be read.

This number (now comprising 15-digits) is held, together with the owner's details, on a national database. Scanners are used by vets, local authority dog wardens and animal welfare groups to check stray cats and dogs; if a chip is in place, and providing the contact details are up-to-date, the owner can quickly and easily be contacted.

Microchipping events

June is National Microchipping Month. This is an initiative started by The Kennel Club (and endorsed by the RSPCA) to promote this method of pet ID. Each year a list of microchipping events, held throughout England, Wales and Scotland, can be found on the Kennel Club's petlog ® website.

Travelling abroad

If you are thinking of taking your pet abroad with you, it is a requirement under the PETS Travel Scheme (see page 19) to have your pet microchipped before your journey. Having fulfilled this particular requirement you can feel reassured that, should your pet go astray, there is more likelihood of a reunion.

*Under the Environmental Protection Act 1990 your stray dog can to be seized and sold, re-homed or destroyed if unclaimed after a seven day period.

Useful websites for further information
www.petlog.org.uk
www.rspca.org.uk
www.nationalpetregister.org
www.petsbureau.co.uk
www.europetnet.com
www.worldpetregister.com

The Pet Travel Scheme (PETS)

Pets are on the move. They now travel more often with their owners in the United Kingdom and, because of changes in quarantine regulations, pets can now be taken abroad and then return to the UK, subject to certain conditions.

The Pets Travel Scheme* gives information about the countries involved in the scheme; regulations; documentation required; microchip ID tags; help finding a vet; guidance on looking after pets during transportation; bringing your pet from a long-haul country; authorised routes; approved transport companies; charges; a latest news section and lots more besides.

Pets that are resident anywhere in the UK can travel unrestricted within Britain, and are not subject to quarantine regulations or to the PETS rules unless they are entering this country from overseas. There are no requirements for pets travelling directly between the UK and the Republic of Ireland.

The PETS scheme, which only applies to dogs (including assistance dogs), cats, ferrets, and certain other pets, enables pets resident in the UK to enter, without quarantine restrictions, certain (listed) countries throughout the world and then return to Britain. Thanks to the relaxation of quarantine controls in this country, they can go straight home on arrival. In order to bring your pet into, or back into, the UK from one of the listed countries the scheme requires that your pet must be fitted with a microchip, be vaccinated against rabies, pass a blood test and be issued with a pet passport. Before entering the UK, your animal will also need to receive both tapeworm and tick treatments. Naturally, careful thought should

be given to the welfare of your pet and whether a holiday abroad is appropriate, but if you decide to go ahead, remember it is necessary for your pet to have passed a satisfactory blood test at least 6 calendar months before travel commences. Your pet cannot travel under this scheme unless this time has elapsed.

*The European Parliament and Council have agreed that existing regulations are applicable until at least 31.12.11

In 2010 The European Parliament and Council introduced a limit of five animals (dogs, cats and ferrets only) per person for all importations into and around the European Union, regardless of the exporting country. This is applicable to all listed countries.

For detailed information about the PETS scheme contact:
PETS Helpline: 0870 241 1710
(8am-6pm (UK time) Monday to Friday)
E-mail: quarantine@ animalhealth.gsi.gov.uk
(Please include your postal address and daytime telephone number in your e-mail).
Website: www.defra.gov.uk/wildlife-pets/pets/travel/pets/index.htm

Remember, whether in the UK or abroad animals can die if left in a vehicle in direct sunlight or high temperatures.

England

ENGLAND

BEDFORDSHIRE

ASPLEY GUISE — Map 4 SP93

Best Western Moore Place

★★★ 77% HOTEL

The Square MK17 8DW
☎ 01908 282000 ▤ 01908 281888
e-mail: manager@mooreplace.com
dir: *M1 junct 13, take A507 signed Aspley Guise & Woburn Sands. Hotel on left in village square*

PETS: Bedrooms (16 GF) ground-floor bedrooms only **Charges** £10 per night **Public areas** except restaurant & bar area on leads **Grounds** on leads disp bin **Exercise area** 10 mins **Facilities** cage storage walks info vet info **On Request** fridge access torch **Stables** nearby **Other** charge for damage max 2 dogs per room **Restrictions** no very large dogs; no St Bernards, Newfoundlands, Alsatians or Mastifs

This impressive Georgian house, set in delightful gardens in the village centre, is very conveniently located for the M1. Bedrooms do vary in size, but consideration has been given to guest comfort, with many thoughtful extras provided. There is a wide range of meeting rooms and private dining options.

Rooms 62 (27 annexe) (16 GF) **S** £65-£109; **D** £79-£145*
Facilities FTV Wi-fi **Parking** 70 **Notes** LB

FLITWICK — Map 4 TL03

MenziesHotels

Menzies Flitwick Manor

★★★★ 73% ◉ COUNTRY HOUSE HOTEL

Church Rd MK45 1AE
☎ 01525 712242 ▤ 01525 718753
e-mail: flitwick@menzieshotels.co.uk
web: www.menzieshotels.co.uk
dir: *M1 junct 12, follow signs for Flitwick, turn left into Church Rd, hotel on left*

PETS: Bedrooms (5 GF) unattended ground-floor bedrooms only **Charges** £20 per night **Public areas** on leads **Grounds** disp bin **Facilities** food (pre-bookable) food bowl water bowl bedding dog chews feeding mat scoop/disp bags leads pet sitting dog walking washing facs dog grooming cage storage walks info vet info **On Request** fridge access torch towels

With its picturesque setting in acres of gardens and parkland, yet only minutes by car from the motorway, this lovely Georgian house combines the best of both worlds, being both accessible and peaceful. Bedrooms are individually decorated and furnished with period pieces; some are air conditioned. Cosy and intimate, the lounge and restaurant help give the hotel a home-from-home feel.

Rooms 18 (1 fmly) (5 GF) (1 smoking) **Facilities** STV ᕽ Putt green ᕽ Xmas New Year Wi-fi **Parking** 18

BERKSHIRE

ASCOT — Map 4 SU96

MACDONALD HOTELS & RESORTS

Macdonald Berystede Hotel & Spa

★★★★ 78% ◉ HOTEL

Bagshot Rd, Sunninghill SL5 9JH
☎ 0844 879 9104 ▤ 01344 872301
e-mail: general.berystede@macdonald-hotels.co.uk
web: www.macdonald-hotels.co.uk/berystede
dir: *A30, B3020 (Windmill Pub). 1.25m to hotel on left just before junct with A330*

PETS: Bedrooms (33 GF) unattended sign **Charges** £10 per night (assist dogs free) **Public areas** except restaurant on leads **Grounds** on leads disp bin **Exercise area** 0.5m **Facilities** dog walking walks info vet info **On Request** fridge access **Stables** 1m **Other** charge for damage **Restrictions** small dogs only

This impressive Victorian mansion, close to Ascot Racecourse, offers executive bedrooms that are spacious, comfortable and particularly well equipped. Public rooms include a cosy bar and an elegant restaurant in which creative dishes are served. An impressive self-contained conference centre and spa facility appeal to both conference and leisure guests.

Rooms 126 (61 fmly) (33 GF) **S** £90-£245; **D** £100-£255*
Facilities Spa STV ᕽ ᕽ Gym Leisure complex (thermal & beauty treatments) Outdoor garden spa Xmas New Year Wi-fi **Services** Lift **Parking** 200 **Notes** LB

BRACKNELL — Map 4 SU86

Coppid Beech

★★★★ 74% ◉ HOTEL

John Nike Way RG12 8TF
☎ 01344 303333 ▤ 01344 301200
e-mail: sales@coppidbeech.com
web: www.coppidbeech.com
dir: *M4 junct 10 take Wokingham/Bracknell onto A329. In 2m take B3408 to Binfield at rdbt. Hotel 200yds on right*

PETS: Bedrooms (16 GF) sign **Charges** £10 per night £70 per week **Public areas** only for access to bedrooms on leads **Grounds** on leads disp bin **Exercise area** 0.5m **Facilities** cage storage walks info vet info **On Request** fridge access towels **Other** charge for damage

This chalet designed hotel offers extensive facilities and includes a ski-slope, ice rink, nightclub, health club and Bier Keller. Bedrooms range from suites to standard rooms - all are impressively equipped. A choice of dining is offered; there's a full bistro menu available in the Keller, and for more formal dining, Rowan's restaurant provides award-winning cuisine.

Rooms 205 (6 fmly) (16 GF) **S** £80-£165; **D** £110-£205 (incl. bkfst) **Facilities** Spa STV ᕽ Gym Ice rink Dry ski slope Snow boarding Freestyle park ♫ New Year Wi-fi **Services** Lift Air con **Parking** 350 **Notes** LB

The Crab at Chieveley

★ ★ ★ ★ @@ GUEST ACCOMMODATION

Wantage Rd RG20 8UE
☎ 01635 247550 📠 01635 247440
e-mail: info@crabatchieveley.com
dir: 1.5m W of Chieveley on B4494

PETS: Bedrooms (7 GF) unattended **Grounds Exercise area**
5 mins **Facilities** food bowl water bowl dog grooming
cage storage walks info vet info **On Request** torch towels
Restrictions small dogs only

The individually themed bedrooms at this former pub have been
appointed to a very high standard and include a full range of
modern amenities. Ground-floor rooms have a small private patio
area complete with a hot tub. The warm and cosy restaurant
offers an extensive and award-winning range of fish and seafood
dishes.

Rooms 8 en suite 5 annexe en suite (7 GF) **Facilities** FTV tea/
coffee Dinner available Direct Dial Cen ht Licensed Wi-fi
Parking 80 **Notes** LB

California Chalet & Touring Park (SU788651)

▶ ▶ ▶

Nine Mile Ride RG40 4HU
☎ 0118 973 3928 📠 0118 932 8720
e-mail: enquiries@californiapark.co.uk
dir: From A321 (S of Wokingham), right onto B3016 to
Finchampstead. Follow Country Park signs on Nine Mile Ride

PETS: Charges 1st dog free, £1 per extra dog per night
Public areas on leads disp bin **Exercise area** adjacent woods
Facilities walks info vet info **Other** prior notice required

Open all year Last arrival flexiblehrs Last departure noon

A simple, peaceful woodland site with secluded pitches among
the trees, adjacent to the country park. Several pitches have a
prime position beside the lake with their own fishing area. Plans
for the future include better hardstanding pitches, refurbished
toilets and more lodges. 5.5 acre site. 44 touring pitches. 44
hardstandings. Tent pitches. Motorhome pitches.

Notes No ground fires, no ball games, no washing of caravans

The Bear Hotel

★ ★ ★ 80% @ HOTEL

41 Charnham St RG17 0EL
☎ 01488 682512 📠 01488 684357
e-mail: info@thebearhotelhungerford.co.uk
web: www.thebearhotelhungerford.co.uk
dir: M4 junct 14, A338 to Hungerford for 3m, left at T-junct onto
A4, hotel on left

PETS: Bedrooms (24 GF) unattended **Public areas** on leads
Grounds Exercise area canal & common nearby **Facilities** food
(pre-bookable) bedding walks info vet info **On Request** fridge
access **Resident Pet:** Bear (cat)

Situated five miles south of the M4 this hotel dates back as far as
early 13th century and was once owned by King Henry VIII. It now
has a contemporary feel throughout. Bedrooms are split between
the main house, the courtyard and Bear Island. The award-
winning restaurant is open for lunch and dinner, and lighter
snacks are available in the bar and lounge. Guests can enjoy the
sun terrace in the summer and log fires in the winter.

Rooms 39 (26 annexe) (2 fmly) (24 GF) **S** £89-£119; **D** £99-£149
(incl. bkfst)* **Facilities** FTV Xmas New Year Wi-fi **Parking** 68
Notes LB

Three Swans Hotel

★ ★ ★ 70% HOTEL

117 High St RG17 0LZ
☎ 01488 682721 📠 01488 681708
e-mail: info@threeswans.net
web: www.threeswans.net
dir: M4 junct 14 follow signs to Hungerford. Hotel half way along
High St on left

PETS: Bedrooms unattended 2 bedrooms only **Charges** £10
per night **Public areas** only in public bar on leads **Grounds**
on leads **Facilities** water bowl dog chews walks info vet info
On Request torch **Stables** 0.75m **Other** charge for damage prior
notice required

Centrally located in the bustling market town of Hungerford
this charming former inn, dating back some 700 years, has
been renovated in a fresh and airy style. Visitors will still see
the original arch under which the horse-drawn carriages once
passed. There is a wood panelled bar, a spacious lounge and
attractive rear garden to relax in. The informal restaurant is
decorated with artwork by local artists. Bedrooms are well
appointed and comfortable.

Rooms 25 (10 annexe) (1 fmly) (5 GF) (3 smoking) **Facilities** FTV
Access to local private gym Xmas New Year Wi-fi **Parking** 30

HUNGERFORD *continued*

The Pheasant Inn

★★★★ ➡ INN
Ermin St, Shefford Woodlands RG17 7AA
☎ 01488 648284 📠 01488 648971
e-mail: enquiries@thepheasant-inn.co.uk
web: www.thepheasant-inn.co.uk
dir: *M4 junct 14, 200yds N on A338 turn left onto B4000 towards Lambourn*

PETS: **Bedrooms** (4 GF) **Public areas Grounds Facilities** food bowl bedding walks info **Other** charge for damage **Resident Pet:** Bailey (Chocolate Labrador)

The Pheasant Inn is a friendly, traditional property conveniently located 400 yards from the M4 and close to the racing centre of Lambourn and also Newbury racecourse. The horseracing theme runs throughout the traditional pub and restaurant where lunch and dinner are served daily. Bedrooms in contrast are contemporary in style providing guests with comfortable accommodation; all feature flat-screen TVs, free Wi-fi and in-room beverage making facilities.

Rooms 11 en suite (4 GF) **Facilities** FTV TVL tea/coffee Dinner available Cen ht Wi-fi **Parking** 100

Hurley Riverside Park *(SU826839)*

▶▶▶▶▶

Park Office SL6 5NE
☎ 01628 824493 & 823501 📠 01628 825533
e-mail: info@hurleyriversidepark.co.uk
dir: *Signed off A4130 (Henley to Maidenhead road), just W of Hurley*

PETS: **Charges** £2 per night **Public areas** on leads disp bin **Exercise area** large riverside picnic grounds adjacent **Facilities** food walks info vet info **Other** pet supplies available in village shop

Open Mar-Oct Last arrival 20.00hrs Last departure noon

A large Thames-side site with a good touring area close to river. Now a quality park following major investment, there are three beautifully refurbished toilet blocks, one of which houses quality, fully-serviced unisex facilities. Level grassy pitches are sited in small, sectioned areas, and this is a generally peaceful setting. There are furnished tents for hire. 15 acre site. 200 touring pitches. 18 hardstandings. Tent pitches. Motorhome pitches. 290 statics.

Notes No unsupervised children, no single sex/young groups, no commercial vehicles, quiet park policy.

Days Inn Membury - M4

BUDGET HOTEL
Membury Service Area RG17 7TZ
☎ 01488 72336 📠 01488 72336
e-mail: membury.hotel@welcomebreak.co.uk
web: www.welcomebreak.co.uk
dir: *M4 between junct 14 & 15*

PETS: **Bedrooms** (17 GF) **Charges** £5 per stay **Public areas** only for access to bedrooms on leads **Grounds** disp bin **Exercise area** adjacent **On Request** fridge access

This modern building offers accommodation in smart, spacious and well-equipped bedrooms, suitable for families and business travellers, and all with en suite bathrooms. Continental breakfast is available and other refreshments may be taken at the nearby family restaurant.

Rooms 38 (32 fmly) (17 GF) (5 smoking) **S** £39.95-£59.95; **D** £49.95-£59.95

Elephant at Pangbourne

★★★ 79% ◉ HOTEL
Church Rd RG8 7AR
☎ 0118 984 2244 📠 0118 976 7346
e-mail: dominic@elephanthotel.co.uk
web: www.elephanthotel.co.uk
dir: *A4 Theale/Newbury, right at 2nd rdbt signed Pangbourne. Hotel on left*

PETS: **Bedrooms** unattended pets allowed in one bedroom only **Charges** £15 per night £105 per week **Public areas** except restaurant on leads **Grounds Exercise area** nearby **Facilities** food bowl water bowl bedding cage storage walks info vet info **On Request** torch towels **Other** charge for damage

Centrally located in this bustling village, just a short drive from Reading. Bedrooms are individual in style but identical in the attention to detail, with handcrafted Indian furniture and rich oriental rugs. Guests can enjoy award-winning cuisine in the restaurant, or there is bistro-style dining in the bar area.

Rooms 22 (8 annexe) (2 fmly) (4 GF) **S** £100-£120; **D** £140-£160 (incl. bkfst)* **Facilities** FTV ⏪ Xmas New Year Wi-fi **Parking** 10 **Notes** LB

Holiday Inn Reading M4 Jct 10

Holiday Inn

★★★★ 76% HOTEL

Wharfedale Rd, Winnersh Triangle RG41 5TS

☎ 0118 944 0444 📠 0118 944 0033

e-mail: reservations@hireadinghotel.com

web: www.meridianleisurehotels.com/reading

dir: *M4 junct 10/A329 (N) towards Reading (E), 1st exit signed Winnersh/Woodley/A329, left at lights into Wharfesale Rd. Hotel on left*

PETS: Bedrooms Charges £10 per night **Grounds** on leads **Other** charge for damage **Restrictions** max weight 7.5kg

Situated in the Winnersh Triangle within close proximity of the M4, Reading, Bracknell and Wokingham, this hotel offers a range of contemporary and stylish bedrooms, eight state-of-the-art meeting rooms and extensive leisure facilities including a 19-metre indoor pool. The Caprice Restaurant offers relaxed dining throughout the day.

Rooms 174 (25 fmly) (16 smoking) **S** £42-£178; **D** £42-£178*
Facilities FTV 🟢 Gym Sauna Steam room Treatment room Xmas New Year Wi-fi **Services** Lift Air con **Parking** 120

Ibis Reading Centre

BUDGET HOTEL

25A Friar St RG1 1DP

☎ 0118 953 3500 📠 0118 953 3510

e-mail: H5431@accor.com

web: www.ibishotel.com

dir: *A329 into Friar St. Hotel near central train station*

PETS: Bedrooms Charges £5 per night **Other** charge for damage dogs are required to be muzzled

Modern, budget hotel offering comfortable accommodation in bright and practical bedrooms. Breakfast is self-service and dinner is available in the restaurant.

Rooms 182 (36 fmly)

Wellington Country Park *(SU728628)*

▶▶▶

Odiham Rd RG7 1SP

☎ 0118 932 6444 📠 0118 932 6445

e-mail: info@wellington-country-park.co.uk

dir: *M4 junct 11, A33 south towards Basingstoke. M3 junct 5, B3349 north towards Reading*

PETS: Charges £2.50 per night **Public areas** except children's play area & animal farm disp bin **Exercise area** nearby **Facilities** food bowl water bowl scoop/disp bags vet info **Stables** 1m **Other** prior notice required dogs must be kept on leads

Open Mar-Nov Last arrival 17.30hrs (16.30hrs low season) Last departure 12.00hrs

A peaceful woodland site set within an extensive country park, which comes complete with lakes and nature trails, and these are accessible to campers after the country park closes. There's also a herd of Red and Fallow deer that roam the meadow area. This site is ideal for those travelling on the M4. 80 acre site. 72 touring pitches. 10 hardstandings. Tent pitches. Motorhome pitches.

Notes No open fires.

The Swan at Streatley

★★★★ 73% ◉◉ HOTEL

High St RG8 9HR

☎ 01491 878800 📠 01491 872554

e-mail: sales@swan-at-streatley.co.uk

web: www.swanatstreatley.co.uk

dir: *From S right at lights in Streatley, hotel on left before bridge*

PETS: Bedrooms (12 GF) unattended **Charges** £15 per night **Public areas** except restaurant on leads **Grounds** disp bin **Facilities** water bowl walks info vet info **Other** charge for damage

A stunning location set beside the Thames, ideal for an English summer's day. The bedrooms are well appointed and many enjoy the lovely views. The hotel offers a range of facilities including meeting rooms, and the Magdalen Barge is moored beside the hotel making an unusual, yet perfect meeting venue. Motor launches are available for hire from April to October. The spa includes an indoor heated mineral pool and offers a range of treatments. Cuisine is accomplished and dining here should not be missed.

Rooms 45 (12 GF) **Facilities** Spa STV 🟢 supervised Fishing 🎣 Gym Electric motor launches for hire Apr-Oct Xmas New Year Wi-fi **Parking** 170

ENGLAND

Christopher Hotel
★★★ 77% HOTEL
110 High St, Eton SL4 6AN
☎ 01753 852359 ☒ 01753 830914
e-mail: reservations@thechristopher.co.uk
web: www.thechristopher.co.uk
dir: *M4 junct 5 (Slough E), Colnbrook Datchet Eton (B470). At rdbt 2nd exit for Datchet. Right at mini rdbt (Eton), left into Eton Rd (3rd rdbt). Left, hotel on right*

PETS: Bedrooms (22 GF) **Charges** £10 per night **Public areas** except restaurant on leads **Grounds** on leads **Exercise area** large field adjacent **Facilities** food (pre-bookable) food bowl water bowl feeding mat washing facs cage storage walks info vet info **On Request** fridge access torch towels **Other** charge for damage **Resident Pets:** Magic (cat)

This hotel benefits from an ideal location in Eton, being only a short stroll across the pedestrian bridge from historic Windsor Castle and the many other attractions the town has to offer. The hotel has comfortable and smartly decorated accommodation, and a wide range of dishes is available in the informal bar and grill. A stylish room is available for private dining or for meetings.

Rooms 34 (23 annexe) (10 fmly) (22 GF) **S** £112-£141;
D £146-£186* **Facilities** FTV Xmas New Year Wi-fi **Parking** 19
Notes LB

Clarence Guest House
★★★ GUEST HOUSE
9 Clarence Rd SL4 5AE
☎ 01753 864436 ☒ 01753 857060
e-mail: clarence.hotel@btconnect.com
web: www.clarence-hotel.co.uk
dir: *M4 junct 6, dual carriageway to Windsor, left at 1st rdbt onto Clarence Rd*

PETS: Bedrooms (2 GF) **Facilities** walks info vet info
On Request towels **Other** charge for damage

This Grade II listed Victorian house is in the heart of Windsor. Space in some rooms is limited, but all are well maintained and offer excellent value for money. Facilities include a lounge with a well-stocked bar, and a steam room. Breakfast is served in the dining room overlooking attractive gardens.

Rooms 20 en suite (6 fmly) (2 GF) (16 smoking) **S** £45-£77;
D £55-£89 **Facilities** FTV TVL tea/coffee Cen ht Licensed Wi-fi
Sauna **Parking** 4

Best Western Reading Moat House
★★★★ 78% HOTEL
Mill Ln, Sindlesham RG41 5DF
☎ 0870 225 0601 ☒ 0118 935 1646
e-mail: ops.reading@qmh-hotels.com
web: www.bestwestern.co.uk/readingmoathouse
dir: *Towards Reading on A329(M), 1st exit to Winnersh. Follow Lower Earley Way North. Hotel on left*

PETS: Bedrooms (22 GF) sign ground-floor bedrooms only
Charges £5 per night £35 per week **Grounds** on leads disp bin
Exercise area 0.5m **Facilities** food bowl water bowl bedding scoop/disp bags walks info vet info **On Request** fridge access torch towels **Stables** approx 3m **Other** charge for damage

Located just off the M4 on the outskirts of Reading, this smart, modern hotel has been sympathetically built around a 19th-century mill house. Bedrooms are stylish and have a contemporary feel to them. Spacious public areas include good conference rooms, a spacious bar and restaurant, as well as a business centre and a small fitness area.

Rooms 129 (12 fmly) (22 GF) **S** £59-£124; **D** £59-£124*
Facilities STV Fishing Gym 🎵 Xmas New Year Wi-fi **Services** Lift
Air con **Parking** 250 **Notes** LB

Hotel du Vin Bristol
★★★★ 74% ⊛ TOWN HOUSE HOTEL
The Sugar House, Narrow Lewins Mead BS1 2NU
☎ 0117 925 5577 ☒ 0117 925 1199
e-mail: info.bristol@hotelduvin.com
web: www.hotelduvin.com
dir: *From A4 follow city centre signs. After 400yds pass Rupert St NCP on right. Hotel on opposite carriageway*

PETS: Bedrooms **Charges** £10 per night **Public areas** except restaurant **Facilities** food bowl water bowl bedding washing facs walks info vet info **On Request** fridge access torch towels **Other** charge for damage

This hotel is part of one of Britain's most innovative hotel groups that offer high standards of hospitality and accommodation. Housed in a Grade II listed, converted 18th-century sugar refinery, it provides great facilities with a modern, minimalist design. The bedrooms are exceptionally well designed and the bistro offers an excellent menu and wine list.

Rooms 40 (10 fmly) **S** £125-£375; **D** £125-£375* **Facilities** STV
FTV Xmas New Year Wi-fi **Services** Lift **Parking** 12 **Notes** LB

Novotel Bristol Centre

★★★★ **70%** HOTEL

Victoria St BS1 6HY
☎ 0117 976 9988 📠 0117 925 5040
e-mail: H5622@accor.com
web: www.novotel.com
dir: At end of M32 follow signs for Temple Meads station to rdbt. Final exit, hotel immediately on right

PETS: Bedrooms Charges £8 per night **Public areas** except food areas (ex assist dogs) muzzled and on leads **Exercise area** 5 mins' walk **Facilities** walks info vet info **On Request** towels

This city centre hotel provides smart, contemporary style accommodation. Most of the bedrooms demonstrate the Novotel 'Novation' style with unique swivel desk, internet access, air-conditioning and a host of extras. The hotel is convenient for the mainline railway station and also has its own car park.

Rooms 131 (20 fmly) **S** £69-£149; **D** £69-£149* **Facilities** STV Gym Wi-fi **Services** Lift **Parking** 120 **Notes** LB

The Berkeley Square

★★★ **78%** ®® HOTEL

15 Berkeley Square, Clifton BS8 1HB
☎ 0117 925 4000 📠 0117 925 2970
e-mail: berkeley@cliftonhotels.com
web: www.cliftonhotels.com/chg.html
dir: M32 follow Clifton signs. 1st left at lights by Nills Memorial Tower (University) into Berkeley Sq

PETS: Bedrooms (4 GF) unattended lower deck double bedrooms only **Public areas** except restaurant on leads **Grounds** on leads **Exercise area** adjacent to park **Facilities** cage storage walks info vet info **On Request** fridge access torch **Other** charge for damage cats must be caged

Set in a pleasant square close to the university, art gallery and Clifton Village, this smart, elegant Georgian hotel has modern, stylishly decorated bedrooms that feature many welcome extras. There is a cosy lounge and stylish restaurant on the ground floor and a smart, contemporary bar in the basement. A small garden is also available at the rear of the hotel.

Rooms 43 (4 GF) **Facilities** Use of local gym & swimming pool **Services** Lift **Parking** 20

Arnos Manor Hotel

★★★ **74%** HOTEL

470 Bath Rd, Arno's Vale BS4 3HQ
☎ 0117 971 1461 📠 0117 971 5507
e-mail: arnos.manor@forestdale.com
web: www.arnosmanorhotel.co.uk
dir: From end of M32 follow signs for Bath. On A4 in 2m hotel on right adjacent to ITV West TV studio

PETS: Bedrooms (7 GF) unattended sign **Charges** £7.50 per night **Public areas** except restaurant & bar on leads **Grounds** disp bin **Exercise area** 50mtrs **Facilities** food (pre-bookable) food bowl water bowl cage storage walks info vet info **On Request** fridge access torch towels **Other** charge for damage **Restrictions** no dangerous dogs (see page 7)

Once the home of a wealthy merchant, this historic 18th-century building is now a comfortable hotel and offers spacious, well-appointed bedrooms with plenty of workspace. The lounge was once the chapel and has many original features, while meals are taken in the atmospheric, conservatory-style restaurant.

Rooms 73 (5 fmly) (7 GF) **Facilities** FTV Xmas New Year Wi-fi **Services** Lift **Parking** 200 **Notes** LB

Rodney Hotel

★★★ **68%** ® HOTEL

4 Rodney Place, Clifton BS8 4HY
☎ 0117 973 5422 📠 0117 946 7092
e-mail: rodney@cliftonhotels.com
dir: Off Clifton Down Rd

PETS: Bedrooms (2 GF) ground-floor bedrooms only **Public areas** except restaurant on leads **Grounds** **Exercise area** park 0.5m **Facilities** vet info **On Request** fridge access **Other** charge for damage **Restrictions** small dogs only

With easy access from the M5, this attractive, listed building in Clifton is conveniently close to the city centre. The individually decorated bedrooms provide a useful range of extra facilities for the business traveller; the public areas include a smart bar and small restaurant offering enjoyable and carefully prepared dishes. A pleasant rear garden provides additional seating in the summer months.

Rooms 31 (1 fmly) (2 GF) **S** £67-£94; **D** £77-£112* **Facilities** FTV Wi-fi **Parking** 10 **Notes** LB Closed 22 Dec-3 Jan RS Sun

BRISTOL *continued*

Clifton

★★ **76%** HOTEL

St Pauls Rd, Clifton BS8 1LX
☎ 0117 973 6882 📠 0117 974 1082
e-mail: clifton@cliftonhotels.com
web: www.cliftonhotels.com/clifton
dir: *M32 follow Bristol/Clifton signs, along Park St. Left at lights into St Pauls Rd*

PETS: Bedrooms (12 GF) unattended **Charges Public areas** except restaurant **Exercise area** 0.5m **Facilities** food (prebookable) walks info vet info **On Request** fridge access torch towels **Other** charge for damage

This popular hotel offers very well equipped bedrooms and relaxed, friendly service. There is a welcoming lounge by the reception, and in summer months drinks and meals can be enjoyed on the terrace. Racks Bar and Restaurant offers an interesting selection of modern dishes in informal surroundings. There is some street parking, but for a small charge, secure garage parking is available.

Rooms 59 (2 fmly) (12 GF) (8 smoking) **S** £41-£75; **D** £50-£91*
Facilities STV FTV Wi-fi **Services** Lift **Parking** 12

The Washington

★★★ GUEST HOUSE

11-15 St Pauls Rd, Clifton BS8 1LX
☎ 0117 973 3980 📠 0117 973 4740
e-mail: washington@cliftonhotels.com
dir: *A4018 into city, right at lights opp BBC, house 200yds on left*

PETS: Bedrooms (10 GF) unattended **Public areas** except breakfast room **Grounds Exercise area** 0.25m **Facilities** food (pre-bookable) vet info **On Request** fridge access torch towels **Other** charge for damage

This large terraced house is within walking distance of the city centre and Clifton Village. The bedrooms, many refurbished, are well equipped for business guests. Public areas include a modern reception lounge and a bright basement breakfast room. The property has secure parking and a rear patio garden.

Rooms 46 rms (40 en suite) (4 fmly) (10 GF) **S** £40-£73;
D £49-£89 **Facilities** FTV tea/coffee Direct Dial Cen ht Licensed Wi-fi **Parking** 16 **Notes** Closed 23 Dec-3 Jan

Hartwell House Hotel, Restaurant & Spa

★★★★ ◉◉◉ HOTEL

Oxford Rd HP17 8NR
☎ 01296 747444 📠 01296 747450
e-mail: info@hartwell-house.com
web: www.hartwell-house.com
dir: *From S: M40 junct 7, A329 to Thame, then A418 towards Aylesbury. After 6m, through Stone, hotel on left. From N: M40 junct 9 for Bicester. A41 to Aylesbury, A418 to Oxford for 2m. Hotel on right*

PETS: Bedrooms unattended Hartwell Court suites only **Grounds** disp bin **Exercise area** nearby **Facilities** food bowl water bowl scoop/disp bags cage storage walks info vet info **On Request** fridge access torch towels **Other** charge for damage **Restrictions** 1 large or 2 small dogs only **Resident Pets:** Inka & Maddy (Labradors)

This beautiful, historic house is set in 90 acres of unspoilt parkland. The grand public rooms are truly magnificent, and feature many fine works of art. The service standards are very high; guests will find that the staff offer attentive and traditional hospitality without stuffiness. There is an elegant, award-winning restaurant where carefully prepared dishes use the best local produce. Bedrooms are spacious, elegant and very comfortable. Most are in the main house, but some, including suites, are in the nearby, renovated coach house, which also houses an excellent spa.

Rooms 46 (16 annexe) (3 fmly) (10 GF) **S** £175; **D** £205-£290 (incl. bkfst)* **Facilities** Spa STV ⓢ supervised ⬛⬛ Gym Sauna Treatment rooms Steam rooms ♬ Xmas New Year Wi-fi **Services** Lift **Parking** 91 **Notes** LB No children 4yrs RS Xmas/New Year

BUCKINGHAM Map 4 SP63

Best Western Buckingham Hotel

★★★ **77%** HOTEL

Buckingham Ring Rd MK18 1RY
☎ 01280 822622 📠 01280 823074
e-mail: info@thebuckinghamhotel.co.uk
dir: *Follow A421 for Buckingham, take ring road S towards Brackley & Bicester. Hotel on left*

PETS: Bedrooms (31 GF) unattended **Charges** £10 per night **Public areas** on leads **Grounds** on leads disp bin **Facilities** vet info **On Request** torch **Restrictions** small dogs only

A purpose-built hotel, which offers comfortable and spacious rooms with well designed working spaces for business travellers. There are also extensive conference facilities. The open-plan restaurant and bar offer a good range of dishes, and the well-equipped leisure suite is popular with guests.

Rooms 70 (6 fmly) (31 GF) **S** £68-£125; **D** £76-£135 (incl. bkfst)* **Facilities** STV FTV ⓢ supervised Gym Sauna Steam room Xmas New Year Wi-fi **Parking** 200 **Notes** LB

CHENIES — Map 4 TQ09

The Bedford Arms Hotel
★★★ 79% ◉ HOTEL

WD3 6EQ
☎ 01923 283301 🖹 01923 284825
e-mail: contact@bedfordarms.co.uk
web: www.bedfordarms.co.uk
dir: *M25 junct 18/A404 towards Amersham, hotel signed after 2m on right*

PETS: Bedrooms (8 GF) **Charges** disp bin **Exercise area** adjacent **Facilities** water bowl walks info vet info **Other** charge for damage **Restrictions** no very large dogs

This attractive, 19th-century country inn enjoys a peaceful rural setting. Comfortable bedrooms are decorated in traditional style and feature a range of thoughtful extras. Each room is named after a relation of the Duke of Bedford, whose family has an historic association with the property. There are two bars, a lounge and a cosy, wood-panelled restaurant.

Rooms 18 (8 annexe) (2 fmly) (8 GF) **S** £60-£110; **D** £95-£140 (incl. bkfst)* **Facilities** STV FTV Wi-fi **Parking** 60 **Notes** RS 27 Dec-4 Jan

MARLOW — Map 4 SU88

 MACDONALD HOTELS & RESORTS

Macdonald Compleat Angler
★★★★ ◉◉◉ HOTEL

Marlow Bridge SL7 1RG
☎ 0844 879 9128 🖹 01628 486388
e-mail: compleatangler@macdonald-hotels.co.uk
web: www.macdonald-hotels.co.uk/compleatangler
dir: *M4 junct 8/9, A404(M) to rdbt, Bisham exit, 1m to Marlow Bridge, hotel on right*

PETS: Bedrooms (6 GF) unattended sign **Charges** on application **Grounds** on leads **Exercise area** 400mtrs **Facilities** cage storage walks info vet info **On Request** fridge access **Stables** 3m **Other** charge for damage

This well-established hotel enjoys an idyllic location overlooking the River Thames and the delightful Marlow weir. The bedrooms, which differ in size and style, are all individually decorated and are equipped with flat-screen satellite TVs, high speed internet and air conditioning; some rooms have balconies with views of the weir and some have four-posters. Aubergine (a sister restaurant to the restaurant of the same name in Chelsea) has three AA rosettes and offers modern French cuisine; Bowaters serves British dishes and has gained two AA rosettes. In summer guests can use two boats that the hotel has moored on the river and the fishing is, of course, a popular activity - a ghillie can accompany guests if prior arranged. Staff throughout are keen to please and nothing is too much trouble.

Rooms 64 (6 fmly) (6 GF) **D** £130-£270 (incl. bkfst) **Facilities** STV Fly & coarse fishing River trips (Apr-Sep) Xmas New Year Wi-fi **Services** Lift **Parking** 100 **Notes** LB

MILTON KEYNES — Map 4 SP83

 NOVOTEL

Novotel Milton Keynes
★★★ 73% HOTEL

Saxon St, Layburn Court, Heelands MK13 7RA
☎ 01908 322212 🖹 01908 322235
e-mail: H3272@accor.com
web: www.novotel.com
dir: *M1 junct 14, follow Childsway signs towards city centre. Right into Saxon Way, straight across all rdbts, hotel on left*

PETS: Bedrooms (40 GF) **Charges** £10 per night **Public areas** only for access to bedrooms on leads **Grounds** on leads disp bin **Exercise area** 50mtrs **Other** charge for damage

Contemporary in style, this purpose-built hotel is situated on the outskirts of the town, just a few minutes' drive from the centre and mainline railway station. Bedrooms provide ample workspace and a good range of facilities for the modern traveller, and public rooms include a children's play area and indoor leisure centre.

Rooms 124 (40 fmly) (40 GF) **Facilities** FTV 🏊 Gym Steam bath Wi-fi **Services** Lift **Parking** 130

 Campanile

Campanile Milton Keynes
BUDGET HOTEL

40 Penn Road (off Watling St), Fenny Stratford, Bletchley MK2 2AU
☎ 01908 649819 🖹 01908 649818
e-mail: miltonkeynes@campanile.com
dir: *M1 junct 14, A4146 to A5. S'bound at 1st rdbt to Fenny Stratford. Hotel 500yds on left*

PETS: Bedrooms (26 GF) **Charges** £5 per night **Public areas** on leads **Exercise area** canal walk nearby **Other** please phone for further details of pet facilities

This modern building offers accommodation in smart, well-equipped bedrooms, all with en suite bathrooms. Refreshments may be taken at the informal bistro.

Rooms 80 (26 GF)

ENGLAND

NEWPORT PAGNELL MOTORWAY SERVICE AREA (M1) Map 4 SP84

Days Inn Milton Keynes East M1

BUDGET HOTEL

Newport Pagnell MK16 8DS
☎ 01908 610878 📄 01908 216539
e-mail: newport.hotel@welcomebreak.co.uk
web: www.daysinn.com
dir: *M1 junct 14-15. In service area - follow signs to Barrier Lodge*

PETS: Bedrooms Public areas muzzled and on leads **Grounds** on leads **Exercise area** nearby **Facilities** walks info vet info **Other** charge for damage

This modern building offers accommodation in smart, spacious and well-equipped bedrooms, suitable for families and business travellers, and all with en suite bathrooms. Refreshments may be taken at the nearby family restaurant.

Rooms 90 (54 fmly) **S** £49.95-£79.95; **D** £49.95-£79.95

TAPLOW Map 4 SU98

Cliveden Country House Hotel

★★★★★ ◉◉ COUNTRY HOUSE HOTEL

SL6 0JF
☎ 01628 668561 📄 01628 661837
e-mail: info@clivedenhouse.co.uk
web: www.clivedenhouse.co.uk
dir: *M4 junct 7, A4 towards Maidenhead, 1.5m, onto B476 towards Taplow, 2.5m, hotel on left*

PETS: Bedrooms (10 GF) **Public areas** except restaurants, spa & walled garden on leads **Grounds** on leads disp bin **Exercise area** woodland walk **Facilities** food (pre-bookable) food bowl water bowl bedding pet sitting dog walking washing facs cage storage walks info vet info **On Request** fridge access **Stables** 2m **Other** charge for damage charge for pet food

This wonderful stately home stands at the top of a gravelled boulevard. Visitors are treated as house-guests and staff recapture the tradition of fine hospitality. Bedrooms have individual quality and style, and reception rooms retain a timeless elegance. Exceptional leisure facilities include cruises along Cliveden Reach and massages in the Pavilion. The Terrace Restaurant with its delightful views has two AA Rosettes. The Rosette award for Waldo's, which offers innovative menus in discreet, luxurious surroundings, is temporarily suspended due to a change of chef; a new award will be in place once our inspectors have completed their assessments of meals cooked by the new kitchen team.

Rooms 39 (10 GF) **Facilities** Spa STV FTV ⊗ ᛏ ❄ ⊛ Gym Squash Full range of beauty treatments 3 vintage boats ♫ Xmas New Year Wi-fi **Services** Lift **Parking** 60

BOXWORTH Map 5 TL36

Days Inn Cambridge - A1

BUDGET HOTEL

Cambridge Extra Services, Junction A14/M11 CB3 8WU
☎ 01954 267176 📄 01954 267864
e-mail: cambridge.hotel@welcomebreak.co.uk
dir: *A14/M11 Cambridge Extra Services*

PETS: Bedrooms (40 GF) unattended certain bedrooms only **Charges** please contact for details **Grounds** on leads disp bin **Exercise area** nearby **Facilities** cage storage walks info vet info **On Request** towels

This modern, purpose built accommodation offers smartly appointed, well-equipped bedrooms, with good power showers. There is a choice of adjacent food outlets where guests may enjoy breakfast, snacks and meals.

Rooms 82 (14 fmly) (40 GF) (19 smoking) **S** £49.95-£69.95; **D** £59.95-£79.95

BURWELL Map 5 TL56

Stanford Park (TL578675)

▶ ▶ ▶

Weirs Drove CB25 0BP
☎ 01638 741547 & 07802 439997
e-mail: enquiries@stanfordcaravanpark.co.uk
dir: *Signed from B1102*

PETS: Public areas disp bin **Exercise area** access from site to many country walks

Open all year **Last arrival** 20.00hrs **Last departure** 11.00hrs

A secluded site on the outskirts of Burwell set in four large fields with several attractive trees. The amenities are modern and well kept, and there are eight hardstandings hedged with privet. 20 acre site. 100 touring pitches. 20 hardstandings. Tent pitches. Motorhome pitches.

Notes No group bookings ⊛

Hotel Felix

★★★★ 80% ◉◉ HOTEL

Whitehouse Ln CB3 0LX
☎ 01223 277977 ▤ 01223 277973
e-mail: help@hotelfelix.co.uk
web: www.hotelfelix.co.uk
dir: M11 junct 13. From A1 N, take A14 onto A1307. At 'City of Cambridge' sign left into Whitehouse Ln

PETS: Bedrooms (26 GF) unattended Grounds on leads Exercise area field behind hotel Facilities cage storage walks info vet info On Request fridge access Other charge for damage please phone for further details of pet facilities

A beautiful Victorian mansion set amidst three acres of landscaped gardens, this property was originally built in 1852 for a surgeon from the famous Addenbrookes Hospital. The contemporary-style bedrooms have carefully chosen furniture and many thoughtful touches; public rooms feature an open-plan bar, the adjacent Graffiti restaurant and a quiet lounge.

Rooms 52 (5 fmly) (26 GF) S £160-£215; D £198-£315 (incl. bkfst)* Facilities STV Xmas New Year Wi-fi Services Lift Parking 90 Notes LB

MenziesHotels

Menzies Cambridge Hotel & Golf Club

★★★★ 77% ◉ HOTEL

Bar Hill CB23 8EU
☎ 01954 249988 ▤ 01954 780010
e-mail: cambridge@menzieshotels.co.uk
web: www.menzieshotels.co.uk
dir: M11 N & S to A14 follow signs for Huntingdon. A14 turn off B1050 Bar Hill, hotel 1st exit on rdbt

PETS: Bedrooms (68 GF) ground-floor bedrooms only Charges £10 per night Grounds on leads disp bin Facilities water bowl Other charge for damage Restrictions max weight 15kg

Ideally situated amidst 200 acres of open countryside, just five miles from the university city of Cambridge. Public rooms include a brasserie restaurant and the popular Gallery Bar. The contemporary-style bedrooms are smartly decorated and equipped with a good range of useful facilities. The hotel also has a leisure club, swimming pool and golf course.

Rooms 136 (35 fmly) (68 GF) (12 smoking) Facilities STV ⊗ ⚓ 18 ⛳ Putt green Gym Hair & beauty salon Steam room Sauna Xmas New Year Wi-fi Services Lift Parking 200

Hotel du Vin Cambridge

★★★★ 75% ◉ TOWN HOUSE HOTEL

15-19 Trumpington St CB2 1QA
☎ 01223 227330 ▤ 01223 227331
e-mail: info.cambridge@hotelduvin.com
web: www.hotelduvin.com
dir: M11 junct 11 Cambridge S, pass Trumpington Park & Ride on left. Hotel 2m on right after double rdbt

PETS: Bedrooms (6 GF) unattended Charges £10 per night Public areas except restaurant & bar on leads Facilities food bowl water bowl bedding feeding mat walks info vet info On Request towels Other charge for damage

This beautiful building, which dates back in part to medieval times, has been transformed to enhance its many quirky architectural features. The bedrooms and suites, some with private terraces, have the company's trademark monsoon showers and Egyptian linen. The French-style bistro has an open-style kitchen and the bar is set in the unusual labyrinth of vaulted cellar rooms. There is also a library, specialist wine tasting room and private dining room.

Rooms 41 (3 annexe) (6 GF) Facilities STV Xmas New Year Wi-fi Services Lift Air con Parking 24

Best Western The Gonville Hotel

★★★ 78% HOTEL

Gonville Place CB1 1LY
☎ 01223 366611 & 221111 ▤ 01223 315470
e-mail: all@gonvillehotel.co.uk
web: www.bw-gonvillehotel.co.uk
dir: M11 junct 11, on A1309 follow city centre signs. At 2nd mini rdbt right into Lensfield Rd, over junct with lights. Hotel 25yds on right

PETS: Bedrooms (8 GF) Grounds on leads Exercise area adjacent Facilities vet info Other charge for damage cats must be caged

A well established hotel situated on the inner ring road, a short walk across the green from the city centre. The air-conditioned public areas are cheerfully furnished, and include a lounge bar and brasserie; bedrooms are well appointed and appealing, offering a good range of facilities for both corporate and leisure guests.

Rooms 80 (2 fmly) (8 GF) S £78-£146; D £78-£156* Facilities FTV New Year Wi-fi Services Lift Parking 80 Notes LB RS 24-29 Dec

Royal Cambridge

★★★ 75% HOTEL

Trumpington St CB2 1PY
☎ 01223 351631 📄 01223 352972
e-mail: royal.cambridge@forestdale.com
web: www.theroyalcambridgehotel.co.uk
dir: *M11 junct 11, signed city centre. At 1st mini rdbt left into Fen Causeway. Hotel 1st right*

PETS: **Bedrooms** (3 GF) sign **Charges** £7.50 per night **Public areas** except restaurant on leads **Facilities** food food bowl water bowl cage storage walks info vet info

This elegant Georgian hotel is situated in the heart of Cambridge. The bedrooms are well equipped and provide great comfort. The stylish restaurant and bar are a popular choice with locals and guests alike. The complimentary parking proves a real benefit in this city centre location.

Rooms 57 (5 fmly) (3 GF) **Facilities** FTV Xmas New Year Wi-fi **Services** Lift **Parking** 80 **Notes** LB

Fields End Water Caravan Park & Fishery

(TL378908)

►►►►

Benwick Rd PE15 0TY
☎ 01354 740199
e-mail: info@fieldsendfishing.co.uk
dir: *Exit A141, follow signs to Doddington. At clock tower in Doddington turn right into Benwick Rd. Site 1.5m on right after sharp bends*

PETS: **Charges** 50p per night £3.50 per week **Public areas** disp bin **Exercise area** public footpath **Facilities** food food bowl water bowl scoop/disp bags washing facs walks info vet info **Other** prior notice required **Resident Pets:** 2 dogs

Open all year Last arrival 20.30hrs Last departure noon

This park has been developed to very high specifications. The 33 fully serviced pitches, all with very generous hardstandings, are on elevated terraces with sweeping views of the surrounding Fenland countryside. The two toilet blocks contain several combined cubicle spaces and there are shady walks through mature deciduous woodland adjacent to two large and appealingly landscaped fishing lakes. 20 acre site. 52 touring pitches. 16 hardstandings. Tent pitches. Motorhome pitches.

Castle Lodge

★★★ GUEST HOUSE

50 New Barns Rd CB7 4PW
☎ 01353 662276 📄 01353 666606
e-mail: castlelodgehotel@supanet.com
dir: *Off B1382 Prickwillow Rd, NE from town centre*

PETS: **Bedrooms** unattended **Charges** £5 per night **Public areas** except restaurant on leads **Grounds** on leads **Exercise area** field nearby **Facilities** food (pre-bookable) food bowl water bowl pet sitting dog walking cage storage walks info **On Request** fridge access torch towels **Other** charge for damage

Located within easy walking distance of the cathedral, this extended Victorian house offers well-equipped bedrooms in a variety of sizes. Public areas include a traditionally furnished dining room and a comfortable air-conditioned bar lounge. Service is friendly and helpful.

Rooms 11 rms (6 en suite) (3 fmly) **Facilities** TVL tea/coffee Dinner available Direct Dial Cen ht Licensed Wi-fi **Parking** 6

The Old Bridge Hotel

★★★ 87% ◉◉ HOTEL

1 High St PE29 3TQ
☎ 01480 424300 📄 01480 411017
e-mail: oldbridge@huntsbridge.co.uk
web: www.huntsbridge.com
dir: *From A14 or A1 follow Huntingdon signs. Hotel visible from inner ring road*

PETS: **Bedrooms** (2 GF) unattended only bedrooms with easy access to car park **Public areas** on leads **Grounds** on leads **Exercise area** adjacent **Facilities** walks info vet info **On Request** towels **Stables** 5m **Other** charge for damage

An imposing 18th-century building situated close to shops and amenities. This charming hotel offers superb accommodation in stylish and individually decorated bedrooms that include many useful extras. Guests can choose from the same menu whether dining in the open-plan terrace, or the more formal restaurant with its bold colour scheme. There is also an excellent business centre.

Rooms 24 (2 fmly) (2 GF) **S** £99-£150; **D** £140-£220 (incl. bkfst)* **Facilities** STV FTV Fishing Private mooring for boats Xmas New Year Wi-fi **Services** Air con **Parking** 50 **Notes** LB

Huntingdon Boathaven & Caravan Park
(TL249706)

▶ ▶ ▶

The Avenue, Godmanchester PE29 2AF
☎ 01480 411977 📄 01480 411977
e-mail: boathaven.hunts@virgin.net
dir: *S of town. Exit A14 at Godmanchester junct, through Godmanchester on B1043 to site (on left by River Ouse)*

PETS: Public areas except toilet block **Exercise area on site** field adjacent **Facilities** vet info **Other** prior notice required

Open all year rs Open in winter when weather permits Last arrival 21.00hrs

A small, well laid out site overlooking a boat marina and the River Ouse, set close to the A14 and within walking distance of Huntingdon town centre. The toilets are clean and well kept. A pretty area has been created for tents beside the marina, with wide views across the Ouse Valley. Weekend family activities are organised throughout the season. 2 acre site. 24 touring pitches. 18 hardstandings. Tent pitches. Motorhome pitches.

The Willows Caravan Park *(TL224708)*

▶ ▶ ▶

Bromholme Ln, Brampton PE28 4NE
☎ 01480 437566
e-mail: willows@willows33.freeserve.co.uk
dir: *Exit A14/A1 signed Brampton, follow Huntingdon signs. Site on right close to Brampton Mill pub*

PETS: Charges 50p per night **Public areas** dogs must be kept on leads disp bin **Exercise area on site** along river bank **Facilities** walks info vet info **Other** prior notice required **Resident Pet:** 1 dog

Open all year Last arrival 20.00hrs Last departure noon

A small, friendly site in a pleasant setting beside the River Ouse, on the Ouse Valley Walk. Bay areas have been provided for caravans and motorhomes, and planting for screening is gradually maturing. There are launching facilities and free river fishing. 4 acre site. 50 touring pitches. 10 hardstandings. Tent pitches. Motorhome pitches.

Notes Ball games on field provided, no generators, no groundsheets, 5mph one-way system. 🐾

Best Western Orton Hall
★★★ 81% 🏵 HOTEL
Orton Longueville PE2 7DN
☎ 01733 391111 📄 01733 231912
e-mail: reception@ortonhall.co.uk
dir: *Off A605 E, opposite Orton Mere*

PETS: Bedrooms (15 GF) **Charges** £15 per night **Public areas** except restaurants on leads **Grounds Exercise area** park 0.25m **Facilities** water bowl **On Request** towels **Other** charge for damage

An impressive country-house hotel set in 20 acres of woodland on the outskirts of town and with easy access to the A1. The spacious and relaxing public areas include the baronial Great Room and the Orton Suite for banqueting and for meetings, and the oak-panelled, award-winning Huntly Restaurant. The on-site pub, Ramblewood Inn, is an alternative, informal dining option.

Rooms 73 (2 fmly) (15 GF) **S** £35-£130; **D** £35-£150*
Facilities STV 🔄 Gym Sauna Steam room Xmas New Year Wi-fi
Parking 200 **Notes** LB

Days Inn Peterborough - A1
BUDGET HOTEL
Peterborough Extra Services, A1 Junction 17, Great North Road, Haddon PE7 3UQ
☎ 01733 371540 📄 01733 391594
e-mail: peterborough.hotel@welcomebreak.co.uk
dir: *A1(M) junct 17*

PETS: Bedrooms (40 GF) **Charges** £5 per stay **Public areas** on leads **Grounds** on leads disp bin **Facilities** cage storage walks info vet info **On Request** towels **Other** charge for damage

This modern, purpose-built accommodation offers smartly appointed, particularly well-equipped bedrooms with good power showers. There is a choice of adjacent food outlets where guests can enjoy breakfast, snacks and meals.

Rooms 82 (13 fmly) (40 GF) (13 smoking) **S** £39.95-£59.95; **D** £49.95-£69.95

ST NEOTS	Map 4 TL16

The George Hotel & Brasserie

★★★ 87% ® HOTEL

High St, Buckden PE19 5XA

☎ 01480 812300 📠 01480 813920

e-mail: mail@thegeorgebuckden.com

web: www.thegeorgebuckden.com

dir: *Just off A1 at Buckden, 2m S of A1 & A14 junct*

PETS: **Bedrooms** standard bedrooms only **Charges** £8 per night **Public areas** only in foyer area on leads **Grounds** on leads **Exercise area** 0.5m **Facilities** food bowl water bowl cage storage walks info vet info **On Request** fridge access

Ideally situated in the heart of this historic town centre and just a short drive from the A1. Public rooms feature a bustling ground-floor brasserie, which offers casual dining throughout the day and evening; there is also an informal lounge bar with an open fire and comfy seating. Bedrooms are stylish, tastefully appointed and thoughtfully equipped.

Rooms 12 (1 fmly) **S** £95-£120; **D** £120-£150 (incl. bkfst)*

Facilities STV Xmas Wi-fi **Services** Lift **Parking** 25 **Notes** LB

UFFORD	Map 4 TF00

The White Hart

★★★★ ⬭ INN

Main St PE9 3BH

☎ 01780 740250 📠 01780 740927

e-mail: info@whitehartufford.co.uk

PETS: **Bedrooms** (2 GF) unattended twin bedrooms only **Charges** £15 per night **Public areas** bar only on leads **Grounds** on leads **Exercise area** 1m **Facilities** water bowl cage storage walks info vet info **On Request** fridge access towels **Stables** 5m **Other** charge for damage

This charming inn is home to Ufford Ales which are served in the bar. The property is built from local stone and retains many of its original features. The delightful bedrooms are split between the main house and a converted block; each one is tastefully furnished and thoughtfully equipped. Public rooms include a lounge bar, conservatory and restaurant.

Rooms 6 en suite (2 GF) **S** £70-£90; **D** £80-£100 **Facilities** tea/coffee Dinner available Cen ht Wi-fi **Parking** 30

WISBECH	Map 5 TF40

Crown Lodge

★★★ 83% ® HOTEL

Downham Rd, Outwell PE14 8SE

☎ 01945 773391 & 772206 📠 01945 772668

e-mail: office@thecrownlodgehotel.co.uk

web: www.thecrownlodgehotel.co.uk

dir: *On A1122, approx 5m from Wisbech*

PETS: **Bedrooms** (10 GF) **Charges** £10 per night **Public areas** except restaurant & food preparation areas on leads **Grounds** on leads **Exercise area** approx 1m **Facilities** cage storage walks info vet info **On Request** fridge access towels **Stables** approx 1m **Other** charge for damage **Resident Pet:** Ella (Rhodesian Ridgeback)

A friendly, privately owned hotel situated in a peaceful location on the banks of Well Creek a short drive from Wisbech. The bedrooms are pleasantly decorated, have co-ordinated fabrics and modern facilities. The public areas are very stylish; they include a lounge bar, brasserie restaurant and a large seating area with plush leather sofas.

Rooms 10 (1 fmly) (10 GF) **S** £79; **D** £99 (incl. bkfst)*

Facilities FTV Squash Wi-fi **Services** Air con **Parking** 55 **Notes** LB Closed 25-26 Dec & 1 Jan

Elme Hall

★★★ 73% HOTEL

Elm High Rd PE14 0DQ

☎ 01945 475566 📠 01945 475666

e-mail: elmehallhotel@btconnect.com

web: www.elmehall.co.uk

dir: *A47 onto A1101 towards Wisbech. Hotel on right*

PETS: **Bedrooms** **Charges** £5 per night £25 per week **Public areas** except restaurant on leads **Grounds** **Facilities** cage storage walks info vet info **On Request** towels **Stables** 5m **Other** charge for damage **Restrictions** single budget bedrooms unsuitable for medium & large dogs

An imposing, Georgian-style property conveniently situated on the outskirts of the town centre just off the A47. Individually decorated bedrooms are tastefully furnished with quality reproduction pieces and equipped to a high standard. Public rooms include a choice of attractive lounges, as well as two bars, meeting rooms and a banqueting suite.

Rooms 8 (3 fmly) **S** £58-£60; **D** £78-£245 (incl. bkfst)*

Facilities FTV 🎵 Wi-fi **Parking** 200

Little Ranch Leisure *(TF456062)*

► ► ►

Begdale, Elm PE14 0AZ
☎ 01945 860066 📠 01945 860114
dir: *From rdbt on A47 (SW of Wisbech) take Redmoor Lane to Begdale*

PETS: Public areas disp bin **Exercise area on site** 10-acre orchard **Facilities** vet info

Open all year

A friendly family site set in an apple orchard, with 25 fully-serviced pitches and a beautifully designed, spacious toilet block. The site overlooks a large fishing lake, and the famous horticultural auctions at Wisbech are nearby. 10 acre site. 25 touring pitches. 25 hardstandings. Tent pitches. Motorhome pitches.

Notes 😑

CHESHIRE

AUDLEM
Map 7 SJ64

Little Heath Farm *(SJ663455)*

★ ★ ★ ★ FARMHOUSE
CW3 0HE
☎ 01270 811324 Mrs H M Bennion
e-mail: littleheath.farm@gmail.com
dir: *Off A525 in village onto A529 towards Nantwich for 0.3m. Farm opposite village green*

PETS: Bedrooms double bedroom only **Charges** £5 per night **Grounds** on leads disp bin **Exercise area** on farm **Other** charge for damage prior notice required

The 200-year-old brick farmhouse retains much original character, including low beamed ceilings. The traditionally furnished public areas include a cosy sitting room and a dining room where guests dine family style. The refurbished bedrooms are stylish, and the friendly proprietors create a relaxing atmosphere.

Rooms 3 en suite (1 fmly) **S** £30-£45; **D** £60-£70 **Facilities** TVL tea/coffee Cen ht **Parking** 6 **Notes** LB 😑 50 acres mixed

BURWARDSLEY
Map 7 SJ55

The Pheasant Inn

★ ★ ★ ★ ★ ⊜ INN

Higher Burwardsley CH3 9PF
☎ 01829 770434 📠 01829 771097
e-mail: info@thepheasantinn.co.uk
web: www.thepheasantinn.co.uk
dir: *From A41, left to Tattenhall, right at 1st junct & left at 2nd Higher Burwardsley. At post office left, signed*

PETS: Bedrooms (5 GF) unattended **Public areas** on leads **Grounds Exercise area** adjacent **Facilities** water bowl washing facs cage storage walks info vet info **On Request** fridge access torch towels

This delightful 300-year-old inn sits high on the Peckforton Hills and enjoys spectacular views over the Cheshire Plain. Well-equipped, comfortable bedrooms are housed in an adjacent converted barn. Creative dishes are served either in the stylish restaurant or in the traditional, beamed bar. Real fires are lit in the winter months.

Rooms 2 en suite 10 annexe en suite (2 fmly) (5 GF) **S** £75-£105; **D** £100-£155 **Facilities** FTV tea/coffee Dinner available Direct Dial Cen ht Wi-fi **Parking** 80

CHESTER
Map 7 SJ46

Grosvenor Pulford Hotel & Spa

★ ★ ★ ★ 74% HOTEL

Wrexham Rd, Pulford CH4 9DG
☎ 01244 570560 📠 01244 570809
e-mail: reservations@grosvenorpulfordhotel.co.uk
web: www.grosvenorpulfordhotel.co.uk
dir: *M53/A55 at junct signed A483 Chester/Wrexham & North Wales. Left onto B5445, hotel 2m on right*

PETS: Bedrooms (21 GF) unattended **Charges** £10 per stay **Public areas** except restaurant on leads **Grounds** disp bin **Exercise area** 100mtrs **Facilities** washing facs cage storage walks info vet info **On Request** fridge access torch towels

Set in rural surroundings, this modern, stylish hotel features a magnificent spa with a large Roman-style swimming pool. Among the bedrooms are several executive suites and others that have spiral staircases leading to the bedroom sections. A smart brasserie restaurant and bar provide a wide range of imaginative dishes in a relaxed atmosphere.

Rooms 73 (10 fmly) (21 GF) (6 smoking) **S** £99-£165; **D** £135-£180 (incl. bkfst)* **Facilities** Spa STV FTV 🏊 ♨ Gym Steam room Sauna Xmas New Year Wi-fi **Services** Lift **Parking** 200

CODDINGTON — Map 7 SJ45

Manor Wood Country Caravan Park
(SJ453553)

▶▶▶▶▶

Manor Wood CH3 9EN
☎ 01829 782990 & 782442 📠 01829 782990
e-mail: info@manorwoodcaravans.co.uk
dir: *From A534 at Barton, turn opposite Cock O'Barton pub signed Coddington. Left in 100yds. Site 0.5m on left*

PETS: Charges £2 per night **Public areas** except swimming pool area, play area & fishing pools disp bin **Exercise area on site** open fields adjacent **Facilities** washing facs vet info **Stables** nearby **Resident Pet:** Scooby Doo (German Shepherd)

Open all year rs Oct-May swimming pool closed Last arrival 19.00hrs Last departure 11.00hrs

A secluded landscaped park in a tranquil country setting with extensive views towards the Welsh Hills across the Cheshire Plain. This park offers fully serviced pitches, modern facilities, a heated outdoor pool and tennis courts. Wildlife is encouraged, and lake fishing with country walks and pubs are added attractions. Generous pitch density provides optimum privacy and the park is immaculately maintained, with a diligent approach to cleanliness throughout. 8 acre site. 45 touring pitches. 38 hardstandings. Tent pitches. Motorhome pitches. 12 statics.

Notes No cycles, no noise after 23.00hrs.

DELAMERE — Map 7 SJ56

Fishpool Farm Caravan Park *(SJ567672)*

▶▶▶▶

Fishpool Rd CW8 2HP
☎ 01606 883970 & 07501 506583 📠 01606 301022
e-mail: enquiries@fishpoolfarmcaravanpark.co.uk
dir: *From Tarporley take A49 towards Cuddington. Left onto B5152. Continue on B5152 (now Fishpool Rd). Site on right*

PETS: Public areas disp bin **Exercise area on site** dog walking area **Facilities** walks info vet info **Other** prior notice required dogs must be kept on leads at all times

Open 15 Feb-15 Jan Last arrival 19.00hrs Last departure mdnt
Developed on a former hay field on the owner's farm, this excellent park has a shop/reception, a superb purpose-built toilet

block with laundry facilities, a picnic area, and 50 spacious pitches, all with electric hook-up. Plans for the future include a lakeside lodge, coarse fishing and a nature walk. 5.5 acre site. 50 touring pitches. Tent pitches. Motorhome pitches.

DISLEY — Map 7 SJ98

Best Western Moorside Grange Hotel & Spa

★★★ 73% HOTEL

Mudhurst Ln, Higher Disley SK12 2AP
☎ 01663 764151 📠 01663 762794
e-mail: sales@moorsidegrangehotel.com
web: www.moorsidegrangehotel.com
dir: *Exit A6 at Rams Head in Disley, onto Buxton Old Rd for 1m, right onto Mudhurst Ln, hotel on left*

PETS: Bedrooms unattended **Charges** £10 per night **Public areas** except restaurants on leads **Grounds** disp bin **Exercise area** nearby **Facilities** water bowl scoop/disp bags walks info vet info **On Request** fridge access torch towels **Other** charge for damage

Situated on the edge of the Peak District National Park, and with spectacular views of the moors above Higher Disley, this large complex is in an area considered a walkers' paradise. The hotel has excellent conference and function facilities, a well-equipped leisure centre and two tennis courts in the extensive grounds. Suites, and bedrooms with four-poster beds, are available.

Rooms 98 (3 fmly) **Facilities** Spa ℜ supervised ⌘ Putt green Gym Squash Xmas New Year Wi-fi **Services** Lift **Parking** 250

KNUTSFORD — Map 7 SJ77

The Longview Hotel & Stuffed Olive Restaurant

★★ 81% HOTEL

55 Manchester Rd WA16 0LX
☎ 01565 632119 📠 01565 652402
e-mail: enquiries@longviewhotel.com
web: www.longviewhotel.com
dir: *M6 junct 19 take A556 W towards Chester. Left at lights onto A5033, 1.5m to rdbt then left. Hotel 200yds on right*

PETS: Bedrooms unattended premier rooms only **Charges** £10 per night **Grounds** on leads **Exercise area** across road **Facilities** vet info

This friendly Victorian hotel offers high standards of hospitality and service. Attractive public areas include a cellar bar and foyer lounge area. The restaurant has a traditional feel and offers an imaginative selection of dishes. Bedrooms, some located in a superb renovation of nearby houses, are individually styled and offer a good range of thoughtful amenities, including broadband internet access.

Rooms 32 (19 annexe) (1 fmly) (5 GF) **S** £92; **D** £112 (incl. bkfst)* **Facilities** FTV Wi-fi **Parking** 20 **Notes** LB RS 19 Dec-4 Jan

The Lymm Hotel
★★★ 73% HOTEL
Whitbarrow Rd WA13 9AQ
☎ 01925 752233   🖷 01925 756035
e-mail: general.lymm@macdonald-hotels.co.uk
web: www.macdonaldhotels.co.uk/lymm
dir: *M6 junct 20, B5158 to Lymm. Left at junct, 1st right, left at mini-rdbt, into Brookfield Rd, 3rd left into Whitbarrow Rd*

PETS: Bedrooms (11 GF) **Charges** £20 per night on leads **Grounds** on leads **Exercise area** nearby **Facilities** walks info vet info **Other** charge for damage

In a peaceful residential area, this hotel benefits from both a quiet setting and convenient access to local motorway networks. It offers comfortable bedrooms equipped for both the business and leisure guest. Public areas include an attractive bar and an elegant restaurant. There is also extensive parking.

Rooms 62 (38 annexe) (5 fmly) (11 GF) **S** £60-£95; **D** £60-£95 **Facilities** STV Xmas New Year Wi-fi **Parking** 75

Crown Hotel & Casa Brasserie
★★ 73% HOTEL
High St CW5 5AS
☎ 01270 625283   🖷 01270 628047
e-mail: info@crownhotelnantwich.com
web: www.crownhotelnantwich.com
dir: *A52 to Nantwich, hotel in town centre*

PETS: Bedrooms unattended **Public areas** except restaurant on leads **Facilities** walks info vet info **On Request** fridge access torch towels **Other** charge for damage **Resident Pet:** Bertie (Shih Tzu)

Ideally set in the heart of this historic and delightful market town, The Crown has been offering hospitality for centuries. It has an abundance of original features and the well-equipped bedrooms retain an old world charm. There is also a bar with live entertainment throughout the week and diners can enjoy Italian food in the atmospheric brasserie.

Rooms 18 (2 fmly) (1 smoking) **S** £55-£76; **D** £60-£88* **Facilities** FTV ♫ Wi-fi **Parking** 18 **Notes** Closed 25 Dec

Campanile Runcorn
BUDGET HOTEL
Lowlands Rd WA7 5TP
☎ 01928 581771   🖷 01928 581730
e-mail: runcorn@campanile.com
dir: *M56 junct 12, A557, follow signs for Runcorn rail station/ Runcorn College*

PETS: Bedrooms (18 GF) **Charges** £5 per night **Grounds** on leads **Exercise area** grassed area **Facilities** walks info vet info **On Request** fridge access towels **Other** charge for damage please phone for further details of pet facilities

This modern building offers accommodation in smart, well-equipped bedrooms, all with en suite bathrooms. Refreshments may be taken at the informal bistro.

Rooms 53 (18 GF)

Nunsmere Hall Hotel
★★★★ ❀❀ COUNTRY HOUSE HOTEL
Tarporley Rd CW8 2ES
☎ 01606 889100   🖷 01606 889055
e-mail: reception@nunsmere.co.uk
web: www.nunsmere.co.uk
dir: *M6 junct 18, A54 to Chester, at x-rds with A49 turn left towards Tarporley, hotel 2m on left*

PETS: Bedrooms (2 GF) unattended ground-floor bedrooms only **Grounds** on leads **Facilities** walks info vet info **On Request** fridge access torch towels **Stables** 0.5m **Other** charge for damage **Resident Pet:** Fritz (Black Labrador)

In an idyllic and peaceful setting of well-kept grounds, including a 60-acre lake, this delightful house dates back to 1900. Spacious bedrooms are individually styled, tastefully appointed to a very high standard and thoughtfully equipped. Guests can relax in the elegant lounges, the library or the oak-panelled bar. Dining in the Crystal Restaurant is a highlight and both a traditional carte and a gourmet menu are offered.

Rooms 36 (2 GF) **Facilities** 🖙 Xmas New Year Wi-fi **Services** Lift **Parking** 80

ENGLAND

The Bear's Paw

★★★★★ ● INN

School Ln CW11 3QN
☎ 01270 526317
e-mail: info@thebearspaw.co.uk
web: www.thebearspaw.co.uk
dir: *M6 junct 17 onto A534/A533 signed Middlewich/Northwich. Continue on A533, left onto Mill Ln, left onto Warmingham Ln. Right onto Plant Ln, left onto Green Ln*

PETS: Bedrooms unattended **Charges** £10 per night
Public areas except restaurant on leads **Grounds**
Exercise area adjacent **Facilities** food bowl water bowl washing facs walks info vet info **On Request** fridge access
Stables 10m **Other** charge for damage

Located beside a small river in a rural Cheshire village, this 19th-century inn, provides very comfortable and well equipped boutique bedrooms with a wealth of thoughtful and practical extras. A friendly team deliver imaginative food, utilising quality seasonal produce, in an attractive open-plan dining room, and a choice of sumptuous lounge areas is also available.

Rooms 17 en suite (4 fmly) **S** £79-£120; **D** £99-£140
Facilities STV FTV tea/coffee Dinner available Direct Dial Cen ht
Wi-fi **Parking** 75 **Notes** LB

The Park Royal

 OHOTELS

★★★★ 78% HOTEL

Stretton Rd, Stretton WA4 4NS
☎ 01925 730706   🖹 01925 730740
e-mail: parkroyalreservations@qhotels.co.uk
web: www.qhotels.co.uk
dir: *M56 junct 10, A49 to Warrington, at lights turn right to Appleton Thorn, 1st right into Spark Hall Close, hotel on left*

PETS: Bedrooms (34 GF) **Charges Grounds** on leads **Facilities**
walks info vet info **On Request** torch **Stables** 2m **Other** charge for damage **Restrictions** small dogs only

This modern hotel enjoys a peaceful setting, yet is conveniently located just minutes from the M56. The bedrooms are modern in style and thoughtfully equipped. Spacious, stylish public areas include extensive conference and function facilities, and a comprehensive leisure centre complete with outdoor tennis courts and an impressive beauty centre.

Rooms 146 (32 fmly) (34 GF) **Facilities** Spa FTV 🔲 🏊 Gym Dance studio Xmas New Year Wi-fi **Services** Lift **Parking** 400

Holiday Inn Warrington

★★★ 73% HOTEL

Woolston Grange Av, Woolston WA1 4PX
☎ 0871 942 9087   🖹 01925 838859
e-mail: nicola.crowley@ihg.com
web: www.holidayinn.co.uk
dir: *M6 junct 21, follow signs for Birchwood*

PETS: Bedrooms (9 GF) **Charges** £10 per night **Grounds** on leads **Exercise area** nearby **Facilities** cage storage walks info vet info **On Request** fridge access towels **Other** charge for damage

Ideally located within the M62 and M56 interchange, this hotel provides the ideal base for all areas of the north-west region for both corporate and leisure guests. Rooms are spacious and well equipped, and a wide choice of meals is available in the comfortable restaurant and cosy bar. Meeting and conference facilities are also available.

Rooms 96 (26 fmly) (9 GF) **Facilities** STV Xmas New Year Wi-fi **Services** Lift Air con **Parking** 101

 VENTURE HOTELS

Paddington House

★★ 74% HOTEL

514 Old Manchester Rd WA1 3TZ
☎ 01925 816767   🖹 01925 816651
e-mail: hotel@paddingtonhouse.co.uk
web: www.paddingtonhouse.co.uk
dir: *1m from M6 junct 21, off A57, 2m from town centre*

PETS: Bedrooms (6 GF) unattended **Charges** £5 per night
Public areas Grounds on leads disp bin **Exercise area** nearby
Facilities water bowl vet info **On Request** fridge access towels
Other charge for damage **Restrictions** no large dogs

This busy, friendly hotel is conveniently situated just over a mile from the M6. Bedrooms are attractively furnished, and include four-poster and ground-floor rooms. Guests can dine in the wood-panelled Padgate Restaurant or in the cosy bar. Conference and function facilities are available.

Rooms 37 (9 fmly) (6 GF) (6 smoking) **Facilities** FTV New Year Wi-fi **Services** Lift **Parking** 50 **Notes** LB

New Farm Caravan Park *(SJ613608)*

▶ ▶ ▶

Long Ln CW7 4DW
☎ 01270 528213 & 07970 221112
e-mail: info@newfarmcheshire.com
dir: *A51 Alpraham near Tarpoley, signed*

PETS: Public areas Exercise area fields for dog walking
Facilities vet info **Other** prior notice required **Resident
Pets:** dogs

Open all year Last arrival 20.00hrs Last departure 14.00hrs

Diversification at New Farm has seen the development of
four fishing lakes, quality AA-listed B&B accommodation in a
converted milking parlour, and the creation of a peaceful small
touring park. The proprietors are to be commended for their
investment to provide a very welcome touring destination within
this peaceful part of Cheshire. Expect good landscaping, 17
generous hardstanding pitches, a spotless toilet block, and good
attention to detail throughout. Please note there is no laundry.
40 acre site. 24 touring pitches. 17 hardstandings. Motorhome
pitches.

Lamb Cottage Caravan Park *(SJ613692)*

▶ ▶ ▶ ▶ ▶

Dalefords Ln CW8 2BN
☎ 01606 882302 📠 01606 888491
e-mail: info@lambcottage.co.uk
dir: *From A556 turn at Sandiway lights into Dalefords Ln, signed
Winsford. Site 1m on right*

PETS: Charges dog £1 per night **Public areas** disp bin
Exercise area on site dog walking area **Facilities** walks info
vet info **Other** prior notice required dogs must be kept on short
leads **Resident Pets:** 2 dogs, 3 cats, 4 horses

Open Mar-Oct Last arrival 20.00hrs Last departure noon

A secluded and attractively landscaped adults-only park in a
glorious location where the emphasis is on peace and relaxation.
The serviced pitches are spacious with wide grass borders for
sitting out and the high quality toilet block is spotlessly clean
and immaculately maintained. A good central base for exploring
this area, with access to nearby woodland walks and cycle trails.
6 acre site. 45 touring pitches. 45 hardstandings. 14 seasonal
pitches. Motorhome pitches. 26 statics.

Notes No tents (except trailer tents), no commercial vehicles.

Lea Farm *(SJ717489)*

★ ★ ★ FARMHOUSE

Wrinehill Rd CW5 7NS
☎ 01270 841429   Mrs J E Callwood
e-mail: leafarm@hotmail.co.uk
dir: *1m E of Wybunbury church on unclassified road*

PETS: Bedrooms Sep accom outdoor kennel, barns **Charges** £2
per night **Public areas** except dining room **Grounds** on leads
disp bin **Exercise area** adjacent **Facilities** food bowl water
bowl bedding feeding mat washing facs cage storage walks
info vet info **On Request** fridge access torch towels **Stables
Other** charge for damage **Resident Pets:** Lucy (Collie), peacocks

This working dairy farm is surrounded by delightful gardens and
beautiful Cheshire countryside. The spacious bedrooms have
modern facilities and there is a cosy lounge. Hearty breakfasts
are served in the attractive dining room, which looks out over the
garden with its resident peacocks.

Rooms 3 rms (2 en suite) (1 fmly) **S** £30-£35; **D** £50-£60
Facilities FTV TVL tea/coffee Cen ht Fishing Pool table **Parking** 24
Notes ⊛ 150 acres dairy/beef

ASHTON — Map 2 SW62

Boscrege Caravan & Camping Park
(SW595305)

►►►

TR13 9TG
☎ 01736 762231   📄 01736 762152
e-mail: enquiries@caravanparkcornwall.com
dir: *From Helston on A394 turn right in Ashton by Post Office into lane. Site in 1.5m, signed*

PETS: Charges £2 per night £14 per week **Public areas** on leads disp bin **Exercise area on site** 6-acre meadow **Exercise area** 200yds **Facilities** walks info vet info **Other** prior notice required **Resident Pets:** Ozzy (German Shepherd), Molly, Topsey, Tilly & Ginge (cats), 12 chickens

Open Mar-Nov Last arrival 22.00hrs Last departure 11.00hrs

A quiet and bright little touring park divided into small paddocks with hedges, and offering plenty of open spaces for children to play in. The family-owned park offers clean, well-painted and refurbished toilets facilities and neatly trimmed grass. In an Area of Outstanding Natural Beauty at the foot of Tregonning Hill. 14 acre site. 50 touring pitches. Tent pitches. Motorhome pitches. 26 statics.

BLACKWATER — Map 2 SW74

Chiverton Park *(SW743468)*

►►►►

East Hill TR4 8HS
☎ 01872 560667 & 07789 377169
e-mail: chivertonpark@btopenworld.com
dir: *Exit A30 at Chiverton rdbt (Starbucks) onto unclass road signed Blackwater (3rd exit). 1st right, site 300mtrs on right*

PETS: Charges £2.50 per night £15 per week **Public areas** except children's play area, shop, reception & toilet block disp bin **Facilities** dog chews walks info vet info **Other** prior notice required **Resident Pet:** Henry (Chocolate Labrador)

Open 3 Mar-3 Nov Last arrival 21.00hrs Last departure noon

A small, well-maintained site with some mature hedges dividing pitches, sited midway between Truro and St Agnes. Facilities include a good toilet block and a steam room, sauna and gym. A games room with pool table, and children's outside play equipment prove popular with families. 4 acre site. 12 touring pitches. 10 hardstandings. Tent pitches. Motorhome pitches. 50 statics.

Notes No ball games.

BODMIN — Map 2 SX06

Trehellas House Hotel & Restaurant
★★★ 74% ◉ SMALL HOTEL
Washaway PL30 3AD
☎ 01208 72700   📄 01208 73336
e-mail: enquiries@trehellashouse.co.uk
web: www.trehellashouse.co.uk
dir: *A389 from Bodmin towards Wadebridge. Hotel on right 0.5m beyond road to Camelford*

PETS: Bedrooms (5 GF) unattended cottage rooms only **Grounds** disp bin **Exercise area** nearby **Facilities** food bowl water bowl leads washing facs cage storage walks info vet info **On Request** fridge access torch towels **Resident Pets:** Bonnie & Clyde (Chocolate Labradors)

This 18th-century former posting inn retains many original features and provides comfortable accommodation. Bedrooms are located in both the main house and adjacent coach house - all provide the same high standards. An interesting choice of cuisine, with an emphasis on locally-sourced ingredients, is offered in the impressive slate-floored restaurant.

Rooms 12 (7 annexe) (2 fmly) (5 GF) **S** £50-£70; **D** £50-£170 (incl. bkfst)* **Facilities** FTV ⬆ Xmas New Year Wi-fi **Parking** 32 **Notes** LB

Westberry
★★ 81% HOTEL
Rhind St PL31 2EL
☎ 01208 72772   📄 01208 72212
e-mail: westberry@btconnect.com
web: www.westberryhotel.net
dir: *On ring road off A30 & A38. St Petroc's Church on right, at mini rdbt turn right. Hotel on right*

PETS: Bedrooms (6 GF) unattended sign courtyard bedrooms only **Charges** £10 per night **Grounds** on leads disp bin **Exercise area** 300yds **Facilities** food bowl water bowl litter tray scoop/disp bags cage storage walks info vet info **On Request** fridge access **Other** charge for damage

This popular hotel is conveniently located for both Bodmin town centre and the A30. The bedrooms are attractive and well equipped. A spacious bar lounge and a billiard room are also provided. The restaurant serves a variety of dishes, ranging from bar snacks to a more extensive carte menu.

Rooms 20 (8 annexe) (2 fmly) (6 GF) **Facilities** STV Full sized snooker table Wi-fi **Parking** 30 **Notes** LB

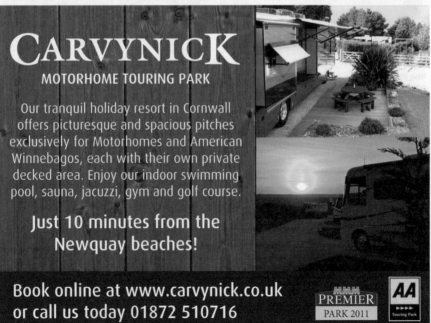

ENGLAND

Mount Pleasant Farm

★★★ GUEST ACCOMMODATION

Mount PL30 4EX

☎ 01208 821342

e-mail: info@mountpleasantcottages.co.uk

dir: *A30 from Bodmin towards Launceston for 4m, right signed Millpool, continue 3m*

PETS: Bedrooms Public areas except dining area on leads **Grounds** on leads disp bin **Exercise area** moorland adjacent **Facilities** pet sitting dog walking washing facs cage storage walks info vet info **On Request** fridge access torch towels **Other** no charge for pets in B&B; £10 per week in cottage **Resident Pets:** Poppy, Penny & Molley (Springer Spaniels), Toffee (cat), Happy & Misty (horses)

Set in 10 acres, this is a wonderfully peaceful base from which to explore the delights of Cornwall. Originally a farmhouse dating back to the 17th century, there is something here for all the family with extensive facilities including a games barn and heated swimming pool. Cosy bedrooms are well furnished, while public areas include a spacious sun lounge and extensive gardens. Breakfast, served in the well-appointed dining room, features local produce and is the highlight of any stay; home-cooked evening meals are available by prior arrangement.

Rooms 6 en suite (3 fmly) **S** £32-£42; **D** £54-£74 **Facilities** FTV TVL tea/coffee Dinner available Cen ht ⓢ Pool table **Parking** 8 **Notes** LB ⊛

Mena Caravan & Camping Park *(SW041626)*

▶ ▶ ▶

PL30 5HW

☎ 01208 831845 📠 01208 831845

e-mail: mena@campsitesincornwall.co.uk

dir: *Exit A30 onto A389 N signed Lanivet & Wadebridge. In 0.5m 1st right & pass under A30. 1st left signed Lostwithiel & Fowey. In 0.25m right at top of hill. 0.5m then 1st right. Entrance 100yds on right*

PETS: Charges £1-£2 per night £7-£14 per week **Public areas** disp bin **Exercise area on site** adjacent fields & woods (11 acres) **Facilities** food food bowl water bowl dog chews leads washing facs walks info vet info **Other** kennels & dog friendly beach nearby, guides available; disposal bags available **Resident Pets:** Molly (Springer Spaniel), Jess (Labrador cross), Daisy (Labrador), Thomas, George, Mildred & Ruby (cats), Rodney & Del (Kune Kune pigs)

Open all year Last arrival 22.00hrs Last departure noon

Set in a secluded, elevated location with high hedges for shelter, and plenty of peace. This grassy site is about four miles from the Eden Project and midway between the north and south Cornish coasts. There is a small coarse fishing lake on site. 15 acre site. 25 touring pitches. 4 hardstandings. Tent pitches. Motorhome pitches. 2 statics.

Colliford Tavern Campsite *(SX171740)*

▶ ▶ ▶

Colliford Lake, St Neot PL14 6PZ

☎ 01208 821335 📠 01208 821661

e-mail: info@colliford.com

dir: *Exit A30 1.25m W of Bolventor onto unclass road signed Colliford Lake. Site 0.25m on left*

PETS: Charges £1 per night **Public areas** except bar & restaurant on leads disp bin **Exercise area on site** dog walking area **Facilities** washing facs walks info vet info **Other** dogs must be kept on leads at all times

Open all year Last arrival 22.00hrs Last departure 11.00hrs

An oasis on Bodmin Moor, a small site with spacious grassy pitches, and the advantage of a comfortable lounge bar and restaurant in the tavern. Attractions for children are greatly enhanced by the merger of the site with the neighbouring children's play park. 3.5 acre site. 40 touring pitches. 8 hardstandings. Tent pitches. Motorhome pitches.

Hell Bay Hotel

★★★ ◎◎◎ HOTEL

TR23 0PR
☎ 01720 422947 📠 01720 423004
e-mail: contactus@hellbay.co.uk
web: www.hellbay.co.uk
dir: *Access by helicopter or boat from Penzance, plane from Bristol, Exeter, Newquay, Southampton or Land's End*

PETS: Bedrooms (15 GF) unattended Charges £12 per night Public areas except bar & lounge Grounds on leads disp bin Exercise area public coastal path adjacent Facilities food bowl water bowl bedding feeding mat cage storage walks info vet info On Request fridge access torch towels Resident Pet: Suzie (Springer Spaniel)

Located on the smallest of the inhabited islands of the Scilly Isles on the edge of the Atlantic, this hotel makes a really special destination. The owners have filled the hotel with original works of art by artists who have connections with the islands, and the interior is decorated in cool blues and greens creating an extremely restful environment. The contemporary bedrooms are equally stylish and many have garden access and stunning sea views. Eating here is a delight, and naturally, seafood features strongly on the award-winning, daily-changing menus.

Rooms 25 (25 annexe) (3 fmly) (15 GF) S £200-£600; D £320-£600 (incl. bkfst & dinner) Facilities STV FTV ₹ ↓7 ④ Gym Wi-fi Notes LB Closed Nov-Feb

Hotel Penarvor

★★ 74% SMALL HOTEL

Crooklets Beach EX23 8NE
☎ 01288 352036 📠 01288 355027
e-mail: stay@hotelpenarvor.co.uk
dir: *A39 towards Bude for 1.5m. At 2nd rdbt turn right, pass shops. Top of hill, left signed Crooklets Beach*

PETS: Bedrooms (3 GF) certain bedrooms only Charges £7 per night Public areas except restaurant on leads Grounds on leads disp bin Exercise area 50yds Facilities vet info On Request fridge access Other charge for damage Resident Pets: Bonnie (Old English/Border Collie cross), Charlie (Cocker Spaniel)

Adjacent to the golf course and overlooking Crooklets Beach, this family owned hotel has a relaxed and friendly atmosphere. Bedrooms vary in size but are all equipped to a similar standard. An interesting selection of dishes, using fresh local produce, is available in the restaurant; bar meals are also provided.

Rooms 16 (6 fmly) (3 GF) S £37-£43; D £74-£86 (incl. bkfst)* Facilities FTV Wi-fi Parking 20 Notes LB Closed 24-28 Dec

The Cliff at Bude

★★★★ GUEST HOUSE

Maer Down, Crooklets Beach EX23 8NG
☎ 01288 353110 & 356833 📠 01288 353110
e-mail: cliff_hotel@btconnect.com
web: www.cliffhotel.co.uk
dir: *A39 through Bude, left at top of High St, pass Sainsburys, 1st right between golf course, over x-rds, premises at end on right*

PETS: Bedrooms (8 GF) unattended sign Charges £2.75 per night Public areas except restaurant & lounge on leads Grounds on leads disp bin Exercise area adjacent to hotel Facilities pet sitting washing facs cage storage walks info vet info On Request torch Stables 2m Other charge for damage Resident Pets: Janus & Crystal (Boxers), 10 rabbits

Overlooking the sea from a clifftop location, this friendly and efficient establishment provides spacious, well-equipped bedrooms. The various public areas include a bar and lounge and an impressive range of leisure facilities. Delicious dinners and tasty breakfasts are available in the attractive dining room.

Rooms 15 en suite (15 fmly) (8 GF) S £39.95-£44.95; D £79.90-£89.90 Facilities FTV TVL tea/coffee Dinner available Direct Dial Cen ht Licensed ③ ⊇ ↓ Gym Pool table Parking 18 Notes LB Closed Nov-Mar

BUDE *continued*

Budemeadows Touring Park *(SS215012)*

▶ ▶ ▶ ▶

Widemouth Bay EX23 0NA
☎ 01288 361646   ▤ 0870 7064825
e-mail: holiday@budemeadows.com
dir: *3m S of Bude on A39. Follow signs after turn to Widemouth Bay. Site accessed via layby*

PETS: Charges £1.50-£2.50 per night **Public areas** except pool & playground disp bin **Exercise area** beach 1m, lane, public footpaths 100mtrs **Facilities** food food bowl water bowl scoop/disp bags walks info vet info **Other** prior notice required max 2 dogs per pitch in high season disposal bags available

Open all year rs mid Sep-late May shop, bar & pool closed Last arrival 21.00hrs Last departure 11.00hrs

A very well kept site of distinction, with good quality facilities, hardstandings and eight fully-serviced pitches. Budemeadows is set on a gentle sheltered slope in acres of naturally landscaped parkland, surrounded by mature hedges. Just one mile from Widemouth Bay, and three miles from the unspoilt resort of Bude. 9 acre site. 145 touring pitches. 24 hardstandings. Tent pitches. Motorhome pitches.

Notes No noise after 23.00hrs.

Willow Valley Holiday Park *(SS236078)*

▶ ▶ ▶ ▶

Bush EX23 9LB
☎ 01288 353104
e-mail: willowvalley@talk21.com
dir: *On A39, 0.5m N of junct with A3072 at Stratton*

PETS: Charges Public areas except children's park disp bin **Exercise area on site** field available **Facilities** vet info **Other** prior notice required max 2 dogs per pitch; dogs must be kept on leads at all times

Open Mar-end Oct Last arrival 21.00hrs Last departure 11.00hrs

A small sheltered park in the Strat Valley with level grassy pitches and a stream running through it. The friendly family owners have improved all areas of this attractive park, including a smart toilet block and a reception/shop. The park has direct access off the A39, and is only two miles from the sandy beaches at Bude. There are four pine lodges for holiday hire. 4 acre site. 41 touring pitches. Tent pitches. Motorhome pitches. 4 statics.

Notes ⊛

Juliot's Well Holiday Park *(SX095829)*

▶ ▶ ▶ ▶

PL32 9RF
☎ 01840 213302   ▤ 01840 212700
e-mail: holidays@juliotswell.com
dir: *Through Camelford, A39 at Valley Truckle turn right onto B3266, then 1st left signed Lanteglos, site 300yds on right*

PETS: Charges £5 per night £30 per week **Public areas** except swimming pool & children's play area disp bin **Exercise area on site** fields, walks around lake **Facilities** food walks info vet info **Other** prior notice required pet shop in town, 1m **Resident Pets:** Rambo (Greyhound), Riley (Labrador)

Open all year Last arrival 20.00hrs Last departure 11.00hrs

Set in the wooded grounds of an old manor house, this quiet site enjoys lovely and extensive views across the countryside. A rustic inn on site offers occasional entertainment, and there is plenty to do, both on the park and in the vicinity. The superb, fully-serviced toilet facilities are very impressive. There are also self-catering pine lodges, static caravans and five cottages. 33 acre site. 39 touring pitches. Tent pitches. Motorhome pitches. 82 statics.

Lakefield Caravan Park *(SX095853)*

▶ ▶ ▶

Lower Pendavey Farm PL32 9TX
☎ 01840 213279
e-mail: lakefieldcaravanpark@btconnect.com
dir: *From A39 in Camelford turn right onto B3266, then right at T-junct, site 1.5m on left*

PETS: Charges stabling £20 per night **Public areas** **Exercise area on site** 5-acre field **Facilities** washing facs vet info **Stables Other** prior notice required full equestrian facilities on site **Resident Pets:** Mo (Border Collie), Bill & Luna (Border Terriers), Spock (Papillon cross), Puss-Puss (cat), 40 horses

Open Etr or Apr-Sep Last arrival 22.00hrs Last departure 11.00hrs

Set in a rural location, this friendly park is part of a specialist equestrian centre, and offers good quality services. Riding lessons and hacks always available, with a BHS qualified instructor. 5 acre site. 40 touring pitches. Tent pitches. Motorhome pitches.

Carlyon Bay Caravan & Camping Park

(SX052526)

▶▶▶▶▶

Bethesda, Cypress Av PL25 3RE
☎ 01726 812735　📠 01726 815496
e-mail: holidays@carlyonbay.net
dir: *Off A390 W of St Blazey, left onto A3092 for Par, right in 0.5m. On private road to Carlyon Bay*

PETS: Charges £3 per night　**Public areas** disp bin
Exercise area on site　Facilities food　food bowl　water bowl　dog chews　scoop/disp bags　leads　walks info　vet info　**Other** prior notice required　**Restrictions** no Pit Bull Terriers, Rottweilers or Akitas; no dangerous dogs (see page 7)

Open Etr-3 Oct rs Etr-mid May & mid Sep-3 Oct swimming pool, takeaway & shop closed; Jul-Aug only - children's entertainment Last arrival 21.00hrs Last departure 11.00hrs

An attractive, secluded site set amongst a belt of trees with background woodland. The spacious grassy park is beautifully landscaped and offers quality toilet and shower facilities together with plenty of on-site attractions, including a well-equipped games room, TV room, café, an inviting swimming pool, and occasional family entertainment. It is less than half a mile from a sandy beach and the Eden Project is only two miles away. 35 acre site. 180 touring pitches. 12 hardstandings. Tent pitches. Motorhome pitches.

Notes No noise after 23.00hrs.

East Crinnis Camping & Caravan Park

(SX062528)

▶▶▶

Lantyan, East Crinnis PL24 2SQ
☎ 01726 813023　& 07950 614780　📠 01726 813023
e-mail: eastcrinnis@btconnect.com
dir: *From A390 (Lostwithiel to St Austell) take A3082 signed Fowey at rdbt by Britannia Inn, site on left*

PETS: Charges £1.50 per night　£10 per week　**Public areas** except children's play area & shower block on leads　disp bin　**Exercise area on site** wildlife area with large pond
Exercise area South West Coastal Path　**Facilities** food bowl　washing facs　walks info　vet info　**Other** prior notice required　disposal bags, ball thrower available **Resident Pets:** Alfie (Labrador), Bonnie (working Collie), Lola (Retriever), Elsa (Rhodesian Ridgeback)

Open Etr-Oct Last arrival 21.00hrs Last departure 11.00hrs

A small rural park with spacious pitches set in individual bays about one mile from the beaches at Carlyon Bay, and just two miles from the Eden Project. The friendly owners keep the site very clean and well maintained and also offer three self-catering holiday lodges. 2 acre site. 25 touring pitches. 6 hardstandings. Tent pitches. Motorhome pitches. 2 bell tents/yurts.

Lavender Fields Touring Park *(SW623377)*

▶▶▶

Penhale Rd TR14 0LU
☎ 01209 832188　& 07855 227773
e-mail: info@lavenderfieldstouring.co.uk
dir: *Exit A30 at Camborne W junct. At top of slip road left at rdbt, 2nd exit through Roseworthy, left after Roseworthy signed Carnhell Green, over level crossing to T-junct, turn left. Site 750yds on right*

PETS: Public areas disp bin　**Exercise area on site** enclosed area (0.25 acre)　**Exercise area** bridlepath (50yds)　**Facilities** washing facs　walks info　vet info　**Other** pet shower; dogs must be kept on leads at all times　pet supply shop within walking distance **Resident Pets:** Troy & Jessica (German Shepherds)

Open all year Last arrival 21.00hrs Last departure 10.00hrs

A family owned and run park in the heart of the Cornish countryside on the outskirts of the idyllic village of Carnhell Green, yet only a short car or bus ride to glorious golden beaches and towns. Developed on an old mine waste site, the park is maturing well and has some good hardstandings for larger units. Dogs are very welcome here. 5 acre site. 45 touring pitches. 21 hardstandings. 5 seasonal pitches. Tent pitches. Motorhome pitches.

Wringford Down

★★★ GUEST ACCOMMODATION
Hat Ln PL10 1LE
☎ 01752 822287
e-mail: andrew@wringford.co.uk
dir: *A374 onto B3247, pass Millbrook, right towards Cawsand & sharp right, 0.5m on right*

PETS: Bedrooms (5 GF) bedrooms with direct outdoor access only　**Charges** £5 per night £35 per week　**Grounds** on leads　disp bin　**Exercise area** many walks adjacent　**Facilities** washing facs　cage storage　walks info　vet info　**On Request** fridge access　torch　towels　**Stables** 0.5m　**Other** charge for damage　paddock available for horses, please phone for details　**Restrictions** no dangerous dogs (see page 7) **Resident Pets:** Daisy (Golden Retriever), Dotty (Springer Spaniel), Baby (cat), Sylvester, Truffle & Toffee (ponies), ducks & peacocks

This family-run establishment has a peaceful location near Rame Head and the South West Coast Path, and is particularly welcoming to families. There is a nursery, swimming pool, games room, and gardens with play areas. A range of bedrooms, suites and self-catering units is available. Breakfast is served in the spacious dining room.

Rooms 5 en suite 2 annexe en suite (4 fmly) (5 GF) **S** £46-£61; **D** £72-£102 **Facilities** FTV TVL tea/coffee Cen ht Licensed Wi-fi 🕙 ⚓ Golf 18 Pool table **Parking** 20 **Notes** LB

ENGLAND

Little Trevothan Caravan & Camping Park
(SW772179)

► ► ►

Trevothan TR12 6SD
☎ 01326 280260
e-mail: sales@littletrevothan.co.uk
dir: *A3083 onto B3293 signed Coverack, approx 2m after Goonhilly ESS, right at Zoar Garage onto unclass road. Approx 1m, 3rd left. Site 0.5m on left*

PETS: Charges £1.50 per night **Public areas** except children's play areas & horse field on leads disp bin **Exercise area on site** fenced area **Exercise area** 0.75m **Facilities** washing facs walks info vet info **Other** prior notice required **Restrictions** no Rottweilers or Pit Bull Terriers **Resident Pets:** 2 Weimaraners, 2 cats, 1 horse

Open Mar-Oct Last arrival 21.00hrs Last departure noon

A secluded site near the unspoilt fishing village of Coverack, with a large recreation area. The nearby sandy beach has lots of rock pools for children to play in, and the many walks both from the park and the village offer stunning scenery. 10.5 acre site. 70 touring pitches. 10 hardstandings. Tent pitches. Motorhome pitches. 40 statics.

Notes 😊

Crantock Plains Touring Park *(SW805589)*

► ► ►

TR8 5PH
☎ 01637 830955 & 07967 956897
e-mail: matthew-milburn@btconnect.com
dir: *Exit Newquay on A3075, 2nd right signed to park & Crantock. Site on left in 0.75m on narrow road*

PETS: Charges £1.20 per night **Public areas** disp bin **Exercise area on site Facilities** walks info vet info **Other** prior notice required dogs must be kept on leads at all times

Open Last arrival 22.00hrs Last departure noon

A small rural park with pitches on either side of a narrow lane, surrounded by mature trees for shelter. This spacious, family-run park has good modern toilet facilities and is ideal for campers who appreciate peace and quiet and is situated approximately 1.2 miles from pretty Crantock, and Newquay is within easy reach. 6 acre site. 60 touring pitches. 20 seasonal pitches. Tent pitches. Motorhome pitches.

Notes No skateboards.

Cottage Farm Touring Park *(SW786589)*

► ► ►

Treworgans TR8 5HH
☎ 01637 831083
dir: *From A392 towards Newquay, left onto A3075 towards Redruth. In 2m right signed Cubert, right again in 1.5m signed Crantock, left in 0.5m*

PETS: Charges £1.50 per night **Public areas** disp bin **Exercise area** country lane adjacent **Facilities** washing facs walks info vet info **Other** prior notice required disposal bags available **Resident Pets:** 1 Jack Russell, 1 cat

Open Apr-end Sep Last arrival 22.30hrs Last departure noon

A small grassy touring park nestling in the tiny hamlet of Treworgans, in sheltered open countryside close to a lovely beach at Holywell Bay. This quiet family-run park boasts very good quality facilities. 2 acre site. 45 touring pitches. 2 hardstandings. Tent pitches. Motorhome pitches. 1 static.

Notes No noise after 23.00hrs

Best Western Falmouth Beach Hotel

★ ★ ★ **78%** HOTEL
Gyllyngvase Beach, Seafront TR11 4NA
☎ 01326 310500 📠 01326 319147
e-mail: info@falmouthbeachhotel.co.uk
web: www.bw-falmouthbeachhotel.co.uk
dir: *A39 to Falmouth, follow seafront signs*

PETS: Bedrooms (4 GF) unattended **Charges** £10 per night **Public areas** in conservatory only on leads **Grounds** on leads **Exercise area** dog field (300yds) **Facilities** walks info vet info **On Request** fridge access

Enjoying wonderful views, this popular hotel is situated opposite the beach and within easy walking distance of Falmouth's attractions and port. A friendly atmosphere is maintained and guests have a good choice of leisure, fitness, entertainment and dining options. Bedrooms, many with balconies and sea views, are well equipped and comfortable.

Rooms 120 (20 fmly) (4 GF) **Facilities** Spa FTV 🕙 supervised ⛳ Gym Sauna Steam room Hair & beauty salon 🎵 Xmas New Year Wi-fi **Services** Lift **Parking** 88

Falmouth

★★★ 77% ◉ HOTEL

Castle Beach TR11 4NZ

☎ 01326 312671 & 0800 019 3121 📠 01326 319533

e-mail: reservations@falmouthhotel.com

web: www.falmouthhotel.com

dir: *A30 to Truro then A390 to Falmouth. Follow signs for beaches, hotel on seafront near Pendennis Castle*

PETS: Bedrooms unattended **Charges** £10 per night **Grounds** on leads **Exercise area** beach (winter only) & countryside **Facilities** walks info vet info **On Request** fridge access torch towels **Other** charge for damage

This spectacular beach-front Victorian property affords wonderful sea views from many of its comfortable bedrooms, some of which have their own balconies. Spacious public areas include a number of inviting lounges, a choice of dining options and an impressive range of leisure facilities.

Rooms 70 (16 fmly) **Facilities** Spa FTV ⊗ Putt green Gym Beauty salon & Therapeutic rooms ♫ Xmas New Year Wi-fi **Services** Lift **Parking** 120

THE INDEPENDENTS
HOTEL ASSOCIATION

Green Lawns

★★★ 77% HOTEL

Western Ter TR11 4QJ

☎ 01326 312734 📠 01326 211427

e-mail: info@greenlawnshotel.com

web: www.greenlawnshotel.com

dir: *On A39*

PETS: Bedrooms (11 GF) unattended **Charges** £12.50 per night **Exercise area** 0.25m **Facilities** cage storage walks info vet info **On Request** fridge access torch towels **Stables** 6m **Restrictions** no large dogs

This attractive property enjoys a convenient location close to the town centre and within easy reach of the sea. Spacious public areas include inviting lounges, an elegant restaurant, conference and meeting facilities and a leisure centre. Bedrooms vary in size and style but all are well equipped and comfortable. The friendly service is particularly noteworthy.

Rooms 39 (8 fmly) (11 GF) **S** £60-£70; **D** £109-£189 (incl. bkfst)* **Facilities** FTV ⊗ ♨ Gym Squash Sauna Steam room Spa bath New Year Wi-fi **Parking** 69 **Notes** LB Closed 24-30 Dec

Penmorvah Manor

★★★ 72% HOTEL

Budock Water TR11 5ED

☎ 01326 250277 📠 01326 250509

e-mail: reception@penmorvah.co.uk

web: www.penmorvah.co.uk

dir: *A39 to Hillhead rdbt, take 2nd exit. Right at Falmouth Football Club, through Budock. Hotel opposite Penjerrick Gardens*

PETS: Bedrooms (10 GF) **Charges** £7.50 per night **Public areas** except restaurant on leads **Grounds** disp bin **Exercise area** nearby **Facilities** water bowl cage storage vet info **On Request** torch towels **Resident Pet:** Millie (Cocker Spaniel)

Situated within two miles of central Falmouth, this extended Victorian manor house is a peaceful hideaway, set in six acres of private woodland and gardens. Penmorvah is well positioned for visiting the local gardens, and offers many garden-tour breaks. Dinner features locally sourced, quality ingredients such as Cornish cheeses, meat, fish and game.

Rooms 27 (1 fmly) (10 GF) **S** fr £55; **D** £105-£160 (incl. bkfst)* **Facilities** FTV Xmas Wi-fi **Parking** 100 **Notes** LB Closed 31 Dec-Jan

The Tudor Court

★★★ GUEST HOUSE

55 Melvill Rd TR11 4DF

☎ 01326 312807

e-mail: enquiries@tudorcourthotel.com

dir: *A39 to Falmouth straight through Dracaena Av, onto Melvill Road. Tudor Court 300yds on right*

PETS: Bedrooms unattended sign **Charges** £2 per night **Public areas** lounge/bar only **Grounds** on leads disp bin **Exercise area** 10 mins **Facilities** walks info vet info **On Request** fridge access torch towels **Other** charge for damage

This mock Tudor establishment offers bright, well-equipped bedrooms, some having the benefit of distant sea views. A comfortable bar/lounge is available for guests and in the dining room, which overlooks the attractive garden, a freshly cooked, full English breakfast is served.

Rooms 10 rms (9 en suite) (1 pri facs) (1 fmly) **S** £30-£45; **D** £60-£80 **Facilities** FTV TVL tea/coffee Cen ht Licensed Wi-fi **Parking** 10 **Notes** LB

FALMOUTH *continued*

Eden Lodge
★★ GUEST HOUSE
54 Melvill Rd TR11 4DQ
☎ 01326 212989 & 07715 696218
e-mail: edenlodge@hotmail.co.uk
dir: *On A39, on left 200yds past Fox Rosehill Gardens*

PETS: Bedrooms (1 GF) unattended **Charges** £10 per stay
Public areas on leads **Grounds** on leads disp bin **Exercise area**
50yds **Facilities** leads walks info vet info **On Request** fridge
access torch towels

Very well located on Melvill Road with off-road parking, Eden
Lodge boasts comfortable rooms and a swimming pool. The
friendly hosts serve dinner by arrangement and do all they can to
ensure a comfortable stay.

Rooms 5 rms (4 en suite) (2 fmly) (1 GF) **Facilities** FTV TVL tea/
coffee Dinner available Cen ht Licensed Wi-fi ✿ Gym **Parking** 9
Notes ⊛

Pennance Mill Farm Touring Park *(SW792307)*
►►►
Maenporth TR11 5HJ
☎ 01326 317431 📠 01326 317431
dir: *From A39 (Truro to Falmouth road) follow brown camping
signs towards Maenporth Beach. At Hill Head rdbt take 2nd exit
for Maenporth Beach*

PETS: Charges dog & cat £2 per night **Public areas** except
playground on leads **Exercise area on site** field & woodland
walk **Facilities** walks info vet info **Other** prior notice required

Open Etr-Xmas Last arrival 22.00hrs Last departure 10.00hrs

Set approximately half a mile from the safe, sandy bay at
Maenporth, accessed by a private woodland walk leading
directly from the park, this is a mainly level, grassy park in a
rural location sheltered by mature trees and shrubs and divided
into three meadows. It has a modern toilet block. 6 acre site.
75 touring pitches. 8 hardstandings. Tent pitches. Motorhome
pitches. 4 statics.

Notes ⊛

Fowey Hall

★★★★ 77% ◉◉ HOTEL
Hanson Dr PL23 1ET
☎ 01726 833866 📠 01726 834100
e-mail: info@foweyhallhotel.co.uk
web: www.foweyhallhotel.co.uk
dir: *In Fowey, over mini rdbt into town centre. Pass school on
right, 400mtrs right into Hanson Drive*

PETS: Bedrooms (6 GF) courtyard bedrooms only **Charges** £10
per night **Public areas** except restaurant on leads **Grounds** on
leads disp bin **Exercise area** beach **Facilities** food bowl water
bowl bedding feeding mat washing facs cage storage walks
info vet info **On Request** fridge access torch towels **Stables**
3m **Other** prior notice required max 2 dogs in hotel at any time
disposal bags available

Built in 1899, this listed mansion looks out on to the English
Channel. The imaginatively designed bedrooms offer charm,
individuality and sumptuous comfort; the Garden Wing rooms
adding a further dimension to staying here. The beautifully
appointed public rooms include the wood-panelled dining room
where accomplished cuisine is served. Enjoying glorious views,
the well-kept grounds have a covered pool and sunbathing area.

Rooms 36 (8 annexe) (30 fmly) (6 GF) **S** £90-£230; **D** £170-£245
(incl. bkfst)* **Facilities** Spa STV FTV ✿ ⛵ Table tennis
Basketball Trampoline Pool table Xmas New Year Wi-fi
Parking 30 **Notes** LB

Trevanion

★★★★ GUEST ACCOMMODATION

70 Lostwithiel St PL23 1BQ
☎ 01726 832602
e-mail: alisteve@trevanionguesthouse.co.uk
web: www.trevanionguesthouse.co.uk
dir: *A3082 into Fowey, down hill, left onto Lostwithiel St, Trevanion on left*

PETS: Bedrooms (1 GF) unattended **Public areas** except dining room **Exercise area** directly across road **Facilities** food (pre-bookable) food bowl water bowl leads pet sitting walks info vet info **On Request** fridge access towels **Other** please phone for further details of pet facilities **Resident Pet:** Poppy (parrot)

This 16th-century merchant's house provides friendly, comfortable accommodation within easy walking distance of the historic town of Fowey and is also convenient for visiting the Eden Project. A hearty farmhouse-style, cooked breakfast, using local produce, is served in the attractive dining room; other menu options are available.

Rooms 5 rms (4 en suite) (1 pri facs) (2 fmly) (1 GF) **S** £40-£45; **D** £60-£70 **Facilities** FTV tea/coffee Dinner available Cen ht Wi-fi **Parking** 6 **Notes** LB

Penmarlam Caravan & Camping Park

(SX134526)

►►►

Bodinnick PL23 1LZ
☎ 01726 870088   📠 01726 870082
e-mail: info@penmarlampark.co.uk
dir: *From A390 at East Taphouse take B3359 signed Looe & Polperro. Follow signs for Bodinnick & Fowey, via ferry. Site on right at entrance to Bodinnick*

PETS: Public areas only assist dogs in toilet/shower block & shop disp bin **Exercise area** adjacent **Facilities** food dog chews cat treats washing facs walks info vet info **Other** all pets must be kept under strict control disposal bags available **Resident Pets:** Rusty (Border Terrier), Pippa (Collie cross), Clive (rabbit), 10 chickens

Open Apr-Oct Last departure noon

This tranquil park set above the Fowey Estuary in an Area of Outstanding Natural Beauty, with access to the water, continues to improve with the addition of six more fully-serviced pitches. Pitches are level, and sheltered by trees and bushes in two paddocks, while the toilets are spotlessly clean and well maintained. 4 acre site. 63 touring pitches. 20 seasonal pitches. Tent pitches. Motorhome pitches. 1 static.

GOONHAVERN　　　　　　　　　　　Map 2 SW75

Silverbow Park *(SW782531)*

►►►►►

Perranwell TR4 9NX
☎ 01872 572347
e-mail: silverbowhols@btconnect.com
dir: *Adjacent to A3075, 0.5m S of village*

PETS: Charges £2 per night **Public areas** except swimming pool area on leads disp bin **Exercise area on site** large field (off lead) **Facilities** food bowl water bowl washing facs walks info vet info **Other** charge for damage prior notice required free biodegradable disposal bags available **Resident Pets:** 1 cat, rabbits & ducks

Open May-end Sep Last arrival 22.00hrs Last departure 10.30hrs

This park has a quiet garden atmosphere, and appeals to families with young children. The superb landscaped grounds and good quality toilet facilities, housed in an attractive chalet-style building, including four family rooms, are maintained to a very high standard with attention paid to detail. Leisure facilities include two inviting swimming pools (outdoor and indoor), a bowling green and a nature reserve. 14 acre site. 100 touring pitches. 2 hardstandings. Tent pitches. Motorhome pitches. 15 statics.

Notes No cycling, no skateboards.

GOONHAVERN *continued*

Penrose Holiday Park *(SW795534)*

►►►►

TR4 9QF

☎ 01872 573185 📠 01872 571972

e-mail: info@penroseholidaypark.com

dir: *From Exeter take A30, past Bodmin & Indian Queens. Just after Wind Farm take B3285 towards Perranporth, site on left on entering Goonhavern*

PETS: Charges Jul-Aug £2; low season £1 per night **Public areas** except office & bathrooms on leads disp bin **Exercise area on site** dog field (off lead) **Exercise area** beach (2m) **Facilities** food walks info vet info **Stables** 2m **Other** prior notice required disposal bags available; shop (300yds) **Resident Pets:** Marley (Springer Spaniel), Kai & Tia (Northern Inuits)

Open Apr-Oct Last arrival 21.30hrs Last departure 10.00hrs

A quiet sheltered park set in five paddocks divided by hedges and shrubs, only a short walk from the village. Lovely floral displays enhance the park's appearance, and the grass and hedges are neatly trimmed. Four cubicled family rooms are very popular, and there is a good laundry, and a smart reception building. 9 acre site. 110 touring pitches. 48 hardstandings. Tent pitches. Motorhome pitches. 24 statics.

Notes Families & couples only.

GORRAN Map 2 SW94

Treveague Farm Caravan & Camping Site

(SX002410)

►►►

PL26 6NY

☎ 01726 842295 📠 01726 842295

e-mail: treveague@btconnect.com

dir: *From St Austell take B3273 towards Mevagissey, past Pentewan at top of hill, turn right signed Gorran. Past Heligan Gardens towards Gorran Churchtown. Follow brown tourist signs from fork in road*

PETS: Public areas on leads disp bin **Exercise area on site** field **Exercise area** surrounding area **Facilities** food food bowl water bowl vet info

Open Apr-Sep Last arrival 21.00hrs Last departure noon

Spectacular panoramic coastal views can be enjoyed from this rural park, which is set on an organic farm and well equipped with modern facilities. A stone-faced toilet block with a Cornish slate roof is an attractive and welcome feature, as is the building that houses the smart reception, café and shop, which sells meat produced on the farm. A footpath leads to the fishing village of Gorran Haven in one direction, and the secluded sandy Vault Beach in the other. 4 acre site. 40 touring pitches. Tent pitches. Motorhome pitches.

Treveor Farm Caravan & Camping Site

(SW988418)

►►►

PL26 6LW

☎ 01726 842387 📠 01726 842387

e-mail: info@treveorfarm.co.uk

dir: *From St Austell bypass left onto B3273 for Mevagissey. On hilltop before descent to village turn right on unclass road for Gorran. Right in 3.5m, site on right*

PETS: Charges £1 per night **Public areas** disp bin **Facilities** walks info vet info

Open Apr-Oct Last arrival 20.00hrs Last departure 11.00hrs

A small family-run camping park set on a working farm, with grassy pitches backing onto mature hedging. This quiet site, with good facilities, is close to beaches and offers a large coarse fishing lake. 4 acre site. 50 touring pitches. Tent pitches. Motorhome pitches.

Notes No hard ball, kites or frizbees.

GORRAN HAVEN Map 2 SX04

Trelispen Caravan & Camping Park

(SX008421)

►►

PL26 6NT

☎ 01726 843501 📠 01726 843501

e-mail: trelispen@care4free.net

dir: *B3273 from St Austell towards Mevagissey, on hilltop at x-roads before descent into Mevagissey turn right on unclass road to Gorran. Through village, 2nd right towards Gorran Haven, site signed on left in 250mtrs*

PETS: Public areas Exercise area 50yds **Facilities** vet info **Other** prior notice required

Open Etr & Apr-Oct Last arrival 22.00hrs Last departure noon

A quiet rural site set in three paddocks, and sheltered by mature trees and hedges. The simple toilets have plenty of hot water, and there is a small laundry. Sandy beaches, pubs and shops are nearby, and Mevagissey is two miles away. 2 acre site. 40 touring pitches. Tent pitches. Motorhome pitches.

Notes

Gwithian Farm Campsite *(SW586412)*

▶ ▶ ▶ ▶

Gwithian Farm TR27 5BX
☎ 01736 753127
e-mail: camping@gwithianfarm.co.uk
dir: *Exit A30 at Hayle rdbt, take 4th exit signed Hayle, 100mtrs. At 1st mini-rdbt turn right onto B3301 signed Portreath. Site 2m on left on entering village*

PETS: Charges £1 per night £7 per week **Public areas** except shop & shower block on leads disp bin **Exercise area** 100mtrs **Facilities** walks info vet info **Stables** 0.5m **Resident Pets:** Charcoal & Barnaby (pygmy goats), Tiggy (cat), guinea pigs, chickens

Open 31 Mar-1 Oct Last arrival 22.00hrs Last departure 17.00hrs

An unspoilt site located behind the sand dunes of Gwithian's golden beach, which can be reached directly by footpath from the site. The site boasts stunning floral displays, a superb toilet block with excellent facilities, including a bathroom and baby-changing unit, and first-class hardstanding pitches. There is a good pub opposite. 7.5 acre site. 87 touring pitches. 26 hardstandings. Tent pitches. Motorhome pitches.

Atlantic Coast Caravan Park *(NW580400)*

▶ ▶ ▶

53 Upton Towans, Gwithian TR27 5BL
☎ 01736 752071 🖷 01736 758100
e-mail: enquiries@atlanticcoastpark.co.uk
dir: *From A30 into Hayle, turn right at double rdbt. Site 1.5m on left*

PETS: Charges Public areas disp bin **Exercise area** adjacent **Facilities** food food bowl water bowl dog chews cat treats leads washing facs walks info vet info **Other** prior notice required contact details of dog sitter available on request disposal bags available; pet shop (5 mins' drive) **Restrictions** no dangerous dogs (see page 7) **Resident Pet:** Bonny (German Shepherd/Flat Coated Retriever cross)

Open Mar-early Jan Last arrival 20.00hrs Last departure 11.00hrs

Fringed by the sand-dunes of St Ives Bay and close to the golden sands of Gwithian Beach, the small, friendly touring area offers fully serviced pitches. There's freshly baked bread, a takeaway and a bar next door. This park is ideally situated for visitors to enjoy the natural coastal beauty and attractions of south-west Cornwall. Static caravans for holiday hire. 4.5 acre site. 15 touring pitches. 5 seasonal pitches. Tent pitches. Motorhome pitches. 50 statics.

Notes No commercial vehicles, gazebos or day tents.

Higher Trevaskis Caravan & Camping Park
(SW611381)

▶ ▶ ▶

Gwinear Rd, Connor Downs TR27 5JQ
☎ 01209 831736
dir: *At Hayle rdbt on A30 take exit signed Connor Downs, in 1m turn right signed Carnhell Green. Site 0.75m just past level crossing*

PETS: Public areas except toilet & shower block, shop & children's play area disp bin **Exercise area** lanes & bridleway adjacent **Facilities** walks info vet info **Other** prior notice required max 2 dogs per pitch **Restrictions** no Pit Bull Terriers, Rottweilers or dangerous dogs (see page 7); if bringing Staffordshire Bull Terriers please call park when booking **Resident Pet:** 1 cat

Open mid Apr-Sep Last arrival 20.00hrs Last departure 10.30hrs

An attractive paddocked park in a sheltered rural position with views towards St Ives. This secluded park is personally run by owners who keep it quiet and welcoming. Three unisex showers are a great hit with visitors. Fluent German is spoken. 6.5 acre site. 82 touring pitches. 3 hardstandings. Tent pitches. Motorhome pitches.

Notes Max speed 5mph, balls on field only. 🚫

Parbola Holiday Park *(SW612366)*

▶ ▶ ▶

Wall, Gwinear TR27 5LE
☎ 01209 831503
e-mail: bookings@parbola.co.uk
dir: *At Hayle rdbt on A30 take Connor Downs exit. In 1m turn right signed Carnhell Green. In village right to Wall. Site in village on left*

PETS: Charges £2 per night £14 per week **Public areas** except swimming pool area, shop, games room, launderette & children's play areas **Exercise area** surrounding area **Facilities** walks info vet info **Other** prior notice required dogs not allowed in Jul & Aug (ex assist dogs) **Restrictions** small & medium size dogs only **Resident Pets:** birds in aviary

Open all year rs Etr-end of Jun & Sep shop closed, pool unheated Last arrival 21.00hrs Last departure 10.00hrs

Pitches are provided in both woodland and open areas in this spacious park in Cornish downland. The park is centrally located for touring the seaside resorts and towns in the area, especially nearby Hayle with its three miles of golden sands. 16.5 acre site. 110 touring pitches. 4 hardstandings. Tent pitches. Motorhome pitches. 28 statics.

ENGLAND

HAYLE *continued*

Treglisson Touring Park *(SW581367)*

▶ ▶ ▶

Wheal Alfred Rd TR27 5JT
☎ 01736 753141
e-mail: enquiries@treglisson.co.uk
dir: *4th exit off rdbt on A30 at Hayle. 100mtrs, left at 1st mini-rdbt. Approx 1.5m past golf course, site sign on left*

PETS: Public areas on leads **Exercise area** adjacent **Facilities** washing facs walks info vet info **Resident Pets:** Poppy (Border Collie), Rosie & Jim (cats)

Open Etr-Sep Last arrival 20.00hrs Last departure 11.00hrs

A small secluded site in a peaceful wooded meadow, a former apple and pear orchard. This quiet rural site has level grass pitches and a well-planned modern toilet block, and is just two miles from the glorious beach at Hayle with its vast stretch of golden sand. 3 acre site. 26 touring pitches. 3 hardstandings. Tent pitches. Motorhome pitches.

Notes Max 6 people to one pitch.

HELSTON   Map 2 SW62

Poldown Caravan Park *(SW629298)*

▶ ▶ ▶

Poldown, Carleen TR13 9NN
☎ 01326 574560
e-mail: stay@poldown.co.uk
dir: *From Helston follow Penzance signs for 1m, right onto B3302 to Hayle, 2nd left to Carleen, 0.5m to site*

PETS: Charges £1 per night **Public areas** on leads
Exercise area footpath leading from site **Facilities** washing facs walks info vet info **Other** prior notice required **Resident Pet:** 1 Retriever

Open Apr-Sep Last arrival 21.00hrs Last departure noon

A small, quiet site set in attractive countryside with bright toilet facilities. All of the level grass pitches have electricity. This sunny park is sheltered by mature trees and shrubs. 2 acre site. 13 touring pitches. 2 hardstandings. Tent pitches. Motorhome pitches. 7 statics. 2 bell tents/yurts.

Notes 🐾

Skyburriowe Farm *(SW698227)*

▶ ▶ ▶

Garras TR12 6LR
☎ 01326 221646
e-mail: bkbenney@hotmail.co.uk
dir: *From Helston A3083 to The Lizard. After Culdrose Naval Airbase continue straight at rdbt, in 1m left at Skyburriowe Ln sign. In 0.5m right at Skyburriowe B&B/Campsite sign. Pass bungalow to farmhouse. Site on left*

PETS: Public areas on leads **Exercise area on site** 0.5m lane on farm **Facilities** walks info vet info **Stables** 4m **Other** prior notice required **Resident Pets:** Finlee & Candy (Golden Retrievers)

Open Apr-Oct Last arrival 22.00hrs Last departure 11.00hrs

A leafy no-through road leads to this picturesque farm park in a rural location on the Lizard Peninsula. The toilet block offers excellent quality facilities, and most pitches have electric hook-ups. There are some beautiful coves and beaches nearby. 4 acre site. 30 touring pitches. 2 hardstandings. Tent pitches. Motorhome pitches.

Notes Quiet after 23.00hrs. 🐾

HOLYWELL BAY   Map 2 SW75

Trevornick Holiday Park (SW776586)

TR8 5PW
☎ 01637 830531 📠 01637 831000
e-mail: info@trevornick.co.uk
dir: *3m from Newquay off A3075 towards Redruth. Follow Cubert & Holywell Bay signs*

PETS: Charges Public areas on leads **Exercise area on site** designated fields for walking dogs **Facilities** walks info vet info **Other** prior notice required owners with dogs allowed on Red & Hay fields only (& Pond Field at Easter). Confirm when booking

Open Etr & mid May-mid Sep Last arrival 21.00hrs Last departure 10.00hrs

A large seaside holiday complex with excellent facilities and amenities. There is plenty of entertainment including a children's club and an evening cabaret, adding up to a full holiday experience for all the family. A sandy beach is just a 15-minute footpath walk away. The park has 68 ready-erected tents for hire. 20 acre site. 593 touring pitches. 6 hardstandings. Tent pitches. Motorhome pitches.

Notes Families & couples only.

Edmore Tourist Park *(SX184955)*

▶ ▶ ▶

Edgar Rd, Wainhouse Corner EX23 0BJ
☎ 01840 230467   🖷 01840 230467
e-mail: enquiries@cornwallvisited.co.uk
dir: *Exit A39 at Wainhouse Corner onto Edgar Rd, site signed on right in 200yds*

PETS: Charges 1st dog free, additional dogs £1 per night
Public areas except play area disp bin **Exercise area** adjacent
Facilities washing facs walks info vet info

Open 1 wk before Etr-Oct Last arrival 21.00hrs Last departure noon

A quiet family-owned site in a rural location with extensive views, set close to the sandy surfing beaches of Bude, and the unspoilt sandy beach and rock pools at Crackington Haven. Friendly owners keep all facilities in a very good condition and improvements have been made to the hardstanding pitches and gravel access roads. 3 acre site. 28 touring pitches. Tent pitches. Motorhome pitches.

Notes 🖻

Gwendreath Farm Holiday Park *(SW738168)*

▶ ▶ ▶

TR12 7LZ
☎ 01326 290666
e-mail: tom.gibson@virgin.net
dir: *From A3083 turn left past Culdrose Naval Air Station onto B3293. Right past Goonhilly Earth Station signed Kennack Sands, left in 1m. At end of lane turn right over cattle grid. Right, through Seaview to 2nd reception*

PETS: Charges contact park for details **Public areas** disp bin
Exercise area adjacent to park **Facilities** walks info vet info
Other prior notice required

Open May-Sep Last arrival 21.00hrs Last departure 10.00hrs

A grassy park in an elevated position with extensive sea and coastal views, and the beach just a short walk through the woods. Campers can use the bar and takeaway at an adjoining site. It is advisable to telephone ahead and book before arrival. 5 acre site. 10 touring pitches. Tent pitches. 17 statics.

Notes 🖻

Silver Sands Holiday Park *(SW727166)*

▶ ▶ ▶

Gwendreath TR12 7LZ
☎ 01326 290631   🖷 01326 290631
e-mail: info@silversandsholidaypark.co.uk
dir: *From Helston follow signs to Future World Goonhilly. After 300yds turn right at x-roads signed Kennack Sands, 1m, left at Gwendreath sign, site 1m*

PETS: Charges camping area £1.80-£2.50 per night
Public areas except toilet block & reception; dogs must be kept on leads in main field disp bin **Exercise area on site** field available **Exercise area** beach (15 mins) **Facilities** food bowl water bowl washing facs walks info vet info **Stables** 2m **Other** prior notice required disposal bags available **Resident Pets:** George (Rough Collie), Whisky (Jack Russell), Alaska (Husky)

Open all year Last arrival 21.00hrs Last departure 11.00hrs

A small park in a remote location, with individually screened pitches providing sheltered suntraps. The owners are gradually upgrading the park, improving the landscaping, access roads, toilets and general detail around the park, notably the lovely floral displays that greet you on arrival. A footpath through the woods from the family-owned park leads to the beach and the local pub. 9 acre site. 16 touring pitches. Tent pitches. Motorhome pitches. 17 statics.

Notes No noise after mdnt.

Upper Tamar Lake *(SS288118)*

▶ ▶

Upper Tamar Lake EX23 9SB
☎ 01288 321712
e-mail: info@swlakestrust.org.uk
dir: *From A39 at Kilkhampton onto B3254, left in 0.5m onto unclass road, follow signs approx 4m to site*

PETS: Public areas except café on leads disp bin **Exercise area on site** around lake, spacious grass areas **Facilities** vet info

Open Apr-Oct

A well-trimmed, slightly sloping site overlooking the lake and surrounding countryside, with several signed walks. The site benefits from the excellent facilities provided for the watersports centre and coarse anglers, with a rescue launch on the lake when the flags are flying. A good family site, with Bude's beaches and surfing waves only eight miles away. 2 acre site. 28 touring pitches. Tent pitches.

Notes No swimming in lake.

ENGLAND

Dolbeare Park Caravan and Camping

(SX363616)

▶ ▶ ▶ ▶

St Ive Rd PL12 5AF
☎ 01752 851332 📄 01752 547871
e-mail: reception@dolbeare.co.uk
dir: *A38 to Landrake, 4m W of Saltash. At footbridge over A38 turn right, follow signs to site (0.75m from A38)*

PETS: Charges £1-£2 per night **Public areas** except shower block, laundry, shop, children's play area & football area on leads **Exercise area on site** dog walk **Exercise area** dog friendly beaches **Facilities** food leads walks info vet info **Other** prior notice required max 2 dogs per pitch except by prior arrangement; dogs must be kept on leads at all times (max length 6') disposal bags available **Restrictions** phone to confirm which breeds are accepted; no dangerous dogs (see page 7)

Open all year Last arrival 18.00hrs Last departure noon

A mainly level grass site with trees and bushes set in meadowland. The keen and friendly owners set high standards, and the park is always neat and clean. The refurbished toilet block with its new inviting interior and spacious family rooms is particularly impressive. 9 acre site. 60 touring pitches. 54 hardstandings. Tent pitches. Motorhome pitches. 1 tipi.

Notes No cycling, no kite flying.

The Crown Inn

★ ★ ★ INN

PL30 5BT
☎ 01208 872707 📄 01208 871208
e-mail: thecrown@wagtailinns.com
web: www.wagtailinns.com
dir: *Signed from A390, 2m W of Lostwithiel. Inn 0.5m down lane into village, opposite church*

PETS: Bedrooms (7 GF) **Public areas** except restaurant on leads **Grounds** on leads **Exercise area** footpath adjacent **Facilities** water bowl dog chews scoop/disp bags washing facs cage storage walks info vet info **On Request** fridge access torch towels **Other** charge for damage

This character inn has a long history, reflected in its worn flagstone floors, aged beams, open fireplaces and ancient well. Dating in part from the 12th century, The Crown has undergone a faithful restoration. Dining is a feature and menus offer a wide choice of fresh fish, local produce and interesting dishes. The attractive bedrooms are more contemporary and are impressively appointed. The garden is a delight.

Rooms 2 en suite 7 annexe en suite (1 fmly) (7 GF) **Facilities** FTV tea/coffee Dinner available Cen ht Wi-fi **Parking** 50

Redgate Smithy

★ ★ ★ ★ 🏠 BED AND BREAKFAST

Redgate, St Cleer PL14 6RU
☎ 01579 321578
e-mail: enquiries@redgatesmithy.co.uk
web: www.redgatesmithy.co.uk
dir: *3m NW of Liskeard. Off A30 at Bolventor/Jamaica Inn onto St Cleer Rd for 7m, B&B just past x-rds*

PETS: Bedrooms unattended **Public areas** except at breakfast **Grounds** disp bin **Exercise area** lane adjacent **Facilities** food bowl bedding dog chews scoop/disp bags pet sitting dog walking washing facs cage storage walks info vet info **On Request** fridge access torch towels **Restrictions** small, friendly dogs only; no Rottweilers, Staffordshire Bull Terriers or Rhodesian Ridgebacks **Resident Pet:** Sinbad (Cocker Spaniel)

This 200-year-old converted smithy is on the southern fringe of Bodmin Moor near Golitha Falls. The friendly accommodation offers smartly furnished, cottage-style bedrooms with many extra facilities. There are several dining options nearby, and the wide choice of freshly cooked breakfasts is served in the conservatory.

Rooms 3 rms (2 en suite) (1 pri facs) **S** £48; **D** £75 **Facilities** FTV tea/coffee Cen ht Wi-fi **Parking** 3 **Notes** LB No Children 12yrs Closed Xmas & New Year

Trelaske Hotel & Restaurant

★ ★ ★ 79% 🏵 HOTEL

Polperro Rd PL13 2JS
☎ 01503 262159 📄 01503 265360
e-mail: info@trelaske.co.uk
dir: *B252 signed Looe. Over Looe bridge signed Polperro. 1.9m, hotel signed on left, turn right*

PETS: Bedrooms (2 GF) unattended sign bedrooms that have direct access to gardens **Charges** £6.50 per night **Grounds** on leads disp bin **Exercise area** nearby **Facilities** food bowl water bowl dog chews cat treats feeding mat dog grooming walks info vet info **On Request** fridge access torch towels

This small and welcoming hotel offers comfortable accommodation, professional yet friendly service and award-winning food. Set in its own very well-tended and pretty grounds, it is only two miles from Polperro and Looe.

Rooms 7 (4 annexe) (2 fmly) (2 GF) **S** £70-£105; **D** £95-£105 (incl. bkfst)* **Facilities** FTV Wi-fi **Parking** 50 **Notes** LB

Hannafore Point

 ★★★ 71% HOTEL

Marine Dr, West Looe PL13 2DG
☎ 01503 263273   📄 01503 263272
e-mail: stay@hannaforepointhotel.com
dir: A38, left onto A385 to Looe. Over bridge turn left. Hotel 0.5m on left

PETS: Bedrooms unattended sign   **Charges** £10 per night **Public areas** except terrace & bar on leads **Exercise area** adjacent **Facilities** water bowl washing facs cage storage walks info **Other** charge for damage dogs accepted by prior arrangement only **Restrictions** small dogs only

With panoramic coastal views of St George's Island around to Rame Head, this popular hotel provides a warm welcome. The wonderful view is certainly a feature of the spacious restaurant and bar, creating a scenic backdrop for both dinners and breakfasts. Additional facilities include a heated indoor pool and a gym.

Rooms 37 (5 fmly) **S** £55-£70; **D** £110-£150 (incl. bkfst)*
Facilities STV ⊗ Gym Spa pool Steam room Sauna 🎵 Xmas New Year Wi-fi **Services** Lift **Parking** 32 **Notes** LB

Fieldhead Hotel & Horizons Restaurant

★★ 80% HOTEL

Portuan Rd, Hannafore PL13 2DR
☎ 01503 262689
e-mail: fieldheadhotel@gmail.com
web: www.fieldhead.co.uk
dir: In Looe pass Texaco garage, cross bridge, left to Hannafore. At Tom Sawyer turn right & right again. Hotel on left

PETS: Bedrooms (2 GF) unattended sign certain bedrooms only **Charges** £7.50 per night **Grounds** **Exercise area** nearby **Stables** nearby

Overlooking the bay, this engaging hotel has a relaxing atmosphere. Bedrooms are furnished with care and many have sea views. Smartly presented public areas include a convivial bar and restaurant, and outside there is a palm-filled garden with a secluded patio and swimming pool. The fixed-price menu changes daily and features quality local produce.

Rooms 16 (2 fmly) (2 GF) **S** £46-£63; **D** £92-£160 (incl. bkfst)*
Facilities FTV ⊀ New Year Wi-fi Child facilities **Parking** 15 **Notes** LB Closed 1 day at Xmas

Coombe Farm

★★★★ GUEST ACCOMMODATION

Widegates PL13 1QN
☎ 01503 240223
e-mail: coombe_farm@hotmail.com
web: www.coombefarmhotel.co.uk
dir: 3.5m E of Looe on B3253 just S of Widegates

PETS: Bedrooms (3 GF) **Charges** £3.50 per night £20 per week **Public areas** **Grounds** on leads **Exercise area** 2m **Facilities** walks info vet info **Other** charge for damage dogs must be on leads immediately outside cottages (be aware there are peacocks in grounds) **Resident Pets:** Lordy & Barney (Shetland/Welsh pony), Piglet & Tigger (guinea pigs), peacocks, rabbits

Set in ten acres of grounds and gardens, Coombe Farm has a friendly atmosphere. The bedrooms are in a converted stone barn, and are comfortable and spacious. Each has a dining area, with breakfast delivered to your room.

Rooms 3 annexe en suite (1 fmly) (3 GF) **S** £45-£55; **D** £75-£82 **Facilities** STV FTV tea/coffee Direct Dial ⊀ Golf 18 **Parking** 20 **Notes** Closed 15 Dec-5 Jan

Little Harbour

★★★ GUEST HOUSE

Church St PL13 2EX
☎ 01503 262474
e-mail: littleharbour@btinternet.com
web: www.looedirectory.co.uk
dir: From harbour at West Looe, right into Princess Sq, guest house on left

PETS: Bedrooms **Public areas** **Facilities** water bowl washing facs walks info vet info **On Request** fridge access towels **Other** charge for damage **Restrictions** no large dogs; no dangerous dogs (see page 7) **Resident Pets:** Katamia Gingerbean (Persian cat), Biscuit (guinea pig)

Little Harbour is situated almost on Looe's harbourside in the historic old town; it has a pleasant and convenient location and parking is available. The proprietors are friendly and attentive and bedrooms are well appointed and attractively decorated. Breakfast is served freshly cooked in the dining room.

Rooms 5 en suite (1 fmly) **Facilities** FTV tea/coffee Cen ht Wi-fi **Parking** 3 **Notes** LB No Children 12yrs

LOOE *continued*

Tencreek Holiday Park *(SX233525)*

Polperro Rd PL13 2JR
☎ 01503 262447 📄 01503 262760
e-mail: reception@tencreek.co.uk
dir: *Take A387 1.25m from Looe. Site on left*

PETS: Charges variable **Public areas** except public buildings
disp bin **Exercise area on site** designated area **Exercise area**
footpath from site **Facilities** food walks info vet info **Other**
prior notice required disposal bags available

Open all year Last arrival 23.00hrs Last departure 10.00hrs

Occupying a lovely position with extensive countryside and sea
views, this holiday centre is in a rural spot but close to Looe and
Polperro. There is a full family entertainment programme, with
indoor and outdoor swimming pools, an adventure playground
and an exciting children's club. The two toilet blocks on the
touring area are exceptional and include two superb family/
disabled cubicles. 24 acre site. 254 touring pitches. 12
hardstandings. 120 seasonal pitches. Tent pitches. Motorhome
pitches. 101 statics.

Notes Families & couples only

Camping Caradon Touring Park *(SX218539)*

▶ ▶ ▶ ▶

Trelawne PL13 2NA
☎ 01503 272388
e-mail: enquiries@campingcaradon.co.uk
dir: *Site signed from B3359 near junct with A387, between Looe &
Polperro. Also signed on junct A387/B3359*

PETS: Charges £1-£2 per night **Public areas** except any indoor
areas & site facilities disp bin **Exercise area** 0.25m **Facilities**
walks info vet info **Other** disposal bags, dog food & dog anchors
available **Resident Pet:** 1 rabbit

Open all year rs Nov-Mar by booking only Last arrival 22.00hrs
Last departure noon

Set in a quiet rural location between the popular coastal resorts
of Looe and Polperro, this family-run and developing eco-friendly
park is just one and half miles from the beach at Talland Bay.
The hands-on owners have upgraded the bar and restaurant (food
can also be delivered to your pitch), and added two fully-serviced
family/disabled wet rooms. 3.5 acre site. 85 touring pitches. 23
hardstandings. Tent pitches. Motorhome pitches.

Notes No noise 23.00hrs-07.00hrs & barrier not operational

Polborder House Caravan & Camping Park
(SX283557)

▶ ▶ ▶

Bucklawren Rd, St Martin PL13 1NZ
☎ 01503 240265
e-mail: reception@polborderhouse.co.uk
dir: *Approach Looe from E on A387, follow B3253 for 1m, left at
Polborder & Monkey Sanctuary sign. Site 0.5m on right*

PETS: Charges £1 per night **Public areas** disp bin
Exercise area adjacent **Facilities** food food bowl water bowl
dog chews cat treats scoop/disp bags leads washing facs
walks info vet info **Stables** 2m **Other** prior notice required
Restrictions no dangerous dogs (see page 7) **Resident Pet:** 1 St
Bernard

Open all year Last arrival 22.00hrs Last departure 11.00hrs

A very neat and well-kept small grassy site on high ground
above Looe in a peaceful rural setting. Friendly and enthusiastic
owners continue to invest in the park, refurbishing the toilet
facilities with upmarket fittings (note the infra-red operated taps
and under floor heating) and adding new roadways. The whole
park looked immaculate at our last inspection. 3.3 acre site.
31 touring pitches. 19 hardstandings. Tent pitches. Motorhome
pitches. 5 statics.

Trelay Farmpark *(SX210544)*

▶ ▶ ▶

Pelynt PL13 2JX
☎ 01503 220900 📄 01503 220902
e-mail: stay@trelay.co.uk
dir: *From A390 at East Taphouse, take B3359 S towards Looe.
After Pelynt, site 0.5m on left*

PETS: Charges £1 per night £7 per week **Public areas** except
children's play area, shower block, toilets, pot wash & laundry
disp bin **Exercise area** 50yds **Facilities** washing facs walks
info vet info **Other** prior notice required

Open Dec-Oct Last arrival 21.00hrs Last departure 11.00hrs

A small site with a friendly atmosphere set in a pretty rural area
with extensive views. The good-size grass pitches are on slightly-
sloping ground, and the toilets are immaculately kept, with the
addition of an excellent washing-up room. Looe and Polperro
are just three miles away. 4.5 acre site. 66 touring pitches. 3
hardstandings. 7 seasonal pitches. Tent pitches. Motorhome
pitches. 45 statics.

Notes No skateboards, ball games or kites

ENGLAND

Best Western Restormel Lodge

★★★ 75% HOTEL
Castle Hill PL22 0DD
☎ 01208 872223 🖷 01208 873568
e-mail: bookings@restormellodgehotel.co.uk
web: www.restormellodgehotel.co.uk
dir: On A390 in Lostwithiel

PETS: Bedrooms (9 GF) **Charges** £10 per night £60 per week
Grounds on leads **Exercise area** 500mtrs **Facilities** washing
facs vet info **On Request** fridge access torch towels **Resident
Pet:** Monster (cat)

A short drive from the Eden Project, this popular hotel offers
a friendly welcome to all visitors and is ideally situated for
exploring the area. The older building houses the bar, restaurant
and lounges, with original features adding to the character.
Bedrooms are comfortably furnished, with a number overlooking
the secluded outdoor pool.

Rooms 36 (12 annexe) (2 fmly) (9 GF) **S** £29-£69; **D** £39-£119
(incl. bkfst) **Facilities** FTV 🐾 Xmas New Year Wi-fi **Parking** 40
Notes LB

Lostwithiel Hotel Golf & Country Club

★★★ 68% HOTEL
Lower Polscoe PL22 0HQ
☎ 01208 873550 🖷 01208 873479
e-mail: reception@golf-hotel.co.uk
web: www.golf-hotel.co.uk
dir: Off A38 at Dobwalls onto A390. In Lostwithiel turn right &
hotel signed

PETS: Bedrooms (16 GF) unattended sign **Charges** £8 per
night **Public areas** except restaurant & sports bar on leads
Grounds on leads **Facilities** washing facs walks info vet info
On Request torch towels **Other** charge for damage

This rural hotel is based around its own golf club and other
leisure activities. The main building offers guests a choice of
eating options, including all-day snacks in the popular Sports
Bar. The bedroom accommodation, designed to incorporate
beamed ceilings, has been developed from old Cornish barns that
are set around a courtyard.

Rooms 27 (2 fmly) (16 GF) (2 smoking) **S** £45-£57; **D** £90-£114
(incl. bkfst)* **Facilities** FTV 🐾 👤 18 ⛳ Putt green Fishing Gym
Undercover floodlit driving range Indoor golf simulator Xmas New
Year Wi-fi **Parking** 120 **Notes** LB

Penrose B&B

★★★★ GUEST ACCOMMODATION
1 The Terrace PL22 0DT
☎ 01208 871417 & 07766 900179 🖷 01208 871101
e-mail: enquiries@penrosebb.co.uk
web: www.penrosebb.co.uk
dir: A390 Edgcumbe Rd, Lostwithiel onto Scrations Ln, 1st right
for parking

PETS: Bedrooms (2 GF) **Public areas** except dining room at
breakfast **Grounds** on leads disp bin **Exercise area** 0.25m
Facilities pet sitting washing facs cage storage walks info
vet info **On Request** fridge access torch towels **Resident Pet:**
Chocky (cat)

Just a short walk from the town centre, this grand Victorian
house offers comfortable accommodation and a genuine homely
atmosphere. Many of the bedrooms have the original fireplaces
and all are equipped with thoughtful extras. Breakfast is a
generous offering and is served in the elegant dining room, with
views over the garden. Wi-fi access is also available.

Rooms 7 en suite (3 fmly) (2 GF); **D** £40-£100 **Facilities** FTV TVL
tea/coffee Cen ht Wi-fi **Parking** 8 **Notes** LB 🚭

ENGLAND

Eden Valley Holiday Park *(SX083593)*

▶▶▶▶

PL30 5BU

☎ 01208 872277   ▤ 01208 871236

e-mail: enquiries@edenvalleyholidaypark.co.uk

dir: *1.5m SW of Lostwithiel on A390 turn right at brown/white sign in 400mtrs*

PETS: Charges £1-£2 per night **Public areas** except children's play area disp bin **Exercise area on site** specific field allocated **Facilities** walks info vet info **Stables** 100yds **Other** prior notice required **Restrictions** no Dobermans, Rottweilers, German Shepherds or Staffordshire Bull Terriers **Resident Pet:** Pippin (Cairn Terrier)

Open Etr or Apr-Oct Last arrival 22.00hrs Last departure 11.30hrs

A grassy park set in attractive paddocks with mature trees. A gradual upgrading of facilities continues, and both buildings and grounds are carefully maintained and contain an impressive children's play area. Improvements include cinder roadways and a large motorhome service point. This park is ideally located for visiting the Eden Project, the nearby golden beaches and sailing at Fowey. There are also two self-catering lodges. 12 acre site. 56 touring pitches. 12 hardstandings. 20 seasonal pitches. Tent pitches. Motorhome pitches. 38 statics.

 Map 2 SX05

Croft Farm Holiday Park *(SX044568)*

▶▶▶

PL30 5EQ

☎ 01726 850228   ▤ 01726 850498

e-mail: enquiries@croftfarm.co.uk

dir: *Exit A30 at Bodmin onto A391 towards St Austell. In 7m left at double rdbt onto unclass road towards Luxulyan/Eden Project, continue to rdbt at Eden, left signed Luxulyan. Site 1m on left. (NB Do not approach any other way as roads are very narrow)*

PETS: Charges £1.50 per night £10.50 per week **Public areas** except public buildings & playing field (dogs must be exercised on dog walk only) disp bin **Exercise area on site** dog walking area; woodland walk **Facilities** washing facs walks info vet info **Other** prior notice required disposal bags available

Open 21 Mar-21 Jan Last arrival 18.00hrs Last departure 11.00hrs

A peaceful, picturesque setting at the edge of a wooded valley, and only one mile from The Eden Project. Facilities include a well-maintained toilet block, a well-equipped dishwashing area, replete with freezer and microwave, and a children's play area reached via an attractive woodland trail. 10.5 acre site. 52 touring pitches. 42 hardstandings. 32 seasonal pitches. Tent pitches. Motorhome pitches. 45 statics.

Notes No skateboarding, ball games only in playing field, quiet between 23.00hrs-07.00hrs

 Map 2 SW53

Godolphin Arms

★★★★ INN

TR17 0EN

☎ 01736 710202

e-mail: enquiries@godolphinarms.co.uk

dir: *From A30 follow Marazion signs for 1m to inn. At end of causeway to St Michael's Mount*

PETS: Bedrooms (2 GF) **Charges** £10 per night **Public areas** on leads **Grounds** on leads disp bin **Exercise area** 100yds **Facilities** water bowl dog chews walks info vet info **On Request** fridge access towels **Stables** 1m **Other** charge for damage

A traditional inn overlooking St Michael's Mount and beyond, The Godolphin Arms is the heart of the community and caters for all ages. Bedrooms are stylish, modern and appointed in pale colours. The staff are friendly. Food is served daily, and there are often special themed evenings. There is reserved parking for guests.

Rooms 10 en suite (2 fmly) (2 GF) **D** £90-£180 **Facilities** STV tea/coffee Dinner available Direct Dial Cen ht Wi-fi Pool table **Parking** 10 **Notes** No coaches

Wheal Rodney Holiday Park *(SW525315)*

▶▶▶

Gwallon Ln TR17 0HL

☎ 01736 710605

e-mail: reception@whealrodney.co.uk

dir: *Exit A30 at Crowlas, signed Rospeath. Site 1.5m on right. From Marazion centre turn opposite Fire Engine Inn, site 500mtrs on left*

PETS: Charges £2 per night **Public areas** except buildings disp bin **Exercise area** 200yds **Facilities** food food bowl water bowl dog chews cat treats washing facs walks info vet info **Stables** nearby **Other** prior notice required; early booking is advised disposal bags available **Resident Pets:** Harry (sheep dog), Naughty Ralph (cat)

Open Etr-Oct Last arrival 20.00hrs Last departure 11.00hrs

Set in a quiet rural location surrounded by farmland, with level grass pitches and well-kept facilities. Within half a mile are the beach at Marazion and the causeway or ferry to St Michael's Mount. A cycle route is just 400 yards away. 2.5 acre site. 30 touring pitches. Tent pitches. Motorhome pitches.

Notes Quiet after 22.00hrs.

Budock Vean-The Hotel on the River

★★★★ 79% ⊛ COUNTRY HOUSE HOTEL

TR11 5LG

☎ 01326 252100 & 0800 833927 📄 01326 250892

e-mail: relax@budockvean.co.uk

web: www.budockvean.co.uk

dir: *From A39 follow tourist signs to Trebah Gardens. 0.5m to hotel*

PETS: Bedrooms sign **Charges** £7.75 per night £43.75 per week **Grounds** on leads disp bin **Exercise area** nearby **Facilities** feeding mat scoop/disp bags walks info vet info **On Request** fridge access torch **Stables** 5m **Other** charge for damage

Set in 65 acres of attractive, well-tended grounds, this peaceful hotel offers an impressive range of facilities. Convenient for visiting the Helford River Estuary and the many local gardens, or simply as a tranquil venue for a leisure break. Bedrooms are spacious and come in a choice of styles; some overlook the grounds and golf course.

Rooms 57 (2 fmly) **S** £69-£134; **D** £138-£268 (incl. bkfst & dinner)* **Facilities** Spa FTV ⊛ ↟ 9 ⊜ Putt green ⛳ Private river boat & foreshore ♫ Xmas New Year Wi-fi **Services** Lift **Parking** 100 **Notes** Closed 3 wks Jan

Meudon

★★★ 85% COUNTRY HOUSE HOTEL

TR11 5HT

☎ 01326 250541 📄 01326 250543

e-mail: wecare@meudon.co.uk

web: www.meudon.co.uk

dir: *From Truro A39 towards Falmouth at Hillhead (Anchor & Cannons) rdbt, follow signs to Maenporth Beach. Hotel on left in 1m*

PETS: Bedrooms (15 GF) unattended **Charges** £12 per night **Public areas** Bridge Lounge only **Grounds** disp bin **Exercise area** 8.5-acre gardens & private beach **Facilities** water bowl bedding walks info **On Request** fridge access

This charming late Victorian mansion is a relaxing place to stay, with friendly hospitality and attentive service. It sits in impressive subtropical gardens that lead down to a private beach. The spacious and comfortable bedrooms are situated in a more modern building. The cuisine features the best local Cornish produce and is served in the conservatory restaurant.

Rooms 29 (2 fmly) (15 GF) **S** £94-£150; **D** £188-£300 (incl. bkfst & dinner)* **Facilities** FTV Fishing Private beach Hair salon Yacht for skippered charter Xmas Wi-fi **Services** Lift **Parking** 50 **Notes** LB Closed 28 Dec-Jan

Seaview International Holiday Park

(SW990412)

▶▶▶▶▶

Boswinger PL26 6LL

☎ 01726 843425 📄 01726 843358

e-mail: holidays@seaviewinternational.com

dir: *From St Austell take B3273 signed Mevagissey. Turn right before entering village. Follow brown tourist signs to site*

PETS: Charges dog £3 per night **Public areas** except swimming pool disp bin **Exercise area on site** dog walk & allocated area **Exercise area** beach (0.5m) **Facilities** food food bowl water bowl dog chews cat treats scoop/disp bags walks info vet info **Other** prior notice required **Restrictions** no dangerous dogs (see page 7)

Open Mar-Oct rs Late May-Early Sep swimming pool opens late Last arrival 21.00hrs Last departure 10.00hrs

An attractive holiday park set in a beautiful environment overlooking Veryan Bay, with colourful landscaping, including attractive flowers and shrubs. It continues to offer an outstanding holiday experience, with its luxury family pitches, super toilet facilities, takeaway and shop and static caravans for holiday hire. The beach and sea are just half a mile away. 28 acre site. 201 touring pitches. 28 hardstandings. 8 seasonal pitches. Tent pitches. Motorhome pitches. 35 statics.

The Plume of Feathers

★★★★ INN

TR8 5AX

☎ 01872 510387 & 511122 📄 01872 511124

e-mail: enquiries@theplume.info

dir: *Just off A30 & A3076, follow signs*

PETS: Bedrooms bedrooms 1 & 2 only **Public areas** on leads **Grounds** on leads disp bin **Exercise area** nearby **Facilities** food bowl water bowl walks info vet info **On Request** fridge access towels **Other** charge for damage

A very popular inn with origins dating back to the 16th century, situated close to Newquay and the beaches. The restaurant offers a varied menu which relies heavily on local produce. The stylish bedrooms are decorated in neutral colours and have wrought-iron beds with quality linens. The garden makes an ideal place to enjoy a meal or a Cornish tea. The staff are very friendly.

Rooms 7 annexe en suite (1 fmly) (5 GF) **S** £60-£90; **D** £80-£120 **Facilities** FTV tea/coffee Dinner available Cen ht Wi-fi **Parking** 40 **Notes** LB No coaches

ENGLAND

Mullion Cove Hotel

★★★ **79%** ◉ HOTEL

TR12 7EP

☎ 01326 240328   📄 01326 240998

e-mail: enquiries@mullion-cove.co.uk

dir: *A3083 towards The Lizard. Through Mullion towards Mullion Cove. Hotel in approx 1m*

PETS: Bedrooms (3 GF) unattended   **Charges** free in low season, otherwise £7 per night   **Public areas** in specific lounge only on leads   **Grounds** on leads   disp bin   **Exercise area** nearby **Facilities** dog chews   scoop/disp bags   washing facs   dog grooming   walks info   vet info   **On Request** fridge access   torch **Stables** 2m   **Other** charge for damage

Built at the turn of the last century and set high above the working harbour of Mullion, this hotel has spectacular views of the rugged coastline; seaward facing rooms are always popular. The stylish restaurant offers some carefully prepared dishes using local produce; an alternative option is to eat less formally in the bar. After dinner guests might like to relax in one of the elegant lounges.

Rooms 30 (3 fmly) (3 GF) **S** £60-£232.50; **D** £120-£310 (incl. bkfst)* **Facilities** FTV ⚡ Xmas New Year Wi-fi **Services** Lift **Parking** 60 **Notes** LB

Polurrian

★★★ **77%** HOTEL

TR12 7EN

☎ 01326 240421   📄 01326 240083

e-mail: relax@polurrianhotel.com

web: www.polurrianhotel.com

dir: *A394 to Helston, then follow The Lizard & Mullion signs, onto A3083. Approx 5m, right onto B3296 to Mullion. Follow one-way system to T-junct, turn left signed Mullion Cove. 0.5m turn right, follow hotel sign. Hotel at end of road*

PETS: Bedrooms (8 GF) sign   ground & first-floor bedrooms only **Charges** £8 per night   **Public areas** except lounge & restaurant on leads   **Grounds** on leads   disp bin   **Exercise area** adjacent **Facilities** water bowl   bedding   feeding mat   scoop/disp bags walks info   vet info   **On Request** fridge access   torch   towels **Stables** 2m   **Other** charge for damage

With spectacular views across St Mount's Bay, this is a well managed and relaxed hotel where guests are assured of a warm

welcome from the friendly team of staff. In addition to the formal eating option, the High Point restaurant offers a more casual approach, open throughout the day and into the evening. The popular leisure club has a good range of equipment. Bedrooms vary in size, and the sea-view rooms are always in demand.

Rooms 39 (4 fmly) (8 GF) **S** £55-£104; **D** £110-£208 (incl. bkfst)* **Facilities** FTV ⚡ ⚡ ☕ Gym Children's games room & outdoor play area Xmas New Year Wi-fi Child facilities **Parking** 60 **Notes** Closed Jan-5 Feb

Mullion Holiday Park *(SW699182)*

Ruan Minor TR12 7LJ

☎ 0844 335 3756   & 01326 240428   📄 01326 241141

e-mail: touringandcamping@parkdeanholidays.com

dir: *A30 onto A39 through Truro towards Falmouth. A394 to Helston, A3083 for The Lizard. Site 7m on left*

PETS: Charges contact holiday park for details   **Public areas** disp bin   **Exercise area on site** small meadow   **Facilities** food   food bowl   water bowl   scoop/disp bags   leads   walks info   vet info **Restrictions** no dangerous dogs (see page 7)

Open Apr-Oct rs 17 May-20 Sep outdoor pool open Last arrival 22.00hrs Last departure 10.00hrs

A comprehensively-equipped leisure park geared mainly for self-catering holidays, and set close to the sandy beaches, coves and fishing villages on The Lizard peninsula. There is plenty of on-site entertainment for all ages, with indoor and outdoor swimming pools and a bar and grill. 49 acre site. 69 touring pitches. 9 hardstandings. Tent pitches. Motorhome pitches. 305 statics.

'Franchis' Holiday Park *(SW698203)*

▶▶▶

Cury Cross Lanes TR12 7AZ

☎ 01326 240301

e-mail: enquiries@franchis.co.uk

dir: *Off A3083 on left 0.5m past Wheel Inn PH, between Helston & The Lizard*

PETS: Charges from £1.50 per night   **Public areas** disp bin **Exercise area on site** small field adjacent to site   **Facilities** scoop/disp bags   walks info   vet info   **Other** prior notice required **Resident Pets:** 2 cats

Open Apr-Oct Last arrival 20.00hrs Last departure 10.30hrs

A grassy site surrounded by hedges and coppices, and divided into two paddocks for tourers, in an ideal position for exploring the Lizard Peninsula. The pitches are a mixture of level and slightly sloping. 16 acre site. 70 touring pitches. Tent pitches. Motorhome pitches. 12 statics.

Hotel California

★★★ 67% HOTEL

Pentire Crescent TR7 1PU

☎ 01637 879292 & 872798 📄 01637 875611

e-mail: info@hotel-california.co.uk

web: www.hotel-california.co.uk

dir: *A392 to Newquay, follow signs for Pentire Hotels & Guest Houses*

PETS: Bedrooms (13 GF) unattended **Charges** £10 per night on leads **Grounds** disp bin **Exercise area** nearby **Facilities** walks info vet info **On Request** fridge access torch **Stables** 1m **Other** charge for damage dogs are only accepted at manager's discretion & may be required to be muzzled

This hotel is tucked away in a delightful location, close to Fistral Beach and adjacent to the River Gannel. Many rooms have views across the river towards the sea, and some have balconies. There is an impressive range of leisure facilities, including indoor and outdoor pools, and ten-pin bowling. Cuisine is enjoyable and menus offer a range of interesting dishes.

Rooms 70 (27 fmly) (13 GF) **S** £40-£56; **D** £80-£107 (incl. bkfst) **Facilities** FTV 🐕 🏊 Squash 4-lane American bowling alley Hairdresser Snooker & pool room Sauna Solarium 🎵 Xmas New Year Wi-fi **Services** Lift **Parking** 66 **Notes** LB Closed 3 wks Jan

Dewolf Guest House

★★★★ GUEST HOUSE

100 Henver Rd TR7 3BL

☎ 01637 874746

e-mail: holidays@dewolfguesthouse.com

dir: *A392 onto A3058 at Quintrell Downs rdbt, guest house on left just past mini-rdbts*

PETS: Bedrooms sign family & single room (1st floor) only **Public areas** except dining room on leads **Exercise area** beach, walks less than 5 mins from house **Facilities** food bowl water bowl dog chews feeding mat walks info vet info **On Request** fridge access towels **Other** charge for damage **Restrictions** no small dogs **Resident Pet:** 1 Siberian Husky

Making guests feel welcome and at home is the priority here. The bedrooms in the main house are bright and well equipped, and there are two more in a separate single storey building at the rear. The cosy lounge has pictures and items that reflect the host's interest in wildlife. The guest house is just a short walk from Porth Beach.

Rooms 4 en suite 2 annexe en suite (1 fmly) (3 GF) **S** £35-£45; **D** £60-£80 **Facilities** FTV tea/coffee Cen ht Licensed **Parking** 6 **Notes** LB

The Three Tees

★★★ GUEST ACCOMMODATION

21 Carminow Way TR7 3AY

☎ 01637 872055 📄 01637 872055

e-mail: greg@3tees.co.uk

web: www.3tees.co.uk

dir: *A30 onto A392 Newquay. Right at Quintrell Downs rdbt signed Porth, over x-rds & 3rd right*

PETS: Bedrooms (2 GF) **Charges** £1 per night **Public areas** except dining room **Grounds** disp bin **Exercise area** 2 mins' walk **Facilities** water bowl dog chews cage storage walks info vet info **Other** dog walking & sitting available locally **Restrictions** no very large dogs **Resident Pets:** Poppy (Border Collie), Sas (Labrador Cross)

Located in a quiet residential area just a short walk from the town and beach, this friendly family-run accommodation is comfortable and well equipped. There is a lounge, bar and a sun lounge for the use of guests. Breakfast is served in the dining room, where snacks are available throughout the day; the bar serves light snacks in the evenings.

Rooms 8 rms (7 en suite) (1 pri facs) 1 annexe en suite (4 fmly) (2 GF); **D** £60-£74 **Facilities** FTV TVL tea/coffee Cen ht Licensed Wi-fi **Parking** 11 **Notes** LB Closed Nov-Feb

Porth Lodge

★★★ GUEST ACCOMMODATION

Porth Bean Rd TR7 3LT

☎ 01637 874483

e-mail: info@porthlodgehotel.co.uk

PETS: Bedrooms unattended bedrooms near exit allocated **Charges** £10 per stay **Public areas** bars only on leads **Grounds** on leads disp bin **Exercise area** 200mtrs **Facilities** water bowl dog walking walks info vet info **On Request** fridge access towels **Other** charge for damage larger dogs may require larger bedrooms, please call to discuss

A popular venue with its own bowling alley. The property has been totally refurbished to provide bedrooms that are even more comfortable and well equipped. Food is served daily and the team are friendly and helpful.

Rooms 16 en suite (1 fmly) **S** £30-£40; **D** £60-£75 **Facilities** FTV tea/coffee Dinner available Cen ht Licensed Wi-fi Golf 18 Pool table **Parking** 20

NEWQUAY *continued*

Hendra Holiday Park *(SW833601)*

TR8 4NY

☎ 01637 875778   📄 01637 879017

e-mail: enquiries@hendra-holidays.com

dir: *A30 onto A392 signed Newquay. At Quintrell Downs over rdbt, signed Lane, site 0.5m on left*

PETS: Charges contact park for details **Public areas** **Exercise area on site** dog walking areas **Facilities** walks info vet info **Other** prior notice required limited number of pitches available for guests with dogs; dogs must be kept on leads at all times **Restrictions** no Pit Bull Terriers, Tosas, Argentino Brazilieros, Rottweilers, Dobermans, Akitas, Rhodesian Ridgebacks, Presa Canaros or wolf hybrids (see also page 7)

Open Apr-Oct rs Apr-Spring BH, Sep-Oct outdoor pool closed Last arrival dusk Last departure 10.00hrs

A large complex with holiday statics and superb facilities including an indoor fun pool and an outdoor pool. There is a children's club for the over 6s, and evening entertainment during high season. The touring pitches are set amongst mature trees and shrubs, and some have fully-serviced facilities. All amenities are open to the public. 80 acre site. 548 touring pitches. 28 hardstandings. Tent pitches. Motorhome pitches. 283 statics. 1 wooden pod.

Notes Families and couples only.

See advert on page 41

Newquay Holiday Park *(SW853626)*

TR8 4HS

☎ 0844 335 3756   📄 01637 850818

e-mail: touringandcamping@parkdeanholidays.com

dir: *From Bodmin on A30, under low bridge, right towards RAF St Mawgan. Take A3059 towards Newquay, site past Treloy Golf Club*

PETS: Charges £2.50 per night **Public areas** except swimming pool, club, arcade & shop **Exercise area on site** field for dog walking **Facilities** food food bowl water bowl dog chews cat treats litter tray scoop/disp bags leads washing facs walks info vet info **Other** prior notice required max of 2 dogs per pitch

Open Mar-Oct rs May-19 Sep outdoor pool complex open Last arrival 21.00hrs Last departure 10.00hrs

A well-maintained park with a wide range of indoor and outdoor activities. A children's playground and bar and grill enhance the facilities, and the club and bars offer quality entertainment. Three heated outdoor pools and a giant waterslide are very popular. 60 acre site. 50 touring pitches. 10 hardstandings. Tent pitches. Motorhome pitches. 262 statics.

Treloy Touring Park *(SW858625)*

▶ ▶ ▶ ▶

TR8 4JN

☎ 01637 872063 & 876279   📄 01637 872063

e-mail: treloy.tp@btconnect.com

dir: *Off A3059 (St Columb Major-Newquay road)*

PETS: Charges £1-£2.50 per night **Public areas** except swimming pool area, children's play area & bar disp bin **Exercise area on site** dog walking area **Facilities** food vet info **Stables** 0.5m **Other** prior notice required dogs must be kept on leads at all times **Restrictions** no Pit Bull Terriers or similar breeds

Open May-15 Sep rs Sep pool, takeaway, shop & bar Last arrival 21.00hrs Last departure 10.00hrs

An attractive site with fine countryside views, that is within easy reach of resorts and beaches. The pitches are set in four paddocks with mainly level but some slightly sloping grassy areas. Maintenance and cleanliness are very high. 18 acre site. 223 touring pitches. 24 hardstandings. Tent pitches. Motorhome pitches.

Trebellan Park *(SW790571)*

▶▶▶

Cubert TR8 5PY

☎ 01637 830522 🖹 01637 830522

e-mail: enquiries@trebellan.co.uk

dir: *4m S of Newquay, turn W off A3075 at Cubert sign. Left in 0.75m onto unclass road*

PETS: Charges £2.50 per night £17.50 per week **Public areas** except swimming pool area on leads disp bin **Exercise area on site** footpaths & open fields **Facilities** washing facs walks info vet info **Other** prior notice required **Resident Pets:** Missus, Bob, Beastie & Ginge (cats), peacocks, ducks, aviary

Open May-Oct Last arrival 21.00hrs Last departure 10.00hrs

A terraced grassy rural park within a picturesque valley with views of Cubert Common, and adjacent to the Smuggler's Den, a 16th-century thatched inn. This park has three well-stocked coarse fishing lakes on site. 8 acre site. 150 touring pitches. Tent pitches. Motorhome pitches. 7 statics.

Notes Families and couples only.

Trethiggey Touring Park *(SW846596)*

▶▶▶

Quintrell Downs TR8 4QR

☎ 01637 877672 🖹 01637 879706

e-mail: enquiries@trethiggey.co.uk

dir: *A30 onto A392 signed Newquay at Quintrell Downs rdbt, left onto A3058, pass Newquay Pearl centre. Site 0.5m on left*

PETS: Charges please phone for pet charges **Public areas** except playground, shop & restaurant on leads disp bin **Exercise area on site** field **Facilities** food food bowl dog chews cat treats scoop/disp bags washing facs walks info vet info **Other** prior notice required **Resident Pets:** Bex (Springer Spaniel), Brook (Border Collie), Cooper (Springer/Collie cross)

Open Mar-Dec Last arrival 22.00hrs Last departure 10.30hrs

A family-owned park in a rural setting that is ideal for touring this part of Cornwall. It is pleasantly divided into paddocks with maturing trees and shrubs, and offering coarse fishing and tackle hire. 15 acre site. 145 touring pitches. 35 hardstandings. Tent pitches. Motorhome pitches. 12 statics.

RICHARDSON

The Metropole

★★★★ 73% ☺ HOTEL

Station Rd PL28 8DB

☎ 01841 532486 🖹 01841 532867

e-mail: info@the-metropole.co.uk

web: www.the-metropole.co.uk

dir: *M5/A30 pass Launceston, follow Wadebridge & N Cornwall signs. Take A39, follow Padstow signs*

PETS: Bedrooms (2 GF) unattended sign **Charges** £10 per night **Public areas** except restaurant & café bar on leads **Grounds** on leads disp bin **Facilities** scoop/disp bags washing facs walks info vet info **On Request** fridge access torch towels **Other** charge for damage can provide details of day care for dogs **Restrictions** well behaved dogs only

This long-established hotel first opened its doors to guests back in 1904 and there is still an air of the sophistication and elegance of a bygone age. Bedrooms are soundly appointed and well equipped; dining options include the informal Met Café Bar, and the main restaurant with its enjoyable cuisine and wonderful views over the Camel estuary.

Rooms 58 (3 fmly) (2 GF) **S** £118; **D** £236 (incl. bkfst) **Facilities** FTV ⚓ Swimming pool open Jul & Aug only Xmas New Year Wi-fi **Services** Lift **Parking** 36 **Notes** LB

St Petroc's Hotel and Bistro

★★ 85% ☺ SMALL HOTEL

4 New St PL28 8EA

☎ 01841 532700 🖹 01841 532942

e-mail: reservations@rickstein.com

dir: *A39 onto A389, follow signs to town centre. Follow one-way system, hotel on right on leaving town*

PETS: Bedrooms (3 GF) unattended **Charges** 1st night £20; thereafter £5 per night **Public areas** except restaurant on leads **Exercise area** beach (2 mins' walk) **Facilities** food bowl water bowl bedding pet sitting dog grooming walks info vet info **On Request** fridge access torch towels **Other** charge for damage dogs accepted by prior arrangement only; take home Chalky Pal blanket (included in price)

One of the oldest buildings in town, this charming establishment is just up the hill from the picturesque harbour. Style, comfort and individuality are all great strengths here, particularly so in the impressively equipped bedrooms. Breakfast, lunch and dinner all reflect a serious approach to cuisine, and the popular restaurant has a relaxed, bistro style. Comfortable lounges, a reading room and lovely gardens complete the picture.

Rooms 14 (4 annexe) (3 fmly) (3 GF) **D** £97–£280 (incl. bkfst)* **Facilities** FTV Cookery school New Year Wi-fi **Services** Lift **Parking** 12 **Notes** LB Closed 1 May & 25-26 Dec RS 24 Dec eve

PADSTOW *continued*

The Old Ship Hotel

★★ 75% HOTEL

Mill Square PL28 8AE

☎ 01841 532357   📠 01841 533211

e-mail: stay@oldshiphotel-padstow.co.uk

web: www.oldshiphotel-padstow.co.uk

dir: *From M5 take A30 to Bodmin then A389 to Padstow, follow brown tourist signs to car park*

PETS: Bedrooms sign   **Charges** £5 per night   **Public areas** on leads   **Grounds** on leads   disp bin   **Exercise area** nearby **Facilities** water bowl   dog chews   washing facs   walks info   vet info   **On Request** fridge access   torch   **Other** charge for damage **Resident Pet:** Sox (cat)

This attractive inn is situated in the heart of the old town's quaint and winding streets, just a short walk from the harbour. A warm welcome is assured, accommodation is pleasant and comfortable, and public areas offer plenty of character. Freshly caught fish features on both the bar and restaurant menus. On site parking is a bonus.

Rooms 14 (4 fmly) **S** £39-£59; **D** £90-£130 (incl. bkfst)* **Facilities** STV ♫ Xmas New Year Wi-fi **Parking** 20

The Seafood Restaurant

★★★★★★ 🏵🏵🏵 🍴 RESTAURANT WITH ROOMS

Riverside PL28 8BY

☎ 01841 532700   📠 01841 532942

e-mail: reservations@rickstein.com

dir: *Into town centre down hill, follow round sharp bend, restaurant on left*

PETS: Bedrooms (3 GF) unattended   **Charges** 1st night £20, thereafter £5 per night   **Public areas** except restaurant   on leads   **Exercise area** beach nearby   **Facilities** food bowl   water bowl   bedding   pet sitting   dog grooming   walks info   vet info **On Request** fridge access   torch   towels   **Other** charge for damage

Food lovers continue to beat a well-trodden path to this legendary establishment. Situated on the edge of the harbour, just a stone's throw from the shops, the Seafood Restaurant offers stylish and comfortable bedrooms that boast numerous thoughtful extras; some have views of the estuary and a couple have stunning private balconies. Service is relaxed and friendly; booking is essential for both accommodation and a table in the restaurant.

Rooms 14 en suite 6 annexe en suite (6 fmly) (3 GF) **Facilities** FTV tea/coffee Dinner available Direct Dial Cen ht Lift Wi-fi **Parking** 12 **Notes** LB Closed 24-26 Dec RS 1 May restaurant closed No coaches

Rick Stein's Café

★★★★ BED AND BREAKFAST

10 Middle St PL28 8AP

☎ 01841 532700   📠 01841 532942

e-mail: reservations@rickstein.com

dir: *A389 into town, one way past church, 3rd right*

PETS: Bedrooms unattended   **Charges** 1st night £20, thereafter £5 per night   **Public areas** except restaurant   on leads   **Exercise area** beach (2 mins' walk)   **Facilities** food bowl water bowl   bedding   pet sitting   dog grooming   walks info   vet info   **On Request** fridge access   torch   towels   **Other** charge for damage

Another Rick Stein success story, this lively café by day, restaurant by night, offers good food, quality accommodation, and is just a short walk from the harbour. Three bedrooms are available - each is quite different but have high standards of cosseting comfort. Friendly and personable staff are always on hand.

Rooms 3 en suite (1 fmly); **D** £97-£145 **Facilities** tea/coffee Dinner available Cen ht Licensed **Notes** LB Closed 1 May BH RS 24-26 Dec

Little Pentyre

★★ BED AND BREAKFAST

6 Moyle Rd PL28 8DG

☎ 01841 532246

e-mail: JujuLloyd@aol.com

dir: *From A389, right onto Dennis Rd, bear right onto Moyle Rd*

PETS: Bedrooms (2 GF) unattended   **Public areas** under control **Grounds** on leads   disp bin   **Exercise area** 50mtrs   **Facilities** food bowl   water bowl   bedding   dog chews   cat treats   feeding mat   scoop/disp bags   leads   washing facs   cage storage   walks info   vet info   **On Request** fridge access   torch   towels   **Other** pets must be under strict control at all times **Resident Pets:** 2 cats, 8 chickens

Within easy, level walking distance of the town centre, Little Pentyre is situated in a quiet residential area, adjacent to the Camel Estuary and Trail. The comfortable bedrooms are well equipped and guests enjoy a freshly cooked breakfast, featuring eggs from the hens in the rear garden.

Rooms 2 en suite (2 GF) **S** fr £30; **D** £55 **Facilities** FTV tea/coffee Cen ht **Parking** 2 **Notes** No Children 10yrs 🐾

Padstow Touring Park (SW913738)

▶▶▶▶▶

PL28 8LE

☎ 01841 532061

e-mail: mail@padstowtouringpark.co.uk

dir: *1m S of Padstow, on E side of A389 (Padstow to Wadebridge road)*

PETS: Charges £1.50 per night £10.50 per week **Public areas** except shop, amenity blocks & children's play area disp bin **Exercise area** adjacent public footpaths **Facilities** food food bowl water bowl dog chews cat treats scoop/disp bags walks info vet info **Other** prior notice required **Resident Pets:** Lottie (Border Terrier), Poppy (Yorkshire Terrier)

Open all year Last arrival 21.00hrs Last departure 11.00hrs

Improvements continue apace at this popular park set in open countryside above the quaint fishing town of Padstow, which can be approached by footpath directly from the park. It is divided into paddocks by maturing bushes and hedges to create a peaceful and relaxing holiday atmosphere. 13.5 acre site. 150 touring pitches. 27 hardstandings. Tent pitches. Motorhome pitches.

Notes No groups

Dennis Cove Camping (SW919743)

▶▶▶

Dennis Ln PL28 8DR

☎ 01841 532349

e-mail: denniscove@freeuk.com

dir: *Approach Padstow on A389, right at Tesco into Sarah's Ln, 2nd right to Dennis Ln, follow to site at end*

PETS: Charges £1.40-£2 per night **Public areas** except shower block on leads disp bin **Exercise area** adjacent **Facilities** walks info vet info **Stables** 2m **Other** prior notice required shop 0.25m **Restrictions** well behaved dogs only

Open Apr-end Sep Last arrival 21.00hrs Last departure 11.00hrs

Set in meadowland with mature trees, this site overlooks Padstow Bay, with access to the Camel Estuary and the nearby beach. The centre of town is just a 10-minute walk away, and bike hire is available on site, with the famous Camel Trail beginning right outside. 3 acre site. 42 touring pitches. Tent pitches. Motorhome pitches.

Notes Arrivals from 14.00hrs.

Sun Valley Holiday Park (SX005486)

▶▶▶▶▶

Pentewan Rd PL26 6DJ

☎ 01726 843266 & 844393 📠 01726 843266

e-mail: reception@sunvalley-holidays.co.uk

dir: *From St Austell take B3273 towards Mevagissey. Site 2m on right*

PETS: Charges contact holiday park for details **Public areas** except restaurant during food service & pool area disp bin **Exercise area on site** separate dog walk **Exercise area** adjacent **Facilities** food washing facs walks info vet info **Other** prior notice required disposal bags available (free of charge) **Resident Pets:** Sunny (cat), Jenny & Joe (donkeys), Milly & Lilly (goats), rabbits

Open all year rs Winter pool, restaurant & touring field Last arrival 22.00hrs Last departure 10.30hrs

In a picturesque valley amongst woodland, this neat park is kept to a high standard. The extensive amenities include tennis courts, indoor swimming pool, licensed clubhouse and restaurant. The sea is just a mile away, and can be accessed via a footpath and cycle path along the river bank. 20 acre site. 29 touring pitches. 13 hardstandings. Tent pitches. Motorhome pitches. 75 statics.

Notes No motorised scooters, skateboards or bikes at night

Heligan Woods (SW998470)

▶▶▶

PL26 6BT

☎ 01726 842714 & 844414 📠 01726 844142

e-mail: info@pentewan.co.uk

dir: *From A390 take B3273 for Mevagissey at x-roads signed 'No caravans beyond this point'. Right onto unclass road towards Gorran, site 0.75m on left*

PETS: Charges £2.50 per night **Public areas** except children's play area, showers, toilets & shop disp bin **Exercise area on site** long lane through woodland **Facilities** food washing facs walks info vet info

Open 16 Jan-26 Nov Last arrival 22.30hrs Last departure 10.30hrs

A pleasant peaceful park adjacent to the Lost Gardens of Heligan, with views over St Austell Bay, and well-maintained facilities. Guests can also use the extensive amenities at the sister park, Pentewan Sands, and there's a footpath with direct access to Heligan Gardens. 12 acre site. 89 touring pitches. 24 hardstandings. 3 seasonal pitches. Tent pitches. Motorhome pitches. 17 statics.

PENZANCE — Map 2 SW43

Hotel Penzance

★★★ 85% ◉◉ HOTEL

Britons Hill TR18 3AE

☎ 01736 363117 🖨 01736 350970

e-mail: reception@hotelpenzance.com

web: www.hotelpenzance.com

dir: *From A30 pass heliport on right, left at next rdbt for town centre. 3rd right onto Britons Hill. Hotel on right*

PETS: Bedrooms (2 GF) **Charges** dog £10 per night **Public areas** except restaurant on leads **Grounds** **Exercise area** 300mtrs **Facilities** feeding mat walks info vet info **On Request** fridge access torch towels **Stables** 5m **Other** charge for damage **Resident Pets:** Tom & Jerry (Birman cats)

This Edwardian house has been tastefully redesigned, particularly in the contemporary Bay Restaurant. The focus on style is not only limited to the decor, but is also apparent in the award-winning cuisine that is based on fresh Cornish produce. Bedrooms have been appointed to modern standards and are particularly well equipped; many have views across Mount's Bay.

Rooms 25 (2 GF) **S** £82-£89; **D** £120-£190 (incl. bkfst)* **Facilities** FTV ⅃ Xmas New Year Wi-fi **Parking** 12 **Notes** LB

Queens

★★★ 73% HOTEL

The Promenade TR18 4HG

☎ 01736 362371 🖨 01736 350033

e-mail: enquiries@queens-hotel.com

web: www.queens-hotel.com

dir: *A30 to Penzance, follow signs for seafront pass harbour into promenade, hotel 0.5m on right*

PETS: Bedrooms sign **Charges** phone for details **Public areas** except restaurant on leads **Facilities** cage storage walks info vet info **On Request** fridge access torch towels **Resident Pets:** Bilbo & Cleo (Jack Russells), Logan & Murphy (Labradors)

With views across Mount's Bay towards Newlyn, this impressive Victorian hotel has a long and distinguished history. Comfortable public areas are filled with interesting pictures and artefacts, and in the dining room guests can choose from the daily-changing menu. Bedrooms, many with sea views, vary in style and size.

Rooms 70 (10 fmly) **S** £60-£92; **D** £100-£180 (incl. bkfst)* **Facilities** FTV Xmas New Year Wi-fi **Services** Lift **Parking** 50 **Notes** LB

See advert on opposite page

Mount View

★★★ INN

Longrock TR20 8JJ

☎ 01736 710416 🖨 01736 710416

dir: *Off A30 at Marazion/Penzance rdbt, 3rd exit signed Longrock. On right after pelican crossing*

PETS: Bedrooms unattended **Public areas** bar only on leads **Exercise area** beach & field 50yds **Facilities** walks info vet info **Resident Pet:** Muppet (Beagle)

This Victorian inn, just a short walk from the beach and half a mile from the Isles of Scilly heliport, is a good base for exploring west Cornwall. Bedrooms are well equipped, including a hospitality tray, and the bar is popular with locals. Breakfast is served in the dining room and a dinner menu is available.

Rooms 5 rms (3 en suite) (2 fmly) (2 smoking) **S** £22-£34.50; **D** £44-£59 **Facilities** FTV tea/coffee Dinner available Wi-fi Pool table **Parking** 8 **Notes** RS Sun closed 4.30-7pm

Penmorvah

★★★ GUEST ACCOMMODATION

61 Alexandra Rd TR18 4LZ

☎ 01736 363711

e-mail: penmorvah_penzance@talktalk.net

dir: *A30 to Penzance, at railway station follow road along harbour front pass Jubilee pool. At mini-rdbt, right onto Alexandra Rd*

PETS: Bedrooms (2 GF) **Public areas** except dining room on leads **Exercise area** park (400yds) **Facilities** food bowl water bowl feeding mat walks info vet info **On Request** fridge access torch towels **Other** charge for damage **Resident Pet:** Marbles (dog)

A well situated property offering comfortable rooms, all of which are en suite. Penmorvah is just a few minutes' walk from the seafront with convenient on-street parking nearby.

Rooms 8 en suite (2 fmly) (2 GF) **S** £30-£45; **D** £60-£70 **Facilities** FTV tea/coffee Cen ht **Notes** LB No Children 5yrs ⊗

Bone Valley Caravan & Camping Park
(SW472316)

▶▶▶

Heamoor TR20 8UJ
☎ 01736 360313 🖹 01736 360313
e-mail: wardmandie@yahoo.co.uk
dir: *Exit A30 at Heamoor/Madron rdbt. 4th on right into Josephs Lane. 800yds left into Bone Valley. Entrance 200yds on left*

PETS: Public areas on leads **Exercise area** field 100yds **Facilities** walks info vet info **Stables** 100yds **Other** prior notice required

Open all year Last arrival 22.00hrs Last departure 10.00hrs

A compact grassy park on the outskirts of Penzance, with well maintained facilities. It is divided into paddocks by mature hedges, and a small stream runs alongside. 1 acre site. 17 touring pitches. 6 hardstandings. Tent pitches. Motorhome pitches. 3 statics.

PERRANPORTH	Map 2 SW75

St Georges Country House
★★★★ GUEST ACCOMMODATION
St Georges Hill TR6 0ED
☎ 01872 572184
e-mail: info@stgeorgescountryhouse.co.uk

PETS: Bedrooms certain bedrooms only **Charges** £5 per night **Public areas** except restaurant on leads **Grounds Exercise area** 500mtrs **Facilities** walks info vet info **Restrictions** very large dogs not accepted **Resident Pet:** Mollie (Border Collie)

Situated in an elevated position above Perranporth, St Georges is a very friendly and comfortable establishment. The owners and staff are attentive and very welcoming. Food is served most evenings and there is also a bar and large sitting room with comfy sofas and lots of books.

Rooms 7 en suite (2 fmly) **Facilities** FTV TVL tea/coffee Dinner available Cen ht Licensed Wi-fi **Parking** 10 **Notes** LB Closed 23-30 Dec

Tollgate Farm Caravan & Camping Park
(SW768547)

▶▶▶▶

Budnick Hill TR6 0AD
☎ 01872 572130 & 0845 166 2126
e-mail: enquiries@tollgatefarm.co.uk
dir: *Off A30 onto B3285 to Perranporth. Site on right 1.5m after Goonhavern*

PETS: Public areas disp bin **Exercise area** beach & sand dunes adjacent **Facilities** food dog chews cat treats scoop/disp bags washing facs walks info vet info **Stables** 1m **Resident Pets:** 5 dogs, 2 ponies, 1 llama, 9 goats, 1 rabbit, guinea pigs, chipmunks, chickens, guineafowl

Open Etr-Sep Last arrival 21.00hrs Last departure 11.00hrs

A quiet site in a rural location with spectacular coastal views. Pitches are divided into four paddocks sheltered and screened by mature hedges. Children will enjoy the play equipment and pets' corner. The three miles of sand at Perran Bay are just a walk away through the sand dunes, or by car it it is a three-quarter mile drive. 10 acre site. 102 touring pitches. 10 hardstandings. 12 seasonal pitches. Tent pitches. Motorhome pitches.

Notes No large groups.

ENGLAND

Talland Bay Hotel

★★★ 87% ◉◉ COUNTRY HOUSE HOTEL

Porthallow PL13 2JB

☎ 01503 272667　📠 01503 272940

e-mail: info@tallandbayhotel.co.uk

web: www.tallandbayhotel.co.uk

dir: *From Looe over bridge towards Polperro on A387, 2nd turn to hotel*

PETS: Bedrooms (5 GF) sign **Charges** £7.50 per night **Public areas** except restaurant on leads **Grounds** on leads disp bin **Exercise area** surrounding countryside **Facilities** bedding feeding mat leads washing facs cage storage walks info vet info **On Request** fridge access torch towels **Other** charge for damage **Resident Pets:** Alfie & Bunnie (dogs), Flo & Jonty (cats)

This hotel has the benefit of a wonderful location, being situated in its own extensive gardens that run down almost to the cliff edge. A warm and friendly atmosphere prevails and many bedrooms have sea views. Public areas and bedrooms have under gone a major refurbishment with impressive and stylish results. Accomplished cooking, with an emphasis on carefully prepared local produce, remains a key feature here.

Rooms 20 (2 fmly) (5 GF) **S** £75-£110; **D** £100-£200 (incl. bkfst) **Facilities** FTV ✈ Xmas New Year Wi-fi **Parking** 22 **Notes** LB

Penryn House

★★★★ GUEST ACCOMMODATION

The Coombes PL13 2RQ

☎ 01503 272157　📠 01503 273055

e-mail: enquiries@penrynhouse.co.uk

web: www.penrynhouse.co.uk

dir: *A387 to Polperro, at mini-rdbt left down hill into village (ignore restricted access). 200yds on left*

PETS: Bedrooms unattended family bedrooms only **Public areas** except restaurant **Grounds** on leads disp bin **Exercise area** 200yds **Facilities** food bowl water bowl leads pet sitting washing facs cage storage walks info vet info **On Request** fridge access torch towels **Stables** 5m **Resident Pet:** Ella (Great Dane)

Penryn House has a relaxed atmosphere and offers a warm welcome. Every effort is made to ensure a memorable stay. Bedrooms are neatly presented and reflect the character of the building. After a day exploring, enjoy a drink at the bar and relax in the comfortable lounge.

Rooms 12 en suite (3 fmly) **S** £41-£46; **D** £72-£102 **Facilities** FTV tea/coffee Licensed Wi-fi **Parking** 13 **Notes** LB

Polruan Holidays-Camping & Caravanning

(SX133509)

▶ ▶ ▶

Polruan-by-Fowey PL23 1QH

☎ 01726 870263

e-mail: polholiday@aol.com

dir: *A38 to Dobwalls, left onto A390 to East Taphouse. Left onto B3359. Right in 4.5m signed Polruan*

PETS: Charges £1 per night **Public areas** except toilet/shower block & laundry room disp bin **Exercise area** adjacent **Facilities** food food bowl water bowl dog chews leads walks info vet info **Stables** 5m **Other** prior notice required day kennels 5m disposal bags available

Open Etr-Oct Last arrival 21.00hrs Last departure noon

A very rural and quiet site in a lovely elevated position above the village, with good views of the sea. The River Fowey passenger ferry is close by, and the site has a good shop, and barbecues to borrow. 3 acre site. 47 touring pitches. 7 hardstandings. Tent pitches. Motorhome pitches. 10 statics.

Notes No skateboards, rollerskates, bikes, water pistols or water bombs

South Winds Caravan & Camping Park

(SW948790)

▶ ▶ ▶

Polzeath Rd PL27 6QU

☎ 01208 863267　📠 01208 869920

e-mail: info@southwindscamping.co.uk

dir: *Exit B3314 onto unclass road signed Polzeath, site on right just past turn to New Polzeath*

PETS: Charges £2 per night **Public areas** on leads **Exercise area** adjacent **Facilities** washing facs walks info vet info **Other** prior notice required shop nearby

Open May-mid Sep Last arrival 21.00hrs Last departure 10.30hrs

A peaceful site with beautiful sea and panoramic rural views, within walking distance of a golf complex, and just three quarters of a mile from beach and village. There is an impressive reception building, replete with tourist information, TV, settees and a range of camping spares. 16 acre site. 165 touring pitches. Tent pitches. Motorhome pitches.

Notes No disposable BBQs, no noise 23.00hrs-07.00hrs, families & couples only.

Tristram Caravan & Camping Park *(SW936790)*

►►►

PL27 6TP

☎ 01208 862215   🖹 01208 869920

e-mail: info@tristramcampsite.co.uk

dir: *From B3314 onto unclassified road signed Polzeath. Through village, up hill, site 2nd right*

PETS: Charges £2-£3 per night **Public areas** disp bin
Exercise area field adjacent **Facilities** walks info vet info
Stables nearby **Other** prior notice required

Open Mar-Nov rs Mid Sep reseeding works Last arrival 21.00hrs Last departure 10.00hrs

An ideal family site, positioned on a gently sloping cliff with grassy pitches and glorious sea views, which are best enjoyed from the terraced premier pitches, or over lunch at the Salt Water Café adjacent to the reception/shop. There is direct, gated access to the beach, where surfing is very popular, and the park has a holiday bungalow for rent. The local amenities of the village are only a few hundred yards away. 10 acre site. 100 touring pitches. Tent pitches. Motorhome pitches.

Notes No ball games, no disposable BBQs, no noise between 23.00hrs-07.00hrs.

PORTHTOWAN   Map 2 SW64

Porthtowan Tourist Park *(SW693473)*

►►►►

Mile Hill TR4 8TY

☎ 01209 890256

e-mail: admin@porthtowantouristpark.co.uk

dir: *Exit A30 at junct signed Redruth/Porthtowan. Take 3rd exit at rdbt. 2m, right at T-junct. Site on left at top of hill*

PETS: Charges peak season £1 per night **Public areas** except buildings & children's play area disp bin **Exercise area on site** fenced area **Facilities** walks info vet info **Other** prior notice required disposal bags available

Open Apr-Sep Last arrival 21.30hrs Last departure 11.00hrs

A neat, level grassy site on high ground above Porthtowan, with plenty of shelter from mature trees and shrubs. The superb toilet facilities considerably enhance the appeal of this peaceful rural park, which is almost midway between the small seaside resorts of Portreath and Porthtowan, with their beaches and surfing. 5 acre site. 80 touring pitches. 2 hardstandings. 8 seasonal pitches. Tent pitches. Motorhome pitches.

Notes No bikes or skateboards during Jul & Aug.

Wheal Rose Caravan & Camping Park *(SW717449)*

►►►►

Wheal Rose TR16 5DD

☎ 01209 891496

e-mail: whealrose@aol.com

dir: *Exit A30 at Scorrier sign, follow signs to Wheal Rose. Site 0.5m on left (Wheal Rose to Porthtowan road)*

PETS: Public areas on leads disp bin **Exercise area** adjacent tram road **Facilities** food food bowl water bowl dog chews cat treats leads cage storage walks info vet info **On Request** fridge access torch **Other** charge for damage prior notice required dogs must be kept on leads at all times & exercised off site

Open Mar-Dec Last arrival 21.00hrs Last departure 11.00hrs

A quiet, peaceful park in a secluded valley setting, central for beaches and countryside, and two miles from the surfing beaches of Porthtowan. The friendly owners work hard to keep this park immaculate, with a bright toilet block and well-trimmed pitches. 6 acre site. 50 touring pitches. 6 hardstandings. Tent pitches. Motorhome pitches. 3 statics.

Notes 5mph speed limit, minimum noise after 23.00hrs, gates locked 23.00hrs.

REDRUTH   Map 2 SW64

Cambrose Touring Park *(SW684453)*

►►►

Portreath Rd TR16 4HT

☎ 01209 890747

e-mail: cambrosetouringpark@supanet.com

dir: *A30 onto B3300 towards Portreath. Approx 0.75m at 1st rdbt right onto B3300. Take unclass road on right signed Porthtowan. Site 200yds on left*

PETS: Charges £1 per night **Public areas** disp bin
Exercise area on site large field **Facilities** walks info vet info
Other prior notice required disposal bags available **Resident Pet:** Pip (Collie)

Open Apr-Oct Last arrival 22.00hrs Last departure 11.30hrs

Situated in a rural setting surrounded by trees and shrubs, this park is divided into grassy paddocks. It is situated about two miles from the harbour village of Portreath. 6 acre site. 60 touring pitches. Tent pitches. Motorhome pitches.

REDRUTH *continued*

Lanyon Holiday Park *(SW684387)*

▶ ▶ ▶

Loscombe Ln, Four Lanes TR16 6LP
☎ 01209 313474
e-mail: info@lanyonholidaypark.co.uk
dir: *Signed 0.5m off B2397 on Helston side of Four Lanes village*

PETS: Bedrooms Charges £1 (£2 high season) per night
Public areas except toilets/showers & launderettes on leads
disp bin **Exercise area on site** large dog walking paddock
Facilities walks info vet info **On Request** fridge access **Stables**
nearby **Other** charge for damage prior notice required

Open Mar-Oct Last arrival 21.00hrs Last departure noon

Small, friendly rural park in an elevated position with fine views
to distant St Ives Bay. This family owned and run park continues
to be upgraded in all areas, with refurbished toilet blocks and two
holiday lodges, and is close to a cycling trail. Stithian's Reservoir
for fishing, sailing and windsurfing is two miles away. 14 acre
site. 25 touring pitches. Tent pitches. Motorhome pitches. 49
statics.

Notes Family park

REJERRAH	Map 2 SW75

Monkey Tree Holiday Park *(SW803545)*

Scotland Rd TR8 5QR
☎ 01872 572032 📠 01872 573577
e-mail: enquiries@monkeytreeholidaypark.co.uk
dir: *Exit A30 onto B3285 to Perranporth, 0.25m right into
Scotland Rd, site on left in 1.5m*

PETS: Charges £3 per night **Public areas** except bar, restaurant,
children's play areas, pool, clubhouse, takeaway & toilet/shower
facilities disp bin **Exercise area on site** dog walking area
Facilities food walks info vet info **Stables** 3m **Other** prior
notice required disposal bags available **Restrictions** no Pit Bull
Terriers, Japanese Tosas, Dogo Argentinos & Fila Brasilieros (see
page 7)

Open all year Last arrival 22.00hrs Last departure 10.00hrs

A busy holiday park with plenty of activities and a jolly holiday
atmosphere. Set close to lovely beaches between Newquay and
Perranporth, it offers an outdoor swimming pool, children's
playground, two bars with entertainment, and a good choice
of eating outlets including a restaurant and a takeaway. 56
acre site. 750 touring pitches. 17 hardstandings. Tent pitches.
Motorhome pitches. 48 statics.

Notes Family & couples park.

Newperran Holiday Park *(SW801555)*

▶ ▶ ▶ ▶

TR8 5QJ
☎ 01872 572407 📠 01872 571254
e-mail: holidays@newperran.co.uk
dir: *4m SE of Newquay & 1m S of Rejerrah on A3075. Or A30
Redruth, exit B3275 Perranporth, at 1st T-junct right onto A3075
towards Newquay, site 300mtrs on left*

PETS: Charges £2.50 per night **Public areas** except children's
play area on leads disp bin **Exercise area on site** dog walks
& field **Facilities** washing facs walks info vet info **Stables** 2m
Other prior notice required **Resident Pet:** Hamish (West Highland
Terrier)

Open Etr-Oct Last arrival mdnthrs Last departure 10.00hrs

A family site in a lovely rural position near several beaches and
bays. This airy park offers screening to some pitches, which are
set in paddocks on level ground. High season entertainment is
available in the park's country inn, and the café has an extensive
menu. 25 acre site. 357 touring pitches. 14 hardstandings. Tent
pitches. Motorhome pitches. 16 statics.

Notes Families & couples only. No skateboards.

ROSUDGEON	Map 2 SW52

Kenneggy Cove Holiday Park *(SW562287)*

▶ ▶ ▶

Higher Kenneggy TR20 9AU
☎ 01736 763453
e-mail: enquiries@kenneggycove.co.uk
dir: *On A394 between Penzance & Helston, turn S into signed lane
to site & Higher Kenneggy*

PETS: Charges dog £3 per night **Public areas** except children's
play area, shop, toilets & laundry disp bin **Exercise area** 50mtrs
Facilities food food bowl water bowl scoop/disp bags washing
facs walks info vet info **Other** dogs allowed on Kenneggy Sands
all year **Restrictions** no dangerous breeds (see page 7) **Resident
Pets:** Hugo & Tickle (Wire Haired Dachshunds), Ginger (cat)

Open 12 May-Sep Last arrival 21.00hrs Last departure 11.00hrs

Set in an Area of Outstanding Natural Beauty with spectacular
sea views, this family-owned park is quiet and well kept, with a
well-equipped children's play area, clean, well maintained toilets,
and a takeaway food facility offering home-cooked meals. A short
walk along a country footpath leads to the Cornish Coastal Path,
and on to the golden sandy beach at Kenneggy Cove. 4 acre site.
45 touring pitches. Tent pitches. Motorhome pitches. 7 statics.

Notes No large or single sex groups. 📷

RUMFORD
Map 2 SW87

ST AGNES
Map 2 SW75

Music Water Touring Park *(SW906685)*

▶ ▶ ▶

PL27 7SJ

☎ 01841 540257

dir: *A39 at Winnards Perch rdbt onto B3274 signed Padstow. Left in 2m onto unclass road signed Rumford & St Eval. Site 500mtrs on right*

PETS: Charges £2-£3 per night **Public areas** except bar disp bin **Exercise area on site** short dog walk **Facilities** walks info vet info **Stables** nearby **Other** prior notice required max 2 dogs per pitch **Restrictions** no Pit Bull Terriers or Rottweilers **Resident Pets:** pets' corner on site (donkeys, dog, chickens, rabbits)

Open Apr-Oct Last arrival 23.00hrs Last departure 11.00hrs

Set in a peaceful location yet only a short drive to the pretty fishing town of Padstow, and many sandy beaches and coves. This family owned and run park has grassy paddocks, and there is a quiet lounge bar and a separate children's games room. 8 acre site. 55 touring pitches. 2 hardstandings. Tent pitches. Motorhome pitches. 2 statics.

Notes Maximum one tent per pitch. ♨

Rose-in-Vale Country House

★★★ 81% ⊚ COUNTRY HOUSE HOTEL

Mithian TR5 0QD

☎ 01872 552202 ▤ 01872 552700

e-mail: reception@rose-in-vale-hotel.co.uk

web: www.rose-in-vale-hotel.co.uk

dir: *A30 S towards Redruth. At Chiverton Cross at rdbt take B3277 signed St Agnes. In 500mtrs follow tourist sign for Rose-in-Vale. Into Mithian, right at Miners Arms, down hill. Hotel on left*

PETS: Bedrooms (6 GF) **Charges** £6 per night **Public areas** except restaurant on leads **Grounds** on leads disp bin **Exercise area** nearby **Facilities** walks info vet info **Stables** 3m **Other** charge for damage **Restrictions** dogs accepted only at manager's discretion **Resident Pets:** Daisey & Rosie (Black Labradors)

Peacefully located in a wooded valley this Georgian manor house has a wonderfully relaxed atmosphere and abundant charm. Guests are assured of a warm welcome. Accommodation varies in size and style; several rooms are situated on the ground floor. An imaginative fixed-price menu featuring local produce is served in the spacious restaurant.

Rooms 23 (3 annexe) (1 fmly) (6 GF) **Facilities** FTV ⚲ ⛵ Xmas New Year Wi-fi **Services** Lift **Parking** 50 **Notes** No children 12yrs

ST AGNES *continued*

Beacon Country House Hotel

★★ 82% HOTEL

Goonvrea Rd TR5 0NW
☎ 01872 552318
e-mail: info@beaconhotel.co.uk
dir: *A30 onto B3277 to St Agnes. At rdbt left into Goonvrea Rd. Hotel 0.75m on right*

PETS: **Bedrooms** (2 GF) ground-floor bedrooms only **Charges** discretionary **Grounds** on leads disp bin **Exercise area** approx 200yds **Facilities** pet sitting dog walking washing facs cage storage walks info vet info **On Request** fridge access torch towels **Other** charge for damage max 2 dogs per room

Set in a quiet and attractive area away from the busy village, this family-run, relaxed hotel has splendid views over the countryside and along the coast to St Ives. Hospitality and customer care are great strengths with guests assured of a very warm and friendly stay. Bedrooms are comfortable and well equipped, and many benefit from glorious views.

Rooms 11 (2 GF) **Facilities** FTV Xmas New Year Wi-fi **Parking** 12 **Notes** LB No children 8yrs Closed 4-31 Jan

Driftwood Spars

★★★★ ⌂ GUEST ACCOMMODATION

Trevaunance Cove TR5 0RT
☎ 01872 552428
e-mail: info@driftwoodspars.co.uk
dir: *A30 to Chiverton rdbt, right onto B3277, through village. Driftwood Spars 200yds before beach*

PETS: **Bedrooms** (5 GF) **Charges** £3 per night £21 per week **Public areas** except restaurant on leads **Grounds** **Exercise area** beach (500yds) **Facilities** vet info **On Request** fridge access **Stables** 3m **Other** charge for damage **Resident Pet:** Treacle (cat)

Partly built from shipwreck timbers, this 18th-century inn attracts locals and visitors alike. The attractive bedrooms, some in an annexe, are decorated in a bright, seaside style with many interesting features. Local produce, including delicious seafood, is served in the informal pub dining room and in the restaurant, together with a range from hand-pulled beers.

Rooms 9 en suite 6 annexe en suite (4 fmly) (5 GF) **S** £45-£66; **D** £86-£102 **Facilities** tea/coffee Dinner available Direct Dial Cen ht Licensed Wi-fi Pool table **Parking** 40 **Notes** LB RS 25 Dec no lunch/dinner, no bar in evening

Penkerris

★★ GUEST HOUSE

Penwinnick Rd TR5 0PA
☎ 01872 552262   📠 01872 552262
e-mail: info@penkerris.co.uk
web: www.penkerris.co.uk
dir: *A30 onto B3277 to village, on right after village sign*

PETS: **Bedrooms** **Grounds** disp bin **Facilities** walks info vet info **On Request** fridge access **Stables** 1m **Resident Pet:** Sylvester (cat)

Close to three surfing beaches and dramatic cliff walks, Penkerris is an elegant Edwardian house with a friendly atmosphere. An ideal place for families, the house has a large, lawned garden with plenty of toys and activities, and drinks can be served outside in warm weather. Bedrooms are comfortable and well appointed, and home-cooked meals are served by arrangement. A beach hut, complete with surf boards, is available for guests at nearby Trevaunance Cove.

Rooms 7 rms (4 en suite) (3 fmly); **D** £40-£70 **Facilities** FTV TVL tea/coffee Dinner available Licensed Wi-fi **Parking** 9 **Notes** LB

Beacon Cottage Farm Touring Park

(SW705502)

▶▶▶▶

Beacon Dr TR5 0NU
☎ 01872 552347 & 07879 413862
e-mail: beaconcottagefarm@lineone.net
dir: *From A30 at Threeburrows rdbt take B3277 to St Agnes, left into Goonvrea Rd, right into Beacon Drive, follow brown sign to site*

PETS: **Charges** £2.50 per night **Public areas** except play area disp bin **Exercise area on site** field available **Facilities** washing facs walks info vet info **Resident Pets:** Rusty (cat), Folly (horse)

Open Apr-Oct rs Etr-Whit shop closed Last arrival 20.00hrs Last departure noon

A neat and compact site on a working farm, utilizing a cottage and outhouses, an old orchard and adjoining walled paddock. The unique location on a headland looking north-east along the coast comes with stunning views towards St Ives, and the keen friendly family owners keep all areas very well maintained. 5 acre site. 70 touring pitches. 2 seasonal pitches. Tent pitches. Motorhome pitches.

Notes No large groups.

Presingoll Farm Caravan & Camping Park
(SW721494)

► ► ►

TR5 0PB
☎ 01872 552333 📄 01872 552333
e-mail: pam@presingollfarm.co.uk
dir: *From A30 Chiverton rdbt take B3277 towards St Agnes. Site 3m on right*

PETS: Public areas dogs must be kept on leads at all times disp bin **Exercise area on site** adjacent meadow with disposal bins **Facilities** walks info vet info **Resident Pets:** working farm with cattle, pigs & horses; family dogs (Collies & Dalmatians)

Open Etr/Apr-Oct Last departure 10.00hrs

An attractive rural park adjoining farmland, with extensive views of the coast beyond. Family owned and run, with level grass pitches, and modernised toilet block in smart converted farm buildings. There is also a campers' room with microwave, freezer, kettle and free coffee and tea, and a children's play area. 5 acre site. 90 touring pitches. 6 hardstandings. Tent pitches. Motorhome pitches.

Notes No large groups. 🐾

ST AUSTELL	Map 2 SX05

The Cornwall Hotel Spa & Estate
★★★★ 78% ◉◉ COUNTRY HOUSE HOTEL
Pentewan Rd, Tregorrick PL26 7AB
☎ 01726 874050 📄 01726 66294
e-mail: enquiries@thecornwall.com
dir: *A391 to St Austell then B3273 towards Mevagissey. Hotel approx 0.5m on right*

PETS: Bedrooms certain bedrooms only **Charges** call hotel for details **Public areas** except restaurant on leads **Grounds** on leads disp bin **Exercise area** nearby **Facilities** scoop/disp bags walks info vet info **On Request** fridge access

Set in 43 acres of wooded parkland, this manor house offers guests a real retreat. The restored White House has suites and traditionally styled bedrooms, and adjoining are the contemporary Woodland rooms ranging from standard, family, accessible, and also deluxe which have private balcony areas looking out to the Pentewan Valley. There are superb leisure facilities including the spa with luxury treatments, an infinity pool and state-of-the-art fitness centre. There is a choice of eating options - The Arboretum and the more informal Acorns plus the Drawing Room and Parkland Terrace for afternoon tea and cocktails. This is an ideal base for visiting The Eden Project, The Lost Gardens of Heligan and south Cornwall fishing villages.

Rooms 65 (4 fmly) **Facilities** Spa STV FTV ◉ 🌊 🏊 Gym Xmas New Year Wi-fi Child facilities **Services** Lift **Parking** 200

Sunnycroft
★★★★ GUEST ACCOMMODATION
28 Penwinnick Rd PL25 5DS
☎ 01726 73351 📄 01726 879409
e-mail: enquiries@sunnycroft.net
dir: *600yds SW of town centre on A390*

PETS: Bedrooms Grounds on leads disp bin **Exercise area** 10-15 mins from house **Facilities** food bowl water bowl dog chews leads washing facs cage storage walks info vet info **On Request** fridge access torch towels **Other** dogs accepted by prior arrangement only **Resident Pet:** Benje (dog)

Just a short walk from the town centre, this 1930s house is conveniently situated for the Eden Project. The bright bedrooms offer good levels of comfort, and ground-floor rooms are available. Tasty and substantial breakfasts are served in the light and airy conservatory dining room. Ample off-road, secure parking is available too.

Rooms 5 en suite **S** £45-£75; **D** £65-£120 **Facilities** FTV tea/coffee Dinner available Cen ht Wi-fi Golf 18 **Parking** 10 **Notes** LB No Children 7yrs Closed 24-26 Dec

River Valley Holiday Park *(SX010503)*
► ► ► ► ►

London Apprentice PL26 7AP
☎ 01726 73533
e-mail: mail@cornwall-holidays.co.uk
dir: *Direct access to site signed on B3273 from St Austell at London Apprentice*

PETS: Charges contact park for details **Public areas** disp bin **Exercise area** woods adjacent **Facilities** food food bowl water bowl walks info vet info **Other** prior notice required

Open Apr-end of Sep Last arrival 21.00hrs Last departure 11.00hrs

A neat, well-maintained family-run park set in a pleasant river valley. The quality toilet block and attractively landscaped grounds make this a delightful base for a holiday. All pitches are hardstanding, mostly divided by low fencing and neatly trimmed hedges, and the park offers a good range of leisure facilities, including an inviting swimming pool, a games room, an internet room, and an excellent children's play area. There is direct access to river walks and the cycle trail to the beach at Pentewan. 2 acre site. 45 touring pitches. 45 hardstandings. Tent pitches. Motorhome pitches. 40 statics.

ENGLAND

ST AUSTELL *continued*

Court Farm Holidays *(SW953524)*

▶ ▶ ▶

St Stephen PL26 7LE
☎ 01726 823684 📄 01726 823684
e-mail: truscott@ctfarm.freeserve.co.uk
dir: *From St Austell take A3058 towards Newquay. Through St Stephen (pass Peugeot garage). Right at St Stephen/Coombe Hay/Langreth/Industrial site sign. 400yds, site on right*

PETS: Charges horse £25 per week **Public areas** on leads disp bin **Exercise area on site** adjacent fields **Facilities** walks info vet info **Other** prior notice required dog grooming nearby please phone for details regarding horses **Resident Pets:** 2 dogs, 2 cats, 16 horses & 1 tortoise

Open Apr-Sep Last arrival by dark Last departure 11.00hrs

Set in a peaceful rural location, this large camping field offers plenty of space, and is handy for the Eden Project and the Lost Gardens of Heligan. Coarse fishing and star-gazing facilities at the Roseland Observatory are among the on-site attractions. 4 acre site. 20 touring pitches. 5 hardstandings. Tent pitches. Motorhome pitches.

Notes No noise after dark.

| ST BLAZEY GATE | Map 2 SX05 |

Doubletrees Farm *(SX060540)*

▶ ▶ ▶

Luxulyan Rd PL24 2EH
☎ 01726 812266
e-mail: doubletrees@eids.co.uk
dir: *On A390 at Blazey Gate. Turn by Leek Seed Chapel, almost opposite BP filling station. After approx 300yds turn right by public bench into site*

PETS: Public areas except showers & toilet blocks on leads disp bin **Exercise area on site** 5 acres **Facilities** walks info vet info **Resident Pets:** Ben (Border Collie), chickens, ducks

Open all year Last arrival 22.30hrs Last departure 11.30hrs

A popular park with terraced pitches offering superb sea and coastal views. Close to beaches, and the nearest park to the Eden Project, it is very well maintained by friendly owners. 1.57 acre site. 32 touring pitches. 6 hardstandings. Tent pitches. Motorhome pitches.

Notes No noise after mdnt.

| ST COLUMB MAJOR | Map 2 SW96 |

Southleigh Manor Naturist Park *(SW918623)*

▶ ▶ ▶

TR9 6HY
☎ 01637 880938 📄 01637 881108
e-mail: enquiries@southleigh-manor.com
dir: *Exit A30 at junct with A39 signed Wadebridge. At Highgate Hill rdbt take A39. At Halloon rdbt take A39. At Trekenning rdbt take 4th exit. Site 500mtrs on right*

PETS: Charges Public areas dogs only allowed adjacent to owner's pitch on leads **Exercise area** surrounding area **Facilities** walks info vet info **Other** dogs must be kept on leads at all times & exercised off site **Restrictions** no dangerous dogeds (see page 7)

Open Etr-Oct rs Peak times shop open Last arrival 20.00hrs Last departure 10.30hrs

A very well maintained, naturist park in the heart of the Cornish countryside, catering for families and couples only. Seclusion and security are very well planned, and the lovely gardens provide a calm setting. There are two lodges and static caravans for holiday hire. 4 acre site. 50 touring pitches. Tent pitches. Motorhome pitches.

Notes

| ST IVES | Map 2 SW54 |

Garrack Hotel & Restaurant

★★★ 77% ⊛ HOTEL

Burthallan Ln, Higher Ayr TR26 3AA
☎ 01736 796199 📄 01736 798955
e-mail: aa@garrack.com
dir: *Exit A30 for St Ives. From B3311 follow brown signs for Tate Gallery, then Garrack signs*

PETS: Bedrooms (3 GF) unattended certain bedrooms only **Charges** max £10 per night **Grounds** on leads disp bin **Exercise area** country lane & cliff walks 15 mins' walk **Facilities** washing facs walks info vet info **On Request** fridge access towels **Other** charge for damage prior notice required

Enjoying a peaceful, elevated position with splendid views across the harbour and Porthmeor Beach, the Garrack sits in its own delightful grounds and gardens. Bedrooms are comfortable and many have sea views. Public areas include a small leisure suite, a choice of lounges and an attractive restaurant, where locally sourced ingredients are used in the enjoyable dishes.

Rooms 18 (2 annexe) (2 fmly) (3 GF) **Facilities** FTV ⊗ Gym New Year Wi-fi **Parking** 30 **Notes** LB

Old Vicarage

★★★★ 🏛 GUEST HOUSE

Parc-an-Creet TR26 2ES
☎ 01736 796124
e-mail: stay@oldvicarage.com
web: www.oldvicarage.com
dir: *From A3074 in town centre take B3306, 0.5m right into Parc-an-Creet*

PETS: Bedrooms Charges £5 per night £35 per week
Public areas except dining room **Grounds** disp bin
Exercise area Exercise area 10 mins **Other** charge for damage pets must be well behaved **Resident Pet:** Tiger (cat)

This former Victorian rectory stands in secluded gardens in a quiet part of St Ives and is convenient for the seaside, town and Tate St Ives. The bedrooms are enhanced by modern facilities. A good choice of local produce is offered at breakfast, plus home-made yoghurt and preserves.

Rooms 6 en suite (4 fmly) **S** £63-£67; **D** £84-£94 **Facilities** FTV TVL tea/coffee Cen ht Licensed Wi-fi 🛆 **Parking** 12 **Notes** LB Closed Dec-Jan

Penderleath Caravan & Camping Park

(SW496375)

▶ ▶ ▶ ▶

Towednack TR26 3AF
☎ 01736 798403 & 07840 208542
e-mail: holidays@penderleath.co.uk
dir: *From A30 take A3074 towards St Ives. Left at 2nd mini-rdbt, approx 3m to T-junct. Left then immediately right. Next left*

PETS: Charges £1.50-£3 per night **Public areas** except toilets, bar area & shop on leads disp bin **Exercise area on site** available except in Aug **Facilities** scoop/disp bags walks info vet info **Other** prior notice required dogs must be well behaved; maximum 2 dogs per pitch disposal bags & pet toys available **Resident Pet:** Buster (Jack Russell)

Open Etr-Oct Last arrival 21.30hrs Last departure 10.30hrs

Set in a rugged rural location, this tranquil park has extensive views towards St Ives Bay and the north coast. Facilities are all housed in modernised granite barns, and include spotless toilets, including fully-serviced shower rooms, and there's a quiet licensed bar with beer garden, breakfast room and bar meals. The owners are welcoming and helpful and have now opened a food takeaway facility. 10 acre site. 75 touring pitches. Tent pitches. Motorhome pitches.

Notes No campfires, no noise after 23.00hrs.

Trevalgan Touring Park *(SW490402)*

▶ ▶ ▶ ▶

Trevalgan TR26 3BJ
☎ 01736 792048
e-mail: recept@trevalgantouringpark.co.uk
dir: *From A30 follow holiday route to St Ives. B3311 through Halsetown to B3306. Left towards Land's End. Site signed 0.5m on right*

PETS: Charges Public areas except children's play area disp bin
Exercise area 100mtrs, beaches from Nov-Easter only **Facilities** food washing facs walks info vet info

Open Etr-Sep Last arrival 22.00hrs Last departure 10.00hrs

An open park next to a working farm in a rural area on the coastal road from St Ives to Zennor. The park is surrounded by mature hedges, but there are extensive views over the sea. There are very good toilet facilities including family rooms, and a large TV lounge and recreation room with drinks machine. 4.9 acre site. 120 touring pitches. Tent pitches. Motorhome pitches.

Balnoon Camping Site *(SW509382)*

▶ ▶

Halsetown TR26 3JA
☎ 01736 795431
e-mail: nat@balnoon.fsnet.co.uk
dir: *From A30 take A3074, at 2nd mini-rdbt 1st left signed Tate/ St Ives. In 3m right after Balnoon Inn*

PETS: Public areas disp bin **Facilities** walks info vet info **Other** prior notice required **Restrictions** no Staffordshire Bull Terriers or similar breeds

Open Etr-Oct Last arrival 20.00hrs Last departure 11.00hrs

Small, quiet and friendly, this sheltered site offers superb views of the adjacent rolling hills. The two paddocks are surrounded by mature hedges, and the toilet facilities are kept spotlessly clean. The beaches of Carbis Bay and St Ives are about two miles away. 1 acre site. 23 touring pitches. Tent pitches. Motorhome pitches.

Notes No noise between 23.00hrs-07.30hrs. 🐾

ST JUST (NEAR LAND'S END) — Map 2 SW33

Trevaylor Caravan & Camping Park
(SW368222)

▶▶▶

Botallack TR19 7PU
☎ 01736 787016
e-mail: trevaylor@cornishcamping.co.uk
dir: *On B3306 (St Just-St Ives road), site on right 0.75m from St Just*

PETS: Public areas dogs must be kept on leads at all times disp bin **Exercise area** 50mtrs **Facilities** food food bowl water bowl dog chews cat treats washing facs walks info vet info **Other** prior notice required disposal bags available

Open Fri before Etr-Oct Last departure 11.00hrs

A sheltered grassy site located off the beaten track in a peaceful location at the western tip of Cornwall. The dramatic coastline and the pretty villages nearby are truly unspoilt. Clean, well-maintained facilities and a good shop are offered along with a bar serving meals. 6 acre site. 50 touring pitches. Tent pitches. Motorhome pitches. 5 statics.

Notes Quiet between 22.30hrs-07.30hrs.

ST JUST-IN-ROSELAND — Map 2 SW83

Trethem Mill Touring Park *(SW860365)*

▶▶▶▶▶

TR2 5JF
☎ 01872 580504 📠 01872 580968
e-mail: reception@trethem.com
dir: *From Tregony on A3078 to St Mawes. 2m after Trewithian, follow signs to site*

PETS: Charges £1 per night **Public areas** except in buildings disp bin **Exercise area on site** 5-acre dog walk **Facilities** food walks info vet info **Other** disposal bags available

Open Apr-mid Oct Last arrival 20.00hrs Last departure 11.00hrs

A quality park in all areas, with upgraded amenities including a reception, shop, laundry, and disabled/family room. This carefully-tended and sheltered park is in a lovely rural setting, with spacious pitches separated by young trees and shrubs. The very keen family who own the site are continually looking for ways to enhance its facilities. 11 acre site. 84 touring pitches. 61 hardstandings. Tent pitches. Motorhome pitches.

Notes No skateboards or rollerblades.

ST KEVERNE — Map 2 SW72

Gallen-Treath Guest House
★★★ GUEST HOUSE
Porthallow TR12 6PL
☎ 01326 280400 📠 01326 280400
e-mail: gallentreath@btclick.com
dir: *1.5m SE of St Keverne in Porthallow*

PETS: Bedrooms (1 GF) unattended **Charges** £3 per night £21 per week **Public areas** except restaurant/dining room **Grounds** disp bin **Exercise area** 2 mins' walk to beach, coastal path & fields **Facilities** food (pre-bookable) food bowl water bowl bedding dog chews cat treats scoop/disp bags washing facs walks info vet info **On Request** fridge access torch towels **Other** charge for damage all pet facilities by prior request only; pets may be left unattended in bedrooms only at meal times **Resident Pet:** J.D.(Bearded Collie/Lurcher cross)

Gallen-Treath has super views over the countryside and sea from its elevated position above Porthallow. Bedrooms are individually decorated and feature many personal touches. Guests can relax in the large, comfortable lounge complete with balcony. Hearty breakfasts and dinners (by arrangement) are served in the bright dining room.

Rooms 5 rms (4 en suite) (1 pri facs) (1 fmly) (1 GF) **S** £27-£34; **D** £54-£68 **Facilities** FTV TVL tea/coffee Dinner available Cen ht Licensed **Parking** 6

ST MAWES — Map 2 SW83

RICHARDSON

Idle Rocks Hotel
★★★ 83% ◉◉ HOTEL
Harbour Side TR2 5AN
☎ 01326 270771 📠 01326 270062
e-mail: reception@idlerocks.co.uk
web: www.idlerocks.co.uk
dir: *A390 onto A3078, 14m to St Mawes. Hotel on left*

PETS: Bedrooms unattended sign 4 cottage rooms only **Charges** £10 per night **Public areas** except restaurant on leads **Exercise area** adjacent **Facilities** water bowl dog chews washing facs cage storage walks info vet info **On Request** fridge access torch towels **Other** charge for damage please phone for further details of pet facilities

This hotel has splendid sea views overlooking the attractive fishing port. The lounge and bar also benefit from the views and in warmer months service is available on the terrace. Bedrooms are individually styled and tastefully furnished to a high standard. The daily-changing menu served in the restaurant features fresh, local produce in imaginative cuisine.

Rooms 27 (4 annexe) (6 fmly) (2 GF) **D** £109-£209 (incl. bkfst)* **Facilities** FTV Xmas New Year Wi-fi **Parking** 4 **Notes** LB

Trevean Caravan & Camping Park (SW875724)

▶▶▶

Trevean Ln PL28 8PR

☎ 01841 520772　🖹 01841 520772

e-mail: trevean.info@virgin.net

dir: *From St Merryn take B3276 to Newquay for 1m. Turn left for Rumford. Site 0.25m on right*

PETS: Charges £1 per night　£7 per week　**Public areas** disp bin
Exercise area on site　Facilities food　washing facs　walks info
vet info　**Stables** 1m　**Other** prior notice required

Open Apr-Oct rs Whit-Sep shop open Last arrival 22.00hrs Last departure 11.00hrs

A small working farm site with level grassy pitches in open countryside. The toilet facilities are clean and well kept, and there is a laundry and good children's playground. 1.5 acre site. 68 touring pitches. Tent pitches. Motorhome pitches. 3 statics.

Tregavone Touring Park (SW898732)

▶▶

Tregavone Farm PL28 8JZ

☎ 01841 520148

e-mail: info@tregavone.co.uk

dir: *From A389 towards Padstow, right after Little Petherick. In 1m just beyond Padstow Holiday Park turn left into unclass road signed Tregavone. Site on left, approx 1m*

PETS: Charges £2 per night　**Public areas** disp bin
Exercise area on site field for dog walking　**Exercise area**
50yds　**Facilities** walks info　vet info　**Other** prior notice required
Resident Pets: Jessy & Millie (Collies), 6 cats

Open Mar-Oct

Situated on a working farm with unspoilt country views, this spacious grassy park, run by friendly family owners, makes an ideal base for exploring the north Cornish coast and the seven local golden beaches with surfing areas, or for enjoying quiet country walks from the park. 3 acre site. 40 touring pitches. Tent pitches. Motorhome pitches.

Notes

Crooked Inn

★★★★ INN

Stoketon Cross, Trematon PL12 4RZ

☎ 01752 848177　🖹 01752 843203

e-mail: info@crooked-inn.co.uk

dir: *1.5m NW of Saltash. A38 W from Saltash, 2nd left to Trematon, sharp right*

PETS: Bedrooms (7 GF)　unattended　sign　**Charges** £5 per
night　**Public areas　Grounds** on leads　disp bin　**Exercise area**
fields　**Facilities** water bowl　pet sitting　dog walking　washing
facs　walks info　vet info　**On Request** fridge access　torch　towels
Other phone for further details of pet facilities　**Resident Pets:**
Bella (Bassett Hound), Mambo & Wilky (Golden Retrievers),
Jimmy, Billy & Pepe (cats), Laddie (pony), 2 Kunu Kune pigs,
geese, ducks

The friendly animals that freely roam the courtyard add to the relaxed country style of this delightful property. The spacious bedrooms are well equipped, and freshly cooked dinners are available in the bar and conservatory. Breakfast is served in the cottage-style dining room.

Rooms 18 annexe rms 15 annexe en suite (5 fmly) (7 GF)
Facilities tea/coffee Dinner available Cen ht 🐾 **Parking** 45
Notes Closed 25 Dec

See advert on page 39

Carvynick Country Club *(SW878564)*

RV ▶▶▶▶

TR8 5AF

☎ 01872 510716   🖷 01872 510172

e-mail: info@carvynick.co.uk

dir: *Off A3058*

PETS: Public areas except swimming pool area   on leads **Exercise area** adjacent lane **Facilities** vet info **Other** dogs must be exercised off site

Open all year rs Jan-early Feb restricted leisure facilities

Set within the gardens of an attractive country estate this spacious dedicated American RV Park (also home to the 'Itchy Feet' retail company) provides all full facility pitches on hardstandings. The extensive on-site amenities, shared by the high quality time share village, include an excellent restaurant with lounge bar, indoor leisure area with swimming pool, fitness suite and badminton court. 47 touring pitches. Motorhome pitches.

See advert on page 41

Donnington Guest House

★★★ GUEST ACCOMMODATION

43 Treyew Rd TR1 2BY

☎ 01872 222552 & 07787 555475

e-mail: info@donnington-guesthouse.co.uk

PETS: Bedrooms (3 GF) unattended   ground-floor bedrooms usually allocated **Public areas** except dining room & hallway on leads **Grounds** on leads   disp bin **Exercise area** 500yds **Facilities** food (pre-bookable) food bowl water bowl scoop/ disp bags cage storage walks info vet info **On Request** fridge access torch

A well located property within 12 minutes' walk of the city centre. This property is actually two houses operating as one with breakfast being taken in the breakfast room of one of them. Well-appointed rooms, a friendly host and good off-road parking make this a very popular venue.

Rooms 14 rms (12 en suite) (2 pri facs) (5 fmly) (3 GF) **S** £30-£35; **D** £55-£65 **Facilities** FTV tea/coffee Cen ht Lift Wi-fi Golf 18 **Parking** 11 **Notes** ⊛

Polsue Manor Farm *(SW858462)*

★★★ FARMHOUSE

Tresillian TR2 4BP

☎ 01872 520234   Mrs G Holliday

e-mail: geraldineholliday@hotmail.com

dir: *2m NE of Truro. Farm entrance on A390 at S end of Tresillian*

PETS: Bedrooms (1 GF) non en suite bedrooms only **Charges** horses only - fee on application **Grounds Exercise area** woods (0.5m) **Facilities** walks info vet info **Stables Resident Pets:** Polly & Penny (Yellow Labradors)

The 190-acre sheep farm is in peaceful countryside a short drive from Truro. The farmhouse provides a relaxing break from the city, with hearty breakfasts and warm hospitality. The spacious dining room has pleasant views and three large communal tables. Bedrooms do not offer televisions but there is a homely lounge equipped with a television and video recorder with a selection of videos for viewing.

Rooms 5 rms (2 en suite) (3 fmly) (1 GF) **S** £30-£35; **D** £54-£60 **Facilities** TVL tea/coffee **Parking** 5 **Notes** Closed 21 Dec-2 Jan 190 acres mixed/sheep/horses

Carnon Downs Caravan & Camping Park *(SW805406)*

▶▶▶▶▶

Carnon Downs TR3 6JJ

☎ 01872 862283   🖷 01872 870820

e-mail: info@carnon-downs-caravanpark.co.uk

dir: *Take A39 from Truro towards Falmouth. Site just off main Carnon Downs rdbt, on left*

PETS: Public areas except toilets, wash-up & showers   disp bin **Exercise area on site** good dog walks **Facilities** walks info vet info **Stables** nearby **Other** walks book provided **Resident Pet:** Jaz (Collie)

Open all year Last arrival 22.00hrs Last departure 11.00hrs

A beautifully upgraded, mature park set in meadowland and woodland close to the village amenities of Carnon Downs. The four toilet blocks provide exceptional facilities in bright modern surroundings. An extensive landscaping programme has been carried out to give more spacious pitch sizes, and there is an exciting children's playground with modern equipment, and a football pitch. 33 acre site. 150 touring pitches. 80 hardstandings. Tent pitches. Motorhome pitches. 1 static.

Notes No children's bikes in Jul & Aug.

Truro Caravan and Camping Park *(SW772452)*

▶▶▶▶▶

TR4 8QN

☎ 01872 560274 ▤ 01872 561413

e-mail: info@trurocaravanandcampingpark.co.uk

dir: *Exit A390 at Threemilestone rdbt onto unclass road towards Chacewater. Site signed on right in 0.5m*

PETS: Public areas disp bin **Exercise area on site Facilities** washing facs walks info vet info **Stables** 2m **Other** prior notice required

Open all year Last arrival 19.00hrs Last departure 10.30hrs

An attractive south-facing and well laid out park with spacious pitches, including hardstandings, and quality modern toilets that are kept spotlessly clean. It is situated on the edge of the city of Truro yet close to many beaches, with St Agnes being just ten minutes away by car. It is equidistant from both the rugged north coast and the calmer south coastal areas. There is a good bus service from the gate of the park to Truro. 8.5 acre site. 51 touring pitches. 26 hardstandings. Tent pitches. Motorhome pitches. 49 statics.

Cosawes Park *(SW768376)*

▶▶▶▶

Perranworthal TR3 7QS

☎ 01872 863724 & 07747 852772 ▤ 01872 870268

e-mail: info@cosawes.com

dir: *Exit A39 midway between Truro & Falmouth. Direct access at site sign after Perranworthal*

PETS: Public areas except residential area disp bin **Exercise area on site** large riverside field **Facilities** washing facs vet info **Other** local kennels will take 'day borders' with valid vaccination certificate; list available of beaches that allow dogs free disposal bags available **Resident Pet:** Daisy (dog)

Open all year Last departure 10.00hrs

A small touring park in a peaceful wooded valley, midway between Truro and Falmouth, with toilet facilities that include two smart family rooms. Its stunning location is ideal for visiting the many nearby hamlets and villages close to the Carrick Roads, a stretch of tidal water, which is a centre for sailing and other boats. 2 acre site. 40 touring pitches. 25 hardstandings. 15 seasonal pitches. Tent pitches. Motorhome pitches.

Summer Valley *(SW800479)*

▶▶▶

Shortlanesend TR4 9DW

☎ 01872 277878

e-mail: res@summervalley.co.uk

dir: *3m NW off B3284*

PETS: Charges 50p per night **Public areas** except toilet block disp bin **Exercise area on site Facilities** food food bowl water bowl walks info vet info **Other** disposal bags available

Open Apr-Oct Last arrival 20.00hrs Last departure noon

A very attractive and secluded site in a rural setting midway between the A30 and the cathedral city of Truro. The keen owners maintain the facilities to a good standard. 3 acre site. 60 touring pitches. Tent pitches. Motorhome pitches.

VERYAN	Map 2 SW93

The Nare Hotel

★★★★ ⊛ COUNTRY HOUSE HOTEL

Carne Beach TR2 5PF

☎ 01872 501111 ▤ 01872 501856

e-mail: stay@narehotel.co.uk

web: www.narehotel.co.uk

dir: *From Tregony follow A3078 for approx 1.5m. Left at Veryan sign, through village towards sea & hotel*

PETS: Bedrooms (7 GF) unattended sign **Sep accom** working dog kennels available **Charges** £16 (small), £21 (medium), £25 (large) per night **Public areas** except food areas & lounge **Grounds** disp bin **Exercise area** 50mtrs **Facilities** food (pre-bookable) food bowl water bowl bedding dog chews feeding mat scoop/disp bags leads pet sitting dog walking washing facs cage storage walks info vet info **On Request** fridge access torch towels **Stables** 0.5m **Other** chef's dish of the day & carte menu **Resident Pets:** Ghillie & Hector (Springer Spaniels), Sammy (Tibetan Spaniel)

This delightful hotel offers a relaxed, country-house atmosphere in a spectacular coastal setting. The elegantly designed bedrooms, many with balconies, have fresh flowers, carefully chosen artwork and antiques that contribute to their engaging individuality. A choice of dining options is available, from light snacks to superb local seafood.

Rooms 37 (7 fmly) (7 GF) **S** £136-£260; **D** £262-£746 (incl. bkfst)* **Facilities** Spa FTV ⊙ ↺ ⌁ ⌁ Gym Health & beauty clinic Sauna Steam room Hotel sailing boat Shooting Xmas New Year Wi-fi **Services** Lift **Parking** 80 **Notes** LB

The Laurels Holiday Park (SW957715)

▶▶▶

Padstow Rd, Whitecross PL27 7JQ
☎ 01209 313474
e-mail: info@thelaurelsholidaypark.co.uk
dir: *Off A389 (Padstow road) near junct with A39, W of Wadebridge*

PETS: **Charges** dog £1-£2 per night **Public areas** except toilets & laundry on leads disp bin **Exercise area on site** fenced exercise area **Facilities** walks info vet info **Other** prior notice required dogs must be kept on leads at all times

Open Apr or Etr-Oct Last arrival 20.00hrs Last departure 11.00hrs

A very smart and well-equipped park with individual pitches screened by hedges and young shrubs. The enclosed dog walk is of great benefit to pet owners, and the Camel cycle trail and Padstow are not far away. 2.2 acre site. 30 touring pitches. 2 hardstandings. Tent pitches. Motorhome pitches.

Notes No group bookings, family park

Little Bodieve Holiday Park (SW995734)

▶▶▶

Bodieve Rd PL27 6EG
☎ 01208 812323
e-mail: info@littlebodieve.co.uk
dir: *From A39 rdbt on Wadebridge by-pass take B3314 signed Rock/Port Isaac, site 0.25m on right*

PETS: **Charges** £4 per night **Public areas** except swimming pool area, shop, bar & games room **Exercise area on site** fenced grass area **Facilities** food vet info **Restrictions** no Pit Bull Terriers

Open Apr-Oct rs Early & late season pool, shop & clubhouse closed Last arrival 21.00hrs Last departure 11.00hrs

Rurally located with pitches in three large grassy paddocks, this family park is close to the Camel Estuary. The licensed clubhouse provides bar meals, with an entertainment programme in high season, and there is a swimming pool with sun terrace plus a separate waterslide and splash pool. 22 acre site. 195 touring pitches. Tent pitches. Motorhome pitches. 75 statics.

Notes Families & couples only.

Watergate Bay Touring Park (SW850653)

▶▶▶▶

TR8 4AD
☎ 01637 860387   ▤ 0871 661 7549
e-mail: email@watergatebaytouringpark.co.uk
dir: *4m N of Newquay on B3276 (coast road)*

PETS: **Charges** Jul-Aug £2 per night **Public areas** except swimming pool area, clubroom, cafeteria & recreational area disp bin **Exercise area on site** 2-acre exercise field **Facilities** food walks info vet info **Other** prior notice required no more than 2 dogs per pitch

Open Mar-Nov rs Mar-Spring BH & Sep-Oct restricted bar, café, shop & pool Last arrival 22.00hrs Last departure noon

A well-established park above Watergate Bay, where acres of golden sand, rock pools and surf are seen as a holidaymakers' paradise. The toilet facilities are appointed to a high standard, and there is a well-stocked shop and café, an inviting swimming pool, and a wide range of activities including tennis courts and outdoor facilities for all ages, and a regular entertainment programme in the clubhouse. 30 acre site. 171 touring pitches. 14 hardstandings. Tent pitches. Motorhome pitches. 2 statics.

Widemouth Bay Caravan Park (SS199008)

EX23 0DF
☎ 01271 866766   ▤ 01271 866791
e-mail: bookings@jfhols.co.uk
dir: *Take Widemouth Bay coastal road off A39, turn left. Site on left*

PETS: **Charges** £3 per night £20 per week **Public areas** except in buildings & specific areas of site disp bin **Exercise area on site** large field **Exercise area** approx 20 mins to Millook Haven beach **Facilities** dog chews walks info vet info **Other** charge for damage prior notice required disposal bags available **Restrictions** no dangerous dogs (see page 7)

Open Etr-Oct Last arrival duskhrs Last departure 10.00hrs

A partly sloping rural site set in countryside overlooking the sea and one of Cornwall's finest beaches. Nightly entertainment in high season with emphasis on children's and family club programmes. This park is located less than half a mile from the sandy beaches of Widemouth Bay. 58 acre site. 220 touring pitches. 90 hardstandings. Tent pitches. Motorhome pitches. 200 statics.

ZENNOR	Map 2 SW43

The Gurnard's Head

★ ★ ★ INN

Treen TR26 3DE
☎ 01736 796928
e-mail: enquiries@gurnardshead.co.uk
dir: *5m from St Ives on B3306, 4.5m from Penzance via New Mill*

PETS: Bedrooms unattended **Public areas** except restaurant
Grounds Exercise area adjacent fields & footpaths **Facilities**
food bowl water bowl **On Request** towels

This inn is ideally located for enjoying the beautiful coastline,
and is very popular with walkers keen to rest their weary legs.
The style is relaxed with a log fire in the bar providing a warm
welcome on colder days, and outside seating ideal for enjoying
the sun. Lunch and dinner are available either in the bar or the
adjoining restaurant area. The dinner menu is not extensive
but there are interesting choices and everything is home made,
including the bread. Breakfast is also a treat with newspapers on
the bar to peruse whilst easing into the day.

Rooms 7 en suite **S** £65–£125; **D** £95–£165 **Facilities** tea/coffee
Dinner available Wi-fi **Parking** 40 **Notes** Closed 25 Dec & 4 days
mid Jan No coaches

CUMBRIA

ALSTON	Map 12 NY74

Lowbyer Manor Country House

★ ★ ★ ★ ≜ GUEST HOUSE

Hexham Rd CA9 3JX
☎ 01434 381230 📠 01434 381425
e-mail: stay@lowbyer.com
web: www.lowbyer.com
dir: *250yds N of village centre on A686. Pass South Tynedale
Railway on left, turn right*

PETS: Bedrooms ground-floor bedrooms only **Charges** £5 per
night **Public areas** except restaurant on leads **Grounds** disp
bin **Exercise area** 0.5m **Facilities** scoop/disp bags washing
facs cage storage walks info vet info **On Request** fridge access
torch towels

Located on the edge of the village, this Grade II listed Georgian
building retains many original features, which are highlighted
by the furnishings and decor. Cosy bedrooms are filled with a
wealth of thoughtful extras and day rooms include an elegant
dining room, a comfortable lounge and bar equipped with lots of
historical artefacts.

Rooms 9 en suite (1 fmly) **S** £36–£60; **D** £72–£86 **Facilities** tea/
coffee Cen ht Licensed **Parking** 9 **Notes** LB

AMBLESIDE	Map 7 NY30

Waterhead Hotel

★ ★ ★ ★ 77% TOWN HOUSE HOTEL

Lake Rd LA22 0ER
☎ 015394 32566 📠 015394 31255
e-mail: waterhead@englishlakes.co.uk
web: www.englishlakes.co.uk
dir: *A591 to Ambleside. Hotel opposite Waterhead Pier*

PETS: Bedrooms (7 GF) certain bedrooms only **Charges** £10
per night **Public areas** bar only on leads **Grounds** on leads
Exercise area 50yds **Facilities** food bowl water bowl bedding
dog chews walks info vet info **On Request** fridge access
torch towels **Other** charge for damage pets accepted by prior
arrangement only **Restrictions** no Rottweilers or dangerous dogs
(see page 7)

With an enviable location opposite the bay, this well-established
hotel offers contemporary and comfortable accommodation with
CD/DVD players, plasma screens and internet access. There is
a bar with a garden terrace overlooking the lake and a stylish
restaurant serving classical cuisine with a modern twist. Staff
are very attentive and friendly. Guests can enjoy full use of the
Low Wood Hotel leisure facilities nearby.

Rooms 41 (3 fmly) (7 GF) **S** £86–£143; **D** £113–£226 (incl. bkfst)*
Facilities FTV Free use of leisure facilities at sister hotel (1m)
Xmas New Year Wi-fi **Parking** 43 **Notes** LB

Skelwith Bridge

★ ★ ★ 75% HOTEL

Skelwith Bridge LA22 9NJ
☎ 015394 32115 📠 015394 34254
e-mail: info@skelwithbridgehotel.co.uk
web: www.skelwithbridgehotel.co.uk
dir: *2.5m W on A593 at junct with B5343 to Langdale*

PETS: Bedrooms (1 GF) **Charges** £5 per night **Public areas**
except restaurant on leads **Grounds Exercise area** 100mtrs
Facilities water bowl pet sitting washing facs cage storage
walks info vet info **On Request** torch towels **Other** charge for
damage

This 17th-century inn is now a well-appointed tourist hotel
located at the heart of the Lake District National Park and
renowned for its friendly and attentive service. Bedrooms include
two rooms with four-poster beds. Spacious public areas include
a choice of lounges and bars, and an attractive restaurant
overlooking the gardens to the bridge from which the hotel takes
its name.

Rooms 28 (6 annexe) (2 fmly) (1 GF) **S** £48–£66; **D** £108–£132
(incl. bkfst)* **Facilities** Xmas New Year Wi-fi **Parking** 60
Notes LB

AMBLESIDE *continued*

Wateredge Inn

★★★★ INN

Waterhead Bay LA22 0EP
☎ 015394 32332 📠 015394 31878
e-mail: rec@wateredgeinn.co.uk
web: www.wateredgeinn.co.uk
dir: *On A59, at Waterhead, 1m S of Ambleside. Inn at end of promenade by lake*

PETS: Bedrooms (3 GF) certain bedrooms only **Public areas** allowed in one public room only on leads **Grounds** on leads **Exercise area** park adjacent **Facilities** water bowl walks info vet info

This modern inn has an idyllic location on the shore of Windermere at Waterhead Bay. The pretty bedrooms are particularly smart and generally spacious, and all offer a high standard of quality and comfort. The airy bar-restaurant opens onto attractive gardens, which have magnificent lake views. There is also a comfortable lounge, bar and dining area.

Rooms 15 en suite 7 annexe en suite (4 fmly) (3 GF) **S** £40-£60; **D** £75-£170 **Facilities** tea/coffee Dinner available Cen ht Wi-fi **Parking** 40 **Notes** LB Closed 25-26 Dec

Skelwith Fold Caravan Park *(NY355029)*

▶ ▶ ▶ ▶

LA22 0HX
☎ 015394 32277 📠 015394 34344
e-mail: info@skelwith.com
dir: *From Ambleside on A593 towards Coniston, left at Clappersgate onto B5286 (Hawkshead road). Site 1m on right*

PETS: Public areas except shop & children's playground disp bin **Exercise area** surrounding area **Facilities** food dog chews washing facs vet info **Other** disposal bags available

Open Mar-15 Nov Last arrival duskhrs Last departure noon

In the grounds of a former mansion, this park is in a beautiful setting close to Lake Windermere. Touring areas are dotted in paddocks around the extensively wooded grounds, and the all-weather pitches are set close to the many facility buildings. The premium pitches are quite superb. There is a five-acre family recreation area, which has spectacular views of Loughrigg Fell. 130 acre site. 150 touring pitches. 150 hardstandings. Motorhome pitches. 300 statics.

Hall Croft

★★★★ 🛏 BED AND BREAKFAST

Dufton CA16 6DB
☎ 017683 52902
e-mail: hallcroft@phonecoop.coop
dir: *3m N of Appleby. In Dufton by village green*

PETS: Bedrooms Public areas except dining room at breakfast **Grounds** disp bin **Exercise area** woods nearby **Facilities** food (pre-bookable) food bowl water bowl pet sitting washing facs cage storage walks info vet info **On Request** fridge access torch towels **Other** charge for damage pet sitting on request **Resident Pets:** Monty (Collie cross), Caio (Border Collie)

Standing at the end of a lime-tree avenue, Hall Croft, built in 1882, has been restored to its original glory. Bedrooms are comfortably proportioned, traditionally furnished and well equipped. Breakfasts, served in the lounge-dining room, are substantial and include a range of home-made produce. Guests can enjoy the lovely garden, which has views of the Pennines.

Rooms 3 rms (2 en suite) (1 pri facs) **Facilities** FTV tea/coffee Cen ht Wi-fi **Parking** 3 **Notes** Closed 24-26 Dec ⊛

Wild Rose Park *(NY698165)*

▶ ▶ ▶ ▶ ▶

Ormside CA16 6EJ
☎ 017683 51077 📠 017683 52551
e-mail: reception@wildrose.co.uk
dir: *Signed on unclass road to Great Ormside, off B6260*

PETS: Charges £1.50 per night **Public areas** except shop & restaurant on leads disp bin **Exercise area on site** fenced exercise area **Facilities** food food bowl water bowl dog chews scoop/disp bags leads washing facs walks info vet info **Other** prior notice required **Restrictions** no Rottweilers, Pit Bull Terriers or Dobermans

Open all year rs Nov-Mar shop closed, restaurant rs, pool closed 6 Sep-27 May Last arrival 22.00hrs Last departure noon

Situated in the Eden Valley, this large family-run park has been carefully landscaped and offers superb facilities maintained to an extremely high standard, including four wooden wigwams for hire. There are several individual pitches, and extensive views from most areas of the park. Traditional stone walls and the planting of lots of indigenous trees help it to blend into the environment, and wildlife is actively encouraged. 85 acre site. 226 touring pitches. 140 hardstandings. Tent pitches. Motorhome pitches. 273 statics.

Notes No unaccompanied teenagers, no group bookings, no noise after 22.30hrs.

AYSIDE
Map 7 SD38

Oak Head Caravan Park *(SD389839)*
▶ ▶ ▶
LA11 6JA
☎ 015395 31475
dir: *M6 junct 36, A590 towards Newby Bridge, 14m. From A590 bypass follow signs for Ayside*

PETS: Public areas disp bin **Exercise area** nearby **Facilities** washing facs walks info vet info **Other** prior notice required disposal bags available **Restrictions** no Rottweilers

Open Mar-Oct Last arrival 22.00hrs Last departure noon

A pleasant terraced site with two separate areas - grass for tents and all gravel pitches for caravans and motorhomes. The site is enclosed within mature woodland and surrounded by hills. This site is located in a less busy area but convenient for all the Lake District attractions. 3 acre site. 60 touring pitches. 30 hardstandings. Tent pitches. Motorhome pitches. 71 statics.

Notes No open fires. 🐾

BASSENTHWAITE
Map 11 NY23

Armathwaite Hall Country House & Spa
★★★★ ⬢ COUNTRY HOUSE HOTEL
CA12 4RE
☎ 017687 76551 ▤ 017687 76220
e-mail: reservations@armathwaite-hall.com
web: www.armathwaite-hall.com
dir: *M6 junct 40/A66 to Keswick rdbt then A591 signed Carlisle. 8m to Castle Inn junct, turn left. Hotel 300yds*

PETS: Bedrooms (8 GF) unattended sign **Charges** £15 per night **Grounds** on leads disp bin **Exercise area** 400-acre estate **Facilities** food (pre-bookable) bedding dog chews cat treats scoop/disp bags pet sitting dog walking washing facs cage storage walks info vet info **On Request** fridge access torch **Other** charge for damage dog grooming can be arranged **Resident Pets:** Ben & Millie (Belgian Shepherds), Chrissy (Labrador)

Enjoying fine views over Bassenthwaite Lake, this impressive mansion, dating from the 17th century, is situated amid 400 acres of deer park. Comfortably furnished bedrooms and refurbished bathrooms are complemented by a choice of public rooms that have many original features. The new spa is an outstanding addition to the leisure facilities; it offers an infinity pool, thermal suite, sauna, state-of-the-art gym, treatments, exercise classes and a hot tub overlooking the landscaped gardens.

Rooms 42 (4 fmly) (8 GF) **S** £135-£170; **D** £270-£380 (incl. bkfst) **Facilities** Spa STV ⓣ supervised ⬥ Fishing ⬥ Gym Archery Clay shooting Quad & mountain bikes Falconry Xmas New Year Wi-fi **Services** Lift **Parking** 100

The Pheasant
★★★ 86% ⬢ HOTEL
CA13 9YE
☎ 017687 76234 ▤ 017687 76002
e-mail: info@the-pheasant.co.uk
web: www.the-pheasant.co.uk
dir: *Midway between Keswick & Cockermouth, signed from A66*

PETS: Bedrooms Garden Lodge bedrooms only **Charges** £5 per night **Public areas** except lounge at meal times on leads **Grounds** on leads disp bin **Exercise area** nearby **Facilities** walks info vet info **On Request** torch towels **Other** please phone for further details of pet facilities

Enjoying a rural setting, within well-tended gardens, on the western side of Bassenthwaite Lake, this friendly 500-year-old inn is steeped in tradition. The attractive oak-panelled bar has seen few changes over the years and features log fires and a great selection of malt whiskies. The individually decorated bedrooms are stylish and thoughtfully equipped.

Rooms 15 (2 annexe) (2 GF) **S** £90-£110; **D** £140-£200 (incl. bkfst)* **Facilities** New Year Wi-fi **Parking** 40 **Notes** LB No children 12yrs Closed 25 Dec

BOOT
Map 7 NY10

Eskdale Camping & Caravanning Club Site
(NY178011)
▶ ▶ ▶ ▶ ▶
CA19 1TH
☎ 019467 23253 & 0845 130 7633
e-mail: eskdale.site@thefriendlyclub.co.uk
dir: *Exit A595 at Gosforth or Holmrook to Eskdale Green & then to Boot. Site on left towards Hardknott Pass after railway & 150mtrs after Brook House Inn*

PETS: Public areas disp bin **Exercise area** wooded area adjacent to site **Facilities** food food bowl water bowl bedding dog chews cat treats scoop/disp bags leads washing facs walks info vet info **Other** dogs must be kept on leads at all times

Open Mar-14 Jan Last arrival 20.00hrs Last departure noon

Stunningly located in Eskdale, a feeling of peace and tranquillity prevails at this top quality Club site, with the sounds of running water and birdsong the only welcome distractions. Although mainly geared to campers, the facilities here are very impressive, with a smart amenities block, equipped with efficient modern facilities including an excellent fully-serviced wet room-style family room with power shower, and the surroundings of mountains, mature trees and shrubs create a wonderful 'back to nature' feeling. There's a nest of camping pods under the trees, with gravel access paths and barbeques, and an adults-only backpackers' area. Expect great attention to detail and a high level of customer care. The park is only a quarter of a mile from Boot station on the Ravenglass/Eskdale railway ('Ratty'). 8 acre site. 80 touring pitches. Tent pitches. Motorhome pitches. 10 wooden pods.

Notes Site gates closed & no noise 23.00hrs-07.00hrs, no open fires.

BORROWDALE — Map 11 NY21

Lodore Falls Hotel
★★★★ 77% HOTEL

CA12 5UX
☎ 017687 77285 & 0800 840 1246 ☐ 017687 77343
e-mail: lodorefalls@lakedistricthotels.net
web: www.lakedistricthotels.net/lodorefalls
dir: *M6 junct 40 take A66 to Keswick, then B5289 to Borrowdale. Hotel on left*

PETS: Bedrooms unattended **Charges** £10 per night
Public areas except restaurant & lounge bar on leads **Grounds** on leads disp bin **Exercise area** nearby **Facilities** food bowl water bowl pet sitting dog walking cage storage walks info vet info **On Request** torch towels **Other** charge for damage

This impressive hotel has an enviable location overlooking Derwentwater. The bedrooms, many with lake or fell views, are comfortably equipped; family rooms and suites are also available. The dining room, bar and lounge areas are appointed to a very high standard. One of the treatments in the hotel's Elemis Spa actually makes use of the Lodore Waterfall!

Rooms 69 (11 fmly) **S** £90-£156; **D** £181-£450 (incl. bkfst)
Facilities Spa STV FTV ⊗ ⌇ 🏊 Fishing Gym Squash Sauna Xmas New Year Wi-fi **Services** Lift **Parking** 93 **Notes** LB

Borrowdale Gates Country House Hotel
★★★ 80% COUNTRY HOUSE HOTEL

CA12 5UQ
☎ 017687 77204 ☐ 017687 77195
e-mail: hotel@borrowdale-gates.com
dir: *From A66 follow B5289 for approx 4m. Turn right over bridge, hotel 0.25m beyond village*

PETS: Bedrooms (10 GF) unattended **Charges** £5 per night **Grounds** on leads disp bin **Exercise area** surrounding countryside **Facilities** walks info vet info **Other** charge for damage

This friendly hotel is peacefully located in the Borrowdale Valley, close to the village but in its own three acres of wooded grounds. Public rooms include comfortable lounges and a restaurant with lovely views. Bedrooms vary in size and style.

Rooms 27 (10 GF) **Facilities** FTV Xmas New Year Wi-fi **Services** Lift **Parking** 29 **Notes** Closed 3 Jan-4 Feb

Borrowdale Hotel
★★★ 78% HOTEL

CA12 5UY
☎ 017687 77224 ☐ 017687 77338
e-mail: borrowdale@lakedistricthotels.net
dir: *3m from Keswick, on B5289 at S end of Lake Derwentwater*

PETS: Bedrooms (2 GF) unattended **Sep accom** small kennel in car park **Charges** £5 per night **Public areas** except restaurant (& bar at lunch) **Grounds Exercise area** 50mtrs **Facilities** water bowl washing facs walks info vet info **On Request** fridge access torch **Restrictions** no Pit Bull Terriers

Situated in the beautiful Borrowdale Valley overlooking Derwentwater, this traditionally styled hotel guarantees a friendly welcome. Extensive public areas include a choice of lounges, traditional dining room, lounge bar and popular conservatory which serves more informal meals. Bedrooms vary in style and size, including two that are suitable for less able guests.

Rooms 36 (2 fmly) (2 GF) **S** £101-£121; **D** £202-£242 (incl. bkfst & dinner)* **Facilities** STV FTV Leisure facilities available at nearby sister hotel Xmas New Year Wi-fi **Parking** 30 **Notes** LB

BRAITHWAITE — Map 11 NY22

The Royal Oak
★★★ INN

CA12 5SY
☎ 017687 78533 📠 017687 78533
e-mail: info@royaloak-braithwaite.co.uk
web: www.royaloak-braithwaite.co.uk
dir: *In village centre*

PETS: Bedrooms unattended **Charges** £3 per night **Public areas**
except in bar/restaurant during food service **Grounds** disp bin
Facilities water bowl leads washing facs walks info vet info
On Request fridge access torch towels

The Royal Oak, in the pretty village of Braithwaite, has delightful
views of Skiddaw and Barrow, and is a good base for tourists
and walkers. Some of the well-equipped bedrooms are furnished
with four-poster beds. Hearty meals and traditional Cumbrian
breakfasts are served in the restaurant, and there is an
atmospheric, well-stocked bar.

Rooms 10 en suite (1 fmly) **S** £43-£46; **D** £78-£92 **Facilities** STV
FTV tea/coffee Dinner available Cen ht Wi-fi 🐾 **Parking** 20
Notes LB

BRAMPTON — Map 12 NY56

Farlam Hall
★★★ ◉◉ HOTEL

CA8 2NG
☎ 016977 46234 📠 016977 46683
e-mail: farlam@relaischateaux.com
web: www.farlamhall.co.uk
dir: *On A689 (Brampton to Alston). Hotel 2m on left (not in Farlam village)*

PETS: Bedrooms (2 GF) **Public areas** except restaurant
Grounds disp bin **Exercise area** 1m **Facilities** food bowl
water bowl washing facs cage storage walks info vet info
On Request fridge access torch towels **Other** charge for
damage max 2 dogs permitted in bedroom; field available for
horses **Resident Pets:** 2 llamas

This delightful country house has a history dating back to 1428,
although the building today is very much the result of alterations
carried out in the mid-19th century. The hotel is run by a friendly
family team and their enthusiastic staff and is set in beautifully
landscaped Victorian gardens complete with an ornamental lake

and stream. Lovingly restored over many years, it provides the
highest standards of comfort and hospitality. Gracious public
rooms invite relaxation, whilst every thought has gone into
the beautiful bedrooms, many of which are simply stunning.
Nearby are Hadrian's Wall and the Northern Pennines Area of
Outstanding Natural Beauty which provide endless opportunities
for walking and sightseeing.

Farlam Hall

Rooms 12 (1 annexe) (2 GF) **S** £160-£190; **D** £300-£360 (incl.
bkfst & dinner)* **Facilities** FTV 🐾 New Year Wi-fi **Parking** 25
Notes LB No children 5yrs Closed 24-30 Dec & 4-13 Jan

CARLISLE — Map 11 NY45

Crown
★★★ 81% ◉ HOTEL

Station Rd, Wetheral CA4 8ES
☎ 01228 561888 📠 01228 561637
e-mail: info@crownhotelwetheral.co.uk
web: www.crownhotelwetheral.co.uk
dir: *M6 junct 42, B6263 to Wetheral, right at village shop, car park at rear of hotel*

PETS: Bedrooms (3 GF) unattended certain bedrooms only
Charges £10 per night **Public areas** except restaurant on leads
Grounds on leads disp bin **Exercise area** 1-2m **Facilities** water
bowl bedding walks info vet info **On Request** fridge access
torch towels **Other** charge for damage **Resident Pets:** Bubble &
Squeak (cats)

Set in the attractive village of Wetheral and with landscaped
gardens to the rear, this hotel is well suited to both business
and leisure guests. Rooms vary in size and style and include two
apartments in an adjacent house ideal for long stays. A choice
of dining options is available, with the popular Waltons Bar an
informal alternative to the main restaurant.

Rooms 51 (2 annexe) (10 fmly) (3 GF) **S** £65-£80; **D** £110-£130
(incl. bkfst)* **Facilities** Spa STV 🕙 supervised Gym Squash
Children's splash pool Steam room Beauty room Sauna Xmas New
Year Wi-fi **Parking** 80 **Notes** LB

The Crown & Mitre

PEEL HOTELS PLC

★★★ 70% HOTEL

4 English St CA3 8HZ

☎ 01228 525491 📠 01228 514553

e-mail: info@crownandmitre-hotel-carlisle.com

web: www.crownandmitre-hotel-carlisle.com

dir: *A6 to city centre, pass station on left. Right into Blackfriars St. Rear entrance at end*

PETS: Bedrooms unattended **Public areas** except restaurant **Exercise area** nearby **Facilities** walks info vet info **Other** charge for damage

Located in the heart of the city, this Edwardian hotel is close to the cathedral and a few minutes' walk from the castle. Bedrooms vary in size and style, from smart executive rooms to more functional standard rooms. Public rooms include a comfortable lounge area and the lovely bar with its feature stained-glass windows.

Rooms 95 (20 annexe) (4 fmly) (11 smoking) **Facilities** FTV 🐾 Xmas New Year Wi-fi **Services** Lift **Parking** 42

Angus House & Almonds Restaurant

★★★ GUEST ACCOMMODATION

14-16 Scotland Rd CA3 9DG

☎ 01228 523546 📠 01228 531895

e-mail: hotel@angus-hotel.co.uk

web: www.angus-hotel.co.uk

dir: *0.5m N of city centre on A7*

PETS: Bedrooms unattended **Charges Public areas** except restaurant **Facilities** walks info vet info **On Request** fridge access **Restrictions** no Rottweilers or Bull Terriers

Situated just north of the city, this family-run establishment is ideal for business and leisure. A warm welcome is assured and the accommodation is well equipped. Almonds Restaurant provides enjoyable food and home baking, and there is also a lounge and a large meeting room.

Rooms 10 en suite (2 fmly) **Facilities** FTV tea/coffee Dinner available Direct Dial Cen ht Licensed Wi-fi **Notes** LB

Green Acres Caravan Park *(NY416614)*

► ► ►

High Knells, Houghton CA6 4JW

☎ 01228 675418

e-mail: info@caravanpark-cumbria.com

dir: *Exit M6 junct 44, A689 towards Brampton for 1m. Left at Scaleby sign. Site 1m on left*

PETS: Public areas disp bin **Exercise area on site** small woodland area **Facilities** vet info **Resident Pet:** Molly (Labrador/Beagle cross)

Open Apr-Oct Last arrival 21.00hrs Last departure noon

A small touring park in rural surroundings close to the M6 with distant views of the fells. A convenient stopover, this pretty park is run by keen, friendly owners who maintain high standards throughout. 3 acre site. 30 touring pitches. 30 hardstandings. 12 seasonal pitches. Tent pitches. Motorhome pitches.

Notes 😿

Aynsome Manor Hotel

★★★ 78% ⚜ COUNTRY HOUSE HOTEL

LA11 6HH

☎ 015395 36653 📠 015395 36016

e-mail: aynsomemanor@btconnect.com

dir: *M6 junct 36, A590 signed Barrow-in-Furness towards Cartmel. Left at end of road, hotel before village*

PETS: Bedrooms Charges £4 per night **Public areas** on leads **Grounds Exercise area** 0.75m **Other** charge for damage guests must bring dog's own bedding; dogs to be kept on leads at all times

Dating back, in part, to the early 16th century, this manor house overlooks the fells and the nearby priory. Spacious bedrooms, including some courtyard rooms, are comfortably furnished. Dinner in the elegant restaurant features local produce whenever possible, and there is a choice of lounges to relax in.

Rooms 12 (2 annexe) (2 fmly) **S** £75-£105; **D** £140-£180 (incl. bkfst & dinner)* **Facilities** FTV New Year **Parking** 20 **Notes** LB Closed 2-31 Jan RS Sun

Ennerdale Country House

OXFORD
HOTELS & INNS

★★★ 74% HOTEL

CA23 3DT

☎ 01946 813907　📄 01946 815260

e-mail: reservations.ennerdale@ohiml.com

web: www.oxfordhotelsandinns.com

dir: *M6 junct 40 to A66, A5086 for 12m, hotel on left*

PETS: Bedrooms (10 GF) unattended **Charges** £10 per night £50 per week **Grounds** on leads **Facilities** walks info vet info **Other** charge for damage **Restrictions** no Rottweilers or Pit Bull Terriers **Resident Pet:** Jack (Cocker Spaniel)

This fine Grade II listed building lies on the edge of the village and has landscaped gardens. Impressive bedrooms, including split-level suites and four-poster rooms, are richly furnished, smartly decorated and offer a range of facilities. Attractive public areas include a stylish restaurant and an American themed bar which offers a good range of bar meals.

Rooms 30 (2 fmly) (10 GF) **Facilities** STV Xmas New Year Wi-fi **Parking** 40

Shepherds Hotel

★★★ 74% HOTEL

Lakeland Sheep & Wool Centre, Egremont Rd CA13 0QX

☎ 0845 459 9770　📄 01301 703327

e-mail: info@argyllholidays.com

web: www.shepherdshotel.co.uk

dir: *At junct of A66 & A5086 S of Cockermouth, entrance off A5086, 200mtrs off rdbt*

PETS: Bedrooms (13 GF) unattended **Charges** £5 per night **Grounds** disp bin **Exercise area** adjacent **Facilities** cage storage walks info vet info **Resident Pets:** dogs, geese

This hotel is modern in style and offers thoughtfully equipped accommodation. It is well situated for the northern lakes area and has good road links. The restaurant, open all day, serves a wide variety of meals and snacks; the Black Rock dishes are recommended. Free Wi-fi is available in the bedrooms.

Rooms 26 (4 fmly) (13 GF) **Facilities** FTV Pool table Small children's play area Wi-fi **Services** Lift **Parking** 100 **Notes** Closed 25-26 Dec & 4-18 Jan

Waters Edge Caravan Park *(SD533838)*

▶▶▶

LA7 7NN

☎ 015395 67708

e-mail: info@watersedgecaravanpark.co.uk

dir: *M6 junct 36 take A65 towards Kirkby Lonsdale, at 2nd rdbt follow signs for Crooklands/Endmoor. Site 1m on right at Crooklands garage, just beyond 40mph limit*

PETS: Public areas except bar & toilets on leads **disp bin** **Exercise area** walks & canal banks 300yds **Facilities** food food bowl water bowl dog chews scoop/disp bags vet info **Other** dog grooming available nearby

Open Mar-14 Nov rs Low season bar not always open on week days Last arrival 22.00hrs Last departure noon

A peaceful, well-run park close to the M6, pleasantly bordered by streams and woodland. A Lakeland-style building houses a shop and bar, and the attractive toilet block is clean and modern. This is ideal either as a stopover or for longer stays. 3 acre site. 26 touring pitches. 26 hardstandings. Tent pitches. Motorhome pitches. 20 statics.

Damson Dene

★★★ 72% HOTEL

LA8 8JE

☎ 015395 68676　📄 015395 68227

e-mail: info@damsondene.co.uk

web: www.bestlakesbreaks.co.uk

dir: *M6 junct 36, A590 signed Barrow-in-Furness, 5m right onto A5074. Hotel on right in 5m*

PETS: Bedrooms (9 GF) unattended certain bedrooms only **Charges** £5 per stay **Public areas** except restaurant & leisure club on leads **Grounds** disp bin **Exercise area** nearby **Facilities** walks info vet info **Resident Pet:** Fly (dog)

A short drive from Lake Windermere, this hotel enjoys a tranquil and scenic setting. Bedrooms include a number with four-poster beds and jacuzzi baths. The spacious restaurant serves a daily-changing menu, with some of the produce coming from the hotel's own kitchen garden. Real fires warm the lounge in the cooler months, and leisure facilities are available.

Rooms 40 (3 annexe) (7 fmly) (9 GF) **S** £79-£99; **D** £118-£148 (incl. bkfst)* **Facilities** Spa ⊗ Gym Beauty salon Xmas New Year Wi-fi **Parking** 45 **Notes** LB

CROSTHWAITE *continued*

Crosthwaite House

★★★★ GUEST HOUSE

LA8 8BP

☎ 015395 68264 📠 015395 68264

e-mail: bookings@crosthwaitehouse.co.uk

web: www.crosthwaitehouse.co.uk

dir: *A590 onto A5074, 4m right to Crosthwaite, 0.5m turn left*

PETS: Bedrooms unattended **Public areas** except lounge & dining room **Grounds** disp bin **Exercise area** many walks nearby **Facilities** leads washing facs cage storage walks info vet info **On Request** fridge access torch towels **Other** charge for damage **Resident Pet:** Bee (cat)

Enjoying stunning views across the Lyth Valley, this friendly Georgian house is a haven of tranquillity. Bedrooms are spacious and offer a host of thoughtful extras. The reception rooms include a comfortable lounge and a pleasant dining room with polished floorboards and individual tables.

Rooms 6 en suite **S** £28-£33; **D** £56-£66 **Facilities** FTV TVL tea/coffee Cen ht Wi-fi **Parking** 10 **Notes** Closed mid Nov-Mar RS early Nov & Feb-Mar

GLENRIDDING	Map 11 NY31

LAKE DISTRICT ■■■■■HOTELS

The Inn on the Lake

★★★ 83% ◉ HOTEL

Lake Ullswater CA11 0PE

☎ 017684 82444 📠 017684 82303

e-mail: innonthelake@lakedistricthotels.net

web: www.lakedistricthotels.com

dir: *M6 junct 40, A66 to Keswick. At rdbt take A592 to Ullswater Lake. Along lake to Glenridding. Hotel on left on entering village*

PETS: Bedrooms (1 GF) unattended certain bedrooms only **Charges** £10 per night **Public areas** bar/conservatory only on leads **Grounds** disp bin **Exercise area** surrounding countryside **On Request** fridge access **Other** dogs accepted at manager's discretion only (please call hotel when booking) **Resident Pet:** Chrissy (Black Labrador)

In a picturesque lakeside setting, this restored Victorian hotel is a popular leisure destination as well as catering for weddings

and conferences. Superb views can be enjoyed from the bedrooms and from the garden terrace where afternoon teas are served during warmer months. There is a popular pub in the grounds, and moorings for yachts are available to guests. Sailing tuition can be arranged.

Rooms 47 (6 fmly) (1 GF) **Facilities** ♨ 9 ⌸ Putt green Fishing 🛶 Gym Sailing 9 hole pitch & putt Bowls Xmas New Year Wi-fi **Services** Lift **Parking** 200

Best Western Glenridding Hotel

★★★ 77% HOTEL

Best Western

CA11 0PB

☎ 017684 82228 & 82289 📠 017684 82555

e-mail: glenridding@bestwestern.co.uk

dir: *N'bound M6 junct 36, A591 Windermere then A592, for 14m. S'bound M6 junct 40, A592 for 13m*

PETS: Bedrooms (8 GF) **Charges** £10 per night **Public areas** except dining room, restaurant, lounge & library on leads **Grounds** on leads disp bin **Exercise area** nearby **Facilities** dog chews walks info vet info **Other** charge for damage **Restrictions** small dogs only

This friendly hotel benefits from a picturesque location in the village centre, and many rooms have fine views of the lake and fells. Public areas are extensive and include a choice of dining options including Ratchers Restaurant and a café. Leisure facilities are available along with a conference room and a garden function room.

Rooms 36 (7 fmly) (8 GF) **Facilities** STV ⊗ Sauna Snooker Table tennis Xmas New Year Wi-fi **Services** Lift **Parking** 30

GRANGE-OVER-SANDS	Map 7 SD47

Hampsfell House

★★ 81% HOTEL

Hampsfell Rd LA11 6BG

☎ 015395 32567 📠 015395 35995

e-mail: enquiries@hampsfellhouse.co.uk

web: www.hampsfellhouse.co.uk

dir: *A590 at junct with B5277, signed to Grange-over-Sands. Left at rdbt into Main St, right at 2nd rdbt & right at x-rds. Hotel on left*

PETS: Bedrooms Charges from £5 per night **Public areas** except restaurant on leads **Grounds** on leads **Exercise area** adjacent **Facilities** pet sitting walks info vet info **On Request** fridge access torch towels **Resident Pets:** Maissie (small Terrier), Pepsi (Whippet), Bertie (Pug)

Dating back to 1800, this owner managed hotel is peacefully set in two acres of private grounds yet is just a comfortable walk from the town centre. Bedrooms are smartly decorated and well maintained. There is a cosy bar where guests can relax and enjoy pre-dinner drinks. Comprehensive and imaginative dinners are taken in an attractive dining room.

Rooms 8 (1 fmly) **S** £35-£60; **D** £50-£90 (incl. bkfst)* **Facilities** FTV New Year Wi-fi **Parking** 20 **Notes** LB

Wordsworth Hotel & Spa

★★★★ **79%** ◉◉ HOTEL

LA22 9SW

☎ 015394 35592 📄 015394 35765

e-mail: enquiry@thewordsworthhotel.co.uk

web: www.thewordsworthhotel.co.uk

dir: *Off A591 centre of village adjacent to St Oswald's Church*

PETS: Bedrooms (2 GF) ground-floor bedrooms only **Charges** £20 per stay **Public areas** Dove Bar & small lounge only on leads **Grounds** disp bin **Exercise area** nearby **Facilities** food bowl water bowl washing facs walks info vet info **On Request** fridge access towels **Other** charge for damage **Restrictions** no very large dogs

Named after the famous poet, this charming hotel is set in two acres of landscaped gardens. Peaceful lounges, furnished with antiques, look out over well-kept lawns and the friendly staff provide professional service. Bedrooms are individually furnished and well equipped. There are comprehensive leisure facilities, and diners have a choice between the popular pub and the more formal Prelude Restaurant.

Rooms 36 (2 fmly) (2 GF) **S** £40–£175; **D** £120–£375 (incl. bkfst)* **Facilities** Spa FTV 🄫 ❧ Gym Treatment room Mixed sauna Nail bar Xmas New Year Wi-fi **Services** Lift **Parking** 60 **Notes** LB

Best Western Grasmere Red Lion [Best Western]

★★★ **80%** HOTEL

Red Lion Square LA22 9SS

☎ 015394 35456 📄 015394 35579

e-mail: reservations@grasmereredlionhotel.co.uk

dir: *Off A591, signed Grasmere Village. Hotel in village centre*

PETS: Bedrooms unattended certain bedrooms only **Charges** £20 per stay **Public areas** except restaurant & main lounge **Exercise area** nearby **Facilities** cage storage walks info vet info **On Request** fridge access torch towels **Stables** 1m **Other** charge for damage

This modernised and extended 18th-century coaching inn, located in the heart of the village, offers spacious well-equipped rooms and a number of meeting and conference facilities. A range of pub meals complement the more formal Courtyard Restaurant. The spacious and comfortable lounge area is ideal for relaxing, and for the more energetic guest there is a pool and gym.

Rooms 47 **Facilities** STV 🄫 Gym Sauna Steam room Spa bath Xmas New Year Wi-fi **Services** Lift **Parking** 35 **Notes** LB

Grasmere

★★ **81%** HOTEL

Broadgate LA22 9TA

☎ 015394 35277

e-mail: enquiries@grasmerehotel.co.uk

web: www.grasmerehotel.co.uk

dir: *From Ambleside take A591 N, 2nd left into Grasmere. Over humpback bridge, past playing field. Hotel on left*

PETS: Bedrooms (2 GF) unattended some bedrooms are not suitable for large dogs **Charges Grounds** on leads **Exercise area** park adjacent **Facilities** washing facs cage storage walks info vet info **On Request** fridge access torch towels **Other** charge for damage **Restrictions** no dangerous dogs (see page 7)

Attentive and hospitable service contribute to the atmosphere at this family-run hotel, set in secluded gardens by the River Rothay. There are two inviting lounges (one with residents' bar) and an attractive dining room looking onto the garden. The thoughtfully prepared dinner menu makes good use of fresh ingredients. Quality antique furniture is featured in most bedrooms, along with welcome personal touches.

Rooms 14 (1 annexe) (2 GF) **S** £55–£63; **D** £90–£125 (incl. bkfst)* **Facilities** Full leisure facilities at nearby country club Fishing permit available Xmas New Year Wi-fi **Parking** 14 **Notes** LB No children 10yrs Closed 3 Jan–early Feb

Moss Grove Organic

★★★★★ 🏠 GUEST ACCOMMODATION

LA22 9SW

☎ 015394 35251 📄 015394 35306

e-mail: enquiries@mossgrove.com

web: www.mossgrove.com

dir: *From S, M6 junct 36 onto A591 signed Keswick, from N M6 junct 40 onto A591 signed Windermere*

PETS: Bedrooms (2 GF) ground-floor bedrooms only **Charges** £20 per night **Facilities** water bowl walks info vet info **On Request** fridge access torch

Located in the centre of Grasmere, this impressive Victorian house has been refurbished using as many natural products as possible with ongoing dedication to causing minimal environmental impact. The stylish bedrooms are decorated with beautiful wallpaper and natural clay paints, featuring handmade beds and furnishings. Bose home entertainment systems, flat screen TVs and luxury bathrooms add further comfort. Extensive continental breakfasts are served in the spacious kitchen, where guests can help themselves and dine at the large wooden dining table in the guest lounge.

Rooms 11 en suite (2 GF) **S** £95–£154; **D** £110–£250 **Facilities** STV tea/coffee Cen ht Licensed Wi-fi **Parking** 11 **Notes** LB No Children 14yrs Closed 24-25 Dec

Kings Arms
★★★ INN

LA22 0NZ
☎ 015394 36372 ᛒ 015394 36006
e-mail: info@kingsarmshawkshead.co.uk
web: www.kingsarmshawkshead.co.uk
dir: M6 junct 36 onto A591, left onto A593 at Waterhead. After 1m onto B5286 to Hawkshead, in main square

PETS: Bedrooms Public areas except restaurant (bar only) on leads Exercise area adjacent Facilities food bowl water bowl washing facs walks info vet info On Request fridge access torch towels Stables 2m

A traditional Lakeland inn in the heart of a conservation area. The cosy, thoughtfully equipped bedrooms retain much character and are traditionally furnished. A good choice of freshly prepared food is available in the lounge bar and the neatly presented dining room.

Rooms 8 en suite (3 fmly) S £52-£65; D £74-£96 Facilities FTV tea/coffee Dinner available Direct Dial Cen ht Wi-fi ⌕ Golf 18 Fishing Riding Notes LB Closed 25 Dec

Overwater Hall
★★★ 86% ◎◎ COUNTRY HOUSE HOTEL

CA7 1HH
☎ 017687 76566 ᛒ 017687 76921
e-mail: welcome@overwaterhall.co.uk
dir: From A591 take turn to Ireby at Castle Inn. Hotel signed after 2m on right

PETS: Bedrooms (1 GF) unattended Public areas except restaurant & drawing room Grounds disp bin Exercise area 18-acre gardens Exercise area adjacent Facilities food bowl water bowl scoop/disp bags pet sitting washing facs cage storage walks info vet info On Request fridge access torch towels Other charge for damage Resident Pets: Oscar & Bafta (Black Labradors), Carina (cat)

This privately owned country house dates back to 1811 and is set in lovely gardens surrounded by woodland. The owners have lovingly restored this Georgian property over the years paying great attention to the authenticity of the original design;

guests will receive warm hospitality and attentive service in a relaxed manner. The elegant and well appointed bedrooms include the more spacious Superior Rooms and the Garden Room; all bedrooms have Wi-fi. Creative dishes are served in the traditional-style dining room.

Rooms 11 (2 fmly) (1 GF) S £100-£175; D £200-£270 (incl. bkfst & dinner)* Facilities FTV Xmas New Year Wi-fi Parking 20 Notes LB

Woodlands Country House
★★★★ ⇔ GUEST HOUSE

CA7 1EX
☎ 016973 71791 ᛒ 016973 71482
e-mail: stay@woodlandsatireby.co.uk
web: www.woodlandsatireby.co.uk
dir: M6 junct 40 onto A66, pass Keswick at rdbt turn right onto A591. At Castle Inn turn right signed Ireby, then 2nd left signed Ireby. Pass church on left, last house in village

PETS: Bedrooms (3 GF) ground-floor bedrooms only Charges £15 per stay Grounds disp bin Facilities washing facs walks info vet info On Request torch Other charge for damage

Previously a vicarage, this lovely Victorian home is set in well tended gardens that attract lots of wildlife. Guests are given a warm welcome by the friendly owners and delicious home-cooked evening meals are available by prior arrangement. A peaceful lounge and cosy bar with snug are also available. Bedrooms are attractively furnished and thoughtfully equipped.

Rooms 4 en suite 3 annexe en suite (3 fmly) (3 GF) S £45-£60; D £75-£105 Facilities FTV TVL tea/coffee Dinner available Cen ht Licensed Wi-fi Parking 11 Notes LB

Riverside Hotel Kendal
★★★ 77% HOTEL

Beezon Rd, Stramongate Bridge LA9 6EL
☎ 01539 734861 ᛒ 01539 734863
e-mail: info@riversidekendal.co.uk
web: www.bestlakesbreaks.co.uk
dir: M6 junct 36 Sedbergh, Kendal 7m, left at end of Ann St, 1st right onto Beezon Rd, hotel on left

PETS: Bedrooms (10 GF) unattended certain bedrooms only Charges £5 per stay Public areas except restaurant & leisure areas on leads Exercise area 100yds Facilities walks info vet info On Request fridge access torch

Centrally located in this market town, and enjoying a peaceful riverside location, this 17th-century former tannery provides a suitable base for both business travellers and tourists. The comfortable bedrooms are well equipped, and open-plan day rooms include the attractive restaurant and bar. Conference facilities are available, and the state-of-the-art leisure club has a heated pool, sauna, steam room, solarium and gym.

Rooms 50 (18 fmly) (10 GF) S £79-£99; D £118-£158 (incl. bkfst)* Facilities STV ⓢ supervised Gym Sauna Steam room Spa bath Xmas New Year Wi-fi Services Lift Parking 60 Notes LB

Stonecross Manor

★★★ 75% HOTEL

Milnthorpe Rd LA9 5HP
☎ 01539 733559 📄 01539 736386
e-mail: info@stonecrossmanor.co.uk
web: www.stonecrossmanor.co.uk
dir: *M6 junct 36, A590, follow signs to Windermere, take exit for Kendal South. Hotel just past 30mph sign on left*

PETS: Bedrooms 2nd floor bedrooms only **Charges** £10 per stay **Public areas** except restaurant on leads **Grounds** on leads **Exercise area** 5 mins' walk **Facilities** water bowl dog chews scoop/disp bags walks info vet info **On Request** towels **Other** charge for damage

Located on the edge of Kendal, this smart hotel offers a good combination of traditional style and modern facilities. Bedrooms are comfortable, well equipped and some feature four-poster beds. Guests can relax in the lounges or bar and enjoy an extensive choice of home cooked meals in the pleasant restaurant. Facilities also include a swimming pool.

Rooms 30 (4 fmly) **S** £87–£145; **D** £98–£156 (incl. bkfst)* **Facilities** FTV 🏊 Xmas New Year Wi-fi **Services** Lift **Parking** 55 **Notes** LB

KESWICK	Map 11 NY22

LAKE DISTRICT
▪▪▪▪▪ HOTELS

Skiddaw

★★★ 77% HOTEL

Main St CA12 5BN
☎ 017687 72071 📄 017687 74850
e-mail: info@skiddawhotel.co.uk
web: www.skiddawhotel.co.uk
dir: *A66 to Keswick, follow town centre signs. Hotel in market square*

PETS: Bedrooms unattended certain bedrooms only **Charges** £10 per night **Public areas** except food areas on leads **Exercise area** nearby **Facilities** food bowl water bowl walks info vet info

Occupying a central position overlooking the market square, this hotel provides smartly furnished bedrooms that include several family suites and a room with a four-poster bed. In addition to the restaurant, food is served all day in the bar and in the conservatory bar. There is also a quiet residents' lounge and two conference rooms.

Rooms 43 (7 fmly) (3 smoking) **Facilities** STV Use of leisure facilities at sister hotels (3m) Xmas New Year Wi-fi **Services** Lift **Parking** 35 **Notes** LB

Cragside

★★★★ GUEST ACCOMMODATION

39 Blencathra St CA12 4HX
☎ 017687 73344 📄 017687 73344
e-mail: cragside-keswick@hotmail.com
dir: *A591 Penrith Rd into Keswick, under rail bridge, 2nd left*

PETS: Bedrooms Charges £3 per night £18 per week **Public areas** except dining room on leads **Exercise area** park (2 mins' walk) **Facilities** walks info vet info **Other** charge for damage **Restrictions** small & medium size dogs only; no dangerous dogs (see page 7)

Expect warm hospitality at this establishment, located within easy walking distance of the town centre. The attractive bedrooms are well equipped, and many have fine views of the fells. Hearty Cumbrian breakfasts are served in the breakfast room, which overlooks the small front garden. Visually or hearing impaired guests are catered for, with Braille information, televisions with teletext, and a loop system installed in the dining room.

Rooms 4 en suite (1 fmly) **S** £40–£60; **D** £50–£70 **Facilities** FTV tea/coffee Cen ht Wi-fi **Notes** No Children 4yrs

The Hollies

★★★★ GUEST HOUSE

Threlkeld CA12 4RX
☎ 017687 79216
e-mail: info@theholliesinlakeland.co.uk
dir: *M6 junct 40 W on A66 towards Keswick. Turn right into Threlkeld, on main village road opposite village hall*

PETS: Bedrooms Charges £5 per night **Grounds** disp bin **Exercise area** adjacent **Facilities** walks info vet info **Resident Pet:** 1 West Highland Terrier

The Hollies is located in the picturesque village of Threlkeld with commanding views up to Blencathra and across to the Helvellyn range. A warm and genuine welcome awaits, along with refreshments and home baking. Bedrooms are well appointed and comfortable with thoughtful extras provided as standard. Quality breakfasts are served on individual tables.

Rooms 4 en suite **S** £43–£58; **D** £66–£86 **Facilities** FTV tea/coffee Cen ht Wi-fi **Parking** 6 **Notes** Closed 25 Dec

KESWICK *continued*

Keswick Lodge
★★★★ INN
Main St CA12 5HZ
☎ 017687 74584
e-mail: relax@keswicklodge.co.uk

PETS: Bedrooms unattended 5 bedrooms only **Charges** dog £15 per night (includes donation to local dog charity) **Public areas** except restaurant **Exercise area** 5 mins' walk **Facilities** food bowl water bowl cage storage walks info vet info **On Request** fridge access towels **Other** charge for damage

Located on the corner of the vibrant market square this large, friendly 18th-century coaching inn offers a wide range of meals throughout the day and evening. There is a fully stocked bar complete with well-kept cask ales. Bedrooms vary in size but all are contemporary, smartly presented and feature quality accessories such as LCD TVs. There is also a drying room.

Rooms 19 en suite (2 fmly) **S** £75-£99; **D** £99-£120 **Facilities** FTV tea/coffee Dinner available Cen ht **Notes** LB

Low Nest Farm B&B
★★★★ GUEST ACCOMMODATION
Castlerigg CA12 4TF
☎ 017687 72378
e-mail: info@lownestfarm.co.uk
dir: *2m S of Keswick, off A591 (Windermere road)*

PETS: Bedrooms (4 GF) unattended **Sep accom** kennel block **Charges** £3 per night **Public areas** Grounds disp bin **Exercise area** 5-acre adjacent field **Facilities** food bowl water bowl bedding dog chews scoop/disp bags leads pet sitting dog walking washing facs cage storage walks info vet info **On Request** fridge access torch towels **Stables** at adjacent farm **Other** charge for damage **Resident Pets:** Billie, Max & Lucy (Weimaraners), Pepsi (Poodle), Jasper (parrot), 3 goats, 2 sheep

Low Nest Farm is a small, family-run farm set in some typically breath-taking Cumbrian scenery. Bedrooms are very comfortable with smart en suites and lovely views. Dog owners are especially well catered for. There are of course, any number of walks available in the area, and Keswick is just two miles away.

Rooms 6 en suite (4 GF) **Facilities** FTV TVL tea/coffee Cen ht Wi-fi **Parking** 8 **Notes** LB No Children 14yrs Closed mid Dec-mid Feb 🐾

The Sun Inn
★★★★★ ⊛ INN
6 Market St LA6 2AU
☎ 015242 71965 📠 015242 72485
e-mail: email@sun-inn.info
web: www.sun-inn.info
dir: *From A65 follow signs to town centre. Inn on main street*

PETS: Bedrooms unattended **Charges** £10 per night **Public areas** except restaurant on leads **Exercise area** adjacent **Facilities** water bowl

A 17th-century inn situated in a historic market town, overlooking St Mary's Church. The atmospheric bar features stone walls, wooden beams and log fires with real ales available. Delicious meals are served in the bar and more formal, modern restaurant. Traditional and modern styles are blended together in the beautifully appointed rooms with excellent en suites.

Rooms 11 en suite (1 fmly) **S** £72-£134; **D** £102-£154 **Facilities** FTV tea/coffee Cen ht Wi-fi ⛳ Golf 18 **Notes** LB No coaches

Woodclose Caravan Park *(SD618786)*
▶ ▶ ▶ ▶ ▶
High Casterton LA6 2SE
☎ 01524 271597 📠 01524 272301
e-mail: info@woodclosepark.com
dir: *On A65, 0.25m after Kirkby Lonsdale towards Skipton, on left*

PETS: Public areas except children's area disp bin **Exercise area** surrounding area **Facilities** food food bowl water bowl dog chews scoop/disp bags washing facs walks info vet info **Other** prior notice required dogs must be kept on leads & exercised off site

Open Mar-Oct Last arrival 21.00hrs Last departure noon

A peaceful park with excellent toilet facilities set in idyllic countryside in the beautiful Lune Valley. Ideal for those seeking quiet relaxation, and for visiting the Lakes and Dales, with the riverside walks at Devil's Bridge, and historic Kirkby Lonsdale both an easy walk from the park. There are three wigwam cabins, and Freeview TV is available via a booster cable from reception. 9 acre site. 29 touring pitches. 8 hardstandings. Tent pitches. Motorhome pitches. 54 statics.

Notes No arrivals before 13.00hrs

New House Caravan Park *(SD628774)*

►►►►

LA6 2HR

☎ 015242 71590

e-mail: colinpreece9@aol.com

dir: *1m SE of Kirkby Lonsdale on A65, turn right into site entrance 300yds past Whoop Hall Inn*

PETS: Public areas except toilet block **Exercise area** adjacent **Facilities** walks info vet info **Other** prior notice required **Resident Pets:** 1 Lurcher, 4 cats, 1 tortoise, 2 cockatiels

Open Mar-Oct Last arrival 20.00hrs

A very pleasant base in which to relax or tour the surrounding area, developed around a former farm. The excellent toilet facilities are purpose built, and there are good roads and hardstandings, all in a lovely rural setting. 3 acre site. 50 touring pitches. 50 hardstandings. Motorhome pitches.

Notes No cycling. 😾

LONGTOWN   Map 11 NY36

Camelot Caravan Park *(NY391666)*

►►

CA6 5SZ

☎ 01228 791248

dir: *M6 junct 44/A7, site 5m N & 1m S of Longtown*

PETS: Public areas on leads disp bin **Exercise area on site** adjacent field **Facilities** washing facs walks info vet info

Open Mar-Oct Last arrival 22.00hrs Last departure noon

A very pleasant level grassy site in a wooded setting near the M6, with direct access from the A7, and simple, clean toilet facilities. The park is an ideal stopover site. 1.5 acre site. 20 touring pitches. Tent pitches. Motorhome pitches. 2 statics.

Notes 😾

LOWESWATER   Map 11 NY12

Grange Country House

★★ **74%** SMALL HOTEL

CA13 0SU

☎ 01946 861211 & 861570

e-mail: info@thegrange-loweswater.co.uk

dir: *Exit A5086 for Mockerkin, through village. After 2m left for Loweswater Lake. Hotel at bottom of hill on left*

PETS: Bedrooms (1 GF) unattended certain bedrooms only **Charges** £5 per night **Public areas** except dining room **Grounds** disp bin **Exercise area** across road **Facilities** food bowl water bowl scoop/disp bags leads washing facs cage storage walks info vet info **On Request** fridge access torch towels **Other** charge for damage paddock available for horses **Resident Pet:** Toby (Labrador/Collie cross)

This delightful country hotel is set in extensive grounds in a quiet valley at the north-western end of Loweswater, and continues to prove popular with guests seeking peace and quiet. It has a friendly and relaxed atmosphere, and the cosy public areas include a small bar, a residents' lounge and an attractive dining room. The bedrooms are well equipped and comfortable, and include four-poster rooms.

Rooms 8 (2 fmly) (1 GF) **Facilities** FTV National Trust boats & fishing Xmas **Parking** 22 **Notes** RS Jan-Feb

---

MEALSGATE   Map 11 NY24

Larches Caravan Park *(NY205415)*

►►►►

CA7 1LQ

☎ 016973 71379 & 71803 📠 016973 71782

dir: *On A595 (Carlisle to Cockermouth road)*

PETS: Charges dog £2 per night **Public areas** except toilet block & swimming pool on leads **Exercise area** surrounding area **Facilities** food litter tray scoop/disp bags dog grooming walks info vet info **Resident Pets:** Nemo (German Shepherd), Tigger, Tibby, Blacky & Sam (cats)

Open Mar-Oct rs Early & late season Last arrival 21.30hrs Last departure noon

This over 18s-only park is set in wooded rural surroundings on the fringe of the Lake District National Park. Touring units are spread out over two sections. The friendly family-run park offers well cared for facilities, and a small indoor swimming pool. 20 acre site. 73 touring pitches. 30 hardstandings. Tent pitches. Motorhome pitches.

Notes 😾

PATTERDALE	Map 11 NY31

Sykeside Camping Park *(NY403119)*

▶▶▶

Brotherswater CA11 0NZ
☎ 017684 82239 🖺 017684 82239
e-mail: info@sykeside.co.uk
dir: *Direct access off A592 (Windermere to Ullswater road) at foot of Kirkstone Pass*

PETS: Charges £2 per night Public areas disp bin
Exercise area on site fenced exercise area Facilities food food bowl water bowl dog chews leads washing facs walks info vet info Stables nearby Other prior notice required disposal bags available

Open all year Last arrival 22.30hrs Last departure 14.00hrs

A camper's delight, this family-run park is sited at the foot of Kirkstone Pass, under the 2,000ft Hartsop Dodd in a spectacular area with breathtaking views. The park has mainly grass pitches with a few hardstandings, an area with tipis for hire, and for those campers without a tent there is bunkhouse accommodation. There's a small campers' kitchen and the bar serves breakfast and bar meals. There is abundant wildlife. 10 acre site. 86 touring pitches. 5 hardstandings. Tent pitches. Motorhome pitches.

PENRITH	Map 12 NY53

LAKE DISTRICT
■■■■■■HOTELS

George

★★★ 77% HOTEL

Devonshire St CA11 7SU
☎ 01768 862696 & 0800 840 1242 🖺 01768 868223
e-mail: georgehotel@lakedistricthotels.net
dir: *M6 junct 40, 1m to town centre. From A6/A66 to Penrith*

PETS: Bedrooms unattended sign standard rooms only Charges £10 per night Public areas except restaurant Exercise area 5 mins' walk Facilities food bowl water bowl dog walking cage storage walks info vet info

This inviting and popular hotel dates back to a time when 'Bonnie' Prince Charlie made a visit. Extended over the years this town centre hotel offers well equipped bedrooms. The spacious public areas retain a timeless charm, and include a choice of lounge areas that make ideal places for morning coffees and afternoon teas.

Rooms 35 (4 fmly) S £80; D £80-£124 (incl. bkfst)* Facilities FTV Xmas New Year Wi-fi Parking 40 Notes LB

Flusco Wood *(NY345529)*

▶▶▶▶

Flusco CA11 0JB
☎ 017684 80020 🖺 017684 80794
e-mail: info@fluscowood.co.uk
dir: *From Penrith to Keswick on A66 turn right signed Flusco. Approx 800mtrs, up short incline to right. Site on left*

PETS: Charges Public areas except children's play area & buildings disp bin Exercise area on site open area for dog walking Facilities food washing facs vet info Other prior notice required Restrictions no breed larger than a Labrador; no dangerous dogs (see page 7)

Open all year rs Etr-Nov tourers & motorhomes. Last arrival 20.00hrs Last departure noon

Flusco Wood is set in mixed woodland with outstanding views towards Blencathra and the fells around Keswick. It combines two distinct areas, one of which has been designed specifically for touring caravans in neat glades with hardstandings, all within close proximity of the excellent log cabin-style toilet facilities. 24 acre site. 53 touring pitches. 53 hardstandings. Motorhome pitches.

Notes Quiet site, not suitable for large groups.

POOLEY BRIDGE	Map 12 NY42

Park Foot Caravan & Camping Park *(NY469235)*

Howtown Rd CA10 2NA
☎ 017684 86309 🖺 017684 86041
e-mail: holidays@parkfootullswater.co.uk
dir: *M6 junct 40, A66 towards Keswick, then A592 to Ullswater. Turn left for Pooley Bridge, right at church, right at x-roads signed Howtown*

PETS: Charges £1 per night Public areas except club house & children's play area Exercise area Lakeland Fells adjacent Facilities food food bowl water bowl scoop/disp bags walks info vet info Other prior notice required Restrictions no dangerous dogs (see page 7)

Open Mar-Oct rs Mar-Apr, mid Sep-Oct clubhouse open wknds only Last arrival 22.00hrs Last departure noon

A lively park with good outdoor sports facilities, and boats can be launched directly onto Lake Ullswater. The attractive mainly tenting park has many mature trees and lovely views across the lake. The Country Club bar and restaurant provides good meals,

as well as discos, live music and entertainment in a glorious location. There are lodges and static caravans for holiday hire. 18 acre site. 323 touring pitches. 32 hardstandings. Tent pitches. Motorhome pitches. 131 statics.

Notes Families & couples only.

Waterfoot Caravan Park *(NY462246)*

► ► ►

CA11 0JF

☎ 017684 86302   🖹 017684 86728

e-mail: enquiries@waterfootpark.co.uk

dir: *M6 junct 40, A66 for 1m, then A592 for 4m, site on right before lake. (NB do not leave A592 until site entrance; Sat Nav not compatible)*

PETS: Public areas except children's area disp bin **Exercise area on site** allocated dog walking area **Exercise area** adjacent **Facilities** food dog chews scoop/disp bags walks info vet info **Other** prior notice required

Open Mar-14 Nov Last arrival duskhrs Last departure noon

A quality touring park with neat, hardstanding pitches in a grassy glade within the wooded grounds of an elegant Georgian mansion. Toilets facilities are clean and well maintained, and the lounge bar with a separate family room enjoys lake views, and there is a path to Ullswater. Aira Force waterfall, Dalemain House and Gardens and Pooley Bridge are all close by. Please note that there is no access via Dacre. 22 acre site. 34 touring pitches. 30 hardstandings. Motorhome pitches. 146 statics.

Notes Families only, no tents, no large RVS.

The Fat Lamb

★★ **75%** HOTEL

Crossbank CA17 4LL

☎ 015396 23242   🖹 015396 23285

e-mail: enquiries@fatlamb.co.uk

dir: *On A683, between Kirkby Stephen & Sedbergh*

PETS: Bedrooms (5 GF)   **Public areas** except restaurant **Grounds** **Exercise area** 100yds **Facilities** water bowl leads cage storage vet info **On Request** fridge access torch

Solid stone walls and open fires feature at this 17th-century inn, set on its own nature reserve. There is a choice of dining options with an extensive menu available in the traditional bar and a more formal dining experience in the restaurant. Bedrooms are bright and cheerful, and include family rooms and easily accessible rooms for guests with limited mobility.

Rooms 12 (4 fmly) (5 GF) **S** £58-£59; **D** £90-£98 (incl. bkfst)* **Facilities** Private 5-acre nature reserve Xmas Wi-fi Child facilities **Parking** 60 **Notes** LB

Royal Oak

★ **75%** SMALL HOTEL

CA12 5XB

☎ 017687 77214 & 77695

e-mail: info@royaloakhotel.co.uk

web: www.royaloakhotel.co.uk

dir: *6m S of Keswick on B5289 in village centre*

PETS: Bedrooms (4 GF) unattended   **Public areas** except dining room **Grounds** **Exercise area** nearby **Facilities** food bowl water bowl leads cage storage walks info vet info **On Request** fridge access torch towels **Resident Pet:** Monty (cat)

Set in a village in one of Lakeland's most picturesque valleys, this family-run hotel offers friendly and obliging service. There is a variety of accommodation styles, with particularly impressive rooms being located in a converted barn across the courtyard and backing onto a stream; family rooms are available. The cosy bar is for residents and diners only, and a set home-cooked dinner is served at 7pm.

Rooms 12 (4 annexe) (5 fmly) (4 GF) **S** £48-£62; **D** £96-£134 (incl. dinner)* **Parking** 15 **Notes** LB Closed 4-21 Jan & 5-28 Dec

The Old Post Office Campsite *(NY110016)*

► ► ►

CA19 1UY

☎ 01946 726286 & 01785 822866

e-mail: enquiries@theoldpostofficecampsite.co.uk

dir: *A595 to Holmrook and Santon Bridge, 2.5m*

PETS: Charges £1.50 per night £10.50 per week **Public areas** disp bin **Exercise area** 100mtrs **Facilities** washing facs walks info vet info **Resident Pet:** George (Labrador)

Open Mar-15 Nov Last departure noon

A family-run campsite in a delightful riverside setting next to an attractive stone bridge, with very pretty pitches. The enthusiastic owner is steadily upgrading the park and has upgraded the toilets. Permits for salmon, sea and brown trout fishing are available, and there is an adjacent pub serving excellent meals. 2.2 acre site. 40 touring pitches. 5 hardstandings. Tent pitches. Motorhome pitches.

Notes 😊

ENGLAND

| SILLOTH | Map 11 NY15 |

Golf Hotel
★★ 71% HOTEL

Criffel St CA7 4AB
☎ 016973 31438 📄 016973 32582
e-mail: info@golfhotelsilloth.co.uk

PETS: Bedrooms sign **Charges** £2-£5 per night **Public areas** on leads **Exercise area** opposite **Facilities** washing facs cage storage walks info vet info **On Request** fridge access torch **Stables** nearby **Other** charge for damage

A friendly welcome waits at this hotel which occupies a prime position in the centre of the historic market town; it is a popular meeting place for the local community. Bedrooms are mostly well proportioned and are comfortably equipped. The lounge bar is a popular venue for dining, with a wide range of dishes on offer.

Rooms 22 (4 fmly) **S** £50-£87.50; **D** £97-£112 (incl. bkfst)* **Facilities** FTV Snooker & Games room **Notes** Closed 25 Dec RS 26 Dec, 1 Jan

Stanwix Park Holiday Centre
(NY108527)

Greenrow CA7 4HH
☎ 016973 32666 📄 016973 32555
e-mail: enquiries@stanwix.com
dir: *1m SW on B5300. From A596 (Wigton bypass), follow signs to Silloth on B5302. In Silloth follow signs to site, approx 1m on B5300*

PETS: Charges £3 per night £21 per week **Public areas** except complex, leisure centre, toilets & launderette **Exercise area** beach 1m **Facilities** food food bowl water bowl bedding dog chews cat treats scoop/disp bags leads walks info vet info **Other** prior notice required max 2 dogs per pitch **Restrictions** no dangerous dogs (see page 7)

Open all year rs Nov-Feb (ex New Year) no entertainment/shop closed Last arrival 21.00hrs Last departure 11.00hrs

A large well-run family park within easy reach of the Lake District. Attractively laid out, with lots of amenities to ensure a lively holiday, including a 4-lane automatic, 10-pin bowling alley. Excellent touring areas with hardstandings, one in a peaceful glade well away from the main leisure complex, and there's a campers' kitchen and clean, well maintained toilet facilities. 4 acre site. 121 touring pitches. 100 hardstandings. Tent pitches. Motorhome pitches. 212 statics.

Notes Families only.

Hylton Caravan Park *(NY113533)*
► ► ► ►

Eden St CA7 4AY
☎ 016973 31707 & 32666 📄 016973 32555
e-mail: enquiries@stanwix.com
dir: *On entering Silloth on B5302 follow signs Hylton Caravan Park, approx 0.5m on left, (end of Eden St)*

PETS: Charges £3 per night £21 per week **Public areas** except toilets, laundrette & leisure complex (except assist dogs) on leads disp bin **Exercise area** beach **Facilities** food walks info **Other** prior notice required max 2 pets per pitch, shop on main park (Stanwix) 1m; disposal bags available **Restrictions** no dangerous dogs (see page 7)

Open Mar-15 Nov Last arrival 21.00hrs Last departure 11.00hrs

A smart, modern touring park with excellent toilet facilities including several bathrooms. This high quality park is a sister site to Stanwix Park, which is just a mile away and offers all the amenities of a holiday centre, which are available to Hylton tourers. 18 acre site. 90 touring pitches. Tent pitches. Motorhome pitches. 213 statics.

Notes Families only.

| TEBAY | Map 7 NY60 |

Westmorland Hotel
★★★ 83% ◉ HOTEL

Westmorland Place, Orton CA10 3SB
☎ 015396 24351 📄 015396 24354
e-mail: reservations@westmorlandhotel.com
web: www.westmorlandhotel.com
dir: *Signed from Westmorland Services between M6 junct 38 & 39 N'bound & S'bound*

PETS: Bedrooms (12 GF) unattended ground-floor bedrooms only **Charges** £8 per night **Grounds** on leads **Facilities** walks info vet info **Other** charge for damage

With fine views over rugged moorland, this modern and friendly hotel is ideal for conferences and meetings. Bedrooms are spacious and comfortable, with the executive rooms being particularly well equipped. Open-plan public areas provide a Tyrolean touch and include a split-level restaurant.

Rooms 51 (5 fmly) (12 GF) **S** £87-£113; **D** £104-£124 (incl. bkfst)* **Facilities** FTV Xmas New Year Wi-fi **Services** Lift **Parking** 60 **Notes** LB RS 1 Jan

Westmorland Caravan Park (NY609060)

▶▶▶

Orton CA10 3SB
☎ 01539 711322 📄 015396 24944
e-mail: caravans@westmorland.com
dir: *Exit M6 at Westmorland Services, 1m from junct 38. Site accessed through service area from either N'bound or S'bound carriageways. Follow park signs*

PETS: **Public areas** disp bin **Exercise area on site** walks around woods & grassland **Exercise area** open countryside (0.5m) **Facilities** food bowl water bowl washing facs walks info vet info **Stables** 3m **Other** disposal bags available

Open Mar-Nov Last arrival anytimehrs Last departure noon

An ideal stopover site adjacent to the Tebay service station on the M6, and handy for touring the Lake District. The park is screened by high grass banks, bushes and trees, and is within walking distance of an excellent farm shop and restaurant. 4 acre site. 70 touring pitches. 70 hardstandings. 43 seasonal pitches. Motorhome pitches. 7 statics.

TEMPLE SOWERBY   Map 12 NY62

The Kings Arms Hotel

★★ 83% HOTEL

CA10 1SB
☎ 017683 62944
e-mail: enquiries@kingsarmstemplesowerby.co.uk
dir: *M6 junct 40, E on A66 to Temple Sowerby. Hotel in town centre*

PETS: **Bedrooms Public areas** except restaurant on leads **Grounds** disp bin **Exercise area** nearby **Facilities** water bowl washing facs cage storage walks info vet info **On Request** torch towels

Located in the peaceful village of Temple Sowerby just a short drive from the A66 by-pass. This historic property dates back over 400 years and has now completed a massive refurbishment. Highly enjoyable food, using quality local produce, and comfortable well-appointed bedrooms are on offer. This is an ideal location to touring the Lake District, Cumbria and Northumberland.

Rooms 9 (5 fmly) **S** £45-£50; **D** £70-£80 (incl. bkfst)* **Facilities** Fishing Xmas New Year Wi-fi **Parking** 20 **Notes** LB

TROUTBECK (NEAR KESWICK)   Map 11 NY32

Troutbeck Camping and Caravanning Club Site (NY365271)

▶▶▶▶▶

Hutton Moor End CA11 0SX
☎ 017687 79149
dir: *M6 junct 40, take A66 towards Keswick. After 9.5m take sharp left for Wallthwaite. Site is 0.5m on the left*

PETS: **Public areas** except in buildings disp bin **Exercise area on site** walks in adjacent fields **Facilities** food food bowl water bowl walks info vet info **Other** prior notice required

Open 9 Mar-11 Nov Last arrival 20.00hrs Last departure noon

Beautifully situated between Penrith and Keswick, this quiet, well managed Lakeland park offers two immaculate touring areas, one a sheltered paddock for caravans and motorhomes, with serviced hardstanding pitches, and a newly developed and maturing lower field, which has spacious hardstanding pitches and a superb and very popular small tenting area that enjoys stunning and extensive views of the surrounding fells. The toilet block is appointed to a very high standard and includes two family cubicles, and the log cabin reception/shop stocks local and organic produce. The enthusiastic franchisees offer high levels of customer care and are constantly improving the park, which is well-placed for visited Keswick, Ullswater and the north lakes. 5 acre site. 54 touring pitches. 36 hardstandings. Tent pitches. Motorhome pitches. 20 statics.

Notes Site gates closed 23.00hrs-07.00hrs.

ENGLAND

Broadoaks Country House

★★★★★ 👄 GUEST ACCOMMODATION

Bridge Ln LA23 1LA

☎ 015394 45566 📠 015394 88766

e-mail: enquiries@broadoakscountryhouse.co.uk

web: www.broadoakscountryhouse.co.uk

dir: *Exit A591 junct 36 pass Windermere. Filing station on left, 1st right 0.5m*

PETS: Bedrooms (4 GF) unattended sign ground-floor & courtyard bedrooms only **Charges** £20 per night **Public areas** only in bar/lounge on leads **Grounds** on leads disp bin **Exercise area** nearby **Facilities** food (pre-bookable) food bowl water bowl dog chews scoop/disp bags leads dog walking washing facs walks info vet info **On Request** fridge access torch towels **Other** charge for damage own dog menu & welcome procedure **Resident Pets:** Molly (Cockapoo), Sofi (cat)

This impressive Lakeland stone house has been restored to its original Victorian grandeur and is set in seven acres of landscaped grounds with stunning views of the Troutbeck Valley. Individually furnished bedrooms are well appointed and en suite bathrooms feature either whirlpool or Victorian roll top baths. Spacious day rooms include the music room, featuring a Bechstein piano. Meals are served by friendly and attentive staff in the elegant dining room.

Rooms 11 en suite 4 annexe en suite (5 fmly) (4 GF) **S** £75-£260; **D** £110-£270 **Facilities** FTV tea/coffee Dinner available Direct Dial Cen ht Licensed Wi-fi 🍴 ⚓ Fishing **Parking** 40 **Notes** LB

See advert on opposite page

Church Walk House

★★★★ BED AND BREAKFAST

Church Walk LA12 7EW

☎ 01229 582211 & 07774 368331

e-mail: martinchadd@btinternet.com

dir: *In town centre opposite Stables furniture shop on corner of Fountain St & Church Walk*

PETS: Bedrooms Public areas except dining room **Grounds** on leads disp bin **Exercise area** 25yds **Facilities** water bowl dog walking cage storage walks info vet info **On Request** fridge access torch **Stables** nearby **Other** charge for damage dog walking can be arranged with prior notice

This Grade II listed 18th-century residence stands in the heart of the historic market town. Stylishly decorated, the accommodation includes attractive bedrooms with a mix of antiques and contemporary pieces. Service is attentive and there is a small herbal garden and patio.

Rooms 3 rms (2 en suite) (1 pri facs) **S** £30-£40; **D** £65-£75 **Facilities** TVL tea/coffee Cen ht **Notes** LB

Bardsea Leisure Park (SD292765)

►►►►

Priory Rd LA12 9QE

☎ 01229 584712 📠 01229 580413

e-mail: reception@bardsealeisure.co.uk

dir: *Off A5087*

PETS: Public areas except toilet blocks disp bin **Exercise area** on site **Exercise area** 10 mins' walk **Facilities** washing facs walks info vet info

Open all year Last arrival 21.00hrs Last departure 18.00hrs

An attractively landscaped former quarry, making a quiet and very sheltered site. Many of the generously-sized pitches offer all-weather full facilities, and a luxury toilet block provides plenty of fully-serviced cubicles. Set on the southern edge of the town, it is convenient for both the coast and the Lake District. Please note that this site no longer accepts tents. 5 acre site. 83 touring pitches. 83 hardstandings. Motorhome pitches. 83 statics.

WATERMILLOCK
Map 12 NY42

Rampsbeck Country House
★★★ ⑳⑳⑳ HOTEL
CA11 0LP
☎ 017684 86442 📠 017684 86688
e-mail: enquiries@rampsbeck.co.uk
web: www.rampsbeck.co.uk
dir: M6 junct 40, A592 to Ullswater, at T-junct (with lake in front) turn right, hotel 1.5m

PETS: Bedrooms (1 GF) unattended 3 bedrooms only **Charges** £5 per night **Public areas** hall only on leads **Grounds** disp bin **Exercise area** meadow adjacent **Facilities** walks info vet info **On Request** fridge access torch towels

This fine country house lies in 18 acres of parkland on the shores of Lake Ullswater, and is furnished with many period and antique pieces. There are three delightful lounges, an elegant restaurant and a traditional bar. Bedrooms come in three grades; the most spacious rooms are spectacular and overlook the lake. Service is attentive and the award-winning cuisine a real highlight.

Rooms 19 (1 fmly) (1 GF) **S** £97.50-£200; **D** £145-£300 (incl. bkfst)* **Facilities** STV FTV Putt green 🚣 Private boat trips on Lake Ullswater Xmas New Year Wi-fi **Parking** 25 **Notes** LB

Brackenrigg
★★★ INN
CA11 0LP
☎ 017684 86206 📠 017684 86945
e-mail: enquiries@brackenrigginn.co.uk
web: www.brackenrigginn.co.uk
dir: M6 junct 40, A66 towards Keswick. In 0.5m take A592 at Rheged Services rdbt towards Ullswater. In 5m right at T-junct at lake. 1m to Watermillock sign. Inn 300yds on right. (NB car park entrance before inn)

PETS: Bedrooms stable rooms only **Charges** £10 per stay **Public areas** except restaurant on leads **Grounds** on leads **Exercise area** surrounding area **Facilities** cage storage walks info vet info **On Request** fridge access torch towels **Other** charge for damage

An 18th-century coaching inn with superb views of Ullswater and the surrounding countryside. Freshly prepared dishes and daily specials are served by friendly staff in the traditional bar and restaurant. The bedrooms include six attractive rooms in the stable cottages.

Rooms 11 en suite 6 annexe en suite (8 fmly) (3 GF) **Facilities** tea/coffee Dinner available Cen ht Wi-fi **Parking** 40 **Notes** LB

The Quiet Site (NY431236)
▶▶▶▶
Ullswater CA11 0LS
☎ 07768 727016
e-mail: info@thequietsite.co.uk
dir: M6 junct 40, A592 towards Ullswater. Right at lake junct, then right at Brackenrigg Hotel. Site 1.5m on right

PETS: Charges £1 per night **Public areas** touring pitch area only disp bin **Exercise area on site** dog walk through meadow **Facilities** food food bowl water bowl bedding dog chews scoop/disp bags washing facs walks info vet info **Stables** 5m **Other** prior notice required dogs must be kept on short leads at all times

Open all year rs Low season park open wknds only Last arrival 22.00hrs Last departure noon

A well-maintained site in a lovely, peaceful location, with good terraced pitches offering great fells views, very good, toilet facilities including family bathrooms, and a charming 'olde-worlde' bar. There are wooden camping pods for hire and a self-catering stone cottage. 10 acre site. 100 touring pitches. 60 hardstandings. Tent pitches. Motorhome pitches. 23 statics.

Notes Quiet from 22.00hrs onwards.

For a trip to the Lakes, you will find Broadoaks Country House Hotel is the perfect place to bring your furry friend. Not only does our delightful boutique hotel welcome dogs, we adore them. With Lake Windermere not far away, the 19th century house stands impressively looking out across 7 acres of land and stunning views of the Lake District – you can even hear the beck that runs through the hotel grounds. Our lovely rooms on the ground floor can cater for pets.

There's an excellent choice of walks straight from the hotel offering an invigorating day's dog walking. On your return, simply collapse by the fire in the music room and enjoy a sumptuous tea, or wait until the evening when our chef will serve up one of his magnificent culinary delights. But we won't forget about our canine friends. There's a welcoming letter for your pet too and a nutritious Four Paws Menu approved by the hotel's resident dog, Molly (right).

Broadoaks Country House, Bridge Lane, Troutbeck, Windermere, Cumbria LA23 1LA
T. 015394 45566 F. 015394 88766
E. enquiries@broadoakscountryhouse.co.uk
www.broadoakscountryhouse.co.uk

WATERMILLOCK *continued*

Cove Caravan & Camping Park *(NY431236)*

▶ ▶ ▶

Ullswater CA11 0LS
☎ 017684 86549   ▤ 017684 86549
e-mail: info@cove-park.co.uk
dir: *M6 junct 40 take A592 for Ullswater. Right at lake junct, then right at Brackenrigg Inn. Site 1.5m on left*

PETS: Charges dog £1 per night **Public areas** on leads disp bin **Exercise area on site** 2 dog walks **Facilities** washing facs walks info vet info **Restrictions** well behaved dogs only **Resident Pet:** Molly (Springer Spaniel)

Open Mar-Oct Last arrival 21.00hrs Last departure noon

A peaceful family site in an attractive and elevated position with extensive fell views and glimpses of Ullswater Lake. The ground is gently sloping grass, but there are also hardstandings for motorhomes and caravans, and simple toilet facilities are fresh, clean and well maintained by enthusiastic and welcoming wardens. 3 acre site. 50 touring pitches. 17 hardstandings. 5 seasonal pitches. Tent pitches. Motorhome pitches. 39 statics.

Notes No open fires, no noise after 22.30hrs

WINDERMERE   **Map 7 SD49**

Holbeck Ghyll Country House Hotel

★★★★ ◉◉◉ COUNTRY HOUSE HOTEL

Holbeck Ln LA23 1LU
☎ 015394 32375   ▤ 015394 34743
e-mail: stay@holbeckghyll.com
dir: *3m N of Windermere on A591, right into Holbeck Lane (signed Troutbeck), hotel 0.5m on left*

PETS: Bedrooms (11 GF) unattended **Charges** £60 per stay **Public areas** front hall only **Grounds** disp bin **Exercise area** adjacent **Facilities** food (pre-bookable) food bowl water bowl bedding dog chews feeding mat scoop/disp bags leads pet sitting dog walking washing facs cage storage walks info vet info **On Request** fridge access torch towels **Stables** 1.5m **Other** charge for damage dog grooming available nearby

Holbeck Ghyll sits high up overlooking the majestic Lake Windermere surrounded by well maintained grounds. The original house was bought in 1888 by Lord Lonsdale, the first president of the AA, who used it as a hunting lodge. Guests today will find that this is a delightful place where the service is professional and attentive. There are beautifully designed, spacious bedrooms situated in the main house and also in lodges in the grounds; each has lake views and some have patios. There are also The Shieling and Miss Potter suites. Each bedroom has Egyptian cotton linens, fresh flowers, LCD satellite TV, CD & DVD players, bathrobes and a decanter of damson gin. The restaurant impresses with its award-winning cuisine. The hotel also has a health spa, gym and boutique store.

Rooms 26 (12 annexe) (5 fmly) (11 GF) **D** £250-£570 (incl. bkfst & dinner) **Facilities** Spa STV ⌁ ⌁ Gym Sauna Steam room Treatment rooms Beauty massage Xmas New Year Wi-fi **Parking** 34 **Notes** LB

Linthwaite House Hotel & Restaurant

★★★★ ◉◉ COUNTRY HOUSE HOTEL

Crook Rd LA23 3JA
☎ 015394 88600   ▤ 015394 88601
e-mail: stay@linthwaite.com
web: www.linthwaite.com
dir: *A591 towards The Lakes for 8m to large rdbt, take 1st exit (B5284), 6m, hotel on left. 1m past Windermere golf club*

PETS: Bedrooms dogs allowed in 2 bedrooms only **Sep accom** outdoor kennel & caged run **Charges** £9 per night **Grounds** **Exercise area** nearby **Facilities** food (pre-bookable) food bowl water bowl bedding scoop/disp bags washing facs cage storage walks info vet info **On Request** fridge access torch towels **Other** charge for damage prior notice required owners are requested to bring dog's own bedding **Restrictions** no breed of similar size, or larger than, a Great Dane

Linthwaite House is set in 14 acres of hilltop grounds and enjoys stunning views over Lake Windermere. Inviting public rooms include an attractive conservatory and adjoining lounge, and an elegant restaurant which occupies three rooms and offers menus based on the finest local ingredients. Bedrooms, which are individually decorated, combine contemporary furnishings with classical styles; all are thoughtfully equipped and include CD players, radios and free Wi-fi. There is also a Garden Suite and the new luxurious Loft Suite which even has a retractable roof and telescope for star gazing. Service and hospitality are attentive and friendly.

Rooms 30 (1 fmly) (7 GF) **S** £129-£160; **D** £189-£531 (incl. bkfst)* **Facilities** STV FTV Putt green Fishing ⌁ Beauty treatments Massage Access to nearby spa with pool & gym Xmas New Year Wi-fi **Parking** 40

Storrs Hall

★★★★ 78% ◉◉ HOTEL

Storrs Park LA23 3LG
☎ 015394 47111   ▤ 015394 47555
e-mail: storrshall@elhmail.co.uk
web: www.elh.co.uk/hotels/storrshall
dir: *On A592, 2m S of Bowness, on Newby Bridge road*

PETS: Bedrooms Charges £10 per night on leads **Grounds** disp bin **Exercise area** adjacent **Facilities** water bowl cage storage walks info vet info **On Request** torch **Other** dogs accepted by prior arrangement only

Set in 17 acres of landscaped grounds by the lakeside, this imposing Georgian mansion is delightful. There are numerous lounges to relax in, furnished with fine art and antiques. Individually styled bedrooms are generally spacious and boast impressive bathrooms. Imaginative cuisine is served in the elegant restaurant, which offers fine views across the lawn to the lake and fells beyond.

Rooms 30 **Facilities** FTV Fishing ⌁ Use of nearby sports/beauty facilities Xmas New Year Wi-fi **Parking** 50 **Notes** LB No children 12yrs

Low Wood Bay

★★★★ 76% HOTEL

LA23 1LP

☎ 015394 33338 & 0845 850 3502   📠 015394 34275

e-mail: lowwood@elhmail.co.uk

dir: *M6 junct 36, A590, A591 to Windermere, then 3m towards Ambleside, hotel on right*

PETS: Bedrooms (21 GF)   **Charges** £10 per night   **Grounds** on leads disp bin   **Exercise area** woods & fells   **Facilities** water bowl bedding dog chews cat treats leads pet sitting dog walking washing facs cage storage walks info vet info   **On Request** fridge access torch towels   **Other** max 2 pets per booking

Benefiting from a lakeside location, this hotel offers an excellent range of leisure and conference facilities. Bedrooms, many with panoramic lake views, are attractively furnished, and include a number of larger executive rooms and suites. There is a choice of bars, a spacious restaurant and the more informal Café del Lago. The poolside bar offers internet access.

Rooms 111 (13 fmly) (21 GF) **S** £79-£160; **D** £98-£260 (incl. bkfst)* **Facilities** Spa ⓢ supervised Fishing Gym Squash Water skiing Canoeing Beauty salon Marina Xmas New Year Wi-fi **Services** Lift **Parking** 204 **Notes** LB

Beech Hill Hotel

★★★★ 74% ⊛ HOTEL

Newby Bridge Rd LA23 3LR

☎ 015394 42137   📠 015394 43745

e-mail: reservations@beechhillhotel.co.uk

web: www.beechhillhotel.co.uk

dir: *M6 junct 36, A591 to Windermere. Left onto A592 towards Newby Bridge. Hotel 4m from Bowness-on-Windermere*

PETS: Bedrooms (4 GF) standard bedrooms only   **Charges** dog £7 per night   **Grounds** on leads disp bin   **Exercise area** adjacent & within 150yds   **Facilities** walks info vet info   **On Request** fridge access   **Stables** 5m   **Other** charge for damage

Located on the edge of Lake Windermere, the panoramic views across the lake to the Cumbrian fells beyond are impressive. The bedrooms are well appointed and some have balconies overlooking the lake. The open areas, for enjoying coffee or drinks, prove very popular in the summer. There are cosy lounges with log fires, a fine restaurant, leisure facilities and landscaped gardens. High standards of service can be expected from the attentive, informative and very friendly staff.

Rooms 57 (4 fmly) (4 GF) **Facilities** FTV ⓢ Fishing Solarium ♫ Xmas New Year Wi-fi **Parking** 70

Miller Howe Hotel

★★★ 86% ⊛⊛ COUNTRY HOUSE HOTEL

Rayrigg Rd LA23 1EY

☎ 015394 42536   📠 015394 45664

e-mail: info@millerhowe.com

dir: *M6 junct 36 , A591 past Windermere, left at rdbt towards Bowness*

PETS: Bedrooms (1 GF) unattended   **Charges** £5 per night   **Public areas** only at management's discretion on leads   **Grounds** **Exercise area** 100yds   **Facilities** food bowl water bowl cage storage walks info vet info   **On Request** fridge access torch towels   **Resident Pets:** Betty & Doris (Cocker Spaniels)

This long established hotel of much character enjoys a lakeside setting amidst delightful landscaped gardens. The bright and welcoming day rooms include sumptuous lounges, a conservatory and an opulently decorated restaurant. Imaginative dinners make use of fresh, local produce where possible and there is an extensive, well-balanced wine list. Stylish bedrooms, many with fabulous lake views, include well-equipped cottage rooms and a number with whirlpool baths.

Rooms 15 (3 annexe) (1 GF) **Facilities** Xmas New Year Wi-fi **Parking** 35

WINDERMERE *continued*

Fairfield House and Gardens

★ ★ ★ ★ ⚲ GUEST HOUSE

Brantfell Rd, Bowness-on-Windermere LA23 3AE
☎ 015394 46565 📄 015394 46564
e-mail: tonyandliz@the-fairfield.co.uk
web: www.the-fairfield.co.uk
dir: *Into Bowness town centre, turn opp St Martin's Church & sharp left by Spinnery restaurant, house 200yds on right*

PETS: Bedrooms (3 GF) unattended ground-floor, standard rooms only **Charges** £10-£20 per night **Public areas** except dining room on leads **Grounds** on leads **Exercise area** 100mtrs **Facilities** food bowl water bowl pet sitting washing facs cage storage walks info vet info **On Request** towels **Other** charge for damage **Restrictions** no dangerous dogs (see page 7)

Situated just above Bowness and Lake Windermere this Lakeland country house is tucked away in a half acre of secluded, peaceful gardens. The house has been beautifully refurbished to combine Georgian and Victorian features with stylish, contemporary design. Guests are shown warm hospitality and can relax in the delightful lounge. Bedrooms are well furnished, varying in size and style with some featuring luxurious bathrooms. Delicious breakfasts are served in the attractive dining room or on the terrace in warmer weather.

Rooms 10 en suite (2 fmly) (3 GF) **Facilities** TVL tea/coffee Dinner available Cen ht Licensed Wi-fi ⛄ **Parking** 10 **Notes** No Children 10yrs

The Wild Boar

★ ★ ★ ★ INN

Crook LA23 3NF
☎ 015394 45225 📄 015394 42498
e-mail: thewildboar@englishlakes.co.uk
dir: *2.5m S of Windermere on B5284. From Crook 3.5m, on right*

PETS: Bedrooms (9 GF) sign **Charges** £10 per night **Public areas** except grill room **Grounds** disp bin **Exercise area** 72-acre wood **Facilities** cage storage walks info vet info **On Request** fridge access torch towels **Other** charge for damage

Steeped in history this former coaching inn enjoys a peaceful rural location close to Windermere. Public areas include a welcoming lounge and a cosy bar where an extensive choice of wines, ales and whiskies are served. The Grill and The Smokehouse feature quality local and seasonal ingredients. Bedrooms, some with four-poster beds, vary in style and size. Leisure facilities are available close by.

Rooms 33 en suite (2 fmly) (9 GF) **S** £70-£110; **D** £80-£160 **Facilities** FTV tea/coffee Dinner available Direct Dial Cen ht **Parking** 60 **Notes** LB

Hill of Oaks & Blakeholme *(SD386899)*

► ► ► ►

LA12 8NR
☎ 015395 31578 📄 015395 30431
e-mail: enquiries@hillofoaks.co.uk
dir: *M6 junct 36 onto A590 towards Barrow. At rdbt signed Bowness turn right onto A592. Site approx 3m on left*

PETS: Public areas except children's play area **Exercise area on site Exercise area** surrounding area **Facilities** food dog chews scoop/disp bags walks info vet info **Other** dogs must be kept on leads at all times

Open Mar-14 Nov Last departure noon

A secluded, heavily wooded park on the shores of Lake Windermere. Pretty lakeside picnic areas, woodland walks and a play area make this a delightful park for families, with excellent serviced pitches, a licensed shop and a heated toilet block. Watersports include sailing and canoeing, with private jetties for boat launching. 31 acre site. 43 touring pitches. Motorhome pitches. 215 statics.

Park Cliffe Camping & Caravan Estate *(SD391912)*

► ► ► ►

Birks Rd, Tower Wood LA23 3PG
☎ 01539 531344 📄 01539 531971
e-mail: info@parkcliffe.co.uk
dir: *M6 junct 36, A590. Right at Newby Bridge onto A592. 3.6m right into site. (NB due to difficult access from main road this is only advised direction for approaching site)*

PETS: Charges £2 per night **Public areas** except bar, shop, restaurant, laundry, toilets & showers disp bin **Exercise area** walks leading from park **Facilities** food leads walks info vet info **Other** prior notice required disposal bags available **Restrictions** no dangerous dogs (see page 7) **Resident Pets:** Chester & Taylor (cats)

Open Mar-11 Nov rs (Wknds/school hols facilities open fully) Last arrival 22.00hrs Last departure noon

A lovely hillside park set in 25 secluded acres of fell land. The camping area is sloping and uneven in places, but well drained and sheltered; some pitches have spectacular views of Lake Windermere and the Langdales. The park is very well equipped for families, and there is an attractive bar lounge. 25 acre site. 60 touring pitches. 60 hardstandings. 25 seasonal pitches. Tent pitches. Motorhome pitches. 55 statics. 4 wooden pods.

Notes No noise 23.00hrs-07.30hrs

DERBYSHIRE

ASHBOURNE
Map 7 SK14

Callow Hall

von Essen hotels
A PRIVATE COLLECTION
www.vonessenhotels.com

★★★ 82% ◉◉ HOTEL

Mappleton Rd DE6 2AA

☎ 01335 300900 📄 01335 300512

e-mail: info@callowhall.co.uk

dir: *A515 through Ashbourne towards Buxton, left at Bowling Green pub, then 1st right*

PETS: Bedrooms (2 GF) **Charges** £25 per stay **Public areas** except restaurants **Grounds** on leads disp bin **Exercise area** nearby **Facilities** dog chews walks info vet info **On Request** fridge access **Other** charge for damage **Restrictions** small dogs only

This delightful, creeper-clad, early Victorian house, set on a 44-acre estate, enjoys views over Bentley Brook and the Dove Valley. The atmosphere is relaxed and welcoming, and some of the spacious bedrooms in the main house have comfortable sitting areas. Public rooms feature high ceilings, ornate plasterwork and antique furniture. There is a good range of dishes offered on both the carte and the fixed-price, daily-changing menus.

Rooms 16 (2 fmly) (2 GF) **Facilities** STV Cycle hire nearby (Tissington Trail) Xmas New Year Wi-fi **Parking** 21 **Notes** LB

Mercaston Hall *(SK279419)*

★★★★ FARMHOUSE

Mercaston DE6 3BL

☎ 01335 360263 & 07836 648102 Mr & Mrs A Haddon

e-mail: mercastonhall@btinternet.com

dir: *Off A52 in Brailsford onto Luke Ln, 1m turn right at 1st x-rds, house 1m on right*

PETS: Bedrooms Charges £2 per night **Public areas** except dining room **Grounds** on leads disp bin **Exercise area** adjacent fields **Facilities** food bowl water bowl leads washing facs cage storage walks info vet info **On Request** fridge access torch towels **Stables Other** charge for damage

Located in a pretty hamlet, this medieval building retains many original features. Bedrooms are homely, and additional facilities include an all-weather tennis court and a livery service. This is a good base for visiting local stately homes, the Derwent Valley mills and Dovedale.

Rooms 3 en suite **S** £50-£55; **D** £70-£75 **Facilities** FTV tea/coffee Cen ht Wi-fi ⌇ **Parking** 3 **Notes** No Children 8yrs Closed Xmas ⌾ 60 acres mixed

Carsington Fields Caravan Park *(SK251493)*
►►

Millfields Ln, Nr Carsington Water DE6 3JS

☎ 01335 372872

dir: *From Belper towards Ashbourne on A517, turn right approx 0.25m past Hulland Ward into Dog Ln. 0.75m right at x-roads signed Carsington. Site on right approx 0.75m*

PETS: Public areas except near toilets disp bin **Exercise area** on site grass dog run **Facilities** vet info **Other** prior notice required

Open end Mar-Sep Last arrival 21.00hrs Last departure 18.00hrs

A very well presented and spacious park with a good toilet block, open views and a large fenced pond that attracts plenty of wildlife. The popular tourist attraction of Carsington Water is a short stroll away, with its variety of leisure facilities including fishing, sailing, windsurfing and children's play area. The park is also a good base for walkers. 6 acre site. 20 touring pitches. 12 hardstandings. Tent pitches. Motorhome pitches.

Notes No large groups or group bookings, no noise after 23.00hrs.

BAKEWELL
Map 8 SK26

Monsal Head Hotel

★★ 83% ◉ HOTEL

Monsal Head DE45 1NL

☎ 01629 640250 📄 01629 640815

e-mail: enquiries@monsalhead.com

web: www.monsalhead.com

dir: *A6 from Bakewell to Buxton. In 2m turn into Ashford-in-the-Water, take B6465 for 1m. Hotel on left through public car park entrance*

PETS: Bedrooms Charges £10 per night **Public areas** only in bar on leads **Grounds** on leads disp bin **Exercise area** 100yds **Facilities** cage storage walks info vet info **On Request** torch **Stables** approx 2.5m **Other** charge for damage please phone for further details of pet facilities

Situated three miles from Bakewell and overlooking the picturesque Monsal Dale in the Peak District National Park, this hotel is full of charm and character. The bedrooms have beautiful views, and public areas include the Ashford Room, a quiet residents' lounge, and Longstone Restaurant. The converted stables bar adjacent to the hotel has an excellent choice of cask ales and lagers.

Rooms 7 (1 fmly) **S** £65-£70; **D** £90-£100 (incl. bkfst)* **Facilities** Xmas New Year **Parking** 20 **Notes** LB RS 25 Dec

BAKEWELL *continued*

Croft Cottages

★★★★ GUEST ACCOMMODATION

Coombs Rd DE45 1AQ

☎ 01629 814101

e-mail: croftco@btinternet.com

dir: *A619 E from town centre over bridge, right onto Station Rd & Coombs Rd*

PETS: Bedrooms unattended Barn Suite only **Grounds** on leads **Exercise area** 100yds **Facilities** walks info vet info **On Request** fridge access towels **Restrictions** no breed larger than a Labrador/Retreiver **Resident Pet:** Steffi (Belgian Shepherd)

A warm welcome is assured at this Grade II listed stone building close to the River Wye and town centre. Thoughtfully equipped bedrooms are available in the main house or in an adjoining converted barn suite. Breakfast is served in a spacious lounge dining room.

Rooms 3 rms (2 en suite) (1 pri facs) 1 annexe en suite (1 fmly); **D** £60-£85 **Facilities** tea/coffee Cen ht **Parking** 2 **Notes** 🚳

Greenhills Holiday Park *(SK202693)*

▶▶▶

Crowhill Ln DE45 1PX

☎ 01629 813052 & 813467 📠 01629 815760

e-mail: info@greenhillsholidaypark.co.uk

dir: *1m NW of Bakewell on A6. Signed before Ashford-in-the-Water, 50yds along unclass road on right*

PETS: Charges dog £1.50 per night **Public areas** disp bin **Exercise area on site** large field **Exercise area** nearby **Facilities** food food bowl water bowl dog chews scoop/disp bags leads walks info vet info

Open Feb-Nov rs Mar, Apr & Oct bar & shop closed Last arrival 22.00hrs Last departure noon

A well-established park set in lovely countryside within the Peak District National Park. Many pitches enjoy uninterrupted views, and there is easy accessibility to all facilities. A clubhouse, shop and children's playground are popular features. 8 acre site. 172 touring pitches. 30 hardstandings. Tent pitches. Motorhome pitches. 63 statics.

Makeney Hall Hotel

★★★★ 73% HOTEL

Makeney, Milford DE56 0RS

☎ 0845 609 9966 📠 01332 842777

e-mail: reservations@akkeron-hotels.com

web: www.akkeron-hotels.com

dir: *Off A6 at Milford, signed Makeney. Hotel 0.25m on left*

PETS: Bedrooms courtyard bedrooms only **Charges** £5 per night **Grounds** on leads **Exercise area** fields adjacent **Facilities** walks info vet info **Other** charge for damage **Restrictions** no dangerous dogs (see page 7)

This restored Victorian mansion stands in six acres of landscaped gardens and grounds above the River Derwent. Bedrooms vary in style and are generally very spacious. They are divided between the main house and the ground-floor courtyard. Comfortable public rooms include a lounge, bar and spacious restaurant with views of the gardens.

Rooms 46 (18 annexe) (4 fmly) **Facilities** STV FTV Xmas New Year Wi-fi **Services** Lift **Parking** 150

Shottle Hall

★★★★★ GUEST ACCOMMODATION

White Ln, Shottle DE56 2EB

☎ 01773 550577 📠 01332 440260

e-mail: Joanne.nicol@shottlehall.co.uk

dir: *M1 junct 25, A52 to Derby follow signs for Matlock. A6 at Duffield take B5023 signed Wirksworth & Hazelwood; from N - M1 junct 28, A6 to Belper onto A517 signed Shottle Hall*

PETS: Bedrooms Charges £15 per night **Grounds** on leads disp bin **Exercise area** 0.5m **Facilities** cage storage walks info vet info **On Request** fridge access torch **Other** charge for damage **Restrictions** no breed larger than a Labrador

Shottle Hall is set on the edge of the Peak District National Park and is part of the Chatsworth House Estate. Standing in beautiful grounds and gardens, the hall is a country house that offers spacious public areas, a feature dining room and individually designed bedrooms. All bedrooms have modern bathrooms, some with roll-top baths. The property is ideal for corporate functions, weddings and business meetings.

Rooms 8 en suite (4 fmly) **S** £78-£98; **D** £115-£128 **Facilities** FTV tea/coffee Direct Dial Cen ht Licensed Wi-fi Golf 18 **Parking** 50 **Notes** Closed 25-28 Dec

Barceló Buxton Palace Hotel

★★★★ 72% HOTEL

Palace Rd SK17 6AG
☎ 01298 22001 🖹 01298 72131
e-mail: palace@barcelo-hotels.co.uk
web: www.barcelo-hotels.co.uk
dir: M6 junct 20, follow M56/M60 signs to Stockport then A6 to Buxton, hotel adjacent to railway station

PETS: Bedrooms unattended sign 3rd floor bedrooms only **Charges** £15 per night **Public areas** except bar & restaurant on leads **Grounds** on leads **Exercise area** park 600mtrs **Facilities** cage storage walks info vet info **On Request** fridge access **Other** charge for damage

This impressive Victorian hotel is located on the hill overlooking the town. Public areas are traditional and elegant in style, and include chandeliers and decorative ceilings. The bedrooms are spacious and equipped with modern facilities, and The Dovedale Restaurant provides modern British cuisine. Good leisure facilities are available.

Rooms 122 (18 fmly) **Facilities** Spa ⊙ supervised Gym Beauty facilities Xmas New Year Wi-fi **Services** Lift **Parking** 180

Lime Tree Park (SK070725)

►►►►

Dukes Dr SK17 9RP
☎ 01298 22988 🖹 01298 22988
e-mail: info@limetreeparkbuxton.co.uk
dir: 1m S of Buxton, between A515 & A6

PETS: Charges £2 per night **Public areas** on leads disp bin **Exercise area on site** field available **Facilities** food food bowl water bowl dog chews cat treats leads walks info vet info **Other** prior notice required disposal bags available

Open Mar-Oct Last arrival 21.00hrs Last departure noon

A most attractive and well-designed site, set on the side of a narrow valley in an elevated location, with separate, neatly landscaped areas for statics, tents, touring caravans and now motorhomes. There's good attention to detail throughout including the clean toilets with refurbished showers. Its backdrop of magnificent old railway viaduct and views over Buxton and the surrounding hills make this a sought-after destination. There are eight static caravans, a pine lodge and two apartments available for holiday lets. 10.5 acre site. 106 touring pitches. 22 hardstandings. Tent pitches. Motorhome pitches. 43 statics.

Clover Fields Touring Caravan Park

(SK075704)

►►►

1 Heath View, Harpur Hill SK17 9PU
☎ 01298 78731
e-mail: cloverfields@tiscali.co.uk
dir: A515, B5053, then immediately right. Site 0.5m on left

PETS: Public areas disp bin **Exercise area on site** fenced area **Facilities** food food bowl water bowl leads walks info vet info **Other** prior notice required disposal bags available

Open all year Last departure 18.00hrs

A developing and spacious adults-only park with very good facilities, including an upmarket, timber chalet-style toilet block, just over a mile from the attractions of Buxton. All pitches are fully serviced including individual barbecues, and are set out on terraces, each with extensive views over the countryside. Swathes of natural meadow grasses and flowers cloak the terraces and surrounding fields. 12 acre site. 25 touring pitches. 25 hardstandings. Tent pitches. Motorhome pitches.

Notes No commercial vehicles.

Beech Croft Farm (SK122720)

►►

Beech Croft, Blackwell in the Peak SK17 9TQ
☎ 01298 85330
e-mail: mail@beechcroftfarm.net
dir: Off A6 midway between Buxton & Bakewell. Site signed

PETS: Public areas except toilets, showers & pot washing area **Exercise area** bridlepath 100yds **Facilities** water bowl walks info vet info

Open all year rs Mar Last arrival 21.30hrs

A small terraced site in an attractive farm setting with lovely views. Hardstandings are provided for caravans, and there is a separate field for tents. An ideal site for those touring or walking in the Peak District. 3 acre site. 30 touring pitches. 30 hardstandings. Tent pitches. Motorhome pitches.

Notes No noise after 23.00hrs.

CHESTERFIELD Map 8 SK37

Ibis Chesterfield

BUDGET HOTEL

Lordsmill St S41 7RW

☎ 01246 221333 📄 01246 221444

e-mail: h3160@accor.com

web: www.ibishotel.com

dir: M1 junct 29/A617 to Chesterfield. 2nd exit at 1st rdbt. Hotel on right at 2nd rdbt

PETS: Bedrooms (8 GF) certain bedrooms only **Charges** £7.50 per night **Public areas** except restaurant on leads **Facilities** walks info vet info **Other** charge for damage

Modern, budget hotel offering comfortable accommodation in bright and practical bedrooms. Breakfast is self-service and dinner is available in the restaurant.

Rooms 86 (21 fmly) (8 GF) **S** £48-£65; **D** £48-£65*

CROMFORD Map 8 SK25

Alison House

★★★★ GUEST ACCOMMODATION

Intake Ln DE4 3RH

☎ 01629 822211 📄 01629 822316

e-mail: info@alison-house-hotel.co.uk

PETS: Bedrooms (4 GF) unattended ground-floor bedrooms only **Charges** £5 per night **Public areas** except restaurant & lounge (in evening) on leads **Grounds** disp bin **Exercise area** 100yds **Facilities** scoop/disp bags washing facs walks info vet info **On Request** fridge access torch towels **Stables** 2m **Other** charge for damage

This very well furnished and spacious 18th-century house stands in seven acres of grounds just a short walk from the village. Public rooms are comfortable and bedrooms are mostly very spacious.

Rooms 16 en suite (1 fmly) (4 GF) **S** fr £55; **D** fr £85 **Facilities** tea/coffee Dinner available Direct Dial Cen ht Licensed Wi-fi ⚄ **Parking** 30 **Notes** LB

DERBY Map 8 SK33

Menzies Mickleover Court

★★★★ 77% HOTEL

Etwall Rd, Mickleover DE3 0XX

☎ 01332 521234 📄 01332 521238

e-mail: mickleovercourt@menzieshotels.co.uk

web: www.menzieshotels.co.uk

dir: A50 towards Derby, exit at junct 5. A516 towards Derby, take exit signed Mickleover

PETS: Bedrooms Grounds on leads **Facilities** walks info vet info **Other** charge for damage **Restrictions** small dogs only

Located close to Derby, this modern hotel is well suited to both the conference and leisure markets. Bedrooms are spacious, air conditioned, well equipped and include some smart executive rooms and suites. The well presented leisure facilities are amongst the best in the region.

Rooms 99 (20 fmly) (5 smoking) **Facilities** STV ⊗ Gym Beauty salon Steam room Xmas New Year Wi-fi **Services** Lift Air con **Parking** 270

Littleover Lodge

★★★ 72% HOTEL

222 Rykneld Rd, Littleover DE23 4AN

☎ 01332 510161 📄 01332 514010

e-mail: enquiries@littleoverlodge.co.uk

web: www.littleoverlodge.co.uk

dir: A38 towards Derby approx 1m on left slip lane signed Littleover/Mickleover/Findon, take 2nd exit off island marked Littleover 0.25m on right

PETS: Bedrooms (6 GF) unattended **Charges** £50 deposit (refunded if no damage) **Grounds** disp bin **Exercise area** 200yds **Facilities** walks info vet info **Other** charge for damage **Restrictions** no breed larger than a Labrador

Situated in a rural location this friendly hotel offers modern bedrooms with direct access from the car park. Two styles of dining are available - an informal carvery operation which is very popular locally, and a more formal restaurant which is open for lunch and dinner each day. Service is excellent with the long serving staff being particularly friendly.

Rooms 16 (3 fmly) (6 GF) **Facilities** STV ♫ Xmas New Year Wi-fi **Parking** 75 **Notes** LB

DERBY SERVICE AREA (A50) — Map 8 SK42

Days Inn Donington - A50

BUDGET HOTEL

Welcome Break Services, A50 Westbound DE72 2WA
☎ 01332 799666 📄 01332 794166
e-mail: derby.hotel@welcomebreak.co.uk
web: www.welcomebreak.co.uk
dir: M1 junct 24/24a, onto A50 towards Stoke/Derby. Hotel between juncts 1 & 2

PETS: Bedrooms (17 GF) unattended **Public areas** except restaurant **Grounds** on leads **Other** pets must either be on leads or in carriers

This modern building offers accommodation in smart, spacious and well-equipped bedrooms, suitable for families and business travellers, and all with en suite bathrooms. Continental breakfast is available and other refreshments may be taken at the nearby family restaurant.

Rooms 47 (39 fmly) (17 GF) (8 smoking) **S** £39.95-£59.95; **D** £49.95-£69.95

FENNY BENTLEY — Map 7 SK14

Bentley Brook Inn

★★★ INN

DE6 1LF
☎ 01335 350278 📄 01335 350422
e-mail: all@bentleybrookinn.co.uk
dir: 2m N of Ashbourne at junct of A515 & B5056

PETS: Bedrooms (2 GF) unattended sign 3 bedrooms only **Charges** £10 per stay **Public areas** except restaurant & breakfast room on leads **Grounds** on leads **Exercise area** surrounded by fields **Facilities** feeding mat scoop/disp bags cage storage walks info vet info **On Request** fridge access torch towels **Other** charge for damage dogs not permitted on beds

This popular inn is located in the Peak District National Park, just north of Ashbourne. It is a charming building with an attractive terrace, sweeping lawns, and nursery gardens. A well-appointed family restaurant dominates the ground floor, where a wide range of dishes is available all day. The character bar serves beer from its own micro-brewery. Bedrooms are well appointed and thoughtfully equipped.

Rooms 11 en suite (1 fmly) (2 GF) **Facilities** TVL tea/coffee Dinner available Direct Dial Cen ht Wi-fi **Parking** 100

FOOLOW — Map 7 SK17

The Bulls Head Inn

★★★★ INN

S32 5QR
☎ 01433 630873 📄 01433 631738
e-mail: wilbnd@aol.com
dir: Off A623 into Foolow

PETS: Bedrooms Charges £5 per night **Public areas** except restaurant **Exercise area** nearby **Facilities** food bowl walks info vet info **Other** charge for damage **Resident Pets:** Jack & Holly (West Highland Terriers)

Located in the village centre, this popular inn retains many original features and offers comfortable, well-equipped bedrooms. Extensive and imaginative bar meals are served in the traditionally furnished dining room or in the cosy bar areas. The inn welcomes well-behaved dogs in the bar (and even muddy boots on the flagstone areas).

Rooms 3 en suite (1 fmly) **Facilities** tea/coffee Dinner available Cen ht Golf 18 **Parking** 20

GRINDLEFORD — Map 8 SK27

Maynard

★★★ 79% ◉◉ HOTEL

Main Rd S32 2HE
☎ 01433 630321 📄 01433 630445
e-mail: info@themaynard.co.uk
dir: From Sheffield take A625 to Castleton. Left into Grindleford on B6521. On left after Fox House Hotel

PETS: Bedrooms sign **Charges** £20 per night **Public areas** except restaurant on leads **Grounds** on leads disp bin **Exercise area** 250mtrs **Facilities** food (pre-bookable) food bowl water bowl cage storage walks info vet info **On Request** fridge access **Other** charge for damage prior notice required cats must be kept in carriers

This building, dating back over 100 years, is situated in a beautiful and tranquil location yet is within easy reach of Sheffield and the M1. The bedrooms are contemporary in style and offer a wealth of accessories. The Peak District views from the restaurant and garden are stunning.

Rooms 10 (1 fmly) **Facilities** STV Wi-fi **Parking** 70 **Notes** LB

Charles Cotton
★★★★ 🍃 INN

SK17 0AL

☎ 01298 84229 📠 01298 84301

e-mail: info@charlescotton.co.uk

dir: *M1 junct 23A/A50 to Sudbury, follow A515 to Ashbourne then follow signs for Buxton. On B5054 1m S of A515 halfway between Buxton & Ashbourne*

PETS: Bedrooms unattended 3 ground-floor, stable block bedrooms only **Charges** £10 per night £70 per week **Public areas** except restaurants on leads **Grounds** on leads **Exercise area** 0.5m **Facilities** water bowl cage storage walks info vet info **On Request** towels **Stables** 3m **Other** charge for damage

A 17th-century inn in the centre of a pretty village in the Peak District. The cosy traditional bar, which features real ales and an open fire, blends with stylish design in the restaurant and attractive bedrooms. Complimentary Wi-fi is available. Food is a highlight and menus feature local ingredients.

Rooms 11 en suite 6 annexe en suite (3 fmly) (3 GF) **S** £55-£75; **D** £65-£105 **Facilities** TVL tea/coffee Dinner available Cen ht Wi-fi Fishing **Parking** 25 **Notes** LB

Underleigh House
★★★★★ 🍃 GUEST ACCOMMODATION

Lose Hill Ln S33 6AF

☎ 01433 621372 📠 01433 621324

e-mail: info@underleighhouse.co.uk

web: www.underleighhouse.co.uk

dir: *From village church on A6187 onto Edale Rd, 1m left onto Losehill Ln*

PETS: Bedrooms (2 GF) ground-floor bedrooms only **Grounds** on leads disp bin **Exercise area** public footpath adjacent **Facilities** washing facs walks info vet info **On Request** fridge access torch towels **Other** dogs are accepted by prior arrangement only **Resident Pet:** Freddie (cat)

Situated at the end of a private lane, surrounded by glorious scenery, Underleigh House was converted from a barn and cottage that dates from 1873, and now offers carefully furnished and attractively decorated bedrooms with modern facilities. One room has a private lounge and others have access to the gardens. There is a very spacious lounge with comfortable chairs and a welcoming log fire. Memorable breakfasts are served at one large table in the dining room.

Rooms 5 en suite (2 GF) **S** £65-£85; **D** £85-£105 **Facilities** TVL tea/coffee Direct Dial Cen ht Licensed Wi-fi **Parking** 6 **Notes** LB No Children 12yrs Closed Xmas, New Year & 23 Jan-23 Feb

Stoney Ridge
★★★★ 🍃 GUEST ACCOMMODATION

Granby Rd, Bradwell S33 9HU

☎ 01433 620538

e-mail: info@stoneyridge.org.uk

web: www.stoneyridge.org.uk

dir: *From N end of Bradwell, Gore Ln uphill past Bowling Green Inn, turn left onto Granby Rd*

PETS: Bedrooms unattended **Public areas** except dining room on leads **Grounds** on leads disp bin **Exercise area** 100mtrs **Facilities** pet sitting dog walking washing facs cage storage walks info vet info **On Request** fridge access torch towels **Resident Pets:** Paddy (cockatiel); Bertie & Boris (cockerels); 18 hens

This large, split-level bungalow stands in attractive mature gardens at the highest part of the village and has extensive views. Hens roam freely in the landscaped garden, and their fresh eggs add to the hearty breakfasts. Bedrooms are attractively furnished and thoughtfully equipped, and there is a spacious comfortable lounge and a superb indoor swimming pool.

Rooms 4 rms (3 en suite) (1 pri facs) **S** £47-£55; **D** £74 **Facilities** STV FTV TVL tea/coffee Cen ht Wi-fi 🏊 **Parking** 3 **Notes** LB No Children 10yrs RS Winter Pool may be closed for maintenance

Round Meadow Barn
★★★ BED AND BREAKFAST

Parsons Ln S33 6RB

☎ 01433 621347 & 07836 689422 📠 01433 621347

e-mail: rmbarn@bigfoot.com

dir: *Off A625 (Hope Rd) N onto Parsons Ln, over rail bridge, in 200yds right into hay barnyard, through gates, across 3 fields, house on left*

PETS: Bedrooms **Charges** dog £3, horse £10 per night **Public areas** except at breakfast on leads **Grounds** disp bin **Exercise area** **Exercise area** nearby **Facilities** water bowl feeding mat washing facs vet info **On Request** towels **Stables** **Restrictions** no Staffordshire Bull Terriers **Resident Pets:** Ellie(Jack Russell), Floss (horse), Lucy (cat)

This converted barn, with original stone walls and exposed timbers, stands in open fields in the picturesque Hope Valley. The bedrooms are large enough for families and there are two modern bathrooms. Breakfast is served at one large table adjoining the family kitchen.

Rooms 3 rms (1 en suite) (2 pri facs) (1 fmly) **S** £35-£45; **D** £60-£66 **Facilities** tea/coffee Cen ht Golf 18 Riding **Parking** 8 **Notes** LB 🚭

Hodgkinsons

★★★★ ⊜ GUEST ACCOMMODATION

150 South Pde, Matlock Bath DE4 3NR
☎ 01629 582170 📠 01629 584891
e-mail: enquiries@hodgkinsons-hotel.co.uk
dir: On A6 in village centre, corner of Waterloo Rd & South Parade

PETS: Bedrooms unattended 1st floor bedrooms only **Charges** £10 per night **Public areas** except restaurant/bar area **Grounds Exercise area** 200yds **Facilities** food bowl water bowl bedding dog chews cat treats feeding mat washing facs cage storage walks info vet info **On Request** fridge access torch towels **Other** charge for damage only 1 dog per room

This fine Georgian building was renovated in the Victorian era and has many interesting and unusual features. Bedrooms are equipped with fine antique furniture and a wealth of thoughtful extras. The elegant dining room is the setting for imaginative dinners and a comfortable lounge is also available.

Rooms 8 en suite (1 fmly) **S** £42-£85; **D** £93-£145 **Facilities** tea/coffee Dinner available Direct Dial Cen ht Licensed Wi-fi **Parking** 5 **Notes** LB Closed 24-26 Dec

Farley (SK294622)

★★★ FARMHOUSE

Farley DE4 5LR
☎ 01629 582533 & 07801 756409 📠 01629 584856
Mrs Brailsford
e-mail: eric.brailsford@btconnect.com
dir: 1m N of Matlock. From A6 rdbt towards Bakewell, 1st right, right at top of hill, left up Farley Hill, 2nd farm on left

PETS: Bedrooms Charges pony £15, horse £20 inc feed/bedding per night **Public areas** except dining room **Grounds Exercise area** fields surrounding farm **Facilities** food (pre-bookable) food bowl water bowl bedding leads pet sitting dog walking washing facs dog grooming cage storage vet info **On Request** fridge access torch towels **Stables** Resident Pets: 5 Border Terriers, 1 Labrador, 1 Boxer, 4 horses

Guests can expect a warm welcome at this traditional stone farmhouse. In addition to farming, the proprietors also breed dogs and horses. The bedrooms are pleasantly decorated and equipped with many useful extras. A hearty farmhouse breakfast offers a good start to any day.

Rooms 2 en suite (3 fmly) **S** £35-£40; **D** £60-£64 **Facilities** TVL tea/coffee Dinner available Cen ht Riding **Parking** 8 **Notes** LB 🐾 165 acres arable/beef/dairy

Lickpenny Caravan Site (SK339597)

►►►►

Lickpenny Ln, Tansley DE4 5GF
☎ 01629 583040 📠 01629 583040
e-mail: lickpenny@btinternet.com
dir: From Matlock take A615 towards Alfreton for 3m. Site signed to left, into Lickpenny Ln, right into site near end of road

PETS: Public areas disp bin **Exercise area on site** woodland area **Facilities** food food bowl water bowl dog chews scoop/disp bags leads walks info vet info

Open all year Last arrival 20.00hrs Last departure noon

A picturesque site in the grounds of an old plant nursery with areas broken up and screened by a variety of shrubs, and spectacular views, which are best enjoyed from the upper terraced areas. Pitches, several fully serviced, are spacious, well screened and well marked, and facilities are to a very good standard. The bistro/coffee shop is popular with visitors. 16 acre site. 80 touring pitches. 80 hardstandings. 20 seasonal pitches. Motorhome pitches.

Newhaven Caravan & Camping Park
(SK167602)

►►►

SK17 0DT
☎ 01298 84300 📠 01332 726027
e-mail: newhavencaravanpark@btconnect.com
dir: Between Ashbourne & Buxton at A515 & A5012 junct

PETS: Public areas except shop disp bin **Exercise area on site** woodland walks **Facilities** food food bowl water bowl dog chews cat treats scoop/disp bags walks info

Open Mar-Oct Last arrival 21.00hrs

Pleasantly situated within the Peak District National Park, this park has mature trees screening the three touring areas. Very good toilet facilities, with updated showers, cater for touring vans and a large tent field, and there's a restaurant adjacent to the site. 30 acre site. 125 touring pitches. 18 hardstandings. 40 seasonal pitches. Tent pitches. Motorhome pitches. 73 statics.

RIPLEY Map 8 SK35

Golden Valley Caravan & Camping Park
(SK408513)

▶ ▶ ▶ ▶

Coach Rd DE55 4ES
☎ 01773 513881 & 746786 ▤ 01773 746786
e-mail: enquiries@goldenvalleycaravanpark.co.uk
dir: *M1 junct 26, A610 to Codnor. Right at lights, then right onto Alfreton Rd. In 1m left onto Coach Rd, park on left. (NB it is advised that Sat Nav is ignored for last few miles & guide directions are followed)*

PETS: Sep accom Charges £2 per night £14 per week
Public areas Exercise area on site Topwood Area or field at rear
Exercise area footpaths adjacent to park **Facilities** dog chews
cat treats washing facs walks info vet info **Stables Other** prior
notice required disposal bags available **Resident Pets:** Roxy
(Labrador), Toby (goat), Gavin (peacock), Brian (goose), rabbits,
ducks, chickens

Open all year rs Wknds only in low season bar/café open Last
arrival 21.00hrs Last departure noon

This superbly landscaped park is set within 30 acres of woodland
in the Amber Valley. The fully-serviced pitches are set out in
informal groups in clearings amongst the trees. The park has
a cosy bar and bistro with outside patio, a fully stocked fishing
lake, an innovative and well-equipped play area, an on-site
jacuzzi and fully equipped fitness suite. There is also a wildlife
pond and a nature trail. 30 acre site. 45 touring pitches. 45
hardstandings. Tent pitches. Motorhome pitches. 1 static.

Notes No open fires or disposable BBQs, no noise after 22.30hrs,
no vehicles on grass.

ROSLISTON Map 8 SK21

Beehive Woodland Lakes (SK249161)

▶ ▶

DE12 8HZ
☎ 01283 763981 ▤ 01283 763981
e-mail: info@beehivefarm-woodlandlakes.co.uk
dir: *Turn S off A444 at Castle Gresley onto Mount Pleasant Rd,
follow Rosliston signs for 3.5m through Linton to T-junct. Turn left
signed Beehive Farms*

PETS: Charges £2 per night **Public areas** except farm & banks
of lakes on leads disp bin **Exercise area on site Facilities**
food food bowl water bowl dog chews scoop/disp bags leads
washing facs dog grooming walks info vet info **Other** prior
notice required **Restrictions** no dangerous dogs (see page 7)

Open Mar-Nov Last arrival 20.00hrs Last departure 10.30hrs

A small, informal and rapidly developing caravan area secluded
from an extensive woodland park in the heart of the National
Forest National Park. Young children will enjoy the on-site animal
farm and playground, whilst anglers will appreciate fishing the
three lakes within the park, and bikes can be hired. The Honey Pot
tearoom provides snacks and is open most days. 2.5 acre site.
25 touring pitches. 12 hardstandings. Tent pitches. Motorhome
pitches.

ROWSLEY Map 8 SK26

The Peacock at Rowsley
★★★ ⊕⊕⊕ HOTEL
Bakewell Rd DE4 2EB
☎ 01629 733518 ▤ 01629 732671
e-mail: reception@thepeacockatrowsley.com
web: www.thepeacockatrowsley.com
dir: *A6, 3m before Bakewell, 6m from Matlock towards Bakewell*

PETS: Bedrooms unattended **Charges** dog £10 per night
Grounds Exercise area 0.25m **Facilities** food (pre-bookable)
water bowl walks info vet info **On Request** torch towels **Other**
charge for damage

Owned by Lord Manners of Haddon Hall, this hotel combines
stylish contemporary design by India Mahdavi with original
period and antique features. Bedrooms are individually designed
and boast DVD players, complimentary Wi-fi and smart marble
bathrooms. Two rooms are particularly special - one with a
four-poster and one with an antique bed originating from Belvoir
Castle in Leicestershire. Imaginative cuisine, using local, seasonal
produce, is a highlight. Guests are warmly welcomed and service
is attentive. Fly fishing is popular in this area and the hotel has its
own fishing rights on seven miles of the Rivers Wye and Derwent.

Rooms 16 (5 fmly) **S** £85-£140; **D** £150-£257.50*
Facilities Fishing 🎣 Free use of Woodlands Fitness Centre Free
membership to Bakewell Golf Club 🎵 New Year Wi-fi **Parking** 25
Notes No children 10yrs

Holiday Inn Derby/Nottingham

Holiday Inn

★★★ **73%** HOTEL

Bostocks Ln NG10 5NJ
☎ 0871 942 9062   📠 0115 949 0469
e-mail: reservations-derby-nottingham@ihg.com
web: www.holidayinn.co.uk
dir: *M1 junct 25 follow Sandiacre signs, hotel on right*

PETS: Bedrooms (53 GF) unattended 2 bedrooms only **Charges** £10 per night £70 per week muzzled and on leads **Grounds** on leads disp bin **Facilities** vet info **On Request** fridge access torch towels **Other** charge for damage

This hotel is conveniently located by the M1, and ideal for exploring Derby and Nottingham. The bedrooms are modern and smart. The restaurant offers a wide range of dishes for breakfast, lunch and dinner. The lounge/bar area is a popular meeting place, with food served all day.

Rooms 92 (31 fmly) (53 GF) **Facilities** STV Xmas New Year Wi-fi **Services** Air con **Parking** 200 **Notes** LB

Izaak Walton

★★★ **80%** HOTEL

Dovedale DE6 2AY
☎ 01335 350555   📠 01335 350539
e-mail: reception@izaakwaltonhotel.com
web: www.izaakwaltonhotel.com
dir: *A515 onto B5054 to Thorpe, over cattle grid & 2 small bridges, 1st right, sharp left*

PETS: Bedrooms (8 GF) unattended **Charges** £10 per night **Public areas** except main restaurant & 1st floor **Grounds** disp bin **Exercise area** adjacent **Facilities** water bowl washing facs walks info vet info **On Request** fridge access torch **Other** charge for damage

Peacefully situated, with magnificent views over the valley of Dovedale to Thorpe Cloud. Many of the bedrooms have lovely views, and executive rooms are particularly spacious; Wi-fi access is available throughout. Food is a highlight, with an appealing choice in the bar area and more formal dining in the Haddon Restaurant. Fishing on the River Dove can be arranged.

Rooms 35 (6 fmly) (8 GF) **D** £70–£200 (incl. bkfst) **Facilities** FTV Fishing Xmas New Year Wi-fi **Parking** 80 **Notes** LB

The Rising Sun

★★★★ INN

Woodland TQ13 7JT
☎ 01364 652544
e-mail: admin@therisingsunwoodland.co.uk
dir: *A38, exit signed Woodland/Denbury, continue straight on for 1.5m, Rising Sun on left*

PETS: Bedrooms (2 GF) unattended **Public areas** on leads **Grounds** disp bin **Exercise area** 50yds **Facilities** cage storage walks info vet info **Resident Pet:** Ruby (rabbit)

Peacefully situated in scenic south Devon countryside, this inn is just a short drive from the A38. A friendly welcome is extended to all guests; business, leisure and families alike. Bedrooms are comfortable and well equipped. Dinner and breakfast feature much local and organic produce. A good selection of homemade puddings, West Country cheeses, local wines and quality real ales are available.

Rooms 5 en suite (2 fmly) (2 GF) **S** £45; **D** £55–£65 **Facilities** FTV tea/coffee Dinner available Cen ht Wi-fi **Parking** 30 **Notes** Closed 25 Dec No coaches

Parkers Farm Holiday Park *(SX779713)*

▶▶▶▶

Higher Mead Farm TQ13 7LJ
☎ 01364 654869   📠 01364 654004
e-mail: parkersfarm@btconnect.com
dir: *From Exeter on A38, take 2nd left after Plymouth 26m sign, signed Woodland-Denbury. From Plymouth on A38 take A383 Newton Abbot exit, turn right across bridge, rejoin A38, then as above*

PETS: Charges £1.50 per night **Public areas** except children's play area & main bar disp bin **Exercise area on site** 2 very large fields for dog walking **Facilities** food food bowl water bowl dog chews leads walks info vet info **Other** prior notice required disposal bags available **Resident Pet:** 1 Collie

Open Etr-end Oct rs Wknds only bar/restaurant open out of season Last arrival 22.00hrs Last departure 10.00hrs

A well-developed site terraced into rising ground. Part of a working farm, this park offers beautifully maintained, good quality facilities. Large family rooms with two shower cubicles, a large sink and a toilet are especially appreciated by families with small children. There are regular farm walks when all the family can meet and feed the various animals. 25 acre site. 100 touring pitches. 20 hardstandings. Tent pitches. Motorhome pitches. 18 statics.

ASHBURTON *continued*

River Dart Country Park *(SX734700)*

▶▶▶▶

Holne Park TQ13 7NP
☎ 01364 652511 📄 01364 652020
e-mail: info@riverdart.co.uk
dir: *M5 junct 31, A38 towards Plymouth. In Ashburton at Peartree junct follow brown site signs. Site 1m on left. (NB Peartree junct is 2nd exit at Ashburton - do not exit at Linhay junct as narrow roads are unsuitable for caravans)*

PETS: Charges £3 per night **Public areas** disp bin
Exercise area on site woodland area **Facilities** vet info **Other** prior notice required toys & disposal bags available

Open Apr-Sep rs Low season café bar restricted opening hours
Last arrival 21.00hrs Last departure 11.00hrs

Set in 90 acres of magnificent parkland that was once part of a Victorian estate, with many specimen and exotic trees, and in spring a blaze of colour from the many azaleas and rhododendrons. There are numerous outdoor activities for all ages including abseiling, caving and canoeing, plus high quality, well-maintained facilities. The open moorland of Dartmoor is only a few minutes away. 90 acre site. 170 touring pitches. 23 hardstandings. Tent pitches. Motorhome pitches.

ASHWATER Map 2 SX39

Blagdon Manor

★ ★ ★ ★ ★ ◎◎ 🍴 RESTAURANT WITH ROOMS

EX21 5DF
☎ 01409 211224 📄 01409 211634
e-mail: stay@blagdon.com
web: www.blagdon.com
dir: *A388 towards Launceston/Holsworthy. Approx 2m N of Chapman's Well take 2nd right for Ashwater. Next right beside Blagdon Lodge, 0.25m to manor*

PETS: Bedrooms Charges £8 per night **Public areas** except restaurant & conservatory on leads **Grounds** disp bin
Exercise area surrounding area **Facilities** food bowl water bowl bedding dog chews feeding mat scoop/disp bags washing facs cage storage walks info vet info **On Request** fridge access torch towels **Stables** livery 0.25m **Other** charge for damage
Resident Pets: Nutmeg, Cassia & Mace (Chocolate Labradors)

Located on the borders of Devon and Cornwall within easy reach of the coast, and set in its own beautifully kept natural gardens, this small and friendly restaurant with rooms offers a charming home-from-home atmosphere. The tranquillity of the secluded setting, the character and charm of the house and its unhurried pace ensure calm and relaxation. High levels of service, personal touches and thoughtful extras are all part of a stay here. Steve Morey cooks with passion and his commitment to using only the finest local ingredients speaks volumes.

Rooms 7 en suite **S** £85-£110; **D** £135-£195 **Facilities** FTV tea/coffee Dinner available Direct Dial Cen ht Wi-fi 🏊 **Parking** 13 **Notes** No Children 12yrs Closed Jan RS Mon & Tue closed No coaches

AXMINSTER Map 3 SY29

Fairwater Head Hotel

★ ★ ★ 75% ◎ HOTEL

Hawkchurch EX13 5TX
☎ 01297 678349 📄 01297 678459
e-mail: stay@fairwaterheadhotel.co.uk
web: www.fairwaterheadhotel.co.uk
dir: *Off B3165 (Crewkerne to Lyme Regis road). Hotel signed to Hawkchurch*

PETS: Bedrooms (8 GF) unattended **Sep accom** cabin with pen **Public areas** except dining room on leads **Grounds** on leads disp bin **Exercise area** surrounding countryside **Facilities** food (pre-bookable) food bowl water bowl dog chews scoop/disp bags leads pet sitting washing facs cage storage walks info vet info **On Request** fridge access torch towels **Stables** 400mtrs **Other** charge for damage **Resident Pets:** Mocca (Springer/Cocker Spaniel cross), Lollipop (Black Labrador)

This elegant Edwardian country house provides a perfect location for anyone looking for a peaceful break. Surrounded by extensive gardens and rolling countryside, the setting guarantees relaxation. Bedrooms are located both within the main house and the garden wing; all provide good levels of comfort. Public areas have much appeal and include lounge areas, a bar and an elegant restaurant. Food is a highlight with excellent local produce prepared with care and skill.

Rooms 16 (4 annexe) (8 GF) **S** £70-£125; **D** £85-£180 (incl. bkfst)* **Facilities** FTV Library Xmas New Year Wi-fi **Parking** 30 **Notes** LB Closed 1-30 Jan

Andrewshayes Caravan Park *(ST248088)*

▶▶▶▶

Dalwood EX13 7DY

☎ 01404 831225 📠 01404 831893

e-mail: info@andrewshayes.co.uk

dir: *On A35, 3m from Axminster. Turn N at Taunton Cross signed Stockland/Dalwood. Site 150mtrs on right*

PETS: Charges seasonal £1.50-£2.50 per night **Public areas** except bar & shop disp bin **Exercise area on site** 2 dog walking fields **Facilities** scoop/disp bags walks info vet info **Other** prior notice required

Open Mar-Nov rs Sep-Nov shop, bar hours limited, pool closed Sep-mid May Last arrival 22.00hrs Last departure 11.00hrs

An attractive family park within easy reach of Lyme Regis, Seaton, Branscombe and Sidmouth in an ideal touring location. This popular park offers modern toilet facilities, an outdoor swimming pool and a quiet, cosy bar with a widescreen TV. 12 acre site. 150 touring pitches. 105 hardstandings. Tent pitches. Motorhome pitches. 80 statics.

The Bark House

★★★★ 🛏 GUEST ACCOMMODATION

Oakfordbridge EX16 9HZ

☎ 01398 351236

dir: *A361 to rdbt at Tiverton onto A396 for Dulverton, then onto Oakfordbridge. House on right*

PETS: Bedrooms Public areas if other guests do not object **Grounds** disp bin **Exercise area** adjacent **Facilities** feeding mat walks info vet info **On Request** towels **Other** charge for damage **Restrictions** well behaved dogs only **Resident Pets:** Jack & Ellie (dogs)

Located in the stunning Exe Valley and surrounded by wonderful unspoilt countryside, this is a perfect place to relax and unwind. Hospitality is the hallmark here and a cup of tea by the fireside is always on offer. Both breakfast and dinner make use of the excellent local produce, and are served in the attractive dining room, overlooking fields and the river. Bedrooms have a homely, cottage-style feel with comfy beds to ensure a peaceful night's sleep.

Rooms 6 rms (5 en suite) (1 pri facs) (1 fmly) **S** £50-£60; **D** £80-£110 **Facilities** tea/coffee Dinner available Cen ht Licensed **Parking** 6

Cedars Lodge

★★★★ INN

Bickington Rd EX31 2HP

☎ 01271 371784 📠 01271 325733

e-mail: cedars.barnstaple@oldenglishinns.co.uk

PETS: Bedrooms unattended certain bedrooms only **Public areas** except restaurant on leads **Grounds** on leads **Exercise area** 0.5m **Other** charge for damage

Once a private country house, this popular establishment stands in three-acre gardens, situated just outside Barnstaple and within easy reach of the M5 and major roads. Bedrooms are located in the adjacent lodge which is set around a courtyard facing the main house; all rooms offer generous levels of comfort and modern facilities. The popular conservatory restaurant serves a wide choice of dishes.

Rooms 2 en suite 32 annexe en suite (7 fmly) **S** £55-£75; **D** £69-£90 **Facilities** FTV TVL tea/coffee Dinner available Direct Dial Cen ht Wi-fi Golf 18 **Parking** 200

Mill Park *(SS559471)*

▶▶▶

Mill Ln EX34 9SH

☎ 01271 882647

e-mail: millparkdevon@btconnect.com

dir: *M5 junct 27 onto A361 towards Barnstaple. Right onto A399 towards Combe Martin. At Sawmills Inn take turn opposite for Berrynarbor*

PETS: Charges low season 50p, high season £2 per night **Public areas** disp bin **Exercise area on site** 1 acre dog exercise field **Exercise area** beach **Facilities** food food bowl water bowl walks info vet info **Other** prior notice required disposal bags available

Open Mar-30 Oct rs High season on-site facilities open Last arrival 22.00hrs Last departure 10.00hrs

This family owned and run park is set in an attractive wooded valley with a stream running into a lake where coarse fishing is available. There is a quiet bar/restaurant with a family room. The park is two miles from Combe Martin and Ilfracombe and just a stroll across the road from the small harbour at Watermouth. 23 acre site. 178 touring pitches. 20 hardstandings. Tent pitches. Motorhome pitches. 1 static. 2 wooden pods.

Notes No large groups.

ENGLAND

Lemonford Caravan Park *(SX793723)*

►►►►

TQ12 6JR
☎ 01626 821242
e-mail: info@lemonford.co.uk
dir: *From Exeter on A38 take A382, then 3rd exit at rdbt, follow Bickington signs*

PETS: Charges dog £1.50 per night **Public areas** except bar & pool area on leads disp bin **Exercise area** adjacent **Facilities** walks info vet info **Other** prior notice required dogs must be kept on short leads **Restrictions** dog breeds must be approved by owner prior to arrival **Resident Pets:** 3 cats

Open all year Last arrival 22.00hrs Last departure 11.00hrs

Small, secluded and well-maintained park with a good mixture of attractively laid out pitches. The friendly owners pay a great deal of attention to detail, and the toilets in particular are kept spotlessly clean. This good touring base is only one mile from Dartmoor and ten miles from the seaside at Torbay. 7 acre site. 82 touring pitches. 55 hardstandings. Tent pitches. Motorhome pitches. 44 statics.

Yeoldon Country House

★★★ 74% SMALL HOTEL
Durrant Ln, Northam EX39 2RL
☎ 01237 474400 📄 01237 476618
e-mail: yeoldonhouse@aol.com
web: www.yeoldonhousehotel.co.uk
dir: *A39 from Barnstaple over River Torridge Bridge. At rdbt right onto A386 towards Northam, 3rd right into Durrant Lane*

PETS: Bedrooms Charges £5 per night **Public areas** lounge only (under strict control) on leads **Grounds** disp bin **Exercise area** North Devon coastal path adjacent **Facilities** washing facs cage storage walks info vet info **On Request** fridge access torch towels **Other** charge for damage **Resident Pet:** Shaz (Collie cross)

In a tranquil location with superb views over attractive grounds and the River Torridge, this is a charming Victorian house. The well-equipped bedrooms are individually decorated and some have balconies with breathtaking views. The public rooms are full of character with many interesting features and artefacts. The daily-changing dinner menu offers imaginative dishes.

Rooms 10 **S** £80-£90; **D** £120-£140 (incl. bkfst) **Facilities** FTV Wi-fi **Parking** 20 **Notes** LB Closed 24-27 Dec

Royal

★★★ 74% HOTEL
Barnstaple St EX39 4AE
☎ 01237 472005 📄 01237 478957
e-mail: reservations@royalbideford.co.uk
web: www.royalbideford.co.uk
dir: *At eastern end of Bideford Bridge*

PETS: Bedrooms (2 GF) standard bedrooms only **Charges** £5 per night **Public areas** only reception **Facilities** cage storage vet info **Stables** 3-5m **Other** charge for damage

A quiet and relaxing hotel, the Royal is set near the river within a five-minute walk of the busy town centre and the quay. The bright, well maintained public areas retain much of the charm and style of its 16th-century origins, particularly in the wood-panelled Kingsley Suite. Bedrooms are well equipped and comfortable. The meals at dinner and the lounge snacks are appetising.

Rooms 32 (2 fmly) (2 GF) **S** £59-£120; **D** £75-£120*
Facilities FTV Xmas New Year Wi-fi **Services** Lift **Parking** 70
Notes LB

Pines at Eastleigh

★★★★ GUEST ACCOMMODATION
The Pines, Eastleigh EX39 4PA
☎ 01271 860561 📄 01271 861689
e-mail: pirrie@thepinesateastleigh.co.uk
dir: *A39 onto A386 signed East-the-Water. 1st left signed Eastleigh, 500yds next left, 1.5m to village, house on right*

PETS: Bedrooms (4 GF) ground-floor bedrooms only **Charges** £5 per night **Public areas** except breakfast room, garden room & bar on leads **Grounds** on leads disp bin **Exercise area** nearby **Facilities** food bowl water bowl leads pet sitting dog walking washing facs cage storage walks info vet info **On Request** fridge access torch towels **Stables** 2m **Other** charge for damage

Friendly hospitality is assured at this Georgian house, set in seven acres of hilltop grounds. Two of the comfortable bedrooms are located in the main house, the remainder in converted barns around a charming courtyard that has a pretty pond and well. A delicious breakfast, featuring local and home-made produce, is served in the dining room, and a lounge and honesty bar are also available.

Rooms 6 en suite (1 fmly) (4 GF) **S** £55-£69; **D** £79-£89
Facilities FTV tea/coffee Direct Dial Cen ht Licensed Wi-fi
Parking 20 **Notes** LB No Children 9yrs

BISHOPSTEIGNTON — Map 3 SX97

THE INDEPENDENTS
HOTEL ASSOCIATION

Cockhaven Manor Hotel
★★ 72% HOTEL

Cockhaven Rd TQ14 9RF
☎ 01626 775252 📄 01626 775572
e-mail: cockhaven@btconnect.com
web: www.cockhavenmanor.com
dir: M5/A380 towards Torquay, then A381 towards Teignmouth. Left at Metro Motors. Hotel 500yds on left

PETS: Bedrooms unattended sign **Public areas** except restaurant, dining room **Grounds** disp bin **Exercise area** garden & river walks 0.25m **Facilities** food (pre-bookable) food bowl water bowl bedding dog chews cat treats feeding mat scoop/disp bags leads pet sitting dog walking washing facs walks info vet info **On Request** fridge access torch towels **Other** charge for damage **Resident Pet:** Bitsi (rescue dog)

A friendly, family-run inn that dates back to the 16th century. Bedrooms are well equipped and many enjoy views across the beautiful Teign estuary. A choice of dining options is offered, and traditional and interesting dishes, along with locally caught fish, prove popular.

Rooms 12 (2 fmly) **S** £50-£65; **D** £75-£90 (incl. bkfst)* **Facilities** FTV Petanque Wi-fi **Parking** 50 **Notes** LB Closed 25-26 Dec

BOVEY TRACEY — Map 3 SX87

The Cromwell Arms
★★★★ INN

Fore St TQ13 9AE
☎ 01626 833473 📄 01626 836873
e-mail: info@thecromwellarms.co.uk
dir: From A38 from Exeter towards Plymouth take A382 at Drumbridges rdbt & follow Bovey Tracey signs. At mini rdbt take 2nd exit, follow town centre signs. At next rdbt take 3rd exit into Station Rd (B3344) & up hill

PETS: Bedrooms bedrooms 11 & 12 only **Charges** dog £5 per night **Public areas** except restaurant & lounge on leads **Grounds** on leads disp bin **Exercise area** 2 mins' walk **Facilities** food bowl water bowl bedding feeding mat scoop/disp bags leads washing facs cage storage walks info vet info **On Request** fridge access torch towels **Resident Pets:** Jasper, Benji & Poppy (Lhasa Apsos), 8 chickens

A traditional country inn situated in the heart of Bovey Tracey, on the southern edge of Dartmoor and approximately three miles from Newton Abbot, The Cromwell dates back from the 1600s, is full of original charm and has been enhanced with 21st-century facilities. This is an atmospheric, friendly pub with lots of character, which is suitable for all ages and is open all day every day.

Rooms 12 en suite (2 fmly) **S** £50-£60; **D** £70-£80 **Facilities** FTV tea/coffee Dinner available Direct Dial Cen ht Wi-fi **Parking** 25

BRAUNTON — Map 2 SS43

Hidden Valley Park (SS499408)
▶▶▶▶

West Down EX34 8NU
☎ 01271 813837
dir: Direct access off A361, 8m from Barnstaple & 2m from Mullacott Cross

PETS: Charges £1.50 per night **Public areas** except shop & coffee shop disp bin **Exercise area on site** exercise field & woods **Facilities** washing facs walks info vet info **Other** dogs must be kept on short leads & not left unattended; tick sticks; disposal bags & ground tethers available **Resident Pet:** Poppy (Dalmatian)

A delightful, well-appointed family site set in a wooded valley, with superb facilities and a café. The park is set in a very rural, natural location not far from the beautiful coastline around Ilfracombe. 25 acre site. 115 touring pitches. Tent pitches. Motorhome pitches.

BRAUNTON *continued*

Lobb Fields Caravan & Camping Park
(SS475378)

►►►

Saunton Rd EX33 1HG
☎ 01271 812090   📠 01271 812090
e-mail: info@lobbfields.com
dir: *At x-rds in Braunton take B3231 to Croyde. Site signed on right leaving Braunton*

PETS: Charges £2 per night **Public areas** except shower, toilets & play area disp bin **Exercise area on site** dog walk with disposal bin **Exercise area** dog friendly beach (0.25m) **Facilities** washing facs walks info vet info **Other** disposal bags available at reception **Restrictions** no Pit Bull Terriers or similar breeds

Open 23 Mar-28 Oct Last arrival 22.00hrs Last departure 10.30hrs

A bright, tree-lined park with the gently-sloping grass pitches divided into two open areas and a camping field in August. Braunton is an easy walk away, and the golden beaches of Saunton Sands and Croyde are within easy reach. 14 acre site. 180 touring pitches. 6 hardstandings. Tent pitches. Motorhome pitches.

Notes No under 18s unless accompanied by an adult.

Hedleywood Caravan & Camping Park
(SS262013)

►►►

EX22 7ED
☎ 01288 381404   📠 01288 382011
e-mail: alan@hedleywood.co.uk
dir: *M5 south to Exeter, follow A30 to Launceston, then B3254 towards Bude. left Widemouth road at the Devon/Cornwall border*

PETS: Sep accom pens for dogs if owners are off site (few hours only) **Public areas** except children's play area disp bin **Exercise area** 1m dog walk & exercise field **Facilities** food food bowl water bowl bedding dog chews scoop/disp bags leads washing facs vet info **Other** toys & balls available **Resident Pets:** Ella & Uira (German Shepherds), Arthur & Martha (Kune Kune pigs), goats, chickens, ducks & aviary birds

Open all year rs Main hols bar/restaurant open Last arrival anytime Last departure anytime

Set in a very rural location about four miles from Bude, this relaxed family-owned site has a peaceful, easy-going atmosphere. Pitches are in separate paddocks, some with extensive views, and this wooded park is quite sheltered in the lower areas. 16.5 acre site. 120 touring pitches. 30 hardstandings. Tent pitches. Motorhome pitches. 16 statics.

Notes 🐾

Highfield House Camping & Caravanning
(SS279035)

► ►

Holsworthy EX22 7EE
☎ 01288 381480
e-mail: njt@btinternet.com
dir: *Exit A3072 at Red Post x-rds onto B3254 towards Launceston. Direct access just over Devon border on right*

PETS: Public areas on leads disp bin **Exercise area on site Facilities** washing facs walks info vet info **Restrictions** no Staffordshire Bull Terriers, German Shepherds or Rottweilers **Resident Pets:** Tilly (West Highland White Terrier), Sparky (Cairn Terrier) & Nevja (English Mastiff), goats, chickens, ducks, geese, pigs

Open all year

Set in a quiet and peaceful rural location, this park has extensive views over the valley to the sea at Bude, five miles away. The friendly young owners, with small children of their own, offer a relaxing holiday for families, with the simple facilities carefully looked after. 4 acre site. 20 touring pitches. Tent pitches. Motorhome pitches. 4 statics.

Notes 🐾

Quayside
★★★ 75% ⊛ HOTEL

41-49 King St TQ5 9TJ
☎ 01803 855751   📠 01803 882733
e-mail: reservations@quaysidehotel.co.uk
web: www.quaysidehotel.co.uk
dir: *A380, at 2nd rdbt at Kinkerswell towards Brixham on A3022*

PETS: Bedrooms Charges £12.50 per night **Public areas** except restaurant, lounge & Main Mast bar on leads **Facilities** food bowl water bowl walks info vet info **On Request** fridge access **Other** charge for damage prior notice required **Restrictions** small dogs only

With views over the harbour and bay, this hotel was formerly six cottages, and the public rooms retain a certain cosiness and intimacy, and include the lounge, residents' bar and Ernie Lister's public bar. Freshly landed fish features on the menus, alongside a number of creative and skilfully prepared dishes, served in the well-appointed restaurant. Good food is also available in the public bar. The owners and their team of local staff provide friendly and attentive service.

Rooms 29 (2 fmly) **Facilities** FTV ♫ Xmas New Year Wi-fi **Parking** 30

Berry Head Hotel
★★★ 75% HOTEL

Berry Head Rd TQ5 9AJ
☎ 01803 853225   📠 01803 882084
e-mail: stay@berryheadhotel.com
dir: *From marina, 1m, hotel on left*

PETS: Bedrooms Charges £10 per night **Public areas** lounge only at certain times on leads **Grounds Exercise area** adjacent **Other** prior notice required **Restrictions** small dogs only

From its stunning cliff-top location, this imposing property that dates back to 1809, has spectacular views across Torbay. Public areas include two comfortable lounges, an outdoor terrace, a swimming pool, together with a bar serving a range of popular dishes. Many of the bedrooms have the benefit of the splendid sea views.

Rooms 32 (7 fmly) **S** £55-£70; **D** £110-£164 (incl. bkfst)* **Facilities** FTV 🕑 ⌣ Petanque Sailing Deep sea fishing Yacht charter ♫ Xmas New Year Wi-fi **Services** Lift **Parking** 200 **Notes** LB

Roadford Lake *(SX421900)*

► ► ►

Lower Goodacre PL16 0JL
☎ 01409 211507   📠 01566 778503
e-mail: info@swlakestrust.org.uk
dir: *Exit A30 between Okehampton & Launceston at Roadford Lake signs, across dam wall, watersports centre 0.25m on right*

PETS: Public areas on leads disp bin **Exercise area on site** lake walks **Facilities** washing facs walks info

Open Apr-Oct

Located right at the edge of Devon's largest inland water, this popular rural park is well screened by mature trees and shrubs. It boasts an excellent watersports school (sailing, windsurfing, rowing and kayaking) with hire and day launch facilities, and is an ideal location for fly fishing for brown trout. 1.5 acre site. 30 touring pitches. 4 hardstandings. Tent pitches. Motorhome pitches.

BUDLEIGH SALTERTON — Map 3 SY08

Hansard House

★ ★ ★ ★ GUEST ACCOMMODATION

3 Northview Rd EX9 6BY
☎ 01395 442773 📠 01395 442475
e-mail: enquiries@hansardhousehotel.co.uk
web: www.hansardhousehotel.co.uk
dir: *500yds W of town centre*

PETS: Bedrooms (3 GF) unattended ground-floor bedrooms only **Charges** £7.50 per night £45 per week **Grounds** disp bin **Exercise area** 100yds **Facilities** food bowl water bowl bedding feeding mat pet sitting dog walking washing facs cage storage walks info vet info **On Request** fridge access torch towels **Other** charge for damage

Hansard House is quietly situated a short walk from the town centre. Many of the well-presented bedrooms have commanding views across the town to the countryside and estuary beyond. Several are located on the ground floor and have easier access. Guests enjoy a varied selection at breakfast including a range of healthy options. The dining room and lounge are both comfortably furnished, and dinners are sometimes available with prior notification.

Rooms 12 en suite (1 fmly) (3 GF) **S** £52-£57; **D** £89-£98 **Facilities** STV TVL tea/coffee Direct Dial Cen ht Lift Licensed Wi-fi **Parking** 11 **Notes** LB

Pooh Cottage Holiday Park *(SY053831)*

▶ ▶ ▶

Bear Ln EX9 7AQ
☎ 01395 442354 & 07928 486938
e-mail: info@poohcottage.co.uk
dir: *M5 junct 30 onto A376 towards Exmouth. Left onto B3179 towards Woodbury & Budleigh Salterton. Left into Knowle on B3178. Through village, at brow of hill take sharp left into Bear Lane. Site 200yds*

PETS: Public areas except woodland walkway **Exercise area** common land (150yds), river & coastal paths **Facilities** food bowl walks info vet info **Stables** 1m **Other** prior notice required **Restrictions** no dangerous dogs (see page 7) **Resident Pet:** Charlie Brown (Chocolate Labrador)

Open 15 Mar-Oct Last arrival 20.00hrs Last departure 11.00hrs

A rural park with widespread views of the sea and surrounding peaceful countryside. Expect a friendly welcome to this attractive site, with its lovely play area, and easy access to plenty of walks, as well as the Buzzard Cycle Way. 8 acre site. 52 touring pitches. 40 seasonal pitches. Tent pitches. Motorhome pitches. 3 statics.

BURRINGTON (NEAR PORTSMOUTH ARMS STATION) — Map 3 SS61

Northcote Manor

★ ★ ★ COUNTRY HOUSE HOTEL

EX37 9LZ
☎ 01769 560501 📠 01769 560770
e-mail: rest@northcotemanor.co.uk
web: www.northcotemanor.co.uk
dir: *Off A377 opposite Portsmouth Arms, into hotel drive. (NB do not enter Burrington village)*

PETS: Bedrooms Charges £10 per night **Public areas** except restaurant, top lounge & conservatory **Grounds Exercise area** beach (12m) **Facilities** food (pre-bookable) food bowl water bowl dog chews washing facs cage storage walks info vet info **On Request** fridge access torch towels **Stables** 5m

A warm and friendly welcome is assured at this beautiful country-house hotel, built in 1716 and surrounded by 20 acres of grounds and woodlands. Guests can enjoy wonderful views over the Taw River Valley whilst relaxing in the delightful environment created by the attentive staff. A meal in either the intimate, more formal Manor House Restaurant or the Walled Garden Restaurant will prove a highlight; each offers menus of the finest local produce used in well-prepared dishes. Bedrooms, including some suites, are individually styled, spacious and well appointed.

Rooms 11 **S** £110-£170; **D** £160-£260 (incl. bkfst)* **Facilities** FTV ⚓ Xmas New Year Wi-fi **Parking** 30 **Notes** LB

CHAGFORD — Map 3 SX78

Mill End Hotel

★ ★ 85% COUNTRY HOTEL

Dartmoor National Park TQ13 8JN
☎ 01647 432282 📠 01647 433106
e-mail: info@millendhotel.com
web: www.millendhotel.com
dir: *From A30 at Whiddon Down take A382 to Moretonhampstead. In 3.5m hump back bridge at Sandy Park, hotel on right*

PETS: Bedrooms (3 GF) unattended **Charges** £7 per night **Public areas** except restaurant **Grounds** disp bin **Exercise area** **Exercise area** adjacent **Facilities** water bowl scoop/disp bags leads washing facs cage storage walks info vet info **On Request** fridge access torch towels **Other** charge for damage **Resident Pet:** Tess (Rhodesian Ridgeback)

Originally an 18th-century working water mill, this engaging hotel sits alongside the River Teign and offers six miles of angling. Surrounded by picturesque Devon countryside, the atmosphere is akin to a family home where guests are encouraged to relax and enjoy the peace and informality. Bedrooms are available in a range of sizes and all are stylishly decorated and thoughtfully equipped. Dining is certainly a highlight of any stay here with the menus offering exciting dishes based on local produce.

Rooms 14 (3 GF) **Facilities** FTV Fishing ⚓ Xmas New Year Wi-fi **Parking** 25 **Notes** LB

CHAPMANS WELL — Map 2 SX39

Chapmanswell Caravan Park *(SX354931)*

▶▶▶

St Giles-on-the-Heath PL15 9SG
☎ 01409 211382 📠 01409 211154
e-mail: george@chapmanswellcaravanpark.co.uk
dir: *Take A338 from Launceston towards Holsworthy, 6m. Site on left at Chapmans Well*

PETS: Public areas except clubhouse, shop & children's play area disp bin **Exercise area** 500yds **Facilities** food dog chews cat treats walks info vet info **Other** prior notice required disposal bags available

Open all year Last arrival anytime by prior agreement Last departure anytime by prior agreement

Set on the borders of Devon and Cornwall in peaceful countryside, this park is just waiting to be discovered. It enjoys extensive views towards Dartmoor from level pitches, and is within easy driving distance of Launceston (7 miles) and the golden beaches at Bude (14 miles). 10 acre site. 50 touring pitches. 35 hardstandings. 32 seasonal pitches. Tent pitches. Motorhome pitches. 50 statics.

COMBE MARTIN — Map 2 SS54

Newberry Valley Park *(SS576473)*

▶▶▶▶

Woodlands EX34 0AT
☎ 01271 882334
e-mail: relax@newberryvalleypark.co.uk
dir: *M5 junct 27, A361 to North Aller rdbt. Right onto A399, through Combe Martin to sea. Left into site*

PETS: Charges peak season £1-£2 per night **Public areas** disp bin **Exercise area on site** exercise field (on lead only) **Exercise area** beach **Facilities** dog chews cat treats walks info vet info **Other** prior notice required disposal bags available **Resident Pets:** Diesel (British Wolfdog), Teyha (Utonagan/Wolfdog), Barney (cross)

Open Apr-Oct Last arrival 20.45hrs Last departure 10.00hrs

A family owned and run touring park on the edge of Combe Martin, with all its amenities just a five-minute walk away. The park is set in a wooded valley with its own coarse fishing lake. The safe beaches of Newberry and Combe Martin are reached by a short footpath opposite the park entrance, where the South West Coast Path is located. 20 acre site. 120 touring pitches. 18 hardstandings. 20 seasonal pitches. Tent pitches. Motorhome pitches.

Notes No camp fires, latest arrival time dusk in winter.

Stowford Farm Meadows *(SS560427)*

▶▶▶▶

Berry Down EX34 0PW
☎ 01271 882476 📠 01271 883053
e-mail: enquiries@stowford.co.uk
dir: *M5 junct 27 onto A361 to Barnstaple. Take A39 from town centre towards Lynton, in 1m turn left onto B3230. Right at garage at Lynton Cross onto A3123, site 1.5m on right*

PETS: Sep accom day crèche (£10 per day) **Charges** £1.60-£2.60 per night **Public areas** except children's play area & swimming pool disp bin **Exercise area on site** woodland walk & exercise fields **Facilities** food food bowl water bowl dog chews cat treats scoop/disp bags leads **Other** prior notice required

Open all year rs Winter bars & catering closed Last arrival 20.00hrs Last departure 10.00hrs

Very gently sloping, grassy, sheltered and south-facing site approached down a wide, well-kept driveway. This large farm park is set in 500 acres, and offers many quality amenities, including a large swimming pool, horse riding and crazy golf. A 60-acre wooded nature trail is an added attraction, as is the mini zoo with its stock of friendly animals. 100 acre site. 700 touring pitches. 115 hardstandings. Tent pitches. Motorhome pitches.

DARTMEET — Map 3 SX67

Brimpts Farm

★★★ GUEST ACCOMMODATION

PL20 6SG
☎ 01364 631450 📠 01364 631179
e-mail: info@brimptsfarm.co.uk
web: www.brimptsfarm.co.uk
dir: *Dartmeet at E end of B3357, establishment signed on right at top of hill*

PETS: Bedrooms (7 GF) **Public areas Grounds Exercise area** adjacent **Facilities** water bowl washing facs walks info vet info **On Request** fridge access torch towels **Stables Other** fenced paddock for horses **Resident Pets:** Matilda (Jack Russell), Charlie & Bertie (Border Collies), Fern & Bramble (cats)

A popular venue for walkers and lovers of the great outdoors, Brimpts is peacefully situated in the heart of Dartmoor and has been a Duchy of Cornwall farm since 1307. Bedrooms are simply furnished and many have wonderful views across Dartmoor. Dinner is served by arrangement. Additional facilities include a sauna and spa, and a children's play area. Brimpts is also home to the Dartmoor Pony Heritage Trust.

Rooms 10 en suite (2 fmly) (7 GF) **S** £35; **D** £60 **Facilities** TVL tea/coffee Dinner available Cen ht Licensed Wi-fi Sauna Pool table **Parking** 50 **Notes** LB

DARTMOUTH
Map 3 SX85

The Dart Marina
★★★★ 80% ◉◉ HOTEL
Sandquay Rd TQ6 9PH
☎ 01803 832580 & 837120 📠 01803 835040
e-mail: reservations@dartmarina.com
web: www.dartmarina.com
dir: *A3122 from Totnes to Dartmouth. Follow road which becomes College Way, before Higher Ferry. Hotel sharp left in Sandquay Rd*

PETS: **Bedrooms** (4 GF) unattended **Charges** £10 per night
Public areas except restaurants on leads **Exercise area** 30yds
Facilities walks info vet info

Boasting a stunning riverside location with its own marina, this is a special place to stay. Bedrooms vary in style, and all have wonderful views; some have private balconies to sit and soak up the atmosphere. The stylish public areas take full advantage of the waterside setting with opportunities to dine alfresco. In addition to the Wildfire Bar & Bistro, the River Restaurant is the venue for accomplished cooking.

Rooms 49 (4 annexe) (4 fmly) (4 GF) **S** £95-£155; **D** £140-£200 (incl. bkfst)* **Facilities** Spa ☺ Gym Canoeing Sailing Xmas New Year Wi-fi **Services** Lift **Parking** 50 **Notes** LB

Royal Castle
★★★ 81% HOTEL
11 The Quay TQ6 9PS
☎ 01803 833033 📠 01803 835445
e-mail: enquiry@royalcastle.co.uk
web: www.royalcastle.co.uk
dir: *In centre of town, overlooking Inner Harbour*

PETS: **Bedrooms** unattended **Charges** **Public areas** except restaurant **Exercise area** 800mtrs **Facilities** bedding dog chews pet sitting walks info vet info **On Request** fridge access torch towels **Other** charge for damage well behaved dogs only **Resident Pet:** Stella (Springer Spaniel)

At the edge of the harbour, this imposing 17th-century former coaching inn is filled with charm and character. Bedrooms are well equipped and comfortable; many have harbour views. A choice of quiet seating areas is offered in addition to both the traditional and contemporary bars. A variety of eating options is available, including the main restaurant which has lovely views.

Rooms 25 (3 fmly) **S** £95-£110; **D** £140-£210 (incl. bkfst)*
Facilities FTV ♫ Xmas New Year Wi-fi **Parking** 15

Stoke Lodge
★★★ 73% HOTEL
Stoke Fleming TQ6 0RA
☎ 01803 770523 📠 01803 770851
e-mail: mail@stokelodge.co.uk
web: www.stokelodge.co.uk
dir: *2m S A379*

PETS: **Bedrooms** (7 GF) unattended **Grounds Exercise area** park (2 mins), beach in winter (20 mins) **Facilities** walks info **On Request** fridge access torch towels

This family-run hotel continues to attract returning guests and is set in three acres of gardens and grounds with lovely views across to the sea. A range of leisure facilities is offered including both indoor and outdoor pools, along with a choice of comfortable lounges. Bedrooms are pleasantly appointed. The restaurant offers a choice of menus and an impressive wine list.

Rooms 25 (5 fmly) (7 GF) **S** £71-£75.50; **D** £99-£129 (incl. bkfst)* **Facilities** FTV ☺ ⚲ ⚲ Putt green Table tennis Pool & Snooker tables Sauna Xmas New Year Wi-fi **Parking** 50 **Notes** LB

DAWLISH
Map 3 SX97

THE INDEPENDENTS
HOTEL ASSOCIATION

Langstone Cliff
★★★ 78% HOTEL
Dawlish Warren EX7 0NA
☎ 01626 868000 📠 01626 868006
e-mail: reception@langstone-hotel.co.uk
web: www.langstone-hotel.co.uk
dir: *1.5m NE off A379 (Exeter road) to Dawlish Warren*

PETS: **Bedrooms** (10 GF) unattended **Public areas** except restaurant & pool area on leads **Grounds** on leads disp bin **Exercise area** woods **Facilities** water bowl scoop/disp bags washing facs cage storage walks info vet info **On Request** torch towels **Resident Pets:** Buster & Sally (dogs)

A family owned and run hotel, this hotel offers a range of leisure, conference and function facilities. Bedrooms, many with sea views and balconies, are spacious, comfortable and well equipped. There are a number of attractive lounges and a well-stocked bar. Dinner is served, often carvery style, in the restaurant.

Rooms 66 (4 annexe) (52 fmly) (10 GF) **S** £81-£95; **D** £148-£212 (incl. bkfst)* **Facilities** STV FTV ☺ ⚲ ⚲ Gym Table tennis Golf practice area Hair & beauty salon Therapy room Ballroom ♫ Xmas New Year Wi-fi Child facilities **Services** Lift **Parking** 200 **Notes** LB

Lady's Mile Holiday Park (SX968784)

 EX7 0LX
☎ 0845 026 7252   📠 01626 888689
e-mail: info@ladysmile.co.uk
dir: *1m N of Dawlish on A379*

PETS: Charges dog £2.50-£4.75 per night **Public areas** except swimming pool, club house & childrens' play area disp bin **Exercise area on site** fenced area **Facilities** food walks info vet info

Open 17 Mar-27 Oct Last arrival 20.00hrs Last departure 11.00hrs

A holiday site with a wide variety of touring pitches, including fully serviced pitches. There are plenty of activities for everyone, including two swimming pools with waterslides, a large adventure playground, 9-hole golf course, and a bar with entertainment in high season all add to the enjoyment of a stay here. Facilities are kept very clean, and the surrounding beaches are easily accessed. Holiday homes are also available. 16 acre site. 243 touring pitches. 30 hardstandings. Tent pitches. Motorhome pitches. 43 statics.

Peppermint Park (SX978788)

Warren Rd EX7 0PQ
☎ 01626 863436   📠 01626 866482
e-mail: peppermint@parkholidaysuk.com
dir: *From A379 at Dawlish follow signs for Dawlish Warren. Site 1m on left at bottom of hill*

PETS: Charges £4 per night **Public areas** except play area, swimming pool & club house disp bin **Exercise area on site** **Exercise area** 750yds **Facilities** walks info vet info **Stables** 2m **Other** please phone for further details of pet facilities dog food available

Open Mar-end Oct Last arrival 18.00hrs Last departure 10.00hrs

Well managed, attractive park close to the coast, with excellent facilities including a club and bar, which are well away from pitches. Nestling close to sandy beaches, the park offers individually marked pitches on level terraces in pleasant, sheltered grassland. The many amenities include a heated swimming pool and water chute, coarse fishing and a launderette. 26 acre site. 25 touring pitches. Tent pitches. Motorhome pitches. 82 statics.

Notes Families & couples only.

Cofton Country Holidays (SX967801)

▶ ▶ ▶ ▶
Starcross EX6 8RP
☎ 01626 890111   & 0800 085 8649   📠 01626 890160
e-mail: info@coftonholidays.co.uk
dir: *On A379 (Exeter/Dawlish road) 3m from Dawlish*

PETS: Charges £2.75-£5 per night **Public areas** except bar, shop & pool area **Exercise area on site** field for dog walking **Exercise area** woodland walk (0.25m) **Facilities** food food bowl water bowl dog chews scoop/disp bags leads walks info vet info **Other** prior notice required

Open all year rs Spring BH-mid Sep; Etr-end Oct pool open; bar & shop open Last arrival 20.00hrs Last departure 11.00hrs

This park is set in a rural location surrounded by spacious open grassland, with plenty of well-kept flowerbeds throughout. Most pitches overlook either the swimming pool complex or the fishing lakes and woodlands. An on-site pub serves drinks, meals and snacks for all the family, and a mini-market caters for most shopping needs. 45 acre site. 450 touring pitches. 30 hardstandings. 110 seasonal pitches. Tent pitches. Motorhome pitches. 76 statics.

DREWSTEIGNTON   Map 3 SX79

Woodland Springs Adult Touring Park
(SX695912)

▶ ▶ ▶ ▶
Venton EX6 6PG
☎ 01647 231695
e-mail: enquiries@woodlandsprings.co.uk
dir: *Exit A30 at Whiddon Down Junction, left onto A382 towards Moretonhampstead. Site 1.5m on left*

PETS: Sep accom day kennels **Charges** 2 dogs free, £1 per extra dog per night **Public areas** disp bin **Exercise area on site** 1-acre open area **Facilities** walks info vet info **Other** disposal bags available **Resident Pets:** Charlie & Suzie (West Highland White Terriers)

Open all year Last arrival 20.00hrs Last departure 11.00hrs

An attractive park in a rural area within Dartmoor National Park. This site is surrounded by woodland and neighbouring farmland, and is very peaceful. There is a toilet block with superb facilities for the disabled. Please note that children are not admitted to this park. 4 acre site. 81 touring pitches. 45 hardstandings. 17 seasonal pitches. Tent pitches. Motorhome pitches.

Notes No fires, no noise 23.00hrs-08.00hrs.

EAST ALLINGTON
Map 3 SX74

Mounts Farm Touring Park (SX757488)
▶ ▶ ▶

The Mounts TQ9 7QJ
☎ 01548 521591
e-mail: mounts.farm@lineone.net
dir: A381 from Totnes towards Kingsbridge (NB ignore signs for East Allington). At 'Mounts', site 0.5m on left

PETS: Public areas except play area disp bin Exercise area public footpaths adjacent Facilities food bowl water bowl dog chews cat treats scoop/disp bags washing facs walks info vet info Resident Pets: Smokie & Dot (cats)

Open 15 Mar-Oct Last arrival anytime Last departure anytime

A neat grassy park divided into four paddocks by mature natural hedges. Three of the paddocks house the tourers and campers, and the fourth is the children's play area. The laundry and well-stocked little shop are in converted farm buildings. 7 acre site. 50 touring pitches. 10 seasonal pitches. Tent pitches. Motorhome pitches.

EAST ANSTEY
Map 3 SS82

Zeacombe House Caravan Park (SS860240)
▶ ▶ ▶ ▶

Blackerton Cross EX16 9JU
☎ 01398 341279
e-mail: enquiries@zeacombeadultretreat.co.uk
dir: M5 junct 27, A361 signed Barnstaple, right at next rdbt onto A396 signed Dulverton & Minehead. In 5m at Exeter Inn left, 1.5m, at Black Cat junct left onto B3227 towards South Molton, site 7m on left

PETS: Public areas except toilet block & shop on leads disp bin Exercise area on site Facilities washing facs walks info vet info Other prior notice required disposal bags available Restrictions no Pit Bull Terriers

Open 7 Mar-Oct Last arrival 21.00hrs Last departure noon

Set on the southern fringes of Exmoor National Park, this 'garden' park is nicely landscaped in a tranquil location, and enjoys panoramic views towards Exmoor. This adult-only park offers a choice of grass or hardstanding pitches, and a unique restaurant-style delivery service allows you to eat an evening meal in the comfort of your own unit. 5 acre site. 50 touring pitches. 12 hardstandings. Tent pitches. Motorhome pitches.

EAST WORLINGTON
Map 3 SS71

Yeatheridge Farm Caravan Park (SS768110)
▶ ▶ ▶ ▶

EX17 4TN
☎ 01884 860330
e-mail: yeatheridge@talk21.com
dir: M5 junct 27, A361, at 1st rdbt at Tiverton take B3137 for 9m towards Witheridge. Fork left 1m past Nomansland onto B3042. Site on left in 3.5m. (NB do not enter East Worlington)

PETS: Charges £1 per night Public areas except swimming pool, children's play area & bar disp bin Exercise area on site dog walking area & woods Exercise area woodland Facilities food water bowl dog chews cat treats leads washing facs walks info vet info Other dog shower (warm water) disposal bags available

Open Etr-Sep Last arrival 22.00hrs Last departure 10.00hrs

Gently sloping grass site with mature trees, set in meadowland in rural Devon. There are good views of distant Dartmoor, and the site is of great appeal to families with its farm animals, horse riding, and two indoor swimming pools, one with flume. There are many attractive villages in this area. 9 acre site. 85 touring pitches. Tent pitches. Motorhome pitches. 12 statics.

EGGESFORD
Map 3 SS61

Fox & Hounds Country Hotel
★ ★ ★ 72% ◉ HOTEL

EX18 7JZ
☎ 01769 580345 📠 01271 410200
e-mail: relax@foxandhoundshotel.co.uk
web: www.foxandhoundshotel.co.uk
dir: M5 junct 27, A361 towards Tiverton. Take B3137 signed Witheridge. After Nomans Land follow signs for Eggesford Station. Hotel 50mtrs up hill from station

PETS: Bedrooms (3 GF) unattended Charges £10 per night £20 per week Public areas except restaurant Grounds disp bin Exercise area 50mtrs Facilities food (pre-bookable) food bowl water bowl bedding dog chews feeding mat scoop/disp bags leads pet sitting dog walking washing facs cage storage walks info vet info On Request fridge access torch towels Stables 2m Resident Pet: Charlie (Hungarian Vizsla)

Situated midway between Exeter and Barnstaple, in the beautiful Taw Valley, this extensively developed hotel was originally a coaching inn dating back to the 1800s. Many of the comfortable, elegant bedrooms have lovely countryside views. Good cooking utilises excellent local produce and can be enjoyed in either restaurant or the convivial bar. For fishing enthusiasts, the hotel has direct access to the River Taw, and equipment and tuition can be provided if required.

Rooms 19 (6 fmly) (3 GF) S £62.50-£75; D £125-£145 (incl. bkfst)* Facilities FTV Fishing Health & beauty suite Xmas New Year Wi-fi Parking 100 Notes LB

EXETER — Map 3 SX99

Best Western Lord Haldon Country Hotel

★★★ 74% HOTEL

Dunchideock EX6 7YF
☎ 01392 832483 📠 01392 833765
e-mail: enquiries@lordhaldonhotel.co.uk
web: www.lordhaldonhotel.co.uk
dir: *M5 junct 31, 1st exit off A30, follow signs through Ide to Dunchideock*

PETS: **Bedrooms** certain bedrooms only **Charges** £7.50 per night **Public areas** except restaurant & lounge **Grounds** disp bin **Exercise area** nearby **Facilities** cage storage walks info vet info **On Request** fridge access torch towels **Stables** 3m **Other** charge for damage

Set amidst rural tranquillity, this attractive country house goes from strength to strength. Guests are assured of a warm welcome from the professional team of staff, and the well-equipped bedrooms are comfortable; many have stunning views. The daily-changing menu features skilfully cooked dishes with most of the produce sourced locally.

Rooms 23 (3 fmly) **S** £49-£160; **D** £60-£200 (incl. bkfst)*
Facilities FTV Xmas New Year Wi-fi **Parking** 120 **Notes** LB

Barton Cross Hotel & Restaurant

★★★ 71% HOTEL

Huxham, Stoke Canon EX5 4EJ
☎ 01392 841245 📠 01392 841942
e-mail: bartonxhuxham@aol.com
dir: *0.5m off A396 at Stoke Canon, 3m N of Exeter*

PETS: **Bedrooms** (2 GF) unattended sign ground-floor bedrooms only **Charges Grounds** on leads disp bin **Exercise area** nearby **Facilities** walks info vet info **On Request** fridge access torch towels **Stables** 1m **Other** charge for damage **Resident Pets:** Alfie (German Shepherd), Purdy (Greyhound)

17th-century charm combined with 21st-century luxury perfectly sums up the appeal of this lovely country hotel. The bedrooms are spacious, tastefully decorated and well maintained. Public areas include the cosy first-floor lounge and the lounge/bar with its warming log fire. The restaurant offers a seasonally changing menu of consistently enjoyable cuisine.

Rooms 9 (2 fmly) (2 GF) (2 smoking) **Facilities** STV FTV Xmas New Year Wi-fi **Parking** 35 **Notes** LB

HAYTOR VALE — Map 3 SX77

Rock Inn

★★ 80% HOTEL

TQ13 9XP
☎ 01364 661305 & 661465 📠 01364 661242
e-mail: inn@rock-inn.co.uk
web: www.rock-inn.co.uk
dir: *A38 onto A382 to Bovey Tracey, in 0.5m left onto B3387 to Haytor*

PETS: **Bedrooms** unattended 3 bedrooms only **Charges** £6.50 per night **Grounds** on leads **Exercise area** woods adjacent **Facilities** washing facs cage storage walks info vet info **On Request** torch towels **Other** charge for damage

Dating back to the 1750s, this former coaching inn is in a pretty hamlet on the edge of Dartmoor. Each named after a Grand National winner, the individually decorated bedrooms have some nice extra touches. Bars are full of character, with flagstone floors and old beams, and offer a wide range of dishes, cooked with imagination.

Rooms 9 (2 fmly) **S** £75-£100; **D** £85-£135 (incl. bkfst)*
Facilities FTV New Year Wi-fi **Parking** 20 **Notes** Closed 25-26 Dec

HOLSWORTHY — Map 2 SS30

Headon Farm Caravan Site *(SS367023)*

▶▶▶

Headon Farm, Hollacombe EX22 6NN
☎ 01409 254477 📠 0870 705 9052
e-mail: reader@headonfarm.co.uk
dir: *Exit A388, 0.75m into Staddon Rd, 1m, right follow Ashwater sign. In 0.75m left follow Hollacombe sign. Site on left in 50yds*

PETS: **Sep accom** please phone for details **Public areas** on leads disp bin **Exercise area on site** adjacent fields (on or off lead) **Exercise area** forest (3m) **Facilities** washing facs dog grooming walks info vet info **Stables** 2m **Other** prior notice required kennels available locally; campsite on working farm with cattle so please seek guidance concerning exercising dogs etc **Resident Pets:** Joey (Border Collie), Treasure (Dartmoor pony)

Open all year Last arrival 19.00hrs Last departure noon

Set on a working farm in a quiet rural location. All pitches have extensive views of the Devon countryside, yet the park is only two and a half miles from the market town of Holsworthy, and within easy reach of roads to the coast and beaches of north Cornwall. 2 acre site. 19 touring pitches. 5 hardstandings. Motorhome pitches.

Notes Breathable groundsheets only.

ENGLAND

Tamarstone Farm *(SS286056)*

►►

Bude Rd, Pancrasweek EX22 7JT
☎ 01288 381734
e-mail: camping@tamarstone.co.uk
dir: *A30 to Launceston, then B3254 towards Bude, approx 14m. Right onto A3072 towards Holsworthy, approx 1.5m, site on left*

PETS: Charges £1 per night £6 per week **Public areas** except wildlife area & woods **Exercise area on site** small field with 'dog loo' **Facilities** washing facs vet info **Other** prior notice required **Resident Pets:** Candy & Toffee (cats), chickens

Open Etr-end Oct Last arrival 22.00hrs Last departure noon

Four acres of river-bordered meadow and woodland providing a wildlife haven for those who enjoy peace and seclusion. The wide, sandy beaches of Bude are just five miles away, and coarse fishing is provided free on site for visitors. 1 acre site. 16 touring pitches. Tent pitches. Motorhome pitches. 1 static.

Notes 🐾

Noteworthy Caravan and Campsite *(SS303052)*

►

Noteworthy, Bude Rd EX22 7JB
☎ 01409 253731
e-mail: enquiries@noteworthy-devon.co.uk
dir: *On A3072 between Holsworthy & Bude. 3m from Holsworthy on right*

PETS: Charges 50p per night **Public areas** except children's play area & farmland disp bin **Exercise area on site** dog walk around field **Facilities** food bowl water bowl washing facs dog grooming walks info vet info **Stables Other** prior notice required **Resident Pets:** 1 dog, cats, horses

Open all year

This campsite is owned by a friendly young couple with their own small children. There are good views from the quiet rural location, and simple toilet facilities. 5 acre site. 5 touring pitches. Tent pitches. Motorhome pitches. 1 static.

Notes No open fires. 🐾

Combe House - Devon

★★★ ◉◉ COUNTRY HOUSE HOTEL
Gittisham EX14 3AD
☎ 01404 540400
e-mail: stay@combehousedevon.com
web: www.combehousedevon.com
dir: *Off A30 1m S of Honiton, follow Gittisham Heathpark signs. From M5 exit 29 for Honiton. Exit Pattesons Cross*

PETS: Bedrooms unattended sign **Charges** £9 per night **Public areas** except restaurants **Grounds** on leads disp bin **Exercise area Exercise area** 1m **Facilities** food bowl water bowl bedding dog chews cat treats feeding mat scoop/disp bags leads washing facs dog grooming cage storage walks info vet info **On Request** fridge access torch towels **Stables Other** charge for damage cottage with dog room & walled garden available dog welcome letter & gift, dog map, dog survival box **Resident Pet:** Maverick (cat)

Standing proudly in an elevated position, this Elizabethan mansion enjoys uninterrupted views over acres of its own woodland, meadow and pasture. Bedrooms are a blend of comfort and quality with relaxation being the ultimate objective; the Linen Room suite combines many original features with contemporary style. A range of atmospheric public rooms retain all the charm and history of the old house. Dining is equally impressive - a skilled kitchen brigade maximises the best of local and home-grown produce, augmented by excellent wines.

Rooms 16 (1 annexe) (1 fmly) **S** £169-£379; **D** £199-£399 (incl. bkfst)* **Facilities** Fishing ⮷ Xmas New Year Wi-fi **Parking** 39 **Notes** LB Closed 3-18 Jan

Ridgeway Farm

★★★★ GUEST ACCOMMODATION

Awliscombe EX14 3PY

☎ 01404 841331 📠 01404 841119

e-mail: jessica@ridgewayfarm.co.uk

dir: 3m NW of Honiton. A30 onto A373, through Awliscombe to near end of 40mph area, right opp Godford Farm, farm 500mtrs up narrow lane, sign on entrance

PETS: Bedrooms Charges charge for horses (on request) **Public areas Grounds** disp bin **Exercise area** surrounding fields **Facilities** washing facs cage storage walks info vet info **On Request** fridge access torch **Stables Other** charge for damage **Restrictions** no large dogs (eg Great Danes etc) **Resident Pets:** Chaos (Labrador), Lettuce & Noodle (Border Terriers), 4 horses

This 18th-century farmhouse has a peaceful location on the slopes of Hembury Hill, and is a good base for exploring nearby Honiton and the east Devon coast. Renovations have brought the cosy accommodation to a high standard and the atmosphere is relaxed and homely. The proprietors and their own family pets assure a warm welcome.

Rooms 2 en suite **S** £34-£38; **D** £60-£66 **Facilities** FTV TVL tea/coffee Dinner available Cen ht Wi-fi **Parking** 4 **Notes** LB 🐾

ILFRACOMBE   Map 2 SS54

Darnley

★★ 72% HOTEL

3 Belmont Rd EX34 8DR

☎ 01271 863955

e-mail: darnleyhotel@yahoo.co.uk

web: www.darnleyhotel.co.uk

dir: A361 to Barnstaple & Ilfracombe. Left at Church Hill, 1st left into Belmont Rd. 3rd entrance on left under walled arch

PETS: Bedrooms (2 GF) unattended **Public areas** except restaurant on leads **Grounds** on leads disp bin **Exercise area** 400yds **Facilities** food bowl water bowl dog chews feeding mat leads cage storage walks info vet info **On Request** fridge access torch towels **Resident Pet:** Pepsi (cat)

Standing in award-winning, mature gardens, with a wooded path to the High Street and the beach (about a five minute stroll away), this former Victorian gentleman's residence offers friendly, informal service. The individually furnished and decorated bedrooms vary in size. Dinners feature honest home cooking, with 'old fashioned puddings' always proving popular.

Rooms 10 (2 fmly) (2 GF) **S** £40-£45; **D** £59-£80 (incl. bkfst)* **Facilities** FTV Xmas New Year Wi-fi **Parking** 10 **Notes** No children 3yrs

Strathmore

★★★★ GUEST ACCOMMODATION

57 St Brannock's Rd EX34 8EQ

☎ 01271 862248 📠 01271 862248

e-mail: info@the-strathmore.co.uk

web: www.the-strathmore.co.uk

dir: A361 from Barnstaple to Ilfracombe, Strathmore 1.5m from Mullacot Cross entering Ilfracombe

PETS: Bedrooms Charges £6.50 per night (breakfast included) **Public areas** in bar & lounge only on leads **Grounds Exercise area** 0.25m **Facilities** water bowl dog chews scoop/disp bags leads washing facs cage storage walks info vet info **On Request** fridge access torch towels **Stables** 1m **Other** charge for damage **Restrictions** small & medium size dogs only no Bullmastiffs, Staffordshire Bull Terriers, German Shepherds or Rottweilers **Resident Pet:** Poppy (Sheltie/Spaniel cross)

Situated within walking distance of the town centre and beach, this charming Victorian property offers a very warm welcome. The attractive bedrooms are comfortably furnished, while public areas include a well-stocked bar, an attractive terraced garden, and an elegant breakfast room.

Rooms 8 en suite (3 fmly) **S** £35-£40; **D** £65-£76 **Facilities** FTV tea/coffee Cen ht Licensed Wi-fi **Parking** 7 **Notes** LB

Hele Valley Holiday Park *(SS533472)*

▶ ▶ ▶ ▶

Hele Bay EX34 9RD

☎ 01271 862460 📠 01271 867926

e-mail: holidays@helevalley.co.uk

dir: M5 junct 27 onto A361. Through Barnstaple & Braunton to Ilfracombe. Then A399 towards Combe Martin. Follow brown Hele Valley signs. 400mtrs sharp right, to T-junct. Park on left

PETS: Charges £2.85-£4 per night £20 per week **Public areas** except children's play area disp bin **Exercise area on site** dog walking area **Exercise area** direct access to walks from site **Facilities** food food bowl water bowl dog chews scoop/disp bags washing facs walks info vet info **Other** prior notice required **Resident Pets:** Anna (Rottweiler), Chalky, Maverick & Cody (cats)

Open Etr-Oct Last arrival 18.00hrs Last departure 11.00hrs

A deceptively spacious park set in a picturesque valley with glorious tree-lined hilly views from most pitches. High quality toilet facilities are provided, and the park is close to a lovely beach, with the harbour and other attractions of Ilfracombe just a mile away. 17 acre site. 50 touring pitches. 18 hardstandings. Tent pitches. Motorhome pitches. 80 statics.

Notes Groups by arrangement only.

ILSINGTON — Map 3 SX77

Ilsington Country House

★★★ 86% ◉◉ COUNTRY HOUSE HOTEL

Ilsington Village TQ13 9RR
☎ 01364 661452 🖩 01364 661307
e-mail: hotel@ilsington.co.uk
web: www.ilsington.co.uk
dir: M5 onto A38 to Plymouth. Exit at Bovey Tracey. 3rd exit from rdbt to 'Ilsington', then 1st right. Hotel in 5m by Post Office

PETS: Bedrooms (6 GF) unattended sign dogs not allowed in Superior Rooms or Suites **Charges** £8 per night **Grounds** on leads disp bin **Exercise area** 5 mins' walk **Facilities** food (pre-bookable) food bowl water bowl dog chews cat treats scoop/disp bags leads washing facs cage storage walks info vet info **On Request** fridge access torch towels **Stables** 5m **Other** charge for damage **Restrictions** well behaved dogs only **Resident Pet:** Bilbo (Springer Spaniel/Collie cross)

This friendly, family owned hotel, offers tranquillity and far-reaching views from its elevated position on the southern slopes of Dartmoor. The stylish suites and bedrooms, some on the ground floor, are individually furnished. The restaurant provides a stunning backdrop for the innovative, daily changing menus which feature local fish, meat and game. Additional facilities include an indoor pool and the Blue Tiger Inn, where a pint, a bite to eat and convivial banter can all be enjoyed.

Rooms 25 (4 fmly) (6 GF) **S** £85-£110; **D** £85-£215 (incl. bkfst)* **Facilities** FTV ⓢ supervised 🏊 Gym Steam room Sauna Beauty treatments Xmas New Year Wi-fi **Services** Lift **Parking** 100 **Notes** LB

KENNFORD — Map 3 SX98

Kennford International Caravan Park

(SX912857)

▶▶▶▶

EX6 7YN
☎ 01392 833046 🖩 01392 833046
e-mail: ian@kennfordinternational.com
dir: At end of M5, take A38, site signed at Kennford slip road

PETS: Charges dog £1 per night **Public areas** on leads disp bin **Exercise area on site** small field **Facilities** walks info vet info **Resident Pets:** Jade (Rottweiler), Alfie (British Bulldog), Tigger (cat), guinea pigs

Open all year rs Winter arrival times change **Last arrival** 21.00hrs **Last departure** 11.00hrs

Screened from the A38 by trees and shrubs, this park offers many pitches divided by hedging for privacy. A high quality toilet block complements the park's facilities. A good, centrally-located base for touring the coast and countryside of Devon, and Exeter is easily accessible via a nearby bus stop. 15 acre site. 96 touring pitches. Tent pitches. Motorhome pitches. 53 statics.

KENTISBEARE — Map 3 ST00

Forest Glade Holiday Park (ST101073)

▶▶▶▶

EX15 2DT
☎ 01404 841381 🖩 01404 841593
e-mail: enquiries@forest-glade.co.uk
dir: Tent traffic: from A373 turn left past Keepers Cottage Inn (2.5m E of M5 junct 28). Touring caravans: via Honiton/Dunkeswell road: please phone for access details

PETS: Charges £2 per night **Public areas** except swimming pool, shop, toilets & play areas disp bin **Exercise area** surrounding woodland **Facilities** food dog chews washing facs walks info vet info **Other** prior notice required **Resident Pet:** Poppy (dog)

Open mid Mar-end Oct rs Low season limited shop hours **Last arrival** 21.00hrs **Last departure** noon

A quiet, attractive park in a forest clearing with well-kept gardens and beech hedge screening. One of the main attractions is the immediate proximity of the forest, which offers magnificent hillside walks with surprising views over the valleys. Please telephone for route details. 15 acre site. 80 touring pitches. 40 hardstandings. 28 seasonal pitches. Tent pitches. Motorhome pitches. 57 statics.

Notes Families and couples only.

LEWDOWN — Map 2 SX48

Lewtrenchard Manor

★★★ ◉◉◉ HOTEL

EX20 4PN
☎ 01566 783256 & 783222 🖩 01566 783332
e-mail: info@lewtrenchard.co.uk
web: www.vonessenhotels.co.uk
dir: A30 from Exeter to Plymouth/Tavistock road. At T-junct turn right, then left onto old A30 (Lewdown road). Left in 6m signed Lewtrenchard

PETS: Bedrooms (3 GF) **Charges** £15 per night **Public areas** except restaurant **Grounds** on leads disp bin **Exercise area** adjacent **Facilities** water bowl washing facs cage storage vet info **On Request** fridge access torch towels **Other** charge for damage

This Jacobean mansion was built in the 1600s, with many interesting architectural features, and is surrounded by its own idyllic grounds in a quiet valley close to the northern edge of Dartmoor. Public rooms include a fine gallery, as well as magnificent carvings and oak panelling. Meals can be taken in the dining room where imaginative and carefully prepared dishes are served using the best of Devon produce. Bedrooms are comfortably furnished and spacious.

Rooms 16 (2 fmly) (3 GF) **S** £125-£255; **D** £155-£395 (incl. bkfst)* **Facilities** FTV Fishing 🏊 Clay pigeon shooting Falconry Beauty therapies Xmas New Year Wi-fi **Parking** 50 **Notes** LB

Arundell Arms

★★★ 80% ◉◉ HOTEL

PL16 0AA

☎ 01566 784666 📠 01566 784494

e-mail: reservations@arundellarms.co.uk

dir: *1m off A30, 3m E of Launceston*

PETS: Bedrooms (4 GF) unattended **Charges** £10 per night
Public areas except restaurant **Grounds** disp bin **Exercise area**
0.5m **Facilities** food water bowl walks info vet info
On Request fridge access torch **Stables** 1m **Other** dogs not
allowed on river bank

This former coaching inn, boasting a long history, sits in the
heart of a quiet Devon village. It is internationally famous for
its country pursuits such as winter shooting and angling. The
bedrooms offer individual style and comfort. Public areas are full
of character with a relaxed atmosphere, particularly around the
open log fire during colder evenings. Award-winning cuisine is a
celebration of local produce.

Rooms 21 (3 fmly) (4 GF) **Facilities** STV Fishing Skittle alley
Game shooting (in winter) Fly fishing school New Year Wi-fi
Parking 70 **Notes** LB

Bath Hotel

★★ 71% HOTEL

Sea Front EX35 6EL

☎ 01598 752238 📠 01598 753894

e-mail: info@bathhotellynmouth.co.uk

dir: *M5 junct 25, follow A39 to Lynmouth*

PETS: Bedrooms unattended **Public areas** except restaurant
Exercise area 200yds **Facilities** food (pre-bookable) food bowl
water bowl bedding walks info vet info **On Request** fridge
access torch towels

This well established, friendly hotel, situated near the harbour
offers lovely views from the attractive, sea-facing bedrooms
and is an excellent starting point for scenic walks. There are two
lounges and a sun lounge. The restaurant menu is extensive and
features daily-changing specials that make good use of fresh
produce and local fish.

Rooms 22 (9 fmly) **S** £45-£55; **D** £75-£115 (incl. bkfst)*
Facilities Wi-fi **Parking** 12 **Notes** Closed Dec & Jan RS Nov & Feb

Lynton Cottage

★★★ 75% ◉◉ HOTEL

Northwalk EX35 6ED

☎ 01598 752342 📠 01598 754016

e-mail: enquiries@lynton-cottage.co.uk

dir: *M5 junct 23 to Bridgwater, A39 to Minehead, follow signs to
Lynton. 1st right after church, right again*

PETS: Bedrooms (1 GF) unattended certain bedrooms only
Public areas except restaurant on leads **Grounds** on leads disp
bin **Exercise area** beach 1.5m **Facilities** water bowl walks
info vet info **Other** charge for damage **Resident Pets:** Chloe &
Charlie (cats)

Boasting breathtaking views, this wonderfully relaxing and
friendly hotel stands some 500 feet above the sea and makes a
peaceful hideaway. Bedrooms are individual in style and size,
with the added bonus of the wonderful views; public areas have
charm and character in equal measure. Accomplished cuisine is
on offer with dishes created with care and skill.

Rooms 16 (1 fmly) (1 GF) **Facilities** FTV Wi-fi **Parking** 20
Notes Closed 2 Dec-12 Jan

Channel View Caravan and Camping Park

(SS724482)

▶▶▶▶

Manor Farm EX35 6LD

☎ 01598 753349 📠 01598 752777

e-mail: relax@channel-view.co.uk

dir: *A39 E for 0.5m on left past Barbrook*

PETS: Public areas Exercise area on site exercise field provided
Exercise area 0.25m **Facilities** food food bowl water bowl
washing facs walks info vet info **Other** prior notice required

Open 15 Mar-15 Nov Last arrival 22.00hrs Last departure noon

On the top of the cliffs overlooking the Bristol Channel, a well-
maintained park on the edge of Exmoor, and close to both Lynton
and Lynmouth. Pitches can be selected from a hidden hedged
area, or with panoramic views over the coast. 6 acre site. 76
touring pitches. 15 hardstandings. Tent pitches. Motorhome
pitches. 31 statics.

Notes Groups by prior arrangement only.

LYNTON *continued*

Sunny Lyn Holiday Park *(SS719486)*

►►►

Lynbridge EX35 6NS
☎ 01598 753384 ▤ 01598 753273
e-mail: info@caravandevon.co.uk
dir: *M5 junct 27, A361 to South Molton. Right onto A399 to Blackmoor Gate, right onto A39, left onto B3234 towards Lynmouth. Site 1m on right*

PETS: Charges dog £2.50, other animals negotiable per night **Public areas** except buildings disp bin **Exercise area** National Trust woodland adjacent **Facilities** food food bowl water bowl bedding leads walks info vet info **Stables** approx 2m **Other** prior notice required disposal bags available

Open Mar-Oct Last arrival 20.00hrs Last departure 11.00hrs

Set in a sheltered riverside location in a wooded combe within a mile of the sea, in Exmoor National Park. This family-run park offers good facilities including an excellent café. 4.5 acre site. 9 touring pitches. 5 hardstandings. Tent pitches. Motorhome pitches. 7 statics.

Notes No wood fires

MORTEHOE	Map 2 SS44

Twitchen House Holiday Village
(SS465447)

Station Rd EX34 7ES
☎ 01271 870343 ▤ 01271 870089
e-mail: goodtimes@woolacombe.com
dir: *From Mullacott Cross rdbt take B3343 (Woolacombe road) to Turnpike Cross junct. Take right fork, site 1.5m on left*

PETS: Charges £1.50 per night £10 per week **Public areas** except main clubhouse & pool areas **Exercise area on site** on site & path to beach **Exercise area** coastal trail & beaches **Facilities** washing facs dog grooming walks info vet info **Other** phone for further details of pet facilities

Open Mar-Oct rs mid May & mid Sep outdoor pool closed Last arrival mdnthrs Last departure 10.00hrs

A very attractive park with good leisure facilities. Visitors can use the amenities at all three of Woolacombe Bay holiday parks, and a bus service connects them all with the beach. The touring area features pitches with either sea views or a woodland countryside outlook. 45 acre site. 334 touring pitches. 110 hardstandings. Tent pitches. Motorhome pitches. 278 statics.

Warcombe Farm Caravan & Camping Park
(SS478445)

►►►►

Station Rd EX34 7EJ
☎ 01271 870690 & 07774 428770 ▤ 01271 871070
e-mail: info@warcombefarm.co.uk
dir: *On B3343 towards Woolacombe turn right towards Mortehoe. Site less than 2m on right*

PETS: Charges 50p-£1.65 per night **Public areas** except play area, toilets & shop disp bin **Exercise area on site** 14-acre field provided **Facilities** food food bowl water bowl dog chews cat treats leads walks info vet info **Other** prior notice required disposal bags available

Open 15 Mar-Oct rs Low season no takeaway food Last arrival 21.00hrs Last departure 11.00hrs

Extensive views over the Bristol Channel can be enjoyed from the open areas of this attractive park, while other pitches are sheltered in paddocks with maturing trees. The superb sandy beach with a Blue Flag award at Woolacombe Bay is only a mile and a half away, and there is a fishing lake with direct access from some pitches. 19 acre site. 250 touring pitches. 10 hardstandings. Tent pitches. Motorhome pitches.

Notes No groups unless booked in advance.

Easewell Farm Holiday Park & Golf Club
(SS465455)

►►►

EX34 7EH
☎ 01271 870343 ▤ 01271 870089
e-mail: goodtimes@woolacombe.com
dir: *B3343 to Mortehoe. Turn right at fork, site 2m on right*

PETS: Charges Public areas except main clubhouse & pool areas disp bin **Exercise area on site** adjacent to camping & touring pitches **Other** please contact site for further details of facilities & charges for pets

Open Mar-Oct rs Etr Last arrival 22.00hrs Last departure 10.00hrs

A peaceful cliff-top park with full facility pitches for caravans and motorhomes, and superb views. The park offers a range of activities including indoor bowling and a 9-hole golf course, and all the facilities at the three other nearby holiday centres within this group are open to everyone. 17 acre site. 302 touring pitches. 50 hardstandings. Tent pitches. Motorhome pitches. 1 static.

North Morte Farm Caravan & Camping Park (SS462455)

▶ ▶ ▶

North Morte Rd EX34 7EG
☎ 01271 870381 📠 01271 870115
e-mail: info@northmortefarm.co.uk
dir: From B3343 into Mortehoe, right at post office. Site 500yds on left

PETS: Charges £1.50-£2 per night **Public areas** on leads disp bin **Exercise area on site** dog walking areas **Exercise area** beach 500yds **Facilities** food dog chews scoop/disp bags leads walks info vet info **Other** disposal bags

Open Apr-Oct Last arrival 22.30hrs Last departure noon

Set in spectacular coastal countryside close to National Trust land and 500 yards from Rockham Beach. This attractive park is very well run and maintained by friendly family owners, and the quaint village of Mortehoe with its cafés, shops and pubs, is just a five-minute walk away. 22 acre site. 180 touring pitches. 25 hardstandings. Tent pitches. Motorhome pitches. 73 statics.

Notes No large groups.

NEWTON ABBOT
Map 3 SX87

Bulleigh Park (SX860660)
★★★★ 🏠 FARMHOUSE

Ipplepen TQ12 5UA
☎ 01803 872254 📠 01803 872254 Mrs A Dallyn
e-mail: bulleigh@lineone.net
dir: 3.5m S of Newton Abbot. Off A381 at Parkhill Cross by petrol station for Compton, continue 1m, signed

PETS: Bedrooms certain bedrooms only **Charges** dog £5 per night £30 per week **Public areas** except restaurant & lounge **Grounds** disp bin **Exercise area** woods 0.5m **Facilities** food (pre-bookable) food bowl water bowl dog chews scoop/disp bags leads washing facs cage storage walks info vet info **On Request** fridge access torch towels **Other** charge for damage **Resident Pet:** Nippy (Jack Russell cross)

Bulleigh Park is a working farm, producing award-winning Aberdeen Angus beef. The owners have also won an award for green tourism by reducing the impact of the business on the environment. Expect a friendly welcome at this family home set in glorious countryside, where breakfasts are notable for the wealth of fresh, local and home-made produce, and the porridge is cooked using a secret recipe.

Rooms 2 en suite 1 annexe en suite (1 fmly) **S** £42-£45; **D** £72-£80 **Facilities** FTV TVL tea/coffee Cen ht Wi-fi **Parking** 6 **Notes** LB Closed Dec-1 Feb 60 acres beef/sheep/hens

Dornafield (SX838683)
▶ ▶ ▶ ▶ ▶

Dornafield Farm, Two Mile Oak TQ12 6DD
☎ 01803 812732 📠 01803 812032
e-mail: enquiries@dornafield.com
dir: Take A381 (Newton Abbot-Totnes) for 2m. At Two Mile Oak Inn turn right, then left at x-roads in 0.5m to site on right

PETS: Charges dog £1-£2 per night **Public areas** disp bin **Exercise area on site** 2 exercise areas provided **Facilities** food food bowl water bowl dog chews cat treats washing facs walks info vet info **Other** prior notice required free disposal bags available

Open 16 Mar-3 Jan Last arrival 22.00hrs Last departure 11.00hrs

An immaculately kept park in a tranquil wooded valley between Dartmoor and Torbay, offering either deluxe or fully-serviced pitches. A lovely 15th-century farmhouse sits at the entrance, and the park is divided into three separate areas, served by two superb, ultra-modern toilet blocks. The friendly family owners are always available. Well positioned for visiting nearby Totnes or the resorts of Torbay. 30 acre site. 135 touring pitches. 119 hardstandings. 13 seasonal pitches. Tent pitches. Motorhome pitches.

Ross Park (SX845671)
▶ ▶ ▶ ▶ ▶

Park Hill Farm, Ipplepen TQ12 5TT
☎ 01803 812983 📠 01803 812983
e-mail: enquiries@rossparkcaravanpark.co.uk
dir: Off A381, 3m from Newton Abbot towards Totnes, signed opposite Texaco garage towards 'Woodland'

PETS: Public areas except restaurant disp bin **Exercise area on site** 3 fields & orchard **Facilities** food washing facs walks info vet info **Other** dog shower room **Restrictions** dog breeds must be approved by manager **Resident Pets:** Monty & Zinzan (Labradors)

Open Mar-2 Jan rs Nov-Jan & 1st 3 wks of Mar restaurant/bar closed (ex Xmas/New Year) Last arrival 21.00hrs Last departure 10.00hrs

A top-class park in every way, with large secluded pitches, high quality toilet facilities and lovely floral displays throughout. The beautiful tropical conservatory also offers a breathtaking show of colour. This very rural park enjoys superb views of Dartmoor, and good quality meals to suit all tastes and pockets are served in the restaurant. A park that manages to get better each year. 32 acre site. 110 touring pitches. 94 hardstandings. Tent pitches. Motorhome pitches.

Notes Bikes, skateboards/scooters only allowed on leisure field.

ENGLAND

Twelve Oaks Farm Caravan Park *(SX852737)*

▶▶▶

Teigngrace TQ12 6QT
☎ 01626 335015
e-mail: info@twelveoaksfarm.co.uk
dir: *A38 from Exeter left signed Teigngrace (only), 0.25m before Drumbridges rdbt. 1.5m, through village, site on left. From Plymouth pass Drumbridges rdbt, take slip road for Chudleigh Knighton. Right over bridge, rejoin A38 towards Plymouth. Left for Teigngrace (only), then as above*

PETS: Charges £2 per night £14 per week **Public areas** on leads **Exercise area on site** dog walking area **Exercise area** 500mtrs **Facilities** washing facs walks info vet info **Stables** 2m **Other** prior notice required dogs must be on leads at all times disposal bags available

Open all year Last arrival 21.00hrs Last departure 10.30hrs

An attractive small park on a working farm close to Dartmoor National Park, and bordered by the River Teign. The tidy pitches are located amongst trees and shrubs, and the modern facilities are very well maintained. Children will enjoy all the farm animals, and nearby is the Templar Way walking route. 2 acre site. 50 touring pitches. 25 hardstandings. Tent pitches. Motorhome pitches.

Notes No noise after 23.00hrs.

White Hart Hotel

★★ 72% HOTEL
Fore St EX20 1HD
☎ 01837 52730 & 54514   📠 01837 53979
e-mail: enquiry@thewhitehart-hotel.com
dir: *In town centre, adjacent to lights, car park at rear of hotel*

PETS: Bedrooms Charges £5 per night **Public areas** except restaurant on leads **Exercise area** 200yds **Facilities** cage storage walks info vet info **Other** charge for damage

Dating back to the 17th century and situated on the edge of the Dartmoor National Park, the White Hart offers modern facilities. Bedrooms are well equipped and spacious. Locally sourced, home-cooked food is on offer in the bars and the Courtney Restaurant; or guests can choose to eat in Vines Pizzeria. Wi-fi is available in public areas.

Rooms 19 (2 fmly) **Facilities** FTV Xmas Wi-fi **Parking** 20

Fluxton Farm

★★ BED AND BREAKFAST
Fluxton EX11 1RJ
☎ 01404 812818   📠 01404 814843
web: www.fluxtonfarm.co.uk
dir: *2m SW of Ottery St Mary. B3174, W from Ottery over river, left, next left to Fluxton*

PETS: Bedrooms Public areas except dining room & lounge **Grounds** on leads **Exercise area** opposite **Facilities** food bowl water bowl cat treats feeding mat washing facs cage storage walks info vet info **On Request** fridge access **Other** cat food available on request **Resident Pets:** the farm is a cat rescue sanctuary; ducks, chickens

A haven for cat lovers, Fluxton Farm offers comfortable accommodation with a choice of lounges and a large garden, complete with pond and ducks. Set in peaceful farmland four miles from the coast, this 16th-century longhouse has a wealth of beams and open fireplaces.

Rooms 7 en suite **S** £27.50-£30; **D** £55-£60 **Facilities** FTV TVL tea/coffee Cen ht **Parking** 15 **Notes** LB No Children 8yrs RS Nov-Apr pre-booked & wknds only ⊛

Merritt House B&B

★★★★ ≡ GUEST ACCOMMODATION
7 Queens Rd TQ4 6AT
☎ 01803 528959
e-mail: bookings@merritthouse.co.uk
dir: *From Paignton seafront, turn right onto Torbay Rd, then 1st left onto Queens Rd, house on right*

PETS: Bedrooms (3 GF) ground-floor bedrooms only Charges £3 per night (may vary) Exercise area 1m Facilities food bowl water bowl bedding dog chews feeding mat litter tray washing facs cage storage walks info vet info On Request fridge access torch towels Other charge for damage Restrictions small dogs only Resident Pets: Pippa (Labrador/Springer Spaniel cross), Sooty, Holly & Crumble (cats)

Just a five-minute stroll from the seafront and town centre, this elegant Victorian property is ideally situated to make the most of this traditional resort. The owners take understandable pride of their establishment and will assist in any way possible to ensure a relaxed and rewarding stay. Bedrooms and bathrooms are thoughtfully furnished and generously equipped to ensure a cosseting and comfortable stay. Breakfast is a real treat with plenty of choice, and an emphasis on local and home-made produce.

Rooms 7 en suite (3 GF) S £27-£34; D £54-£72 Facilities FTV tea/coffee Cen ht Wi-fi Parking 4 Notes No Children 14yrs Closed 20 Dec-7 Jan

The Wentworth Guest House

★★★★ GUEST HOUSE
18 Youngs Park Rd, Goodrington TQ4 6BU
☎ 01803 557843
e-mail: enquiries@wentworthguesthouse.co.uk
dir: *Through Paignton on A378, 1m left at rdbt, sharp right onto Roundham Rd, right & right again onto Youngs Park Rd*

PETS: Bedrooms (1 GF) unattended 1 bedroom only (with own front door) Charges £4 per night Exercise area park opposite, beach 250mtrs Facilities food bowl water bowl bedding dog chews feeding mat walks info vet info On Request torch towels Other charge for damage Restrictions well behaved, small & meduim size dogs only Resident Pet: Blue (Staffordshire Bull Terrier cross)

Quietly located opposite a pretty park, this is an ideal location for exploring the many and varied attractions of the English Riviera. Goodrington's lovely beaches are just a short stroll away and the town centre is a 10-15 minute walk away. The caring owners make every effort to ensure guests enjoy a relaxing break, and are always on hand to assist with local information. Bedrooms offer good levels of comfort and include both a dog-friendly room and family rooms. Breakfast is served in the informal dining room with a cosy guest lounge also provided.

Rooms 10 en suite (2 fmly) (1 GF) S £26-£30; D £52-£70 Facilities FTV TVL tea/coffee Cen ht Licensed Wi-fi Parking 5 Notes LB Closed 16 Dec-2 Jan

The Park

★★★ GUEST ACCOMMODATION
Esplanade Rd TQ4 6BQ
☎ 01803 557856 📠 01803 555626
e-mail: stay@parkhotel.me.uk
web: www.theparkhotel.net
dir: *On Paignton seafront, nearly opp pier*

PETS: Bedrooms (3 GF) Charges £2 per night £10 per week Grounds on leads Exercise area seafront 50yds Facilities cage storage walks info On Request fridge access Other charge for damage

This large establishment has a prominent position on the seafront with excellent views of Torbay. The pleasant bedrooms are spacious and available in a number of options, and several have sea views. Entertainment is provided on some evenings in the lounge. Dinner and breakfast are served in the spacious dining room, which overlooks the attractive front garden.

Rooms 47 en suite (5 fmly) (3 GF) Facilities tea/coffee Dinner available Cen ht Lift Licensed Wi-fi Pool table Parking 38

Duke of Cornwall Hotel

★★★ 77% ◉ HOTEL
Millbay Rd PL1 3LG
☎ 01752 275850 & 275855 📠 01752 275854
e-mail: enquiries@thedukeofcornwall.co.uk
web: www.thedukeofcornwall.co.uk
dir: *Follow city centre, then Plymouth Pavilions Conference & Leisure Centre signs. Hotel opposite Plymouth Pavilions*

PETS: Bedrooms unattended sign Exercise area park 50yds Facilities food bowl water bowl bedding cage storage walks info vet info On Request fridge access torch towels

A historic landmark, this city centre hotel is conveniently located. The spacious public areas include a popular bar, comfortable lounge and multi-functional ballroom. Bedrooms, many with far reaching views, are individually styled and comfortably appointed. The range of dining options includes meals in the bar, or the elegant dining room for a more formal atmosphere.

Rooms 71 (6 fmly) (20 smoking) S £65-£110; D £75-£130 (incl. bkfst) Facilities STV FTV Xmas New Year Wi-fi Services Lift Parking 50 Notes LB

ENGLAND

PLYMOUTH *continued*

The Legacy Plymouth International Hotel

★★★ **64%** HOTEL

Marsh Mills PL6 8NH

☎ 08444 119 097 📄 08444 119 098

e-mail: res-plymouthinternational@legacy-hotels.co.uk

web: www.legacy-hotels.co.uk

dir: *Exit A38 at Marsh Mills, follow Plympton signs, hotel on left*

PETS: Bedrooms (18 GF) ground-floor bedrooms only **Charges** £10 per night **Public areas** except restaurant on leads **Grounds** on leads disp bin **Exercise area** 0.25m **Facilities** water bowl cage storage walks info vet info **On Request** torch towels **Other** charge for damage

Conveniently located on the outskirts of the city, close to Marsh Mills roundabout, this modern hotel offers good value accommodation. All bedrooms are spacious and designed with flexibility for family use. Public areas are open-plan with meals available throughout the day in either the Garden Brasserie, the bar, or from room service.

Rooms 100 (17 fmly) (18 GF) **Facilities** STV FTV ✇ Xmas New Year **Services** Lift **Parking** 140 **Notes** LB

The Cranbourne

★★★ GUEST ACCOMMODATION

278-282 Citadel Rd, The Hoe PL1 2PZ

☎ 01752 263858 & 224646 & 661400 📄 01752 263858

e-mail: info@cranbournehotel.co.uk

web: www.cranbournehotel.co.uk

dir: *Behind the Promenade, Plymouth Hoe*

PETS: Bedrooms (2 GF) **Public areas** except dining room on leads **Exercise area** 60yds **Facilities** scoop/disp bags leads walks info vet info **On Request** fridge access towels **Other** pets accepted by prior arrangement only

This attractive Georgian terrace house is located just a short walk from The Hoe, The Barbican and the city centre. Bedrooms are practically furnished and well equipped. Hearty breakfasts are served in the elegant dining room and there is also a cosy bar.

Rooms 40 rms (28 en suite) (5 fmly) (2 GF) **S** £27-£40; **D** £48-£60 **Facilities** FTV TVL tea/coffee Cen ht Licensed Wi-fi **Parking** 14

The Firs Guest Accommodation

★★★ GUEST ACCOMMODATION

13 Pier St, West Hoe PL1 3BS

☎ 01752 262870 & 300010

e-mail: thefirsguesthouse@hotmail.co.uk

PETS: Bedrooms Public areas except dining room on leads **Exercise area** 100yds **Facilities** walks info vet info **On Request** fridge access torch **Restrictions** well behaved dogs only; must have up-to-date vaccinations **Resident Pets:** Rosie, Jessica, Tabitha & Fluffy (cats)

A well-located-and-well established house on the West Hoe with convenient on-street parking. Friendly owners and comfortable rooms make it a popular destination.

Rooms 7 rms (2 en suite) (2 fmly) **S** £25-£35; **D** £45-£65 **Facilities** FTV tea/coffee Dinner available Cen ht Wi-fi **Notes** LB

The Lamplighter

★★★ GUEST ACCOMMODATION

103 Citadel Rd, The Hoe PL1 2RN

☎ 01752 663855 & 07793 360815

e-mail: stay@lamplighterplymouth.co.uk

web: www.lamplighterplymouth.co.uk

dir: *Near war memorial*

PETS: Bedrooms Charges min £5 per night **Public areas** except dining room on leads **Exercise area** 50mtrs **Facilities** cage storage walks info vet info **Other** charge for damage

With easy access to The Hoe, The Barbican and the city centre, this comfortable house provides a good base for leisure or business. Bedrooms, including family rooms, are light and airy and furnished to a consistent standard. Breakfast is served in the dining room, which has an adjoining lounge area.

Rooms 9 rms (7 en suite) (2 pri facs) (2 fmly) **S** £30-£40; **D** £50-£60 **Facilities** FTV TVL tea/coffee Cen ht Wi-fi **Parking** 4

PRINCETOWN Map 2 SX57

The Plume of Feathers Inn (SX592734)

►►

PL20 6QQ

☎ 01822 890240

dir: *Site accessed directly from B3212 rdbt (beside Plume of Feathers Inn) in centre of Princetown*

PETS: Public areas except carvery & B&B disp bin **Exercise area on site** paddock & field **Exercise area** Dartmoor National Park adjacent **Facilities** food food bowl water bowl dog chews walks info vet info **Other** prior notice required paddock available for horses, prior booking essential pet menu available at the bar **Resident Pets:** Bonnie (West Highland Terrier), Dribbles (cat)

Open all year Last arrival 23.30hrs Last departure 11.00hrs

Set amidst the rugged beauty of Dartmoor not far from the notorious prison, this campsite boasts good toilet facilities and all the amenities of the inn. The Plume of Feathers is Princetown's oldest building, and serves all day food in an atmospheric setting - try the 'camp and breakfast' deal that's on offer. The campsite is mainly for tents. 3 acre site. 85 touring pitches. Tent pitches. Motorhome pitches.

Notes No caravans

SALCOMBE Map 3 SX73

Tides Reach

★★★ 82% ⊛ HOTEL

South Sands TQ8 8LJ

☎ 01548 843466   ▤ 01548 843954

e-mail: enquire@tidesreach.com

web: www.tidesreach.com

dir: *Off A38 at Buckfastleigh to Totnes. Then A381 to Salcombe, follow signs to South Sands*

PETS: Bedrooms unattended certain bedrooms only **Charges** £9 per night **Public areas** except bar, restaurant & 2 lounges on leads **Grounds** on leads disp bin **Exercise area** adjacent **Facilities** food (pre-bookable) bedding cage storage walks info vet info **On Request** torch towels **Other** charge for damage dogs accepted by prior arrangement only; please phone for further details of pet facilities

Superbly situated at the water's edge, this personally run, friendly hotel has splendid views of the estuary and beach. Bedrooms,

many with balconies, are spacious and comfortable. In the bar and lounge, attentive service can be enjoyed along with the view, and the Garden Room restaurant serves appetising and accomplished cuisine.

Rooms 32 (5 fmly) **S** £85-£144; **D** £140-£332 (incl. bkfst & dinner)* **Facilities** Spa STV FTV ✆ supervised Gym Squash Windsurfing Sailing Kayaking Scuba diving Hair & beauty treatment Wi-fi **Services** Lift **Parking** 100 **Notes** LB No children 8yrs Closed Dec-early Feb

Bolberry House Farm Caravan & Camping Park (SX687395)

►►►

Bolberry TQ7 3DY

☎ 01548 561251

e-mail: enquiries@bolberryparks.co.uk

dir: *At Malborough on A381 turn right signed Hope Cove/Bolberry. Take left fork after village signed Soar/Bolberry. 0.6m right again. Site signed in 0.5m*

PETS: Charges high season & Whitsun weekend £1 per night **Public areas** except toilet block on leads disp bin **Exercise area on site** separate dog walk **Other** well behaved dogs only disposal bags available

Open Etr-Oct Last arrival 20.00hrs Last departure 11.30hrs

A very popular park in a peaceful setting on a coastal farm with sea views, fine cliff walks and nearby beaches. There's a discount in low season for senior citizens. Customers are assured of a warm welcome. 6 acre site. 70 touring pitches. Tent pitches. Motorhome pitches. 10 statics.

Notes ⊛

Karrageen Caravan & Camping Park
(SX686395)

►►►

Bolberry, Malborough TQ7 3EN

☎ 01548 561230   ▤ 01548 560192

e-mail: phil@karrageen.co.uk

dir: *At Malborough on A381, turn sharp right through village, after 0.6m right again, after 0.9m site on right*

PETS: Charges £1 per night **Public areas** except toilets **Exercise area on site** available in high season **Facilities** food vet info

Open Etr-Sep Last arrival 21.00hrs Last departure 11.30hrs

A small friendly, family-run park with terraced grass pitches giving extensive sea and country views. There is a varied takeaway menu available every evening, and a well-stocked shop. This park is just one mile from the beach and pretty hamlet of Hope Cove. 7.5 acre site. 70 touring pitches. Tent pitches. Motorhome pitches. 25 statics.

Notes ⊛

SAMPFORD PEVERELL — Map 3 ST01

Minnows Touring Park *(SS042148)*

▶ ▶ ▶ ▶

Holbrook Ln EX16 7EN
☎ 01884 821770   📄 01884 829199
dir: *M5 junct 27 take A361 signed Tiverton & Barnstaple. In 600yds take 1st slip road, then right over bridge, site ahead*

PETS: Charges 2 dogs free, £1 per extra dog per night **Public areas** except in buildings **Exercise area** canal towpath (with disposal bins) adjacent **Facilities** washing facs walks info vet info **Other** prior notice required water at reception, dog tethers by buildings

Open 5 Mar-28 Oct Last arrival 20.00hrs Last departure 11.30hrs

A small, well-sheltered park, peacefully located amidst fields and mature trees. The toilet facilities are of a high quality in keeping with the rest of the park, and there is a good laundry. The park has direct gated access to the canal towpath. All pitches have hardstandings. 5.5 acre site. 59 touring pitches. 59 hardstandings. Tent pitches. Motorhome pitches. 1 static.

Notes No cycling, no groundsheets on grass.

SHALDON — Map 3 SX97

Coast View Holiday Park *(SX935716)*

Torquay Rd TQ14 0BG
📄 01626 872719
e-mail: info@coastview.co.uk
dir: *M5 junct 31, A38 then A380 towards Torquay. Then A381 towards Teignmouth. Right in 4m at lights, over Shaldon Bridge. 0.75m, up hill, site on right*

PETS: Charges £2.50 per night **Public areas** except swimming pool, shop & restaurant disp bin **Exercise area on site** specific dog walking area **Facilities** walks info vet info **Other** prior notice required

Open 15 Mar-1 Nov Last arrival 21.00hrs Last departure 10.30hrs

This park has stunning sea views from its spacious pitches. The family-run park has a full entertainment programme every night for all the family, plus outdoor and indoor activities for children; this site will certainly appeal to lively families. 17 acre site. 110 touring pitches. 6 hardstandings. Tent pitches. Motorhome pitches. 86 statics.

SIDMOUTH — Map 3 SY18

Royal Glen

★★★ 75% HOTEL

Glen Rd EX10 8RW
☎ 01395 513221 & 513456   📄 01395 514922
e-mail: info@royalglenhotel.co.uk
dir: *A303 to Honiton, A375 to Sidford, follow seafront signs, right onto esplanade, right at end into Glen Rd*

PETS: Bedrooms (3 GF) unattended certain bedrooms only **Charges** £5 per night **Grounds** on leads **Facilities** walks info

This historic 17th-century, Grade I listed hotel has been owned by the same family for several generations. The comfortable bedrooms are furnished in period style. Guests may use the well-maintained gardens and a heated indoor pool, and can enjoy well-prepared food in the elegant dining room.

Rooms 32 (3 fmly) (3 GF) **S** £48-£72; **D** £96-£144 (incl. bkfst)* **Facilities** FTV ⓢ Gym Wi-fi **Services** Lift **Parking** 22 **Notes** LB Closed Dec-1 Feb

Kingswood & Devoran Hotel

★★★ 73% HOTEL

The Esplanade EX10 8AX
☎ 01395 516367 & 08000 481731   📄 01395 513185
e-mail: kingswoodanddevoran@hotels-sidmouth.co.uk
web: www.hotels-sidmouth.co.uk
dir: *M5 junct 30, A3052 signed Sidmouth on right, follow Station Rd down to Esplanade*

PETS: Bedrooms (2 GF) unattended **Charges** £7 per night

This seafront hotel continues to offer friendly hospitality and service. Many bedrooms enjoy the sea views; all are well appointed and have smart bathrooms. Cuisine is pleasant and offers enjoyable dining featuring freshly prepared dishes.

Rooms 50 (8 fmly) (2 GF) **S** £85-£101; **D** £118-£168 (incl. bkfst & dinner)* **Facilities** FTV Xmas Wi-fi **Services** Lift **Parking** 23 **Notes** LB Closed 27 Dec-10 Feb

Royal York & Faulkner

★★ **80%** HOTEL

The Esplanade EX10 8AZ

☎ 01395 513043 & 0800 220714 📠 01395 577472

e-mail: stay@royalyorkhotel.co.uk

web: www.royalyorkhotel.co.uk

dir: *M5 junct 30 take A3052, 10m to Sidmouth, hotel in centre of Esplanade*

PETS: Bedrooms (5 GF) unattended **Charges** £5 per night **Exercise area** 250mtrs **Facilities** food (pre-bookable) food bowl water bowl walks info vet info **On Request** fridge access torch towels **Other** charge for damage

This seafront hotel, owned and run by the same family for over 60 years, maintains its Regency charm and grandeur. The attractive bedrooms vary in size, and many have balconies and sea views. Public rooms are spacious and traditional dining is offered, alongside Blinis Café-Bar, which is more contemporary in style and offers morning coffee, lunch and afternoon tea. The spa facilities include a hydrotherapy pool, steam room, sauna and a variety of treatments.

Rooms 70 (2 annexe) (8 fmly) (5 GF) **S** £57.50-£90.50; **D** £115-£181 (incl. bkfst & dinner)* **Facilities** Spa FTV 🏊 Steam cabin Snooker table Sauna 🎵 Xmas New Year Wi-fi **Services** Lift **Parking** 20 **Notes** LB Closed Jan

The Woodlands Hotel

★★ **74%** HOTEL

Cotmaton Cross EX10 8HG

☎ 01395 513120 📠 01395 513348

e-mail: info@woodlands-hotel.com

web: www.woodlands-hotel.com

dir: *Follow signs for Sidmouth*

PETS: Bedrooms unattended sign 1 bedroom only **Exercise area** 200yds **Facilities** cage storage walks info vet info **Other** prior notice required **Restrictions** no breed larger than a Labrador

Located in the heart of the town and ideally situated for exploring Devon and Dorset, this listed property has numerous character features. There is a spacious bar and a lounge where guests may relax. Freshly prepared dinners can be enjoyed in the smart dining room. Families with children are made very welcome and may dine early.

Rooms 20 (4 fmly) (8 GF) **S** £43-£73; **D** £74-£126 (incl. bkfst)* **Facilities** Wi-fi **Parking** 20 **Notes** LB Closed 20 Dec-15 Jan

The Salty Monk

★★★★★ ◎◎ 🍴 RESTAURANT WITH ROOMS

Church St, Sidford EX10 9QP

☎ 01395 513174

e-mail: saltymonk@btconnect.com

web: www.saltymonk.co.uk

dir: *On A3052 opposite church*

PETS: Bedrooms 2 ground-floor bedrooms only **Charges** £20 per stay **Public areas** on leads **Grounds** on leads disp bin **Exercise area** adjacent **Facilities** food (pre-bookable) food bowl water bowl bedding dog chews scoop/disp bags leads cage storage walks info vet info **On Request** fridge access torch towels **Other** charge for damage **Resident Pets:** Finn (Irish Water Spaniel) & Isca (Italian Spinone)

Set in the village of Sidford, this attractive property dates from the 16th century. There's oodles of style and appeal here and each bedroom has a unique identity. Bathrooms are equally special with multi-jet showers, spa baths and cosseting robes and towels. The output from the kitchen is impressive with excellent local produce very much in evidence, served in the elegant surroundings of the restaurant. A mini spa facility is available.

Rooms 5 en suite 1 annexe en suite (3 GF) **S** £70-£150 **Facilities** FTV tea/coffee Dinner available Cen ht Wi-fi Golf 18 Sauna **Parking** 20 **Notes** LB Closed 2wks Nov & 3wks Jan No coaches

Bramley Lodge Guest House

★★★ GUEST HOUSE

Vicarage Rd EX10 8UQ

☎ 01395 515710

e-mail: bramleyowner@btinternet.com

dir: *0.5m N of seafront on A375*

PETS: Bedrooms **Charges** £1 per night **Public areas** except dining room **Grounds** disp bin **Exercise area** Byes Park (30mtrs), beach Oct-Apr (600mtrs) **Facilities** water bowl walks info vet info **On Request** fridge access torch towels **Other** charge for damage prior notice required **Restrictions** small & medium size dogs only; only one dog accepted at a time

Guests are assured of a warm and friendly welcome at this family-run, small guest house, located about a half mile from the sea. The neatly furnished bedrooms vary in size, and all are equipped to a good standard. Home-cooked evening meals are available, by prior arrangement, with special diets on request.

Rooms 6 rms (5 en suite) (1 fmly) **S** £32-£36; **D** £64-£72 **Facilities** FTV tea/coffee Dinner available Cen ht **Parking** 6 **Notes** Closed mid Nov-mid Feb RS 1st wk Aug week-long bookings only 🐾

SIDMOUTH *continued*

Oakdown Country Holiday Park *(SY167902)*

►►►►►

Gatedown Ln, Weston EX10 0PT
☎ 01297 680387 📄 01297 680541
e-mail: enquiries@oakdown.co.uk
dir: *Off A3052, 2.5m E of junct with A375*

PETS: Charges dog £2.30 per night **Public areas** except
amenities & children's play area disp bin **Exercise area on site**
field trails **Exercise area** adjacent **Facilities** walks info vet
info **Other** prior notice essential in high season disposal bags
available

Open Apr-Oct Last arrival 22.00hrs Last departure 10.30hrs

A quality, friendly, well-maintained park with good landscaping
and plenty of maturing trees that makes it well screened from the
A3502. Pitches are grouped in paddocks surrounded by shrubs,
with a new 50-pitch development replete with an upmarket
toilet block. The park's conservation areas, with their natural
flora and fauna, offer attractive walks, and there is a hide by the
Victorian reed bed for both casual and dedicated bird watchers. A
delightful park in every respect. 16 acre site. 150 touring pitches.
90 hardstandings. Tent pitches. Motorhome pitches. 62 statics.

Notes No bikes/skateboards or kite flying

Salcombe Regis Caravan & Camping Park
(SY153892)

►►►

Salcombe Regis EX10 0JH
☎ 01395 514303 📄 01395 514314
e-mail: contact@salcombe-regis.co.uk
dir: *Off A3052 1m E of junct with A375. From opposite direction
turn left past Donkey Sanctuary*

PETS: Charges £1.50 per night £10.50 per week **Public areas**
except shower & toilet block disp bin **Exercise area on site** dog
exercise area (off lead) with clear-up facilities **Facilities** walks
info vet info **Other** prior notice required disposal bags available

Open Etr-end Oct Last arrival 20.15hrs Last departure 10.30hrs

Set in quiet countryside with glorious views, this spacious park
has well-maintained facilities, and a good mix of grass and
hardstanding pitches. There is a self-catering holiday cottage
and static caravans for hire. A footpath runs from the park to the
coastal path and the beach. 16 acre site. 100 touring pitches. 40
hardstandings. Tent pitches. Motorhome pitches. 10 statics.

Collaven Manor

★★ **79%** COUNTRY HOUSE HOTEL

EX20 4HH
☎ 01837 861522 📄 01837 861614
e-mail: collavenmanor@supanet.com
dir: *A30 onto A386 to Tavistock, hotel 2m on right*

PETS: Bedrooms unattended **Charges** £5 per night
Public areas except restaurant on leads **Grounds** disp bin
Exercise area accessed directly from grounds **Facilities** food
bowl water bowl cat treats washing facs cage storage walks
info vet info **On Request** fridge access torch towels **Stables**
5m **Other** food available by prior arrangement **Restrictions** no
Dobermans, Rottweilers or Pit Bull Terriers **Resident Pets:** Willow,
Jas & Jack (cats)

This delightful 15th-century manor house is quietly located in
five acres of well-tended grounds. The friendly proprietors provide
attentive service and ensure a relaxing environment. Charming
public rooms have old oak beams and granite fireplaces, and
provide a range of comfortable lounges and a well stocked bar. In
the restaurant, a daily-changing menu offers interesting dishes.

Rooms 9 (1 fmly) **S** £59-£65; **D** £98-£146 (incl. bkfst)*
Facilities FTV 🏌 Bowls Wi-fi **Parking** 50 **Notes** LB Closed
Dec-Jan

Bundu Camping & Caravan Park *(SX546916)*

►►►

EX20 4HT
☎ 01837 861611
e-mail: frances@bundu.plus.com
dir: *W on A30, past Okehampton. Take A386 to Tavistock. Take 1st
left & left again*

PETS: Charges Public areas disp bin **Exercise area** adjacent
Facilities food washing facs walks info vet info **Resident Pet:**
Sophie (German Shepherd)

Open all year Last arrival 23.30hrs Last departure 14.00hrs

Welcoming, friendly owners set the tone for this well-maintained
site, ideally positioned on the border of the Dartmoor National
Park. Along with fine views and level grassy pitches, the Granite
Way cycle track from Lydford to Okehampton along the old railway
line (part of the Devon Coast to Coast cycle trail) passes the edge
of the park. 4.5 acre site. 38 touring pitches. 11 hardstandings.
Tent pitches. Motorhome pitches.

SOUTH BRENT — Map 3 SX66

Glazebrook House Hotel

★★ 78% ⚫ HOTEL

TQ10 9JE

☎ 01364 73322 🖹 01364 72350

e-mail: enquiries@glazebrookhouse.com

web: www.glazebrookhouse.com

dir: *Exit A38 at South Brent, follow brown signs to hotel*

PETS: Bedrooms unattended **Charges** £5 per night
Public areas except restaurant **Grounds** disp bin **Exercise area**
0.5m **Facilities** leads dog walking washing facs cage storage
walks info vet info **On Request** fridge access torch towels
Stables 2m **Other** charge for damage **Restrictions** only well
behaved dogs accepted **Resident Pets:** Bobsy (Pointer/Collie
cross), hens

Enjoying a tranquil and convenient location next to the Dartmoor
National Park and set within four acres of gardens, this 18th-
century former gentleman's residence offers a friendly welcome
and comfortable accommodation. Elegant public areas provide
ample space to relax and enjoy the atmosphere, whilst bedrooms
are well appointed and include a number with four-poster
beds. The dishes on the menus are created from interesting
combinations of fresh, locally-sourced produce.

Rooms 10 **S** £50-£55; **D** £80-£137.50 (incl. bkfst)* **Facilities** FTV
Reflexology Holistic therapies Xmas New Year Wi-fi **Parking** 40
Notes LB Closed 2-18 Jan RS 1 wk Aug

SOUTH MOLTON — Map 3 SS72

Riverside Caravan & Camping Park

(SS723274)

▶▶▶▶

Marsh Ln, North Molton Rd EX36 3HQ

☎ 01769 579269 🖹 01769 574853

e-mail: relax@exmoorriverside.co.uk

dir: *M5 junct 27 onto A361 towards Barnstaple. Site signed 1m
before South Molton on right*

PETS: Public areas assist dogs only disp bin **Exercise area**
on site wooded field **Facilities** food food bowl water bowl dog
chews cat treats leads washing facs walks info vet info
Stables 1m **Other** prior notice required disposal bags available

Open all year Last arrival 22.00hrs Last departure 11.00hrs

A newly-developed family-run park, set alongside the River Mole,
where supervised children can play, and fishing is available. This
is an ideal base for exploring Exmoor, as well as north Devon's
golden beaches. The site has an award for the excellence of the
toilets. 40 acre site. 42 touring pitches. 42 hardstandings. Tent
pitches. Motorhome pitches.

STOKE GABRIEL — Map 3 SX85

Broadleigh Farm Park *(SX851587)*

▶▶▶

Coombe House Ln, Aish TQ9 6PU

☎ 01803 782422

e-mail: enquiries@broadleighfarm.co.uk

dir: *From Exeter on A38 then A380 towards Torbay. Right onto
A385 for Totnes. In 0.5m right at Whitehill Country Park. Site
approx 0.75m on left*

PETS: Public areas except facility block (ex assist dogs) disp bin
Exercise area field adjacent **Facilities** walks info vet info **Other**
prior notice required dogs must be on leads at all times **Resident
Pets:** 2 Border Collies (working dogs), 2 cats

Open Mar-Oct Last arrival 21.00hrs Last departure 11.30hrs

Set in a very rural location on a working farm bordering Paignton
and Stoke Gabriel. The large sloping field with a timber-clad
toilet block in the centre is sheltered and peaceful, surrounded
by rolling countryside but handy for the beaches. There is also an
excellent rally field with good toilets and showers. 7 acre site. 80
touring pitches. Tent pitches. Motorhome pitches.

Notes

STOKE GABRIEL *continued*

Higher Well Farm Holiday Park *(SX857577)*

► ► ►

Waddeton Rd TQ9 6RN
☎ 01803 782289
e-mail: higherwell@talk21.com
dir: *From Exeter A380 to Torbay, turn right onto A385 for Totnes, in 0.5m left for Stoke Gabriel, follow signs*

PETS: Public areas disp bin **Exercise area on site** fenced area **Facilities** food vet info **Other** dog tether pegs available

Open 31 Mar-4 Nov Last arrival 22.00hrs Last departure 10.00hrs

Set on a quiet farm yet only four miles from Paignton, this rural holiday park is on the outskirts of the picturesque village of Stoke Gabriel. A toilet block, with some en suite facilities, is an excellent amenity, and tourers are housed in an open field with some very good views. 10 acre site. 80 touring pitches. 3 hardstandings. Tent pitches. Motorhome pitches. 19 statics.

Notes No commercial vehicles.

STOKENHAM   Map 3 SX84

Old Cotmore Farm *(SX804417)*

► ► ►

TQ7 2LR
☎ 01548 580240
e-mail: info@holiday-in-devon.com
dir: *From Kingsbridge take A379 towards Dartmouth, through Frogmore & Chillington to mini rdbt at Stokenham. Right towards Beesands, site 1m on right*

PETS: Charges max £2 per night **Public areas** disp bin **Exercise area on site** mown field for dogs **Facilities** food food bowl water bowl scoop/disp bags washing facs walks info vet info **Stables** nearby **Resident Pet:** Megan (Springer/Labrador cross)

Open 15 Mar-Oct Last arrival 20.00hrs Last departure 11.00hrs

A small and peaceful, family run touring caravan and camp site well located in the South Hams region of Devon, close to Slapton and within easy reach of Salcombe and Dartmouth. Facilities are very clean and well maintained and there is a basic shop and small play area. Pebble and sandy beaches with cliff walks through woods and fields are within walking distance. Self-catering cottages are available. 22 acre site. 30 touring pitches. 25 hardstandings. Tent pitches. Motorhome pitches.

STOWFORD   Map 2 SX48

Townleigh Farm *(SX425876)*

★ ★ ★ ★ FARMHOUSE

EX20 4DE
☎ 01566 783186 Mr Stubbs
e-mail: mail@townleigh.com
dir: *M5 junct 31, A30 southbound Roadford, left, left again, follow lane for approx 2m*

PETS: Charges contact owner for details **Stables Other** charge for damage

This 19th-century farmhouse, in 350 acres of picturesque countryside, has something to offer just about everyone. The Victorian architecture, complemented by all the expected modern luxuries, creates an understated grandeur. Bedrooms have much charm, comfort and character together with lovely views, and public areas are equally special with a sumptuous drawing room and elegant dining room. The estate also has a number of self-catering cottages, fishing lakes, an equestrian centre and, in season, pheasant shoots.

Rooms 3 rms (2 en suite) (1 pri facs) **S** £60; **D** £80 **Facilities** TVL tea/coffee Dinner available Cen ht Wi-fi 🏊 Fishing **Parking** 8 **Notes** 250 acres country sports/horses

---

STRETE   Map 3 SX84

Strete Barton House

★ ★ ★ ★ ★ GUEST HOUSE

Totnes Rd TQ6 0RU
☎ 01803 770364 🖷 01803 771182
e-mail: info@stretebarton.co.uk
web: www.stretebarton.co.uk
dir: *Off A379 coastal road into village, just below church*

PETS: Bedrooms cottage suite only **Charges** £7 per night £49 per week **Grounds** disp bin **Exercise area** dog chews cage storage walks info vet info **On Request** fridge access torch towels **Other** charge for damage

This delightful 16th-century farmhouse has been refurbished to blend stylish accommodation with its original character. Bedrooms are very comfortably furnished and well equipped with useful extras. Breakfast utilises quality local produce and is served in the spacious dining room. Guests are also welcome to use the very comfortable lounge, complete with log burning stove for the cooler months. The village lies between Dartmouth and Kingsbridge and has easy access to the natural beauty of the South Hams as well as local pubs and restaurants.

Rooms 5 rms (4 en suite) (1 pri facs) 1 annexe en suite; **D** £100-£150 **Facilities** FTV tea/coffee Cen ht Wi-fi **Parking** 4 **Notes** LB No Children 8yrs

TAVISTOCK
Map 2 SX47

Horn of Plenty

★★★ 85% HOTEL

Gulworthy PL19 8JD
☎ 01822 832528 🖹 01822 834390
e-mail: enquiries@thehornofplenty.co.uk
web: www.thehornofplenty.co.uk
dir: From Tavistock take A390 W for 3m. Right at Gulworthy Cross. In 400yds turn left, hotel in 400yds on right

PETS: Bedrooms unattended garden bedrooms only **Charges** £10 per night **Grounds** disp bin **Exercise area** 0.25m **Facilities** walks info vet info **On Request** torch towels **Other** charge for damage

With stunning views over the Tamar Valley, The Horn of Plenty maintains a good reputation as an excellent country-house hotel. Bedrooms are well equipped and have many thoughtful extras, with garden rooms offering impressive levels of both quality and comfort. Award-winning cuisine is prepared with skill and there is a passion to use the best ingredients the area has to offer.

Rooms 10 (6 annexe) (3 fmly) (4 GF) **S** £85-£215; **D** £95-£225 (incl. bkfst)* **Facilities** FTV Xmas New Year Wi-fi **Parking** 25 **Notes** LB

Sampford Manor

★★★ BED AND BREAKFAST

Sampford Spiney PL20 6LH
☎ 01822 853442
e-mail: manor@sampford-spiney.fsnet.co.uk
web: www.sampford-spiney.fsnet.co.uk
dir: B3357 towards Princetown, right at 1st x-rds. Next x-rds Warren Cross left for Sampford Spiney. 2nd right, house below church

PETS: Bedrooms Sep accom stable **Charges** £3 per night **Public areas** except dining room on leads **Grounds** disp bin **Exercise area** 200yds **Facilities** food bowl water bowl feeding mat leads washing facs cage storage walks info vet info **On Request** fridge access torch towels **Stables Other** charge for damage **Resident Pets:** Spin (Springer/Terrier cross), Cleo (Springer/Collie cross), Monty (cat), 31 alpacas, 2 horses

Once owned by Sir Francis Drake, this manor house is tucked away in a tranquil corner of Dartmoor National Park. The family home is full of character, with exposed beams and slate floors, while outside, a herd of award-winning alpacas graze in the fields. Genuine hospitality is assured together with scrumptious breakfasts featuring home-produced eggs. Children, horses and pets are all equally welcome.

Rooms 3 rms (2 pri facs) (1 fmly) **S** £27-£35; **D** £50-£70 **Facilities** FTV tea/coffee Cen ht **Parking** 3 **Notes** Closed Xmas

Langstone Manor Camping & Caravan Park
(SX524738)

▶▶▶▶

Moortown PL19 9JZ
☎ 01822 613371 🖹 01822 613371
e-mail: jane@langstone-manor.co.uk
dir: Take B3357 from Tavistock to Princetown. Approx 1.5m turn right at x-rds, follow signs. Over bridge, cattle grid, up hill, left at sign, left again. Follow lane to park

PETS: Public areas disp bin **Exercise area** moor adjacent **Facilities** leads washing facs walks info vet info **Other** prior notice required disposal bags available **Resident Pets:** Izzy (Collie), Murphy (Springer Spaniel), Mercury (Russian Blue cat)

Open 15 Mar-Oct Last arrival 22.00hrs Last departure 11.00hrs

A secluded site set in the well-maintained grounds of a manor house in Dartmoor National Park. Many attractive mature trees provide a screen within the park, and there is a popular lounge bar with an excellent menu of reasonably priced evening meals. Plenty of activities and places of interest can be found within the surrounding moorland. 6.5 acre site. 40 touring pitches. 10 hardstandings. 5 seasonal pitches. Tent pitches. Motorhome pitches. 25 statics. 3 wooden pods.

Notes No skateboards, scooters, cycles, ball games.

Woodovis Park *(SX431745)*

▶▶▶▶

Gulworthy PL19 8NY
☎ 01822 832968 🖹 01822 832948
e-mail: info@woodovis.com
dir: A390 from Tavistock signed Callington & Gunnislake. At hill top right at rdbt signed Lamerton & Chipshop. Site 1m on left

PETS: Public areas except buildings & swimming pool disp bin **Exercise area on site** dog walks & woods **Exercise area** 1.5m **Facilities** washing facs walks info vet info **Other** prior notice required ground tether for dog leads by tents & disposal bags available **Resident Pets:** Maddie & Molly (Springer Spaniels), Zimba (cat)

Open 23 Mar-2 Nov Last arrival 20.00hrs Last departure 11.00hrs

A well-kept park in a remote woodland setting on the edge of the Tamar Valley. This peacefully-located park is set at the end of a private, half-mile, tree-lined road, and has lots of on-site facilities. The toilets are excellent, and there is an indoor swimming pool, all in a friendly, purposeful atmosphere. 14.5 acre site. 50 touring pitches. 20 hardstandings. 8 seasonal pitches. Tent pitches. Motorhome pitches. 35 statics. 1 wooden pod.

ENGLAND

Harford Bridge Holiday Park *(SX504767)*

▶▶▶

Peter Tavy PL19 9LS
☎ 01822 810349 & 07773 251457 📠 01822 810028
e-mail: stay@harfordbridge.co.uk
dir: *2m N of Tavistock, off A386 Okehampton Rd, take Peter Tavy turn, entrance 200yds on right*

PETS: Charges dog £1.70 per night **Public areas** on leads disp bin **Exercise area on site** field opposite **Facilities** walks info vet info **Other** prior notice required max 3 dogs per pitch

Open all year rs Nov-Mar statics only & 5 hardstandings Last arrival 21.00hrs Last departure noon

This beautiful spacious park is set beside the River Tavy in the Dartmoor National Park. Pitches are located beside the river and around the copses, and the park is very well equipped for the holidaymaker. An adventure playground and games room entertain children, and there is fly-fishing and a free tennis court. 16 acre site. 120 touring pitches. 5 hardstandings. Tent pitches. Motorhome pitches. 80 statics.

Notes No large groups.

Cliffden Hotel

★★★ 74% HOTEL

Dawlish Rd TQ14 8TE
☎ 01626 770052 📠 01626 770594
e-mail: cliffden.hotel@actionforblindpeople.org.uk
dir: *M5 junct 31, A380, B3192 to Teignmouth. Down hill on Exeter Rd to lights, left to rdbt (station on left). Left, follow Dawlish signs. Up hill. Hotel next right*

PETS: Bedrooms (10 GF) unattended sign **Sep accom**
Charges £3 per night £21 per week **Grounds** on leads disp bin
Facilities food (pre-bookable) food bowl water bowl bedding washing facs dog grooming walks info vet info **On Request** fridge access towels **Other** charge for damage guide dog specialists **Restrictions** no dangerous dogs (see page 7)

Whilst this hotel mainly caters for visually impaired guests, their families, friends and guide dogs, it offers a warm welcome to all. This establishment is a listed Victorian building set in six acres of delightful gardens overlooking a small valley. Bedrooms are comfortable, very spacious and thoughtfully equipped. There's also leisure facilities and, of course, special provision for guide dogs.

Rooms 47 (5 fmly) (10 GF) **Facilities** FTV 🕲 supervised 🎵 Xmas New Year Wi-fi **Services** Lift **Parking** 25

Thurlestone Hotel

★★★★ 83% ⚛ HOTEL

TQ7 3NN
☎ 01548 560382 📠 01548 561069
e-mail: enquiries@thurlestone.co.uk
web: www.thurlestone.co.uk
dir: *A38, A384 into Totnes, A381 towards Kingsbridge, A379 towards Churchstow, onto B3197. Into lane signed to Thurlestone*

PETS: Bedrooms unattended sign except family & premier bedrooms **Charges** £6 per night **Public areas** front foyer only
Grounds on leads **Exercise area** nearby **Facilities** food bowl water bowl pet sitting dog walking washing facs cage storage walks info vet info **On Request** fridge access torch towels
Stables 5m **Other** charge for damage

This perennially popular hotel has been in the same family-ownership since 1896 and continues to go from strength to strength. A vast range of facilities is available for all the family including indoor and outdoor pools, a golf course and a beauty salon. Bedrooms are equipped to ensure a comfortable stay with many having wonderful views of the south Devon coast. The range of eating options includes the elegant and stylish restaurant with its stunning views.

Rooms 66 (23 fmly) **S** £75-£205; **D** £150-£410 (incl. bkfst)*
Facilities STV 🕲 ⚓ supervised ⚓ 9 ⛳ Putt green ⚑ Gym Squash Badminton courts Games room Toddler room Snooker room 🎵 Xmas New Year Wi-fi Child facilities **Services** Lift **Parking** 121 **Notes** LB Closed 1-2 wks Jan

Barceló Torquay Imperial Hotel

★★★★ **80%** HOTEL

Park Hill Rd TQ1 2DG

☎ 01803 294301 📠 01803 298293

e-mail: imperialtorquay@barcelo-hotels.co.uk

web: www.barcelo-hotels.co.uk

dir: *A380 towards seafront. Turn left to harbour, right at clocktower. Hotel 300yds on right*

PETS: Bedrooms unattended certain bedrooms only **Charges** £15 per night **Public areas** muzzled and on leads **Grounds** on leads disp bin **Exercise area** 100yds **Facilities** food bowl water bowl dog chews scoop/disp bags cage storage walks info vet info **On Request** fridge access torch towels **Other** charge for damage **Restrictions** small & medium size dogs only

This hotel has an enviable location with extensive views of the coastline. Traditional in style, the public areas are elegant and offer a choice of dining options including the Regatta Restaurant, with its stunning views over the bay. Bedrooms are spacious, most with private balconies, and the hotel has an extensive range of indoor and outdoor leisure facilities.

Rooms 152 (14 fmly) **Facilities** Spa STV 🕙 ₹ supervised 🏊 Gym Squash Beauty salon Hairdresser Steam room 🎵 Xmas New Year Wi-fi **Services** Lift **Parking** 140

Corbyn Head Hotel & Orchid Restaurant

★★★ **77%** ◉◉◉ HOTEL

Torbay Rd, Sea Front TQ2 6RH

☎ 01803 213611 📠 01803 296152

e-mail: info@corbynhead.com

web: www.corbynhead.com

dir: *Follow signs to Torquay seafront, turn right on seafront. Hotel on right with green canopies*

PETS: Bedrooms (9 GF) **Charges** £7 per night £49 per week **Exercise area** 400mtrs **Facilities** vet info **Other** charge for damage

This hotel occupies a prime position overlooking Torbay, and offers well-equipped bedrooms, many with sea views and some with balconies. The staff are friendly and attentive, and a well-stocked bar and comfortable lounge are available. Guests can enjoy fine dining in the award-winning Orchid Restaurant or more traditional dishes in the Harbour View Restaurant.

Rooms 45 (4 fmly) (9 GF) **Facilities** FTV ₹ Gym Squash 🎵 Xmas New Year Wi-fi **Parking** 50

Best Western Livermead Cliff

★★★ **72%** HOTEL

Torbay Rd TQ2 6RQ

☎ 01803 299666 📠 01803 294496

e-mail: enquiries@livermeadcliff.co.uk

web: www.livermeadcliff.co.uk

dir: *A379, A3022 to Torquay, towards seafront, turn right towards Paignton. Hotel 600yds on seaward side*

PETS: Bedrooms unattended sign **Charges** £8 per night **Public areas** except restaurant & lounge on leads **Grounds** on leads **Exercise area** 1-min walk **Facilities** food (pre-bookable) water bowl dog walking washing facs cage storage vet info **On Request** fridge access torch towels **Other** charge for damage pet food available if pre-booked; disposal bags available, dog walking can be arranged **Restrictions** small dogs preferred (larger dogs accepted at manager's discretion)

Situated at the water's edge, this long-established hotel offers friendly service and traditional hospitality. The splendid views can be enjoyed from the lounge, bar and dining room. Alternatively, guests can take advantage of refreshment on the wonderful terrace and enjoy one of the best outlooks in the bay. Bedrooms, many with sea views and some with balconies, are comfortable and well equipped; a range of room sizes is available.

Rooms 65 (21 fmly) **S** £30-£97; **D** £60-£250 (incl. bkfst) **Facilities** FTV Fishing Use of facilities at sister hotel Xmas New Year Wi-fi **Services** Lift **Parking** 80 **Notes** LB

TORQUAY *continued*

Red House Hotel

★★ 72% HOTEL

Rousdown Rd, Chelston TQ2 6PB

☎ 01803 607811 📄 0871 5289455

e-mail: stay@redhouse-hotel.co.uk

web: www.redhouse-hotel.co.uk

dir: *Follow signs for seafront & Chelston, turn into Avenue Rd, right at 1st lights. Pass shops & church, next left. Hotel on right*

PETS: Bedrooms unattended **Charges** £3 per night **Public areas** except restaurant on leads **Grounds** on leads **Exercise area** 300yds **Facilities** vet info **Other** charge for damage **Restrictions** small & medium size dogs only

Set just a few minutes' drive from the town and seafront, this hotel is in an ideal location for exploring the Torbay area. The hotel offers comfortably appointed bedrooms, and facilities include indoor and outdoor swimming pools, plus a gym, sauna, steam room and a treatment room.

Rooms 9 (3 fmly) **Facilities** 🎱 🏊 Gym Sun shower Beauty room Sauna Xmas New Year Wi-fi **Parking** 9 **Notes** LB

Shelley Court

★★ 68% HOTEL

29 Croft Rd TQ2 5UD

☎ 01803 295642 📄 01803 215793

e-mail: shelleycourthotel@hotmail.com

dir: *From B3199 up Shedden Hill Rd, 1st left into Croft Rd*

PETS: Bedrooms (6 GF) unattended sign **Charges** £10 per night **Public areas** except dining room **Grounds** disp bin **Exercise area** adjacent **Facilities** scoop/disp bags leads washing facs cage storage walks info vet info **On Request** fridge access torch towels **Other** charge for damage **Resident Pets:** Jack (Parson Jack Russell), Vera (Jack Russell)

This hotel, popular with groups, is located in a pleasant, quiet area that overlooks the town towards Torbay. With a friendly team of staff, many guests return here time and again. Entertainment is provided most evenings in the season. Bedrooms come in a range of sizes and there is a large and comfortable lounge bar.

Rooms 27 (3 fmly) (6 GF) **Facilities** FTV 🏊 Pool table Indoor skittle alley 🎵 Xmas New Year **Parking** 20 **Notes** LB Closed 4 Jan-10 Feb

The Cary Arms

★★★★★ INN

Babbacombe Beach TQ1 3LX

☎ 01803 327110 📄 01803 323221

e-mail: enquiries@caryarms.co.uk

web: www.caryarms.co.uk

dir: *A380 at Ashcombe Cross onto B3192 to Teignmouth. Right at lights to Torquay on A379, left at lights to Babbacombe. Left into Babbacombe Downs Rd, left into Beach Rd*

PETS: Bedrooms 2 ground-floor bedrooms only **Charges** £10 per night **Public areas** on leads **Grounds** on leads disp bin **Exercise area** dog friendly beach & coastal path (100mtrs) **Facilities** food bowl water bowl bedding dog chews scoop/disp bags pet sitting dog walking washing facs dog grooming walks info vet info **On Request** fridge access torch towels **Other** charge for damage

Located on the water's edge at Babbacombe, this seaside retreat has been refurbished to the highest of standards; the rooms have sea views and nearly all have terraces or balconies. A dedicated team of hosts who will assist in planning your day, or simply impart local knowledge. Bedrooms and bathrooms are fitted to a high standard with many thoughtful extras and unique touches to make a stay memorable. This is a popular dining venue whether eating inside, or on the terraces that lead down to the water's edge; in summer there's a BBQ and wood-fired oven.

Rooms 8 en suite (1 fmly) (3 GF) **S** £105-£210; **D** £155-£260 **Facilities** FTV tea/coffee Dinner available Cen ht Wi-fi Golf 18 Pool table **Parking** 15 **Notes** LB No coaches

Blue Conifer

★★★★ GUEST ACCOMMODATION

Higher Downs Rd, The Seafront, Babbacombe TQ1 3LD

☎ 01803 327637

dir: *Signs for Babbacombe & seafront, premises 500yds from model village, opp cliff railway*

PETS: Bedrooms (1 GF) unattended **Charges** £2 per night **Grounds Exercise area** 100yds **Facilities** walks info vet info **Other** charge for damage

Surrounded by neat gardens with splendid views across beaches to the bay, this attractive property provides a relaxed and friendly atmosphere. Bedrooms, many with sea views, are well equipped and one is on the ground floor. A relaxing lounge and spacious car park are welcome additions.

Rooms 7 en suite (3 fmly) (1 GF) **S** £37-£43; **D** £58-£74 **Facilities** FTV tea/coffee Cen ht **Parking** 9 **Notes** LB Closed Nov-Feb

The Downs, Babbacombe

★★★★ GUEST ACCOMMODATION

41-43 Babbacombe Downs Rd, Babbacombe TQ1 3LN

☎ 01803 328543

e-mail: manager@downshotel.co.uk

PETS: Bedrooms unattended seaview & rear bedrooms only **Charges** £5 per night **Public areas** except restaurant on leads **Exercise area** adjacent **Facilities** water bowl bedding feeding mat cage storage walks info vet info **On Request** fridge access torch towels **Other** charge for damage dogs can accompany guests if breakfast or dinner is served in lounge/bar (prior notice required)

Originally built in the 1850s, this elegant building forms part of a seafront terrace with direct access to the promenade and Babbacombe Downs. The warmth of welcome is matched by attentive service, with every effort made to ensure a rewarding and relaxing stay. Bedrooms offer impressive levels of comfort and most have spectacular views across Lyme Bay with balconies being an added bonus. For guests with limited mobility, assisted access is available to the first floor. Additional facilities include the convivial lounge/bar and spacious restaurant where enjoyable dinners and breakfasts are offered.

Rooms 12 en suite (4 fmly) **S** £50-£64; **D** £65-£79 **Facilities** FTV TVL tea/coffee Dinner available Direct Dial Cen ht Licensed Wi-fi **Parking** 8 **Notes** LB

Robin Hill

★★★★ GUEST ACCOMMODATION

74 Braddons Hill Road East TQ1 1HF

☎ 01803 214518 📠 01803 291410

e-mail: stay@robinhillhotel.co.uk

dir: *From A38 to seafront then left to Babbacombe. Pass theatre to Clock Tower rdbt, take 1st exit & through 2 sets of lights, Braddons Hill Road East on left*

PETS: Bedrooms one 1st-floor bedroom only **Public areas** lounge only on leads **Grounds** on leads disp bin **Exercise area** 50yds **Facilities** walks info vet info **On Request** towels **Other** charge for damage **Restrictions** small dogs only; no Rottweilers, Dobermans, Staffordshire Bull Terriers, Huskies or Alsatians

Dating back to 1896, this fascinating building has character in abundance and is located a short stroll from the harbour and shops. Every effort is made to ensure a stay is enjoyable; assistance is readily available at all times. Bedrooms, in varying styles, provide all the expected necessities; a number have now been impressively refurbished. Public areas include the inviting lounge and light and airy dining room where breakfast can be enjoyed.

Rooms 10 en suite (2 fmly) (1 GF) **S** £35-£40; **D** £65-£78 **Facilities** FTV TVL tea/coffee Cen ht Licensed Wi-fi Golf 18 **Parking** 10 **Notes** LB Closed Nov-Mar

Torcroft

★★★★ GUEST ACCOMMODATION

28-30 Croft Rd TQ2 5UE

☎ 01803 298292 📠 01803 291799

e-mail: info@torcrofthotel.co.uk

dir: *A390 onto A3022 to Avenue Rd, follow seafront signs, turn left. Cross lights, up Shedden Hill,1st left onto Croft Rd*

PETS: Bedrooms unattended sign larger bedrooms only **Public areas** except restaurant on leads **Grounds Exercise area** Torre Meadow (8 mins) **Facilities** water bowl pet sitting dog walking cage storage vet info **On Request** fridge access **Restrictions** small, well-behaved dogs only no Pit Bull Terriers or similar breeds

Located a short stroll away from the seafront, within a quiet residential area, this elegant establishment is well situated for exploring this area. Bedrooms have good levels of comfort and some have the added bonus of balconies with sea views. Public areas include a spacious dining room and stylish bar/lounge where drinks can be enjoyed. A lovely, secluded garden is available with ample space to sit and enjoy some summer sunshine.

Rooms 15 en suite (1 fmly) **S** £40-£45; **D** £71-£81 **Facilities** FTV TVL tea/coffee Cen ht Licensed Wi-fi Golf 18 **Parking** 10 **Notes** LB Closed Jan-Feb

TORQUAY *continued*

Widdicombe Farm Touring Park *(SX876643)*

▶▶▶▶

Marldon TQ3 1ST
☎ 01803 558325 🖷 01803 559526
e-mail: info@widdicombefarm.co.uk
dir: *On A380, midway between Torquay & Paignton ring road*

PETS: Charges £1.50 per night £10.50 per week Public areas
except buildings on leads disp bin Exercise area on site small
field Facilities food food bowl water bowl dog chews cat
treats scoop/disp bags walks info vet info Other prior notice
required dogs must be on short leads at all times Restrictions
no Alsatians, Dobermans, Rottweilers, Bull Terriers or Ridgebacks
Resident Pets: 2 Border Collies, 3 Jack Russells

Open mid Mar-end Oct Last arrival 20.00hrs Last departure
11.00hrs

A friendly family-run park on a working farm with good quality
facilities and extensive views. The level pitches are terraced to
take advantage of the views towards the coast and Dartmoor.
This is the only adult touring park within Torquay, and is also
handy for Paignton and Brixham. Wi-fi is available and there's
a bus service from the park to the local shopping centre and
Torquay's harbour. There is a small shop, a restaurant and
a lounge bar with entertainment from Easter to the end of
September. 8 acre site. 180 touring pitches. 180 hardstandings.
20 seasonal pitches. Tent pitches. Motorhome pitches. 3 statics.

TWO BRIDGES   Map 2 SX67

Two Bridges Hotel

★★★ 78% ◉ HOTEL

PL20 6SW
☎ 01822 890581 🖷 01822 892306
e-mail: enquiries@twobridges.co.uk
web: www.twobridges.co.uk
dir: *At junct of B3212 & B3357*

PETS: Bedrooms (6 GF) unattended Public areas except
restaurant on leads Grounds on leads disp bin Exercise area
Dartmoor Facilities water bowl washing facs cage storage
walks info vet info On Request fridge access torch towels
Resident Pet: Mousehound (cat)

This wonderfully relaxing hotel is set in the heart of the Dartmoor
National Park, in a beautiful riverside location. Three standards
of comfortable rooms provide every modern convenience, and
include four-poster rooms. There is a choice of lounges and fine
dining is available in the restaurant, where menus feature local
game and other seasonal produce.

Rooms 33 (2 fmly) (6 GF) Facilities STV Fishing Xmas New Year
Parking 100 Notes LB

WOOLACOMBE   Map 2 SS44

Woolacombe Bay Holiday Village
(SS465442)

Sandy Ln EX34 7AH
☎ 01271 870343 🖷 01271 870089
e-mail: goodtimes@woolacombe.com
dir: *From Mullacott Cross rdbt take B3343 (Woolacombe road)
to Turnpike Cross junct. Right towards Mortehoe, site approx 1m
on left*

PETS: Charges £1.50 per night £10 per week Public areas
except main clubhouse & pool areas disp bin Exercise area on
site field Exercise area 0.5m to Tarka Trail, beach & coastal
path Facilities food food bowl water bowl bedding dog chews
cat treats litter tray scoop/disp bags leads washing facs
walks info vet info Other max 3 dogs per pitch free pet pack,
toys, Woof Guide available Restrictions no dangerous dogs (see
page 7)

Open Mar-Oct rs Mar-mid May, mid Sep-Oct no touring, camping
only available Last arrival mdnt Last departure 10.00hrs

A well-developed touring section in a holiday complex with a full
entertainment and leisure programme. This park offers excellent
facilities including a steam room and sauna. For a small charge
a bus takes holidaymakers to the other Woolacombe Bay holiday
centres where they can take part in any of the activities offered,
and there is also a bus to the beach. 8.5 acre site. 180 touring
pitches. Tent pitches. Motorhome pitches. 237 statics.

Woolacombe Sands Holiday Park
(SS471434)

Beach Rd EX34 7AF
☎ 01271 870569 🖷 01271 870606
e-mail: lifesabeach@woolacombe-sands.co.uk
dir: *M5 junct 27, A361 to Barnstaple. Follow Ilfracombe signs to
Mullacott Cross. Left onto B3343 to Woolacombe. Site on left*

PETS: Charges £5 per night £35 per week Public areas except
shop & pools disp bin Exercise area on site dog trail & dog
exercise area Exercise area footpath to beach Facilities food
food bowl water bowl dog chews scoop/disp bags leads walks
info vet info Stables Woolacombe riding stables Other prior
notice required lead tether pegs & toys available

Open Apr-Oct Last arrival 22.00hrs Last departure 10.00hrs

Set in rolling countryside with grassy terraced pitches, most with
spectacular views overlooking the sea at Woolacombe. The lovely
Blue Flag beach can be accessed directly by footpath in 10-15
minutes, and there is a full entertainment programme for all
the family in high season. 20 acre site. 200 touring pitches. 75
hardstandings. 40 seasonal pitches. Tent pitches. Motorhome
pitches. 80 statics.

Europa Park *(SS475435)*

▶▶▶

Beach Rd EX34 7AN
☎ 01271 871425 📠 01271 871425
e-mail: europaparkwoolacombe@yahoo.co.uk
dir: *M5 junct 27, A361 through Barnstaple to Mullacott Cross. Left onto B3343 signed Woolacombe. Site on right at Spa shop/ garage*

PETS: Charges £3 per night **Public areas Exercise area**
Woolacombe Beach (1m) **Facilities** food food bowl water bowl dog chews leads vet info **Other** disposal bags & dog toys available

Open all year Last arrival 23.00hrs Last departure 10.00hrs

A very lively family-run site handy for the beach at Woolacombe, and catering well for surfers but maybe not suitable for a quieter type of stay (please make sure the site is suitable for you before making your booking). Set in a stunning location high above the bay, it provides a wide range of accommodation including surf cabins, and generous touring pitches. Visitors can enjoy the indoor pool and sauna, games room, restaurant/café/bar and clubhouse. 16 acre site. 200 touring pitches. 20 hardstandings. Tent pitches. Motorhome pitches. 22 statics.

YELVERTON   Map 2 SX56

Moorland Garden Hotel

★★★ 77% HOTEL
PL20 6DA
☎ 01822 852245 📠 01822 855004
e-mail: moorland.links@forestdale.com
web: www.moorlandlinkshotel.co.uk
dir: *A38 from Exeter to Plymouth, then A386 towards Tavistock. 5m onto open moorland, hotel 1m on left*

PETS: Bedrooms (17 GF) sign certain bedrooms only **Charges** £7.50 per night **Public areas** except restaurant on leads **Grounds** on leads disp bin **Exercise area** open moorland **Facilities** food (pre-bookable) water bowl walks info vet info **On Request** torch towels **Other** charge for damage **Restrictions** small dogs only

Set in nine acres in the Dartmoor National Park, this hotel offers spectacular views from many of the rooms across open moorland and the Tamar Valley. Bedrooms are well equipped and comfortably furnished, and some rooms have open balconies. The stylish restaurant looks out over the oak fringed lawns.

Rooms 44 (4 fmly) (17 GF) **Facilities** FTV Xmas New Year Wi-fi **Parking** 120 **Notes** LB

ALDERHOLT   Map 4 SU11

Hill Cottage Farm Camping and Caravan Park *(SU119133)*

▶▶▶▶▶

Sandleheath Rd SP6 3EG
☎ 01425 650513 & 07714 648690 📠 01425 652339
e-mail: hillcottagefarmcaravansite@supanet.com
dir: *Take B3078 W of Fordingbridge. Exit at Alderholt, site 0.25m on left after railway bridge*

PETS: Charges £1 per night **Public areas** except children's play area & farm fields disp bin **Exercise area on site** dog walks **Exercise area** adjacent woodlands **Facilities** washing facs dog grooming walks info vet info **Stables** nearby

Open Mar-Nov Last arrival 19.00hrs Last departure 11.00hrs

Set within extensive grounds this rural, beautifully landscaped park offers all fully-serviced pitches set in individual hardstanding bays with mature hedges between giving adequate pitch privacy. The modern toilet block is kept immaculately clean, and there's a good range of leisure facilities. In high season there is an area available for tenting plus a rally field. 40 acre site. 35 touring pitches. 35 hardstandings. Tent pitches. Motorhome pitches.

Notes No noise after 22.30hrs.

BEAMINSTER   Map 3 ST40

BridgeHouse

★★★ 81% ◉◉ HOTEL
3 Prout Bridge DT8 3AY
☎ 01308 862200 📠 01308 863700
e-mail: enquiries@bridge-house.co.uk
web: www.bridge-house.co.uk
dir: *Off A3066, 100yds from town square*

PETS: Bedrooms (4 GF) coach house bedrooms only **Charges** £15 per night **Public areas** except dining areas, bar, lounge (at food service times) **Grounds Exercise area** 500yds **Facilities** food bowl water bowl pet sitting washing facs cage storage walks info **On Request** fridge access torch towels **Other** charge for damage

Dating back to the 13th century, this property offers friendly and attentive service. The stylish bedrooms feature finest Italian cotton linens, flat-screen TVs and Wi-fi. There are five types of room to choose from including four-poster and coach house rooms. Smartly presented public areas include the Georgian dining room, cosy bar and adjacent lounge, and a breakfast room together with the Beaminster Brasserie with its alfresco eating area under a canopy overlooking the attractive walled garden.

Rooms 13 (4 annexe) (2 fmly) (4 GF) **S** £86-£120; **D** £126-£215 (incl. bkfst)* **Facilities** FTV Xmas New Year Wi-fi Child facilities **Parking** 20 **Notes** LB

BLANDFORD FORUM — Map 3 ST80

The Anvil Inn
★★★★ INN

Salisbury Rd, Pimperne DT11 8UQ
☎ 01258 453431 📠 01258 480182
e-mail: theanvil.inn@btconnect.com
dir: *2m NE of Blandford on A354 in Pimperne*

PETS: Bedrooms Charges £10 per night (varies) **Public areas** only in bar on leads **Grounds** on leads **Exercise area** 2 mins' walk **Facilities** water bowl dog chews walks info vet info **On Request** fridge access torch **Other** charge for damage

Located in a village near Blandford, this 16th-century thatched inn provides a traditional country welcome. Bedrooms have been appointed to high standards. Dinner is a varied selection of home-made dishes, plus there is a tempting variety of hand-pulled ales and wines by the glass.

Rooms 12 en suite **Facilities** STV tea/coffee Dinner available Direct Dial Cen ht **Parking** 18 **Notes** LB No coaches

The Inside Park *(ST869046)*
▶ ▶ ▶ ▶

Down House Estate DT11 9AD
☎ 01258 453719 📠 01258 459921
e-mail: inspark@aol.com
dir: *From town, over River Stour, follow Winterborne Stickland signs. Site in 1.5m*

PETS: Sep accom day kennels **Charges** 60p–£1 per night **Public areas** except allocated dog-free areas disp bin **Exercise area on site** private woods & farm walks (6m) **Facilities** food food bowl water bowl walks info vet info **Other** prior notice required

Open Etr-Oct Last arrival 22.00hrs Last departure noon

An attractive, well-sheltered and quiet park, half a mile off a country lane in a wooded valley. Spacious pitches are divided by mature trees and shrubs, and amenities are housed in an 18th-century coach house and stables. There are some lovely woodland walks within the park and an excellent fenced play area for children. 12 acre site. 125 touring pitches. Tent pitches. Motorhome pitches.

BOURNEMOUTH — Map 4 SZ09

Hallmark Bournemouth
★★★★ 71% HOTEL

Durley Chine Rd, West Cliff BH2 5JS
☎ 01202 751000 📠 01202 757585
e-mail: bournemouth.sales@hallmarkhotels.co.uk
dir: *A338 follow signs to West Cliff & BIC, hotel on right*

PETS: Bedrooms Charges £25 per night **Exercise area** 10 mins **Facilities** walks info vet info **On Request** fridge access torch **Stables** 8m **Other** charge for damage **Restrictions** small & medium size dogs only

This refurbished property is conveniently located and offers a friendly atmosphere and attentive service. The comfortable bedrooms are tastefully appointed and are suitable for both business and leisure guests. The restaurant and bar serve a good choice of dishes, and the well-appointed leisure area is popular with both residents and locals alike. There is also a good range of conference facilities and meeting rooms.

Rooms 78 (12 annexe) **Facilities** Spa FTV ⏱ Gym Sauna Steam room Aromatherapy Ice zone Xmas New Year Wi-fi **Services** Lift **Parking** 80

Cumberland
★★★ 85% HOTEL

East Overcliff Dr BH1 3AF
☎ 01202 290722 & 298350 📠 01202 311394
e-mail: info@cumberlandbournemouth.co.uk
dir: *A35 towards East Cliff & beaches, right onto Holdenhurst Rd, straight over 2 rdbts, left at junct to East Overcliff Drive, hotel on seafront*

PETS: Bedrooms Charges £10 per night £70 per week **Exercise area** gardens 10 mins' walk **Facilities** walks info vet info **Other** charge for damage **Restrictions** small dogs only

A purpose built, art deco hotel where many of the bedrooms are appointed in keeping with the hotel's original character. Front-facing bedrooms have balconies with superb sea views. The comfortable public areas are spacious and striking in their design. The Mirabelle Restaurant and the Red Door Brasserie offer cuisine prepared from local produce.

Rooms 102 (20 fmly) **S** £25-£85; **D** £50-£170 (incl. bkfst)* **Facilities** FTV ⏱ Gym Squash Sauna Xmas New Year Wi-fi **Services** Lift **Parking** 50 **Notes** LB

Langtry Manor - Lovenest of a King

★★★ 82% ⊛ HOTEL

Derby Rd, East Cliff BH1 3QB

☎ 0844 3725 432   📠 01202 290115

e-mail: lillie@langtrymanor.com

web: www.langtrymanor.co.uk

dir: *A31/A338, 1st rdbt by rail station turn left. Over next rdbt, 1st left into Knyveton Rd. Hotel opposite*

PETS: Bedrooms (3 GF) **Public areas** except restaurant & main lounge **Grounds** disp bin **Exercise area** beach & gardens (5 mins) **Facilities** washing facs dog grooming cage storage walks info vet info **On Request** fridge access torch towels **Other** charge for damage **Resident Pet:** Tyson (Boxer)

Retaining a stately air, this property was originally built in 1877 by Edward VII for his mistress Lillie Langtry. The individually furnished and decorated bedrooms include several with four-poster beds. Enjoyable cuisine is served in the magnificent dining hall, that displays several large Tudor tapestries. There is an Edwardian banquet on Saturday evenings.

Rooms 20 (8 annexe) (2 fmly) (3 GF) **Facilities** FTV Free use of health club (200yds) ♫ Xmas New Year Wi-fi **Parking** 30 **Notes** LB

The Riviera

★★★ 79% HOTEL

Burnaby Rd, Alum Chine BH4 8JF

☎ 01202 763653   📠 01202 768422

e-mail: info@rivierabournemouth.co.uk

web: www.rivierabournemouth.co.uk

dir: *A338, follow signs to Alum Chine*

PETS: Bedrooms (11 GF) ground-floor bedrooms only **Charges** £7.50 per night £52.50 per week **Public areas** except restaurant & main bar on leads **Exercise area** 5 mins' walk **Facilities** vet info **Other** charge for damage **Restrictions** small dogs only

The Riviera offers a range of comfortable, well-furnished bedrooms and bathrooms. Welcoming staff provide efficient service delivered in a friendly manner. In addition to a spacious lounge with regular entertainment, there is an indoor and an outdoor pool, and all just a short walk from the beach.

Rooms 73 (4 annexe) (25 fmly) (11 GF) **S** £37-£78; **D** £74-£156 (incl. bkfst)* **Facilities** FTV ⊗ ⚲ Games room Sauna Spa bath Treatments available ♫ Xmas New Year Wi-fi **Services** Lift **Parking** 45 **Notes** LB

Carrington House

★★★ 77% HOTEL

31 Knyveton Rd BH1 3QQ

☎ 01202 369988   📠 01202 292221

e-mail: carrington.house@forestdale.com

web: www.carringtonhousehotel.co.uk

dir: *A338 at St Paul's rdbt, 200mtrs & left into Knyveton Rd. Hotel 400mtrs on right*

PETS: Bedrooms (2 GF) unattended **Charges** £7.50 per night **Public areas** except restaurant & bar on leads **Grounds** on leads **Exercise area** beach (15 mins' walk) **Facilities** food (pre-bookable) food bowl walks info vet info **Other** charge for damage

This hotel occupies a prominent position on a tree-lined avenue and a short walk from the seafront. The bedrooms are comfortable, well equipped and include many purpose-built family rooms. There are two dining options, Mortimers restaurant, and the Kings bar which serves light meals and snacks. Guests can relax in the comfortable lounge areas whilst the leisure complex offers a whole host of activities including a heated swimming pool.

Rooms 145 (42 fmly) (2 GF) **Facilities** FTV ⊗ Children's play area Xmas New Year Wi-fi **Services** Lift **Parking** 85 **Notes** LB

Wessex

★★★ 77% HOTEL

West Cliff Rd BH2 5EU

☎ 01202 551911   📠 01202 297354

e-mail: wessex@forestdale.com

web: www.thewessexhotel.co.uk

dir: *Follow M27/A35 or A338 from Dorchester & A347 N. Hotel on West Cliff side of town*

PETS: Bedrooms (17 GF) unattended **Charges** £7.50 per night **Public areas** except restaurant **Grounds** **Facilities** food (pre-bookable) feeding mat

Centrally located and handy for the beach, the Wessex is a popular, relaxing hotel. Bedrooms are well equipped and comfortable with a range of modern amenities. The Lulworth Restaurant provides a range of appetizing dishes. The excellent leisure facilities include both indoor and outdoor pools, sauna, ample function rooms and an open-plan bar and lounge.

Rooms 109 (32 fmly) (17 GF) **Facilities** FTV ⊗ ⚲ Gym Table tennis Sauna Steam room Xmas New Year Wi-fi **Services** Lift **Parking** 160 **Notes** LB

BOURNEMOUTH *continued*

Suncliff

★★★ **75%** HOTEL

29 East Overcliff Dr BH1 3AG

☎ 01202 291711 & 298350 📠 01202 293788

e-mail: info@suncliffbournemouth.co.uk

dir: *A338/A35 towards East Cliff & beaches, right into Holdenhurst Rd, straight over 2 rdbts, left at junct into East Overcliff Drive, hotel on seafront*

PETS: Bedrooms (14 GF) **Charges** £10 per night **Exercise area** 0.5m **Facilities** walks info vet info **Other** charge for damage **Restrictions** small dogs only

Enjoying splendid views from the East Cliff and catering mainly for leisure guests, this friendly hotel offers a range of facilities and services. Bedrooms are well equipped and comfortable, and many have sea views. Public areas include a large conservatory, an attractive bar and pleasant lounges.

Rooms 97 (29 fmly) (14 GF) **S** £22-£75; **D** £44-£150 (incl. bkfst)* **Facilities** ③ ⅄ Gym Squash ♫ Xmas New Year Wi-fi **Services** Lift **Parking** 62 **Notes** LB

Hotel Collingwood

★★★ **70%** HOTEL

11 Priory Rd, West Cliff BH2 5DF

☎ 01202 557575 📠 01202 293219

e-mail: info@hotel-collingwood.co.uk

web: www.hotel-collingwood.co.uk

dir: *A338 left at West Cliff sign, over 1st rdbt, left at 2nd rdbt. Hotel 500yds on left*

PETS: Bedrooms (6 GF) unattended ground-floor bedrooms only **Charges** £8 per night £56 per week **Exercise area** park & beach (5 mins) **Facilities** cage storage walks info vet info **On Request** fridge access towels **Other** charge for damage **Restrictions** small, well behaved dogs only

This privately owned and managed hotel is situated close to the BIC. Bedrooms are airy, with the emphasis on comfort. An excellent range of leisure facilities is available and the public areas are spacious and welcoming. Pinks Restaurant offers carefully prepared cuisine and a fixed-price, five-course dinner.

Rooms 53 (16 fmly) (6 GF) **S** £39-£65; **D** £78-£130 (incl. bkfst) **Facilities** FTV ③ Gym Steam room Sauna Games room Snooker room ♫ Xmas New Year Wi-fi **Services** Lift **Parking** 55

Burley Court

★★★ **61%** HOTEL

Bath Rd BH1 2NP

☎ 01202 552824 & 556704 📠 01202 298514

e-mail: info@burleycourthotel.co.uk

dir: *Exit A338 at St Paul's rdbt, take 3rd exit at next rdbt into Holdenhurst Rd. 3rd exit at next rdbt into Bath Rd, over crossing, 1st left*

PETS: Bedrooms (4 GF) unattended sign **Charges** £10 per night **Exercise area** 50mtrs **Facilities** food (pre-bookable) food bowl water bowl washing facs walks info vet info **On Request** fridge access torch towels **Other** charge for damage

Located on the West Cliff, this well-established hotel is well located and convenient for the town and beaches. Bedrooms are pleasantly furnished and decorated in bright colours. A daily-changing menu is served in the spacious dining room.

Rooms 38 (8 fmly) (4 GF) **Facilities** ⅄ Xmas **Services** Lift **Parking** 35 **Notes** Closed 30 Dec-14 Jan RS 15-31 Jan

The Whitehall

★★ **78%** HOTEL

Exeter Park Rd BH2 5AX

☎ 01202 554682 📠 01202 292637

e-mail: reservations@thewhitehallhotel.co.uk

web: www.thewhitehallhotel.co.uk

dir: *Follow BIC signs, turn into Exeter Park Rd (off Exeter Rd)*

PETS: Bedrooms (3 GF) unattended **Charges** £2 per night **Grounds** on leads **Exercise area** green (less than 50mtrs) **Facilities** vet info **Other** charge for damage **Restrictions** small, well behaved dogs only

This friendly hotel enjoys an elevated position overlooking the park and is also close to the town centre and seafront. The spacious public areas include a choice of lounges, a cosy bar and a well-presented restaurant. The well-equipped and inviting bedrooms are spread over three floors.

Rooms 46 (5 fmly) (3 GF) **Facilities** ♫ Xmas **Services** Lift **Parking** 25

Ullswater

★★ **71%** HOTEL

West Cliff Gardens BH2 5HW

☎ 01202 555181 📠 01202 317896

e-mail: enquiries@ullswater-hotel.co.uk

web: www.ullswater-hotel.co.uk

dir: *In Bournemouth follow signs to West Cliff. Hotel just off Westcliff Rd*

PETS: Bedrooms (2 GF) unattended sign certain bedrooms only **Charges** £5 per night **Grounds** on leads **Exercise area** beach & cliff top walks (150yds) **Other** charge for damage **Restrictions** well behaved dogs only

A welcoming family run hotel conveniently located for the city and the seafront. This popular establishment attracts a loyal

following. The well-equipped bedrooms vary in size, and the charming lounge bar and dining room are very smart. Cuisine is hearty and homemade offering a good choice from the daily-changing menu.

Rooms 42 (8 fmly) (2 GF) **S** £43-£56; **D** £86-£110 (incl. bkfst)*
Facilities FTV Snooker room Table tennis ♫ Xmas New Year Wi-fi
Services Lift **Parking** 12 **Notes** LB

Bourne Hall Hotel

★★ 63% HOTEL

14 Priory Rd, West Cliff BH2 5DN
☎ 01202 299715 📄 01202 552669
e-mail: info@bournehall.co.uk
web: www.bournehall.co.uk
dir: *M27/A31 from Ringwood into Bournemouth on A338, Wessex Way. Follow signs to BIC, onto West Cliff. Hotel on right*

PETS: Bedrooms (5 GF) **Charges** £10 per night £50 per week **Public areas** except restaurant muzzled and on leads **Exercise area** 2 mins' walk **Facilities** food (pre-bookable) pet sitting dog walking cage storage walks info vet info **On Request** fridge access torch towels **Other** charge for damage

This friendly, comfortable hotel is conveniently located close to the Bournemouth International Centre and the seafront. Bedrooms are well equipped, some located on the ground floor and some with sea views. In addition to the spacious lounge, there are two bars and a meeting room. A daily-changing menu is offered in the dining room.

Rooms 48 (9 fmly) (5 GF) **S** £29-£55; **D** £58-£110 (incl. bkfst)*
Facilities STV Free leisure facilities for guests at Marriott Highcliff Hotel ♫ Xmas New Year Wi-fi **Services** Lift **Parking** 35

Wood Lodge

★★★★ GUEST ACCOMMODATION

10 Manor Rd, East Cliff BH1 3EY
☎ 01202 290891 📄 01202 290892
e-mail: enquiries@woodlodgehotel.co.uk
web: www.woodlodgehotel.co.uk
dir: *A338 to St Pauls rdbt, 1st exit left. Straight over next 2 rdbts, immediate left*

PETS: Bedrooms (4 GF) standard bedrooms only **Charges** up to £5 per night up to £35 per week **Public areas** only allowed in halls for access to bedrooms on leads **Grounds** on leads disp bin **Exercise area** many walks nearby **Facilities** vet info **On Request** fridge access torch towels **Other** charge for damage **Restrictions** small & medium size dogs only **Resident Pet:** Buster (Yorkshire Terrier)

Expect a warm welcome from this family-run establishment. Set in beautiful gardens minutes from the seafront and a 10-minute walk from the town centre. Bedrooms, which vary in size, are well presented. Home-cooked evening meals and hearty breakfasts are served in the smart dining room.

Rooms 15 rms (14 en suite) (1 pri facs) (1 fmly) (4 GF)
S £35-£50; **D** £70-£100 **Facilities** TVL tea/coffee Dinner available Cen ht Licensed Wi-fi 🐾 🦴 Pool table **Parking** 12 **Notes** LB

ENGLAND

THE INDEPENDENTS
HOTEL ASSOCIATION

Bridge House
★★ 76% HOTEL
115 East St DT6 3LB
☎ 01308 423371   🖥 01308 459573
e-mail: info@bridgehousebridport.co.uk
dir: *From A35 follow town centre signs, hotel 200mtrs on right*

PETS: Bedrooms Public areas except restaurant, must be
well behaved on leads **Grounds** disp bin **Exercise area** park
adjacent **Facilities** walks info vet info **On Request** fridge
access **Other** charge for damage

A short stroll from the town centre, this 18th-century Grade II
listed property offers well-equipped bedrooms that vary in size.
In addition to the main lounge, there is a small bar-lounge and
a separate breakfast room. An interesting range of home-cooked
meals is provided in the wine bar and brasserie.

Rooms 10 (3 fmly) **S** £69-£105; **D** £98-£148 (incl. bkfst)*
Facilities FTV New Year Wi-fi **Parking** 13 **Notes** LB

The Shave Cross Inn
★★★★★ 🍴 INN
Marshwood Vale DT6 6HW
☎ 01308 868358   🖥 01308 867064
e-mail: roy.warburton@virgin.net
web: www.theshavecrossinn.co.uk
dir: *From B3165 turn at Birdsmoorgate & follow brown signs*

PETS: Bedrooms (3 GF) unattended **Charges** £15 per stay
Public areas except restaurant on leads **Grounds** on leads
Exercise area nearby **Facilities** washing facs cage storage
walks info vet info **On Request** fridge access torch towels
Stables Other charge for damage **Resident Pets:** Lulu, Liddy,
Lotty (Great Danes), Libby (horse)

This historic inn has been providing refreshment to weary
travellers for centuries and continues to offer a warm and
genuine welcome. The snug bar is dominated by a wonderful
fireplace with crackling logs creating just the right atmosphere.
Bedrooms are located in a separate Dorset flint and stone
building. Quality is impressive throughout with wonderful stone
floors and oak beams, combined with feature beds and luxurious
bathrooms. Food, using excellent local produce, has a distinct

Caribbean and international slant, including a number of
authentic dishes.

Rooms 7 en suite (1 fmly) (3 GF) **Facilities** STV FTV tea/coffee
Dinner available Direct Dial Cen ht Wi-fi Pool table **Parking** 29
Notes No Children RS Mon (ex BH) closed for lunch & dinner No
coaches

Britmead House
★★★★ GUEST ACCOMMODATION
West Bay Rd DT6 4EG
☎ 01308 422941 & 07973 725243
e-mail: britmead@talk21.com
web: www.britmeadhouse.co.uk
dir: *1m S of town centre, off A35 onto West Bay Rd*

PETS: Bedrooms (2 GF) **Public areas** except dining room &
lounge on leads **Grounds** on leads disp bin **Exercise area**
100mtrs **Facilities** water bowl washing facs walks info vet
info **On Request** fridge access torch towels **Other** charge
for damage **Restrictions** no Pit Bull Terriers, Rottweilers or
Staffordshire Bull Terriers

Britmead House is located south of Bridport, within easy reach
of the town centre and West Bay harbour. Family-run, the
atmosphere is friendly and the accommodation well appointed
and comfortable. As it is suitable for both business and leisure,
many guests return regularly. A choice of breakfast is served in
the light and airy dining room.

Rooms 8 en suite (2 fmly) (2 GF) **S** £40-£58; **D** £64-£80
Facilities FTV TVL tea/coffee Cen ht Wi-fi **Parking** 12 **Notes** LB
Closed 24-27 Dec

🐾 🐕

Bingham Grange Touring & Camping Park
(SY478963)
▶▶▶▶▶
Melplash DT6 3TT
☎ 01308 488234   🖥 01308 488426
e-mail: enquiries@binghamsfarm.co.uk
dir: *From A35 at Bridport take A3066 N towards Beaminster. Site
on left after 3m*

PETS: Charges £2 per night **Public areas** except washrooms,
shop, office, bar & restaurant disp bin **Exercise area on site**
long woodland trail leading to river bank **Exercise area** park
& footpaths adjacent **Facilities** food leads walks info vet
info **Stables** nearby **Other** disposal bags, tennis balls & dog
ground tether spikes available **Restrictions** no dangerous dogs
(see page 7) **Resident Pets:** Acorn, Wesley, Conker & Bracken
(Spaniels), Snoopy (Beagle), Bonzo (Smooth Terrier), Oscar
(Golden Labrador) chickens, ducks, geese

Open 16 Mar-Oct rs Wed (high season), Tue & Wed (low season)
restaurant & bar closed Last departure 11.00hrs

Set in a quiet rural location but only five miles from the Jurassic
Coast, this adults-only park enjoys views over the west Dorset
countryside. The mostly level pitches are attractively set amongst
shrub beds and ornamental trees. There is an excellent restaurant
with lounge bar and takeaway, and all facilities are of a high

quality. The bottom section of the park has been transformed with new roads and spacious new pitch areas. 20 acre site. 150 touring pitches. 83 hardstandings. Tent pitches. Motorhome pitches.

Notes No under 18's to stay or visit, no noise after 23.00hrs.

CERNE ABBAS   Map 3 ST60

Lyons Gate Caravan and Camping Park
(ST660062)

► ► ►

Lyons Gate DT2 7AZ
☎ 01300 345260
e-mail: info@lyons-gate.co.uk
dir: *Signed with direct access from A352, 3m N of Cerne Abbas*

PETS: Charges £1 per night **Public areas** disp bin
Exercise area on site bridle path **Facilities** walks info vet info
Other prior notice required

Open all year Last arrival 20.00hrs Last departure 11.30hrs

A peaceful park with pitches set out around the four attractive coarse fishing lakes. It is surrounded by mature woodland, with many footpaths and bridleways. Other easily accessible attractions include the Cerne Giant carved into the hills, the old market town of Dorchester, and the superb sandy beach at Weymouth. Holiday homes are available for sale. 10 acre site. 90 touring pitches. 24 hardstandings. Tent pitches. Motorhome pitches. 14 statics.

Giants Head Caravan & Camping Park
(ST675029)

► ►

Giants Head Farm, Old Sherborne Rd DT2 7TR
☎ 01300 341242
e-mail: holidays@giantshead.co.uk
dir: *From Dorchester into town avoiding by-pass, at Top O'Town rdbt take A352 (Sherborne road), in 500yds right fork at BP (Loder's) garage, site signed*

PETS: Charges dog £2 per night **Public areas** except dog-free areas on leads disp bin **Exercise area** adjacent **Facilities** walks info vet info **Other** prior notice required

Open Etr-Oct rs Etr shop & bar closed Last arrival anytimehrs Last departure 13.00hrs

A pleasant, though rather basic, park set in Dorset downland near the Cerne Giant (the famous landmark figure cut into the chalk) with stunning views. This is a good stopover site, ideal for tenters and backpackers on the Ridgeway route. 4 acre site. 50 touring pitches. Tent pitches. Motorhome pitches.

Notes

CHARMOUTH   Map 3 SY39

Wood Farm Caravan & Camping Park
(SY356940)

► ► ► ► ►

Axminster Rd DT6 6BT
☎ 01297 560697   📠 01297 561243
e-mail: holidays@woodfarm.co.uk
dir: *Site entered directly off A35 rdbt, on Axminster side of Charmouth*

PETS: Charges dog £2 per night **Public areas** except buildings & play area on leads disp bin **Exercise area on site** 2-acre area **Facilities** food food bowl water bowl walks info vet info **Other** prior notice required cats not allowed to roam free; dogs must be kept on leads at all times

Open Etr-Oct Last arrival 19.00hrs Last departure noon

This top quality park is set amongst mature native trees with the various levels of the site falling away into a beautiful valley below. The park offers excellent facilities including family rooms and fully serviced pitches. The facilities throughout the park are spotless. At the bottom end of the site there is an excellent indoor swimming pool and leisure complex, plus the licensed, conservatory-style Offshore Café. There's a good children's play room plus tennis courts and a well-stocked, coarse-fishing lake. The park is well positioned on the Heritage Coast near Lyme Regis. Static holiday homes are also available for hire. 13 acre site. 216 touring pitches. 175 hardstandings. 20 seasonal pitches. Tent pitches. Motorhome pitches. 92 statics.

Notes No skateboards, scooters, roller skates or bikes.

Manor Farm Holiday Centre *(SY368937)*

► ► ►

DT6 6QL
☎ 01297 560226
e-mail: enquiries@manorfarmholidaycentre.co.uk
dir: *W on A35 to Charmouth, site 0.75m on right*

PETS: Charges low season £1, high season £3 per night **Public areas** except swimming pool, club, shop, children's play area, toilets & showers disp bin **Exercise area on site** large open field **Facilities** vet info **Other** prior notice required

Open all year rs End Oct-mid Mar statics only Last arrival 20.00hrs Last departure 10.00hrs

Set just a short walk from the safe sand and shingle beach at Charmouth, this popular family park offers a good range of facilities. Children enjoy the activity area and outdoor swimming pool (so do their parents!), and the park also offers a lively programme in the extensive bar and entertainment complex. 30 acre site. 400 touring pitches. 80 hardstandings. Tent pitches. Motorhome pitches. 29 statics.

Notes No skateboards.

CHRISTCHURCH Map 4 SZ19

Captain's Club Hotel and Spa
★★★★ 81% @@ HOTEL

Wick Ferry, Wick Ln BH23 1HU
☎ 01202 475111 📄 01202 490111
e-mail: enquiries@captainsclubhotel.com
web: www.captainsclubhotel.com
dir: B3073 to Christchurch. On Fountain rdbt take 5th exit (Sopers Ln) 2nd left (St Margarets Ave) 1st right onto Wick Ln

PETS: Bedrooms unattended sign smaller suites only **Public areas** outside terrace area only **Grounds** on leads disp bin **Exercise area** 2 mins' walk **Facilities** food bowl water bowl bedding walks info vet info **On Request** fridge access torch towels **Stables** 5m **Other** charge for damage **Restrictions** small & medium size dogs only

Situated in the heart of the town on the banks of the River Stour at Christchurch Quay, and only ten minutes from Bournemouth. All bedrooms, including the suites and apartments have views overlooking the river. Guests can relax in the hydrotherapy pool, enjoy a spa treatment or enjoy the cuisine in Tides Restaurant.

Rooms 29 (12 fmly) **Facilities** Spa STV FTV Hydro-therapy pool Sauna 🎵 Xmas New Year Wi-fi **Services** Lift Air con **Parking** 41

CORFE CASTLE Map 3 SY98

Corfe Castle Camping & Caravanning Club Site *(SY953818)*

▶ ▶ ▶ ▶

Bucknowle BH20 5PQ
☎ 01929 480280 & 0845 130 7633
dir: From Wareham A351 towards Swanage. In 4m turn right at foot of Corfe Castle signed Church Knowle. 0.75m right to site on left at top of lane

PETS: Public areas except facility blocks (ex assist dogs) disp bin **Exercise area** surrounding countryside **Facilities** food vet info **Other** prior notice required

Open Mar-Oct Last arrival 20.00hrs Last departure noon

This lovely park is set in woodland near to the famous Corfe Castle. It has modern toilet and shower facilities which are spotless. Although the site is sloping, pitches are level and include spacious hardstandings. The site is perfect for visiting the many attractions of the Purbeck area including Swanage and Studland, as well as having the nearby station at Corfe for the Swanage Steam Railway. 5 acre site. 80 touring pitches. 33 hardstandings. 80 seasonal pitches. Tent pitches. Motorhome pitches.

Notes Site gates closed between 23.00hrs-07.00hrs, latest arrival time after 20.00hrs by prior arrangement.

EVERSHOT Map 3 ST50

THE
RED CARNATION
HOTEL COLLECTION
CHATEAUX

Summer Lodge Country House Hotel, Restaurant & Spa
★★★★ @@@ COUNTRY HOUSE HOTEL

DT2 0JR
☎ 01935 482000 📄 01935 482040
e-mail: summer@relaischateaux.com
dir: 1m W of A37 halfway between Dorchester & Yeovil

PETS: Bedrooms unattended sign coach house & cottages only **Charges** £20 per night (negotiable) **Public areas** except restaurant & drawing room **Grounds** disp bin **Exercise area** adjacent **Facilities** food (pre-bookable) food bowl water bowl bedding dog chews feeding mat scoop/disp bags leads pet sitting dog walking washing facs dog grooming cage storage walks info vet info **On Request** fridge access torch towels **Stables** 5m **Other** charge for damage **Resident Pets:** William & Felix (cats)

This picturesque hotel is situated in the heart of Dorset and is the ideal retreat for getting 'away from it all', and it's worth arriving in time for the excellent afternoon tea. Bedrooms are appointed to a very high standard; each is individually designed with upholstered walls and come with a wealth of luxurious facilities. Expect plasma screen TVs, DVD players, radios, air conditioning and Wi-fi access, plus little touches such as homemade shortbread, fresh fruit and scented candles. The delightful public areas include a sumptuous lounge complete with an open fire, and the elegant restaurant where the cuisine continues to be the high point of any stay.

Rooms 24 (14 annexe) (6 fmly) (2 GF) (1 smoking) **S** £185-£535; **D** £210-£560 (incl. bkfst)* **Facilities** Spa STV FTV 🕸 🌊 🌿 Gym Sauna Xmas New Year Wi-fi **Services** Air con **Parking** 41 **Notes** LB

The Acorn Inn
★★★★ @ INN

DT2 0JW
☎ 01935 83228 📄 01935 83707
e-mail: stay@acorn-inn.co.uk
web: www.acorn-inn.co.uk
dir: 0.5m off A37 between Yeovil & Dorchester, signed Evershot & Holywell

PETS: Bedrooms unattended **Charges** £10 per night **Public areas** except restaurant on leads **Grounds** on leads **Exercise area** 400yds **Facilities** water bowl dog chews walks info vet info **On Request** torch **Other** charge for damage **Resident Pet:** Dougall (Labrador cross)

This delightful 16th-century coaching inn is located in the heart of the village. Several of the bedrooms feature interesting four-poster beds, and all the rooms have been individually decorated and furnished. The public rooms retain many original features including oak panelling, open fires and stone-flagged floors. Fresh local produce is included on the varied menu.

Rooms 10 en suite (2 fmly) **S** £79-£89; **D** £99-£149 **Facilities** FTV TVL tea/coffee Dinner available Direct Dial Cen ht Wi-fi Pool table **Parking** 40 **Notes** LB

LOWER ANSTY
Map 3 ST70

The Fox Inn
★★★★ INN

DT2 7PN
☎ 01258 880328 📠 01258 881440
e-mail: fox@anstyfoxinn.co.uk
web: www.anstyfoxinn.co.uk
dir: Off A354 at Millbourne St Andrew, follow brown signs to Ansty

PETS: Bedrooms unattended standard bedrooms only
Public areas bar only **Grounds** on leads disp bin **Exercise area**
public footpath (200yds) **Facilities** food bowl water bowl cage
storage walks info vet info **On Request** fridge access torch
towels **Other** charge for damage **Resident Pet:** Reggie (Labrador)

This popular inn has a long and interesting history including
strong links to the Hall & Woodhouse Brewery. Surrounded by
beautiful Dorset countryside, this is a great base for exploring the
area. Bedrooms are smartly appointed and offer high levels of
comfort. The interesting menu focuses on excellent local produce,
with a choice of dining options including the oak-panelled dining
room. An extensive garden and patio area are also available.

Rooms 11 en suite (7 fmly) **S** £50-£75; **D** £60-£125 **Facilities** FTV
TVL tea/coffee Dinner available Direct Dial Cen ht Wi-fi
Parking 30 **Notes** LB

LYME REGIS
Map 3 SY39

Hook Farm Caravan & Camping Park
(SY323930)

►►►

Gore Ln, Uplyme DT7 3UU
☎ 01297 442801 📠 01297 442801
e-mail: information@hookfarm-uplyme.co.uk
dir: A35 onto B3165 towards Lyme Regis & Uplyme at Hunters
Lodge pub. In 2m right into Gore Ln, site 400yds on right

PETS: Charges £1.50 per night **Public areas** except shop,
reception & washroom facilities disp bin **Exercise area on site**
apple orchard **Facilities** leads walks info vet info **Other** tether
spikes for sale, tether hook at shop, disposal bags available
Restrictions no Dobermans, Bullmastiffs, Pit Bull Terriers,
Staffordshire Bull Terriers or Rottweilers **Resident Pets:** 4 cats

Open 15 Mar-Oct rs Low season shop closed Last arrival 21.00hrs
Last departure 11.00hrs

Set in a peaceful and very rural location, the popular farm site
enjoys lovely views of Lym Valley and is just a mile from the
seaside at Lyme Regis. There are modern toilet facilities and
good on-site amenities. Most pitches are level due to excellent
terracing - a great site for tents. 5.5 acre site. 100 touring
pitches. 4 hardstandings. Tent pitches. Motorhome pitches. 17
statics.

Notes No groups of 6 adults or more.

LYTCHETT MATRAVERS
Map 3 SY99

Huntick Farm Caravan Park *(SY955947)*

►►►

Huntick Rd BH16 6BB
☎ 01202 622222
e-mail: huntickcaravans@btconnect.com
dir: Site between Lytchett Minster & Lytchett Matravers. From
A31 take A350 towards Poole. Follow Lytchett Minster signs, then
Lytchett Matravers signs. Huntick Rd by Red Cow pub

PETS: Charges £1 per night **Public areas** disp bin
Exercise area on site Facilities vet info

Open Apr-Oct Last arrival 21.00hrs Last departure noon

A really attractive little park nestling in rural surroundings
edged by woodland, a mile from the village amenities of Lytchett
Matravers. This neat grassy park is divided into three paddocks
offering a peaceful location, yet it is close to the attractions of
Poole and Bournemouth. 4 acre site. 30 touring pitches. Tent
pitches. Motorhome pitches.

Notes No ball games on site.

South Lytchett Manor Caravan & Camping Park (SY954926)

►►►►►

Dorchester Rd BH16 6JB
☎ 01202 622577
e-mail: info@southlytchettmanor.co.uk
dir: On B3067, off A35, 1m E of Lytchett Minster, 600yds on right after village

PETS: Charges £1 per night £7 per week **Public areas** except play area & toilet blocks disp bin **Exercise area on site** around pond & woods in adjoining fields **Facilities** food food bowl water bowl dog chews cat treats washing facs walks info vet info **Other** prior notice required disposal bags available **Restrictions** no Rottweilers **Resident Pets:** 2 Labradors, 1 Jack Russell, 1 cat, chickens

Open Mar-2 Jan Last arrival 21.00hrs Last departure 11.00hrs

Situated in the grounds of a historic manor house the park has modern facilities, which are spotless and well maintained. A warm and friendly welcome awaits at this lovely park which is well located for visiting Poole and Bournemouth; the Jurassic X53 bus route (Exeter to Poole) has a stop just outside the park. This park continues to improve each year. 20 acre site. 150 touring pitches. 80 hardstandings. Tent pitches. Motorhome pitches.

Notes No camp fires or Chinese lanterns.

Fishmore Hill Farm (ST799013)

★★★ FARMHOUSE

DT11 0DL
☎ 01258 881122 & 07708 003561   📄 01258 881122
Mr & Mrs N Clarke
e-mail: sarah@fishmorehillfarm.com
dir: Off A354 signed Milton Abbas, 3m left on sharp bend, up steep hill, 1st left

PETS: Sep accom kennel suitable for larger dogs barn **Charges** dog £5, horse £10 per night **Public areas** on leads **Grounds** on leads disp bin **Exercise area** National Trust/Forestry Commission 500yds **Facilities** food bowl water bowl cage storage walks info **On Request** fridge access torch **Stables** **Other** pets only accepted with prior notice; on-site veterinary practice; paddock for horses **Restrictions** contact owner to establish which breeds are accepted **Resident Pets:** Jack Russells, horses & sheep

This working sheep farm and family home is surrounded by beautiful Dorset countryside, close to historic Milton Abbas and only a short drive from the coast. Bedrooms, which vary in size, are comfortable and have useful extras. The atmosphere is friendly and relaxed. Breakfast is served in the smart dining room around a communal table.

Rooms 3 en suite **S** £35; **D** £70 **Facilities** TVL tea/coffee Cen ht **Parking** 4 **Notes** Closed Xmas & New Year 🐾 50 acres sheep/ horses

The Coppleridge Inn

★★★ INN

SP7 9HW
☎ 01747 851980   📄 01747 851858
e-mail: thecoppleridgeinn@btinternet.com
web: www.coppleridge.com
dir: Off A350 to Motcombe, under railway bridge, 400yds right to Mere, inn 300yds on left

PETS: Bedrooms (10 GF) unattended **Charges** £5 per stay **Public areas** except restaurant on leads **Grounds** disp bin **Facilities** food food bowl water bowl dog chews litter tray scoop/disp bags walks info vet info **On Request** fridge access **Stables** 1m **Other** paddock available for horses **Resident Pet:** 1 cat

This village inn set within its own 15 acres of land offers ten en suite bedrooms located in a pretty courtyard. All have been appointed to a very high standard providing a very comfortable stay. Staff offer a warm welcome, and the inn serves good food with many daily specials. There are tennis courts and boules, plus a children's play area. Clay pigeon shooting can also be arranged.

Rooms 10 en suite (2 fmly) (10 GF) **S** £50; **D** £90 **Facilities** FTV TVL tea/coffee Dinner available Direct Dial Cen ht Wi-fi 🏊 Pool table **Parking** 100 **Notes** LB

Hotel du Vin Poole

★★★★ 78% 🏅 HOTEL

Thames St BH15 1JN
☎ 01202 785570   📄 01202 785571
e-mail: info.poole@hotelduvin.com
web: www.hotelduvin.com
dir: A31 to Poole, follow channel ferry signs. Left at Poole bridge onto Poole Quay, 1st left into Thames St. Hotel opposite St James Church

PETS: Bedrooms (4 GF) ground-floor bedrooms only **Charges** £10 per night **Public areas** except bistro (restaurant) on leads **Exercise area** 0.25m **Facilities** cage storage walks info vet info **On Request** fridge access torch **Other** charge for damage

Offering a fresh approach to the well established company style, this property boasts some delightful rooms packed with comfort and all the expected Hotel du Vin features. Situated near the harbour the hotel offers nautically-themed bedrooms and suites that have plasma TVs, DVD players and bathrooms with power showers. The public rooms are light, open spaces, and as with the other hotels in this group, the bar and restaurant form centre stage.

Rooms 38 (4 GF) **Facilities** STV Xmas New Year Wi-fi **Services** Air con

Thistle Poole

★★★ **80%** HOTEL

The Quay BH15 1HD

☎ 0871 376 9032 📠 0871 376 9132

e-mail: poole@thistle.co.uk

web: www.thistlehotels.com/poole

dir: *On quay adjacent to Dolphin Marina*

PETS: Bedrooms (22 GF) ground-floor bedrooms only **Charges** £5 per night **Exercise area** 100mtrs **Facilities** vet info **On Request** towels **Other** charge for damage **Restrictions** no large dogs

Situated on the quayside overlooking the harbour, this modern hotel is situated close to the ferry terminal and is also a good base for exploring the beautiful Dorset countryside. Many of the bedrooms have views of Poole harbour. There is a restaurant and two bars, plus two meeting rooms are available. Thistle Hotels - AA Hotel Group of the Year 2011-12.

Rooms 70 (22 GF) **Facilities** Xmas New Year Wi-fi **Services** Lift **Parking** 120

The Burleigh

★★★ GUEST ACCOMMODATION

76 Wimborne Rd BH15 2BZ

☎ 01202 673889 📠 01202 685283

dir: *Off A35 onto A349*

PETS: Bedrooms Public areas except dining room on leads **Exercise area** fields nearby **Facilities** walks info vet info **Other** charge for damage guests must provide dog's own bedding **Restrictions** contact proprietor to confirm which dogs are accepted **Resident Pets:** Alfie (Tibetan Terrier), Cassie & Jazz (cats)

Suited to business and leisure, this well-kept guest accommodation is close to the town centre and ferry terminal. The individually furnished and decorated bedrooms are of a good standard. Breakfast is served at separate tables and there is a small, attractive lounge.

Rooms 8 rms (4 en suite) (1 fmly) **Facilities** TVL tea/coffee Cen ht Wi-fi **Parking** 5

PORTESHAM   **Map 3 SY68**

Portesham Dairy Farm Campsite *(SY602854)*

▶▶▶▶

Weymouth DT3 4HG

☎ 01305 871297

e-mail: info@porteshamdairyfarm.co.uk

dir: *From Dorchester on A35 towards Bridport. In 5m left at Winterbourne Abbas, follow Portesham signs. Through village, left at Kings Arms pub, site 350yds on right*

PETS: Charges £1 per night **Public areas** except children's play area, farmyard & facilities buildings disp bin **Exercise area on site** dog walking area **Exercise area** public footpaths **Facilities** vet info **Other** dogs must be kept on leads at all times & never left unattended

Open mid Mar-Oct Last arrival 21.00hrs Last departure 16.00hrs

Located at the edge of the picturesque village of Portesham, this family run, level park is part of a small working farm in a quiet rural location. Near the site entrance is a pub where meals are served, and that has a garden for children. 8 acre site. 90 touring pitches. 61 hardstandings. Tent pitches. Motorhome pitches.

Notes No commercial vehicles, minimal noise after 22.00hrs.

PUNCKNOWLE   **Map 3 SY58**

Offley Bed & Breakfast

★★★★ GUEST ACCOMMODATION

Looke Ln DT2 9BD

☎ 01308 897044 & 07792 624977

dir: *Off B3157 into village centre, left after Crown Inn into Looke Ln, 2nd house on right*

PETS: Bedrooms Public areas on leads **Grounds** disp bin **Exercise area** woods & fields adjacent **Facilities** food bowl water bowl feeding mat leads washing facs cage storage walks info vet info **On Request** fridge access torch towels

With magnificent views over the Bride Valley, this village house provides comfortable, quality accommodation. Guests are assured of a warm, friendly welcome; an ideal venue to enjoy the numerous local attractions. There are several local inns, one in the village which is just a gentle stroll away.

Rooms 3 rms (2 en suite) (1 pri facs) **Facilities** FTV TVL tea/coffee Cen ht **Parking** 3 **Notes** LB ⊜

ENGLAND

ST LEONARDS — Map 4 SU10

Shamba Holidays (SU105029)

▶ ▶ ▶ ▶ ▶

230 Ringwood Rd BH24 2SB
☎ 01202 873302 🖷 01202 873392
e-mail: enquiries@shambaholidays.co.uk
dir: Off A31, from Poole, left into Eastmoors Lane, 100yds after 2nd rdbt from Texaco garage. Site 0.25m on right (just past Woodman Inn)

PETS: Charges Public areas except buildings disp bin
Exercise area woods 0.5 Facilities food walks info vet info
Other dogs must be kept on leads at all times

Open Mar-Oct rs Low season some facilities only open at wknds
Last arrival 22.00hrs Last departure 11.00hrs

This top quality park has excellent modern facilities particularly suited to families. There'll certainly be a warm welcome from the friendly staff. There is a really good indoor/outdoor heated pool, plus a tasteful bar supplying a good range of meals. The park is well located for visiting the south coast, which is just a short drive away, and also for the New Forest National Park. 7 acre site. 150 touring pitches. Tent pitches. Motorhome pitches.

Notes No large groups, no commercial vehicles.

Back of Beyond Touring Park (SU103034)

▶ ▶ ▶ ▶

234 Ringwood Rd BH24 2SB
☎ 01202 876968 🖷 01202 876968
e-mail: melandsuepike@aol.com
dir: From E: on A31 over Little Chef rdbt, pass St Leonard's Hotel, at next rdbt U-turn into lane immediately left to site at end of lane. From W: on A31 pass Texaco garage & Woodman Inn, immediately left to site

PETS: Charges £1 per night Public areas disp bin
Exercise area on site 18-acre wood Facilities food food bowl
water bowl walks info vet info Other prior notice required
Resident Pets: Dusty & Gabby (Dalmatians)

Open Mar-Oct Last arrival 19.00hrs Last departure noon

Set well off the beaten track in natural woodland surroundings, with its own river and lake, yet close to many attractions. This tranquil park is run by keen, friendly owners, and the quality facilities are for adults only. 28 acre site. 80 touring pitches. 20 seasonal pitches. Tent pitches. Motorhome pitches.

Notes No commercial vehicles.

Forest Edge Touring Park (SU104024)

▶ ▶ ▶

229 Ringwood Rd BH24 2SD
☎ 01590 648331 🖷 01590 645610
e-mail: holidays@shorefield.co.uk
dir: From E: on A31 over 1st rdbt (Little Chef), pass St Leonards Hotel, left at next rdbt into Boundary Ln, site 100yds on left. From W: on A31 pass Texaco garage & Woodman Inn, right at rdbt into Boundary Ln

PETS: Charges £1.50 per night Public areas disp bin
Exercise area adjacent Facilities food water bowl bedding dog chews cat treats scoop/disp bags washing facs walks info vet info Stables nearby Other 1 dog only per pitch free disposal bags

Open Feb-3 Jan rs School & summer hols pool open Last arrival 21.00hrs Last departure 10.00hrs

A tree-lined park set in grassland with plenty of excellent amenities for all the family, including an outdoor heated swimming pool and toddlers' pool, an adventure playground, and two launderettes. Visitors are invited to use the superb leisure club plus all amenities and entertainment at the sister site of Oakdene Forest Park, which is less than a mile away. Some pitches may experience some traffic noise from the nearby A31. 9 acre site. 72 touring pitches. 29 seasonal pitches. Tent pitches. Motorhome pitches. 30 statics.

Notes Families & couples only. 1 car per pitch, no gazebos. Rallies welcome.

SHAFTESBURY — Map 3 ST82

Best Western Royal Chase

★ ★ ★ 70% ⊛ HOTEL

Royal Chase Roundabout SP7 8DB
☎ 01747 853355 🖷 01747 851969
e-mail: reception@theroyalchasehotel.co.uk
web: www.theroyalchasehotel.co.uk
dir: A303 to A350 signed Blandford Forum. Avoid town centre, follow road to 3rd rdbt

PETS: Bedrooms (6 GF) unattended Charges £6.50 per night Public areas except bar & restaurant Grounds disp bin Facilities cage storage walks info vet info On Request fridge access towels Other pets can only be left unattended in bedrooms if owners are in hotel

Equally suitable for both leisure and business guests, this well-known local landmark is situated close to the famous Gold Hill. Both Standard and Crown bedrooms offer good levels of comfort and quality. In addition to the fixed-price menu in the Byzant Restaurant, guests have the option of eating more informally in the convivial bar.

Rooms 33 (13 fmly) (6 GF) S £50-£95; D £50-£95 Facilities ⊗ Turkish steam room New Year Wi-fi Parking 100 Notes LB

Blackmore Vale Caravan & Camping Park

(ST835233)

►►

Sherborne Causeway SP7 9PX
☎ 01747 851523 & 851497 📠 01747 851671
e-mail: info@dche.co.uk
dir: *From Shaftesbury's Ivy Cross rdbt take A30 signed Sherborne. Site 2m on right*

PETS: Charges £1 per night **Public areas** on leads disp bin **Exercise area on site** large field adjacent **Facilities** walks info vet info **Other** prior notice required **Restrictions** no Rottweilers, Dobermans or Pit Bull Terriers **Resident Pets:** cats & chickens

Open all year Last arrival 21.00hrs

A pleasant touring park with spacious pitches and well-maintained facilities. A fully-equipped gym is the latest addition to this park, and is open to visitors. Blackmore Vale, about two miles from Shaftesbury, is set behind a caravan sales showground and dealership. 5 acre site. 26 touring pitches. 6 hardstandings. Tent pitches. Motorhome pitches. 20 statics.

SHERBORNE Map 3 ST61

Munden House

★★★★★ 🛏 GUEST ACCOMMODATION

Munden Ln, Alweston DT9 5HU
☎ 01963 23150
e-mail: stay@mundenhouse.co.uk
dir: *A352 from Sherborne, left onto A3030 to Alweston, pass village shop on right, 250yds on left at Oxfords Bakery sign*

PETS: Bedrooms 3 self contained units only **Charges** £10 per stay **Public areas** except dining room on leads **Grounds** disp bin **Exercise area** numerous walks nearby **Facilities** food bowl water bowl dog chews leads washing facs walks info vet info **On Request** fridge access torch towels **Other** charge for damage **Resident Pets:** Cassie (Border Collie), Sausage (cat)

Delightful property set in a quiet lane away from the main road with pleasant views over the surrounding countryside. Bedrooms and bathrooms come in a variety of shapes and styles but all are very well decorated and furnished; the beds are especially comfortable. Guests are welcome to use to lounge and garden, and delicious home-cooked dinners (accompanied by an Italian wine list) are available by prior arrangement. Breakfast includes a selection of high quality hot and cold dishes, all carefully prepared to order.

Rooms 4 en suite 3 annexe en suite (3 fmly) (4 GF) **S** £70-£95; **D** £80-£130 **Facilities** FTV tea/coffee Dinner available Cen ht Licensed Wi-fi 🐾 **Parking** 14 **Notes** LB

SWANAGE Map 4 SZ07

The Pines

★★★ **78%** HOTEL

Burlington Rd BH19 1LT
☎ 01929 425211 📠 01929 422075
e-mail: reservations@pineshotel.co.uk
web: www.pineshotel.co.uk
dir: *A351 to seafront, left then 2nd right. Hotel at end of road*

PETS: Bedrooms (6 GF) unattended certain bedrooms only **Grounds** on leads disp bin **Exercise area** nearby **Facilities** walks info vet info **On Request** torch towels **Stables** 4m

Enjoying a peaceful location with spectacular views over the cliffs and sea, The Pines is a pleasant place to stay. Many of the comfortable bedrooms have sea views. Guests can take tea in the lounge, enjoy appetising bar snacks in the attractive bar, and interesting cuisine in the restaurant.

Rooms 41 (26 fmly) (6 GF) **S** £66; **D** £132-£176 (incl. bkfst)*
Facilities FTV 🎵 Xmas New Year Wi-fi **Services** Lift **Parking** 60 **Notes** LB

Grand

★★★ **70%** HOTEL

Burlington Rd BH19 1LU
☎ 01929 423353 📠 01929 427068
e-mail: reservations@grandhotelswanage.co.uk
web: www.grandhotelswanage.co.uk

PETS: Bedrooms unattended sign inland view bedrooms only **Charges** £10 per night **Public areas** except restaurant muzzled and on leads **Grounds** on leads **Exercise area** nearby **Facilities** water bowl walks info **Other** charge for damage **Resident Pets:** 1 dog, 1 cat

Dating back to 1898, this hotel is located on the Isle of Purbeck and has spectacular views across Swanage Bay and Peveril Point. Bedrooms are individually decorated and well equipped; public rooms offer a number of choices from relaxing lounges to extensive leisure facilities. The hotel also has its own private beach.

Rooms 30 (2 fmly) **S** £45-£85; **D** £90-£170 (incl. bkfst)*
Facilities FTV 🐾 supervised Fishing Gym Table tennis Treatment room Xmas New Year Wi-fi **Services** Lift **Parking** 15 **Notes** LB Closed 10 days in Jan (dates on application)

SWANAGE *continued*

Railway Cottage

★★★ BED AND BREAKFAST

26 Victoria Av BH19 1AP

☎ 01929 425542

e-mail: foxysh@btinternet.com

PETS: Bedrooms (1 GF) unattended **Grounds** on leads **Exercise area** adjacent **Facilities** food bowl water bowl washing facs walks info vet info **On Request** fridge access torch **Other** charge for damage **Restrictions** well behaved dogs only **Resident Pets:** Terrence & Pickles (Patterdale Terrier cross)

Ideally located and only a short stroll from both the town centre and the seafront, this is a relaxed and welcoming family-run establishment with bedrooms of varying sizes. Breakfast is served in the pleasant dining room; parking is available either to the rear of the property or in the main car park opposite.

Rooms 6 en suite (1 fmly) (1 GF) **S** £30-£60; **D** £60-£90 **Facilities** tea/coffee Cen ht Wi-fi **Parking** 5 **Notes** LB 🐾

Ulwell Cottage Caravan Park (SZ019809)

▶ ▶ ▶ ▶

Ulwell Cottage, Ulwell BH19 3DG

☎ 01929 422823 📠 01929 421500

e-mail: enq@ulwellcottagepark.co.uk

dir: *From Swanage N for 2m on unclass road towards Studland*

PETS: Charges Public areas on leads disp bin **Exercise area** 100yds **Facilities** food food bowl water bowl bedding dog chews scoop/disp bags leads walks info vet info **Other** dogs must be kept on leads at all times

Open Mar-7 Jan rs Mar-Spring BH & mid Sep-early Jan takeaway closed, shop open variable hrs Last arrival 22.00hrs Last departure 11.00hrs

Nestling under the Purbeck Hills and surrounded by scenic walks, this park is only two miles from the beach. A family-run park that caters well for families and couples, and offers a refurbished toilet and shower block complete with good family rooms, all appointed to a high standard. There is a good indoor swimming pool and village inn offering a good range of meals. 13 acre site. 77 touring pitches. 19 hardstandings. Tent pitches. Motorhome pitches. 140 statics.

Herston Caravan & Camping Park (SZ018785)

▶ ▶ ▶

Washpond Ln BH19 3DJ

☎ 01929 422932 📠 01929 423888

e-mail: office@herstonleisure.co.uk

dir: *From Wareham on A351 towards Swanage. Washpond Ln on left just after 'Welcome to Swanage' sign*

PETS: Charges £3 per night £21 per week **Public areas** except shop, bar & restaurant **Exercise area on site** public footpath across farmland & country walks **Exercise area** adjacent to park **Facilities** walks info vet info **Other** prior notice required dogs must be kept on leads at all times

Open all year

Set in a rural area, with extensive views of the Purbecks, this tree-lined park has many full facility pitches and quality toilet facilities. Herston Halt is within walking distance, a stop for the famous Swanage steam railway between the town centre and Corfe Castle. There are also yurts available for hire. 10 acre site. 100 touring pitches. 71 hardstandings. Tent pitches. Motorhome pitches. 5 statics. 6 bell tents/yurts.

Notes No noise after 23.00hrs.

Acton Field Camping Site (SY991785)

▶

Acton Field, Langton Matravers BH19 3HS

☎ 01929 424184 & 439424 📠 01929 424184

e-mail: enquiries@actonfieldcampsite.co.uk

dir: *From A351 right after Corfe Castle onto B3069 to Langton Matravers, 2nd right after village sign (bridleway)*

PETS: Public areas except children's play areas disp bin **Exercise area** nearby **Facilities** walks info vet info **Stables** 5m **Other** prior notice required

Open mid Jul-early Sep rs Apr-Oct open for organised groups Last arrival 22.00hrs Last departure noon

An informal campsite bordered by farmland on the outskirts of Langton Matravers. There are superb views of the Purbeck Hills and towards the Isle of Wight, and a footpath leads to the coastal path. The site was once a stone quarry, and rock pegs may be required. 7 acre site. 80 touring pitches. Tent pitches. Motorhome pitches.

Notes No open fires, no noise after mdnt. 🐾

The Langton Arms

★★★★ INN

DT11 8RX

☎ 01258 830225 📄 01258 830053

e-mail: info@thelangtonarms.co.uk

dir: *Off A354 in Tarrant Hinton to Tarrant Monkton, through ford, Langton Arms opp*

PETS: Bedrooms (6 GF) unattended **Charges** £10 per night **Public areas** small bar only on leads **Grounds Exercise area** adjacent **Facilities** walks info vet info **On Request** fridge access torch towels **Stables** 1m **Other** paddock available for horses

Tucked away in this sleepy Dorset village, the Langton Arms offers stylish, light and airy accommodation and is a good base for touring this attractive area. Bedrooms, all on the ground-floor level in the modern annexe, are very well equipped and comfortable. There is a choice of dining options - the relaxed bar-restaurant or the more formal Stables Restaurant, offering innovative and appetising dishes. Breakfast is served in the conservatory dining room just a few steps through the pretty courtyard.

Rooms 6 annexe en suite (6 fmly) (6 GF) **S** £70; **D** £90 **Facilities** tea/coffee Dinner available Direct Dial Cen ht Wi-fi **Parking** 100

Luckford Wood House *(SY872864)*

★★★★ FARMHOUSE

East Stoke BH20 6AW

☎ 01929 463098 & 07888 719002 Mr & Mrs Barnes

e-mail: luckfordleisure@hotmail.co.uk

web: www.luckfordleisure.co.uk

dir: *3m W of Wareham. Off A352, take B3070 to Lulworth, turn right onto Holme Ln, signed East Stoke. 1m right onto Church Ln*

PETS: Bedrooms (1 GF) **Charges** £6 per night £35 per week **Public areas** except dining room & lounge on leads **Exercise area** lane adjacent **Facilities** cage storage walks info vet info **On Request** fridge access towels **Stables Other** paddock & stables available for horses, please phone for charges **Resident Pet:** Sammy (cat)

Rurally situated about three miles west of Wareham, this family home offers comfortable accommodation. Situated on the edge of woodland, there is abundant wildlife to see. Guests can be assured of a friendly welcome and an extensive choice at breakfast.

Rooms 6 rms (5 en suite) (1 pri facs) (3 fmly) (1 GF) **S** £40-£65; **D** £70-£85 **Facilities** FTV TVL tea/coffee Cen ht Wi-fi Golf 27 **Parking** 6 **Notes** LB 122 acres sheep

Wareham Forest Tourist Park *(SY894912)*

▶▶▶▶▶

North Trigon BH20 7NZ

☎ 01929 551393 📄 01929 558321

e-mail: holiday@warehamforest.co.uk

dir: *Telephone for directions*

PETS: Charges max £1.50 per night **Public areas** except buildings on leads disp bin **Exercise area on site** woodland walks **Facilities** washing facs walks info vet info **Restrictions** well behaved dogs only

Open all year rs Off-peak season limited services Last arrival 21.00hrs Last departure 11.00hrs

A woodland park within the tranquil Wareham Forest, with its many walks and proximity to Poole, Dorchester and the Purbeck coast. Two luxury blocks, with combined washbasin and toilets for total privacy, maintain a high standard of cleanliness. A heated outdoor swimming pool, off licence, shop and games room add to the pleasure of a stay on this top quality park. 55 acre site. 200 touring pitches. 70 hardstandings. 70 seasonal pitches. Tent pitches. Motorhome pitches.

Notes Couples & families only, no group bookings.

Birchwood Tourist Park *(SY896905)*

▶▶▶

Bere Rd, Coldharbour BH20 7PA

☎ 01929 554763 📄 01929 556635

dir: *From Poole (A351) or Dorchester (A352) on N side of railway line at Wareham, follow road signed Bere Regis (unclassified). 2nd tourist park after 2.25m*

PETS: Charges high season only £1 per night **Public areas** except paddling pool area & games field disp bin **Exercise area** Wareham Forest adjacent **Facilities** food food bowl water bowl dog chews cat treats scoop/disp bags leads walks info vet info **Other** prior notice required

Open 13 Dec-23 Nov rs 31 Oct-1 Mar shop/reception open for 2-3 hrs daily in winter Last arrival 21.00hrs Last departure 11.30hrs

Set in 50 acres of parkland located within Wareham Forest, this site offers direct access into ideal areas for walking, mountain biking, and horse and pony riding. The modern facilities are in two central locations and are very clean. There is a good security barrier system. 25 acre site. 175 touring pitches. 25 hardstandings. Tent pitches. Motorhome pitches.

Notes No generators, no groups on BH, no camp fires.

WAREHAM *continued*

East Creech Farm Campsite *(SY928827)*

▶ ▶ ▶

East Creech Farm, East Creech BH20 5AP
☎ 01929 480519 & 481312 📠 01929 480519
e-mail: east.creech@virgin.net
dir: *From Wareham on A351 S towards Swanage. On bypass at 3rd rdbt take Furzebrook/Blue Pool Rd exit, approx 2m site on right*

PETS: **Public areas** except children's play area & toilet facilities disp bin **Exercise area** surrounding area **Facilities** walks info vet info **Other** prior notice required working farm - dogs must be under strict control at all times **Resident Pets:** dogs, cats, cows, goats, horses, ducks, geese & chickens

Open Apr-Oct Last arrival 20.00hrs Last departure noon

A grassy park set in a peaceful location beneath the Purbeck Hills, with extensive views towards Poole and Brownsea Island. The park boasts a woodland play area, bright, clean toilet facilities, and a farm shop selling milk, eggs and bread. There are also three coarse fishing lakes teeming with fish. The park is close to the Norden Station on the Swanage to Norden steam railway, and is well located for visiting Corfe Castle, Swanage and the Purbeck coast. 4 acre site. 80 touring pitches. Tent pitches. Motorhome pitches.

Notes No camp fires. 🐾

Cromwell House

★★ 75% HOTEL

Lulworth Cove BH20 5RJ
☎ 01929 400253 & 400332 📠 01929 400566
e-mail: catriona@lulworthcove.co.uk
web: www.lulworthcove.co.uk
dir: *200yds beyond end of West Lulworth, left onto high slip road, hotel 100yds on left opposite beach car park*

PETS: **Bedrooms** (2 GF) unattended sign **Charges** £5 per night **Public areas** except dining room on leads **Grounds** disp bin **Exercise area** adjacent **Facilities** water bowl washing facs cage storage walks info vet info **On Request** fridge access torch towels **Resident Pet:** Douglas (Bearded Collie cross)

Built in 1881 by the Mayor of Weymouth, specifically as a guest house, this family-run hotel now provides visitors with an ideal

base for touring the area and for exploring the beaches and coast. The house enjoys spectacular views across the sea and countryside. Bedrooms, many with sea views, are comfortable and some have been specifically designed for family use.

Rooms 18 (1 annexe) (3 fmly) (2 GF) **S** £45-£65; **D** £90-£120 (incl. bkfst) **Facilities** ⅊ Access to Dorset coastal footpath & Jurassic Coast Wi-fi **Parking** 17 **Notes** LB Closed 22 Dec-3 Jan RS Xmas & New Year

Moonfleet Manor

★★★ 77% ◉◉ COUNTRY HOUSE HOTEL

Fleet DT3 4ED
☎ 01305 786948 📠 01305 774395
e-mail: info@moonfleetmanorhotel.co.uk
web: www.moonfleetmanor.com
dir: *A354 to Weymouth, right on B3157 to Bridport. At Chickerell left at mini rdbt to Fleet*

PETS: **Bedrooms** unattended **Public areas** except restaurant on leads **Grounds** on leads disp bin **Exercise area** 30mtrs **Facilities** scoop/disp bags washing facs walks info vet info **On Request** fridge access torch towels

This enchanting hideaway, where children are especially welcome, is peacefully located at the end of the village of Fleet and enjoys a wonderful sea-facing position. The hotel is furnished with style and panache, particularly in the sumptuous lounges, and many of the well-equipped bedrooms overlook Chesil Beach. Accomplished cuisine is served in the beautiful restaurant.

Rooms 36 (6 annexe) (26 fmly) **Facilities** STV FTV 🕙 supervised ⊗ 🏊 Squash Child facilities including nursery Xmas Child facilities **Services** Lift **Parking** 50

East Fleet Farm Touring Park *(SY640797)*

▶ ▶ ▶ ▶ ▶

Chickerell DT3 4DW
☎ 01305 785768
e-mail: enquiries@eastfleet.co.uk
dir: *On B3157 (Weymouth-Bridport road), 3m from Weymouth*

PETS: **Charges** peak season £1.50 per night **Public areas** except children's play area & shop disp bin **Exercise area on site** **Exercise area** nearby **Facilities** food food bowl water bowl dog chews cat treats scoop/disp bags leads walks info vet info **Other** prior notice required **Resident Pets:** George & Clem (donkeys)

Open 16 Mar-Oct Last arrival 22.00hrs Last departure 10.30hrs

Set on a working organic farm overlooking Fleet Lagoon and Chesil Beach, with a wide range of amenities and quality toilet facilities with family rooms in a Scandinavian log cabin. The friendly owners are welcoming and helpful, and their family bar serving meals and takeaway food is open from Easter, with glorious views from the patio area. There is also a good accessory shop. 21 acre site. 400 touring pitches. 50 hardstandings. Tent pitches. Motorhome pitches.

Bagwell Farm Touring Park (SY627816)

▶▶▶▶

Knights in the Bottom, Chickerell DT3 4EA
☎ 01305 782575 📠 01305 780554
e-mail: aa@bagwellfarm.co.uk
dir: 4m W of Weymouth on B3157 (Weymouth-Bridport), past Chickerell, turn left into site 500yds after Victoria Inn

PETS: Charges Public areas except washrooms & one eating area on leads Exercise area on site field available (dogs on leads) Facilities food food bowl water bowl dog chews scoop/disp bags leads walks info vet info Other prior notice required dogs must be kept on short leads (2mtrs max) & not left unattended

Open all year rs Winter bar closed Last arrival 21.00hrs Last departure 11.00hrs

An idyllically placed, terraced site on a hillside of a valley overlooking Chesil Beach. The park is well equipped with fully-serviced pitches, a mini-supermarket, children's play area, pets' corner and a bar and grill serving food in high season. 14 acre site. 320 touring pitches. 10 hardstandings. Tent pitches. Motorhome pitches.

Notes Families only.

WIMBORNE MINSTER   Map 3 SZ09

Les Bouviers Restaurant with Rooms

★★★★★ ◉◉ 🍴 RESTAURANT WITH ROOMS
Arrowsmith Rd, Canford Magna BH21 3BD
☎ 01202 889555 📠 01202 639428
e-mail: info@lesbouviers.co.uk
web: www.lesbouviers.co.uk
dir: A31 onto A349. In 0.6m turn left. In approx 1m right onto Arrowsmith Rd. Establishment approx 100yds on right

PETS: Bedrooms sign Charges £25 per stay Public areas except restaurant on leads Grounds on leads disp bin Exercise area 2 mins' walk Facilities food (pre-bookable) food bowl water bowl dog chews feeding mat cage storage walks info vet info On Request fridge access torch Other charge for damage Restrictions no breed of similar size, or larger than, a Great Dane

An excellent restaurant with rooms in a great location, set in five and a half acres of grounds. Food is a highlight of any stay here as is the friendly, attentive service. Chef patron James Coward's team turn out impressive cooking, which has been recognised with 2 AA Rosettes. Bedrooms are extremely well equipped and beds are supremely comfortable. Cream tea can be taken on the terrace.

Rooms 6 en suite (4 fmly) S £88-£183; D £94-£215 Facilities FTV tea/coffee Dinner available Direct Dial Cen ht Wi-fi Parking 50 Notes LB RS Sun eve restricted opening & restaurant closed

Wilksworth Farm Caravan Park (SU004018)

▶▶▶▶▶

Cranborne Rd BH21 4HW
☎ 01202 885467 📠 01202 885467
e-mail: rayandwendy@wilksworthfarmcaravanpark.co.uk
dir: 1m N of Wimborne on B3078

PETS: Charges £2 per night £14 per week Public areas except coffee shop, shop, pool & play area disp bin Exercise area on site dog exercise paddock & walk Facilities walks info vet info Other prior notice required Restrictions max 2 pets per pitch

Open Apr-Oct rs Oct no shop Last arrival 20.00hrs Last departure 11.00hrs

A popular and attractive park peacefully set in the grounds of a listed house in the heart of rural Dorset. The spacious site has much to offer visitors, including an excellent heated swimming pool, takeaway and café, plus a games room. The modern toilet facilities contain en suite rooms and good family rooms. 11 acre site. 85 touring pitches. 20 hardstandings. Tent pitches. Motorhome pitches. 77 statics.

Charris Camping & Caravan Park (SY992988)

▶▶▶

Candy's Ln, Corfe Mullen BH21 3EF
☎ 01202 885970
e-mail: bookings@charris.co.uk
dir: From E, exit Wimborne bypass (A31) W end. 300yds after Caravan Sales, follow brown sign. From W on A31, over A350 rdbt, take next turn after B3074, follow brown signs

PETS: Public areas except toilet & shop disp bin Exercise area 0.25m Facilities food bowl water bowl washing facs walks info vet info Other prior notice required Resident Pets: Spike (cat), 12 doves

Open all year Last arrival 21.00hrs Last departure 11.00hrs

A sheltered park of grassland lined with trees on the edge of the Stour Valley. The owners are friendly and welcoming, and they maintain the park facilities to a good standard. Barbecues are a popular occasional event. 3.5 acre site. 45 touring pitches. 12 hardstandings. Tent pitches. Motorhome pitches.

Notes Earliest arrival time 11.00hrs.

CO DURHAM

BARNARD CASTLE
Map 12 NZ01

The Morritt
★★★★ 78% HOTEL

Greta Bridge DL12 9SE
☎ 01833 627232 📄 01833 627392
e-mail: relax@themorritt.co.uk
web: www.themorritt.co.uk
dir: Exit A1(A1(M)) at Scotch Corner onto A66 W'bound towards Penrith. Greta Bridge 9m on left

PETS: Bedrooms Silver Courtyard rooms only **Charges** £10 per night **Public areas** except restaurants on leads **Grounds** on leads disp bin **Exercise area** surrounding countryside **Facilities** washing facs cage storage walks info vet info **On Request** fridge access torch towels **Stables** 5m **Other** charge for damage guests are requested to bring dog's own bed

Set off the main road at Greta Bridge, this 17th-century former coaching house provides comfortable public rooms full of character. The bar, with its interesting Dickensian mural, is very much focused on food, but in addition a fine dining is offered in the oak-panelled restaurant. Bedrooms come in individual styles and of varying sizes. The attentive service is noteworthy.

Rooms 27 (6 annexe) (3 fmly) (4 GF) **S** £85-£155; **D** £95-£200 (incl. bkfst) **Facilities** FTV Xmas New Year Wi-fi **Parking** 40 **Notes** LB

CONSETT
Map 12 NZ15

Best Western Derwent Manor
OXFORD
HOTELS & INNS

★★★ 75% HOTEL

Allensford DH8 9BB
☎ 01207 592000 📄 01207 502472
e-mail: reservations.derwentmanor@ohiml.com
web: www.oxfordhotelsandinns.com
dir: On A68

PETS: Bedrooms (26 GF) **Charges** £15 per night **Grounds** **Exercise area** surrounding countryside **Facilities** walks info vet info **On Request** torch **Other** charge for damage dogs accepted by prior arrangement only

This hotel, built in the style of a manor house, is set in open grounds overlooking the River Derwent. Spacious bedrooms, including a number of suites, are comfortably equipped. A popular wedding venue, there are also extensive conference facilities and an impressive leisure suite. The Grouse & Claret bar serves a wide range of drinks and light meals, and Guinevere's restaurant offers the fine dining option.

Rooms 48 (29 fmly) (26 GF) **S** £55-£125; **D** £70-£150 (incl. bkfst)* **Facilities** STV FTV 🏊 supervised Gym Xmas New Year Wi-fi **Services** Lift **Parking** 100 **Notes** LB

DARLINGTON
Map 8 NZ21

Headlam Hall
★★★★ 77% ⚜ HOTEL

Headlam, Gainford DL2 3HA
☎ 01325 730238 📄 01325 730790
e-mail: admin@headlamhall.co.uk
web: www.headlamhall.co.uk
dir: 2m N of A67 between Piercebridge & Gainford

PETS: Bedrooms (10 GF) unattended ground-floor mews rooms only **Grounds** on leads disp bin **Exercise area** village green (50yds) **Facilities** water bowl washing facs cage storage walks info vet info **On Request** fridge access torch **Stables Other** charge for damage **Restrictions** small & medium size dogs only (eg Terriers, Spaniels & Labradors) no Rottweilers, Dobermans, Alsatians or similar breeds **Resident Pets:** Freda, Harold, Perdie & Meg (dogs), Connor & Rupert (horses)

This impressive Jacobean hall lies in farmland north-east of Piercebridge and has its own 9-hole golf course. The main house retains many historical features, including flagstone floors and a pillared hall. Bedrooms are well proportioned and traditionally styled; a converted coach house contains the more modern rooms. There are extensive conference facilities, and the hotel is popular as a wedding venue. There is a stunning spa complex with a 14-metre pool, an outdoor hot spa, drench shower, sauna and steam room. There is also a gym with the latest cardio and resistance equipment, and five treatment rooms offering a range of therapies and beauty treatments.

Rooms 40 (22 annexe) (4 fmly) (10 GF) **S** £95-£130; **D** £120-£195 (incl. bkfst)* **Facilities** Spa STV FTV 🏊 ⅃ 9 ⛳ Putt green Fishing 🏋 Gym New Year Wi-fi **Services** Lift **Parking** 80 **Notes** LB Closed 24-26 Dec

The Blackwell Grange Hotel

★★★ 79% HOTEL

Blackwell Grange DL3 8QH
☎ 0870 609 6121 & 01325 509955 📠 01325 380899
e-mail: blackwell.grange@forestdale.com
web: www.blackwellgrangehotel.com
dir: *On A167, 1.5m from central ring road*

PETS: Bedrooms (36 GF) **Charges** £7.50 per night **Public areas** except restaurant **Other** please phone for further details of pet facilities

This beautiful 17th-century mansion is peacefully situated in nine acres of its own grounds yet is convenient for the motorway network. The pick of the bedrooms are in a courtyard building or the impressive feature rooms in the original house. The Havelock Restaurant offers a range of traditional and continental menus.

Rooms 108 (11 annexe) (3 fmly) (36 GF) **Facilities** FTV Ⓢ Gym Beauty room Xmas New Year Wi-fi **Services** Lift **Parking** 250 **Notes** LB

Durham Marriott Hotel, Royal County

★★★★ 78% HOTEL

Old Elvet DH1 3JN
☎ 0191 386 6821 📠 0191 386 0704
e-mail: mhrs.xvudm.frontdesk@marriotthotels.com
web: www.durhammarriottroyalcounty.co.uk
dir: *From A1(M) junct 62, then A690 to Durham, over 1st rdbt, left at 2nd rdbt left at lights, hotel on left*

PETS: Bedrooms (15 GF) **Public areas** except restaurant & bar on leads **Exercise area** 100mtrs **Facilities** vet info **Other** charge for damage **Restrictions** small dogs only

In a wonderful position on the banks of the River Wear, the hotel's central location makes it ideal for visiting the attractions of this historic city. The building was developed from a series of Jacobean town houses. The bedrooms are tastefully styled. Eating options include the County Restaurant, for formal dining, and the Cruz Restaurant.

Rooms 150 (8 annexe) (10 fmly) (15 GF) (4 smoking) **S** £99-£140; **D** £99-£140 (incl. bkfst)* **Facilities** STV FTV Ⓢ supervised Gym Turkish steam room Plunge pool Sanarium Tropical fun shower Wi-fi **Services** Lift **Parking** 76 **Notes** LB

The Teesdale Hotel

★★ 65% HOTEL

Market Place DL12 0QG
☎ 01833 640264 📠 01833 640651
e-mail: enquiries@teesdalehotel.co.uk
web: www.teesdalehotel.co.uk
dir: *From Barnard Castle take B6278, follow signs for Middleton-in-Teesdale & Highforce. Hotel in town centre*

PETS: Bedrooms certain bedrooms only **Charges** £5 per night **Public areas** bar only on leads **Exercise area** 50mtrs **Facilities** walks info vet info **Restrictions** small & medium size dogs only

Located in the heart of the popular village, this family-run hotel offers a relaxed and friendly atmosphere. Bedrooms and bathrooms are well equipped and offer a good standard of quality and comfort. Public areas include a residents' lounge on the first floor, a spacious restaurant and a lounge bar which is popular with locals.

Rooms 14 (1 fmly) **S** £30-£45; **D** £55-£80 (incl. bkfst)* **Facilities** Wi-fi **Parking** 20 **Notes** LB

Barceló

Barceló Redworth Hall Hotel

★★★★ 79% ⊚ COUNTRY HOUSE HOTEL

DL5 6NL
☎ 01388 770600 📠 01388 770654
e-mail: redworthhall@barcelo-hotels.co.uk
web: www.barcelo-hotels.co.uk
dir: *From A1(M) junct 58/A68 signed Corbridge. Follow hotel signs*

PETS: Bedrooms Charges £15 per stay **Public areas** only for access to bedrooms on leads **Grounds** disp bin **Facilities** food (pre-bookable) food bowl water bowl bedding feeding mat dog grooming walks info vet info **On Request** fridge access **Other** charge for damage

This imposing Georgian building includes a health club with state-of-the-art equipment and impressive conference facilities making this hotel a popular destination for business travellers. There are several spacious lounges to relax in along with the Conservatory Restaurant. Bedrooms are very comfortable and well equipped.

Rooms 143 (12 fmly) **Facilities** STV Ⓢ ⌇ ⌇ Gym Bodysense Health & Leisure Club ♫ Xmas New Year Wi-fi **Services** Lift **Parking** 300

ENGLAND

Rose & Crown

★★★ **86%** ◉◉ HOTEL

DL12 9EB

☎ 01833 650213   🖷 01833 650828

e-mail: hotel@rose-and-crown.co.uk

web: www.rose-and-crown.co.uk

dir: *6m NW from Barnard Castle on B6277*

PETS: Bedrooms (5 GF) **Charges** £5 per night **Public areas** except restaurant/brasserie on leads **Facilities** walks info vet info **On Request** fridge access torch **Stables** 0.5m **Other** charge for damage

This charming 18th-century country inn is located in the heart of the village, overlooking fine dale scenery. The attractively furnished bedrooms, including suites, are split between the main house and the rear courtyard. Guests might like to have a drink in the cosy bar with its log fire, after returning from a long walk. Good local produce features extensively on the menus that can be enjoyed in the oak-panelled restaurant, or in the brasserie and bar. Service is both friendly and attentive.

Rooms 12 (5 annexe) (1 fmly) (5 GF) **S** £95-£125; **D** £135-£210 (incl. bkfst)* **Facilities** STV New Year Wi-fi **Parking** 20 **Notes** LB Closed 24-26 Dec

The Manor House Hotel

★★★ **80%** HOTEL

The Green DL14 9HW

☎ 01388 834834   🖷 01388 833566

e-mail: enquiries@manorhousehotelcountydurham.co.uk

web: www.manorhousehotelcountydurham.co.uk

dir: *A1(M) junct 58, A68 to West Auckland. At T-junct left, hotel 150yds on right*

PETS: Bedrooms unattended courtyard bedrooms only **Public areas** only in public bar on leads **Grounds** on leads disp bin **Exercise area** 100mtrs **Facilities** water bowl bedding cage storage walks info vet info **On Request** fridge access

This historic manor house, dating back to the 14th century, is full of character. Welcoming log fires await guests on cooler evenings. Comfortable bedrooms are individual in style, tastefully furnished and well equipped. The brasserie and Juniper's restaurant both offer an interesting selection of freshly prepared dishes. Well-equipped leisure facilities are available.

Rooms 35 (11 annexe) (6 fmly) (3 GF) **S** £55-£75; **D** £70-£140 (incl. bkfst)* **Facilities** FTV ⊗ Gym Steam room Sauna Xmas New Year Wi-fi **Parking** 150 **Notes** LB

Days Inn Bishop's Stortford - M11

BUDGET HOTEL

CM23 5QZ

☎ 01279 656477   🖷 01279 656590

e-mail: birchanger.hotel@welcomebreak.co.uk

web: www.welcomebreak.co.uk

dir: *M11 junct 8*

PETS: Bedrooms Charges £10 deposit on arrival (refunded if no damage) **Public areas** on leads **Grounds** on leads **Exercise area** grass area **On Request** towels **Other** charge for damage

This modern building offers accommodation in smart, spacious and well-equipped bedrooms, suitable for families and business travellers, and all with en suite bathrooms. Continental breakfast is available and other refreshments may be taken at the nearby family restaurant.

Rooms 60 (57 fmly) (10 smoking) **S** £49.95-£69.95; **D** £59.95-£79.95

Riverside Village Holiday Park *(TQ929951)*

▶▶▶

Creeksea Ferry Rd, Wallasea Island SS4 2EY

☎ 01702 258297   🖷 01702 258555

e-mail: riversidevillage@tiscali.co.uk

dir: *M25 junct 29, A127, towards Southend-on-Sea. Take B1013 towards Rochford. Follow signs for Wallasea Island & Baltic Wharf*

PETS: Charges £2 per night £12 per week **Public areas** except children's play area on leads disp bin **Exercise area on site** long lakeside 'run', designated dog walk **Facilities** food washing facs walks info vet info **Other** prior notice required free disposal bags available **Restrictions** dogs not permitted in tents **Resident Pets:** Amber (Red Setter), Mazsie (Terrier cross)

Open Mar-Oct

Next to a nature reserve beside the River Crouch, this holiday park is surrounded by wetlands but only eight miles from Southend. A modern toilet block with disabled facilities is provided for tourers and there's a handsome reception area. Several restaurants and pubs are within a short distance. 25 acre site. 60 touring pitches. Tent pitches. Motorhome pitches. 159 statics.

GREAT CHESTERFORD
Map 5 TL54

The Crown House
★★★ 72% HOTEL

CB10 1NY
☎ 01799 530515 📠 01799 530683
e-mail: reservations@crownhousehotel.com
web: www.crownhousehotel.com
dir: *From N: M11 at junct 9 (from S junct 10) follow signs for Saffron Walden, then Great Chesterford (B1383)*

PETS: Bedrooms (5 GF) unattended **Charges** £5 per night **Public areas** lounge only on leads **Grounds** on leads disp bin **Facilities** washing facs walks info vet info **On Request** fridge access torch towels **Other** charge for damage

This Georgian coaching inn, situated in a peaceful village close to the M11, has been sympathetically restored and retains much original character. The bedrooms are well equipped and individually decorated; some rooms have delightful four-poster beds. Public rooms include an attractive lounge bar, an elegant oak-panelled restaurant and an airy conservatory.

Rooms 18 (10 annexe) (1 fmly) (5 GF) **S** £69.50-£79.50; **D** £99.50-£145 (incl. bkfst)* **Facilities** FTV New Year Wi-fi **Parking** 30 **Notes** LB Closed 27-30 Dec

MERSEA ISLAND
Map 5 TM01

Waldegraves Holiday Park *(TM033133)*
CO5 8SE
☎ 01206 382898 📠 01206 385359
e-mail: holidays@waldegraves.co.uk
dir: *A12 junct 26, B1025 to Mersea Island across The Strood. Left to East Mersea, 2nd turn on right, follow tourist signs to site*

PETS: Charges dog £2 per night **Public areas** except restaurant, shop, clubhouse & pool on leads disp bin **Exercise area on site** field & beach **Exercise area** 3m **Facilities** food food bowl water bowl dog chews cat treats litter tray walks info vet info **Other** prior notice required disposal bags available **Resident Pets:** Daisy (Boxer), Charley (Jack Russell)

Open Mar-Nov rs Mar-Jun & Sep-Nov (excl Bank Holidays & school half terms) pool, shop & clubhouse reduced opening hrs low season, pool open May-Sep (weather permitting) Last arrival 22.00hrs Last departure 15.00hrs

A spacious and pleasant site, located between farmland and its own private beach on the Blackwater Estuary. Facilities include two freshwater fishing lakes, heated swimming pool, club, amusements, café and golf, and there is generally good provision for families. 25 acre site. 60 touring pitches. 30 seasonal pitches. Tent pitches. Motorhome pitches. 250 statics.

Notes No large groups or groups of under 21s.

ST LAWRENCE
Map 5 TL90

Waterside St Lawrence Bay *(TL953056)*
 Main Rd CM0 7LY
☎ 0871 664 9794
e-mail: waterside@park-resorts.com
dir: *A12 towards Chelmsford, A414 signed Maldon. Follow B1010 & signs to Latchingdon, then signs for Mayland/Steeple/ St Lawrence. Left towards St Lawrence. Site on right*

PETS: Charges phone for charges **Public areas** except complex & swimming pool disp bin **Exercise area on site** dog walks **Exercise area** public footpaths **Facilities** food food bowl water bowl scoop/disp bags walks info vet info **Other** prior notice required **Restrictions** no dangerous dogs (see page 7)

Open Apr-Oct rs Wknds Last arrival 22.00hrs Last departure 10.00hrs

Waterside occupies a scenic location overlooking the Blackwater estuary. In addition to the range of on-site leisure facilities there are opportunities for beautiful coastal walks and visits to the attractions of Southend. Tents are welcome on this expansive site, which has some touring pitches with electricity and good toilet facilities. The park has its own boat storage and slipway onto the Blackwater. 72 touring pitches. Tent pitches. Motorhome pitches. 271 statics.

SOUTHEND-ON-SEA
Map 5 TQ88

Terrace Guest House
★★★ GUEST ACCOMMODATION

8 Royal Ter SS1 1DY
☎ 01702 348143 📠 01702 348143
e-mail: info@terraceguesthouse.co.uk
dir: *From pier up Pier Hill onto Royal Terrace*

PETS: Bedrooms Charges £10 per night **Public areas** with other guests' agreement on leads **Exercise area** adjacent **Facilities** cage storage walks info vet info **On Request** fridge access torch towels **Other** charge for damage **Restrictions** no dangerous dogs (see page 7) **Resident Pet:** Victor (cat)

Set on a terrace above the Western Esplanade, this comfortable guest house has an informal atmosphere. There is a cosy bar, and an elegant sitting room and breakfast room. The spacious, well-planned bedrooms include four en suite front and rear-facing rooms, and several front-facing rooms that share two bathrooms.

Rooms 9 rms (6 en suite) (2 fmly) **S** £39-£45; **D** £59-£65 **Facilities** FTV TVL tea/coffee Cen ht Wi-fi **Notes** LB Closed 21 Dec-4 Jan

GLOUCESTERSHIRE

ALDERTON   Map 3 SP03

Tally Ho Bed & Breakfast

★★★★ BED AND BREAKFAST

20 Beckford Rd GL20 8NL

☎ 01242 621482 & 07966 593169

e-mail: tallyhobb@aol.com

dir: M5 junct 9, A46 signed Evesham, through Ashchurch. Take B4077 signed Stow-on-the-Wold & Alderton. Left in 1.5m opposite garage signed Alderton

PETS: Bedrooms (2 GF) ground-floor bedrooms only **Exercise area** 200yds **Facilities** walks info vet info **Other** charge for damage **Resident Pets:** Springer Spaniels, Fox Terriers

Convenient for the M5, this friendly establishment stands in a delightful quiet village. Bedrooms, including two on the ground floor, offer modern comforts and attractive co-ordinated furnishings. Breakfast is served in the stylish dining room, and for dinner, the village pub is just a stroll away.

Rooms 3 en suite (1 fmly) (2 GF) **S** £35-£45; **D** £65-£70 **Facilities** FTV tea/coffee Cen ht Wi-fi **Parking** 3 **Notes** LB

ALVESTON   Map 3 ST68

Alveston House Hotel

★★★ 81% @ HOTEL

Davids Ln, Alveston BS35 2LA

☎ 01454 415050   01454 415425

e-mail: info@alvestonhousehotel.co.uk

web: www.alvestonhousehotel.co.uk

dir: M5 junct 14 from N or junct 16 from S, on A38

PETS: Bedrooms (6 GF) **Public areas** except restaurant on leads **Grounds Exercise area** 0.5m **Facilities** water bowl cage storage walks info vet info **On Request** fridge access torch towels **Stables** 5m **Other** charge for damage

In a quiet area with easy access to the city and a short drive from both the M4 and M5, this smartly presented hotel provides an impressive combination of good service, friendly hospitality and a relaxed atmosphere. The comfortable bedrooms are well equipped for both business and leisure guests. The restaurant offers carefully prepared fresh food, and the pleasant bar and conservatory area is perfect for enjoying a pre-dinner drink.

Rooms 30 (1 fmly) (6 GF) **S** £80-£95; **D** £110-£120 (incl. bkfst)* **Facilities** FTV Beauty treatments Xmas New Year Wi-fi **Parking** 75 **Notes** LB

BERKELEY   Map 3 ST69

Hogsdown Farm Caravan & Camping Park

(ST710974)

►►►

Hogsdown Farm, Lower Wick GL11 6DD

☎ 01453 810224

dir: M5 junct 14 (Falfield), take A38 towards Gloucester, turn right for site

PETS: Charges dog £2 per night **Public areas** except children's play area, wash rooms & toilet/shower blocks **Exercise area** adjacent **Facilities** food bowl water bowl washing facs walks info vet info **Other** prior notice required disposal bags available **Restrictions** no dangerous dogs (see page 7)

Open all year Last arrival 21.00hrs Last departure 16.00hrs

A pleasant site with good toilet facilities, located between Bristol and Gloucester. It is well positioned for visiting Berkeley Castle and the Cotswolds, and makes an excellent overnight stop when travelling to or from the West Country. 5 acre site. 45 touring pitches. 12 hardstandings. Tent pitches. Motorhome pitches.

Notes No skateboards or bicycles. 🖂

BIBURY   Map 4 SP10

Bibury Court

★★★ 85% @@ COUNTRY HOUSE HOTEL

GL7 5NT

☎ 01285 740337 & 741171   01285 740660

e-mail: info@biburycourt.com

web: www.biburycourt.com

dir: On B4425, 6m N of Cirencester (A4179). 8m S of Burford (A40), entrance by River Coln

PETS: Bedrooms certain bedrooms only **Charges** £10 per night **Public areas** except dining room, bar & conservatory on leads **Grounds** disp bin **Facilities** food (pre-bookable) food bowl water bowl bedding dog chews walks info vet info **On Request** fridge access torch **Other** charge for damage max 2 dogs per guest room; phone to check on pet policy

Dating back to Tudor times, this elegant manor is the perfect antidote to the hustle and bustle of the modern world. Public areas have abundant charm and character. Bedrooms are spacious and offer traditional quality with modern comforts. A choice of interesting dishes is available in the conservatory at lunchtime, whereas dinner is served in the more formal restaurant. Staff are friendly and helpful.

Rooms 18 (3 fmly) (1 GF) **S** £150-£410; **D** £150-£425 (incl. bkfst)* **Facilities** FTV Fishing Xmas New Year Wi-fi **Parking** 40 **Notes** LB

Swan

Cotswold
Inns & Hotels

★★★ 83% ⊛ HOTEL

GL7 5NW

☎ 01285 740695 📄 01285 740473

e-mail: info@swanhotel.co.uk

web: www.cotswold-inns-hotels.co.uk/swan

dir: *9m S of Burford A40 onto B4425. 6m N of Cirencester A4179 onto B4425*

PETS: Bedrooms unattended certain bedrooms only **Charges** £15 per night **Public areas** except eating areas on leads **Exercise area** surrounding fields & paths **Facilities** walks info vet info **On Request** fridge access torch towels **Other** charge for damage

This hotel, built in the 17th century as a coaching inn, is set in peaceful and picturesque surroundings. It provides well-equipped and smartly presented accommodation, including four luxury cottage suites set just outside the main hotel. The elegant public areas are comfortable and have feature fireplaces. There is a choice of dining options to suit all tastes.

Rooms 22 (4 annexe) (1 fmly) **S** £140-£200; **D** £160-£200 (incl. bkfst)* **Facilities** Fishing Xmas New Year Wi-fi **Services** Lift **Parking** 22 **Notes** LB

BOURTON-ON-THE-WATER   Map 4 SP12

Chester House

★★★ 72% SMALL HOTEL

Victoria St GL54 2BU

☎ 01451 820286 📄 01451 820471

e-mail: info@chesterhousehotel.com

dir: *On A429 between Northleach & Stow-on-the-Wold*

PETS: Bedrooms (8 GF) unattended **Public areas** except main house & lounge/bar on leads **Grounds** on leads **Exercise area** 300mtrs **Facilities** cage storage walks info vet info **On Request** fridge access **Other** charge for damage dogs are accepted by prior arrangement only

This hotel occupies a secluded but central location in this delightful Cotswold village. Bedrooms, some at ground floor level, are situated in the main house and adjoining coach house. The public areas are stylish, light and airy. Breakfast is taken in the main building whereas dinner is served in the attractive restaurant just a few yards away.

Rooms 22 (10 annexe) (3 fmly) (8 GF) **S** £80-£125; **D** £90-£125 (incl. bkfst)* **Facilities** FTV Beauty therapist New Year Wi-fi **Parking** 18 **Notes** Closed 7 Jan-1 Feb

CHELTENHAM   Map 3 SO92

Hotel du Vin Cheltenham

Hotel du Vin
&
Bistro

★★★★ 80% ⊛ HOTEL

Parabola Rd GL50 3AQ

☎ 01242 588450 📄 01242 588455

e-mail: info@cheltenham.hotelduvin.com

web: www.hotelduvin.com

dir: *M5 junct 11, follow signs for city centre. At rdbt opposite Morgan Estate Agents take 2nd left, 200mtrs to Parabola Rd*

PETS: Bedrooms (5 GF) unattended **Public areas** except bistro on leads **Exercise area** 10 mins' walk **Facilities** walks info **Other** bowl & basket available at a charge

This hotel, in the Montpellier area of the town, has spacious public areas that are packed with stylish features. The pewter-topped bar has comfortable seating and the spacious restaurant has the Hotel du Vin trademark design; alfresco dining is possible on the extensive terrace area. Bedrooms are very comfortable, with Egyptian linen, deep baths and power showers. The spa is the ideal place to relax and unwind. Although parking is limited, it is a definite bonus. Service is friendly and attentive.

Rooms 49 (2 fmly) (5 GF) **Facilities** Spa STV Wi-fi **Services** Lift Air con **Parking** 26

The Greenway Spa Hotel

von Essen hotels
A PRIVATE COLLECTION
www.vonessenhotels.com

★★★ 86% ⊛⊛ COUNTRY HOUSE HOTEL

Shurdington GL51 4UG

☎ 01242 862352 📄 01242 862780

e-mail: info@thegreenway.co.uk

web: www.thegreenway.co.uk

dir: *From Cheltenham centre 2.5m S on A46*

PETS: Bedrooms unattended **Charges** £5 per night **Grounds** **Exercise area** adjacent countryside **Facilities** food bowl water bowl washing facs walks info vet info **On Request** fridge access torch **Other** charge for damage

This hotel, with a wealth of history, is peacefully located in a delightful setting close within easy reach of the many attractions of the Cotswolds and also the M5. The Manor House bedrooms are luxuriously appointed - traditional in style yet with plasma TVs and internet access. The tranquil Coach House rooms, in the converted stable block, have direct access to the beautiful grounds. The attractive dining room overlooks the sunken garden and is the venue for excellent food, proudly served by dedicated and attentive staff. The Elan Spa opened in 2011.

Rooms 17 (6 annexe) (4 fmly) **Facilities** Spa FTV ⛳ Clay pigeon shooting Horse riding Mountain biking Archery Xmas New Year Wi-fi **Parking** 50

CHELTENHAM *continued*

Charlton Kings

★★★ 74% SMALL HOTEL

London Rd, Charlton Kings GL52 6UU
☎ 01242 231061 📠 01242 241900
e-mail: enquiries@charltonkingshotel.co.uk
dir: *From E (London or Oxford) on A40, hotel 1st building on left on entering Cheltenham. From M5 towards town centre follow Oxford/A40 signs. Through town, hotel last building on right on exiting Cheltenham*

PETS: Bedrooms (3 GF) unattended **Public areas** except restaurant **Grounds** disp bin **Exercise area** 100yds **Facilities** walks info vet info **On Request** fridge access **Resident Pet:** Charlie (Collie cross)

Personally run by the resident proprietors, the relatively small size of this hotel enables a good deal of individual guest care and attention. Bedrooms are very well decorated and furnished and include some welcome extras. Breakfast and dinner, served in the comfortable conservatory-style restaurant, offer a good selection of carefully prepared ingredients. There's a pleasant garden and rear car park.

Rooms 14 (3 GF) **Facilities** STV FTV Wi-fi **Parking** 15

Cotswold Grange

★★ 78% HOTEL

Pittville Circus Rd GL52 2QH
☎ 01242 515119 📠 01242 241537
e-mail: info@cotswoldgrange.co.uk
dir: *From town centre, follow Prestbury signs. Right at 1st rdbt, next rdbt straight over, hotel 100yds on left*

PETS: Bedrooms Charges £5 per night **Public areas** except restaurant on leads **Grounds Exercise area** park nearby **Facilities** walks info vet info **On Request** fridge access torch **Other** charge for damage **Restrictions** no very large dogs; no dangerous dogs (see page 7)

A delightful building located in a quieter, mainly residential area of Cheltenham, near Pitville Park and just a short walk to the town centre. The hotel offers a relaxed and welcoming atmosphere; there are many useful extras such as Wi-fi in the bedrooms. A range of carefully cooked and presented dishes is served in the comfortable restaurant.

Rooms 24 (2 fmly) **Facilities** Wi-fi **Parking** 20 **Notes** Closed 25 Dec-1 Jan

Hope Orchard

★★★★ GUEST ACCOMMODATION

Gloucester Rd, Staverton GL51 0TF
☎ 01452 855556 📠 01452 530037
e-mail: info@hopeorchard.com
web: www.hopeorchard.com
dir: *A40 onto B4063 at Arlecourt rdbt, Hope Orchard 1.25m on right*

PETS: Bedrooms (8 GF) unattended **Public areas** except in breakfast room **Grounds** disp bin **Exercise area** nearby **Facilities** food bowl water bowl scoop/disp bags washing facs cage storage walks info vet info **On Request** fridge access torch towels **Other** charge for damage local kennel can provide day sitting service **Resident Pets:** Toby (Staffordshire Bull Terrier), Jessie, Jasper & Louis (cats)

Situated midway between Gloucester and Cheltenham, Hope Orchard is a good base for exploring the area. The comfortable bedrooms are next to the main house, and all are on the ground floor and have their own separate entrances. There is a large garden, and ample off-road parking is available.

Rooms 8 en suite (8 GF) **Facilities** FTV tea/coffee Direct Dial Cen ht Wi-fi **Parking** 10

White Lodge

★★★★ GUEST ACCOMMODATION

Hatherley Ln GL51 6SH
☎ 01242 242347 📠 01242 242347
e-mail: pamela@whitelodgebandb.co.uk
dir: *M5 junct 11, A40 to Cheltenham, 1st rdbt 4th exit Hatherley Ln, White Lodge 1st on right*

PETS: Bedrooms (1 GF) unattended **Charges** £5 per night **Public areas** except dining room **Grounds** disp bin **Exercise area** nearby **Facilities** pet sitting washing facs cage storage walks info vet info **On Request** fridge access torch towels

Built around 1900, this well cared for, smart and friendly establishment is very convenient for access to the M5. Bedrooms, of varying sizes, offer quality and many extra facilities, including fridges and Wi-fi. The very comfortable dining room, where breakfast is served around a grand table, looks out across the pleasant and extensive gardens.

Rooms 4 en suite (1 GF) **S** £42-£45; **D** £60-£65 **Facilities** FTV tea/coffee Cen ht Wi-fi **Parking** 6 **Notes** 🐾

Three Ways House

★★★ 82% ⓦ HOTEL

Mickleton GL55 6SB
☎ 01386 438429 📠 01386 438118
e-mail: reception@puddingclub.com
web: www.threewayshousehotel.com
dir: In Mickleton centre, on B4632 (Stratford-upon-Avon to Broadway road)

PETS: Bedrooms (14 GF) unattended Charges £5 per night
Public areas except restaurant on leads Grounds on leads
Exercise area 100mtrs Facilities water bowl walks info vet info
On Request fridge access Restrictions well behaved dogs only

Built in 1870, this charming hotel has welcomed guests for over 100 years and is home to the world famous Pudding Club, formed in 1985 to promote traditional English puddings. Individuality is a hallmark here, as reflected in a number of the bedrooms that have been designed around to a pudding theme. Public areas are stylish and include the air-conditioned restaurant, lounges and meeting rooms.

Rooms 48 (7 fmly) (14 GF) S £85-£90; D £145-£250 (incl. bkfst)*
Facilities ♪ Xmas New Year Wi-fi Services Lift Parking 37
Notes LB

Noel Arms

★★★ 78% HOTEL

High St GL55 6AT
☎ 01386 840317 📠 01386 841136
e-mail: reception@noelarmshotel.com
web: www.noelarmshotel.com
dir: Off A44 onto B4081 to Chipping Campden, 1st right down hill into town. Hotel on right

PETS: Bedrooms (8 GF) unattended Charges £15 per stay
Public areas except restaurant on leads Exercise area 0.25m
Facilities vet info On Request fridge access Stables approx 5m
Restrictions small & medium size dogs preferred

This historic 14th-century hotel has a wealth of character and charm, and retains some of its original features. Bedrooms are very individual in style, and all have high levels of comfort and interesting interior design. Such distinctiveness is also evident throughout the public areas, which include the popular bar, conservatory lounge and attractive restaurant.

Rooms 28 (1 fmly) (8 GF) Facilities Use of spa at sister hotel (charged) Xmas New Year Wi-fi Parking 28 Notes LB

Staddlestones

★★★★★ BED AND BREAKFAST

7 Aston Rd GL55 6HR
☎ 01386 849288
e-mail: info@staddle-stones.com
web: www.staddle-stones.com
dir: From Chipping Campden take B4081 signed Mickleton, 200mtrs. House on right opposite gravel lane

PETS: Bedrooms garden bedroom only Charges £5 per night
Public areas except breakfast room & main house on leads
Grounds on leads disp bin Exercise area track adjacent
Facilities walks info vet info On Request fridge access torch
towels Other charge for damage Restrictions no very large dogs
Resident Pet: Phoebe (Border Collie)

A warm welcome can be expected from host Pauline Kirton at this delightful property, situated just a short walk from the Cotswold village of Chipping Campden; this makes an ideal base for walking, cycling, golf or just relaxing. There are three bedrooms offering quality and comfort plus some thoughtful extras. A hearty breakfast is served in the dining room around the communal table, and there's a good choice of mostly organic produce sourced from local farms.

Rooms 2 en suite 1 annexe en suite (1 fmly); D £65-£85
Facilities FTV tea/coffee Cen ht Wi-fi Parking 6 Notes No
Children 12yrs ⓦ

Best Western Stratton House

★★★ 77% HOTEL

Gloucester Rd GL7 2LE
☎ 01285 651761 📠 01285 640024
e-mail: stratton.house@forestdale.com
web: www.strattonhousehotel.co.uk
dir: M4 junct 15, A419 to Cirencester. Hotel on left on A417 or M5 junct 11 to Cheltenham onto B4070 to A417. Hotel on right

PETS: Bedrooms (9 GF) unattended Charges £7.50 per night
Public areas except restaurant

This attractive 17th-century manor house is quietly situated about half a mile from the town centre. Bedrooms are well presented, and spacious, stylish premier rooms are available. The comfortable drawing rooms and restaurant have views over well-tended gardens - the perfect place to enjoy pre-dinner drinks on a summer evening.

Rooms 39 (9 GF) Facilities FTV Xmas New Year Wi-fi Parking 100
Notes LB

CIRENCESTER *continued*

The Crown of Crucis

★★★ **73%** HOTEL

Ampney Crucis GL7 5RS

☎ 01285 851806   📠 01285 851735

e-mail: reception@thecrownofcrucis.co.uk

web: www.thecrownofcrucis.co.uk

dir: *A417 to Fairford, hotel 2.5m on left*

PETS: Bedrooms (13 GF) unattended ground-floor bedrooms only
Charges £6 per night **Public areas** in bar only **Grounds** disp bin
Exercise area over bridge (adjacent) **Facilities** walks info vet
info **On Request** fridge access torch **Stables** stable in village,
please phone for details **Other** charge for damage

This delightful hotel consists of two buildings; one a 16th-century
coaching inn, which houses the bar and restaurant, and a more
modern bedroom block which surrounds a courtyard. Rooms are
attractively appointed and offer modern facilities; the restaurant
serves a range of imaginative dishes.

Rooms 25 (2 fmly) (13 GF) (4 smoking) **D** £80–£105 (incl. bkfst)*
Facilities FTV Wi-fi **Parking** 82 **Notes** LB RS 25-26 Dec

Wyndham Arms

★★★ **68%** ◉ HOTEL

GL16 8JT

☎ 01594 833666   📠 01594 836450

e-mail: nigel@thewyndhamhotel.co.uk

dir: *Off B4228, in village centre on B4231*

PETS: Bedrooms (6 GF) unattended certain bedrooms only
Charges £5 per night **Public areas** except restaurant on
leads **Grounds** disp bin **Exercise area** field at top of car park
Exercise area 0.25m **Facilities** dog chews scoop/disp bags
washing facs cage storage walks info vet info **On Request**
fridge access torch towels **Other** charge for damage **Resident
Pets:** Ruby & Poppy (Irish Red Setters)

The history of this charming village inn can be traced back over
600 years. It has exposed stone walls, original beams and an
impressive inglenook fireplace in the friendly bar. Most bedrooms
are in a modern extension, whilst the other rooms, in the main
house, are more traditional in style. A range of dishes is offered in
the bar or restaurant.

Rooms 18 (12 annexe) (3 fmly) (6 GF) **S** £45–£55; **D** £75–£175
(incl. bkfst) **Facilities** FTV Xmas Wi-fi **Parking** 52 **Notes** LB

Dryslade Farm *(SO581147)*

★★★★ FARMHOUSE

English Bicknor GL16 7PA

☎ 01594 860259   📠 01594 860259 Mrs D Gwilliam

e-mail: daphne@drysladefarm.co.uk

web: www.drysladefarm.co.uk

dir: *3m N of Coleford. Off A4136 onto B4432, right towards
English Bicknor, farm 1m*

PETS: Bedrooms (1 GF) ground-floor bedrooms only
Public areas except conservatory at breakfast **Grounds** disp
bin **Exercise area** on farm **Facilities** scoop/disp bags leads
washing facs cage storage walks info vet info **On Request**
fridge access torch towels **Other** charge for damage **Resident
Pets:** Milly (Cocker Spaniel), Jasmin (Cavalier King Charles
Spaniel)

Visitors are warmly welcomed at this 184-acre working farm,
which dates from 1780 and has been in the same family for
almost 100 years. The en suite bedrooms are attractively
furnished in natural pine and are well equipped. The lounge leads
onto a conservatory where hearty breakfasts are served.

Rooms 3 en suite (1 GF); **D** £66–£72 **Facilities** FTV TVL tea/coffee
Cen ht Wi-fi **Parking** 6 **Notes** LB 🏵 184 acres beef

The Rock B&B

★★★★ GUEST ACCOMMODATION

GL16 7NY

☎ 01594 837893

e-mail: chris@stayattherock.com

web: www.stayattherock.com

dir: *A40 at Monmouth onto A4136, in 5m left at Five Acres
into Park Rd. At Christchurch right & immediately left towards
Symonds Yat Rock. 0.75m S of Symonds Yat Rock*

PETS: Bedrooms (5 GF) sign certain bedrooms only **Charges**
£10 per stay **Grounds** on leads disp bin **Exercise area** Forest
of Dean adjacent **Facilities** scoop/disp bags washing facs
cage storage walks info vet info **On Request** fridge access
torch towels **Other** some pet facilities available on request
Restrictions well behaved & quiet dogs only

The Rock offers stylish modern accommodation and is located
on the outskirts of Coleford, near the famous Symonds Yat Rock.
Bedrooms are attractively presented and very comfortable, with
the new garden rooms making the most of the spectacular views
over the Wye Valley. Very popular with walkers, the Rock also
caters well for business guests. Breakfasts are served in the
spacious dining room overlooking the garden.

Rooms 7 annexe en suite (5 GF) **S** £40–£45; **D** £50–£95
Facilities FTV tea/coffee Cen ht Lift Wi-fi **Parking** 20 **Notes** LB No
Children 12yrs

CORSE LAWN
Map 3 SO83

Corse Lawn House
★★★ ◉◉ HOTEL

GL19 4LZ
☎ 01452 780771 📠 01452 780840
e-mail: enquiries@corselawn.com
web: www.corselawn.com
dir: On B4211 5m SW of Tewkesbury

PETS: Bedrooms (5 GF) unattended sign Public areas except restaurant on leads Grounds disp bin Exercise area 100yds Facilities food (pre-bookable) washing facs walks info vet info On Request fridge access torch Resident Pets: Sugar & Spice (Black Labradors), Donna & Gigi (horses)

This gracious Grade II listed Queen Anne house, in 12-acre grounds, has been home to the Hine family for 33 years. Aided by an enthusiastic and committed team, the family continues to preside over all aspects of the hotel, creating a wonderfully relaxed environment. Bedrooms offer a reassuring mix of comfort and quality, and include four-poster rooms. In both The Restaurant and The Bistro the impressive cuisine is based on excellent produce, much of it locally sourced.

Rooms 19 (2 fmly) (5 GF) S £100; D £160 (incl. bkfst)*
Facilities STV FTV ⊗ ⓢ ⛳ Badminton Table tennis New Year Wi-fi Parking 62 Notes LB Closed 24-26 Dec

EWEN
Map 3 SU09

The Wild Duck
★★ 71% HOTEL

Drakes Island GL7 6BY
☎ 01285 770310 📠 01285 770492
e-mail: duckreservations@aol.com
dir: From Cirencester take A429 towards Malmesbury. At Kemble left to Ewen. Inn in village centre

PETS: Bedrooms (8 GF) unattended ground-floor bedrooms only Charges £10 per stay Public areas except restaurant on leads Grounds on leads disp bin Exercise area country park & lakes (15 mins' walk) Facilities dog chews walks info vet info On Request fridge access Stables 5m Resident Pets: Daisy & Bertie (Spaniels), Archie (Scottish Deerhound)

This lovely 16th-century, family run inn sits in a delightful Cotswold location and offers a wealth of character and interest. Log fires crackle and there are heaps of nooks and crannies in the bar and restaurant where guests can enjoy the hearty cuisine and an extensive choice of beers and wines. There is a lovely courtyard for alfresco dining in the warmer weather. The individually designed bedrooms have a contemporary look, and each has a black lacquered four-poster; the Chinese Suite is in the oldest part of the building.

Rooms 12 (8 GF) S £50-£70; D £85-£165 (incl. bkfst)
Facilities FTV Wi-fi Parking 50 Notes Closed 25 Dec evening

FOSSEBRIDGE — Map 4 SP01

The Inn at Fossebridge
★★★★ 😊 INN
GL54 3JS
☎ 01285 720721
e-mail: info@fossebridgeinn.co.uk
dir: On A429, 3m S of A40 & 6m N of Cirencester

PETS: Bedrooms Charges £10 per night **Public areas** on leads **Grounds** on leads disp bin **Exercise area** nearby **Facilities** water bowl dog chews feeding mat walks info vet info **On Request** fridge access towels **Other** charge for damage

Located not too far from Stratford-upon-Avon, Cheltenham and Cirencester this inn is around 300 years old, and was once a coaching inn on the old Fosse Way. Today it is a beautiful Cotswold retreat with wonderful accommodation and grounds. Fine food is served in the character bar and dining areas, and a warm welcome awaits all visitors.

Rooms 9 en suite (1 fmly) **D** £110-£165 **Facilities** FTV TVL tea/coffee Dinner available Cen ht Wi-fi Fishing **Parking** 40 **Notes** LB

GLOUCESTER — Map 3 SO81

Hatherley Manor
★★★ 78% HOTEL
Down Hatherley Ln GL2 9QA
☎ 01452 730217 📠 01452 731032
e-mail: reservations@hatherleymanor.com
web: www.hatherleymanor.com
dir: Off A38 into Down Hatherley Lane, signed. Hotel 600yds on left

CLASSIC BRITISH HOTELS

PETS: Bedrooms (18 GF) unattended sign ground-floor bedrooms only **Charges** £10 per stay **Public areas** lounge bar only **Grounds Exercise area** nearby **Other** charge for damage

Within easy striking distance of the M5, Gloucester, Cheltenham and the Cotswolds, this stylish 17th-century manor, set in attractive grounds, remains popular with both business and leisure guests. Bedrooms are well appointed and offer contemporary comforts. A particularly impressive range of meeting and function rooms is available.

Rooms 50 (5 fmly) (18 GF) **Facilities** FTV Xmas New Year Wi-fi **Parking** 250 **Notes** LB

Hatton Court
★★★ 75% HOTEL
Upton Hill, Upton St Leonards GL4 8DE
☎ 01452 617412 📠 01452 612945
e-mail: res@hatton-court.co.uk
web: www.hatton-court.co.uk
dir: From Gloucester on B4073 (Painswick road). Hotel at top of hill on right

PETS: Bedrooms Exercise area Painswick Beacon 2m **Facilities** walks info vet info **Other** charge for damage

Built in the style of a 17th-century Cotswold manor house, and set in seven acres of well-kept gardens this hotel is popular with both business and leisure guests. It stands at the top of Upton Hill and commands truly spectacular views of the Severn Valley. Bedrooms are comfortable and tastefully furnished with many extra facilities. The elegant Carringtons Restaurant offers a varied choice of menus, and there is also a bar and foyer lounge.

Rooms 45 (28 annexe) **Facilities** 🏊 Gym Xmas New Year Wi-fi **Parking** 80 **Notes** LB

Red Lion Caravan & Camping Park (SO849258)
▶ ▶ ▶
Wainlode Hill, Norton GL2 9LW
☎ 01452 730251 & 731810 📠 01452 730251
dir: Exit A38 at Norton, follow road to river

PETS: Charges 1st dog free, 2nd dog £1.50 per night **Public areas** on leads **Exercise area** river bank adjacent **Facilities** food walks info vet info **Stables** nearby **Other** prior notice required pets must not roam free

Open all year Last arrival 22.00hrs Last departure 11.00hrs

An attractive meadowland park, adjacent to a traditional pub, with the River Severn just across a country lane. This is an ideal touring and fishing base. 24 acre site. 60 touring pitches. 10 hardstandings. Tent pitches. Motorhome pitches. 85 statics.

Notes 📵

LOWER SLAUGHTER — Map 4 SP12

Washbourne Court
★★★ 88% ◎◎ COUNTRY HOUSE HOTEL

GL54 2HS
☎ 01451 822143 📠 01451 821045
e-mail: info@washbournecourt.co.uk
web: www.vonessenhotels.co.uk
dir: Exit A429 at `The Slaughters' sign, between Stow-on-the-Wold & Bourton-on-the-Water. Hotel in village centre

PETS: Bedrooms (9 GF) unattended Charges £30 per stay Public areas except restaurant on leads Grounds on leads Exercise area 50mtrs Facilities food (pre-bookable) food bowl water bowl dog walking dog grooming cage storage walks info vet info On Request fridge access torch towels Other charge or damage contact hotel for details of charges

Beamed ceilings, log fires and flagstone floors are some of the attractive features of this part 17th-century hotel, set in four acres of immaculate grounds beside the River Eye. The hotel has an elegant, contemporary style and boasts stunning bedrooms with up-to-the-minute technology and marble bathrooms. Dining, whether in the restaurant or bar is memorable and utilises fine local produce.

Rooms 30 (9 GF) Facilities FTV Xmas New Year Wi-fi Parking 40

MARSHFIELD — Map 3 ST77

Lord Nelson Inn
★★★ INN

SN14 8LP
☎ 01225 891820
e-mail: thelordnelsoninn@btinternet.com
web: www.thelordnelsoninn.info
dir: M4 junct 18 onto A46 towards Bath. Left at Cold Ashton rdbt towards Marshfield

PETS: Bedrooms Public areas on leads Grounds on leads Exercise area nearby Facilities food bowl water bowl walks info vet info Stables nearby Other charge for damage

Located at one end of the pleasant village of Marshfield, the Lord Nelson is a traditional coaching inn with a pleasant ambience. The spacious bar provides a good opportunity to mix with the locals, while the candlelit restaurant offers a quieter environment in which to enjoy the excellent selection of carefully prepared home-made dishes. Bedrooms and bathrooms are all well decorated and furnished.

Rooms 3 en suite S £35-£47.50; D £65-£77.50 Facilities FTV tea/coffee Dinner available Cen ht Notes LB

MICHAEL WOOD MOTORWAY SERVICE AREA (M5) Map 3 ST79

Days Inn Michaelwood - M5
BUDGET HOTEL

Michaelwood Service Area, Lower Wick GL11 6DD
☎ 01454 261513 📠 01454 269150
e-mail: michaelwood.hotel@welcomebreak.co.uk
web: www.welcomebreak.co.uk
dir: M5 N'bound between junct 13 & 14

PETS: Bedrooms unattended Charges £5 per stay Public areas Grounds on leads disp bin Facilities walks info vet info On Request fridge access torch towels Other charge for damage Restrictions no dangerous dogs (see page 7)

This modern building offers accommodation in smart, spacious and well-equipped bedrooms, suitable for families and business travellers, and all with en suite bathrooms. Continental breakfast is available and other refreshments may be taken at the nearby family restaurant.

Rooms 38 (34 fmly) (5 smoking) S £39.95-£59.95; D £49.95-£69.95

MORETON-IN-MARSH — Map 4 SP23

White Hart Royal Hotel
★★★ 79% HOTEL

High St GL56 0BA
☎ 01608 650731 📠 01608 650880
e-mail: whr@bpcmail.co.uk
web: www.whitehartroyal.co.uk
dir: On High St at junct with Oxford Rd

PETS: Bedrooms (9 GF) sign ground-floor bedrooms only Charges £10 per night Public areas except public bar & courtyard on leads Grounds on leads disp bin Exercise area 1m Facilities food bowl water bowl walks info vet info On Request fridge access torch towels Other charge for damage

This historic hotel has been providing accommodation for hundreds of years and has now completed a major refurbishment programme that has resulted in high standards of quality and comfort. Public areas are full of character, and the bedrooms, in a wide range of shapes and sizes, include several very spacious and luxurious rooms situated adjacent to the main building. A varied range of well prepared dishes is available throughout the day and evening in the main bar and the relaxing restaurant.

Rooms 28 (8 annexe) (2 fmly) (9 GF) Facilities STV FTV Xmas New Year Wi-fi Notes LB

MORETON-IN-MARSH *continued*

Red Lion Inn

★★★ ⊜ INN

Little Compton GL56 0RT

☎ 01608 674397

e-mail: info@theredlionlittlecompton.co.uk

dir: *On A44 between Chipping Norton & Moreton-in-Marsh*

PETS: Public areas except restaurant on leads **Grounds** on leads disp bin **Exercise area** adjacent **Facilities** feeding mat scoop/disp bags leads washing facs cage storage walks info vet info **On Request** torch towels **Stables** 1m **Other** charge for damage **Restrictions** no very large dogs

Built in 1748 as a coaching inn the Red Lion retains much of the charm and character of a friendly country pub. It has been sympathetically restored and the inglenook fireplaces, stone walls and oak beams remain a real feature. The comfortable bedrooms are stylishly presented and overlook the neat gardens with the beautiful Cotswold countryside beyond. Comprehensive breakfast choices are available, and evening meals should not to be missed.

Rooms 2 en suite **Facilities** FTV tea/coffee Dinner available Cen ht Wi-fi Pool table **Parking** 15 **Notes** LB

NEWENT — Map 3 SO72

Pelerine Caravan and Camping *(SO645183)*

▶▶▶

Ford House Rd GL18 1LQ

☎ 01531 822761

e-mail: pelerine@hotmail.com

dir: *1m from Newent*

PETS: Charges £1 per night **Public areas** disp bin **Exercise area** adjacent **Facilities** washing facs vet info **Stables** 1m **Other** prior notice required **Resident Pets:** Buttons & Tom (cats)

Open Mar-Nov Last arrival 22.00hrs Last departure 16.00hrs

A pleasant site divided into two areas, one of which is for adults only, with some hardstandings and electric hook-ups in each area. Facilities are very good, especially for families. It is close to several vineyards, and well positioned in the north of the Forest of Dean with Tewkesbury, Cheltenham and Ross-on-Wye within easy reach. 5 acre site. 35 touring pitches. 2 hardstandings. Tent pitches. Motorhome pitches.

Notes ⊛

OLD SODBURY — Map 3 ST78

The Cross Hands

★★★ INN

BS37 6RJ

☎ 01454 313000 📄 01454 324409

e-mail: 6435@greeneking.co.uk

dir: *M4 junct 18 signed to Cirencester/Stroud on A46. After 1.5m, on right at 1st lights*

PETS: Bedrooms (9 GF) unattended ground-floor bedrooms only **Public areas** except in restaurant on leads **Grounds** on leads **Facilities** water bowl walks info vet info **On Request** fridge access

The Cross Hands is a former posting house dating back to the 14th century that is just off the main road, and within easy reach of both Bath and Bristol. The bedrooms are well equipped and some are at ground-floor level. The public areas include a bar, comfortable seating area and a spacious split-level restaurant which offers a selection of home-cooked dishes. Alternatively, guests may choose to eat from the extensive menu in the bar area.

Rooms 21 en suite (1 fmly) (9 GF) **Facilities** tea/coffee Dinner available Direct Dial Cen ht Wi-fi **Parking** 120

PAINSWICK — Map 3 SO80

Hambutts Mynd Guest House

★★★ GUEST ACCOMMODATION

Edge Rd GL6 6UP

☎ 01452 812352

e-mail: ewarland@supanet.com

PETS: Bedrooms Public areas on leads disp bin **Exercise area** 50yds **Facilities** food bowl water bowl feeding mat scoop/disp bags pet sitting washing facs walks info vet info **On Request** fridge access torch towels **Other** charge for damage owners must bring their own pet food

Built in the 1700s as a corn mill, this property has an interesting history. In 1801 it was converted into a school, and much later it commenced its role of offering guest accommodation. Homely and welcoming hospitality is delivered and the bedrooms benefit from delightful views over the valley and the hills. A number of pleasant Cotswold walks start directly from the house and Painswick itself is a just a five-minute stroll away.

Rooms 3 en suite **S** £36-£42; **D** £65 **Facilities** STV FTV TVL tea/coffee Cen ht **Parking** 3 **Notes** No Children 10yrs Closed Jan RS Mar ⊛

RANGEWORTHY — Map 3 ST68

Rangeworthy Court

★★ 72% HOTEL

Church Ln, Wotton Rd BS37 7ND

☎ 01454 228347 📄 01454 65089

e-mail: reception@rangeworthycourt.com

dir: *Signed from B4058. Hotel at end of Church Lane*

PETS: Bedrooms unattended **Charges** £3 per night
Public areas except restaurant on leads **Grounds** disp bin
Facilities food bowl water bowl walks info vet info **Other**
charge for damage dogs accepted by prior arrangement only
Restrictions well behaved dogs only **Resident Pets:** Bennie
(German Shepherd/Corgi cross) Davey (Jack Russell)

This welcoming manor house hotel is peacefully located in its
own grounds, and is within easy reach of the motorway network.
The character bedrooms come in a variety of sizes and there is
a choice of comfortable lounges in which to enjoy a drink before
dinner. The relaxing restaurant offers a selection of carefully
prepared, enjoyable dishes.

Rooms 13 (4 fmly) **S** £45-£82.25; **D** £60-£100* **Facilities** FTV ⚲
Wi-fi **Parking** 30 **Notes** Closed 24-30 Dec

SLIMBRIDGE — Map 3 SO70

Tudor Caravan & Camping *(SO728040)*

▶▶▶▶

Shepherds Patch GL2 7BP

☎ 01453 890483

e-mail: aa@tudorcaravanpark.co.uk

dir: *From M5 junct 13/14 follow signs for WWT Wetlands Wildlife
Centre-Slimbridge. Site at rear of Tudor Arms pub*

PETS: Charges £1 per night **Public areas** except toilet, shower,
laundry & reception buildings on leads disp bin **Exercise area**
on site rally field available when not in use **Exercise area**
canal towpath adjacent **Facilities** walks info vet info **Stables**
2m **Other** prior notice required local pet sitter/walker available
(please contact for details) dog tethers available

Open all year Last arrival 20.00hrs Last departure noon

An orchard-style park sheltered by mature trees and shrubs, set
in an attractive meadow beside the Sharpness to Gloucester
canal. A facility block has been added in the more open area of
the site. This tidy site offers both level grass and gravel pitches
complete with electric hook-ups, and there is a separate adults-
only area. The Wildfowl and Wetlands Trust at Slimbridge is close
by, and there is much scope locally for birdwatching. 8 acre site.
75 touring pitches. 48 hardstandings. Tent pitches. Motorhome
pitches.

Notes Debit cards only accepted (not credit cards)

STOW-ON-THE-WOLD — Map 4 SP12

Old Stocks

★★ 72% SMALL HOTEL

The Square GL54 1AF

☎ 01451 830666 📄 01451 870014

e-mail: aa@oldstockshotel.co.uk

web: www.oldstockshotel.co.uk

dir: *Exit A429 to town centre. Hotel facing village green*

PETS: Bedrooms (4 GF) unattended patio garden bedrooms
most suitable **Charges Public areas** except restaurant on
leads **Grounds** on leads **Exercise area** 500yds **Facilities**
walks info vet info **On Request** torch **Other** charge for damage
Restrictions well behaved dogs only; no dangerous dogs (see
page 7) **Resident Pet:** Alfie (Golden Retriever)

Overlooking the old market square, this Grade II listed, mellow
Cotswold-stone building is a comfortable and friendly base from
which to explore this picturesque area. There's lots of character
throughout, and the bedrooms offer individuality and charm.
Facilities include a guest lounge, restaurant and bar, whilst
outside, the patio is a popular summer venue for refreshing
drinks and good food.

Rooms 18 (3 annexe) (5 fmly) (4 GF) **S** £36-£56; **D** £72-£112
(incl. bkfst)* **Facilities** FTV New Year Wi-fi **Parking** 12 **Notes** LB

STROUD — Map 3 SO80

COTSWOLD
INNS & HOTELS

The Bear of Rodborough

★★★ 79% HOTEL

Rodborough Common GL5 5DE

☎ 01453 878522 📄 01453 872523

e-mail: info@bearofrodborough.info

web: www.cotswold-inns-hotels.co.uk/bear

dir: *M5 junct 13, A419 to Stroud. Follow signs to Rodborough. Up
hill, left at top at T-junct. Hotel on right*

PETS: Bedrooms unattended Woodchester House bedrooms only
Charges £10 per night **Public areas** except restaurant & lounge
on leads **Grounds** disp bin **Exercise area** 2 mins **Facilities**
water bowl walks info vet info **Other** charge for damage

This popular 17th-century coaching inn is situated high above
Stroud in acres of National Trust parkland. Character abounds
in the lounges and cocktail bar, and in the Box Tree Restaurant
where the cuisine utilises fresh local produce. Bedrooms offer
equal measures of comfort and style with plenty of extra touches.
There is also a traditional and well-patronised public bar.

Rooms 46 (2 fmly) **S** £80-£90; **D** £130-£140 (incl. bkfst)*
Facilities STV Putt green 🏌 Xmas New Year Wi-fi **Parking** 70
Notes LB

STROUD *continued*

Hyde Crest

★★★★ BED AND BREAKFAST

Cirencester Rd GL6 8PE

☎ 01453 731631

e-mail: stay@hydecrest.co.uk

dir: *Off A419, 5m E of Stroud, signed Minchinhampton & Aston Down, house 3rd right opp Ragged Cot pub*

PETS: Bedrooms (3 GF) unattended **Public areas Grounds** disp bin **Exercise area** 500-acre common (1m) **Facilities** washing facs walks info vet info **On Request** fridge access torch towels **Resident Pet:** Harry (Cocker Spaniel)

Hyde Crest lies on the edge of the picturesque Cotswold village of Minchinhampton. Bedrooms are located at ground floor level, each with a private patio where welcome refreshments are enjoyed upon arrival (weather permitting). Guests are attentively cared for and scrumptious breakfasts are served in the small lounge-dining room around a communal table.

Rooms 3 en suite (3 GF) **S** fr £45; **D** fr £70 **Facilities** FTV TVL tea/coffee Cen ht Wi-fi **Parking** 6 **Notes** No Children 10yrs RS Xmas & New Year no meals available 🐾

TETBURY	Map 3 ST89

Cotswold Inns & Hotels

Hare & Hounds

★★★★ 78% ◉◉ HOTEL

Westonbirt GL8 8QL

☎ 01666 880233 & 881000 📠 01666 880241

e-mail: reception@hareandhoundshotel.com

web: www.hareandhoundshotel.com

dir: *2.5m SW of Tetbury on A433*

PETS: Bedrooms (13 GF) unattended **Charges** £5 per night **Public areas** except restaurant on leads **Grounds** disp bin **Exercise area** nearby **Facilities** water bowl walks info vet info **Other** charge for damage

This popular hotel, set in extensive grounds, is situated close to Westonbirt Arboretum and has remained under the same ownership for over 50 years. Bedrooms are individual in style; those in the main house are more traditional and the stylish

cottage rooms are contemporary in design. Public rooms include the informal bar and light, airy lounges - one with a log fire in colder months. Guests can eat either in the bar or the attractive restaurant.

Rooms 42 (21 annexe) (8 fmly) (13 GF) **S** £95-£105; **D** £145-£179 (incl. bkfst)* **Facilities** FTV 🏊 🌳 Xmas New Year Wi-fi **Parking** 85 **Notes** LB

UPPER SLAUGHTER	Map 4 SP12

Lords of the Manor

★★★★ ◉◉◉ COUNTRY HOUSE HOTEL

GL54 2JD

☎ 01451 820243 📠 01451 820696

e-mail: reservations@lordsofthemanor.com

web: www.lordsofthemanor.com

dir: *2m W of A429. Exit A40 onto A429, take 'The Slaughters' turn. Through Lower Slaughter for 1m to Upper Slaughter. Hotel on right*

PETS: Bedrooms (9 GF) unattended certain bedrooms only **Charges** £30 per night **Public areas** except restaurant on leads **Grounds** disp bin **Exercise area** adjacent **Facilities** food (pre-bookable) dog chews cage storage walks info vet info **On Request** torch towels **Other** charge for damage

This wonderfully welcoming 17th-century manor house hotel sits in eight acres of gardens and parkland surrounded by Cotswold countryside. A relaxed atmosphere, underpinned by professional and attentive service is the hallmark here, so that guests are often reluctant to leave. The hotel has elegant public rooms that overlook the immaculate lawns, and the restaurant is the venue for consistently impressive cuisine. Bedrooms have much character and charm, combined with the extra touches expected of a hotel of this stature.

Rooms 26 (4 fmly) (9 GF) **Facilities** FTV Fishing 🌳 Xmas New Year Wi-fi **Parking** 40

GREATER LONDON

HARROW WEALD
Map 4 TQ19

Grim's Dyke Hotel
★★★ 82% ◉◉ HOTEL

Old Redding HA3 6SH
☎ 020 8385 3100 & 020 8954 4227   📠 020 8954 4560
e-mail: reservations@grimsdyke.com
web: www.grimsdyke.com
dir: *A410 onto A409 north towards Bushey, at top of hill at lights turn left into Old Redding*

PETS: Bedrooms (17 GF)   **Charges** £30 per night   **Grounds** on leads   **Exercise area** woodland   **Facilities** cage storage   vet info **Stables** 5m   **Other** charge for damage   **Restrictions** small dogs & assist dogs only

Once home to Sir William Gilbert, this Grade II mansion contains many references to well-known Gilbert and Sullivan productions. The house is set in over 40 acres of beautiful parkland and gardens. Bedrooms in the main house are elegant and traditional, while those in the adjacent lodge are aimed more at the business guest.

Rooms 46 (37 annexe) (4 fmly) (17 GF) **S** £60-£125; **D** £70-£150 (incl. bkfst)* **Facilities** STV 🏊 Gilbert & Sullivan opera dinner Murder mystery & Sabrage evenings 🎵 Xmas New Year Wi-fi **Parking** 97 **Notes** LB RS 24-31 Dec

KINGSTON UPON THAMES
Map 4 TQ16

Chase Lodge House
★★★ GUEST ACCOMMODATION

10 Park Rd, Hampton Wick KT1 4AS
☎ 020 8943 1862   📠 020 8943 9363
e-mail: info@chaselodgehotel.com
web: www.chaselodgehotel.com
dir: *A308 onto A310 signed Twickenham, 1st left onto Park Rd*

PETS: Bedrooms sign   **Exercise area** nearby   **Facilities** food food bowl water bowl bedding dog chews cat treats feeding mat litter tray scoop/disp bags leads dog walking cage storage walks info vet info   **On Request** fridge access torch towels **Other** charge for damage

This independent establishment is set in a quiet residential area, a short walk from Kingston town centre, Bushey Park and the River Thames. The individually decorated rooms vary in size and are all well-appointed and feature a range of useful extras. An attractive lounge-bar-restaurant is provided where breakfast, snacks and dinner by pre-arrangement are served. Children and dogs are most welcome, and on-road parking is available.

Rooms 13 en suite (2 smoking) **Facilities** FTV Direct Dial Wi-fi **Notes** LB

GREATER MANCHESTER

BOLTON
Map 7 SD70

Broomfield House
★★★ GUEST HOUSE

33-35 Wigan Rd, Deane BL3 5PX
☎ 01204 61570   📠 01204 650932
e-mail: contact@broomfieldhotel.co.uk
dir: *M61 junct 5, A58 to 1st lights, straight onto A676, premises on right*

PETS: Bedrooms (2 GF) unattended   **Public areas   Exercise area** across road   **Facilities** cage storage vet info   **On Request** fridge access torch towels   **Other** charge for damage

A friendly relaxed atmosphere prevails at Broomfield House, close to the motorway and west of the town centre. There is a comfy lounge and separate bar area. Hearty breakfasts are served in the dining room.

Rooms 20 en suite (2 fmly) (2 GF) (6 smoking) **S** £33-£43; **D** £48-£58 **Facilities** FTV TVL tea/coffee Cen ht Licensed Wi-fi **Parking** 12

BURY
Map 7 SD81

Red Hall Hotel
★★★ 80% HOTEL

Manchester Rd, Walmersley BL9 5NA
☎ 01706 822476   📠 01706 828086
e-mail: info@red-hall.co.uk
dir: *M66 junct 1, A56. Over motorway bridge, hotel approx 300mtrs on right*

PETS: Bedrooms (18 GF) unattended certain bedrooms only **Charges** £15 per night   **Public areas** except bar & restaurants on leads   **Facilities** walks info vet info   **Other** charge for damage prior notice required owners must bring dog's own food, bowls & bedding   **Restrictions** small dogs only

Originally a farmhouse this hotel, located in the picturesque village of Warmersley on the outskirts of Ramsbottom, is just off the M66 making it ideal for both business and leisure guests alike. Bedrooms are contemporary and well equipped. There is a restaurant and lounge bar, plus meeting and event facilities.

Rooms 37 (2 fmly) (18 GF) **Facilities** STV Xmas New Year Wi-fi **Services** Lift **Parking** 100

DELPH

Map 7 SD90

Wellcroft House

★★★★ ⊜ GUEST ACCOMMODATION

Bleak Hey Nook OL3 5LY

☎ 01457 875017

e-mail: wellcrofthouse@hotmail.co.uk

web: www.wellcrofthouse.co.uk

dir: Off A62 on Standedge Foot Rd near A670 junct

PETS: **Bedrooms** ground-floor bedroom only **Charges** £5 per night **Public areas Grounds Exercise area** 100mtrs **Facilities** food (pre-bookable) water bowl bedding washing facs vet info **On Request** torch towels **Other** charge for damage

Commanding superb views down the valley below, this former weaver's cottage offers warm traditional hospitality to walkers on the Pennine Way and those touring the Pennine towns and villages. Modern comforts in all bedrooms and transport from local railway or walks is routinely provided by the friendly proprietors.

Rooms 3 rms (2 en suite) (1 GF) **S** £30-£65; **D** £50-£65 **Facilities** FTV TVL tea/coffee Dinner available Cen ht Wi-fi Pool table **Parking** 1 **Notes** LB ⊛

MANCHESTER

Map 7 SJ89

Novotel Manchester Centre

★★★ 79% HOTEL

21 Dickinson St M1 4LX

☎ 0161 235 2200 ▤ 0161 235 2210

e-mail: H3145@accor.com

web: www.novotel.com

dir: From Oxford St, into Portland St, left into Dickinson St. Hotel on right

PETS: **Bedrooms** unattended **Charges** £15 per night disp bin **Exercise area** adjacent **Facilities** walks info vet info **On Request** fridge access **Other** charge for damage

This smart, modern property enjoys a central location convenient for theatres, shops, China Town and Manchester's business district. Spacious bedrooms are thoughtfully equipped and brightly decorated. Open-plan, contemporary public areas include an all-day restaurant and a stylish bar. Extensive conference and meeting facilities are available.

Rooms 164 (15 fmly) (10 smoking) **Facilities** STV FTV Gym Steam room Sauna Aromatherapy Wi-fi **Services** Lift Air con **Notes** LB

Ibis Manchester Charles Street

BUDGET HOTEL

Charles St, Princess St M1 7DL

☎ 0161 272 5000 ▤ 0161 272 5010

e-mail: H3143@accor.com

web: www.ibishotel.com

dir: M62, M602 towards Manchester Centre, follow signs for UMIST(A34)

PETS: **Bedrooms On Request** towels

Modern, budget hotel offering comfortable accommodation in bright and practical bedrooms. Breakfast is self-service and dinner is available in the restaurant.

Rooms 126

Ibis Manchester City Centre

BUDGET HOTEL

96 Portland St M1 4GY

☎ 0161 234 0600 ▤ 0161 234 0610

e-mail: H3142@accor.com

web: www.ibishotel.com

dir: In city centre, between Princess St & Oxford St

PETS: **Bedrooms Charges Public areas** except restaurant & bars on leads **Restrictions** small & medium size dogs only

Rooms 127 (16 fmly) (7 smoking)

ROCHDALE

Map 7 SD81

Best Western Broadfield Park Hotel

★★★ 77% HOTEL

Sparrow Hill OL16 1AF

☎ 01706 639000 ▤ 01706 759398

e-mail: reservations@broadfieldparkhotel.co.uk

web: www.broadfieldparkhotel.co.uk

dir: M60 junct 20, follow signs for Rochdale & town centre. A640 onto Drake St, hotel signed 0.5m on left

PETS: **Bedrooms** unattended **Grounds** on leads **Exercise area** nearby **Facilities** vet info **On Request** torch towels **Other** charge for damage

Overlooking historic Broadfield Park and the town centre and only minutes away from the M60 and M62. Bedrooms are comfortably furnished and attractively decorated. The hotel offers a range of carefully prepared meals and snacks in either the formal restaurant, or the lounge bar. Service is friendly and attentive.

Rooms 29 (4 fmly) **S** £59-£89; **D** £59-£89 **Facilities** FTV Xmas New Year Wi-fi **Parking** 30 **Notes** RS 24-26 Dec

Gelderwood Country Park (SD852127)

►►►

Ashworth Rd OL11 5UP
☎ 01706 364858 & 620300 📠 01706 364858
e-mail: gelderwood@aol.com
dir: *Signed midway from B6222 (Bury/Rochdale road). Turn into Ashworth Rd, continue past mill. Uphill for 800yds, site on right*

PETS: Charges £1.50 dog per night **Public areas** disp bin **Exercise area** adjacent **Facilities** walks info vet info

Open all year Last departure noon

A very rural site in a peaceful private country park with excellent facilities. All pitches have extensive views of the moor, and this is a popular base for walkers and birdwatchers. The park is for adults only. 10 acre site. 34 touring pitches. 26 hardstandings. Motorhome pitches.

Notes 😊

Novotel Manchester West

★★★ **72%** HOTEL
Worsley Brow M28 2YA
☎ 0161 799 3535 📠 0161 703 8207
e-mail: H0907@accor.com
web: www.novotel.com
dir: *Adjacent to M60 junct 13*

PETS: Bedrooms (41 GF) **Charges** £10.25 per night **Grounds** on leads disp bin **Exercise area** 100yds **Facilities** walks info vet info **Other** charge for damage

Well placed for access to the Peak District and the Lake District, as well as Manchester, this modern hotel successfully caters for both families and business guests. The spacious bedrooms have sofa beds and a large work area; the hotel has an outdoor swimming pool, children's play area and secure parking.

Rooms 119 (10 fmly) (41 GF) **S** £60-£130; **D** £60-£130* **Facilities** STV 🏌 Gym Xmas New Year Wi-fi **Services** Lift **Parking** 95

The Anchor Inn

★★★★★ 🎖🎖 INN
Lower Froyle GU34 4NA
☎ 01420 23261
e-mail: info@anchorinnatlowerfroyle.co.uk
dir: *On A31, exit towards Bentley*

PETS: Bedrooms unattended **Public areas** except restaurant **Grounds** disp bin **Facilities** water bowl dog chews walks info vet info **Other** charge for damage

The Anchor Inn is located in the tranquil village of Lower Froyle. Luxury rooms are designed to reflect the traditional English inn style with charming decor, pictures and a selection of books. The restaurant welcomes residents and the local population with classic pub cooking, and impressive surroundings, with wooden floors and period furnishings.

Rooms 5 en suite **S** £110-£140; **D** £110-£140 **Facilities** STV FTV tea/coffee Dinner available Direct Dial Cen ht Wi-fi **Parking** 30 **Notes** Closed 25 Dec

Esseborne Manor

★★★ **80%** 🎖🎖 HOTEL
Hurstbourne Tarrant SP11 0ER
☎ 01264 736444 📠 01264 736725
e-mail: info@esseborne-manor.co.uk
web: www.esseborne-manor.co.uk
dir: *Halfway between Andover & Newbury on A343, 1m N of Hurstbourne Tarrant*

PETS: Bedrooms unattended sign courtyard bedrooms only **Grounds** disp bin **Exercise area** nearby **Facilities** food bowl water bowl washing facs walks info vet info **On Request** fridge access torch **Other** charge for damage

Set in two acres of well-tended gardens, this attractive manor house is surrounded by the open countryside of the North Wessex Downs. Bedrooms are delightfully individual and are split between the main house, an adjoining courtyard and separate garden cottage. There's a wonderfully relaxed atmosphere throughout, and public rooms combine elegance with comfort.

Rooms 19 (8 annexe) (2 fmly) (6 GF) **S** £80-£110; **D** £100-£180 (incl. bkfst)* **Facilities** STV FTV 🏌🏌 Xmas New Year Wi-fi **Parking** 50 **Notes** LB

ENGLAND

The Hampshire Court Hotel
★★★★ **79%** HOTEL

Centre Dr, Chineham RG24 8FY
☎ 01256 319700 📠 01256 319730
e-mail: hampshirecourt@qhotels.co.uk
web: www.qhotels.co.uk
dir: Off A33 (Reading road) behind Chineham Shopping Centre via Great Binfields Rd

PETS: Bedrooms sign **Charges** dog £15 per night **Public areas** except food service areas on leads **Exercise area** adjacent **Facilities** cage storage walks info vet info **On Request** fridge access torch **Other** charge for damage

This hotel boasts a range of smart, comfortable and stylish bedrooms, and leisure facilities that are unrivalled locally. Facilities include indoor and outdoor tennis courts, two swimming pools, a gym and a number of treatment rooms.

Rooms 90 (6 fmly) **Facilities** Spa STV 🕲 🏊 Gym Steam room Beauty salon Sauna Exercise studios Xmas New Year Wi-fi **Services** Lift **Parking** 220

Barceló Basingstoke Country Hotel
★★★★ **75%** HOTEL

Scures Hill, Nately Scures, Hook RG27 9JS
☎ 01256 764161 📠 01256 768341
e-mail: basingstokecountry.mande@barcelo-hotels.co.uk
web: www.barcelo-hotels.co.uk
dir: M3 junct 5, A287 towards Newnham. Left at lights. Hotel 200mtrs on right

PETS: Bedrooms (26 GF) sign **Charges** £15 per stay **Grounds** on leads disp bin **Exercise area** 100mtrs **Facilities** cage storage walks info vet info **On Request** fridge access torch **Stables** 7m **Other** charge for damage

This popular hotel is close to Basingstoke and its country location ensures a peaceful stay. Bedrooms are available in a number of styles - all have air conditioning, Wi-fi, in-room safes and hairdryers. Guests have a choice of dining in the formal restaurant, or for lighter meals and snacks there is a relaxed café and a smart bar. Extensive wedding, conference and leisure facilities complete the picture.

Rooms 100 (26 GF) **Facilities** Spa STV 🕲 supervised Gym Sauna Solarium Steam room Dance studio Beauty treatments New Year Wi-fi **Services** Lift Air con **Parking** 200 **Notes** RS 24 Dec-2 Jan

The Master Builders at Bucklers Hard
★★★ **79%** ◉ HOTEL

Buckler's Hard SO42 7XB
☎ 01590 616253 📠 01590 616297
e-mail: enquiries@themasterbuilders.co.uk
web: www.themasterbuilders.co.uk
dir: M27 junct 2, follow Beaulieu signs. At T-junct left onto B3056, 1st left to Buckler's Hard. Hotel 2m on left before village

PETS: Bedrooms unattended standard rooms in Henry Adams wing only **Charges** £20 per night £140 per week **Public areas** except restaurant & lounge on leads **Grounds** on leads disp bin **Facilities** food (pre-bookable) food bowl water bowl bedding **On Request** towels **Other** charge for damage

A tranquil historic riverside setting creates the backdrop for this delightful property. The main house bedrooms are full of historical features and of individual design, and in addition there are some bedrooms in the newer wing. Public areas include a popular bar and guest lounge, whilst grounds are an ideal location for alfresco dining in the summer months. Award-winning cuisine is served in the stylish dining room.

Rooms 25 (17 annexe) (4 fmly) (8 GF) **S** fr £95; **D** fr £105 (incl. bkfst)* **Facilities** FTV Xmas New Year Wi-fi **Parking** 40

Beaulieu Hotel
★★★ **78%** ◉ HOTEL

Beaulieu Rd SO42 7YQ
☎ 023 8029 3344 📠 023 8029 2729
e-mail: beaulieu@newforesthotels.co.uk
web: www.newforesthotels.co.uk
dir: M27 junct 1, A337 towards Lyndhurst. Left at lights, through Lyndhurst, right onto B3056, hotel in 3m

PETS: Bedrooms (4 GF) unattended certain bedrooms only (please check when booking) **Charges** £7.50 per night **Public areas** except food areas on leads **Grounds** **Exercise area** adjacent **Facilities** water bowl walks info vet info **On Request** fridge access **Other** dogs may only be left unattended in bedrooms if owners are on premises & reception staff have been informed

Located in the heart of the beautiful New Forest and close to Beaulieu Road railway station, this popular, small hotel provides an ideal base for exploring this remarkable area. Once a coaching inn, the hotel now particularly welcomes families; children will delight in seeing the ponies on the doorstep! Bedrooms, all with free Wi-fi and flat-screen TVs with Freeview, range from cosy Keeper rooms to Crown rooms which also have four-posters and iPod docking stations. The relaxing Exbury Restaurant has doors that lead out onto the patio area and the landscaped gardens, and alfresco eating is possible in the summer. Facilities include an indoor swimming pool and an adjoining pub.

Rooms 28 (7 annexe) (5 fmly) (4 GF) **D** £120-£190 (incl. bkfst)* **Facilities** FTV 🕲 Steam room Xmas New Year Wi-fi **Services** Lift **Parking** 60 **Notes** LB

ENGLAND

Balmer Lawn

★★★★ 74% HOTEL

Lyndhurst Rd SO42 7ZB

☎ 01590 623116 📄 01590 623864

e-mail: info@balmerlawnhotel.com

dir: *Just off A337 from Brockenhurst towards Lymington*

PETS: Bedrooms unattended certain bedrooms only **Charges** 1st night £20, subsequent nights £15 £80 per week **Public areas** except restaurant & function rooms on leads **Grounds** on leads disp bin **Exercise area** direct access to New Forest National Park **Facilities** food food bowl water bowl feeding mat washing facs cage storage walks info vet info **On Request** fridge access torch towels **Stables** 0.5m **Other** charge for damage

Situated in the heart of the New Forest, this peacefully located hotel provides comfortable public rooms and a wide range of bedrooms. A selection of carefully prepared and enjoyable dishes is offered in the spacious restaurant. The extensive function and leisure facilities make this popular with both families and conference delegates.

Rooms 54 (10 fmly) **Facilities** FTV ⓢ ⌁ ⌘ Gym Squash Indoor leisure suite Treatment room Sauna ♫ Xmas New Year Wi-fi **Services** Lift **Parking** 100

The Pig

★★★ ◉◉ COUNTRY HOUSE HOTEL

Beaulieu Rd SO42 7QL

☎ 01590 622354 📄 01590 622856

dir: *At Brockenhurst onto B3055 Beaulieu Road. 1m on left up private road*

PETS: Bedrooms unattended The Stableyard bedrooms only **Grounds** on leads disp bin **Exercise area** The New Forest **Facilities** food bowl water bowl bedding scoop/disp bags washing facs cage storage walks info vet info **On Request** torch towels **Stables** nearby **Other** charge for damage **Resident Pets:** pigs, chickens

Rebranded as The Pig and opening its doors in July 2011, this country house has undergone a complete change. Now, the focus will be very much on the food with the chef, gardener and forager working as a team to create menus of seasonal, locally sourced produce; all ingredients will be found within a 15-mile radius. The result of such a policy is that menus will change daily, and sometimes even more frequently! The stylish dining room is an authentically reproduced Victorian greenhouse, and alfresco eating is possible as there is a wood-fired oven in the courtyard. The bedrooms have eclectic furnishings, good beds and views of either the forest or the garden; two suites with private courtyards are available.

Rooms 26

New Park Manor

★★★ 80% ◉◉ COUNTRY HOUSE HOTEL

Lyndhurst Rd SO42 7QH

☎ 01590 623467 📄 01590 622268

e-mail: info@newparkmanorhotel.co.uk

web: www.newparkmanorhotel.co.uk

dir: *M27 junct 1, A337 to Lyndhurst & Brockenhurst. Hotel 1.5m on right*

PETS: Bedrooms unattended **Charges** £10 per night **Public areas** except restaurant & spa on leads **Grounds** disp bin **Exercise area** 100yds **Facilities** water bowl walks info vet info **Stables** 2m **Other** charge for damage

Once the favoured hunting lodge of King Charles II, this well presented hotel enjoys a peaceful setting in the New Forest and comes complete with an equestrian centre. The bedrooms are divided between the old house and a purpose-built wing. Food in the restaurant is based on seasonally available produce, including game and venison. An impressive spa offers a range of treatments.

Rooms 24 (6 fmly) **S** £155-£325; **D** £185-£325 (incl. bkfst)* **Facilities** Spa STV FTV ⓢ ⌁ ⌘ Gym Mountain biking Xmas New Year Wi-fi **Parking** 70

Forest Park

★★★ 71% HOTEL

Rhinefield Rd SO42 7ZG

☎ 01590 622844 📄 01590 623948

e-mail: forest.park@forestdale.com

web: www.forestparkhotel.co.uk

dir: *A337 to Brockenhurst into Meerut Rd, through Waters Green. Right at T-junct into Rhinefield Rd*

PETS: Bedrooms (7 GF) unattended sign **Charges** £7.50 per night **Public areas** except restaurant on leads **Grounds** disp bin **Exercise area** across road **Facilities** food (pre-bookable) walks info vet info **On Request** fridge access torch towels **Stables** 10m

Situated in the heart of the New Forest, this former vicarage and war field hospital is now a hotel which offers a warm and friendly welcome to all its guests. The hotel has a heated pool, riding stables, a log cabin sauna and tennis courts. The bedrooms and public areas are comfortable and stylish.

Rooms 38 (2 fmly) (7 GF) **Facilities** FTV ⌁ ⌘ Horse riding stables Sauna Xmas New Year Wi-fi **Parking** 80 **Notes** LB

BROCKENHURST *continued*

Watersplash

★★ **63%** HOTEL

The Rise SO42 7ZP

☎ 01590 622344

e-mail: bookings@watersplash.co.uk

web: www.watersplash.co.uk

dir: *M3 junct 13/M27 junct 1/A337 S through Lyndhurst & Brockenhurst. The Rise on left, hotel on left*

PETS: Bedrooms (3 GF) unattended **Charges** dog £5 per night **Grounds** disp bin **Facilities** walks info vet info **Other** phone to further details of pet facilities

This popular, welcoming hotel that dates from Victorian times has been in the same family for over 40 years. Bedrooms have co-ordinated decor and good facilities. The restaurant overlooks the neatly tended garden and there is also a comfortably furnished lounge, separate bar and an outdoor pool.

Rooms 23 (6 fmly) (3 GF) **Facilities** ⤳ Xmas New Year **Parking** 29

BURLEY
Map 4 SU20

NEW FOREST HOTELS

Moorhill House

★★★ **78%** ◉ COUNTRY HOUSE HOTEL

BH24 4AH

☎ 01425 403285 📄 01425 403715

e-mail: moorhill@newforesthotels.co.uk

web: www.newforesthotels.co.uk

dir: *M27, A31, follow signs to Burley, through village, up hill, right opposite school & cricket grounds*

PETS: Bedrooms (3 GF) unattended certain bedrooms only (please check when booking) **Charges** £7.50 per night £52.50 per week **Public areas** except restaurant & bar on leads **Grounds Exercise area** nearby **Facilities** water bowl dog chews walks info vet info **On Request** fridge access towels **Stables** 2m **Other** dogs may only be left unattended in bedrooms if owners are on premises & reception staff have been informed

Situated deep in the heart of the New Forest and formerly a grand gentleman's residence, this charming hotel offers a relaxed and friendly environment. Bedrooms, of varying sizes, are smartly decorated. A range of facilities is provided and guests can relax by walking around the extensive grounds. Both dinner and breakfast offer a choice of interesting and freshly prepared dishes.

Rooms 31 (13 fmly) (3 GF) **S** £60-£65; **D** £120-£170 (incl. bkfst)* **Facilities** FTV ◔ Putt green ⛳ Badminton (Apr-Sep) Sauna Xmas New Year Wi-fi **Parking** 50 **Notes** LB

Burley Manor

★★★ **76%** HOTEL

Ringwood Rd BH24 4BS

☎ 01425 403522 📄 01425 403227

e-mail: burley.manor@forestdale.com

web: www.theburleymanorhotel.co.uk

dir: *Exit A31 at Burley sign, hotel 3m on left*

PETS: Bedrooms (17 GF) unattended **Charges** £7.50 per night **Public areas** except restaurant on leads **Grounds** on leads disp bin **Facilities** water bowl scoop/disp bags cage storage walks info vet info **Stables**

Set in extensive grounds, this 18th-century mansion house enjoys a relaxed ambience and a peaceful setting. Half of the well-equipped, comfortable bedrooms, including several with four-posters, are located in the main house. The remainder, many with balconies, are in the adjacent converted stable block overlooking the outdoor pool. Cosy public rooms benefit from log fires in winter.

Rooms 38 (17 annexe) (2 fmly) (17 GF) **Facilities** FTV ⤳ Horse riding stables Xmas New Year Wi-fi **Parking** 60 **Notes** LB

CADNAM
Map 4 SU31

NEW FOREST HOTELS

Bartley Lodge Hotel

★★★ **80%** ◉ HOTEL

Lyndhurst Rd SO40 2NR

☎ 023 8081 2248 📄 023 8081 2075

e-mail: bartley@newforesthotels.co.uk

web: www.newforesthotels.co.uk

dir: *M27 junct 1 at 1st rdbt 1st exit, at 2nd rdbt 3rd exit onto A337. Hotel sign on left*

PETS: Bedrooms (4 GF) unattended certain bedrooms only (please check when booking) **Charges** £7.50 per night **Public areas** except restaurant & bar on leads **Grounds** on leads **Exercise area** nearby **Facilities** water bowl walks info vet info **On Request** fridge access **Stables** 5m **Other** dogs may only be left unattended in bedrooms if owners are on premises & reception staff have been informed

This 18th-century former hunting lodge is very quietly situated, yet is just minutes from the M27. Bedrooms vary in size but all are well equipped. There is a selection of small lounge areas, a cosy bar and an indoor pool, together with a small fitness suite. The Crystal dining room offers a tempting choice of well prepared dishes.

Rooms 40 (15 fmly) (4 GF) **S** £60-£75; **D** £120-£160 (incl. bkfst)* **Facilities** FTV ◔ Sauna Xmas New Year Wi-fi **Parking** 60 **Notes** LB

DOGMERSFIELD — Map 4 SU75

Four Seasons Hotel Hampshire
★★★★★ HOTEL

Dogmersfield Park, Chalky Ln RG27 8TD
☎ 01252 853000 📠 01252 853010
e-mail: reservations.ham@fourseasons.com
dir: M3 junct 5 onto A287 Farnham. After 1.5m left for Dogmersfield, hotel 0.6m on left

PETS: Bedrooms (23 GF) **Charges** £35 per stay **Public areas** except spa & dining areas on leads **Grounds** on leads disp bin **Exercise area** 500-acre grounds **Facilities** food bowl water bowl bedding dog chews feeding mat scoop/disp bags pet sitting cage storage walks info vet info **On Request** fridge access torch towels **Other** charge for damage **Restrictions** no breed larger than a Labrador

This Georgian manor house, set in 500 acres of rolling grounds and English Heritage listed gardens, offers the upmost in luxury and relaxation, just an hour from London. The spacious and stylish bedrooms are particularly well appointed and offer up-to-date technology. Fitness and spa facilities include nearly every conceivable indoor and outdoor activity, in addition to luxurious pampering. An elegant restaurant, a healthy eating spa café and a trendy bar are popular venues.

Rooms 133 (23 GF) **Facilities** Spa STV 🅮 ♨ Fishing 🏊 Gym Clay pigeon shooting Bikes Canal boat Falconry Horse riding Jogging trails 🎵 Xmas New Year Wi-fi **Services** Lift Air con **Parking** 165

EAST TYTHERLEY — Map 4 SU22

The Star Inn
★★★★ INN

SO51 0LW
☎ 01794 340225
e-mail: info@starinn.co.uk
dir: 1m S of East Tytherley

PETS: Bedrooms (3 GF) unattended **Public areas** except restaurant on leads **Grounds** on leads disp bin **Exercise area** 500mtrs **Facilities** water bowl dog chews leads washing facs cage storage walks info vet info **On Request** fridge access torch towels **Other** charge for damage **Resident Pets:** Jake (Jack Russell), Gray (cat)

This charming coaching inn offers bedrooms in a purpose-built annexe, separate from the main pub. The spacious rooms have high levels of quality and comfort, and an outdoor children's play area is available. There is a loyal following of locals and visitors alike, drawn especially by the excellent food.

Rooms 3 annexe en suite (3 GF) **Facilities** FTV tea/coffee Dinner available Wi-fi **Parking** 50 **Notes** RS Sun eve & Mon

FAREHAM — Map 4 SU50

Bembridge House
★★★★ GUEST ACCOMMODATION

32 Osborn Rd PO16 7DS
☎ 01329 317050
e-mail: bembridgehouse@live.co.uk
web: www.bembridge-house.co.uk
dir: M27 junct 11 follow signs to Fareham town centre, then signs to Ferneham Hall, Bembridge House opposite

PETS: Bedrooms unattended sign 2 bedrooms only please phone for charges **Public areas** except dining room **Grounds** on leads disp bin **Exercise area** 1m **Facilities** food bowl water bowl litter tray scoop/disp bags leads washing facs cage storage vet info **On Request** fridge access torch towels **Other** charge for damage

Bembridge House is a haven of tranquillity yet it is located within walking distance of the town centre with its varied choice of restaurants and shops. The house has been sympathetically restored and offers well appointed accommodation. Breakfast is served in the attractive dining room, which overlooks the front garden.

Rooms 4 en suite (4 fmly) **S** £60-£70; **D** £100-£120 **Facilities** FTV tea/coffee Cen ht Wi-fi **Parking** 9 **Notes** 🐾

FARNBOROUGH — Map 4 SU85

Holiday Inn Farnborough
★★★ 80% HOTEL

Lynchford Rd GU14 6AZ
☎ 0871 942 9029 & 01252 894300 📠 01252 523166
e-mail: reservations-farnborough@ihg.com
web: www.holidayinn.co.uk
dir: M3 junct 4, follow A325 through Farnborough towards Aldershot. Hotel on left at The Queen's rdbt

PETS: Bedrooms (35 GF) sign ground-floor bedrooms (with access to garden) only **Charges** **Grounds** on leads disp bin **Exercise area** 500yds **Facilities** cage storage walks info vet info **On Request** fridge access torch **Stables** approx 5m **Other** charge for damage

This hotel occupies a perfect location for events in Aldershot and Farnborough with ample parking on site and easy access to the M3. Modern bedrooms provide good comfort levels, and internet access is provided throughout. Leisure facilities comprise a swimming pool, gym and beauty treatment rooms. Smart meeting rooms are also available.

Rooms 142 (31 fmly) (35 GF) (7 smoking) **Facilities** Spa STV 🅮 supervised Gym Sauna Steam room Beauty room 🎵 Xmas New Year Wi-fi **Services** Air con **Parking** 170

FLEET MOTORWAY SERVICE AREA (M3)　　Map 4 SU75

Days Inn Fleet - M3
BUDGET HOTEL

Fleet Services GU51 1AA
☎ 01252 815587　📄 01252 815587
e-mail: fleet.hotel@welcomebreak.co.uk
web: www.welcomebreak.co.uk
dir: *Between junct 4a & 5 southbound on M3*

PETS: Bedrooms Charges £5 per night **Public areas Grounds**
on leads **Exercise area** surrounding woodland **Facilities** walks
info vet info **Other** charge for damage cats must be caged

This modern building offers accommodation in smart, spacious
and well-equipped bedrooms, suitable for families and business
travellers, and all with en suite bathrooms. Continental breakfast
is available and other refreshments may be taken at the nearby
family restaurant.

Rooms 58 (46 fmly) (5 smoking) **S** £39.95-£59.95;
D £49.95-£69.95

FORDINGBRIDGE　　Map 4 SU11

Sandy Balls Holiday Centre *(SU167148)*
Sandy Balls Estate Ltd, Godshill SP6 2JZ
☎ 0845 270 2248　📄 01425 653067
e-mail: post@sandyballs.co.uk
dir: *M27 junct 1 onto B3078/B3079, W 8m to Godshill. Site 0.25m
after cattle grid*

PETS: Charges pet friendly touring pitches/dog £4 per night
Public areas disp bin **Exercise area on site** dog exercise field,
woodland **Facilities** food food bowl water bowl dog chews litter
tray scoop/disp bags leads washing facs walks info vet info
Other prior notice required max 2 dogs per booking

Open all year rs Nov-Feb pitches reduced, no activities Last
arrival 21.00hrs Last departure 11.00hrs

A large, mostly wooded New Forest holiday complex with good
provision of touring facilities on terraced, well-laid-out fields.
Pitches are fully serviced with shingle bases, and groups can
be sited beside the river and away from the main site. There are
excellent sporting, leisure and entertainment facilities for the
whole family, a bistro and information centre, and also four tipis
and eight ready-erected tents for hire. 120 acre site. 233 touring
pitches. 233 hardstandings. Tent pitches. Motorhome pitches.
233 statics. 4 bell tents/yurts.

Notes Groups by arrangement, no gazebos.

HARTLEY WINTNEY　　Map 4 SU75

The Elvetham Hotel
★★★ 79% HOTEL

RG27 8AR
☎ 01252 844871　📄 01252 844161
e-mail: enq@theelvetham.co.uk
web: www.theelvetham.co.uk
dir: *M3 junct 4A W, junct 5 E (or M4 junct 11, A33, B3011). Hotel
signed from A323 between Hartley Wintney & Fleet*

PETS: Bedrooms (7 GF) unattended **Charges** £15 per night
Public areas Grounds disp bin **Exercise area Facilities** water
bowl feeding mat washing facs cage storage walks info vet
info **On Request** fridge access torch towels **Other** charge for
damage **Resident Pets:** Harvey (Golden Retriever), Chess (Golden
Labrador)

A spectacular 19th-century mansion set in 35 acres of grounds
with an arboretum. All bedrooms are individually styled and
many have views of the manicured gardens. A popular venue for
weddings and conferences, the hotel lends itself to team building
events and outdoor pursuits.

Rooms 72 (29 annexe) (10 fmly) (7 GF) **S** £80-£120; **D** £100-£140
(incl. bkfst)* **Facilities** STV ⚲ Putt green ⚑ Gym Badminton
Boules Volleyball New Year Wi-fi **Parking** 200 **Notes** Closed 24-27

HURSLEY　　Map 4 SU42

Kings Head
★★★★ INN

SO21 2JW
☎ 01962 775208　📄 01962 775954
e-mail: info@kingsheadhursley.co.uk
dir: *M3 junct 11 onto A3090. Pass through Standon, Kings Head
on left in centre of Hursley opposite church*

PETS: Bedrooms unattended **Public areas** except restaurant on
leads **Grounds** on leads **Exercise area** adjacent **Facilities** food
bowl water bowl washing facs cage storage walks info vet info
On Request fridge access towels

A traditional coaching inn refurbished to its former glory with
modern amenities and stylish interior decor sympathetic to its
historical past. Bedrooms are deeply comfortable, individually
designed and named after previous incumbents of the Hursley
Estate. The cosy bar features changing guest ales and a very
good wine list. The varied and interesting menus take inspiration
from the locally available produce, and prove popular with
residents and locals alike.

Rooms 7 en suite 1 annexe en suite (1 fmly) **S** £55-£65;
D £85-£115 **Facilities** FTV tea/coffee Dinner available Cen ht
Wi-fi **Parking** 30 **Notes** RS 24-25 Dec no accommodation
available No coaches

LINWOOD — Map 4 SU10

Red Shoot Camping Park (SU187094)

▶ ▶ ▶

BH24 3QT
☎ 01425 473789 📠 01425 471558
e-mail: enquiries@redshoot-campingpark.com
dir: *A31 onto A338 towards Fordingbridge & Salisbury. Right at brown signs for caravan park towards Linwood on unclassified roads, site signed*

PETS: Charges £1 per night £7 per week **Public areas** except shop & toilets disp bin **Exercise area** New Forest adjacent **Facilities** food scoop/disp bags leads walks info vet info **Stables** 2m **Other** prior notice required dogs must be on leads at all times & not left unattended **Restrictions** no Pit Bull Terriers

Open Mar-Oct Last arrival 20.30hrs Last departure 13.00hrs

Located behind the Red Shoot Inn in one of the most attractive parts of the New Forest, this park is in an ideal spot for nature lovers and walkers. It is personally supervised by friendly owners, and offers many amenities including a children's play area. There are modern and spotless facilities including a reception and shop. 3.5 acre site. 130 touring pitches. Tent pitches. Motorhome pitches.

Notes Quiet after 22.30hrs

LYMINGTON — Map 4 SZ39

Stanwell House

★★★ 86% ◉ HOTEL
14-15 High St SO41 9AA
☎ 01590 677123 📠 01590 677756
e-mail: enquiries@stanwellhouse.com
dir: *M27 junct 1, follow signs to Lyndhurst then Lymington*

PETS: Bedrooms unattended garden bedrooms only **Charges** £15 per night **Public areas** except restaurant **Grounds** on leads disp bin **Exercise area** 2 mins' walk **Facilities** water bowl dog chews scoop/disp bags washing facs walks info vet info **On Request** fridge access torch towels **Other** dog walking can be arranged **Restrictions** small, well behaved dogs only **Resident Pets:** Louis & Lola (Terriers)

A privately owned Georgian house situated on the wide high street only a few minutes from the marina, and a short drive from the New Forest. Styling itself as a boutique hotel, the bedrooms are individually designed; there are Terrace rooms with garden access, four-poster rooms, and Georgian rooms in the older part of the building. The four suites include two with their own roof terrace. Dining options include the informal bistro and the intimate Seafood Restaurant. Service is friendly and attentive. A meeting room is available.

Rooms 30 (6 fmly) (5 GF) **S** £89-£99; **D** £99-£140 (incl. bkfst)*
Facilities FTV Xmas New Year Wi-fi **Parking** 12 **Notes** LB

Passford House

★★★ 83% HOTEL
Mount Pleasant Ln SO41 8LS
☎ 01590 682398 📠 01590 683494
e-mail: sales@passfordhousehotel.co.uk
web: www.passfordhousehotel.co.uk
dir: *From A337 at Lymington over 2 mini rdbts. 1st right at Tollhouse pub, 1m right into Mount Pleasant Lane*

PETS: Bedrooms (10 GF) certain rooms only **Charges** £10 per night **Public areas** on leads **Grounds** on leads disp bin **Exercise area** nearby **Facilities** vet info **Stables** 0.5m **Other** charge for damage stabling for horses can be arranged

A peaceful hotel set in attractive grounds on the edge of town. Bedrooms vary in size but all are comfortably furnished and well equipped. Extensive public areas include lounges, a smartly appointed restaurant and bar plus leisure facilities. The friendly and well motivated staff provide attentive service.

Rooms 51 (2 annexe) (10 GF) **S** £95-£115; **D** £135-£225 (incl. bkfst)* **Facilities** ◉ ⚡ Putt green 🏊 Gym Petanque Table tennis Pool table Xmas New Year **Parking** 100 **Notes** LB

Gorse Meadow Guest House

★★★★ GUEST HOUSE
Sway Rd SO41 8LR
☎ 01590 673354 📠 01590 673336
e-mail: gorsemeadow@btconnect.com
web: www.gorsemeadow.co.uk
dir: *Off A337 from Brockenhurst, right onto Sway Rd before Toll House pub, Gorse Meadow 1.5m on right*

PETS: Bedrooms (2 GF) **Charges** £10 per night **Grounds** on leads **Facilities** cage storage walks info vet info **On Request** fridge access torch towels **Other** charge for damage **Resident Pets:** Camilla & Igor (Great Danes)

This imposing Edwardian house is situated in 14 acres of grounds, and most of the bedrooms enjoy views across the gardens and paddocks. Situated just one mile from Lymington, this is an excellent base for enjoying the many leisure pursuits that the New Forest has to offer. Meals are also available here, and Mrs Tee often uses the local wild mushrooms in her dishes.

Rooms 5 en suite (2 fmly) (2 GF) **S** £35-£50; **D** £70-£120
Facilities tea/coffee Dinner available Cen ht Licensed Wi-fi **Parking** 20

ENGLAND

NEW FOREST HOTELS

Best Western Forest Lodge

★★★ 83% HOTEL

Pikes Hill, Romsey Rd SO43 7AS
☎ 023 8028 3677 📄 023 8028 2940
e-mail: forest@newforesthotels.co.uk
web: www.newforesthotels.co.uk
dir: *M27 junct 1, A337 towards Lyndhurst. In village, with police station & courts on right, take 1st right into Pikes Hill*

PETS: Bedrooms (10 GF) certain bedrooms only (please check when booking) **Charges** £7.50 per night **Public areas** except restaurant & bar on leads **Grounds** on leads **Exercise area** adjacent **Facilities** water bowl dog chews walks info vet info **On Request** fridge access towels **Other** charge for damage dogs may only be left unattended in bedrooms if owners are on premises & reception staff have been informed

Situated on the edge of Lyndhurst, this hotel is set well back from the main road. The smart, contemporary bedrooms include four-poster rooms and family rooms; children are very welcome here. The eating options are the Forest Restaurant and the fine-dining Glasshouse Restaurant. There is an indoor swimming pool and Nordic sauna.

Rooms 36 (11 fmly) (10 GF) **D** £120-£170 (incl. bkfst)*
Facilities FTV ⊗ Xmas New Year Wi-fi **Parking** 50 **Notes** LB

Lyndhurst Park

★★★ 74% HOTEL

High St SO43 7NL
☎ 023 8028 3923 📄 023 8028 3019
e-mail: lyndhurst.park@forestdale.com
web: www.lyndhurstparkhotel.co.uk
dir: *M27 junct 1-3 to A35 to Lyndhurst. Hotel at bottom of High St*

PETS: Bedrooms unattended **Charges** £7.50 per night **Public areas** except restaurant **Grounds** on leads disp bin **Exercise area** less than 5 mins from hotel **Facilities** food (pre-bookable) food bowl water bowl washing facs cage storage walks info vet info **On Request** fridge access

Although it is just by the High Street, this hotel is afforded seclusion and tranquillity from the town due to its five acres of mature grounds. The comfortable bedrooms include home-from-home touches. The bar offers a stylish setting for a snack whilst the oak-panelled Tudor restaurant provides a more formal dining venue.

Rooms 59 (3 fmly) **Facilities** FTV ⊰ ⊗ Sauna Xmas New Year Wi-fi **Services** Lift **Parking** 100 **Notes** LB

Westover Hall Hotel

★★★ 88% COUNTRY HOUSE HOTEL

Park Ln SO41 0PT
☎ 01590 643044 📄 01590 644490
e-mail: info@westoverhallhotel.com
dir: *M3 & M27 W onto A337 to Lymington, follow signs to Milford on Sea onto B3058, hotel outside village centre towards cliff*

PETS: Bedrooms (2 GF) unattended **Charges** £12 per night **Public areas** except restaurants & bar on leads **Grounds** on leads **Exercise area** beach 100mtrs **Facilities** washing facs walks info vet info **On Request** torch towels **Other** charge for damage **Resident Pet:** Lancelot (Manx cat)

Just a few moments' walk from the beach and boasting uninterrupted views across Christchurch Bay to the Isle of Wight in the distance, this late-Victorian mansion offers a relaxed, informal and friendly atmosphere together with efficient standards of hospitality and service. Bedrooms do vary in size and aspect, but all have been decorated with flair and style. Architectural delights include dramatic stained-glass windows, extensive oak panelling and a galleried entrance hall. The cuisine is prepared with much care and attention to detail.

Rooms 15 (3 annexe) (2 fmly) (2 GF) **S** £99-£210; **D** £120-£270 (incl. bkfst)* **Facilities** Xmas New Year Wi-fi **Parking** 50 **Notes** LB

South Lawn

★★★ 67% HOTEL

Lymington Rd SO41 0RF
☎ 01590 643911 📄 01590 645843
e-mail: reservations.southlawn@ohiml.com
web: www.oxfordhotelsandinns.com
dir: *M27 junct 1, A337 to Lymington, follow signs for Christchurch, in 3m left on B3058 signed Milford on Sea, hotel 1m on right*

PETS: Bedrooms (3 GF) sign **Charges** £8.50 per night **Public areas** except at food service times **Grounds** on leads **Exercise area** 0.5m **Facilities** walks info vet info **Other** charge for damage

Close to the coast and enjoying a quiet location, this pleasant hotel is set in well tended and spacious grounds this hotel is a comfortable place to stay. Bedrooms are spacious and well appointed. Guests can relax or take afternoon tea in the lounge; the restaurant menu offers a good range of choice. Staff are friendly and attentive.

Rooms 24 (3 fmly) (3 GF) **S** £55-£85; **D** £90-£120 (incl. bkfst)* **Facilities** FTV Xmas New Year **Parking** 60 **Notes** LB

Lytton Lawn Touring Park *(SZ293937)*

▶ ▶ ▶ ▶

Lymore Ln SO41 0TX

☎ 01590 648331 📠 01590 645610

e-mail: holidays@shorefield.co.uk

dir: *From Lymington A337 to Christchurch for 2.5m to Everton.
Left onto B3058 to Milford on Sea. 0.25m, left onto Lymore Lane*

PETS: Charges Public areas except shop, play area, games room
& toilet blocks disp bin **Exercise area on site** exercise field
Facilities food walks info vet info **Other** prior notice required
max 2 pets per pitch disposal bags available **Restrictions** no
Rottweilers or Staffordshire Bull Terriers

Open 6 Feb-2 Jan rs Low season shop/reception limited hrs. No
grass pitches Last arrival 22.00hrs Last departure 10.00hrs

A pleasant well-run park with good facilities, located near the
coast. The park is peaceful and quiet, but the facilities of a
sister park 2.5 miles away are available to campers, including
swimming pool, tennis courts, bistro and bar/carvery, and large
club with family entertainment. Fully-serviced pitches provide
good screening, and standard pitches are on gently-sloping
grass. 8 acre site. 136 touring pitches. 53 hardstandings. Tent
pitches. Motorhome pitches.

Notes Families & couples only. Rallies welcome.

THE INDEPENDENTS
HOTEL ASSOCIATION

Swan

★★ 68% HOTEL

11 West St SO24 9AD

☎ 01962 732302 & 734427 📠 01962 735274

e-mail: swanhotel@btinternet.com

web: www.swanhotelalresford.com

dir: *Off A31 onto B3047*

PETS: Bedrooms (5 GF) ground-floor, annexe bedrooms only
Charges £20 per stay **Public areas** except dining room on leads
Exercise area approx 450yds **Facilities** cage storage walks info
vet info **On Request** fridge access **Other** charge for damage
Restrictions no Pit Bull Terriers or Staffordshire Bull Terriers

This former coaching inn dates back to the 18th century and
remains a busy and popular destination for travellers and locals
alike. Bedrooms are situated in both the main building and the
more modern wing. The lounge bar and adjacent restaurant
are open all day; for more traditional dining there is another
restaurant which overlooks the busy village street.

Rooms 23 (12 annexe) (3 fmly) (5 GF) **S** £45-£55; **D** £75-£85
(incl. bkfst)* **Facilities** FTV New Year Wi-fi **Parking** 25 **Notes** LB
RS 25 Dec

The Woolpack Inn

★ ★ ★ ★ ◉◉ INN

Totford SO24 9TJ

☎ 01962 734184 & 0845 293 8066 📠 0845 293 8055

e-mail: info@thewoolpackinn.co.uk

web: www.thewoolpackinn.co.uk

dir: *M3 junct 6 take A339 towards Alton, turn right onto B3046.
In Totford on left*

PETS: Bedrooms (4 GF) unattended ground-floor bedrooms only
Public areas on leads **Grounds** on leads **Exercise area** many
walks within 200mtrs **Facilities** food bowl water bowl bedding
walks info vet info **On Request** fridge access towels **Stables**
1m **Other** charge for damage fenced area on-site suitable for
exercising dogs **Resident Pets:** Buster, Stella & Olive (dogs)

Situated in the small village of Totford, a tranquil and
picturesque location that is within easy reach of main
transport routes. This traditional establishment has benefited
from extensive refurbishment resulting in a fine balance of
contemporary styling and traditional features. The bedrooms
(named after game birds) and the bathrooms are well appointed
with many thoughtful extras making guest comfort a top priority.
The award-winning dining room showcases local produce with
regularly changing specials enhancing the carte options.

Rooms 7 en suite (1 fmly) (4 GF) **S** £85-£105; **D** £85-£105
Facilities FTV tea/coffee Dinner available Direct Dial Cen ht Wi-fi
Pool table **Parking** 20 **Notes** Closed 25 Dec eve

Green Pastures Farm *(SU321158)*

▶ ▶ ▶

SO51 6AJ

☎ 023 8081 4444

e-mail: enquiries@greenpasturesfarm.com

dir: *M27 junct 2. Follow Salisbury signs for 0.5m. Then follow
brown tourist signs for Green Pastures. Also signed from A36 &
A3090 at Ower*

PETS: Sep accom day kennels **Public areas Exercise area**
track leading to common **Facilities** walks info vet info **Other**
prior notice required **Resident Pets:** Pudsey (Collie), Nipper (Jack
Russell), Molly (cat)

Open 15 Mar-Oct Last departure 11.00hrs

A pleasant site on a working farm, with good screening of trees
and shrubs around the perimeter. The touring area is divided by a
border of shrubs and, at times, colourful foxgloves. This peaceful
location is close to the M27 and the New Forest, and is also very
convenient for visiting Paultons Family Theme Park. 5 acre site.
45 touring pitches. 2 hardstandings. Tent pitches. Motorhome
pitches.

Langrish House

★★★ **75%** HOTEL

Langrish GU32 1RN
☎ 01730 266941 📄 01730 260543
e-mail: frontdesk@langrishhouse.co.uk
web: www.langrishhouse.co.uk
dir: A3 onto A272 towards Winchester. Hotel signed, 2.5m on left

PETS: Bedrooms (3 GF) unattended **Charges** £10 per night
Public areas except restaurant **Grounds** on leads **Exercise area**
surrounding area **Facilities** food bowl bedding scoop/disp bags
walks info vet info **On Request** torch towels **Other** pet pack
for dogs (welcome letter, blanket, poop scoop, biscuits & towel)
Resident Pets: Tonga (Black Labrador), Constanza, Redolfo &
Aurora (Siamese cats), chickens, ducks, guineafowl

Langrish House has been in the same family for seven
generations. It is located in an extremely peaceful area just a few
minutes' drive from Petersfield, halfway between Guildford and
Portsmouth. Bedrooms are comfortable and well equipped with
stunning views across the gardens to the hills. Guests can eat in
the intimate Frederick's Restaurant with views over the lawn, or
in the Old Vaults which have an interesting history dating back
to 1644. The hotel is licensed for civil ceremonies and various
themed events take place throughout the year.

Rooms 13 (1 fmly) (3 GF) **S** £45-£100; **D** £65-£170 (incl. bkfst)*
Facilities 🏊 Xmas New Year Wi-fi **Parking** 80 **Notes** LB Closed
2 weeks in Jan

Marriott.
HOTELS & RESORTS

Portsmouth Marriott Hotel

★★★★ **79%** HOTEL

Southampton Rd PO6 4SH
☎ 0870 400 7285 📄 0870 400 7385
web: www.portsmouthmarriott.co.uk
dir: M27 junct 12, keep left off slip road & at lights. Hotel on left

PETS: Bedrooms Public areas on leads **Grounds** on leads
Exercise area 20 mins **Other** charge for damage **Restrictions**
small & medium size dogs only

Close to the motorway and ferry port, this hotel is well suited to
the business trade. The comfortable and well laid-out bedrooms
provide a comprehensive range of facilities including up-to-date
workstations. The leisure club offers a pool, a gym, and a health
and beauty salon.

Rooms 174 (77 fmly) (9 smoking) **D** £95-£170* **Facilities** STV
FTV 🏊 supervised Gym Exercise studio Beauty salon Treatment
room Xmas New Year Wi-fi **Services** Lift Air con **Parking** 196
Notes LB

Best Western Royal Beach

★★★ **78%** HOTEL

South Pde, Southsea PO4 0RN
☎ 023 9273 1281 📄 023 9281 7572
e-mail: enquiries@royalbeachhotel.co.uk
web: www.royalbeachhotel.co.uk
dir: M27 to M275, follow signs to seafront. Hotel on seafront

PETS: Bedrooms Public areas except restaurant **Exercise area**
nearby park & green **Facilities** walks info vet info

This former Victorian seafront hotel is a smart and comfortable
venue suitable for leisure and business guests alike. Bedrooms
and public areas are well presented and generally spacious, and
the smart Coast Bar is an ideal venue for a relaxing drink.

Rooms 124 (18 fmly) **Facilities** STV Xmas New Year Wi-fi
Services Lift **Parking** 50 **Notes** LB

Seacrest

★★ **80%** HOTEL

11/12 South Pde, Southsea PO5 2JB
☎ 023 9273 3192 📄 023 9283 2523
e-mail: office@seacresthotel.co.uk
dir: From M27/M275 follow signs for seafront, Pyramids & Sea
Life Centre. Hotel opposite Rock Gardens & Pyramids

PETS: Bedrooms (3 GF) unattended specific bedrooms allocated
Charges £6 per night £42 per week **Public areas** except
restaurant **Restrictions** small & medium size dogs only

In a premier seafront location, this smart hotel provides the ideal
base for exploring the town. Bedrooms, many benefiting from
sea views, are decorated to a high standard with good facilities.
Guests can relax in either the south-facing lounge, furnished
with large leather sofas, or the adjacent bar; there is also a cosy
dining room popular with residents.

Rooms 28 (3 fmly) (3 GF) **S** £55-£79; **D** £65-£145 (incl. bkfst)
Facilities STV FTV Wi-fi **Services** Lift **Parking** 12 **Notes** LB Closed
24 Dec-2 Jan

ENGLAND

Moortown Lodge

★ ★ ★ ★ GUEST ACCOMMODATION

244 Christchurch Rd BH24 3AS
☎ 01425 471404 📠 01425 476527
e-mail: enquiries@moortownlodge.co.uk
dir: *1m S of Ringwood. Off A31 at Ringwood onto B3347, signs to Sopley, Lodge next to David Lloyds Leisure Club*

PETS: Bedrooms (2 GF) certain bedrooms only **Exercise area** 50yds **Facilities** food bowl water bowl dog chews feeding mat leads washing facs walks info vet info **On Request** fridge access torch towels **Other** charge for damage **Restrictions** small & medium size dogs only; no aggressive breeds (see page 7)

The light and airy accommodation is finished to a very high standard, with digital TV and broadband in each room. Two of the well-equipped bedrooms are at ground-floor level, and one features a four-poster bed. Breakfast is served at separate tables in the smart lounge-dining room.

Rooms 7 en suite (3 fmly) (2 GF); **D** £86–£96 **Facilities** FTV tea/coffee Direct Dial Cen ht Wi-fi **Parking** 9 **Notes** LB

Little Forest Lodge

★ ★ ★ ★ GUEST HOUSE

Poulner Hill BH24 3HS
☎ 01425 478848 📠 01425 473564
dir: *1.5m E of Ringwood on A31*

PETS: Bedrooms (1 GF) **Charges** £5 per night **Public areas** except dining room **Grounds** disp bin **Exercise area** nearby **Facilities** food bowl water bowl dog chews feeding mat washing facs cage storage walks info vet info **On Request** fridge access torch towels **Resident Pets:** Ollie (Flat Coat Retriever), Millie (Doberman/Whippet cross), Harry & Spike (cats), ducks, chickens

A warm welcome is given to guests, and their pets, at this charming Edwardian house set in two acres of woodland. Bedrooms are pleasantly decorated and equipped with thoughtful extras. Both the attractive wood-panelled dining room and the delightful lounge, with bar and wood-burning fire, overlook the gardens.

Rooms 6 en suite (3 fmly) (1 GF) **S** £45–£50; **D** £70 **Facilities** tea/coffee Cen ht Licensed ⇒ **Parking** 10

Hill Farm Caravan Park *(SU287238)*

▶ ▶ ▶ ▶ ▶

Branches Ln, Sherfield English SO51 6FH
☎ 01794 340402 📠 01794 342358
e-mail: gjb@hillfarmpark.com
dir: *Signed from A27 (Salisbury to Romsey road) in Sherfield English, 4m NW of Romsey & M27 junct 2*

PETS: Charges Public areas disp bin **Exercise area on site** dog walk with disposal bin **Facilities** food washing facs dog grooming walks info vet info **Other** prior notice required dogs must be kept on leads at all times & not left unattended; max 2 dogs per pitch disposal bags available

Open Mar-Oct Last arrival 20.00hrs Last departure noon

A small, well-sheltered park peacefully located amidst mature trees and meadows. The two toilet blocks offer smart unisex showers as well as a fully en suite family/disabled room and plenty of privacy in the washrooms. Bramleys is a good restaurant, with an outside patio, that serves a wide range of snacks and meals. This attractive park is well placed for visiting Salisbury and the New Forest National Park, and the south coast is only a short drive away, making it an appealing holiday location. 10.5 acre site. 70 touring pitches. 60 hardstandings. Tent pitches. Motorhome pitches. 6 statics.

Notes Minimum noise at all times & no noise after 23.00hrs. One unit per pitch. Unsuitable for teenagers. 🐾

ENGLAND

ROTHERWICK — Map 4 SU75

Tylney Hall Hotel

★★★★ ◎◎ HOTEL

RG27 9AZ

☎ 01256 764881   📠 01256 768141

e-mail: sales@tylneyhall.com

web: www.tylneyhall.com

dir: *M3 junct 5, A287 to Basingstoke, over junct with A30, over rail bridge, towards Newnham. Right at Newnham Green. Hotel 1m on left*

PETS: Bedrooms (40 GF) unattended garden bedrooms only **Charges** £25 per night **Grounds** on leads disp bin **Exercise area** fields (approx 0.5m) **Facilities** water bowl bedding dog chews cat treats feeding mat vet info **On Request** fridge access torch towels **Stables** nearby

A grand Victorian country house set in 66 acres of beautiful parkland. The hotel offers high standards of comfort in relaxed yet elegant surroundings, featuring magnificently restored water gardens, originally laid out by the famous gardener, Gertrude Jekyll. Spacious public rooms include Italian and Wedgwood styled drawing rooms and the panelled Oak Room Restaurant, filled with stunning flower arrangements and warmed by log fires, that offers cuisine based on locally sourced ingredients. The spacious bedrooms are traditionally furnished and offer individual style and high degrees of comfort. The excellent leisure facilities include indoor and outdoor swimming pools, tennis courts, jogging trails, croquet lawns and a spa.

Rooms 112 (77 annexe) (1 fmly) (40 GF) **S** £190–£470; **D** £220–£500 (incl. bkfst)* **Facilities** Spa STV FTV ◎ ⚘ 🏊 🏌 Gym Clay pigeon shooting Archery Falconry Balloon rides Laser shooting Xmas New Year Wi-fi **Parking** 120 **Notes** LB

SOUTHAMPTON — Map 4 SU41

The Legacy Botleigh Grange Hotel

★★★★ 75% ◎ HOTEL

Grange Rd, Hedge End SO30 2GA

☎ 08444 119050 & 0330 333 2850   📠 08444 119051

e-mail: res-botleighgrange@legacy-hotels.co.uk

web: www.legacy-hotels.co.uk

dir: *M27 junct 7, A334 to Botley, hotel 0.5m on left*

PETS: Bedrooms (9 GF) unattended east wing ground floor bedrooms only **Charges** £10 per night £70 per week **Grounds** on leads **Exercise area** 5 mins **Facilities** vet info **Other** charge for damage

This impressive mansion, situated close to the M27, displays good quality throughout. The bedrooms are spacious with a good range of facilities. Public areas include a large conference room and a pleasant terrace with views overlooking the gardens and lake. The restaurant offers interesting menus using fresh, local produce.

Rooms 56 (8 fmly) (9 GF) **Facilities** Spa STV FTV ◎ Putt green Fishing Gym Sauna Steam room Relaxation room Xmas New Year Wi-fi **Services** Lift **Parking** 200

Southampton Park

★★★ 71% HOTEL

Cumberland Place SO15 2WY

☎ 023 8034 3343   📠 023 8033 2538

e-mail: southampton.park@forestdale.com

web: www.southamptonparkhotel.com

dir: *At north end of Inner Ring Road, opposite Watts Park & Civic Centre*

PETS: Bedrooms sign **Charges** £7.50 per night **Public areas** except food area & bar on leads **Exercise area** across road **Facilities** food (pre-bookable) food bowl cage storage **On Request** towels **Other** charge for damage

This modern hotel, in the heart of the city, provides well-equipped, smartly appointed and comfortable bedrooms. It boasts a well equipped spa with all modern facilities and a beauty salon for those who wish to pamper themselves. The public areas are spacious and include the popular MJ's Brasserie. Parking is available in a multi-storey behind the hotel.

Rooms 72 (10 fmly) **Facilities** Spa FTV ◎ supervised Gym New Year Wi-fi **Services** Lift **Notes** Closed 25 & 26 Dec nights

THE INDEPENDENTS
HOTEL ASSOCIATION

Elizabeth House

★★ 78% HOTEL

42-44 The Avenue SO17 1XP

☎ 023 8022 4327   📠 023 8033 9651

e-mail: mail@elizabethhousehotel.com

web: www.elizabethhousehotel.com

dir: *On A33, hotel on left after Southampton Common, before main lights*

PETS: Bedrooms (8 GF) **Grounds** disp bin **Exercise area** 200yds **Facilities** cage storage walks info vet info **On Request** fridge access torch towels **Resident Pet:** Henry (West Highland Terrier)

This hotel is conveniently situated close to the city centre, so provides an ideal base for both business and leisure guests. The bedrooms are well equipped and are attractively furnished with comfort in mind. There is also a cosy and atmospheric bistro in the cellar where evening meals are served.

Rooms 27 (7 annexe) (9 fmly) (8 GF) **S** £60-£67.50; **D** £70-£79.95 (incl. bkfst)* **Facilities** FTV Wi-fi **Parking** 31

Holiday Inn Express Southampton M27 Jct 7

BUDGET HOTEL

Botley Rd, West End SO30 3XA
☎ 023 8060 6060 & 8060 6040 📠 023 8060 6050
e-mail: reservations@expressbyholidayinn.uk.net
web: www.meridianleisurehotels.com/southampton
dir: M27 junct 7, follow brown Rose Bowl signs. Hotel 1m at entrance to The Rose Bowl

PETS: Bedrooms (38 GF) **Charges** £10 per night **Grounds** on leads **Exercise area** nearby **Facilities** cage storage walks info vet info **Stables** 1.5m **Other** charge for damage no charge for assist dogs **Restrictions** max weight 7kg

This hotel, adjacent to the Rose Bowl, is conveniently located for Southampton Airport and Docks and has ample free parking. There is an air-conditioned restaurant serving conference lunches, evening meals and complimentary hot breakfast, a fully licensed bar and lounge area with a 42" plasma TV with freeview channels. The hotel offers high speed Wi-fi throughout. Leisure facilities are available at the adjacent Esporta Leisure Centre for a nominal fee.

Rooms 176 (129 fmly) (38 GF) (18 smoking) **S** £49.46-£109; **D** £49.46-£109 (incl. bkfst)*

SOUTHSEA

See Portsmouth & Southsea

STOCKBRIDGE　　　　　　　　Map 4 SU33

York Lodge

★★★★ BED AND BREAKFAST

Five Bells Ln, Nether Wallop SO20 8HE
☎ 01264 781313
e-mail: bradley@york-lodge.co.uk
web: www.york-lodge.co.uk
dir: Exit A30, or A343, onto B3084, into Hosketts Ln, left into Five Bells Ln, 1st house on right

PETS: Bedrooms (2 GF) **Public areas Grounds** disp bin **Exercise area** 2 mins' walk **Facilities** washing facs cage storage walks info vet info **On Request** fridge access torch towels **Resident Pet:** Ella (Boston Terrier/Pug cross)

Located in the picturesque village used as one of the sets for Agatha Christie's *Miss Marple* TV series, this charming house has comfortable accommodation in a self-contained wing. Bedrooms are stylishly presented with many thoughtful extra facilities. The dining room overlooks peaceful gardens.

Rooms 2 en suite (2 GF) **S** £35-£55; **D** £70-£75 **Facilities** FTV tea/coffee Cen ht Wi-fi **Parking** 4 **Notes** No Children 8yrs 🐾

The Three Cups Inn

★★★ INN

High St SO20 6HB
☎ 01264 810527
e-mail: manager@the3cups.co.uk

PETS: Bedrooms unattended **Charges** £10 per night **Public areas** bar & lounge only on leads **Grounds** on leads **Exercise area** adjacent **Facilities** food bowl water bowl cage storage walks info vet info **On Request** fridge access torch **Other** charge for damage **Resident Pet:** Tommy (cat)

A former coaching inn on the high street in a popular town, with its own parking. Bedrooms are comfortable and well equipped, and food is available every evening.

Rooms 8 en suite (3 fmly) **S** £72-£79; **D** £79-£89 **Facilities** tea/coffee Dinner available Cen ht Wi-fi Fishing **Parking** 15

The Grosvenor

★★★ INN

23 High St SO20 6EU
☎ 01264 810606 📠 01264 810747
e-mail: 9180@greeneking.co.uk

PETS: Bedrooms sign ground-floor bedrooms 2, 3 & 4 only **Public areas** except restaurant on leads **Grounds** on leads **Exercise area** 150yds **Facilities** walks info vet info **Other** charge for damage

Located between the historic cathedral cities of Winchester and Salisbury and a stone's throw from the River Test, The Grosvenor provides en suite accommodation within the traditional setting of this Georgian building. Bedrooms have been refurbished and have been designed with guest comfort in mind. The Tom Cannon Restaurant is popular with both residents and locals alike, and provides a good range of locally sourced produce, and game when in season.

Rooms 14 en suite 12 annexe en suite (6 GF) **S** £59; **D** £79-£89 **Facilities** tea/coffee Dinner available Direct Dial Cen ht Wi-fi Fishing **Parking** 16

SUTTON SCOTNEY — Map 4 SU43

Norton Park
★★★★ 76% HOTEL

SO21 3NB

☎ 0845 074 0055 & 01962 763000 📠 01962 760860

e-mail: nortonpark@qhotels.co.uk

web: www.qhotels.co.uk

dir: *From A303 & A34 junct follow signs to Sutton Scotney. Hotel on Micheldever Station Rd (old A30), 1m from Sutton Scotney*

PETS: Bedrooms (80 GF) unattended sign ground-floor bedrooms only **Sep accom** 2 kennels **Charges** £15 per night **Public areas** except food service areas on leads **Grounds** on leads disp bin **Exercise area** nearby **Facilities** food food bowl water bowl bedding dog chews cat treats scoop/disp bags cage storage walks info vet info **On Request** fridge access torch towels **Stables** 0.5m **Other** charge for damage

Set in 54 acres of beautiful parkland in the heart of Hampshire, Norton Park offers both business and leisure guests a great range of amenities. Dating from the 16th century, the hotel is complemented by extensive buildings housing the bedrooms, and public areas which include a superb leisure club and numerous conference facilities. Ample parking is available.

Rooms 175 (11 fmly) (80 GF) **Facilities** Spa ⓣ supervised 🏊 Gym Steam room Sauna Experience shower Ice fountain Xmas New Year Wi-fi **Services** Lift **Parking** 220 **Notes** LB

WARNFORD — Map 4 SU62

George & Falcon
★★★★ INN

Warnford Rd SO32 3LB

☎ 01730 829623 📠 01730 352222

e-mail: reservations@georgeandfalcon.com

web: www.georgeandfalcon.com

dir: *Adjacent to A32 in village*

PETS: Bedrooms 2 specific bedrooms only **Public areas** except restaurant on leads **Grounds** on leads disp bin **Exercise area** 200mtrs **Facilities** water bowl washing facs cage storage walks info vet info **On Request** torch towels **Stables** adjacent farm **Other** charge for damage please phone for stabling charges

Set within the picturesque village of Warnford located close to major transport links to Winchester, Portsmouth and Southampton. Bedrooms are tastefully appointed following a refurbishment, featuring modern appointments yet keeping the charm and character of this old coaching inn. Traditional fayre is served in the popular restaurant and bar, whilst the large decking area is a welcome addition for summer months.

Rooms 6 en suite (1 fmly) **S** £59-£99; **D** £59-£109 **Facilities** FTV tea/coffee Dinner available Cen ht Wi-fi Golf 18 Fishing Riding **Parking** 47 **Notes** LB Closed Xmas & 1 Jan

WINCHESTER — Map 4 SU42

Lainston House
★★★★ ◉◉◉ COUNTRY HOUSE HOTEL

Sparsholt SO21 2LT

☎ 01962 776088 📠 01962 776672

e-mail: enquiries@lainstonhouse.com

web: www.exclusivehotels.co.uk

dir: *2m NW off B3049 towards Stockbridge*

PETS: Bedrooms (18 GF) **Charges** £50 per night **Public areas** lounge only on leads **Grounds Facilities** food (pre-bookable) water bowl bedding dog chews cat treats feeding mat dog walking cage storage walks info vet info **On Request** fridge access torch towels **Other** charge for damage dog menu

This graceful example of a William and Mary House enjoys a countryside location amidst mature grounds and gardens. Staff provide good levels of courtesy and care with a polished, professional service. Bedrooms are tastefully appointed and include some spectacular, spacious rooms with stylish handmade beds and stunning bathrooms. Public rooms include a cocktail bar built entirely from a single cedar and stocked with an impressive range of rare drinks and cigars.

Rooms 49 (6 fmly) (18 GF) **D** £245-£745* **Facilities** STV FTV 🎣 Fishing 🏋 Gym Archery Clay pigeon shooting Cycling Hot air ballooning Falconry 🎵 Xmas New Year Wi-fi **Parking** 200 **Notes** LB

Mercure Wessex
★★★★ 69% HOTEL

Paternoster Row SO23 9LQ

☎ 01962 861611 📠 01962 841503

e-mail: H6619@accor.com

web: www.mercure.com

dir: *M3 junct 10, 2nd exit at rdbt signed Winchester/B3330. Right at lights. Left at 2nd rdbt. Over small bridge, on at next rdbt into Broadway. Left at Guildhall Tavern into Colebrook St. Hotel 50yds on right*

PETS: Bedrooms east wing bedrooms only **Charges** £10 per night £70 per week **Exercise area** 0.5m **Facilities** cage storage walks info vet info **Other** charge for damage

Occupying an enviable location in the centre of this historic city and adjacent to the spectacular cathedral, this hotel is quietly situated on a side street. Inside, the atmosphere is restful and welcoming, with public areas and some bedrooms enjoying unrivalled views of the hotel's centuries-old neighbour.

Rooms 94 (6 fmly) **S** £75-£147; **D** £85-£157* **Facilities** STV Gym Xmas New Year Wi-fi **Services** Lift **Parking** 42 **Notes** LB

The Winchester Royal Hotel

★★★ 78% HOTEL

St Peter St SO23 8BS

☎ 01962 840840 📠 01962 841582

e-mail: winchester.royal@forestdale.com

web: www.thewinchesterroyalhotel.co.uk

dir: *M3 junct 9 to Winnall Trading Estate. Follow to city centre, cross river, left, 1st right. Onto one-way system, take 2nd right. Hotel immediately on right*

PETS: Bedrooms (27 GF) unattended **Charges** £7.50 per night **Public areas** except restaurant on leads **Grounds** disp bin **Exercise area** few mins' walk **Facilities** food food bowl water bowl walks info vet info **On Request** fridge access **Other** charge for damage please phone for further details of pet facilities **Restrictions** well behaved dogs only

Situated in the heart of the former capital of England, a warm welcome awaits at this friendly hotel, which in parts, dates back to the 16th century. The bedrooms may vary in style but all are comfortable and well equipped; the modern annexe rooms overlook the attractive well-tended gardens. The conservatory restaurant makes a very pleasant setting for enjoyable meals.

Rooms 75 (56 annexe) (1 fmly) (27 GF) **Facilities** FTV Xmas New Year Wi-fi **Parking** 50 **Notes** LB

HEREFORDSHIRE

EARDISLAND — Map 3 SO45

Arrow Bank Holiday Park *(SO419588)*

►►►

Nun House Farm HR6 9BG

☎ 01544 388312 📠 01544 388312

e-mail: enquiries@arrowbankholidaypark.co.uk

dir: *From Leominster A44 towards Rhayader. Right to Eardisland, follow signs*

PETS: Charges £1 per night **Public areas** disp bin **Exercise area on site** fully enclosed exercise area **Facilities** washing facs walks info vet info **Other** prior notice required **Restrictions** no dangerous dogs (see page 7)

Open Mar-7 Jan

This peaceful, adults-only park is set in the beautiful 'Black and White' village of Eardisland with its free exhibitions, tea rooms and heritage centre. The park is well positioned for visiting the many local attractions, as well as those further afield such as Ludlow Castle, Ross-on-Wye, Shrewsbury and Wales. The modern toilet facilities are spotlessly clean. 45 touring pitches. 36 hardstandings. 16 seasonal pitches. Tent pitches. Motorhome pitches. 62 statics.

Notes No ball games, no skateboards/cycles in park.

HEREFORD — Map 3 SO54

Three Counties Hotel

★★★ 75% HOTEL

Belmont Rd HR2 7BP

☎ 01432 299955 📠 01432 275114

e-mail: enquiries@threecountieshotel.co.uk

web: www.threecountieshotel.co.uk

dir: *On A465 (Abergavenny road)*

PETS: Bedrooms (46 GF) certain bedrooms only **Grounds** on leads **Facilities** vet info

Just a mile west of the city centre, this large, privately owned, modern complex has well-equipped, spacious bedrooms; many are located in separate single-storey buildings around the extensive car park. There is a spacious, comfortable lounge, a traditional bar and an attractive restaurant.

Rooms 60 (32 annexe) (4 fmly) (46 GF) **S** £67-£71.50; **D** £77-£92.50 (incl. bkfst)* **Facilities** STV FTV Wi-fi **Parking** 250 **Notes** LB

Holly House Farm *(SO456367)*

★★★★ FARMHOUSE

Allensmore HR2 9BH

☎ 01432 277294 & 07889 830223 Mrs D Sinclair

e-mail: hollyhousefarm@aol.com

web: www.hollyhousefarm.org.uk

dir: *A465 S to Allensmore, right signed Cobhall Common, at small x-rds right into lane, house on right*

PETS: Bedrooms Sep accom **Public areas** except dining room on leads **Grounds** on leads disp bin **Exercise area** field adjacent **Facilities** pet sitting dog walking washing facs cage storage walks info vet info **On Request** fridge access torch **Stables Resident Pets:** Daisy (Labrador), Popsie (cat), Sam & Tommy (horses)

Surrounded by open countryside, this spacious farmhouse is a relaxing base for those visiting this beautiful area. The homely and comfortable bedrooms have lovely views over the fields. Breakfast makes use of local produce together with home-made jams and marmalade. Pets are very welcome here and the proprietor is happy to look after them during the day if required.

Rooms 2 rms (1 en suite) (1 pri facs); **D** £50-£70 **Facilities** FTV tea/coffee Cen ht **Parking** 32 **Notes** Closed 25-26, 31 Dec & 1 Jan 11 acres horses

HEREFORD *continued*

Sink Green *(SO542377)*

★★★★ FARMHOUSE

Rotherwas HR2 6LE

☎ 01432 870223 📠 01432 870223 Mr D E Jones

e-mail: enquiries@sinkgreenfarm.co.uk

web: www.sinkgreenfarm.co.uk

dir: *3m SE of city centre. Off A49 onto B4399 for 2m*

PETS: Bedrooms Public areas Grounds disp bin **Exercise area** adjoining fields **Facilities** water bowl washing facs walks info vet info **On Request** fridge access torch towels **Other** charge for damage **Resident Pet:** Max (Sheepdog)

This charming 16th-century farmhouse stands in attractive countryside and has many original features, including flagstone floors, exposed beams and open fireplaces. Bedrooms are traditionally furnished and one has a four-poster bed. The pleasant garden has a comfortable summer house, hot tub and barbecue.

Rooms 3 en suite **S** £35-£40; **D** £70-£80 **Facilities** FTV TVL tea/coffee Cen ht Wi-fi Fishing **Parking** 10 **Notes** LB 🐾 180 acres beef

Ridge Hill Caravan and Campsite *(SO509355)*

▶

HR2 8AG

☎ 01432 351293

e-mail: ridgehill@fsmail.net

dir: *From Hereford on A49, then B4399 signed Rotherwas. At 1st rdbt follow Dinedor/Little Dewchurch signs, in 1m signed Ridge Hill/Twyford turn right, then right at phone box, 200yds, site on right*

PETS: Charges dog £2 per night **Public areas Exercise area on site Exercise area** 1.05m **Facilities** walks info vet info **Other** dogs must be kept on leads at all times

Open Mar-Oct Last departure noon

A simple, basic site set high on Ridge Hill a few miles south of Hereford. This peaceful site offers outstanding views over the countryside. It does not have toilets or showers, and therefore own facilities are essential, although toilet tents can be supplied on request at certain times of the year. Please do not rely on Sat Nav directions to this site - guidebook directions should be used for caravans and motorhomes. 1.3 acre site. 5 touring pitches. Tent pitches. Motorhome pitches.

Notes 🐾

Cuckoo's Corner Campsite *(SO501456)*

▶ ▶

Cuckoo's Corner HR4 8AH

☎ 01432 760234

e-mail: cuckooscorner@gmail.com

dir: *Direct access from A49. From Hereford 2nd left after Moreton on Lugg sign. From Leominster 1st right (non gated road) after brown sign. Right just before island*

PETS: Public areas disp bin **Exercise area** public footpath from site **Facilities** washing facs walks info vet info **Other** prior notice required dogs must be quiet & kept on leads at all times

Open all year Last arrival 21.00hrs Last departure 13.00hrs

This small, adults-only site is well positioned just north of Hereford, with easy access to the city. The site is in two areas, and offers hardstandings and some electric pitches. It is an ideal spot for an overnight stop or longer stay to visit the attractions of the area. There's a bus stop just outside the site and a full timetable is available from the reception office. 3 acre site. 19 touring pitches. 15 hardstandings. Tent pitches. Motorhome pitches.

Notes No large groups, no noise after 22.30hrs. 🐾

Townsend Touring Park *(SO395583)*

▶ ▶ ▶ ▶ ▶

Townsend Farm HR6 9HB

☎ 01544 388527

e-mail: info@townsend-farm.co.uk

dir: *A44 through Pembridge. Site 40mtrs from 30mph on E side of village*

PETS: Charges dog £2 per night **Public areas Exercise area on site Exercise area** 0.5m **Facilities** walks info vet info **Other** dogs must be kept on leads at all times

Open Mar-mid Jan Last arrival 22.00hrs Last departure noon

This outstanding park is spaciously located on the edge of one of Herefordshire's most beautiful Black and White villages. The park offers excellent facilities, and all hardstanding pitches are fully serviced, and it has its own award-winning farm shop and butchery. It also makes an excellent base from which to explore the local area, including Ludlow Castle and Ironbridge. There's a camping pod available for hire. 12 acre site. 60 touring pitches. 23 hardstandings. Tent pitches. Motorhome pitches.

ROSS-ON-WYE   Map 3 SO62

Glewstone Court

★★★ **74%** @ COUNTRY HOUSE HOTEL

Glewstone HR9 6AW

☎ 01989 770367   🖹 01989 770282

e-mail: glewstone@aol.com

web: www.glewstonecourt.com

dir: *From Ross-on-Wye market palce follow A40/A49 Monmouth/ Hereford signs, over Wilton Bridge to rdbt, left onto A40 towards Monmouth, in 1m right for hotel*

PETS: Bedrooms (1 GF) unattended   **Charges** £7 per night **Public areas** except restaurant   on leads   **Grounds** disp bin **Exercise area** 50mtrs   **Facilities** food (pre-bookable) food bowl water bowl   bedding   feeding mat   litter tray   scoop/disp bags leads   washing facs   cage storage   walks info   vet info   **On Request** fridge access   torch   towels   **Stables** 3m   **Other** charge for damage **Resident Pets:** Brecon (Golden Retriever), Barney (Long Haired Miniature Dachshund), Benji (working Cocker Spaniel), Tilly (cat)

This charming hotel enjoys an elevated position with views over Ross-on-Wye, and is set in well-tended gardens. Informal service is delivered with great enthusiasm by Bill Reeve-Tucker, whilst the kitchen is the domain of Christine Reeve-Tucker who offers an extensive menu of well executed dishes. Bedrooms come in a variety of sizes and are tastefully furnished and well equipped.

Rooms 8 (2 fmly) (1 GF) **S** £60-£85; **D** £100-£125 (incl. bkfst)* **Facilities** FTV 🏊 New Year Wi-fi **Parking** 25 **Notes** LB Closed 25-27 Dec

Pengethley Manor

★★★ **74%** HOTEL

Pengethley Park HR9 6LL

☎ 01989 730211   🖹 01989 730238

e-mail: reservations@pengethleymanor.co.uk

web: www.pengethleymanor.co.uk

dir: *4m N on A49 (Hereford road), from Ross-on-Wye*

PETS: Bedrooms unattended   courtyard bedrooms only **Public areas** except restaurant & bar   on leads   **Grounds** on leads disp bin   **Exercise area** 100yds   **Facilities** washing facs   walks info   vet info   **On Request** fridge access   torch   towels   **Stables** 5m   **Other** charge for damage   prior arrangement must be made for pets to ensure correct room is allocated

This fine Georgian mansion is set in extensive grounds with glorious views and two successful vineyards that produce over

1,000 bottles a year. The bedrooms are tastefully appointed and come in a wide variety of styles; all are well equipped. The elegant public rooms are furnished in a style that is in keeping with the character of the house. Dinner provides a range of enjoyable options and is served in the spacious restaurant.

Rooms 25 (14 annexe) (3 fmly) (4 GF) **Facilities** 🏌 ♨ 9 🏊 Golf improvement course Xmas New Year Wi-fi **Parking** 70

King's Head

★★★ **68%** HOTEL

8 High St HR9 5HL

☎ 01989 763174   🖹 01989 769578

e-mail: enquiries@kingshead.co.uk

web: www.kingshead.co.uk

dir: *In town centre, past market building on right*

PETS: Bedrooms unattended   certain bedrooms only **Public areas** bar only   on leads   **Grounds** on leads   **Exercise area** 200yds   **Facilities** food (pre-bookable) food bowl water bowl cage storage   walks info   vet info   **On Request** torch

This establishment dates back to the 14th century and has a wealth of charm and character. Bedrooms are well equipped and comfortable with thoughtful guest extras provided; both four-poster and family rooms are available. The restaurant offers menus and a specials board that reflect a varied selection of local produce including fresh fish, free range beef and lamb. There is a well-stocked bar serving hand-pulled, real ales and along with the restaurant is popular with locals and visitors alike.

Rooms 15 (1 fmly) **S** £56; **D** £95 (incl. bkfst)* **Facilities** FTV Wi-fi **Parking** 13 **Notes** LB

Chasedale

★★ **74%** SMALL HOTEL

Walford Rd HR9 5PQ

☎ 01989 562423 & 565801   🖹 01989 567900

e-mail: chasedale@supanet.com

web: www.chasedale.co.uk

dir: *From town centre, S on B4234, hotel 0.5m on left*

PETS: Bedrooms (1 GF) unattended   **Public areas** except restaurant   **Grounds** disp bin   **Exercise area** 300mtrs   **Facilities** food bowl   water bowl   cage storage   walks info   vet info **On Request** fridge access   towels   **Resident Pet:** Cassis (Black Labrador)

This large, mid-Victorian property is situated on the south-west outskirts of the town. Privately owned and personally run, it provides spacious, well-proportioned public areas and extensive grounds. The accommodation is well equipped and includes ground floor and family rooms, whilst the restaurant offers a wide selection of wholesome food.

Rooms 10 (2 fmly) (1 GF) **S** £45; **D** £90* **Facilities** FTV Xmas Wi-fi **Parking** 14 **Notes** LB

ROSS-ON-WYE *continued*

Wilton Court Restaurant with Rooms

★★★★★ ◉◉ 🏠 RESTAURANT WITH ROOMS

Wilton Ln HR9 6AQ
☎ 01989 562569 📠 01989 768460
e-mail: info@wiltoncourthotel.com
dir: *M50 junct 4, A40 towards Monmouth at 3rd rdbt left signed Ross-on-Wye, 1st right, on right*

PETS: Bedrooms unattended **Charges** £10 per night
Public areas bar only on leads **Grounds** on leads disp bin
Exercise area nearby **Facilities** washing facs walks info vet
info **On Request** fridge access torch **Other** charge for damage
Restrictions no very large dogs

Dating back to the 16th century, this establishment has great charm and a wealth of character. Standing on the banks of the River Wye and just a short walk from the town centre, there is a genuinely relaxed, friendly and unhurried atmosphere created by hosts Roger and Helen Wynn and their reliable team. Bedrooms are tastefully furnished and well equipped, while public areas include a comfortable lounge, traditional bar and pleasant restaurant with a conservatory extension overlooking the garden. High standards of food, using fresh, locally sourced ingredients, are offered.

Rooms 10 en suite (1 fmly) **S** £100-£155; **D** £125-£175
Facilities FTV TVL tea/coffee Dinner available Direct Dial Cen ht
Wi-fi 🔌 Golf 18 Fishing **Parking** 20 **Notes** LB Closed 3-15 Jan

Orles Barn

★★★★★ ◉◉ 🏠 RESTAURANT WITH ROOMS

Wilton HR9 6AE
☎ 01989 562155 📠 01989 768470
e-mail: reservations@orles-barn.co.uk
web: www.orles-barn.co.uk
dir: *A49/A40 rdbt outside Ross-on-Wye, take slip road between petrol station & A40 to Monmouth. 100yds on left*

PETS: Bedrooms sign one bedroom only **Charges** £5 per
night **Public areas** except at food service times **Grounds** disp
bin **Exercise area** 200mtrs **Facilities** water bowl dog chews
feeding mat scoop/disp bags walks info vet info **On Request**
towels **Other** charge for damage **Resident Pets:** William (Black
Labrador), Twiglet (Jack Russell)

The proprietors of this character property offer a warm welcome to all their guests. Older sections of the property date back to the 14th and 17th centuries when it was a farmhouse with a barn. The property offers comfortable bedrooms, a smart cosy lounge with a bar and a spacious restaurant. Dinner and Sunday lunch are offered on a balanced menu of fresh local and seasonal ingredients. Breakfast also utilises quality local produce and makes a good start to the day.

Rooms 5 en suite (1 fmly) (1 GF) **S** £95-£135; **D** £135-£175
Facilities FTV tea/coffee Dinner available Cen ht Wi-fi **Parking** 20
Notes LB

Lumleys

★★★★ BED AND BREAKFAST

Kern Bridge, Bishopswood HR9 5QT
☎ 01600 890040 📠 0870 706 2378
e-mail: helen@lumleys.force9.co.uk
web: www.thelumleys.co.uk
dir: *Off A40 onto B4229 at Goodrich, over Kern Bridge, right at Inn On The Wye, 400yds opposite picnic ground*

PETS: Bedrooms unattended **Public areas** except dining room
Grounds disp bin **Exercise area** adjacent **Facilities** water bowl
washing facs cage storage walks info vet info **On Request**
fridge access torch towels **Resident Pets:** Hector & Barnaby
(Cocker Spaniel/Poodle cross)

This pleasant and friendly bed and breakfast overlooks the River Wye, and has been a hostelry since Victorian times. It offers the character of a bygone era combined with modern comforts and facilities. Bedrooms are individually and carefully furnished and one has a four-poster bed and its own patio. Comfortable public areas include a choice of sitting rooms. Helen Mattis and Judith Mills-Haworth were finalists in the AA's Friendliest Landlady of the Year award 2011-12.

Rooms 3 en suite; **D** £70-£75 **Facilities** STV FTV TVL tea/coffee
Direct Dial Cen ht Wi-fi 🔌 **Parking** 15 **Notes** Closed Nov-end
Mar ◉

Lea House

★★★★ GUEST ACCOMMODATION

Lea HR9 7JZ
☎ 01989 750652 📄 01989 750652
e-mail: enquiries@leahouse.co.uk
web: www.leahouse.co.uk
dir: *4m SE of Ross on A40 towards Gloucester in Lea*

PETS: Bedrooms Charges £7.50 per stay **Public areas**
except dining room during meals on leads **Grounds** disp bin
Exercise area 30yds **Facilities** washing facs cage storage
walks info vet info **On Request** torch towels **Resident Pets:**
Jellybean (Jack Russell), Lilli (cat)

This former coaching inn, near Ross-on-Wye, makes a good
base for exploring the Forest of Dean and the Wye Valley, and
the atmosphere is relaxed and comfortable. The individually
furnished bedrooms are thoughtfully equipped and very homely.
Breakfast in the oak-beamed dining room offers homemade
breads, freshly squeezed juice, fresh fruit platters, local sausages
and fish choices. Home-cooked dinners are available by prior
arrangement.

Rooms 3 rms (2 en suite) (1 pri facs) (1 fmly) **S** £40-£55;
D £65-£75 **Facilities** FTV TVL tea/coffee Dinner available Cen ht
Wi-fi **Parking** 4 **Notes** LB

Thatch Close

★★★★ GUEST ACCOMMODATION

Llangrove HR9 6EL
☎ 01989 770300
e-mail: info@thatchclose.co.uk
web: www.thatchclose.co.uk
dir: *Off A40 at Symonds Yat West/Whitchurch junct to Llangrove,
right at x-rds after Post Office & before school. Thatch Close 0.6m
on left*

PETS: Bedrooms Charges £2.50 per night £10 per week
Public areas at discretion of other guests **Grounds** disp bin
Exercise area adjacent **Facilities** food food bowl water bowl
dog chews feeding mat leads washing facs cage storage
walks info vet info **On Request** fridge access torch towels
Resident Pets: Oliver & Tilly (Spaniel/Collie cross), Aku & Zippy
(African Grey Parrots),

Standing in 13 acres, this sturdy 18th-century farmhouse is
full of character. Expect a wonderfully warm atmosphere with
a genuine welcome from your hosts. The homely bedrooms are
equipped for comfort with many thoughtful extras. Breakfast is
served in the elegant dining room, and a lounge is available. The
extensive patios and gardens are popular in summer, providing
plenty of space to find a quiet corner and relax with a good book.

Rooms 3 en suite **S** £45-£55; **D** £70-£80 **Facilities** TVL tea/coffee
Cen ht Wi-fi **Parking** 8 **Notes** LB 🐾

ROSS-ON-WYE *continued*

The Whitehouse Guest House
★★★ GUEST HOUSE
Wye St HR9 7BX
☎ 01989 763572
e-mail: whitehouseross@aol.com
dir: *Exit A40 dual-carriageway at Wilton, pass over bridge, take 1st left White House on right*

PETS: **Bedrooms** sign **Charges** dog £4 per night **Public areas** except dining room on leads **Exercise area** adjacent **Facilities** food bowl water bowl dog chews feeding mat scoop/disp bags leads washing facs walks info vet info **On Request** torch towels **Stables** 4.5m **Other** charge for damage **Resident Pet:** Pip (Springer Spaniel)

A warm welcome awaits at this 18th-century guest house which is located adjacent to the River Wye and just a short walk to the town centre. The bedrooms are tastefully appointed and provide a thoughtful range of extras including Wi-fi access. There are four-poster rooms and single rooms. A hearty breakfast is provided at individual tables in the dining room; evening meals are available with prior notice. Parking is on the road to the front.

Rooms 7 en suite (2 fmly) **S** £40-£45; **D** £60-£70 **Facilities** tea/coffee Dinner available Cen ht Licensed Wi-fi **Notes** No Children 12yrs Closed 24-25 Dec

The Bateman Arms
★★★★ INN
HR6 9LX
☎ 01568 708374   📠 08701 236418
e-mail: diana@batemanarms.co.uk
web: www.batemanarms.co.uk
dir: *On B4362 in Shobdon*

PETS: **Bedrooms** (3 GF) **Charges** **Public areas** except restaurant & bar on leads **Grounds** on leads disp bin **Exercise area** 50mtrs **Facilities** food (pre-bookable) food bowl water bowl scoop/disp bags leads pet sitting dog walking washing facs cage storage walks info vet info **On Request** fridge access torch towels **Stables** 1.5m **Other** charge for damage **Restrictions** no long haired dogs or dogs likely to moult heavily **Resident Pets:** Bing & Lui (Shih Tzus)

Located in the village, parts of this inn date back over 400 years; Bill and Diana Mahood offer a warm welcome to all their guests. The accommodation comprises six modern bedrooms located in a separate building, all are comfortable and well appointed. There are plenty of oak beams and a large log fire adds to the warm ambience of the public areas. In addition to the friendly welcome, the food, using carefully prepared local produce, is a key feature.

Rooms 6 annexe en suite (2 fmly) (3 GF) **S** £55-£60; **D** £85-£95 **Facilities** FTV tea/coffee Dinner available Cen ht Wi-fi Pool table **Parking** 40 **Notes** LB

Boyce Caravan Park *(SO692528)*
►►►
WR6 5UB
☎ 01886 884248   📄 01886 884187
e-mail: enquiries@boyceholidaypark.co.uk
dir: *From A44 take B4220. In Stanford Bishop take 1st left signed Linley Green, then 1st right down private driveway*

PETS: **Public areas** except buildings & play areas disp bin **Exercise area on site** dog walking area **Facilities** walks info vet info **Other** prior notice required **Restrictions** no Dobermans, German Shepherds, Bull Terriers, Rottweilers, Japanese Tosa or similar cross breeds

Open Feb-Dec (static) rs Mar-Oct (touring) tourers Last arrival 18.00hrs Last departure noon

A friendly and peaceful park with access allowed onto the 100 acres of farmland. Coarse fishing is also available in the grounds, and there are extensive views over the Malvern and Suckley Hills. There are many walks to be enjoyed. 10 acre site. 14 touring pitches. 3 hardstandings. 18 seasonal pitches. Tent pitches. Motorhome pitches. 200 statics.

The Oak Inn
★★★★ INN
HR8 1NP
☎ 01531 640954
e-mail: oakinn@wyenet.co.uk
dir: *2m N of Ledbury on B4214*

PETS: **Bedrooms** unattended **Charges** £5 per stay **Public areas** except restaurant on leads **Grounds** disp bin **Exercise area** 50yds **Facilities** dog chews scoop/disp bags washing facs cage storage walks info vet info **On Request** fridge access torch towels **Stables** 100yds **Other** horses accepted only by prior arrangement, please phone for charges **Resident Pets:** 3 dogs

A privately owned, delightful country inn surrounded by a cider apple orchard. Situated north of the market town of Ledbury, yet within easy access of the Malvern Hills, this 17th-century building has been totally renovated. The bedrooms are modern, spacious and well appointed with under-floor heating and beds that have quality pocket-sprung mattresses. The public areas feature log-burning fires, flagstone floors and wooden beams. Dining is available seven days a week, and the open-plan kitchen allows diners to see their meals being prepared. Wi-fi is accessible throughout.

Rooms 4 en suite (1 fmly) **S** £55-£60; **D** £80-£90 **Facilities** FTV tea/coffee Dinner available Cen ht Wi-fi **Notes** No coaches

The Royal Lodge
★★★★ 🔲 GUEST ACCOMMODATION
HR9 6JL
☎ 01600 890238 📠 01600 891425
e-mail: info@royalhotel-symondsyat.com
web: www.royallodgesymondsyat.co.uk
dir: Midway between Ross and Monmouth exit A40 at signs for Goodrich & B4229 to Symonds Yat East

PETS: Bedrooms unattended standard bedrooms only Charges Public areas except restaurant on leads Grounds on leads disp bin Exercise area adjacent Facilities water bowl cage storage walks info vet info On Request torch Other charge for damage

The Royal Lodge stands at the top end of the village overlooking the River Wye. The bedrooms are spacious and comfortable, and have flat-screen TVs and many guest extras; the bathrooms offer modern facilities. There is a cosy lounge with an open fireplace and two bars are available. Meals are offered in the welcoming restaurant which provides carefully prepared meals, using fresh and local ingredients. The staff are pleasant and friendly.

Rooms 20 en suite (5 fmly) S £39-£55; D £49-£99 Facilities TVL tea/coffee Dinner available Direct Dial Cen ht Licensed Wi-fi Parking 150 Notes LB

Portland House Guest House
★★★★ 🔲 GUEST ACCOMMODATION
HR9 6DB
☎ 01600 890757
e-mail: info@portlandguesthouse.co.uk
web: www.portlandguesthouse.co.uk
dir: Off A40 between Monmouth & Ross-on-Wye. Follow signs for Whitchurch/Symonds Yat West

PETS: Bedrooms ground-floor bedroom only Charges £5 per night Grounds disp bin Exercise area 250yds Facilities scoop/disp bags washing facs walks info vet info On Request fridge access torch towels Other charge for damage

Portland House is an impressive property, dating in part to the 17th century, and situated in the picturesque Wye Valley. Comfortable bedrooms include a large family room, an accessible bedroom on the ground floor, and a four-poster suite. All have a thoughtful range of extras. Walkers can use the Boot Room and guests have use of the laundry, the terrace garden area, and the attractive lounge. Breakfast, with home-made bread and up to eight kinds of home-made preserve, is served around the shared dining table, or at a separate table in the dining room. With prior arrangement, evening meals can be provided.

Rooms 6 en suite (2 fmly) (1 GF) S £55-£70; D £70-£95 Facilities FTV TVL tea/coffee Dinner available Cen ht Licensed Wi-fi 🏊 Parking 6 Notes LB Closed 25-26 Dec

Garford Farm (SO600435)
★★★★ FARMHOUSE
HR1 3ST
☎ 01432 890226 📠 01432 890707 Mrs H Parker
e-mail: garfordfarm@btconnect.com
dir: Off A417 at Newtown x-rds onto A4103 for Hereford, farm 1.5m on left

PETS: Bedrooms Sep accom Charges dog £4 per night Public areas Grounds disp bin Exercise area adjacent Facilities food bowl water bowl bedding leads washing facs cage storage walks info vet info On Request fridge access torch towels Stables Other charge for damage Resident Pets: Sooty & Berry (Black Labradors), Cokie & Soda (cats)

This black and white timber-framed farmhouse, set on a large arable holding, dates from the 17th century. Its character is enhanced by period furnishings, and fires burn in the comfortable lounge during colder weather. The traditionally furnished bedrooms, including a family room, have modern facilities.

Rooms 2 en suite (1 fmly) S fr £35; D fr £60 Facilities tea/coffee Cen ht 🏊 Fishing Parking 6 Notes No Children 2yrs Closed 25-26 Dec 🏡 700 acres arable

Down Hall Country House
★★★★ 75% ◉◉ HOTEL
Hatfield Heath CM22 7AS
☎ 01279 731441 📠 01279 730416
e-mail: reservations@downhall.co.uk
web: www.downhall.co.uk
dir: A1060, at Hatfield Heath keep left. Right into lane opposite Hunters Meet restaurant, left at end, follow signs

PETS: Bedrooms (20 GF) unattended ground-floor bedrooms only Charges £5 per night Public areas only in snooker/games room Grounds disp bin Exercise area nearby Facilities food bowl water bowl dog chews scoop/disp bags cage storage vet info On Request fridge access torch Other welcome pack on arrival; dogs can only be left unattended when owners are on premises

Imposing country-house hotel set amidst 100 acres of mature grounds in a peaceful location just a short drive from Stansted Airport. Bedrooms are generally quite spacious; each one is pleasantly decorated, tastefully furnished and equipped with modern facilities. Public rooms include a choice of restaurants, a cocktail bar, two lounges and leisure facilities.

Rooms 99 (20 GF) Facilities FTV ⓢ ♨ 🏊 Giant chess Whirlpool Sauna Snooker room Gym equipment Xmas New Year Wi-fi Services Lift Parking 150

BISHOP'S STORTFORD *continued*

Broadleaf Guest House
★★★ BED AND BREAKFAST
38 Broadleaf Av CM23 4JY
☎ 01279 835467
e-mail: b-pcannon@sky.com
dir: *1m SW of town centre. Off B1383 into Whittinton Way & Friedburge Ave, Broadleaf Ave 6th left*

PETS: Bedrooms Charges Exercise area surrounding countryside Facilities washing facs walks info vet info On Request fridge access torch Other charge for damage

A delightful detached house situated in a peaceful residential area close to the town centre, and within easy striking distance of the M11 and Stansted Airport. The pleasantly decorated bedrooms are carefully furnished and equipped with many thoughtful touches. Breakfast is served in the smart dining room, which overlooks the pretty garden.

Rooms 2 rms (1 fmly) Facilities FTV tea/coffee Cen ht Parking 2 Notes ⊛

HEMEL HEMPSTEAD   Map 4 TL00

The Bobsleigh Hotel
★★★ 75% ❀ HOTEL
Hempstead Rd, Bovingdon HP3 0DS
☎ 0844 879 9033   🖹 01442 832471
e-mail: bobsleigh@macdonald-hotels.co.uk
web: www.macdonald-hotels.co.uk
dir: *M1 junct 8, A414 signed Hemel Hempstead. At Plough Rdbt follow railway station signs. Pass rail station on left, straight on at rdbt, under 2 bridges. Left onto B4505 (Box Lane) signed Chesham. Hotel 1.5m on left*

PETS: Bedrooms unattended sign garden bedrooms only Charges £10 per night Grounds disp bin Exercise area 2 mins Facilities washing facs walks info vet info On Request fridge access torch towels Other charge for damage

Located just outside the town, the hotel enjoys a pleasant rural setting, yet is within easy reach of local transport links and the motorway network. Bedrooms vary in size; all are modern in style. There is an open-plan lobby, a bar area and an attractive dining room with views over the garden.

Rooms 47 (15 annexe) (8 fmly) (29 GF) S £45-£120; D £45-£120* Facilities STV Xmas New Year Wi-fi Parking 60 Notes LB

SOUTH MIMMS SERVICE AREA (M25)   Map 4 TL20

Days Inn South Mimms - M25
BUDGET HOTEL
Bignells Corner EN6 3QQ
☎ 01707 665440   🖹 01707 660189
e-mail: south.mimms@welcomebreak.co.uk
web: www.welcomebreak.co.uk
dir: *M25 junct 23, at rdbt follow signs*

PETS: Bedrooms (18 GF) unattended Charges £5 per stay Public areas on leads Grounds on leads disp bin Facilities walks info vet info Other charge for damage well behaved dogs only

This modern building offers accommodation in smart, spacious and well-equipped bedrooms, suitable for families and business travellers, and all with en suite bathrooms. Continental breakfast is available and other refreshments may be taken at the nearby family restaurant.

Rooms 74 (55 fmly) (18 GF) (8 smoking) S £49.95-£69.95; D £59.95-£79.95

STEVENAGE   Map 4 TL22

Novotel Stevenage
★★★ 78% HOTEL
Knebworth Park SG1 2AX
☎ 01438 346100   🖹 01438 723872
e-mail: H0992@accor.com
web: www.novotel.com
dir: *A1(M) junct 7, at entrance to Knebworth Park*

PETS: Bedrooms (30 GF) Charges £6 per night Public areas except restaurant on leads Grounds disp bin Exercise area nearby Other charge for damage

Ideally situated just off the A1(M) is this purpose built hotel, which is a popular business and conference venue. Bedrooms are pleasantly decorated and equipped with a good range of useful extras. Public rooms include a large open plan lounge bar serving a range of snacks, and a smartly appointed restaurant.

Rooms 101 (20 fmly) (30 GF) Facilities STV Use of local health club New Year Wi-fi Services Lift Parking 120

ENGLAND

WARE
Map 5 TL31

Hanbury Manor, A Marriott Hotel & Country Club

★★★★★ 81% ◉◉ COUNTRY HOUSE HOTEL

SG12 0SD
☎ 01920 487722 & 0870 400 7222 ▤ 01920 487692
e-mail: mhrs.stngs.guestrelations@marriotthotels.com
web: www.marriotthanburymanor.co.uk
dir: M25 junct 25, A10 N for 12m, take A1170, right at rdbt, hotel on left

PETS: Bedrooms Charges £40 per stay **Grounds** on leads **Exercise area** 100mtrs **Facilities** food bowl water bowl walks info vet info **On Request** torch **Other** charge for damage

Set in 200 acres of landscaped grounds, this impressive Jacobean-style mansion boasts an enviable range of leisure facilities, including an excellent health club and championship golf course. Bedrooms are traditionally and comfortably furnished in the country-house style and have lovely marbled bathrooms. There are a number of food and drink options, including the renowned Zodiac and Oakes restaurants.

Rooms 161 (27 annexe) (60 fmly) **Facilities** Spa STV FTV ⊗ supervised ⚹ 18 ⛳ Putt green ⚽ Gym Health & beauty treatments Aerobics Yoga Dance class Xmas New Year Wi-fi **Services** Lift **Parking** 200

Roebuck

★★★ 72% HOTEL

Baldock St SG12 9DR
☎ 01920 409955 ▤ 01920 468016
e-mail: roebuck@forestdale.com
web: www.theroebuckhotel.co.uk
dir: A10 onto B1001, left at rdbt, 1st left behind fire station

PETS: Bedrooms (16 GF) unattended sign **Charges** £7.50 per night **Public areas** except restaurant on leads **Facilities** food (pre-bookable) food bowl water bowl feeding mat walks info vet info **On Request** fridge access **Other** charge for damage

The Roebuck is a comfortable and friendly hotel situated close to the old market town of Ware, it is also within easy reach of Stansted Airport, Cambridge and Hertford. The hotel has spacious bedrooms, a comfortable lounge, bar and conservatory restaurant. There is also a range of air-conditioned meeting rooms.

Rooms 47 (1 fmly) (16 GF) **Facilities** FTV Wi-fi **Services** Lift **Parking** 64 **Notes** LB

KENT

ASHFORD
Map 5 TR04

Ashford International Hotel

★★★★ 80% HOTEL

Simone Weil Av TN24 8UX
☎ 01233 219988 ▤ 01233 647743
e-mail: ashford@qhotels.co.uk
web: www.qhotels.co.uk
dir: M20 junct 9, exit for Ashford/Canterbury. Left at 1st rdbt, hotel 200mtrs on left

PETS: Bedrooms (57 GF) **Charges** £15 per stay **Public areas** except food & beverage outlets on leads **Grounds Exercise area** 200yds **Facilities** washing facs cage storage walks info vet info **On Request** fridge access towels **Restrictions** 1 medium size, or 2 small dogs per room

Situated just off the M20 and with easy links to the Eurotunnel, Eurostar and ferry terminals, this hotel has been stunningly appointed. The slick, stylishly presented bedrooms are equipped with the latest amenities. Public areas include the spacious Horizons Wine Bar and Restaurant serving a competitively priced menu, and Quench Sports Bar for relaxing drinks. The Reflections leisure club boasts a pool, fully-equipped gym, spa facilities and treatment rooms.

Rooms 179 (29 fmly) (57 GF) **S** £75-£250; **D** £85-£260 (incl. bkfst)* **Facilities** Spa ⊗ Gym Aroma steam room Rock sauna Feature shower Ice fountain Xmas New Year Wi-fi **Services** Lift Air con **Parking** 400 **Notes** LB

Broadhembury Caravan & Camping Park

(TR009387)

▶▶▶▶▶

Steeds Ln, Kingsnorth TN26 1NQ
☎ 01233 620859 ▤ 01233 620918
e-mail: holidaypark@broadhembury.co.uk
dir: From M20 junct 10 take A2070. Left at 2nd rdbt signed Kingsnorth, then left at 2nd x-roads in village

PETS: Public areas except toilets & play area on leads disp bin **Exercise area on site** 200-yard walk **Exercise area** public footpaths & woods adjacent **Facilities** water bowl washing facs walks info vet info **Other** prior notice required max 2 dogs per pitch disposal bags available **Resident Pets:** Henry (Cavalier King Charles Spaniel), Scooby (cross), chickens

Open all year Last arrival 22.00hrs Last departure noon

A well-run and well-maintained small family park surrounded by open pasture; it is neatly landscaped with pitches sheltered by mature hedges. There is a well-equipped campers' kitchen adjacent to the spotless toilet facilities and children will love the play areas, games room and football pitch. An adults-only area, close to the excellent reception building, has been developed to include some popular fully serviced hardstanding pitches. 10 acre site. 110 touring pitches. 20 hardstandings. Tent pitches. Motorhome pitches. 25 statics.

Notes No noise after 23.00hrs.

Yorke Lodge

★ ★ ★ ★ ★ GUEST ACCOMMODATION

50 London Rd CT2 8LF
☎ 01227 451243   📠 01227 462006
e-mail: info@yorkelodge.com
web: www.yorkelodge.com
dir: *From London M2/A2, 1st exit signed Canterbury. At 1st rdbt left onto London Rd*

PETS: Bedrooms unattended **Exercise area** 100yds **Facilities** walks info vet info **On Request** fridge access torch towels **Other** charge for damage **Resident Pet:** Fleur (Dalmatian/Collie cross)

The charming Victorian property stands in a tree-lined road just a ten-minute walk from the town centre and railway station. The spacious bedrooms are thoughtfully equipped and carefully decorated; some rooms have four-poster beds. The stylish dining room leads to a conservatory-lounge, which opens onto a superb terrace.

Rooms 8 en suite (1 fmly) **S** £58-£70; **D** £90-£130 **Facilities** FTV tea/coffee Cen ht Wi-fi **Parking** 5 **Notes** LB No Children 5yrs

Bridgewood Manor

★ ★ ★ ★ 74% HOTEL

Bridgewood Roundabout, Walderslade Woods ME5 9AX
☎ 01634 201333   📠 01634 201330
e-mail: bridgewoodmanor@qhotels.co.uk
web: www.qhotels.co.uk
dir: *Adjacent to Bridgewood rdbt on A229. Take 3rd exit signed Walderslade & Lordswood. Hotel 50mtrs on left*

PETS: Bedrooms (26 GF) unattended **Charges** £15 per stay **Public areas** except bar, leisure areas & restaurant on leads **Exercise area** woods adjacent **Other** charge for damage

A modern, purpose-built hotel situated on the outskirts of Rochester. Bedrooms are pleasantly decorated, comfortably furnished and equipped with many thoughtful touches. The hotel has an excellent range of leisure and conference facilities. Guests can dine in the informal Terrace Bistro or experience fine dining in the more formal Squires restaurant, where the service is both attentive and friendly.

Rooms 100 (12 fmly) (26 GF) **S** £69-£149; **D** £89-£169 (incl. bkfst) **Facilities** Spa STV 🏊 supervised 🏋 Gym Beauty treatments Xmas New Year Wi-fi **Services** Lift **Parking** 170 **Notes** LB

Campanile Dartford

BUDGET HOTEL

1 Clipper Boulevard West, Crossways Business Park DA2 6QN
☎ 01322 278925   📠 01322 278948
e-mail: dartford@campanile.com
dir: *Follow signs for Ferry Terminal from Dartford Bridge*

PETS: Bedrooms Charges £5 per night **Public areas** muzzled and on leads **Grounds** on leads disp bin **Facilities** water bowl vet info **On Request** towels **Other** charge for damage

This modern building offers accommodation in smart, well-equipped bedrooms, all with en suite bathrooms. Refreshments may be taken at the informal bistro.

Rooms 125 (14 fmly)

Sutherland House

★ ★ ★ ★ ★ GUEST ACCOMMODATION

186 London Rd CT14 9PT
☎ 01304 362853   📠 01304 381146
e-mail: info@sutherlandhouse.fsnet.co.uk
dir: *0.5m W of town centre/seafront on A258*

PETS: Bedrooms (1 GF) unattended sign **Public areas** with consideration for other guests' comfort **Grounds** disp bin **Exercise area** nearby **Facilities** water bowl washing facs walks info vet info **On Request** fridge access torch towels **Other** charge for damage **Restrictions** small dogs only

This stylish accommodation demonstrates impeccable taste with its charming, well-equipped bedrooms and a comfortable lounge. A fully stocked bar, books, free Wi-fi, Freeview TV and radio are some of the many amenities offered. The elegant dining room is the venue for a hearty breakfast and dinner is available by prior arrangement.

Rooms 4 en suite (1 GF) **S** £60-£75; **D** £70-£85 **Facilities** FTV tea/coffee Dinner available Direct Dial Cen ht Licensed Wi-fi **Parking** 7 **Notes** LB No Children 5yrs

Wallett's Court Country House Hotel & Spa
★★★★ 74% HOTEL

West Cliffe, St Margarets-at-Cliffe CT15 6EW
☎ 01304 852424 & 0800 035 1628 📠 01304 853430
e-mail: wc@wallettscourt.com
web: www.wallettscourt.com
dir: *From Dover take A258 towards Deal. 1st right to St Margarets-at-Cliffe & West Cliffe, 1m on right opposite West Cliffe church*

PETS: Bedrooms (7 GF) **Charges Public areas** except restaurant on leads **Grounds** on leads **Exercise area** 1m **Facilities** walks info vet info **On Request** fridge access

A lovely Jacobean manor situated in a peaceful location on the outskirts of town. Bedrooms in the original house are traditionally furnished whereas the rooms in the courtyard buildings are more modern; all are equipped to a high standard. Public rooms include a smart bar, a lounge and a restaurant that utilises local organic produce. An impressive spa facility is housed in converted barn buildings in the grounds.

Rooms 16 (13 annexe) (2 fmly) (7 GF) **S** £110-£140; **D** £140-£250 (incl. bkfst)* **Facilities** Spa FTV Putt green Gym Treatment suite Aromatherapy massage Beauty therapy Golf pitching range New Year Wi-fi **Parking** 30 **Notes** LB Closed 24-26 Dec

Hubert House Guesthouse & Bistro
★★★★ GUEST HOUSE

9 Castle Hill Rd CT16 1QW
☎ 01304 202253 📠 01304 210142
e-mail: stay@huberthouse.co.uk
web: www.huberthouse.co.uk
dir: *On A258 by Dover Castle*

PETS: Bedrooms 2 bedrooms only **Charges** £7.50 per night **Exercise area** 300mtrs **Facilities** walks info vet info **On Request** fridge access torch **Other** charge for damage **Resident Pet:** Tullah (Slovakian Pointer)

This charming Georgian house is within walking distance of the ferry port and the town centre. Bedrooms are sumptuously decorated and furnished with an abundance of practical extras. Breakfast, including full English and healthy options, is served in the smart coffee house, which is open all day. Families are especially welcome.

Rooms 6 en suite (4 fmly) **S** fr £45; **D** fr £60 **Facilities** FTV tea/coffee Dinner available Cen ht Licensed Wi-fi **Parking** 6 **Notes** LB

Langhorne Garden
★★★ GUEST ACCOMMODATION

10-12 Langhorne Gardens CT20 2EA
☎ 01303 257233 📠 01303 242760
e-mail: info@langhorne.co.uk
web: www.langhorne.co.uk
dir: *Exit M20 junct 13, follow signs for The Leas, 2m*

PETS: Bedrooms unattended **Public areas** except restaurant on leads **Exercise area** 100yds **Facilities** cage storage walks info vet info **On Request** fridge access torch towels

Once a Victorian villa, Langhorne Garden is close to the seafront, shops and restaurants. Bright spacious bedrooms are traditionally decorated with plenty of original charm. Public rooms include a choice of comfortable lounges and a bar, a spacious dining room and a popular local bar in the basement with billiards, darts and table football.

Rooms 29 en suite (8 fmly) **S** fr £37; **D** fr £60 **Facilities** STV FTV tea/coffee Dinner available Direct Dial Cen ht Lift Licensed Wi-fi Pool table **Notes** LB Closed Xmas RS Jan-Etr no evening meal

Little Satmar Holiday Park *(TR260390)*
▶ ▶ ▶

Winehouse Ln, Capel Le Ferne CT18 7JF
☎ 01303 251188 📠 01303 251188
e-mail: satmar@keatfarm.co.uk
dir: *Signed off B2011*

PETS: Charges £1.50 per night **Public areas Exercise area** 100mtrs **Facilities** food dog chews washing facs walks info vet info **Other** 1 dog per pitch (contact site if more than 1 dog)

Open Mar-Nov Last arrival 21.00hrs Last departure 12.00hrs

A quiet, well-screened site well away from the road and statics, with clean and tidy facilities. A useful base for visiting Dover and Folkestone, or as an overnight stop for the Channel Tunnel and ferry ports, and it's just a short walk from cliff paths with their views of the Channel, and sandy beaches below. 5 acre site. 47 touring pitches. Tent pitches. Motorhome pitches. 75 statics.

Notes No noise after 22.00hrs.

ENGLAND

FOLKESTONE *continued*

Little Switzerland Camping & Caravan Site
(TR248380)

►►

Wear Bay Rd CT19 6PS
☎ 01303 252168
e-mail: btony328@aol.com
dir: *Signed from A20 E of Folkestone. Approaching from A259 or B2011 on E outskirts of Folkestone follow signs for Wear Bay/ Martello Tower, then tourist sign to site, follow signs to country park*

PETS: Public areas disp bin **Exercise area on site** dog walks, cliff path **Facilities** food bowl water bowl washing facs walks info vet info **Stables** 1m **Resident Pet:** Fluffy (cat)

Open Mar-Oct Last arrival mdnt Last departure noon

Set on a narrow plateau below the white cliffs, this unusual site has sheltered camping in secluded dells and enjoys fine views across Wear Bay and the Strait of Dover. The licensed café with an alfresco area is popular; please note that the basic toilet facilities are unsuitable for disabled visitors. 3 acre site. 32 touring pitches. Tent pitches. Motorhome pitches. 13 statics.

Notes No open fires.

HYTHE	Map 5 TR13

Mercure Hythe Imperial
★★★★ 71% HOTEL

Princes Pde CT21 6AE
☎ 01303 267441 📠 01303 264610
e-mail: h6862@accor.com
web: www.mercure.com
dir: *M20, junct 11 onto A261. In Hythe follow Folkestone signs. Right into Twiss Rd to hotel*

PETS: Bedrooms (6 GF) unattended sign **Charges** £12.50 per night **Public areas** except restaurant, bar & lounge on leads **Grounds** disp bin **Exercise area** 1m **Facilities** cage storage walks info vet info **On Request** fridge access torch **Other** charge for damage

This imposing seafront hotel is enhanced by impressive grounds including a 13-hole golf course, tennis court and extensive gardens. Bedrooms are varied in style but all offer modern facilities, and many enjoy stunning sea views. The elegant restaurant, bar and lounges are traditional in style and retain many original features. The leisure club includes a gym, a squash court, an indoor pool, and the spa offers a range of luxury treatments.

Rooms 80 (6 fmly) (6 GF) **S** £60-£90; **D** £70-£135* **Facilities** Spa STV ⊗ ⬩ 13 ⬨ Putt green Gym Squash Snooker & pool table Aerobic studio Table tennis Sauna Steam room Xmas New Year Wi-fi **Services** Lift **Parking** 207

KINGSGATE	Map 5 TR37

The Fayreness
★★★ 79% HOTEL

Marine Dr CT10 3LG
☎ 01843 868641 & 861103 📠 01843 608750
e-mail: info@fayreness.co.uk
web: www.fayreness.co.uk
dir: *A28 onto B2051 which becomes B2052. Pass Holy Trinity Church on right & '19th Hole' public house. Next left, into Kingsgate Ave, hotel at end on left*

PETS: Bedrooms (5 GF) unattended **Charges** £5 per night £20 per week **Public areas** except restaurant & conservatory on leads **Grounds** on leads disp bin **Exercise area** clifftop & beach adjacent **Facilities** food bowl water bowl dog chews cage storage walks info vet info **On Request** fridge access torch towels **Stables** 5m **Other** charge for damage

Situated on the cliff top overlooking the English Channel, just a few steps from a sandy beach and adjacent to the North Foreland Golf Club. The spacious bedrooms are tastefully furnished with many thoughtful touches including free Wi-fi; some rooms have stunning sea views. Public rooms include a large open-plan lounge/bar, a function room, dining room and conservatory restaurant.

Rooms 29 (3 fmly) (5 GF) (4 smoking) **Facilities** STV New Year Wi-fi **Parking** 70

LEYSDOWN-ON-SEA	Map 5 TR07

Priory Hill *(TR038704)*

►►►

Wing Rd ME12 4QT
☎ 01795 510267
e-mail: touringpark@prioryhill.co.uk
dir: *Take A249 signed Sheerness then B2231 to Leysdown, follow brown tourist signs*

PETS: Public areas except club area & swimming pool **Exercise area** coastal park adjacent **Facilities** walks info vet info **Other** prior notice required dogs must be kept on leads & exercised off site

Open Mar-Oct rs Low season shorter opening times for pool & club Last arrival 20.00hrs Last departure noon

A small well-maintained touring area on an established family-run holiday park close to the sea, with views of the north Kent coast. Amenities include a clubhouse and a swimming pool. The pitch price includes membership of the clubhouse with live entertainment, and use of indoor swimming pool. 1.5 acre site. 37 touring pitches. Tent pitches. Motorhome pitches.

The Black Horse Inn

★★★★ ⌖ INN

Pilgrims Way, Thurnham ME14 3LD
☎ 01622 737185 & 630830 📠 01622 739170
e-mail: info@wellieboot.net
web: www.wellieboot.net/home_blackhorse.htm
dir: M20 junct 7, N onto A249. Right into Detling, opp pub onto Pilgrims Way for 1m

PETS: Bedrooms (30 GF) unattended sign **Charges** £6 per night **Public areas** in bar area only on leads **Grounds** on leads disp bin **Exercise area** North Downs Way adjacent **Facilities** scoop/disp bags walks info vet info **On Request** fridge access torch towels **Other** charge for damage **Restrictions** no Pit Bull Terriers **Resident Pets:** Sam (Pointer cross), Boston (Staffordshire Terrier), Snowball (cat)

This charming inn dates from the 17th century, and the public areas have a wealth of oak beams, exposed brickwork and open fireplaces. The stylish bedrooms are in a series of cosy cabins behind the premises; each one is attractively furnished and thoughtfully equipped.

Rooms 30 annexe en suite (8 fmly) (30 GF) **Facilities** FTV tea/coffee Dinner available Cen ht Wi-fi **Parking** 40 **Notes** LB No coaches

Aylesbury House

★★★★ GUEST ACCOMMODATION

56-58 London Rd ME16 8QL
☎ 01622 762100 📠 01622 664673
e-mail: mail@aylesburyhouse.co.uk
dir: M20 junct 5, A20 to Maidstone. Aylesbury House on left before town centre

PETS: Bedrooms unattended **Grounds** on leads **Facilities** walks info vet info **Resident Pet:** Kami (cat)

Located just a short walk from the town centre, this smartly maintained establishment offers a genuine welcome. The carefully decorated bedrooms have co-ordinated soft fabrics and many thoughtful touches. Breakfast is served in the smart dining room overlooking a walled garden.

Rooms 8 en suite **S** £58-£65; **D** £69-£80 **Facilities** FTV tea/coffee Cen ht Wi-fi **Parking** 8

Honeychild Manor Farmhouse *(TR062276)*

★★★★ ⌂ FARMHOUSE

St Mary In The Marsh TN29 0DB
☎ 01797 366180 & 07951 237821 📠 01797 366925
Mrs V Furnival
e-mail: honeychild@farming.co.uk
dir: 2m N of New Romney off A259. S of village centre

PETS: Bedrooms Charges horse £15 per night **Grounds** on leads disp bin **Exercise area** approx 100yds **Facilities** cage storage walks info vet info **On Request** fridge access torch towels **Stables Resident Pets:** Georgie (Labrador), Molly (Collie), Charlie & Eddie (horses)

This imposing Georgian farmhouse is part of a working dairy farm on Romney Marsh. Walkers and dreamers alike will enjoy the stunning views and can relax in the beautifully landscaped gardens or play tennis on the full-sized court. A hearty breakfast is served in the elegant dining room and features quality local produce. Bedrooms are pleasantly decorated, well furnished and thoughtfully equipped.

Rooms 3 rms (1 en suite) (2 pri facs) (1 fmly) **S** £40; **D** fr £85 **Facilities** tea/coffee Dinner available Cen ht Wi-fi ⌖ **Parking** 10 **Notes** LB ✿ 1500 acres arable/dairy

The Bell

★★★ 83% ⚜ HOTEL

The Quay CT13 9EF
☎ 01304 613388 📠 01304 615308
e-mail: reservations@bellhotelsandwich.co.uk
web: www.bellhotelsandwich.co.uk
dir: In town centre

PETS: Bedrooms unattended sign lower level bedrooms only **Charges** £5 per night **Public areas** except restaurant & bar on leads **Exercise area** adjacent **Facilities** food (pre-bookable) food bowl water bowl bedding dog chews cat treats feeding mat litter tray scoop/disp bags leads pet sitting dog walking washing facs cage storage walks info vet info **On Request** fridge access torch towels **Stables** nearby **Other** charge for damage

The Bell has been welcoming travellers since the 14th century, when it looked out over a harbour, now the River Stour; the existing building dates mainly from the 19th century. The bedrooms to offer guests much style and comfort, and some have balconies with river views. The contemporary Old Dining Room Restaurant offers a seasonally changing menu that highlights locally caught fish and seafood, salt marsh lamb and produce from nearby farms. Dating from the Georgian era, the elegant Regency Room is ideal for conferences, wedding receptions and parties. Wi-fi is available throughout.

Rooms 37 (4 fmly) (3 GF) **S** £85-£120; **D** £110-£220 (incl. bkfst)* **Facilities** FTV Xmas New Year Wi-fi **Parking** 7 **Notes** LB

SITTINGBOURNE — Map 5 TQ96

Hempstead House Country Hotel

★★★ 86% ⊛ HOTEL

London Rd, Bapchild ME9 9PP
☎ 01795 428020 📠 01795 436362
e-mail: info@hempsteadhouse.co.uk
web: www.hempsteadhouse.co.uk
dir: *1.5m from town centre on A2 towards Canterbury*

PETS: Bedrooms (1 GF) unattended **Public areas** except restaurant (ex assist dogs) **Grounds** disp bin **Exercise area** adjacent **Facilities** food (pre-bookable) food bowl water bowl scoop/disp bags pet sitting dog walking washing facs cage storage walks info vet info **On Request** fridge access torch towels **Stables** 1.5m **Resident Pets:** 2 Toy Poodles, 1 Yorkshire Terrier & 1 Labrador

Expect a warm welcome at this charming detached Victorian property, situated amidst four acres of mature landscaped gardens. Bedrooms are attractively decorated with lovely co-ordinated fabrics, tastefully furnished and equipped with many thoughtful touches. Public rooms feature a choice of elegant lounges as well as a superb conservatory dining room. In summer guests can eat on the terraces. There is a spa and fitness suite.

Rooms 34 (7 fmly) (1 GF) **Facilities** Spa STV FTV 🐾 Gym Fitness studio Steam room Sauna Hydrotherapy pool Xmas New Year Wi-fi **Services** Lift **Parking** 100 **Notes** LB

The Beaumont

★★★★ ≜ GUEST ACCOMMODATION

74 London Rd ME10 1NS
☎ 01795 472536 📠 01795 425921
e-mail: info@thebeaumont.co.uk
web: www.thebeaumont.co.uk
dir: *From M2 or M20 take A249 N. Exit at A2, 1m on left towards Sittingbourne*

PETS: Bedrooms (3 GF) unattended **Public areas** on leads **Grounds** on leads disp bin **Exercise area** 5 mins' walk **Facilities** water bowl scoop/disp bags walks info vet info **On Request** fridge access torch towels **Restrictions** no large dogs **Resident Pet:** Scooby (Cocker Spaniel)

This Georgian farmhouse is a charming family-run property that offers the best hospitality and service. Comfortable bedrooms and bathrooms are well equipped for business and leisure guests. Breakfast in the bright, spacious conservatory makes good use of local produce and home-made preserves. Off-road parking is available.

Rooms 9 rms (6 en suite) (3 pri facs) (3 GF) **S** £44-£70; **D** £66-£84 **Facilities** STV TVL tea/coffee Cen ht Wi-fi **Parking** 9 **Notes** Closed 24 Dec-1 Jan

STELLING MINNIS — Map 5 TR14

Heathwood Lodge B&B

★★★★ ≜ BED AND BREAKFAST

Wheelbarrow Town CT4 6AH
☎ 01227 709315 & 07831 347395 📠 01227 709475
e-mail: enquiries@heathwoodlodge.co.uk
dir: *B2068 from Canterbury, left into Stelling Minnis. Right at T-junct, pass village hall, after 0.5m round right-hand corner, last yellow house on left*

PETS: Bedrooms Rose Room only **Charges** small & medium dogs free, large dogs £10 per night **Grounds** on leads disp bin **Exercise area** adjacent **Facilities** water bowl feeding mat scoop/disp bags leads washing facs cage storage walks info vet info **On Request** fridge access torch towels **Stables Other** charge for damage **Restrictions** small & medium size dogs only in B&B; larger dogs in stables only phone to check which breeds are accepted **Resident Pets:** Molly (Labrador), Twinkle & Tumble (Jack Russells), Getty, Maggie & Benny (horses)

Heathwood Lodge is located in a quiet village area of Stelling Minnis. Boasting scenic views, spacious gardens for guests to enjoy during summer months, it is easily accessed from both Canterbury and Dover. Bedrooms are tastefully appointed, comfortable and have en suite facilities. The guest lounge provides additional space for guests to relax and features an open fireplace. The traditionally styled dining room serves both a cooked and continental breakfast using high quality ingredients sourced from the surrounding area.

Rooms 3 en suite **S** £50-£85; **D** £60-£100 **Facilities** FTV TVL tea/coffee Cen ht Wi-fi **Parking** 8 **Notes** LB ⊛

TUNBRIDGE WELLS (ROYAL) — Map 5 TQ53

Hotel du Vin Bistro

Hotel du Vin Tunbridge Wells

★★★★ 71% ⊛ TOWN HOUSE HOTEL

Crescent Rd TN1 2LY
☎ 01892 526455 📠 01892 512044
e-mail: reception.tunbridgewells@hotelduvin.com
web: www.hotelduvin.com
dir: *Follow town centre, to main junct of Mount Pleasant Rd & Crescent Rd/Church Rd. Hotel 150yds on right just past Phillips House*

PETS: Bedrooms unattended **Public areas** except bistro on leads **Grounds** on leads **Exercise area** 200yds **Facilities** food bowl water bowl cage storage walks info vet info **On Request** fridge access torch towels **Stables** 3m **Other** charges may apply for some pet supplies

This impressive Grade II listed building dates from 1762, and as a princess, Queen Victoria often stayed here. The spacious bedrooms are available in a range of sizes, beautifully and individually appointed, and equipped with a host of thoughtful extras. Public rooms include a bistro-style restaurant, two elegant lounges and a small bar.

Rooms 34 **Facilities** STV Boules court in garden Wi-fi **Services** Lift **Parking** 30

WESTERHAM Map 5 TQ45

Corner Cottage

★★★★ GUEST ACCOMMODATION

Toys Hill TN16 1PY
☎ 01732 750362 📄 01732 750754
e-mail: cornercottagebandb@jshmanco.com
dir: *A25 to Brasted, into Chart Ln signed Fox & Hounds. Turn right into Puddledock Ln, 1st house on left*

PETS: Bedrooms Public areas Grounds disp bin **Exercise area** adjacent **Facilities** food (pre-bookable) food bowl water bowl pet sitting dog walking washing facs cage storage walks info vet info **On Request** fridge access torch towels **Resident Pet:** Softie (cat)

Set in a charming village this property offers a spacious, well-equipped annexe bedroom that is comfortably furnished and includes many thoughtful touches. In the main cottage a hearty Aga-cooked breakfast is served in the rustic dining room with stunning views of the countryside.

Rooms 1 annexe en suite (1 fmly) **S** fr £60; **D** fr £80
Facilities tea/coffee Dinner available Cen ht Wi-fi **Parking** 2
Notes ⊗

WHITSTABLE Map 5 TR16

 Seaview Holiday Park *(TR145675)*
St John's Rd CT5 2RY
☎ 01227 792246 📄 01227 792247
e-mail: info@parkholidaysuk.com
dir: *A299 onto A2990 then B2205 to Swalecliffe, site between Herne Bay & Whitstable*

PETS: Charges Public areas except club house & café disp bin **Exercise area on site Facilities** food dog chews vet info **Stables** 5m

Open Mar-Oct Last arrival 21.30hrs Last departure noon

A pleasant open site on the edge of Whitstable, set well away from the static area, with a smart, modern toilet block and both super and hardstanding pitches. Developments at this popular holiday centre include an excellent bar, restaurant, clubhouse (with entertainment) and games room complex, and an outdoor swimming pool area. 12 acre site. touring pitches. 16 hardstandings. 25 seasonal pitches. Tent pitches. Motorhome pitches. 523 statics.

LANCASHIRE

ACCRINGTON Map 7 SD72

The Maple Lodge

★★★★ GUEST ACCOMMODATION

70 Blackburn Rd, Clayton-le-Moors BB5 5JH
☎ 01254 301284 📄 0560 112 5380
e-mail: info@stayatmaplelodge.co.uk
dir: *M65 junct 7, signs for Clitheroe, right at T-junct onto Blackburn Rd*

PETS: Bedrooms 1 double & 1 twin (lodge only) **Charges** £5 per stay **Exercise area** 50yds **Facilities** walks info vet info **Other** charge for damage

This welcoming house is convenient for the M65, and provides comfortable, well-equipped bedrooms, as well as an inviting lounge with well-stocked bar. Freshly cooked dinners (by arrangement) and hearty breakfasts are served in the attractive dining room.

Rooms 4 en suite 4 annexe en suite (1 fmly) (4 GF) **S** £40-£44; **D** £58-£62 **Facilities** FTV TVL tea/coffee Dinner available Direct Dial Cen ht Licensed Wi-fi **Parking** 6 **Notes** LB

BLACKBURN Map 7 SD62

Mercure Blackburn Foxfields Country Hotel

★★★ 76% HOTEL

Whalley Rd, Billington BB7 9HY
☎ 01254 822556 📄 01254 824613
e-mail: enquiries@hotels-blackburn.com
dir: *Just off A59*

PETS: Bedrooms (13 GF) unattended sign **Charges** £10 per night **Public areas** except restaurant on leads **Grounds** on leads **Exercise area** 2m **Facilities** food bowl water bowl walks info vet info **On Request** torch **Resident Pet:** Cassie (cat)

This modern hotel is easily accessible from major road networks. Bedrooms are comfortable and spacious, and include some suites and others with separate dressing areas. Facilities include a good-sized swimming pool, a small gym and conference suites. The traditional restaurant serves an interesting range of cuisine.

Rooms 44 (16 annexe) (27 fmly) (13 GF) (8 smoking) **S** £55-£125; **D** £65-£135 **Facilities** STV FTV 🏊 Gym Sauna Steam room Xmas New Year Wi-fi **Parking** 194 **Notes** LB

Barceló Blackpool Imperial Hotel
★★★★ 73% HOTEL

North Promenade FY1 2HB
☎ 01253 623971 📄 01253 751784
e-mail: imperialblackpool@barcelo-hotels.co.uk
web: www.barcelo-hotels.co.uk
dir: *M55 junct 2, take A583 North Shore, follow signs to North Promenade. Hotel on seafront, north of tower*

PETS: Bedrooms unattended sign standard bedrooms only
Charges £15 per night **Public areas** only in lobby area on leads
Grounds on leads **Exercise area** beach adjacent **Facilities** vet
info **Other** charge for damage

Enjoying a prime seafront location, this grand Victorian hotel offers smartly appointed, well-equipped bedrooms and spacious, elegant public areas. Facilities include a smart leisure club, a comfortable lounge, the No.10 bar and an attractive split-level restaurant that overlooks the seafront. Conferences and functions are extremely well catered for.

Rooms 180 (16 fmly) **Facilities** Spa STV Ⓢ supervised Gym Xmas
New Year Wi-fi **Services** Lift **Parking** 150

Headlands
★★ 71% HOTEL

611-613 South Promenade FY4 1NJ
☎ 01253 341179 📄 01253 342657
e-mail: headlandshotel@aol.com
dir: *From end of M55 follow South Promenade signs*

PETS: Bedrooms unattended **Charges** £10 per night
Exercise area 50mtrs **Facilities** water bowl cage storage walks
info vet info **On Request** fridge access torch towels **Resident
Pet:** Charlie (Cavalier King Charles Spaniel)

This friendly, family owned hotel stands on the South Promenade, close to the Pleasure Beach and many of the town's major attractions. Bedrooms are traditionally furnished and many enjoy sea views. There is a choice of lounges and live entertainment is provided regularly. Home cooked food is served in the panelled dining room.

Rooms 41 (10 fmly) **S** £25-£51.95; **D** £50-£103.90 (incl. bkfst)*
Facilities Darts Games room Pool Snooker 🎵 Xmas New Year
Services Lift **Parking** 46 **Notes** LB Closed 2-15 Jan

Red Bank Farm *(SD472681)*
▶▶▶

LA5 8JR
☎ 01524 823196 📄 01524 824981
e-mail: mark.archer@hotmail.co.uk
dir: *Take A5105 (Morecambe road), after 200mtrs right on Shore Lane. At rail bridge turn right to site*

PETS: Public areas Exercise area 50mtrs **Facilities** vet info

Open Mar-Oct

A gently sloping grassy field with mature hedges, close to the sea shore and a RSPB reserve. This farm site has smart toilet facilities, a superb view across Morecambe Bay to the distant Lake District hills, and is popular with tenters. 3 acre site. 60 touring pitches. Tent pitches. Motorhome pitches.

Old Hall Caravan Park *(SD533716)*
▶▶▶

LA6 1AD
☎ 01524 733276 📄 01524 734488
e-mail: info@oldhallcaravanpark.co.uk
dir: *M6 junct 35 follow signs to Over Kellet, left onto B6254, left at village green signed Capernwray. Site 1.5m on right*

PETS: Public areas except children's play area disp bin
Exercise area on site woodland walk **Exercise area** canal path
(0.25m) **Facilities** cage storage walks info

Open Mar-Oct rs Nov-Jan Last departure noon

A lovely secluded park set in a clearing amongst trees at the end of a half-mile long drive. This peaceful park is home to a wide variety of wildlife, and there are marked walks in the woods. The facilities are well maintained by friendly owners, and booking is advisable. 3 acre site. 38 touring pitches. 38 hardstandings. Motorhome pitches. 220 statics.

Notes No skateboards, roller blades or roller boots.

CHARNOCK RICHARD MOTORWAY SERVICE AREA (M6) Map 7 SD51

Days Inn Charnock Richard - M6
BUDGET HOTEL
Welcome Break Service Area PR7 5LR
☎ 01257 791746 📄 01257 793596
e-mail: charnockhotel@welcomebreak.co.uk
web: www.welcomebreak.co.uk
dir: *Between junct 27 & 28 of M6 N'bound. 500yds from Camelot Theme Park via Mill Lane*

PETS: Bedrooms (32 GF) certain bedrooms only **Charges** £5 per night **Grounds** disp bin **Exercise area** large field **Facilities** cage storage vet info **Other** charge for damage

This modern building offers accommodation in smart, spacious and well-equipped bedrooms, suitable for families and business travellers, and all with en suite bathrooms. Continental breakfast is available and other refreshments may be taken at the nearby family restaurant.

Rooms 100 (68 fmly) (32 GF) (20 smoking) **S** £39.95-£59.95; **D** £49.95-£69.95

COCKERHAM Map 7 SD45

Moss Wood Caravan Park *(SD456497)*
▶ ▶ ▶ ▶
Crimbles Ln LA2 0ES
☎ 01524 791041 📄 01524 792444
e-mail: info@mosswood.co.uk
dir: *Approx 4m from A6/M6 junct 33, 1m W of Cockerham on A588*

PETS: Public areas except children's play area, office, shop & toilets disp bin **Exercise area on site** 4-acre field (50yds) **Facilities** food food bowl water bowl walks info vet info **Other** dogs permitted by prior arrangement only

Open Mar-Oct Last arrival 20.00hrs Last departure 16.00hrs

A tree-lined grassy park with sheltered, level pitches, located on peaceful Cockerham Moss. The modern toilet block is attractively clad in stained wood, and the facilities include cubicled washing facilities and a launderette. 25 acre site. 25 touring pitches. 25 hardstandings. Tent pitches. Motorhome pitches. 143 statics.

CROSTON Map 7 SD51

Royal Umpire Caravan Park *(SD504190)*
▶ ▶ ▶
Southport Rd PR26 9JB
☎ 01772 600257 📄 01704 505886
e-mail: info@royalumpire.co.uk
dir: *From Chorley take A581, 3.5m towards Croston, site on right*

PETS: Charges dog £1.50 per stay **Public areas** disp bin **Exercise area on site** small fenced grass area **Facilities** washing facs walks info vet info **Other** prior notice required **Restrictions** no Pit Bull Terriers or dangerous dogs (see page 7)

Open all year Last arrival 20.00hrs Last departure 16.00hrs

A pleasant level site set in open countryside, with an attractive sunken garden and seating area. Plenty of leisure opportunities include an interesting children's playground, and a large playing field. The toilets, laundry and dishwashing area are of a very good quality. An ongoing upgrade programme is underway. A restaurant and a pub are within walking distance. 60 acre site. 195 touring pitches. 180 hardstandings. Tent pitches. Motorhome pitches.

GARSTANG Map 7 SD44

Claylands Caravan Park *(SD496485)*
▶ ▶ ▶ ▶
Cabus PR3 1AJ
☎ 01524 791242 📄 01524 792406
e-mail: alan@claylands.com
dir: *From M6 junct 33 S to Garstang, approx 6m pass Quattros Restaurant, signed off A6 into Weavers Lane, follow lane to end, over cattle grid*

PETS: Charges £1.50 per night £7 per week **Public areas** except bar & restaurant on leads disp bin **Exercise area on site** walkway near river **Facilities** food scoop/disp bags washing facs walks info vet info **Stables** 5m

Open Mar-Jan Last arrival 23.00hrs Last departure noon

A well-maintained site with lovely river and woodland walks and good views over the River Wyre towards the village of Scorton. This friendly park is set in delightful countryside where guests can enjoy fishing, and the atmosphere is very relaxed. The quality facilities and amenities are of a high standard, and everything is immaculately maintained. 14 acre site. 30 touring pitches. 30 hardstandings. Tent pitches. Motorhome pitches. 68 statics.

Notes No roller blades or skateboards.

ENGLAND

Stirk House
★★★ **80%** @ HOTEL

BB7 4LJ
☎ 01200 445581   📄 01200 445744
e-mail: reservations@stirkhouse.co.uk
dir: W of village, on A59. Hotel 0.5m on left

PETS: Bedrooms (12 GF) unattended **Public areas** except
restaurant **Grounds** disp bin **Facilities** food bowl water bowl
washing facs walks info vet info **On Request** fridge access
torch towels **Other** charge for damage

This delightful historic hotel enjoys a peaceful location in its own
grounds, amid rolling countryside. Extensive public areas include
excellent conference and banqueting facilities, a leisure centre
and an elegant restaurant. The stylish bedrooms and suites
vary in size and style but all are comfortable and well equipped.
Hospitality is warm and friendly, and service attentive.

Rooms 30 (10 annexe) (2 fmly) (12 GF) **S** £100-£180;
D £130-£210 (incl. bkfst)* **Facilities** STV 🔍 supervised 🏊 Gym
Aromatherapy Personal training Kick boxing Xmas New Year Wi-fi
Parking 400 **Notes** LB

CLASSIC
BRITISH HOTELS

Lancaster House
★★★★ **76%** @ HOTEL

Green Ln, Ellel LA1 4GJ
☎ 01524 844822   📄 01524 844766
e-mail: lancaster@elhmail.co.uk
web: www.elh.co.uk/hotels/lancaster
dir: M6 junct 33 N towards Lancaster. Through Galgate into Green
Ln. Hotel before university on right

PETS: Bedrooms (44 GF) **Charges** £10 per night
Public areas except restaurant & bar on leads **Grounds** on
leads **Exercise area** 500mtrs **Facilities** walks info vet info
On Request fridge access towels **Other** charge for damage

This modern hotel enjoys a rural setting south of the city and
close to the university. The attractive open-plan reception and
lounge boast a roaring log fire in colder months. Bedrooms
are spacious, and include 19 rooms that are particularly well
equipped for business guests. There are leisure facilities with a
hot tub and a function suite.

Rooms 99 (29 fmly) (44 GF) **Facilities** Spa STV 🔍 supervised
Gym Beauty salon Xmas New Year Wi-fi **Parking** 120 **Notes** LB

The Royal Kings Arms
★★★ **70%** HOTEL

OXFORD
HOTELS & INNS

Market St LA1 1HP
☎ 01524 32451   📄 01524 841698
e-mail: reservations.lancaster@ohiml.com
web: www.oxfordhotelsandinns.com
dir: M6 junct 33, A6 to city centre, 1st left, after Market Hotel.
Hotel at lights before Lancaster Castle

PETS: Bedrooms unattended **Public areas** except restaurant
on leads **Exercise area** 0.5m **Facilities** walks info vet info
On Request fridge access torch **Other** charge for damage

A distinctive period building located in the town centre, close
to the castle. Bedrooms are comfortable and suitable for both
business and leisure guests. Public areas include a small lounge
on the ground floor and The Castle Bar and Brasserie Restaurant
on the first floor. The hotel also has a private car park.

Rooms 55 (14 fmly) **Facilities** FTV Xmas Wi-fi **Services** Lift
Parking 26

Clarendon
★★★ **71%** HOTEL

76 Marine Road West, West End Promenade LA4 4EP
☎ 01524 410180   📄 01524 421616
e-mail: clarendon@mitchellshotels.co.uk
dir: M6 junct 34 follow Morecambe signs. At rdbt (with 'The
Shrimp' on corner) 1st exit to Westgate, follow to seafront. Right
at lights, hotel 3rd block

PETS: Bedrooms unattended **Exercise area** 40mtrs **Facilities**
cage storage walks info vet info **Other** charge for damage
Restrictions small & medium size dogs only

This traditional seafront hotel offers views over Morecambe Bay,
modern facilities and convenient parking. An extensive fish and
grill menu is offered in the contemporary Waterfront Restaurant
and guests can relax in the comfortable lounge bar. Davy Jones
Locker in the basement has a more traditional pub atmosphere
and offers cask ales and regular live entertainment.

Rooms 29 (4 fmly) **S** £60; **D** £90 (incl. bkfst)* **Facilities** Xmas
New Year Wi-fi **Services** Lift **Parking** 22

Beach Mount

★★★ GUEST ACCOMMODATION

395 Marine Road East LA4 5AN

☎ 01524 420753

e-mail: beachmounthotel@aol.com

dir: *M6 junct 34/35, follow signs to Morecambe. Beach Mount 0.5m from town centre on E Promenade*

PETS: Bedrooms (1 GF) unattended **Public areas** except restaurant on leads **Facilities** vet info **On Request** fridge access towels **Resident Pet:** Lola (Labradoodle)

This spacious property overlooks the bay and features a range of room styles that includes a family room and a junior suite. Guests have use of a comfortable lounge with fully licensed bar, and breakfasts are served in a pleasant separate dining room.

Rooms 10 en suite (1 GF) (10 smoking) **S** £25.50-£28.75; **D** £52.50-£59.50 **Facilities** FTV tea/coffee Cen ht Licensed **Notes** LB Closed Nov-Mar

Venture Caravan Park *(SD436633)*

▶▶▶

Langridge Way, Westgate LA4 4TQ

☎ 01524 412986 📠 01524 422029

e-mail: mark@venturecaravanpark.co.uk

dir: *From M6 junct 34 follow Morecambe signs. At rdbt take road towards Westgate & follow site signs. 1st right after fire station*

PETS: Public areas except children's play areas on leads disp bin **Exercise area** nearby **Facilities** food dog chews cat treats litter tray vet info **Other** prior notice required

Open all year rs Winter one toilet block open Last arrival 22.00hrs Last departure noon

A large family park with good modern facilities, including a small indoor heated pool, a licensed clubhouse and a family room with children's entertainment. The site has many statics, some of which are for holiday hire, and is close to the town centre. 17.5 acre site. 56 touring pitches. 40 hardstandings. Tent pitches. Motorhome pitches. 304 statics.

Abbey Farm Caravan Park *(SD434098)*

▶▶▶▶

Dark Ln L40 5TX

☎ 01695 572686 📠 01695 572686

e-mail: abbeyfarm@yahoo.com

dir: *M6 junct 27 onto A5209 to Burscough. 4m left onto B5240. Immediate right into Hobcross Lane. Site 1.5m on right*

PETS: Charges £1 per night **Public areas** except recreation field on leads disp bin **Exercise area on site** field **Facilities** walks info vet info

Open all year Last arrival 21.00hrs Last departure noon

Delightful hanging baskets and flower beds brighten this garden-like rural park which is sheltered by hedging and mature trees. Modern, very clean facilities include a family bathroom, and there are suitable pitches, close to the toilet facilities, for disabled visitors. A superb recreation field caters for children of all ages, and there is an indoor games room, large library, fishing lake and dog walk. Tents have their own area with BBQ and picnic tables. 6 acre site. 56 touring pitches. Tent pitches. Motorhome pitches. 44 statics.

Notes No camp fires

Ibis Preston North

BUDGET HOTEL

Garstang Rd, Broughton PR3 5JE

☎ 01772 861800 📠 01772 861900

e-mail: H3162@accor.com

web: www.ibishotel.com

dir: *M6 junct 32, then M55 junct 1. Left lane onto A6. Left at slip road, left again at mini-rdbt. 2nd turn, hotel on right past pub*

PETS: Bedrooms 3rd floor bedrooms only **Grounds** on leads **Facilities** walks info vet info **On Request** torch towels **Other** charge for damage

Modern, budget hotel offering comfortable accommodation in bright and practical bedrooms. Breakfast is self-service and dinner is available in the restaurant.

Rooms 82 (27 fmly) (16 GF) (12 smoking)

ENGLAND

WHITEWELL · Map 7 SD64

The Inn at Whitewell
★★★★★ ⊚ INN

Forest of Bowland, Clitheroe BB7 3AT
☎ 01200 448222 📄 01200 448298
e-mail: reception@innatwhitewell.com
dir: *M6 junct 31a, B6243 to Longridge. Left at mini-rdbt. After 3 rdbts & approx 3m, sharp left bend (with white railings), then right. Approx 1m left, right at T-junct. Next left, 3m to Whitewell*

PETS: Bedrooms (2 GF) unattended **Public areas** except restaurant **Grounds** disp bin **Exercise area** 50yds **Facilities** water bowl washing facs walks info vet info **On Request** towels **Stables** 1m **Other** stabling can be arranged

This long-established culinary destination is hidden away in quintessential Lancashire countryside just 20 minutes from the M6. The fine dining restaurant is complemented by two historic and cosy bars with roaring fires, real ales and polished service. Bedrooms are richly furnished with antiques and eye-catching bijouterie, while many of the bathrooms have Victorian brass showers.

Rooms 19 en suite 4 annexe en suite (1 fmly) (2 GF) **S** £88-£187; **D** £120-£231 **Facilities** STV FTV tea/coffee Dinner available Direct Dial Cen ht Wi-fi Golf 18 Fishing **Parking** 60 **Notes** No coaches

LEICESTERSHIRE

HINCKLEY · Map 4 SP49

CLASSIC BRITISH HOTELS

Sketchley Grange
★★★★ 81% ⊚⊚ HOTEL

Sketchley Ln, Burbage LE10 3HU
☎ 01455 251133 📄 01455 631384
e-mail: info@sketchleygrange.co.uk
web: www.sketchleygrange.co.uk
dir: *SE of town, off A5/M69 junct 1, take B4109 to Hinckley. Left at 2nd rdbt. 1st right onto Sketchley Lane*

PETS: Bedrooms (6 GF) unattended **Charges** £10 per night **Public areas** except restaurant & lounge on leads **Grounds** on leads disp bin **Exercise area** nearby **Facilities** walks info vet info **On Request** torch towels **Other** charge for damage **Restrictions** small dogs only

Close to motorway connections, this hotel is peacefully set in its own grounds, and enjoys open country views. Extensive leisure facilities include a stylish health and leisure spa. Modern meeting facilities, a choice of bars, and two dining options, together with comfortable bedrooms furnished with many extras, make this a special hotel.

Rooms 94 (9 fmly) (6 GF) **S** £65-£130; **D** £65-£130* **Facilities** Spa STV FTV ⊛ Gym Steam room Sauna Xmas New Year Wi-fi **Services** Lift **Parking** 270 **Notes** LB

LEICESTER FOREST MOTORWAY SERVICE AREA (M1) · Map 4 SK50

Welcome Break

Days Inn Leicester Forest East - M1
BUDGET HOTEL

Leicester Forest East, M1 Junct 21 LE3 3GB
☎ 0116 239 0534 📄 0116 239 0546
e-mail: leicester.hotel@welcomebreak.co.uk
web: www.welcomebreak.co.uk
dir: *On M1 N'bound between junct 21 & 21A*

PETS: Bedrooms certain bedrooms only **Public areas** on leads **Grounds** on leads

This modern building offers accommodation in smart, spacious and well-equipped bedrooms, suitable for families and business travellers, and all with en suite bathrooms. Continental breakfast is available, and other refreshments may be taken at the nearby family restaurant.

Rooms 92 (71 fmly) (10 smoking) **S** £39.95-£59.95; **D** £49.95-£69.95

MARKET HARBOROUGH · Map 4 SP78

Best Western

Best Western Three Swans
★★★ 77% HOTEL

21 High St LE16 7NJ
☎ 01858 466644 📄 01858 433101
e-mail: sales@threeswans.co.uk
web: www.bw-threeswanshotel.co.uk
dir: *M1 junct 20, A304 to Market Harborough. Through town centre on A6 from Leicester, hotel on right*

PETS: Bedrooms (20 GF) unattended **Charges** £10 per night **Public areas** except restaurant **Grounds** on leads disp bin **Exercise area** 0.75m **Facilities** water bowl dog chews cat treats washing facs cage storage walks info vet info **On Request** fridge access torch towels **Stables** nearby **Other** charge for damage

Public areas in this former coaching inn include an elegant fine dining restaurant and cocktail bar, a smart foyer lounge

and popular public bar areas. Bedroom styles and sizes vary, but are very well appointed and equipped. Those in the wing are particularly impressive, offering high quality and spacious accommodation.

Rooms 61 (48 annexe) (8 fmly) (20 GF) **S** £50–£79; **D** £50–£90.50 (incl. bkfst) **Facilities** STV Xmas New Year Wi-fi **Services** Lift **Parking** 100 **Notes** LB

MELTON MOWBRAY   **Map 8 SK71**

Stapleford Park

★★★★ ◉◉ COUNTRY HOUSE HOTEL

Stapleford LE14 2EF

☎ 01572 787000   📠 01572 787651

e-mail: reservations@stapleford.co.uk

web: www.staplefordpark.com

dir: *1m SW of B676, 4m E of Melton Mowbray & 9m W of Colsterworth*

PETS: Bedrooms Charges £15 per night **Public areas** except dining areas & pool area **Grounds** disp bin **Exercise area** nearby **Facilities** food bowl water bowl bedding dog chews feeding mat pet sitting walks info vet info **On Request** fridge access torch towels **Other** charge for damage treats for cats on request; no dogs on golf course

This stunning mansion, dating back to the 14th century, sits in over 500 acres of beautiful grounds. Spacious, sumptuous public rooms include a choice of lounges and an elegant restaurant; an additional brasserie-style restaurant is located in the golf complex. The hotel also boasts a spa with health and beauty treatments and gym, plus horseriding and many other country pursuits. Bedrooms are individually styled and furnished to a high standard. Attentive service is delivered with a relaxed yet professional style. Dinner, in the impressive dining room, is a highlight of any stay.

Rooms 55 (7 annexe) (10 fmly) **Facilities** Spa STV FTV ⊛ ♨ 18 ⌣ Putt green Fishing ♨ Gym Archery Croquet Falconry Horseriding Petanque Shooting Billiards Xmas New Year Wi-fi **Services** Lift **Parking** 120

Sysonby Knoll

★★★ 78% HOTEL

Asfordby Rd LE13 0HP

☎ 01664 563563   📠 01664 410364

e-mail: reception@sysonby.com

web: www.sysonby.com

dir: *0.5m from town centre on A6006*

PETS: Bedrooms (7 GF) all bedrooms except annexe & four-poster rooms **Charges** 1st pet free, additonal pet £5 per stay **Public areas** except restaurant on leads **Grounds** on leads disp bin **Exercise area** exercise field **Exercise area** adjacent **Facilities** leads washing facs cage storage walks info vet info **On Request** fridge access torch towels **Other** charge for damage **Resident Pets:** Stalky & Twiglet (Miniature Dachshunds)

Built in the 19th century and set in five acres of parkland and lawns, the main house still retains much of the elegance of an English mansion. The garden restaurant serves traditional English cuisine. Modern, comfortable bedrooms complement the traditional, spacious lounges now used for conferences, meetings and other special occasions.

Rooms 30 (7 annexe) (1 fmly) (7 GF) **S** £75–£103; **D** £95–£130 (incl. bkfst)* **Facilities** FTV Fishing ♨ Wi-fi **Parking** 48 **Notes** LB Closed 25 Dec–1 Jan

Bryn Barn

★★★★ GUEST ACCOMMODATION

38 High St, Waltham-on-the-Wolds LE14 4AH

☎ 01664 464783 & 07914 222407

e-mail: glenarowlands@onetel.com

web: www.brynbarn.co.uk

dir: *4.5m NE of Melton. Off A607, in Waltham-on-the-Wolds centre*

PETS: Bedrooms (1 GF) 1 bedroom only **Charges** £5 per night **Grounds** on leads disp bin **Exercise area** 500mtrs **Facilities** food bowl water bowl feeding mat scoop/disp bags cage storage walks info vet info **On Request** fridge access torch towels **Other** charge for damage **Restrictions** no very large dogs; no Alsatians, Pit Bull Terriers, Newfoundlands or Rottweilers

A warm welcome awaits at this attractive, peacefully located cottage within easy reach of Melton Mowbray, Grantham, Rutland Water and Belvoir Castle. Bedrooms are smartly appointed and comfortably furnished, while public rooms include an inviting lounge overlooking a wonderful courtyard garden. Meals are available at one of the nearby village pubs.

Rooms 4 rms (3 en suite) (1 pri facs) (2 fmly) (1 GF) **S** £35–£50; **D** £60–£70 **Facilities** FTV TVL tea/coffee Cen ht Wi-fi **Parking** 4 **Notes** LB Closed 21 Dec–4 Jan

ENGLAND

RAVENSTONE — Map 8 SK41

Ravenstone Guesthouse
★★★★ 🏠 GUEST HOUSE
Church Lane Farm House LE67 2AE
☎ 01530 810536
e-mail: annthorne@ravenstone-guesthouse.co.uk
web: www.ravenstone-guesthouse.co.uk
dir: *1.5m W of Coalville. Off A447 onto Church Ln for Ravenstone, 2nd house on left*

PETS: Bedrooms sign **Sep accom** raised, heated kennel with small run **Public areas** at proprietor's discretion **Grounds** disp bin **Exercise area** 40yds **Facilities** food bowl water bowl bedding feeding mat scoop/disp bags leads washing facs cage storage walks info vet info **On Request** fridge access torch towels **Stables** in village (DIY livery) **Other** charge for damage no charge but contribution to Dogs Trust charity invited **Restrictions** no puppies; no Pit Bull Terriers or fighting dogs (see page 7) **Resident Pet:** Russet (Labrador)

Situated in the heart of Ravenstone village, this early 18th-century house is full of character. The bedrooms are individually decorated and feature period furniture. Local produce is used for dinner and in the extensive breakfast menu. The beamed dining room has an honesty bar and there is also a cosy lounge.

Rooms 4 en suite **Facilities** FTV TVL tea/coffee Dinner available Cen ht Licensed Wi-fi **Parking** 6 **Notes** Closed 23-30 Dec & 1 Jan RS 31 Dec

LINCOLNSHIRE

ANCASTER — Map 8 SK94

Woodland Waters *(SK979435)*
▶ ▶ ▶
Willoughby Rd NG32 3RT
☎ 01400 230888 📠 01400 230888
e-mail: info@woodlandwaters.co.uk
dir: *On A153 W of x-roads with B6403*

PETS: Charges £2 per night £14 per week **Public areas** except bar on leads disp bin **Exercise area on site** lake & park walks **Facilities** walks info vet info **Other** dog bowls at outdoor eating areas on request **Resident Pets:** 2 Black Labradors

Open all year Last arrival 21.00hrs Last departure noon

Peacefully set around five impressive fishing lakes, with a few log cabins in a separate area, this is a pleasant open park. The access road is through mature woodland, and there is an excellent heated toilet block, and a pub/club house with restaurant. 72 acre site. 62 touring pitches. 2 hardstandings. Tent pitches. Motorhome pitches.

BARTON-UPON-HUMBER — Map 8 TA02

Best Western Reeds Country Hotel
★★★ 77% HOTEL
Westfield Lakes, Far Ings Rd DN18 5RG
☎ 01652 632313 📠 01652 636361
e-mail: info@reedshotel.co.uk
dir: *At A15 rdbt take 2nd exit (Humber Bridge) & exit at Barton-upon-Humber, left at rdbt. In 200yds right at hotel sign, down hill & hotel at junct*

PETS: Bedrooms smaller bedrooms not suitable for large dogs **Charges** £10 per night **Grounds** on leads **Exercise area** Viking Way adjacent **Facilities** cage storage walks info vet info **Other** charge for damage

This hotel is situated in a quiet wildlife sanctuary just upstream from the Humber Bridge. A very attractive lakeside restaurant commands tranquil views, and there is a health spa offering various alternative therapies. Bedrooms are comfortable and well equipped, and service is both friendly and helpful.

Rooms 26 (5 fmly) **Facilities** Spa STV FTV Xmas New Year Wi-fi **Services** Lift **Parking** 100 **Notes** LB

BOSTON — Map 8 TF34

Long Acre Caravan Park *(TF385535)*
▶ ▶ ▶ ▶
Station Rd, Old Leake PE22 9RF
☎ 01205 871555 📠 01205 871555
e-mail: lacp@btconnect.com
dir: *From A16 take B1184 at Sibsey (by church); approx 1m at T-junct turn left. 1.5m, after level crossing take next right into Station Rd. Park entrance approx 0.5m on left*

PETS: Charges £1 per night **Public areas Exercise area on site** small area available **Exercise area** approx 0.5m **Facilities** walks info vet info **Other** prior notice required **Resident Pet:** Max (Mastif/Ridgeback cross)

Open Mar-Oct Last arrival 20.00hrs Last departure 11.00hrs

A small rural adults-only park in an attractive setting within easy reach of Boston, Spalding and Skegness. There is a very clean toilet block with an appealing interior and modern, upmarket fittings. Excellent shelter is provided by the high, mature boundary hedging. A holiday cottage is available to let. 40 touring pitches. 40 hardstandings. Tent pitches. Motorhome pitches.

Notes Washing lines not permitted.

Orchard Park *(TF274432)*

▶▶▶▶

Frampton Ln, Hubbert's Bridge PE20 3QU
☎ 01205 290328   📠 01205 290247
e-mail: info@orchardpark.co.uk
dir: *On B1192, between A52 (Boston-Grantham) & A1121 (Boston-Sleaford)*

PETS: Public areas except café & bar disp bin **Exercise area** adjacent **Facilities** food washing facs walks info vet info **Stables** 1.5m **Other** disposal bags available

Open all year rs Dec-Feb bar, shop & café closed Last arrival 22.30hrs Last departure 16.00hrs

Ideally located for exploring the unique fenlands, this rapidly-improving park has two lakes - one for fishing and the other set aside for conservation. The very attractive restaurant and bar prove popular with visitors. 51 acre site. 87 touring pitches. 15 hardstandings. Tent pitches. Motorhome pitches. 164 statics.

Notes Washing lines not permitted. 🐾

Pilgrims Way Caravan & Camping Park *(TF358434)*

▶▶▶▶

Church Green Rd, Fishtoft PE21 0QY
☎ 01205 366646   & 07973 941955   📠 01205 366646
e-mail: pilgrimsway@caravanandcampingpark.com
dir: *E from Boston on A52. In 1m, after junct with A16, at Ball House pub turn right. Follow tourist signs to site*

PETS: Sep accom Public areas except play area & toilet block **Exercise area** 0.5m **Facilities** food bowl water bowl washing facs walks info vet info **Stables** 1m **Other** local grooming & dog wash service can visit the site local pet shop delivery service **Resident Pets:** 1 Bernese Mountain Dog, 2 Jack Russells, 3 cats, 2 horses

Open all year Last arrival 22.00hrs Last departure noon

A peaceful and relaxing park situated in the heart of the south Lincolnshire countryside, yet only a mile from the centre of Boston. After a change of ownership a couple of years ago, the enthusiastic, hands-on owners have done a superb job in upgrading the facilities. The park offers quality toilet facilities, 22 electric hook-ups and hardstandings, and tents are welcome in a separate grassy area. 2.5 acre site. 22 touring pitches. 15 hardstandings. Tent pitches. Motorhome pitches.

Notes Last arrival time 21.00hrs summer 🐾

West End Farm *(TF418842)*

▶▶▶

Salterns Way LN11 8BF
☎ 01507 450949   & 07766 278740
e-mail: westendfarm@talktalkbusiness.net
dir: *From A157 turn towards Great Carlton at Gayton Top. Brown sign for West End Farm in 0.5m, turn right into site*

PETS: Public areas except toilet & shower block **Exercise area** adjacent **Facilities** walks info vet info

Open 28 Mar-2 Oct Last arrival 20.30hrs Last departure 14.00hrs

A neat and well-maintained four-acre touring park situated on the edge of the Lincolnshire Wolds. Surrounded by mature trees and bushes and well away from the busy main roads, yet connected by footpaths ideal for walking and cycling, it offers enjoyable peace and quiet close to the popular holiday resort of Mablethorpe. Good clean facilities throughout. 4 acre site. 35 touring pitches. 4 seasonal pitches. Tent pitches. Motorhome pitches.

Herons Cottage Touring Park *(TF364204)*

▶▶▶

Frostley Gate PE12 8SR
☎ 01406 540435
e-mail: simon@satleisure.co.uk
dir: *Site 4m S of Holbeach on B1165 between Sutton St James & Whaplode St Catherine*

PETS: Public areas disp bin **Exercise area on site** riverside dog walks

Open all year Last arrival 20.00hrs Last departure 11.00hrs

Under the same ownership as Heron's Mead Touring Park in Orby (see entry), this rapidly improving park is situated in the heart of the Fens beside the Little South Holland Drain, with its extremely good coarse fishing. There's excellent supervision and 18 fully-serviced pitches. 4.5 acre site. 52 touring pitches. 48 hardstandings. 40 seasonal pitches. Tent pitches. Motorhome pitches. 9 statics.

Notes Strictly no children under 12yrs. 🐾

LINCOLN   Map 8 SK97

Washingborough Hall

★★★ **79%** ⊛ COUNTRY HOUSE HOTEL

Church Hill, Washingborough LN4 1BE
☎ 01522 790340   📄 01522 792936
e-mail: enquiries@washingboroughhall.com
dir: *B1190 into Washingborough. Right at rdbt, hotel 500yds on left*

PETS: Bedrooms Charges Public areas main hall, reception & bar areas only on leads **Grounds** disp bin **Exercise area** 500yds **Facilities** food bowl water bowl leads walks info vet info **On Request** torch **Other** charge for damage **Restrictions** well behaved, non barking dogs only **Resident Pets:** Teasel & Higgins (Jack Russells), Thomas (cat)

This Georgian manor stands on the edge of the quiet village of Washingborough and is set in attractive gardens. Public rooms are pleasantly furnished and comfortable, while the restaurant offers interesting menus. Bedrooms are individually designed and most have views out over the grounds to the countryside beyond.

Rooms 12 (3 fmly) **S** £50-£85; **D** £80-£135 (incl. bkfst)*
Facilities FTV ⛳ Bicycles for hire New Year Wi-fi **Parking** 40
Notes LB

LOUTH   Map 8 TF38

Best Western Kenwick Park

★★★ **77%** HOTEL

Kenwick Park Estate LN11 8NR
☎ 01507 608806   📄 01507 608027
e-mail: enquiries@kenwick-park.co.uk
web: www.kenwick-park.co.uk
dir: *A16 from Grimsby, then A157 Mablethorpe/Manby Rd. Hotel 400mtrs down hill on right*

PETS: Bedrooms unattended **Charges Public areas** on leads **Grounds** on leads disp bin **Facilities** water bowl washing facs walks info vet info **On Request** fridge access torch towels **Other** charge for damage please phone for further details of pet facilities

This elegant Georgian house is situated on the 320-acre Kenwick Park estate, overlooking its own golf course. Bedrooms are spacious, comfortable and provide modern facilities. Public areas include a restaurant and a conservatory bar that overlook the grounds. There is also an extensive leisure centre and state-of-the-art conference and banqueting facilities.

Rooms 34 (5 annexe) (10 fmly) **Facilities** Spa ⓢ supervised ⚓ 18 ⛳ Putt green Gym Squash Health & beauty centre Xmas New Year Wi-fi **Parking** 100

MABLETHORPE   Map 9 TF58

Park View Guest House

★★★ GUEST HOUSE

48 Gibraltar Rd LN12 2AT
☎ 01507 477267 & 07906 847841   📄 01507 477267
e-mail: malcolm@pvgh.freeserve.co.uk
dir: *Take A1104, at beach turn right onto Gibraltar Rd*

PETS: Bedrooms (3 GF) sign ground-floor bedrooms only **Charges** £10 per stay **Public areas** allowed in bar but not dining room on leads **Grounds** disp bin **Exercise area** adjacent to beach & park **Facilities** feeding mat walks info vet info **On Request** fridge access torch **Stables** 3m **Other** charge for damage **Restrictions** 1 small dog only **Resident Pet:** Parker (Shih Tzu)

This well-established guest house is ideally situated just beside Mablethorpe's golden beach and the Queens Park, and also within easy walking distance of the main town centre amenities. Service is both helpful and friendly, provided by the resident proprietors, Debbie and Malcolm. The accommodation is soundly presented and of varying sizes, the ground-floor bedrooms proving particularly popular.

Rooms 5 rms (2 en suite) (1 fmly) (3 GF) **S** £25-£27.50; **D** £50-£55 **Facilities** FTV TVL tea/coffee Dinner available Cen ht Licensed Wi-fi **Parking** 6 **Notes** LB ⊛

Golden Sands Holiday Park (TF501861)

Quebec Rd LN12 1QJ
☎ 01507 477871   📄 01507 472066
e-mail: naomi.mcintosh@bourne-leisure.co.uk
dir: *From centre of Mablethorpe turn left on seafront road towards north end. Site on left*

PETS: Charges Public areas except complex area **Exercise area** beach adjacent (dogs must be on leads) **Other** prior notice required max 2 dogs per group **Restrictions** certain breeds not accepted (check when booking)

Open mid Mar-Oct Last arrival anytime Last departure 10.00hrs

A large, well-equipped seaside holiday park with separate touring facilities on two sites, including a refurbished toilet block, additional portaloo facilities, and a much improved shop at reception. The first-floor entertainment rooms are only accessible via stairs (no lifts). 23 acre site. 214 touring pitches. 20 hardstandings. Tent pitches. Motorhome pitches. 1500 statics.

MARTON (VILLAGE) Map 8 SK88

Black Swan Guest House

★★★ GUEST ACCOMMODATION

High St DN21 5AH
☎ 01427 718878
e-mail: info@blackswanguesthouse.co.uk
web: www.blackswanguesthouse.co.uk
dir: On A156 in village centre at junct A1500

PETS: Bedrooms (4 GF) unattended **Public areas** only assist dogs allowed in dining room **Grounds** disp bin **Exercise area** 200yds **Facilities** washing facs cage storage walks info vet info **On Request** fridge access torch **Stables** 4m **Other** charge for damage **Resident Pets:** Scooby & Patch (cats)

Centrally located in the village, this 18th-century former coaching inn retains many original features, and offers good hospitality and homely bedrooms with modern facilities. Tasty breakfasts are served in the cosy dining room and a comfortable lounge with Wi-fi access is available. Transport to nearby pubs and restaurants can be provided.

Rooms 6 en suite 4 annexe en suite (3 fmly) (4 GF) **S** £45-£50; **D** £68 **Facilities** FTV TVL tea/coffee Cen ht Licensed Wi-fi **Parking** 10 **Notes** LB

ORBY Map 9 TF46

Heron's Mead Fishing Lake & Touring Park
(TF508673)

▶▶▶▶

Marsh Ln PE24 5JA
☎ 01754 811340
e-mail: mail@heronsmeadtouringpark.co.uk
dir: From A158 (Lincoln to Skegness road) turn left at rdbt, through Orby for 0.5m

PETS: Charges £1 per night £5 per week **Public areas** except lakeside disp bin **Exercise area on site** woodland walk **Facilities** walks info vet info

Open Mar-1 Nov Last arrival 21.00hrs Last departure noon

A pleasant fishing and touring park with coarse fishing and an eight-acre woodland walk. The owners have made many improvements to the facilities, which prove particularly appealing to quiet couples and more elderly visitors. 16 acre site. 21 touring pitches. 21 hardstandings. 10 seasonal pitches. Tent pitches. Motorhome pitches. 35 statics.

Notes No ball games, no motorbikes.

SALTFLEETBY ST PETER Map 9 TF48

Saltfleetby Fisheries *(TF425892)*

▶▶▶

Main Rd LN11 7SS
☎ 01507 338272
e-mail: saltfleetbyfish@btinternet.com
dir: On B1200, 6m E of junct with A16. 3m W of A103

PETS: Charges £1 per night **Public areas** on leads disp bin **Exercise area on site** field for dog walking **Facilities** washing facs vet info **Other** prior notice required **Resident Pets:** Jack & Whisky (Jack Russells)

Open Mar-Nov Last arrival 21.00hrs Last departure 10.00hrs

An excellent small site with just 12 touring pitches, each with gravel hardstanding and electric hook-up, set in a sheltered area close to two large and very popular fishing lakes. A spacious, upmarket Swedish chalet doubles as a reception and a well-furnished café with open-plan kitchen. The purpose-built toilet block is light, airy and well maintained. 14 acre site. 12 touring pitches. 12 hardstandings. Tent pitches. Motorhome pitches. 3 statics.

Notes 🐾

SCUNTHORPE — Map 8 SE81

Forest Pines Hotel & Golf Resort

★★★★ 79% ⊛ HOTEL

Ermine St, Broughton DN20 0AQ
☎ 01652 650770 📠 01652 650495
e-mail: forestpines@qhotels.co.uk
web: www.qhotels.co.uk
dir: 200yds from M180 junct 4, on Brigg-Scunthorpe rdbt

PETS: Bedrooms (67 GF) unattended **Charges** £20 per night
Exercise area 0.5m **Facilities** vet info **Other** charge for damage
prior notice required **Restrictions** small, well behaved dogs only

This smart hotel provides a comprehensive range of leisure
facilities. Extensive conference rooms, a modern health and
beauty spa, and a championship golf course ensure that it is
a popular choice with both corporate and leisure guests. The
well-equipped bedrooms are modern, spacious, and appointed
to a good standard. Extensive public areas include a choice of
dining options, with fine dining available in The Eighteen57 fish
restaurant, and more informal eating in the Grill Bar.

Rooms 188 (66 fmly) (67 GF) **Facilities** Spa STV FTV ⊛
supervised ↕ 27 Putt green Gym Mountain bikes Jogging track
Xmas New Year Wi-fi **Services** Lift **Parking** 400

SKEGNESS — Map 9 TF56

Best Western Vine

★★★ 70% HOTEL

Vine Rd, Seacroft PE25 3DB
☎ 01754 763018 & 610611 📠 01754 769845
e-mail: info@thevinehotel.com
dir: A52 to Skegness, S towards Gibraltar Point, right into
Drummond Rd, 0.5m, right into Vine Rd

PETS: Bedrooms unattended **Charges** £5 per night
Public areas except restaurant **Grounds** disp bin **Exercise area**
surrounding area **Facilities** cage storage walks info vet info
On Request fridge access torch towels

Reputedly the second oldest building in Skegness, this traditional
style hotel offers two character bars that serve excellent local
beers. Freshly prepared dishes are served in both the bar
and the restaurant; service is both friendly and helpful. The
smartly decorated bedrooms are well equipped and comfortably
appointed.

Rooms 25 (3 fmly) **Facilities** FTV Xmas New Year Wi-fi **Parking** 50

STAMFORD — Map 4 TF00

The George of Stamford

★★★★ 77% ⊛ HOTEL

71 St Martins PE9 2LB
☎ 01780 750750 & 750700 (res) 📠 01780 750701
e-mail: reservations@georgehotelofstamford.com
web: www.georgehotelofstamford.com
dir: A1, 15m N of Peterborough onto B1081, hotel 1m on left

PETS: Bedrooms certain bedrooms only **Public areas** except
restaurant (assist dogs only) **Grounds Exercise area** meadow
500yds **Facilities** water bowl bedding dog chews feeding mat
vet info **On Request** towels **Resident Pets:** Sooty & Sweep (cats)

Steeped in hundreds of years of history, this delightful coaching
inn provides spacious public areas that include a choice of dining
options, inviting, lounges, a business centre and a range of
quality shops. A highlight is afternoon tea, taken in the colourful
courtyard when the weather permits. Bedrooms are stylishly
appointed and range from traditional to contemporary in design.

Rooms 47 (24 fmly) **S** £95-£100; **D** £150-£230 (incl. bkfst)*
Facilities STV ⛵ Complimentary membership to local gym Xmas
New Year Wi-fi **Parking** 110 **Notes** LB

SUTTON ON SEA — Map 9 TF58

The Grange & Links

★★★ 73% HOTEL

Sea Ln, Sandilands LN12 2RA
☎ 01507 441334 📠 01507 443033
e-mail: grangeandlinkshotel@btconnect.com
web: www.grangeandlinkshotel.co.uk
dir: A1111 to Sutton-on-Sea, follow signs to Sandilands

PETS: Bedrooms (3 GF) unattended sign **Sep accom Charges**
phone for charges per night **Public areas** except eating area &
bar **Grounds Exercise area** 5 mins **Facilities** food bowl water
bowl litter tray scoop/disp bags leads walks info vet info
On Request towels **Other** charge for damage **Resident Pet:** 1
Chocolate Labrador

This friendly, family-run hotel sits in five acres of grounds,
close to both the beach and its own 18-hole links golf course.
Bedrooms are pleasantly appointed and are well equipped for
both business and leisure guests. Public rooms include ample
lounge areas, a formal restaurant and a traditional bar, serving a
wide range of meals and snacks.

Rooms 23 (10 fmly) (3 GF) **S** £69.50; **D** £94 (incl. bkfst)*
Facilities ↕ 18 ⚲ Putt green ⛵ Gym Xmas New Year Wi-fi
Parking 60 **Notes** LB

WADDINGHAM — Map 8 SK99

Brandy Wharf Leisure Park *(TF014968)*

► ► ►

Brandy Wharf DN21 4RT
☎ 01673 818010 📠 01673 818010
e-mail: brandywharflp@freenetname.co.uk
dir: *From A15 onto B1205 through Waddingham. Site 3m from Waddingham*

PETS: Public areas disp bin **Exercise area on site** river bank **Facilities** washing facs walks info vet info **Stables** 5m **Other** prior notice required **Restrictions** well behaved dogs only

Open all year rs Etr-Oct for tents Last arrival dusk Last departure 17.00hrs

A delightful site in a very rural area on the banks of the River Ancholme, where fishing is available. The toilet block has unisex rooms with combined facilities as well as a more conventional ladies and gents with wash hand basins and toilet. All of the grassy pitches have electricity, and there's a playing and picnic area. The site attracts a lively clientele at weekends, and music round open fires is allowed until 1am. Advance booking is necessary for weekend pitches. 5 acre site. 50 touring pitches. Tent pitches. Motorhome pitches.

Notes No disposable BBQs on grass, no music after 01.00hrs. 🐾

WINTERINGHAM — Map 8 SE92

Winteringham Fields

★ ★ ★ ★ ★ ◉◉ 🍴 RESTAURANT WITH ROOMS

DN15 9ND
☎ 01724 733096 📠 01724 733898
e-mail: reception@winteringhamfields.co.uk
dir: *In village centre at x-rds*

PETS: Bedrooms (3 GF) courtyard rooms recommended **Charges** £10 per night **Grounds** disp bin **Exercise area** 20mtrs **Facilities** food (pre-bookable) food bowl water bowl bedding dog chews scoop/disp bags leads washing facs dog grooming cage storage walks info vet info **On Request** fridge access torch towels **Stables Other** charge for damage dog grooming by prior arrangement; barns & stables available **Resident Pets:** Uma & Peri (Labradors), Azerah (Great Dane), Puggly (Pug)

This highly regarded restaurant with rooms, located deep in the countryside in Winteringham village, is six miles west of the Humber Bridge. Public rooms and bedrooms, some of which are housed in renovated barns and cottages, are delightfully inviting. Award-winning food is served in the restaurant.

Rooms 4 en suite 7 annexe en suite (2 fmly) (3 GF) **S** £140-£180; **D** £165-£220 **Facilities** tea/coffee Dinner available Direct Dial Cen ht **Parking** 14 **Notes** LB Closed 25 Dec for 2 wks, last wk Oct, 2 wks Aug No coaches

WOODHALL SPA — Map 8 TF16

The Claremont Guest House

★ ★ ★ GUEST HOUSE

9/11 Witham Rd LN10 6RW
☎ 01526 352000
e-mail: claremontgh@live.co.uk
web: www.theclaremontguesthouse.co.uk
dir: *In town centre on B1191 near mini-rdbt*

PETS: Bedrooms (2 GF) unattended sign **Public areas** except restaurant & not before 10am on leads **Grounds** disp bin **Exercise area** 50mtrs **Facilities** water bowl bedding dog chews feeding mat scoop/disp bags leads washing facs cage storage walks info vet info **On Request** fridge access torch towels **Other** charge for damage **Resident Pets:** 2 Miniature Schnauzers

A Victorian townhouse with a lovely dining room, guest lounge and Wi-fi access. Having benefited from a refurbishment by the friendly owners, bedrooms are well equipped and vary in size from cosy singles to family rooms. The house has lock up facilities for cycling and golfing equipment.

Rooms 11 rms (6 en suite) (5 pri facs) (3 fmly) (2 GF) **S** £30-£35; **D** £55-£60 **Facilities** FTV TVL tea/coffee Cen ht Wi-fi **Parking** 4

LONDON

E14

Four Seasons Hotel London at Canary Wharf

★ ★ ★ ★ ★ ◉ HOTEL

Westferry Circus, Canary Wharf E14 8RS
☎ 020 7510 1999 📠 020 7510 1998
e-mail: reservations.caw@fourseasons.com
web: www.fourseasons.com/canarywharf
dir: *From A13 follow Canary Wharf, Isle of Dogs & Westferry Circus signs. Hotel off 3rd exit of Westferry Circus rdbt*

PETS: Bedrooms Exercise area 5 mins' walk to waterfront **Facilities** food (pre-bookable) food bowl water bowl bedding dog chews litter tray pet sitting dog walking dog grooming cage storage walks info vet info **On Request** fridge access torch towels **Other** charge for damage concierge will assist in arranging kennel space for larger pets **Restrictions** max weight 15lbs

With superb views over the London skyline, this stylish modern hotel enjoys a delightful riverside location. Spacious contemporary bedrooms are particularly thoughtfully equipped. Public areas include the Italian Quadrato Bar and Restaurant, an impressive business centre and a gym. Guests also have complimentary use of the impressive Holmes Place health club and spa. Welcoming staff provide exemplary levels of service and hospitality.

Rooms 142 (20 smoking) **S** £160-£330; **D** £160-£330*
Facilities Spa STV FTV 🏊 supervised ⌚ Gym Fitness centre Xmas New Year Wi-fi **Services** Lift Air con **Parking** 54

EC1

Malmaison Charterhouse Square

★★★ 88% ◉◉ HOTEL

18-21 Charterhouse Square, Clerkenwell EC1M 6AH
☎ 020 7012 3700 📄 020 7012 3702
e-mail: london@malmaison.com
web: www.malmaison.com
dir: Exit Barbican Station turn left, take 1st left. Hotel on far left corner of Charterhouse Square

PETS: Bedrooms (5 GF) **Charges** £10 per night **Public areas** except restaurant (assist dogs only) muzzled and on leads **Facilities** food bowl water bowl bedding cage storage vet info **On Request** fridge access torch towels **Other** charge for damage

Situated in a leafy and peaceful square, Malmaison Charterhouse maintains the same focus on quality service and food as the other hotels in the group. The bedrooms, stylishly decorated in calming tones, have all the expected facilities including power showers, CD players and free internet access. The brasserie and bar at the hotel's centre has a buzzing atmosphere and offers traditional French cuisine.

Rooms 97 (5 GF) **S** £255-£365; **D** £275-£385* **Facilities** STV Gym Wi-fi **Services** Lift Air con **Notes** LB

EC3

Novotel London Tower Bridge

★★★★ 73% HOTEL

10 Pepys St EC3N 2NR
☎ 020 7265 6000 & 7265 6002 📄 020 7265 6060
e-mail: H3107@accor.com
web: www.novotel.com

PETS: Bedrooms Charges £8 per night **Public areas** except restaurant & bar on leads **Exercise area** park 30mtrs **Facilities** cage storage walks info vet info **Other** charge for damage

Located near the Tower of London, this smart hotel is convenient for Docklands, the City, Heathrow and London City airports. Air-conditioned bedrooms are spacious, modern, and offer a great range of facilities. There is a smart bar and restaurant, a small gym, children's play area and extensive meeting and conference facilities.

Rooms 203 (130 fmly) **Facilities** STV FTV Gym Steam room Sauna Fitness room Xmas New Year Wi-fi **Services** Lift

N9

Lee Valley Camping & Caravan Park
(TQ360945)

►►►

Meridian Way N9 0AR
☎ 020 8803 6900 📄 020 8884 4975
e-mail: leisurecomplex@leevalleypark.org.uk
dir: M25 junct 25, A10 S, 1st left onto A1055, approx 5m to Leisure Complex. From A406 (North Circular), N on A1010, left after 0.25m, right (Pickets Lock Ln)

PETS: Charges £1.90 per night £13.30 per week **Public areas** except toilets, showers, laundry & shop disp bin **Exercise area** adjacent **Facilities** food **Other** dogs must be under strict control at all times & not enter the water

Open all year rs Xmas & New Year Last arrival 22.00hrs Last departure noon

A pleasant, open site within easy reach of London yet peacefully located close to two large reservoirs. The very good toilet facilities are beautifully kept by dedicated wardens, and the site has the advantage of being adjacent to a restaurant and bar, and a multi-screen cinema. 4.5 acre site. 160 touring pitches. 41 hardstandings. Tent pitches. Motorhome pitches.

Notes No commercial vehicles

NW1

Ibis London Euston St Pancras

BUDGET HOTEL

3 Cardington St NW1 2LW
☎ 020 7388 7777 📄 020 7388 0001
e-mail: H0921@accor-hotels.com
web: www.ibishotel.com
dir: From Euston Rd or station, right to Melton St & into Cardington St

PETS: Bedrooms unattended **Charges** £5 per night **Public areas Exercise area** Regents Park **Facilities** food bowl water bowl **On Request** towels

Modern, budget hotel offering comfortable accommodation in bright and practical bedrooms. Breakfast is self-service and dinner is available in the restaurant.

Rooms 380 **S** £80-£159; **D** £80-£159*

SE1

Novotel London City South

 ★★★★ 74% HOTEL

Southwark Bridge Rd SE1 9HH
☎ 020 7089 0400 🖹 020 7089 0410
e-mail: H3269@accor.com
web: www.novotel.com
dir: At junct at Thrale St, off Southwark St

PETS: Bedrooms Charges £8 per night Public areas except restaurant & bar on leads Facilities walks info vet info Other charge for damage

Conveniently located for both business and leisure guests, with The City just across the Thames; other major attractions are also easily accessible. The hotel is contemporary in design with smart, modern bedrooms and spacious public rooms. There is a gym, sauna and steam room on the 6th floor, and limited parking is available at the rear of the hotel.

Rooms 182 (139 fmly) Facilities STV FTV Gym Steam room Sauna Wi-fi Services Lift Air con Parking 80

SW1

RED CARNATION
HOTEL COLLECTION

No 41

★★★★★ TOWN HOUSE HOTEL

41 Buckingham Palace Rd SW1W 0PS
☎ 020 7300 0041 🖹 020 7300 0141
e-mail: book41@rchmail.com
web: www.41hotel.com
dir: Opposite Buckingham Palace Mews entrance

PETS: Bedrooms sign Charges £500 damage deposit required Public areas on mezzanine area except at food service Exercise area St James's Park (5 mins' walk) Facilities food (pre-bookable) food bowl water bowl bedding dog chews cat treats feeding mat litter tray scoop/disp bags leads pet sitting dog walking dog grooming cage storage walks info vet info On Request fridge access torch towels Other charge for damage pets are accepted by prior arrangement only; pet menus; dedicated staff member for pets

Small, intimate and very private, this stunning town house is located opposite the Royal Mews. Decorated in stylish black and white, bedrooms successfully combine comfort with state-of-the-art technology such as iPod docking stations, interactive TV and free high speed internet access. Thoughtful touches such as fresh fruit, flowers and scented candles add to the very welcoming atmosphere. The large lounge is the focal point; food and drinks are available as are magazines and newspapers from around the world plus internet access. Attentive personal service and a host of thoughtful extra touches make No 41 really special.

Rooms 30 (2 fmly) D £323-£467* Facilities STV Local health club Beauty treatments In-room spa Xmas New Year Wi-fi Services Lift Air con Notes LB

The Rubens at the Palace

THE
RED CARNATION
HOTEL COLLECTION

★★★★ 83% ◉◉ HOTEL

39 Buckingham Palace Rd SW1W 0PS
☎ 020 7834 6600 🖹 020 7233 6037
e-mail: bookrb@rchmail.com
web: www.rubenshotel.com
dir: Opposite Royal Mews, 100mtrs from Buckingham Palace

PETS: Bedrooms sign Charges £500 damage deposit required Public areas except food service area (except assist dogs) on leads Exercise area St James's Park & Green Park 0.5m Facilities food (pre-bookable) food bowl water bowl dog chews cat treats feeding mat litter tray scoop/disp bags leads pet sitting dog walking dog grooming cage storage walks info vet info On Request fridge access torch towels Other charge for damage pets are accepted by prior arrangement only; dedicated staff member for pets

This hotel enjoys an enviable location close to Buckingham Palace. Stylish, air-conditioned bedrooms include the pinstripe-walled Savile Row rooms, which follow a tailoring theme, and the opulent Royal rooms, named after different monarchs. Public rooms include The Library fine dining restaurant and a comfortable stylish cocktail bar and lounge. The team here pride themselves on their warmth and friendliness.

Rooms 161 (13 fmly) (14 smoking) S £167-£299; D £179-£311* Facilities STV Health club & beauty treatment available nearby ♫ Xmas New Year Wi-fi Services Lift Air con Notes LB

SW3

Egerton House

THE
RED CARNATION
HOTEL COLLECTION

★★★★★ 84% TOWN HOUSE HOTEL

17 Egerton Ter, Knightsbridge SW3 2BX
☎ 020 7589 2412 🖹 020 7584 6540
e-mail: bookeg@rchmail.com
web: www.egertonhousehotel.com
dir: Just off Brompton Rd, between Harrods & Victoria & Albert Museum, opposite Brompton Oratory

PETS: Bedrooms (2 GF) unattended sign Public areas except restaurant on leads Exercise area Hyde Park (10 mins' walk) Facilities food (pre-bookable) food bowl water bowl bedding dog chews cat treats litter tray scoop/disp bags leads pet sitting dog walking dog grooming cage storage walks info vet info On Request fridge access torch towels Other charge for damage 24-hour notice required for all pet provisions

This delightful town house enjoys a prestigious Knightsbridge location, a short walk from Harrods and close to the Victoria & Albert Museum. Air-conditioned bedrooms and public rooms are appointed to the highest standards, with luxurious furnishings and quality antique pieces; an exceptional range of facilities include iPods, safes, mini bars and flat-screen TVs. Staff offer the highest levels of personalised, attentive service.

Rooms 28 (5 fmly) (2 GF) D £280-£895* Facilities STV Xmas New Year Wi-fi Services Lift Air con

SW7

Baglioni Hotel

★★★★★ 88% HOTEL

60 Hyde Park Gate, Kensington Rd, Kensington SW7 5BB
☎ 020 7368 5700 ▤ 020 7368 5701
e-mail: baglioni.london.@baglionihotels.com
dir: *On corner of Hyde Park Gate & De Vere Gardens*

PETS: Bedrooms sign **Exercise area** adjacent **Facilities** cage storage walks info vet info **On Request** towels **Other** charge for damage **Restrictions** small dogs only (max 5kg)

Located in the heart of Kensington and overlooking Hyde Park, this small hotel buzzes with Italian style and chic. Bedrooms, mostly suites, are generously sized and designed in bold dark colours; they have espresso machines, interactive plasma-screen TVs and a host of other excellent touches. Service is both professional and friendly, with personal butlers for the bedrooms. Public areas include the main open-plan space with bar, lounge and Brunello restaurant, all merging together with great elan; there is a small health club and a fashionable private club bar downstairs.

Rooms 67 (7 fmly) (30 smoking) **S** £334-£474; **D** £334-£474
Facilities Spa STV FTV Gym Xmas New Year Wi-fi **Services** Lift Air con **Parking** 2 **Notes** LB

SW10

Wyndham Grand London Chelsea Harbour

★★★★★ 84% HOTEL

Chelsea Harbour SW10 0XG
☎ 020 7823 3000 ▤ 020 7351 6525
e-mail: wyndhamlondon@wyndham.com
web: www.wyndham.com
dir: *A4 to Earls Court Rd S towards river. Right into Kings Rd, left into Lots Rd. Chelsea Harbour facing*

PETS: Bedrooms bedrooms with wooden floors only **Charges** contact hotel for details of pet charges **Public areas** except restaurant on leads **Grounds** on leads disp bin **Exercise area** 5 mins' walk **Facilities** food (pre-bookable) food bowl water bowl bedding dog chews cat treats feeding mat pet sitting dog walking dog grooming cage storage walks info vet info **On Request** fridge access towels **Other** charge for damage max 2 pets per bedroom **Restrictions** max weight 20lbs

Against the picturesque backdrop of Chelsea Harbour's small marina, this modern hotel offers spacious, comfortable accommodation. All rooms are suites, which are superbly equipped; many enjoy splendid views of the marina. In addition, there are also several luxurious penthouse suites. Public areas include a modern bar and restaurant, excellent leisure facilities and extensive meeting and function rooms.

Rooms 158 (36 fmly) (46 smoking) **Facilities** Spa STV FTV 🐕 Gym Sauna Steam room 🎵 Xmas New Year Wi-fi **Services** Lift Air con **Parking** 2000 **Notes** LB

SW15

The Lodge Hotel

★★★ 75% METRO HOTEL

52-54 Upper Richmond Rd, Putney SW15 2RN
☎ 020 8874 1598 ▤ 020 8874 0910
e-mail: res@thelodgehotellondon.com
dir: *M25 junct 10/A3 towards central London. A219 to Putney, right to Upper Richmond, left at lights after 0.5m*

PETS: Bedrooms (15 GF) **Public areas** on leads **Grounds** disp bin **Exercise area** Wandsworth Park & River Thames walk (250yds) **Facilities** food bowl water bowl scoop/disp bags walks info vet info **On Request** fridge access torch towels **Other** charge for damage

This friendly hotel is conveniently located for East Putney tube station. Public areas include a bar/lounge with satellite TV and conference and banqueting facilities. A buffet breakfast is served in the garden conservatory. Thoughtfully equipped, comfortable bedrooms include a selection of executive rooms and suites. Parking for residents is an asset.

Rooms 60 (5 fmly) (15 GF) (4 smoking) **Facilities** STV FTV Wi-fi **Parking** 35

W1

Chesterfield Mayfair

★★★★ HOTEL

35 Charles St, Mayfair W1J 5EB
☎ 020 7491 2622 ▤ 020 7491 4793
e-mail: bookch@rchmail.com
web: www.chesterfieldmayfair.com
dir: *Hyde Park Corner along Piccadilly, left into Half Moon St. At end left & 1st right into Queens St, then right into Charles St*

PETS: Bedrooms Charges Public areas except restaurant & conservatory on leads **Exercise area** Berkely Square (4 mins), Hyde Park (10 mins) **Facilities** food (pre-bookable) food bowl water bowl bedding dog chews cat treats leads pet sitting dog walking cage storage walks info vet info **On Request** fridge access torch towels **Other** charge for damage all pet facilities available on request

Quiet elegance and an atmosphere of exclusivity characterise this stylish Mayfair hotel where attentive, friendly service is paramount. The bedrooms, each with a marble-clad bathroom, have contemporary styles - perhaps with floral fabric walls, an African theme or with Savile Row stripes. In addition to these deluxe bedrooms there are 13 individually designed suites; some with four-poster beds and some with jacuzzis. The Butler's Restaurant is the fine dining option, and The Conservatory, with views over the garden, is just the place for cocktails, light lunches and afternoon teas. The hotel is air conditioned throughout.

Rooms 107 (7 fmly) **S** £168-£330; **D** £192-£450* **Facilities** STV 🎵 Xmas Wi-fi **Services** Lift Air con

W8

THE
RED CARNATION
HOTEL COLLECTION

Milestone Hotel

★★★★★ ◎◎ HOTEL

1 Kensington Court W8 5DL
☎ 020 7917 1000 📠 020 7917 1010
e-mail: bookms@rchmail.com
web: www.milestonehotel.com
dir: *From Warwick Rd right into Kensington High St. Hotel 400yds past Kensington tube station*

PETS: Bedrooms (1 GF) **Charges Public areas** except restaurant **Exercise area** Kensington Gardens (30mtrs) **Facilities** food (pre-bookable) food bowl water bowl bedding dog chews cat treats feeding mat litter tray scoop/disp bags leads pet sitting dog walking washing facs dog grooming cage storage walks info vet info **On Request** fridge access torch towels **Other** charge for damage **Restrictions** small & medium size dogs only; no Great Danes

This delightful town house enjoys a wonderful location opposite Kensington Palace and is near the elegant shops. The individually themed bedrooms include a selection of stunning suites that are equipped with every conceivable extra - fruit, cookies, chocolates, complimentary newspapers and even the next day's weather forecast. Up-to-the-minute technology includes high speed Wi-fi and interactive TV. Public areas include the luxurious Park Lounge where afternoon tea is served, the delightful split-level Stables Bar, a conservatory, the sumptuous Cheneston's restaurant and a fully equipped small gym, resistance pool and a spa treatment room.

Rooms 62 (3 fmly) (1 GF) (5 smoking) **S** £300-£432; **D** £336-£492* **Facilities** STV FTV ⊛ Gym Health club 🎵 Xmas New Year Wi-fi **Services** Lift Air con **Parking** 1 **Notes** LB

WC1

THE
RED CARNATION
HOTEL COLLECTION

The Montague on the Gardens

★★★★ 85% ◎ HOTEL

15 Montague St, Bloomsbury WC1B 5BJ
☎ 020 7637 1001 📠 020 7637 2516
e-mail: bookmt@rchmail.com
web: www.montaguehotel.com
dir: *Just off Russell Square, adjacent to British Museum*

PETS: Bedrooms (19 GF) sign **Public areas** except food service areas on leads **Exercise area** 100mtrs **Facilities** food bowl water bowl bedding dog chews cat treats pet sitting dog walking cage storage walks info vet info **On Request** fridge access torch towels **Other** charge for damage please phone for further details of pet facilities

This stylish hotel is situated right next to the British Museum. A special feature is the alfresco terrace overlooking a delightful garden. Other public rooms include the Blue Door Bistro and Chef's Table, a bar, a lounge and a conservatory where traditional afternoon teas are served. The bedrooms are beautifully

appointed and range from split-level suites to more compact rooms.

Rooms 100 (10 fmly) (19 GF) (5 smoking) **S** £174-£306; **D** £198-£330* **Facilities** STV Gym 🎵 Xmas New Year Wi-fi **Services** Lift Air con **Notes** LB

WC2

The Savoy

★★★★★ ◎◎ HOTEL

Strand WC2R 0EU
☎ 020 7836 4343 📠 020 7240 6040
e-mail: savoy@fairmont.com
dir: *Halfway along The Strand between Trafalgar Sq & Aldwych*

PETS: Bedrooms unattended sign **Charges** assist dog free; other dog £25 per night **Facilities** food food bowl water bowl bedding feeding mat pet sitting dog walking cage storage walks info vet info **On Request** towels **Other** charge for damage **Restrictions** max weight 20lb

The Savoy Hotel has been at the fore of the London hotel scene since it opened in 1889. Now taken over by the Fairmont Group, the hotel has benefited from some loving restoration with much of its art deco and Edwardian heritage kept intact. The bedrooms, including an extensive range of stunning suites, vary in style and size, and many overlook the Thames. The famous River Restaurant, Savoy Grill and American Bar remain as well loved favourites, the Thames Foyer is well known for its afternoon teas and the newly created Beaufort Bar offers a comprehensive range of champagnes. Immaculately presented staff offer excellent standards of hospitality and service. AA Hotel of the Year for London 2011-12.

Rooms 268 (5 fmly) **D** £350-£10,000* **Facilities** STV FTV ⊛ supervised Gym Fitness gallery Health & beauty treatments Personal training 🎵 Xmas New Year Wi-fi **Services** Lift Air con **Parking** 65

LONDON GATEWAY MOTORWAY SERVICE AREA (M1)   Map 4 TQ29

Days Hotel London North - M1

★★★ 67% HOTEL

Welcome Break Service Area NW7 3HU
☎ 020 8906 7000 📠 020 8906 7011
e-mail: lgw.hotel@welcomebreak.co.uk
web: www.welcomebreak.co.uk
dir: *On M1 between junct 2/4 N'bound & S'bound*

PETS: Bedrooms (80 GF) **Charges** £5 per night **Public areas** except restaurant & bar area **Facilities** walks info vet info **Other** charge for damage pets accepted by prior arrangement only (confirm when booking)

This modern building offers accommodation in smart, spacious and well-equipped bedrooms, suitable for families and business travellers, and all with en suite bathrooms. Continental breakfast is available and other refreshments may be taken at the nearby family restaurant.

Rooms 200 (190 fmly) (80 GF) (20 smoking) **S** £59.95-£89.95; **D** £69.95-£99.95 **Facilities** FTV Wi-fi **Services** Lift Air con **Parking** 160 **Notes** LB

ENGLAND

HAYDOCK
Map 7 SJ59

thistle

Thistle Haydock
★★★★ 76% HOTEL

Penny Ln WA11 9SG
☎ 0871 376 9044 📠 0871 376 9144
e-mail: haydock@thistle.co.uk
web: www.thistle.com/haydock
dir: *M6 junct 23, follow Haydock Racecourse signs (A49) N towards Ashton-in-Makerfield, 1st left, after bridge 1st turn left*

PETS: Bedrooms (65 GF) **Charges** £15 per night **Public areas** assist dogs only on leads **Grounds** on leads disp bin **Facilities** walks info vet info **Other** charge for damage **Restrictions** small dogs only

A smart, purpose-built hotel which offers an excellent standard of thoughtfully equipped accommodation. It is conveniently situated between Liverpool and Manchester, just off the M6. The wide range of leisure and meeting facilities prove popular with guests. Thistle Hotels - AA Hotel Group of the Year 2011-12.

Rooms 137 (10 fmly) (65 GF) **Facilities** STV FTV ⏱ supervised Gym Children's play area Sauna Steam room Wi-fi **Parking** 210 **Notes** LB

LIVERPOOL
Map 7 SJ39

Hope Street Hotel
★★★★ 78% ⑧⑧ HOTEL

40 Hope St L1 9DA
☎ 0151 709 3000 📠 0151 709 2454
e-mail: sleep@hopestreethotel.co.uk
dir: *Follow Cathedral & University signs on entering city. Telephone for detailed directions*

PETS: Bedrooms (5 GF) unattended **Charges** £30 per stay **Public areas** except restaurant & bar **Exercise area** 4 mins' walk **Facilities** food (pre-bookable) food bowl water bowl bedding dog chews cat treats feeding mat litter tray scoop/disp bags leads pet sitting dog walking cage storage walks info vet info **On Request** fridge access torch towels **Other** charge for damage

This stylish property is located within easy walking distance of the city's cathedrals, theatres, major shops and attractions. Stylish bedrooms and suites are appointed with flat-screen TVs, DVD players, internet access and comfy beds with Egyptian cotton sheets; the bathrooms have rain showers and deep tubs. The London Carriage Works Restaurant specialises in local, seasonal produce and the adjacent lounge bar offers lighter all-day dining and wonderful cocktails.

Rooms 89 (16 fmly) (5 GF) **S** £89-£650; **D** £89-£650* **Facilities** STV FTV Gym Massage & beauty rooms ♫ New Year Wi-fi **Services** Lift Air con **Parking** 14

Novotel Liverpool
★★★★ 71% HOTEL

40 Hanover St L1 4LY
☎ 0151 702 5100 📠 0151 702 5110
e-mail: h6495@accor.com

PETS: Bedrooms Charges £10 per night **Public areas** except restaurant **Exercise area** town centre area **Facilities** walks info vet info **On Request** fridge access torch towels **Other** charge for damage

This attractive and stylish city centre hotel is convenient for Liverpool Echo Arena, Liverpool One shopping centre and the Albert Dock; it is adjacent to a town centre car park. The hotel has a range of conference and leisure facilities which include an indoor heated pool and fitness suite. The restaurant offers a contemporary style menu. Bedrooms are comfortable and stylishly designed.

Rooms 209 (127 fmly) **S** £75-£195; **D** £75-£195* **Facilities** STV FTV ⏱ Gym Steam room Wi-fi **Services** Lift Air con

Campanile

Campanile Liverpool
BUDGET HOTEL

Chaloner St, Queens Dock L3 4AJ
☎ 0151 709 8104 📠 0151 709 8725
e-mail: liverpool@campanile.com
dir: *Follow tourist signs marked Albert Dock. Hotel on waterfront*

PETS: Bedrooms (33 GF) **Charges** £5 per night **Public areas** except bar & restaurant **Grounds** on leads disp bin **Other** charge for damage

This modern building offers accommodation in smart, well-equipped bedrooms, all with en suite bathrooms. Refreshments may be taken at the informal bistro.

Rooms 100 (4 fmly) (33 GF) **S** £62-£100; **D** £62-£100*

MORETON
Map 7 SJ28

Leasowe Castle
★★★ 78% HOTEL

Leasowe Rd CH46 3RF
☎ 0151 606 9191 📠 0151 678 5551
e-mail: reservations@leasowecastle.com
web: www.leasowecastle.com
dir: *M53 junct 1, 1st exit from rdbt onto A551. Hotel 0.75m on right*

PETS: Bedrooms Charges £10 per night **Grounds** disp bin **Exercise area** beach (40yds) **Facilities** cage storage walks info vet info **On Request** fridge access towels **Other** charge for damage

Located adjacent to Leasowe Golf Course and within easy reach of Liverpool, Chester and all of the Wirral's attractions, this historic hotel dates back to 1592. Bedrooms are smartly appointed and well equipped, many enjoying ocean views. Public areas retain

many original features. Weddings and functions are well catered for.

Rooms 47 (3 fmly) **S** £60-£95; **D** £85-£120 (incl. bkfst)*
Facilities FTV Gym Water sports Sea fishing Sailing Health club Xmas New Year Wi-fi **Services** Lift **Parking** 200

Balmoral Lodge Hotel

★★ 74% HOTEL

41 Queens Rd PR9 9EX
☎ 01704 544298 📠 01704 501224
e-mail: balmorallg@aol.com
dir: *On edge of town on A565 (Preston road). E at rdbt at North Lord St, left at lights, hotel 200yds on left*

PETS: Bedrooms (4 GF) sign **Charges** £5 per night £35 per week **Grounds** on leads disp bin **Exercise area** park (5 mins' walk) **Facilities** walks info vet info **Other** charge for damage

Situated in a quiet residential area, this popular friendly hotel is ideally situated just 50 yards from Lord Street. Bedrooms are comfortably appointed and family rooms are available. In addition to the restaurant which offers freshly prepared dishes, there is a choice of lounges including a comfortable lounge bar.

Rooms 15 (4 annexe) (3 fmly) (4 GF) **S** £30-£50; **D** £40-£90 (incl. bkfst) **Facilities** STV FTV Wi-fi **Parking** 12 **Notes** LB

Bay Tree House B & B

★★★★ 🛏 GUEST ACCOMMODATION

No1 Irving St, Marine Gate PR9 0HD
☎ 01704 510555 📠 0870 753 6318
e-mail: baytreehouseuk@aol.com
web: www.baytreehousesouthport.co.uk
dir: *Off Leicester St*

PETS: Bedrooms unattended **Charges** £5 per stay **Public areas Exercise area** 100mtrs **Facilities** walks info vet info **On Request** fridge access **Other** charge for damage

A warm welcome is assured at this immaculately maintained house, located a short walk from the promenade and central attractions. Bedrooms are equipped with a wealth of thoughtful extras, and delicious imaginative breakfasts are served in an attractive dining room overlooking the pretty front patio garden.

Rooms 6 en suite **S** £45-£69; **D** £68-£110 **Facilities** FTV tea/coffee Dinner available Direct Dial Cen ht Licensed Wi-fi **Parking** 2 **Notes** Closed 14 Dec-1 Feb

Riverside Holiday Park *(SD405192)*

Southport New Rd PR9 8DF
☎ 01704 228886 📠 01704 505886
e-mail: reception@harrisonleisureuk.com
dir: *M6 junct 27, A5209 towards Parbold/Burscough, right onto A59. Left onto A565 at lights in Tarleton. Continue to dual carriageway. At rdbt straight across, site 1m on left*

PETS: Charges £1.50 per night **Public areas** disp bin **Exercise area on site Facilities** food food bowl water bowl dog chews litter tray leads walks info vet info **Stables** 2m **Other** prior notice required dog toys available **Restrictions** No Rottweilers, Pit Bull Terriers or Dobermans

Open 14 Feb-Jan Last arrival 17.00hrs Last departure 11.00hrs

A large, spacious park with a lively family entertainment complex for cabaret, dancing and theme nights. Children have their own club and entertainer plus games and food. A superb health and leisure centre next door is available at an extra charge. 80 acre site. 260 touring pitches. 130 hardstandings. Tent pitches. Motorhome pitches. 355 statics.

Notes One car per pitch.

Willowbank Holiday Home & Touring Park
(SD305110)

► ► ►

Coastal Rd, Ainsdale PR8 3ST
☎ 01704 571566 📠 01704 571576
e-mail: info@willowbankcp.co.uk
dir: *From A565 between Formby & Ainsdale exit at Woodvale lights onto coast road, site 150mtrs on left. From N: M6 junct 31, A59 towards Preston, A565, through Southport & Ainsdale, right at Woodvale lights*

PETS: Charges £1.35 per night **Public areas** except play area disp bin **Exercise area on site** enclosed area (with disposal bins) **Exercise area** woodland walk (1m) **Facilities** washing facs walks info vet info **Stables** approx 5m **Other** prior notice required dogs must be kept on short leads **Restrictions** no Dobermans, Rottweilers, or dangerous dogs (see page 7)

Open Mar-Jan Last arrival 21.00hrs Last departure noon

Set in a wooded clearing on a nature reserve next to the beautiful sand dunes, this attractive park is just off the coastal road to Southport. The immaculate toilet facilities are well equipped. 8 acre site. 87 touring pitches. 61 hardstandings. Motorhome pitches. 228 statics.

Notes Cannot site continental door entry units.

NORFOLK

NORFOLK

BARNEY
Map 9 TF93

The Old Brick Kilns *(TG007328)*

▶▶▶▶

Little Barney Ln NR21 0NL
☎ 01328 878305   📄 01328 878948
e-mail: enquiries@old-brick-kilns.co.uk
dir: *From A148 (Fakenham-Cromer) follow brown tourist signs to Barney, left into Little Barney Lane. Site at end of lane*

PETS: Charges £1 per night £7 per week Public areas except children's play area disp bin Exercise area on site dog walk around perimeter of site Exercise area 500yds Facilities food food bowl water bowl dog chews scoop/disp bags leads washing facs walks info vet info Stables 2m Other prior notice required Restrictions no Rottweilers or Pit Bull Terriers

Open mid Mar-6 Jan rs Low season bar food/takeaway selected nights only Last arrival 21.00hrs Last departure 11.00hrs

A secluded and peaceful park approached via a quiet leafy country lane. The park is on two levels with its own boating and fishing pool and many mature trees. Excellent, well-planned toilet facilities can be found in two blocks. Due to a narrow access road, no arrivals are accepted until after 1pm. B&B accommodation is available and there are four self-catering holiday cottages. 12.73 acre site. 65 touring pitches. 65 hardstandings. Tent pitches. Motorhome pitches.

Notes No gazebos.

BELTON
Map 5 TG40

Rose Farm Touring & Camping Park
(TG488033)

▶▶▶▶

Stepshort NR31 9JS
☎ 01493 780896   📄 01493 780896
dir: *Follow signs to Belton off A143, right at lane signed Stepshort, site 1st on right*

PETS: Public areas except washing areas, toilet blocks & lounge on leads disp bin Exercise area on site Facilities walks info vet info Other prior notice required Restrictions no dangerous dogs (see page 7)

Open all year

A former railway line is the setting for this very peaceful site which enjoys rural views and is beautifully presented throughout. The ever-improving toilet facilities are spotlessly clean and inviting to use, and the park is brightened with many flower and herb beds. The customer care here is truly exceptional. 10 acre site. 145 touring pitches. 20 hardstandings. Tent pitches. Motorhome pitches.

BLAKENEY
Map 9 TG04

Morston Hall
★★★ ◉◉◉ HOTEL
Morston, Holt NR25 7AA
☎ 01263 741041   📄 01263 740419
e-mail: reception@morstonhall.com
web: www.morstonhall.com
dir: *1m W of Blakeney on A149 (King's Lynn to Cromer road)*

PETS: Bedrooms (7 GF) unattended Sep accom 2 kennels with runs (no charge) Charges £5 per night Grounds Exercise area adjacent Facilities feeding mat cage storage walks info vet info On Request fridge access torch towels Other charge for damage

This delightful 17th-century country-house hotel enjoys a tranquil setting amid well-tended gardens. The comfortable public rooms offer a choice of attractive lounges and a sunny conservatory, while the elegant dining room is the perfect setting to enjoy Galton Blackiston's award-winning cuisine. The spacious bedrooms are individually decorated and stylishly furnished with room opulence.

Rooms 13 (6 annexe) (7 GF) S £200-£270; D £310-£360 (incl. bkfst & dinner)* Facilities STV FTV ⬥ New Year Wi-fi Parking 40 Notes Closed 1 Jan-last Fri in Jan & 2 days Xmas

BRANCASTER STAITHE
Map 9 TF74

White Horse
★★★ 79% ◉◉ HOTEL
PE31 8BY
☎ 01485 210262   📄 01485 210930
e-mail: reception@whitehorsebrancaster.co.uk
web: www.whitehorsebrancaster.co.uk
dir: *On A149 (coast road) midway between Hunstanton & Wells-next-the-Sea*

PETS: Bedrooms (8 GF) annexe bedrooms only Charges £10 per night Public areas except restaurant & guest lounge on leads Grounds on leads disp bin Exercise area Norfolk Coastal Path at end of garden Facilities washing facs walks info vet info On Request fridge access torch towels Other charge for damage water bowls are placed outside

A charming hotel situated on the north Norfolk coast with contemporary bedrooms in two wings, some featuring an interesting cobbled fascia. Each room is attractively decorated and thoughtfully equipped. There is a large bar and a lounge area leading through to the conservatory restaurant, with stunning tidal marshland views across to Scolt Head Island.

Rooms 15 (8 annexe) (4 fmly) (8 GF) S £77-£125; D £94-£190 (incl. bkfst)* Facilities Xmas New Year Wi-fi Parking 60 Notes LB

Hoste Arms
★★★ 87% ◉◉ HOTEL

The Green PE31 8HD
☎ 01328 738777   📠 01328 730103
e-mail: reception@hostearms.co.uk
web: www.hostearms.co.uk
dir: Signed on B1155, 5m W of Wells-next-the-Sea

PETS: Bedrooms (7 GF) unattended sign certain bedrooms only
Charges £10 per stay **Public areas** bar & lounge only **Grounds**
on leads disp bin **Exercise area** green opposite **Facilities**
food (pre-bookable) food bowl water bowl bedding walks info
vet info **On Request** torch towels **Other** charge for damage
Resident Pets: Shaka & Tala (Labradors)

A stylish, privately-owned inn situated in the heart of a bustling
village close to the north Norfolk coast. The extensive public
rooms feature a range of dining areas that include a conservatory
with plush furniture, a sunny patio and a traditional pub. The
tastefully furnished and thoughtfully equipped bedrooms are
generally very spacious and offer a high degree of comfort.

Rooms 34 (7 GF) **S** £122-£241; **D** £149-£241 (incl. bkfst)*
Facilities Spa STV Beauty treatment rooms Xmas New Year Wi-fi
Services Air con **Parking** 45 **Notes** LB

See advert on this page

Clippesby Hall *(TG423147)*
▶ ▶ ▶ ▶ ▶

Hall Ln NR29 3BL
☎ 01493 367800   📠 01493 367809
e-mail: holidays@clippesby.com
dir: *From A47 follow tourist signs for The Broads. At Acle rdbt
take A1064, after 2m left onto B1152, 0.5m turn left opposite
village sign, site 400yds on right*

PETS: Charges £3.75 per night **Public areas** except The
Pinewoods area on leads disp bin **Exercise area on site** dog
walk **Exercise area** 0.5m **Facilities** food food bowl water bowl
dog chews walks info vet info **Other** prior notice required

Open all year Last arrival 17.30hrs Last departure 11.00hrs

A lovely country house estate with secluded pitches hidden
among the trees or in sheltered sunny glades. The toilet facilities
are appointed to a very good standard, providing a wide choice
of cubicles. Amenities include a coffee shop with Wi-fi and wired
internet access, family bar and restaurant and family golf. There
are four pine lodges and 13 holiday cottages available for holiday
lets. 30 acre site. 120 touring pitches. 9 hardstandings. Tent
pitches. Motorhome pitches.

The Cliftonville

★★★ 75% HOTEL

Seafront NR27 9AS

☎ 01263 512543 📠 01263 515700

e-mail: reservations@cliftonvillehotel.co.uk

web: www.cliftonvillehotel.co.uk

dir: *From A149 (coast road), 500yds from town centre, N'bound on clifftop by sunken gardens*

PETS: Bedrooms unattended **Charges** £5 per night
Public areas except restaurants on leads **Exercise area** 50mtrs
Facilities food (pre-bookable) food bowl water bowl bedding washing facs cage storage walks info vet info **On Request** fridge access towels **Other** charge for damage

An imposing Edwardian hotel situated on the main coast road with stunning views of the sea. Public rooms feature a magnificent staircase, minstrels' gallery, coffee shop, lounge bar, a further residents' lounge, Boltons Bistro and an additional restaurant. The pleasantly decorated bedrooms are generally quite spacious and have lovely sea views.

Rooms 30 (5 fmly) **S** £62-£75; **D** £124-£150 (incl. bkfst)*
Facilities Xmas New Year Wi-fi **Services** Lift **Parking** 21

White Horse Overstrand

★★★★ ◉◉ INN

34 High St, Overstrand NR27 0AB

☎ 01263 579237

e-mail: reservations@whitehorseoverstrand.co.uk

dir: *From A140, before Cromer, right into Mill Rd. At bottom right into Station Rd. After 2m, left into High St, White Horse on left*

PETS: Bedrooms unattended certain bedrooms only
Public areas bar only on leads **Grounds** on leads **Exercise area** nearby **Facilities** food bowl water bowl cage storage walks info vet info **Other** charge for damage

A smartly appointed inn ideally situated in the heart of this popular village on the north Norfolk coastline. The modern bedrooms are tastefully appointed and equipped with a good range of useful extras. Public rooms include a large open-plan lounge bar with comfortable seating and a relaxed dining area.

Rooms 7 en suite (1 fmly) **S** £65-£79; **D** £72-£99 **Facilities** TVL tea/coffee Dinner available Cen ht Wi-fi Pool table **Parking** 6

The Red Lion Food and Rooms

★★★★ ⊜ INN

Brook St NR27 9HD

☎ 01263 514964 📠 01263 512834

e-mail: info@redlion-cromer.co.uk

PETS: Bedrooms unattended sign **Charges** £5 per night
Public areas except restaurant on leads **Exercise area** beach (100yds) from end Sep-Apr only **Facilities** water bowl bedding walks info vet info

A charming Victorian inn situated in an elevated position in the heart of the town centre overlooking the beach and the sea. The open-plan public areas include a billiard room, lounge bar, a popular restaurant, a sunny conservatory and a first-floor residents' lounge with superb sea views. The spacious bedrooms are tastefully decorated with co-ordinated soft furnishings and include many thoughtful touches.

Rooms 12 en suite **S** £60-£70; **D** £100-£150 **Facilities** FTV tea/coffee Dinner available Direct Dial Cen ht Wi-fi Snooker **Parking** 20 **Notes** LB

Glendale

★★★ GUEST HOUSE

33 Macdonald Rd NR27 9AP

☎ 01263 513278

e-mail: glendalecromer@btconnect.com

dir: *A149 (coast road) from Cromer centre, 4th left*

PETS: Bedrooms unattended **Public areas** except breakfast room on leads **Grounds** on leads disp bin **Exercise area** 200mtrs **Facilities** walks info vet info **On Request** fridge access torch towels **Other** pets may only be left unattended at breakfast **Resident Pets:** Daisy & Megan (Jack Russells), Jess (Collie/ Springer Spaniel cross)

Victorian property situated in a peaceful side road adjacent to the seafront, just a short walk from the town centre. Bedrooms are pleasantly decorated, well maintained and equipped with a good range of useful extras. Breakfast is served at individual tables in the smart dining room.

Rooms 5 rms (1 en suite) **S** £25-£40; **D** £50-£80 **Facilities** FTV tea/coffee **Parking** 2 **Notes** LB Closed 20 Oct-6 Apr

Manor Farm Caravan & Camping Site
(TG198416)

▶▶▶▶

East Runton NR27 9PR
☎ 01263 512858
e-mail: manor-farm@ukf.net
dir: *1m W of Cromer, exit A148 or A149 at Manor Farm sign*

PETS: Charges £1 per night **Public areas** except dog-free areas **Exercise area** farmland & public footpaths adjacent **Facilities** walks info vet info **Other** prior notice required max 2 dogs per pitch; dogs permitted on Moll's Meadow only & must not be left unattended

Open Etr-Sep Last arrival 20.30hrs Last departure noon

A well-established family-run site on a working farm enjoying panoramic sea views. There are good modern facilities across the site, including three smart toilet blocks; there are two quality family rooms and privacy cubicles. The site has two good play areas and a large expanse of grass for games making it very popular with families. 17 acre site. 250 touring pitches. Tent pitches. Motorhome pitches.

Notes 😾

DOWNHAM MARKET   Map 5 TF60

Crosskeys Riverside House
★★★ BED AND BREAKFAST
Bridge St, Hilgay PE38 0LD
☎ 01366 387777 📠 01366 387777
e-mail: crosskeyshouse@aol.com
web: www.crosskeys.info
dir: *2m S of Downham Market. Off A10 into Hilgay, Crosskeys on bridge*

PETS: Bedrooms (2 GF) unattended **Charges** £5 per night **Public areas** except dining room on leads **Grounds** disp bin **Exercise area** 500yds **Facilities** leads walks info vet info **On Request** fridge access torch towels **Stables Resident Pets:** 3 Shih Tzus, 3 horses

Situated in the small village of Hilgay on the banks of the River Wissey, this former coaching inn offers comfortable accommodation that includes a number of four-poster bedrooms; many rooms have river views. Public rooms include a dining room with oak beams and inglenook fireplace, plus a small, rustic residents' bar.

Rooms 4 en suite (1 fmly) (2 GF) **S** £30-£55; **D** £55-£60
Facilities FTV tea/coffee Cen ht Wi-fi Fishing **Parking** 10

Lakeside Caravan Park & Fisheries
(TF608013)

▶▶▶

Sluice Rd, Denver PE38 0DZ
☎ 01366 387074 & 07790 272978 📠 01366 387074
e-mail: richesflorido@aol.com
dir: *Off A10 towards Denver, follow signs to Denver Windmill*

PETS: Public areas except club room, showers & toilets on leads disp bin **Exercise area on site** large field **Exercise area** nearby **Facilities** scoop/disp bags washing facs walks info vet info **Stables Other** quiet lanes & country rides for horses

Open Mar-Oct Last arrival 21.00hrs Last departure noon

A peaceful, rapidly improving park set around four pretty fishing lakes. Several grassy touring areas are sheltered by mature hedging and trees. There is a function room, shop and laundry. 30 acre site. 100 touring pitches. Tent pitches. Motorhome pitches. 1 static.

FAKENHAM   Map 9 TF92

Abbott Farm *(TF975390)*
★★★ FARMHOUSE
Walsingham Rd, Binham NR21 0AW
☎ 01328 830519 📠 01328 830519 Mrs E Brown
e-mail: abbot.farm@btinternet.com
web: www.abbottfarm.co.uk
dir: *NE of Fakenham. From Binham SW onto Walsingham Rd, farm 0.6m on left*

PETS: Bedrooms (2 GF) sign **Public areas Grounds** on leads disp bin **Exercise area** fields adjacent **Facilities** food bowl water bowl bedding feeding mat leads washing facs cage storage walks info vet info **On Request** fridge access torch towels **Stables** approx 3m **Other** charge for damage **Resident Pet:** Buster (Retriever/Labrador cross), Joss (cat)

A detached red-brick farmhouse set amidst 190 acres of arable farmland and surrounded by open countryside. The spacious bedrooms are pleasantly decorated and thoughtfully equipped; they include a ground-floor room with a large en suite shower. Breakfast is served in the attractive conservatory, which has superb views of the countryside.

Rooms 3 en suite (2 GF) **S** £30; **D** £60 **Facilities** TVL tea/coffee Cen ht **Parking** 20 **Notes** Closed 24-26 Dec 😾 190 acres arable

FAKENHAM *continued*

Caravan Club M.V.C. Site *(TF926288)*

▶▶▶

Fakenham Racecourse NR21 7NY
☎ 01328 862388   📄 01328 855908
e-mail: caravan@fakenhamracecourse.co.uk
dir: *From B1146, S of Fakenham follow brown Racecourse signs (with tent & caravan symbols) leads to site entrance*

PETS: Public areas disp bin **Exercise area on site** allocated field **Facilities** food bowl water bowl dog chews washing facs walks info vet info **Stables Other** prior notice required max 2 dogs per pitch disposal bags available

Open all year Last arrival 21.00hrs Last departure noon

A very well laid-out site set around the racecourse, with a grandstand offering smart modern toilet facilities. Tourers move to the centre of the course on race days, and enjoy free racing, and there's a wide range of sporting activities in the club house. 11.4 acre site. 120 touring pitches. 25 hardstandings. Tent pitches. Motorhome pitches.

Fakenham Campsite *(TF907310)*

▶▶▶

Burnham Market Rd, Sculthorpe NR21 9SA
☎ 01328 856614
e-mail: fakenham.campsite@gmail.com
dir: *From Fakenham take A148 towards King's Lynn then B1355 Burnham Market road. Site on right in 400yds*

PETS: Charges £1 per night £7 per week **Public areas** except club house & children's play area disp bin **Exercise area on site Facilities** vet info **Other** prior notice required **Resident Pet:** Tilly (Retriever)

Open all year Last arrival 22.00hrs Last departure noon

Enthusiastic owners run this peaceful site that is surrounded by tranquil countryside and which is part of a par 3, 9-hole golf complex and driving range. The toilet facilities are of good quality, and there is a golf shop and licensed bar. Please note there is no laundry. 4 acre site. 50 touring pitches. 11 hardstandings. Tent pitches. Motorhome pitches. 2 statics.

Notes No noise after 22.30hrs.

Crossways Caravan & Camping Park
(TF961321)

▶▶

Crossways, Holt Rd, Little Snoring NR21 0AX
☎ 01328 878335
e-mail: joyholland@live.co.uk
dir: *From Fakenham take A148 towards Cromer. After 3m pass exit for Little Snoring. Site on A148 on left behind Post Office*

PETS: Charges £1 per night **Public areas** disp bin **Exercise area** adjacent **Facilities** food dog chews cat treats litter tray scoop/disp bags walks info vet info **Other** prior notice required

Open all year Last arrival 22.00hrs Last departure noon

Set on the edge of the peaceful hamlet of Little Snoring, this level site enjoys views across the fields towards the North Norfolk coast some seven miles away. Visitors can use the health suite for a small charge, and there is a shop on site, and a good village pub. 2 acre site. 26 touring pitches. 10 hardstandings. Tent pitches. Motorhome pitches. 1 static.

GORLESTON ON SEA   Map 5 TG50

Jennis Lodge

★★★★ GUEST HOUSE
63 Avondale Rd NR31 6DJ
☎ 01493 662840
e-mail: bookings@jennis-lodge.co.uk
dir: *A12, past James Paget Hospital, rdbt 2nd exit, next rdbt 2nd exit, left & 2nd right*

PETS: Bedrooms certain bedrooms only **Public areas** except dining room on leads **Facilities** bedding walks info vet info **On Request** fridge access towels **Stables** nearby **Other** dogs accepted by prior arrangement only **Resident Pet:** 1 Greyhound/Labrador cross

Jennis Lodge is a friendly, family-run guest house situated close to the seafront, marine gardens and town centre. The smartly decorated bedrooms have pine furniture and many thoughtful touches that include TV, DVD or video plus broadband connection. Breakfast and dinner are served in the smart dining room and guests have the use of a cosy lounge with comfy sofas.

Rooms 8 en suite (2 fmly) **S** £30; **D** £55 **Facilities** FTV TVL tea/coffee Dinner available Cen ht **Notes** LB

Kings Head
★★★ 86% HOTEL
PE31 6RJ
☎ 01485 578265 🖹 01485 578635
e-mail: welcome@the-kings-head-bircham.co.uk
web: www.the-kings-head-bircham.co.uk
dir: *From King's Lynn take A149 towards Fakenham. After Hillington, turn left onto B1153, to Great Bircham*

PETS: Bedrooms unattended sign **Charges** £10 per stay **Public areas** except restaurant **Grounds** disp bin **Exercise area** nearby **Facilities** food (pre-bookable) food bowl water bowl bedding feeding mat scoop/disp bags washing facs cage storage walks info vet info **On Request** fridge access torch towels **Stables** nearby **Other** charge for damage

This inn is situated in a peaceful village location close to the north Norfolk coastline. The spacious, individually decorated bedrooms are tastefully appointed with superb co-ordinated furnishings and many thoughtful touches. The contemporary, public rooms include a brasserie restaurant, a relaxing lounge, a smart bar and a private dining room.

Rooms 12 (2 fmly) **Facilities** Xmas Wi-fi **Parking** 25

Barnard House
★★★★ BED AND BREAKFAST
2 Barnard Crescent NR30 4DR
☎ 01493 855139
e-mail: enquiries@barnardhouse.com
dir: *0.5m N of town centre. Off A149 onto Barnard Crescent*

PETS: Bedrooms Charges Public areas with other guests' approval **Grounds** on leads **Exercise area** beach (500yds) **Facilities** walks info vet info **On Request** fridge access torch **Other** charge for damage **Resident Pet:** Flora (Field Spaniel)

A friendly, family-run bed and breakfast, set in mature landscaped gardens in a residential area. The smartly decorated bedrooms are thoughtfully equipped. Breakfast is served in the stylish dining room and there is an elegant lounge with comfy sofas. A warm welcome is assured.

Rooms 3 rms (2 en suite) (1 pri facs) **S** £45-£50; **D** £65-£75 **Facilities** FTV TVL tea/coffee Cen ht Wi-fi **Parking** 3 **Notes** LB Closed Xmas & New Year

Swiss Cottage B&B
Exclusively for Non Smokers
★★★★ GUEST ACCOMMODATION
31 North Dr NR30 4EW
☎ 01493 855742 & 07986 399857 🖹 01493 843547
e-mail: info@swiss-cottage.info
dir: *0.5m N of town centre. Off A47 or A12 to to seafront, 750yds N of pier. Turn left at Britannia Pier. Swiss Cottage on left opposite Water Gardens*

PETS: Bedrooms (2 GF) except bedrooms 5, 8 & 9 **Public areas** except breakfast room **Exercise area** adjacent **Facilities** walks info vet info **On Request** fridge access **Other** charge for damage dogs must not be left unattended in bedrooms at any time **Restrictions** small & medium size dogs only; no dangerous dogs (see page 7)

A charming detached property situated in the peaceful part of town overlooking the Venetian waterways and the sea beyond. The comfortable bedrooms are pleasantly decorated with co-ordinated fabrics and have many useful extras. Breakfast is served in the smart dining room and guests have use of an open-plan lounge area.

Rooms 8 en suite 1 annexe en suite (2 GF) **S** £33-£42; **D** £55-£83 **Facilities** FTV tea/coffee Cen ht Wi-fi **Parking** 9 **Notes** LB No Children 11yrs Closed Nov-Feb

The Grange Touring Park *(TG510142)*
►►►►
Yarmouth Rd, Ormesby St Margaret NR29 3QG
☎ 01493 730306 & 730023 🖹 01493 730188
e-mail: info@grangetouring.co.uk
dir: *From A419, 3m N of Great Yarmouth. Site at junct of A419 & B1159. Signed*

PETS: Charges 1st dog free, 2nd dog £3.50 per night £24.50 per week **Public areas** except toilets, showers & laundry room disp bin **Exercise area** 100yds **Facilities** water bowl walks info vet info **Stables** 2m **Other** prior notice required information available on dog-friendly beaches & local attractions **Restrictions** no Rottweilers, Pit Bull Terriers or Dobermans

Open Etr-Oct Last arrival 21.00hrs Last departure 11.00hrs

A mature, ever improving park with plenty of trees, located just one mile from the sea, within easy reach of both coastal attractions and the Norfolk Broads. The level pitches have electric hook-ups and include hardstanding pitches, and there are clean, modern toilets including three spacious new family rooms. All pitches have Wi-fi access. 3.5 acre site. 70 touring pitches. 7 hardstandings. Tent pitches. Motorhome pitches.

Notes No football, no gazebos, no open fires.

HUNSTANTON — Map 9 TF64

Caley Hall
★★★ 83% HOTEL

Old Hunstanton Rd PE36 6HH
☎ 01485 533486 📠 01485 533348
e-mail: mail@caleyhallhotel.co.uk
web: www.caleyhallhotel.co.uk
dir: *1m from Hunstanton, on A149*

PETS: Bedrooms (30 GF) unattended sign certain bedrooms only **Charges** £5 per night **Public areas** except restaurant & lounge on leads **Grounds** on leads disp bin **Exercise area** 150mtrs **Facilities** food bowl water bowl feeding mat leads washing facs cage storage walks info vet info **On Request** fridge access torch towels **Other** charge for damage **Resident Pet:** Basil (Cocker Spaniel)

Situated within easy walking distance of the seafront. The tastefully decorated bedrooms are in a series of converted outbuildings; each is smartly furnished and thoughtfully equipped. Public rooms feature a large open-plan lounge/bar with plush leather seating, and a restaurant offering an interesting choice of dishes.

Rooms 39 (20 fmly) (30 GF) **S** £50-£200; **D** £80-£200 (incl. bkfst) **Facilities** STV Wi-fi Child facilities **Parking** 50 **Notes** LB Closed 18 Dec-20 Jan

Claremont
★★★★ GUEST HOUSE

35 Greevegate PE36 6AF
☎ 01485 533171
e-mail: claremontgh@tiscali.co.uk
dir: *Off A149 onto Greevegate, house before St Edmund's Church*

PETS: Bedrooms (1 GF) certain bedrooms only **Public areas** except dining room **Exercise area** adjacent **Facilities** walks info vet info **Other** charge for damage

This Victorian guest house, close to the shops, beach and gardens, has individually decorated bedrooms with a good range of useful extras. There are also a ground-floor room, two feature rooms, one with a four-poster, and another with a canopied bed.

Rooms 7 en suite (1 fmly) (1 GF) **Facilities** TVL tea/coffee Cen ht **Parking** 4 **Notes** LB No Children 5yrs Closed 15 Nov-15 Mar

Searles Leisure Resort (TF671400)

South Beach Rd PE36 5BB
☎ 01485 534211 📠 01485 533815
e-mail: bookings@searles.co.uk
dir: *A149 from King's Lynn to Hunstanton. At rdbt follow signs for South Beach. Straight on at 2nd rdbt. Site on left*

PETS: Charges Public areas except shop, club, plaza & toilets **Exercise area on site** field (dogs on leads) **Exercise area** beach (200mtrs) **Facilities** food food bowl water bowl washing facs walks info vet info **Stables** 5m **Other** prior notice required max 1 dog per pitch (school hols & BHs); 2 dogs at other times disposal bags available **Restrictions** no Rottweilers, Pit Bull Terriers, Staffordshire Bull Terriers, German Shepherds, Alsatians, Dobermans or similar breeds (see page 7)

Open all year rs 25 Dec & Feb-May limited entertainment & restaurant Last arrival 20.45hrs Last departure 11.00hrs

A large seaside holiday complex with well-managed facilities, adjacent to sea and beach. The tourers have their own areas, including two excellent toilet blocks, and pitches are individually marked by small maturing shrubs for privacy. The bars and entertainment, restaurant, bistro and takeaway, heated indoor and outdoor pools, golf, fishing and bowling green make this park popular throughout the year. 50 acre site. 332 touring pitches. 100 hardstandings. Tent pitches. Motorhome pitches. 460 statics.

Notes No dangerous dog breeds

KING'S LYNN — Map 9 TF62

King's Lynn Caravan and Camping Park
(TF645160)

▶▶▶▶

New Rd, North Runcton PE33 0RA
☎ 01553 840004
e-mail: klcc@btconnect.com
dir: *From King's Lynn take A47 signed Swaffham & Norwich, right in 1.5m to North Runcton. Site 100yds on left*

PETS: Charges £1 per stay **Public areas** disp bin **Exercise area on site** fields **Exercise area** 200mtrs **Facilities** food dog chews cat treats washing facs walks info vet info **Stables** 0.5m **Other** stabling for horses can be arranged pet shops nearby

Open all year Last arrival flexible Last departure flexible

Set in approximately 10 acres of parkland, this developing camping park is situated on the edge of North Runcton, just a few miles south of the historic town of King's Lynn. There is a new and very handsome, eco-friendly toilet block which is powered by solar panels and an air-sourced heat pump, plus it also recycles rainwater. In itself this a source of great interest on this attractive park. The three very extensive touring fields are equipped with 150 electric hook-ups and one field is reserved for rallies. 9 acre site. 150 touring pitches. 2 hardstandings. Tent pitches. Motorhome pitches.

Notes No skateboards or fires.

Beechwood Hotel

★★★ ◉◉ HOTEL

Cromer Rd NR28 0HD

☎ 01692 403231   🖨 01692 407284

e-mail: info@beechwood-hotel.co.uk

web: www.beechwood-hotel.co.uk

dir: *B1150 from Norwich. At North Walsham left at 1st lights, then right at next*

PETS: Bedrooms (4 GF) unattended sign 3 bedrooms only **Charges** £10 per night **Public areas** except restaurant on leads **Grounds** disp bin **Exercise area** park 400yds **Facilities** food bowl water bowl dog chews leads pet sitting dog walking cage storage walks info vet info **On Request** fridge access torch towels **Resident Pet:** Tess (Airedale Terrier)

Expect a warm welcome at this elegant 18th-century house, situated just a short walk from the town centre. The individually styled bedrooms are tastefully furnished with well chosen antique pieces, attractive co-ordinated soft fabrics and many thoughtful touches. The spacious public areas include a lounge bar with plush furnishings, a further lounge and a smartly appointed restaurant.

Rooms 17 (4 GF) **S** fr £82; **D** £90-£150 (incl. bkfst) **Facilities** FTV ⛄ New Year Wi-fi **Parking** 20 **Notes** LB No children 10yrs

Chimneys

★★★★ 🏠 BED AND BREAKFAST

51 Cromer Rd NR28 0HB

☎ 01692 406172 & 07952 117701

e-mail: jenny.harmer8@virgin.net

dir: *0.5m NW of town centre on A149*

PETS: Bedrooms Public areas on leads **Grounds** on leads disp bin **Exercise area** 1m **Facilities** washing facs cage storage walks info vet info **On Request** fridge access torch towels **Restrictions** no large dogs or long haired dogs **Resident Pet:** 1 small terrier cross

A delightful Edwardian-style town house set amidst mature secluded grounds close to the town centre. Bedrooms are tastefully furnished and thoughtfully equipped, the superior room has a jacuzzi bath. Breakfast is served in the smart dining room and guests are welcome to sit on the balcony, which overlooks the garden. Dinner is available by prior arrangement.

Rooms 3 en suite (1 fmly) **S** £40-£55; **D** £60-£75 **Facilities** FTV tea/coffee Dinner available Cen ht Wi-fi **Parking** 6

Two Mills Touring Park *(TG291286)*

▶▶▶▶

Yarmouth Rd NR28 9NA

☎ 01692 405829   🖨 01692 405829

e-mail: enquiries@twomills.co.uk

dir: *1m S of North Walsham on Old Yarmouth road past police station & hospital on left*

PETS: Charges 75p per night **Public areas** except in buildings disp bin **Exercise area on site** dog walks **Exercise area** 200yds **Facilities** food washing facs walks info vet info **Other** prior notice required max 2 dogs per pitch disposal bags available **Resident Pet:** Pusscat (cat)

Open Mar-3 Jan Last arrival 20.30hrs Last departure noon

An intimate, beautifully presented park set in superb countryside in a peaceful, rural spot, which is also convenient for touring. A 'Top Acre' section features an additional 26 fully serviced pitches, offering panoramic views over the site, an immaculate toilet block and good planting, plus the layout of pitches and facilities is excellent. The very friendly and helpful owners keep the park in immaculate condition. Please note this park does not accept children. 7 acre site. 81 touring pitches. 81 hardstandings. Tent pitches. Motorhome pitches.

 SPROWSTON MANOR

Sprowston Manor, A Marriott Hotel & Country Club

★★★★ 82% ◉◉ HOTEL

Sprowston Park, Wroxham Rd, Sprowston NR7 8RP

☎ 01603 410871   🖨 01603 423911

e-mail: mhrs.nwigs.frontdesk@marriotthotels.com

web: www.marriottsprowstonmanor.co.uk

dir: *From NE of Norwich take A1151 (Wroxham road). 2m, follow signs to Sprowston Park*

PETS: Bedrooms (5 GF) unattended ground-floor bedrooms only **Charges** £15 per night **Public areas** except restaurants & bar on leads **Grounds** on leads disp bin **Facilities** food bowl water bowl dog chews cage storage walks info vet info **On Request** fridge access torch

Surrounded by open parkland, this imposing property is set in attractively landscaped grounds and is just a short drive from the city centre. Bedrooms are spacious and feature a variety of decorative styles. The hotel also has extensive conference, banqueting and leisure facilities. Other public rooms include an array of seating areas and the elegant Manor Restaurant.

Rooms 94 (3 fmly) (5 GF) (8 smoking) **S** £105-£135; **D** £140-£145 (incl. bkfst)* **Facilities** Spa FTV 🏊 supervised ♪ 18 Putt green Gym Steam room Sauna Xmas New Year Wi-fi **Services** Lift **Parking** 150 **Notes** LB

ENGLAND

NORWICH *continued*

Stower Grange

★★ 85% ® HOTEL

School Rd, Drayton NR8 6EF
☎ 01603 860210 📄 01603 860464
e-mail: enquiries@stowergrange.co.uk
web: www.stowergrange.co.uk
dir: *Norwich ring road N to Asda supermarket. Take A1067 (Fakenham road) at Drayton, right at lights into School Rd. Hotel 150yds on right*

PETS: **Bedrooms** unattended **Public areas** except restaurant **Grounds** disp bin **Exercise area** adjacent **Facilities** food (pre-bookable) food bowl water bowl dog chews cat treats pet sitting dog walking washing facs cage storage walks info vet info **On Request** torch towels **Other** charge for damage

Expect a warm welcome at this 17th-century, ivy-clad property situated in a peaceful residential area close to the city centre and airport. The individually decorated bedrooms are generally quite spacious; each is tastefully furnished and equipped with many thoughtful touches. Public rooms include a smart open-plan lounge bar and an elegant restaurant.

Rooms 11 (1 fmly) **S** fr £80; **D** £100-£150 (incl. bkfst) **Facilities** FTV 🌊 New Year Wi-fi **Parking** 40 **Notes** LB

Edmar Lodge

★★★ GUEST ACCOMMODATION

64 Earlham Rd NR2 3DF
☎ 01603 615599 📄 01603 495599
e-mail: mail@edmarlodge.co.uk
web: www.edmarlodge.co.uk
dir: *Exit A47 (S bypass) onto B1108 Earlham Rd, follow university & hospital signs*

PETS: **Bedrooms Grounds** on leads **Exercise area** small wooded area (approx 100yds) **Facilities** food bowl water bowl washing facs walks info vet info **On Request** fridge access towels **Other** please phone for further details of pet facilities

Located just a ten-minute walk from the city centre, this friendly family-run establishment offers a convenient location and ample private parking. Individually decorated bedrooms are smartly appointed and well equipped. Freshly prepared breakfasts are served in the cosy dining room; a microwave and a fridge are also available.

Rooms 5 en suite (1 fmly) **S** £38-£45; **D** £48-£55 **Facilities** FTV tea/coffee Cen ht Wi-fi **Parking** 6

REEPHAM Map 9 TG12

Old Brewery House

★★★ 68% HOTEL

Market Place NR10 4JJ
☎ 01603 870881 📄 01603 870969
e-mail: reservations.oldbreweryhouse@ohiml.com
web: www.oxfordhotelsandinns.com
dir: *A1067, right at Bawdeswell onto B1145 into Reepham*

PETS: **Bedrooms** (7 GF) unattended sign certain bedrooms only **Charges** £5 per night **Public areas** except restaurant & breakfast room on leads **Grounds** on leads **Exercise area** woods (1m) **Facilities** water bowl cage storage walks info vet info **On Request** fridge access torch towels **Other** prior notice required

This Grade II listed Georgian building is situated in the heart of this bustling town centre. Public areas include a cosy lounge, a bar, a conservatory and a smart restaurant. Bedrooms come in a variety of styles; each one is pleasantly decorated and equipped with a good range of facilities.

Rooms 23 (2 fmly) (7 GF) **Facilities** 🏊 Gym Squash Xmas **Parking** 40

The Gin Trap Inn
★★★★ INN

6 High St PE36 5JU
☎ 01485 525264
e-mail: thegintrap@hotmail.co.uk
dir: *A149 from King's Lynn towards Hunstanton. In 15m right at Heacham for Ringstead, into village centre*

PETS: Bedrooms Public areas except conservatory & dining room **Grounds Exercise area** 500mtrs **Facilities** water bowl dog chews walks info vet info **On Request** fridge access torch

This delightful 17th-century inn is in a quiet village just a short drive from the coast. The public rooms include a large open-plan bar and a cosy restaurant. The accommodation is luxurious. Each individually appointed bedroom has been carefully decorated and thoughtfully equipped.

Rooms 3 en suite **S** £49-£70; **D** £78-£140 **Facilities** tea/coffee Dinner available Cen ht Wi-fi **Parking** 20 **Notes** No Children No coaches

Virginia Lake Caravan Park *(TF538113)*
▶ ▶ ▶ ▶

Smeeth Rd PE14 8JF
☎ 01945 430585 & 430167
e-mail: louise@virginialake.co.uk
dir: *From A47 E of Wisbech follow tourist signs to Terrington St John. Site on left*

PETS: Public areas except lakeside disp bin **Exercise area on site** dog walk **Exercise area** 100 mtrs **Facilities** food food bowl water bowl litter tray scoop/disp bags leads washing facs walks info vet info **Other** prior notice required **Restrictions** no Pit Bull Terriers, Staffordshire Bull Terriers, Rottweilers or Dobermans **Resident Pets:** 4 Labradors & 2 cats

Open all year Last arrival 21.00hrs Last departure 15.00hrs

A well-established park beside a two-acre fishing lake with good facilities for both anglers and tourers. The toilet facilities are very good, and security is carefully observed throughout the park. A clubhouse serves a selection of meals. 7 acre site. 97 touring pitches. 20 hardstandings. Tent pitches. Motorhome pitches.

Notes No camp fires

Scratby Hall Caravan Park *(TG501155)*
▶ ▶ ▶

NR29 3SR
☎ 01493 730283
e-mail: scratbyhall@aol.com
dir: *5m N of Great Yarmouth. Exit A149 onto B1159, site signed*

PETS: Public areas except children's play area, buildings & swimming pool disp bin **Exercise area** direct access to footpaths & bridleways **Facilities** food food bowl water bowl bedding dog chews scoop/disp bags leads washing facs walks info vet info **Stables** 0.5m **Other** max 2 pets per pitch pet toys available

Open Spring BH-mid Sep Last arrival 22.00hrs Last departure noon

A neatly-maintained site with a popular children's play area, well-equipped shop and outdoor swimming pool with sun terrace. The toilets are kept very clean. The beach and the Norfolk Broads are close by. 5 acre site. 97 touring pitches. Tent pitches. Motorhome pitches.

Notes No commercial vehicles

The Rickels Caravan & Camping Park
(TF794355)
▶ ▶ ▶

Bircham Rd PE31 8PU
☎ 01485 518671
dir: *A148 from King's Lynn to Hillington. B1153 to Great Bircham. B1155 to x-rds, straight over, site on left*

PETS: Charges £1 per night **Public areas** disp bin **Exercise area on site** small field available (morning & evening) **Facilities** walks info vet info **Other** prior notice required max 2 dogs per pitch; all dogs must be kept on leads at all times

Open Mar-Oct Last arrival 21.00hrs Last departure 11.00hrs

Set in three acres of grassland, with sweeping country views and a pleasant, relaxing atmosphere fostered by being for adults only. The meticulously maintained grounds and facilities are part of the attraction, and the slightly sloping land has some level areas and sheltering for tents. 3 acre site. 30 touring pitches. Tent pitches. Motorhome pitches. 1 static.

Notes No ground sheets. 🐾

SWAFFHAM — Map 5 TF80

Breckland Meadows Touring Park *(TF809094)*

▶ ▶ ▶

Lynn Rd PE37 7PT
☎ 01760 721246
e-mail: info@brecklandmeadows.co.uk
dir: *1m W of Swaffham on old A47*

PETS: Charges 50p per night £3.50 per week **Public areas** disp bin **Exercise area on site Facilities** washing facs walks info vet info **Stables** 5m

Open all year Last arrival 21.00hrs Last departure 12.00hrs

An immaculate, well-landscaped little park on the edge of Swaffham. The impressive toilet block is well equipped, and there are hardstandings, full electricity and laundry equipment. Plentiful planting is now resulting in attractive screening. 3 acre site. 45 touring pitches. 35 hardstandings. 5 seasonal pitches. Tent pitches. Motorhome pitches.

SYDERSTONE — Map 9 TF83

The Garden Caravan Site *(TF812337)*

▶ ▶ ▶

Barmer Hall Farm PE31 8SR
☎ 01485 578220 & 578178
e-mail: nigel@gardencaravansite.co.uk
dir: *Signed from B1454 at Barmer between A148 & Docking, 1m W of Syderstone*

PETS: Public areas Exercise area adjacent **Facilities** walks info vet info **Other** prior notice required max 2 dogs per pitch

Open Mar-Nov Last arrival 21.00hrs Last departure noon

In the tranquil setting of a former walled garden beside a large farmhouse, with mature trees and shrubs, a secluded site surrounded by woodland. The site is run mainly on trust, with a daily notice indicating which pitches are available, and an honesty box for basic foods. An ideal site for the discerning camper, and well placed for touring north Norfolk. 3.5 acre site. 30 touring pitches. Tent pitches. Motorhome pitches.

Notes 🐾

THURSFORD — Map 9 TF93

The Old Forge Seafood Restaurant

★★★★ ❀ RESTAURANT WITH ROOMS

Seafood Restaurant, Fakenham Rd NR21 0BD
☎ 01328 878345
e-mail: sarah.goldspink@btconnect.com
dir: *On A148 (Fakenham to Holt road)*

PETS: Bedrooms Charges horse £10 per night **Grounds** on leads disp bin **Exercise area** adjacent **Facilities** leads pet sitting dog walking cage storage walks info vet info **On Request** fridge access torch towels **Stables Other** charge for damage **Resident Pets:** 3 Labradors, 1 Miniature Schnauzer, 2 horses

Expect a warm welcome at this delightful relaxed restaurant with rooms. The open-plan public areas include a lounge bar area with comfy sofas, and an intimate restaurant with pine tables. Bedrooms are pleasantly decorated and equipped with a good range of useful facilities.

Rooms 3 en suite **S** £35-£55; **D** £65 **Facilities** STV FTV tea/coffee Dinner available Cen ht Wi-fi Riding **Parking** 14 **Notes** No Children 5yrs No coaches

TITCHWELL — Map 9 TF74

Titchwell Manor

★★★ 86% ❀❀ HOTEL

PE31 8BB
☎ 01485 210221 📠 01485 210104
e-mail: margaret@titchwellmanor.com
web: www.titchwellmanor.com
dir: *On A149 (coast road) between Brancaster & Thornham*

PETS: Bedrooms (16 GF) unattended sign **Sep accom Charges** £8 per night **Public areas** except conservatory restaurant on leads **Grounds** on leads disp bin **Exercise area** 1m **Facilities** food bowl water bowl bedding dog chews cat treats feeding mat litter tray scoop/disp bags leads pet sitting washing facs cage storage walks info vet info **On Request** fridge access torch towels **Stables** 2m **Other** charge for damage

Friendly family-run hotel ideally placed for touring the north Norfolk coastline. The tastefully appointed bedrooms are very comfortable; some in the adjacent annexe offer ground floor access. Smart public rooms include a lounge area, relaxed informal bar and a delightful conservatory restaurant, overlooking

the walled garden. Imaginative menus feature quality local produce and fresh fish.

Rooms 26 (18 annexe) (4 fmly) (16 GF) **S** £45-£125; **D** £90-£250 (incl. bkfst)* **Facilities** FTV Xmas New Year Wi-fi **Parking** 50 **Notes** LB

WATTON   Map 5 TF90

Broom Hall Country Hotel
★★★ **77%** COUNTRY HOUSE HOTEL

Richmond Rd, Saham Toney IP25 7EX
☎ 01953 882125 📠 01953 885325
e-mail: enquiries@broomhallhotel.co.uk
web: www.broomhallhotel.co.uk
dir: *From A11 at Thetford onto A1075 to Watton (12m), B1108 towards Swaffham, in 0.5m at rdbt turn right to Saham Toney, hotel 0.5m on left. From A47 take A1075, left onto B1108*

PETS: Bedrooms (5 GF) unattended certain bedrooms only **Sep accom** by arrangement **Charges** £5 per night (£10 for 2 nights or more) **Public areas** only bar & reception **Grounds** disp bin **Exercise area** adjacent **Facilities** bedding leads washing facs walks info vet info **On Request** fridge access torch **Stables** 6m **Other** charge for damage **Resident Pets:** Maggie & Toby (Jack Russells), Berti (Cavalier King Charles Spaniel)

A delightful Victorian country house situated down a private drive and set in mature landscaped gardens surrounded by parkland. The well-equipped bedrooms are split between the main house and an adjacent building. Public rooms include a relaxing lounge, a brasserie restaurant, a lounge bar, a conservatory and a smart restaurant. There is an indoor swimming pool.

Rooms 15 (5 annexe) (3 fmly) (5 GF) **S** £78-£150; **D** £95-£200 (incl. bkfst) **Facilities** FTV ⊗ Massage Reflexology Beauty treatments Wi-fi **Parking** 30 **Notes** LB Closed 24 Dec-4 Jan

---

WORSTEAD   Map 9 TG32

The Ollands
★★★★ 🏠 🍽 GUEST HOUSE

Swanns Yard NR28 9RP
☎ 01692 535150 📠 01692 535150
e-mail: theollands@btinternet.com
dir: *Off A149 to village x-rds, off Back St*

PETS: Bedrooms (1 GF) **Charges** £3 per night **Public areas** except dining room **Grounds** disp bin **Exercise area** nearby **Facilities** walks info vet info **On Request** torch **Other** charge for damage **Restrictions** small & medium size dogs only **Resident Pets:** Candy, Mouse & Abbs (Burmese cats), Storm (cat)

This charming detached property is set in the heart of the picturesque village of Worstead. The well-equipped bedrooms are pleasantly decorated and carefully furnished, and breakfasts served in the elegant dining room feature local produce.

Rooms 3 en suite (1 GF) **S** £40-£42.50; **D** £66-£70 **Facilities** TVL tea/coffee Dinner available Cen ht Wi-fi **Parking** 8 **Notes** LB

CASTLE ASHBY   Map 4 SP85

The Falcon
★★★ INN

NN7 1LF
☎ 01604 696200 📠 01604 696673
e-mail: 6446@greeneking.co.uk
dir: *Off A428*

PETS: Bedrooms sign certain bedrooms only **Charges Public areas** except restaurant on leads **Grounds** on leads **Exercise area** 5 mins **Facilities** food bowl water bowl walks info vet info **On Request** torch towels **Other** charge for damage **Restrictions** no Great Danes

Set in the heart of a peaceful village, the inn consists of a main house and a neighbouring cottage. Bedrooms are all individually decorated and provide a wealth of thoughtful extras. Character public rooms, in the main house, include a cellar bar, a choice of lounges and a pretty restaurant serving good quality cuisine.

Rooms 5 en suite 10 annexe en suite (1 fmly) **Facilities** TVL tea/coffee Dinner available Cen ht Wi-fi **Parking** 75 **Notes** LB

CRICK   Map 4 SP57

Holiday Inn Rugby/Northampton
★★★ **72%** HOTEL

M1 Junction 18 NN6 7XR
☎ 0871 942 9059 & 01788 824800 📠 01788 823 8955
e-mail: rugbyhi@ihg.com
web: www.holidayinn.co.uk
dir: *0.5m from M1 junct 18*

PETS: Bedrooms (42 GF) sign standard bedrooms only **Charges** £10 per night **Public areas** except eating areas on leads **Grounds** on leads **Facilities** walks info vet info **Other** charge for damage

Situated in pleasant surroundings, located just off the M1, this modern hotel offers well-equipped and comfortable bedrooms. Public areas include the popular Traders restaurant and a comfortable lounge where an all-day menu is available. The Spirit Health Club provides indoor swimming and a good fitness facility.

Rooms 90 (19 fmly) (42 GF) (12 smoking) **Facilities** STV ⊗ Gym New Year Wi-fi **Services** Lift Air con **Parking** 250

CRICK *continued*

Ibis Rugby

BUDGET HOTEL

Parklands NN6 7EX

☎ 01788 824331 📄 01788 824332

e-mail: H3588@accor.com

web: www.ibishotel.com

dir: *M1 junct 18, follow Daventry/Rugby A5 signs. At rdbt 3rd exit signed DIRFT East. Hotel on right*

PETS: Bedrooms (12 GF) **Charges** £10 per night **Public areas** except restaurant on leads **Grounds** on leads **Facilities** vet info

Modern, budget hotel offering comfortable accommodation in bright and practical bedrooms. Breakfast is self-service and dinner is available in the restaurant.

Rooms 111 (47 fmly) (12 GF)

DAVENTRY

Map 4 SP56

Fawsley Hall

★★★★ HOTEL

Fawsley NN11 3BA

☎ 01327 892000 📄 01327 892001

e-mail: reservations@fawsleyhall.com

web: www.fawsleyhall.com

dir: *A361 S of Daventry, between Badby & Charwelton, hotel signed (single track lane)*

PETS: Bedrooms (2 GF) Club Rooms only **Grounds** on leads **Exercise area** 1m **Facilities** water bowl bedding vet info **On Request** fridge access torch towels **Other** charge for damage

Dating back to the 15th century, this delightful hotel is peacefully located in beautiful gardens designed by 'Capability' Brown. Spacious, individually designed bedrooms and stylish public areas are beautifully furnished with antique and period pieces. Afternoon tea is served in the impressive Great Hall. Dinner is available in the fine-dining Equilibrium Restaurant while a more relaxed style is found in Bess's Brasserie. The Grayshot Spa features an ozone pool, treatment rooms and fitness studio. The AA Rosette award for the cuisine is temporarily suspended due to a change of chef. An award will be in place once our inspectors have assessed the food cooked by the new kitchen brigade.

Rooms 58 (14 annexe) (2 GF) **S** fr £185; **D** £185-£495 (incl. bkfst)* **Facilities** Spa STV 🖲 🏊 🦢 Gym Health & beauty treatment rooms Fitness studio 29-seat cinema Xmas New Year Wi-fi **Parking** 140 **Notes** LB

Barceló Daventry Hotel

★★★★ 71% HOTEL

Sedgemoor Way NN11 0SG

☎ 01327 307000 📄 01327 706313

e-mail: daventry@barcelo-hotels.co.uk

web: www.barcelo-hotels.co.uk

dir: *M1 junct 16/A45 to Daventry, at 1st rdbt turn right to Kilsby/M1(N). Hotel on right in 1m*

PETS: Bedrooms unattended **Charges** £15 per night **Public areas** except restaurant & bar **Grounds** on leads **Exercise area** parks nearby **Facilities** washing facs cage storage walks info vet info **On Request** fridge access torch **Other** charge for damage

This modern, striking hotel overlooking Drayton Water boasts spacious public areas that include a good range of banqueting, meeting and leisure facilities. It is a popular venue for conferences. Bedrooms are suitable for both business and leisure guests.

Rooms 155 (17 fmly) **Facilities** STV 🖲 supervised Gym Steam room Health & beauty salon Xmas New Year Wi-fi **Services** Lift **Parking** 350

HELLIDON

Map 4 SP55

Hellidon Lakes Golf & Spa Hotel

★★★★ 74% HOTEL

NN11 6GG

☎ 01327 262550 📄 01327 262559

e-mail: hellidonlakes@qhotels.co.uk

web: www.qhotels.co.uk

dir: *Off A361 between Daventry & Banbury, signed*

PETS: Bedrooms unattended sign **Charges** contact hotel for details **Public areas** muzzled and on leads **Grounds** on leads disp bin **Exercise area** nearby **Facilities** food (pre-bookable) food bowl water bowl bedding feeding mat scoop/disp bags leads pet sitting dog walking washing facs dog grooming cage storage walks info vet info **On Request** fridge access torch towels **Stables** less than 10m **Other** charge for damage

Some 220 acres of beautiful countryside, which include 27 holes of golf and 12 lakes, combine to form a rather spectacular backdrop to this impressive hotel. Bedroom styles vary, from ultra smart, modern rooms through to those in the original wing that offer superb views. There is an extensive range of facilities available from meeting rooms to a swimming pool, gym and ten-pin bowling. Golfers of all levels can try some of the world's most challenging courses on the indoor golf simulator.

Rooms 110 (5 fmly) **S** £65-£120; **D** £75-£130 (incl. bkfst)* **Facilities** Spa STV 🖲 ⚑ 27 🏊 Putt green Fishing 🦢 Gym Beauty therapist Indoor smart golf 10-pin bowling Steam room Coarse fishing lake Xmas New Year Wi-fi **Services** Lift **Parking** 200 **Notes** LB

NORTHAMPTON
Map 4 SP76

Campanile Northampton
★★★ 67% HOTEL

Cheaney Dr, Grange Park NN4 5FB
☎ 01604 662599 ▤ 01604 622598
e-mail: northampton@campanile.com
dir: M1 junct 15, A508 towards Northampton. 2nd exit at 1st rdbt, 2nd exit at 2nd rdbt into Grange Park

PETS: Bedrooms Charges £5 per night on leads **Exercise area** nearby **Other** charge for damage

This modern building offers accommodation in smart, well-equipped bedrooms, all with en suite bathrooms. Refreshments may be taken at the informal bistro.

Rooms 87 (18 fmly) **Facilities** STV FTV Xmas New Year Wi-fi **Services** Lift Air con **Parking** 100

WELLINGBOROUGH
Map 4 SP86

ibis
HOTEL

Ibis Wellingborough
BUDGET HOTEL

Enstone Court NN8 2DR
☎ 01933 228333 ▤ 01933 228444
e-mail: H3164@accor-hotels.com
web: www.ibishotel.com
dir: At junct of A45 & A509 towards Kettering, SW outskirts of Wellingborough

PETS: Bedrooms (2 GF) unattended **Public areas** except lounge & dining room **Exercise area** field nearby **Facilities** vet info

Modern, budget hotel offering comfortable accommodation in bright and practical bedrooms. Breakfast is self-service and dinner is available in the restaurant.

Rooms 78 (20 fmly) (2 GF)

NORTHUMBERLAND

BAMBURGH
Map 12 NU13

Waren House
★★★ 82% ◉ COUNTRY HOUSE HOTEL

Waren Mill NE70 7EE
☎ 01668 214581 ▤ 01668 214484
e-mail: enquiries@warenhousehotel.co.uk
web: www.warenhousehotel.co.uk
dir: 2m E of A1 turn onto B1342 to Waren Mill, at T-junct turn right, hotel 100yds on right

PETS: Bedrooms (3 GF) ground-floor bedrooms only **Grounds** on leads disp bin **Exercise area** adjacent **Facilities** water bowl walks info vet info **On Request** torch towels **Other** charge for damage

This delightful Georgian mansion is set in six acres of woodland and offers a welcoming atmosphere and views of the coast. The individually themed bedrooms and suites include many with large bathrooms. Good, home-cooked food is served in the elegant dining room. A comfortable lounge and library are also available.

Rooms 15 (4 annexe) (3 GF) **S** £95-£130; **D** £130-£185 (incl. bkfst) **Facilities** FTV Xmas New Year Wi-fi **Parking** 20 **Notes** No children 14yrs

BAMBURGH *continued*

Waren Caravan Park *(NU155343)*

▶ ▶ ▶ ▶

Waren Mill NE70 7EE
☎ 01668 214366 📠 01668 214224
e-mail: waren@meadowhead.co.uk
dir: *2m E of town. From A1 onto B1342 signed Bamburgh. Take unclass road past Waren Mill, signed Budle*

PETS: Charges £3 per night **Public areas** except public buildings & play areas disp bin **Exercise area on site** open field & dog walk areas **Facilities** food food bowl water bowl dog chews feeding mat scoop/disp bags leads washing facs walks info vet info **Other** prior notice required anchor pegs, shampoo & feeding mat available **Restrictions** no Rottweilers, Pit Bull Terriers or Dobermans

Open Apr-Oct Last arrival 20.00hrs Last departure noon

Attractive seaside site with footpath access to the beach, surrounded by a slightly sloping grassy embankment giving shelter to caravans. The park offers excellent facilities including several family bathrooms. 4 acre site. 150 touring pitches. 24 hardstandings. Tent pitches. Motorhome pitches. 300 statics. 4 tipis.

Glororum Caravan Park *(NU166334)*

▶ ▶ ▶

Glororum Farm NE69 7AW
☎ 01668 214457 📠 01688 214484
dir: *Exit A1 at junct with B1341 (Purdy's Lodge). In 3.5m left onto unclass road. Site 300yds on left*

PETS: Public areas except children's play area on leads disp bin **Exercise area on site** dog walks **Facilities** food food bowl water bowl scoop/disp bags washing facs walks info vet info **Stables** 5m **Other** prior notice required dogs must be kept on leads at all times **Restrictions** well behaved dogs only

Open Mar-end Oct Last arrival 18.00hrs Last departure noon

A pleasantly situated site where tourers have their own well-established facilities. The open countryside setting affords good views of Bamburgh Castle and surrounding farmland. 6 acre site. 100 touring pitches. Motorhome pitches. 150 statics.

Purdy Lodge

★ ★ **76%** HOTEL

Adderstone Services NE70 7JU
☎ 01668 213000 📠 01668 213111
e-mail: stay@purdylodge.co.uk
web: www.purdylodge.co.uk
dir: *A1 onto B1341 then immediately left*

PETS: Bedrooms (10 GF) **Public areas** except restaurant & bar on leads **Grounds** on leads **Exercise area** adjacent **Other** charge for damage

Situated off the A1, this family-owned lodge provides modern bedrooms that look out over the fields towards Bamburgh Castle.

Food is readily available in the attractive restaurant, Café One, and the lounge bar. This is a great stop-off hotel where a friendly welcome is guaranteed.

Rooms 20 (4 fmly) (10 GF) **Facilities** FTV New Year Wi-fi **Parking** 60 **Notes** Closed 25 Dec

Bellingham Camping & Caravanning Club Site *(NY835826)*

▶ ▶ ▶ ▶

Brown Rigg NE48 2JY
☎ 01434 220175 & 0845 130 7633 📠 01434 220175
dir: *From A69 take A6079 N to Chollerford & B6320 to Bellingham. Pass Forestry Commission land, site 0.5m S of Bellingham*

PETS: Public areas except public buildings & children's play area disp bin **Exercise area** 0.5m **Facilities** leads walks info vet info **Other** free disposal bags

Open 11 Mar-Oct Last arrival 20.00hrs Last departure noon

A beautiful and peaceful site set in the glorious Northumberland National Park. This is a perfect base for exploring this undiscovered part of England, and it is handily placed for visiting the beautiful Northumberland coast. This is an exceptionally well-managed park that continues to improve. There are four camping pods for hire. 5 acre site. 64 touring pitches. 42 hardstandings. Tent pitches. Motorhome pitches. 4 wooden pods.

Notes Site gates closed & quiet time 23.00hrs-07.00hrs.

Lindisfarne Inn

★ ★ ★ INN

Beal TD15 2PD
☎ 01289 381223 📠 01289 381223
e-mail: enquiries@lindisfarneinn.co.uk
dir: *On A1, turn off for Holy Island*

PETS: Bedrooms (10 GF) unattended **Charges** £5 per night **Grounds** disp bin **Exercise area** 2m **On Request** fridge access torch towels **Stables** 3m **Other** charge for damage

The Lindisfarne Inn stands on the site of the old Plough Hotel at Beal, on the road leading to Holy Island. Now totally refurbished and re-opened with a traditional bar, rustic style restaurant and comfortably equipped courtyard bedrooms in the adjacent wing. Food is available all day.

Rooms 21 annexe en suite (20 fmly) (10 GF) **S** £60; **D** £80 **Facilities** FTV TVL tea/coffee Dinner available Cen ht Wi-fi **Parking** 25

Ord House Country Park *(NT982515)*

▶ ▶ ▶ ▶ ▶

East Ord TD15 2NS
☎ 01289 305288 📄 01289 330832
e-mail: enquiries@ordhouse.co.uk
dir: *On A1, Berwick bypass, turn off at 2nd rdbt at East Ord, follow 'Caravan' signs*

PETS: Charges max £1.50 per night **Public areas** except club house (assist dogs only) **Exercise area on site** 2km walk **Facilities** food food bowl water bowl bedding dog chews cat treats walks info vet info **Other** prior notice required scoop available; dog tents for sale **Restrictions** max 1 large & 2 small dogs per family; no Rottweilers, Dobermans or dangerous dogs (see page 7)

Open all year Last arrival 23.00hrs Last departure noon

A very well run park set in the pleasant grounds of an 18th-century country house. Touring pitches are marked and well spaced, some of them fully-serviced. The very modern toilet facilities include family bath and shower suites, and first class disabled rooms. There is an outdoor leisure shop with a good range of camping and caravanning spares, as well as clothing and equipment, and an attractive licensed club selling bar meals. 42 acre site. 79 touring pitches. 46 hardstandings. Tent pitches. Motorhome pitches. 255 statics.

Tillmouth Park Country House

★ ★ ★ 86% ⬢ COUNTRY HOUSE HOTEL

TD12 4UU
☎ 01890 882255 📄 01890 882540
e-mail: reception@tillmouthpark.f9.co.uk
web: www.tillmouthpark.co.uk
dir: *Exit A1(M) at East Ord rdbt at Berwick-upon-Tweed. Take A698 signed Cornhill & Coldstream. Hotel 9m on left*

PETS: Bedrooms unattended **Charges** £3 per night **Public areas** bar only on leads **Grounds** on leads disp bin **Exercise area** less than 1m **Facilities** water bowl cage storage walks info vet info **Stables** 4m **Resident Pets:** Carter & Teal (Black Labradors)

An imposing mansion set in landscaped grounds by the River Till. Gracious public rooms include a stunning galleried lounge with a drawing room adjacent. The quiet, elegant dining room overlooks the gardens, whilst lunches and early dinners are available in the bistro. Bedrooms retain much traditional character and include several magnificent master rooms.

Rooms 14 (2 annexe) (4 smoking) **S** £79-£205; **D** £158-£225 (incl. bkfst)* **Facilities** FTV 🏊 Game shooting Fishing New Year Wi-fi **Parking** 50 **Notes** LB Closed 3 Jan-1 Apr

Dunstanburgh Castle Hotel

★ ★ 82% HOTEL

NE66 3UN
☎ 01665 576111 📄 0870 706 0394
e-mail: stay@dunstanburghcastlehotel.co.uk
web: www.dunstanburghcastlehotel.co.uk
dir: *From A1, take B1340 to Denwick past Rennington & Masons Arms. Take next right signed Embleton*

PETS: Bedrooms unattended **Grounds** disp bin **Exercise area** adjacent **Facilities** scoop/disp bags walks info vet info **On Request** fridge access torch towels **Resident Pet:** Uncle Bob (dog)

The focal point of the village, this friendly, family-run hotel has a dining room and grill room that offer different menus, plus a cosy bar and two lounges. In addition to the main bedrooms, a barn conversion houses three stunning suites, each with a lounge and gallery bedroom above.

Rooms 32 (12 annexe) (6 fmly) **S** £45.50-£68.50; **D** £91-£137 (incl. bkfst)* **Facilities** Wi-fi **Parking** 33 **Notes** LB Closed Dec-Jan

ENGLAND

FALSTONE — Map 12 NY78

The Blackcock Country Inn and Restaurant
★★★★ INN

NE48 1AA
☎ 01434 240200
e-mail: thebcinn@yahoo.co.uk
dir: *From Hexham take A6079 to Bellingham, then left at church. In village centre, towards Kielder Water*

PETS: Bedrooms unattended **Public areas** except restaurant on leads **Grounds** on leads disp bin **Exercise area** adjacent **Facilities** food (pre-bookable) food bowl water bowl bedding dog chews cat treats feeding mat litter tray scoop/disp bags leads washing facs cage storage walks info vet info **On Request** fridge access torch towels **Stables** adjacent **Other** charge for damage doggy dinner menus, squeaky toys available **Resident Pets:** Pooch (dog), Banjo & Sno (cats), Rosso (rabbit), Cheese (fish)

This traditional family-run village inn lies close to Kielder Water. A cosy pub, it has a very homely atmosphere, with welcoming fires in the colder weather. The bedrooms are very comfortable and well equipped. Evening meals are served here or in the restaurant. The inn is closed during the day on Wednesday throughout winter.

Rooms 6 rms (4 en suite) (2 pri facs) (1 fmly) **S** £45-£62; **D** £85 **Facilities** STV tea/coffee Dinner available Cen ht Wi-fi Fishing Riding Pool table **Parking** 15 **Notes** LB RS Wed closed during low season

HEXHAM — Map 12 NY96

Hexham Racecourse Caravan Site *(NY919623)*
▶▶▶

Hexham Racecourse NE46 2JP
☎ 01434 606847 & 606881 📄 01434 605814
e-mail: hexrace.caravan@btconnect.com
dir: *From Hexham take B6305 signed Allendale/Alston. Left in 3m signed to racecourse. Site 1.5m on right*

PETS: Public areas disp bin **Exercise area on site** part of car park just outside site gate **Facilities** vet info

Open May-Sep Last arrival 20.00hrs Last departure noon

A part-level and part-sloping grassy site situated on a racecourse overlooking Hexhamshire Moors. The facilities are functional. 4 acre site. 50 touring pitches. Tent pitches. Motorhome pitches.

MATFEN — Map 12 NZ07

PRIMA

Matfen Hall
★★★★ 81% @@ HOTEL

NE20 0RH
☎ 01661 886500 & 855708 📄 01661 886055
e-mail: info@matfenhall.com
web: www.matfenhall.com
dir: *Off A69 to B6318. Hotel just before village*

PETS: Bedrooms unattended **Charges** £10 per night **Public areas** except restaurant, juice bar & conservatory on leads **Grounds** on leads **Exercise area** surrounding area **Other** charge for damage

This fine mansion lies in landscaped parkland overlooking its own golf course. Bedrooms are a blend of contemporary and traditional, but all are very comfortable and well equipped. Impressive public rooms include a splendid drawing room and the elegant Library and Print Room Restaurant, as well as a conservatory bar and very stylish spa, leisure and conference facilities.

Rooms 53 (11 fmly) **Facilities** Spa STV FTV ⊗ supervised ⌁ 27 Putt green Gym Sauna Steam room Salt grotto Ice fountain Aerobics Driving range Golf academy Xmas Wi-fi **Services** Lift **Parking** 150

OTTERBURN
Map 12 NY89

The Otterburn Tower Hotel
★★★ 78% ◉◉ HOTEL

NE19 1NS
☎ 01830 520620 📠 01830 521504
e-mail: info@otterburntower.com
web: www.otterburntower.com
dir: *In village, on A696 (Newcastle to Edinburgh road)*

PETS: Bedrooms (2 GF) sign ground-floor bedrooms only
Charges £10 per night **Public areas** except restaurant on leads
Grounds on leads disp bin **Exercise area Facilities** food (pre-bookable) food bowl water bowl scoop/disp bags dog walking washing facs cage storage walks info vet info **On Request** fridge access torch towels **Stables** at adjacent stud farm **Other** gun dog training days **Resident Pets:** Pete (Jack Russell), Logan (Springer Spaniel)

Built by a cousin of William the Conqueror, this mansion is set in its own wooded grounds. The property is steeped in history, and Sir Walter Scott stayed here in 1812. Bedrooms come in a variety of sizes and some have huge ornamental fireplaces; though furnished in period style, they are equipped with all modern amenities. The restaurant features 16th-century oak panelling.

Rooms 18 (2 fmly) (2 GF) **Facilities** STV FTV Fishing 🎣
Clay target shooting 🎵 Xmas New Year Wi-fi Child facilities
Parking 70

SEAHOUSES
Map 12 NU23

Bamburgh Castle Inn
★★★ INN

NE68 7SQ
☎ 01665 720283 📠 01665 720284
e-mail: enquiries@bamburghcastleinn.co.uk
web: www.bamburghcastleinn.co.uk
dir: *A1 onto B1341 to Bamburgh, B1340 to Seahouses, follow signs to harbour*

PETS: (8 GF) **Charges** £5 per night **Public areas** except bar area on leads **Grounds** on leads disp bin **Exercise area** nearby **Facilities** water bowl cage storage walks info **On Request** fridge access torch towels

Situated in a prime location on the quayside in the popular coastal resort of Seahouses, this establishment has arguably the best viewpoint along the coast. Dating back to the 18th century, the inn has been transformed in recent years and has superb dining and bar areas, with outside seating available in warmer weather. There are smart, comfortable bedrooms, many with views of the Farne Islands and the inn's famous namesake Bamburgh Castle.

Rooms 27 en suite 2 annexe en suite (6 fmly) (8 GF)
Facilities FTV TVL tea/coffee Dinner available Cen ht Sauna
Solarium Gym **Parking** 35 **Notes** LB

NOTTINGHAMSHIRE

HOLME PIERREPONT
Map 8 SK63

Holme Grange Cottage
★★★ GUEST ACCOMMODATION

Adbolton Ln NG12 2LU
☎ 0115 981 0413
e-mail: jean.colinwightman@talk21.com
dir: *Off A52 SE of Nottingham, opp National Water Sports Centre main entrance*

PETS: Bedrooms Charges £2 per night **Public areas** except dining room on leads **Grounds Exercise area** adjacent **Facilities** cage storage vet info **Restrictions** no Rottweilers, Pit Bull Terriers or Rhodesian Ridgebacks **Resident Pet:** Peggy (Cavalier King Charles Spaniel)

A stone's throw from the National Water Sports Centre, this establishment with its own all-weather tennis court is ideal for the active guest. Indeed, when not providing warm hospitality and freshly cooked breakfasts, the proprietor is usually on the golf course.

Rooms 3 rms (1 en suite) (1 fmly) **S** £32-£36; **D** £52-£58
Facilities TVL tea/coffee Cen ht Wi-fi 🐾 **Parking** 6 **Notes** LB
Closed Xmas 🐾

MANSFIELD
Map 8 SK56

Tall Trees Touring Park *(SK551626)*
▶▶▶

Old Mill Ln, Forest Town NG19 0JP
☎ 01623 626503 & 07770 661957
e-mail: info@talltreestouringpark.co.uk
dir: *A60 from Mansfield towards Worksop. After 1m turn right at lights into Old Mill Lane. Site approx 0.5m on left*

PETS: Charges £1 per night **Public areas** disp bin
Exercise area on site

Open all year Last arrival anytime

A very pleasant park situated just on the outskirts of Mansfield and within easy walking distance of shops and restaurants. It is surrounded on three sides by trees and shrubbery, and securely set at the back of the residential park. At the time of our inspection the small touring area was undergoing a major redevelopment, with the addition of a new facilities block, a fishing lake to the rear of the site and an extra grassed area to give more space for caravans and tents. 3 acre site. 15 touring pitches. 15 hardstandings. Tent pitches. Motorhome pitches.

NOTTINGHAM — Map 8 SK54

Hart's Hotel
★★★★ 82% ⊛⊛ HOTEL
Standard Hill, Park Row NG1 6FN
☎ 0115 988 1900 📄 0115 947 7600
e-mail: reception@hartsnottingham.co.uk
web: www.hartsnottingham.co.uk
dir: At junct of Park Row & Ropewalk

PETS: Bedrooms (7 GF) **Charges** £5 per night **Exercise area** local walks **Facilities** walks info vet info **On Request** fridge access torch towels **Other** charge for damage **Restrictions** certain breeds may not be accepted, please phone for details

This outstanding modern building stands on the site of the ramparts of the medieval castle, overlooking the city. Many of the bedrooms enjoy splendid views. Rooms are well appointed and stylish, while the Park Bar is the focal point of the public areas; service is professional and caring. Fine dining is offered at nearby Hart's Restaurant. Secure parking and private gardens are an added bonus.

Rooms 32 (1 fmly) (7 GF) **D** £125-£260* **Facilities** STV FTV Xmas New Year Wi-fi **Services** Lift **Parking** 16

Best Western Bestwood Lodge
★★★ 71% HOTEL
Bestwood Country Park, Arnold NG5 8NE
☎ 0115 920 3011 📄 0115 964 9678
e-mail: enquiries@bestwoodlodgehotel.co.uk
web: www.bw-bestwoodlodge.co.uk
dir: 3m N off A60. Left at lights into Oxclose Ln, right at next lights into Queens Bower Rd. 1st right. Keep right at fork in road

PETS: Bedrooms unattended **Charges** £10 per night **Public areas** except restaurant on leads **Grounds** disp bin **Exercise area** nearby country park **Facilities** cage storage walks info vet info **On Request** fridge access **Other** charge for damage **Restrictions** well behaved dogs only

Set in 700 acres of parkland this Victorian building, once a hunting lodge, has stunning architecture that includes Gothic features and high vaulted ceilings. Bedrooms include all the modern comforts, suitable for both business and leisure guests, and the popular restaurant serves an extensive menu.

Rooms 39 (5 fmly) **Facilities** FTV ☝ Guided walks Xmas Wi-fi **Parking** 120 **Notes** RS 25 Dec & 1 Jan

Nottingham Gateway
★★★ 68% HOTEL
Nuthall Rd, Cinderhill NG8 6AZ
☎ 0115 979 4949 📄 0115 979 4744
e-mail: sales@nottinghamgatewayhotel.co.uk
web: www.nottinghamgatewayhotel.co.uk
dir: M1 junct 26, A610, hotel on 3rd rdbt on left

PETS: Bedrooms unattended **Grounds** on leads disp bin **Exercise area** 0.25m **Facilities** cage storage vet info **On Request** fridge access **Other** charge for damage

Located approximately three miles from the city centre, and with easy access to the M1. This modern hotel provides spacious public areas, with the popular Bows Gallery Restaurant and lounge bar, and the contemporary accommodation is suitably well equipped. Ample parking is a bonus.

Rooms 108 (18 fmly) (6 smoking) **S** £49.95-£85; **D** £54.95-£100 (incl. bkfst)* **Facilities** STV FTV Xmas New Year **Services** Lift **Parking** 250 **Notes** LB

Rutland Square Hotel
★★★ 68% HOTEL
St James St NG1 6FJ
☎ 0115 941 1114 📄 0115 941 0014
e-mail: rutland.square@forestdale.com
web: www.rutlandsquarehotel.co.uk
dir: Follow signs to castle. Hotel on right 50yds beyond castle

PETS: Bedrooms sign **Charges** £7.50 per night **Public areas** except bar & restaurant on leads **Facilities** food (pre-bookable) food bowl water bowl vet info **On Request** fridge access towels **Other** charge for damage

The enviable location in the heart of the city adjacent to the castle makes this hotel a popular choice with both leisure and business travellers. The hotel is modern and comfortable with excellent business facilities. Bedrooms offer a host of thoughtful extras to guests and the penthouse has its own jacuzzi. The contemporary Woods Restaurant offers a full range of dining options.

Rooms 87 (3 fmly) **Facilities** FTV Discounted day passes to nearby gym Xmas Wi-fi **Services** Lift **Parking** 30 **Notes** LB

Fairhaven

★★ GUEST ACCOMMODATION

19 Meadow Rd, Beeston NG9 1JP
☎ 0115 922 7509 📄 0115 922 5344
e-mail: info@fairhavennottingham.com
web: www.fairhavennottingham.com
dir: *A52 onto B6005 for Beeston station, 200yds after bridge*

PETS: Bedrooms (1 GF) certain rooms only **Charges** £5 per night **Exercise area** 10 mins' walk **Restrictions** no Rottweilers **Resident Pet:** Kevin (dog)

This well-established guest accommodation is in the quiet residential suburb of Beeston on the outskirts of Nottingham. The public rooms offer a stylish reception lounge, and breakfast is served in the cosy dining room. The bedrooms vary in style and size.

Rooms 14 rms (10 en suite) (1 fmly) (1 GF) **S** £30-£42; **D** £52
Facilities tea/coffee Cen ht Licensed Wi-fi **Parking** 13

Thornton's Holt Camping Park *(SK638377)*

▶▶▶

Stragglethorpe Rd, Stragglethorpe NG12 2JZ
☎ 0115 933 2125 & 933 4204 📄 0115 933 3318
e-mail: camping@thorntons-holt.co.uk
dir: *Take A52, 3m E of Nottingham. Turn S at lights towards Cropwell Bishop. Site 0.5m on left. Or A46 SE of Nottingham. N at lights. Site 2.5m on right*

PETS: Public areas except swimming pool & central toilet block **Exercise area** public footpaths **Facilities** washing facs walks info vet info **Other** disposal bags available **Resident Pets:** Pickle (Border Terrier), Sprocket, Perkins & Scrabble (cats), Eric (horse)

Open Apr-6 Nov rs Nov-Mar pool & shop closed Last arrival 20.00hrs Last departure noon

A well-run family site in former meadowland, with pitches located among young trees and bushes for a rural atmosphere and outlook. The toilets are housed in converted farm buildings, and an indoor swimming pool is a popular attraction. 13 acre site. 155 touring pitches. 35 hardstandings. 20 seasonal pitches. Tent pitches. Motorhome pitches.

Notes Noise curfew at 22.00hrs.

Teversal Camping & Caravanning Club Site

(SK472615)

▶▶▶▶▶

Silverhill Ln NG17 3JJ
☎ 01623 551838
dir: *M1 junct 28 onto A38 towards Mansfield. Left at lights onto B6027. At top of hill straight over at lights & left at Tesco Express. Right onto B6014, left at Craven Arms, site on left*

PETS: Public areas except facility block (ex assist dogs) **Exercise area** surrounding countryside **Facilities** food dog chews cat treats washing facs walks info vet info **Other** prior notice required **Resident Pet:** Tommy (Springer Spaniel)

Open all year Last arrival 20.00hrs Last departure noon

A top notch park with excellent purpose-built facilities and innovative, hands-on owners. Each pitch is spacious, the excellent toilet facilities are state-of-the-art, and there are views of, and access to, the countryside and nearby Silverhill Community Woods. The attention to detail and all-round quality are truly exceptional. 6 acre site. 126 touring pitches. 92 hardstandings. Tent pitches. Motorhome pitches. 1 static. 2 bell tents/yurts.

Notes Site gates closed 23.00hrs-07.00hrs.

Riverside Caravan Park *(SK582790)*

▶▶▶

Central Av S80 1ER
☎ 01909 474118
dir: *From A57 E of town, take B6040 signed Town Centre at rdbt. Follow international camping sign to site*

PETS: Public areas except toilet block **Exercise area** Clumber Park 4m; Chesterfield canal walk 0.25 **Facilities** washing facs vet info **Resident Pet:** Thomas (cat)

Open all year Last arrival 18.00hrs Last departure noon

A very well maintained park within the attractive market town of Worksop and next door to the cricket and bowls club where Riverside customers are made welcome. This is an ideal park for those wishing to be within walking distance of all amenities yet also within a 10-minute car journey of the extensive Clumber Park and numerous good garden centres. The towpath of the adjacent Chesterfield Canal provides excellent walking opportunities. 4 acre site. 60 touring pitches. 59 hardstandings. Tent pitches. Motorhome pitches.

Notes No bikes around reception or in toilet block.

ENGLAND

ENGLAND

OXFORDSHIRE

BANBURY
Map 4 SP44

Fairlawns

★★★ GUEST ACCOMMODATION

60 Oxford Rd OX16 9AN
☎ 01295 262461 & 07831 330220 📠 01295 261296
e-mail: fairlawnsgh@aol.com
dir: 0.5m S of Banbury Cross on A4260 opp Horton Hospital

PETS: Bedrooms (9 GF) **Grounds** disp bin **Exercise area** park nearby **Facilities** vet info **On Request** fridge access torch towels **Other** charge for damage **Resident Pets:** Rosie (Boxer), Harley (cat)

This extended Edwardian house retains many original features and has a convenient location. Bedrooms are mixed in size, and all are neatly furnished, some with direct access to the car park. A comprehensive breakfast is served in the traditional dining room and a selection of soft drinks and snacks is also available.

Rooms 11 rms (10 en suite) 6 annexe en suite (5 fmly) (9 GF)
S £54; **D** £64 **Facilities** FTV tea/coffee Direct Dial Cen ht Wi-fi **Parking** 17

Barnstones Caravan & Camping Site
(SP455454)

▶ ▶ ▶ ▶

Great Bourton OX17 1QU
☎ 01295 750289
dir: Take A423 from Banbury signed Southam. In 3m turn right signed Gt Bourton/Cropredy, site 100yds on right

PETS: Public areas disp bin **Exercise area on site** fenced area (off lead) **Facilities** washing facs dog grooming walks info vet info

Open all year

A popular, neatly-laid-out site with plenty of hardstandings, some fully serviced pitches, a smart up-to-date toilet block, and excellent rally facilities. Well run by a very personable owner, this is an excellent value park. 3 acre site. 49 touring pitches. 44 hardstandings. Tent pitches. Motorhome pitches.

Notes

Bo Peep Farm Caravan Park (SP481348)

▶ ▶ ▶ ▶

Bo Peep Farm, Aynho Rd, Adderbury OX17 3NP
☎ 01295 810605 📠 01295 810605
e-mail: warden@bo-peep.co.uk
dir: 1m E of Adderbury & A4260, on B4100 (Aynho road)

PETS: Charges £2 per stay **Public areas** on leads disp bin **Exercise area on site** extensive walks **Facilities** food food bowl water bowl dog chews cat treats scoop/disp bags leads washing facs walks info vet info **Resident Pets:** 3 cats

Open Mar-Oct Last arrival 20.00hrs Last departure noon

A delightful park with good views and a spacious feel. Four well laid out camping areas including two with hardstandings and a separate tent field are all planted with maturing shrubs and trees. The two facility blocks are built in attractive Cotswold stone. Unusually there is a bay in which you can clean your caravan or motorhome. There are four miles of on-site walks including through woods and on the river bank. 13 acre site. 104 touring pitches. Tent pitches. Motorhome pitches.

BLETCHINGDON
Map 4 SP51

The Oxfordshire Inn

★★★ 64% HOTEL

Heathfield Village OX5 3DX
☎ 01869 351444 📠 01869 351555
e-mail: staff@oxfordshireinn.co.uk
web: www.oxfordshireinn.co.uk
dir: M40 junct 9, A34 towards Oxford, then A4027 towards Bletchingdon. Hotel signed 0.7m on right

PETS: Bedrooms (15 GF) unattended certain bedrooms only **Charges** £10 per night **Grounds** on leads disp bin **Exercise area** large grounds & fields surrounding **Facilities** vet info **Stables** adjacent **Other** charge for damage

A converted farmhouse with additional outbuildings that is located close to major motorway networks. Accommodation is set around an open courtyard, and includes suites that have four-poster beds. There is a spacious bar and restaurant.

Rooms 28 (4 fmly) (15 GF) **Facilities** Putt green Golf driving range Xmas New Year Wi-fi **Parking** 50 **Notes** LB

Greenhill Leisure Park (SP488178)

▶▶▶▶

Greenhill Farm, Station Rd OX5 3BQ
☎ 01869 351600 📄 01869 350918
e-mail: info@greenhill-leisure-park.co.uk
dir: M40 junct 9, A34 south for 3m. Take B4027 to Bletchingdon.
Site 0.5m after village on left

PETS: Charges dog £3 per night Public areas except play area,
shower area & games room disp bin Exercise area on site field
with fenced area Exercise area 1m Facilities food dog chews
cat treats leads walks info vet info Other dogs accepted from
1 Feb to 30 Sep only disposal bags available

Open all year rs Oct-Mar no dogs, shop & games room closed
Last arrival 21.00hrs Last departure noon

An all-year round park set in open countryside near the village
of Bletchingdon. Fishing is available in the nearby river or in the
parks two well stocked lakes. Pitches are very spacious and the
park is very family orientated and in keeping with the owner's
theme of 'Where fun meets the countryside'. The facilities are also
very good. 7 acre site. 92 touring pitches. 30 hardstandings. 20
seasonal pitches. Tent pitches. Motorhome pitches.

Notes No camp fires, latest arrival time 20.00hrs in winter.

BURFORD Map 4 SP21

The Lamb Inn

★★★ 83% ◉◉ SMALL HOTEL

Sheep St OX18 4LR
☎ 01993 823155 📄 01993 822228
e-mail: info@lambinn-burford.co.uk
web: www.cotswold-inns-hotels.co.uk/lamb
dir: A40 into Burford, downhill, 1st left into Sheep St, hotel last
on right

PETS: Bedrooms (4 GF) unattended ground-floor bedrooms
only Public areas except eating areas Grounds on leads
Exercise area footpaths Facilities food bowl water bowl cage
storage walks info vet info On Request fridge access torch
towels Other charge for damage

This enchanting old inn is just a short walk from the centre
of this delightful Cotswold village. Inside an abundance of
character and charm is found in the cosy lounge with log fire,
and intimate bar with flagged floors. An elegant restaurant offers
locally sourced produce in carefully prepared dishes. Bedrooms,
some with original features, are comfortable and well appointed.

Rooms 17 (1 fmly) (4 GF) S £120-£155; D £155-£180 (incl.
bkfst)* Facilities Xmas New Year Wi-fi Notes LB

The Bay Tree Hotel

★★★ 81% ◉ HOTEL

Sheep St OX18 4LW
☎ 01993 822791 📄 01993 823008
e-mail: info@baytreehotel.info
web: www.cotswold-inns-hotels.co.uk/bay-tree
dir: A40 or A361 to Burford. From High St turn into Sheep St, next
to old market square. Hotel on right

PETS: Bedrooms (3 GF) Garden & Superior Garden bedrooms
only Charges £10-£30 per night Public areas except eating
areas Grounds Facilities cage storage walks info vet info
On Request torch towels Other charge for damage

The modern decorative style combines seamlessly with features
from this delightful inn's long history. Bedrooms are tastefully
furnished and some have four-poster and half-tester beds. Public
areas consist of a character bar, a sophisticated airy restaurant,
a selection of meeting rooms and an attractive walled garden.

Rooms 21 (13 annexe) (2 fmly) (3 GF) S £120-£130; D £170-£180
(incl. bkfst)* Facilities ◈ Xmas New Year Wi-fi Parking 50
Notes LB

The Bull at Burford

★★★★ ◉◉ 🍴 RESTAURANT WITH ROOMS

105 High St OX18 4RG
☎ 01993 822220 📄 01993 824055
e-mail: info@bullatburford.co.uk
dir: In town centre

PETS: Bedrooms unattended certain bedrooms only
Public areas except restaurant on leads Exercise area 200mtrs
Facilities walks info vet info Other charge for damage

Situated in the heart of a pretty Cotswold town, The Bull has
undergone major refurbishment. Originally built in 1475 as a
rest house for the local priory, it now has stylish, attractively
presented bedrooms that still reflect charm and character. Dinner
should not be missed and the award-winning restaurant has an
imaginative menu along with an excellent choice of wines. Lunch
is served daily and afternoon tea is popular. There is a residents'
lounge, and free Wi-fi is available.

Rooms 12 en suite (1 fmly) S £60-£105; D £70-£140
Facilities FTV tea/coffee Dinner available Cen ht Wi-fi Parking 6
Notes LB

BURFORD *continued*

The Inn For All Seasons

★★★ RESTAURANT WITH ROOMS

The Barringtons OX18 4TN
☎ 01451 844324 📄 01451 844375
e-mail: sharp@innforallseasons.com
web: www.innforallseasons.com
dir: *3m W of Burford on A40 towards Cheltenham*

PETS: Bedrooms unattended sign **Charges** £5 per night £15 per week **Public areas** except restaurant & breakfast room **Grounds** disp bin **Exercise area** adjacent **Facilities** food (pre-bookable) food bowl water bowl leads dog walking washing facs cage storage walks info vet info **On Request** fridge access torch towels **Other** charge for damage prior notice required **Resident Pets:** Bob (Black Labrador), Guscot (Springer Spaniel), Ted (German Shepherd)

This charming 16th-century coaching inn is close to the pretty village of Burford. The individually styled bedrooms are comfortable, and include a four-poster room, as well as a family room that sleeps four. The public areas include a cosy bar with oak beams and real fires. There is a good choice on the bar menu, and evening meals feature the best of local Cotswold produce. The inn is certainly a dog-friendly establishment and there are ground-floor bedrooms with direct access to the garden and an exercise area.

Rooms 10 en suite (1 fmly) **Facilities** Dinner available

Best Western Sudbury House Hotel & Conference Centre

★★★ 74% ⊛ HOTEL

London St SN7 8AA
☎ 01367 241272 📄 01367 242346
e-mail: stay@sudburyhouse.co.uk
web: www.sudburyhouse.co.uk
dir: *Off A420, signed Folly Hill*

PETS: Bedrooms (10 GF) unattended ground-floor bedrooms only **Charges** £10 per night **Public areas** except restaurant & bar area **Grounds** disp bin **Exercise area** nearby **Facilities** food bowl water bowl washing facs cage storage walks info vet info **On Request** fridge access torch towels **Other** charge for damage

Situated on the edge of the Cotswolds and in nine acres of pleasant grounds, this hotel offers spacious and well-equipped bedrooms that are attractively decorated in warm colours. Dining options include the comfortable restaurant for a good selection of carefully presented dishes, and the bar for lighter options; a comprehensive room-service menu is also available.

Rooms 49 (2 fmly) (10 GF) (2 smoking) **S** £72-£140; **D** £92-£160 (incl. bkfst)* **Facilities** STV 🏊 Gym Boules New Year Wi-fi **Services** Lift **Parking** 100 **Notes** LB

Chowle Farmhouse Bed & Breakfast *(SU272925)*

★★★★ FARMHOUSE

SN7 7SR
☎ 01367 241688 Mr & Mrs Muir
e-mail: info@chowlefarmhouse.co.uk
web: www.chowlefarmhouse.co.uk
dir: *From Faringdon rdbt on A420, 2m W on right. From Watchfield rdbt 1.5m E on left*

PETS: Bedrooms (1 GF) ground-floor bedroom only **Public areas** except dining rooms & upstairs on leads **Grounds** on leads disp bin **Exercise area** fields adjacent **Facilities** feeding mat scoop/disp bags leads washing facs cage storage walks info vet info **On Request** fridge access torch towels **Stables** 0.5m **Other** paddock available for horses (stabling can be arranged) **Resident Pets:** Susie (Yellow Labrador), Winston (Black Labrador), Angus, Lulu, Marvin, Denzel & Lola (cats), Dexter cows, guinea pigs, ferrets, chickens, guinea fowl, quail, tropical fish

Chowle is a delightful modern farmhouse in a quiet setting, just off the A420 and ideally placed for visiting Oxford and Swindon. Bedrooms are very well equipped, and there is a charming and airy downstairs breakfast room. An outdoor pool and hot tub are available to guests. There is ample parking space.

Rooms 4 en suite (1 GF) **Facilities** FTV tea/coffee Cen ht Wi-fi 🏌 Golf 9 Fishing Riding Sauna Gym **Parking** 10 **Notes** LB 10 acres pedigree beef cattle

The Trout at Tadpole Bridge
★★★★ ⊚ INN
Buckland Marsh SN7 8RF
☎ 01367 870382 🖷 01367 870912
e-mail: info@troutinn.co.uk
web: www.troutinn.co.uk
dir: A420 Swindon to Oxford road, turn signed Bampton. Inn 2m on right

PETS: Bedrooms (4 GF) unattended Public areas Grounds on leads disp bin Facilities food bowl water bowl dog chews walks info vet info On Request fridge access towels Other charge for damage

The Trout is located 'where the River Thames meets the Cotswolds'. The peaceful location offers riverside walks from the door and berthing for up to six boats. Bedrooms and bathrooms are located adjacent to the inn and all rooms are very comfortable and well equipped with welcome extras. The main bar and restaurant offer an excellent selection of carefully prepared local produce at both lunch and dinner, together with cask ales and a varied choice of wines by the glass.

Rooms 3 en suite 3 annexe en suite (1 fmly) (4 GF) Facilities FTV tea/coffee Dinner available Cen ht Wi-fi Fishing Parking 40 Notes LB Closed 25-26 Dec No coaches

The Miller of Mansfield
★★★★★ ⊚ RESTAURANT WITH ROOMS
High St RG8 9AW
☎ 01491 872829 🖷 01491 873100
e-mail: reservations@millerofmansfield.com
web: www.millerofmansfield.com
dir: M40 junct 7, S on A329 towards Benson, A4074 towards Reading, B4009 towards Goring. Or M4 junct 12, S on A4 towards Newbury. 3rd rdbt onto A340 to Pangbourne. A329 to Streatley, right at lights onto B4009 into Goring

PETS: Bedrooms unattended Charges Public areas except restaurant Grounds Exercise area approx 0.5m Facilities water bowl cage storage walks info vet info On Request torch towels Other charge for damage

The frontage of this former coaching inn hides sumptuous rooms with a distinctive and individual style, an award-winning restaurant that serves appealing dishes using locally sourced ingredients, and a comfortable bar, which serves real ales, fine wines, afternoon tea and a bar menu for a quick bite to eat.

Rooms 13 en suite (2 fmly) Facilities FTV tea/coffee Dinner available Direct Dial Cen ht Wi-fi Parking 2 Notes LB

Hotel du Vin Henley-on-Thames
★★★★ 76% ⊚⊚ TOWN HOUSE HOTEL
New St RG9 2BP
☎ 01491 848400 🖷 01491 848401
e-mail: info.henley@hotelduvin.com
web: www.hotelduvin.com
dir: M4 junct 8/9 signed High Wycombe, 2nd exit onto A404 in 2m. A4130 into Henley, over bridge, through lights, up Hart St, right onto Bell St, right onto New St, hotel on right

PETS: Bedrooms (4 GF) Charges £10 per night £70 per week Public areas except restaurant on leads Grounds on leads Exercise area nearby Facilities food bowl water bowl bedding vet info On Request torch

Situated just 50 yards from the water's edge, this hotel retains the character and much of the architecture of the former brewery. Food, and naturally wine, take on a strong focus here and guests will find an interesting mix of dishes to choose from; there are three private dining rooms where the fermentation room and old malt house once were; alfresco dining is popular when the weather permits. Bedrooms provide comfort, style and a good range of facilities including power showers. Parking is available and there is a drop-off point in the courtyard.

Rooms 43 (4 fmly) (4 GF) S £110-£435; D £110-£435* Facilities STV Use of local spa & gym Xmas New Year Wi-fi Services Air con Parking 36 Notes LB

The Baskerville
★★★★ INN
Station Rd, Lower Shiplake RG9 3NY
☎ 0118 940 3332
e-mail: enquiries@thebaskerville.com
web: www.thebaskerville.com
dir: 2m S of Henley in Lower Shiplake. Off A4155 onto Station Rd, inn signed

PETS: Bedrooms unattended Charges Public areas except public bar on leads Grounds on leads Exercise area village lanes & riverbanks nearby Facilities water bowl cage storage vet info Stables nearby Other charge for damage

Located close to Shiplake station and just a short drive from Henley, this smart accommodation is perfect for a business or leisure break. It is a good base for exploring the Oxfordshire countryside, and the enjoyable hearty meals served in the cosy restaurant use good local produce.

Rooms 4 en suite (1 fmly) S £77.50; D £87.50 Facilities STV tea/coffee Dinner available Cen ht Wi-fi Parking 15 Notes No coaches

The Kingham Plough

★★★★ ◉◉ ⌂ INN

The Green OX7 6YD
☎ 01608 658327
e-mail: book@thekinghamplough.co.uk
dir: *On the green in Kingham Village*

PETS: Bedrooms unattended annexe bedrooms only **Charges** £10 per stay **Public areas** only in bar area on leads **Grounds** disp bin **Exercise area** nearby **Facilities** food bowl water bowl bedding dog chews scoop/disp bags walks info vet info **Stables** 0.5m **Other** charge for damage

The Kingham Plough is a quintessential Cotswold inn, sympathetically refurbished and set in the pretty village of Kingham, just minutes away from the well known Daylesford Organic estate. The seven en suite bedrooms have Cotswold character and offer impressive quality and comfort. Dining is memorable both for evening meals and at breakfast; the team here deliver excellence using locally sourced produce.

Rooms 7 en suite (2 fmly) **S** £75-£105; **D** £90-£130 **Facilities** FTV tea/coffee Dinner available Cen ht Wi-fi **Parking** 25 **Notes** Closed 25 Dec

Moat End

★★★★ ⌂ BED AND BREAKFAST

The Moat OX7 6XZ
☎ 01608 658090 & 07765 278399
e-mail: moatend@gmail.com
web: www.moatend.co.uk
dir: *Off B4450/A436 into village centre*

PETS: Bedrooms Charges £10 per stay **Public areas** on leads **Grounds** on leads disp bin **Facilities** washing facs cage storage walks info vet info **On Request** fridge access torch towels **Stables Other** horses £15 per night (stabling, turn out & hay) **Resident Pets:** Domino (cat), Heather, Cobweb & Rolo (ponies)

This converted barn lies in a peaceful Cotswold village and has splendid country views. Its well-appointed bedrooms either have a jacuzzi or large shower cubicles, one with hydro-massage jets. The attractive dining room leads to a comfortable beamed sitting room with a stone fireplace. Quality local ingredients are used in the wholesome breakfasts. The owner has won an award for green tourism by reducing the impact of the business on the environment.

Rooms 3 en suite (1 fmly) **S** £55-£60; **D** £70-£80 **Facilities** TVL tea/coffee Cen ht Wi-fi **Parking** 4 **Notes** LB Closed Xmas & New Year 🐾

The Tollgate Inn & Restaurant

★★★★ ⌂ INN

Church St OX7 6YA
☎ 01608 658389
e-mail: info@thetollgate.com

PETS: Bedrooms (4 GF) unattended ground-floor bedrooms only **Charges** £10 per stay **Public areas** except restaurant & lounge on leads **Grounds** disp bin **Exercise area Exercise area** 200mtrs **Facilities** walks info vet info **On Request** fridge access **Other** please phone for further details of pet facilities **Resident Pets:** Guinness (Black Labrador), Tinker (cat)

Situated in the idyllic Cotswold village of Kingham, this Grade II listed Georgian building has been lovingly restored to provide a complete home-from-home among some of the most beautiful countryside in Britain. The Tollgate provides comfortable, well-equipped accommodation in pleasant surroundings. A good choice of menu for lunch and dinner is available with fine use made of fresh and local produce. Guests can also be sure of a hearty breakfast which is served in the modern, well-equipped dining room.

Rooms 5 en suite 4 annexe en suite (1 fmly) (4 GF) **Facilities** tea/coffee Dinner available Cen ht Wi-fi **Parking** 12

Fallowfields Country House Hotel & Restaurant

★★★ **73%** HOTEL

Faringdon Rd OX13 5BH
☎ 01865 820416 📠 01865 821275
e-mail: stay@fallowfields.com
web: www.fallowfields.com
dir: A34 (Oxford Ring Rd) take A420 towards Swindon. At junct with A415 left for 100yds then turn at mini rdbt. Hotel on left after 1m

PETS: Bedrooms unattended sign **Charges** £5 per night **Public areas** except restaurant **Grounds** disp bin **Facilities** food bowl water bowl washing facs dog grooming cage storage walks info vet info **On Request** fridge access torch **Stables** 800mtrs **Other** charge for damage **Resident Pets:** Phoebe & Kasper (cats)

Located in rural Oxfordshire just ten miles from Oxford city centre, this small family-run hotel offers the personal touch. The bedrooms are generous in size and some have delightful views over the croquet lawn. The grounds are home to several breeds of cattle, pigs and chickens along with the kitchen garden where much of the produce for the menus is sourced.

Rooms 10 (2 fmly) **S** £75-£125; **D** £125-£175 (incl. bkfst)*
Facilities FTV ⚓ Xmas New Year Wi-fi **Parking** 50

Barceló Oxford Hotel

★★★★ **77%** ⊛ HOTEL

Godstow Rd, Wolvercote Roundabout OX2 8AL
☎ 01865 489988 📠 01865 489952
e-mail: oxford@barcelo-hotels.co.uk
web: www.barcelo-hotels.co.uk
dir: Adjacent to A34/A40, 2m from city centre

PETS: Bedrooms (89 GF) sign **Charges** £15 per night **Grounds** on leads disp bin **Exercise area** at rear of hotel, canal walk (1m) **Facilities** walks info vet info **Other** charge for damage **Restrictions** small dogs only

Conveniently located on the northern edge of the city centre, this purpose-built hotel offers bedrooms that are bright, modern and well equipped. Guests can eat in the Medio Restaurant or try the Cappuccino Lounge menu. There is the option to eat alfresco on the Patio Terrace when the weather is fine. The hotel offers impressive conference, business and leisure facilities.

Rooms 168 (11 fmly) (89 GF) **Facilities** Spa STV ⊛ supervised Gym Squash Steam room Beauty treatments New Year Wi-fi **Parking** 250

Old Parsonage

★★★★ **75%** ⊛ TOWN HOUSE HOTEL

1 Banbury Rd OX2 6NN
☎ 01865 310210 📠 01865 311262
e-mail: info@oldparsonage-hotel.co.uk
web: www.oldparsonage-hotel.co.uk
dir: From Oxford ring road to city centre via Summertown. Hotel last building on right before entering St Giles

PETS: Bedrooms (10 GF) unattended **Public areas** except restaurant on leads **Grounds Exercise area** 2 mins' walk **Facilities** water bowl bedding walks info vet info **Other** charge for damage dog baskets available & special menus on request, pet sitting on request **Restrictions** well behaved dogs only

Dating back in parts to the 16th century, this stylish hotel offers great character and charm and is conveniently located at the northern edge of the city centre. Bedrooms are attractively styled and particularly well appointed. The focal point of the operation is the busy all-day bar and restaurant; the small garden areas and terraces prove popular in summer months.

Rooms 30 (4 fmly) (10 GF) **D** £132.50-£225* **Facilities** STV FTV In room beauty treatments Free use of nearby leisure facilities & house bikes ♫ Xmas New Year Wi-fi **Services** Air con **Parking** 14 **Notes** LB

Westwood Country Hotel

★★★ **78%** HOTEL

Hinksey Hill, Boars Hill OX1 5BG
☎ 01865 735408 📠 01865 736536
e-mail: reservations@westwoodhotel.co.uk
web: www.westwoodhotel.co.uk
dir: Off Oxford ring road at Hinksey Hill junct towards Boars Hill & Wootton. At top of hill road bends to left. Hotel on right

PETS: Bedrooms (7 GF) **Charges** £100 deposit + £15 per night **Grounds** on leads **Exercise area** 50mtrs **Other** charge for damage **Restrictions** small dogs only

This Edwardian country-house hotel is prominently set in terraced landscaped grounds and is within easy reach of the city centre by car. The hotel is modern in style with very comfortable, well-equipped and tastefully decorated bedrooms. Public areas include a contemporary bar, a cosy lounge and a restaurant overlooking the pretty garden.

Rooms 20 (5 fmly) (7 GF) **Facilities** FTV Arrangement with local health club, golf club & riding school Xmas New Year Wi-fi **Parking** 50 **Notes** LB

OXFORD *continued*

Bath Place Hotel

★★ **65%** METRO HOTEL

4-5 Bath Place, Holywell St OX1 3SU

☎ 01865 791812 📄 01865 791834

e-mail: info@bathplace.co.uk

dir: *On S side of Holywell St (parallel to High St)*

PETS: Bedrooms (5 GF) **Charges** £10 per night **Public areas** except dining room on leads **Exercise area** park 500mtrs **Facilities** water bowl walks info vet info **Other** charge for damage **Resident Pet:** Hamish (Border Terrier)

The hotel has been created from a group of 17th-century cottages originally built by Flemish weavers who were permitted to settle outside the city walls. This lovely hotel is very much at the heart of the city today and offers individually designed bedrooms, including some with four-posters.

Rooms 16 (3 fmly) (5 GF) **S** £89-£105; **D** £118-£148 (incl. bkfst)* **Facilities** FTV Wi-fi **Parking** 16

STANDLAKE   Map 4 SP30

Lincoln Farm Park Oxfordshire *(SP395028)*

►►►►►

High St OX29 7RH

☎ 01865 300239 📄 01865 300127

e-mail: info@lincolnfarmpark.co.uk

dir: *In village of Standlake off A415 between Abingdon & Witney, 5m SE of Witney*

PETS: Charges £1.25 per night **Public areas** except children's play area disp bin on leads **Exercise area on site** 2 small dog runs **Facilities** food food bowl water bowl bedding dog chews cat treats litter tray scoop/disp bags leads walks info vet info **Other** prior notice required **Resident Pets:** Chance (Border Collie), 2 Giant Continental rabbits, 4 rabbits, free range chickens

Open Feb-Nov Last arrival 20.00hrs Last departure noon

An attractively landscaped park in a quiet village setting, with superb facilities and a high standard of maintenance. Family rooms, fully serviced pitches, two indoor swimming pools and a fully-equipped gym are part of the comprehensive amenities.

Overall, an excellent top quality park and the perfect base for visiting the Oxfordshire area and the Cotswolds. A warm welcome is assured from the friendly staff. 9 acre site. 90 touring pitches. 75 hardstandings. Tent pitches. Motorhome pitches.

Notes No gazebos, no noise after 23.00hrs.

UPPER HEYFORD   Map 4 SP42

Heyford Leys Camping Park *(SP518256)*

►►►

Camp Rd OX25 5LX

☎ 01869 232048

e-mail: heyfordleys@aol.com

dir: *M40 junct 10 take B430 towards Middleton Stoney. Right after 1.5m marked The Heyford, follow brown signs to site*

PETS: Charges dog £1.02 per night £7.14 per week **Public areas** disp bin **Exercise area on site Exercise area** surrounding area **Facilities** walks info vet info **Other** prior notice required **Resident Pet:** Wilson (dog)

Open all year Last arrival 22.00hrs Last departure 11.00hrs

This small peaceful park near the Cherwell Valley and the village of Upper Heyford is well positioned for visiting nearby Bicester, Oxford and Banbury, as well as being about a 15-minute drive from Silverstone. The facilities are very clean and guests will be assured of a warm welcome. A small fishing lake is also available to customers. 5 acre site. 25 touring pitches. 5 hardstandings. Tent pitches. Motorhome pitches.

Notes No groups, no noise after 20.00hrs.

WALLINGFORD   Map 4 SU68

The Springs Hotel & Golf Club

★★★ **80%** ◉ HOTEL

Wallingford Rd, North Stoke OX10 6BE

☎ 01491 836687 📄 01491 836877

e-mail: info@thespringshotel.com

web: www.thespringshotel.com

dir: *Off A4074 (Oxford-Reading road) onto B4009 (Goring). Hotel approx 1m on right*

PETS: Bedrooms (10 GF) certain bedrooms only (with direct garden access) **Charges** £10 per night **Grounds** on leads **Exercise area** nearby **Facilities** vet info **Other** charge for damage dogs are only accepted by prior arrangement

Set on its own 18-hole, par 72 golf course, this Victorian mansion has a timeless and peaceful atmosphere. The generously equipped, individually styled bedrooms vary in size but many are spacious. Some bedrooms overlook the pool and grounds while others have views of the spring-fed lake as does the elegant restaurant. There is also a comfortable lounge, with original features, to relax in.

Rooms 32 (3 fmly) (10 GF) **Facilities** FTV ⟋ ♨ 18 Putt green Fishing ⛵ Boat trips on Thames Xmas New Year Wi-fi **Parking** 150

⌖ ⌖

Hill Barn (SU337852)

★★★ FARMHOUSE

Sparholt Firs OX12 9XB

☎ 01235 751236 & 07885 368918   Mrs Joanna Whittington

e-mail: jmw@hillbarn.plus.com

dir: W of B4001 on The Ridgeway, 4m N of Wantage

PETS: Bedrooms unattended **Charges** dog £5, horse £10 per night **Public areas Grounds** disp bin **Exercise area** adjacent **Facilities** food (pre-bookable) food bowl water bowl scoop/disp bags leads pet sitting dog walking washing facs cage storage walks info vet info **On Request** fridge access torch towels **Stables Other** charge for damage **Resident Pets:** Ella (Border Terrier), Chillie & Pepper (Labradors)

This working farm offers en suite bedrooms with beautiful distant views over the countryside. The atmosphere is friendly, and guests are able to relax either in the sitting room or in the garden. Breakfast is a highlight with home-made jams and produce from the farm, when available.

Rooms 2 en suite **Facilities** TVL tea/coffee Dinner available Cen ht **Parking** 3 **Notes** LB ⊕ 100 acres horses

The Fleece

★★★ ⌖ INN

11 Church Green OX28 4AZ

☎ 01993 892270 📠 0871 8130458

e-mail: fleece@peachpubs.com

dir: A40 to Witney town centre, on Church Green

PETS: Bedrooms (1 GF) unattended **Charges** £10 per night £70 per week **Public areas Grounds** disp bin **Exercise area** village green **Facilities** water bowl washing facs cage storage walks info vet info **On Request** fridge access towels **Other** please call if there are any specific pet requirements

Set in the centre of Witney overlooking the church green, The Fleece offers ten well equipped en suite modern bedrooms. The popular destination pub offers food all day including breakfast, and a great selection of wines and real ales.

Rooms 7 en suite 3 annexe en suite (1 fmly) (1 GF) **Facilities** tea/coffee Dinner available Direct Dial Cen ht Wi-fi **Parking** 12 **Notes** Closed 25 Dec

⌖ 🐾 ⌖

The Feathers Hotel

★★★★ **79%** ◉◉ TOWN HOUSE HOTEL

Market St OX20 1SX

☎ 01993 812291 📠 01993 813158

e-mail: enquiries@feathers.co.uk

dir: From A44 (Oxford to Woodstock), 1st left after lights. Hotel on left

PETS: Bedrooms (2 GF) unattended certain bedrooms only **Charges** £15 per night **Public areas** except restaurant on leads **Grounds** on leads disp bin **Exercise area** 0.5m **Facilities** food bowl water bowl bedding washing facs cage storage walks info vet info **On Request** fridge access torch towels **Stables** 1m **Other** charge for damage **Resident Pet:** Johann (African Grey parrot)

This intimate and unique hotel enjoys a town centre location with easy access to nearby Blenheim Palace. Public areas are elegant and full of traditional character from the cosy drawing room to the atmospheric restaurant. Individually styled bedrooms are appointed to a high standard and are furnished with attractive period and reproduction furniture.

Rooms 21 (5 annexe) (4 fmly) (2 GF) **S** £104-£189; **D** £104-£349 (incl. bkfst)* **Facilities** FTV Xmas New Year Wi-fi **Notes** LB

WOODSTOCK *continued*

Macdonald Bear

★★★★ 77% ◉◉ HOTEL

Park St OX20 1SZ

☎ 0844 879 9143   🖩 01993 813380

e-mail: gm.bear@macdonaldhotels.co.uk

web: www.macdonaldhotels.co.uk

dir: *M40 junct 9 follow signs for Oxford & Blenheim Palace. A44 to town centre, hotel on left*

PETS: Bedrooms (8 GF) unattended sign ground-floor bedrooms only **Charges** £10 per night **Public areas** except restaurant on leads disp bin **Exercise area** nearby **Facilities** water bowl bedding cage storage walks info **On Request** fridge access **Other** charge for damage **Restrictions** small dogs only

With its ivy-clad façade, oak beams and open fireplaces, this 13th-century coaching inn exudes charm and cosiness. The bedrooms are decorated in a modern style that remains in keeping with the historic character of the building. Public rooms include a variety of function rooms, an intimate bar area and an attractive restaurant where attentive service and good food are offered.

Rooms 54 (18 annexe) (1 fmly) (8 GF) **Facilities** STV Xmas New Year Wi-fi **Parking** 40

RUTLAND

CLIPSHAM
Map 8 SK91

Beech House

★★★★★ ◉◉ 🛏 INN

Main St LE15 7SH

☎ 01780 410355   🖩 01780 410000

e-mail: rooms@theolivebranchpub.com

dir: *From A1 take B668 signed Stretton & Clipsham*

PETS: Bedrooms (3 GF) ground-floor bedrooms only **Charges** £10 per night **Public areas** bar only on leads **Grounds** on leads **Exercise area** field 200mtrs **Facilities** water bowl washing facs walks info vet info **On Request** fridge access towels **Other** charge for damage

Beech House stands over the road from the Olive Branch restaurant. It offers very well furnished bedrooms which include DVD players. Breakfasts are served in the Olive Branch. Excellent lunches and dinners are also available.

Rooms 5 en suite 1 annexe en suite (2 fmly) (3 GF) **S** £97.50-£180; **D** £115-£195 **Facilities** FTV tea/coffee Dinner available Direct Dial Cen ht Wi-fi **Parking** 10 **Notes** LB No coaches

---

EMPINGHAM
Map 4 SK90

The White Horse Inn

★★★ INN

Main St LE15 8PS

☎ 01780 460221   🖩 01780 460521

e-mail: info@whitehorserutland.co.uk

web: www.whitehorserutland.co.uk

dir: *On A606 (Oakham to Stamford road)*

PETS: Bedrooms (5 GF) unattended **Charges** £5 per night **Grounds Exercise area** 10 mins' walk **Facilities** cage storage walks info vet info **On Request** fridge access **Resident Pets:** Tia & Toby (Chocolate Labradors)

This attractive stone-built inn, offering bright, comfortable accommodation, is conveniently located just minutes from the A1. Bedrooms in the main building are spacious and include a number of family rooms. Public areas include a well-stocked bar, a bistro and restaurant where a wide range of meals is served.

Rooms 4 en suite 9 annexe en suite (4 fmly) (5 GF) **S** £53-£63; **D** £70 **Facilities** TVL tea/coffee Dinner available Direct Dial **Parking** 60 **Notes** Closed 25 Dec

---

GREETHAM
Map 8 SK91

Rutland Caravan & Camping *(SK925148)*

►►►►

Park Ln LE15 7FN

☎ 01572 813520

e-mail: info@rutlandcaravanandcamping.co.uk

dir: *From A1 onto B668 towards Greetham. Before Greetham turn right at x-rds, 2nd left to site*

PETS: Charges Public areas except children's play area on leads disp bin **Exercise area on site** 2.5-acre area for dog walking **Facilities** food scoop/disp bags washing facs walks info vet info

Open all year Last arrival 20.00hrs

This pretty caravan park, built to a high specification and surrounded by well-planted banks, continues to improve due to the enthusiasm and vision of its owner. Everything is of a very high standard. The spacious grassy site is close to the Viking Way and other footpath networks, and well sited for visiting Rutland Water.

The Marquess of Exeter
★★★★ ⊜ INN
52 Main St LE15 9LT
☎ 01572 822477 📄 08082 801159
e-mail: info@marquessexeter.co.uk
dir: *M1 junct 19 onto A14 to Kettering, then A6003 to Caldecott. Turn right onto Lyddington Rd, 2m to village*

PETS: Bedrooms (10 GF) **Charges** £10 per night **Public areas** except restaurant (accompanied at all times) on leads **Grounds** on leads disp bin **Exercise area** fields adjacent **Facilities** vet info **On Request** fridge access **Resident Pets:** Sammy & Winston (cats)

Situated in the picturesque Rutland countryside, the inn has been refurbished with a contemporary touch whilst retaining many original features such as timber beam ceilings, open log fires and flagstone floors. The stylish bedrooms, situated across a courtyard, are individually decorated and comfortable. The food is imaginative with the chef's 'sharing dishes' being particularly noteworthy.

Rooms 18 en suite (2 fmly) (10 GF) **Facilities** FTV tea/coffee Dinner available Direct Dial Cen ht Wi-fi **Parking** 60 **Notes** No coaches

Best Western Normanton Park
★★★ 70% HOTEL
Oakham LE15 8RP
☎ 01780 720315 📄 01780 721086
e-mail: info@normantonpark.co.uk
web: www.normantonpark.com
dir: *From A1 follow A606 towards Oakham, 5m. Turn left, 1.5m. Hotel on right*

PETS: Bedrooms (11 GF) sign **Charges** £10 per night £50 per week **Public areas** except restaurant on leads **Grounds** on leads disp bin **Exercise area** nearby **Facilities** food bowl water bowl bedding dog chews cat treats feeding mat litter tray scoop/disp bags leads walks info vet info **On Request** fridge access torch towels **Other** charge for damage **Resident Pet:** Jake (Jack Russell)

This hotel offers some of Rutland Water's best views over the south shore. The comfortable bedrooms are located in the main house and the courtyard. Public rooms include a conservatory dining room overlooking the water, and a cosy lounge is available for guests to relax in.

Rooms 30 (7 annexe) (6 fmly) (11 GF) **Facilities** FTV Xmas New Year Wi-fi **Parking** 100 **Notes** LB

Hambleton Hall
★★★★ ⊛⊛⊛⊛ COUNTRY HOUSE HOTEL
Hambleton LE15 8TH
☎ 01572 756991 📄 01572 724721
e-mail: hotel@hambletonhall.com
web: www.hambletonhall.com
dir: *3m E off A606*

PETS: Bedrooms Charges £10 per night £70 per week on leads **Grounds** on leads **Exercise area** 5 mins from hotel **Facilities** vet info **On Request** torch **Stables** 10m

Established 30 years ago by Tim and Stefa Hart this delightful country house enjoys tranquil and spectacular views over Rutland Water. The beautifully manicured grounds are a delight to walk in. The bedrooms in the main house are stylish, individually decorated and equipped with a range of thoughtful extras. A two-bedroom folly, with its own sitting and breakfast room, is only a short walk away. Day rooms include a cosy bar and a sumptuous drawing room, both featuring open fires. The elegant restaurant serves very accomplished, award-winning cuisine with menus highlighting locally sourced, seasonal produce - some grown in the hotel's own grounds.

Rooms 17 (2 annexe) **S** £195-£215; **D** £235-£625 (incl. bkfst)* **Facilities** STV FTV ↻ ⊜⊜ Private access to lake Xmas New Year Wi-fi **Services** Lift **Parking** 40 **Notes** LB

OAKHAM *continued*

Barnsdale Lodge Hotel
★★★ 75% ® HOTEL

The Avenue, Rutland Water, North Shore LE15 8AH
☎ 01572 724678 🖺 01572 724961
e-mail: enquiries@barnsdalelodge.co.uk
web: www.barnsdalelodge.co.uk
dir: *Off A1 onto A606. Hotel 5m on right, 2m E of Oakham*

PETS: Bedrooms (15 GF) unattended ground-floor bedrooms only
Charges £10 per night **Public areas** in bar area only on leads
Grounds disp bin **Exercise area** adjacent **Facilities** food bowl
water bowl bedding scoop/disp bags leads dog chews cage
storage walks info vet info **On Request** fridge access torch
towels **Other** charge for damage paddock available for horses
Resident Pets: Coco & Maisie (Norfolk Terriers), Willow (Black
Labrador)

A popular and interesting hotel converted from a farmstead
overlooking Rutland Water. The public areas are dominated by
a successful food operation with a good range of appealing
meals on offer for either formal or informal dining. Bedrooms
are comfortably appointed with excellent beds enhanced by
contemporary soft furnishings and thoughtful extras.

Rooms 44 (2 fmly) (15 GF) **S** £85-£90; **D** £100-£110 (incl. bkfst)*
Facilities FTV Fishing 🛶 Archery Beauty treatments Golf Sailing
Shooting Xmas New Year Wi-fi **Parking** 200 **Notes** LB

BRIDGNORTH Map 7 SO79

Bearwood Lodge Guest House
★★★★ GUEST ACCOMMODATION

10 Kidderminster Rd WV15 6BW
☎ 01746 762159
e-mail: dawnjones604@yahoo.co.uk
dir: *On A442, 50yds S of Bridgnorth bypass island*

PETS: Bedrooms (1 GF) unattended **Public areas Exercise area**
100yds to riverside walk & park **Facilities** pet sitting washing
facs walks info vet info

This friendly guest accommodation is situated on the outskirts
of Bridgnorth. It provides soundly maintained modern bedrooms,
including one on the ground floor. The bright and pleasant
breakfast room has an adjacent conservatory, which opens onto
the attractive and colourful garden. There is also a comfortable
lounge.

Rooms 4 en suite (1 GF) **S** £45; **D** £65 **Facilities** FTV TVL tea/
coffee Cen ht Wi-fi **Parking** 8 **Notes** LB ®

The Halfway House Inn
★★★ INN

Cleobury Mortimer Rd WV16 5LS
☎ 01746 762670 🖺 01746 768063
e-mail: info@halfwayhouseinn.co.uk
web: www.halfwayhouseinn.co.uk
dir: *1m from town centre on B4363 to Cleobury Mortimer*

PETS: Bedrooms (6 GF) ground-floor bedrooms only **Charges** £5
per night £25 per week **Public areas** except bar & restaurant
on leads **Grounds** on leads disp bin **Exercise area** 200mtrs
Facilities leads cage storage walks info **On Request** fridge
access torch **Stables Other** charge for damage 2 weeks notice
required for horses **Restrictions** no Great Danes, Pit Bull Terriers
or Rottweilers

Located in a rural area, this 16th-century inn has been renovated
to provide good standards of comfort, while retaining its original
character. The bedrooms, most of which are in converted stables
and cottages, are especially suitable for families and groups.

Rooms 10 en suite (10 fmly) (6 GF) **S** £50-£75; **D** £60-£95
Facilities FTV TVL tea/coffee Dinner available Cen ht Wi-fi Golf
18 Fishing Pool table **Parking** 30 **Notes** LB Closed 25-26 Dec RS
Sun eve (ex BHs)

Stanmore Hall Touring Park *(SO742923)*

▶▶▶▶▶

Stourbridge Rd WV15 6DT
☎ 01746 761761   📠 01746 768069
e-mail: stanmore@morris-leisure
dir: 2m E of Bridgnorth on A458

PETS: Charges £1 per night **Public areas** disp bin
Exercise area on site 2 dog walks **Facilities** food food bowl
water bowl leads walks info vet info **Other** max 2 dogs per
pitch disposal bags available

Open all year Last arrival 20.00hrs Last departure noon

An excellent park in peaceful surroundings offering outstanding
facilities. The pitches, many fully serviced, are arranged around
the lake close to Stanmore Hall, home of the Midland Motor
Museum. Handy for touring Ironbridge and the Severn Valley
Railway, while Bridgnorth itself is an attractive old market town.
12.5 acre site. 131 touring pitches. 53 hardstandings. Tent
pitches. Motorhome pitches.

CHURCH STRETTON   Map 7 SO49

Longmynd Hotel

★★★ **73%** HOTEL

Cunnery Rd SY6 6AG
☎ 01694 722244   📠 01694 722718
e-mail: info@longmynd.co.uk
web: www.longmynd.co.uk
*dir: A49 into town centre on Sandford Ave, left at Lloyds TSB, over
mini-rdbt, 1st right into Cunnery Rd, hotel at top of hill on left*

PETS: Bedrooms unattended **Charges** £6 per night
Public areas except restaurant, bar, lounge & pool area **Grounds**
disp bin **Exercise area** nearby **Facilities** food (pre-bookable)
scoop/disp bags washing facs cage storage walks info vet
info **On Request** fridge access torch towels **Other** charge for
damage **Restrictions** well behaved dogs only

Built in 1901 as a spa, this family-run hotel overlooks the town,
and the views from many of the rooms and public areas are
breathtaking. The attractive wooded grounds include a unique
wood sculpture trail. Bedrooms, with smart modern bathrooms,
are comfortable and well equipped; suites are available. Facilities
include a choice of relaxing lounges. An ethical approach to
climatic issues is observed, and a warm welcome is assured.

Rooms 50 (3 fmly) **S** £44-£59; **D** £88-£118 (incl. bkfst)*
Facilities FTV ⚜ Putt green Sauna Xmas New Year Wi-fi
Services Lift **Parking** 100 **Notes** LB

Belvedere

★★★★ GUEST HOUSE

Burway Rd SY6 6DP
☎ 01694 722232   📠 01694 722232
e-mail: info@belvedereguesthouse.co.uk
dir: Off A49 into town centre, over x-rds onto Burway Rd

PETS: Bedrooms Public areas except restaurant & lounge
Grounds on leads disp bin **Exercise area** 100mtrs **Facilities**
food bowl water bowl washing facs cage storage walks info
vet info **On Request** fridge access torch towels **Resident Pet:**
rabbit

Popular with walkers and cyclists and located on the lower slopes
of the Long Mynd, this impressive, well-proportioned Edwardian
house has a range of homely bedrooms, equipped with practical
extras and complemented by modern bathrooms. Ground-floor
areas include a cottage-style dining room overlooking the pretty
garden and a choice of lounges.

Rooms 7 rms (6 en suite) (2 fmly) **S** £33-£40; **D** £58-£68
Facilities TVL tea/coffee Cen ht Wi-fi **Parking** 9 **Notes** LB

North Hill Farm

★★★★ BED AND BREAKFAST

Cardington SY6 7LL
☎ 01694 771532
e-mail: cbrandon@btinternet.com
*dir: From Cardington village S onto Church Stretton road, right
signed Cardington Moor, farm at top of hill on left*

PETS: Bedrooms (2 GF) courtyard bedrooms only **Sep accom**
unheated, outdoor kennel with inner bunk barn **Charges** £3
per night **Public areas** except dining room on leads **Grounds**
on leads disp bin **Exercise area** adjacent **Facilities** feeding
mat scoop/disp bags leads washing facs cage storage walks
info vet info **On Request** fridge access torch towels **Stables**
Other charge for damage giant breeds must stay in kennels
Restrictions no dangerous dogs (see page 7) **Resident Pets:**
Saffron & Kitty (Gordon Setters), Millie & Tilly (Springer Spaniels)

This delightful house has been modernised to provide comfortable
accommodation. It is located on a fairly remote 20-acre
sheep-rearing holding amid the Shropshire hills. The lounge, with
exposed beams, has log fires in colder weather. Guests share
one large table in the breakfast room. There are two bedrooms in
the main house and two in different buildings, one newly built to
provide high quality spacious accommodation.

Rooms 2 rms (2 pri facs) 2 annexe en suite (2 GF) **S** £35;
D £56-£80 **Facilities** FTV tea/coffee Cen ht Wi-fi **Parking** 6
Notes LB Closed Xmas 🏠

Castle View

★★★★ BED AND BREAKFAST

Stokesay SY7 9AL

☎ 01588 673712

e-mail: castleviewb_b@btinternet.com

dir: *On A49 S of Craven Arms opp turning to Stokesay Castle*

PETS: Bedrooms unattended **Charges** £5 per stay **Public areas** only assist dogs in dining room **Grounds** disp bin **Exercise area** nearby **Facilities** food (pre-bookable) food bowl water bowl bedding feeding mat leads washing facs cage storage walks info vet info **On Request** fridge access torch towels **Other** charge for damage

This Victorian cottage, extended about 20 years ago, stands in delightful gardens on the southern outskirts of Craven Arms, close to Stokesay Castle. Bedrooms are thoughtfully furnished, and breakfasts, featuring local produce, are served in the cosy, traditionally furnished dining room.

Rooms 3 rms (1 en suite) (2 pri facs) **S** £35-£40; **D** £60-£68 **Facilities** tea/coffee Cen ht **Parking** 4 **Notes** LB No Children 3yrs

Fishmore Hall

★★★ ◉◉◉ SMALL HOTEL

Fishmore Rd SY8 3DP

☎ 01584 875148   01584 877907

e-mail: reception@fishmorehall.co.uk

web: www.fishmorehall.co.uk

dir: *A49 into Henley Rd. 1st right, Weyman Rd, at bottom of hill right into Fishmore Rd*

PETS: Bedrooms (1 GF) unattended **Charges** £30 per stay **Public areas** except restaurant **Grounds** **Exercise area** adjacent **Facilities** food bowl water bowl washing facs cage storage walks info vet info **On Request** fridge access torch towels **Stables** approx 10m **Other** charge for damage

Located in a rural area within easy reach of town centre, this Palladian style Georgian house has been sympathetically renovated and extended to provide high standards of comfort and facilities. The contemporary interior highlights many period features, and public areas include a comfortable lounge and restaurant, the setting for imaginative cooking.

Rooms 15 (1 GF) **S** £100-£210; **D** £150-£250 (incl. bkfst)* **Facilities** FTV 🏊 In room beauty treatments & massage Xmas New Year Wi-fi **Services** Lift **Parking** 48 **Notes** LB

Cliffe

★★ **80%** SMALL HOTEL

Dinham SY8 2JE

☎ 01584 872063   01584 873991

e-mail: thecliffehotel@hotmail.com

web: www.thecliffehotel.co.uk

dir: *In town centre turn left at castle gates to Dinham, follow over bridge. Take right fork, hotel 200yds on left*

PETS: Bedrooms certain bedrooms only **Charges** £5 per night **Public areas** except during food service on leads **Grounds** on leads disp bin **Exercise area** fields surrounding hotel **Facilities** washing facs cage storage walks info vet info **On Request** torch towels **Restrictions** no Pit Bull Terriers **Resident Pet:** Megan (Black Labrador)

Built in the 19th century and standing in extensive grounds and gardens, this privately owned and personally run hotel is quietly located close to the castle and the river. It provides well-equipped accommodation, and facilities include a lounge bar, a pleasant restaurant and a patio overlooking the garden.

Rooms 9 (2 fmly) **S** £50-£65; **D** £65-£90 (incl. bkfst)* **Facilities** FTV Wi-fi **Parking** 22 **Notes** LB

Angel House

★★★★ BED AND BREAKFAST

Angel Bank, Bitterley SY8 3HT

☎ 01584 891377   08723 520921

e-mail: angelhousebandb@googlemail.com

dir: *On A4117, 4m E of Ludlow on Clee Hill*

PETS: Bedrooms **Charges** £5 per stay **Public areas** except breakfast room if other guests are present **Grounds** on leads disp bin **Exercise area** adjacent **Facilities** food bowl water bowl feeding mat scoop/disp bags cage storage walks info vet info **On Request** fridge access torch towels

Located in an elevated position four miles from Ludlow, this sympathetically renovated 17th-century former pub provides high standards of comfort and facilities. Thoughtfully furnished bedrooms have stunning rural views, and comprehensive breakfasts are served in the attractive dining room. A guest lounge is also available and a warm welcome is assured.

Rooms 2 en suite (1 fmly) **S** fr £68; **D** fr £78 **Facilities** FTV tea/coffee Dinner available Cen ht Wi-fi **Parking** 7 **Notes** No Children 7yrs

The Charlton Arms
★★★★ ⏺ INN

Ludford Bridge SY8 1PJ

☎ 01584 872813

dir: *From town centre onto Broad St, over Ludford Bridge, Charlton Arms on right*

PETS: Bedrooms unattended **Charges Public areas** except top terrace, restaurant & eating area **Grounds** disp bin **Exercise area** adjacent **Facilities** water bowl cage storage walks vet info **On Request** fridge access torch towels **Other** charge for damage

The accommodation at this riverside inn reflects the character of the historic building whilst offering all the comforts of modern living. The restaurant provides fresh locally-sourced ingredients, and as a free house also offers a fine selection of local beers. There is one bedroom which has a private terrace and a hot tub, and there are decking areas to enjoy drinks or a meal on warmer days.

Rooms 10 en suite (2 fmly) **Facilities** tea/coffee Dinner available Cen ht Wi-fi Fishing **Parking** 25

Church Inn
★★★★ INN

The Buttercross SY8 1AW

☎ 01584 872174   📠 01584 877146

web: www.thechurchinn.com

dir: *In town centre at top of Broad St, behind Buttercross*

PETS: Bedrooms unattended **Charges Public areas** except in breakfast area on leads **Facilities** water bowl dog chews **Other** charge for damage prior notice required owners must bring dog's own bedding if required

Set right in the heart of the historic town, this Grade II listed inn has been renovated to provide quality accommodation with smart modern bathrooms, some with spa baths. Other areas include a small lounge, a well-equipped meeting room, and cosy bar areas where imaginative food and real ales are served.

Rooms 8 en suite (3 fmly) **Facilities** TVL tea/coffee Dinner available Direct Dial Cen ht **Notes** No coaches

Haynall Villa *(SO543674)*
★★★★ FARMHOUSE

Little Hereford SY8 4BG

☎ 01584 711589   📄 01584 711589 Mrs R Edwards

e-mail: rachelmedwards@hotmail.com

web: www.haynallvilla.co.uk

dir: *A49 onto A456, at Little Hereford right signed Leysters & Middleton on the Hill. Villa 1m on right*

PETS: Bedrooms Charges £5 per night **Public areas** except dining room on leads **Grounds** on leads **Exercise area** adjacent **Facilities** leads walks info vet info **On Request** torch **Stables** 300yds **Other** charge for damage food & water bowl available on request; dogs allowed in lounge only with other guests' approval **Resident Pet:** Gerry (Springer Spaniel)

Located in immaculate gardens in the pretty hamlet of Little Hereford, this Victorian house retains many original features, which are enhanced by the furnishings and decor. Bedrooms are filled with lots of homely extras and the lounge has an open fire.

Rooms 3 rms (2 en suite) (1 pri facs) (1 fmly); **D** fr £554 **Facilities** FTV TVL tea/coffee Dinner available Cen ht Wi-fi Fishing **Parking** 3 **Notes** No Children 6yrs Closed mid Dec-mid Jan 🐾 72 acres arable

Moor Hall
★★★★ GUEST HOUSE

Cleedownton SY8 3EG

☎ 01584 823209

e-mail: enquiries@moorhall.co.uk

dir: *From A4117 (Ludlow to Kidderminster) left to Bridgnorth. B4364, 3.2m, Moor Hall on right*

PETS: Bedrooms unattended **Public areas** except dining room, other areas if agreed **Grounds** disp bin **Exercise area** surrounding fields **Facilities** washing facs cage storage walks info vet info **On Request** fridge access torch towels **Resident Pets:** 2 dogs & 4 cats

This impressive Georgian house, once the home of Lord Boyne, is surrounded by extensive gardens and farmland. Bedrooms are richly decorated, well equipped, and one room has a sitting area. Public areas are spacious and comfortably furnished. There is a choice of sitting rooms and a library bar. Guests dine family-style in an elegant dining room.

Rooms 3 en suite **S** £40-£45; **D** £60-£70 **Facilities** tea/coffee Dinner available Cen ht Licensed **Parking** 7 **Notes** LB Closed 25-26 Dec 🐾

LYNEAL (NEAR ELLESMERE) — Map 7 SJ43

Fernwood Caravan Park (SJ445346)

▶ ▶ ▶ ▶

SY12 0QF

☎ 01948 710221   📄 01948 710324

e-mail: enquiries@fernwoodpark.co.uk

dir: *From A495 in Welshampton take B5063, over canal bridge, turn right as signed*

PETS: Public areas except children's play area disp bin **Exercise area on site** 40-acre woods (adjacent) **Facilities** food food bowl water bowl washing facs walks info vet info **Other** prior notice required disposal bags available **Resident Pet:** Poppy (Border Collie)

Open Mar-Nov rs Apr-Oct shop open Last arrival 21.00hrs Last departure 17.00hrs

A peaceful park set in wooded countryside, with a screened, tree-lined touring area and coarse fishing lake. The approach is past colourful flowerbeds, and the static area which is tastefully arranged around an attractive children's playing area. There is a small child-free touring area for those wanting complete relaxation, and the park has woodland walks. 26 acre site. 60 touring pitches. 8 hardstandings. Motorhome pitches. 165 statics.

MINSTERLEY — Map 7 SJ30

The Old School Caravan Park (SO322977)

▶ ▶

Shelve SY5 0JQ

☎ 01588 650410   📄 01588 650410

dir: *6.5m SW of Minsterley on A488, site on left 2m after village sign for Hope*

PETS: Public areas disp bin **Exercise area** adjacent to site **Facilities** vet info **Other** prior notice required disposal bags available

Open Mar-Jan Last arrival 21.00hrs Last departure 11.00hrs

Situated in the Shropshire hills with many excellent walks direct from the site, as well as being close to many cycle trails. There's also a shooting range and leisure centre within six miles. Near Snailbreach Mine, one of the most complete disused mineral mines in the country, and just a 45-minute drive from Ironbridge. This is a really beautiful small park with excellent facilities. 1.5 acre site. 22 touring pitches. 10 hardstandings. 6 seasonal pitches. Tent pitches. Motorhome pitches.

Notes No ball games or cycle riding. ⊛

MUCH WENLOCK — Map 7 SO69

Yew Tree (SO543958)

★ ★ ★ ★ 🏠 FARMHOUSE

Longville In The Dale TF13 6EB

☎ 01694 771866   Mr & Mrs Hilbery

e-mail: enquiries@yewtreefarmshropshire.co.uk

dir: *5m SW of Much Wenlock. N off B4371 at Longville, left at pub, right at x-rds, farm 1.2m on right*

PETS: Bedrooms Charges £5 per stay **Public areas** except dining room on leads **Grounds** disp bin **Exercise area** adjacent **Facilities** food bowl water bowl scoop/disp bags leads washing facs cage storage walks info vet info **On Request** fridge access torch towels **Other** charge for damage **Resident Pets:** Saffy & Tuli (Norfolk Terriers/Jack Russell cross), sheep, pigs, chickens

Yew Tree is peacefully located between Much Wenlock and Church Stretton in ten acres of unspoiled countryside, where pigs, sheep and chickens are reared, and own produce is a feature on the comprehensive breakfast menu. Bedrooms are equipped with thoughtful extras and a warm welcome is assured.

Rooms 2 rms (1 en suite) (1 pri facs) **S** £35-£45; **D** £50-£70 **Facilities** FTV TVL tea/coffee Cen ht Wi-fi **Parking** 4 **Notes** LB Closed 24-30 Dec ⊛ 10 acres smallholding/sheep/pigs

OSWESTRY — Map 7 SJ22

Pen-y-Dyffryn Country Hotel

★ ★ ★ 83% ⊛⊛ HOTEL

Rhydycroesau SY10 7JD

☎ 01691 653700   📄 01978 211004

e-mail: stay@peny.co.uk

web: www.peny.co.uk

dir: *A5 into town centre. Follow signs to Llansilin on B4580, hotel 3m W of Oswestry before Rhydycroesau*

PETS: Bedrooms (1 GF) unattended **Public areas** not after 6pm **Grounds** disp bin **Exercise area** nearby **Facilities** food bowl water bowl scoop/disp bags leads washing facs cage storage walks info vet info **On Request** fridge access torch towels **Stables**

Peacefully situated in five acres of grounds, this charming old house dates back to around 1840, when it was built as a rectory. The tastefully appointed public rooms have real fires during cold weather, and the accommodation includes several mini-cottages, each with its own patio. This hotel attracts many guests for its food and attentive, friendly service.

Rooms 12 (4 annexe) (1 fmly) (1 GF) **S** £85-£92; **D** £120-£180 (incl. bkfst)* **Facilities** STV FTV Guided walks Wi-fi **Parking** 18 **Notes** LB No children 3yrs Closed 18 Dec-19 Jan

The Bradford Arms
★★★★ INN

Llanymynech SY22 6EJ
☎ 01691 830582 📠 01691 839009
e-mail: catelou@tesco.net
dir: *5.5m S of Oswestry on A483 in Llanymynech*

PETS: Bedrooms (2 GF) unattended **Public areas** except restaurant & conservatory on leads **Grounds** on leads disp bin **Exercise area** 200yds **Facilities** water bowl bedding dog chews washing facs cage storage walks info vet info **On Request** fridge access torch towels **Stables** 2m **Other** charge for damage **Resident Pet:** Charlie (cat)

Once a coaching inn on the Earl of Bradford's estate, the Bradford Arms provides a range of carefully furnished bedrooms with a wealth of thoughtful extras. The elegant ground-floor areas include lounges, bars, and a choice of formal or conservatory restaurants, the settings for imaginative food and fine wines.

Rooms 5 en suite (2 fmly) (2 GF) **S** £40; **D** £60 **Facilities** FTV tea/coffee Dinner available Direct Dial Cen ht Wi-fi Golf 18 Fishing Riding Pool table **Parking** 20

Park House
★★★★ 77% ◉ HOTEL

Park St TF11 9BA
☎ 01952 460128 📠 01952 461658
e-mail: reception@parkhousehotel.net
dir: *M54 junct 4, A464 (Wolverhampton road) for approx 2m, under railway bridge, hotel 100yds on left*

PETS: Bedrooms (8 GF) unattended **Charges** £10 per night **Grounds Exercise area** 500yds **Facilities** walks info vet info **On Request** fridge access **Restrictions** no breed larger than a Labrador

This hotel was created from what were originally two country houses of very different architectural styles. Located on the edge of the historic market town, it offers guests easy access to motorway networks, a choice of banqueting and meeting rooms, plus leisure facilities. Butlers Bar and Restaurant is the setting for imaginative food. Service is friendly and attentive.

Rooms 54 (16 annexe) (4 fmly) (8 GF) (4 smoking) **Facilities** STV FTV ⓢ Gym Steam room Sauna Xmas New Year Wi-fi **Services** Lift **Parking** 90

Albright Hussey Manor Hotel & Restaurant
★★★★ 75% ◉◉ HOTEL

Ellesmere Rd SY4 3AF
☎ 01939 290571 & 290523 📠 01939 291143
e-mail: info@albrighthussey.co.uk
web: www.albrighthussey.co.uk
dir: *2.5m N of Shrewsbury on A528, follow signs for Ellesmere*

PETS: Bedrooms (8 GF) unattended **Charges** £5 per night **Public areas** disp bin **Exercise area** nearby **Facilities** walks info vet info **On Request** torch **Other** charge for damage contact hotel for details of facilities for dogs

First mentioned in the Domesday Book, this enchanting medieval manor house is complete with a moat. Bedrooms are situated in either the sumptuously appointed main house or in the more modern wing. The intimate restaurant displays an abundance of original features and there is also a comfortable cocktail bar and lounge.

Rooms 26 (4 fmly) (8 GF) **Facilities** ⌣ Xmas New Year Wi-fi **Parking** 100

Mytton & Mermaid
★★★ 77% ◉◉ HOTEL

Atcham SY5 6QG
☎ 01743 761220 📠 01743 761292
e-mail: reception@myttonandmermaid.co.uk
web: www.myttonandmermaid.co.uk
dir: *From Shrewsbury over old bridge in Atcham. Hotel opposite main entrance to Attingham Park*

PETS: Bedrooms (6 GF) unattended ground-floor bedrooms only **Charges** £10 per night **Grounds** disp bin **Exercise area** National Trust park opposite **Facilities** food bowl water bowl cage storage walks info vet info **On Request** fridge access

Convenient for Shrewsbury, this former coaching inn enjoys a pleasant location beside the River Severn. Some bedrooms, including family suites, are in a converted stable block adjacent to the hotel. There is a large lounge bar, a comfortable lounge, and a brasserie that has gained a well-deserved local reputation for the quality of its food.

Rooms 18 (7 annexe) (1 fmly) (6 GF) **S** £85-£90; **D** £110-£175 (incl. bkfst)* **Facilities** Fishing ⌢ New Year Wi-fi **Parking** 50 **Notes** LB Closed 25 Dec

SHREWSBURY *continued*

Oxon Hall Touring Park *(SJ455138)*

▶▶▶▶▶

Welshpool Rd SY3 5FB
☎ 01743 340868   📠 01743 340869
e-mail: oxon@morris-leisure.co.uk
dir: *Exit A5 (ring road) at junct with A458. Site shares entrance with 'Oxon Park & Ride'*

PETS: Charges Public areas Exercise area on site 2 dog walks **Facilities** washing facs walks info vet info **Other** prior notice required max 2 dogs per pitch

Open all year Last arrival 21.00hrs

A delightful park with quality facilities, and a choice of grass and fully-serviced pitches. A warm welcome is assured from the friendly staff. An adults-only section proves very popular, and there is an inviting patio area next to the reception and the shop, overlooking a small lake. This site is ideally located for visiting Shrewsbury and the surrounding countryside, and the site also benefits from the Oxon Park & Ride, a short walk through the park. 15 acre site. 105 touring pitches. 72 hardstandings. Tent pitches. Motorhome pitches. 60 statics.

TELFORD	Map 7 SJ60

Telford Hotel & Golf Resort

★★★★ **75%** HOTEL
Great Hay Dr, Sutton Heights TF7 4DT
☎ 01952 429977   📠 01952 586602
e-mail: telford@qhotels.co.uk
web: www.qhotels.co.uk
dir: *M54 junct 4, A442. Follow signs for Telford Golf Club*

PETS: Bedrooms (50 GF) sign **Charges** £15 per night **Public areas** only for access to bedrooms (ex assist dogs) on leads **Grounds** disp bin **Exercise area** public footpath through grounds **Facilities** walks info vet info **Stables** 8m **Other** charge for damage 1 medium or large dog or max 2 small dogs per bedroom; dogs are not allowed on golf course **Restrictions** no breed larger than a Labrador

Set on the edge of Telford with panoramic views of the famous Ironbridge Gorge, this hotel offers excellent standards. Smart bedrooms are complemented by spacious public areas, large conference facilities, a spa with treatment rooms, a golf course and a driving range. Ample parking is available.

Rooms 114 (8 fmly) (50 GF) **S** £75-£165; **D** £95-£185 (incl. bkfst)* **Facilities** Spa STV 🐾 ⚓ 18 Putt green Gym Xmas New Year Wi-fi **Services** Lift **Parking** 200 **Notes** LB

Church Farm Guest House

★★★★ 🏵 🔒 GUEST ACCOMMODATION
Wrockwardine Village, Wellington TF6 5DG
☎ 01952 251927 & 07976 897528   📠 01952 427511
e-mail: info@churchfarm-shropshire.co.uk
dir: *M54 junct 7 towards Wellington, 1st left, 1st right, right at end of road. 0.5m on left opposite St Peters Church*

PETS: Bedrooms garden annexe only **Charges** £10 per stay **Public areas** except restaurant on leads **Grounds** disp bin **Exercise area** 2m **Facilities** food bowl water bowl dog chews feeding mat scoop/disp bags leads washing facs cage storage walks info vet info **On Request** fridge access torch towels **Other** charge for damage **Resident Pet:** Basil (Staffordshire Bull Terrier)

Located in the pretty rural village of Wrockwardine, this impressive period former farmhouse provides high standards of comfort and good facilities. Attractive bedrooms, furnished in minimalist style, offer a wealth of thoughtful extras including complimentary Wi-fi. The spacious day rooms include a comfortable lounge and an elegant dining room, the setting for imaginative cooking.

Rooms 4 rms (3 en suite) (1 pri facs) (1 fmly) **S** £55-£65; **D** £70-£80 **Facilities** FTV tea/coffee Dinner available Cen ht Wi-fi Golf 18 ⚓ Sauna Solarium Gym **Parking** 12

Severn Gorge Park *(SJ705051)*

▶▶▶▶▶

Bridgnorth Rd, Tweedale TF7 4JB
☎ 01952 684789   📠 01952 587299
e-mail: info@severngorgepark.co.uk
dir: *Signed off A442, 1m S of Telford*

PETS: Charges contact for details **Public areas** on leads disp bin **Exercise area on site Facilities** walks info vet info **Other** prior notice required max 2 dogs per pitch & must be kept on leads at all times **Restrictions** well behaved dogs only

Open all year Last arrival 22.00hrs Last departure 18.00hrs

A very pleasant wooded site in the heart of Telford, well-screened and well-maintained. The sanitary facilities are fresh and immaculate, and landscaping of the grounds is carefully managed. Although the touring section is small, this is a really delightful park to stay on, and it is also well positioned for visiting nearby Ironbridge and its museums. 6 acre site. 10 touring pitches. 10 hardstandings. Motorhome pitches. 120 statics.

Days Inn Telford - M54

BUDGET HOTEL

Telford Services, Priorslee Rd TF11 8TG
☎ 01952 238400 📄 01952 238410
e-mail: telford.hotel@welcomebreak.co.uk
web: www.welcomebreak.co.uk
dir: At M54 junct 4

PETS: Bedrooms (21 GF) ground-floor bedrooms only **Charges** £5 per stay **Public areas** on leads **Grounds** disp bin **Facilities** food bowl water bowl scoop/disp bags vet info

This modern building offers accommodation in smart, spacious and well-equipped bedrooms, suitable for families and business travellers, and all with en suite bathrooms. Continental breakfast is available, and other refreshments may be taken at the nearby family restaurant.

Rooms 48 (45 fmly) (21 GF) (8 smoking) **S** £39.95-£59.95; **D** £49.95-£69.95

Soulton Hall

★★★★ 🛏 GUEST ACCOMMODATION

Soulton SY4 5RS
☎ 01939 232786 📄 01939 234097
e-mail: enquiries@soultonhall.co.uk
web: www.soultonhall.co.uk
dir: From A49 between Shrewsbury & Whitchurch take B5065 towards Wem. Soulton Hall 2m E of Wem

PETS: Bedrooms (3 GF) carriage house rooms only **Charges** £10 per night **Grounds** on leads **Exercise area** adjacent **Facilities** leads washing facs dog grooming cage storage walks info vet info **On Request** torch towels **Stables** 9m **Other** charge for damage dogs, on leads, allowed in Carriage House & Cedar Lodge only (not in Soulton Hall)

Located two miles from historic Wem, this 16th-century manor house incorporates part of an even older building. The house stands in 560 acres and provides high levels of comfort. Bedrooms are equipped with homely extras and the ground-floor areas include a spacious hall sitting room, lounge-bar and an attractive dining room, the setting for imaginative dinners.

Rooms 4 en suite 3 annexe en suite (2 fmly) (3 GF) **S** £44-£131; **D** £88-£142 **Facilities** FTV tea/coffee Dinner available Direct Dial Cen ht Licensed Wi-fi 🏌 Golf 18 Fishing **Parking** 52 **Notes** LB

Lower Lacon Caravan Park (SJ534304)

▶ ▶ ▶

SY4 5RP
☎ 01939 232376 📄 01939 233606
e-mail: info@llcp.co.uk
dir: Take A49 to B5065. Site 3m on right

PETS: Public areas except swimming pool area, toilets & licensed premises disp bin **Exercise area on site** dog walk **Facilities** food dog chews vet info **Other** prior notice required dogs must be kept on leads at all times & not left unattended disposal bags available **Resident Pets:** 1 Shetland Pony, Kune Kune pigs, alpacas, sheep, chickens & ducks

Open all year **Last arrival** anytime **Last departure** 16.00hrs

A large, spacious park with lively club facilities and an entertainments barn, set safely away from the main road. The park is particularly suited to families, with an outdoor swimming pool and farm animals. 52 acre site. 270 touring pitches. 30 hardstandings. Tent pitches. Motorhome pitches. 50 statics.

Notes No skateboards, no commercial vehicles, no sign written vehicles.

The Green Caravan Park (SO380932)

▶ ▶ ▶

SY9 5EF
☎ 01588 650605
e-mail: karen@greencaravanpark.co.uk
dir: 1m NE of Bishop's Castle on A489. Right at brown tourist sign

PETS: Charges £1 per night **Public areas** disp bin **Exercise area on site** dog walk & small field for exercising **Facilities** food scoop/disp bags walks info vet info **Other** charge for damage **Resident Pets:** Ronnie (pygmy goat), Sophie, Lily, Bonnie & Molly (cats)

Open Etr-Oct **Last arrival** 21.00hrs **Last departure** 13.00hrs

A pleasant site in a peaceful setting convenient for visiting Ludlow or Shrewsbury. Very family orientated, with good facilities. The grassy pitches are mainly level, and some hardstandings are available. 15 acre site. 140 touring pitches. 5 hardstandings. Tent pitches. Motorhome pitches. 20 statics.

ENGLAND

WESTON-UNDER-REDCASTLE — Map 7 SJ52

Hawkstone Park Hotel
★★★ 75% HOTEL
SY4 5UY
☎ 01948 841700 📄 01939 200335
e-mail: enquiries@hawkstone.co.uk
dir: 1m E of A49 between Shrewsbury & Whitchurch

PETS: Bedrooms (26 GF) unattended **Charges** £10 per night **Public areas** except restaurant & dining areas muzzled and on leads **Grounds** on leads disp bin **Exercise area** 50mtrs **Facilities** food bowl water bowl bedding cage storage walks info vet info **On Request** fridge access torch towels

Built in the 1700 this splendid former coaching inn is set in 400 acres of lovely scenery which includes two championship golf courses and the much remarked upon, 18th-century follies. The bedrooms are comfortably appointed and well equipped for both leisure and business guests, and the public areas include conference facilities and a pleasant dining room.

Rooms 67 (19 annexe) (2 fmly) (26 GF) **S** £42-£99; **D** £62-£129 (incl. bkfst)* **Facilities** STV ⅃ 42 Putt green ⍦ Xmas New Year **Parking** 200 **Notes** LB

SOMERSET

BATH — Map 3 ST76

The Royal Crescent
★★★★★ 85% ◉◉ HOTEL
16 Royal Crescent BA1 2LS
☎ 01225 823333 📄 01225 339401
e-mail: info@royalcrescent.co.uk
web: www.vonessenhotels.co.uk
dir: From A4, right at lights. 2nd left into Bennett St, into The Circus, 2nd exit into Brock St

PETS: Bedrooms (7 GF) unattended Garden Villa bedrooms only **Public areas** except restaurant on leads **Grounds Exercise area** park adjacent **Facilities** food (pre-bookable) food bowl water bowl bedding pet sitting dog walking cage storage walks info vet info **Other** charge for damage please contact hotel to confirm which pets are accepted **Resident Pets:** Tilly & Toby (cats)

John Wood's masterpiece of fine Georgian architecture provides the setting for this elegant hotel in the centre of the world famous Royal Crescent. Spacious, air-conditioned bedrooms are individually designed and furnished with antiques. Delightful central grounds lead to a second house, which is home to further rooms, the award-winning Dower House restaurant and the Bath House which offers therapies and treatments.

Rooms 45 (8 fmly) (7 GF) **S** £179-£325; **D** £199-£345 (incl. bkfst)* **Facilities** Spa STV FTV ⍰ ⍦ Gym 1920s river launch Xmas New Year Wi-fi **Services** Lift Air con **Parking** 27 **Notes** LB

Best Western The Cliffe
★★★ 83% ◉ HOTEL
Cliffe Dr, Crowe Hill, Limpley Stoke BA2 7FY
☎ 01225 723226 📄 01225 723871
e-mail: cliffe@bestwestern.co.uk
dir: A36 S from Bath onto B3108 at lights left towards Bradford-on-Avon, 0.5m. Right before bridge through village, 2nd hotel on right

PETS: Bedrooms (4 GF) **Charges** £8 per night **Grounds** on leads disp bin **Exercise area** adjacent **Facilities** water bowl washing facs walks info vet info **On Request** fridge access torch towels **Other** charge for damage

With stunning countryside views, this attractive country house is just a short drive from the City of Bath. Bedrooms vary in size and style but are well equipped; several are particularly spacious and a number of rooms are on the ground floor. The restaurant overlooks the well-tended garden and offers a tempting selection of carefully prepared dishes. Wi-fi is available throughout.

Rooms 11 (3 annexe) (2 fmly) (4 GF) **Facilities** FTV ⍺ Xmas New Year Wi-fi **Parking** 20

Pratt's Hotel
★★★ 72% HOTEL
South Pde BA2 4AB
☎ 01225 460441 📄 01225 448807
e-mail: pratts@forestdale.com
web: www.prattshotel.co.uk
dir: A46 into city centre. Left at 1st lights (Curfew Pub), right at next lights. 2nd exit at next rdbt, right at lights, left at next lights, 1st left into South Pde

PETS: Bedrooms unattended sign **Charges** £7.50 per night **Public areas** except restaurant & bar on leads **Exercise area** 2 mins' walk **Facilities** food food bowl water bowl cage storage walks info vet info

Built in 1743 this popular Georgian hotel still has many original features and is centrally placed for exploring Bath. The bedrooms, each with their own individual character and style, offer great comfort. The lounge has original open fireplaces and offers a relaxing venue for afternoon tea.

Rooms 46 (2 fmly) **Facilities** FTV Xmas New Year Wi-fi **Services** Lift **Notes** LB

Eagle House

★★★★ GUEST ACCOMMODATION

Church St, Bathford BA1 7RS
☎ 01225 859946 📄 01225 859430
e-mail: jonap@eagleho.demon.co.uk
web: www.eaglehouse.co.uk
dir: Off A363 onto Church St

PETS: Bedrooms (2 GF) **Charges** £5 per night **Public areas** except dining room (drawing room on request) **Grounds** disp bin **Exercise area** 400yds **Facilities** water bowl washing facs cage storage walks info vet info **On Request** fridge access torch towels **Stables** 2m **Resident Pets:** Aquilla (Labrador), Inka (cat)

Set in attractive gardens, this delightful Georgian house is pleasantly located on the outskirts of the city. Bedrooms are individually styled, and each has a thoughtful range of extra facilities. The impressive lounge is adorned with attractive pictures, and the dining room has views of the grounds and tennis court.

Rooms 6 en suite 2 annexe en suite (2 fmly) (2 GF) **S** £48-£88.50; **D** £64-£115 **Facilities** FTV tea/coffee Direct Dial Cen ht Wi-fi 🔌 ✈ **Parking** 10 **Notes** LB Closed 12 Dec-15 Jan

Newton Mill Holiday Park *(ST715649)*

▶▶▶▶

Newton Rd BA2 9JF
☎ 08442 729503
e-mail: enquiries@newtonmillpark.co.uk
dir: From Bath W on A4 to rdbt by Globe Inn, immediate left, site 1m on left

PETS: Charges Public areas except children's play area, toilets & washrooms disp bin **Exercise area on site** dog walk **Exercise area** playing fields **Facilities** food food bowl water bowl leads washing facs walks info vet info **Other** prior notice required disposal bags available **Restrictions** no dangerous dogs (see page 7)

Open all year rs Wknds low season restaurant open Last arrival 21.30hrs Last departure 11.30hrs

An attractive, high quality park set in a sheltered valley and surrounded by woodland, with a stream running through. It offers excellent toilet facilities with private cubicles and family rooms, and there is an appealing restaurant and bar offering a wide choice of menus throughout the year. Additional hardstandings have been put in on the top area of the park. The city of Bath is easily accessible by bus or via the Bristol to Bath cycle path. 42 acre site. 106 touring pitches. 67 hardstandings. Tent pitches. Motorhome pitches.

Notes No noise after 22.00hrs.

 Warren Farm Holiday Centre *(ST297564)*

Brean Sands TA8 2RP
☎ 01278 751227
e-mail: enquiries@warren-farm.co.uk
dir: M5 junct 22 , B3140 through Burnham-on-Sea to Berrow & Brean. Site 1.5m past Brean Leisure Park

PETS: Public areas except buildings, Sunnyside area & field 6 disp bin **Exercise area on site** farm walk **Facilities** food food bowl water bowl dog chews litter tray scoop/disp bags walks info vet info **Other** prior notice required

Open Apr-Oct Last arrival 20.00hrs Last departure noon

A large family-run holiday park close to the beach, divided into several fields each with its own designated facilities. Pitches are spacious and level, and enjoy panoramic views of the Mendip Hills and Brean Down. A bar and restaurant are part of the complex, which provide entertainment for all the family, and there is also separate entertainment for children. The park has excellent modern facilities. 100 acre site. 575 touring pitches. Tent pitches. Motorhome pitches. 400 statics.

Notes No commercial vehicles.

Northam Farm Caravan & Touring Park *(ST299556)*

▶▶▶▶

TA8 2SE
☎ 01278 751244 📄 01278 751150
e-mail: enquiries@northamfarm.co.uk
dir: From M5 junct 22 to Burnham-on-Sea, Brean, Northam Farm on right 0.5m past Brean Leisure Park

PETS: Public areas except fields on leads disp bin **Exercise area on site** dog walks & exercise field **Facilities** food dog chews scoop/disp bags leads washing facs walks info vet info **Other** prior notice required allocated camping areas for owners who bring their dogs

Open Mar-Oct rs Mar & Oct shop/café/takeaway open limited hours Last arrival 20.00hrs Last departure 10.30hrs

An attractive site a short walk from the sea and a long sandy beach. This quality park also has lots of children's play areas, and also owns the Seagull Inn about 600 yards away, which includes a restaurant and entertainment. There is a fishing lake on the site, which proves very popular. Facilities on this park are excellent. A DVD of the site is available free of charge. 30 acre site. 350 touring pitches. 252 hardstandings. Tent pitches. Motorhome pitches.

Notes Families & couples only, no motorcycles or commercial vehicles.

BRIDGETOWN · Map 3 SS93

Exe Valley Caravan Site *(SS923333)*

▶ ▶ ▶ ▶

Mill House TA22 9JR

☎ 01643 851432

e-mail: paul@paulmatt.fsnet.co.uk

dir: *Take A396 (Tiverton to Minehead road). Turn W in centre of Bridgetown, site 40yds on right*

PETS: Charges contact for details **Public areas** on leads disp bin **Exercise area on site** riverside walks **Facilities** food dog chews scoop/disp bags leads walks info vet info

Open 16 Mar-15 Oct Last arrival 22.00hrs

Set in the Exmoor National Park, this adults-only park occupies an enchanting, peaceful spot in a wooded valley alongside the River Exe. There is free fly-fishing, and an abundance of wildlife, with excellent walks directly from the park. The inn opposite serves lunchtime and evening meals. 4 acre site. 50 touring pitches. 10 hardstandings. Tent pitches. Motorhome pitches.

Notes 🐾

BURTLE · Map 3 ST34

Orchard Camping *(ST397434)*

▶

Ye Olde Burtle Inn, Catcott Rd TA7 8NG

☎ 01278 722269 & 722123 📠 01278 722269

e-mail: food@theinn.eu

dir: *M5 junct 23, A39, in approx 4m left onto unclass road to Burtle, site by pub in village centre*

PETS: Public areas Exercise area surrounding open countryside 0.25m **Facilities** washing facs walks info vet info **Stables** 0.25m **Other** prior notice required enclosed orchard available for horses

Open all year Last arrival anytime

A simple campsite set in an orchard at the rear of a lovely 17th-century family inn in the heart of the Somerset Levels. The restaurant offers a wide range of meals, and breakfast can be pre-ordered by campers. A shower and disabled toilet have been added and these facilities are available to campers outside pub opening hours. Free internet access and Wi-fi are available. 0.75 acre site. 30 touring pitches. Tent pitches.

CASTLE CARY · Map 3 ST63

The George Hotel

★★ 67% HOTEL

Market Place BA7 7AH

☎ 01963 350761 📠 01963 350035

e-mail: castlecarygeorge@aol.co.uk

dir: *A303 onto A371. Signed Castle Cary, 2m on left*

PETS: Bedrooms (5 GF) sign ground-floor bedrooms only **Public areas** on leads **Grounds** disp bin **Exercise area** nearby **Facilities** food (pre-bookable) food bowl water bowl dog chews cat treats feeding mat leads pet sitting dog walking washing facs dog grooming cage storage walks info vet info **On Request** torch towels **Stables** 3m **Other** charge for damage

This 15th-century coaching inn provides well-equipped bedrooms that are generally spacious. Most bedrooms are at the back of the house, enjoying a quiet aspect, and some are on the ground floor; one is suitable for less able guests. Diners can choose to eat in the more formal dining room, or in one of the two cosy bars.

Rooms 17 (5 annexe) (1 fmly) (5 GF) **S** fr £65; **D** fr £85 (incl. bkfst) **Facilities** Xmas New Year Wi-fi **Parking** 7 **Notes** LB

CHARD · Map 3 ST30

Lordleaze

★★★ 77% HOTEL

Henderson Dr, Forton Rd TA20 2HW

☎ 01460 61066 📠 01460 66468

e-mail: info@lordleazehotel.com

web: www.lordleazehotel.com

dir: *A358 from Chard, left at St Mary's Church to Forton & Winsham on B3162. Follow signs to hotel*

PETS: Bedrooms (7 GF) unattended **Charges** £5 per night **Grounds** disp bin **Exercise area** surrounding fields **Facilities** vet info **On Request** fridge access

Conveniently and quietly located, this hotel is close to the Devon, Dorset and Somerset borders, and only minutes from Chard. All bedrooms are well equipped and comfortable. The friendly lounge bar has a wood-burning stove and serves tempting bar meals. The conservatory restaurant offers more formal dining.

Rooms 25 (2 fmly) (7 GF) **S** £75-£78; **D** £115-£120 (incl. bkfst)* **Facilities** FTV Xmas New Year Wi-fi **Parking** 55 **Notes** LB

Broadway House Holiday Park
(ST448547)

Axbridge Rd BS27 3DB
☎ 08442 729501 📠 01934 744950
e-mail: enquiries@broadwayhousepark.co.uk
dir: *From M5 junct 22 follow signs to Cheddar Gorge & Caves (8m). Site midway between Cheddar & Axbridge on A371*

PETS: Charges £2.50 per night **Public areas** except swimming pool, children's play area & shower/toilet blocks disp bin **Exercise area on site** dog walks **Exercise area** open space within easy reach of site **Facilities** food food bowl water bowl walks info vet info **Other** prior notice is not required for touring pitches disposal bags available **Restrictions** no dangerous dogs (see page 7)

Open Mar-Oct rs Mar-end May & Oct bar & pool closed, limited shop hours Last arrival 22.00hrs Last departure 11.00hrs

A well-equipped holiday park on the slopes of the Mendips with an exceptional range of activities for all ages. This is a busy and lively park in the main holiday periods, but can be quiet and peaceful off-peak. Broadway has its own competition standard BMX track, which is used for National and European Championships, plus a skateboard park and many other activities. The slightly-terraced pitches face south, and are backed by the Mendips. 30 acre site. 342 touring pitches. 70 hardstandings. Tent pitches. Motorhome pitches. 35 statics.

Notes Children to be supervised at all times.

Cheddar Bridge Touring Park *(ST459529)*
▶▶▶▶

Draycott Rd BS27 3RJ
☎ 01934 743048 📠 01934 743048
e-mail: enquiries@cheddarbridge.co.uk
dir: *M5 junct 22 (Burnham-on-Sea), A38 towards Cheddar & Bristol, approx 5m. Right onto A371 at Cross, follow Cheddar signs. Through Cheddar village towards Wells, site on right just before Caravan Club site*

PETS: Charges dog £2 per night **Public areas** on leads disp bin **Exercise area** riverside walk adjacent **Facilities** vet info

Open Mar-Oct Last arrival 22.00hrs Last departure 11.00hrs

A peaceful adults-only park on the edge of the village of Cheddar, with the River Yeo passing attractively through its grounds. It is handy for exploring Cheddar Gorge and Wookey Hole, Wells and Bath. The toilet and shower facilities are very good. 4 acre site. 45 touring pitches. 10 hardstandings. Tent pitches. Motorhome pitches. 4 statics.

Notes Quiet 23.00hrs-08.00hrs

The Hunters Rest
★★★★ INN

King Ln, Clutton Hill BS39 5QL
☎ 01761 452303 📠 01761 453308
e-mail: paul@huntersrest.co.uk
web: www.huntersrest.co.uk
dir: *Off A37 onto A368 towards Bath, 100yds right onto lane, left at T-junct, inn 0.25m on left*

PETS: Bedrooms unattended certain bedrooms only **Charges** £10 per stay **Public areas** on leads **Grounds** disp bin **Exercise area** adjacent **Facilities** food (pre-bookable) food bowl water bowl dog chews feeding mat scoop/disp bags leads washing facs cage storage walks info vet info **On Request** fridge access torch **Stables** adjacent **Other** charge for damage phone for details of stabling arrangements **Resident Pet:** Reg (Black Labrador)

This establishment was originally built around 1750 as a hunting lodge for the Earl of Warwick. Set in delightful countryside, it is ideally located for Bath, Bristol and Wells. Bedrooms and bathrooms are furnished and equipped to excellent standards, and the ground floor combines the character of a real country inn with an excellent range of home-cooked meals.

Rooms 5 en suite (1 fmly) **S** £67.50-£77.50; **D** £95-£130 **Facilities** FTV tea/coffee Dinner available Direct Dial Cen ht Wi-fi Golf 18 **Parking** 90 **Notes** LB

Manor Farm
★★★ GUEST ACCOMMODATION

Wayford TA18 8QL
☎ 01460 78865 & 0776 7620031 📠 01460 78865
e-mail: theresaemery@hotmail.com
web: www.manorfarm.biz
dir: *B3165 from Crewkerne to Lyme Regis, 3m in Clapton right onto Dunsham Ln, Manor Farm 0.5m up hill on right*

PETS: Sep accom stable block, barns **Public areas Grounds** disp bin **Exercise area** woods 0.25m **Facilities** food bowl water bowl bedding leads washing facs cage storage walks info vet info **On Request** fridge access torch **Stables Other** pet food on request **Resident Pets:** Charlie & Ginger (cats), Rosie (Highland cow)

Located off the beaten track, this fine Victorian country house has extensive views over Clapton towards the Axe Valley. The comfortably furnished bedrooms are well equipped, and front-facing rooms enjoy splendid views. Breakfast is served at separate tables in the dining room, and a spacious lounge is also provided.

Rooms 4 en suite 1 annexe en suite (2 fmly) **S** £35-£40; **D** £70-£75 **Facilities** STV FTV TVL tea/coffee Cen ht Fishing Riding **Parking** 14 **Notes** ⊛

CROWCOMBE · Map 3 ST13

Quantock Orchard Caravan Park *(ST138357)*

▶ ▶ ▶ ▶

Flaxpool TA4 4AW
☎ 01984 618618
e-mail: member@flaxpool.freeserve.co.uk
dir: *Take A358 from Taunton, signed Minehead & Wiliton. In 8m turn left just past Flaxpool Garage. Park immediately on left*

PETS: Charges Public areas except swimming pool & toilet block **Exercise area** adjacent **Facilities** food food bowl water bowl washing facs walks info vet info **Other** disposal bags available; pet chews & treats can be ordered

Open all year rs 10 Sep-20 May swimming pool closed Last arrival 22.00hrs Last departure noon

This small family run park is set at the foot of the beautiful Quantock Hills and makes an ideal base for touring Somerset, Exmoor and North Devon. It is also close to the West Somerset Railway. It has excellent facilities and there is a lovely heated outdoor swimming pool, plus gym and fitness centre; bike hire is also available. There are static homes for hire. 3.5 acre site. 69 touring pitches. 30 hardstandings. Tent pitches. Motorhome pitches. 8 statics.

DULVERTON · Map 3 SS92

Tarr Farm Inn

★ ★ ★ ★ ★ ◉ INN

Tarr Steps, Exmoor National Park TA22 9PY
☎ 01643 851507 📠 01643 851111
e-mail: enquiries@tarrfarm.co.uk
web: www.tarrfarm.co.uk
dir: *4m NW of Dulverton. Off B3223 signed Tarr Steps, signs to Tarr Farm Inn*

PETS: Bedrooms (4 GF) **Charges** £8 per night £56 per week **Public areas** except restaurant & lounge on leads **Grounds** on leads disp bin **Exercise area** adjacent **Facilities** food bowl water bowl bedding dog chews leads cage storage walks info vet info **On Request** fridge access torch towels **Stables** 0.5m **Other** charge for damage prior notice required

Tarr Farm, dating from the 16th century, nestles on the lower slopes of Exmoor overlooking the famous old clapper bridge, Tarr Steps. The majority of rooms are in the bedroom block that provides very stylish and comfortable accommodation with an impressive selection of thoughtful touches. Tarr Farm Inn, with much character and traditional charm, draws the crowds for cream teas and delicious dinners which are prepared from good local produce.

Rooms 9 en suite (4 GF) **S** £95; **D** £150 **Facilities** STV tea/coffee Dinner available Direct Dial Cen ht Wi-fi Fishing Riding **Parking** 10 **Notes** LB No Children 14yrs No coaches

DUNSTER · Map 3 SS94

The Luttrell Arms Hotel

★ ★ ★ **73%** HOTEL

High St TA24 6SG
☎ 01643 821555 📠 01643 821567
e-mail: info@luttrellarms.fsnet.co.uk
web: www.luttrellarms.co.uk/main.htm
dir: *A39/A396 S towards Tiverton. Hotel on left opposite Yarn Market*

PETS: Bedrooms unattended **Charges** dog £5 per night **Public areas** except restaurant on leads **Grounds** on leads **Exercise area** adjacent **Facilities** walks info vet info **On Request** fridge access torch **Resident Pets:** Merlin & Mordred (cats)

Occupying an enviable position on the high street, this 15th-century hotel looks up towards the town's famous castle. Beautifully renovated and decorated, high levels of comfort can be found throughout. Some of the spacious bedrooms have four-poster beds. The warm and friendly staff provide attentive service in a relaxed atmosphere.

Rooms 28 (3 fmly) **Facilities** FTV Exmoor safaris Historic tours Walking tours New Year **Notes** LB

EMBOROUGH · Map 3 ST65

Old Down Touring Park *(ST628513)*

▶ ▶ ▶

Old Down House BA3 4SA
☎ 01761 232355 📠 01761 232355
e-mail: jsmallparkhomes@aol.com
dir: *A37 from Farrington Gurney through Ston Easton. In 2m left onto B3139 to Radstock. Site opposite Old Down Inn*

PETS: Charges £1 per night **Public areas** disp bin **Exercise area** on site **Facilities** food bowl water bowl walks info vet info **Other** prior notice required dogs must be kept on leads at all times

Open all year Last arrival 20.00hrs Last departure noon

A small family-run site set in open parkland, surrounded by well-established trees. The excellent toilet facilities are well maintained as is every other aspect of the park. Children are welcome. 4 acre site. 30 touring pitches. 15 hardstandings. 6 seasonal pitches. Tent pitches. Motorhome pitches.

Map 3 SS83

Crown
★★★ **79%** ® HOTEL

TA24 7PP
☎ 01643 831554 📄 01643 831665
e-mail: info@crownhotelexmoor.co.uk
web: www.crownhotelexmoor.co.uk
dir: M5 junct 25, follow Taunton signs. Take A358 from Taunton, then B3224 via Wheddon Cross to Exford

PETS: Bedrooms unattended **Sep accom** stables available for kenneling **Charges** £12 per stay **Public areas** except restaurant **Grounds** disp bin **Exercise area** 25mtrs **Facilities** water bowl dog chews pet sitting washing facs walks info vet info **On Request** fridge access torch towels **Stables Other** charge for damage **Resident Pet:** Oscar (Patterdale Terrier)

Guest comfort is certainly the hallmark here. Afternoon tea is served in the lounge beside a roaring fire, and tempting menus in the bar and restaurant are all part of the charm of this delightful old coaching inn that specialises in breaks for shooting and other country sports. Bedrooms retain a traditional style yet offer a range of modern comforts and facilities, many have views of this pretty moorland village.

Rooms 16 (3 fmly) **S** £69-£77; **D** £119-£155 (incl. bkfst)*
Facilities Xmas New Year Wi-fi **Parking** 30 **Notes** LB

 Map 3 ST53

The Old Oaks Touring Park (ST521394)
▶▶▶▶▶

Wick Farm, Wick BA6 8JS
☎ 01458 831437
e-mail: info@theoldoaks.co.uk
dir: On A361 from Glastonbury towards Shepton Mallet. In 1.75m turn left at Wick sign, site on left in 1m

PETS: Charges £1.50 per night **Public areas** except shop & cabins disp bin **Exercise area on site** enclosed area (with seating) **Exercise area** 100mtrs **Facilities** food food bowl water bowl dog chews cat treats leads washing facs walks info vet info **Other** prior notice required dog shower; dog minding service (chargeable); dog grooming can be arranged disposal bags available

Open 10 Feb-12 Nov rs Low season reduced shop & reception hours Last arrival 20.00hrs Last departure noon

An idyllic park on a working farm with panoramic views towards the Mendip Hills. Old Oaks offers sophisticated services whilst retaining a farming atmosphere, and there are some 'super' pitches as well as en suite toilet facilities. Glastonbury's two famous 1,000-year-old oak trees, Gog and Magog, are on site. This is an adult-only park, and three camping cabins are available for hire. 10 acre site. 100 touring pitches. 90 hardstandings. Tent pitches. Motorhome pitches.

Notes Group or block bookings only at owners' discretion, latest arrival time 18.00hrs in low season

---

 Map 3 ST57

Days Inn Bristol West - M5
BUDGET HOTEL

BS20 7XG
☎ 01275 373709 & 373624 📄 01275 374104
e-mail: gordano.hotel@welcomebreak.co.uk
web: www.welcomebreak.co.uk
dir: M5 junct 19, follow signs for Gordano Services

PETS: Bedrooms (29 GF) ground-floor bedrooms only **Charges** £5 per stay **Public areas** except food service areas **Grounds** on leads disp bin **Facilities** vet info **On Request** torch towels **Other** please phone for further details of pet facilities

This modern building offers accommodation in smart, spacious and well-equipped bedrooms, suitable for families and business travellers, and all with en suite bathrooms. Continental breakfast is available and other refreshments may be taken at the nearby family restaurant.

Rooms 60 (52 fmly) (29 GF) (10 smoking) **S** £39.95-£59.95; **D** £49.95-£69.95

HIGHBRIDGE — Map 3 ST34

The Greenwood

★★★★ GUEST ACCOMMODATION

76 Main Rd, West Huntspill TA9 3QU
☎ 01278 795886 📠 01278 795886
e-mail: info@the-greenwood.co.uk
web: www.the-greenwood.co.uk
dir: *On A38 in West Huntspill, between Orchard Inn & Sundowner Hotel*

PETS: Bedrooms (1 GF) unattended **Public areas** except restaurant on leads **Grounds** on leads disp bin **Exercise area** adjacent **Facilities** water bowl scoop/disp bags washing facs cage storage walks info **On Request** fridge access torch **Stables** 2m **Other** charge for damage paddock available for horses (stabling can be arranged) **Resident Pets:** Paddy & Guinness (Siberian Husky cross)

Set in two acres of land, this 18th-century former farmhouse and family home offers comfortable accommodation in a friendly environment. Breakfast, featuring home-made preserves, is served in the dining room and home-cooked dinners are available by arrangement. There is a lounge for relaxation.

Rooms 7 rms (6 en suite) (1 pri facs) (3 fmly) (1 GF)
S £45-£49.50; **D** £65-£72 **Facilities** FTV TVL tea/coffee Dinner available Cen ht Licensed Wi-fi **Parking** 8 **Notes** LB

HINTON CHARTERHOUSE — Map 3 ST75

von Essen hotels
A PRIVATE COLLECTION
www.vonessenhotels.com

Homewood Park

★★★ COUNTRY HOUSE HOTEL

BA2 7TB
☎ 01225 723731 📠 01225 723820
e-mail: info@homewoodpark.co.uk
web: www.homewoodpark.co.uk
dir: *6m SE of Bath on A36, turn left at 2nd sign for Freshford*

PETS: Bedrooms (2 GF) **Charges** contact for details
Public areas except restaurant on leads **Grounds** disp bin **Facilities** food (pre-bookable) food bowl water bowl bedding dog chews feeding mat scoop/disp bags leads pet sitting washing facs cage storage walks info vet info **On Request** fridge access torch towels **Other** charge for damage prior notice required

Homewood Park, an unassuming yet stylish Georgian house set in delightful grounds, offers relaxed surroundings and maintains high standards of quality and comfort throughout. Bedrooms, all individually decorated, include thoughtful extras to ensure a comfortable stay. The hotel has a reputation for excellent cuisine. The Rosette award has been suspended due to a change of chef. A new award will be in place once the AA inspectors have assessed the food cooked by the new kitchen brigade.

Rooms 21 (2 annexe) (3 fmly) (2 GF) **Facilities** Spa FTV ↖ ⌕ ⌣ Sauna Steam room Xmas New Year Wi-fi **Parking** 30

HOLFORD — Map 3 ST14

Combe House

★★★ 75% ◉ HOTEL

TA5 1RZ
☎ 01278 741382 & 741213 📠 01278 741322
e-mail: enquiries@combehouse.co.uk
web: www.combehouse.co.uk
dir: *From A39 W left in Holford then left at T-junct. Left at fork, 0.25m to Holford Combe*

PETS: Bedrooms (2 GF) **Charges** £5 per night **Public areas** except dining areas on leads **Grounds** on leads disp bin **Facilities** food (pre-bookable) food bowl water bowl leads washing facs cage storage walks info vet info **On Request** fridge access torch towels **Other** charge for damage dogs must not be left unattended in bedrooms unless caged

Located in a peaceful wooded valley with four acres of tranquil gardens to explore, the atmosphere here is relaxed and welcoming. The individually styled bedrooms have lots of comfort - all are designed for a cosseted and pampered stay. Public areas have equal charm with traditional features interwoven with contemporary style. Food comes highly recommended with a dedicated kitchen team producing accomplished, seasonal dishes.

Rooms 18 (1 annexe) (3 fmly) (2 GF) **Facilities** ⊗ ⌣ Sauna Small gym Beauty therapy treatments Xmas New Year Wi-fi **Parking** 36

KILVE — Map 3 ST14

Hood Arms Inn

★★★★ INN

TA5 1EA
☎ 01278 741210 & 741969 📠 01278 741210
e-mail: info@thehoodarms.com
web: www.thehoodarms.com
dir: *W of Bridgwater on A39, halfway between Bridgwater & Minehead*

PETS: Bedrooms (2 GF) **Charges** £5 per night £25 per week **Public areas** except dining areas on leads **Grounds** on leads disp bin **Exercise area** adjacent **Facilities** food (pre-bookable) food bowl water bowl bedding dog chews scoop/disp bags leads washing facs cage storage walks info vet info **On Request** torch towels **Stables** 0.25m **Other** stabling for horses can be arranged **Resident Pet:** Jenny (Terrier)

A traditional inn providing good food, comfortable bedrooms and a range of local beers in the bar. Bedrooms are well equipped, and both the bar and restaurant have a cosy feel enhanced by the

pen fire. Food is available daily and fresh local produce features
n the extensive menu.

Hood Arms Inn

Rooms 8 en suite 4 annexe en suite (2 GF) **S** £75; **D** £95
Facilities FTV TVL tea/coffee Dinner available Direct Dial Wi-fi
Riding **Parking** 11

LANGPORT — Map 3 ST42

Thorney Lakes Caravan Park *(ST430237)*
►►►

Thorney Lakes, Muchelney TA10 0DW
☎ 01458 250811
e-mail: enquiries@thorneylakes.co.uk
dir: *From A303 at Podimore rdbt take A372 to Langport. At Huish
Episcopi Church turn left for Muchelney. In 100yds left (signed
Muchelney & Crewkerne). Site 300yds after John Leach Pottery*

PETS: Public areas disp bin **Exercise area on site** 2m walks in
fields **Facilities** walks info vet info **Stables**

Open Etr-Oct

A small, basic but very attractive park set in a cider apple
orchard, with coarse fishing in the three well-stocked, on-site
lakes. The famous John Leach pottery shop is close at hand,
and The Lowland Games are held nearby in July. 6 acre site. 36
touring pitches. Tent pitches. Motorhome pitches.

Notes 🐾

MARTOCK — Map 3 ST41

Southfork Caravan Park *(ST448188)*
►►►►

Parrett Works TA12 6AE
☎ 01935 825661 📠 01935 825122
e-mail: southforkcaravans@btconnect.com
dir: *8m NW of Yeovil, 2m off A303. From E, take exit after
Cartgate rdbt. From W, 1st exit off rdbt signed South Petherton,
follow camping signs*

PETS: Charges £1 per night **Public areas** except children's play
area & toilet/shower block disp bin **Exercise area on site** small
area at bottom of park **Exercise area** 200yds **Facilities** walks
info vet info **Other** prior notice required disposal bags available
Resident Pet: Tommy (Border Collie)

Open all year Last arrival 22.30hrs Last departure noon

A neat, level mainly grass park in a quiet rural area, just outside
the pretty village of Martock. Excellent, spacious hardstandings
are available. The facilities are always spotless and the whole
site well cared for by the friendly owners, who will ensure
your stay is a happy one, a fact borne out by the many repeat
customers. The park is unique in that it also has a fully-approved
caravan repair and servicing centre with accessory shop. There
are also static caravans for hire. 2 acre site. 27 touring
pitches. 2 hardstandings. Tent pitches. Motorhome pitches. 3
statics.

MINEHEAD — Map 3 SS94

Best Western Northfield

Best Western

★★★ 74% HOTEL
Northfield Rd TA24 5PU
☎ 01643 705155 & 0845 1302678 📠 01643 707715
e-mail: reservations@northfield-hotel.co.uk
web: www.northfield-hotel.co.uk
dir: *M5 junct 23, follow A38 to Bridgwater then A39 to Minehead*

PETS: Bedrooms (4 GF) unattended **Charges** £8 per night
Public areas except restaurant, bar & lounge on leads **Grounds**
on leads disp bin **Exercise area** 75mtrs **Facilities** washing facs
walks info vet info **On Request** fridge access torch towels

Located conveniently close to the town centre and the seafront,
this hotel is set in delightfully maintained gardens and has a
loyal following. A range of comfortable sitting rooms and leisure
facilities, including an indoor, heated pool is provided. A fixed-
price menu is served every evening in the oak-panelled dining
room. The attractively co-ordinated bedrooms vary in size and are
equipped to a good standard.

Rooms 30 (7 fmly) (4 GF) (6 smoking) **Facilities** STV FTV ⊛
Putt green Gym Steam room Xmas New Year Wi-fi **Services** Lift
Parking 34 **Notes** LB

MINEHEAD *continued*

Alcombe House Hotel

★★ 85% HOTEL

Bircham Rd, Alcombe TA24 6BG

☎ 01643 705130

e-mail: alcombehouse@talktalkbusiness.net

web: www.alcombehouse.co.uk

dir: *On A39 on outskirts of Minehead opposite West Somerset Community College*

PETS: Bedrooms unattended **Grounds** on leads disp bin **Exercise area** 0.25m **Facilities** water bowl cage storage walks info vet info **On Request** fridge access torch towels **Stables** 2m **Other** prior notice required

Located midway between Minehead and Dunster on the coastal fringe of Exmoor National Park, this Grade II listed, Georgian hotel offers a delightful combination of efficient service and genuine hospitality delivered by the very welcoming resident proprietors. Public areas include a comfortable lounge and a candlelit dining room where a range of carefully prepared dishes is offered from a daily-changing menu.

Rooms 7 **S** £45.50; **D** £71 (incl. bkfst)* **Facilities** FTV Xmas Wi-fi **Parking** 9 **Notes** No children 15yrs Closed 8 Nov-18 Mar

Minehead & Exmoor Caravan & Camping Park *(SS950457)*

▶▶▶

Porlock Rd TA24 8SW

☎ 01643 703074

dir: *1m W of Minehead town centre, take A39 towards Porlock. Site on right*

PETS: Public areas except children's play area & toilet block disp bin **Exercise area** 30mtrs **Facilities** walks info vet info **Other** vet available on-site on certain days

Open Mar-Oct rs Nov-Feb open certain weeks only (phone to check) Last arrival 22.00hrs Last departure noon

A small terraced park on the edge of Exmoor, spread over five small paddocks and screened by the mature trees that surround it. The level pitches provide a comfortable space for each unit on this family-run park. There is a laundrette in nearby Minehead. 3 acre site. 50 touring pitches. 10 hardstandings. 9 seasonal pitches. Tent pitches. Motorhome pitches.

Notes No open fires.

OARE
Map 3 SS74

Cloud Farm *(SS794467)*

▶▶▶

EX35 6NU

☎ 01598 741278

e-mail: stay@cloudfarmcamping.co.uk

dir: *M5 junct 24/A39 towards Minehead/Porlock then Lynton. Left in 6.5m, follow signs to Oare then right & site signed*

PETS: Charges dog £2, horse £12 per night **Public areas** disp bin **Exercise area on site Facilities** food food bowl water bowl bedding washing facs walks info vet info **Stables**

Open all year

Set in the heart of Exmoor's Doone Valley, this quiet, sheltered park is arranged over four riverside fields, with modern toilet facilities. It offers a good shop and café serving all day food, including breakfasts, with a large garden for outdoor eating, and there are self-catering holiday cottages. 110 acre site. 70 touring pitches. Tent pitches. Motorhome pitches.

PORLOCK
Map 3 SS84

Porlock Caravan Park *(SS882469)*

▶▶▶▶▶

TA24 8ND

☎ 01643 862269 🖳 01643 862269

e-mail: info@porlockcaravanpark.co.uk

dir: *Through village fork right signed Porlock Weir, site on right*

PETS: Charges £1 per night £7 per week **Public areas** except toilets, shower, dishwash area, laundry & nature garden disp bin **Exercise area** 30yds **Facilities** walks info vet info **Other** prior notice required organised walks with dogs **Resident Pets:** Sid & Alfie (cats)

Open 15 Mar-Oct Last arrival 20.00hrs Last departure 11.00hrs

A sheltered touring park, attractively laid-out in the centre of lovely countryside, on the edge of the village of Porlock. The famous Porlock Hill which starts a few hundred yards from the site, takes you to some spectacular parts of Exmoor with stunning views. The toilet facilities are superb, and there's a popular kitchen area with microwave and freezer. Holiday statics for hire. 3 acre site. 40 touring pitches. 14 hardstandings. Tent pitches. Motorhome pitches. 55 statics.

Notes No fires.

Burrowhayes Farm Caravan & Camping Site *(SS897460)*

►►►►

West Luccombe TA24 8HT
☎ 01643 862463
e-mail: info@burrowhayes.co.uk
dir: *A39 from Minehead towards Porlock for 5m. Left at Red Post to Horner & West Luccombe, site 0.25m on right, immediately before humpback bridge*

PETS: Public areas disp bin Exercise area adjacent woods Facilities food dog chews cat treats scoop/disp bags leads walks info vet info Stables 2m Other ground anchors available

Open 15 Mar-Oct Last arrival 22.00hrs Last departure noon

A delightful site on the edge of Exmoor, sloping gently down to Horner Water. The farm buildings have been converted into riding stables, from where escorted rides onto the moors can be taken, and the excellent toilet facilities are housed in timber-clad buildings. There are many walks into the surrounding countryside that can be directly accessed from the site. Additional hardstandings are now available. 8 acre site. 120 touring pitches. 10 hardstandings. Tent pitches. Motorhome pitches. 20 statics.

PRIDDY   Map 3 ST55

Cheddar Camping & Caravanning Club Site *(ST522519)*

►►►►

Townsend BA5 3BP
☎ 01749 870241 & 0845 130 7633
dir: *From A39 take B3135 to Cheddar. After 4.5m turn left. Site 200yds on right*

PETS: Public areas except facility blocks (ex assist dogs) disp bin Exercise area surrounding countryside Facilities walks info Other prior notice required

Open 15 Mar-5 Nov Last arrival 20.00hrs Last departure noon

A gently sloping site set high on the Mendip Hills and surrounded by trees. This excellent site offers really good facilities, which have now been upgraded with even more family rooms and private cubicles; these are spotlessly maintained. Fresh bread is baked daily and available from the well-stocked shop. The site is well positioned for visiting local attractions such as Cheddar, Wookey Hole, Wells and Glastonbury, and is popular with walkers. 4.5 acre site. 90 touring pitches. 37 hardstandings. Tent pitches. Motorhome pitches. 2 statics.

Notes Site gates closed 23.00hrs-07.00hrs.

SEDGEMOOR MOTORWAY SERVICE AREA (M5)   Map 3 ST35

Days Inn Sedgemoor - M5

BUDGET HOTEL

Sedgemoor BS24 0JL
☎ 01934 750831 📠 01934 750808
e-mail: sedgemoor.hotel@welcomebreak.co.uk
web: www.welcomebreak.co.uk
dir: *M5 northbound junct 21/22*

PETS: Bedrooms (19 GF) ground-floor bedrooms only Charges £5 per stay Public areas Grounds on leads Facilities vet info

This modern building offers accommodation in smart, spacious and well-equipped bedrooms, suitable for families and business travellers, and all with en suite bathrooms. Continental breakfast is available and other refreshments may be taken at the nearby family restaurant.

Rooms 40 (39 fmly) (19 GF) (8 smoking) S £39.95-£59.95; D £49.95-£69.95

SPARKFORD   Map 3 ST62

Long Hazel Park *(ST602262)*

►►►

High St BA22 7JH
☎ 01963 440002
e-mail: longhazelpark@hotmail.com
dir: *Exit A303 at Hazlegrove rdbt, follow signs for Sparkford. Site 400yds on left*

PETS: Charges dog £1 per night Public areas only on pitch occupied by dog owner disp bin Exercise area 200yds Facilities walks info vet info Other prior notice required dogs must be exercised off site shop 300mtrs; disposal bags available Restrictions no Pit Bull Terriers, Rottweilers, Dobermans or dangerous dogs (see page 7) Resident Pet: Lola (Jack Russell)

Open all year Last arrival 22.00hrs Last departure 11.00hrs

A very neat, adults-only park next to the village inn in the high street. This attractive park is run by friendly owners to a very good standard. Spacious pitches, many with hardstandings. There are also luxury lodges on site for hire or purchase. 3.5 acre site. 50 touring pitches. 30 hardstandings. 21 seasonal pitches. Tent pitches. Motorhome pitches. 1 static.

Notes 🚭

ENGLAND

STANTON DREW — Map 3 ST56

Greenlands *(ST597636)*

★★★★ FARMHOUSE

BS39 4ES

☎ 01275 333487 📄 01275 331211 Mrs J Cleverley

dir: *A37 onto B3130, on right before Stanton Drew Garage*

PETS: Bedrooms Public areas except dining room on leads **Grounds** on leads disp bin **Exercise area** adjacent **Facilities** washing facs cage storage walks info vet info **On Request** fridge access torch **Resident Pet:** Magic (Labrador)

Situated near the ancient village of Stanton Drew in the heart of the Chew Valley, Greenlands is convenient for Bristol Airport and Bath, Bristol and Wells. There are comfortable, well-equipped bedrooms and a downstairs lounge, and breakfast is the highlight of any stay here.

Rooms 4 en suite **S** £30; **D** £60 **Facilities** STV FTV TVL tea/coffee Cen ht Wi-fi **Parking** 8 **Notes** No Children 12yrs 🐾 3 acres hobby farm/poultry

STON EASTON — Map 3 ST65

🐾 von Essen hotels
A PRIVATE COLLECTION
www.vonessenhotels.co.uk

Ston Easton Park

★★★★ ⚜⚜ COUNTRY HOUSE HOTEL

BA3 4DF

☎ 01761 241631 📄 01761 241377

e-mail: info@stoneaston.co.uk

web: www.stoneaston.co.uk

dir: *On A37*

PETS: Bedrooms Charges £10 per night **Public areas** except restaurant & at manager's discretion **Grounds** disp bin **Exercise area Exercise area** woodland **Facilities** food (pre-bookable) food bowl water bowl bedding dog chews feeding mat scoop/disp bags leads washing facs dog grooming cage storage walks info vet info **On Request** fridge access torch towels **Stables** 0.5m **Other** charge for damage

Surrounded by The Mendips this outstanding Palladian mansion lies in extensive parklands that were landscaped by Humphrey Repton. The architecture and decorative features are stunning; the state rooms include one of England's earliest surviving Print Rooms, and the Palladian Saloon considered one of Somerset's finest rooms. There is even an Edwardian kitchen that guests might like to take a look at. The helpful and attentive team provide a very efficient service, and the award-winning cuisine

uses organic produce from the hotel's own kitchen garden. The bedrooms and bathrooms are all appointed to an excellent standard.

Rooms 22 (3 annexe) (2 fmly) **Facilities** STV 🎣 Fishing 🎣 Archery Clay pigeon shooting Quad bikes Hot air ballooning Xmas New Year Wi-fi **Parking** 120 **Notes** LB

TAUNTON — Map 3 ST22

🐾 von Essen hotel
A PRIVATE COLLECTION
www.vonessenhotels.co.uk

The Mount Somerset

★★★ 83% ⚜⚜ HOTEL

Lower Henlade TA3 5NB

☎ 01823 442500 📄 01823 442900

e-mail: info@mountsomersethotel.co.uk

web: www.vonessenhotels.co.uk

dir: *M5 junct 25, A358 towards Chard/Ilminster, at Henlade right into Stoke Rd, left at T-junct at end, then right into drive*

PETS: Bedrooms unattended **Charges** £10 per night **Public areas** except restaurant, conservatory & conference room on leads **Grounds Exercise area** 1.5m **Facilities** food bowl water bowl pet sitting dog walking cage storage walks info **On Request** fridge access torch towels **Other** charge for damage pet sitting & dog walking can be arranged (1 week notice required); charge for towels.

From its elevated and rural position, this impressive Regency house has wonderful views over Taunton Vale. Refurbishment has resulted in impressive quality and comfort levels throughout in the stylish bedrooms and bathrooms. The elegant public rooms combine elegance and flair with an engaging and intimate atmosphere. In addition to the daily-changing, fixed-price menu, a carefully selected seasonal carte is available in the restaurant.

Rooms 11 (1 fmly) **Facilities** 🎣 Beauty treatments Xmas New Year Wi-fi **Services** Lift **Parking** 100

Farthings Country House Hotel and Restaurant

★★★ 74% ⚜ SMALL HOTEL

Village Rd, Hatch Beauchamp TA3 6SG

☎ 01823 480664 & 0785 668 8128 📄 01823 481118

e-mail: farthingshotel@yahoo.co.uk

web: www.farthingshotel.co.uk

dir: *From A358 (between Taunton & Ilminster) into Hatch Beauchamp. Hotel in village centre*

PETS: Bedrooms (3 GF) **Public areas** on leads **Grounds** on leads disp bin **Exercise area** adjacent **Facilities** food (pre-bookable) food bowl water bowl dog chews scoop/disp bags leads washing facs cage storage walks info vet info **On Request** fridge access torch towels **Other** charge for damage please phone for further details of pet facilities; dog grooming available locally **Resident Pets:** Sasha (Cocker Spaniel), Borris, Dorothy & Lucy (pigs) chickens, ducks, geese

This delightful hotel, set in its own extensive gardens in a peaceful village location, offers comfortable accommodation, combined with all the character and charm of a building dating back over 200 years. The calm atmosphere makes this a great place to relax and unwind. Dinner service is attentive, and menus

feature best quality local ingredients prepared and presented with care.

Rooms 12 (2 annexe) (2 fmly) (3 GF) **S** £110-£155; **D** £130-£195 (incl. bkfst) **Facilities** FTV ✦ Xmas New Year Wi-fi **Parking** 25 **Notes** LB

Express by Holiday Inn Taunton M5 Jct 25

BUDGET HOTEL

Blackbrook Business Park, Blackbrook Park Av TA1 2PX
☎ 01823 624000 📠 01823 624024
e-mail: managertaunton@expressholidayinn.co.uk
web: www.hiexpress.com/taunton
dir: M5 junct 25. Follow signs for Blackbrook Business Park. Hotel 100yds on right

PETS: Bedrooms (22 GF) **Public areas** except breakfast area **Grounds** on leads **Exercise area** nearby **On Request** torch **Other** charge for damage well behaved pets only, must be supervised at all times

A modern hotel ideal for families and business travellers. Fresh and uncomplicated, the spacious rooms include Sky TV, power shower and tea and coffee-making facilities. Continental buffet breakfast is included in the room rate; other meals may be taken at the nearby family pub or restaurant.

Rooms 92 (55 fmly) (22 GF) (8 smoking)

Cornish Farm Touring Park (ST235217)
▶ ▶ ▶ ▶

Shoreditch TA3 7BS
☎ 01823 327746 📠 01823 354946
e-mail: info@cornishfarm.com
dir: M5 junct 25 towards Taunton. Left at lights. 3rd left into Ilminster Rd (follow Corfe signs). Right at rdbt, left at next. Right at T-junct, left into Killams Dr, 2nd left into Killams Ave. Over motorway bridge. Site on left, take 2nd entrance

PETS: Charges £1 per night £7 per week **Public areas** disp bin **Exercise area** public footpath adjacent **Facilities** walks info vet info **Resident Pets:** 2 German Shepherds, cats

Open all year Last arrival anytime Last departure 11.30hrs

This smart park provides really top quality facilities throughout. Although only two miles from Taunton, it is set in open countryside and is a very convenient base for visiting the many attractions of the area such as Clarks Village, Glastonbury and Cheddar Gorge. 3.5 acre site. 50 touring pitches. 25 hardstandings. Tent pitches. Motorhome pitches.

Ashe Farm Camping & Caravan Site
(ST279229)
▶ ▶ ▶

Thornfalcon TA3 5NW
☎ 01823 443764 & 07891 989482
e-mail: info@ashefarm.co.uk
dir: M5 junct 25, A358 E for 2.5m. Right at Nags Head pub. Site 0.25m on right

PETS: Public areas Exercise area on site dog walk around fields **Facilities** walks info vet info

Open Apr-Oct Last arrival 22.00hrs Last departure noon

A well-screened site surrounded by mature trees and shrubs, with two large touring fields. A modern facilities block includes toilets and showers plus a separate laundry room. Not far from the bustling market town of Taunton, and handy for both south and north coasts. 7 acre site. 30 touring pitches. 11 hardstandings. Tent pitches. Motorhome pitches. 3 statics.

Notes ⊛

WATCHET   Map 3 ST04

Home Farm Holiday Centre (ST106432)
▶ ▶ ▶

St Audries Bay TA4 4DP
☎ 01984 632487 📠 01984 634687
e-mail: dib@homefarmholidaycentre.co.uk
dir: Follow A39 towards Minehead, right onto B3191 at West Quantoxhead after St Audries garage, then right in 0.25m

PETS: Charges dog £2 per night **Public areas** except bar building, shop & swimming pool disp bin **Exercise area on site** 2 open grass areas, beach & woodland walk **Facilities** food leads walks info vet info **Other** max 2 dogs per pitch disposal bags & pet toys available

Open all year rs mid Nov-Etr shop & bar closed Last arrival dusk Last departure noon

In a hidden valley beneath the Quantock Hills, this park overlooks its own private beach. The atmosphere is friendly and quiet, and there are lovely sea views from the level pitches. Flowerbeds, woodland walks, and a Koi carp pond all enhance this very attractive site, along with a lovely indoor swimming pool and a beer garden. 45 acre site. 40 touring pitches. 35 hardstandings. Tent pitches. Motorhome pitches. 230 statics.

Notes No noise after mdnt.

WELLINGTON — Map 3 ST12

Greenacres Touring Park *(ST156001)*

▶ ▶ ▶ ▶

Haywards Ln, Chelston TA21 9PH
☎ 01823 652844
e-mail: enquiries@wellington.co.uk
dir: *M5 junct 26, right at rdbt signed Wellington, approx 1.5m. At Chelston rdbt, take 1st left, signed A38 West Buckland Rd. In 500mtrs follow sign for site*

PETS: Public areas disp bin **Exercise area** walks nearby **Facilities** walks info vet info **Other** dogs must be kept on leads at all times **Restrictions** no dangerous dogs (see page 7)

Open Apr-end Sep Last arrival 20.00hrs Last departure 11.00hrs

This attractively landscaped adults-only park is situated close to the Somerset/Devon border in a peaceful setting with great views of the Blackdown and Quantock Hills. It is in a very convenient location for overnight stays, being just one and a half miles from the M5. It is also close to a local bus route. It has excellent facilities, which are spotlessly clean and well maintained. 2.5 acre site. 40 touring pitches. 30 hardstandings. Motorhome pitches.

Notes No RVs.

Gamlins Farm Caravan Park *(ST083195)*

▶ ▶ ▶

Gamlins Farm House, Greenham TA21 0LZ
☎ 01823 672859 & 07967 683738
e-mail: nataliehowe@hotmail.com
dir: *M5 junct 26, A38 towards Tiverton & Exeter. 5m, right for Greenham, site 1m on right*

PETS: Charges dog or cat 50p, horse £6-£10 per night **Public areas** except laundry & wash rooms **Exercise area on site** field available **Facilities** washing facs walks info vet info **Stables Other** prior notice required sand school (80 x 20mtrs) available

Open Mar-Oct

A well-planned site in a secluded position with panoramic views. The friendly owners keep the toilet facilities to a good standard of cleanliness. 4 acre site. 35 touring pitches. 6 hardstandings. Tent pitches. Motorhome pitches. 3 statics.

Notes No loud noise after 22.00hrs.

WELLS — Map 3 ST54

Coxley Vineyard

★★ 71% HOTEL

Coxley BA5 1RQ
☎ 01749 670285 🖷 01749 679708
e-mail: max@orofino.freeserve.co.uk
dir: *A39 from Wells signed Coxley. Village halfway between Wells & Glastonbury. Hotel at end of village*

PETS: Bedrooms (8 GF) unattended **Public areas** except restaurant & lounge bar **Grounds** disp bin **Exercise area** surrounding area **Facilities** water bowl washing facs cage storage walks info vet info **On Request** fridge access towels **Stables** 3m

This privately owned and personally run hotel was built on the site of an old cider farm. It was later part of a commercial vineyard and some of the vines are still in evidence. It provides well equipped, modern bedrooms; most are situated on the ground floor. There is a comfortable bar and a spacious restaurant with an impressive lantern ceiling. The hotel is a popular venue for conferences and other functions.

Rooms 9 (5 fmly) (8 GF) **Facilities** FTV ⚡ Xmas Wi-fi **Parking** 50

The Crown at Wells

★★★★ INN

Market Place BA5 2RP
☎ 01749 673457 🖷 01749 679792
e-mail: stay@crownatwells.co.uk
web: www.crownatwells.co.uk
dir: *On entering Wells follow signs for Hotels & Deliveries, in Market Place, car park at rear*

PETS: Bedrooms Charges £5 per night **Grounds** on leads **Exercise area** 200yds **Facilities** walks info **On Request** fridge access torch **Other** charge for damage

Retaining its original features and period charm, this historic inn is situated in the heart of the city, just a short stroll from the cathedral. The building's frontage has been used in many film productions. Bedrooms, all with modern facilities, vary in size and style. Public areas focus around Anton's, the popular bistro, which offers a light and airy environment and relaxed atmosphere. The Penn Bar offers an alternative eating option and real ales.

Rooms 15 en suite (2 fmly) **S** £65-£95; **D** £95-£115 **Facilities** FTV tea/coffee Dinner available Cen ht Wi-fi Golf 18 **Parking** 10 **Notes** LB

Infield House

★★★★ BED AND BREAKFAST

36 Portway BA5 2BN
☎ 01749 670989   📠 01749 679093
e-mail: infield@talk21.com
web: www.infieldhouse.co.uk
dir: *500yds W of city centre on A371 Portway*

PETS: Bedrooms Public areas on leads **Grounds** on leads
disp bin **Exercise area** 0.5m **Facilities** leads washing facs
walks info vet info **On Request** fridge access torch towels
Restrictions no dogs under 1 year **Resident Pet:** Pepper
(Pembroke Corgi)

This charming Victorian house offers comfortable, spacious
rooms of elegance and style. The friendly hosts are very
welcoming and provide a relaxing home-from-home. Guests may
bring their pets, by arrangement. Dinners, also by arrangement,
are served in the pleasant dining room where good home cooking
ensures an enjoyable and varied range of options.

Rooms 3 en suite; **D** £68-£70 **Facilities** FTV tea/coffee Dinner
available Cen ht Wi-fi **Parking** 3 **Notes** No Children 12yrs

Homestead Park *(ST532474)*

▶ ▶

Wookey Hole BA5 1BW
☎ 01749 673022   📠 01749 673022
e-mail: homesteadpark@onetel.com
dir: *0.5m NW off A371 (Wells to Cheddar road). (NB weight limit
on bridge into touring area now 1 tonne)*

PETS: Charges 50p per night **Public areas** disp bin
Exercise area 50mtrs **Facilities** walks info vet info

Open Etr-Sep Last arrival 20.00hrs Last departure noon

This attractive, small site for tents only is set on a wooded
hillside and meadowland with access to the river and Wookey
Hole. This park is for adults only and the statics are residential
caravans. Please note that this site only accepts tents. 2 acre
site. 30 touring pitches. Tent pitches. 28 statics.

Notes

WESTON-SUPER-MARE   Map 3 ST36

Lauriston Hotel

★★★ **70%** HOTEL

6-12 Knightstone Rd BS23 2AN
☎ 01934 620758   📠 01934 621154
e-mail: lauriston.hotel@actionforblindpeople.org.uk
dir: *1st right after Winter Gardens, hotel entrance opposite Cabot
public house*

PETS: Bedrooms (8 GF) unattended **Charges** £3 per night
Grounds on leads disp bin **Exercise area** nearby **Facilities**
food (pre-bookable) food bowl water bowl bedding feeding mat
washing facs dog grooming cage storage walks info vet info
On Request fridge access torch towels **Stables** 2m

A friendly welcome is assured at this pleasant hotel, located right
on the seafront, just a few minutes' stroll from the pier. The hotel
extends a warm welcome to everyone but caters especially for the
visually impaired, their families, friends and guide dogs. There
are comfortable and well-appointed bedrooms; special facilities
for the guide dogs are, of course, available.

Rooms 37 (2 fmly) (8 GF) **Facilities** FTV ♫ Xmas New Year
Services Lift **Parking** 16

WESTON-SUPER-MARE *continued*

Camellia Lodge

★★★★ BED AND BREAKFAST

76 Walliscote Rd BS23 1ED
☎ 01934 613534 📠 01934 613534
e-mail: dachefs@aol.com
dir: *200yds from seafront*

PETS: Bedrooms unattended **Exercise area** beach & parks (400yds) **Facilities** walks info vet info **On Request** torch **Other** charge for damage **Resident Pets:** Jack (dog), Rosie & Riley (cats)

Guests return regularly for the warm welcome at this immaculate Victorian family home, which is just off the seafront and within walking distance of the town centre. Bedrooms have a range of thoughtful touches, and carefully prepared breakfasts are served in the relaxing dining room. Home-cooked dinners are also available by prior arrangement.

Rooms 5 en suite (2 fmly) **S** £30-£40; **D** £60-£80 **Facilities** FTV tea/coffee Dinner available Cen ht Wi-fi

Country View Holiday Park *(ST335647)*

▶▶▶

Sand Rd, Sand Bay BS22 9UJ
☎ 01934 627595
e-mail: info@cvhp.co.uk
dir: *M5 junct 21, A370 towards Weston-Super-Mare. Immediately into left lane, follow Kewstoke/Sand Bay signs. Straight over 3 rdbts onto Lower Norton Ln. At Sand Bay right into Sand Rd, site on right*

PETS: Charges £2 per night £14 per week **Public areas** bar disp bin **Exercise area** 200yds **Facilities** walks info vet info **Stables** 1m **Other** prior notice required

Open Mar-Jan Last arrival 20.00hrs Last departure noon

A pleasant open site in a rural area a few hundred yards from Sandy Bay and beach. The park is also well placed for energetic walks along the coast at either end of the beach and is only a short drive away from Weston-Super-Mare. The facilities are excellent and well maintained. 8 acre site. 120 touring pitches. 90 hardstandings. 90 seasonal pitches. Tent pitches. Motorhome pitches. 65 statics.

North Wheddon Farm *(SS923385)*

★★★★ 🛏 ⌂ FARMHOUSE

TA24 7EX
☎ 01643 841791 Mrs R Abraham
e-mail: rachael@go-exmoor.co.uk
dir: *500yds S of village x-rds on A396. Pass Moorland Hall on left, driveway next right*

PETS: Bedrooms Charges dog £5 per night **Public areas** except dining areas at meal times on leads **Grounds** on leads disp bin **Exercise area** 0.25m **Facilities** washing facs cage storage walks info vet info **On Request** torch towels **Other** charge for damage **Resident Pets:** Poppy & Mingming (Border/Lakeland Terrier cross), sheep, pigs, chickens, ducks, goats, geese, tortoise

North Wheddon Farm is a delightfully friendly and comfortable environment with great views, a perfect base for exploring the delights of Exmoor. The tranquil grounds include a pleasant garden and guests are welcome to roam the fields and say hello to the pigs, sheep, goats and any other new arrivals. Memorable dinners and breakfasts feature excellent produce, much of it straight from the farm. The bedrooms are thoughtfully equipped and individual in style with lovely comfy beds.

Rooms 3 rms (2 en suite) (1 pri facs) **S** £33-£38.50; **D** £66-£77 **Facilities** FTV tea/coffee Dinner available Cen ht Licensed Wi-fi Riding **Parking** 5 **Notes** LB 20 acres mixed

The White House
★★★★ GUEST ACCOMMODATION
11 Long St TA4 4QW
☎ 01984 632306   📠 0118 900 7881
e-mail: whitehouselive@btconnect.com
dir: A39 Bridgwater to Minehead, in Williton on right prior to Watchet turning

PETS: Bedrooms (6 GF) unattended courtyard bedrooms only Exercise area 2 mins' walk Facilities washing facs cage storage walks info vet info On Request fridge access torch towels Other charge for damage Resident Pet: 1 Standard Poodle

This Grade II listed Georgian house is in a perfect location for guests wishing to explore this beautiful countryside and coast. Many original features have been retained which add to the character of this charming establishment. Bedrooms are located both in the main house and an adjacent courtyard; all are impressive and have Egyptian cotton linen and fluffy towels. Breakfast is served in the elegant dining room, and there is a guest lounge for relaxation.

Rooms 8 rms (7 en suite) (1 pri facs) 6 annexe en suite (2 fmly) (6 GF) S £39-£49; D £78-£98 Facilities FTV TVL tea/coffee Cen ht Licensed Wi-fi Parking 12 Notes LB

Holbrook House
★★★ 82% ◉◉ COUNTRY HOUSE HOTEL
Holbrook BA9 8BS
☎ 01963 824466 & 828844   📠 01963 32681
e-mail: enquiries@holbrookhouse.co.uk
web: www.holbrookhouse.co.uk
dir: From A303 at Wincanton left onto A371 towards Castle Cary & Shepton Mallet

PETS: Bedrooms (5 GF) unattended Charges £10 per night Public areas except restaurant areas on leads Grounds on leads Exercise area 50mtrs Facilities food bowl water bowl leads cage storage walks info vet info On Request fridge access torch towels Other charge for damage

This handsome country house offers a unique blend of quality and comfort combined with a friendly atmosphere. Set in 17 acres of peaceful gardens and wooded grounds, Holbrook House makes a perfect retreat. The restaurant provides a selection of innovative dishes prepared with enthusiasm and served by a team of caring staff.

Rooms 21 (5 annexe) (2 fmly) (5 GF) S £95-£150; D £95-£250 (incl. bkfst)* Facilities Spa FTV ⊙ ♨ ♒ Gym Beauty treatment Exercise classes Sauna Steam room Fitness suite ♫ Xmas New Year Wi-fi Parking 100 Notes LB

The Royal Oak Inn
★★★★ ⬤ INN
TA24 7QP
☎ 01643 831506   📠 01643 831659
e-mail: enquiries@royaloakwithypool.co.uk
dir: 7m N of Dulverton, off B3223

PETS: Bedrooms Sep accom 1 outdoor kennel Charges £8 per night £56 per week Public areas except restaurant on leads Exercise area 500mtrs Facilities food bowl water bowl bedding dog chews leads walks info vet info On Request torch towels Stables 1m

Set at the heart of Exmoor, this long established and popular inn continues to provide rest and sustenance for weary travellers. The atmosphere is warm and engaging with the bar always frequented by cheery locals. Bedrooms and bathrooms are stylish and very well appointed with added touches of luxury such as Egyptian cotton linen, bath robes and cosseting towels. Menus feature local produce and can be enjoyed either in the bars or in the elegant restaurant.

Rooms 8 rms (7 en suite) (1 pri facs); D £120 Facilities tea/coffee Dinner available Direct Dial Cen ht Parking 10 Notes LB No Children 10yrs No coaches

Waterrow Touring Park (ST053251)
▶▶▶▶▶
TA4 2AZ
☎ 01984 623464
e-mail: waterrowpark@yahoo.co.uk
dir: M5 junct 25, A358 (signed Minehead) bypassing Taunton, B3227 through Wiveliscombe. Site in 3m at Waterrow, 0.25m past Rock Inn

PETS: Sep accom day kennel only Charges £1.50 per night £10.50 per week Public areas except on-site facilities disp bin Exercise area on site dog exercise field & river walks Exercise area many walks from site Facilities walks info vet info Other prior notice required max 2 dogs per pitch tick removing tools & disposal bags available Resident Pets: Acer (Yellow Labrador), Basil & Smokey (cats)

Open all year Last arrival 19.00hrs Last departure 11.30hrs

This really delightful park for adults only has spotless facilities and plenty of spacious hardstandings. The River Tone runs along a valley beneath the park, accessed by steps to a nature area created by the owners, where fly-fishing is permitted. Painting workshops and other activities are available, and the local pub is a short walk away. 6 acre site. 45 touring pitches. 38 hardstandings. Tent pitches. Motorhome pitches. 1 static.

Notes No gazebos.

YEOVIL
Map 3 ST51

Little Barwick House

★★★★★ @@@ 🍽 RESTAURANT WITH ROOMS

Barwick Village BA22 9TD
☎ 01935 423902 🖷 01935 420908
e-mail: littlebarwick@hotmail.com
dir: From Yeovil A37 towards Dorchester, left at 1st rdbt, 1st left, 0.25m on left

PETS: Bedrooms unattended **Charges Public areas** except restaurant **Grounds Exercise area** fields & footpaths accessed from house **Facilities** leads pet sitting dog walking washing facs cage storage walks info vet info **On Request** torch towels **Other** charge for damage dogs allowed in lounge if acceptable to other guests **Resident Pets:** Ellie (Pointer), Max & Casey (cats), Pip (Hanovarian horse), Maverick (Welsh Pony)

Situated in a quiet hamlet in three and half acres of gardens and grounds, this listed Georgian dower house is an ideal retreat for those seeking peaceful surroundings and good food. Just one of the highlights of a stay here is a meal in the restaurant, where good use is made of local ingredients. Each of the bedrooms has its own character, and a range of thoughtful extras such as fresh flowers, bottled water and magazines is provided.

Rooms 6 en suite **S** £80-£100; **D** £100-£140 **Facilities** FTV tea/coffee Dinner available Direct Dial Cen ht **Parking** 30 **Notes** No Children 5yrs RS Sun eve & Mon closed No coaches

The Masons Arms

★★★★ 🍽 ➾ INN

41 Lower Odcombe BA22 8TX
☎ 01935 862591 🖷 01935 862591
e-mail: paula@masonsarmsodcombe.co.uk
web: www.masonsarmsodcombe.co.uk
dir: From A303 take A3088 to Yeovil, follow signs to Montacute after village, 3rd turn on right

PETS: Bedrooms (6 GF) unattended **Charges** £5 per night **Public areas** on leads **Grounds** disp bin **Exercise area** 025m **Facilities** food (pre-bookable) food bowl water bowl bedding dog chews cat treats feeding mat litter tray scoop/disp bags leads washing facs cage storage walks info vet info **On Request** fridge access torch towels **Other** charge for damage **Resident Pets:** Ruff (Border Collie), Blake (Jack Russell/Chihuahua cross), Rolo (Jack Russell/Poodle cross), Harley, Duke & Morgan (cats), PJ & Moppet (rabbits), chickens

Dating back to the 16th century, this charming inn claims to be the oldest building in this small country village on the outskirts of Yeovil. The spacious bedrooms are contemporary in style, with clean lines, a high level of comfort and a wide range of considerate extras. The friendly hosts run their own micro-brewery, and their ales are available at the bar along with others. Public areas include the bar/restaurant, which offers a full menu of freshly prepared dishes, along with a choice of lighter snacks. There is a small caravan/touring park at the rear of the inn.

Rooms 6 en suite (1 fmly) (6 GF) **S** £55-£70; **D** £75-£85 **Facilities** FTV tea/coffee Dinner available Direct Dial Cen ht Wi-fi **Parking** 35 **Notes** No coaches

The Helyar Arms

★★★★ @ INN

Moor Ln, East Coker BA22 9JR
☎ 01935 862332 🖷 01935 864129
e-mail: info@helyar-arms.co.uk
dir: 3m S of Yeovil. Off A30 or A37 into East Coker

PETS: Bedrooms unattended **Charges** £10 per night **Public areas** on leads **Grounds** disp bin **Exercise area** 0.5m **Facilities** walks info vet info **Stables** 1m **Other** charge for damage

A charming 15th-century inn, serving real food in the heart of a pretty Somerset village. The traditional friendly bar with hand-drawn ales retains many original features while the bedrooms offer well equipped, attractive accommodation and modern facilities.

Rooms 6 en suite (3 fmly) **Facilities** tea/coffee Dinner available Direct Dial Cen ht Wi-fi **Parking** 40

The Halfway House Inn Country Lodge

★★★ INN

Ilchester Rd BA22 8RE
☎ 01935 840350 & 849005 🖷 01935 849006
e-mail: paul@halfwayhouseinn.com
web: www.halfwayhouseinn.com
dir: A303 onto A37 Yeovil road at Ilchester, inn 2m on left

PETS: Bedrooms sign bedrooms 2-10 only **Charges** £5 per night **Public areas** except restaurant/main bar (ex assist dogs) on leads **Grounds** on leads disp bin **Exercise area** 2m **Facilities** walks info vet info **On Request** fridge access **Other** charge for damage

This roadside inn offers comfortable accommodation, which consists of bedrooms in the main house and other contemporary style rooms, each having its own front door, in the annexe. All rooms are bright and well equipped. Meals are available in the cosy restaurant and bar where friendly staff ensure a warm welcome.

Rooms 11 en suite 9 annexe en suite (7 fmly) **S** £51.95-£64.95; **D** £62.95-£72.95 **Facilities** STV tea/coffee Dinner available Cen ht Wi-fi Fishing Pool table **Parking** 49 **Notes** LB

At Your Service B&B

 ★★★ BED AND BREAKFAST

102 West Coker Rd BA20 2JG
☎ 01935 706932 & 07590 960339
e-mail: randall9ee@btinternet.com

PETS: Bedrooms (4 GF) **Public areas** except dining room on leads **Grounds** on leads disp bin **Exercise area** 200yds **Facilities** feeding mat cage storage walks info vet info **On Request** fridge access **Resident Pet:** Misty (Chocolate Labrador)

Conveniently located on the main through road, this relaxed bed and breakfast makes an ideal base from which to explore the various nearby attractions. Bedrooms come in a range of shapes and sizes including some on the ground floor. Guests have use of the lounge and there is a car park to the rear of the property.

Rooms 4 en suite (4 GF) **S** £35-£50; **D** £55-£70 **Facilities** FTV Cen ht **Parking** 4 **Notes** LB Closed 24-27 Dec

Halfway Caravan & Camping Park (ST530195)

▶▶

Trees Cottage, Halfway, Ilchester Rd BA22 8RE
☎ 01935 840342
e-mail: halfwaycaravanpark@earthlink.net
dir: On A37 between Ilchester & Yeovil

PETS: Charges £1 per night £7 per week **Public areas** disp bin **Exercise area** public footpath **Facilities** washing facs walks info vet info **Restrictions** no large dogs; no Rottweilers, Mastiffs, Pit Bull Terriers or Dobermans

Open Mar-Oct Last arrival 19.00hrs Last departure noon

An attractive little park near the Somerset and Dorset border, and next to the Halfway House pub and restaurant, which also has excellent AA-graded accommodation. It overlooks a fishing lake and is surrounded by attractive countryside, with free fishing for people staying at the park. 2 acre site. 20 touring pitches. 10 hardstandings. Tent pitches. Motorhome pitches.

Notes 🐕

STAFFORDSHIRE

CHEADLE — Map 7 SK04

Quarry Walk Park (SK045405)

▶▶▶▶

Coppice Ln, Croxden Common, Freehay ST10 1RQ
☎ 01538 723412
e-mail: quarry@quarrywalkpark.co.uk
dir: From A522 (Uttoxeter-Cheadle road) turn at Crown Inn at Mabberley signed Freehay. In 1m at rdbt by Queen pub turn to Great Gate. Site signed on right in 1.25m

PETS: Charges £1.50 per night **Public areas** except children's play area **Exercise area on site Facilities** vet info **Other** prior notice required 1 dog per pitch only

Open all year Last arrival 18.00hrs Last departure 11.00hrs

A pleasant park, close to Alton Towers, developed in an old quarry with well-screened pitches, all with water and electricity, and mature trees and shrubs, which enhance the peaceful ambience of the park. There are seven glades of varying sizes used exclusively for tents, one with ten electric hook-ups. There are timber lodges and a camping pod for hire, each with its own hot tub. Expect good toilet facilities, which include two family rooms in the reception building. 46 acre site. 16 touring pitches. 16 hardstandings. 13 seasonal pitches. Tent pitches. Motorhome pitches. 1 wooden pod.

PENKRIDGE — Map 7 SJ91

Mercure Stafford South Hatherton House Hotel

★★★ 66% HOTEL

Pinfold Ln ST19 5QP
☎ 01785 712459 📠 01785 715532
e-mail: enquiries@hotels-stafford.com
dir: A449 to Wolverhampton. In Penkridge turn right into Pinfold Ln. Hotel on left in 300yds

PETS: Bedrooms (18 GF) **Grounds** on leads disp bin **Exercise area** 0.25m **Facilities** water bowl cage storage vet info **On Request** fridge access towels **Stables** 1.5m **Other** charge for damage

The hotel offers comfortable accommodation to both leisure and business guests. The leisure facilities consist of a pool, steam room and jacuzzi with a well-equipped gym and two squash courts. Conference facilities are also available. There is free parking and easy access to the city and countryside.

Rooms 51 (4 fmly) (18 GF) (4 smoking) **Facilities** FTV 🏊 Gym Squash Sauna Steam room Xmas New Year Wi-fi **Parking** 200 **Notes** LB

ENGLAND

STAFFORD Map 7 SJ92

Old School

★★★ BED AND BREAKFAST
Newport Rd, Haughton ST18 9JH
☎ 01785 780358 📄 01785 780358
e-mail: info@theoldsc.co.uk
dir: A518 W from Stafford, 3m to Haughton, Old School next to church

PETS: Bedrooms (3 GF) on leads **Grounds** disp bin
Exercise area 2 mins' walk **Facilities** walks info vet info
On Request fridge access torch

Located in the heart of Haughton, this Grade II listed former Victorian school has been renovated to provide a range of modern bedrooms equipped with thoughtful extras. The three rooms include a single, a double and a twin. All three have colour TV. Breakfast is served at a family table in a cosy lounge-dining room.

Rooms 3 rms (3 GF) **S** £25; **D** £50 **Facilities** FTV tea/coffee Cen ht Wi-fi **Parking** 3 **Notes** No Children 14yrs 🐾

TAMWORTH Map 7 SK20

Oak Tree Farm

★★★★★ GUEST ACCOMMODATION
Hints Rd, Hopwas B78 3AA
☎ 01827 56807 📄 01827 67271
e-mail: oaktreefarm1@aol.com
web: www.oaktreefarmhotel.co.uk
dir: 2m NW of Tamworth. Off A51 in Hopwas

PETS: Bedrooms (7 GF) sign barn bedrooms only **Grounds**
Exercise area woods (5 mins) **Facilities** cage storage walks info
On Request fridge access **Other** charge for damage **Resident Pet:** Holly (Lhaso Apso)

A warm welcome is assured at this sympathetically restored farmhouse, located in peaceful rural surroundings yet only a short drive from the NEC. Spacious bedrooms are filled with homely extras. The elegant dining room, adorned with Oriental artefacts, is the setting for memorable breakfasts. A small conference room is available.

Rooms 4 en suite 10 annexe en suite (4 fmly) (7 GF) **S** £35-£70;
D £50-£85 **Facilities** FTV TVL tea/coffee Cen ht Wi-fi 🎣 Fishing
Sauna **Parking** 20

SUFFOLK

ALDEBURGH Map 5 TM45

Brudenell Hotel

★★★★ 85% ◉◉ HOTEL
The Parade IP15 5BU
☎ 01728 452071 📄 01728 454082
e-mail: info@brudenellhotel.co.uk
web: www.brudenellhotel.co.uk
dir: A12, A1094. In town, right into High St. Hotel on seafront adjoining Fort Green car park

PETS: Bedrooms unattended **Charges** £10 per night
Public areas only on terrace on leads **Exercise area** nearby
Facilities food bowl water bowl dog chews vet info **On Request** fridge access torch **Other** charge for damage **Restrictions** well behaved dogs only

Situated at the far end of the town centre just a step away from the beach, this hotel has a contemporary appearance, enhanced by subtle lighting and quality soft furnishings. Many of the bedrooms have superb sea views; they include deluxe rooms with king-sized beds and superior rooms suitable for families. The informal restaurant showcases skilfully prepared dishes that use fresh, seasonal produce especially local fish, seafood and game.

Rooms 44 (17 fmly) **S** £80-£117; **D** £147-£314 (incl. bkfst)
Facilities Xmas New Year Wi-fi **Services** Lift **Parking** 18
Notes LB

Wentworth

★★★ 88% ◉◉ HOTEL
Wentworth Rd IP15 5BD
☎ 01728 452312 📄 01728 454343
e-mail: stay@wentworth-aldeburgh.co.uk
web: www.wentworth-aldeburgh.com
dir: Off A12 onto A1094, 6m to Aldeburgh, with church on left, left at bottom of hill

PETS: Bedrooms (5 GF) unattended **Charges** £2 per night
Public areas except restaurant **Exercise area** beach (300mtrs)
Facilities food bowl water bowl walks info vet info **On Request** fridge access torch **Other** charge for damage **Restrictions** no breed larger than a Labrador

A delightful privately owned hotel overlooking the beach. The attractive, well-maintained public rooms include three stylish

lounges as well as a cocktail bar and elegant restaurant. Bedrooms are smartly decorated with co-ordinated fabrics and have many thoughtful touches; some rooms have superb sea views. Several very spacious Mediterranean-style rooms are located across the road.

Rooms 35 (7 annexe) (2 fmly) (5 GF) **S** £83-£129; **D** £141-£290 (incl. bkfst & dinner)* **Facilities** FTV Xmas New Year Wi-fi **Parking** 30 **Notes** LB

BILDESTON
Map 5 TL94

Bildeston Crown

★★★ ◉◉◉ HOTEL

104 High St IP7 7EB
☎ 01449 740510 📠 01449 741843
e-mail: hayley@thebildestoncrown.co.uk
web: www.thebildestoncrown.co.uk
dir: A12 junct 31, turn right onto B1070 & follow signs to Hadleigh. At T-junct turn left onto A1141, then immediately right onto B1115. Hotel 0.5m

PETS: Bedrooms unattended **Charges** £10 per stay
Public areas except restaurant **Grounds** on leads disp bin
Exercise area nearby **Facilities** food bowl water bowl **Stables** 1m **Other** charge for damage

A charming inn situated in a peaceful village close to the historic town of Lavenham. Public areas feature beams, exposed brickwork and oak floors, with contemporary style decor; they include a choice of bars, a lounge and a restaurant. The tastefully decorated bedrooms have lovely co-ordinated fabrics and modern facilities that include Yamaha music systems and LCD TVs. Food here is the real focus and draw; guests can expect fresh, high-quality local produce and accomplished technical skills in both modern and classic dishes.

Rooms 13 **Facilities** STV FTV Xmas New Year Wi-fi **Services** Lift **Parking** 30

BUCKLESHAM
Map 5 TM24

Westwood Caravan Park (TM253411)

▶▶▶▶

Old Felixstowe Rd IP10 0BN
☎ 01473 659637 & 07814 570973
e-mail: caroline.pleace@westwoodcaravanpark.co.uk
dir: A14 towards Felixstowe, after junct 58 take 1st exit signed to Kirton. Follow road to Bucklesham for 1.5m. Site on right

PETS: Public areas on leads disp bin **Exercise area on site** walking area around perimeter of site **Facilities** vet info **Other** prior notice required dogs must be kept on leads at all times; max 2 dogs per pitch

Open Mar-15 Jan Last arrival 22.00hrs Last departure 15.00hrs

This site is in the heart of rural Suffolk in an idyllic, peaceful setting. All buildings are of traditional Suffolk style, and the toilet facilities are of outstanding quality. There is also a spacious room for disabled visitors, and plenty of space for children to play. 4.5 acre site. 100 touring pitches. 35 hardstandings. Tent pitches. Motorhome pitches.

BURY ST EDMUNDS
Map 5 TL86

Angel Hotel

★★★★ 83% ◉◉ TOWN HOUSE HOTEL

Angel Hill IP33 1LT
☎ 01284 714000 📠 01284 714001
e-mail: staying@theangel.co.uk
web: www.theangel.co.uk
dir: From A134, left at rdbt into Northgate St. Continue to lights, right into Mustow St, left into Angel Hill. Hotel on right

PETS: Bedrooms (15 GF) unattended **Charges** £5 per night
Public areas lounge only on leads **Exercise area** Abbey Gardens, 1 min walk **Facilities** walks info vet info **Other** charge for damage

An impressive building situated just a short walk from the town centre. One of the Angel's more notable guests over the last 400 years was Charles Dickens who is reputed to have written part of *The Pickwick Papers* whilst in residence. The hotel offers a range of individually designed bedrooms that includes a selection of four-poster rooms and a suite.

Rooms 75 (5 fmly) (15 GF) **D** £125-£170 (incl. bkfst)*
Facilities FTV Xmas Wi-fi **Services** Lift **Parking** 20

Ravenwood Hall

★★★ 88% ◉◉ COUNTRY HOUSE HOTEL

Rougham IP30 9JA
☎ 01359 270345 📠 01359 270788
e-mail: enquiries@ravenwoodhall.co.uk
web: www.ravenwoodhall.co.uk
dir: 3m E off A14, junct 45. Hotel on left

PETS: Bedrooms (5 GF) unattended **Public areas** except restaurant on leads **Grounds Facilities** walks info vet info **Other** charge for damage please phone for further details of pet facilities **Resident Pet:** Minx (Labrador)

Delightful 15th-century property set in seven acres of woodland and landscaped gardens. The building has many original features including carved timbers and inglenook fireplaces. The spacious bedrooms are attractively decorated, tastefully furnished with well-chosen pieces and equipped with many thoughtful touches. Public rooms include an elegant restaurant and a smart lounge bar with an open fire.

Rooms 14 (7 annexe) (5 GF) **S** £102-£136; **D** £125-£175 (incl. bkfst)* **Facilities** 🎾 🏌 Shooting, fishing & horse riding can be arranged Xmas New Year Wi-fi Child facilities **Parking** 150 **Notes** LB

BURY ST EDMUNDS *continued*

Best Western Priory

★★★ 83% ◉◉ HOTEL

Mildenhall Rd IP32 6EH
☎ 01284 766181 📄 01284 767604
e-mail: reservations@prioryhotel.co.uk
web: www.prioryhotel.co.uk
dir: *From A14 take Bury St Edmunds W slip road. Follow signs to Brandon. At mini-rdbt turn right. Hotel 0.5m on left*

PETS: Bedrooms (30 GF) unattended sign **Charges** £10 per night **Public areas Grounds** on leads disp bin **Facilities** washing facs cage storage walks info vet info **On Request** fridge access torch towels **Other** charge for damage bedding available on request

An 18th-century Grade II listed building set in landscaped grounds on the outskirts of town. The attractively decorated, tastefully furnished and thoughtfully equipped bedrooms are split between the main house and garden wings, which have their own sun terraces. Public rooms feature a smart restaurant, a conservatory dining room and a lounge bar.

Rooms 36 (29 annexe) (1 fmly) (30 GF) **Facilities** FTV Xmas New Year Wi-fi **Parking** 60

Grange

★★★ 74% COUNTRY HOUSE HOTEL

Barton Rd, Thurston IP31 3PQ
☎ 01359 231260 📄 01359 231387
e-mail: info@grangecountryhousehotel.com
web: www.grangecountryhousehotel.com
dir: *A14 junct 45 towards Gt Barton, right at T-junct. At x-rds left into Barton Rd to Thurston. At rdbt, left after 0.5m, hotel on right*

PETS: Bedrooms (3 GF) **Charges** £15 per night **Exercise area** surrounding countryside **Facilities** walks info vet info **Other** charge for damage **Restrictions** no Rottweilers

A Tudor-style country-house hotel situated on the outskirts of town. The individually decorated bedrooms have co-ordinated fabrics and many thoughtful touches; some rooms have nice views of the gardens. Public areas include a smart lounge bar, two private dining rooms, the Garden Restaurant and banqueting facilities.

Rooms 18 (5 annexe) (1 fmly) (3 GF) **S** £79.50; **D** £110 (incl. bkfst)* **Facilities** FTV Xmas New Year Wi-fi **Parking** 100 **Notes** LB

6 Orchard Street

★★★ BED AND BREAKFAST

IP33 1EH
☎ 01284 750191 & 07946 590265
e-mail: mariellascarlett@me.com
dir: *In town centre near St John's Church on one-way system; Northgate St turn right onto Looms Ln, 2nd right onto Well St, straight on onto Orchard St*

PETS: Bedrooms Exercise area 10 mins' walk **Facilities** water bowl vet info **On Request** torch towels **Other** dogs accepted by prior arrangement only **Restrictions** small & medium size dogs only

Expect a warm welcome from the caring hosts at this terrace property situated just a short walk from the town centre. The pleasant bedrooms are comfortably appointed and have a good range of useful extras. Breakfast is served at a large communal table in the cosy dining room.

Rooms 2 rms (1 en suite) (1 pri facs) **S** £30-£35; **D** £45-£55 **Facilities** FTV tea/coffee Cen ht Wi-fi **Notes** No Children 6yrs ⊗

Dell Touring Park *(TL928640)*

▶▶▶▶

Beyton Rd, Thurston IP31 3RB
☎ 01359 270121
e-mail: thedellcaravanpark@btinternet.com
dir: *Signed from A14 at Beyton/Thurston (4m E of Bury St Edmunds) & from A143 at Barton/Thurston*

PETS: Public areas disp bin **Facilities** cage storage walks info **Stables Other** prior notice required

Open all year Last arrival 20.00hrs Last departure noon

A small site with enthusiastic owners that has been developed to a high specification with more improvements planned. Set in a quiet spot with lots of mature trees, the quality purpose-built toilet facilities include family rooms, dishwashing and laundry. This is an ideal base for exploring this picturesque area. 6 acre site. 60 touring pitches. 12 hardstandings. Tent pitches. Motorhome pitches.

Notes No footballs, no noise after 23.00hrs.

The Ship Inn

★★ 80% ◉ SMALL HOTEL

St James St IP17 3DT

☎ 01728 648219 & 07921 061060

e-mail: info@shipatdunwich.co.uk

dir: *From N: A12, exit at Blythburgh onto B1125, then left to village. Inn at end of road. From S: A12, turn right to Westleton. Follow signs for Dunwich*

PETS: Bedrooms (4 GF) unattended **Charges** £5 per night **Public areas Grounds** disp bin **Exercise area** adjacent **Facilities** food bowl water bowl dog chews scoop/disp bags cage storage walks info vet info **On Request** fridge access torch towels **Other** charge for damage

A delightful inn situated in the heart of this quiet village, surrounded by nature reserves and heathland, and just a short walk from the beach. Public rooms feature a smart lounge bar with an open fire and real ales on tap. The comfortable bedrooms are traditionally furnished; some rooms have lovely views across the sea or marshes.

Rooms 15 (4 annexe) (4 fmly) (4 GF) **D** £95-£125 (incl. bkfst)* **Facilities** FTV Xmas New Year **Parking** 15

Haw Wood Farm Caravan Park (TM421717)

▶▶

Hinton IP17 3QT

☎ 01986 784248

dir: *Exit A12, 1.5m N of Darsham level crossing at Little Chef. Site 0.5m on right*

PETS: Public areas on leads disp bin **Exercise area on site** large field **Exercise area** adjoining site (2.5 acres) **Facilities** food food bowl water bowl dog chews scoop/disp bags leads washing facs walks info vet info **Stables** 3m **Resident Pets:** Dyson (Yellow Lab), Rabies (cat)

Open Mar-14 Jan Last arrival 21.00hrs Last departure noon

An unpretentious family-orientated park set in two large fields surrounded by low hedges. The toilets are clean and functional, and there is plenty of space for children to play. 8 acre site. 65 touring pitches. Tent pitches. Motorhome pitches. 25 statics.

Notes 🐾

Kiln Farm Guest House

★★★★ GUEST HOUSE

Kiln Ln IP30 9QR

☎ 01359 240442

e-mail: davejankilnfarm@btinternet.com

dir: *Exit A14 junct 47 for A1088. Entrance to Kiln Ln off E'bound slip road*

PETS: Bedrooms (6 GF) courtyard bedrooms only **Public areas Grounds** disp bin **Exercise area** adjacent **Facilities** feeding mat cage storage vet info **On Request** fridge access torch towels **Other** charge for damage **Resident Pets:** Barney & Milo (cats)

A delightful Victorian farmhouse situated in a peaceful rural location amid three acres of landscaped grounds. The bedrooms are housed in converted farm buildings; each one is smartly decorated and furnished in country style. Breakfast is served in the smart conservatory and there is also a cosy lounge and bar area. David Copeman was a finalist in the AA Friendliest Landlady of the Year award 2011-12.

Rooms 2 en suite 6 annexe en suite (2 fmly) (6 GF) **S** £35-£40; **D** £70-£80 **Facilities** FTV TVL tea/coffee Dinner available Cen ht Licensed Wi-fi **Parking** 20

Peewit Caravan Park (TM290338)

▶▶▶

Walton Av IP11 2HB

☎ 01394 284511

e-mail: peewitpark@aol.com

dir: *Signed from A14 in Felixstowe, 100mtrs past Dock Gate 1, 1st on left*

PETS: Public areas except shower/toilet block & children's play area disp bin **Exercise area on site** grass walkway **Facilities** walks info vet info **Other** dogs must be kept on leads **Restrictions** well behaved dogs only **Resident Pet:** Bonnie (Dalmatian)

Open Apr (or Etr)-Oct Last arrival 21.00hrs Last departure 11.00hrs

A grass touring area fringed by trees, with well-maintained grounds and a colourful floral display. This handy urban site is not overlooked by houses, and the toilet facilities are clean and well cared for. A function room contains a TV and library. The beach is a few minutes away by car. 13 acre site. 45 touring pitches. 4 hardstandings. Tent pitches. Motorhome pitches. 200 statics.

Notes Only foam footballs are permitted.

FRAMLINGHAM — Map 5 TM26

Church Farm (TM605267)

★★★★ FARMHOUSE

Church Rd, Kettleburgh IP13 7LF
☎ 01728 723532   Mrs A Bater
e-mail: jbater@suffolkonline.net
dir: Off A12 to Wickham Market, signs to Easton Farm Park & Kettleburgh 1.25m, house behind church

PETS: Bedrooms (3 GF) **Charges** £1 per night **Public areas** if other guests approve on leads **Grounds** on leads **Exercise area** nearby **Facilities** leads cage storage walks info vet info
On Request fridge access torch towels **Resident Pets:** Minnie (Jack Russell), Jessie (Labrador)

A charming 300-year-old farmhouse situated close to the village church amid superb grounds with a duck pond, mature shrubs and sweeping lawns. The converted property retains exposed beams and open fireplaces. Bedrooms are pleasantly decorated and equipped with useful extras, and ground-floor rooms are available.

Rooms 2 rms (1 en suite) (1 pri facs) 2 annexe rms 1 annexe en suite (1 pri facs) (3 GF) **Facilities** TVL tea/coffee Dinner available Cen ht Wi-fi Fishing **Parking** 10 **Notes** ⊛ 70 acres mixed

HINTLESHAM — Map 5 TM04

Hintlesham Hall Hotel

★★★★ ◉◉ HOTEL

George St IP8 3NS
☎ 01473 652334   🖨 01473 652463
e-mail: reservations@hintleshamhall.com
web: www.hintleshamhall.com
dir: 4m W of Ipswich on A1071 to Hadleigh & Sudbury

PETS: Bedrooms (10 GF) **Public areas** on leads **Grounds** disp bin **Exercise area** nearby **Facilities** water bowl feeding mat scoop/disp bags pet sitting dog walking cage storage walks info vet info **On Request** torch towels **Other** charge for damage dogs to be muzzled at owner's discretion

Hospitality and service are key features at this imposing Grade I listed country-house hotel, situated in 175 acres of grounds and landscaped gardens. Originally a manor house dating from the Elizabethan era, the building was extended in the 17th and 18th centuries. It was a Red Cross hospital in World War II and has been a hotel for nearly forty years. Individually decorated bedrooms offer a high degree of comfort; each one is tastefully furnished and equipped with many thoughtful touches. The spacious public rooms include a series of comfortable lounges, and an elegant restaurant which serves fine classical cuisine based on top-notch ingredients. Wi-fi is available throughout.

Rooms 33 (10 GF) **S** £119-£149; **D** £129-£199 (incl. bkfst)*
Facilities FTV ⚄ ♨ 18 ⛳ Putt green ⚐ Gym Health & Beauty services Clay pigeon shooting ♫ Xmas New Year Wi-fi **Parking** 60 **Notes** LB RS Sat

HOLLESLEY — Map 5 TM34

Run Cottage Touring Park (TM350440)

▶▶▶

Alderton Rd IP12 3RQ
☎ 01394 411309
e-mail: info@run-cottage.co.uk
dir: From A12 (Ipswich-Saxmundham) onto A1152 at Melton. 1.5m, right at rdbt onto B1083. 0.75m, left to Hollesley. In Hollesley right into The Street, through village, down hill, over bridge, site 100yds on left

PETS: Public areas on leads disp bin **Exercise area on site**
Facilities washing facs walks info vet info **Restrictions** max 2 large dogs or 3 small dogs **Resident Pets:** Harvey (Sussex Spaniel), Dudley (Clumber Spaniel)

Open all year Last arrival 20.00hrs Last departure 11.00hrs

Located in the peaceful village of Hollesley on the Suffolk coast, this landscaped park is set behind the owners' house. The generously-sized pitches are serviced by a well-appointed and immaculately maintained toilet block. This site is handy for the National Trust's Sutton Hoo, and also by travelling a little further north, the coastal centre and beach at Dunwich Heath, and the RSPB bird reserve at Minsmere. 2.5 acre site. 20 touring pitches. 6 hardstandings. Tent pitches. Motorhome pitches.

Notes No groundsheets, ball games or cycles.

HORRINGER — Map 5 TL86

The Ickworth Hotel & Apartments

★★★★ 75% ◉◉ COUNTRY HOUSE HOTEL

IP29 5QE
☎ 01284 735350   🖨 01284 736300
e-mail: info@ickworthhotel.co.uk
web: www.ickworthhotel.co.uk
dir: A14 exit for Bury St Edmunds, follow brown signs for Ickworth House, 4th exit at rdbt, cross staggered x-rds. Then onto T-junct, right into village, almost immediately right into Ickworth Estate

PETS: Bedrooms (4 GF) unattended **Charges** £15 per night
Public areas except restaurant & food areas on leads **Grounds** on leads **Facilities** walks info vet info **On Request** fridge access torch towels **Other** charge for damage prior notice required please contact hotel to confirm which dog breeds are accepted

Gifted to the National Trust in 1956 this stunning property is in part a luxurious hotel that combines the glorious design and atmosphere of the past with a reputation for making children very welcome. The staff are friendly and easy going, there is a children's play area, crèche, horses and bikes to ride, and wonderful 'Capability' Brown gardens to roam in. Plus tennis, swimming, beauty treatments and an impressive dining room.

Rooms 39 (12 annexe) (35 fmly) (4 GF) **S** £229.50-£526.50; **D** £255-£585 (incl. bkfst & dinner)* **Facilities** Spa FTV ⚄ ♨ ⚐ Children's crèche Massage Manicures Adventure playground Vineyard Xmas New Year Wi-fi Child facilities **Services** Lift **Parking** 40 **Notes** LB

Map 5 TM14

Salthouse Harbour
★★★★ ◉◉ TOWN HOUSE HOTEL
No 1 Neptune Quay IP4 1AX
☎ 01473 226789 📠 01473 226927
e-mail: staying@salthouseharbour.co.uk
dir: From A14 junct 56 follow signs for town centre, then
Salthouse signs

PETS: Bedrooms unattended Charges £5 per night
Public areas except in food areas on leads disp bin
Exercise area 5 mins' walk Facilities water bowl walks info vet
info On Request fridge access Other charge for damage

Situated just a short walk from the town centre, this waterfront
warehouse conversion is a clever mix of contemporary styles and
original features. The hotel is stylish designed throughout with
modern art, sculptures, interesting artefacts and striking colours.
The spacious bedrooms provide luxurious comfort; some have
feature bathrooms and some have balconies. Two air-conditioned
penthouse suites, with stunning views, have extras such as
state-of-the-art sound systems and telescopes. Award-winning
food is served in the busy, ground-floor brasserie, and alfresco
eating is possible in warmer weather.

Rooms 70 (6 fmly) D £125-£170 (incl. bkfst)* Facilities FTV Wi-fi
Services Lift Parking 30

milsoms Kesgrave Hall
★★★★ 76% ◉ HOTEL
Hall Rd, Kesgrave IP5 2PU
☎ 01473 333741 📠 01473 617614
e-mail: reception@kesgravehall.com
web: www.milsomshotels.com
dir: A12 N of Ipswich, left at Ipswich/Woodbridge rdbt onto
B1214. Right after 0.5m into Hall Rd. Hotel 200yds on left

PETS: Bedrooms (8 GF) unattended 'outside' bedrooms only
Charges £20 per night £140 per week Grounds Exercise area
2m Other charge for damage

A superb 18th-century, Grade II listed Georgian mansion set
amidst 38 acres of mature grounds. Appointed in a contemporary
style, the large open-plan public areas include a smart bar, a
lounge with plush sofas, and a restaurant where guests can
watch the chefs in action. Bedrooms are tastefully appointed and
thoughtfully equipped.

Rooms 23 (8 annexe) (4 fmly) (8 GF) S £97-£184; D £122-£250*
Facilities STV FTV ᜂ Xmas Wi-fi Parking 100 Notes LB

Novotel Ipswich Centre
★★★ 82% HOTEL
Greyfriars Rd IP1 1UP
☎ 01473 232400 📠 01473 232414
e-mail: h0995@accor.com
web: www.novotel.com
dir: From A14 towards Felixstowe. Left onto A137, 2m into town
centre. Hotel on double rdbt by Stoke Bridge

PETS: Bedrooms unattended sign Charges £6 per night
Public areas except restaurant on leads Grounds on leads
Exercise area marina area & parks nearby Facilities cage
storage walks info vet info Other charge for damage

A modern, red brick hotel perfectly placed in the centre of town
close to shops, bars and restaurants. The open-plan public areas
include a Mediterranean-style restaurant and a bar with a small
games area. The bedrooms are smartly appointed and have many
thoughtful touches; three rooms are suitable for less mobile
guests.

Rooms 101 (8 fmly) Facilities STV Gym Xmas New Year Wi-fi
Services Lift Air con Parking 53

Map 5 TL94

The Swan
★★★★ 83% ◉◉ HOTEL
High St CO10 9QA
☎ 01787 247477 📠 01787 248286
e-mail: info@theswanatlavenham.co.uk
web: www.theswanatlavenham.co.uk
dir: From Bury St Edmunds take A134 (S), then A1141 to
Lavenham

PETS: Bedrooms (13 GF) unattended Charges £10 per night
Public areas except food service areas on leads Grounds on
leads Exercise area 400yds Facilities water bowl walks info
vet info On Request fridge access torch towels Other charge
for damage well behaved dogs only

A delightful collection of listed buildings dating back to the 14th
century, lovingly restored to retain their original charm. Public
rooms include comfortable lounge areas, a charming rustic bar,
an informal brasserie and a fine-dining restaurant. Bedrooms are
tastefully furnished and equipped with many thoughtful touches.
The friendly staff are helpful, attentive and offer professional
service.

Rooms 45 (11 fmly) (13 GF) S £95-£155; D £180-£300 (incl.
bkfst)* Facilities STV FTV Xmas New Year Wi-fi Parking 62

LEISTON — Map 5 TM46

Cakes & Ale *(TM432637)*

▶▶▶

Abbey Ln, Theberton IP16 4TE
☎ 01728 831655
e-mail: cakesandalepark@gmail.com
dir: *From Saxmundham E on B1119. 3m follow minor road over level crossing, turn right, in 0.5m straight on at x-rds, entrance 0.5m on left*

PETS: Charges £2 per night **Public areas** disp bin
Exercise area on site 5-acre field & small copse **Facilities** food washing facs walks info vet info **Other** charge for damage prior notice required **Resident Pet:** Jasper (Blue Merle Border Collie)

Open Apr-Oct rs Low season club, shop & reception limited hours Last arrival 20.00hrs Last departure 13.00hrs

A large, well spread out and beautifully maintained site with many trees and bushes on a former Second World War airfield. The spacious touring area includes plenty of hardstandings and super pitches, and there is a good bar and a well-maintained toilet block, which has now been extended to house ladies' showers, a fully-serviced family/disabled room and a washing-up room. Wi-fi access is available on site. 45 acre site. 50 touring pitches. 50 hardstandings. Tent pitches. Motorhome pitches. 200 statics.

Notes No group bookings, no noise between 21.00hrs-08.00hrs.

LONG MELFORD — Map 5 TL84

The Black Lion
★★★ 80% HOTEL
Church Walk, The Green CO10 9DN
☎ 01787 312356 📠 01787 374557
e-mail: enquiries@blacklionhotel.net
web: www.blacklionhotel.net
dir: *At junct of A134 & A1092*

PETS: Bedrooms unattended **Public areas** except restaurant on leads **Grounds Exercise area** green opposite **Facilities** water bowl walks info vet info **Other** charge for damage **Resident Pet:** Melford (Labrador/Poodle cross)

This charming 15th-century hotel is situated on the edge of this bustling town overlooking the green. Bedrooms are generally spacious and each is attractively decorated, tastefully furnished and equipped with useful extras. An interesting range of dishes is served in the lounge bar or guests may choose to dine from the same innovative menu in the more formal restaurant.

Rooms 10 (1 fmly) **Facilities** Xmas New Year Wi-fi **Parking** 10

LOWESTOFT — Map 5 TM59

Ivy House Country Hotel
★★★ 85% ⧆⧆ HOTEL
Ivy Ln, Beccles Rd, Oulton Broad NR33 8HY
☎ 01502 501353 & 588144 📠 01502 501539
e-mail: aa@ivyhousecountryhotel.co.uk
web: www.ivyhousecountryhotel.co.uk
dir: *On A146 SW of Oulton Broad turn into Ivy Ln beside Esso petrol station. Over railway bridge, follow private drive*

PETS: Bedrooms (17 GF) sign **Charges** £15 per stay
Public areas except restaurant on leads **Grounds** on leads disp bin **Exercise area** hotel's fields **Facilities** food bowl bedding dog chews scoop/disp bags washing facs walks info vet info **On Request** fridge access torch towels

A peacefully located, family-run hotel set in three acres of mature landscaped grounds and just a short walk from Oulton Broad. Public rooms include an 18th-century thatched barn restaurant where an interesting choice of dishes is served. The attractively decorated bedrooms are housed in garden wings, and many have lovely views of the grounds to the countryside beyond.

Rooms 20 (20 annexe) (1 fmly) (17 GF) **S** £99-£109; **D** £135-£175 (incl. bkfst)* **Facilities** FTV Wi-fi **Parking** 50 **Notes** LB Closed 23 Dec-6 Jan

Somerton House
★★★★ GUEST ACCOMMODATION
7 Kirkley Cliff NR33 0BY
☎ 01502 565665
e-mail: pippin.somerton@btinternet.com
dir: *On old A12, 100yds from Claremont Pier*

PETS: Bedrooms (1 GF) **Charges** £5 per stay **Public areas** except dining room **Exercise area** beach (out of season) 50yds **Facilities** cage storage walks info vet info **On Request** torch **Stables** 2m **Other** charge for damage

Somerton House is a Grade II Victorian terrace situated in a peaceful area of town overlooking the sea. Bedrooms are smartly furnished in a period style and have many thoughtful touches; some rooms have four poster or half-tester beds. Breakfast is served in the smart dining room and there's a cosy lounge.

Rooms 7 rms (4 en suite) (2 pri facs) (1 fmly) (1 GF) **S** £36-£46; **D** £57-£62 **Facilities** FTV TVL tea/coffee Cen ht Licensed Wi-fi **Notes** LB Closed 25-26 Dec

ENGLAND

Tuddenham Mill

★★★★ **81%** ◉◉ HOTEL

High St, Tuddenham St Mary IP28 6SQ

☎ 01438 713552

e-mail: info@tuddenhammill.co.uk

PETS: Bedrooms unattended Meadow & Millstream bedrooms only **Charges** £15 per night £105 per week **Public areas Grounds** on leads **Facilities** food bowl water bowl walks info vet info **On Request** fridge access torch towels **Other** charge for damage

A beautifully converted old watermill set amidst landscaped grounds between Newmarket and Bury St Edmunds. The contemporary style bedrooms are situated in separate buildings adjacent to the main building, each one is tastefully appointed with co-ordinated fabrics and soft furnishings. The public areas have a wealth of original features such as the water wheel and exposed beams; they include a lounge bar, a smart restaurant, a meeting room and choice of terraces.

Rooms 15 **D** £185-£395 (incl. bkfst)*

Best Western Heath Court

Best Western

★★★ **78%** HOTEL

Moulton Rd CB8 8DY

☎ 01638 667171   🖷 01638 666533

e-mail: quality@heathcourthotel.com

dir: Exit A14 for Newmarket & Ely onto A142. Follow town centre signs over mini rdbt. At clocktower left into Moulton Rd

PETS: Bedrooms unattended sign **Grounds** on leads disp bin **Exercise area** 200yds **Facilities** food (pre-bookable) food bowl water bowl bedding feeding mat pet sitting dog walking washing facs dog grooming cage storage walks info vet info **On Request** fridge access torch towels **Stables** 5m **Other** charge for damage

A modern red-brick hotel situated close to Newmarket Heath and perfectly placed for the town centre. Public rooms include a choice of dining options - informal meals can be taken in the lounge bar or a modern carte menu is offered in the restaurant. The smartly presented bedrooms are mostly spacious and some have air conditioning.

Rooms 41 (2 fmly) **S** £35-£89.50; **D** £40-£182* **Facilities** STV FTV New Year Wi-fi **Services** Lift **Parking** 70 **Notes** LB

Cadogan

★★★ **73%** SMALL HOTEL

Fordham Rd CB8 7AA

☎ 01638 663814 & 07776 258688   🖷 01638 561480

e-mail: kgreed@btinternet.com

dir: A14, A142 to Newmarket. Over 2 rdbts signed Town Centre. 1.5m. At 30mph limit hotel 500mtrs on left

PETS: Bedrooms (1 GF) **Charges** £7.50 per night **Public areas** on leads **Exercise area** 250yds **Other** charge for damage

This small, friendly, family run hotel is situated just a short walk from the town centre within easy reach of Newmarket racecourse. Public rooms include an open-plan lounge bar with plush seating and a smart dining room. The bedrooms are pleasantly decorated with co-ordinated fabrics and have a good range of facilities.

Rooms 12 (2 fmly) (1 GF) **S** £65-£95; **D** £85-£145 (incl. bkfst) **Facilities** FTV Wi-fi **Parking** 18 **Notes** LB Closed 24 Dec-2 Jan

The Garden Lodge

★★★★ BED AND BREAKFAST

11 Vicarage Ln, Wooditton CB8 9SG

☎ 01638 731116

e-mail: swedishgardenlodge@hotmail.com

web: www.gardenlodge.net

dir: 3m S of Newmarket in Wooditton

PETS: Bedrooms (3 GF) unattended **Public areas Grounds** disp bin **Facilities** food bowl water bowl vet info **On Request** torch towels **Restrictions** no Bull Terriers

A warm welcome is assured in this home-from-home, not far from the famous racecourse. The accommodation, in quality chalets, is very well equipped and features a wealth of thoughtful extras. Freshly prepared home-cooked breakfasts are served in an elegant dining room in the main house.

Rooms 3 en suite (3 GF) **S** £35-£40; **D** £60-£70 **Facilities** FTV tea/coffee Dinner available Cen ht Wi-fi **Parking** 6 **Notes** ☺

ENGLAND

The Crown & Castle
★★★ 86% ◉◉ HOTEL
IP12 2LJ
☎ 01394 450205
e-mail: info@crownandcastle.co.uk
web: www.crownandcastle.co.uk
dir: Turn right from B1084 on entering village, towards castle

PETS: Bedrooms (11 GF) unattended certain bedrooms only
Charges £5.50 per night Public areas Grounds on leads disp
bin Exercise area nearby Facilities bedding dog chews scoop/
disp bags leads washing facs walks info vet info On Request
fridge access torch towels Other 1 dog friendly table in
restaurant Resident Pets: Teddy & Anle (Wire-Haired Fox Terriers)

A delightful inn situated adjacent to the Norman castle keep.
Contemporary style bedrooms are spilt between the main house
and the garden wing; the latter are more spacious and have
patios with access to the garden. The restaurant has an informal
atmosphere with polished tables and local artwork; the menu
features quality, locally sourced produce.

Rooms 19 (12 annexe) (1 fmly) (11 GF) D £130-£235 (incl.
bkfst)* Facilities Xmas New Year Wi-fi Parking 20 Notes LB
No children 8yrs

Sandpit Farm
★★★★ BED AND BREAKFAST
Bruisyard IP17 2EB
☎ 01728 663445
e-mail: smarshall@aldevalleybreaks.co.uk
web: www.aldevalleybreaks.co.uk
dir: 4m W of Saxmundham. A1120 onto B1120, 1st left for
Bruisyard, house 1.5m on left

PETS: Bedrooms sign twin room only Charges £5 per night £35
per week Public areas except dining room on leads Grounds
on leads disp bin Exercise area nearby Facilities cage storage
walks info vet info On Request fridge access towels Stables
Other charge for damage outbuilding by barn available Resident
Pets: Twiggy & Inca (Black Labradors), chickens, guinea fowl

Sandpit Farm is a delightful Grade II listed farmhouse set in 20
acres of grounds. Bedrooms have many thoughtful touches and
lovely country views, and there are two cosy lounges to enjoy.
Breakfast features quality local produce and freshly laid
free-range eggs.

Rooms 2 en suite S £40-£60; D £65-£90 Facilities TVL tea/coffee
Cen ht Wi-fi ⌁ Parking 4 Notes LB Closed 24-26 Dec 🐾

Whitearch Touring Caravan Park (TM379610)
►►►
Main Rd, Benhall IP17 1NA
☎ 01728 604646 & 603773
dir: At junct of A12 & B1121

PETS: Public areas Exercise area on site Facilities walks info
vet info

Open Apr-Oct Last arrival 20.00hrs

A small, maturing park set around an attractive coarse-fishing
lake, with good quality toilet facilities and secluded pitches
tucked away among trees and shrubs. The park is popular with
anglers; there is some traffic noise from the adjacent A12. 14.5
acre site. 50 touring pitches. 50 hardstandings. Tent pitches.
Motorhome pitches.

Notes No bicycles. 🐾

Swan Hotel
★★★★ 78% ◉◉ HOTEL
Market Place IP18 6EG
☎ 01502 722186 🖷 01502 724800
e-mail: swan.hotel@adnams.co.uk
dir: A1095 to Southwold. Hotel in town centre. Parking via
archway to left of building

PETS: Bedrooms (17 GF) Lighthouse bedrooms only Charges
£10 per night Grounds disp bin Facilities food bowl water bowl
bedding dog chews feeding mat scoop/disp bags washing
facs cage storage walks info vet info On Request fridge access
Other charge for damage

A charming 17th-century coaching inn situated in the heart of
this bustling town centre overlooking the market place. Public
rooms feature an elegant restaurant, a comfortable drawing
room, a cosy bar and a lounge where guests can enjoy afternoon
tea. The spacious bedrooms are attractively decorated, tastefully
furnished and thoughtfully equipped.

Rooms 42 (17 annexe) (11 fmly) (17 GF) S £95-£110.50;
D £135-£252 (incl. bkfst)* Facilities STV FTV Treatment room
Xmas New Year Wi-fi Services Lift Parking 42 Notes LB

The Blyth Hotel

★★ 85% ◉ SMALL HOTEL

Station Rd IP18 6AY

☎ 01502 722632 & 0845 348 6867

e-mail: reception@blythhotel.com

PETS: Bedrooms unattended **Charges** £5 per night
Public areas except restaurant & lounge on leads **Grounds** on leads disp bin **Exercise area** 5 mins **Facilities** food bowl water bowl dog chews vet info **Other** charge for damage

Expect a warm welcome at this delightful family run hotel which is situated just a short walk from the town centre. The spacious public rooms include a smart residents' lounge, an open-plan bar and a large restaurant. Bedrooms are tastefully appointed with co-ordinated fabrics and have many thoughtful touches.

Rooms 13 **S** £65-£80; **D** £95-£150 (incl. bkfst)* **Facilities** FTV Xmas New Year Wi-fi **Parking** 8 **Notes** LB

WESTLETON | Map 5 TM46

Westleton Crown

★★★ 79% ◉◉ HOTEL

The Street IP17 3AD

☎ 01728 648777   📠 01728 648239

e-mail: reception@westletoncrown.co.uk

web: www.westletoncrown.co.uk

dir: A12 N, turn right for Westleton just after Yoxford. Hotel opposite on entering Westleton

PETS: Bedrooms (13 GF) unattended **Charges** £7.50 per night **Public areas** except main dining room **Grounds Exercise area** outside hotel **Facilities** food bowl water bowl dog chews walks info vet info **On Request** fridge access torch **Resident Pet:** Stopit (Lurcher)

A charming coaching inn situated in a peaceful village location just a few minutes from the A12. Public rooms include a smart, award-winning restaurant, comfortable lounge, and busy bar with exposed beams and open fireplaces. The stylish bedrooms are tastefully decorated and equipped with many thoughtful little extras.

Rooms 34 (22 annexe) (5 fmly) (13 GF) **S** £80-£100; **D** £90-£215 (incl. bkfst)* **Facilities** FTV Xmas New Year Wi-fi **Parking** 34 **Notes** LB

WOODBRIDGE | Map 5 TM24

Best Western Ufford Park Hotel Golf & Spa

★★★ 82% HOTEL

Yarmouth Rd, Ufford IP12 1QW

☎ 01394 383555   📠 0844 4773727

e-mail: mail@uffordpark.co.uk

web: www.uffordpark.co.uk

dir: A12 N to A1152, in Melton left at lights, follow B1438, hotel 1m on right

PETS: Bedrooms (32 GF) unattended sign **Charges** from £10 per night **Public areas** except restaurant on leads **Grounds** on leads **Exercise area** 0.5m **Facilities** food bowl water bowl washing facs cage storage walks info vet info **On Request** fridge access torch towels **Other** charge for damage

A modern hotel set in open countryside boasting superb leisure facilities including a challenging golf course. The spacious public rooms provide a wide choice of areas in which to relax and include a busy lounge bar, a carvery restaurant and the Vista Restaurant. Bedrooms are smartly appointed and pleasantly decorated; each is thoughtfully equipped and many overlook the golf course.

Rooms 87 (20 fmly) (32 GF) **Facilities** Spa FTV ⓣ supervised ⅃ 18 Putt green Fishing ⛳ Gym Golf Academy with PGA tuition 2 storey floodlit driving range Dance Studio Xmas New Year Wi-fi **Services** Lift **Parking** 250

Moon & Sixpence (TM263454)

►►►►►

Newbourn Rd, Waldringfield IP12 4PP

☎ 01473 736650   📠 01473 736270

e-mail: info@moonandsixpence.eu

dir: Follow caravan & Moon & Sixpence signs from A12 Ipswich (east bypass). 1.5m, left at x-roads

PETS: Charges £1 per night £7 per week **Public areas** except bar, restaurant & beach disp bin **Exercise area on site** trail around perimeter **Facilities** walks info vet info **Other** prior notice required pet centre & store at nearby retail park **Resident Pet:** 1 Collie

Open Apr-Oct rs Low season club, shop, reception open limited hours Last arrival 20.00hrs Last departure noon

A well-planned site, with tourers occupying a sheltered valley position around an attractive boating lake with a sandy beach. Toilet facilities are housed in a smart Norwegian-style cabin, and there is a laundry and dishwashing area. Leisure facilities include two tennis courts, a bowling green, fishing, boating and a games room. There is an adult-only area, and a strict 'no groups and no noise after 9pm' policy. 5 acre site. 65 touring pitches. Tent pitches. Motorhome pitches. 225 statics.

Notes No group bookings or commercial vehicles, quiet 21.00hrs-08.00hrs.

ENGLAND

WORLINGWORTH
Map 5 TM26

Pond Farm B&B *(TM219697)*
★★★ FARMHOUSE
Fingal St IP13 7PD
☎ 01728 628565 & 0798 0914768 Mrs S Bridges
e-mail: enquiries@featherdown.co.uk

PETS: Bedrooms (2 GF) unattended sign ground-floor bedrooms only **Sep accom** **Public areas** except dining area & lounge **Grounds** disp bin **Exercise area** field on farm **Facilities** water bowl leads pet sitting dog walking washing facs cage storage walks info vet info **On Request** torch towels **Stables Other** charge for damage

A Grade II listed farmhouse set in twelve acres of grounds, close to the market towns of Framlingham and Woodbridge. The property is part of a working farm with Aberdeen Angus cattle, horse livery and free-range chickens. The well-equipped bedrooms are situated in an annexe adjacent to the main building. Breakfast is served at a large communal table in the cosy dining room.

Rooms 2 en suite (2 fmly) (2 GF) **S** fr £35; **D** fr £70 **Facilities** STV FTV TVL tea/coffee Dinner available Direct Dial Cen ht Fishing **Parking** 10 **Notes** LB 100 acres beef/pigs

YOXFORD
Map 5 TM36

Satis House
★★★ 88% ◉◉ COUNTRY HOUSE HOTEL
IP17 3EX
☎ 01728 668418 📠 01728 668640
e-mail: enquiries@satishouse.co.uk
web: www.satishouse.co.uk
dir: *Off A12 between Ipswich & Lowestoft. 9m E Aldeburgh & Snape*

PETS: Bedrooms (2 GF) **Charges** £10 per night £30 per week **Public areas** except restaurant & lounge on leads **Grounds** on leads **Exercise area** walled garden adjacent **Facilities** food (pre-bookable) food bowl water bowl cage storage walks info vet info **On Request** fridge access torch towels **Other** charge for damage prior notice required **Restrictions** small & medium size dogs only

Expect a warm welcome from the caring hosts at this delightful 18th-century, Grade II listed property set in three acres of parkland. The stylish public areas have a really relaxed atmosphere; they include a choice of dining rooms, a smart bar and a cosy lounge. The individually decorated bedrooms are tastefully appointed and thoughtfully equipped.

Rooms 10 (2 annexe) (1 fmly) (2 GF) **S** £65-£130; **D** £75-£210 (incl. bkfst)* **Facilities** STV FTV Xmas New Year Wi-fi **Parking** 30 **Notes** LB

SURREY

BAGSHOT
Map 4 SU96

Pennyhill Park Hotel & The Spa
★★★★★ ◉◉◉◉◉ COUNTRY HOUSE HOTEL
London Rd GU19 5EU
☎ 01276 471774 📠 01276 473217
e-mail: enquiries@pennyhillpark.co.uk
web: www.exclusivehotels.co.uk
dir: *M3 junct 3, follow signs to Camberley. On A30 between Bagshot & Camberley*

PETS: Bedrooms (26 GF) unattended **Charges** **Public areas** except restaurant, bar & spa on leads **Grounds** **Exercise area** 2m **Facilities** food (pre-bookable) food bowl water bowl bedding dog chews cat treats feeding mat leads pet sitting dog walking washing facs cage storage walks info vet info **On Request** fridge access torch towels **Stables** 5m **Other** charge for damage

This delightful country-house hotel, set in 120-acre grounds, provides every modern comfort. The stylish bedrooms are individually designed and have impressive bathrooms. Leisure facilities include a jogging trail, a golf course and a state-of-the-art spa with a thermal sequencing experience, ozone treated swimming and hydrotherapy pools along with a comprehensive range of therapies and treatments. The Latymer restaurant, overseen by chef Michael Wignall, has become a true dining destination in its own right. The cooking is outstanding and great care is made to source first-rate ingredients, much from local suppliers. There is an eight-seater chef's table for enjoying the tasting menu while watching the action in the kitchen. In addition there are other eating options, and lounges and bars to relax in.

Rooms 123 (97 annexe) (6 fmly) (26 GF) **S** £315-£1375; **D** £315-£1375* **Facilities** Spa STV ⊕ ⚡ ♨ 9 ⛳ Fishing 🏊 Gym Archery Clay shooting Plunge pool Turkish steam room Rugby/football pitch 🎵 Xmas New Year Wi-fi **Services** Lift **Parking** 500 **Notes** LB

CAMBERLEY
Map 4 SU86

Burwood House
★★★★ ⬤ GUEST ACCOMMODATION
15 London Rd GU15 3UQ
☎ 01276 685686 📠 01276 62220
e-mail: enquiries@burwoodhouse.co.uk
dir: On A30 between Camberley and Bagshot

PETS: Bedrooms (7 GF) Charges £15 per night Exercise area woods (50mtrs) Facilities food (pre-bookable) cage storage walks info vet info On Request fridge access torch towels Other charge for damage Resident Pets: Luna (Pyrenean Mountain Dog), Caramel (cat)

Burwood House is a very stylish establishment with individually designed bedrooms that offer all modern conveniences including Wi-fi. Every Monday to Thursday evening the kitchen offers a varied menu full of traditional favourites, as well as seasonal house specialties. Breakfast can be taken either buffet-style or as a fresh-cooked meal prepared upon request. Public areas include a lounge, bar and garden.

Rooms 22 en suite (3 fmly) (7 GF) Facilities tea/coffee Dinner available Direct Dial Cen ht Licensed Wi-fi ↘ Golf 18 Parking 22 Notes Closed 22 Dec-4 Jan

CHOBHAM
Map 4 SU96

Pembroke House
★★★★ GUEST ACCOMMODATION
Valley End Rd GU24 8TB
☎ 01276 857654 📠 01276 856080
e-mail: pembroke_house@btinternet.com
dir: A30 onto B383 signed Chobham, 3m right onto Valley End Rd, 1m on left

PETS: Bedrooms Public areas except dining room & kitchen Grounds disp bin Exercise area adjacent Facilities food bowl water bowl bedding leads pet sitting washing facs cage storage walks info vet info On Request fridge access torch towels Resident Pets: Puzzle, Carrie, Pandora (Jack Russells)

Proprietor Julia Holland takes obvious pleasure in welcoming guests to her beautifully appointed and spacious home. The elegantly proportioned public areas include an imposing entrance hall and dining room with views over the surrounding countryside. Bedrooms are restful and filled with thoughtful extras.

Rooms 4 rms (2 en suite) (2 pri facs) (1 fmly) S £40-£60; D £80-£150 Facilities STV tea/coffee Cen ht Wi-fi ⬤ Parking 10 Notes ⬤

DORKING
Map 4 TQ14

Mercure

Mercure White Horse
★★★ 68% HOTEL
High St RH4 1BE
☎ 01306 881138 📠 01306 887241
e-mail: h6637@accor.com
web: www.mercure.com
dir: M25 junct 9, A24 S towards Dorking. Hotel in town centre

PETS: Bedrooms (5 GF) unattended sign Charges £10 per night Public areas except restaurant on leads Grounds on leads disp bin Exercise area 100yds Facilities walks info vet info On Request fridge access torch towels Restrictions small dogs only due to size of bedrooms

The hotel was first established as an inn in 1750, although parts of the building date back as far as the 15th century. Its town centre location and Dickensian charm have long made this a popular destination for travellers. There's beamed ceilings, open fires and four-poster beds; more contemporary rooms can be found in the garden wing.

Rooms 78 (41 annexe) (2 fmly) (5 GF) S £60-£90; D £65-£140 (incl. bkfst)* Facilities FTV Discount for at local leisure centre Xmas Wi-fi Parking 73 Notes LB

HASLEMERE
Map 4 SU93

CLASSIC
BRITISH HOTELS

Lythe Hill Hotel and Spa
★★★★ 74% ⬤ HOTEL
Petworth Rd GU27 3BQ
☎ 01428 651251 📠 01428 644131
e-mail: lythe@lythehill.co.uk
web: www.lythehill.co.uk
dir: From High St onto B2131. Hotel 1.25m on right

PETS: Bedrooms (18 GF) Charges £20 per night £140 per week Public areas except restaurant, bar & lounge Grounds on leads disp bin Facilities food (pre-bookable) food bowl water bowl bedding dog chews dog grooming cage storage walks info vet info On Request fridge access torch towels Stables 10 mins Other charge for damage

This privately owned hotel sits in 30 acres of attractive parkland with lakes, complete with roaming geese. The hotel has been described as a hamlet of character buildings, each furnished in a style that complements the age of the property; the oldest one dating back to 1475. Cuisine in the adjacent 'Auberge de France' offers interesting, quality dishes, whilst breakfast is served in the hotel dining room. The bedrooms are split between a number of 15th-century buildings and vary in size. The stylish spa includes a 16-metre swimming pool.

Rooms 41 (8 fmly) (18 GF) Facilities Spa FTV ⬤ ⬤ Fishing ⬤ Gym Boules Giant chess ♫ Xmas New Year Wi-fi Parking 200

ENGLAND

Wheatsheaf
★★★ INN

Grayswood Rd, Grayswood GU27 2DE
☎ 01428 644440 📄 01428 641285
e-mail: ken@thewheatsheafgrayswood.co.uk
web: www.thewheatsheafgrayswood.co.uk
dir: *1m N of Haslemere on A286 in Grayswood*

PETS: Bedrooms (6 GF) unattended accommodation not
suitable for large dogs **Public areas** except restaurant on leads
Exercise area 50yds **Facilities** water bowl walks info vet info
On Request fridge access torch

Situated in a small village just outside Haslemere, this well-
presented inn has a friendly atmosphere. The smart conservatory
restaurant is a new addition, which complements the attractive
dining area and popular bar. Bedrooms are furnished to a good
standard, all but one on the ground floor.

Rooms 7 en suite (6 GF) **S** £59; **D** £79 **Facilities** tea/coffee Dinner
available Direct Dial Cen ht Wi-fi **Parking** 21 **Notes** No coaches

STAINES
Map 4 TQ07

Mercure Thames Lodge
★★★ **73%** HOTEL

Thames St TW18 4SJ
☎ 01784 464433 📄 01784 454858
e-mail: h6620@accor.com
web: www.mercure.com
dir: *M25 junct 13. Follow A30/town centre signs (bus station on
right). Hotel straight ahead*

PETS: Bedrooms (23 GF) **Charges** £15 per night **Public areas**
except restaurant (ex assist dogs) on leads **Grounds** on leads
Facilities food bowl water bowl cage storage **On Request** towels
Stables 5m **Other** charge for damage **Restrictions** small dogs
only

Located on the banks of the River Thames in a bustling town, this
hotel is well positioned for both business and leisure travellers.
Meals are served in the Riverside Restaurant, and snacks are
available in the spacious lounge/bar; weather permitting the
terrace provides a good place for a drink on a summer evening.
Onsite parking is an additional bonus.

Rooms 79 (17 fmly) (23 GF) **S** £79-£200; **D** £82-£210*
Facilities STV Moorings New Year Wi-fi **Parking** 40

SUSSEX, EAST

ALFRISTON
Map 5 TQ50

Deans Place
★★★ **86%** 🏵🏵 HOTEL

Seaford Rd BN26 5TW
☎ 01323 870248 📄 01323 870918
e-mail: mail@deansplacehotel.co.uk
web: www.deansplacehotel.co.uk
dir: *From A27 (between Eastbourne & Brighton) follow signs for
Alfriston & Drusillas Zoo Park. S through village towards Seaford.
Hotel on left*

PETS: Bedrooms (8 GF) unattended sign **Charges** £5 per
night **Public areas** except restaurant & function rooms on leads
Grounds Exercise area fields adjacent **Facilities** water bowl
washing facs cage storage walks info vet info **On Request**
fridge access torch towels

Situated on the southern fringe of the village, this friendly hotel
is set in attractive gardens. Bedrooms vary in size and are well
appointed with good facilities. A wide range of food is offered
including an extensive bar menu and a fine dining option in
Harcourt's Restaurant.

Rooms 36 (4 fmly) (8 GF) **S** £80-£95; **D** £120-£185 (incl. bkfst)*
Facilities STV FTV 🎾 Putt green ⛵ Boules Xmas New Year Wi-fi
Parking 100 **Notes** LB

The Star Alfriston
★★★ **77%** 🏵 HOTEL

BN26 5TA
☎ 01323 870495 📄 01323 870922
e-mail: bookings@thestaralfriston.co.uk
dir: *2m off A27, at Drusillas rdbt follow Alfriston signs. Hotel on
right in centre of High St*

PETS: Bedrooms (11 GF) unattended sign **Charges** £5 per
night **Public areas** except restaurant on leads **Exercise area**
0.2m **Facilities** water bowl bedding dog chews cage storage
vet info **On Request** fridge access torch towels **Other** charge
for damage

Built in the 13th century and reputedly one of the country's
oldest inns, this charming establishment is ideally situated
for walking the South Downs or exploring the Sussex coast.
Bedrooms, including two feature rooms and a mini suite, are
traditionally decorated but with comfortable, modern facilities.
Public areas include cosy lounges with open log fires, a bar and a
popular restaurant serving a wide choice of dishes using mainly
local produce. Guests can also enjoy luxury spa treatments by
appointment.

Rooms 37 (1 fmly) (11 GF) **S** £70-£90; **D** £110-£135 (incl. bkfst)
Facilities Xmas New Year Wi-fi **Parking** 35 **Notes** LB Closed
3-31 Jan

BATTLE
Map 5 TQ71

Powder Mills
★★★ **80%** ◉ HOTEL

Powdermill Ln TN33 0SP
☎ 01424 775511 📠 01424 774540
e-mail: powdc@aol.com
web: www.powdermillshotel.com
dir: *M25 junct 5, A21 towards Hastings. At St Johns Cross take A2100 to Battle. Pass Abbey on right, 1st right into Powdermills Ln. 1m, hotel on right*

PETS: Bedrooms (5 GF) unattended sign ground-floor bedrooms only **Charges** £10 per night **Public areas** except restaurant **Grounds** disp bin **Facilities** leads washing facs cage storage walks info vet info **On Request** fridge access torch towels **Stables Other** charge for damage **Resident Pets:** Amy & Gemma (English Springer Spaniels)

A delightful 18th-century country-house hotel set amidst 150 acres of landscaped grounds with lakes and woodland. The individually decorated bedrooms are tastefully furnished and thoughtfully equipped; some rooms have sun terraces with lovely views over the lake. Public rooms include a cosy lounge bar, music room, drawing room, library, restaurant and conservatory.

Rooms 40 (10 annexe) (5 GF) **S** £95-£115; **D** £140-£350 (incl. bkfst)* **Facilities** STV FTV ᴿ ᴥ Fishing Jogging trails Woodland walks Clay pigeon shooting Xmas New Year Wi-fi **Parking** 101 **Notes** LB

Brakes Coppice Park *(TQ765134)*
▶▶▶

Forewood Ln TN33 9AB
☎ 01424 830322
e-mail: brakesco@btinternet.com
dir: *From Battle on A2100 towards Hastings. After 2m turn right for Crowhurst. Site 1m on left*

PETS: Charges 25p per night **Public areas** disp bin **Exercise area on site** woodland walk **Facilities** walks info vet info **Stables** 3m **Other** prior notice required **Resident Pet:** Marlie (Doberman)

Open Mar-Oct Last arrival 21.00hrs Last departure noon

A secluded farm site in a sunny meadow deep in woodland with a small stream and a coarse fishing lake. The toilet block has been revamped and modernised with quality fittings and there's a washing-up area and a good fully-serviced family/disabled room. Hardstanding pitches are neatly laid out on a terrace, and tents are pitched on grass edged by woodland. A peaceful base for exploring Battle and the south coast. 3 acre site. 30 touring pitches. 10 hardstandings. Tent pitches. Motorhome pitches.

Notes No fires, footballs or kite flying.

Senlac Wood *(TQ722153)*
▶▶▶

Catsfield Rd, Catsfield TN33 9LN
☎ 01424 773969
e-mail: senlacwood@xlninternet.co.uk
dir: *A271 from Battle onto B2204 signed Bexhill. Site on left*

PETS: Charges 75p per night **Public areas** except children's play area disp bin **Exercise area on site Exercise area** 5 mins **Facilities** food dog chews cat treats **Other** disposal bags available in the shop

Open Mar-Oct Last arrival 22.00hrs Last departure noon

An improving woodland site with many secluded bays with hardstanding pitches, and two peaceful grassy glades for tents. The functional toilet facilities are clean, and the site is ideal for anyone looking for seclusion and shade. Well placed for visiting Battle and the south coast beaches. 20 acre site. 35 touring pitches. 16 hardstandings. Tent pitches. Motorhome pitches.

Notes No camp fires.

BEXHILL
Map 5 TQ70

Cooden Beach Hotel
★★★ **80%** HOTEL

Cooden Beach TN39 4TT
☎ 01424 842281 📠 01424 846142
e-mail: rooms@thecoodenbeachhotel.co.uk
web: www.thecoodenbeachhotel.co.uk
dir: *A259 towards Cooden. Signed at rdbt in Little Common Village. Hotel at end of road*

PETS: Bedrooms (4 GF) unattended **Public areas** except restaurant (tavern/bar only) **Grounds Exercise area** beach adjacent **Facilities** water bowl walks info vet info **On Request** fridge access **Other** dogs only to be left unattended for short periods **Restrictions** well behaved dogs only

This privately owned hotel is situated in private gardens which have direct access to the beach. With a train station within walking distance the location is perfectly suited for both business and leisure guests. Bedrooms are comfortably appointed, and public areas include a spacious restaurant, lounge, bar and leisure centre with swimming pool.

Rooms 41 (8 annexe) (10 fmly) (4 GF) **Facilities** FTV ⊗ Gym Sauna Steam room Spa bath ♫ Xmas New Year Wi-fi **Parking** 60

ENGLAND

Best Western Princes Marine

★★★ 75% HOTEL

153 Kingsway BN3 4GR

☎ 01273 207660 📄 01273 325913

e-mail: princesmarine@bestwestern.co.uk

dir: Right at Brighton Pier, follow seafront for 2m. Hotel 200yds from King Alfred leisure centre

PETS: Bedrooms certain bedrooms only **Charges** £5 per stay **Public areas** except restaurant on leads **Grounds** on leads disp bin **Exercise area** across road **Facilities** water bowl washing facs walks info vet info **On Request** fridge access torch towels **Stables** 4m

This friendly hotel enjoys a seafront location and offers spacious, comfortable bedrooms equipped with a good range of facilities including free Wi-fi. There is a stylish restaurant, modern bar and selection of roof-top meeting rooms with sea views. Limited parking is available at the rear.

Rooms 48 (4 fmly) **Facilities** Xmas **Services** Lift **Parking** 30

Brighton Pavilions

★★★★ GUEST ACCOMMODATION

7 Charlotte St BN2 1AG

☎ 01273 621750 📄 01273 622477

e-mail: sanchez-crespo@lineone.net

web: www.brightonpavilions.com

dir: A23 to Brighton Pier, left onto A259 Marine Parade, 15th left

PETS: Bedrooms (1 GF) unattended **Charges** £10 per night **Public areas** except dining room on leads **Exercise area** 200mtrs **Facilities** walks info vet info **On Request** fridge access **Other** charge for damage **Restrictions** no large dogs

This well-run operation is in one of Brighton's Regency streets, a short walk from the seafront and town centre. Bedrooms have themes such as Mikado or Pompeii, and are very smartly presented with many thoughtful extras including room service breakfast in superior rooms and free Wi-fi. The bright breakfast room has doors opening out onto a patio.

Rooms 10 rms (7 en suite) (1 fmly) (1 GF) **S** £45-£47; **D** £86-£148 **Facilities** FTV tea/coffee Direct Dial Cen ht Wi-fi **Notes** LB

New Steine

★★★★ 🛏 ☕ GUEST ACCOMMODATION

10-11 New Steine BN2 1PB

☎ 01273 695415 & 681546 📄 01273 622663

e-mail: reservation@newsteinehotel.com

dir: A23 to Brighton Pier, left onto Marine Parade, New Steine on left after Wentworth St

PETS: Bedrooms (2 GF) terraced bedrooms only **Charges** £5 per night £35 per week **Exercise area** 5 mins' walk **Facilities** walks info vet info **On Request** fridge access towels **Other** charge for damage **Restrictions** small & medium size dogs only

Close to the seafront off the Esplanade, the New Steine provides spacious bedrooms. There is a cosy lounge, where a wide choice of English, vegetarian, vegan or continental breakfasts is served. There is street parking in front of the property.

Rooms 20 rms (16 en suite) (4 pri facs) (4 fmly) (2 GF) **S** £29.50-£59; **D** £57.50-£119 **Facilities** FTV tea/coffee Dinner available Direct Dial Cen ht Licensed Wi-fi **Notes** LB No Children 4yrs

Ambassador Brighton

★★★★ GUEST ACCOMMODATION

22-23 New Steine, Marine Pde BN2 1PD

☎ 01273 676869 📄 01273 689988

e-mail: info@ambassadorbrighton.co.uk

web: www.ambassadorbrighton.co.uk

dir: A23 to Brighton Pier, left onto A259, 9th left, onto Garden Sq, 1st left

PETS: Bedrooms (3 GF) **Public areas** except restaurant **Grounds** disp bin **Exercise area** beach nearby **Facilities** dog walking cage storage walks info vet info **On Request** fridge access torch towels **Other** charge for damage

At the heart of bustling Kemp Town, overlooking the attractive garden square next to the seaside, this well-established property has a friendly and relaxing atmosphere. Bedrooms are well equipped and vary in size, with the largest having the best views. A small lounge with a separate bar is available.

Rooms 24 en suite (9 fmly) (3 GF) (8 smoking) **S** £50-£77; **D** £75.50-£128 **Facilities** tea/coffee Direct Dial Cen ht Licensed **Notes** LB

The Oriental

★★★★ GUEST ACCOMMODATION

9 Oriental Place BN1 2LJ
☎ 01273 205050 📠 01273 205050
e-mail: info@orientalbrighton.co.uk
dir: A23 right onto A259 at seafront, right into Oriental Place,
on right

PETS: Bedrooms (1 GF) unattended bedrooms with wood floors
only **Public areas** except restaurant at meal times on leads
Exercise area 50mtrs **Facilities** food bowl water bowl walks
info vet info **On Request** torch towels **Other** charge for damage
Restrictions well behaved dogs only

The Oriental is situated close to the seafront and enjoys easy
access to all areas. The accommodation is comfortable and
modern, and there is a licensed bar. A tasty Sussex breakfast
using locally sourced produce is offered in a friendly, relaxed
atmosphere.

Rooms 9 en suite (4 fmly) (1 GF) **S** £45-£79; **D** £75-£150
Facilities FTV tea/coffee Cen ht Licensed Wi-fi

Avalon

★★★ GUEST ACCOMMODATION

7 Upper Rock Gardens BN2 1QE
☎ 01273 692344 📠 01273 692344
e-mail: info@avalonbrighton.co.uk
dir: A23 to Brighton Pier, left onto Marine Parade, 300yds at
lights left onto Lower Rock Gdns, over lights, Avalon on left

PETS: Bedrooms (1 GF) unattended **Public areas Exercise area**
parks & beach nearby **Facilities** food bowl water bowl feeding
mat walks info vet info **Other** charge for damage maps, list of
dog friendly restaurants & bars available

A warm welcome is assured at this guest accommodation just
a short walk from the seafront and The Lanes. The en suite
bedrooms vary in size and style but all are attractively presented
with plenty of useful accessories including free Wi-fi. Parking
vouchers are available for purchase from the proprietor.

Rooms 7 en suite (3 fmly) (1 GF) **Facilities** FTV tea/coffee Cen ht
Wi-fi

Camber Sands (TQ972184)

New Lydd Rd TN31 7RT
☎ 0871 664 9719
e-mail: camber.sands@park-resorts.com
dir: M20 junct 10 (Ashford International Station), A2070 signed
Brenzett. Follow Hastings & Rye signs on A259. 1m before Rye,
left signed Camber. Site in 3m

PETS: Public areas except swimming pool, bars & complex
Exercise area adjacent **Facilities** food food bowl water bowl
dog chews litter tray scoop/disp bags leads walks info vet info
Other prior notice required phone for details of charges for dogs
Restrictions no dangerous dogs (see page 7)

Open Apr-Oct Last arrival anytime Last departure 10.00hrs

Located opposite Camber's vast sandy beach, this large holiday
centre offers a good range of leisure and entertainment facilities.
The touring area is positioned close to the reception and
entrance, and is served by a clean and functional toilet block.
110 acre site. 40 touring pitches. 6 hardstandings. Tent pitches.
Motorhome pitches. 921 statics.

Notes Quiet between 23.00hrs-7.00hrs.

The Grand Hotel

★★★★★ 84% ◉◉ HOTEL

King Edward's Pde BN21 4EQ
☎ 01323 412345 📠 01323 412233
e-mail: reservations@grandeastbourne.com
web: www.grandeastbourne.com
dir: On seafront W of Eastbourne, 1m from railway station

PETS: Bedrooms (4 GF) **Charges** £7 per night **Exercise area**
park & beach adjacent **Facilities** food (pre-bookable) food bowl
water bowl bedding dog chews dog walking dog grooming vet
info **On Request** fridge access **Other** footballs & toys available

This famous Victorian hotel offers high standards of service and
hospitality, and is in close proximity to both the beach and the
South Downs National Park. The extensive public rooms feature a
magnificent Great Hall, with marble columns and high ceilings,
where guests can relax and enjoy afternoon tea. The spacious
bedrooms provide high levels of comfort; many with stunning sea
views and a number with private balconies. Guests can choose to
eat in the fine dining The Mirabelle or the Garden Restaurant and
there are bars as well as superb spa and leisure facilities.

Rooms 152 (20 fmly) (4 GF) **S** £169-£425; **D** £199-£455 (incl.
bkfst)* **Facilities** Spa STV 🟦 supervised 🥅 Putt green Gym
Hairdressing Beauty therapy 🎵 Xmas New Year Child facilities
Services Lift **Parking** 80 **Notes** LB

EASTBOURNE *continued*

Congress

★★ 75% HOTEL

31-41 Carlisle Rd BN21 4JS

☎ 01323 732118 📠 01323 720016

e-mail: reservations@congresshotel.co.uk

web: www.congresshotel.co.uk

dir: *From Eastbourne seafront W towards Beachy Head. Right at Wishtower into Wilmington Sq, cross Compton St, hotel on left*

PETS: Bedrooms (8 GF) unattended sign **Grounds Exercise area** 200yds **Facilities** walks info vet info **On Request** fridge access

An attractive Victorian property ideally located close to the seafront, Wish Tower and Congress Theatre. The bedrooms are bright and spacious. Family rooms are available plus facilities for less able guests. Entertainment is provided in a large dining room that has a dance floor and bar.

Rooms 62 (6 fmly) (8 GF) **S** £33-£48; **D** £66-£96 (incl. bkfst) **Facilities** FTV Games room ♬ Xmas New Year Wi-fi **Services** Lift **Parking** 12 **Notes** LB RS Jan-Feb

The Mowbray

★★★★ GUEST ACCOMMODATION

2 Lascelles Ter BN21 4BJ

☎ 01323 720012 📠 01323 733579

e-mail: info@themowbray.com

dir: *Opposite Devonshire Park Theatre*

PETS: Bedrooms (1 GF) unattended **Public areas** except lounge **Exercise area** seafront (adjacent) **Facilities** walks info vet info **On Request** torch **Other** charge for damage **Restrictions** small dogs only

This elegant townhouse is located opposite The Devonshire Park Theatre and a few minutes' walk from the seafront. Bedrooms are accessible by a lift to all floors, and vary in size, but all are attractively furnished and comfortable. There are a spacious well presented lounge, small modern bar and a stylish dining room. Breakfast is home-cooked, as are evening meals, available by prior arrangement

Rooms 13 en suite (2 fmly) (1 GF) **S** £38-£43; **D** £75-£102 **Facilities** FTV TVL tea/coffee Dinner available Cen ht Lift Licensed Wi-fi **Notes** LB

Arden House

★★★★ GUEST ACCOMMODATION

17 Burlington Place BN21 4AR

☎ 01323 639639 📠 01323 417840

e-mail: info@theardenhotel.co.uk

dir: *On seafront, towards W, 5th turn after pier*

PETS: Bedrooms Charges Exercise area 100mtrs **Facilities** food bowl water bowl scoop/disp bags leads walks info vet info **On Request** torch towels

This attractive Regency property sits just minutes away from the seafront and town centre. Bedrooms are comfortable and bright, many with new en suite bathrooms. Guests can enjoy a hearty breakfast at the beginning of the day then relax in the cosy lounge in the evening.

Rooms 11 rms (10 en suite) (1 pri facs) (1 fmly) **S** £38-£42; **D** £62-£68 **Facilities** STV FTV TVL tea/coffee Cen ht Wi-fi **Parking** 3 **Notes** LB

The Royal

★★★★ GUEST ACCOMMODATION

8-9 Marine Pde BN21 3DX

☎ 01323 649222 📠 0560 1500 065

e-mail: info@royaleastbourne.org.uk

dir: *On seafront 100mtrs E of pier*

PETS: Bedrooms (1 GF) unattended sign **Public areas** except breakfast room on leads **Exercise area** beach adjacent **Facilities** food (pre-bookable) food bowl water bowl bedding feeding mat scoop/disp bags leads pet sitting dog walking cage storage walks info vet info **On Request** fridge access towels **Other** charge for damage

This property enjoys a central seafront location close to the pier and within easy walking distance of the town centre. Spectacular uninterrupted sea views are guaranteed. Now fully renovated and eco-friendly, the comfortable bedrooms are modern with flat-screen TVs and free Wi-fi. One of the ten rooms has private facilities, while the others are fully en suite. A substantial continental breakfast is served.

Rooms 10 rms (9 en suite) (1 pri facs) (1 fmly) (1 GF) **S** £35-£55; **D** £59-£90 **Facilities** STV FTV tea/coffee Cen ht Wi-fi **Notes** LB No Children 12yrs

Beachy Rise
★★★ GUEST HOUSE
5 Beachy Head Rd BN20 7QN
☎ 01323 639171 📠 01323 645006
e-mail: susanne234@hotmail.co.uk
dir: 1m SW of town centre. Off B2103 Upper Dukes Rd

PETS: Bedrooms Charges £5 per stay **Grounds** on leads
Exercise area 200yds **Facilities** walks info vet info **On Request**
fridge access towels **Other** charge for damage **Resident Pets:**
Tipsy & Tigo (cats)

This friendly family-run guest house has a quiet residential
location close to Meads Village. Bedrooms are individually styled
with co-ordinated soft furnishings and feature some useful
extras. Breakfast is served in the light and airy dining room
overlooking the garden, which guests are welcome to use.

Rooms 4 en suite (2 fmly) **S** £35-£45; **D** £55-£70
Facilities tea/coffee Cen ht Wi-fi

Ashdown Park Hotel & Country Club
★★★★ ◉◉ HOTEL
Wych Cross RH18 5JR
☎ 01342 824988 📠 01342 826206
e-mail: reservations@ashdownpark.com
web: www.ashdownpark.com
dir: A264 to East Grinstead, then A22 to Eastbourne. 2m S of
Forest Row at Wych Cross lights. Left to Hartfield, hotel on right
0.75m

PETS: Bedrooms (16 GF) unattended ground-floor Fairway
Suites only **Charges** £30 per night **Grounds** disp bin **Facilities**
food (pre-bookable) food bowl water bowl bedding dog chews
feeding mat washing facs cage storage walks info vet info
On Request fridge access torch towels **Stables** 3m **Other**
charge for damage charge includes pet dinner & toy

Situated in 186 acres of landscaped gardens and parkland, this
impressive country house enjoys a peaceful countryside setting in
the heart of the Ashdown Forest. Bedrooms are individually styled
and decorated. Public rooms include a restored 18th-century
chapel, ideal for exclusive meetings and wedding parties, plus
three drawing rooms, a cocktail bar and the award-winning
Anderida Restaurant. The extensive indoor and outdoor leisure
facilities include the Country Club and Spa plus an 18-hole,
par 3 golf course and driving range.

Rooms 106 (16 GF) **D** £199-£465 (incl. bkfst)* **Facilities** Spa
FTV ⊗ ♨ 18 ♨ Putt green ⛳ Gym Beauty salon Aerobics studio
Treatment rooms Steam room Mountain bike hire ♫ Xmas New
Year Wi-fi **Parking** 200 **Notes** LB

Heaven Farm *(TQ403264)*
▶▶
TN22 3RG
☎ 01825 790226 📠 01825 790881
e-mail: heavenfarmleisure@btinternet.com
dir: On A275 between Lewes & East Grinstead, 1m N of Sheffield
Park Gardens

PETS: Public areas on leads **Exercise area on site** meadow
Exercise area adjacent **Facilities** walks info vet info **Other**
prior notice required dogs must not worry resident poultry &
ducks, & must be kept on leads at all times **Resident Pets:** 3 cats

Open Apr-Oct Last arrival 21.00hrs Last departure noon

A delightful, small, rural site on a popular farm complex
incorporating a farm museum, craft shop, organic farm shop,
tea room and nature trail. Good clean toilet facilities are housed
in well-converted outbuildings. Ashdown Forest, the Bluebell
Railway and Sheffield Park Garden are nearby. 1.5 acre site.
25 touring pitches. 2 hardstandings. Tent pitches. Motorhome
pitches.

Notes The site prefers no children between 6-18yrs. ♨

The Olde Forge Hotel & Restaurant
★★ 79% HOTEL
Magham Down BN27 1PN
☎ 01323 842893 📠 01323 842893
e-mail: theoldeforgehotel@tesco.net
web: www.theoldeforgehotel.co.uk
dir: Off Boship Rdbt on A271 to Bexhill & Herstmonceux. Hotel
3m on left

PETS: Bedrooms sign **Charges** £5 per night **Public areas**
except restaurant & guest lounge **Grounds** on leads disp bin
Exercise area opposite **Facilities** food (pre-bookable) food
bowl water bowl bedding dog chews feeding mat scoop/
disp bags leads washing facs cage storage walks info vet
info **On Request** fridge access torch towels **Other** charge
for damage please phone for further details of pet facilities
Resident Pet: Diesel (Boxer)

In the heart of the countryside, this family-run hotel offers a
friendly welcome and an informal atmosphere. The bedrooms are
attractively decorated with thoughtful extras. The restaurant,
with its timbered beams and log fires, was a forge in the 16th
century; today it has a good local reputation for both its cuisine
and service.

Rooms 7 **S** fr £48; **D** fr £85 (incl. bkfst)* **Facilities** Wi-fi
Parking 11 **Notes** LB

HEATHFIELD
Map 5 TQ52

Holly Grove

★ ★ ★ ★ BED AND BREAKFAST

Little London TN21 0NU

☎ 01435 863375 & 07811 963193

e-mail: joedance@btconnect.com

dir: A267 to Horam, turn right at Little London garage, proceed to bottom of lane

PETS: Bedrooms (2 GF) **Charges** charge for horses (livery) **Public areas** except restaurant **Grounds** disp bin **Exercise area** adjacent **Facilities** food (pre-bookable) food bowl water bowl bedding dog chews cat treats feeding mat litter tray leads pet sitting dog walking washing facs cage storage walks info vet info **On Request** fridge access torch towels **Stables Other** charge for damage **Resident Pets:** Annie, Oscar & Golly (Spaniels), Plessi, Chopin & Sophie (cats), Apache & Josh (horses)

Holly Grove is set in a quiet rural location with heated outdoor swimming pool, satellite TV, Wi-fi and parking facilities. Bedrooms are appointed to a very high standard. There is a separate lounge available for guests, and breakfast is served in the dining room or on the terrace, weather permitting.

Rooms 3 rms (2 en suite) (1 pri facs) (1 fmly) (2 GF) **Facilities** STV TVL tea/coffee Dinner available Cen ht Wi-fi ⌇ Pool table **Parking** 7

HERSTMONCEUX
Map 5 TQ61

Cleavers Lyng Country House

★ ★ ★ ★ GUEST ACCOMMODATION

Church Rd BN27 1QJ

☎ 01323 833644

e-mail: cleaverslyng@btinternet.com

web: www.cleaverslyng.co.uk

dir: From A271 at Herstmonceux, turn into Chapel Row leading into Church Rd, 1.5m on right

PETS: Bedrooms Public areas on leads **Grounds** disp bin **Exercise area** adjacent **Facilities** food (pre-bookable) food bowl water bowl bedding dog chews feeding mat leads washing facs cage storage walks info vet info **On Request** fridge access torch towels **Stables** 1m **Other** charge for damage

Expect a warm welcome at this Grade II listed country house, parts of which date back to 1577. A spacious downstairs lounge

and breakfast room offers the perfect place to relax with its log burning fireplace. Alternatively guests can enjoy the peaceful, landscaped gardens with fantastic views of beautiful Sussex countryside. Rooms are well appointed with LCD TVs, free Wi-fi and many with amazing scenic views.

Rooms 4 en suite (1 fmly) **S** £50–£90; **D** £75–£110 **Facilities** tea/coffee Cen ht Wi-fi **Parking** 10

HOVE

See Brighton & Hove

NEWICK
Map 5 TQ42

Newick Park Hotel & Country Estate

★ ★ ★ ◉◉ HOTEL

BN8 4SB

☎ 01825 723633 📄 01825 723969

e-mail: bookings@newickpark.co.uk

web: www.newickpark.co.uk

dir: Exit A272 at Newick Green, 1m, pass church & pub. Turn left, hotel 0.25m on right

PETS: Bedrooms (1 GF) unattended sign ground-floor & granary bedrooms only **Charges** £5 per night **Grounds Facilities** food (pre-bookable) food bowl water bowl feeding mat washing facs walks info vet info **On Request** fridge access torch towels **Resident Pets:** Maddy (Black Labrador), Tibby (Cocker Spaniel)

Delightful Grade II listed Georgian country house set amid 250 acres of Sussex parkland and landscaped gardens. The spacious, individually decorated bedrooms are tastefully furnished, thoughtfully equipped and have superb views of the grounds; many rooms have huge American king-size beds. The comfortable public rooms include a study, a sitting room, lounge bar and an elegant restaurant.

Rooms 16 (3 annexe) (5 fmly) (1 GF) **Facilities** FTV ⌇ ⛳ Fishing ⛳ Badminton Clay pigeon shooting Helicopter rides Quad biking Tank driving Xmas Wi-fi **Parking** 52 **Notes** LB

PEASMARSH
Map 5 TQ82

Flackley Ash Hotel & Restaurant

★ ★ ★ 78% HOTEL

TN31 6YH

☎ 01797 230651 📄 01797 230510

e-mail: enquiries@flackleyashhotel.co.uk

web: www.flackleyashhotel.co.uk

dir: Exit A21 onto A268 to Newenden, next left A268 to Rye. Hotel on left on entering Peasmarsh

PETS: Bedrooms (19 GF) unattended **Charges** £8.50 per night **Public areas** except restaurant on leads **Grounds** disp bin **Exercise area** nearby **Facilities** walks info vet info **On Request** fridge access torch towels **Other** charge for damage

Five acres of beautifully kept grounds make a lovely setting for this elegant Georgian country house. The hotel is superbly situated for exploring the many local attractions, including the ancient Cinque Port of Rye. Stylishly decorated bedrooms are comfortable and boast many thoughtful touches. A sunny

conservatory dining room, luxurious beauty spa and a swimming pool are available.

Rooms 45 (5 fmly) (19 GF) (10 smoking) **Facilities** Spa STV ⊕ supervised ❧ Gym Beauty salon Steam room Saunas Xmas New Year Wi-fi **Parking** 80

PEVENSEY BAY   Map 5 TQ60

Bay View Park *(TQ648028)*

▶▶▶

Old Martello Rd BN24 6DX
☎ 01323 768688   📠 01323 769637
e-mail: holidays@bay-view.co.uk
dir: *Signed from A259 W of Pevensey Bay. On sea side of A259 along private road towards beach*

PETS: Charges £1 per night **Public areas** except children's play area disp bin **Exercise area** shingle beach (50yds) **Facilities** food bowl walks info vet info **Other** prior notice required max 3 dogs per pitch **Restrictions** no dangerous dogs (see page 7)

Open Mar-Oct Last arrival 20.00hrs Last departure noon

A pleasant well-run site just yards from the beach, in an area east of Eastbourne town centre known as 'The Crumbles'. The level grassy site is very well maintained and the toilet facilities feature fully-serviced cubicles. 6 acre site. 94 touring pitches. 10 hardstandings. Tent pitches. Motorhome pitches. 8 statics.

Notes Families & couples only, no commercial vehicles.

RYE   Map 5 TQ92

Rye Lodge Hotel

★★★★ **75%** METRO HOTEL
Hilders Cliff TN31 7LD
☎ 01797 223838 & 226688   📠 01797 223585
e-mail: info@ryelodge.co.uk
web: www.ryelodge.co.uk
dir: *On one-way system follow signs for town centre, through Landgate arch, hotel 100yds on right*

PETS: Bedrooms (5 GF) sign certain rooms only **Charges** £8 per night **Public areas** except restaurant **Grounds** disp bin **Exercise area** 150mtrs **Facilities** food (pre-bookable) food bowl water bowl dog chews cage storage walks info vet info **On Request** fridge access torch towels **Other** charge for damage

Standing in an elevated position, Rye Lodge has panoramic views across Romney Marshes and the Rother Estuary. Traditionally styled bedrooms come in a variety of sizes; they are attractively decorated and thoughtfully equipped. Public rooms feature indoor leisure facilities and the Terrace Room Restaurant where home-made dishes are offered. Lunch and afternoon tea are served on the flower-filled outdoor terrace in warmer months.

Rooms 19 (5 GF) **S** £75-£125; **D** £95-£195* **Facilities** STV FTV ⊕ Aromatherapy Steam cabinet Sauna Exercise machines Wi-fi **Parking** 20 **Notes** LB

Jeake's House

★★★★★ ▤ GUEST ACCOMMODATION
Mermaid St TN31 7ET
☎ 01797 222828
e-mail: stay@jeakeshouse.com
web: www.jeakeshouse.com
dir: *Approach from High St or The Strand*

PETS: Bedrooms Charges £5 per night **Public areas** except dining room (welcome in bar) **Exercise area** 5-10 mins' walk **Facilities** walks info vet info **On Request** fridge access torch towels **Resident Pets:** Princess Yum Yum & Monte (Tonkinese cats)

Previously a 17th-century wool store and then a 19th-century Baptist school, this delightful house stands on a cobbled street in one of the most beautiful parts of this small, bustling town. The individually decorated bedrooms combine elegance and comfort with modern facilities. Breakfast is served at separate tables in the galleried dining room, and there is an oak-beamed lounge as well as a stylish book-lined bar with old pews. Jenny Hadfield was a finalist in the AA Friendliest Landlady of the Year award 2011-12.

Rooms 11 rms (10 en suite) (1 pri facs) (2 fmly) **S** £70-£80; **D** £90-£140 **Facilities** FTV tea/coffee Direct Dial Cen ht Licensed Wi-fi **Parking** 20 **Notes** LB No Children 5yrs

RYE *continued*

Little Saltcote

★★★★ GUEST ACCOMMODATION

22 Military Rd TN31 7NY
☎ 01797 223210 & 07940 742646 📄 01797 224474
e-mail: info@littlesaltcote.co.uk
web: www.littlesaltcote.co.uk
dir: *0.5m N of town centre. Off A268 onto Military Rd signed Appledore, house 300yds on left*

PETS: Bedrooms (1 GF) ground-floor bedrooms preferred **Charges** £5 per night **Public areas** except dining room on leads **Exercise area** 0.5m **Facilities** food bowl water bowl cage storage walks info vet info **On Request** fridge access torch towels **Other** charge for damage **Restrictions** no breed larger than a Labrador **Resident Pet:** Bracken (Labrador/Poodle cross)

This delightful family-run establishment stands in quiet surroundings within walking distance of Rye town centre. The bright and airy en suite bedrooms are equipped with modern facilities including Wi-fi, and guests can enjoy afternoon tea in the garden conservatory. A hearty breakfast is served at individual tables in the dining room.

Rooms 4 en suite (2 fmly) (1 GF) **S** £40-£75; **D** £70-£80 **Facilities** FTV tea/coffee Cen ht Wi-fi **Parking** 5 **Notes** LB

Little Tidebrook Farm *(TQ621304)*

★★★★ FARMHOUSE

Riseden TN5 6NY
☎ 01892 782688 & 07970 159988 Mrs Sally Marley-Ward
e-mail: info@littletidebrook.co.uk
web: www.littletidebrook.co.uk
dir: *A267 from Tunbridge Wells to Mark Cross, left onto B2100, 2m turn right at Best Beech Inn, left after 1m into Riseden Rd, farm on left*

PETS: Sep accom indoor, heated, (safe & secure) **Charges** £5 per night **Public areas** not during meal times on leads **Grounds** on leads disp bin **Exercise area** farmland **Facilities** water bowl scoop/disp bags leads washing facs cage storage walks info vet info **On Request** fridge access torch towels **Stables Resident Pets:** 2 Labradors, 1 Jack Russell, 2 cats, 17 horses

This traditional farmhouse has cosy log fires in winter and wonderful garden dining in warm months. The imaginative decor

combines with modern amenities such as Wi-fi to provide leisure and business travellers with the ideal setting. Close to Bewl Water and Royal Tunbridge Wells.

Rooms 3 rms (2 en suite) (1 pri facs) **S** £50-£75; **D** £50-£75 **Facilities** TVL tea/coffee Cen ht Wi-fi **Parking** 8 **Notes** No Children 12yrs 🐾 50 acres horses

Norfolk Arms

★★★ 74% HOTEL

High St BN18 9AB
☎ 01903 882101 📄 01903 884275
e-mail: norfolk.arms@forestdale.com
web: www.norfolkarmshotel.com
dir: *On High St in centre*

PETS: Bedrooms (8 GF) unattended **Charges** £7.50 per night **Public areas** except restaurant **Facilities** food (pre-bookable) food bowl water bowl feeding mat cage storage walks info vet info **On Request** torch **Other** charge for damage

Built by the 10th Duke of Norfolk, this Georgian coaching inn enjoys a superb setting beneath the battlements of Arundel Castle. Bedrooms vary in sizes and character - all are comfortable and well equipped. Public areas include two bars serving real ales, comfortable lounges with roaring log fires, a traditional restaurant and a range of meeting and function rooms.

Rooms 33 (13 annexe) (4 fmly) (8 GF) **Facilities** FTV Xmas New Year Wi-fi **Parking** 34 **Notes** LB

Comfort Inn

★★ 65% HOTEL

Crossbush BN17 7QQ
☎ 01903 840840 📄 01903 849849
e-mail: reservations@comfortinnarundel.co.uk
dir: *A27/A284, 1st right into services*

PETS: Bedrooms (25 GF) certain bedrooms only **Charges** £5 per night £35 per week **Public areas** except restaurant & bar on leads **Facilities** vet info

This modern, purpose-built hotel provides a good base for exploring the nearby historic town. Good access to local road networks and a range of meeting rooms, all air-conditioned, also make this an ideal venue for business guests. Bedrooms are spacious, smartly decorated and well equipped.

Rooms 53 (4 fmly) (25 GF) (12 smoking) **Facilities** STV FTV Xmas New Year Wi-fi **Parking** 53

Ship & Anchor Marina *(TQ002040)*

►►

Station Rd, Ford BN18 0BJ
☎ 01243 551262 🖷 01243 555256
e-mail: enquiries@shipandanchormarina.co.uk
dir: *From A27 at Arundel take road S signed Ford. Site 2m on left after level crossing*

PETS: Public areas disp bin **Exercise area on site** riverside walks **Facilities** food dog chews cat treats walks info vet info **Resident Pets:** 1 dog & 4 cats

Open Mar-Oct Last arrival 21.00hrs Last departure noon

A neat and tidy site with dated but spotlessly clean toilet facilities enjoying a pleasant position beside the Ship & Anchor pub and the tidal River Arun. There are good walks from the site to Arundel and the coast. 12 acre site. 120 touring pitches. 11 hardstandings. Tent pitches. Motorhome pitches.

Notes No music audible to others.

Sumners Ponds Fishery & Campsite
(TQ125268)

►►►►

Chapel Rd RH13 0PR
☎ 01403 732539
e-mail: sumnersponds@dsl.co.uk
dir: *From A272 at Coolham x-rds, N towards Barns Green. In 1.5m take 1st left at small x-rds. 1m, over level crossing. Site on left just after right bend*

PETS: Public areas disp bin **Exercise area on site Facilities** food bowl water bowl walks info vet info **Stables** 2m **Other** disposal bags available **Resident Pet:** Skippy (Jack Russell)

Open all year Last arrival 20.00hrs Last departure noon

Diversification towards high quality camping continues apace at this working farm set in attractive surroundings on the edge of the quiet village of Barns Green. There are now three touring areas; the site has excellent pitches on the banks of one of the well-stocked fishing lakes. Camping pods are now available. A woodland walk has direct access to miles of footpaths, and both Horsham and Brighton are within easy reach. 40 acre site. 85 touring pitches. 45 hardstandings. Tent pitches. Motorhome pitches.

Notes Only one car per pitch.

Limeburners Arms Camp Site *(TQ072255)*

►►

Lordings Rd, Newbridge RH14 9JA
☎ 01403 782311
e-mail: chippy.sawyer@virgin.net
dir: *From A29 take A272 towards Petworth for 1m, left onto B2133. Site 300yds on left*

PETS: Public areas Exercise area adjacent walks **Facilities** vet info

Open Apr-Oct Last arrival 22.00hrs Last departure 14.00hrs

A secluded site in rural West Sussex, at the rear of the Limeburners Arms public house, and surrounded by fields. It makes a pleasant base for touring the South Downs and the Arun Valley. The toilets are basic but very clean. 2.75 acre site. 40 touring pitches. Tent pitches. Motorhome pitches.

Tawny Touring Park *(SZ818991)*

►

Tawny Nurseries, Bell Ln PO20 7HY
☎ 01243 512168
e-mail: tawny@pobox.co.uk
dir: *From A27 at Stockbridge rdbt take A286 towards The Witterings. 5m to mini rdbt in Birdham. 1st exit onto B2198. Site 300mtrs on left*

PETS: Public areas disp bin **Exercise area on site** fenced area **Facilities** washing facs walks info vet info **Other** prior notice required **Resident Pet:** 1 Labrador

Open all year Last arrival 21.00hrs Last departure 19.00hrs

A small site for the self-contained tourer only, on a landscaped field adjacent to the owners' nurseries. There are six hardstanding pitches for American RVs but no toilet facilities. The beach is just one mile away. 4.5 acre site. 30 touring pitches. 7 hardstandings. Motorhome pitches.

BOGNOR REGIS
Map 4 SZ99

The Russell Hotel
★★★ 77% HOTEL

King's Pde PO21 2QP
☎ 01243 871300 🖨 01243 871301
e-mail: russell.hotel@actionforblindpeople.org.uk
dir: A27 follow signs for town centre, hotel on seafront

PETS: Bedrooms unattended sign **Exercise area** nearby **Facilities** food bowl water bowl bedding washing facs walks info vet info **On Request** fridge access torch towels **Other** charge for damage **Resident Pet:** Pebbles (cat)

Situated in a pleasant location close to the seafront, the Russell Hotel offers large and well-appointed bedrooms; some are fully accessible and many have sea views. This hotel also caters for visually impaired people, their families, friends and their guide dogs, as well as offering a warm welcome to business and leisure guests. There are of course special facilities for the guide dogs. Leisure facilities are also available.

Rooms 40 (5 fmly) **S** £39.90-£99; **D** £49.90-£110 (incl. bkfst) **Facilities** FTV ⊗ supervised Gym ♫ Xmas New Year **Services** Lift **Parking** 6 **Notes** LB

CHICHESTER
Map 4 SU80

Crouchers Country Hotel & Restaurant
★★★ 81% ◉◉ HOTEL

Birdham Rd PO20 7EH
☎ 01243 784995 🖨 01243 539797
e-mail: crouchers@btconnect.com
dir: From A27 Chichester bypass onto A286 towards West Wittering, 2m, hotel on left between Chichester Marina & Dell Quay

PETS: Bedrooms (15 GF) **Charges** £10 per night £70 per week **Public areas** except restaurant & lounge on leads **Grounds** on leads disp bin **Exercise area** nearby **Facilities** walks info vet info **On Request** fridge access torch towels **Other** charge for damage **Restrictions** max 2 (small or medium size) dogs only

This friendly, family-run hotel, situated in open countryside, is just a short drive from the harbour. The stylish and well-equipped bedrooms are situated in a separate barn, coach house and stable block, and include four-poster rooms and rooms with patios that overlook the fields. The modern oak-beamed restaurant, with country views, serves award-winning cuisine.

Rooms 26 (23 annexe) (2 fmly) (15 GF) **Facilities** STV FTV Xmas New Year Wi-fi **Parking** 80

Old Chapel Forge
★★★★ ⏚ BED AND BREAKFAST

Lower Bognor Rd, Lagness PO20 1LR
☎ 01243 264380
e-mail: info@oldchapelforge.co.uk
dir: 4m SE of Chichester. Off A27 Chichester bypass at Bognor rdbt signed Pagham/Runcton, onto B2166 Pagham Rd & Lower Bognor Rd, Old Chapel Forge on right

PETS: Bedrooms chapel suite & king-size suite only **Charges** donation to nature reserve (min £10 per stay) **Public areas** except breakfast area on leads **Grounds** on leads disp bin **Exercise area** 80 acres adjacent & beach 1m **Facilities** walks info vet info **On Request** fridge access torch towels **Stables** 0.25m **Other** charge for damage pets accepted by prior arrangement only; minimum 2 night stay **Restrictions** no dogs under 1 year; dogs must be house-trained **Resident Pets:** Jade (Labrador), 4 donkeys, geese

Great local produce features in the hearty breakfasts at this comfortable, eco-friendly property, an idyllic 17th-century house and chapel set in mature gardens with panoramic views of the South Downs. Old Chapel Forge is a short drive from Chichester, Goodwood, Pagham Harbour Nature Reserve and the beach. Bedrooms, including suites in the chapel, are luxurious, and all have internet access.

Rooms 4 annexe en suite (2 fmly) (4 GF) **S** £45-£90; **D** £50-£120 **Facilities** tea/coffee Dinner available Cen ht Wi-fi Golf 18 **Parking** 6 **Notes** LB

Ellscott Park (SU829995)
▶▶▶

Sidlesham Ln, Birdham PO20 7QL
☎ 01243 512003 🖨 01243 512003
e-mail: camping@ellscottpark.co.uk
dir: Take A286 (Chichester/Wittering road) for approx 4m, left at Butterfly Farm sign, site 500yds right

PETS: Public areas on leads disp bin **Exercise area on site** 3-acre field **Facilities** washing facs walks info vet info **Stables** 1m **Other** prior notice required **Restrictions** no German Shepherds or dangerous dogs (see page 7) **Resident Pet:** Luckie (Springer Spaniel)

Open Apr-3rd wk in Oct Last arrival daylight Last departure variable

A well-kept park set in meadowland behind the owners' nursery and van storage area. The park attracts a peace-loving clientele, and is handy for the beach, Chichester, Goodwood House and Races, walking on the South Downs, and other local attractions. Home-grown produce is for sale. 2.5 acre site. 50 touring pitches. 25 seasonal pitches. Tent pitches. Motorhome pitches.

Notes ☺

CLIMPING
Map 4 SU90

Bailiffscourt Hotel & Spa
★★★ ◉◉ HOTEL

Climping St BN17 5RW
☎ 01903 723511 ▤ 01903 723107
e-mail: bailiffscourt@hshotels.co.uk
web: www.hshotels.co.uk
dir: A259, follow Climping Beach signs. Hotel 0.5m on right

PETS: Bedrooms (16 GF) unattended **Charges** £13.50 per night **Public areas** except restaurant on leads **Grounds** on leads disp bin **Exercise area** 200mtrs to beach. Hotel in 30-acre grounds **Facilities** food (pre-bookable) food bowl water bowl dog chews feeding mat scoop/disp bags washing facs walks info vet info **On Request** fridge access torch towels **Other** charge for damage room service menu for dogs

This delightful moated 'medieval manor' dating back only to the 1920s has the appearance of having been in existence for centuries. In fact it was built for Lord Moyne, a member of the Guinness family, who wanted to create an ancient manor house. It became a hotel just over 60 years ago and sits in 30 acres of delightful parkland that leads to the beach. Bedrooms vary from atmospheric feature rooms with log fires, oak beams and four-poster beds to spacious, stylish and contemporary rooms located in the grounds. The Tapestry Restaurant serves award-winning classic European cuisine, and in summer the Courtyard is the place for informal light lunches and afternoon tea. Superb facilities are to be found in the health spa.

Rooms 39 (30 annexe) (25 fmly) (16 GF) **S** £158-£398; **D** £210-£530 (incl. bkfst)* **Facilities** Spa STV FTV ⊕ ⌇ ⊰⇘ Gym Sauna Steam room Dance/fitness studio Yoga/Pilates/gym inductions Xmas New Year Wi-fi **Parking** 100 **Notes** LB

CUCKFIELD
Map 4 TQ32

Ockenden Manor
★★★ ◉◉◉ HOTEL

Ockenden Ln RH17 5LD
☎ 01444 416111 ▤ 01444 415549
e-mail: reservations@ockenden-manor.com
web: www.hshotels.co.uk
dir: A23 towards Brighton. 4.5m left onto B2115 towards Haywards Heath. Cuckfield 3m. Ockenden Lane off High St. Hotel at end

PETS: Bedrooms (4 GF) unattended ground-floor bedrooms only **Charges** £10 per night **Grounds Exercise area** countryside walks **Facilities** washing facs walks info vet info **On Request** fridge access torch towels **Other** charge for damage

This charming 16th-century property enjoys fine views of the South Downs. The individually designed bedrooms and suites offer high standards of accommodation, some with unique historic features. Public rooms, retaining much original character, include an elegant sitting room with all the elements for a relaxing afternoon in front of the fire. Imaginative, noteworthy cuisine is the highlight to any stay. The beautiful rooms and lovely garden make Ockenden a popular wedding venue. The hotel has a new spa, situated in a walled garden, that offers a pool, hot tub, spa bath, rain shower, floatation room, gym, sauna, steam room plus health and beauty treatments.

Rooms 28 (6 annexe) (4 fmly) (4 GF) **S** £113-£210; **D** £190-£395 (incl. bkfst)* **Facilities** Spa STV FTV ⊕ ⌇ ⊰⇘ Gym Floatation tank Xmas New Year Wi-fi **Parking** 98 **Notes** LB

DIAL POST
Map 4 TQ11

Honeybridge Park (TQ152183)
▶ ▶ ▶ ▶

Honeybridge Ln RH13 8NX
☎ 01403 710923 ▤ 01403 712815
e-mail: enquiries@honeybridgepark.co.uk
dir: 10m S of Horsham, just off A24 at Dial Post. Behind Old Barn Nursery

PETS: Charges dog £1.35 per night **Public areas** on leads disp bin **Exercise area** adjacent **Facilities** food walks info vet info **Other** prior notice required disposal bags available

Open all year Last arrival 19.00hrs Last departure noon

An attractive and very popular park on gently-sloping ground surrounded by hedgerows and mature trees. A comprehensive amenities building houses upmarket toilet facilities including luxury family and disabled rooms, as well as a laundry, shop and off-licence. There are plenty of hardstandings and electric hook-ups, and an excellent children's play area. 15 acre site. 130 touring pitches. 70 hardstandings. 20 seasonal pitches. Tent pitches. Motorhome pitches. 50 statics.

Notes No open fires.

GATWICK AIRPORT (LONDON) — Map 4 TQ24

The Lawn Guest House
★★★★ GUEST HOUSE
30 Massetts Rd RH6 7DF
☎ 01293 775751 📠 01293 821803
e-mail: info@lawnguesthouse.co.uk
web: www.lawnguesthouse.co.uk
dir: M25 junct 7, M23 S towards Brighton/Gatwick Airport. Exit at junct 9. At either South or North Terminal rdbts take A23 towards Redhill. At 3rd rdbt (Esso garage on left) take 3rd exit. (Texaco garage on right). In 200yds right at lights onto Massetts Rd. Guest house 400yds on left

PETS: Bedrooms certain bedrooms only **Charges** £5 per night **Public areas** muzzled **Grounds** on leads **Facilities** walks info **On Request** fridge access towels **Other** charge for damage dogs are required to be muzzled **Restrictions** quiet dogs only; no dangerous dogs (see page 7)

Once a Victorian school, this friendly guest house is well-positioned on a quiet leafy street close to Gatwick. Bedrooms are spacious with thoughtful amenities such as free Wi-fi, and fans for use in warm weather. Airport parking is available.

Rooms 12 en suite (4 fmly) **S** £40-£50; **D** £50-£65 **Facilities** STV tea/coffee Direct Dial Cen ht Wi-fi **Parking** 4

GOODWOOD — Map 4 SU81

The Goodwood Hotel
★★★★ 79% ◉◉ HOTEL
PO18 0QB
☎ 01243 775537 📠 01243 520120
e-mail: reservations@goodwood.com
web: www.goodwood.com
dir: Off A285, 3m NE of Chichester

PETS: Bedrooms (48 GF) unattended sign £25 per stay **Charges Public areas** except restaurants on leads **Grounds** on leads **Exercise area** 5m **Facilities** food bowl water bowl bedding scoop/disp bags washing facs cage storage walks info vet info **On Request** fridge access torch towels **Other** charge for damage

Set at the centre of the 12,000-acre Goodwood Estate, this attractive hotel boasts extensive indoor and outdoor leisure facilities, along with a range of meeting rooms plus conference and banqueting facilities. Bedrooms are furnished to a consistently high standard, including a luxury suite located in the old coaching inn, and Executive rooms, each with a patio. Eating options are varied - the Richmond Arms sourcing produce extensively from the estate farm, The Richmond Arms Bar, and the Goodwood Bar and Grill. Overnight guests can also choose to dine in The Kennels, a private members' clubhouse.

Rooms 91 (48 GF) **S** £105-£300 (incl. bkfst) **Facilities** Spa STV FTV ◉⚹ 18 ⛳ Putt green Gym Golf driving range Sauna Steam room Fitness studio Xmas New Year Wi-fi **Parking** 350 **Notes** LB

MIDHURST — Map 4 SU82

Spread Eagle Hotel and Spa
★★★ 81% ◉◉ HOTEL
South St GU29 9NH
☎ 01730 816911 📠 01730 815668
e-mail: spreadeagle@hshotels.co.uk
web: www.hshotels.co.uk/spread/spreadeagle-main.htm
dir: M25 junct 10, A3 to Milford, take A286 to Midhurst. Hotel adjacent to market square

PETS: Bedrooms (8 GF) unattended **Charges** £15 per night **Public areas** except restaurant **Grounds Exercise area** nearby **Facilities** food (pre-bookable) food bowl water bowl bedding walks info vet info **On Request** fridge access torch **Stables** 3m **Other** charge for damage pets not allowed on beds **Restrictions** no very large dogs **Resident Pet:** Poppy (Boxer)

Offering accommodation since 1430, this historic property is full of character, evident in its sloping floors and inglenook fireplaces. Individually styled bedrooms provide modern comforts; those in the main house have oak panelling and include some spacious feature rooms. The hotel also boasts a well-equipped spa and offers noteworthy food in the oak beamed restaurant.

Rooms 38 (4 annexe) (8 GF) **S** £95-£340; **D** £125-£340 (incl. bkfst)* **Facilities** Spa STV FTV ◉ Gym Health & beauty treatment rooms Steam room Sauna Fitness trainer Xmas New Year Wi-fi **Parking** 75 **Notes** LB

TILLINGTON — Map 4 SU92

The Horse Guards Inn
★★★★ ◉ INN
GU28 9AF
☎ 01798 342332 📠 01798 345126
e-mail: info@thehorseguardsinn.co.uk
dir: Off A272 to Tillington, up hill opposite All Hallows church

PETS: Bedrooms cottage bedrooms only **Charges** £10 per stay **Public areas** on leads **Grounds** on leads **Exercise area** 200yds **Facilities** food bowl water bowl bedding dog chews feeding mat washing facs cage storage walks info vet info **On Request** fridge access torch towels **Stables** 0.5km **Other** charge for damage **Resident Pets:** Sasha (Siamese cat), Marvin (Russian Blue cat)

This inn is conveniently located close to Petworth and Midhurst in a quiet village setting opposite the quaint church, which makes it perfect for exploring the beautiful surrounding countryside. The comfortable bedrooms are simply decorated, and delicious breakfasts are prepared to order using the finest local ingredients. The same principles apply to the substantial and flavoursome meals served in the cosy restaurant/bar dining areas.

Rooms 2 en suite 1 annexe en suite (1 fmly) **S** £80-£145; **D** £80-£145 **Facilities** FTV tea/coffee Dinner available Cen ht Wi-fi

WEST MARDEN — Map 4 SU71

Grandwood House
★★★★ GUEST ACCOMMODATION
Watergate PO18 9EG
☎ 07971 845153 & 023 9263 1436
e-mail: info@grandwoodhouse.co.uk
web: www.grandwoodhouse.co.uk

PETS: Bedrooms (4 GF) unattended certain bedrooms only **Public areas** on leads **Grounds** on leads disp bin **Exercise area** adjacent **Facilities** scoop/disp bags washing facs cage storage walks info vet info **On Request** fridge access torch towels **Stables** 1m **Other** charge for damage **Restrictions** please phone to check which size of dog is acceptable **Resident Pet:** Prince (German Shepherd)

Set in the South Downs and built in 1907, Grandwood House was originally a lodge belonging to Watergate House, which was accidentally burnt down by troops during WWII. Only a short walk away is the local pub in nearby Walderton which serves lunches and evening meals. All rooms are en suite and enjoy views of the garden, open farmland or both. Large security gates leading onto the driveway ensure secure parking at all times.

Rooms 4 annexe en suite (4 GF) **S** £40-£60; **D** £50-£85 **Facilities** FTV tea/coffee Cen ht Wi-fi **Parking** 8 **Notes** LB

WORTHING — Map 4 TQ10

Kingsway
★★ 71% HOTEL
Marine Pde BN11 3QQ
☎ 01903 237542 01903 204173
e-mail: kingsway-hotel@btconnect.com
dir: A27 to Worthing seafront follow signs 'Hotel West'. Hotel 0.75m west of pier

PETS: Bedrooms (3 GF) unattended sign **Charges** £10 per stay **Public areas** except restaurant **Grounds Exercise area** beach (adjacent) **Facilities** walks info vet info

Ideally located on the seafront and close to the town centre, this family-owned property extends a warm welcome to guests. Bedrooms vary in size, and some are very spacious with impressive sea views. Comfortable public areas include two modern lounges, a bright, stylish bar and well appointed restaurant.

Rooms 36 (7 annexe) (4 fmly) (3 GF) **Facilities** FTV Xmas Wi-fi **Services** Lift **Parking** 9

NEWCASTLE UPON TYNE — Map 12 NZ26

Marriott HOTELS & RESORTS

Newcastle Marriott Hotel Gosforth Park
★★★★ 78% HOTEL
High Gosforth Park, Gosforth NE3 5HN
☎ 0191 236 4111 0191 236 8192
web: www.newcastlemarriottgosforthpark.co.uk
dir: Onto A1056 to Killingworth & Wideopen. 3rd exit to Gosforth Park, hotel ahead

PETS: Bedrooms Grounds on leads disp bin **Exercise area** nearby **Facilities** walks info vet info **Other** pets only accepted by prior agreement with General Manager (when booking)

Set within its own grounds, this modern hotel offers extensive conference and banqueting facilities, along with indoor and outdoor leisure. There is a choice of dining in the more formal Plate Restaurant or the relaxed Chat's lounge bar. Many of the air-conditioned bedrooms have views over the park. The hotel is conveniently located for the bypass, airport and racecourse.

Rooms 178 (17 smoking) **Facilities** Spa STV supervised Gym Squash Jogging trail New Year Wi-fi **Services** Lift Air con **Parking** 340

Kenilworth Hotel
★★ 76% SMALL HOTEL
44 Osborne Rd, Jesmond NE2 2AL
☎ 0191 281 8111 & 281 9111 0191 281 9476
e-mail: info@thekenilworthhotel.co.uk
web: www.thekenilworthhotel.co.uk
dir: A1058 signed Tynemouth for 1m. Left at lights onto Osborne Rd, hotel 0.5m on right

PETS: Bedrooms sign **Exercise area** 0.5m **Facilities** food bowl water bowl cage storage walks info vet info **On Request** torch **Other** charge for damage

This family-run hotel in the Jesmond area of the city features wooden floors and leather furniture. The smart bedrooms have satellite TVs, DVD players, beverage trays and hairdryers. There is relaxed and informal restaurant, and exterior seating in the summer allows guests to enjoy the café culture which is popular in this area.

Rooms 11 (5 fmly) **S** £45-£58; **D** £65-£90 (incl. bkfst) **Facilities** FTV Access to leisure centre (1.5km) Xmas New Year Wi-fi **Parking** 11

ENGLAND

WHICKHAM — Map 12 NZ26

Gibside
★★★ 80% HOTEL

Front St NE16 4JG
☎ 0191 488 9292 📠 0191 488 8000
e-mail: reception@gibside-hotel.co.uk
web: www.gibside-hotel.co.uk
dir: Off A1(M) towards Whickham on B6317, onto Front St, hotel 2m on right

PETS: Bedrooms (13 GF) unattended **Grounds** on leads disp bin **Exercise area** adjacent **Facilities** food (pre-bookable) food bowl water bowl dog grooming cage storage walks info vet info **On Request** fridge access torch **Other** pet sitting & dog walking can be arranged **Restrictions** well behaved dogs only

Conveniently located in the village centre, this hotel is close to the Newcastle by-pass and its elevated position affords views over the Tyne Valley. Bedrooms come in two styles, classical and contemporary. Public rooms include the Egyptian-themed Sphinx bar and a more formal restaurant. Secure garage parking is available.

Rooms 44 (2 fmly) (13 GF) **S** £75-£110; **D** £85-£120*
Facilities FTV Golf Academy at The Beamish Park ♫ New Year Wi-fi **Services** Lift **Parking** 18 **Notes** LB

WARWICKSHIRE

ALCESTER — Map 4 SP05

Kings Court
★★★ 73% HOTEL

Kings Coughton B49 5QQ
☎ 01789 763111 📠 01789 400242
e-mail: info@kingscourthotel.co.uk
web: www.kingscourthotel.co.uk
dir: 1m N on A435

PETS: Bedrooms (32 GF) sign **Charges Public areas** on leads **Grounds** on leads disp bin **Exercise area** nearby **Facilities** food bowl water bowl walks info vet info **On Request** fridge access torch towels **Other** charge for damage

This privately owned hotel dates back to Tudor times and the bedrooms in the original house have oak beams. Most guests are accommodated in the well-appointed modern wings. The bar and restaurant offer very good dishes on interesting menus. The hotel is licensed to hold civil ceremonies and the pretty garden is ideal for summer weddings.

Rooms 62 (58 annexe) (3 fmly) (32 GF) **S** £58-£68; **D** £58-£90 (incl. bkfst)* **Facilities** STV Gym Wi-fi **Parking** 200

BAGINTON — Map 4 SP37

The Oak
★★★ INN

Coventry Rd CV8 3AU
☎ 024 7651 8855 📠 024 7651 8866
e-mail: thebagintonoak@aol.com
web: http://theoak.greatpubs.net

PETS: Bedrooms (6 GF) unattended **Charges** £5 per night £35 per week **Public areas** on leads **Grounds** disp bin **Exercise area** adjacent **Facilities** water bowl dog chews dog walking washing facs cage storage walks info vet info **On Request** fridge access torch towels **Stables** 0.5m **Other** charge for damage pet washing facilities on request, dog grooming available nearby **Resident Pets:** Beau & Jasper (Border Collies)

Located close to major road links and Coventry Airport, this popular inn provides a wide range of food throughout the themed, open-plan public areas. Families are especially welcome. Modern, well-equipped bedrooms are situated in a separate accommodation building.

Rooms 13 annexe en suite (1 fmly) (6 GF) **S** £45-£60; **D** £45-£60 **Facilities** FTV tea/coffee Dinner available Cen ht Wi-fi **Parking** 110

ENGLAND

BARFORD · Map 4 SP26

The Glebe at Barford
★★★ 71% HOTEL
Church St CV35 8BS
☎ 01926 624218 📠 01926 624625
e-mail: sales@glebehotel.co.uk
dir: M40 junct 15/A429 (Stow). At mini island turn left, hotel 500mtrs on right

PETS: Bedrooms (4 GF) unattended **Public areas** except bar, restaurant & leisure club **Grounds Exercise area** 5 mins **Facilities** walks info vet info **Other** charge for damage

The giant Lebanese cedar tree in front of this hotel was ancient even in 1820, when the original rectory was built. Public rooms within the house include a lounge bar and the aptly named Cedars Conservatory Restaurant which offers interesting cuisine. Individually appointed bedrooms are tastefully decorated in soft pastel fabrics, with coronet, tented ceiling or four-poster style beds.

Rooms 39 (3 fmly) (4 GF) **S** £75-£105; **D** £80-£140 (incl. bkfst)* **Facilities** STV 🏊 Gym Beauty salon Xmas New Year Wi-fi **Services** Lift **Parking** 60 **Notes** LB

COLESHILL · Map 4 SP28

Grimstock Country House
★★★ 71% COUNTRY HOUSE HOTEL
Gilson Rd, Gilson B46 1LJ
☎ 01675 462121 📠 01675 467646
e-mail: enquiries@grimstockhotel.co.uk
web: www.grimstockhotel.co.uk
dir: Off A446 at rdbt onto B4117 to Gilson, hotel 100yds on right

PETS: Bedrooms (13 GF) unattended sign certain bedrooms only **Charges Public areas** except bar & restaurant on leads **Grounds** on leads disp bin **Exercise area** adjacent field **Facilities** walks info vet info **On Request** fridge access **Other** charge for damage

This privately owned hotel is convenient for Birmingham International Airport and the NEC, and benefits from a peaceful rural setting. Bedrooms are spacious and comfortable. Public rooms include two restaurants, a wood-panelled bar, good conference facilities and a gym featuring the latest cardiovascular equipment.

Rooms 44 (1 fmly) (13 GF) **S** £62-£95; **D** £70-£109 (incl. bkfst) **Facilities** STV Gym Xmas New Year Wi-fi **Parking** 100 **Notes** LB

CORLEY MOTORWAY SERVICE AREA (M6) · Map 4 SP38

Days Inn Corley - NEC - M6
BUDGET HOTEL
Junction 3-4, M6 North, Corley CV7 8NR
☎ 01676 543800 & 540111 📠 01676 540128
e-mail: corley.hotel@welcomebreak.co.uk
dir: On M6 between juncts 3 & 4 N'bound

PETS: Bedrooms (24 GF) unattended **Charges** £5 per stay **Public areas** except main service area on leads **Grounds** on leads disp bin **Exercise area** nearby **Facilities** water bowl feeding mat washing facs cage storage walks info vet info **On Request** fridge access torch towels **Stables** 2m **Other** charge for damage

This modern building offers accommodation in smart, spacious and well-equipped bedrooms, suitable for families and business travellers, and all with en suite bathrooms. Continental breakfast is available and other refreshments may be taken at the nearby family restaurant.

Rooms 50 (13 fmly) (24 GF) (8 smoking) **S** £39.95-£59.95; **D** £49.95-£69.95

HARBURY · Map 4 SP35

Harbury Fields (SP352604)
►►►►
Harbury Fields Farm CV33 9JN
☎ 01926 612457
e-mail: rdavis@harburyfields.co.uk
dir: M40 junct 12, B4451 (signed Kenton/Gaydon). 0.75m, right signed Lightborne. 4m, right at rdbt onto B4455 (signed Harbury). 3rd right by petrol station, site in 700yds (by two cottages)

PETS: Public areas except washrooms disp bin **Exercise area** on site farm walk **Facilities** walks info vet info **Other** prior notice required

Open 2 Jan-19 Dec Last arrival 21.30hrs Last departure noon

This developing park is in a peaceful farm setting with lovely countryside views. All pitches have hardstandings with electric and the facilities are spotless. It is well positioned for visiting Warwick and Leamington Spa as well as the exhibition centres at NEC Birmingham, and the National Agricultural Centre at Stoneleigh Park. 3 acre site. 32 touring pitches. 31 hardstandings. Motorhome pitches.

Notes 🐾

Chesford Grange

★★★★ 79% HOTEL

Chesford Bridge CV8 2LD
☎ 01926 859331 📠 01926 859272
e-mail: chesfordreservations@qhotels.co.uk
web: www.qhotels.co.uk
dir: *0.5m SE of junct A46/A452. At rdbt turn right signed Leamington Spa, follow signs to hotel*

PETS: Bedrooms (43 GF) **Charges** £15 per stay **Grounds** on leads **Exercise area** woods (800yds) **Facilities** scoop/disp bags cage storage walks info vet info **On Request** fridge access **Other** prior notice required well behaved dogs only

This much-extended hotel set in 17 acres of private grounds is well situated for Birmingham International Airport, the NEC and major routes. Bedrooms range from traditional style to contemporary rooms featuring state-of-the-art technology. Public areas include a leisure club and extensive conference and banqueting facilities.

Rooms 205 (20 fmly) (43 GF) **S** £95-£140; **D** £100-£150 (incl. bkfst)* **Facilities** Spa STV 🏊 supervised Gym Steam room Solarium Xmas New Year Wi-fi **Services** Lift **Parking** 650 **Notes** LB

Tame View Caravan Site *(SP209979)*

▶

Cliff B78 2DR
☎ 01827 873853
dir: *400yds off A51 (Tamworth-Kingsbury road), 1m N of Kingsbury opposite pub. Signed Cliff Hall Lane*

PETS: Public areas dogs must be kept on leads at all times disp bin **Exercise area on site** woodland walk **Exercise area** 100yds **Other** prior notice required dog grooming available nearby

Open all year Last arrival 23.00hrs Last departure 23.00hrs

A secluded spot overlooking the Tame Valley and river, sheltered by high hedges. Sanitary facilities are minimal but clean on this small park. The site is popular with many return visitors who like a peaceful basic site. 5 acre site. 5 touring pitches. Tent pitches. Motorhome pitches.

Notes 🌐

The Red Lion

★★★★ ◉ INN

Main St CV36 5JS
☎ 01608 684221 📠 01608 684968
e-mail: info@redlion-longcompton.co.uk
dir: *5m S of Shipston on Stour on A3400*

PETS: Bedrooms sign certain bedrooms only **Public areas** except restaurant on leads **Grounds** on leads disp bin **Exercise area** 5 mins' walk **Facilities** water bowl walks info vet info **On Request** torch **Stables** 5 mins **Other** charge for damage **Resident Pet:** Cocoa (Chocolate Labrador)

Located in a pretty village, this mid 18th-century posting house retains many original features which are complemented by rustic furniture. A good range of ales is offered, and interesting menus make good use of quality local produce. The bedrooms are well appointed and have a good range of facilities.

Rooms 5 en suite (1 fmly) **S** £55-£75; **D** £85-£185 **Facilities** tea/coffee Dinner available Cen ht Wi-fi **Parking** 60 **Notes** No coaches

Best Western Weston Hall

★★★ 73% HOTEL

Weston Ln, Bulkington CV12 9RU
☎ 024 7631 2989 📠 024 7664 0846
e-mail: info@westonhallhotel.co.uk
dir: *M6 junct 2, B4065 through Ansty. Left in Shilton, from Bulkington follow Nuneaton signs, into Weston Ln at 30mph sign*

PETS: Bedrooms (14 GF) **Charges** £10 per night **Public areas** only front bar on leads **Grounds** **Exercise area** 400yds **Facilities** food bowl water bowl bedding washing facs cage storage walks info vet info **On Request** torch towels **Other** charge for damage food available by prior arrangement

This Grade II listed hotel, with origins dating back to the reign of Elizabeth I, sits within seven acres of peaceful grounds. The original three-gabled building retains many original features, such as the carved wooden fireplace in the library. Friendly service is provided; and the bedrooms, that vary in size, are thoughtfully equipped.

Rooms 40 (1 fmly) (14 GF) **Facilities** FTV 🐾 New Year Wi-fi **Parking** 300

Number Seven Guest House
★★★ GUEST HOUSE

7 Eastfield Place CV21 3AT

☎ 01788 541010   📄 01788 544996

dir: *Follow signs to town centre & Rugby school, onto Hillmorton Rd then Littlechurch St. 1st right onto Eastfield Pl, before black & white pub*

PETS: Bedrooms (4 GF) unattended **Public areas** except dining area **Grounds** disp bin **Exercise area** 100yds **Facilities** water bowl feeding mat scoop/disp bags dog walking washing facs cage storage walks info vet info **On Request** fridge access torch towels

Located in a quiet side road, just minutes from Rugby town centre, this guest house, originally a private residence, offers good quality accommodation, some with en suite facilities. Ground-floor areas include a comfortable lounge in addition to an open plan kitchen/dining room where hearty breakfasts are served.

Rooms 7 rms (1 en suite) (6 pri facs) 3 annexe en suite (1 fmly) (4 GF) **S** £36-£70; **D** £55-£70 **Facilities** FTV TVL tea/coffee Cen ht Wi-fi **Notes** LB ☺

Lodge Farm Campsite *(SP476748)*
▶▶

Bilton Ln, Long Lawford CV23 9DU

☎ 01788 560193

e-mail: jane@lodgefarm.com

dir: *From Rugby take A428 (Lawford road), towards Coventry, 1.5m. At Sheaf & Sickle pub left into Bilton Ln, site 500yds*

PETS: Public areas disp bin **Exercise area** disused railway line & bridleway (0.25m) **Facilities** food bowl water bowl scoop/disp bags washing facs walks info vet info **Stables** 3m **Other** dogs must be kept on leads, under control at all times & exercised off site **Resident Pets:** 1 Collie, 1 Jack Russell, 1 German Shorthaired Pointer, 3 cats, chickens

Open all year rs Winter - extreme weather conditions limit access Last arrival 22.00hrs

A small, simple farm site set behind the friendly owner's home and self-catering cottages, with converted stables housing the toilet facilities. Rugby is only a short drive away, and the site is tucked well away from the main road. Wi-fi is now available. 2.5 acre site. 35 touring pitches. 3 hardstandings. 10 seasonal pitches. Tent pitches. Motorhome pitches.

Barceló Billesley Manor Hotel
★★★★ 79% ◉◉ HOTEL

Billesley, Alcester B49 6NF

☎ 01789 279955   📄 01789 764145

e-mail: billesleymanor@barcelo-hotels.co.uk

web: www.barcelo-hotels.co.uk

dir: *A46 towards Evesham. Over 3 rdbts, right for Billesley after 2m*

PETS: Bedrooms (5 GF) unattended sign **Charges** £15 per night **Grounds** on leads disp bin **Exercise area** 100yds **Facilities** cage storage walks info vet info **On Request** fridge access torch towels **Other** charge for damage

This 16th-century manor is set in peaceful grounds and parkland with a delightful yew topiary garden and fountain. The spacious bedrooms and suites, most in traditional country-house style, are thoughtfully designed and well equipped. Conference facilities and some of the bedrooms are found in the cedar barns. Public areas retain many original features, such as oak panelling, fireplaces and exposed stone.

Rooms 72 (29 annexe) (5 GF) **Facilities** Spa ⟲ supervised ♨♨ Gym Steam room Beauty treatments Yoga studio Xmas New Year **Parking** 100

Mercure Shakespeare
★★★★ 71% ◉ HOTEL

Chapel St CV37 6ER

☎ 01789 294997   📄 01789 415411

e-mail: h6630@accor.com

web: www.mercure.com

dir: *M40 junct 15. Follow signs for Stratford town centre on A439. Follow one-way system onto Bridge St. Left at rdbt, hotel 200yds on left opp HSBC bank*

PETS: Bedrooms (3 GF) unattended **Charges** £10 per night **Public areas** disp bin **Exercise area** park (300yds) **Other** charge for damage

Dating back to the early 17th century, The Shakespeare is one of the oldest hotels in this historic town. The hotel name represents one of the earliest exploitations of Stratford as the birthplace of one of the world's leading playwrights. With exposed beams and open fires, the public rooms retain an ambience reminiscent of this era. Bedrooms are appointed to a good standard and remain in keeping with the style of the property.

Rooms 73 (11 annexe) (3 GF) **D** £79-£230 (incl. bkfst)* **Facilities** Xmas New Year Wi-fi **Services** Lift **Parking** 34

WARWICK MOTORWAY SERVICE AREA (M40) Map 4 SP35

Days Inn Warwick North - M40

BUDGET HOTEL

Warwick Services, M40 Northbound Junction 12-13, Banbury Rd CV35 0AA

☎ 01926 651681 📠 01926 651634

e-mail: warwick.north.hotel@welcomebreak.co.uk
web: www.welcomebreak.co.uk
dir: *M40 northbound between junct 12 & 13*

PETS: Bedrooms certain bedrooms only **Charges** £5 per night **Public areas** on leads **Grounds** on leads disp bin **Exercise area** large grassed area **On Request** torch **Other** prior notice required **Restrictions** small & medium size dogs only

This modern building offers accommodation in smart, spacious and well-equipped bedrooms, suitable for families and business travellers, and all with en suite bathrooms. Continental breakfast is available and other refreshments may be taken at the nearby family restaurant.

Rooms 54 (45 fmly) (8 smoking) **S** £39.95-£59.95; **D** £49.95-£69.95

Days Inn Warwick South - M40

BUDGET HOTEL

Warwick Services, M40 Southbound, Banbury Rd CV35 0AA
☎ 01926 650168 📠 01926 651601
e-mail: warwick.south.hotel@welcomebreak.co.uk
web: www.welcomebreak.co.uk
dir: *M40 southbound between junct 14 & 12*

PETS: Bedrooms sign certain bedrooms only **Charges** £5 per night **Public areas** on leads **Grounds** on leads disp bin **Exercise area** adjacent **Facilities** vet info **On Request** fridge access **Other** charge for damage

Rooms 40 (38 fmly) (5 smoking) **S** £39.95-£59.95; **D** £49.95-£69.95

WOLVEY Map 4 SP48

Wolvey Villa Farm Caravan & Camping Site
(SP428869)

▶ ▶ ▶

LE10 3HF
☎ 01455 220493 & 220630
dir: *M6 junct 2, B4065 follow Wolvey signs. Or M69 junct 1 & follow Wolvey signs*

PETS: Charges dog £1 per night **Public areas** except shop disp bin **Exercise area on site** field **Facilities** food vet info **Stables**

Open all year Last arrival 22.00hrs Last departure noon

A level grass site surrounded by trees and shrubs, on the borders of Warwickshire and Leicestershire. This quiet country site has its own popular fishing lake, and is convenient for visiting the cities of Coventry and Leicester. 7 acre site. 110 touring pitches. 24 hardstandings. Tent pitches. Motorhome pitches.

Notes No twin axles.

WEST MIDLANDS

BALSALL COMMON Map 4 SP27

Haigs Hotel

★★★ **73%** HOTEL

Kenilworth Rd CV7 7EL
☎ 01676 533004 📠 01676 535132
e-mail: info@haigshotel.co.uk
dir: *A45 towards Coventry, at Stonebridge Island turn right, 4m S of M42 junct 6*

PETS: Bedrooms (5 GF) unattended **Charges** £5 per night **Public areas** except restaurant **Grounds** disp bin **Exercise area** 500yds **Facilities** water bowl walks info vet info **On Request** torch **Stables** 1m **Other** charge for damage

Conveniently located just five miles from Birmingham Airport and twelve miles from Stratford-upon-Avon. This small family-run hotel offers its guests a comfortable stay. Enjoyable meals on a monthly changing menu can be taken in McKee's Restaurant.

Rooms 23 (2 fmly) (5 GF) (incl. bkfst) **Facilities** Xmas New Year Wi-fi **Parking** 23

Hotel du Vin Birmingham

★★★★ 76% ⚫ TOWN HOUSE HOTEL

25 Church St B3 2NR
☎ 0121 200 0600   📄 0121 236 0889
e-mail: info@birmingham.hotelduvin.com
web: www.hotelduvin.com
dir: *M6 junct 6/A38(M) to city centre, over flyover. Keep left & exit at St Chads Circus signed Jewellery Quarter. At lights & rdbt take 1st exit, follow signs for Colmore Row, opposite cathedral. Right into Church St, across Barwick St. Hotel on right*

PETS: Bedrooms unattended **Sep accom Charges** £10 per night **Public areas** except bar & bistro on leads **Facilities** food bowl water bowl bedding cage storage walks info vet info **Other** charge for damage dog bed, blanket & bowls available

The former Birmingham Eye Hospital has become a chic and sophisticated hotel. The stylish, high-ceilinged rooms, all with a wine theme, are luxuriously appointed and feature stunning bathrooms, sumptuous duvets and Egyptian cotton sheets. The Bistro offers relaxed dining and a top-notch wine list, while other attractions include a champagne bar, a wine boutique and a health club.

Rooms 66 **Facilities** Spa STV Gym Treatment rooms Steam room Sauna Xmas New Year Wi-fi **Services** Lift Air con **Notes** LB

Novotel Birmingham Centre

★★★★ 71% HOTEL

70 Broad St B1 2HT
☎ 0121 643 2000   📄 0121 643 9786
e-mail: h1077@accor.com
web: www.novotel.com
dir: *A38/A456, hotel on right beyond International Convention Centre*

PETS: Bedrooms Charges £10 per night **Public areas** only assist dogs in restaurant & bar on leads **Facilities** walks info vet info **On Request** towels **Other** charge for damage **Restrictions** small dogs only

This large, modern, purpose-built hotel benefits from an excellent city centre location, with the bonus of secure parking. Bedrooms are spacious, modern and well equipped especially for business users; four rooms have facilities for less able guests. Public areas include the Garden Brasserie, function rooms and a fitness room.

Rooms 148 (148 fmly) (11 smoking) **Facilities** Gym Fitness room Cardio-vascular equipment Sauna Steam room Wi-fi **Services** Lift Air con **Parking** 53 **Notes** LB

Holiday Inn Birmingham M6 Jct 7

★★★ 72% HOTEL

Chapel Ln, Great Barr B43 7BG
☎ 0871 942 9009 & 0121 357 7303   📄 0121 357 7503
e-mail: birminghamgreatbarr@ihg.com
web: www.holidayinn.co.uk
dir: *M6 junct 7, A34 signed Walsall. Hotel 200yds on right across carriageway in Chapel Ln*

PETS: Bedrooms (67 GF) unattended **Charges** £25 per night **Public areas** except restaurant muzzled and on leads **Grounds** on leads **Exercise area** nearby **Facilities** cage storage walks info vet info **On Request** fridge access towels **Stables** 2m **Other** charge for damage

Situated in pleasant surroundings, this modern hotel offers well-equipped and comfortable bedrooms. Public areas include the popular Traders restaurant and a comfortable lounge where a menu is available to guests all day. There is also 24-hour room service; a courtyard patio and a garden.

Rooms 190 (45 fmly) (67 GF) (12 smoking) **S** £59-£119; **D** £69-£129 (incl. bkfst)* **Facilities** STV FTV ⛱ supervised Gym Xmas New Year Wi-fi **Services** Air con **Parking** 250 **Notes** LB

Ibis Birmingham Bordesley Circus

BUDGET HOTEL

1 Bordesley Park Rd, Bordesley B10 0PD
☎ 0121 506 2600   📄 0121 506 2610
e-mail: H2178@accor.com
web: www.ibishotel.com

PETS: Bedrooms (16 GF) unattended sign **Charges** £5 per night **Grounds** on leads **Facilities** food bowl water bowl **Other** charge for damage

Modern, budget hotel offering comfortable accommodation in bright and practical bedrooms. Breakfast is self-service and dinner is available in the restaurant.

Rooms 87 (16 GF)

Ibis Birmingham City Centre

BUDGET HOTEL

Arcadian Centre, Ladywell Walk B5 4ST
☎ 0121 622 6010   📄 0121 622 6020
e-mail: h1459@accor-hotels.com
web: www.ibishotel.com
dir: *From motorways follow city centre signs. Then follow Bullring or Indoor Market signs. Hotel adjacent to market*

PETS: Bedrooms Charges £10 per night **Facilities** walks info vet info **Other** charge for damage **Restrictions** small dogs only

Rooms 159 (5 fmly)

BIRMINGHAM *continued*

Ibis Birmingham Holloway Circus

BUDGET HOTEL
55 Irving St B1 1DH
☎ 0121 622 4925 📠 0121 622 4195
e-mail: H2092@accor.com
web: www.ibishotel.com
dir: *From M6 take A38/City Centre, left after 2nd tunnel. Right at rdbt, 4th left (Sutton St) into Irving St. Hotel on left*

PETS: Bedrooms (26 GF) Charges £5 per night Public areas except restaurant on leads Grounds on leads

Rooms 51 (2 fmly) (26 GF) S £52-£125; D £52-£125*

Westbourne Lodge

★★★★★ ⬤ GUEST ACCOMMODATION
25-31 Fountain Rd, Edgbaston B17 8NJ
☎ 0121 429 1003 📠 0121 429 7436
e-mail: info@westbournelodge.co.uk
web: www.westbournelodge.co.uk
dir: *100yds from A456*

PETS: Bedrooms (2 GF) Grounds disp bin Exercise area 200mtrs Facilities food (pre-bookable) food bowl water bowl dog chews leads washing facs cage storage walks info On Request fridge access torch towels

Located on a quiet residential avenue close to Hagley Road, this well-maintained property provides a range of no-smoking, thoughtfully furnished bedrooms; two are on the ground floor. Breakfasts (and dinner by arrangement) are served in an attractive dining room overlooking a pretty patio garden. A comfortable sitting room and lounge bar are also available.

Rooms 18 en suite (4 fmly) (2 GF) S £49.50-£69.50; D £69.50-£89.50 Facilities FTV TVL tea/coffee Dinner available Cen ht Licensed Wi-fi Parking 12 Notes Closed 24 Dec-1 Jan

Rollason Wood

★★ GUEST ACCOMMODATION
130 Wood End Rd, Erdington B24 8BJ
☎ 0121 373 1230 📠 0121 382 2578
e-mail: rollwood@globalnet.co.uk
dir: *M6 junct 6, A5127 to Erdington, right onto A4040, house 0.25m on left*

PETS: Bedrooms sign Exercise area 200yds Facilities cage storage walks info vet info

Well situated for many road networks and the city centre, this owner-managed establishment is popular with contractors. The choice of three different bedroom styles suits most budgets, and rates include full English breakfasts. Ground-floor areas include a popular bar, cosy TV lounge and a dining room.

Rooms 35 rms (11 en suite) (5 fmly) (9 smoking) S £21.50-£39.95; D £38-£49.50 Facilities TVL tea/coffee Dinner available Cen ht Licensed Wi-fi Pool table Parking 35

Novotel Birmingham Airport

★★★★ 71% HOTEL
B26 3QL
☎ 0121 782 7000 & 782 4111 📠 0121 782 0445
e-mail: H1158@accor.com
web: www.novotel.com
dir: *M42 junct 6/A45 to Birmingham, signed to airport. Hotel opposite main terminal*

PETS: Bedrooms Charges £20 per night Other charge for damage dogs are required to be muzzled

This smartly decorated hotel with air conditioning throughout its public areas and bedrooms benefits from being less than a minute's walk from the main terminal of Birmingham International Airport. Spacious bedrooms are comfortable and modern bathrooms are stylish with powerful showers. The Elements bar and restaurant provides a great atmosphere for meals and a fitness room is available on site. Long stay car parking packages can be arranged at this location.

Rooms 195 (24 fmly) Facilities STV Gym Fitness room Wi-fi Services Lift Air con

Arden Hotel & Leisure Club

★★★ 73% HOTEL
Coventry Rd, Bickenhill B92 0EH
☎ 01675 443221 📠 01675 445604
e-mail: enquiries@ardenhotel.co.uk
dir: *M42 junct 6/A45 towards Birmingham. Hotel 0.25m on right, just off Birmingham International railway island*

PETS: Bedrooms (6 GF) twin bedrooms only Charges £10 per night Grounds on leads disp bin Exercise area Facilities vet info On Request fridge access Other charge for damage

This smart hotel neighbouring the NEC offers modern rooms and well-equipped leisure facilities. After dinner in the formal restaurant, the place to relax is the spacious lounge area. A buffet breakfast is served in the bright and airy Meeting Place.

Rooms 216 (6 fmly) (6 GF) (12 smoking) Facilities Spa STV ⊗ supervised Gym Sports therapy Beautician ♫ Xmas New Year Wi-fi Services Lift Parking 300 Notes Closed 25-28 Dec

COVENTRY — Map 4 SP37

Novotel Coventry

★★★ 75% HOTEL

Wilsons Ln CV6 6HL
☎ 024 7636 5000   📠 024 7636 2422
e-mail: h0506@accor-hotels.com
web: www.novotel.com
dir: M6 junct 3. Follow signs for B4113 towards Longford & Bedworth. 3rd exit on large rdbt

PETS: Bedrooms (25 GF) ground-floor bedrooms only **Charges** £12 per night £60 per week **Public areas** except restaurant & bar areas on leads **Grounds** on leads disp bin **Facilities** scoop/disp bags walks info vet info **On Request** towels **Other** charge for damage disposal bags available

A modern hotel convenient for Birmingham, Coventry and the motorway network, offering spacious, well-equipped accommodation. The bright brasserie has extended dining hours, and alternatively there is an extensive room-service menu. Family rooms and a play area make this a child-friendly hotel, and there is also a selection of meeting rooms.

Rooms 98 (25 GF) **Facilities** STV Wi-fi **Services** Lift **Parking** 120

Ibis Coventry Centre

BUDGET HOTEL

Mile Ln, St John's Ringway CV1 2LN
☎ 024 7625 0500   📠 024 7655 3548
e-mail: H2793@accor.com
web: www.ibishotel.com
dir: A45, A4114 signed Jaguar Assembly Plant. At inner ring road S. Exit junct 5 for Mile Lane

PETS: Bedrooms (25 GF) ground-floor bedrooms only **Charges** £5 per night **Exercise area** 0.5m **Other** charge for damage **Restrictions** small & medium size dogs only

Modern, budget hotel offering comfortable accommodation in bright and practical bedrooms. Breakfast is self-service and dinner is available in the restaurant.

Rooms 89 (15 fmly) (25 GF) **D** £54-£65*

Ibis Coventry South

BUDGET HOTEL

Abbey Rd, Whitley CV3 4BJ
☎ 024 7663 9922   📠 024 7630 6898
e-mail: H2094@accor.com
web: www.ibishotel.com
dir: Signed from A46/A423 rdbt. Take A423 towards A45. Follow signs for Racquets Health Club & Jaguar Engineering Plant. 1st exit from Jaguar rdbt, hotel at end of lane by The Racquets

PETS: Bedrooms (25 GF) unattended **Public areas** except restaurant on leads **Grounds** disp bin **Exercise area** 0.1m **Facilities** walks info vet info **On Request** fridge access towels **Other** charge for damage

Rooms 51 (51 annexe) (25 GF) **S** £44-£74; **D** £44-£74*

MERIDEN — Map 4 SP28

Manor Hotel

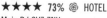

★★★★ 73% ◉ HOTEL

Main Rd CV7 7NH
☎ 01676 522735   📠 01676 522186
e-mail: reservations@manorhotelmeriden.co.uk
web: www.manorhotelmeriden.co.uk
dir: M42 junct 6, A45 towards Coventry then A452 signed Leamington. At rdbt take B4102 signed Meriden, hotel on left

PETS: Bedrooms (20 GF) unattended **Public areas** assist dogs only on leads **Grounds** on leads disp bin **Exercise area** nearby **Facilities** vet info **On Request** fridge access **Stables** 3m **Other** charge for damage

A sympathetically extended Georgian manor in the heart of a sleepy village is just a few minutes away from the M6, M42 and National Exhibition Centre. The Regency Restaurant offers modern dishes, while Houston's serves lighter meals and snacks. The bedrooms are smart and well equipped.

Rooms 110 (20 GF) **S** £55-£150; **D** £55-£150* **Facilities** FTV Wi-fi **Services** Lift **Parking** 200 **Notes** LB RS 24 Dec-2 Jan

Somers Wood Caravan Park (SP225824)

▶ ▶ ▶ ▶

Somers Rd CV7 7PL
☎ 01676 522978   📠 01676 522978
e-mail: enquiries@somerswood.co.uk
dir: M42 junct 6, A45 signed Coventry. Keep left (do not take flyover). Then right onto A452 signed Meriden/Leamington. At next rdbt left onto B4102, Hampton Lane. Site in 0.5m on left

PETS: Charges 2 pets free; £1 per extra pet per night **Public areas Exercise area** adjacent **Facilities** washing facs walks info vet info **Other** prior notice required

Open all year Last arrival variable Last departure variable

A peaceful adults-only park set in the heart of England with spotless facilities. The park is well positioned for visiting the National Exhibition Centre (NEC), the NEC Arena and National Indoor Arena (NIA) and Birmingham is only 12 miles away. The park also makes an ideal touring base for Warwick, Coventry and Stratford-upon-Avon just 22 miles away. Please note that tents are not accepted. 4 acre site. 48 touring pitches. 48 hardstandings. Motorhome pitches.

ENGLAND

Novotel Wolverhampton

NOVOTEL

★★★ **78%** HOTEL

Union St WV1 3JN

☎ 01902 871100   🖷 01902 870054

e-mail: H1188@accor.com

web: www.novotel.com

dir: *6m from M6 junct 10. A454 to Wolverhampton. Hotel on main ring road*

PETS: Bedrooms unattended   **Charges** small dog £5, large dog £10 per night **Public areas** on leads **Grounds** on leads   disp bin **Exercise area** 1m **Facilities** water bowl   cage storage   walks info vet info **On Request** fridge access **Stables** 2m **Other** charge for damage

This large, modern, purpose-built hotel stands close to the town centre. It provides spacious, smartly presented and well-equipped bedrooms, all of which contain convertible bed settees for family occupancy. In addition to the open-plan lounge and bar area, there is an attractive brasserie-style restaurant, which overlooks an attractive patio garden.

Rooms 132 (9 fmly) (6 smoking) **S** £59–£145; **D** £59–£145* **Facilities** STV Wi-fi **Services** Lift **Parking** 120 **Notes** LB RS 23 Dec–4 Jan

Mercure Wolverhampton Goldthorn Hotel

Mercure

★★★ **68%** HOTEL

126 Penn Rd WV3 0ER

☎ 01902 429216   🖷 01902 710419

e-mail: enquiries@hotels-wolverhampton.com

dir: *A454 then A449 signed Kidderminster. Hotel 1m on right*

PETS: Bedrooms (4 GF) **Grounds** on leads   disp bin **Facilities** vet info **On Request** towels **Other** charge for damage

This hotel is situated just on the outskirts of the old town and offers easy access to major motorway networks. Bedrooms are comfortable and well equipped, with free Wi-fi available throughout. Leisure facilities include a swimming pool, steam and sauna. There is also free on-site parking.

Rooms 74 (16 annexe) (12 fmly) (4 GF) **Facilities** FTV 🏊 Gym Sauna Steam room Xmas New Year Wi-fi **Parking** 100

Blandings

★★★★ BED AND BREAKFAST

Horringford PO30 3AP

☎ 01983 865720 & 865331   🖷 01983 862099

e-mail: robin.oulton@horringford.com

web: www.horringford.com/bedandbreakfast.htm

dir: *S through Arreton (B3056), pass Stickworth Hall on right, 300yds on left farm entrance signed Horringford Gdns. U-turn to left, at end of poplar trees turn right. Blandings on left*

PETS: Bedrooms (1 GF) **Charges** **Public areas** **Grounds** on leads   disp bin **Exercise area** nearby **Facilities** washing facs cage storage   walks info   vet info **Stables** nearby **Other** charge for damage   dogs to be kept off furniture

This newly-built detached home stands in the grounds of Horringford Gardens. One bedroom has private access and a decking area for warm summer evenings. Breakfast is a highlight with local island produce gracing the table.

Rooms 2 en suite (1 GF) **Facilities** FTV tea/coffee Cen ht **Parking** 3 **Notes** LB ⊕

The Lake

★★★★ GUEST ACCOMMODATION

Shore Rd PO38 1RF

☎ 01983 852613

e-mail: enquiries@lakehotel.co.uk

dir: *0.5m E of Ventnor. Off A3055 to Bonchurch, opposite village pond*

PETS: Bedrooms (4 GF) **Charges** £6.50 per night **Public areas** in one sun lounge only   on leads **Grounds** on leads   disp bin **Exercise area** beach (400yds) **Facilities** cage storage   vet info **On Request** fridge access   torch   towels **Other** pet food on request

A warm welcome is assured at this friendly, family-run property set in two acres of well-tended gardens close to the sea. Bedrooms are equipped with modern facilities and the elegant public rooms offer a high standard of comfort. The breakfast menu offers a good choice of cold and hot options.

Rooms 11 en suite 9 annexe en suite (7 fmly) (4 GF) **S** £36–£47; **D** £72–£94 **Facilities** TVL tea/coffee Cen ht Licensed Wi-fi Golf 9 **Parking** 20 **Notes** LB No Children 3yrs Closed 20 Dec–2 Jan

COWES — Map 4 SZ49

Best Western New Holmwood
★★★ 72% HOTEL

Queens Rd, Egypt Point PO31 8BW
☎ 01983 292508 ▤ 01983 295020
e-mail: reception@newholmwoodhotel.co.uk
dir: From A3020 at Northwood Garage lights, left & follow to rdbt. 1st left then sharp right into Baring Rd, 4th left into Egypt Hill. At bottom turn right, hotel on right

PETS: Bedrooms (9 GF) unattended **Public areas** except restaurant on leads **Exercise area** beach opposite **Facilities** water bowl **Other** charge for damage please contact for details of charges

Just by the Esplanade, this hotel has an enviable outlook. Bedrooms are comfortable and very well equipped, and the light and airy, glass-fronted restaurant looks out to sea and serves a range of interesting meals. The sun terrace is delightful in the summer and there is a small pool area.

Rooms 26 (1 fmly) (9 GF) **Facilities** STV Xmas New Year Wi-fi **Parking** 20

Duke of York
★★★ INN

Mill Hill Rd PO31 7BT
☎ 01983 295171 ▤ 01983 295047
e-mail: dukeofyorkcowes@btconnect.com

PETS: Bedrooms (1 GF) ground-floor bedrooms only **Public areas** on leads **Exercise area** nearby **Facilities** bedding walks info vet info **On Request** fridge access torch towels **Stables** 2m **Other** dog grooming can be arranged

This family-run inn is situated very close to the town centre of Cowes. Comfortable bedrooms are divided between the main building and a separate building only seconds away. Home-cooked meals, with a number of fish and seafood dishes, feature on the menu every evening and are served in the bar and dining area. Parking is a bonus at this location, and outdoor, covered dining is also an option.

Rooms 8 en suite 5 annexe en suite (1 fmly) (1 GF) **Facilities** FTV tea/coffee Dinner available Wi-fi **Parking** 10

The Fountain Inn
★★★ INN

High St PO31 7AW
☎ 01983 292397 ▤ 01983 299554
e-mail: fountain.cowes@oldenglishinns.co.uk
dir: Adjacent to Red Jet passenger ferry in town centre

PETS: Bedrooms Public areas except coffee shop on leads **Grounds** on leads **Exercise area** 1m **Facilities** water bowl walks info vet info **Stables** 3m **Other** charge for damage

The Fountain Inn, located in the heart of this harbourside town, offers a number of bedrooms that have beautiful views across the water. Bedrooms, and bathrooms, are modern in design and provide comfortable accommodation. Substantial bar meals are served in the public areas, and breakfast offers a wide range of options. There is a regular transport service with a convenient drop-off point at the rear of the inn; a pay-and-display car park is a short walk away.

Rooms 20 en suite **Facilities** STV FTV tea/coffee Dinner available Direct Dial Cen ht Wi-fi **Notes** LB No coaches

FRESHWATER — Map 4 SZ38

Heathfield Farm Camping (SZ335879)
▶ ▶ ▶ ▶

Heathfield Rd PO40 9SH
☎ 01983 407822
e-mail: web@heathfieldcamping.co.uk
dir: 2m W from Yarmouth ferry port on A3054, left to Heathfield Rd, entrance 200yds on right

PETS: Charges £2 per night **Public areas** disp bin **Exercise area** adjacent meadow **Facilities** water bowl vet info **Stables** 600mtrs **Other** prior notice required 2 dogs per pitch (low season), 1 dog per pitch (high season)

Open May-Sep Last arrival 20.00hrs Last departure 11.00hrs

A very good quality park with friendly and welcoming staff. There are lovely views across the Solent to Hurst Castle. The upgraded toilet facilities, amenities and grounds are very well maintained, and this park is now amongst the best on the island. 10 acre site. 60 touring pitches. Tent pitches. Motorhome pitches.

Notes Family camping only.

NEWBRIDGE — Map 4 SZ48

The Orchards Holiday Caravan Park
(SZ411881)
▶ ▶ ▶ ▶ ▶

Main Rd PO41 0TS
☎ 01983 531331 & 531350 ▤ 01983 531666
e-mail: info@orchards-holiday-park.co.uk
dir: 4m E of Yarmouth; 6m W of Newport on B3401. Take A3054 from Yarmouth, after 3m turn right at Horse & Groom Inn. Follow signs to Newbridge. Entrance opposite Post Office

PETS: Charges £1.50-£2.50 per night **Public areas** disp bin **Exercise area on site** fenced field **Facilities** food dog chews scoop/disp bags washing facs walks info vet info **Other** prior notice required

Open 11 Feb-2 Jan rs Mar-Oct takeaway, shop, outdoor pool open Last arrival 23.00hrs Last departure 11.00hrs

A really excellent, well-managed park set in a peaceful village location amid downs and meadowland, with glorious downland views. Pitches are terraced and offer a good provision of hardstandings, including water serviced pitches. There is a new high quality facility centre offering excellent spacious showers and family rooms, plus there is access for disabled visitors to all site facilities and disabled toilets. The park has indoor and outdoor swimming pools, a shop, takeaway and licensed coffee shop. 15 acre site. 171 touring pitches. 74 hardstandings. Tent pitches. Motorhome pitches. 65 statics.

Notes No cycling.

NEWPORT Map 4 SZ58

Riverside Paddock Camp Site (SZ503911)

▶▶▶▶

Dodnor Ln PO30 5TE
☎ 01983 821367 & 07962 400533
e-mail: enquiries@riversidepaddock.co.uk
dir: *From Newport take dual carriageway towards Cowes. At 1st rdbt take 3rd exit, immediately left at next rdbt. Follow until road meets National Cycle Route. Site on left*

PETS: Charges £1 per night £7 per week Public areas disp bin Exercise area public footpath from site Facilities washing facs walks info vet info Other prior notice required

Open all year Last arrival 20.00hrs Last departure 11.00hrs

Although fairly close to Newport this quiet campsite offers a really peaceful environment and has direct access to the national cycle route from Newport to Cowes.The Medina River with its riverside walks is also nearby. The park has good hardstandings many with electric plus spotless facilities. The location of the park makes it perfect for people who like to walk or ride their bikes. 8 acre site. 28 touring pitches. 18 hardstandings. Tent pitches. Motorhome pitches. 5 tipis.

Notes No loud music, no generators. 🐾

RYDE Map 4 SZ59

Yelf's Hotel

★★★ 73% HOTEL

Union St PO33 2LG
☎ 01983 564062 📠 01983 563937
e-mail: manager@yelfshotel.com
web: www.yelfshotel.com
dir: *From Esplanade into Union St. Hotel on right*

PETS: Bedrooms (3 GF) Charges £10 per night Public areas Grounds on leads disp bin Exercise area beach (0.5m) Facilities water bowl cage storage walks info vet info On Request fridge access torch towels

This former coaching inn has smart public areas including a busy bar, a separate lounge and an attractive dining room. Bedrooms are comfortably furnished and well equipped; some are located in an adjoining wing and some in an annexe. A conservatory lounge bar and stylish terrace are ideal for relaxing.

Rooms 40 (9 annexe) (5 fmly) (3 GF) (6 smoking) Facilities STV Spa & treatments at sister hotel nearby Wi-fi Services Lift Parking 23

Whitefield Forest Touring Park (SZ604893)

▶▶▶▶▶

Brading Rd PO33 1QL
☎ 01983 617069
e-mail: pat&louise@whitefieldforest.co.uk
dir: *From Ryde follow A3055 towards Brading, after Tesco rdbt site 0.5m on left*

PETS: Charges £1-£1.50 per night Public areas except toilets disp bin Exercise area nearby Facilities walks info vet info Other prior notice required Resident Pets: Izzy (West Highland White Terrier), Scooby (Black Labrador)

Open Etr-Oct Last arrival 21.00hrs Last departure 11.00hrs

This park is beautifully laid out in Whitefield Forest, and offers a wide variety of pitches, all of which have electricity. It offers excellent modern facilities, which are spotlessly clean. The park takes great care in retaining the natural beauty of the forest, and is a haven for wildlife, including red squirrels , which may be seen on the park's nature walk. 23 acre site. 80 touring pitches. 20 hardstandings. Tent pitches. Motorhome pitches.

Roebeck Camping and Caravan Park (SZ581903)

▶▶▶

Gatehouse Rd, Upton Cross PO33 4BP
☎ 01983 611475 & 07930 992080
e-mail: info@roebeck-farm.co.uk
dir: *Turn right from Fishbourne ferry terminal (west of Ryde). At lights turn left onto A3054 towards Ryde. In outskirts straight on at 'All Through Traffic' sign. At end of Pellhurst Rd right into Upton Rd. Site 50yds beyond mini-rdbt*

PETS: Public areas Facilities walks info vet info Other prior notice required

Open Apr-Nov

A quiet park in a country setting on the outskirts of Ryde offering very nice facilities, especially for campers, including a dishwashing/kitchen cabin. The unique, ready-erected tipis, which are available for hire, add to the ambience of the site. There is also an excellent fishing lake. 4 acre site. 37 touring pitches. Tent pitches.

SANDOWN
Map 4 SZ58

The Wight Montrene
★★ 74% HOTEL
11 Avenue Rd PO36 8BN
☎ 01983 403722 📄 01983 405553
e-mail: enquiries@wighthotel.co.uk
web: www.wighthotel.co.uk
dir: *100yds after mini-rdbt between High St & Avenue Rd*

PETS: Bedrooms (21 GF) unattended sign **Grounds** on leads **Exercise area** 300yds **Facilities** cage storage walks info vet info **Stables** 8m **Other** charge for damage dogs must be exercised off site **Resident Pets:** Magnum (Pyrenean Mountain Dog), Diva & Gizmo (cats)

A family hotel, set in secluded grounds, that is only a short walk from Sandown's beach and high street shops. Bedrooms provide comfort and are either on the ground or first floor. Guests can relax in the heated swimming pool and enjoy the spa facility; there's also evening entertainment in the bar. The dinner menu changes nightly, and a plentiful breakfast is served in the colourful dining room.

Rooms 41 (18 fmly) (21 GF) **Facilities** Spa 🏊 Gym Steam room Sauna Solarium Table tennis Full size snooker table 🎵 Xmas New Year Wi-fi **Parking** 40

Old Barn Touring Park *(SZ573833)*
▶ ▶ ▶ ▶
Cheverton Farm, Newport Rd, Apse Heath PO36 9PJ
☎ 01983 866414 📄 01983 865988
e-mail: oldbarn@weltinet.com
dir: *On A3056 from Newport, site on left after Apse Heath rdbt*

PETS: Charges 1st dog free, £1.50 per extra dog per night **Public areas Exercise area** adjacent **Facilities** walks info vet info **Other** prior notice required **Resident Pets:** cows, ferrets, geese, chickens

Open May-Sep Last arrival 21.00hrs Last departure noon

A terraced site with good quality facilities, bordering onto open farmland. The spacious pitches are secluded and fully serviced, and there is a decent, modern toilet block. 5 acre site. 60 touring pitches. 9 hardstandings. 6 seasonal pitches. Tent pitches. Motorhome pitches.

Queenbower Dairy Caravan Park *(SZ567846)*
▶
Alverstone Rd, Queenbower PO36 0NZ
☎ 01983 403840 📄 01983 409671
e-mail: queenbowerdairy@aol.com
dir: *3m N of Sandown off A3056 turn right towards Alverstone Rd, site 1m on left*

PETS: Charges £1 per night **Public areas** disp bin **Exercise area** 200yds **Other** prior notice required dogs must be kept on leads at all times & exercised off site

Open May-Oct

A small site with basic amenities that will appeal to campers keen to escape the crowds and the busy larger sites. The enthusiastic owners keep the facilities very clean. 2.5 acre site. 20 touring pitches. Tent pitches. Motorhome pitches.

Notes 😊

SHANKLIN
Map 4 SZ58

Melbourne Ardenlea Hotel
★★ 76% HOTEL
4-6 Queens Rd PO37 6AP
☎ 01983 862596 📄 01983 868927
e-mail: reservations@mahotel.co.uk
web: www.mahotel.co.uk
dir: *A3055 to Shanklin, then follow signs to Ventnor via A3055 (Queens Rd). Hotel just before end of road on right*

PETS: Bedrooms (6 GF) unattended sign **Charges** £4 per night **Public areas** except dining room (ex assist dogs) on leads **Grounds** disp bin **Exercise area** 50mtrs **Facilities** food (pre-bookable) dog chews washing facs cage storage walks info vet info **On Request** fridge access torch towels **Other** charge for damage all pets except dogs must be caged

This quietly located hotel is within easy walking distance of the town centre and the lift down to the promenade. Bedrooms are traditionally furnished and guests can enjoy the various spacious public areas including a welcoming bar and a large heated indoor swimming pool.

Rooms 54 (5 fmly) (6 GF) **S** £45-£80; **D** £70-£120 (incl. bkfst)* **Facilities** 🏊 Sauna 🎵 New Year Wi-fi **Services** Lift **Parking** 26 **Notes** LB Closed 21-28 Dec

ENGLAND

SHANKLIN *continued*

Rowborough

★★★★ GUEST ACCOMMODATION

32 Arthurs Hill PO37 6EX

☎ 01983 866072 & 863070 ▤ 01983 867703

e-mail: susanpatricia@btconnect.com

web: www.rowboroughhotel.com

dir: *Between Sandown & Shanklin*

PETS: Bedrooms (1 GF) **Charges** £10 per week **Public areas** except restaurant at meal times on leads **Grounds** disp bin **Exercise area** 300yds **Facilities** walks info vet info **On Request** fridge access torch towels **Other** charge for damage **Resident Pet:** Penny (Lhasa Apso)

Located on the main road into town, this charming, family-run establishment provides comfortable bedrooms with many extra facilities. The non-smoking conservatory overlooks the garden, along with a lounge and a bar. Dinner is available by arrangement.

Rooms 9 en suite (5 fmly) (1 GF) **S** £46-£52; **D** £92-£104 **Facilities** TVL tea/coffee Dinner available Cen ht Licensed Wi-fi **Parking** 5 **Notes** LB

 Lower Hyde Holiday Park *(SZ575819)*

Landguard Rd PO37 7LL

☎ 01983 866131 ▤ 01983 862532

e-mail: holidaysales.lowerhyde@park-resorts.com

dir: *From Fishbourne ferry terminal follow A3055 to Shanklin. Site signed just past lake*

PETS: Charges £1 per night **Public areas** except swimming pool & children's play areas disp bin **Exercise area on site** field, dog walk trails **Facilities** food walks info vet info **Other** prior notice required **Restrictions** no dangerous dogs (see page 7)

Open Apr-Oct Last arrival anytime Last departure 10.00hrs

A popular holiday park on the outskirts of Shanklin, close to the sandy beaches. There is an outdoor swimming pool and plenty of organised activities for youngsters of all ages. In the evening there is a choice of family entertainment. The touring facilities are located in a quiet area away from the main complex, with good views over the downs. 65 acre site. 148 touring pitches. 25 hardstandings. Tent pitches. Motorhome pitches. 313 statics.

The Hermitage

★★★ GUEST ACCOMMODATION

Cliff Rd PO39 0EW

☎ 01983 752518

e-mail: blake_david@btconnect.com

web: www.thehermitagebnb.co.uk

dir: *Church Hill B3322, right onto Eden Rd, left onto Cliff Rd, 0.5m on right*

PETS: Bedrooms unattended **Public areas** except dining area **Grounds Exercise area** 5 mins' walk **Facilities** water bowl washing facs cage storage walks info vet info **On Request** fridge access torch towels **Other** charge for damage **Resident Pets:** 1 German Shepherd, 3 cats, 2 lovebirds

The Hermitage is an extremely pet and people friendly establishment which occupies a stunning and unspoilt location near to the cliff top in Totland Bay. Extensive gardens are well maintained and off-road parking is a bonus. Accommodation is comfortable and guests are assured of a genuinely warm welcome at this traditionally styled establishment. A range of delicious items at breakfast provide a substantial start to the day.

Rooms 6 rms (5 en suite) (1 pri facs) (1 fmly) **Facilities** TVL tea/coffee Dinner available **Parking** 6 **Notes** LB

Eversley

★★★ 74% HOTEL

Park Av PO38 1LB

☎ 01983 852244 & 852462 ▤ 01983 856534

e-mail: eversleyhotel@yahoo.co.uk

web: www.eversleyhotel.com

dir: *On A3055 W of Ventnor, next to Ventnor Park*

PETS: Bedrooms (2 GF) **Charges** £10 per stay **Public areas** except restaurant on leads **Grounds** on leads **Exercise area** private access to Ventor Park & coastal walks **Facilities** water bowl walks info vet info **Other** charge for damage

Located west of Ventnor, this hotel enjoys a quiet location and has some rooms with garden and pool views. The spacious

restaurant is sometimes used for local functions, and there is a bar, television room, lounge area, a card room as well as a jacuzzi and gym. Bedrooms are generally a good size.

Rooms 30 (8 fmly) (2 GF) **Facilities** ⚡ Gym Pool table Xmas **Parking** 23 **Notes** Closed 30 Nov-22 Dec & 2 Jan-8 Feb

See advert on this page

Ventnor Towers Hotel

★★★ **72%** HOTEL

54 Madeira Rd PO38 1QT
☎ 01983 852277 📄 01983 855536
e-mail: reservations@ventnortowers.com
web: www.ventnortowers.com
dir: *From E, 1st left off A3055 just before pelican crossing*

PETS: Bedrooms (6 GF) unattended ground-floor bedrooms only **Charges** £7.50 per night on leads **Grounds** on leads disp bin **Facilities** walks info vet info **Other** charge for damage **Resident Pets:** Wirzell (dog), Felix (cat)

This mid-Victorian hotel, set in spacious grounds from where a path leads down to the shore, is high above the bay and enjoys splendid sea views. Many potted plants and fresh flowers grace the day rooms, which include two lounges and a spacious bar. Bedrooms include two four-poster rooms and some that have their own balconies.

Rooms 25 (4 fmly) (6 GF) **S** £55-£85; **D** £65-£110 (incl. bkfst)* **Facilities** ⚡ ⛴ 9 ⛳ Putt green Xmas New Year Wi-fi **Parking** 20 **Notes** LB

Whitecliff Bay Holiday Park *(SZ637862)*

Hillway Rd, Bembridge PO35 5PL
☎ 01983 872671 📄 01983 872941
e-mail: holiday@whitecliff-bay.com
dir: *1m S of Bembridge, signed off B3395 in village*

PETS: Charges dog £1 (low season), £3 (high season) per night **Public areas** on leads disp bin **Exercise area on site** dog field & walkway through park **Facilities** vet info **Other** prior notice required max 2 dogs per pitch; dogs must wear collar with ID tag & on leads at all times **Restrictions** no dangerous dogs (see page 7)

Open Mar-Oct Last arrival 21.00hrs Last departure 10.30hrs

A large seaside complex on two sites, with camping on one and self-catering chalets and statics on the other. There is an indoor pool with flume and spa pool, and an outdoor pool with a kiddies' pool, a family entertainment club, and plenty of traditional on-site activities including crazy golf, a soft play area and table tennis, plus a restaurant and a choice of bars. A Canvas Village has been introduced with 12 ready-erected tents for hire. There is easy access to Whitecliff beach. 49 acre site. 400 touring pitches. 50 hardstandings. Tent pitches. Motorhome pitches. 227 statics. 12 bell tents/yurts.

Notes Adults & families only.

ENGLAND

Kite Hill Farm Caravan & Camping Park
(SZ549906)

►►►

Firestone Copse Rd PO33 4LE
☎ 01983 882543 & 883261   📄 01983 883883
e-mail: welcome@kitehillfarm.co.uk
dir: *Signed off A3054 at Wootton Bridge, between Ryde & Newport*

PETS: Public areas disp bin **Exercise area on site** 2 acres of uncut meadow, with mown path **Facilities** walks info vet info

Open all year Last arrival anytime Last departure anytime

The park, on a gently sloping field, is tucked away behind the owners' farm, just a short walk from the village and attractive river estuary. The refurbished facilities are very clean. This park provides a nice relaxing atmosphere to stay on the island. 12.5 acre site. 50 touring pitches. 10 hardstandings. Tent pitches. Motorhome pitches.

Appuldurcombe Gardens Holiday Park
(SZ546804)

►►►►

Appuldurcombe Rd PO38 3EP
☎ 01983 852597   📄 01983 856225
e-mail: info@appuldurcombegardens.co.uk
dir: *From Newport take A3020 towards Shanklin & Ventnor. Through Rookley & Godshill. Right at Whiteley Bank rdbt towards Wroxall village, then follow brown signs*

PETS: Charges £4.30 per night £30 per week **Public areas** except pool area & café **Exercise area** 150yds **Facilities** food washing facs walks info vet info **Other** prior notice required disposal bags available **Restrictions** no Pit Bull Terriers, Rottweilers or Dobermans

Open Mar-Nov Last arrival 21.00hrs Last departure 11.00hrs

This well-appointed park is set in a unique setting fairly close to the town of Ventnor. It has modern and spotless facilities plus a very tasteful lounge bar and function room. There is an excellent, screened outdoor pool and paddling pool plus café and shop. Static caravans and apartments are also available for hire. The site is close to cycle routes and is only 150 yards from the bus stop making it perfect for those with a motorhome or those not wanting to take the car out. 14 acre site. 100 touring pitches. 2 hardstandings. Tent pitches. Motorhome pitches.

Notes No skateboards.

Park House Motel
★★★★ GUEST ACCOMMODATION

SP4 0EG
☎ 01980 629256   📄 01980 629256
e-mail: info@parkhousemotel.com
dir: *5m E of Amesbury. Junct A303 & A338*

PETS: Bedrooms (25 GF) sign **Charges Public areas Grounds** on leads disp bin **Exercise area** nearby **Facilities** walks info vet info **On Request** fridge access torch towels **Other** charge for damage **Restrictions** small dogs only **Resident Pets:** Bernard & Max (Lhasa Apsos), Arnie (Yorkshire Terrier)

This family-run establishment offers a warm welcome and is extremely convenient for the A303. Bedrooms are practically equipped with modern facilities and come in a variety of sizes. There is a large dining room where dinner is served during the week, and a cosy bar in which to relax.

Rooms 30 rms (27 en suite) (1 pri facs) (9 fmly) (25 GF) **S** £56-£65; **D** £75 **Facilities** STV FTV TVL tea/coffee Dinner available Cen ht Licensed Wi-fi **Parking** 40

Stonehenge Touring Park *(SU061456)*
►►►

SP3 4SH
☎ 01980 620304
e-mail: stay@stonehengetouringpark.com
dir: *From A360 towards Devizes turn right, follow lane, site at bottom of village on right*

PETS: Public areas except facility block & shop **Exercise area** 50mtrs **Facilities** walks info vet info **Other** prior notice required **Resident Pets:** 1 dog

Open all year Last arrival 21.00hrs Last departure 11.00hrs

A quiet site adjacent to the small village of Orcheston near the centre of Salisbury Plain and four miles from Stonehenge. There's an excellent on-site shop. 2 acre site. 30 touring pitches. 12 hardstandings. Tent pitches. Motorhome pitches.

Notes No noise after 23.00hrs.

BRADFORD-ON-AVON   Map 3 ST86

von Essen hotels
A PRIVATE COLLECTION
www.vonessenhotels.com

Woolley Grange
★★★ 82% ◉◉ HOTEL

Woolley Green BA15 1TX
☎ 01225 864705 📠 01225 864059
e-mail: info@woolleygrangehotel.co.uk
web: www.woolleygrangehotel.co.uk
dir: A4 onto B3109. Bradford Leigh, left at x-roads, hotel 0.5m on right at Woolley Green

PETS: Bedrooms (3 GF) unattended Charges £25 per stay Public areas except dining areas Grounds disp bin Exercise area 14-acre grounds Exercise area canal walk (2m) Facilities food bowl water bowl bedding dog chews scoop/disp bags leads walks info vet info On Request fridge access torch towels Other charge for damage dog owners are advised to keep dogs on leads due to children staying at hotel Resident Pet: Peanut (Cocker Spaniel)

This splendid Cotswold manor house is set in beautiful countryside. Children are made especially welcome; there is a trained nanny on duty in the nursery. Bedrooms and public areas are charmingly furnished and decorated in true country-house style, with many thoughtful touches and luxurious extras. The hotel offers a varied and well-balanced menu selection, including ingredients from the hotel's own garden.

Rooms 26 (14 annexe) (20 fmly) (3 GF) D £120-£490 (incl. bkfst)* Facilities Spa FTV ⊗ ⅃ ⅃ Beauty treatments Football Table tennis Trampoline Boules Cricket Steam room Xmas New Year Wi-fi Child facilities Parking 40

BROMHAM   Map 3 ST96

Wayside
★★★ BED AND BREAKFAST

Chittoe Heath SN15 2EH
☎ 01380 850695 & 07770 774460 📠 01380 850696
e-mail: mail@waysideofwiltshire.co.uk
web: www.waysideofwiltshire.co.uk
dir: From A342 take road signed Spye Park & Chittoe, Wayside 1st on right

PETS: Bedrooms (1 GF) Charges pet £5, horse £15 per night pet £30 per week, phone for weekly charge for horse Public areas on leads Grounds disp bin Exercise area 12-acre woods adjacent Facilities cage storage walks info vet info On Request fridge access torch towels Stables Other excellent riding & walks in the area Resident Pets: 4 dogs, horses

Peacefully located yet only just off the main road, Wayside offers relaxed and comfortable accommodation in a range of shapes and sizes. Guests are welcome to use the lounge and there is woodland to the rear of the property where they can take a walk. Good quality ingredients are offered at breakfast; for dinner there is a wide choice of local inns and restaurants.

Rooms 2 en suite (1 fmly) (1 GF) (2 smoking) S £40; D £70 Facilities STV FTV TVL Cen ht Wi-fi Golf 18 Riding Parking 3 Notes LB ⊛

CALNE   Map 3 ST97

Blackland Lakes Holiday & Leisure Centre
(ST973687)

▶▶▶

Stockley Ln SN11 0NQ
☎ 01249 810943 📠 01249 811346
e-mail: blacklandlakes.bookings@btconnect.com
dir: From Calne take A4 E for 1.5m, right at camp sign. Site 1m on left

PETS: Charges £1.50 per night £10.50 per week Public areas disp bin Exercise area on site dog walk approx 1m around perimeter Facilities food scoop/disp bags washing facs vet info Stables Other prior notice required

Open all year rs 30 Oct-1 Mar pre-paid bookings only Last arrival 22.00hrs Last departure noon

A rural site surrounded by the North and West Downs. The park is divided into several paddocks separated by hedges, trees and fences, and there are two well-stocked carp fisheries for the angling enthusiast. There are some excellent walks close by, and the interesting market town of Devizes is just a few miles away. 15 acre site. 180 touring pitches. 25 hardstandings. Tent pitches. Motorhome pitches.

CASTLE COMBE   Map 3 ST87

Manor House Hotel and Golf Club
★★★★ ◉◉◉ COUNTRY HOUSE HOTEL

SN14 7HR
☎ 01249 782206 📠 01249 782159
e-mail: enquiries@manorhouse.co.uk
web: www.exclusivehotels.co.uk
dir: M4 junct 17 follow Chippenham signs onto A420 Bristol, then right onto B4039. Through village, right after bridge

PETS: Bedrooms (12 GF) unattended dogs allowed in cottage bedrooms only Charges please contact hotel for details Public areas except food service areas on leads Grounds on leads Exercise area nearby Facilities food (pre-bookable) food bowl water bowl bedding dog chews cat treats cage storage walks info vet info On Request fridge access towels Resident Pets: 1 cat, 6 pigs, 6 chickens

This delightful hotel is situated in a secluded valley adjacent to a picturesque village, where there have been no new buildings for 300 years. There are 365 acres of grounds to enjoy, complete with an Italian garden and an 18-hole golf course. Bedrooms, some in the main house and some in a row of stone cottages, have been superbly furnished, and public rooms include a number of cosy lounges with roaring fires. Service is a pleasing blend of professionalism and friendliness. The award-winning food utilises top quality local produce.

Rooms 48 (26 annexe) (8 fmly) (12 GF) S £245-£650; D £245-£650 (incl. bkfst)* Facilities STV ⅃ 18 ⅁ Putt green Fishing ⅃ Jogging track Hot air ballooning Xmas New Year Wi-fi Parking 100 Notes LB

ENGLAND

The Lamb Inn
★★★★ ◉ INN

SP3 6DP
☎ 01747 820573 📄 01747 820605
e-mail: info@thelambathindon.co.uk
dir: *Off B3089 in village centre*

PETS: Bedrooms (3 GF) **Charges** £10 per night **Public areas** except restaurant (can dine in bar with dogs) on leads **Grounds** on leads disp bin **Exercise area** 100yds **Facilities** food bowl water bowl cage storage walks info vet info **On Request** towels

This 17th-century coaching inn is in a pretty village within easy reach of Salisbury and Bath. It has been appointed in an eclectic style, and some of the well-equipped bedrooms have four-poster beds. Enjoyable, freshly prepared dishes are available at lunch and dinner in the restaurant or bar, where log fires provide a welcoming atmosphere on colder days.

Rooms 19 rms (13 en suite) 6 annexe en suite (1 fmly) (3 GF) **S** £115; **D** £175 **Facilities** FTV tea/coffee Dinner available Direct Dial Cen ht Wi-fi **Parking** 16

At the Sign of the Angel
★★★★ GUEST ACCOMMODATION

6 Church St SN15 2LB
☎ 01249 730230 📄 01249 730527
e-mail: angel@lacock.co.uk
dir: *Off A350 into Lacock, follow 'Local Traffic' sign*

PETS: Bedrooms (4 GF) unattended sign bedrooms 1-6 only (main building) **Public areas** except restaurant **Grounds** on leads **Exercise area** surrounding area **Facilities** water bowl walks info vet info **On Request** fridge access **Other** charge for damage

Visitors will surely be impressed by the character of this 15th-century former wool merchant's house, set in the National Trust village of Lacock. Bedrooms come in a range of sizes and styles including the atmospheric rooms in the main house and others in an adjacent building. Excellent dinners and breakfasts are served in the beamed dining rooms, and there is also a first-floor lounge and a pleasant rear garden.

Rooms 6 en suite 5 annexe en suite (4 GF) **S** £85; **D** £129-£159 **Facilities** FTV tea/coffee Dinner available Direct Dial Cen ht Licensed Wi-fi **Parking** 6 **Notes** Closed 23-27 Dec RS Mon (ex Bank Holidays) Closed for lunch

Compasses Inn
★★★★ ◉ INN

SP3 6NB
☎ 01722 714318 📄 01722 714318
e-mail: thecompasses@aol.com
web: www.thecompassesinn.com
dir: *Off A30 signed Lower Chicksgrove, 1st left onto Lagpond Ln, single-track lane to village*

PETS: Bedrooms unattended **Public areas Grounds** disp bin **Exercise area** adjacent **Facilities** food bowl water bowl cage storage walks info vet info **On Request** fridge access torch towels

This charming 17th-century inn, within easy reach of Bath, Salisbury, Glastonbury and the Dorset coast, offers comfortable accommodation in a peaceful setting. Carefully prepared dinners are enjoyed in the warm atmosphere of the bar-restaurant, while breakfast is served in a separate dining room.

Rooms 5 en suite (2 fmly) **S** £50-£65; **D** £65-£85 **Facilities** FTV tea/coffee Dinner available Cen ht Wi-fi **Parking** 40 **Notes** LB Closed 25-26 Dec

Whatley Manor
★★★★★ ◉◉◉◉ HOTEL

Easton Grey SN16 0RB
☎ 01666 822888 📄 01666 826120
e-mail: reservations@whatleymanor.com
web: www.whatleymanor.com
dir: *M4 junct 17, follow signs to Malmesbury, continue over 2 rdbts. Follow B4040 & signs for Sherston, hotel 2m on left*

PETS: Bedrooms unattended bedrooms 3 & 4 only **Charges** £30 per night **Public areas** except restaurants on leads **Grounds** on leads disp bin **Exercise area** nearby **Facilities** food (pre-bookable) food bowl water bowl bedding dog chews scoop/disp bags leads pet sitting washing facs walks info **On Request** fridge access torch towels **Other** charge for damage welcome letter, guidelines, luxury dog basket, treats, walk routes & maps

Sitting in 12 acres of beautiful countryside, this impressive country house provides the most luxurious surroundings. Spacious bedrooms, most with views over the attractive gardens, are individually decorated with splendid features such as Bang & Olufsen sound and vision systems and unique works of art. Several eating options are available: Le Mazot, a Swiss-style brasserie, The Dining Room that serves classical French cuisine with a contemporary twist via carte and tasting menus, plus the Kitchen Garden Terrace for alfresco breakfasts, lunches and dinners. Guests might even like to take a hamper and a picnic rug and find a quiet spot in the grounds. The old Loggia Barn is ideal for wedding ceremonies, and the Aquarius Spa is magnificent.

Rooms 23 (4 GF) **D** £305-£865 (incl. bkfst)* **Facilities** Spa STV Fishing Gym Cinema Hydro pool (indoor/outdoor) Xmas New Year Wi-fi **Services** Lift **Parking** 100 **Notes** LB No children 12yrs

Old Bell
★★★ 81% ◉◉ HOTEL
Abbey Row SN16 0BW
☎ 01666 822344 📠 01666 825145
e-mail: info@oldbellhotel.com
web: www.oldbellhotel.com
dir: M4 junct 17, follow A429 north. Left at 1st rdbt. Left at T-junct. Hotel next to Abbey

PETS: Bedrooms (7 GF) unattended sign Charges £10 per night Public areas except restaurants on leads Grounds on leads Exercise area 250mtrs Facilities water bowl bedding cage storage walks info vet info Other charge for damage Restrictions no large dogs (eg Newfoundlands, Great Danes, Irish Wolfhounds)

Dating back to 1220, the wisteria-clad Old Bell is reputed to be the oldest purpose-built hotel in England. Bedrooms vary in size and style; those in the main house tend to be more spacious and are traditionally furnished with antiques, while the newer bedrooms in the coach house have a contemporary feel. Guests have a choice of comfortable sitting areas and dining options, including the main restaurant where the award-winning cuisine is based on high quality ingredients.

Rooms 33 (15 annexe) (7 GF) S £89.55; D £115-£245 (incl. bkfst)* Facilities FTV Xmas New Year Wi-fi Parking 33 Notes LB

Best Western Mayfield House
★★★ 72% ◉ HOTEL
Crudwell SN16 9EW
☎ 01666 577409 📠 01666 577977
e-mail: reception@mayfieldhousehotel.co.uk
web: www.mayfieldhousehotel.co.uk
dir: M4 junct 17, A429 to Cirencester. 2m N of Malmesbury on left in Crudwell

PETS: Bedrooms (8 GF) unattended ground-floor bedrooms only Charges £15 per stay Public areas except restaurant & lounge on leads Exercise area water meadow opposite Facilities water bowl dog chews feeding mat scoop/disp bags washing facs cage storage walks info vet info On Request torch towels Stables 0.25m Other charge for damage Restrictions no dangerous dogs (see page 7)

This popular hotel is in an ideal location for exploring the many attractions that Wiltshire and The Cotswolds have to offer. Bedrooms come in a range of shapes and sizes, and include some on the ground-floor level in a cottage adjacent to the main building. In addition to outdoor seating, guests can relax with a drink in the comfortable lounge area where orders are taken for the carefully prepared dinner to follow.

Rooms 28 (8 annexe) (4 fmly) (8 GF) S £60-£75; D £83-£103 (incl. bkfst)* Facilities FTV Xmas New Year Wi-fi Parking 50 Notes LB

The Castle & Ball
OldEnglish
★★★ 70% HOTEL
High St SN8 1LZ
☎ 01672 515201 📠 01672 515895
e-mail: castleandballmarlboroughreservations@greeneking.co.uk
web: www.oldenglish.co.uk
dir: A338 and A4 to Marlborough

PETS: Bedrooms unattended Public areas except restaurant on leads Grounds on leads Exercise area 5 mins Facilities cage storage walks info vet info On Request fridge access torch towels

This traditional coaching inn in the town centre offers contemporary and very well equipped bedrooms. Open-plan public areas include a comfortable bar/lounge area and a smartly appointed restaurant, which serves food all day. Meeting rooms are also available.

Rooms 35 (1 annexe) (5 fmly) Facilities Xmas New Year Wi-fi Parking 48

The Lamb Inn
★★★ ⬭ INN
The Parade SN8 1NE
☎ 01672 512668 & 07885 275568 📠 01672 512668
e-mail: thelambinnmarlboro@fsmail.net
dir: From High St, right onto Parade, 50yds on left

PETS: Bedrooms unattended Public areas Grounds disp bin Exercise area 0.25m Facilities food bowl water bowl washing facs walks info vet info On Request fridge access towels

Located in a quieter area of Marlborough, yet just a couple of minutes from the bustle of the main street, this traditional inn provides a friendly welcome and relaxed ambience. Bedrooms vary in size and are located above the main inn, and in modernised stables adjacent to the pleasant rear garden. Dinner here is a highlight with a good selection of very well cooked and presented dishes using fresh ingredients.

Rooms 6 en suite (1 fmly) S fr £50; D fr £75 Facilities tea/coffee Dinner available Cen ht Wi-fi Golf 18 Notes No coaches

Beechfield House Hotel, Restaurant & Gardens

★★★ **79%** COUNTRY HOUSE HOTEL

Beanacre SN12 7PU
☎ 01225 703700 📄 01225 790118
e-mail: reception@beechfieldhouse.co.uk
web: www.beechfieldhouse.co.uk
dir: *M4 junct 17, A350 S, bypass Chippenham, towards Melksham. Hotel on left after Beanacre*

PETS: Bedrooms (4 GF) unattended main house bedrooms only **Charges** £15 per night **Grounds** disp bin **Exercise area** fields accessed from grounds **Facilities** cage storage walks info vet info **Other** charge for damage **Restrictions** no large dogs **Resident Pets:** Misty (Black Labrador), Lola & Daisy (cats)

This is a charming, privately owned hotel set within eight acres of beautiful grounds that has its own arboretum. Bedrooms are individual styled and include four-poster rooms, and ground-floor rooms in the coach house. Relaxing public areas are comfortably furnished and there is a beauty salon with a range of pampering treatments available. At dinner there is a very good selection of carefully prepared dishes with an emphasis on seasonal and local produce.

Rooms 24 (6 fmly) (4 GF) **D** £125-£175 (incl. bkfst)*
Facilities FTV 🎾 🏊 Beauty treatment room Xmas New Year Wi-fi **Parking** 70 **Notes** LB

Shaw Country

★★ **76%** SMALL HOTEL

Bath Rd, Shaw SN12 8EF
☎ 01225 702836 & 790321 📄 01225 790275
e-mail: info@shawcountryhotel.com
web: www.shawcountryhotel.com
dir: *1m from Melksham, 9m from Bath on A365*

PETS: Bedrooms Grounds on leads **Exercise area** 500yds **Facilities** walks info vet info **On Request** fridge access torch **Other** charge for damage **Resident Pets:** 2 cats

Located within easy reach of both Bath and the M4, this relaxed and friendly hotel sits in its own gardens and includes a patio area ideal for enjoying a drink during the summer months. The house boasts very well-appointed bedrooms, a comfortable lounge and bar, and the Mulberry Restaurant, where a wide selection of innovative dishes make up both carte and set menus. A spacious function room is a useful addition.

Rooms 13 (2 fmly) **S** £65-£90; **D** £90-£110 (incl. bkfst)*
Facilities FTV Wi-fi **Parking** 30 **Notes** RS 26-27 Dec & 1 Jan

Fosse Farmhouse Chambre d'Hote

★★★★ 🍽 BED AND BREAKFAST

Nettleton Shrub SN14 7NJ
☎ 01249 782286 📄 01249 783066
e-mail: caroncooper@fossefarmhouse.com
web: www.fossefarmhouse.com
dir: *1.5m N from Castle Combe on B4039, left at Gib, 1m on right*

PETS: Bedrooms sign farmhouse bedrooms only **Charges** £20 per night £100 per week **Grounds** on leads disp bin **Exercise area** adjacent **Facilities** food bowl water bowl feeding mat scoop/disp bags walks info vet info **On Request** torch towels **Other** charge for damage

Set in quiet countryside not far from Castle Combe, this bed and breakfast has well-equipped bedrooms decorated in keeping with its 18th-century origins. Excellent dinners are served in the farmhouse, and cream teas can be enjoyed in the old stables or the delightful garden.

Rooms 2 en suite (1 fmly) **S** £70-£80; **D** £95-£125 **Facilities** tea/coffee Dinner available Cen ht Licensed Wi-fi Golf 18 **Parking** 12 **Notes** LB

The Pear Tree at Purton

★★★ **81%** 🍽🍽 HOTEL

Church End SN5 4ED
☎ 01793 772100 📄 01793 772369
e-mail: stay@peartreepurton.co.uk
dir: *M4 junct 16 follow signs to Purton, at Best One shop turn right. Hotel 0.25m on left*

PETS: Bedrooms 2 bedrooms with courtyards only **Public areas** except restaurant **Grounds** disp bin **Exercise area** adjacent **Facilities** food bowl water bowl dog chews cat treats scoop/disp bags leads washing facs walks info vet info **On Request** fridge access torch towels **Resident Pets:** Smudge (dog), Poppy & Cosmos (cats)

A charming 15th-century, former vicarage set amidst extensive landscaped gardens in a peaceful location in the Vale of the

White Horse and near the Saxon village of Purton. The resident proprietors and staff provide efficient, dedicated service and friendly hospitality. The spacious bedrooms are individually decorated and have a good range of thoughtful extras such as fresh fruit, sherry and shortbread. Fresh ingredients feature on the award-winning menus.

The Pear Tree at Purton

Rooms 17 (2 fmly) (6 GF) **S** £120-£150; **D** £120-£180 (incl. bkfst) **Facilities** STV FTV 🏊 Outdoor giant chess Vineyard Wi-fi **Parking** 60 **Notes** LB

SALISBURY   Map 4 SU12

THE INDEPENDENTS
HOTEL ASSOCIATION

Grasmere House Hotel
★★★ 68% HOTEL

Harnham Rd SP2 8JN
☎ 01722 338388   📄 01722 333710
e-mail: info@grasmerehotel.com
web: www.grasmerehotel.com
dir: On A3094 on S side of Salisbury adjacent to Harnham church

PETS: Bedrooms (9 GF) ground-floor bedrooms only **Charges** £10 per night **Public areas** except restaurant & bar muzzled and on leads **Grounds** on leads **Exercise area** adjacent to park **Facilities** walks info vet info **Other** charge for damage **Restrictions** no dangerous dogs (see page 7)

This popular hotel, dating from 1896, has gardens that overlook the water meadows and the cathedral. The attractive bedrooms vary in size, some offer excellent quality and comfort, and some rooms are specially equipped for less mobile guests. In summer there is the option of dining on the pleasant outdoor terrace.

Rooms 38 (31 annexe) (16 fmly) (9 GF) **Facilities** STV FTV Fishing 🏊 Xmas New Year Wi-fi **Parking** 64 **Notes** LB

Coombe Touring Park *(SU099282)*
▶▶▶▶

Race Plain, Netherhampton SP2 8PN
☎ 01722 328451   📄 01722 328451
e-mail: enquiries@coombecaravanpark.co.uk
dir: Exit A36 onto A3094, 2m SW, site adjacent to Salisbury racecourse

PETS: Charges 20p per night **Public areas** except toilet, shower, laundry blocks & shop disp bin **Exercise area** adjacent **Facilities** washing facs walks info vet info **Resident Pets:** Alfie (Labrador/Collie cross), Charlie (cat)

Open 3 Jan-20 Dec rs Oct-May shop closed Last arrival 21.00hrs Last departure noon

A very neat and attractive site adjacent to the racecourse with views over the downs. The park is well landscaped with shrubs and maturing trees, and the very colourful beds are stocked from the owner's greenhouse. A comfortable park with a superb luxury toilet block, and four static holiday homes for hire. 3 acre site. 50 touring pitches. Tent pitches. Motorhome pitches. 4 statics.

Notes No disposable BBQs or fires, no mini motorbikes, no noise between 23.00hrs-07.00hrs. 🐾

SWINDON   Map 4 SU18

Campanile
HOTEL RESTAURANT

Campanile Swindon
BUDGET HOTEL

Delta Business Park, Great Western Way SN5 7XG
☎ 01793 514777   📄 01793 514570
e-mail: swindon@campanile.com
web: www.campanile-swindon.co.uk
dir: M4 junct 16, A3102 towards Swindon. After 2nd rdbt, 2nd exit onto Welton Rd (Delta Business Park), 1st left

PETS: Bedrooms (22 GF) unattended **Charges** £5 per night **Public areas** except restaurant & bar on leads **Grounds** on leads disp bin **Exercise area** nearby **Facilities** cage storage walks info vet info **Other** charge for damage pets may be left unattended in bedrooms for short periods only **Restrictions** no large dogs

This modern building offers accommodation in smart, well-equipped bedrooms, all with en suite bathrooms. Refreshments may be taken at the informal bistro.

Rooms 120 (6 fmly) (22 GF)

SWINDON *continued*

Portquin Guest House
★★★★ GUEST ACCOMMODATION
Broadbush, Broad Blunsdon SN26 7DH
☎ 01793 721261
e-mail: portquin@msn.com
dir: *A419 onto B4019 at Blunsdon signed Highworth, continue 0.5m*

PETS: Bedrooms (4 GF) ground-floor/patio bedrooms only
Public areas except dining room & upstairs **Grounds** disp bin
Exercise area adjacent **Facilities** washing facs cage storage
walks info vet info **On Request** fridge access torch towels
Restrictions no breeds of similar size to Great Dane

This friendly guest house, situated not far from Swindon, offers
a warm welcome and views of the Lambourn Downs. The rooms
vary in shape and size, with six in the main house and three in an
adjacent annexe. Full English breakfasts are served at two large
tables in the kitchen-dining area.

Rooms 6 en suite 3 annexe en suite (2 fmly) (4 GF) **S** £45-£50;
D £55-£80 **Facilities** FTV tea/coffee Cen ht Wi-fi **Parking** 12

WARMINSTER	Map 3 ST84

von Essen hotels
A PRIVATE COLLECTION
www.vonessenhotels.com

Bishopstrow House Hotel
★★★★ 78% ◉◉ HOTEL
BA12 9HH
☎ 01985 212312 ▤ 01985 216769
e-mail: info@bishopstrow.co.uk
web: www.vonessenhotels.co.uk
dir: *A303, A36, B3414, hotel 2m on right*

PETS: Bedrooms (7 GF) unattended **Charges** £20 per
night **Public areas** except restaurant, conservatory & pool
area **Grounds** on leads **Facilities** food (pre-bookable) food
bowl water bowl washing facs cage storage walks info vet
info **On Request** fridge access torch towels **Other** charge for
damage please contact hotel to confirm which pets are accepted;
pet sitting/dog walking can be arranged (charged)

This is a fine example of a Georgian country home, situated in 27
acres of grounds. Public areas are traditional in style and feature
antiques and open fires. Most bedrooms offer DVD players. A
spa, a tennis court and several country walks ensure there is
something for all guests. The restaurant serves top quality,
contemporary cuisine.

Rooms 32 (2 annexe) (2 fmly) (7 GF) **Facilities** Spa ⊕ ⊰ ⊱
Fishing ⊱ Gym Clay pigeon shooting Archery Cycling Xmas New
Year Wi-fi **Parking** 100

The Dove Inn
★★★ ◉ INN
Corton BA12 0SZ
☎ 01985 850109 ▤ 01985 851041
e-mail: info@thedove.co.uk
dir: *5m SE of Warminster. Off A36 to Corton village*

PETS: Bedrooms (5 GF) standard double bedrooms only **Charges**
£10 per night **Public areas** except restaurant on leads **Grounds**
on leads disp bin **Exercise area** 100yds **Facilities** food bowl
water bowl dog chews cage storage walks info vet info **Stables**
stabling can be arranged **Other** charge for damage chocolates &
dog biscuits **Resident Pet:** Pepper (Alsatian/Collie cross)

Quietly located in the village of Corton, this traditional inn has
undergone many changes and now provides plenty of quality and
comfort together with a friendly welcome. In addition to lighter
options, a range of well sourced, quality produce is used to create
the enjoyable dinners, served in the main restaurant. There are
standard bedrooms situated adjacent to the inn and two more
luxurious rooms in a cottage appointed to high standards.

Rooms 7 annexe en suite (1 fmly) (5 GF) **S** £60-£80; **D** £80-£120
Facilities FTV tea/coffee Dinner available Cen ht Wi-fi **Parking** 24
Notes LB

WESTBURY	Map 3 ST85

The Cedar Hotel & Restaurant
★★★ 66% HOTEL
114 Warminster Rd BA13 3PR
☎ 01373 822753 ▤ 01373 858423
e-mail: info@cedarhotel-wiltshire.co.uk
dir: *On A350, 0.5m S of town towards Warminster*

PETS: Bedrooms Charges £10 per night **£**70 per week **Grounds**
Exercise area 500yds **Facilities** water bowl cage storage walks
info vet info **On Request** torch towels **Stables** 2m **Other**
charge for damage

Popular with both business and leisure guests, this hotel is
located on the main Warminster Road with easy access to many
local attractions. Bedrooms and bathrooms offer a variety of
shapes and sizes and the hotel has a relaxed and traditional
feel. A good range of options is available at dinner from the
well chosen restaurant menu with a range of bar snacks also
available. The hotel has a car park and pleasant garden to the
rear.

Rooms 20 (12 annexe) **Notes** LB Closed 25 Dec-2 Jan

Brokerswood Country Park *(ST836523)*

▶▶▶▶

Brokerswood BA13 4EH
☎ 01373 822238 📠 01373 858474
e-mail: info@brokerswoodcountrypark.co.uk
dir: *M4 junct 17, S on A350. Right at Yarnbrook to Rising Sun pub at North Bradley, left at rdbt. Left on bend approaching Southwick, 2.5m, site on right*

PETS: Charges dog £1 per night **Public areas** except children's adventure play area disp bin **Exercise area on site** 80-acre country park **Facilities** food bowl water bowl dog chews scoop/disp bags leads walks info vet info **Other** prior notice required dog/cat balls, toys & dog pegs available **Restrictions** no dangerous dogs (see page 7)

Open all year Last arrival 21.30hrs Last departure 11.00hrs

A popular park on the edge of an 80-acre woodland park with nature trails and fishing lakes. An adventure playground offers plenty of fun for all ages, and there is a miniature railway, an indoor play centre, and a café. There are high quality toilet facilities and fully-equipped, ready-erected tents are available for hire. 5 acre site. 69 touring pitches. 21 hardstandings. Tent pitches. Motorhome pitches.

Notes Families only.

WORCESTERSHIRE

ABBERLEY
Map 7 SO76

von Essen hotels
A PRIVATE COLLECTION
www.vonessenhotels.com

The Elms Hotel

★★★ 88% @@ HOTEL

Stockton Rd WR6 6AT
☎ 01299 896666 📠 01299 896804
e-mail: info@theelmshotel.co.uk
web: www.theelmshotel.co.uk
dir: *On A443, 2m beyond Great Witley*

PETS: Bedrooms (3 GF) unattended Coach House rooms only **Charges** £7 per night **Public areas** except restaurants on leads **Grounds** on leads **Facilities** cage storage walks info vet info **On Request** fridge access torch towels **Other** charge for damage **Resident Pets:** Tickle (Chocolate Labrador), George (cat)

This imposing Queen Anne mansion, set in delightful grounds, dates back to 1710 and offers a sophisticated yet relaxed atmosphere throughout. The spacious public rooms and generously proportioned bedrooms offer elegance and charm. The hotel is particularly well geared for families, with a host of child-friendly facilities including a crèche, a play area and wonderful high teas. Imaginative cooking is served in the elegant restaurant.

Rooms 23 (6 annexe) (1 fmly) (3 GF) **D** £185-£515 (incl. bkfst) **Facilities** Spa FTV ⓢ ♨ ⚽ Gym Xmas New Year Wi-fi Child facilities **Parking** 100 **Notes** LB

BEWDLEY
Map 7 SO77

Royal Forester Country Inn

★★★★ @ INN

Callow Hill DY14 9XW
☎ 01299 266286
e-mail: contact@royalforesterinn.co.uk

PETS: Bedrooms unattended **Charges** dog £10, horse £30 per night **Public areas** bar only on leads disp bin **Exercise area** 100mtrs **Facilities** food (pre-bookable) dog walking washing facs dog grooming cage storage walks info vet info **On Request** fridge access towels **Stables** limited stabling available (livery) **Other** charge for damage

Located opposite The Wyre Forest on the town's outskirts, this inn dates back to 1411 and has been sympathetically restored to provide high standards of comfort. Stylish modern bedrooms are complemented by smart bathrooms, and equipped with many thoughtful extras. Decor styles throughout the public areas highlight the many period features, and the restaurant serves imaginative food featuring locally sourced produce.

Rooms 7 en suite (2 fmly) **S** £55; **D** £79 **Facilities** STV FTV tea/coffee Dinner available Cen ht Wi-fi **Parking** 40 **Notes** No coaches

Woodcolliers Arms

★★★ INN

76 Welch Gate DY12 2AU
☎ 01299 400589
e-mail: roger@woodcolliers.co.uk
web: www.woodcolliers.co.uk
dir: *Exit A456, follow road behind church, left into Welch Gate (B4190)*

PETS: Bedrooms **Charges** £5 per night £15 per week **Public areas** except restaurant on leads **Exercise area** 200mtrs **Facilities** water bowl walks info vet info **On Request** fridge access **Other** charge for damage **Restrictions** small & medium size dogs only **Resident Pet:** Oliver (Jack Russell)

Dating from before 1780, the Woodcolliers Arms is a family-run establishment located in the renowned Georgian town of Bewdley. This is a traditional inn offering an interesting menu with both traditional British pub food and a speciality Russian menu. Accommodation is comfortable and rooms are well equipped.

Rooms 5 rms (4 en suite) (1 pri facs) **S** £26-£36; **D** £51-£61 **Facilities** FTV tea/coffee Dinner available Cen ht Wi-fi **Parking** 2 **Notes** LB

Broadway

★★★ 78% HOTEL

Cotswold Inns & Hotels

The Green, High St WR12 7AA
☎ 01386 852401   🖹 01386 853879
e-mail: info@broadwayhotel.info
web: www.cotswold-inns-hotels.co.uk/broadway
dir: Follow signs to Evesham, then Broadway

PETS: Bedrooms (3 GF) unattended certain bedrooms only **Charges** £10 per night **Public areas** except main restaurant **Grounds Facilities** water bowl cage storage walks info vet info **On Request** fridge access torch towels **Other** charge for damage

A half-timbered Cotswold stone property, built in the 15th century as a retreat for the Abbots of Pershore. The hotel combines modern, attractive decor with original charm and character. Bedrooms are tastefully furnished and well equipped while public rooms include a relaxing lounge, cosy bar and charming restaurant; alfresco all-day dining in summer months proves popular.

Rooms 19 (1 fmly) (3 GF) **S** £115-£155; **D** £155-£175 (incl. bkfst)* **Facilities** Xmas New Year Wi-fi **Parking** 20 **Notes** LB

Cowley House

★★★★ GUEST ACCOMMODATION

Church St WR12 7AE
☎ 01386 858148
e-mail: cowleyhouse.broadway@tiscali.co.uk
dir: Follow signs for Broadway. Church St adjacent to village green, 3rd on left

PETS: Bedrooms ground-floor bedroom with private garden **Charges** £5 per night **Public areas** lounge only on leads **Grounds** disp bin **Exercise area** approx 100yds **Facilities** dog chews feeding mat scoop/disp bags washing facs walks info vet info **On Request** torch **Other** charge for damage **Restrictions** small, well behaved dogs only **Resident Pets:** Holly & Purdey (West Highland Terriers)

A warm welcome is assured at this 18th-century Cotswold-stone house, just a stroll from the village green. Fine period furniture enhances the interior, and the elegant hall has a polished flagstone floor. Tastefully equipped bedrooms include thoughtful extras and smart modern shower rooms. Comprehensive breakfasts feature local produce.

Rooms 7 rms (6 en suite) (1 pri facs) (2 fmly) (2 GF) **S** £50-£75; **D** £69-£110 **Facilities** FTV tea/coffee Cen ht Wi-fi **Parking** 7 **Notes** LB

Horse & Hound

★★★★ INN

54 High St WR12 7DT
☎ 01386 852287   🖹 01386 853784
e-mail: djttruesdale@msn.com
dir: Off A46 to Evesham

PETS: Bedrooms unattended **Charges** £10 per night **Public areas** except restaurant on leads **Exercise area** 100yds **Facilities** dog chews walks info vet info **Other** charge for damage **Restrictions** small dogs only **Resident Pets:** Stella & Gracie (Black Labradors)

The Horse & Hound is at the heart of the beautiful Cotswold village of Broadway. There are many areas of interest to visit within easy distance of this well established inn. A warm welcome is guaranteed from hosts David and Diane whether dining in the inviting pub or staying overnight in attractive and well-appointed bedrooms. Breakfast and dinner provide quality ingredients which are freshly prepared.

Rooms 5 en suite (1 fmly) **S** £60-£70; **D** £70-£80 **Facilities** tea/coffee Dinner available Cen ht Wi-fi **Parking** 15 **Notes** LB RS Winter

The Evesham

★★★ 77% HOTEL

Coopers Ln, Off Waterside WR11 1DA
☎ 01386 765566 & 0800 716969 (Res)   🖹 01386 765443
e-mail: reception@eveshamhotel.com
web: www.eveshamhotel.com
dir: M5 junct 9, A46 to Evesham. At rdbt on entering Evesham, take B4184 towards town, right at new bridge lights, 800yds, right into Coopers Ln

PETS: Bedrooms (11 GF) unattended **Grounds Exercise area** 400yds **Facilities** vet info **Other** please phone for details of pet facilities

Dating from 1540 and set in extensive grounds, this delightful hotel has well-equipped accommodation that includes a selection of quirkily themed rooms - Alice in Wonderland, Egyptian, and Aquarium (which has a tropical fish tank in the bathroom). A reputation for food is well deserved, with a particularly strong choice for vegetarians. Children are welcome and toys are always available.

Rooms 40 (1 annexe) (3 fmly) (11 GF) **S** £77-£89; **D** £123-£126 (incl. bkfst)* **Facilities** FTV Putt green New Year Wi-fi Child facilities **Parking** 50 **Notes** LB Closed 25-26 Dec

The Swan Inn
★★★★ INN

Worcester Rd WR8 0EA
☎ 01684 311870
e-mail: info@theswanhanleyswan.co.uk
web: www.theswanhanleyswan.co.uk
dir: M5 junct 7, follow signs for Three Counties Showground, inn 1m before showground

PETS: Bedrooms Public areas except restaurant on leads **Grounds** on leads disp bin **Exercise area** 200yds **Facilities** water bowl cage storage walks info vet info **On Request** fridge access **Other** charge for damage **Resident Pet:** Klaus (German Shepherd)

This 17th-century property, often described as a quintessential country inn, is located right on the village green, and has a warm, cosy, home-from-home atmosphere. Ideally situated at the foot of the beautiful Malvern Hills, it has five en suite bedrooms that are pleasantly furnished, modern and comfortable. Dining, particularly on warmer days in the garden and the patio, is a delight. There is ample parking to the rear of the property.

Rooms 5 en suite (2 fmly) **S** £62; **D** £84 **Facilities** tea/coffee Dinner available Cen ht Wi-fi **Parking** 30

Walter de Cantelupe Inn
★★★ INN

Main Rd WR5 3NA
☎ 01905 820572
e-mail: walter.depub@fsbdial.co.uk
web: www.walterdecantelupeinn.com
dir: On A38 in village centre

PETS: Bedrooms sign **Charges** £5 per stay **Public areas** bar only on leads **Grounds** on leads **Exercise area** 0.5m **Facilities** water bowl washing facs cage storage walks info vet info **On Request** fridge access torch towels **Stables** 1.5m **Other** charge for damage dog grooming available nearby **Restrictions** small dogs only

This inn provides cosy bedrooms with smart bathrooms, and is convenient for the M5 and Worcester. The intimate, open-plan public areas are the setting for a range of real ales, and imaginative food featuring local produce and a fine selection of British cheeses.

Rooms 3 rms (2 en suite) (1 pri facs) **Facilities** tea/coffee Dinner available Cen ht Wi-fi **Parking** 24 **Notes** No coaches

The Cottage in the Wood Hotel
★★★ 85% ◉◉ HOTEL

Holywell Rd, Malvern Wells WR14 4LG
☎ 01684 588860   📠 01684 560662
e-mail: reception@cottageinthewood.co.uk
web: www.cottageinthewood.co.uk
dir: 3m S of Great Malvern off A449, 500yds N of B4209, on opposite side of road

PETS: Bedrooms (9 GF) unattended downstairs bedrooms only **Charges** £9 per night **Grounds** disp bin **Exercise area** hill walks adjacent **Facilities** food bowl water bowl bedding dog chews cage storage walks info vet info **On Request** fridge access torch **Stables** 1.5m **Other** charge for damage

Sitting high up on a wooded hillside, this delightful, family-run hotel boasts lovely views over the Severn Valley. The bedrooms are divided between the main house, Beech Cottage and the Pinnacles. The public areas are very stylishly decorated, and imaginative food is served in an elegant dining room, overlooking the immaculate grounds.

Rooms 30 (23 annexe) (9 GF) **S** £79-£121; **D** £99-£198 (incl. bkfst)* **Facilities** FTV Xmas New Year Wi-fi **Parking** 40 **Notes** LB

MALVERN *continued*

The Great Malvern Hotel

★★ 71% HOTEL

Graham Rd WR14 2HN
☎ 01684 563411 📠 01684 560514
e-mail: sutton@great-malvern-hotel.co.uk
dir: *From Worcester on A449, left after fire station into Graham Rd. Hotel at end on right*

PETS: **Bedrooms** **Public areas** except at food service times in bar & restaurant on leads **Exercise area** 0.5m **Facilities** feeding mat pet sitting dog walking washing facs cage storage walks info vet info **On Request** fridge access torch towels **Other** charge for damage **Restrictions** no large dogs (eg Dobermans, German Shepherds, Rottweilers)

Close to the town centre this privately owned and managed hotel is ideally situated for many of Malvern's attractions. The accommodation is spacious and well equipped. Public areas include a quiet lounge area and a cosy bar area, popular with locals.

Rooms 13 (1 fmly) **S** £59.50-£65; **D** £79.50 (incl. bkfst)*
Facilities STV FTV 🎵 Wi-fi **Services** Lift **Parking** 9 **Notes** LB

Wyche Inn

★★★★ INN

74 Wyche Rd WR14 4EQ
☎ 01684 575396
e-mail: thewycheinn@googlemail.com
web: www.thewycheinn.co.uk
dir: *1.5m S of Malvern. On B4218 towards Malvern & Colwall. Off A449 (Worcester to Ross/Ledbury road)*

PETS: **Bedrooms** unattended **Public areas** except restaurant **Grounds** on leads disp bin **Exercise area** 100yds **Facilities** dog chews washing facs walks info vet info **On Request** fridge access torch towels

Located in an elevated position on the outskirts of Malvern, this inn is popular with locals and visiting walkers. The thoughtfully furnished bedrooms, all with stunning countryside views, provide good levels of comfort; all bathrooms have a bath and shower. The menus offer a choice of home-cooked dishes and a good range of real ales is available from the bar.

Rooms 4 en suite 1 annexe rm (1 pri facs) **Facilities** FTV tea/coffee Dinner available Cen ht Wi-fi Pool table **Parking** 6 **Notes** LB No coaches

Portocks End House

★★★ BED AND BREAKFAST

Little Clevelode WR13 6PE
☎ 01684 310276
e-mail: email@portocksendbandb.co.uk
dir: *On B4424, 4m N of Upton upon Severn, opposite Riverside Caravan Park*

PETS: **Bedrooms** **Public areas** except dining room **Grounds** disp bin **Facilities** food bowl water bowl scoop/disp bags leads washing facs cage storage walks info vet info **On Request** fridge access torch towels **Resident Pet:** Benji (English Springer Spaniel)

Peacefully located, yet convenient for the showground and major road links, this period house retains many original features; the traditional furnishings and decor highlight its intrinsic charm. The bedrooms are equipped with lots of thoughtful extras, and breakfasts are taken in a cosy dining room overlooking the pretty garden.

Rooms 2 rms (1 en suite) (1 pri facs) (1 fmly) **S** £30; **D** £50 **Facilities** tea/coffee **Parking** 4 **Notes** Closed Dec-Feb 🐾

Sidney House

★★★ GUEST ACCOMMODATION

40 Worcester Rd WR14 4AA
☎ 01684 574994 📠 01684 574994
e-mail: info@sidneyhouse.co.uk
web: www.sidneyhouse.co.uk
dir: *On A449, 200yds N from town centre*

PETS: **Bedrooms** bedrooms 3, 4 & 8 only **Public areas** except dining room on leads **Grounds** disp bin **Exercise area** 50yds **Facilities** leads walks info vet info **On Request** fridge access torch towels

This impressive Grade II listed Georgian house is close to the central attractions and has stunning views. Bedrooms are filled with thoughtful extras, and some have small, en suite shower rooms. The spacious dining room overlooks the Cotswold escarpment and a comfortable lounge is also available.

Rooms 8 rms (6 en suite) (2 pri facs) (1 fmly) **S** £25-£55; **D** £59-£75 **Facilities** FTV TVL tea/coffee Cen ht Licensed Wi-fi **Parking** 9 **Notes** Closed 24 Dec-3 Jan

Four Hedges

★★ GUEST ACCOMMODATION

The Rhydd, Hanley Castle WR8 0AD
☎ 01684 310405
e-mail: fredgies@aol.com
dir: 4m E of Malvern at junct of B4211 & B4424

PETS: Bedrooms unattended **Public areas Grounds** disp
bin **Exercise area** adjacent **Facilities** food bowl water bowl
leads pet sitting washing facs cage storage walks info vet
info **On Request** fridge access torch towels **Other** charge for
damage **Resident Pets:** Max (Golden Retriever), Machu & Pichu
(cats)

Situated in a rural location, this detached house stands in
mature grounds with wild birds in abundance. The bedrooms are
equipped with thoughtful extras. Tasty English breakfasts, using
free-range eggs, are served in a cosy dining room at a table made
from a 300-year-old elm tree.

Rooms 4 rms (2 en suite) **S** £25; **D** £50 **Facilities** TVL tea/coffee
Cen ht ➍ Fishing **Parking** 5 **Notes** No Children 1yr Closed Xmas
⊕

Holiday Inn Express Birmingham - Redditch

BUDGET HOTEL

2 Hewell Rd, Enfield B97 6AE
☎ 01527 584658 📄 01527 597905
e-mail: reservations@express.gb.com
web: www.meridianleisurehotels.com/redditch
dir: M42 junct 2/A441 follow signs to rail station. Before station
turn right into Hewell Rd, 1st left into Gloucester Close

PETS: Bedrooms (10 GF) **Charges** £10 per night **Exercise area**
1m **Facilities** walks info vet info **Other** charge for damage
Restrictions max weight 7.5kg

A modern hotel ideal for families and business travellers.
Fresh and uncomplicated, the spacious rooms include Satellite
channels, power shower and tea and coffee-making facilities.
Complimentary hot breakfast is included in the room rate; with
freshly prepared meals served in the GR Restaurant daily from
18:00-22:00.

Rooms 100 (75 fmly) (10 GF) (14 smoking) **S** £50-£99; **D** £50-£99
(incl. bkfst)*

MenziesHotels

Menzies Stourport Manor

★★★★ 77% HOTEL

35 Hartlebury Rd DY13 9JA
☎ 01299 289955 📄 01299 878520
e-mail: stourport@menzieshotels.co.uk
web: www.menzieshotels.co.uk
dir: M5 junct 6, A449 towards Kidderminster, B4193 towards
Stourport. Hotel on right

PETS: Bedrooms (31 GF) **Charges** £12 per night **Grounds** on
leads **Exercise area** 500yds **Facilities** washing facs vet info
Stables 0.5m **Other** charge for damage **Restrictions** small dogs
only

Once the home of Prime Minister Sir Stanley Baldwin, this much
extended country house is set in attractive grounds. A number
of bedrooms and suites are located in the original building,
although the majority are in a more modern, purpose-built
section. Spacious public areas include a range of lounges, a
popular restaurant, a leisure club and conference facilities.

Rooms 68 (17 fmly) (31 GF) (10 smoking) **Facilities** ⊛ ॐ Putt
green Gym Squash Xmas New Year Wi-fi **Parking** 300

White Lion Hotel

★★★ 71% ⊛ HOTEL

21 High St WR8 0HJ
☎ 01684 592551 📄 01684 593333
e-mail: reservations@whitelionhotel.biz
dir: A422, A38 towards Tewkesbury. In 8m take B4104, after 1m
cross bridge, turn left to hotel, past bend on left

PETS: Bedrooms (2 GF) unattended **Charges** £5 per night
Public areas except restaurant on leads **Exercise area** 2 mins'
walk **Facilities** water bowl washing facs walks info vet info
Other charge for damage please phone for further details of pet
facilities; pets may only be left in bedrooms for short periods
Resident Pets: Oscar (Giant Schnauzer), 2 cats

Famed for being the inn depicted in Henry Fielding's novel *Tom
Jones*, this 16th-century hotel is a reminder of 'Old England' with
features such as exposed beams and wall timbers still remaining.
The quality furnishing and the decor throughout enhance its
character; the bedrooms are smart and include one four-poster
room.

Rooms 13 (2 annexe) (2 fmly) (2 GF) **Facilities** FTV Wi-fi
Parking 14 **Notes** Closed 1 Jan RS 25 Dec

ENGLAND

The Dewdrop Inn

★★★★ INN

Bell Ln, Lower Broadheath WR2 6RR
☎ 01905 640012 📠 01905 640265
e-mail: enquiries@thedewdrop-inn.co.uk
dir: From A44 follow signs for Elgar Birthplace Museum, 0.5m past museum turn right at x-rds. 800yds on left

PETS: Bedrooms ground-floor room 7 only **Charges** dog £5 per night **Public areas** except restaurant & bar area on leads **Grounds** on leads disp bin **Exercise area** 800yds **Facilities** walks info vet info **On Request** torch **Stables** nearby **Other** charge for damage **Resident Pets:** 1 Toy Poodle, 1 Cockapoo

This country pub with rooms is set in the pretty village of Lower Broadheath on the outskirts of Worcester. The accommodation offers seven comfortable, en suite bedrooms that are well equipped with thoughtful extras. Dining in the open-plan contemporary bar and restaurant is especially popular at weekends for the carvery, however a full menu of enticing options is available at other times. Alfresco dining is available in the summer months.

Rooms 7 en suite (7 GF) **S** £69; **D** £90 **Facilities** FTV tea/coffee Dinner available Direct Dial Cen ht Wi-fi **Parking** 40 **Notes** LB

Oaklands B&B

★★★★ GUEST ACCOMMODATION

Claines WR3 7RS
☎ 01905 458871 📠 01905 759362
e-mail: barbara.gadd@zoom.co.uk
dir: M5 junct 6 onto A449. At rdbt take 1st exit signed Claines. 1st left onto School Bank. Oaklands 1st house on right

PETS: Bedrooms Charges Public areas except breakfast room **Grounds** disp bin **Exercise area** paddock **Exercise area** approx 200yds **Facilities** washing facs cage storage walks info vet info **On Request** fridge access torch towels **Stables Other** charge for damage **Restrictions** no dangerous dogs (see page 7)

A warm welcome is guaranteed at this converted stable, which is well located in a peaceful setting just a short drive from major routes. The property stands in abundant mature gardens, and the well-appointed bedrooms are mostly spacious. There is also a snooker room. Parking is available.

Rooms 4 en suite (2 fmly) **Facilities** tea/coffee Cen ht Wi-fi Snooker **Parking** 7 **Notes** LB Closed Xmas & New Year 🐾

Peachley Leisure Touring Park (SO807576)

▶ ▶ ▶

Peachley Ln, Lower Broadheath WR2 6QX
☎ 01905 641309 📠 01905 641854
e-mail: info@peachleyleisure.com
dir: M5 junct 7, A44 (Worcester ring road) towards Leominster. Exit at sign for Elgar's Birthplace Museum. Pass museum, at x-roads turn right. In 0.75m at T-junct turn left. Park signed on right

PETS: Charges £1.50 dog per night **Public areas** disp bin **Exercise area on site** fields **Exercise area** adjacent **Facilities** food bowl water bowl walks info vet info **Other** disposal bags

Open all year **Last arrival** 21.30hrs **Last departure** noon

The park is set in its own area in the grounds of Peachley Farm. It has all hardstanding and fully-serviced pitches. There is also a fishing lake, and a really excellent quad bike course. The park provides a peaceful haven, and is an excellent base from which to explore the area, which includes the Elgar Museum. 8 acre site. 82 touring pitches. 82 hardstandings. Tent pitches. Motorhome pitches.

Notes No skateboards, no riding of motorbikes or scooters

Marton Grange

★★★★★ GUEST ACCOMMODATION

Flamborough Rd, Marton cum Sewerby YO15 1DU
☎ 01262 602034 & 07891 682687 📠 01262 602034
e-mail: info@marton-grange.co.uk
web: www.marton-grange.co.uk
dir: 2m NE of Bridlington. On B1255, 600yds W of Links golf club

PETS: Bedrooms (3 GF) ground-floor bedrooms only **Charges** £5 per night **Public areas** conservatory only on leads **Grounds** on leads disp bin **Exercise area** own paddock **Facilities** cage storage walks info vet info **On Request** fridge access torch **Other** charge for damage no more than 2 small dogs or 1 medium to large dog per room **Resident Pets:** 1 cat, chickens

This Grade II listed former farmhouse is set in well maintained gardens offering high levels of comfort, service and hospitality. Bedrooms are well appointed with quality fixtures and fittings. Public areas offer wonderful views of the gardens. Thoughtful extras, provided as standard, help create a delightful guest experience.

Rooms 11 en suite (3 GF) **Facilities** FTV tea/coffee Cen ht Lift Licensed Wi-fi Golf 18 **Parking** 11 **Notes** LB RS Dec-Jan Restricted opening for refurbishments

The Tennyson

★★★ GUEST ACCOMMODATION

19 Tennyson Av YO15 2EU

☎ 01262 604382 & 07729 149729

e-mail: dianew2@live.co.uk

web: www.thetennyson-brid.co.uk

dir: *500yds NE of town centre. B1254 (Promenade) from town centre towards Flamborough, Tennyson Ave on left*

PETS: Bedrooms (1 GF) **Charges** £5 per stay **Public areas** except dining room on leads disp bin **Exercise area** 300yds **Facilities** food bowl water bowl bedding feeding mat walks info vet info **On Request** fridge access towels **Resident Pets:** Shandy & Jerry (dogs)

Situated in a quiet side road close to the town centre and attractions, this friendly establishment offers attentive service and comfortable bedrooms. Dinner is also available by prior arrangement.

Rooms 8 rms (7 en suite) (1 pri facs) (2 fmly) (1 GF); **D** £56-£65 **Facilities** FTV tea/coffee Dinner available Cen ht Wi-fi **Notes** LB

Portland

★★★★ 73% HOTEL

Paragon St HU1 3JP

☎ 01482 326462 📄 01482 213460

e-mail: info@portland-hotel.co.uk

web: www.portland-hull.com

dir: *M62 junct 38, A63, to 1st main rdbt. Left at 2nd lights, over x-rds. Right at next junct into Carr Ln, follow one-way system*

PETS: Bedrooms Exercise area 5 mins **Facilities** cage storage vet info **On Request** fridge access torch towels **Restrictions** small & medium size dogs only

A modern hotel situated adjacent to the City Hall providing a good range of accommodation. Most of the public rooms are on the first floor and Wi-fi is available. The Bay Tree Café, at street level, is open during the day and evening. Staff are friendly and helpful and take care of parking cars for their guests.

Rooms 126 (4 fmly) **Facilities** STV FTV Complimentary use of nearby health & fitness centre Xmas New Year Wi-fi **Services** Lift **Notes** LB

Robeanne House

★★★ GUEST ACCOMMODATION

Towthorpe Ln, Shiptonthorpe YO43 3PW

☎ 01430 873312 & 07720 468811 📄 01430 879142

e-mail: enquiries@robeannehouse.co.uk

web: www.robeannehouse.co.uk

dir: *1.5m NW on A614*

PETS: Bedrooms (3 GF) log cabins (ground-floor) only **Sep accom** kennel in stable **Charges** dog £5, horse £15 per night **Public areas** except lounge & dining room **Grounds** on leads disp bin **Exercise area** nearby **Facilities** food (pre-bookable) food bowl water bowl bedding dog chews cat treats feeding mat litter tray scoop/disp bags leads pet sitting dog walking washing facs cage storage walks info vet info **On Request** fridge access torch towels **Stables Other** charge for damage **Resident Pets:** Max (Labrador), Beatty, Josie & Nina (horses), Megan & Dylan (ponies), (Jack, Guinness & Poppy - visiting dogs)

Set back off the A614 in a quiet location, this delightful modern family home was built as a farmhouse. York, the coast, and the Yorkshire Moors and Dales are within easy driving distance. All bedrooms have country views and include a large family room. A charming wooden chalet is available in the garden.

Rooms 2 en suite 6 annexe en suite (2 fmly) (3 GF) **S** £35-£45; **D** £60-£75 **Facilities** FTV TVL tea/coffee Dinner available Cen ht Wi-fi **Parking** 10 **Notes** LB

Hallmark Hotel Hull

★★★★ 71% HOTEL

Ferriby High Rd HU14 3LG

☎ 01482 645212 📄 01482 643332

dir: *M62 onto A63 towards Hull. Follow North Ferriby signs, through village, hotel 0.5m on right*

PETS: Bedrooms (16 GF) **Charges** £15 per stay **Grounds** on leads disp bin **Exercise area** nearby **Facilities** cage storage walks info vet info **On Request** fridge access **Other** charge for damage

This fully refurbished property is situated just outside Hull city centre, with breathtaking views of the Humber Bridge. Service is attentive with a friendly atmosphere. The comfortable bedrooms are tastefully appointed and are suitable for both business and leisure guests. The restaurant and bar serve a good choice of dishes. Conference facilities are available along with free Wi-fi and private parking.

Rooms 95 (3 fmly) (16 GF) **S** £59-£89; **D** £69-£99* **Facilities** STV FTV Xmas New Year Wi-fi **Parking** 150 **Notes** LB

ENGLAND

RUDSTON
Map 8 TA06

Thorpe Hall Caravan & Camping Site
(TA108677)

▶ ▶ ▶

Thorpe Hall YO25 4JE
☎ 01262 420393 & 420574
e-mail: caravansite@thorpehall.co.uk
dir: *5m from Bridlington on B1253 (West)*

PETS: Public areas except games room & toilets disp bin
Exercise area on site dog walk **Facilities** food food bowl water bowl dog chews cat treats walks info **Other** disposal bags available **Restrictions** well behaved dogs only

Open Mar-Oct rs Limited opening hours reception & shop Last arrival 22.00hrs Last departure noon

A delightful, peaceful small park within the walled gardens of Thorpe Hall yet within a few miles of the bustling seaside resort of Bridlington. The site offers a games field, its own coarse fishery, pitch and putt, and a games and TV lounge, and there are numerous walks locally. 4.5 acre site. 90 touring pitches. Tent pitches. Motorhome pitches.

Notes No ball games (field provided).

SPROATLEY
Map 8 TA13

Burton Constable Holiday Park & Arboretum *(TA186357)*

▶ ▶ ▶ ▶

Old Lodges HU11 4LN
☎ 01964 562508   01964 563420
e-mail: info@burtonconstable.co.uk
dir: *Off A165 onto B1238 to Sproatley. Follow signs to site*

PETS: Public areas Exercise area 400mtrs **Facilities** food dog chews walks info vet info **Stables** 3m **Other** disposal bags available

Open Mar-Jan (Mar-Oct tourers/tents) Last arrival 22.00hrs Last departure 14.00hrs

A very attractive parkland site overlooking the fishing lakes, in the grounds of Burton Constable Hall. The toilet facilities are kept very clean, and the Lakeside Club provides a focus for relaxing in the evening. Children will enjoy the extensive adventure playground. 90 acre site. 140 touring pitches. 14 hardstandings. 14 seasonal pitches. Tent pitches. Motorhome pitches. 350 statics.

Notes No skateboards/rollerblades.

WILLERBY
Map 8 TA03

Best Western Willerby Manor Hotel

★★★ 83% ⊛ HOTEL

Well Ln HU10 6ER
☎ 01482 652616   01482 653901
e-mail: willerbymanor@bestwestern.co.uk
web: www.willerbymanor.co.uk
dir: *Off A63, signed Humber Bridge. Right at rdbt by Waitrose. At next rdbt hotel signed*

PETS: Bedrooms (20 GF) ground-floor bedrooms only **Charges** £10 per night **Public areas** outside terrace only **Grounds** on leads **Exercise area** 5 mins **Facilities** feeding mat walks info vet info **On Request** fridge access torch towels **Other** charge for damage

Set in a quiet residential area, amid well-tended gardens, this hotel was originally a private mansion; it has now been thoughtfully extended to provide very comfortable bedrooms, equipped with many useful extras. There are extensive leisure facilities and a wide choice of meals offered in the contemporary Figs Brasserie which has an impressive heated outdoor area.

Rooms 63 (6 fmly) (20 GF) (1 smoking) **S** £65-£98; **D** £106-£126 (incl. bkfst)* **Facilities** STV FTV ⊙ supervised ⚒ Gym Steam room Beauty therapist Aerobic classes New Year Wi-fi **Parking** 300 **Notes** LB Closed 24-26 Dec

WITHERNSEA
Map 8 TA23

 # Withernsea Sands *(TA335289)*
Waxholme Rd HU19 2BS
☎ 0871 664 9803
e-mail: withernsea.sands@park-resorts.com
dir: *M62 junct 38, A63 through Hull. At end of dual carriageway, turn right onto A1033, follow Withernsea signs. Through village, left at mini-rdbt onto B1242. Next right at lighthouse. Site 0.5m on left*

PETS: Charges £1-£3 per night **Public areas** except swimming pool, children's play area & restaurant disp bin **Exercise area on site** dog walking area **Exercise area** 3 mins from site **Facilities** food food bowl water bowl dog chews cat treats litter tray walks info vet info **Other** prior notice required disposal bags available

Open Apr-Oct rs BH & peak wknds sports available Last arrival 22.00hrs Last departure noon

Touring is very much at the heart of this holiday park's operation, with 100 all-electric pitches and additional space for tents. The owners, Park Resorts, are planning to upgrade the facilities and attractions, and the leisure complex with its futuristic design is especially impressive. 115 touring pitches. Tent pitches. Motorhome pitches. 400 statics.

Notes No noise between 23.00hrs & 07.00hrs.

YORKSHIRE, NORTH

ALLERSTON
Map 8 SE88

Vale of Pickering Caravan Park (SE879808)
▶▶▶▶▶

Carr House Farm YO18 7PQ
☎ 01723 859280 📠 01723 850060
e-mail: tony@valeofpickering.co.uk
dir: On B1415, 1.75m off A170 (Pickering-Scarborough road)

PETS: Charges dog 50p per night Public areas on leads disp bin Exercise area on site large dog walk Facilities food leads walks info vet info Other prior notice required disposal bags available

Open 5 Mar-3 Jan rs Mar Last arrival 21.00hrs Last departure 11.30hrs

A well-maintained, spacious family park with excellent facilities including a well-stocked shop and immaculate toilet facilities. Younger children will enjoy the attractive play area, while the large ball sports area will attract older ones. The park is set in open countryside bounded by hedges, has manicured grassland, a woodland walk and stunning seasonal floral displays, and is handy for the North Yorkshire Moors and the attractions of Scarborough. 13 acre site. 120 touring pitches. 100 hardstandings. Tent pitches. Motorhome pitches.

ALNE
Map 8 SE46

Alders Caravan Park (SE497654)
▶▶▶▶

Home Farm YO61 1RY
☎ 01347 838722 📠 01347 838722
e-mail: enquiries@homefarmalne.co.uk
dir: From A19 exit at Alne sign, in 1.5m turn left at T-junct, 0.5m site on left in village centre

PETS: Sep accom 2 kennels Public areas Exercise area on site Facilities walks info vet info Stables 0.5m Other max 2 dogs per pitch disposal bags available Resident Pets: Digby (Labrador), Spot & Jess (Collies), Molly & Kelly (horses)

Open Mar-Oct Last arrival 21.00hrs Last departure 14.00hrs

A tastefully developed park on a working farm with screened pitches laid out in horseshoe-shaped areas. This well designed park offers excellent toilet facilities including a bathroom and fully-serviced washing and toilet cubicles. A woodland area and a water meadow are pleasant places to walk. 12 acre site. 87 touring pitches. 6 hardstandings. 71 seasonal pitches. Tent pitches. Motorhome pitches. 2 wooden pods.

APPLETREEWICK
Map 7 SE06

Knowles Lodge
★★★★★ 🏠 BED AND BREAKFAST
BD23 6DQ
☎ 01756 720228 📠 01756 720381
e-mail: pam@knowleslodge.com
web: www.knowleslodge.com
dir: From Bolton Abbey take B6160, 3.5m, turn right after Barden Tower 1.5m, entrance on left

PETS: Bedrooms (3 GF) Charges £5 per night £30 per week Public areas except dining room Grounds disp bin Exercise area adjacent Facilities water bowl bedding washing facs walks info vet info On Request fridge access torch towels

Located in the heart of Wharfedale and surrounded by 17 acres of meadow and woodland, this delightful Canadian-style ranch has been lovingly restored. The house is attractively furnished, with well appointed bedrooms, and whether guests are there to walk, cycle, fish, or simply relax and enjoy the scenery, they are sure to be given a warm welcome. Delicious breakfasts featuring home-made dishes are served around a large table.

Rooms 4 en suite (1 fmly) (3 GF) S £60-£65; D £100 Facilities TVL tea/coffee Cen ht Wi-fi 🎣 Fishing Parking 6 Notes No Children 8yrs

AUSTWICK
Map 7 SD76

The Traddock
★★★★ ◉◉ 🏠 RESTAURANT WITH ROOMS
LA2 8BY
☎ 015242 51224 📠 015242 51796
e-mail: info@austwicktraddock.co.uk
dir: From Skipton take A65 towards Kendal, 3m after Settle turn right signed Austwick, cross hump back bridge, 100yds on left

PETS: Bedrooms (1 GF) unattended Charges £5 per stay Public areas except restaurants Grounds on leads disp bin Exercise area National Park land adjacent Facilities water bowl scoop/disp bags washing facs walks info vet info On Request fridge access torch towels Other charge for damage

Situated within the Yorkshire Dales National Park and a peaceful village environment, this fine Georgian country house with well-tended gardens offers a haven of calm and good hospitality. There are two comfortable lounges with real fires and fine furnishings, as well as a cosy bar and an elegant dining room serving fine cuisine. Bedrooms are individually styled with many homely touches.

Rooms 12 en suite (2 fmly) (1 GF) S £85-£95; D £95-£185 Facilities FTV tea/coffee Dinner available Direct Dial Cen ht Wi-fi 🎣 Golf 18 Parking 20 Notes LB No coaches

ENGLAND

BEDALE
Map 8 SE28

Castle Arms
★★★★ ⊖ INN

Snape DL8 2TB
☎ 01677 470270   📄 01677 470837
e-mail: castlearms@aol.com
dir: *2m S of Bedale. Off B6268 into Snape*

PETS: Bedrooms (8 GF) Charges £5 per stay Public areas
except restaurant on leads Grounds on leads disp bin
Exercise area 100mtrs Facilities walks info vet info Other
charge for damage

Nestled in the quiet village of Snape, this former coaching inn
is full of character. Bedrooms, in a converted barn, are very
comfortable and carefully furnished. The restaurant and public
bar offer a good selection of fine ales, along with an interesting
selection of freshly-prepared dishes.

Rooms 9 annexe en suite (8 GF) S £60-£65; D £70-£80
Facilities FTV tea/coffee Dinner available Cen ht Wi-fi Parking 15
Notes LB No coaches

BISHOP MONKTON
Map 8 SE36

Church Farm Caravan Park *(SE328660)*
▶▶▶

Knaresborough Rd HG3 3QQ
☎ 01765 676578   & 07861 770164   📄 01765 676578
e-mail: churchfarmcaravan@btinternet.com
dir: *From A61 at x-rds turn E, follow Bishop Monkton sign. 1.25m
to village. At x-rds turn right into Knaresborough Rd, site approx
500mtrs on right*

PETS: Public areas on leads Exercise area adjacent Facilities
washing facs walks info vet info Stables 1m Other prior notice
required Resident Pets: 1 Cocker Spaniel, 1 cat, 3 horses

Open Mar-Oct Last arrival 22.30hrs Last departure 15.30hrs

A very pleasant rural site on a working farm, on the edge of
the attractive village of Bishop Monkton with its well-stocked
shop and pubs. Whilst very much a place to relax, there are
many attractions close by, including Fountains Abbey, Newby
Hall, Ripon and Harrogate. 4 acre site. 45 touring pitches. 3
hardstandings. Tent pitches. Motorhome pitches. 3 statics.

Notes No ball games. 🐾

BOLTON ABBEY
Map 7 SE05

The Devonshire Arms Country House Hotel & Spa
★★★★ ◉◉◉◉ HOTEL

BD23 6AJ
☎ 01756 710441   & 718111   📄 01756 710564
e-mail: res@thedevonshirehotels.co.uk
web: www.thedevonshirearms.co.uk
dir: *On B6160, 250yds N of junct with A59*

PETS: Bedrooms (17 GF) unattended sign Charges £10 per
night Public areas except dining rooms Grounds on leads disp
bin Exercise area nearby Facilities food (pre-bookable) food
bowl water bowl bedding dog chews scoop/disp bags leads
pet sitting dog walking washing facs cage storage walks info
vet info On Request fridge access torch towels Resident Pets:
Dexter & Lila (Cocker Spaniels)

With stunning views of the Wharfedale countryside this beautiful
hotel, owned by the Duke and Duchess of Devonshire, dates back
to the 17th century. Bedrooms are elegantly furnished; those in
the old part of the house are particularly spacious and have four-
posters and fine antiques. The sitting rooms are delightfully cosy
with log fires, and the dedicated staff deliver service with a blend
of friendliness and professionalism. The Burlington Restaurant
offers award-winning, highly accomplished cuisine together with
an impressive wine list, while the Brasserie provides a lighter
alternative.

Rooms 40 (1 fmly) (17 GF) S fr £206; D £248-£457 (incl. bkfst)*
Facilities Spa STV 🦢 supervised ⤳ Fishing 💪 Gym Classic cars
Falconry Laser pigeon shooting Fly fishing Cricket Xmas New Year
Wi-fi Parking 150 Notes LB

BURNSALL
Map 7 SE06

The Devonshire Fell
★★★★ @@ RESTAURANT WITH ROOMS
BD23 6BT
☎ 01756 729000 🖹 01756 729009
e-mail: manager@devonshirefell.co.uk
web: www.devonshirefell.co.uk
dir: On B6160, 6m from Bolton Abbey rdbt, A59 junct

PETS: Bedrooms certain bedrooms only **Grounds** on leads
Facilities food food bowl water bowl bedding dog chews
scoop/disp bags cage storage walks info **On Request** fridge
access torch towels **Other** goody bag available

Located on the edge of the attractive village of Burnsall, this
establishment offers comfortable, well-equipped accommodation
in a relaxing atmosphere. There is an extensive menu featuring
local produce, and meals can be taken either in the bar area or
the more formal restaurant. A function room with views over the
valley is also available.

Rooms 12 en suite (2 fmly) **S** £134-£176; **D** £165-£206 (incl.
dinner) **Facilities** STV FTV tea/coffee Dinner available Direct Dial
Cen ht Wi-fi Fishing **Parking** 30 **Notes** LB

CATTERICK
Map 8 SE29

Rose Cottage
★★★ GUEST ACCOMMODATION
26 High St DL10 7LJ
☎ 01748 811164
dir: Off A1 in village centre, opp village pharmacy

PETS: Bedrooms unattended **Exercise area** 5 mins' walk to
river, 10 mins to racecourse **Facilities** food bowl water bowl
walks info vet info **On Request** torch

Convenient for exploring the Dales and Moors, this well-
maintained guest accommodation lies in the middle of Catterick.
Bedrooms are nicely presented and comfortable. The cosy
public rooms include a cottage-style dining room adorned with
Mrs Archer's paintings, and a lounge. Dinner is available by
arrangement during the summer.

Rooms 3 rms (2 en suite) (1 pri facs) (1 fmly) (3 smoking)
S £30-£36; **D** £48-£54 **Facilities** tea/coffee Dinner available
Cen ht **Parking** 3 **Notes** Closed 24-26 Dec 🐾

FILEY
Map 8 TA18

  ## Flower of May Holiday Park *(TA085835)*
Lebberston Cliff YO11 3NU
☎ 01723 584311 🖹 01723 585716
e-mail: info@flowerofmay.com
dir: Signed off A165 on Scarborough side of Filey

PETS: Charges £1 per night **Public areas** except children's play
area, buildings & super pitches disp bin **Exercise area** clifftop
access to paths & beach (0.5m) **Facilities** food food bowl water
bowl dog chews vet info **Other** prior notice required 1 dog per
pitch disposal bags available

Open Etr-Oct rs Early & late season restricted opening in café,
shop & bars Last arrival dusk Last departure noon

A well-run, high quality family holiday park with top class
facilities. This large landscaped park offers a full range of
recreational activities, with plenty to occupy everyone. Grass and
hard pitches are available, all on level ground, and arranged
in avenues screened by shrubs. 13 acre site. 300 touring
pitches. 250 hardstandings. 100 seasonal pitches. Tent pitches.
Motorhome pitches. 193 statics.

Notes No noise after mdnt.

Reighton Sands Holiday Park
(TA142769)
Reighton Gap YO14 9SH
☎ 01723 890476 🖹 01723 891043
e-mail: jon.cussins@bourne-leisure.co.uk
dir: On A165, 5m S of Filey at Reighton Gap, signed

PETS: Charges £1 (ex assist dogs) per night **Public areas** except
main complex disp bin **Exercise area** 200mtrs **Facilities** food
food bowl water bowl dog chews scoop/disp bags walks info
vet info **Other** prior notice required check when booking which
dates dogs are allowed; max 2 dogs per pitch **Restrictions** no
dangerous dogs (see page 7)

Open mid Mar-Oct rs mid Mar-May & Sep-Oct some facilities may
be reduced Last arrival 22.00hrs Last departure 10.00hrs

A large, lively holiday centre with a wide range of entertainment
and all-weather leisure facilities, located just a 10-minute walk
from a long sandy beach. There are good all-weather pitches
and a large tenting field. The site is particularly geared towards
families with young children. 229 acre site. 83 touring pitches. 83
hardstandings. Tent pitches. Motorhome pitches. 800 statics.

FILEY *continued*

Centenary Way Camping & Caravan Park

(TA115798)

▶ ▶ ▶

Muston Grange YO14 0HU
☎ 01723 516415 & 512313
dir: *Just off A1039 near A165 junct towards Bridlington*

PETS: Public areas except toilet block disp bin **Exercise area on site** fenced dog walk **Exercise area** 5 mins **Facilities** vet info **Other** pet shop in town **Resident Pets:** Fudge (Staffordshire Terrier cross), Clarisa, Jessica & Kevin (cats)

Open Mar-Oct Last arrival 21.00hrs Last departure noon

A well set-out family-owned park, with footpath access to nearby beach. Close to the seaside resort of Filey, and caravan pitches enjoy views over open countryside. 3 acre site. 75 touring pitches. 25 hardstandings. Tent pitches. Motorhome pitches.

Notes No group bookings in peak period, no 9-12 berth tents, no gazebos. 🐾

| HARROGATE | Map 8 SE35 |

Barceló
HOTELS & RESORTS

Barceló Harrogate Majestic Hotel

★★★★ 75% HOTEL

Ripon Rd HG1 2HU
☎ 01423 700300 🖥 01423 502283
e-mail: majestic@barcelo-hotels.co.uk
web: www.barcelo-hotels.co.uk
dir: *M1 onto A1(M) at Wetherby. Take A661 to Harrogate. Hotel in town centre adjacent to Royal Hall*

PETS: Bedrooms sign **Charges** £15 per stay **Grounds** on leads **Facilities** vet info **Other** charge for damage some bedrooms may not be suitable for larger breeds (please check when booking) **Restrictions** no Rottweilers, Dobermans or Pit Bull Terriers

Popular for conferences and functions, this grand Victorian hotel is set in 12 acres of landscaped grounds that is within walking distance of the town centre. It benefits from spacious public areas, and the comfortable bedrooms, including some spacious suites, come in a variety of sizes.

Rooms 174 (8 fmly) **Facilities** Spa STV 🟦 supervised 🏊 Gym Golf practice net Xmas New Year Wi-fi **Services** Lift **Parking** 250

The Kimberley Hotel

★★★★ 74% HOTEL

11-19 Kings Rd HG1 5JY
☎ 01423 505613 & 0800 783 7642 🖥 01423 530276
e-mail: info@thekimberley.co.uk
dir: *A661 Wetherby Road into town centre. Over 1st rdbt onto Skipton Rd. Kings Rd is 4th turn on left at Natwest Bank*

PETS: Bedrooms (18 GF) **Charges** £10 per night **Public areas** except restaurant & bar on leads **Exercise area** 100yds **Facilities** cage storage walks info vet info **On Request** fridge access torch **Other** charge for damage

This independently owned hotel is located close to the centre of the town and only a short walk from the Harrogate International Centre. Bedrooms, all now refurbished, are well equipped for both business and leisure guests and have a thoughtful range of extras including Wi-fi. There is a stylish lounge-bar and a contemporary bistro offering an extensive choice of dishes.

Rooms 93 (21 annexe) (3 fmly) (18 GF) **S** £49-£125; **D** £79-£250*
Facilities STV FTV Xmas New Year Wi-fi **Services** Lift **Parking** 42
Notes LB

The Boar's Head

★★★ 83% ◉◉ HOTEL

Ripley Castle Estate HG3 3AY
☎ 01423 771888 🖥 01423 771509
e-mail: reservations@boarsheadripley.co.uk
dir: *On A61 (Harrogate to Ripon road). Hotel in town centre*

PETS: Bedrooms unattended **Charges** £10 per night **Public areas** except restaurant disp bin **Exercise area** adjacent **Facilities** food bowl water bowl bedding dog chews washing facs walks info vet info **On Request** fridge access torch **Stables**

Part of the Ripley Castle estate, this delightful and popular hotel is renowned for its warm hospitality and as a dining destination. Bedrooms offer many comforts, and the luxurious day rooms feature works of art from the nearby castle. The banqueting suites in the castle are very impressive.

Rooms 25 (6 annexe) (2 fmly) **S** £105-£125; **D** £125-£150 (incl. bkfst)* **Facilities** 🏊 Fishing 🎱 Xmas New Year Wi-fi **Parking** 50
Notes LB

Alexa House

★ ★ ★ GUEST HOUSE

26 Ripon Rd HG1 2JJ

☎ 01423 501988

e-mail: enquiries@alexa-house.co.uk

web: www.alexa-house.co.uk

dir: On A61, 0.25m from junct A59

PETS: Bedrooms (4 GF) sign **Public areas** except main building
Grounds disp bin **Exercise area** 200yds **Facilities** feeding mat
washing facs cage storage walks info vet info **On Request**
fridge access torch **Other** charge for damage

This popular establishment has stylish, well-equipped bedrooms
split between the main house and cottage rooms. All rooms come
with homely extras. The opulent day rooms include an elegant
lounge with honesty bar, and a bright dining room. The hands-on
proprietors ensure high levels of customer care.

Rooms 9 en suite 4 annexe en suite (2 fmly) (4 GF) **S** £47-£62;
D £82-£94 **Facilities** tea/coffee Cen ht Licensed Wi-fi **Parking** 10
Notes Closed 23-26 Dec

Rudding Holiday Park (SE333531)

► ► ► ► ►

Follifoot HG3 1JH

☎ 01423 871350   📄 01423 870859

e-mail: holiday-park@ruddingpark.com

dir: From A1 take A59 to A658 signed Bradford. 4.5m then right,
follow signs

PETS: Charges £2.75 per night **Public areas** except pub,
swimming pool & play areas disp bin **Exercise area on site**
grass areas **Exercise area** public footpaths adjacent **Facilities**
food food bowl water bowl dog chews scoop/disp bags vet info
Stables 1m

Open Mar-Jan rs Nov-Jan shop & Deer House Pub - limited
opening, summer open times only for outdoor swimming pool Last
arrival 23.00hrs Last departure 11.00hrs

A spacious park set in the stunning 200 acres of mature
parkland and walled gardens of Rudding Park. The setting has
been tastefully enhanced with terraced pitches and dry-stone
walls. A separate area houses super pitches where all services
are supplied including a picnic table and TV connection, and
there are excellent toilets. An 18-hole golf course, a 6-hole short
course, driving range, golf academy, heated outdoor swimming
pool, the Deer House Pub, and a children's play area complete the
amenities. 55 acre site. 109 touring pitches. 20 hardstandings.
Tent pitches. Motorhome pitches. 57 statics.

Notes Under 18s must be accompanied by an adult.

High Moor Farm Park (SE242560)

► ► ► ►

Skipton Rd HG3 2LT

☎ 01423 563637 & 564955   📄 01423 529449

e-mail: highmoorfarmpark@btconnect.com

dir: 4m W of Harrogate on A59 towards Skipton

PETS: Public areas except swimming pool, shop, bar &
indoor areas disp bin **Exercise area on site** dog walk area
Facilities food walks info vet info **Other** prior notice required
Restrictions no Pit Bull Terriers

Open Etr or Apr-Oct Last arrival 23.30hrs Last departure 15.00hrs

An excellent site with very good facilities, set beside a small
wood and surrounded by thorn hedges. The numerous touring
pitches are located in meadowland fields, each area with its own
toilet block. A large heated indoor swimming pool, games room,
9-hole golf course, full-sized crown bowling green, and a bar
serving meals and snacks are all popular. Please note that this
park does not accept tents. 15 acre site. 320 touring pitches. 51
hardstandings. 57 seasonal pitches. Motorhome pitches. 158
statics.

Bilton Park (SE317577)

► ► ►

Village Farm, Bilton Ln HG1 4DH

☎ 01423 863121

e-mail: welcome@biltonpark.co.uk

dir: In Harrogate exit A59 (Skipton Rd) at Skipton Inn into Bilton
Lane. Site approx 1m

PETS: Public areas Exercise area on site 8 acres of fields &
walks **Facilities** food food bowl water bowl walks info vet info
Other kennels within 100yds

Open Apr-Oct

An established family-owned park in open countryside yet
only two miles from the shops and tearooms of Harrogate. The
spacious grass pitches are complemented by a well-appointed
toilet block with private facilities. The Nidd Gorge is right on the
doorstep. 4 acre site. 50 touring pitches. Tent pitches. Motorhome
pitches.

Notes 🚭

HAWES | Map 7 SD88

Bainbridge Ings Caravan & Camping Site

(SD879895)

►►

DL8 3NU

☎ 01969 667354

e-mail: janet@bainbridge-ings.co.uk

dir: *Approaching Hawes from Bainbridge on A684, left at Gayle sign, site 300yds on left*

PETS: Public areas disp bin **Exercise area** public footpath accessed from site **Facilities** walks info vet info **Resident Pets:** Gem & Tigger (cats)

Open Apr-Oct Last arrival 22.00hrs Last departure noon

A quiet, well-organised site in open countryside close to Hawes in the heart of Upper Wensleydale, popular with ramblers. Pitches are sited around the perimeter of several fields, each bounded by traditional stone walls. 5 acre site. 70 touring pitches. 8 hardstandings. Tent pitches. Motorhome pitches. 15 statics.

Notes No noise after 23.00hrs. ⊛

HAWNBY | Map 8 SE58

Laskill Grange

★★★★ GUEST ACCOMMODATION

YO62 5NB

☎ 01439 798268

e-mail: laskillgrange@tiscali.co.uk

web: www.laskillgrange.co.uk

dir: *From York A19 to Thirsk, A170 to Helmsley then B1257 N, after 6m sign on left to Laskill Grange*

PETS: Bedrooms (3 GF) sign **Public areas** except dining room & lounge **Grounds** on leads disp bin **Exercise area** adjacent **Facilities** food bowl water bowl feeding mat pet sitting dog walking washing facs cage storage walks info vet info **On Request** fridge access torch towels **Stables Other** charge for damage paddock available for horses **Resident Pets:** Tosh (dog), horses, swans, ducks & 1 peacock

Lovers of the countryside will enjoy this charming 19th-century farmhouse. Guests can take a walk in the surrounds, fish the

River Seph, which runs through the grounds, or visit nearby Rievaulx Abbey. The comfortable, well furnished bedrooms are in the main house and are supplied with many thoughtful extras.

Rooms 3 rms (2 en suite) (1 pri facs) (3 GF) **S** £40-£50; **D** £80-£90 **Facilities** FTV TVL tea/coffee Dinner available Cen ht Licensed Wi-fi Fishing Riding **Parking** 20 **Notes** LB

HELMSLEY | Map 8 SE68

Feversham Arms Hotel & Verbena Spa

★★★★ ◉◉◉ HOTEL

1 High St YO62 5AG

☎ 01439 770766 📠 01439 770346

e-mail: info@fevershamarmshotel.com

web: www.fevershamarmshotel.com

dir: *A168 (signed Thirsk) from A1 then A170 or A64 (signed York) from A1 to York North, then B1363 to Helmsley. Hotel 125mtrs from Market Place*

PETS: Bedrooms (8 GF) unattended sign **Grounds** on leads **Exercise area** 100yds **Facilities** food bowl water bowl washing facs walks info vet info **On Request** fridge access torch towels **Stables** 2m **Other** charge for damage

This long established hotel lies just round the corner from the main square, and under its caring ownership proves to be a refined operation, yet without airs and graces. There are several lounge areas and a high-ceilinged conservatory restaurant where good local ingredients are prepared with skill and minimal fuss. The bedrooms, including four poolside suites, have their own individual character and decor.

Rooms 33 (9 fmly) (8 GF) **S** £193-£473; **D** £240-£520 (incl. bkfst & dinner)* **Facilities** Spa STV FTV ⤶ Sauna Saunarium Spa Xmas New Year Wi-fi **Services** Lift **Parking** 50 **Notes** LB

Black Swan Hotel

★★★ 81% ◉◉ HOTEL

Market Place YO62 5BJ
☎ 01439 770466 📠 01439 770174
e-mail: enquiries@blackswan-helmsley.co.uk
web: www.blackswan-helmsley.co.uk
dir: A1 junct 49, A168, A170 east, hotel 14m from Thirsk

PETS: Bedrooms unattended sign ground-floor bedrooms
only Charges £10 per night Public areas except restaurant
& brasserie Grounds Exercise area 0.5m Facilities food
bowl water bowl bedding dog chews cat treats feeding mat
washing facs dog grooming cage storage walks info vet
info On Request fridge access torch towels Other charge for
damage

People have been visiting this establishment for over 200 years
and it has become a landmark that dominates the market square.
The hotel is renowned for its hospitality and friendliness; many
of the staff are long-serving and dedicated. The bedrooms are
stylish and include a junior suite and feature rooms. Dinner in the
award-winning restaurant is the highlight of any stay. The hotel
has a Tearoom and Patisserie that is open daily.

Rooms 45 (4 fmly) S £92-£157; D £132-£197 (incl. bkfst)*
Facilities STV Xmas New Year Wi-fi Parking 50

Golden Square Touring Caravan Park

(SE604797)

▶▶▶▶▶

Oswaldkirk YO62 5YQ
☎ 01439 788269 📠 01439 788236
e-mail: reception@goldensquarecaravanpark.com
dir: From Thirsk A19 towards York turn left onto Caravan Route to
Helmsley (1m out of Ampleforth village). From York B1363, turn
off B1257 to Ampleforth, 0.5m on right

PETS: Charges £1.50 per night Public areas except playground,
shop & toilets on leads disp bin Exercise area on site field
& wood Facilities walks info vet info Stables 3m Other prior
notice required max 2 dogs per pitch Restrictions no dangerous
dogs (see page 7)

Open Mar-Oct Last arrival 21.00hrs Last departure noon

An excellent, popular and spacious site with very good facilities.
This friendly, immaculately maintained park is set in a quiet rural
situation with lovely views over the North York Moors. Terraced on
three levels and surrounded by mature trees, it caters particularly
for families, with excellent play areas and space for ball games.
Country walks and mountain bike trails start here. 12 acre site.
129 touring pitches. 10 hardstandings. Tent pitches. Motorhome
pitches. 10 statics.

Notes No skateboards or fires. 🐾

Foxholme Caravan Park (SE658828)

▶▶▶

Harome YO62 5JG
☎ 01439 771904
dir: A170 from Helmsley towards Scarborough, right signed
Harome, left at church, through village, follow signs

PETS: Public areas on leads disp bin Exercise area on site dog
walking area (off lead) Facilities washing facs walks info vet
info Other prior notice required

Open Etr-Oct Last arrival 23.00hrs Last departure noon

A quiet park set in secluded wooded countryside, with well-
shaded pitches in individual clearings divided by mature trees.
The facilities are well maintained, and the site is ideal as a
touring base or a place to relax. Please note that caravans
are prohibited on the A170 at Sutton Bank between Thirsk and
Helmsley. 6 acre site. 60 touring pitches. Tent pitches. Motorhome
pitches.

Notes 🐾

HINDERWELL — Map 8 NZ71

Serenity Touring and Camping Park

(NZ792167)

▶▶▶

26A High St TS13 5JH
☎ 01947 841122
e-mail: patandni@aol.com
dir: Off A174 in Hinderwell

PETS: Charges 50p per night Public areas except laundry,
washrooms & toilet areas on leads disp bin Exercise area cliff
walks (0.5m) Facilities walks info vet info Other prior notice
required Resident Pet: D.J. (Black Labrador)

Open Mar-Oct Last arrival 21.00hrs Last departure noon

A charming park mainly for adults, being developed by
enthusiastic owners. It lies behind the village of Hinderwell with
its two pubs and store, and is handy for backpackers on the
Cleveland Way. The sandy Runswick Bay and old fishing port of
Staithes are close by, whilst Whitby is a short drive away. 5.5 acre
site. 20 touring pitches. 3 hardstandings. 10 seasonal pitches.
Tent pitches. Motorhome pitches.

Notes Mainly adult site, no ball games, kites or frisbees. 🐾

ENGLAND

Worsley Arms

★★★ 73% HOTEL

High St YO62 4LA
☎ 01653 628234 📠 01653 628130
e-mail: worsleyarms@aol.co.uk
dir: A64, signed York, towards Malton. At dual carriageway left to Hovingham. At Slingsby left, then 2m

PETS: Bedrooms (4 GF) unattended **Charges** £5 per night
Public areas lounge only **Grounds** disp bin **Exercise area** nearby **Facilities** dog chews walks info vet info **On Request** fridge access torch towels **Stables** 5m

Overlooking the village green, this hotel has relaxing and attractive lounges with welcoming open fires. Bedrooms are also comfortable and several are contained in cottages across the green. The restaurant provides interesting, quality cooking, with less formal dining in the Cricketers' Bar and Bistro to the rear.

Rooms 20 (8 annexe) (2 fmly) (4 GF) **Facilities** FTV ⛳ Shooting Xmas New Year Wi-fi **Parking** 25

The New Inn Motel

★★★ GUEST ACCOMMODATION

Main St YO61 1HQ
☎ 01347 810219 📠 01347 810219
e-mail: enquiries@newinnmotel.freeserve.co.uk
web: www.newinnmotel.co.uk
dir: Off A19 E into village centre, motel on left

PETS: Bedrooms (8 GF) sign **Charges** £5 per night (reduced rate for multiple nights stay) **Public areas** except dining room on leads **Grounds** on leads **Exercise area** 150mtrs **Facilities** leads washing facs cage storage walks info vet info **On Request** fridge access torch towels **Other** charge for damage pets accepted by prior arrangement only **Restrictions** well behaved dogs only

Just nine miles north of York and situated in a quiet location behind the New Inn, this establishment offers modern motel-style accommodation. Comfortable bedrooms are spacious and neatly furnished, and breakfast is served in the cosy dining room. The reception area has an array of tourist information and the resident owners provide a friendly and helpful service.

Rooms 8 en suite (3 fmly) (8 GF) **S** £40-£50; **D** £70-£80 **Facilities** FTV tea/coffee Cen ht **Parking** 8 **Notes** LB Closed mid Nov-mid Dec & part Feb

Gale Green Cottage

★★★★ BED AND BREAKFAST

Westhouse LA6 3NJ
☎ 015242 41245 & 077867 82088
e-mail: jill@galegreen.com
dir: 2m NW of Ingleton. S of A65 at Masongill x-rds

PETS: Bedrooms Public areas except dining room on leads **Grounds** on leads disp bin **Exercise area** adjacent **Facilities** food bowl water bowl bedding feeding mat scoop/disp bags leads washing facs cage storage walks info vet info **On Request** fridge access torch towels **Other** fields & barn available for horses dog agility equipment available (under supervision) **Resident Pets:** Jaffa (Red Border Collie), Beau (Golden Retriever), Soxs (cat), ducks, hens

Peacefully located in a rural hamlet, this 300-year-old house has been lovingly renovated to provide modern facilities without compromising original charm and character. Thoughtfully furnished bedrooms feature smart modern en suite shower rooms and a guest lounge is also available.

Rooms 3 en suite (1 fmly) **S** £35-£39; **D** £58-£64 **Facilities** FTV TVL tea/coffee Cen ht **Parking** 6 **Notes** Closed Xmas & New Year

River House

★★★★ GUEST HOUSE

BD23 4DA
☎ 01729 830315
e-mail: info@riverhousehotel.co.uk
web: www.riverhousehotel.co.uk
dir: Off A65, N to Malham

PETS: Bedrooms (1 GF) **Charges** £5 per stay **Public areas** except lounge bar & restaurant (snug only) **Exercise area** 50yds **Facilities** water bowl leads washing facs cage storage walks info vet info **On Request** fridge access torch towels **Other** charge for damage dogs accepted by prior arrangement only; dogs must not be left unattended if owners leave the house **Resident Pets:** Poppy (Weimaraner), Archie (Jack Russell), Heidi (British Shorthair cat)

A warm welcome awaits guests at this attractive house, which dates from 1664. The bedrooms are bright and comfortable, with one on the ground floor. Public areas include a cosy lounge and a large, well-appointed dining room. Breakfasts and evening meals offer choice and quality above expectation.

Rooms 8 en suite (1 GF) **S** £45-£75; **D** £70-£80 **Facilities** FTV tea/coffee Dinner available Cen ht Licensed Wi-fi Fishing **Parking** 5 **Notes** LB No Children 9yrs

ENGLAND

Beck Hall

★★★ GUEST HOUSE

Cove Rd BD23 4DJ

☎ 01729 830332

e-mail: alice@beckhallmalham.com

web: www.beckhallmalham.com

dir: A65 to Gargrave, turn right to Malham. Beck Hall 100yds on right after mini rdbt

PETS: Bedrooms (4 GF) unattended sign certain bedrooms only **Public areas** with other guests' approval **Grounds** disp bin **Exercise area** adjacent **Facilities** food bowl water bowl pet sitting dog walking washing facs cage storage walks info vet info **On Request** fridge access torch towels

A small stone bridge over Malham Beck leads to this delightful property. Dating from 1710, the house has true character, with bedrooms carefully furnished with four-poster beds. Delicious afternoon teas are available in the colourful garden in warmer months, while roaring log fires welcome the guests in the winter.

Rooms 11 en suite 7 annexe en suite (4 fmly) (4 GF) **S** £25-£65; **D** £50-£90 **Facilities** STV tea/coffee Dinner available Cen ht Licensed Wi-fi Fishing **Parking** 40 **Notes** LB

Hob Green Hotel

★★★ 82% COUNTRY HOUSE HOTEL

HG3 3PJ

☎ 01423 770031   📄 01423 771589

e-mail: info@hobgreen.com

web: www.hobgreen.com

dir: From A61, 4m N of Harrogate, left at Wormald Green, follow hotel signs

PETS: Bedrooms unattended **Charges** on leads **Exercise area** 800 acres of woodland **Facilities** food bowl water bowl walks info vet info **Other** charge for damage pets may only be left in bedrooms when guests are dining

This hospitable country house is set in delightful gardens amidst rolling countryside midway between Harrogate and Ripon. The inviting lounges boast open fires in season and there is an elegant restaurant with a small private dining room. The individually designed bedrooms are very comfortable and come with a host of thoughtful extras.

Rooms 12 (1 fmly) **S** £95-£100; **D** £120-£135 (incl. bkfst) **Facilities** FTV ➷ Xmas New Year Wi-fi **Parking** 40 **Notes** LB

Swinton Park
★★★★ ⑳⑳⑳ HOTEL
HG4 4JH
☎ 01765 680900　📠 01765 680901
e-mail: reservations@swintonpark.com
web: www.swintonpark.com
dir: *A1 onto B6267/8 to Masham. Follow signs through town centre & turn right into Swinton Terrace. 1m past golf course, over bridge, up hill. Hotel on right*

PETS: Bedrooms Charges £25 per night on leads **Grounds** disp bin **Exercise area** nearby **Facilities** food (pre-bookable) food bowl water bowl bedding dog chews feeding mat leads pet sitting dog walking washing facs cage storage walks info vet info **On Request** fridge access torch towels **Stables** 1.5m **Other** charge for damage please phone for further details of pet facilities **Resident Pet:** Myrtle (Golden Labrador)

Although extended during the Victorian and Edwardian eras, the original part of this welcoming castle dates from the 17th century. Bedrooms are luxuriously furnished and come with a host of thoughtful extras. Samuel's restaurant (built by the current owner's great-great-great grandfather) is very elegant and serves imaginative dishes using local produce. The majority of the food is sourced from the 20,000-acre Swinton Estate, as the hotel, winner of several green awards, is committed to keeping the 'food miles' to a minimum. The gardens, including a four-acre walled garden, have been gradually restored. The Deerhouse is the venue for the hotel's alfresco food festivals, summer BBQs and weddings.

Rooms 30 (5 fmly) **D** £180-£375 (incl. bkfst)* **Facilities** Spa FTV ⚘ 9 Putt green Fishing ⚘ Gym Shooting Falconry Pony trekking Cookery school Off-road driving Xmas New Year Wi-fi Child facilities **Services** Lift **Parking** 50 **Notes** LB

The Grey House
★★★★ GUEST ACCOMMODATION
79 Cambridge Rd, Linthorpe TS5 5NL
☎ 01642 817485　📠 01642 817485
e-mail: denistaylor-100@btinternet.com
web: www.greyhousehotel.co.uk
dir: *A19 N onto A1130 & A1032 Acklam Rd, right at lights*

PETS: Bedrooms Charges £5 per night **Public areas** except breakfast room muzzled and on leads **Grounds** on leads **Facilities** vet info **On Request** fridge access towels **Other** charge for damage

This Edwardian mansion stands in mature gardens in a quiet residential area, and is lovingly maintained to provide a relaxing retreat. The master bedrooms are well sized, and the upper rooms, though smaller, also offer good comfort. Downstairs there is an attractive lounge and the breakfast room.

Rooms 9 en suite (1 fmly) **Facilities** FTV TVL tea/coffee Direct Dial Cen ht Wi-fi **Parking** 10

Monk Fryston Hall
★★★ 81% COUNTRY HOUSE HOTEL
LS25 5DU
☎ 01977 682369　📠 01977 683544
e-mail: reception@monkfrystonhallhotel.co.uk
web: www.monkfrystonhallhotel.co.uk
dir: *A1(M) junct 42, A63 towards Selby. Monk Fryston 2m, hotel on left*

PETS: Bedrooms (5 GF) unattended **Charges** £5 per night **Public areas** except restaurant **Grounds Exercise area** **Facilities** cage storage vet info **On Request** fridge access torch towels

This delightful 16th-century mansion house enjoys a peaceful location in 30 acres of grounds, yet is only minutes' drive from the A1. Many original features have been retained and the public rooms are furnished with antique and period pieces. Bedrooms are individually styled and thoughtfully equipped for both business and leisure guests.

Rooms 29 (2 fmly) (5 GF) **S** £65-£79; **D** £115-£135 (incl. bkfst)* **Facilities** STV ⚘ Xmas New Year Wi-fi **Parking** 80 **Notes** LB

Cote Ghyll Caravan & Camping Park
(SE459979)

▶ ▶ ▶ ▶ ▶
DL6 3AH
☎ 01609 883425
e-mail: hills@coteghyll.com
dir: *Exit A19 dual carriageway at A684 (Northallerton junct). Follow signs to Osmotherley. Left in village centre. Site entrance 0.5m on right*

PETS: Public areas on leads disp bin **Exercise area on site** dog walk **Exercise area** surrounding area **Facilities** food food bowl water bowl walks info vet info **Other** dogs must be kept on leads at all times disposal bags available

Open Mar-Oct Last arrival 22.00hrs Last departure noon

A quiet, peaceful site in a pleasant valley on the edge of moors, close to the village. The park is divided into terraces bordered by woodland, and the extra well-appointed amenity block is a welcome addition to this attractive park. Mature trees, shrubs and an abundance of fresh seasonal floral displays create a relaxing and peaceful atmosphere and the whole park is immaculately maintained. Major investment has delivered high standards in landscaping and facilities. There are pubs and shops nearby and holiday statics for hire. 7 acre site. 77 touring pitches. 22 hardstandings. Tent pitches. Motorhome pitches. 18 statics.

Notes Family park

The White Swan Inn

★★★ 80% ◉ HOTEL

Market Place YO18 7AA

☎ 01751 472288 📠 01751 475554

e-mail: welcome@white-swan.co.uk

web: www.white-swan.co.uk

dir: In town, between church & steam railway station

PETS: Bedrooms (8 GF) unattended **Charges** £12.50 per stay **Public areas Grounds** disp bin **Exercise area** 200mtrs **Facilities** food (pre-bookable) food bowl water bowl pet sitting dog walking washing facs cage storage walks info vet info **On Request** fridge access torch towels **Stables** 4m

This 16th-century coaching inn offers well-equipped, comfortable bedrooms, including suites, either of a more traditional style in the main building or modern in the annexe. Service is friendly and attentive. Good food is served in the attractive restaurant, in the cosy bar and the lounge, where a log fire burns in cooler months. A comprehensive wine list focuses on many fine vintages. A private dining room is also available.

Rooms 21 (9 annexe) (3 fmly) (8 GF) **D** £150-£260 (incl. bkfst)* **Facilities** FTV Xmas New Year Wi-fi **Parking** 45 **Notes** LB

Fox & Hounds Country Inn

★★ 82% ◉ HOTEL

Main St, Sinnington YO62 6SQ

☎ 01751 431577 📠 01751 432791

e-mail: fox.houndsinn@btconnect.com

web: www.thefoxandhoundsinn.co.uk

dir: 3m W of Pickering, off A170, between Pickering & Helmsley

PETS: Bedrooms (4 GF) **Charges** £8 per night **Public areas** except restaurant & lounge bar **Grounds Exercise area** 10 mins' walk **Facilities** washing facs walks info vet info **On Request** fridge access **Stables** nearby **Resident Pets:** Bracken (Hungarian Vizsla), Flax & Charlie (Labradors)

This attractive inn lies in the quiet village of Sinnington just off the main road. The smartly maintained, yet traditional public areas are cosy and inviting. The menu offers a good selection of freshly cooked, modern British dishes and is available in the restaurant or informally in the bar. Bedrooms and bathrooms are well equipped and offer a good standard of quality and comfort. Service throughout is friendly and attentive.

Rooms 10 (4 GF) **Facilities** New Year Wi-fi **Parking** 40 **Notes** Closed 25-26 Dec

17 Burgate

★★★★★ 🏠 GUEST ACCOMMODATION

17 Burgate YO18 7AU

☎ 01751 473463

e-mail: info@17burgate.co.uk

dir: From A170 follow sign to Castle. 17 Burgate on right

PETS: Bedrooms studio bedroom only **Charges** £5 per stay **Grounds** on leads disp bin **Exercise area** 200yds **Facilities** walks info vet info **On Request** fridge access towels **Other** charge for damage **Resident Pet:** Koshka (cat)

An elegant market town house close to the centre and the castle, offering comfortable individually designed bedrooms with all modern facilities, including free broadband. Public areas include a comfortable lounge bar, and breakfast includes a wide choice of local, healthy foods.

Rooms 5 en suite **S** £70-£110; **D** £83-£120 **Facilities** FTV tea/coffee Cen ht Licensed Wi-fi **Parking** 7 **Notes** LB No Children 10yrs Closed Xmas

Raven Hall Country House

★★★ 78% HOTEL

YO13 0ET

☎ 01723 870353 📠 01723 870072

e-mail: enquiries@ravenhall.co.uk

web: www.ravenhall.co.uk

dir: A171 towards Whitby. At Cloughton turn right onto unclassified road to Ravenscar

PETS: Bedrooms (5 GF) **Charges** contact for details **Public areas** except lounge, bar & restaurant on leads **Grounds** on leads disp bin **Exercise area** 50yds **Facilities** food (pre-bookable) food bowl water bowl bedding dog chews feeding mat scoop/disp bags leads washing facs cage storage walks info vet info **On Request** fridge access torch towels **Stables** 3m **Other** charge for damage

This impressive cliff top mansion enjoys breathtaking views over Robin Hood's Bay. Extensive well-kept grounds include tennis courts, putting green, swimming pools and historic battlements. The bedrooms vary in size but all are comfortably equipped, many offer panoramic views. There are also eight environmentally-friendly Finnish lodges that have been furnished to a high standard.

Rooms 60 (8 annexe) (20 fmly) (5 GF) **S** £24-£51; **D** £48-£102 (incl. bkfst)* **Facilities** 🕲 ♨ 9 🏌 Putt green 🎳 Bowls Table tennis Xmas New Year Wi-fi **Services** Lift **Parking** 200 **Notes** LB

RICCALL — Map 8 SE63

The Park View

★★★★ GUEST ACCOMMODATION

20 Main St YO19 6PX
☎ 01757 248458 🗎 01757 249211
e-mail: mail@parkviewriccall.co.uk
web: www.parkviewriccall.co.uk
dir: *A19 from Selby, left for Riccall by water tower, house 100yds on right*

PETS: Bedrooms Public areas except dining room & bar **Grounds** disp bin **Exercise area** 150yds **Facilities** leads walks info vet info **On Request** fridge access **Other** charge for damage **Resident Pets:** Merty & Elki (Mini Schnauzers), Dougie (Lhasa Apso)

The well-furnished and comfortable Park View stands in grounds and offers well-equipped bedrooms. There is a cosy lounge plus a small bar, while breakfasts are served in the dining room. Dinner is available midweek.

Rooms 7 en suite (1 fmly) **S** fr £52; **D** fr £74 **Facilities** FTV TVL tea/coffee Dinner available Cen ht Licensed Wi-fi **Parking** 10

RICHMOND — Map 7 NZ10

Brompton Caravan Park *(NZ199002)*

►►►►

Brompton-on-Swale DL10 7EZ
☎ 01748 824629 🗎 01748 826383
e-mail: brompton.caravanpark@btinternet.com
dir: *Exit A1 signed Catterick. Take B6271 to Brompton-on-Swale, site 1m on left*

PETS: Charges £1 per night **Public areas** on leads disp bin **Exercise area on site** field **Facilities** food scoop/disp bags dog grooming walks info vet info **Stables** 100mtrs **Other** prior notice required pet shop adjacent **Resident Pets:** Deefur & Barkley (Bassett Hounds), Marley & Penny (Staffordshire Terriers), Cleo (Greyhound), Marmie (cat)

Open mid Mar-Oct Last arrival 21.00hrs Last departure noon

An attractive and well-managed family park where pitches have an open outlook across the River Swale. There is a good children's playground, an excellent family recreation room, a takeaway food service, and fishing is available on the river. Holiday apartments are also available. 14 acre site. 177 touring pitches. 2 hardstandings. Tent pitches. Motorhome pitches. 22 statics.

Notes No gazebos, no motor or electric cars or scooters, no open fires or wood burners, quiet at midnight.

Swale View Caravan Park *(NZ134013)*

►►►

Reeth Rd DL10 4SF
☎ 01748 823106 & 07736 820283 🗎 01748 823123
e-mail: swaleview@teesdaleonline.co.uk
dir: *3m W of Richmond on A6108 (Reeth to Leyburn road)*

PETS: Charges £1 per night **Public areas** disp bin **Exercise area on site** large field **Facilities** washing facs cage storage walks info **Stables** nearby **Other** prior notice required 1 dog per pitch **Restrictions** no dangerous dogs (see page 7)

Open Mar-15 Jan Last arrival 21.00hrs Last departure noon

Shaded by trees and overlooking the River Swale is this attractive, mainly grassy site, which has a number of attractive holiday homes and seasonal tourers. The facilities continue to be improved by enthusiastic owners and the park offers facilities for 30 tourers, all with electric and hardstandings. It is a short distance from Richmond, and well situated for exploring Swaledale and Wensleydale. 13 acre site. 30 touring pitches. 30 hardstandings. 15 seasonal pitches. Tent pitches. Motorhome pitches. 100 statics.

RIPON — Map 8 SE37

The Ripon Spa Hotel

★★★ 81% HOTEL

Park St HG4 2BU
☎ 01765 602172 🗎 01765 690770
e-mail: sales@spahotelripon.co.uk
web: www.riponspa.com
dir: *From A61 to Ripon, follow Fountains Abbey signs. Hotel on left after hospital. Or from A1(M) junct 48, B6265 to Ripon, straight on at 2 rdbts. Right at lights towards city centre. Left at hill top. Left at Give Way sign. Hotel on left*

PETS: Bedrooms (4 GF) unattended **Public areas** except food areas on leads **Grounds** on leads disp bin **Exercise area** adjacent **Facilities** food bowl water bowl dog chews cat treats feeding mat litter tray scoop/disp bags leads washing facs cage storage walks info vet info **On Request** fridge access torch towels **Resident Pet:** Finlay (Black Labrador)

This privately owned hotel is set in extensive and attractive gardens just a short walk from the city centre. The bedrooms

are well equipped to meet the needs of leisure and business travellers alike, while the comfortable lounges are complemented by the convivial atmosphere of the Turf Bar.

Rooms 40 (5 fmly) (4 GF) **S** £75-£134; **D** £84-£155 (incl. bkfst) **Facilities** FTV ⬥ Xmas New Year Wi-fi **Services** Lift **Parking** 60 **Notes** LB

The George at Wath
★★★★ INN
Main St, Wath HG4 5EN
☎ 01765 641324
e-mail: richard@thegeorgeatwath.co.uk
web: www.thegeorgeatwath.co.uk
dir: From A1 (dual carriageway) N'bound turn left signed Melmerby & Wath. From A1 S'bound exit at slip road signed A61. At T-junct right (signed Ripon). Approx 0.5m turn right for Melmerby & Wath

PETS: Bedrooms Charges £10 per stay **Public areas** except restaurant on leads **Grounds** disp bin **Exercise area** 100mtrs **Facilities** washing facs cage storage walks info vet info **On Request** fridge access **Other** charge for damage **Resident Pet:** Bailey (dog)

Located in the centre of the beautiful North Yorkshire village of Wath, this popular village inn provides well-equipped and pleasantly decorated accommodation. The public areas include a spacious lounge bar complete with log burning stove, and a relaxed dining area where a varied selection of dishes is available. Wi-fi connection available throughout.

Rooms 5 en suite (1 fmly) **S** £60-£65; **D** £75-£120 **Facilities** FTV tea/coffee Dinner available Cen ht Wi-fi Pool table **Parking** 25

Hunley Hotel & Golf Club
★★★ 75% HOTEL
Ings Ln, Brotton TS12 2QQ
☎ 01287 676216   📠 01287 678250
e-mail: enquiries@hunleyhotel.co.uk
dir: From A174 bypass left at rdbt with monument, left at T-junct, pass church, turn right. 50yds right, through housing estate, hotel approx 0.5m

PETS: Bedrooms (17 GF) unattended Classic bedrooms only **Charges** £10 per night **Grounds Exercise area** 5m **Facilities** walks info vet info **On Request** fridge access torch towels **Other** charge for damage

Spectacularly situated, this hotel overlooks the 27-hole golf course and beyond to the coastline. The members' bar is licensed and serves snacks all day, and the restaurant offers a wide choice of interesting dishes. The bedrooms are very comfortably equipped and some are particularly spacious.

Rooms 27 (2 fmly) (17 GF) **S** £66-£86; **D** £77-£102* **Facilities** STV FTV ⌁ 27 Putt green Driving range Xmas New Year Wi-fi **Parking** 100 **Notes** LB

Best Western Ox Pasture Hall Country Hotel
★★★★ 75% ◉◉ COUNTRY HOUSE HOTEL
Lady Edith's Dr, Raincliffe Woods YO12 5TD
☎ 01723 365295   📠 01723 355156
e-mail: oxpasture.hall@btconnect.com
web: www.oxpasturehall.com
dir: A171, left onto Lady Edith's Drive, 1.5m, hotel on right

PETS: Bedrooms (14 GF) **Charges** £10 per night **Public areas** except restaurant; allowed in brasserie area **Grounds** disp bin **Exercise area** nearby **Facilities** vet info **Other** charge for damage

This charming country hotel is set in the North Riding Forest Park and has a very friendly atmosphere. Bedrooms (split between the main house, townhouse and the delightful courtyard) are stylish, comfortable and well equipped. Public areas include a split-level bar, quiet lounge and an attractive restaurant. There is also an extensive banqueting area licensed for civil weddings.

Rooms 21 (1 fmly) (14 GF) **S** £79-£129; **D** £89-£199 (incl. bkfst) **Facilities** FTV Xmas New Year Wi-fi **Parking** 100 **Notes** LB

Delmont
★★ 65% HOTEL
18/19 Blenheim Ter YO12 7HE
☎ 01723 364500   📠 01723 363554
e-mail: enquiries@delmonthotel.co.uk
dir: Follow signs to North Bay. At seafront to top of cliff. Hotel near castle

PETS: Bedrooms (5 GF) unattended **Charges Public areas** except restaurant on leads **Grounds** on leads disp bin **Exercise area** adjacent **Facilities** vet info **On Request** fridge access **Other** charge for damage

Popular with groups, a friendly welcome is found at this hotel on the North Bay. Bedrooms are comfortable, and many have sea views. There are two lounges, a bar and a spacious dining room in which good-value, traditional food is served along with entertainment on most evenings.

Rooms 51 (18 fmly) (5 GF) **S** £20-£43; **D** £40-£86 (incl. bkfst)* **Facilities** FTV Games Room Pool table ♫ Xmas New Year **Services** Lift **Parking** 2 **Notes** LB

SCARBOROUGH *continued*

Warwick House

★★ GUEST ACCOMMODATION

70 Westborough YO11 1TS
☎ 01723 374343 📠 01723 374343
e-mail: warwick-house@talktalk.net
dir: *On outskirts of town centre, just before railway station on left*

PETS: Bedrooms Charges £4 per night **Facilities** vet info
Restrictions small dogs only **Resident Pets:** Buddy & Holly (cats)

Close to the Stephen Joseph Theatre, station and shops, this
friendly guest accommodation has some en suite and some
shared facility rooms. Hearty breakfasts are served in the
pleasant basement dining room. Private parking is available.

Rooms 6 rms (2 en suite) (4 fmly) **S** £18.50-£24.50; **D** £37-£49
Facilities FTV tea/coffee Cen ht Wi-fi **Parking** 5 **Notes** LB 😊

Jacobs Mount Caravan Park *(TA021868)*

►►►►►

Jacobs Mount, Stepney Rd YO12 5NL
☎ 01723 361178 📠 01723 361178
e-mail: jacobsmount@yahoo.co.uk
dir: *Direct access from A170*

PETS: Charges £2.50 per night £17.50 per week **Public areas**
except toilet block & public house disp bin **Exercise area on site**
woods & field walks **Facilities** food food bowl water bowl dog
chews cat treats scoop/disp bags washing facs walks info vet
info **Stables** 1.5m **Resident Pets:** 2 Dobermans (working dogs)

Open Mar-Nov rs Mar-May & Oct limited hours at shop/bar Last
arrival 22.00hrs Last departure noon

An elevated family-run park surrounded by woodland and open
countryside, yet only two miles from the beach. Touring pitches
are terraced gravel stands with individual services. The Jacobs
Tavern serves a wide range of appetising meals and snacks, and
there is a separate well-equipped games room for teenagers. 18
acre site. 156 touring pitches. 131 hardstandings. Tent pitches.
Motorhome pitches. 60 statics.

Killerby Old Hall *(TA063829)*

►►►

Killerby YO11 3TW
☎ 01723 583799 📠 01723 581608
e-mail: killerbyhall@btconnect.com
dir: *Direct access via B1261 at Killerby, near Cayton*

PETS: Charges £1 per night **Public areas** except cottage
areas on leads disp bin **Exercise area on site** adjacent field
Facilities walks info vet info **Other** pets allowed on caravan site
area only

Open 14 Feb-4 Jan Last arrival 20.00hrs Last departure noon

A small secluded park, well sheltered by mature trees and
shrubs, located at the rear of the old hall. Use of the small
indoor swimming pool is shared by visitors to the hall's holiday
accommodation. There is a children's play area. 2 acre site. 20
touring pitches. 20 hardstandings. Motorhome pitches.

Scotch Corner Caravan Park *(NZ210054)*

►►►

DL10 6NS
☎ 01748 822530 📠 01748 822530
e-mail: marshallleisure@aol.com
dir: *From Scotch Corner junct of A1 & A66 take A6108 towards
Richmond. 250mtrs, cross central reservation, return 200mtrs to
site entrance*

PETS: Charges £2 per night **Public areas** except toilets,
wash-up area, children's play area & reception area disp bin
Exercise area on site 3-acre dog walk **Facilities** vet info **Other**
prior notice required disposal bags available **Resident Pet:** 1
Labrador

Open Etr-Oct Last arrival 22.30hrs Last departure noon

A well-maintained site with good facilities, ideally situated as a
stopover, and an equally good location for touring. The Vintage
Hotel, which serves food, can be accessed from the rear of the
site. 7 acre site. 96 touring pitches. 4 hardstandings. Tent
pitches. Motorhome pitches.

Notes 😊

The Ranch Caravan Park *(SE664337)*

►►►

Cliffe Common YO8 6EF
☎ 01757 638984 📠 01757 630089
e-mail: contact@theranchcaravanpark.co.uk
dir: *Exit A63 at Cliffe signed Skipwith. Site 1m N on left*

PETS: Public areas except toilet block & bar disp bin
Exercise area surrounding countryside, public footpaths
Facilities walks info vet info **Other** disposal bags available
Resident Pets: Molly, Frieda, K.C & Lottie (Scottish Terriers)

Open 5 Feb-5 Jan Last arrival 20.00hrs Last departure noon

A compact, sheltered park in open countryside offering excellent
amenities. The enthusiastic and welcoming family owners have
created a country club feel, with a tasteful bar serving food
at weekends. There are timber lodge holiday homes for sale. 7
acre site. 50 touring pitches. 50 hardstandings. Tent pitches.
Motorhome pitches.

Notes No ball games, no campfires, no hanging of washing from
trees.

SETTLE
Map 7 SD86

The Lion at Settle
★★★★ INN

Duke St BD24 9DU
☎ 01729 822203
e-mail: relax@thelionsettle.co.uk
dir: In town centre opp Barclays Bank

PETS: Bedrooms unattended 2 hard floor rooms only Charges £25 per stay Public areas except restaurant Grounds on leads disp bin Exercise area 5 mins Facilities water bowl bedding walks info vet info On Request fridge access torch towels Other charge for damage

Located in the heart of the market town of Settle, this is a traditional coaching inn with an inglenook fireplace. The accommodation is comfortable and well equipped. A wide selection of imaginative dishes together with real ales and fine wines is served in the busy bar, and also the restaurant where the atmosphere is relaxed and comfortable; alfresco dining is possible in the courtyard.

Rooms 14 en suite (2 fmly) S £65-£100; D £90-£120
Facilities FTV tea/coffee Dinner available Cen ht Wi-fi Notes LB

SKIPTON
Map 7 SD95

The Coniston
★★★★ 77% HOTEL

Coniston Cold BD23 4EA
☎ 01756 748080 ▤ 01756 749487
e-mail: info@theconistonhotel.com
dir: On A65, 6m NW of Skipton

PETS: Bedrooms (25 GF) certain bedrooms only Charges £10 per night Public areas except restaurant areas on leads Grounds on leads disp bin Exercise area surrounding area Facilities food (pre-bookable) food bowl water bowl cage storage walks info vet info On Request fridge access torch towels Stables 2m Other charge for damage paddock available for horses

This privately owned hotel set in 1,500 acres of prime country estate is a haven for guests staying or just visiting the hotel. All bedrooms and bathrooms are appointed to a very high standard; the bedroom wing offers large rooms with balconies. The reception, bar and restaurant have style and elegance, and the stunning spa adds to the impressive list of activities for guests.

Rooms 50 (13 fmly) (25 GF) Facilities STV Fishing Clay pigeon shooting Falconry Off-road Land Rover driving Archery Target golf Xmas New Year Wi-fi Parking 120 Notes LB

SLINGSBY
Map 8 SE67

Robin Hood Caravan & Camping Park
(SE701748)

▶▶▶▶

Green Dyke Ln YO62 4AP
☎ 01653 628391 ▤ 01653 628392
e-mail: info@robinhoodcaravanpark.co.uk
dir: Access from B1257 (Malton to Helmsley road)

PETS: Public areas except children's play area disp bin Exercise area on site Facilities food leads walks info vet info Other prior notice required disposal bags available Resident Pets: Oscar & Felix (cats)

Open Mar-Oct Last arrival 18.00hrs Last departure noon

A pleasant, well-maintained grassy park, in a good position for touring North Yorkshire. Situated on the edge of the village of Slingsby, the park has hardstandings and electricity for every pitch. 2 acre site. 32 touring pitches. 22 hardstandings. Tent pitches. Motorhome pitches. 35 statics.

Notes No noise after 23.00hrs.

STILLINGFLEET
Map 8 SE54

Home Farm Caravan & Camping (SE595427)
▶▶▶

Moreby YO19 6HN
☎ 01904 728263 ▤ 01904 720059
e-mail: home_farm@hotmail.co.uk
dir: 6m from York on B1222, 1.5m N of Stillingfleet

PETS: Public areas on leads disp bin Exercise area on site fields & woodland Facilities washing facs walks info vet info Other prior notice required Resident Pets: cats

Open Feb-Dec Last arrival 22.00hrs

A traditional meadowland site on a working farm bordered by parkland on one side and the River Ouse on another. Facilities are in converted farm buildings, and the family owners extend a friendly welcome to tourers. An excellent site for relaxing and unwinding in, yet only a short distance from the attractions of York. There are four log cabins for holiday hire. 5 acre site. 25 touring pitches. Tent pitches. Motorhome pitches.

Notes ⓔ

SUTTON-ON-THE-FOREST	Map 8 SE56

Goosewood Caravan Park *(SE595636)*

▶▶▶▶▶

YO61 1ET

☎ 01347 810829 📠 01347 811498

e-mail: enquiries@goosewood.co.uk

dir: *From A1237 take B1363. After 5m turn right. Take right turn after 0.5m & site on right*

PETS: Charges dog £1 per night **Public areas** except children's play areas disp bin **Exercise area on site Facilities** food food bowl water bowl vet info **Other** prior notice required disposal bags available

Open Mar-2 Jan Last arrival dusk Last departure noon

A relaxing and immaculately maintained park with its own lake and seasonal fishing, set in attractive woodland just six miles north of York. Mature shrubs and stunning seasonal floral displays at the entrance create an excellent first impression and the well located toilet facilities are kept spotlessly clean. The generous patio pitches are randomly spaced throughout the site, providing optimum privacy, and there's a good adventure play area for younger children, with a recreation barn for teenagers, plus a health spa. 20 acre site. 100 touring pitches. 75 hardstandings. Motorhome pitches. 35 statics.

Notes No noise after mdnt.

THIRSK	Map 8 SE48

Sowerby Caravan Park *(SE437801)*

▶▶▶

Sowerby YO7 3AG

☎ 01845 522753 📠 01845 574520

e-mail: sowerbycaravans@btconnect.com

dir: *From A19 approx 3m S of Thirsk, turn W for Sowerby. Turn right at junct. Site 1m on left*

PETS: Public areas except children's play area **Exercise area** field adjacent **Facilities** food

Open Mar-Oct Last arrival 22.00hrs

A grassy site beside a tree-lined river bank, with basic but functional toilet facilities. Tourers enjoy a separate grassed area with an open outlook, away from the statics. 1 acre site. 25 touring pitches. 5 hardstandings. Motorhome pitches. 85 statics.

Notes 🐾

Thirkleby Hall Caravan Park *(SE472794)*

▶▶▶

Thirkleby YO7 3AR

☎ 01845 501360 & 07799 641815

e-mail: greenwood.parks@virgin.net

dir: *3m S of Thirsk on A19. Turn E through arched gatehouse into site*

PETS: Public areas on leads disp bin **Exercise area on site** adjacent wood & field **Other** dogs must be under strict control at all times

Open Mar-Oct Last arrival 20.00hrs Last departure 14.30hrs

A long-established site in the grounds of the old hall, with statics in wooded areas around a fishing lake and tourers based on slightly sloping grassy pitches. The site has a quality amenities block and laundry. This well-screened park has superb views of the Hambledon Hills. 53 acre site. 50 touring pitches. 3 hardstandings. 20 seasonal pitches. Tent pitches. Motorhome pitches. 185 statics.

Notes No noise after 23.00hrs. 🐾

THORNTON WATLASS	Map 8 SE28

Buck Inn

★★★ INN

HG4 4AH

☎ 01677 422461 📠 01677 422447

e-mail: innwatlass1@btconnect.com

web: www.thebuckinn.net

dir: *From A1 at Leeming Bar take A684 towards Bedale, B6268 towards Masham 2m, turn right at x-rds to Thornton Watlass*

PETS: Bedrooms (1 GF) unattended **Charges** dog £5 per night **Public areas** in residents' lounge only **Grounds** disp bin **Exercise area** 300yds **Facilities** water bowl cage storage walks info vet info **On Request** fridge access torch towels

This traditional country inn is situated on the edge of the village green overlooking the cricket pitch. Cricket prints and old photographs are found throughout, and an open fire in the bar adds to the warm and intimate atmosphere. Wholesome lunches and dinners, from an extensive menu, are served in the bar and dining room. Bedrooms are brightly decorated and well equipped.

Rooms 7 rms (5 en suite) (1 fmly) (1 GF) **Facilities** TVL tea/coffee Dinner available Cen ht Wi-fi Fishing Pool table **Parking** 10 **Notes** RS 24-25 Dec No accommodation, no food 25 Dec

York Touring Caravan Site *(SE648584)*

 ▶▶▶▶

Greystones Farm, Towthorpe Moor Ln YO32 9ST
☎ 01904 499275   🖹 01904 499271
e-mail: info@yorkcaravansite.co.uk
dir: *Exit A64 at turn for Strensall/Haxby, site 1.5m on left*

PETS: Public areas except shower & toilet block   disp bin
Exercise area separate dog walking area on adjoining site
Facilities walks info   vet info   **Other** dogs must be kept on leads
at all times

Open all year Last arrival 21.00hrs Last departure noon

This purpose-built golf complex and caravan park is situated just
over five miles from York. There is a 9-hole golf course, driving
range and golf shop with a coffee bar/café. The generous sized,
level pitches are set within well-manicured grassland with a
backdrop of trees and shrubs. 6 acre site. 44 touring pitches. 12
hardstandings. Tent pitches. Motorhome pitches.

Wolds Way Caravan and Camping (SE896743)

▶▶▶▶

West Farm YO17 8JE
☎ 01944 728463 & 728180
e-mail: knapton.wold.farms@farming.co.uk
dir: *Signed between Rillington & West Heslerton on A64 (Malton
to Scarborough road). Site 1.5m*

PETS: Sep accom kennel & run   **Public areas** disp bin
Exercise area on site   walks on 200-acre farm   **Facilities**
food   food bowl   water bowl   dog chews   cat treats   scoop/disp
bags   leads   washing facs   walks info   vet info   **Stables Other**
max 2 dogs per pitch; more than 2 dogs by arrangement only
Restrictions no Rottweilers

Open Mar-Oct Last arrival 22.30hrs Last departure 19.00hrs

A park on a working farm in a peaceful, high position on the
Yorkshire Wolds, with magnificent views over the Vale of
Pickering. This is an excellent walking area, with the Wolds Way
passing the entrance to the park. A pleasant one and a half mile
path leads to a lavender farm, with its first-class coffee shop.
7.5 acre site. 70 touring pitches. 5 hardstandings. Tent pitches.
Motorhome pitches.

The Wensleydale Heifer

★★★★ ◉◉ RESTAURANT WITH ROOMS

Main St DL8 4LS
☎ 01969 622322
web: www.wensleydaleheifer.co.uk
dir: *A1 to Leeming Bar junct, A684 towards Bedale for approx
10m to Leyburn, then towards Hawes 3.5m to West Witton*

PETS: Bedrooms (2 GF)   unattended   superior bedrooms only
Charges £10 per night   **Public areas** except bar & lounge   on
leads   **Grounds** disp bin   **Exercise area** adjacent   **Facilities** food
bowl   water bowl   bedding   dog chews   walks info   **On Request**
fridge access   towels

Describing itself as 'boutique style', this 17th-century former
coaching inn is very much in the 21st century. The bedrooms, with
Egyptian cotton linen and Molton Brown toiletries as standard,
are each designed with a unique and interesting theme - for
example, Black Sheep, Night at the Movies, True Romantics and
Shooters, and for chocolate lovers there's a bedroom where they
can eat as much chocolate as they like! The food is very much
the focus here in both the informal fish bar and the contemporary
style restaurant. The kitchen prides itself on sourcing the freshest
fish and locally reared meats. The Wensleydale Heifer is the AA's
Funkiest B&B of the Year (2011-2012).

Rooms 9 en suite 4 annexe en suite (2 GF) **S** £100-£140;
D £120-£190 **Facilities** FTV tea/coffee Dinner available Direct
Dial Cen ht Wi-fi **Parking** 20 **Notes** LB

Cliffemount

★★★ 80% ◉◉ SMALL HOTEL

Bank Top Ln, Runswick Bay TS13 5HU
☎ 01947 840103   🖹 01947 841025
e-mail: info@cliffemounthotel.co.uk
dir: *Exit A174, 8m N of Whitby, 1m to end*

PETS: Bedrooms (5 GF)   **Charges** £7.50 per night   **Public areas**
bar only & not during food service   on leads   **Grounds** on leads
disp bin   **Exercise area** adjacent   **Facilities** walks info   vet info
On Request towels   **Other** charge for damage   **Restrictions** no
breed larger than a Spaniel **Resident Pet:** Rosie (Bedlington)

Overlooking Runswick Bay this property offers a relaxed and
romantic atmosphere with open fires and individual, carefully
designed bedrooms; some have a private balcony overlooking the
bay. Dining is recommended; the food is modern British in style
and uses locally sourced fresh seafood, and game from nearby
estates.

Rooms 20 (4 fmly) (5 GF) **S** £80-£180; **D** £115-£180 (incl. bkfst)*
Facilities FTV Xmas New Year Wi-fi **Parking** 25 **Notes** LB

ENGLAND

WHITBY *continued*

Chiltern Guest House

★★★★ GUEST HOUSE

13 Normanby Ter, West Cliff YO21 3ES
☎ 01947 604981
e-mail: Jjchiltern@aol.com
dir: *Telephone for detailed directions*

PETS: Bedrooms sign **Charges Public areas Grounds** on leads
disp bin **Exercise area** 300mtrs **Facilities** leads walks info vet
info **On Request** torch **Other** charge for damage **Restrictions**
no very large dogs

This Victorian terrace house offers a warm welcome and
comfortable accommodation within walking distance of the town
centre and seafront. Public areas include a smartly decorated
lounge and a bright, attractive dining room. Bedrooms are
thoughtfully equipped and many have modern en suites.

Rooms 9 en suite (2 fmly) **S** fr £30; **D** £60-£70 **Facilities** TVL tea/
coffee Cen ht Wi-fi Golf 18

Arundel House

★★★ GUEST ACCOMMODATION

Bagdale YO21 1QJ
☎ 01947 603645 🖷 08703 121974
e-mail: arundel_house@hotmail.com
dir: *A171 town centre, onto Arundel Pl at bottom of hill*

PETS: Bedrooms (2 GF) **Charges** £5 per night £35 per week
Exercise area 500mtrs **Facilities** cage storage walks info vet
info

In a prime location within walking distance of all the attractions,
Arundel House's bedrooms are simply furnished and offer good
value for money. Expect a helping of true Yorkshire hospitality,
and look out for the unique collection of walking canes on show
in the house.

Rooms 12 en suite (2 fmly) (2 GF) **S** £40-£45; **D** £60-£90
Facilities tea/coffee Cen ht Wi-fi **Parking** 6 **Notes** LB

Ladycross Plantation Caravan Park

(NZ821080)

▶ ▶ ▶ ▶

Egton YO21 1UA
☎ 01947 895502
e-mail: enquiries@ladycrossplantation.co.uk
dir: *On unclassified road (signed) off A171 (Whitby-Teesside road)*

PETS: Charges 1st dog free; additional dog £1 per night
Public areas except reception & shop (ex assist dogs) disp bin
Exercise area on site heath & woodland **Facilities** walks info
vet info **Other** prior notice required

Open Mar-Oct Last arrival 20.30hrs Last departure noon

A unique forest setting creates an away-from-it-all feeling at this
peaceful touring park, which has enthusiastic owners. Pitches
are sited in small groups in clearings around an amenities block,
while an additional toilet block offers excellent facilities. Children
will enjoy exploring the woodland around the site. The site is well
placed for visiting Whitby and exploring the Moors. 30 acre site.
130 touring pitches. 18 hardstandings. 60 seasonal pitches. Tent
pitches. Motorhome pitches.

YORK   **Map 8 SE65**

Hotel du Vin York

★★★★ 81% ⊛ HOTEL

89 The Mount YO24 1AX
☎ 01904 557350 🖷 01904 557351
e-mail: info.york@hotelduvin.com
web: www.hotelduvin.com
dir: *A1036 towards city centre, 6m. Hotel on right through lights.*

PETS: Bedrooms (14 GF) unattended **Charges** £10 per night
Public areas except restaurant on leads **Grounds** on leads
disp bin **Exercise area** 500mtrs **Facilities** food bowl water
bowl bedding washing facs cage storage walks info vet info
On Request torch towels

This Hotel du Vin offers luxury and quality that will cosset even
the most discerning guest. Bedrooms are decadent in design and
the bathrooms have huge monsoon showers and feature baths.
Dinner in the bistro provides a memorable highlight thanks to
exciting menus and a superb wine list. Staff throughout are
naturally friendly, nothing is too much trouble.

Rooms 44 (3 fmly) (14 GF) **Facilities** STV FTV Wi-fi **Services** Lift
Air con **Parking** 18

The Grange

★★★★ 77% ◎◎ HOTEL

1 Clifton YO30 6AA

☎ 01904 644744 📄 01904 612453

e-mail: info@grangehotel.co.uk

web: www.grangehotel.co.uk

dir: *On A19 York/Thirsk road, approx 500yds from city centre*

PETS: Bedrooms (6 GF) unattended **Charges** £10 per night **Exercise area** 5 mins' walk **Facilities** walks info vet info **On Request** fridge access torch towels **Other** charge for damage **Restrictions** small & medium size dogs only

This bustling Regency town house is just a few minutes' walk from the centre of York. A professional service is efficiently delivered by caring staff in a very friendly and helpful manner. Public rooms are comfortable and have been stylishly furnished; these include two dining options, the popular and informal Cellar Bar, and main hotel restaurant The Ivy Brasserie, which offers fine dining in a lavishly decorated environment. The individually designed bedrooms are comfortably appointed and have been thoughtfully equipped.

Rooms 36 (6 GF) **S** £123-£198; **D** £137-£235 (incl. bkfst)*
Facilities STV FTV Use of nearby health club Xmas New Year Wi-fi **Parking** 26

The Churchill Hotel

★★★ 81% ◎◎ HOTEL

65 Bootham YO30 7DQ

☎ 01904 644456 📄 01904 663322

e-mail: info@churchillhotel.com

dir: *On A19 (Bootham), W from York Minster, hotel 250yds on right*

PETS: Bedrooms (5 GF) unattended **Charges** £10 per stay **Public areas** except restaurant **Grounds Facilities** walks info vet info **Other** charge for damage **Restrictions** small & medium size dogs only (phone to check which breeds are accepted) **Resident Pet:** Milo (Toy Poodle)

A late Georgian manor house set in its own grounds, just a short walk from the Minster and other attractions. Period features and interesting artefacts relating to Winston Churchill are incorporated into smart contemporary design and up-to-date technology. Public areas include the Piano Bar & Restaurant, where innovative menus feature high quality, local produce.

Rooms 32 (4 fmly) (5 GF) **Facilities** ♬ Xmas New Year Wi-fi **Services** Lift **Parking** 40 **Notes** LB

Best Western Monkbar

★★★ 80% HOTEL

Monkbar YO31 7JA

☎ 01904 638086 📄 01904 629195

e-mail: sales@monkbarhotel.co.uk

dir: *A64 onto A1079 to city, turn right at city walls, take middle lane at lights. Hotel on right*

PETS: Bedrooms (2 GF) unattended sign courtyard bedrooms only **Charges** £7.50 per night **Public areas** except bar/restaurant on leads **Grounds** on leads disp bin **Exercise area** 100yds **Facilities** food food bowl water bowl bedding dog chews cat treats scoop/disp bags leads pet sitting dog walking cage storage walks info vet info **On Request** fridge access torch towels **Other** charge for damage **Resident Pet:** Misty Monkbar (Golden Labrador)

This smart hotel enjoys a prominent position adjacent to the city walls, and just a few minutes' walk from the cathedral. Individually styled bedrooms are well equipped for both business and leisure guests. Spacious public areas include comfortable lounges, an American-style bar, an airy restaurant and impressive meeting and training facilities.

Rooms 99 (8 fmly) (2 GF) **S** £95-£120; **D** £110-£175 (incl. bkfst) **Facilities** STV FTV Xmas New Year Wi-fi **Services** Lift **Parking** 66 **Notes** LB

Holiday Inn York

Holiday Inn

★★★ 80% HOTEL

Tadcaster Rd YO24 1QF

☎ 0871 942 9085 📄 01904 702804

e-mail: reservations-york@ihg.com

web: www.holidayinn.co.uk

dir: *From A1(M) take A64 towards York. In 7m take A1036 to York. Straight over at rdbt to city centre. Hotel 0.5m on right*

PETS: Bedrooms (12 GF) **Public areas** assist dogs only **Grounds Exercise area** York racecourse adjacent **On Request** fridge access **Stables** adjacent

Located in a suburban area close to the city centre and overlooking York race course, this modern hotel caters equally well for business and leisure guests. Public areas include the spacious family friendly Junction Restaurant, lounge bar and the Cedar Tree Terrace. Function rooms are available.

Rooms 142 (50 fmly) (12 GF) **Facilities** STV Xmas New Year Wi-fi **Services** Lift Air con **Parking** 200

ENGLAND

YORK *continued*

Ascot House

★★★★ GUEST ACCOMMODATION

80 East Pde YO31 7YH

☎ 01904 426826 📄 01904 431077

e-mail: admin@ascothouseyork.com

web: www.ascothouseyork.com

dir: *0.5m NE of city centre. Off A1036 Heworth Green onto Mill Ln, 2nd left*

PETS: Bedrooms (2 GF) unattended **Public areas** except dining room **Grounds** disp bin **Exercise area** 300yds **Facilities** dog chews feeding mat leads pet sitting washing facs cage storage walks info vet info **On Request** fridge access torch towels **Other** charge for damage **Resident Pets:** Millie, Holly & Chloe (Black Labradors)

June and Keith Wood provide friendly service at the 1869 Ascot House, a 15-minute walk from the town centre. Bedrooms are thoughtfully equipped, many with four-poster or canopy beds and other period furniture. Reception rooms include a cosy lounge that also retains its original features.

Rooms 12 en suite (3 fmly) (2 GF) **S** £60-£80; **D** £70-£90 **Facilities** FTV TVL tea/coffee Cen ht Licensed Wi-fi **Parking** 13 **Notes** LB Closed 21-28 Dec

Greenside

★★★ GUEST HOUSE

124 Clifton YO30 6BQ

☎ 01904 623631 📄 01904 623631

e-mail: greenside@onebillnet.co.uk

web: www.greensideguesthouse.co.uk

dir: *A19 N towards city centre, over lights for Greenside, on left opp Clifton Green*

PETS: Bedrooms (3 GF) unattended ground-floor, courtyard bedrooms only **Public areas** except breakfast room & lounge on leads **Exercise area** 50yds **Facilities** food bowl water bowl bedding leads walks info vet info **On Request** towels **Resident Pet:** Jessie (Labrador)

Overlooking Clifton Green, this detached house is just within walking distance of the city centre. Accommodation consists of simply furnished bedrooms and there is a cosy lounge and a dining room, where traditional breakfasts are served. It is a family home, and other families are welcome.

Rooms 6 rms (3 en suite) (2 fmly) (3 GF) **S** fr £30; **D** fr £58 **Facilities** TVL tea/coffee Cen ht Wi-fi **Parking** 6 **Notes** LB Closed Xmas & New Year 🐾

YORKSHIRE, SOUTH

BARNSLEY Map 8 SE30

Best Western Ardsley House Hotel

★★★ 79% HOTEL

Doncaster Rd, Ardsley S71 5EH

☎ 01226 309955 📄 01226 205374

e-mail: ardsley.house@forestdale.com

web: www.ardsleyhousehotel.co.uk

dir: *On A635, 0.75m from Stairfoot rdbt*

PETS: Bedrooms (14 GF) unattended **Charges** £7.50 per night **Public areas** except restaurant & lounge bar on leads **Exercise area** 0.5m **Facilities** food (pre-bookable) food bowl water bowl washing facs cage storage walks info vet info **On Request** fridge access torch towels **Other** charge for damage pet blankets available

This late 18th-century building has retained many of its original Georgian features. Bedrooms are both comfortable and well equipped. The excellent leisure facilities including a gym, pool and beauty salon. The Allendale Restaurant, with views of the nearby woodlands, offers an extensive menu.

Rooms 75 (12 fmly) (14 GF) **Facilities** Spa 🕑 supervised Gym 🎵 Xmas New Year Wi-fi **Parking** 200

DONCASTER
Map 8 SE50

Danum
★★★ 68% HOTEL

High St DN1 1DN
☎ 01302 342261 📠 01302 329034
e-mail: info@danumhotel.com
dir: M18 junct 3, A6182 to Doncaster. Over rdbt, right at next. Right at 'give way' sign, left at mini rdbt, hotel ahead

PETS: Bedrooms unattended **Public areas** except restaurant on leads **Exercise area** 0.25m **Facilities** vet info **Other** charge for damage

Situated in the centre of the town, this Edwardian hotel offers well equipped conference rooms together with comfortable bedrooms. A contemporary lounge area provides modern dining; specially negotiated rates at a local leisure centre are offered.

Rooms 64 (5 fmly) **Facilities** STV FTV Special rates at Cannons Health Club ♫ Xmas New Year Wi-fi **Services** Lift **Parking** 36 **Notes** RS 26-30 Dec

Campanile Doncaster
BUDGET HOTEL

Doncaster Leisure Park, Bawtry Rd DN4 7PD
☎ 01302 370770 📠 01302 370813
e-mail: doncaster@campanile.com
dir: Follow signs to Doncaster Leisure Centre, left at rdbt before Dome complex

PETS: Bedrooms (25 GF) unattended sign **Charges** £5 per night **Public areas** except restaurant (assist dogs only) on leads **Grounds** disp bin **Exercise area** surrounding area **Facilities** walks info vet info **On Request** fridge access **Stables** 1m **Other** charge for damage

This modern building offers accommodation in smart, well-equipped bedrooms, all with en suite bathrooms. Refreshments may be taken at the informal bistro.

Rooms 50 (25 GF)

ROTHERHAM
Map 8 SK49

PRIMA

Hellaby Hall
★★★★ 71% HOTEL

Old Hellaby Ln, Hellaby S66 8SN
☎ 01709 702701 📠 01709 700979
e-mail: reservations@hellabyhallhotel.co.uk
web: www.hellabyhallhotel.co.uk
dir: 0.5m off M18 junct 1, onto A631 towards Maltby. Hotel in Hellaby. (NB do not use postcode for Sat Nav)

PETS: Bedrooms (17 GF) unattended **Public areas** except restaurant & bar on leads **Grounds** on leads **Exercise area** adjacent **Facilities** food (pre-bookable) food bowl water bowl bedding feeding mat cage storage walks info vet info **On Request** fridge access towels **Other** charge for damage **Resident Pet:** Savah (cat)

This 17th-century house was built to a Flemish design with high, beamed ceilings, staircases which lead off to private meeting rooms and a series of oak-panelled lounges. Bedrooms are elegant and well equipped, and guests can dine in the formal Attic Restaurant. There are extensive leisure facilities and conference areas, and the hotel holds a licence for civil weddings.

Rooms 90 (2 fmly) (17 GF) **S** £49-£106; **D** £49-£127* **Facilities** Spa STV FTV ⊗ supervised Gym Beauty salon Exercise studio Spinning bike studio Xmas New Year Wi-fi **Services** Lift **Parking** 250 **Notes** LB

Best Western

Best Western Elton House Hotel
★★★ 80% HOTEL

Main St, Bramley S66 2SF
☎ 01709 545681 📠 01709 549100
e-mail: reception@eltonhotel.co.uk
web: www.eltonhotel.co.uk
dir: M18 junct 1 follow A631 Rotherham signs, turn right to Ravenfield, hotel at end of Bramley, follow brown signs

PETS: Bedrooms (11 GF) unattended **Grounds** on leads **Exercise area** 10 mins **Facilities** walks info vet info **On Request** torch

A stone-built hotel set in well-tended gardens in a quiet village setting but less than a mile from the M18. Bedrooms are modern and well equipped with complimentary Wi-fi also provided. The stylish and contemporary bar and restaurant offer a good range of food. Function rooms are available for conferences, weddings or other special occasions.

Rooms 29 (16 annexe) (4 fmly) (11 GF) **S** fr £57; **D** fr £66 (incl. bkfst) **Facilities** STV FTV ♫ Wi-fi **Parking** 48 **Notes** LB

ENGLAND

SHEFFIELD — Map 8 SK38

Novotel Sheffield Centre
★★★★ 70% HOTEL

50 Arundel Gate S1 2PR
☎ 0114 278 1781 📠 0114 278 7744
e-mail: h1348-re@accor.com
web: www.novotel.com
dir: Between Registry Office & Crucible/Lyceum Theatres, follow signs to Town Hall/Theatres & Hallam University

PETS: Bedrooms Charges £10 per night **Public areas** except restaurant on leads **Facilities** feeding mat walks info vet info **On Request** torch towels **Other** charge for damage **Restrictions** no dangerous dogs (see page 7)

In the heart of the city centre, this hotel has stylish public areas including a very modern restaurant, indoor swimming pool and a range of meeting rooms. Spacious bedrooms are suitable for family occupation, and the Novation rooms are ideal for business users.

Rooms 144 (136 fmly) **Facilities** STV FTV ⏊ Gym Steam room Xmas New Year Wi-fi **Services** Lift Air con **Parking** 60

Best Western Plus Mosborough Hall Hotel
★★★ 80% HOTEL

High St, Mosborough S20 5EA
☎ 0114 248 4353 📠 0114 247 9759
e-mail: hotel@mosboroughhall.co.uk
web: www.mosboroughhall.co.uk
dir: M1 junct 30, A6135 towards Sheffield. Follow Eckington/ Mosborough signs 2m. Sharp bend at top of hill, hotel on right

PETS: Bedrooms (16 GF) ground-floor bedrooms only **Charges** £20 per night £140 per week **Grounds** on leads **Exercise area** 800yds **Facilities** cage storage walks info **On Request** fridge access towels **Stables** 2m **Other** charge for damage **Restrictions** phone to check which breeds are accepted

This 16th-century, Grade II listed manor house is set in gardens not far from the M1 and is convenient for the city centre. The bedrooms offer very high quality and good amenities; some are very spacious. There is a galleried lounge and conservatory bar, and freshly prepared dishes are served in the traditional style dining room.

Rooms 43 (4 fmly) (16 GF) **S** £56-£95; **D** £56-£95* **Facilities** FTV Spa & beauty treatments Xmas New Year Wi-fi **Parking** 100 **Notes** LB

Ibis Sheffield City Centre
BUDGET HOTEL

Shude Hill S1 2AR
☎ 0114 241 9600 📠 0114 241 9610
e-mail: H2891@accor.com
web: www.ibishotel.com
dir: M1 junct 33, follow signs to Sheffield City Centre (A630/A57), at rdbt take 5th exit, signed Ponds Forge, for hotel

PETS: Bedrooms (3 GF) **Charges** £20 per night **Public areas** on leads **Facilities** water bowl **On Request** towels **Other** charge for damage **Restrictions** well behaved dogs only

Modern, budget hotel offering comfortable accommodation in bright and practical bedrooms. Breakfast is self-service and dinner is available in the restaurant.

Rooms 95 (15 fmly) (3 GF) (8 smoking) **S** £40-£89; **D** £40-£89*

TANKERSLEY — Map 8 SK39

QHOTELS

Tankersley Manor
★★★★ 77% HOTEL

Church Ln S75 3DQ
☎ 01226 744700 📠 01226 745405
e-mail: tankersleymanor@qhotels.co.uk
web: www.qhotels.co.uk
dir: M1 junct 36, A61 (Sheffield road

PETS: Bedrooms (16 GF) unattended **Charges** £15 per stay **Grounds** on leads disp bin **Exercise area** 50mtrs **Facilities** food bowl water bowl cage storage walks info vet info **On Request** fridge access towels **Other** charge for damage

High on the moors with views over the countryside, this 17th-century residence is well located for major cities, tourist attractions and motorway links. Where appropriate, bedrooms retain original features such as exposed beams or Yorkshire-stone window sills. The hotel has its own traditional country pub, complete with old beams and open fires, alongside the more formal restaurant and bar. A well-equipped leisure centre is also available.

Rooms 99 (10 fmly) (16 GF) **S** £65-£149; **D** £65-£149* **Facilities** Spa STV FTV ⏊ Gym Swimming lessons Beauty treatments Xmas New Year Wi-fi **Services** Lift **Parking** 350 **Notes** LB

WOODALL MOTORWAY SERVICE AREA (M1)   Map 8 SK48

Days Inn Sheffield - M1
BUDGET HOTEL
Woodall Service Area S26 7XR
☎ 0114 248 7992   📠 0114 248 5634
e-mail: woodall.hotel@welcomebreak.co.uk
web: www.welcomebreak.co.uk
dir: *M1, between juncts 30 & 31 S'bound, at Woodall Services*

PETS: Bedrooms (16 GF) unattended **Charges** £5 per night
Public areas on leads **Grounds** disp bin **Facilities** food bowl
water bowl walks info vet info **On Request** fridge access **Other**
charge for damage

This modern building offers accommodation in smart, spacious
and well-equipped bedrooms, suitable for families and business
travellers, and all with en suite bathrooms. Continental breakfast
is available and other refreshments may be taken at the nearby
family restaurant.

Rooms 38 (32 fmly) (16 GF) (6 smoking) **S** £39.95-£59.95;
D £49.95-£69.95

WORSBROUGH   Map 8 SE30

Greensprings Touring Park *(SE330020)*
►►

Rockley Abbey Farm, Rockley Ln S75 3DS
☎ 01226 288298   📠 01226 288298
dir: *M1 junct 36, A61 to Barnsley. Left after 0.25m signed Pilley.
Site 1m at bottom of hill*

PETS: Public areas except toilets disp bin **Exercise area on**
site dog walking area **Exercise area** 300yds **Facilities** walks
info vet info **Stables Other** prior notice required max 2 dogs
per pitch

Open Apr-Oct Last arrival 21.00hrs Last departure noon

A secluded and attractive farm site set amidst woods and
farmland, with access to the river and several good local walks.
There are two touring areas, one gently sloping. Although not
far from the M1, there is almost no traffic noise, and this site
is convenient for exploring the area's industrial heritage, as
well as the Peak District. 4 acre site. 65 touring pitches. 5
hardstandings. 22 seasonal pitches. Tent pitches. Motorhome
pitches.

Notes 🐾

YORKSHIRE, WEST

BINGLEY   Map 7 SE13

Five Rise Locks Hotel & Restaurant
★★★ 75% ◉ SMALL HOTEL
Beck Ln BD16 4DD
☎ 01274 565296   📠 01274 568828
e-mail: info@five-rise-locks.co.uk
dir: *Off Main St into Park Rd, 0.5m turn left into Beck Ln*

PETS: Bedrooms (2 GF) unattended **Charges** £5.50 per night
Grounds disp bin **Exercise area** 300yds **Facilities** scoop/
disp bags washing facs cage storage walks info vet info
On Request fridge access torch towels **Stables** 3m **Other**
charge for damage **Resident Pets:** Ruby & Tilly (Bassett Hounds)

A warm welcome and comfortable accommodation awaits guests
at this impressive Victorian building. Bedrooms are of a good
size and feature homely extras. The restaurant offers imaginative
dishes and the bright breakfast room overlooks open countryside.

Rooms 9 (2 GF) **S** £60-£67; **D** £89-£110 (incl. bkfst)*
Facilities FTV Wi-fi **Parking** 20 **Notes** LB

BRADFORD   Map 7 SE13

PEEL HOTELS PLC

Midland Hotel
★★★ 80% HOTEL
Forster Square BD1 4HU
☎ 01274 735735   📠 01274 720003
e-mail: info@midland-hotel-bradford.com
web: www.midland-hotel-bradford.com
dir: *M62 junct 26/M606, left opposite ASDA, left at rdbt onto
A650. Through 2 rdbts & 2 lights. Follow A6181/Haworth signs.
Up hill, next left into Manor Row. Hotel 400mtrs*

PETS: Bedrooms Grounds on leads disp bin **Exercise area**
nearby **Other** charge for damage

Ideally situated in the heart of the city, this grand Victorian
hotel provides modern, very well equipped accommodation and
comfortable, spacious day rooms. Ample parking is available in
what was once the city's railway station, and a Victorian walkway
linking the hotel to the old platform can still be used today.

Rooms 90 (5 fmly) (10 smoking) **S** £65-£110; **D** £75-£165 (incl.
bkfst) **Facilities** STV FTV Xmas New Year Wi-fi **Services** Lift
Parking 60 **Notes** LB

ENGLAND

BRADFORD *continued*

Best Western Guide Post Hotel

★★★ 75% HOTEL

Common Rd, Low Moor BD12 0ST
☎ 0845 409 1362 & 01274 607866 📠 01274 671085
e-mail: sue.barnes@guideposthotel.net
web: www.guideposthotel.net
dir: *From M606 rdbt take 2nd exit. At next rdbt take 1st exit (Cleckheaton Rd). 0.5m, turn right at bollard into Common Rd*

PETS: Bedrooms (13 GF) unattended **Public areas** except restaurant & bar on leads **Exercise area** 2 mins **Facilities** washing facs cage storage vet info **On Request** fridge access torch towels **Other** charge for damage

Situated south of the city, this hotel offers attractively styled, modern, comfortable bedrooms. The restaurant offers an extensive range of food using fresh, local produce; lighter snack meals are served in the bar. There is also a choice of well-equipped meeting and function rooms. There is disabled access to the hotel, restaurant and one function room.

Rooms 42 (10 fmly) (13 GF) (8 smoking) **Facilities** STV FTV Complimentary use of nearby swimming & gym facilities Wi-fi **Parking** 100

Campanile Bradford

★★★ 73% HOTEL

6 Roydsdale Way, Euroway Estate BD4 6SA
☎ 01274 683683 📠 0844 800 5769
e-mail: bradford@campanile.com
web: www.campanile.com
dir: *M62 junct 26 onto M606. Exit Euroway Estate East onto Merrydale Rd, right onto Roydsdale Way*

PETS: Bedrooms (22 GF) **Charges** £5 per night **Public areas** except restaurant (ex assist dogs) **Grounds Exercise area** wooded area with large ponds (10 mins) **Facilities** cage storage vet info **On Request** fridge access **Other** disposal bags available **Restrictions** no Great Danes or similar sized breeds

This modern building offers accommodation in smart, well-equipped bedrooms, all with en suite bathrooms. Refreshments may be taken at the informal bistro.

Rooms 130 (37 fmly) (22 GF) (8 smoking) **S** £63; **D** £69*
Facilities STV FTV Wi-fi **Services** Lift **Parking** 200

Best Western Milford Hotel

★★★ 83% HOTEL

A1 Great North Rd, Peckfield LS25 5LQ
☎ 01977 681800 📠 01977 681245
e-mail: enquiries@mlh.co.uk
web: www.mlh.co.uk
dir: *On A63, 1.5m W of A1(M) junct 42 & 4.5m E of M1 junct 46*

PETS: Bedrooms (13 GF) unattended standard bedrooms only **Charges** £7.50 per night **Exercise area** 200yds **Facilities** food (pre-bookable) walks info vet info **On Request** torch **Stables** 3m **Other** charge for damage

This friendly, family owned and run hotel is conveniently situated, and provides very comfortable, modern accommodation. The air-conditioned bedrooms are particularly spacious and well equipped, and ten boutique-style superior rooms are available. Public areas include a relaxing lounge area, the contemporary Watermill Restaurant and lounge bar which has a working waterwheel.

Rooms 46 (13 GF) (6 smoking) **Facilities** FTV Xmas New Year Wi-fi **Services** Air con **Parking** 80 **Notes** LB

Holiday Inn Leeds Garforth

★★★ 83% HOTEL

Wakefield Rd LS25 1LH
☎ 0113 286 6556 📠 0113 286 8326
e-mail: reservations@hileedsgarforth.com
web: www.holidayinn.co.uk
dir: *At junct of A63/A642. Hotel opposite rdbt*

PETS: Bedrooms (35 GF) unattended **Charges** £10 per night **Public areas** except restaurant **Grounds** on leads disp bin **Exercise area** 200yds **Facilities** walks info vet info **Other** charge for damage

Located just outside Leeds, this hotel has excellent access to the M1 and M62 making it an ideal base for exploring the area. Well-equipped accommodation includes executive bedrooms. Public areas are attractively designed and include meeting rooms and leisure club. Aioli's Restaurant serves contemporary cuisine.

Rooms 144 (30 fmly) (35 GF) (15 smoking) **Facilities** FTV 🛇 supervised Gym New Year Wi-fi **Services** Air con **Parking** 250

GOMERSAL
Map 8 SE22

CLASSIC
BRITISH HOTELS

Gomersal Park
★★★ 79% HOTEL

Moor Ln BD19 4LJ
☎ 01274 869386   📄 01274 861042
e-mail: enquiries@gomersalparkhotel.com
web: www.gomersalparkhotel.com
dir: A62 to Huddersfield. At junct with A65, by Greyhound Pub right, after 1m take 1st right after Oakwell Hall

PETS: Bedrooms (32 GF) unattended Charges Public areas except restaurant & bar on leads Grounds disp bin Exercise area 100yds Facilities food bowl water bowl washing facs cage storage walks info vet info On Request fridge access torch towels Other charge for damage Resident Pet: Teal (English Pointer)

Constructed around a 19th-century house, this stylish, modern hotel enjoys a peaceful location and pleasant grounds. Deep sofas ensure comfort in the open-plan lounge and imaginative meals are served in the popular Brasserie 101. The well-equipped bedrooms provide high quality and comfort. Extensive public areas include a well-equipped leisure complex and pool, and a wide variety of air-conditioned conference rooms.

Rooms 100 (3 fmly) (32 GF) Facilities FTV ☜ supervised Gym Wi-fi Services Lift Parking 150 Notes LB

HALIFAX
Map 7 SE02

Holdsworth House
★★★ 86% ◉◉ HOTEL

Holdsworth HX2 9TG
☎ 01422 240024   📄 01422 245174
e-mail: info@holdsworthhouse.co.uk
web: www.holdsworthhouse.co.uk
dir: From town centre take A629 (Keighley road). Right at garage up Shay Ln after 1.5m. Hotel on right after 1m

PETS: Bedrooms (15 GF) unattended Charges £10 per night Public areas except restaurant area on leads Grounds on leads disp bin Exercise area 500yds Facilities walks info vet info On Request fridge access Restrictions well behaved, small & medium size dogs only

This delightful 17th-century Jacobean manor house, set in well tended gardens, offers individually decorated, thoughtfully equipped bedrooms. Public rooms, adorned with beautiful paintings and antique pieces, include a choice of inviting lounges and superb conference and function facilities. Dinner provides the highlight of any stay and is served in the elegant restaurant by friendly, attentive staff.

Rooms 40 (2 fmly) (15 GF) S £80-£100; D £100-£150 (incl. bkfst)* Facilities FTV New Year Wi-fi Parking 60

HARTSHEAD MOOR MOTORWAY SERVICE AREA (M62)
Map 8 SE12

Days Inn Bradford - M62
BUDGET HOTEL

Hartshead Moor Service Area, Clifton HD6 4JX
☎ 01274 851706   📄 01274 855169
e-mail: hartshead.hotel@welcomebreak.co.uk
web: www.welcomebreak.co.uk
dir: M62 between junct 25 & 26

PETS: Bedrooms (16 GF) unattended ground-floor bedrooms only Charges Public areas except restaurant on leads Grounds on leads disp bin Exercise area surrounding fields Facilities vet info On Request fridge access Other charge for damage

This modern building offers accommodation in smart, spacious and well-equipped bedrooms, suitable for families and business travellers, and all with en suite bathrooms. Continental breakfast is available and other refreshments may be taken at the nearby family restaurant.

Rooms 38 (33 fmly) (16 GF) S £39.95-£59.95; D £49.95-£69.95

HUDDERSFIELD
Map 7 SE11

Cedar Court
★★★★ 71% HOTEL

Ainley Top HD3 3RH
☎ 01422 375431   📄 01422 314050
e-mail: sales@cedarcourthotels.co.uk
web: www.cedarcourthotels.co.uk
dir: 500yds from M62 junct 24

PETS: Bedrooms (9 GF) Grounds on leads disp bin Facilities walks info vet info On Request fridge access towels Other charge for damage

Sitting adjacent to the M62, this hotel is an ideal location for business travellers and for those touring the West Yorkshire area. Bedrooms are comfortably appointed; there is a busy lounge with snacks available all day, as well as a modern restaurant and a fully equipped leisure centre. In addition, the hotel has extensive meeting and banqueting facilities.

Rooms 113 (6 fmly) (9 GF) S £50-£120; D £60-£130 (incl. bkfst) Facilities STV FTV ☜ supervised Gym Steam room Sauna Wi-fi Services Lift Parking 250

HUDDERSFIELD *continued*

The Huddersfield Central Lodge

★★★★ GUEST ACCOMMODATION

11/15 Beast Market HD1 1QF
☎ 01484 515551 ▤ 01484 432349
e-mail: angela@centrallodge.com
web: www.centrallodge.com
dir: *In town centre off Lord St, follow signs for Beast Market from ring road*

PETS: Bedrooms unattended **Public areas** except breakfast room during breakfast **Grounds** on leads disp bin **Exercise area** 500mtrs **Facilities** washing facs cage storage walks info vet info **On Request** fridge access torch towels **Other** charge for damage

This friendly, family-run operation offers smart spacious bedrooms with modern en suites. Some rooms are in the main building, while new rooms, many with kitchenettes, are situated across a courtyard. Public rooms include a bar and a conservatory, and there are arrangements for local restaurants to charge meals to guests' accounts. Secure complimentary parking.

Rooms 9 en suite 13 annexe en suite (2 fmly) (6 smoking) **S** £53-£59; **D** £70 **Facilities** FTV TVL tea/coffee Direct Dial Cen ht Licensed Wi-fi **Parking** 50

Griffin Lodge Guest House

★★★ GUEST HOUSE

273 Manchester Rd HD4 5AG
☎ 01484 431042 ▤ 01484 431043
e-mail: info@griffinlodge.co.uk
web: www.griffinlodge.co.uk

PETS: Bedrooms (6 GF) **Public areas Grounds** on leads disp bin **Facilities** walks info vet info

Located on the outskirts of Huddersfield and close to the villages of Holmfirth and Marsden, Griffin Lodge is family run and offers comfortable well appointed accommodation. Either continental or a full cooked breakfast is served in the small dining room and there is parking to the rear.

Rooms 6 en suite (4 fmly) (6 GF) **S** £35-£45; **D** fr £45 **Facilities** FTV tea/coffee Cen ht Wi-fi **Parking** 10

ILKLEY Map 7 SE14

Best Western Rombalds Hotel & Restaurant

★★★ 83% ◉ HOTEL

11 West View, Wells Rd LS29 9JG
☎ 01943 603201 ▤ 01943 816586
e-mail: reception@rombalds.demon.co.uk
web: www.rombalds.co.uk
dir: *A65 from Leeds. Left at 3rd main lights, follow Ilkley Moor signs. Right at HSBC Bank onto Wells Rd. Hotel 600yds on left*

PETS: Bedrooms sign **Charges** £10 per night £50 per week **Grounds** on leads disp bin **Exercise area** adjacent **Facilities** water bowl walks info vet info **On Request** fridge access torch **Stables** 6m

This elegantly furnished Georgian townhouse is located in a peaceful terrace between the town and the moors. Delightful day rooms include a choice of comfortable lounges and an attractive restaurant that provides a relaxed venue in which to sample the skilfully prepared, imaginative meals. The bedrooms are tastefully furnished, well equipped and include several spacious suites.

Rooms 15 (2 fmly) **Facilities** STV Xmas Wi-fi **Parking** 28 **Notes** Closed 28 Dec-2 Jan

ENGLAND

KEIGHLEY — Map 7 SE04

Dalesgate
★★ 70% HOTEL

406 Skipton Rd, Utley BD20 6HP
☎ 01535 664930 📠 01535 611253
e-mail: stephen.e.atha@btinternet.com
dir: *In town centre follow A629 over rdbt onto B6265. Right after 0.75m into St. John's Rd. 1st right into hotel car park*

PETS: Bedrooms (3 GF) unattended Charges Public areas except bar & restaurant Exercise area 300yds Facilities food bowl water bowl leads washing facs cage storage walks info vet info On Request fridge access torch towels Other charge for damage Resident Pets: Dan & Silk (German Shepherds)

Originally the residence of a local chapel minister, this modern, well-established hotel provides well-equipped, comfortable bedrooms. It also boasts a cosy bar and pleasant restaurant, serving an imaginative range of dishes. A large car park is provided to the rear.

Rooms 20 (2 fmly) (3 GF) Parking 25 Notes RS 22 Dec-4 Jan

LEEDS — Map 8 SE33

Malmaison Leeds
★★★ 83% ⊛ HOTEL

1 Swinegate LS1 4AG
☎ 0113 398 1000 📠 0113 398 1002
e-mail: leeds@malmaison.com
web: www.malmaison.com
dir: *M621/M1 junct 3, follow city centre signs. At KPMG building, right into Sovereign Street. Hotel at end on right*

PETS: Bedrooms unattended Charges £10 per night Public areas except bar & restaurant on leads Facilities food (pre-bookable) food bowl water bowl bedding dog chews cat treats feeding mat vet info On Request fridge access torch towels Other charge for damage

Close to the waterfront, this stylish property offers striking bedrooms with CD players and air conditioning. The popular bar and brasserie feature vaulted ceilings, intimate lighting and offer a choice of a full three-course meal or a substantial snack. Service is both willing and friendly. A small fitness centre and impressive meeting rooms complete the package.

Rooms 100 (4 fmly) Facilities STV Gym Xmas New Year Wi-fi Services Lift Air con Notes LB

OSSETT — Map 8 SE22

Heath House
★★★★ GUEST ACCOMMODATION

Chancery Rd WF5 9RZ
☎ 01924 260654 & 07890 385622 📠 01924 263131
e-mail: bookings@heath-house.co.uk
web: www.heath-house.co.uk
dir: *M1 junct 40, A638 towards Dewsbury, at end dual carriageway exit rdbt 2nd left, house 20yds on right*

PETS: Bedrooms sign Sep accom barn Public areas Grounds disp bin Exercise area 600yds Facilities food (pre-bookable) food bowl water bowl bedding feeding mat litter tray scoop/ disp bags leads pet sitting dog walking washing facs cage storage walks info vet info On Request fridge access torch towels Other charge for damage Resident Pets: Sally (Greyhound), Diesel (Japanese Akita), Denby (cat)

The spacious Victorian family home stands in four acres of tranquil gardens a short distance from the M1. It has elegant en suite bedrooms, and the courteous and friendly owners provide healthy, freshly-cooked breakfasts.

Rooms 2 en suite (1 fmly) S £35-£39; D £49-£52 Facilities tea/ coffee Cen ht Wi-fi Parking 16

OTLEY — Map 7 SE24

Chevin Country Park Hotel & Spa
★★★ 74% HOTEL

Yorkgate LS21 3NU
☎ 01943 467818 📠 01943 850335
e-mail: chevin@crerarhotels.com
dir: *From Leeds/Bradford Airport rdbt take A658 N towards Harrogate, 0.75m to lights. Left, 2nd left into Yorkgate. Hotel 0.5m on left*

PETS: Bedrooms (45 GF) unattended lodge rooms only Charges £10 per night Grounds on leads Facilities walks info vet info On Request towels Other 44 acres of woodland available

Peacefully located in its own woodland yet convenient for major road links and the airport. Bedrooms are split between the original main log building and chalet-style accommodation in the extensive grounds. Public areas include a bar and several lounges. The Lakeside Restaurant provides views over the small lake and good leisure facilities are available.

Rooms 49 (30 annexe) (7 fmly) (45 GF) Facilities Spa FTV ⊗ ♨ Fishing Gym Steam room Xmas New Year Wi-fi Parking 100

WAKEFIELD Map 8 SE32

Cedar Court Hotel Wakefield

 THE INDEPENDENTS

★★★★ 73% HOTEL

Denby Dale Rd WF4 3QZ
☎ 01924 276310 📠 01924 280221
e-mail: sales@cedarcourthotels.co.uk
web: www.cedarcourthotels.co.uk
dir: Adjacent to M1 junct 39

PETS: Bedrooms (74 GF) ground-floor bedrooms only **Grounds** on leads **Exercise area** 10 mins' walk **Facilities** walks info vet info

This hotel enjoys a convenient location just off the M1. Traditionally styled bedrooms offer a good range of facilities while open-plan public areas include a busy bar and restaurant operation. Conferences and functions are extremely well catered for and a modern leisure club completes the picture.

Rooms 149 (2 fmly) (74 GF) (6 smoking) **Facilities** FTV 🏊 supervised Gym Xmas New Year Wi-fi **Services** Lift **Parking** 350 **Notes** LB

Holiday Inn Leeds - Wakefield

 Holiday Inn

★★★ 75% HOTEL

Queen's Dr, Ossett WF5 9BE
☎ 0871 942 9082 📠 01924 230613
e-mail: reception-wakefield@ihg.com
web: www.holidayinn.co.uk/wakefield
dir: M1 junct 40 follow signs for Wakefield. Hotel on right in 200yds

PETS: Bedrooms (35 GF) sign **Charges** £7 per night
Public areas except restaurant on leads **Grounds** on leads
Exercise area field adjacent **Other** charge for damage

Situated close to major motorway networks, this modern hotel offers well-equipped and comfortable bedrooms. Public areas include the popular Traders restaurant and a comfortable lounge where a menu is available throughout the day. Conference facilities are also available.

Rooms 104 (32 fmly) (35 GF) (9 smoking) **S** £39-£99; **D** £39-£99* **Facilities** STV Xmas New Year Wi-fi **Services** Lift Air con **Parking** 105 **Notes** LB

Stanley View Guest House

★★★ GUEST HOUSE

226-230 Stanley Rd WF1 4AE
☎ 01924 376803 📠 01924 369123
e-mail: enquiries@stanleyviewguesthouse.co.uk
dir: M62 junct 30, follow Aberford Rd 3m. Signed on left

PETS: Bedrooms (7 GF) ground-floor bedrooms only
Public areas except dining area on leads **Exercise area** nearby
Facilities vet info **Other** charge for damage

Part of an attractive terrace, this well-established guest house is just half a mile from the city centre and has private parking at the rear. The well equipped bedrooms are brightly decorated, and there is a licensed bar and comfortable lounge. Hearty home-cooked meals are served in the attractive dining room.

Rooms 17 rms (13 en suite) (6 fmly) (7 GF) **Facilities** STV TVL tea/coffee Dinner available Direct Dial Cen ht Licensed Wi-fi **Parking** 10

WETHERBY Map 8 SE44

Days Inn Wetherby

 DAYS INN

BUDGET HOTEL

Junction 46 A1(M), Kirk Deighton LS22 5GT
☎ 01937 547557 📠 01937 547559
e-mail: reservations@daysinnwetherby.co.uk
dir: A1(M) junct 46 at Moto Service Area

PETS: Bedrooms (35 GF) unattended 1st floor bedrooms only **Charges** £10 (per room) per night on leads **Grounds** on leads disp bin **Facilities** vet info **Other** charge for damage **Restrictions** small dogs only

This modern building offers accommodation in smart, spacious and well-equipped bedrooms, suitable for families and business travellers, and all with en suite bathrooms. Continental breakfast is available and other refreshments may be taken at the nearby family restaurant.

Rooms 129 (33 fmly) (35 GF)

ENGLAND

CASTEL Map 16

Fauxquets Valley Campsite

▶ ▶ ▶

GY5 7QL

☎ 01481 236951 & 07781 413333

e-mail: info@fauxquets.co.uk

dir: *From pier, take 2nd exit off rdbt. At top of hill left into Queens Rd. 2m. Right into Candie Rd. Site opposite sign for German Occupation Museum*

PETS: Public areas on leads disp bin **Exercise area on site** field **Facilities** washing facs walks info vet info **Other** prior notice required **Resident Pet:** Morley (Chocolate Labrador)

Open mid Jun-Aug

A beautiful, quiet farm site in a hidden valley close to the sea. The friendly and helpful owners, who understand campers' needs, offer good quality facilities and amenities, including upgraded toilets, an outdoor swimming pool, bar/restaurant, a nature trail and sports areas. Fully equipped tents for hire. 3 acre site. 120 touring pitches. Tent pitches.

ROZEL Map 16

Château la Chaire

★★★ ◉◉ HOTEL

Rozel Bay JE3 6AJ

☎ 01534 863354 ▤ 01534 865137

e-mail: res@chateau-la-chaire.co.uk

web: www.chateau-la-chaire.co.uk

dir: *From St Helier on B38 turn left in village by Rozel Bay Inn, hotel 100yds on right*

PETS: Bedrooms (1 GF) ground-floor bedrooms only **Charges** £10 per night **Grounds Exercise area** 50yds **Facilities** food bowl water bowl walks info vet info **On Request** fridge access torch towels **Other** charge for damage **Resident Pet:** Jasmine (Labrador)

Built as a gentleman's residence in 1843, Château la Chaire is a haven of peace and tranquillity, set in a secluded wooded valley. Picturesque Rozel Harbour is within easy walking distance and the house is surrounded by terraced gardens and woods. There is a wonderful atmosphere here and the helpful staff deliver high standards of guest care. Imaginative menus, making the best use of local produce, are served in the oak-panelled dining room, in the conservatory or on the terrace when the weather permits. Bedroom and suite styles and sizes vary, but all are beautifully appointed and include many nice touches such as towelling robes, slippers, flowers and DVD players. Free Wi-fi is available throughout the hotel.

Rooms 14 (2 fmly) (1 GF) **Facilities** FTV Xmas New Year Wi-fi **Parking** 30 **Notes** No children 7yrs

ST BRELADE Map 16

Hotel Miramar

★★ **72%** HOTEL

Mont Gras d'Eau JE3 8ED

☎ 01534 743831 ▤ 01534 745009

e-mail: reservations@miramarjersey.com

dir: *From airport take B36 at lights, turn left onto A13, 1st right into Mont Gras d'Eau*

PETS: Bedrooms (12 GF) unattended **Public areas** on leads disp bin **Exercise area** 100yds **Facilities** cage storage walks info vet info

A friendly welcome awaits at this family-run hotel set in delightful sheltered gardens, overlooking the beautiful bay. Accommodation is comfortable with well-appointed bedrooms; some are on the ground floor, and there are two on the lower ground with their own terrace overlooking the outdoor heated pool. The restaurant offers a varied set menu.

Rooms 38 (2 fmly) (12 GF) (4 smoking) **Facilities** ⚡ Wi-fi **Parking** 30 **Notes** Closed Oct-mid Apr

ST MARTIN Map 16

Beuvelande Camp Site

▶ ▶ ▶ ▶ ▶

Beuvelande JE3 6EZ

☎ 01534 853575 ▤ 01534 857788

e-mail: info@campingjersey.com

dir: *Take A6 from St Helier to St Martin & follow signs to site before St Martins Church*

PETS: Charges dog £2 per night **Public areas** on leads disp bin **Exercise area on site Facilities** walks info **Other** prior notice required **Restrictions** no Staffordshire Bull Terriers or Rottweilers

Open Apr-Sep rs Apr-May & Sep pool & restaurant closed, shop hours limited

A well-established site with excellent toilet facilities, accessed via narrow lanes in peaceful countryside close to St Martin. An attractive bar/restaurant is the focal point of the park, especially in the evenings, and there is a small swimming pool and playground. Motorhomes and towed caravans will be met at the ferry and escorted to the site if requested when booking. 6 acre site. 150 touring pitches. Tent pitches. 75 statics.

ENGLAND

ST SAVIOUR — Map 16

Longueville Manor
★★★★★ ◉◉◉ HOTEL
JE2 7WF
☎ 01534 725501 📠 01534 731613
e-mail: info@longuevillemanor.com
web: www.longuevillemanor.com
dir: A3 E from St Helier towards Gorey. Hotel 1m on left

PETS: Bedrooms (7 GF) unattended **Grounds** disp bin
Exercise area beach 0.5m **Facilities** feeding mat cage storage
walks info vet info **On Request** fridge access torch towels

Dating back to the 13th century, there is something very special about Longueville Manor, which is why so many guests return time and again. It is set in 17 acres of grounds including woodland walks, a spectacular rose garden and a lake. Bedrooms have great style and individuality boasting fresh flowers, fine embroidered bed linen and a host of extras. The committed team of staff create a welcoming atmosphere and every effort is made to ensure a memorable stay. The very accomplished cuisine is also a highlight of any stay.

Rooms 30 (1 annexe) (7 GF) (6 smoking) **S** £195-£370;
D £220-£630 (incl. bkfst)* **Facilities** STV ♜ 🌊🍴 Xmas New Year Wi-fi **Services** Lift **Parking** 40 **Notes** LB

ISLE OF MAN

PORT ERIN — Map 6 SC16

Falcon's Nest
★★ 71% HOTEL
The Promenade IM9 6AF
☎ 01624 834077 📠 01624 835370
e-mail: falconsnest@enterprise.net
web: www.falconsnesthotel.co.uk
dir: Follow coast road S from airport or ferry. Hotel on seafront, immediately after steam railway station

PETS: Bedrooms unattended sign certain bedrooms only
Public areas except food areas, bars & restaurant on leads
Grounds on leads disp bin **Exercise area** beach & park (50mtrs)
Facilities walks info vet info **On Request** fridge access towels
Resident Pets: Spot (dog)

Situated overlooking the bay and harbour, this Victorian hotel offers generally spacious bedrooms. There is a choice of bars, one of which attracts many locals. Meals can be taken in the lounge bar, the conservatory or in the attractively decorated main restaurant.

Rooms 39 (9 fmly) (15 smoking) **Facilities** FTV Xmas New Year Wi-fi **Parking** 20

Scotland

CITY OF ABERDEEN

ABERDEEN
Map 15 NJ90

MILLENNIUM
HOTELS AND RESORTS
MILLENNIUM • COPTHORNE

Copthorne Hotel Aberdeen
★★★★ 73% HOTEL
122 Huntly St AB10 1SU
☎ 01224 630404 📠 01224 640573
e-mail: reservations.aberdeen@millenniumhotels.co.uk
web: www.millenniumhotels.co.uk/aberdeen
dir: West end of city centre, off Union St, up Rose St, hotel 0.25m on right on corner with Huntly St

PETS: Bedrooms sign **Charges** £30 per stay **Facilities** walks info **On Request** fridge access towels **Other** charge for damage

Situated just outside of the city centre, this hotel offers friendly, attentive service. The smart bedrooms are well proportioned and guests will appreciate the added quality of the Connoisseur rooms. Mac's bar provides a relaxed atmosphere in which to enjoy a drink or to dine informally, whilst Poachers Restaurant offers a slightly more formal dining experience.

Rooms 89 (15 fmly) **S** £55-£300; **D** £55-£300* **Facilities** STV FTV New Year Wi-fi **Services** Lift **Parking** 15 **Notes** LB RS 24-26 Dec

Malmaison Aberdeen
★★★ 86% ⊛ HOTEL
49-53 Queens Rd AB15 4YP
☎ 01224 327370 📠 01224 327371
e-mail: info.aberdeen@malmaison.com
dir: A90, 3rd exit into Queens Rd at 3rd rdbt, hotel on right

PETS: Bedrooms (10 GF) unattended **Charges Public areas** except restaurant on leads **Exercise area** 2m **Facilities** food bowl water bowl bedding cage storage walks info vet info **On Request** fridge access torch towels **Stables** 2m

Popular with business travellers and as a function venue, this well-established hotel lies east of the city centre. Public areas include a reception lounge and an intimate restaurant, plus the extensive bar menu which remains a popular choice for many regulars. There are two styles of accommodation, with the superior rooms being particularly comfortable and well equipped.

Rooms 79 (8 fmly) (10 GF) **Facilities** Spa STV FTV Gym Steam room Xmas New Year Wi-fi **Services** Lift **Parking** 50 **Notes** LB

ABERDEENSHIRE

ABOYNE
Map 15 NO59

Aboyne Loch Caravan Park (NO538998)
▶ ▶ ▶
AB34 5BR
☎ 013398 86244 & 82589 📠 013398 86244
e-mail: heatherreid24@yahoo.co.uk
dir: On A93, 1m E of Aboyne

PETS: Public areas disp bin **Exercise area on site** dog walks **Facilities** walks info vet info

Open 31 Mar-Oct Last arrival 20.00hrs Last departure 11.00hrs

An attractively sited caravan park set amidst woodland on the shores of the lovely Aboyne Loch in scenic Deeside. The facilities are modern and immaculately maintained, and amenities include boat-launching, boating and fishing. An ideally situated park for touring Royal Deeside and the Aberdeenshire uplands. 6 acre site 20 touring pitches. 25 hardstandings. Tent pitches. Motorhome pitches. 120 statics.

Notes ⊛

BALLATER
Map 15 NO39

Darroch Learg
★★★ ⊛⊛⊛ SMALL HOTEL
Braemar Rd AB35 5UX
☎ 013397 55443 📠 013397 55252
e-mail: enquiries@darrochlearg.co.uk
web: www.darrochlearg.co.uk
dir: On A93, W of Ballater

PETS: Bedrooms (1 GF) **Public areas** except restaurant & drawing room **Grounds** disp bin **Exercise area** adjacent **Facilities** food bowl water bowl bedding walks info vet info **On Request** fridge access torch towels **Stables** 1m **Resident Pet:** Isla (Black Labrador)

Set high above the road in extensive wooded grounds, this long-established hotel offers superb views over the hills and countryside of Royal Deeside. Nigel and Fiona Franks are caring and attentive hosts who improve their hotel every year. Bedrooms some with four-poster beds, are individually styled, bright and spacious. Food is a highlight of any visit, whether it is a freshly prepared breakfast or the fine cuisine served in the delightful conservatory restaurant.

Rooms 12 (1 GF) **S** £120-£195; **D** £190-£320 (incl. bkfst & dinner)* **Facilities** New Year **Parking** 15 **Notes** LB Closed Xmas & Jan (ex New Year)

SCOTLAND

he Green Inn

★★★★ ◉◉◉ 🍴 RESTAURANT WITH ROOMS

Victoria Rd AB35 5QQ
☎ 013397 55701
mail: info@green-inn.com
eb: www.green-inn.com
r: *In village centre*

ETS: Bedrooms unattended **Exercise area** adjacent **Facilities** age storage walks info vet info **On Request** fridge access wels **Other** charge for damage **Resident Pet:** Molly (Labrador)

former temperance hotel, the Green Inn enjoys a central cation in the pretty village of Ballater. Bedrooms are of a high andard and attractively presented. The kitchen has a strong putation for its fine cuisine, which can be enjoyed in the stylish onservatory restaurant. The head chef is Chris O'Halloran, son owners Trevor and Evelyn. Breakfast is equally enjoyable and nould not be missed. Genuine hospitality from the enthusiastic roprietors is a real feature of any stay.

ooms 2 en suite **S** £59.50; **D** £79 **Facilities** FTV TVL tea/coffee inner available Cen ht Wi-fi **Notes** Closed 1st 2wks Nov, last vks Jan No coaches

---

FORDOUN
Map 15 NO77

rownmuir Caravan Park *(NO740772)*

►►

330 1SJ
☎ 01561 320786 📠 01561 320786
mail: brownmuircaravanpark@talk21.com
r: *From N: A90 take B966 signed Fettercairn, site 1.5m on left. rom S: A90, exit 4m N of Laurencekirk signed Fordoun, site 1m n right*

ETS: Public areas except children's play area disp bin **xercise area on site Facilities** walks info vet info

pen Apr-Oct Last arrival 23.00hrs Last departure noon

mainly static site set in a rural location with level pitches and ood touring facilities. The area is ideal for cyclists, walkers and olfers, as well as those wanting to visit Aberdeen, Banchory, allater, Balmoral, Glamis and Dundee. 7 acre site. 11 touring tches. 7 hardstandings. 7 seasonal pitches. Tent pitches. lotorhome pitches. 49 statics.

otes 🚐

Gordon Arms Hotel

★★ **65%** SMALL HOTEL

The Square AB54 8AF
☎ 01466 792288 📠 01466 794556
e-mail: reception@gordonarms.demon.co.uk
dir: *Off A96 (Aberdeen to Inverness road) at Huntly. Hotel immediately on left after entering town square*

PETS: Bedrooms Charges £5 per night **Facilities** cage storage walks info vet info **On Request** fridge access torch towels **Stables** 2m **Other** charge for damage

This friendly, family-run hotel is located in the town square and offers a good selection of tasty, well-portioned dishes served in the bar, and also in the restaurant at weekends or midweek by appointment. Bedrooms come in a variety of sizes, but all have a good range of accessories.

Rooms 13 (3 fmly) **Facilities** FTV 🎵 Wi-fi

Huntly Castle Caravan Park *(NJ525405)*

►►►►►

The Meadow AB54 4UJ
☎ 01466 794999
e-mail: enquiries@huntlycastle.co.uk
dir: *From Aberdeen on A96 to Huntly. 0.75m after rdbt (on outskirts of Huntly) right towards town centre, left into Riverside Drive*

PETS: Public areas Exercise area adjacent **Facilities** walks info vet info **Other** prior notice required

Open Apr-Oct rs Wknds & school hols indoor activity centre open Last arrival 20.00hrs Last departure noon

A quality parkland site within striking distance of the Speyside Malt Whisky Trail, the beautiful Moray coast, and the Cairngorm Mountains. The park provides exceptional toilet facilities, and there are some fully serviced pitches. The indoor activity centre provides a wide range of games; the attractive town of Huntly is only a five-minute walk away, with its ruined castle plus a wide variety of restaurants and shops. 15 acre site. 90 touring pitches. 51 hardstandings. Tent pitches. Motorhome pitches. 40 statics.

SCOTLAND

SCOTLAND

KILDRUMMY
Map 15 NJ41

Kildrummy Castle Hotel
★★★★ 75% COUNTRY HOUSE HOTEL
AB33 8RA
☎ 019755 71288 📠 019755 71345
e-mail: kildrummy@btconnect.com
web: www.kildrummycastlehotel.co.uk
dir: Off A97 (Huntly to Ballater road)

PETS: **Bedrooms** sign certain bedrooms only **Exercise area** nearby **Facilities** cage storage walks info vet info **On Request** fridge access torch towels **Other** charge for damage owners must bring dog's own bedding; disposal bags available, owners must clean up after their dogs **Restrictions** 1 large dog or 2 small dogs per bedroom; check which breeds are accepted before booking

Set in landscaped gardens and accessed via a tree lined drive, Kildrummy Castle enjoys a peaceful rural location in the heart of the beautiful Grampian Highlands, yet is only a 35-minute drive from Aberdeen. The comfortable bedrooms have fabulous views, often with the ruin of the original castle as a backdrop. The current owners have sympathetically restored much of the original features, and the cosy lounges provide a perfect setting for afternoon tea or a post dinner drink. Dinner features the best of local produce, along with an extensive wine list. The relaxed atmosphere, supported by friendly service, is an obvious attraction here.

Rooms 16 (2 fmly) **S** £97.50; **D** £134-£217 (incl. bkfst)
Facilities FTV Fishing Xmas New Year Wi-fi **Parking** 25 **Notes** LB Closed 3-24 Jan RS 5-15 Nov

NORTH WATER BRIDGE
Map 15 NO66

Dovecot Caravan Park (NO648663)
▶ ▶ ▶
AB30 1QL
☎ 01674 840630 📠 01674 840630
e-mail: adele@dovecotcaravanpark.co.uk
dir: Take A90, 5m S of Laurencekirk. At Edzell Woods sign turn left. Site 500yds on left

PETS: **Public areas** disp bin **Exercise area on site** riverside dog walk **Facilities** walks info vet info **Other** dogs must be kept on leads at all times

Open Apr-Oct Last arrival 20.00hrs Last departure noon

A level grassy site in a country area close to the A90, with mature trees screening one side and the River North Esk on the other. The immaculate toilet facilities make this a handy overnight stop in a good touring area. 6 acre site. 25 touring pitches. 8 hardstandings. 8 seasonal pitches. Tent pitches. Motorhome pitches. 44 statics.

PETERHEAD
Map 15 NK14

Palace
★★★ 81% HOTEL
Prince St AB42 1PL
☎ 01779 474821 📠 01779 476119
e-mail: info@palacehotel.co.uk
web: www.palacehotel.co.uk
dir: A90 from Aberdeen, follow signs to Peterhead, on entering town turn into Prince St, then right into main car park

PETS: **Bedrooms** (14 GF) **Public areas** except restaurant & bar on leads **Grounds Exercise area** beach (10 mins) **Facilities** walks info vet info **Restrictions** small & medium size dogs only **Resident Pet:** Keira (Boxer)

This town centre hotel is popular with business travellers and for social events. Bedrooms come in two styles, with the executive rooms being particularly smart and spacious. Public areas include a themed bar, an informal diner reached via a spiral staircase, and a brasserie restaurant and cocktail bar.

Rooms 64 (1 fmly) (14 GF) **S** £70-£85; **D** £80-£95 (incl. bkfst)*
Facilities Snooker & Pool table ♬ New Year Wi-fi **Services** Lift **Parking** 50

ANGUS

MONIFIETH
Map 11 NO43

Riverview Caravan Park (NO502322)
▶ ▶ ▶ ▶
Marine Dr DD5 4NN
☎ 01382 535471 & 01382 817979 📠 01382 811525
e-mail: info@riverview.co.uk
dir: From Dundee on A930 follow signs to Monifieth, past supermarket, right signed golf course, left under rail bridge. Site signed on left

PETS: **Public areas** except toilets & showers disp bin **Exercise area** park & field adjacent **Facilities** food bowl water bowl leads dog grooming walks info vet info **Other** dog grooming available nearby disposal bags available

Open Mar-Jan Last arrival 22.00hrs Last departure 12.30hrs

A well-landscaped seaside site with individual hedged pitches, and direct access to the beach. The modernised toilet block has excellent facilities which are immaculately maintained. Amenities include a multi-gym, sauna and steam rooms. 5.5 acre site. 40 touring pitches. 40 hardstandings. Motorhome pitches. 46 statics.

ARDUAINE
Map 10 NM71

och Melfort
★★★ 83% ◉◉ HOTEL
A34 4XG
☎ 01852 200233 📠 01852 200214
-mail: reception@lochmelfort.co.uk
eb: www.lochmelfort.co.uk
ir: On A816, midway between Oban & Lochgilphead

ETS: Bedrooms (10 GF) unattended ground-floor bedrooms
nly Charges £8.50 per night Grounds disp bin Exercise area
rge field Facilities washing facs cage storage walks info vet
fo On Request fridge access torch towels Stables 3m Other
harge for damage Resident Pets: Hector (Springer), Toby (Cocker
paniel)

njoying one of the finest locations on the West Coast, this
opular, family-run hotel has outstanding views across
sknish Bay towards the Islands of Jura, Scarba and Shuna.
ccommodation is provided in either the balconied rooms of
e Cedar wing or the more traditional rooms in the main hotel.
ining options include the main restaurant with stunning views
the more informal bistro.

ooms 25 (20 annexe) (2 fmly) (10 GF) S £102-£128;
£144-£196 (incl. bkfst)* Facilities 4 moorings ♫ Xmas New
ear Wi-fi Parking 50 Notes Closed 4-20 Jan RS Winter

BARCALDINE
Map 10 NM94

arcaldine House
★★★★ ◉◉ GUEST ACCOMMODATION
A37 1SG
☎ 01631 720219
-mail: enquiries@barcaldinehouse.co.uk
eb: www.barcaldinehouse.co.uk

ETS: Bedrooms Charges £10 per night Public areas Grounds
isp bin Exercise area 50yds Facilities food (pre-bookable)
ood bowl water bowl bedding dog chews scoop/disp bags
eads pet sitting dog walking washing facs cage storage
alks info vet info On Request fridge access torch towels
tables 5m Other charge for damage Restrictions well behaved
ogs only

riginally built in 1709 by Patrick Campbell IV of Barcaldine,
his fine country house enjoys a peaceful location on lands that
ere once part of the extensive estates of the Campbells of
readalbane. The house has been sympathetically restored, and
he attractive bedrooms are spacious and very well equipped.
he award-winning restaurant serves the best in local produce
nd has a well deserved reputation. Guests have a choice of
omfortable lounges with real fires and the billiard room is a
opular feature. The house is an ideal base when exploring Argyll
Bute, the Highlands and the islands of Scotland.

ooms 8 en suite (1 fmly) S £100-£140; D £120-£190
acilities STV FTV tea/coffee Dinner available Direct Dial Cen ht
icensed Snooker Parking 16

CARRADALE
Map 10 NR83

Carradale Bay Caravan Park *(NR815385)*
►►►
PA28 6QG
☎ 01583 431665
e-mail: info@carradalebay.com
dir: A83 from Tarbert towards Campbeltown, left onto B842
(Carradale road), right onto B879. Site 0.5m

PETS: Charges 1st pet free, 2nd pet £1 per night Public areas
except shower block disp bin Exercise area on site walks &
beach Facilities walks info vet info

Open Apr-Sep Last arrival 22.00hrs Last departure noon

A beautiful, natural site on the sea's edge with superb views over
Kilbrannan Sound to the Isle of Arran. Pitches are landscaped
into small bays broken up by shrubs and bushes, and backed
by dunes close to the long sandy beach. Toilet facilities have
now been appointed to a very high standard. Lodges and static
caravans for holiday hire. 8 acre site. 75 touring pitches. Tent
pitches. Motorhome pitches. 12 statics.

CONNEL
Map 10 NM93

THE INDEPENDENTS
HOTEL ASSOCIATION

Falls of Lora Hotel
★★★ 77% HOTEL
PA37 1PB
☎ 01631 710483 📠 01631 710694
e-mail: enquiries@fallsoflora.com
web: www.fallsoflora.com
dir: From Glasgow take A82, A85. Hotel 0.5m past Connel sign
(5m before Oban)

PETS: Bedrooms (4 GF) Public areas except dining areas &
lounge on leads Grounds disp bin Exercise area 100mtrs
Facilities washing facs cage storage On Request fridge access
torch towels Other charge for damage

Personally run and welcoming, this long-established and thriving
holiday hotel enjoys inspiring views over Loch Etive. The spacious
ground floor takes in a comfortable, traditional lounge and a
cocktail bar with over a hundred whiskies and an open log fire.
Guests can eat in the popular, informal bistro, which is open all
day. Bedrooms come in a variety of styles, ranging from the cosy
standard rooms to high quality luxury rooms.

Rooms 30 (4 fmly) (4 GF) (30 smoking) S £29.50-£69.50;
D £55-£151 (incl. bkfst)* Facilities FTV Wi-fi Child facilities
Parking 40 Notes LB Closed mid Dec & Jan

SCOTLAND

SCOTLAND

Isle of Eriska Hotel, Spa & Golf

★★★★★ COUNTRY HOUSE HOTEL

Eriska PA37 1SD
☎ 01631 720371   📠 01631 720531
e-mail: office@eriska-hotel.co.uk
dir: Exit A85 at Connel, onto A828, 4m, follow hotel signs from N of Benderloch

PETS: Bedrooms (2 GF) **Sep accom** dog run kennel **Grounds** disp bin **Exercise area** 50mtrs **Facilities** food (pre-bookable) food bowl water bowl dog chews leads washing facs walks info vet info **On Request** fridge access torch towels **Other** charge for damage **Resident Pets:** Marti, Dibley & Sula (Labradors)

Situated on its own private island with delightful beaches and walking trails, this hotel is in a tranquil setting, perfect for total relaxation. The spacious bedrooms are very comfortable and boast some fine antique pieces. Local seafood, meats and game feature prominently on the award-winning menu, as do vegetables and herbs grown in the hotel's kitchen garden. Leisure facilities include an indoor pool, gym and spa treatment rooms. As this guide went to press, we learnt that there was a change of chef. The AA Rosette award will be in place once our team of inspectors has assessed the food created by the new kitchen brigade.

Rooms 23 (6 fmly) (2 GF) **S** £250-£460; **D** £330-£460 (incl. bkfst)* **Facilities** Spa FTV 🦢 supervised ⛳9 ⛳ Putt green Fishing 🎣 Gym Squash Sauna Steam room Skeet shooting Nature trails Xmas New Year Wi-fi **Parking** 40 **Notes** Closed Jan

Glendaruel Caravan Park (NR005865)

▶▶▶

PA22 3AB
☎ 01369 820267
e-mail: mail@glendaruelcaravanpark.com
dir: A83 onto A815 to Strachur, 13m to site on A886. By ferry from Gourock to Dunoon then B836, then A886 for approx 4m N. (NB this route not recommended for towing vehicles - 1:5 uphill gradient on B836)

PETS: Public areas except reception, shop, toilets & children's play area on leads disp bin **Exercise area on site** woodland walk **Facilities** food food bowl water bowl washing facs vet info **Other** prior notice required disposal bags available **Resident Pet:** 1 Black Labrador

Open Apr-Oct Last arrival 22.00hrs Last departure noon

A very pleasant, well-established site in the beautiful Victorian gardens of Glendaruel House. The level grass and hardstanding pitches are set in 23 acres of wooded parkland in a valley surrounded by mountains, with many rare specimen trees. The owners are hospitable and friendly. Static caravans are available for hire. 6 acre site. 27 touring pitches. 15 hardstandings. 12 seasonal pitches. Tent pitches. Motorhome pitches. 32 statics. 1 wooden pod.

Taychreggan

★★★★ 76% @@ COUNTRY HOUSE HOTEL

PA35 1HQ
☎ 01866 833211 & 833366   📠 01866 833244
e-mail: info@taychregganhotel.co.uk
dir: W from Crianlarich on A85 to Taynuilt, S for 7m on B845 (single track) to Kilchrenan

PETS: Bedrooms certain bedrooms only **Charges** £10 per night **Public areas** except restaurant & bar **Grounds** on leads disp bin **Exercise area** lochside area **Facilities** walks info vet info **On Request** torch towels **Other** charge for damage

Surrounded by stunning Highland scenery this stylish and superbly presented hotel, once a drover's cottage, enjoys an idyllic setting in 40 acres of wooded grounds on the shores of Loch Awe. The hotel has a smart bar with adjacent courtyard Orangerie and a choice of quiet lounges with deep, luxurious sofas. A well earned reputation has been achieved by the kitchen for the skilfully prepared dinners that showcase the local and seasonal Scottish larder. Families, and also dogs and their owners, are very welcome.

Rooms 18 (1 fmly) **S** £91-£176; **D** £122-£292 (incl. bkfst) **Facilities** FTV Fishing 🎣 Air rifle range Archery Clay pigeon shooting Falconry Mock deer stalk Xmas New Year Wi-fi Child facilities **Parking** 40 **Notes** Closed 3 Jan-9 Feb

The Ardanaiseig

★★★ @@@ COUNTRY HOUSE HOTEL

by Loch Awe PA35 1HE
☎ 01866 833333   📠 01866 833222
e-mail: ardanaiseig@clara.net
dir: A85 at Taynuilt onto B845 to Kilchrenan. Left in front of pub (road very narrow) signed 'Ardanaiseig Hotel' & 'No Through Road'. Continue for 3m

PETS: Bedrooms (5 GF) unattended **Charges** £15 per stay **Grounds** disp bin **Facilities** pet sitting washing facs walks info vet info **On Request** fridge access torch towels **Resident Pet:** Flo (Jack Russell)

Set amid lovely gardens and breathtaking scenery beside the shore of Loch Awe, this peaceful country-house hotel was built in a Scottish baronial style in 1834. Many fine pieces of furniture are evident in the bedrooms and charming day rooms, which include a drawing room, a library bar and an elegant dining room. The bedrooms are individually designed including some with four posters, some with loch views and some with access to the garden; standing on its own by the water is the Boat Shed, a delightful one bedroom suite. Guests can certainly look forward to the award-winning, skilfully cooked dishes that make excellent use of local, seasonal produce.

Rooms 18 (4 fmly) (5 GF) **S** £73-£113; **D** £146-£226 (incl. bkfst)* **Facilities** FTV Fishing 🎣 Boating Clay pigeon shooting Bikes for hire Xmas New Year Wi-fi **Parking** 20 **Notes** LB Closed 2 Jan-1 Fe.

Machrihanish Caravan Park *(NR647208)*

►►►►

East Trodigal PA28 6PT

☎ 01586 810366

e-mail: mail@campkintyre.co.uk

dir: *A82 from Glasgow to Tarbet, A83 to Inveraray, then to Campbeltown. Take B843 to Machrihanish. Site 300yds before village on right*

PETS: Public areas Exercise area on site enclosed flood-lit dog walk **Exercise area** 700yds **Facilities** food food bowl water bowl dog chews cat treats scoop/disp bags leads washing facs walks info vet info **Other** pet toys available

Open Mar-Oct & Dec Last arrival 22.00hrs Last departure 11.30hrs

Machrihanish is an open and breezy coastal site close to the Mull of Kintyre and a glorious three mile sandy beach. There is a campers' room, static caravans and four wooden wigwams for hire and great sea views to the isles of Jura and Islay. The park is adjacent to a fine links golf course, and Campbeltown, with its shops and restaurants, is five miles away. 8 acre site. 90 touring pitches. 12 hardstandings. 7 seasonal pitches. Tent pitches. Motorhome pitches. 5 statics.

Notes No campfires, 10mph speed limit. ♿

Manor House

★★★ **83%** ◉ HOTEL

Gallanach Rd PA34 4LS

☎ 01631 562087   📠 01631 563053

e-mail: info@manorhouseoban.com

web: www.manorhouseoban.com

dir: *Follow MacBrayne Ferries signs, pass ferry entrance for hotel on right*

PETS: Bedrooms (1 GF) **Grounds** on leads disp bin **Exercise area** 100mtrs **Facilities** walks info vet info **On Request** torch

Handy for the ferry terminal and with views of the bay and harbour, this elegant Georgian residence was built in 1780 as the dower house for the family of the Duke of Argyll. Comfortable and attractive public rooms invite relaxation, whilst most of the well-equipped bedrooms are furnished with period pieces.

Rooms 11 (1 GF) **Facilities** New Year Wi-fi **Parking** 20 **Notes** No children 12yrs Closed 25-26 Dec

Lancaster

★★ GUEST ACCOMMODATION

Corran Esplanade PA34 5AD

☎ 01631 562587   📠 01631 562587

e-mail: lancasteroban@btconnect.com

dir: *On seafront next to Columba's Cathedral*

PETS: Bedrooms unattended **Public areas** except dining room on leads **Exercise area** beach & woods adjacent **Facilities** leads cage storage walks info vet info **On Request** fridge access torch towels **Resident Pets:** Yosi (Akita), Tara (Springer Spaniel), Salem (cat), ferrets, guinea pig, budgie, fish

A family-run establishment on the esplanade that offers budget accommodation; many bedrooms boast lovely views out over the bay towards the Isle of Mull. Public areas include a choice of lounges and bars that also benefit from the panoramic views. A swimming pool, sauna and jacuzzi are added benefits.

Rooms 27 rms (24 en suite) (3 fmly) (10 smoking) **Facilities** FTV TVL tea/coffee Cen ht Licensed ⊗ Sauna Pool table **Parking** 20 **Notes** LB

Airds Hotel

★★★★ SMALL HOTEL

PA38 4DF

☎ 01631 730236   📠 01631 730535

e-mail: airds@airds-hotel.com

web: www.airds-hotel.com

dir: *From A828 (Oban to Fort William road), turn at Appin signed Port Appin. Hotel 2.5m on left*

PETS: Bedrooms (2 GF) **Charges** £10 per night **Grounds Exercise area** surrounding area **Facilities** bedding walks info vet info **On Request** fridge access torch towels **Other** charge for damage

The views are stunning from this small, luxury hotel on the shores of Loch Linnhe and where the staff are delightful and nothing is too much trouble. The well-equipped bedrooms provide style and luxury whilst many bathrooms are furnished in marble and have power showers. Expertly prepared dishes, utilising the finest of ingredients, are served in the elegant dining room. Comfortable lounges with deep sofas and roaring fires provide the ideal retreat for relaxation. A real get-away-from-it-all experience. As this guide went to press, we learnt that there was a change of chef. The AA Rosette award will be in place once our team of inspectors has assessed the food created by the new kitchen brigade.

Rooms 11 (3 fmly) (2 GF) **D** £260-£460 (incl. bkfst & dinner)* **Facilities** FTV Putt green ⛵ Xmas New Year Wi-fi **Parking** 20 **Notes** LB RS Nov-Jan

SCOTLAND

SCOTLAND

PORT APPIN *continued*

Pierhouse

★★★ **80%** SMALL HOTEL

PA38 4DE

☎ 01631 730302 & 730622 🖺 01631 730509

e-mail: reservations@pierhousehotel.co.uk

web: www.pierhousehotel.co.uk

dir: *A828 from Ballachulish to Oban. In Appin right at Port Appin & Lismore ferry sign. After 2.5m left after post office, hotel at end of road*

PETS: Bedrooms (6 GF) **Charges** £10 per night £70 per week **Public areas** except restaurant & bar at food service on leads **Grounds** on leads **Exercise area** adjacent **Facilities** food bowl water bowl washing facs cage storage walks info vet info **On Request** fridge access torch towels **Other** charge for damage **Restrictions** no very large dogs, no noisy dogs; no Dobermans, Rottweilers, Pit Bull Terriers, Bulldogs (see page 7)

Originally the residence of the Pier Master, with parts of the building dating back to the 19th century, this hotel is located on the shores of Loch Linnhe with picture-postcard views to the islands of Lismore and Mull. The beautifully appointed, individually designed bedrooms have Wi-fi access and include Arran Aromatics toiletries. The hotel has a Finnish sauna, and also offers a range of treatments. Babysitting can be arranged.

Rooms 12 (3 fmly) (6 GF) **Facilities** FTV Aromatherapy Massage Sauna New Year Wi-fi **Parking** 20 **Notes** LB Closed 25-26 Dec

STRACHUR
Map 10 NN00

Creggans Inn

★★★ **82%** HOTEL

PA27 8BX

☎ 01369 860279 🖺 01369 860637

e-mail: info@creggans-inn.co.uk

web: www.creggans-inn.co.uk

dir: *A82 from Glasgow, at Tarbet take A83 towards Cairndow, left onto A815 to Strachur*

PETS: Bedrooms **Public areas** bar only **Grounds** disp bin **Exercise area** adjacent **Facilities** food bowl water bowl scoop/disp bags leads washing facs cage storage walks info vet info **On Request** fridge access torch towels **Other** charge for damage **Resident Pet:** Hector (Long Haired Jack Russell)

Benefiting from a superb location on the shores of Loch Fyne, this well established family-run hotel caters well for both the leisure and corporate market. Many of the bedrooms are generous in size and enjoy wonderful views of the loch. During the cooler months open log fires are lit in the bar lounge and restaurant. Wi-fi is available throughout.

Rooms 14 (2 fmly) **Facilities** New Year Wi-fi **Parking** 16

TARBERT LOCH FYNE
Map 10 NR86

Stonefield Castle

OXFORD
HOTELS & INNS

★★★★ **73%** HOTEL

PA29 6YJ

☎ 01880 820836 🖺 01880 820929

e-mail: reservations.stonefieldcastle@ohiml.com

web: www.oxfordhotelsandinns.com

dir: *From Glasgow take M8 towards Erskine Bridge onto A82, follow Loch Lomond signs. From Arrochar follow A83 signs through Inveraray & Lochgilphead, hotel on left 2m before Tarbert*

PETS: Bedrooms (10 GF) unattended **Charges** £10 per night **Public areas** except restaurant & bar on leads **Grounds** on leads disp bin **Facilities** food bowl water bowl walks info vet info **On Request** fridge access torch towels **Other** charge for damage

This fine baronial castle commands a superb lochside setting amidst beautiful woodland gardens renowned for their rhododendrons - visit in late spring to see them at their best. Elegant public rooms are a feature, and the picture-window restaurant offers unrivalled views across Loch Fyne. Bedrooms are split between the main house and a purpose-built wing.

Rooms 32 (2 fmly) (10 GF) **Facilities** Xmas New Year Wi-fi **Services** Lift **Parking** 50

DUMFRIES & GALLOWAY

AUCHENCAIRN
Map 11 NX75

Balcary Bay Hotel

★★★ **86%** HOTEL

DG7 1QZ

☎ 01556 640217 & 640311 🖺 01556 640272

e-mail: reservations@balcary-bay-hotel.co.uk

web: www.balcary-bay-hotel.co.uk

dir: *On A711 between Dalbeattie & Kirkcudbright, hotel 2m from village*

PETS: Bedrooms (3 GF) unattended **Public areas** except restaurant, lounges & cocktail bar **Grounds** disp bin **Exercise area** beach adjacent **Facilities** food bowl water bowl scoop/disp bags leads washing facs cage storage walks info vet info **On Request** fridge access torch towels **Other** charge for damage **Resident Pets:** Rusty & Barney (Irish Red Setters)

Taking its name from the bay on which it lies, this hotel has lawns running down to the shore. The larger bedrooms enjoy

stunning views over the bay, whilst others overlook the gardens. The comfortable public areas invite relaxation. Imaginative dishes feature at dinner, accompanied by a good wine list.

Rooms 20 (1 fmly) (3 GF) **S** £65-£75; **D** £134-£164 (incl. bkfst)* **Facilities** FTV **Parking** 50 **Notes** LB Closed 1st Sun Dec-last Fri in Jan

BARGRENNAN
Map 10 NX37

Glentrool Holiday Park (NX350769)
▶ ▶ ▶

DG8 6RN
☎ 01671 840280 📠 01671 840342
e-mail: enquiries@glentroolholidaypark.co.uk
dir: Exit Newton Stewart on A714 towards Girvan, right at Bargrennan towards Glentrool. Site on left before village

PETS: Charges £2 per night £14 per week **Public areas** except children's play area, showers/toilets & shop **Exercise area** 200yds **Facilities** walks info vet info **Other** prior notice required phone to check which breeds are accepted **Resident Pet:** 1 cat

Open Mar-Oct Last arrival 21.00hrs Last departure noon

A small park close to the village of Glentrool, and bordered by the Galloway Forest Park. Both the touring and static area with vans for hire are immaculately presented and the amenity block is clean and freshly painted. The on-site shop is well stocked. 6.75 acre site. 14 touring pitches. 12 hardstandings. 3 seasonal pitches. Tent pitches. Motorhome pitches. 26 statics.

Notes No ball games, no groups.

BRIGHOUSE BAY
Map 11 NX64

Brighouse Bay Holiday Park (NX628453)
▶ ▶ ▶ ▶ ▶

DG6 4TS
☎ 01557 870267 📠 01557 870319
e-mail: info@brighouse-bay.co.uk
dir: Off B727 (Kirkcudbright to Borgue) or take A755 (Kirkcudbright) off A75 2m W of Twynholm. Site signed

PETS: Charges £5 per night **Public areas** except wildlife area, leisure club & children's play area disp bin **Exercise area on site** woods **Exercise area** beach (250yds) **Facilities** food food bowl water bowl dog chews cat treats leads washing facs walks info vet info **Other** prior notice required disposal bags available **Restrictions** no dangerous dogs (see page 7)

Open all year rs Nov-Mar leisure club closed 2 days each week Last arrival 21.30hrs Last departure 11.30hrs

This top class park has a country club feel and enjoys a marvellous coastal setting adjacent to the beach and with superb sea views. Pitches have been imaginatively sculpted into the meadowland, with stone walls and hedges blending in with the site's mature trees. These features, together with the large range of leisure activities, make this an excellent park for families who enjoy an active holiday. Many of the facilities are at an extra charge. A range of self-catering units is available for hire. 30 acre site. 190 touring pitches. 100 hardstandings. Tent pitches. Motorhome pitches. 120 statics.

Notes No motorised scooters, jet skis or own quad bikes

DALBEATTIE
Map 11 NX86

Glenearly Caravan Park (NX838628)
▶ ▶ ▶ ▶

DG5 4NE
☎ 01556 611393 📠 01556 612058
e-mail: glenearlycaravan@btconnect.com
dir: From Dumfries take A711 towards Dalbeattie. Site entrance after Edingham Farm on right (200yds before boundary sign)

PETS: Public areas except children's play area disp bin **Exercise area on site** mowed woodland walk **Exercise area** forests & park in Dalbeattie **Facilities** walks info vet info **Other** prior notice required

Open all year Last arrival 19.00hrs Last departure noon

An excellent small park set in open countryside with panoramic views of Long Fell, Maidenpap and Dalbeattie Forest. The park is located in 84 beautiful acres of farmland which visitors are invited to enjoy. The attention to detail here is of the highest standard and this is most notable in the presentation of the amenity block. Static holiday caravans for hire. 10 acre site. 39 touring pitches. 33 hardstandings. Tent pitches. Motorhome pitches. 74 statics.

Notes No commercial vehicles.

ECCLEFECHAN
Map 11 NY17

Hoddom Castle Caravan Park (NY154729)
▶ ▶ ▶ ▶ ▶

Hoddom DG11 1AS
☎ 01576 300251 📠 01576 300757
e-mail: hoddomcastle@aol.com
dir: M74 junct 19, follow signs to site. From A75, W of Annan, take B723 for 5m, follow signs to site

PETS: Charges £1.50 per night **Public areas** except bar & restaurant on leads disp bin **Exercise area on site** woodland walk **Exercise area** adjacent **Facilities** food food bowl water bowl walks info vet info **Other** prior notice required disposal bags available **Resident Pet:** Oscar (Jack Russell)

Open Etr or Apr-Oct rs Early season cafeteria closed Last arrival 21.00hrs Last departure 14.00hrs

The peaceful, well-equipped park can be found on the banks of the River Annan, and offers a good mix of grassy and hard pitches, beautifully landscaped and blending into the surroundings. There are signed nature trails, maintained by the park's countryside ranger, a 9-hole golf course, trout and salmon fishing, and plenty of activity ideas for children. 28 acre site. 200 touring pitches. 150 hardstandings. Tent pitches. Motorhome pitches. 54 statics.

Notes No electric scooters, no gazebos, no fires.

SCOTLAND

GATEHOUSE OF FLEET — Map 11 NX55

Anwoth Caravan Site *(NX595563)*

▶▶▶▶

DG7 2JU

☎ 01557 814333 & 01556 506200 📄 01557 814333

e-mail: enquiries@auchenlarie.co.uk

dir: *From A75 into Gatehouse of Fleet, site on right towards Stranraer. Signed from town centre*

PETS: Public areas disp bin **Exercise area** 300yds **Facilities** washing facs walks info vet info **Other** charge for damage prior notice required disposal bags available

Open Mar-Oct Last arrival 20.00hrs Last departure noon

A very high quality park in a peaceful sheltered setting within easy walking distance of the village, ideally placed for exploring the scenic hills, valleys and coastline. Grass, hardstanding and fully serviced pitches are available and guests may use the leisure facilities at the sister site, Auchenlarie Holiday Park. 2 acre site. 28 touring pitches. 13 hardstandings. Tent pitches. Motorhome pitches. 44 statics.

GRETNA — Map 11 NY36

King Robert the Bruce's Cave Caravan & Camping Park *(NY266705)*

▶▶▶▶

Cove Estate, Kirkpatrick Fleming DG11 3AT

☎ 01461 800285 & 07779 138694 📄 01461 800269

e-mail: enquiries@brucescave.co.uk

dir: *Exit A74(M) junct 21 for Kirkpatrick Fleming, follow N through village, pass Station Inn, left at Bruce's Court. Over rail crossing to site*

PETS: Public areas except toilet block, shop & children's play area disp bin **Exercise area on site** riverside walk **Facilities** food scoop/disp bags washing facs walks info vet info **Resident Pets:** Scamp, Cally, Bruce & Bruno (dogs), Silver & Buttercup (cats), Daisy (Shetland pony), Silver & Prince (horses), ducks

Open Apr-Nov rs Nov shop closed, water restriction Last arrival 22.00hrs Last departure 16.00hrs

The lovely wooded grounds of an old castle and mansion are the setting for this pleasant park. The mature woodland is a haven for wildlife, and there is a riverside walk to Robert the Bruce's Cave. A toilet block with en suite facilities is of special appeal to families. 80 acre site. 75 touring pitches. 60 hardstandings. Tent pitches. Motorhome pitches. 35 statics.

GRETNA SERVICE AREA (A74(M)) — Map 11 NY36

Days Inn Gretna Green - M74

BUDGET HOTEL

Welcome Break Service Area DG16 5HQ

☎ 01461 337566 📄 01461 337823

e-mail: gretna.hotel@welcomebreak.co.uk

web: www.welcomebreak.co.uk

dir: *Between junct 21/22 on M74 - accessible from both N'bound & S'bound carriageway*

PETS: Bedrooms (64 GF) **Charges** £5 per stay **Public areas** on leads **Grounds** on leads disp bin **Exercise area** adjacent **Facilities** walks info vet info **On Request** torch **Other** charge for damage

This modern building offers accommodation in smart, spacious and well-equipped bedrooms suitable for families and business travellers, and all with en suite bathrooms. Continental breakfast is available and other refreshments may be taken at the nearby family restaurant.

Rooms 64 (54 fmly) (64 GF) **S** £39.95-£59.95; **D** £49.95-£69.95

KIRKBEAN — Map 11 NX95

Cavens

★★★ ◉ COUNTRY HOUSE HOTEL

DG2 8AA

☎ 01387 880234 📄 01387 880467

e-mail: enquiries@cavens.com

web: www.cavens.com

dir: *Enter Kirkbean on A710, hotel signed*

PETS: Bedrooms (1 GF) certain bedrooms only **Sep accom** please enquire when booking **Charges Grounds** disp bin **Exercise area** adjacent **Facilities** walks info vet info **Stables** 1m **Other** charge for damage **Resident Pet:** Hamish (Labrador)

Set in six acres of parkland gardens, Cavens encapsulates all the virtues of an intimate country-house hotel. Quality is the keynote, and the proprietors spared no effort when they renovated the house. Bedrooms are delightfully individual and very comfortably equipped; there are Country rooms or the more spacious Estate rooms. The charming lounges invite peaceful relaxation. The menu at dinner offers dishes using the best local and home-made produce.

Rooms 6 (2 fmly) (1 GF) **S** £80-£130; **D** £80-£180 (incl. bkfst)* **Facilities** FTV 🛥 Shooting Fishing Horse riding New Year Wi-fi **Parking** 20 **Notes** LB Closed Jan

SCOTLAND

Arden House Hotel

★★ 75% HOTEL

Tongland Rd DG6 4UU

☎ 01557 330544 📠 01557 330742

dir: Exit A57, 4m W of Castle Douglas onto A711. Follow Kirkcudbright signs, over Telford Bridge. Hotel 400mtrs on left

PETS: Bedrooms unattended sign **Public areas** except restaurant at meal times **Grounds** disp bin **Exercise area** nearby **Facilities** vet info

Set well back from the main road in extensive grounds on the northeast side of town, this spotlessly maintained hotel offers attractive bedrooms, a lounge bar and adjoining conservatory serving a range of popular dishes, which are also available in the dining room. It boasts an impressive function suite in its grounds.

Rooms 9 (7 fmly) (5 smoking) **S** £60; **D** £80 (incl. bkfst)*
Parking 70

Dryfesdale Country House

★★★★ 73% HOTEL

Dryfebridge DG11 2SF

☎ 01576 202427 📠 01576 204187

e-mail: reception@dryfesdalehotel.co.uk

web: www.dryfesdalehotel.co.uk

dir: From M74 junct 17 follow Lockerbie North signs, 3rd left at 1st rdbt, 1st exit left at 2nd rdbt, hotel 200yds on left

PETS: Bedrooms (20 GF) unattended sign **Charges** £5 per night £15 per week **Public areas Grounds** disp bin **Facilities** food (pre-bookable) food bowl water bowl bedding dog chews feeding mat scoop/disp bags washing facs cage storage walks info vet info **On Request** fridge access torch towels **Stables** 100yds **Other** charge for damage **Resident Pet:** Buddy (Long Haired German Shepherd)

Conveniently situated for the M74, yet discreetly screened from it, this friendly hotel provides attentive service. Bedrooms, some with access to patio areas, vary in size and style; all offer good levels of comfort and are well equipped. Creative, good value dinners make use of local produce and are served in the airy restaurant that overlooks the manicured gardens and rolling countryside.

Rooms 29 (5 fmly) (20 GF) **S** £65-£89; **D** £99-£129*
Facilities STV FTV Putt green ⛳ Clay pigeon shooting Fishing ♬ Xmas New Year Wi-fi **Parking** 60

Kings Arms Hotel

★★ 78% HOTEL

High St DG11 2JL

☎ 01576 202410 📠 01576 202410

e-mail: reception@kingsarmshotel.co.uk

web: www.kingsarmshotel.co.uk

dir: A74(M), 0.5m into town centre, hotel opposite town hall

PETS: Bedrooms unattended **Public areas** except restaurant & 1 bar on leads **Exercise area** 1 min walk **Facilities** food bowl water bowl washing facs cage storage walks info vet info **On Request** fridge access torch towels **Resident Pet:** Bailey (Yellow Labrador)

Dating from the 17th century this former inn lies in the town centre. Now a family-run hotel, it provides attractive well-equipped bedrooms with Wi-fi access. At lunch a menu ranging from snacks to full meals is served in both the cosy bars and the restaurant at dinner.

Rooms 13 (2 fmly) **S** £50; **D** £83 (incl. bkfst) **Facilities** FTV Xmas New Year Wi-fi **Parking** 8

SCOTLAND

LOCKERBIE *continued*

Ravenshill House

★★ 74% HOTEL

12 Dumfries Rd DG11 2EF

☎ 01576 202882

e-mail: aaenquiries@ravenshillhotellockerbie.co.uk

web: www.ravenshillhotellockerbie.co.uk

dir: *From A74(M) Lockerbie junct onto A709. Hotel 0.5m on right*

PETS: Bedrooms max 3 bedrooms available **Grounds** disp bin **Exercise area** 400yds **Facilities** walks info vet info **On Request** fridge access **Other** pets must be supervised at all times

Set in spacious gardens on the fringe of the town, this friendly, family-run hotel offers cheerful service and good value, home-cooked meals. Bedrooms are generally spacious and comfortably equipped, including a two-room unit ideal for families.

Rooms 8 (2 fmly) **S** £40-£65; **D** £78-£85 (incl. bkfst)*
Facilities FTV Wi-fi **Parking** 35 **Notes** LB Closed 1-3 Jan

---

MOFFAT   **Map 11 NT00**

Annandale Arms Hotel

★★★ 78% ⊛ HOTEL

High St DG10 9HF

☎ 01683 220013 📠 01683 221395

e-mail: reception@annandalearmshotel.co.uk

web: www.annandalearmshotel.co.uk

dir: *M74 junct 15/A701. Hotel on west side of central square that forms High St*

PETS: Bedrooms (5 GF) unattended courtyard bedrooms only **Public areas** except restaurant on leads **Grounds** disp bin **Exercise area** 0.5m **Facilities** walks info vet info **Other** charge for damage **Resident Pets:** Jago (Labrador), Zach (Cocker Spaniel)

With a history dating back 250 years old, this family run hotel in the heart of Moffat provides well-appointed, modern bedrooms and bathrooms, located away from the hustle and bustle of the high street. There is a welcoming bar and restaurant serving real ales and quality food. Wi-fi and off-road parking are added benefits.

Rooms 16 (2 fmly) (5 GF) (5 smoking) **S** £70; **D** £110 (incl. bkfst) **Facilities** FTV New Year Wi-fi **Parking** 20 **Notes** LB Closed 25-26 Dec

---

Limetree House

★★★★ GUEST ACCOMMODATION

Eastgate DG10 9AE

☎ 01683 220001

e-mail: info@limetreehouse.co.uk

web: www.limetreehouse.co.uk

dir: *Off High St onto Well St, left onto Eastgate, house 100yds on left*

PETS: Bedrooms (1 GF) **Public areas** except dining room on leads **Exercise area** 0.25m **Facilities** cage storage walks info vet info **On Request** fridge access torch **Other** charge for damage 1 dog per guest, max 2 dogs in house **Restrictions** no large dogs **Resident Pets:** Sully, Mike & Beattie (cats)

A warm welcome is assured at this well-maintained guest accommodation, quietly situated behind the main high street. Recognisable by its colourful flower baskets in season, it provides an inviting lounge and a bright cheerful breakfast room. Bedrooms are smartly furnished and include a large family room.

Rooms 6 en suite (1 fmly) (1 GF) **S** £40-£45; **D** £60-£80 **Facilities** FTV TVL tea/coffee Cen ht Wi-fi Golf 18 **Parking** 3 **Notes** LB No Children 5yrs RS Xmas & New Year

---

Barnhill Springs Country Guest House

★★ GUEST ACCOMMODATION

DG10 9QS

☎ 01683 220580

e-mail: barnhillsprings@yahoo.co.uk

dir: *A74(M) junct 15, A701 towards Moffat. Barnhill Rd 50yds on right*

PETS: Bedrooms (1 GF) unattended **Public areas** except dining room **Grounds** disp bin **Facilities** food bowl water bowl dog chews scoop/disp bags leads washing facs cage storage walks info vet info **On Request** fridge access torch towels **Resident Pet:** Kim (Collie cross)

This former farmhouse is in a quiet, rural location south of the town and within easy reach of the M74. Bedrooms are well proportioned; and have private bathrooms. There is a comfortable lounge and separate dining room. Barnhill Spring continues to welcome pets.

Rooms 5 rms (5 pri facs) (1 fmly) (1 GF) **S** £35-£36; **D** £70-£72 **Facilities** TVL tea/coffee Dinner available Cen ht **Parking** 10 **Notes** LB ⊛

NEWTON STEWART Map 10 NX46

The Bruce Hotel
★★★ 73% HOTEL

88 Queen St DG8 6JL
☎ 01671 402294 📠 01671 402294
e-mail: mail@the-bruce-hotel.com
web: www.the-bruce-hotel.com
dir: Exit A75 at Newton Stewart rdbt towards town. Hotel 800mtrs on right

PETS: Bedrooms unattended Public areas except restaurant on leads Grounds on leads Exercise area nearby Facilities walks info Other charge for damage Restrictions please phone to confirm which breeds are accepted

Named after the Scottish patriot Robert the Bruce, this welcoming hotel is just a short distance from the A75. One of the well-appointed bedrooms features a four-poster bed, and popular family suites contain separate bedrooms for children. Public areas include a traditional lounge, a formal restaurant and a lounge bar, both offering a good choice of dishes.

Rooms 20 (3 fmly) S £50-£70; D £60-£90 (incl. bkfst) Facilities FTV New Year Wi-fi Parking 14 Notes LB

Creebridge Caravan Park (NX415656)
► ► ►

Minnigaff DG8 6AJ
☎ 01671 402324 & 402432 📠 01671 402324
e-mail: john_sharples@btconnect.com
dir: 0.25m E of Newton Stewart at Minnigaff on bypass, signed off A75

PETS: Charges £5 per night £30 per week Public areas disp bin Exercise area 500mtrs Facilities food bowl water bowl washing facs cage storage walks info vet info Stables 0.5m Other charge for damage prior notice required

Open all year rs Mar only one toilet block open Last arrival 20.00hrs Last departure 10.30hrs

A small family-owned site a short walk from the town's amenities. The site is surrounded by mature trees, and the toilet facilities are clean and functional. 5.5 acre site. 36 touring pitches. 12 hardstandings. Tent pitches. Motorhome pitches. 50 statics.

PALNACKIE Map 11 NX85

Barlochan Caravan Park (NX819572)
► ► ►

DG7 1PF
☎ 01556 600256 & 01557 870267 📠 01557 870319
e-mail: aa@barlochan.co.uk
dir: On A711, N of Palnackie, signed

PETS: Charges £2.50 per night Public areas except swimming pool, children's play area, putting green, games room, shop & toilet block Exercise area on site dog walk at top of park Exercise area adjacent to site (2 min's walk) Facilities walks info vet info Other disposal bags available

Open Apr-Oct rs end May-beg Sep swimming pool open Last arrival 21.30hrs Last departure 11.30hrs

A small terraced park with quiet landscaped pitches in a level area backed by rhododendron bushes. There are spectacular views over the River Urr estuary, and the park has its own coarse fishing loch nearby. The amenity block has been upgraded to include combined wash facilities. The leisure facilities at Brighouse Bay are available to visitors. 9 acre site. 20 touring pitches. 3 hardstandings. Tent pitches. Motorhome pitches. 65 statics.

PARTON Map 11 NX67

Loch Ken Holiday Park (NX687702)
► ► ►

DG7 3NE
☎ 01644 470282
e-mail: office@lochkenholidaypark.co.uk
dir: On A713, N of Parton

PETS: Charges £2 per night £10 per week Public areas except shop on leads disp bin Exercise area on site field provided Exercise area 50mtrs Facilities food leads walks info vet info Other prior notice required

Open Mar-mid Nov rs Mar (ex Etr) & Nov restricted shop hours Last departure noon

Much improved following a huge injection of energy, enthusiasm and commitment from the hands-on Bryson family, this busy and popular park, with a natural emphasis on water activities, is set on the eastern shores of Loch Ken, with superb views. It is in a peaceful and beautiful spot opposite the RSPB reserve, with direct access to the loch for fishing and boat launching. The park offers a variety of watersports, as well as farm visits and nature trails. Static caravans for hire. 15 acre site. 40 touring pitches. 12 hardstandings. 12 seasonal pitches. Tent pitches. Motorhome pitches. 35 statics.

Notes No noise after 22.00hrs.

SCOTLAND

Knockinaam Lodge

★★★ ◉◉◉ HOTEL

DG9 9AD

☎ 01776 810471 📠 01776 810435

e-mail: reservations@knockinaamlodge.com

web: www.knockinaamlodge.com

dir: *From A77 or A75 follow signs to Portpatrick. Through Lochans. After 2m left at signs for hotel*

PETS: Bedrooms unattended 3 allocated bedrooms only **Charges** £20 per stay **Grounds** **Exercise area** beach (20mtrs) **Other** owners requested to bring dog's own bedding **Resident Pet:** Jerry (Black Labrador)

Any tour of Dumfries & Galloway would not be complete without a stay at this haven of tranquillity and relaxation. Knockinaam Lodge is an extended Victorian house set in an idyllic cove with its own pebble beach, ideal for a private swim in the summer, and sheltered by majestic cliffs and woodlands. Surrounded by 30 acres of delightful grounds, the lodge was the location for a meeting between Churchill and General Eisenhower in World War II. Today, a warm welcome is assured from the proprietors and their committed team, and much emphasis is placed on providing a sophisticated but intimate home-from-home experience. There are just ten suites - each individually designed and all with flat-screen TVs with DVD players, luxury toiletries and complimentary bottled water. The cooking is a real treat and showcases prime Scottish produce treated with respect on the daily-changing, four-course set menus; guests can always discuss the choices in advance if they wish.

Rooms 10 (1 fmly) **Facilities** FTV Fishing ⤵ Shooting Walking Sea fishing Clay pigeon shooting Xmas New Year Wi-fi **Parking** 20

Sands of Luce Holiday Park (NX103510)

►►►►

Sands of Luce DG9 9JN

☎ 01776 830456 📠 01776 830477

e-mail: info@sandsofluceholidaypark.co.uk

dir: *From S & E: A75 onto B7084 signed Drummore. Site signed at junct with A716. From N: A77 through Stranraer towards Portpatrick, 2m, A716 signed Drummore, site signed in 5m*

PETS: Public areas disp bin **Exercise area on site** part of tent field **Exercise area** beach & park **Facilities** washing facs walks info vet info **Stables** 5m **Other** prior notice required **Resident Pets:** Penny (Springer Spaniel), Skye (Labrador), Noosa & Whinn (cats), chickens

Open Mar-Jan Last arrival 20.00hrs Last departure noon

This is a large, well managed park with a balance of static and touring caravans and enjoys a stunning position with direct access to a sandy beach and with views across Luce Bay. It has its own boat storage area and boasts an excellent static hire fleet and a tastefully decorated well-managed club. 30 acre site. 100 touring pitches. Tent pitches. Motorhome pitches. 190 statics.

Notes No quad bikes.

Blackaddie House Hotel

★★★ 79% ◉◉ COUNTRY HOUSE HOTEL

Blackaddie Rd DG4 6JJ

☎ 01659 502700

e-mail: ian@blackaddiehotel.co.uk

dir: *Exit A76 just N of Sanquhar at Burnside Service Station. Take private road to hotel 300mtrs on right*

PETS: Bedrooms (3 GF) unattended **Charges** £5 per night £25 per week **Public areas** except restaurant on leads **Grounds** disp bin **Exercise area** adjacent **Facilities** food (pre-bookable) food bowl water bowl dog chews leads cage storage walks info vet info **On Request** fridge access torch towels **Other** charge for damage **Resident Pets:** 2 Cocker Spaniels, 1 cat

Overlooking the River Nith and in two acres of secluded gardens, this family run country house hotel offers friendly and attentive hands-on service. The bedrooms and suites, including family accommodation, are all well presented and comfortable with many useful extras provided as standard. The award-winning food, served in the restaurant, with its lovely garden views, is based on prime Scottish ingredients.

Rooms 9 (3 annexe) (2 fmly) (3 GF) **Facilities** Xmas New Year Wi-fi **Parking** 20

Southerness Holiday Village (NX976545)

Off Sandy Ln DG2 8AZ

☎ 0844 335 3756 📠 01387 880429

e-mail: touringandcamping@parkdeanholidays.com

dir: *From S: A75 from Gretna to Dumfries. From N: A74, exit at A701 to Dumfries. Take A710 (coast road), approx 16m, site easily visible*

PETS: Charges £2-£3 per night **Public areas** except indoor venues & outdoor play areas **Facilities** food food bowl water bowl dog chews scoop/disp bags walks info vet info **Other** prior notice required **Restrictions** no American Pitbull Terriers, Japanese Akita, Wolfhound Hybrid, Japanese Tosa, Neapolitan Mastiff, Dogo Argentina or Fila Brasiliero. (see page 7) **Resident Pets:** Lissie (lizard), Sid (seagull)

Open Mar-Oct Last arrival 21.00hrs Last departure 10.00hrs

There are stunning views across the Solway Firth from this holiday park at the foot of the Galloway Hills. A sandy beach on the Solway Firth is accessible directly from the park. The emphasis is on family entertainment, and facilities include an indoor pool, show bar, coast bar and kitchen. A very well organised park with excellent all-weather, fully-serviced pitches available. 50 acre site. 100 touring pitches. 60 hardstandings. Tent pitches. Motorhome pitches. 611 statics.

SCOTLAND

Corsewall Lighthouse Hotel

★★★ 80% HOTEL

Corsewall Point, Kirkcolm DG9 0QG
☎ 01776 853220 ▤ 01776 854231
e-mail: lighthousehotel@btinternet.com
web: www.lighthousehotel.co.uk
dir: *A718 from Stranraer to Kirkcolm (approx 8m). Follow hotel signs for 4m*

PETS: Bedrooms (2 GF) sign certain suites only **Charges** £10 per night **Public areas** except restaurant on leads **Grounds** disp bin **Exercise area** surrounding area **Facilities** washing facs walks info vet info **On Request** torch towels **Other** charge for damage **Restrictions** no breed larger than a Labrador

Looking for something completely different? This is a unique hotel converted from buildings that adjoin a Grade A listed, 19th-century lighthouse set on a rocky coastline. Situated on the headland to the west of Loch Ryan, the lighthouse beam still functions to warn approaching ships. Bedrooms come in a variety of sizes, some reached by a spiral staircase, and like the public areas, are cosy and atmospheric. The cottage suites in the grounds offer greater space. The restaurant menus are based on Scottish produce such as venison and salmon.

Rooms 11 (5 annexe) (4 fmly) (2 GF) (3 smoking) **Facilities** FTV Xmas New Year Wi-fi **Parking** 20

Aird Donald Caravan Park *(NX075605)*

▶▶▶▶

London Rd DG9 8RN
☎ 01776 702025
e-mail: enquiries@aird-donald.co.uk
dir: *From A75 left on entering Stranraer (signed). Opposite school, site 300yds*

PETS: Public areas disp bin **Exercise area on site** wooded area **Exercise area** 0.25m **Facilities** walks info vet info

Open all year Last departure 16.00hrs

A spacious touring site, mainly grass but with tarmac hardstanding areas, with pitches large enough to accommodate a car and caravan overnight without unhitching. On the fringe of town screened by mature shrubs and trees. Ideal stopover en route to Northern Irish ferry ports. 12 acre site. 100 touring pitches. 30 hardstandings. Tent pitches. Motorhome pitches.

Notes Tents Apr-Sep. 🚭

Drumroamin Farm Camping & Touring Site

(NX444512)

▶▶▶

1 South Balfern DG8 9DB
☎ 01988 840613 & 07752 471456
e-mail: enquiry@drumroamin.co.uk
dir: *A75 towards Newton Stewart, onto A714 for Wigtown. Left on B7005 through Bladnock, A746 through Kirkinner. Take B7004 signed Garlieston, 2nd left opposite Kilsture Forest, site 0.75m at end of lane*

PETS: Public areas except shower block disp bin **Exercise area on site** woodland walk **Facilities** washing facs walks info vet info **Resident Pet:** Maggie (Chocolate Labrador)

Open all year Last arrival 21.00hrs Last departure noon

An open, spacious park in a quiet spot a mile from the main road, and close to Wigtown Bay. A superb toilet block offers spacious showers, and there's a lounge/games room and plenty of room for children to play. 5 acre site. 48 touring pitches. Tent pitches. 3 statics.

Notes No fires. 🚭

The Fenwick Hotel

★★★ 82% HOTEL

Fenwick KA3 6AU
☎ 01560 600478 ▤ 01560 600334
e-mail: info@thefenwickhotel.co.uk
web: www.thefenwickhotel.co.uk
dir: *M77 junct 8, B7061 towards Fenwick, follow hotel signs*

PETS: Bedrooms (9 GF) **Charges** £10 per night £70 per week **Grounds** disp bin **Exercise area** nearby **Facilities** walks info vet info **On Request** fridge access towels **Other** charge for damage

Benefiting from a great location alongside the M77 and offering easy links to Ayr, Kilmarnock and Glasgow. The spacious bedrooms are thoughtfully equipped; complimentary Wi-fi is available throughout the hotel. The bright restaurant offers both formal and informal dining and there are two bars to choose from.

Rooms 30 (1 fmly) (9 GF) **Facilities** STV Xmas New Year Wi-fi **Parking** 64

SCOTLAND

EAST LOTHIAN

DUNBAR Map 12 NT67

Thurston Manor Leisure Park *(NT712745)*

▶ ▶ ▶ ▶ ▶

Innerwick EH42 1SA
☎ 01368 840643 📄 01368 840261
e-mail: holidays@thurstonmanor.co.uk
dir: *4m S of Dunbar, signed off A1*

PETS: Charges contact park for details **Public areas** except buildings & children's play area disp bin **Facilities** food food bowl water bowl dog chews litter tray leads vet info **Other** prior notice required max 2 dogs per unit; contact site for details of charges disposal bags available **Restrictions** no dangerous dogs (see page 7)

Open Mar-7 Jan rs 1-22 Dec site open wknds only Last arrival 23.00hrs Last departure noon

A pleasant park set in 250 acres of unspoilt countryside. The touring and static areas of this large park are in separate areas. The main touring area occupies an open, level position, and the toilet facilities are modern and exceptionally well maintained. The park boasts a well-stocked fishing loch, a heated indoor swimming pool, steam room, sauna, jacuzzi, mini-gym and fitness room and seasonal entertainment. 175 acre site. 100 touring pitches. 45 hardstandings. Tent pitches. Motorhome pitches. 500 statics.

Belhaven Bay Caravan & Camping Park
(NT661781)

▶ ▶ ▶

Belhaven Bay EH42 1TS
☎ 01368 865956 📄 01368 865022
e-mail: belhaven@meadowhead.co.uk
dir: *A1 onto A1087 towards Dunbar. Site (1m) in John Muir Park*

PETS: Charges £3 per night **Public areas** except play area on leads disp bin **Exercise area on site** lakeside grass area **Exercise area** adjacent **Facilities** food bowl water bowl washing facs walks info vet info **Other** prior notice required disposal bags available **Restrictions** no dangerous dogs (see page 7)

Open Mar-13 Oct Last arrival 20.00hrs Last departure noon

Small, well-maintained park in a sheltered location and within walking distance of the beach. This is an excellent spot for seabird watching, and there is a good rail connection with Edinburgh from Dunbar. There is a children's play area. 40 acre site. 52 touring pitches. 11 hardstandings. Tent pitches. 64 statics.

MUSSELBURGH Map 11 NT37

Drum Mohr Caravan Park *(NT373734)*

▶ ▶ ▶ ▶

Levenhall EH21 8JS
☎ 0131 665 6867 📄 0131 653 6859
e-mail: admin@drummohr.org
dir: *Exit A1 at A199 junct through Wallyford, at rdbt onto B1361 signed Prestonpans. 1st left, site 400yds*

PETS: Charges £2 per night **Public areas** except children's play area on leads disp bin **Exercise area on site** perimeter walk **Facilities** food vet info **Other** max 2 dogs per pitch disposal bags available

Open all year rs Winter arrivals by arrangement Last arrival 17.00hrs Last departure noon

This attractive park is sheltered by mature trees on all sides, and carefully landscaped within. The park is divided into separate areas by mature hedging and planting of trees and ornamental shrubs. Pitches are generous in size, and there are a number of fully serviced pitches plus first-class amenities. There are five bothys for hire. 9 acre site. 120 touring pitches. 50 hardstandings. Tent pitches. Motorhome pitches. 12 statics. 10 wooden pods.

CITY OF EDINBURGH

EDINBURGH Map 11 NT27

Prestonfield

★★★★★ @@ TOWN HOUSE HOTEL

Priestfield Rd EH16 5UT
☎ 0131 225 7800 📄 0131 220 4392
e-mail: reservations@prestonfield.com
web: www.prestonfield.com
dir: *A7 towards Cameron Toll. 200mtrs beyond Royal Commonwealth Pool, into Priestfield Rd*

PETS: Bedrooms (6 GF) unattended **Charges Public areas** on leads **Grounds** disp bin **Facilities** food (pre-bookable) food bowl water bowl dog chews dog walking cage storage walks info vet info **On Request** torch towels **Other** charge for damage **Resident Pets:** Archie & Brodie (Jack Russells), Highland cattle, peacocks

This centuries-old landmark has been lovingly restored and enhanced to provide deeply comfortable and dramatically furnished bedrooms. The building demands to be explored: from the tapestry lounge and the whisky room to the restaurant, where the walls are adorned with pictures of former owners. Facilities and services are up-to-the-minute, and carefully prepared meals are served in the award-winning Rhubarb restaurant.

Rhubarb is the winner of the AA Wine Award for Scotland 2011-12.

Rooms 23 (6 GF) **D** £295-£365 (incl. bkfst)* **Facilities** STV FTV ⅃ 18 Putt green ⚘ Free bike hire Xmas New Year Wi-fi **Services** Lift **Parking** 250

Novotel Edinburgh Park

★★★★ 77% HOTEL

15 Lochside Av EH12 9DJ
☎ 0131 446 5600 📠 0131 446 5610
e-mail: h6515@accor.com
dir: *Near Hermiston Gate shopping area*

PETS: Bedrooms unattended **Charges** £10 per night **Grounds** on leads **Stables** 3m **Other** charge for damage **Restrictions** no Pit Bull Terriers

Located just off the city by-pass and within minutes of the airport, this modern hotel offers bedrooms that are spacious and comfortable. The public areas include the open-plan lobby, bar and a restaurant where some tables have their own TVs.

Rooms 170 (130 fmly) **Facilities** 🕙 Gym Wi-fi **Services** Lift **Parking** 96

Novotel Edinburgh Centre

★★★★ 76% HOTEL

Lauriston Place, Lady Lawson St EH3 9DE
☎ 0131 656 3500 📠 0131 656 3510
e-mail: H3271@accor.com
web: www.novotel.com
dir: *From Edinburgh Castle right onto George IV Bridge from Royal Mile. Follow to junct, then right into Lauriston Place. Hotel 700mtrs on right*

PETS: Bedrooms unattended **Charges** £10 per night
Public areas except restaurant on leads **Exercise area** park (5 mins' walk) **Facilities** walks info **Other** charge for damage

This modern hotel is located in the centre of the city, close to Edinburgh Castle. Smart and stylish public areas include a cosmopolitan bar, brasserie-style restaurant and indoor leisure facilities. The air-conditioned bedrooms feature a comprehensive range of extras and bathrooms with baths and separate shower cabinets.

Rooms 180 (146 fmly) **Facilities** STV 🕙 Gym Sauna Steam room Xmas Wi-fi **Services** Lift Air con **Parking** 15

Dalhousie Castle and Aqueous Spa

★★★ 82% ◉◉ HOTEL

Bonnyrigg EH19 3JB
☎ 01875 820153 📠 01875 821936
e-mail: info@dalhousiecastle.co.uk
web: www.dalhousiecastle.co.uk
dir: *A7 S from Edinburgh through Lasswade/Newtongrange, right at Shell Garage (B704), hotel 0.5m from junct*

PETS: Bedrooms standard rooms & The Dower House only
Public areas except library & food/beverage areas on leads
Grounds on leads disp bin **Exercise area** 500yds **Facilities** vet info **On Request** fridge access **Stables** 5m **Other** charge for damage **Restrictions** well behaved dogs only

A popular wedding venue, this imposing medieval castle sits amid lawns and parkland and even has a falconry. Bedrooms offer a mix of styles and sizes, including richly decorated themed rooms named after various historical figures. The Dungeon restaurant provides an atmospheric setting for dinner, and the less formal Orangery serves food all day. The spa offers many relaxing and therapeutic treatments and hydro facilities.

Rooms 36 (7 annexe) (3 fmly) **Facilities** Spa FTV Fishing Falconry Clay pigeon shooting Archery Laserday Xmas New Year Wi-fi **Parking** 110

Best Western Kings Manor

★★★ 79% HOTEL

100 Milton Road East EH15 2NP
☎ 0131 669 0444 & 468 8003 📠 0131 669 6650
e-mail: reservations@kingsmanor.com
web: www.kingsmanor.com
dir: *A720 E to Old Craighall junct, left into city, right at A1/A199 junct, hotel 400mtrs on right*

PETS: Bedrooms (13 GF) **Charges** £5 per night **Public areas** except dining areas on leads **Grounds** disp bin **Exercise area** 600yds **Facilities** washing facs vet info **On Request** fridge access torch towels **Other** charge for damage

Lying on the eastern side of the city and convenient for the by-pass, this hotel is popular with business guests, tour groups and for conferences. It boasts a fine leisure complex and a bright modern bistro, which complements the quality, creative cooking in the main restaurant.

Rooms 95 (8 fmly) (13 GF) **S** £60-£125; **D** £70-£180
Facilities Spa STV FTV 🕙 ♨ Gym Health & beauty salon Steam room Sauna Wi-fi **Services** Lift **Parking** 130 **Notes** LB

SCOTLAND

SCOTLAND

EDINBURGH *continued*

Arden Guest House

★★★ GUEST HOUSE

126 Old Dalkeith Rd EH16 4SD

☎ 0131 664 3985 📠 0131 621 0866

e-mail: ardenguesthouse@btinternet.com

dir: *2m SE of city centre near Craigmillar Castle. On A7, 200yds W of hospital*

PETS: Bedrooms (3 GF) unattended certain bedrooms only **Public areas Grounds** disp bin **Exercise area** 0.25m **Facilities** scoop/disp bags pet sitting cage storage walks info vet info **On Request** fridge access torch towels **Other** charge for damage

Arden Guest House is well situated on the south-east side of the city, close to the hospital, and benefits from off-road parking. Many thoughtful extras are provided as standard, including Wi-fi. Attentive and friendly service enhances the guest experience.

Rooms 8 en suite (2 fmly) (3 GF) **S** £30-£45; **D** £50-£90 **Facilities** STV tea/coffee Cen ht Wi-fi **Parking** 8 **Notes** Closed 22-27 Dec

---

FIFE

DUNFERMLINE
Map 11 NT08

Pitbauchlie House

★★★ 79% HOTEL

Aberdour Rd KY11 4PB

☎ 01383 722282 📠 01383 620738

e-mail: info@pitbauchlie.com

web: www.pitbauchlie.com

dir: *M90 junct 2, A823, then B916. Hotel 0.5m on right*

PETS: Bedrooms (19 GF) unattended sign **Grounds Exercise area** nearby **Facilities** dog walking walks info vet info **On Request** fridge access torch towels

Situated in three acres of wooded grounds this hotel is just a mile south of the town and has a striking modern interior. The bedrooms are well equipped, and the deluxe rooms have 32-inch LCD satellite TVs and CD micro systems; there is one bedroom designed for less able guests. The eating options include Harvey's Conservatory bistro and Restaurant 47 where Scottish and French influenced cuisine is offered.

Rooms 50 (3 fmly) (19 GF) **Facilities** STV FTV Gym Wi-fi **Parking** 80

LUNDIN LINKS
Map 12 NO40

Woodland Gardens Caravan & Camping Site *(NO418031)*

▶ ▶ ▶

Blindwell Rd KY8 5QG

☎ 01333 360319

e-mail: enquiries@woodland-gardens.co.uk

dir: *Off A915 (coast road) at Largo at E end of Lundin Links, turn N off A915, 0.5m signed*

PETS: Charges £1 per night **Public areas** except public wash facilities on leads disp bin **Exercise area** 100yds **Facilities** walks info vet info **Other** prior notice required 1 dog per pitch; dogs may not roam free - tether available on site disposal bags available **Restrictions** no dangerous dogs (see page 7)

Open Apr-Oct Last arrival 21.00hrs Last departure noon

A secluded and sheltered little jewel of a site in a small orchard under the hill called Largo Law. This very attractive site is family owned and run to an immaculate standard, and pitches are grouped in twos and threes by low hedging and gorse. 1 acre site. 20 touring pitches. 12 hardstandings. 6 seasonal pitches. Tent pitches. Motorhome pitches. 5 statics.

Notes

ST ANDREWS
Map 12 NO51

The Inn at Lathones

★★★★ ◉◉ INN

Largoward KY9 1JE

☎ 01334 840494 📠 01334 840694

e-mail: lathones@theinn.co.uk

web: www.theinn.co.uk

dir: *5m S of St Andrews on A915, 0.5m before village of Largoward on left just after hidden dip*

PETS: Bedrooms (18 GF) unattended **Charges** £10 per stay **Grounds Exercise area** 5m **Facilities** vet info **On Request** fridge access torch **Other** charge for damage

This lovely country inn, parts of which are 400 years old, is full of character and individuality. The friendly staff help to create a relaxed atmosphere. Smart contemporary bedrooms are in two separate wings. The colourful, cosy restaurant is the main focus, where the menu offers modern interpretations of Scottish and European dishes.

Rooms 21 annexe en suite (1 fmly) (18 GF) **S** £99-£129; **D** £120-£180 **Facilities** STV TVL tea/coffee Dinner available Direct Dial Cen ht Wi-fi **Parking** 35 **Notes** Closed 26 Dec & 3-16 Jan RS 24 Dec

CITY OF GLASGOW

GLASGOW
Map 11 NS56

Malmaison Glasgow
★★★ 82% ◉ HOTEL

278 West George St G2 4LL
☎ 0141 572 1000 📠 0141 572 1002
e-mail: glasgow@malmaison.com
web: www.malmaison.com
dir: From S & E: M8 junct 18 (Charing Cross). From W & N: M8 city centre

PETS: Bedrooms (19 GF) unattended Charges £10 per night Public areas except restaurant on leads Exercise area 50yds Facilities food bowl water bowl bedding cage storage walks info vet info On Request fridge access torch towels Other charge for damage pet food only available by prior request

Built around a former church in the historic Charing Cross area, this hotel is a smart, contemporary establishment offering impressive levels of service and hospitality. Bedrooms are spacious and feature a host of modern facilities, such as CD players and mini bars. Dining is a treat here, with French brasserie-style cuisine, backed up by an excellent wine list, served in the original crypt.

Rooms 72 (4 fmly) (19 GF) Facilities STV Gym Cardiovascular equipment New Year Wi-fi Services Lift Notes LB

Georgian House
★★★ GUEST HOUSE

29 Buckingham Ter, Great Western Rd G12 8ED
☎ 0141 339 0008 & 07973 971563
e-mail: thegeorgianhouse@yahoo.com
web: www.thegeorgianhousehotel.com
dir: M8 junct 17 towards Dumbarton, through 4 sets of lights & right onto Queen Margaret Dr, then right onto Buckingham Ter

PETS: Bedrooms (3 GF) sign ground-floor bedrooms only Charges £10 per night Public areas except dining room Grounds on leads disp bin Exercise area large park across road Facilities food bowl water bowl dog walking washing facs walks info vet info On Request torch towels Stables 7m Other charge for damage

Georgian House offers good value accommodation at the west end of the city in a peaceful tree-lined Victorian terrace near the Botanic Gardens. Bedrooms vary in size and are furnished in modern style. A continental style breakfast is served in the first-floor lounge-dining room.

Rooms 11 rms (10 en suite) (1 pri facs) (4 fmly) (3 GF)
S £40-£60; D £70-£110 Facilities FTV tea/coffee Cen ht Wi-fi Parking 6 Notes LB

The Kelvin
★★★ GUEST HOUSE

15 Buckingham Ter, Great Western Rd, Hillhead G12 8EB
☎ 0141 339 7143 📠 0141 339 5215
e-mail: enquiries@kelvinhotel.com
web: www.kelvinhotel.com
dir: M8 junct 17, A82 Kelvinside/Dumbarton, 1m on right before Botanic Gardens

PETS: Bedrooms (2 GF) Public areas except dining room on leads Grounds disp bin Exercise area 2 mins' walk Facilities walks info vet info On Request fridge access torch towels Other charge for damage

Two substantial Victorian terrace houses on the west side of the city have been combined to create this friendly establishment close to the Botanic Gardens. The attractive bedrooms are comfortably proportioned and well equipped with flat-screen TVs offering an array of channels, and Wi-fi available also. The dining room on the first floor is the setting for breakfasts served at individual tables.

Rooms 21 rms (9 en suite) (4 fmly) (2 GF) (14 smoking)
S £30-£48; D £60-£68 Facilities FTV tea/coffee Cen ht Wi-fi Parking 5

HIGHLAND

ARISAIG
Map 13 NM68

Cnoc-na-Faire
★★★★★ ◉ 🍴 INN

Back of Keppoch PH39 4NS
☎ 01687 450249 📠 01687 450249
e-mail: cnocnafaire@googlemail.com
dir: A830 1m past Arisaig, turn left onto B0080, 0.5m on left into driveway

PETS: Bedrooms unattended Charges donations requested to SSPCA Public areas except restaurant on leads Grounds disp bin Exercise area 500yds Facilities food bowl water bowl dog chews feeding mat scoop/disp bags leads washing facs cage storage walks info vet info On Request fridge access torch towels Stables 1m Restrictions no dangerous dogs (see page 7) Resident Pets: Harris & Lewis (Cocker Spaniels)

The name is Gaelic for 'Hill of Vigil', and the property boasts picture-postcard views down to the white sandy beach and further afield to the Inner Hebridean isles. Modern bedrooms and bathrooms cater well for guests' needs. Award-winning food is served in the cosy bar and restaurant, and the warm and genuine hospitality creates a wonderful atmosphere.

Rooms 6 en suite S £85-£95; D £90-£125 Facilities STV tea/coffee Dinner available Cen ht Wi-fi Golf 9 Parking 15 Notes Closed 23-27 Dec No coaches

SCOTLAND

BALLACHULISH
Map 14 NN55

The Isles of Glencoe Hotel & Leisure Centre
★★★ 72% HOTEL
PH49 4HL
☎ 0845 906 9966 & 0844 855 9134 📠 01855 811 770
e-mail: reservations@akkeronhotels.com
web: www.akkeronhotels.com
dir: *A82 N, slip road on left into village, 1st right, hotel in 600yds*

PETS: Bedrooms (21 GF) unattended sign **Charges** £10 per night **Public areas** except restaurant on leads **Grounds** on leads disp bin **Exercise area Facilities** food bowl water bowl bedding dog chews cat treats scoop/disp bags washing facs cage storage walks info vet info **On Request** fridge access torch towels **Other** charge for damage

This hotel enjoys a spectacular setting beside Loch Leven. This friendly modern establishment has spacious bedrooms and guests have a choice of Loch or Mountain View rooms. Public areas include a popular restaurant and a family friendly leisure centre.

Rooms 59 (21 fmly) (21 GF) **S** £59-£155; **D** £59-£165 (incl. bkfst)* **Facilities** STV ⓣ Gym Hydroseat Bio-sauna ♫ Xmas New Year Wi-fi **Parking** 100 **Notes** LB

Lyn-Leven
★★★★ GUEST HOUSE
West Laroch PH49 4JP
☎ 01855 811392 📠 01855 811600
e-mail: macleodcilla@aol.com
web: www.lynleven.co.uk
dir: *Off A82 signed on left West Laroch*

PETS: Bedrooms (12 GF) **Charges** £5 per night **Public areas Exercise area** nearby **Facilities** walks info

Genuine Highland hospitality and high standards are part of the appeal of this comfortable guest house. The attractive bedrooms vary in size, are well equipped, and offer many thoughtful extra touches. There is a spacious lounge, and a smart dining room where delicious home-cooked breakfasts are served at individual tables.

Rooms 8 en suite 4 annexe en suite (3 fmly) (12 GF) **S** £45-£55; **D** £56-£70 **Facilities** TVL tea/coffee Cen ht Licensed **Parking** 12 **Notes** LB Closed Xmas

BALMACARA
Map 14 NG82

Reraig Caravan Site *(NG815272)*
▶ ▶ ▶
IV40 8DH
☎ 01599 566215
e-mail: warden@reraig.com
dir: *On A87 3.5m E of Kyle, 2m W of junct with A890*

PETS: Public areas except toilet block disp bin **Exercise area** adjacent **Facilities** walks info vet info

Open May-Sep Last arrival 22.00hrs Last departure noon

Set on level, grassy ground surrounded by trees, the site is located on the saltwater Sound of Sleet, and looks south towards Loch Alsh and Skye. Very nicely organised with a high standard of maintenance, and handy for the bridge crossing to the Isle of Skye. 2 acre site. 45 touring pitches. 34 hardstandings. Tent pitches. Motorhome pitches.

Notes No awnings Jul & Aug. Only small tents permitted.

BEAULY
Map 14 NH54

Lovat Arms
★★★ 73% HOTEL
IV4 7BS
☎ 01463 782313 📠 01463 782862
e-mail: info@lovatarms.com
web: www.lovatarms.com
dir: *From The Square past Royal Bank of Scotland, hotel on right*

PETS: Bedrooms (6 GF) **Charges** small dog £15 per stay; medium & large dog £25 per stay **Public areas** except brasserie & dining room on leads **Exercise area** 2 mins **Facilities** water bowl cage storage walks info vet info **On Request** fridge access torch **Stables** 3m **Other** charge for damage

This fine family run hotel enjoys a prominent position in this charming town which is a short drive from Inverness. The bedrooms are comfortable and well appointed. The spacious foyer has a real fire and comfortable seating, while the Strubag lounge is ideal for informal dining.

Rooms 33 (12 annexe) (4 fmly) (6 GF) **Facilities** STV FTV Xmas New Year Wi-fi **Parking** 25

BOAT OF GARTEN
Map 14 NH91

Boat Hotel
★★★ 80% @@ HOTEL

PH24 3BH

☎ 01479 831258 & 831696 📠 01479 831414

e-mail: info@boathotel.co.uk

dir: Off A9 N of Aviemore onto A95, follow signs to Boat of Garten

PETS: Bedrooms unattended sign certain bedrooms only
Charges £10 per night **Public areas** except restaurant &
bar on leads **Grounds** disp bin **Exercise area** river walk (10
mins) **Facilities** walks info vet info **Other** charge for damage
Restrictions small & medium dogs only

A well established hotel situated in the heart of this pretty
village. Public areas include a choice of comfortable lounges and
The Osprey Bistro & Bar is inviting and relaxed, with appealing
menus and a well deserved reputation for food. Individually
styled bedrooms reflect the unique character of the hotel; all are
comfortable and well equipped.

Rooms 34 (2 fmly) **Facilities** FTV Xmas New Year Wi-fi **Parking** 36

BRORA
Map 14 NC90

Royal Marine Hotel, Restaurant & Spa

★★★★ 75% @ HOTEL

Golf Rd KW9 6QS

☎ 01408 621252 📠 01408 621181

e-mail: info@royalmarinebrora.com

web: www.royalmarinebrora.com

dir: Off A9 in village towards beach & golf course

PETS: Bedrooms (2 GF) sign **Charges** £10 per stay **Grounds**
disp bin **Exercise area** beach (300mtrs) **Facilities** washing
facs cage storage walks info vet info **On Request** fridge access
towels **Other** charge for damage

A distinctive Edwardian residence sympathetically extended,
the Royal Marine attracts a mixed market. Its leisure centre
is popular, and the restaurant, Hunters Lounge and café bar
offer three contrasting eating options. A modern bedroom wing
complements the original bedrooms, which retain period style.
There are also luxury apartments just a short walk away.

Rooms 21 (1 fmly) (2 GF) **Facilities** FTV ⊗ ≋ Putt green Fishing
≋ Gym Steam room Sauna Xmas New Year Wi-fi **Parking** 40

CORPACH
Map 14 NN07

Linnhe Lochside Holidays *(NN074771)*
▶▶▶▶▶

PH33 7NL

☎ 01397 772376 📠 01397 772007

e-mail: relax@linnhe-lochside-holidays.co.uk

dir: On A830, 1m W of Corpach, 5m from Fort William

PETS: Charges Public areas except pet-free areas disp bin
Exercise area on site dog walk area & long beach **Facilities**
washing facs walks info vet info **Other** prior notice required
pets must be kept on leads & not left unattended

Open Dec-Oct rs Dec-Etr shop closed out of season, unisex
showers during peak season Last arrival 21.00hrs Last departure
11.00hrs

An excellently maintained site in a beautiful setting on the shores
of Loch Eil, with Ben Nevis to the east and the mountains and
Sunart to the west. The owners have worked in harmony with
nature to produce an idyllic environment, where the highest
standards of design and maintenance are evident. 5.5 acre site.
85 touring pitches. 63 hardstandings. 20 seasonal pitches. Tent
pitches. Motorhome pitches. 20 statics.

Notes No large groups.

FORT WILLIAM
Map 14 NN17

Moorings
★★★ 82% @ HOTEL

Banavie PH33 7LY

☎ 01397 772797 📠 01397 772441

e-mail: reservations@moorings-fortwilliam.co.uk

web: www.moorings-fortwilliam.co.uk

dir: Take A830 (N from Fort William), cross Caledonian Canal,
1st right

PETS: Bedrooms standard bedrooms only **Charges** £7 per stay
Grounds on leads disp bin **Exercise area** canal bank walk
direct from hotel grounds **Facilities** bedding washing facs cage
storage walks info **On Request** torch towels **Other** charge
for damage pet blanket provided; dogs only accepted by prior
arrangement, confirm when booking

Located on the Caledonian Canal next to a series of locks
known as Neptune's Staircase and close to Thomas Telford's
house, this hotel with its dedicated team offers friendly service.
Accommodation comes in two distinct styles and the newer rooms
are particularly appealing. Meals can be taken in the bars or the
spacious dining room.

Rooms 27 (2 fmly) (1 GF) **S** £49-£138; **D** £70-£148 (incl. bkfst)*
Facilities STV Gym New Year Wi-fi **Parking** 60 **Notes** LB Closed
24-26 Dec

FORT WILLIAM *continued*

Lime Tree Hotel & Restaurant

★★★ 78% ◉◉ SMALL HOTEL

Lime Tree Studio, Achintore Rd PH33 6RQ
☎ 01397 701806 🖹 01397 701806
e-mail: info@limetreefortwilliam.co.uk
dir: *On A82 at entrance to Fort William*

PETS: Bedrooms (4 GF) **Charges** £5 per night **Public areas** except restaurant on leads **Grounds** disp bin **Exercise area** 100mtrs **Other** charge for damage **Restrictions** small & medium size dogs only; no puppies **Resident Pet:** Maggie (dog)

A charming small hotel with an inspirational art gallery on the ground floor, with lots of original artwork displayed throughout. Evening meals can be enjoyed in the restaurant which has a loyal following. The hotel's comfortable lounges with their real fires are ideal for pre or post dinner drinks or maybe just to relax in. Individually designed bedrooms are spacious with some nice little personal touches courtesy of the artist owner.

Rooms 9 (4 fmly) (4 GF) **S** £110; **D** £110 (incl. bkfst)* **Facilities** New Year Wi-fi **Parking** 9 **Notes** Closed 24-26 Dec

Glen Nevis Caravan & Camping Park

(NN124722)

▶▶▶▶

Glen Nevis PH33 6SX
☎ 01397 702191 🖹 01397 703904
e-mail: holidays@glen-nevis.co.uk
dir: *On northern outskirts of Fort William follow A82 to mini-rdbt. Exit for Glen Nevis. Site 2.5m on right*

PETS: Public areas on leads disp bin **Exercise area on site** designated area **Facilities** walks info vet info **Other** dogs must be kept on leads at all times **Restrictions** well behaved dogs only

Open 13 Mar-9 Nov rs Mar & mid Oct-Nov limited shop & restaurant facilities Last arrival 22.00hrs Last departure noon

A tasteful site with well-screened enclosures, at the foot of Ben Nevis in the midst of some of the most spectacular Highland scenery; an ideal area for walking and touring. The park boasts a restaurant which offers a high standard of cooking and provides good value for money. 30 acre site. 380 touring pitches. 150 hardstandings. Tent pitches. Motorhome pitches. 30 statics.

Notes Quiet 23.00hrs-08.00hrs

Craigdarroch House

★★★★ ⊜ RESTAURANT WITH ROOMS

IV2 6XU
☎ 01456 486400 🖹 01456 486444
e-mail: info@hotel-loch-ness.co.uk
dir: *Take B862 from either end of loch, then B852 signed Foyers*

PETS: Bedrooms Charges £10 per stay **Grounds** on leads disp bin **Exercise area** adjacent **Facilities** walks info vet info **On Request** towels **Other** charge for damage **Resident Pets:** 2 Border Collies, 1 Harris Hawk

Craigdarroch is located in an elevated position high above Loch Ness on the south side. Bedrooms vary in style and size but all are comfortable and well equipped; those that are front-facing have wonderful views. Dinner is well worth staying in for, and breakfast is also memorable.

Rooms 8 en suite (1 fmly) **S** £65-£95; **D** £99-£160 **Facilities** FTV TVL tea/coffee Dinner available Direct Dial Cen ht Wi-fi **Parking** 24 **Notes** No coaches

Gairloch Caravan Park *(NG798773)*

▶▶▶

Strath IV21 2BX
☎ 01445 712373
e-mail: info@gairlochcaravanpark.com
dir: *From A832 take B8021 signed Melvaig towards Strath. In 0.5m turn right, just after Millcroft Hotel. Immediately right again*

PETS: Public areas disp bin **Exercise area** 50mtrs from tent field **Facilities** washing facs walks info vet info **Other** dog-sitting service available disposal bags available

Open Etr-Oct Last arrival 21.00hrs Last departure noon

A clean, well-maintained site on flat coastal grassland close to Loch Gairloch. The owners and managers are hard working and well organised and continued investment in recent years has seen significant improvements around the park, including the hardstandings, good shrub and flower planting, and a bunkhouse that provides accommodation for families. 6 acre site. 70 touring pitches. 13 hardstandings. 8 seasonal pitches. Tent pitches. Motorhome pitches.

GLENCOE
Map 14 NN15

Invercoe Caravan & Camping Park
(NN098594)

▶▶▶▶

PH49 4HP
☎ 01855 811210 📠 01855 811210
e-mail: holidays@invercoe.co.uk
dir: *Exit A82 at Glencoe Hotel onto B863 for 0.25m*

PETS: Public areas disp bin **Exercise area** 100yds **Facilities** food food bowl water bowl walks info vet info

 Open all year Last departure noon

A level grass site set on the shore of Loch Leven, with excellent mountain views. The area is ideal for both walking and climbing, and also offers a choice of several freshwater and saltwater lochs. Convenient for the good shopping in Fort William. 5 acre site. 60 touring pitches. Tent pitches. Motorhome pitches. 4 statics.

Notes No large group bookings.

GLENFINNAN
Map 14 NM98

The Prince's House
★★★ **75%** ◉◉ SMALL HOTEL
PH37 4LT
☎ 01397 722246 📠 01397 722323
e-mail: princeshouse@glenfinnan.co.uk
web: www.glenfinnan.co.uk
dir: *On A830, 0.5m on right past Glenfinnan Monument. 200mtrs from railway station*

PETS: Bedrooms unattended standard bedrooms only **Charges** £5 per stay **Public areas** except restaurant **Grounds** disp bin **Exercise area** 250mtrs **Facilities** walks info vet info **On Request** torch towels **Other** charge for damage **Restrictions** no breed larger than a Labrador **Resident Pet:** Floren (cat)

This delightful hotel enjoys a well deserved reputation for fine food and excellent hospitality. The hotel has inspiring views and sits close to where 'Bonnie' Prince Charlie raised the Jacobite standard. Comfortably appointed bedrooms offer pleasing

decor. Excellent local game and seafood can be enjoyed in the restaurant and the bar.

Rooms 9 **S** £65-£75; **D** £95-£140 (incl. bkfst)* **Facilities** STV FTV Fishing New Year Wi-fi **Parking** 18 **Notes** LB Closed Xmas & Jan-Feb (ex New Year) RS Nov-Dec & Mar

GOLSPIE
Map 14 NC80

Granite Villa Guest House
★★★★ GUEST ACCOMMODATION
Fountain Rd KW10 6TH
☎ 01408 633146
e-mail: info@granite-villa.co.uk
dir: *Left from A9 (N'bound) onto Fountain Rd, immediately before pedestrian crossing lights*

PETS: Bedrooms (1 GF) **Charges** £5 per stay **Public areas** except dining room on leads **Grounds** on leads disp bin **Exercise area** 500yds **Facilities** washing facs walks info vet info **On Request** towels **Other** charge for damage **Resident Pets:** Indi & Keera (Labradors)

Originally built in 1892 for a wealthy local merchant, this traditional Victorian house has been sympathetically restored in recent years. Bedrooms are comfortable and all come with a range of thoughtful extras. Guests can relax in the large lounge, with its views over the landscaped garden where complimentary tea and coffee is often served. A warm welcome is assured in this charming period house.

Rooms 5 en suite (1 fmly) (1 GF) (2 smoking) **S** £45-£50; **D** £70 **Facilities** FTV tea/coffee Cen ht Wi-fi Golf 18 **Parking** 6 **Notes** ⊛

GRANTOWN-ON-SPEY
Map 14 NJ02

Grant Arms Hotel
★★★ **79%** HOTEL
25-27 The Square PH26 3HF
☎ 01479 872526 📠 01479 873589
e-mail: info@grantarmshotel.com
web: www.grantarmshotel.com
dir: *Exit A9 N of Aviemore onto A95*

PETS: Bedrooms unattended sign **Charges** £10 per stay **Public areas** except restaurant on leads **Grounds** disp bin **Exercise area** 5 mins' walk **Facilities** food bowl water bowl dog chews scoop/disp bags leads washing facs cage storage walks info vet info **On Request** fridge access torch towels **Other** charge for damage **Resident Pets:** Giglia, Chico & Aslia (Collie Cross) & Paddy (Labrador)

Conveniently located in the centre of the town, this fine hotel has now been refurbished and upgraded to a high standard yet still retains the building's traditional character. The spacious bedrooms are stylishly presented and very well equipped. The Garden Restaurant is a popular venue for dinner, and lighter snacks can be enjoyed in the comfortable bar. The hotel is very popular with birdwatchers and wildlife enthusiasts.

Rooms 50 (4 fmly) **S** £45-£80; **D** £90-£160 (incl. bkfst) **Facilities** STV FTV Birdwatching & Wildlife Club ♫ Xmas New Year Wi-fi **Services** Lift **Notes** LB

INVERNESS Map 14 NH64

Culloden House
★★★★ 80% ◉◉ HOTEL
Culloden IV2 7BZ
☎ 01463 790461 ᐧ 01463 792181
e-mail: info@cullodenhouse.co.uk
web: www.cullodenhouse.co.uk
dir: A96 from Inverness, right for Culloden. 1m after 2nd lights, left at church

PETS: Bedrooms (3 GF) sign Public areas except restaurant & bar on leads Grounds disp bin Exercise area 500mtrs Facilities food food bowl water bowl bedding feeding mat washing facs cage storage walks info vet info On Request fridge access torch towels Stables 6m Other charge for damage

Dating from the late 1700s this impressive mansion is set in extensive grounds close to the famous Culloden Battlefield. High ceilings and intricate cornices are particular features of the public rooms, including the elegant Adam dining room. Bedrooms come in a range of sizes and styles, with a number situated in a separate house.

Rooms 28 (5 annexe) (1 fmly) (3 GF) S £95-£175; D £125-£270 (incl. bkfst)* Facilities FTV ⛳ Putt green ⚓ Boules Badminton Golf driving net Putting green New Year Wi-fi Parking 50 Notes LB No children 10yrs Closed 24-28 Dec

Loch Ness Country House Hotel
★★★★ 79% ◉ SMALL HOTEL
Loch Ness Rd IV3 8JN
☎ 01463 230512 ᐧ 01463 224532
e-mail: info@lochnesscountryhousehotel.co.uk
web: www.lochnesscountryhousehotel.co.uk
dir: On A82, 1m from Inverness town boundary

PETS: Bedrooms (3 GF) garden cottages only Charges £10 per night £70 per week Grounds on leads Exercise area nearby Facilities cage storage walks info vet info On Request fridge access torch towels Other charge for damage

Built in the Georgian era, this fine house is perfectly situated in its own six acre private Highland estate. The hotel has luxurious bedrooms, four of which are in the garden suite cottages. The stylish restaurant serves the best of local produce and guests have a choice of cosy well-appointed lounges for after dinner drinks. The garden terrace is ideal for relaxing and has splendid views over the landscaped gardens towards Inverness.

Rooms 13 (2 annexe) (8 fmly) (3 GF) S £85-£165; D £125-£215 (incl. bkfst)* Facilities FTV Xmas New Year Wi-fi Parking 50

Best Western Palace Hotel & Spa

★★★ 75% HOTEL
8 Ness Walk IV3 5NG
☎ 01463 223243 ᐧ 01463 236865
e-mail: palace@miltonhotels.com
web: www.invernesspalacehotel.co.uk
dir: A82 into Ness Walk. Hotel 300yds on right

PETS: Bedrooms unattended (only if staff are aware) Public areas except restaurant on leads Exercise area 5-10 mins Facilities cage storage walks info vet info On Request fridge access torch towels Other charge for damage

Set on the north side of the River Ness close to the Eden Court theatre and a short walk from the town, this hotel has a contemporary look. Bedrooms offer good levels of comfort and equipment, and a smart leisure centre attracts a mixed market.

Rooms 88 (48 annexe) (3 fmly) (5 smoking) S £69.90-£189.90; D £99.90-£249.90 Facilities Spa FTV ◌ supervised Gym Beautician Sauna Steam room Xmas New Year Wi-fi Services Lift Parking 38 Notes LB

Express by Holiday Inn Inverness

BUDGET HOTEL
Stoneyfield IV2 7PA
☎ 01463 732700 ᐧ 01463 732732
e-mail: inverness@expressholidayinn.co.uk
web: www.hiexpress.com/inverness
dir: From A9 follow A96 & Inverness Airport signs, hotel on right

PETS: Bedrooms (24 GF) certain bedrooms only Charges £10 per night Public areas except lounge on leads Grounds Facilities walks info vet info Other charge for damage

A modern hotel ideal for families and business travellers. Fresh and uncomplicated, the spacious rooms include Sky TV, power shower and tea and coffee-making facilities. Continental buffet breakfast is included in the room rate; other meals may be taken at the nearby family pub or restaurant.

Rooms 94 (43 fmly) (24 GF) (10 smoking)

Westbourne
★★★★ ᐧ GUEST ACCOMMODATION
50 Huntly St IV3 5HS
☎ 01463 220700 ᐧ 01463 220700
e-mail: richard@westbourne.org.uk
dir: From A82 rdbt into Wells Rd, right into St Huntly Rd

PETS: Bedrooms unattended large bedrooms only Grounds disp bin Exercise area 50mtrs Facilities dog chews cage storage walks info vet info On Request fridge access torch towels

The immaculately maintained Westbourne looks across the River Ness to the city centre. This friendly, family-run house has bright modern bedrooms of varying size, all attractively furnished in pine and very well equipped. A relaxing lounge with internet access, books, games and puzzles is available.

Rooms 9 en suite (2 fmly) S £45-£55; D £80-£90 Facilities FTV tea/ coffee Cen ht Wi-fi Parking 6 Notes LB Closed Xmas & New Year

JOHN O'GROATS Map 15 ND37

John O'Groats Caravan Site (ND382733)

►►►

KW1 4YR
☎ 01955 611329 & 07762 336359
e-mail: info@johnogroatscampsite.co.uk
dir: At end of A99

PETS: Public areas on lead **Exercise area** adjacent **Facilities** washing facs walks info vet info **Other** shop (0.25m)

Open Apr-Sep Last arrival 22.00hrs Last departure 11.00hrs

An attractive site in an open position above the seashore and looking out towards the Orkney Islands. Nearby is the passenger ferry that makes day trips to the Orkneys, and there are grey seals to watch, and sea angling can be organised by the site owners. 4 acre site. 90 touring pitches. 30 hardstandings. Tent pitches. Motorhome pitches.

Notes 🐾

LOCHINVER Map 14 NC02

Inver Lodge

★★★★ ◉◉ HOTEL

IV27 4LU
☎ 01571 844496 📠 01571 844395
e-mail: stay@inverlodge.com
web: www.inverlodge.com
dir: A835 to Lochinver, through village, left after village hall, follow private road for 0.5m

PETS: Bedrooms (11 GF) unattended **Public areas** front foyer lounge only **Grounds Exercise area** nearby **Facilities** washing facs cage storage walks info vet info **On Request** fridge access torch towels **Other** charge for damage **Resident Pet:** Sam (Cairn Terrier)

Genuine hospitality is a noteworthy at this delightful, purpose-built hotel, set high on the hillside above the village. All bedrooms and public rooms enjoy stunning views. There is a choice of lounges and a restaurant where the chefs make use of the abundant local produce. Bedrooms are spacious, stylish and come with an impressive range of accessories. There is no night service between 11pm and 7am.

Rooms 21 (11 GF) **S** £115-£150; **D** £215-£480 (incl. bkfst)*
Facilities FTV Sauna Wi-fi **Parking** 30 **Notes** LB Closed Nov-Mar

---

MUIR OF ORD Map 14 NH55

THE CIRCLE

Ord House

★★ 72% ◉ SMALL HOTEL

IV6 7UH
☎ 01463 870492 📠 01463 870297
e-mail: admin@ord-house.co.uk
dir: Off A9 at Tore rdbt onto A832. 5m, through Muir of Ord. Left towards Ullapool (A832). Hotel 0.5m on left

PETS: Bedrooms (3 GF) unattended **Public areas** except restaurant **Grounds** disp bin **Exercise area** adjacent **Facilities** food (pre-bookable) food bowl water bowl bedding scoop/disp bags leads pet sitting washing facs cage storage walks info vet info **On Request** fridge access torch towels **Stables** 1m **Other** charge for damage **Resident Pet:** Poppy (Black Labrador)

Dating back to 1637, this country-house hotel is situated peacefully in wooded grounds and offers brightly furnished and well-proportioned accommodation. Comfortable day rooms reflect the character and charm of the house, with inviting lounges, a cosy snug bar and an elegant dining room where wide-ranging, creative menus are offered.

Rooms 12 (3 GF) **S** £60-£85; **D** £100-£150 (incl. bkfst)*
Facilities Putt green 🏌 Clay pigeon shooting Wi-fi **Parking** 30
Notes LB Closed Nov-Apr

NAIRN
Map 14 NH85

Boath House
★★★ ◉◉◉◉ HOTEL

Auldearn IV12 5TE
☎ 01667 454896 📱 01667 455469
e-mail: info@boath-house.com
web: www.boath-house.com
dir: *2m past Nairn on A96, E towards Forres, signed on main road*

PETS: Bedrooms (1 GF) certain bedrooms only **Grounds** on leads disp bin **Exercise area** 1m **Facilities** water bowl dog chews scoop/disp bags washing facs cage storage walks info vet info **On Request** fridge access torch **Stables** 1m **Other** charge for damage pet policy which owners are required to sign **Restrictions** contact hotel to confirm which dog breeds are accepted **Resident Pet:** Pippin (Jack Russell)

Standing in its own grounds, this splendid Georgian mansion has been lovingly restored. Hospitality is first class. The owners are passionate about what they do, and have an ability to establish a special relationship with their guests that will be particularly remembered. The food is also memorable here - the five-course dinners are a culinary adventure, matched only by the excellence of breakfasts. The house itself is delightful, with inviting lounges and a dining room overlooking a trout loch. Bedrooms are striking, comfortable, and include many fine antique pieces.

Rooms 8 (1 fmly) (1 GF) **S** £260-£330; **D** £345-£450 (incl. bkfst & dinner) **Facilities** FTV Fishing 🦌 Beauty salon Xmas New Year Wi-fi **Parking** 20 **Notes** LB

NEWTONMORE
Map 14 NN79

Crubenbeg House
★ ★ ★ ★ GUEST HOUSE

Falls of Truim PH20 1BE
☎ 01540 673300
e-mail: enquiries@crubenbeghouse.com
web: www.crubenbeghouse.com
dir: *4m S of Newtonmore. Off A9 for Crubenmore, over railway bridge & right, signed*

PETS: Bedrooms (1 GF) **Public areas** except kitchen & dining room **Grounds** disp bin **Exercise area** adjacent **Facilities** food (pre-bookable) food bowl water bowl dog chews feeding mat scoop/disp bags leads pet sitting dog walking washing facs cage storage walks info vet info **On Request** fridge access torch towels **Resident Pet:** Rajah (Saluki/Alsatian cross)

Set in a peaceful rural location, Crubenbeg House has stunning country views and is well located for touring the Highlands, The attractive bedrooms are individually styled and well equipped, while the ground-floor bedroom provides easier access. Guests can enjoy a dram in front of the fire in the inviting lounge, while breakfast features the best of local produce in the adjacent dining room.

Rooms 4 rms (3 en suite) (1 pri facs) (1 GF) **S** £33-£40; **D** £55-£87 **Facilities** STV tea/coffee Dinner available Cen ht Licensed Wi-fi **Parking** 10 **Notes** LB No Children 12yrs

SCOURIE
Map 14 NC14

Scourie
★★★ 73% SMALL HOTEL

IV27 4SX
☎ 01971 502396 📱 01971 502423
e-mail: patrick@scourie-hotel.co.uk
dir: *N'bound on A894. Hotel in village on left*

PETS: Bedrooms (5 GF) unattended **Public areas** except dining areas **Grounds** disp bin **Exercise area** 1m **Facilities** cage storage walks info vet info **On Request** fridge access **Other** charge for damage **Resident Pets:** Tilly (Springer Spaniel), Jessie & Clemmie (cats)

This well-established hotel is an angler's paradise with extensive fishing rights available on a 25,000-acre estate. Public areas include a choice of comfortable lounges, a cosy bar and a smart dining room offering wholesome fare. The bedrooms are comfortable and generally spacious. The resident proprietors and their staff create a relaxed and friendly atmosphere.

Rooms 20 (2 annexe) (2 fmly) (5 GF) **S** £43-£54; **D** £82-£102 (incl. bkfst)* **Facilities** Fishing Wi-fi **Parking** 30 **Notes** LB Closed mid Oct-end Mar RS winter evenings

SHIEL BRIDGE
Map 14 NG91

Grants at Craigellachie
★★★★ ◉ RESTAURANT WITH ROOMS

Craigellachie, Ratagan IV40 8HP
☎ 01599 511331
e-mail: info@housebytheloch.co.uk
dir: *From A87 exit for Glenelg, 1st right to Ratagan, opposite Youth Hostel sign*

PETS: Bedrooms (3 GF) **Charges** £7.50 per night £35 per week **Grounds** on leads disp bin **Exercise area** 200mtrs **Facilities** leads cage storage walks info vet info **On Request** torch **Stables** 1m **Other** charge for damage **Resident Pets:** Morgan & Magda (Boxers)

Sitting on the tranquil shores of Loch Duin and overlooked by the Five Sisters Mountains, Grants really does occupy a stunning location. The restaurant has a well deserved reputation for its cuisine, and the bedrooms are stylish and have all the creature comforts. Guests are guaranteed a warm welcome at this charming house.

Rooms 2 en suite 2 annexe en suite (3 GF) **S** £92.50-£112.50; **D** £155-£240 (incl.dinner) **Facilities** STV tea/coffee Dinner available Cen ht Wi-fi Riding **Parking** 8 **Notes** LB No Children 12yrs Closed Dec-mid Feb RS Oct-Apr reservation only No coaches

Tigh an Eilean

★ SMALL HOTEL

IV54 8XN

☎ 01520 755251   📠 01520 755321

e-mail: tighaneilean@keme.co.uk

dir: *Exit A896 into Shieldaig, hotel in village centre*

PETS: Bedrooms unattended sign **Public areas** except eating areas & at busy times **Grounds** disp bin **Exercise area** 400mtrs **Facilities** food (pre-bookable) food bowl water bowl bedding dog chews feeding mat scoop/disp bags leads washing facs cage storage walks info vet info **On Request** fridge access torch towels **Stables** 400yds **Other** please phone for details regarding horses **Restrictions** well-behaved dogs only **Resident Pets:** Ella & Katy (Black Labradors)

A splendid location by the sea, with views over the bay, is the icing on the cake for this delightful small hotel. It can be a long drive to reach Sheildaig but guests remark that the journey is more than worth the effort. The brightly decorated bedrooms are comfortable though don't expect television, except in one of the lounges. For many, it's the food that attracts, with fish and seafood featuring strongly.

Rooms 11 (1 fmly) **S** fr £70; **D** fr £140 (incl. bkfst)*
Facilities Birdwatching Kayaks Astronomical telescope Xmas New Year Wi-fi **Parking** 15 **Notes** LB RS late Oct–mid Mar

Smiddy House

★★★★★ 🍴 RESTAURANT WITH ROOMS

Roy Bridge Rd PH34 4EU

☎ 01397 712335   📠 01397 712043

e-mail: enquiry@smiddyhouse.co.uk

web: www.smiddyhouse.co.uk

dir: *In village centre, A82 onto A86*

PETS: Bedrooms twin-bedded rooms only **Charges** £5 per night **Exercise area** 200yds **Facilities** food (pre-bookable) food bowl water bowl walks info vet info **Other** charge for damage **Restrictions** small dogs only

Set in the Great Glen which stretches from Fort William to Inverness, this was once the village smithy, and is now a very friendly establishment. The attractive bedrooms, named after places in Scotland, are comfortably furnished and well equipped. A relaxing garden room is available for guest use. Delicious evening meals are served in Russell's restaurant.

Rooms 4 en suite (1 fmly) **S** £55–£80; **D** £60–£85 **Facilities** tea/coffee Dinner available Wi-fi **Parking** 15 **Notes** No coaches

Achnabobane *(NN195811)*

★★★ FARMHOUSE

PH34 4EX

☎ 01397 712919   Mr and Mrs N Ockenden

e-mail: enquiries@achnabobane.co.uk

web: www.achnabobane.co.uk

dir: *2m S of Spean Bridge on A82*

PETS: Bedrooms (1 GF) **Charges** £5 per stay **Public areas** except lounge & restaurant on leads **Grounds** on leads disp bin **Facilities** scoop/disp bags cage storage walks info vet info **On Request** fridge access torch towels **Other** charge for damage **Resident Pets:** Morse (Cavalier King Charles Spaniel), Bea, Posy & Rupert (cats), chickens, 2 cockerels

With breathtaking views of Ben Nevis, Aonach Mhor and the Grey Corries, the farmhouse offers comfortable, good-value accommodation in a friendly family environment. Bedrooms are traditional in style and well equipped. Breakfast and evening meals are served in the conservatory-dining room.

Rooms 4 rms (1 en suite) (1 fmly) (1 GF) **S** £30–£34; **D** £60–£68 **Facilities** TVL tea/coffee Dinner available Cen ht Wi-fi **Parking** 5 **Notes** Closed Xmas red deer/woodland

SCOTLAND

STRONTIAN
Map 14 NM86

Kilcamb Lodge
★★★ ⊛⊛ COUNTRY HOUSE HOTEL
PH36 4HY
☎ 01967 402257 📄 01967 402041
e-mail: enquiries@kilcamblodge.co.uk
web: www.kilcamblodge.co.uk
dir: Off A861, via Corran Ferry

PETS: Bedrooms sign certain bedrooms only **Charges** dog £12 per night dog £30 per week **Grounds** disp bin **Exercise area** accessed from hotel grounds **Facilities** food (pre-bookable) water bowl dog chews scoop/disp bags washing facs dog walking cage storage walks info vet info **On Request** fridge access torch towels **Other** charge for damage max 2 dogs per bedroom

This historic house on the shores of Loch Sunart was one of the first stone buildings in the area, and was used as military barracks around the time of the Jacobite uprising. It is situated on the beautiful and peaceful Ardamurchan Peninsula where otters, red squirrels and eagles can be spotted. The suites and bedrooms, with either loch or garden views, are stylishly decorated using designer fabrics and have flat-screen TVs, DVD/CD players, plus bath robes, iced water and even guest umbrellas. Accomplished cooking, utilising much local produce, can be enjoyed in the stylish dining room. Warm hospitality is assured.

Rooms 10 (2 fmly) **S** £145-£208; **D** £229-£369 (incl. bkfst & dinner)* **Facilities** FTV Fishing Boating Hiking Bird/whale/otter watching Stalking Clay pigeon shooting Xmas New Year Wi-fi **Parking** 20 **Notes** LB No children 10yrs Closed 2 Jan-1 Feb

TORRIDON
Map 14 NG95

The Torridon
★★★★ ⊛⊛⊛ COUNTRY HOUSE HOTEL
By Achnasheen, Wester Ross IV22 2EY
☎ 01445 791242 📄 01445 712253
e-mail: info@thetorridon.com
web: www.thetorridon.com
dir: From A832 at Kinlochewe, A896 towards Torridon. (NB do not turn into village) 1m, hotel on right

PETS: Bedrooms one suite only **Grounds** on leads **Exercise area** 1m **Facilities** food food bowl water bowl walks info vet info **On Request** fridge access towels **Other** charge for damage **Resident Pets:** Talisker (Pointer), Pippa (Black Labrador), Bailey, Barney & Baxter (Cocker Spaniels)

Delightfully set amidst inspiring loch and mountain scenery, this elegant Victorian shooting lodge has been beautifully restored to make the most of its many original features. The attractive bedrooms are all individually furnished and most enjoy stunning Highland views. Comfortable day rooms feature fine wood panelling and roaring fires in cooler months. The first class, modern Scottish cuisine of 'Bruno' Birkbeck can be enjoyed in the restaurant which has magnificent oak-panelling and views to match. The whisky bar is aptly named, boasting over 300 malts and in-depth tasting notes. Outdoor activities include shooting, cycling and walking.

Rooms 19 **S** £140; **D** £215-£425 (incl. bkfst)* **Facilities** STV Fishing 🏊 Abseiling Archery Climbing Falconry Kayaking Mountain biking Xmas New Year Wi-fi **Services** Lift **Parking** 20 **Notes** Closed 2 Jan-9 Feb RS Nov-14 Mar

The Torridon Inn
★★★ ⊜ INN
IV22 2EY
☎ 01445 791242 📄 01445 712253
e-mail: inn@thetorridon.com

PETS: Bedrooms sign 1 ground-floor courtyard room only **Public areas** except restaurant **Grounds** on leads disp bin **Exercise area** 10 mins **Facilities** food (pre-bookable) food bowl water bowl washing facs walks info vet info **On Request** fridge access torch towels **Other** charge for damage **Resident Pets:** Talisker (Pointer), Pippa (Black Labrador) Bailey, Barney & Baxter (Cocker Spaniels)

The Torridon Inn enjoys an idyllic location and is set in 58 acres of parkland overlooking Loch Torridon and surrounded by steep mountains on all sides. The inn is very popular with walkers, and guests can also avail themselves of the many outdoor pursuits that are provided at the Torridon Hotel. Each of the spacious bedrooms are well equipped and comfortable. Evening meals and lunches are available at the inn where over 80 whiskies, and several real ales including a local Torridon Ale are firm favourites.

Rooms 12 en suite (3 fmly) (5 GF) **S** £99; **D** £99 **Facilities** STV tea/coffee Dinner available Cen ht Wi-fi 🏊 Fishing Pool table **Parking** 12 **Notes** LB Closed Jan

ULLAPOOL
Map 14 NH19

Broomfield Holiday Park (NH123939)
▶ ▶ ▶

West Shore St IV26 2UT
☎ 01854 612020 & 612664 📄 01854 613151
e-mail: sross@broomfieldhp.com
dir: Take 2nd right past harbour

PETS: Public areas except toilet facilities & children's play area
disp bin **Exercise area on site** beach **Facilities** washing facs
walks info vet info

Open Etr/Apr-Sep Last departure noon

Set right on the water's edge of Loch Broom and the open sea,
with lovely views of the Summer Isles. The clean, well maintained
and managed park is close to the harbour and town centre with
their restaurants, bars and shops. 12 acre site. 140 touring
pitches. Tent pitches. Motorhome pitches.

Notes No noise at night.

WHITEBRIDGE
Map 14 NH41

Whitebridge Hotel
★★ 69% HOTEL

IV2 6UN
☎ 01456 486226 📄 01456 486413
e-mail: info@whitebridgehotel.co.uk
dir: A9 onto B851, follow signs to Fort Augustus. Or A82 onto
B862 at Fort Augustus

PETS: Bedrooms Public areas except restaurant on leads
Grounds Exercise area nearby **Facilities** water bowl walks
info vet info

Close to Loch Ness and set amid rugged mountain and moorland
scenery, this hotel is popular with tourists, fishermen and
deerstalkers. Guests have a choice of more formal dining in the
restaurant or lighter meals in the popular cosy bar. Bedrooms are
thoughtfully equipped and brightly furnished.

Rooms 12 (3 fmly) **S** £50-£60; **D** £75-£85 (incl. bkfst)*
Facilities Fishing Wi-fi **Parking** 32 **Notes** Closed 11 Dec-9 Jan

MIDLOTHIAN

ROSLIN
Map 11 NT26

The Original Rosslyn Inn
★★★★ INN

4 Main St EH25 9LE
☎ 0131 440 2384 📄 0131 440 2514
e-mail: enquiries@theoriginalhotel.co.uk
dir: From A701 at rdbt take B7003 signed Roslin & Rosewell, into
Roslin. At T-junct, inn opposite. Or from mini rdbt on A701 at
Bilston take B7006 to Roslin. Inn on left

PETS: Bedrooms Charges Public areas bar only **Grounds
Exercise area** adjacent **Facilities** food bowl water bowl cage
storage walks info vet info **On Request** towels **Other** charge
for damage

Whether on the Da Vinci Code trail or in the area on business,
this property is a very short walk from the famous Rosslyn
Chapel which is well worth visiting. This delightful village inn
offers well-equipped bedrooms with upgraded en suites. Four
of the bedrooms have four-poster beds. The Grail Restaurant,
the lounge and conservatory offer a comprehensive selection of
dining options.

Rooms 6 en suite (2 fmly) (1 smoking) **Facilities** STV tea/coffee
Dinner available Cen ht Wi-fi **Parking** 8

MORAY

ABERLOUR
Map 15 NJ24

Aberlour Gardens Caravan Park (NJ282434)
▶ ▶ ▶

AB38 9LD
☎ 01340 871586 📄 01340 871586
e-mail: info@aberlourgardens.co.uk
dir: Midway between Aberlour & Craigellachie on A95 turn onto
unclass road. Site signed. (NB vehicles over 10' 6" use A941
Dufftown to Craigellachie road where park is signed)

PETS: Public areas disp bin **Exercise area** numerous walks
accessed from park **Facilities** food bowl water bowl washing
facs walks info vet info **Other** pets must be either on leads or in
cages as appropriate

Open Mar-27 Dec rs Winter park opening dates weather
dependant Last arrival 19.00hrs Last departure noon

This attractive parkland site is set in the five-acre walled garden
of the Victorian Aberlour House, surrounded by the full range of
spectacular scenery from the Cairngorm National Park, through
pine clad glens, to the famous Moray coastline; the park is also
well placed for the world renowned Speyside Malt Whisky Trail.
It offers a small, well-appointed toilet block, laundry and small
licensed shop. 5 acre site. 34 touring pitches. 16 hardstandings.
10 seasonal pitches. Tent pitches. Motorhome pitches. 32 statics.

Notes No ball games, max 5mph speed limit, no noise after
23.00hrs.

SCOTLAND

ALVES
Map 15 NJ16

North Alves Caravan Park (NJ122633)

►►►

IV30 8XD

☎ 01343 850223

dir: *From Elgin towards Forres on A96, follow signs for site (sign in Alves), turn right onto unclassified road. Approx 1m site on right*

PETS: Public areas Exercise area surrounding area, beach (3m) **Facilities** vet info **Other** dogs must be kept on leads at all times

Open Apr-Oct Last arrival 23.00hrs Last departure noon

A quiet rural site in attractive rolling countryside within three miles of a good beach. The site is on a former farm, and the stone buildings are quite unspoilt. 10 acre site. 45 touring pitches. Tent pitches. Motorhome pitches. 45 statics.

Notes

LOSSIEMOUTH
Map 15 NJ27

Silver Sands Leisure Park (NJ205710)

►►►►

Covesea, West Beach IV31 6SP

☎ 01343 813262 📄 01343 815205

e-mail: enquiries@silver-sands.co.uk

dir: *From Lossiemouth follow B9040, 2m W to site*

PETS: Public areas except main complex & office disp bin **Exercise area on site** beach **Facilities** food food bowl water bowl dog chews walks info vet info **Other** dog toys & disposal bags available

Open 15 Feb-15 Jan rs 15 Feb-Jun & Oct-15 Jan shops & entertainment restricted Last arrival 22.00hrs Last departure noon

A large holiday park with entertainment during the peak season, set on the links beside the shore of the Moray Firth. Touring campers and caravans are catered for in three areas: one offers de-luxe, fully-serviced facilities, while the others are either unserviced or include electric hook-ups and water. There's a well-stocked shop, a clubroom and bar, and takeaway food outlet. 60 acre site. 140 touring pitches. 30 hardstandings. Tent pitches. Motorhome pitches. 200 statics.

Notes Over 16yrs only in bar.

NORTH LANARKSHIRE

CUMBERNAULD
Map 11 NS77

The Westerwood Hotel & Golf Resort

★★★★ 81% ◉ HOTEL

1 St Andrews Dr, Westerwood G68 0EW

☎ 01236 457171 📄 01236 738478

e-mail: westerwood@qhotels.co.uk

web: www.qhotels.co.uk

PETS: Bedrooms (49 GF) unattended **Charges** £15 per stay **Public areas** except leisure club & restaurant **Grounds** on leads disp bin **Exercise area Facilities** walks info **Other** charge for damage pet food on request

This stylish, contemporary hotel enjoys an elevated position within 400 acres at the foot of the Campsie Hills. Accommodation is provided in spacious, bright bedrooms, many with super bathrooms, and day rooms include sumptuous lounges and an airy restaurant; extensive golf, fitness and conference facilities are available.

Rooms 148 (15 fmly) (49 GF) **Facilities** Spa STV ⓣ ♨ 18 ♨ Putt green Gym Beauty salon Relaxation room Sauna Steam room Xmas New Year Wi-fi **Services** Lift **Parking** 250

PERTH & KINROSS

ALYTH
Map 15 NO24

Tigh Na Leigh Guesthouse

★★★★★ ♨ ◉ GUEST ACCOMMODATION

22-24 Airlie St PH11 8AJ

☎ 01828 632372 📄 01828 632279

e-mail: bandcblack@yahoo.co.uk

web: www.tighnaleigh.co.uk

dir: *In town centre on B952*

PETS: Bedrooms (1 GF) unattended **Charges** £7.50 per stay **Public areas** except dining room on leads **Grounds** on leads **Exercise area** 200yds **Facilities** food bowl water bowl dog chews scoop/disp bags washing facs cage storage walks info vet info **On Request** fridge access torch towels **Resident Pets:** Tom & Bunny (cats)

Situated in the heart of this country town, Tigh Na Leigh is Gaelic for 'The House of the Doctor'. Its location and somewhat sombre façade are in stunning contrast to what lies inside. The house has been completely restored to blend its Victorian architecture with contemporary interior design. Bedrooms, including a superb suite, have state-of-the-art bathrooms. There are three entirely different lounges, while delicious meals are served in the conservatory/dining room overlooking a spectacular landscaped garden.

Rooms 5 en suite (1 GF) **S** £42-£48; **D** £84-£122.50 **Facilities** FTV TVL tea/coffee Dinner available Cen ht Licensed Wi-fi Golf 18 **Parking** 5 **Notes** No Children 12yrs Closed Dec-Feb

BLAIR ATHOLL
Map 14 NN86

Atholl Arms Hotel

★★★ 72% HOTEL

Old North Rd PH18 5SG

☎ 01796 481205 📠 01796 481550

e-mail: hotel@athollarms.co.uk

web: www.athollarmshotel.co.uk

dir: Off A9 to B8079, 1m into Blair Atholl, hotel near entrance to Blair Castle

PETS: Bedrooms Charges £5 per night £35 per week **Public areas** except restaurant on leads **Grounds** on leads disp bin **Exercise area** village green adjacent **Facilities** cage storage walks info vet info **Stables** 1m **Other** charge for damage

Situated close to Blair Castle and conveniently adjacent to the railway station, this stylish hotel has historically appointed public rooms that include a choice of bars, and a splendid baronial-style dining room. Bedrooms vary in size and style. Staff throughout are friendly and very caring.

Rooms 30 (3 fmly) **S** £51.50-£67; **D** £82-£97 (incl. bkfst)* **Facilities** Fishing Rough shooting 🎵 New Year Wi-fi **Parking** 103 **Notes** LB

Blair Castle Caravan Park (NN874656)

▶ ▶ ▶ ▶

PH18 5SR

☎ 01796 481263 📠 01796 481587

e-mail: mail@blaircastlecaravanpark.co.uk

dir: From A9 junct with B8079 at Aldclune, then NE to Blair Atholl. Site on right after crossing bridge in village

PETS: Charges £1 per night **Public areas** except reception, toilet blocks & children's play area disp bin **Exercise area** dog walk adjacent **Facilities** food food bowl water bowl walks info vet info **Other** prior notice required disposal bags available **Restrictions** no dangerous dogs (see page 7)

Open Mar-Nov Last arrival 21.30hrs Last departure noon

An attractive site set in impressive seclusion within the Atholl Estate, surrounded by mature woodland and the River Tilt. Although a large park, the various groups of pitches are located throughout the extensive parkland, and each has its own sanitary block with all-cubicled facilities of a very high standard. There is a choice of grass pitches, hardstandings, or fully-serviced pitches. This park is particularly suitable for the larger type of motorhome. 32 acre site. 248 touring pitches. Tent pitches. Motorhome pitches. 109 statics.

Notes Family park, no noise after 23.00hrs.

COMRIE
Map 11 NN72

Royal

★★★ 83% ◉ HOTEL

Melville Square PH6 2DN

☎ 01764 679200 📠 01764 679219

e-mail: reception@royalhotel.co.uk

web: www.royalhotel.co.uk

dir: Off A9 on A822 to Crieff, then B827 to Comrie. Hotel in main square on A85

PETS: Bedrooms unattended **Public areas Grounds** disp bin **Exercise area** 500yds **Facilities** food bowl water bowl scoop/disp bags leads washing facs walks info vet info **On Request** fridge access torch towels **Stables** 3m **Other** charge for damage

A traditional façade gives little indication of the style and elegance inside this long-established hotel located in the village centre. Public areas include a bar and library, a bright modern restaurant and a conservatory-style brasserie. Bedrooms are tastefully appointed and furnished with smart reproduction antiques.

Rooms 13 (2 annexe) **Facilities** STV Fishing Shooting arranged New Year Wi-fi **Parking** 22 **Notes** LB Closed 25-26 Dec

---

DUNKELD
Map 11 NO04

Inver Mill Farm Caravan Park (NO015422)

▶ ▶ ▶

Inver PH8 0JR

☎ 01350 727477 📠 01350 727477

e-mail: invermill@talk21.com

dir: A9 onto A822 then immediately right to Inver

PETS: Public areas dogs must be kept on leads at all times **Exercise area** woodland adjacent **Facilities** washing facs walks info vet info **Other** prior notice required **Resident Pet:** Tummel (Black Labrador)

Open end Mar-Oct Last arrival 22.00hrs Last departure noon

A peaceful park on level former farmland, located on the banks of the River Braan and surrounded by mature trees and hills. The active resident owners keep the park in very good condition. 5 acre site. 65 touring pitches. Tent pitches. Motorhome pitches.

Notes 🚭

SCOTLAND

KENMORE · Map 14 NN74

Kenmore Hotel
★★★ 78% HOTEL
The Square PH15 2NU
☎ 01887 830205 📠 01887 830262
e-mail: reception@kenmorehotel.co.uk
web: www.kenmorehotel.com
dir: *Off A9 at Ballinluig onto A827, through Aberfeldy to Kenmore, hotel in village centre*

PETS: Bedrooms (7 GF) annexe bedrooms only Charges £7.50 per night £52.50 per week Public areas except restaurant on leads Grounds on leads disp bin Exercise area 0.5m Facilities food (pre-bookable) food bowl water bowl dog chews cat treats scoop/disp bags washing facs cage storage walks info vet info On Request fridge access torch towels Stables 1m Other charge for damage Restrictions no dangerous dogs (see page 7)

Dating back to 1572, this riverside hotel is Scotland's oldest inn and has a rich and interesting history. Bedrooms have tasteful decor, and meals can be enjoyed in the restaurant which has panoramic views of the River Tay. The choice of bars includes one with real fires.

Rooms 40 (13 annexe) (4 fmly) (7 GF) S £69.50-£79.50; D £109-£129 (incl. bkfst)* Facilities STV Salmon fishing on River Tay Xmas New Year Wi-fi Services Lift Parking 40 Notes LB

KINCLAVEN · Map 11 NO13

Ballathie House Hotel
★★★★ 78% COUNTRY HOUSE HOTEL
PH1 4QN
☎ 01250 883268 📠 01250 883396
e-mail: email@ballathiehousehotel.com
web: www.ballathiehousehotel.com
dir: *From A9, 2m N of Perth, take B9099 through Stanley, follow signs. Or from A93 at Beech Hedge follow signs for hotel, 2.5m*

PETS: Bedrooms (10 GF) Charges Public areas Grounds disp bin Exercise area nearby Facilities food bowl water bowl dog chews vet info On Request fridge access towels Other charge for damage

Set in delightful grounds, this splendid Scottish mansion house combines classical grandeur with modern comfort. Bedrooms range from well-proportioned master rooms to modern

standard rooms, and many boast antique furniture and art deco bathrooms. It might be worth requesting one of the Riverside Rooms, a purpose-built development right on the banks of the river, complete with balconies and terraces. The elegant restaurant has views over the River Tay.

Rooms 41 (16 annexe) (2 fmly) (10 GF) S £65-£130; D £130-£29 (incl. bkfst)* Facilities FTV Putt green Fishing 🛶 Xmas New Yea Wi-fi Services Lift Parking 50

KINLOCH RANNOCH · Map 14 NN65

Dunalastair Hotel
★★★ 78% HOTEL
PH16 5PW
☎ 01882 632323 & 632218 📠 01882 632371
e-mail: info@dunalastair.co.uk
dir: *A9 to Pitlochry, on N side take B8019 to Tummel Bridge then A846 to Kinloch Rannoch*

PETS: Bedrooms (9 GF) unattended sign Charges £10 per night Public areas except restaurant on leads Grounds disp bin Exercise area adjacent Facilities food (pre-bookable) food bowl water bowl dog chews feeding mat scoop/disp bags walks info vet info Other charge for damage Resident Pets: Kiita (Blue Merle Border Collie)

Surrounded by unspoilt and beautiful countryside, this family-owned hotel, offers a warm and friendly welcome and great hospitality. The public areas are inviting, and fires are lit on colder days. The restaurant offers a fine dining experience whilst the lounge and conservatory have a more informal and relaxed atmosphere. The bedrooms are well appointed.

Rooms 28 (4 fmly) (9 GF) Facilities Fishing 4x4 safaris Rafting Clay pigeon shooting Bike hire Archery Xmas New Year Parking 33

Macdonald Loch Rannoch Hotel
★★★ 75% HOTEL
PH16 5PS
☎ 0844 879 9059 & 01882 632201 📠 01882 632203
e-mail: loch_rannoch@macdonald-hotels.co.uk
web: www.macdonald-hotels.co.uk
dir: *Off A9 onto B847 Calvine. Follow signs to Kinloch Rannoch, hotel 1m from village*

PETS: Bedrooms unattended Charges £10 per stay Public areas except lounge, bar & restaurant on leads Grounds on leads disp bin Exercise area 100yds Facilities walks info vet info On Request fridge access torch towels Other charge for damage

Set deep in the countryside with elevated views across Loch Rannoch, this hotel is built around a 19th-century hunting lodge and provides a great base for exploring this beautiful area. The superior bedrooms have views over the loch. There is a choice of eating options - The Ptarmigan Restaurant and the Schiehallan Bar for informal eating. The hotel provides both indoor and outdoor activities.

Rooms 48 (25 fmly) Facilities FTV 🏊 Fishing Gym Xmas New Year Wi-fi Services Lift Parking 52

KINROSS　　　　　　　　　　**Map 11 NO10**

The Green Hotel Golf & Leisure Resort

★★★★ **73%** ⊛ HOTEL

The Muirs KY13 8AS
☎ 01577 863467　📠 01577 863180
e-mail: reservations@green-hotel.com
web: www.green-hotel.com
dir: *M90 junct 6, follow Kinross signs onto A922 for hotel*

PETS: Bedrooms (14 GF)　**Public areas** except restaurant, lounge & bar on leads　**Grounds** on leads　**Exercise area** adjacent
Facilities cage storage walks info vet info　**On Request** fridge access towels　**Stables** 4m

A long-established hotel offering a wide range of indoor and outdoor activities. Public areas include a classical restaurant, a choice of bars and a well-stocked gift shop. The comfortable, well-equipped bedrooms, most of which are generously proportioned, boast attractive colour schemes and smart modern furnishings.

Rooms 46 (3 fmly) (14 GF) **S** £62-£92; **D** £72-£132 (incl. bkfst)*
Facilities STV ⊛ supervised ⚓ 36 🏌 Putt green Fishing 🎣 Gym Petanque Curling (Sep-Apr) Cycling Shooting 🎵 Xmas New Year Wi-fi **Parking** 60 **Notes** LB

PERTH　　　　　　　　　　**Map 11 NO12**

Murrayshall House Hotel & Golf Course

★★★★ **76%** ⊛⊛ HOTEL

New Scone PH2 7PH
☎ 01738 551171　📠 01738 552595
e-mail: info@murrayshall.co.uk
web: www.murrayshall.co.uk
dir: *From Perth take A94 (Coupar Angus), 1m from Perth, right to Murrayshall just before New Scone*

PETS: Bedrooms (5 GF)　unattended　ground-floor bedrooms only
Sep accom dog pen in grounds　**Public areas** except food service areas　**Grounds**　**Facilities** cage storage walks info vet info
On Request fridge access torch **Resident Pet:** Jasper (cat)

This imposing country house is set in 350 acres of grounds, including two golf courses, one of which is of championship

standard. Bedrooms come in two distinct styles: modern suites in a purpose-built building contrast with more classic rooms in the main building. The Clubhouse bar serves a range of meals all day, whilst more accomplished cooking can be enjoyed in the Old Masters Restaurant.

Rooms 41 (14 annexe) (17 fmly) (5 GF) **S** £77-£100; **D** £120-£150 (incl. bkfst)* **Facilities** STV ⚓ 36 🏌 Putt green Driving range New Year Wi-fi **Parking** 120 **Notes** LB

The Anglers Inn

★★★ INN

Main Rd, Guildtown PH2 6BS
☎ 01821 640329
e-mail: info@theanglersinn.co.uk
dir: *6m N of Perth on A93*

PETS: Bedrooms unattended　**Public areas** in bar only　on leads
Grounds on leads　disp bin　**Exercise area** adjacent　**Facilities** water bowl dog chews scoop/disp bags washing facs cage storage walks info vet info　**On Request** fridge access torch towels　**Other** charge for damage disposal bags available

This charming country inn enjoys a peaceful rural setting and yet is only a short drive from Perth city centre and is popular with fishing and shooting parties along with race goers. The inn has been tastefully refurbished and the accommodation consists of en suite bedrooms that vary in size, each equipped with flat-screenTV. The restaurant offers local produce, and a daily changing blackboard.

Rooms 6 en suite (1 fmly) **S** £40-£75; **D** £100-£150 **Facilities** FTV TVL tea/coffee Dinner available Cen ht Wi-fi 🎱 Pool table **Parking** 40 **Notes** LB No Children

PITLOCHRY　　　　　　　　　　**Map 14 NN95**

Green Park

★★★ **87%** ⊛ COUNTRY HOUSE HOTEL

Clunie Bridge Rd PH16 5JY
☎ 01796 473248　📠 01796 473520
e-mail: bookings@thegreenpark.co.uk
web: www.thegreenpark.co.uk
dir: *Exit A9 at Pitlochry, follow signs 0.25m through town*

PETS: Bedrooms (16 GF)　unattended　**Grounds** disp bin
Exercise area adjacent　**Facilities** food bowl water bowl bedding scoop/disp bags leads washing facs cage storage walks info vet info　**On Request** fridge access torch towels **Resident Pets:** Dan (Golden Retriever), Squeaky & Speedy (guinea pigs)

Guests return year after year to this lovely hotel that is situated in a stunning setting on the shores of Loch Faskally. Most of the thoughtfully designed bedrooms, including a splendid wing, the restaurant and the comfortable lounges enjoy these views. Dinner utilises fresh produce, much of it grown in the kitchen garden.

Rooms 51 (3 fmly) (16 GF) **S** £66-£103; **D** £132-£206 (incl. bkfst & dinner)* **Facilities** FTV Putt green New Year Wi-fi **Services** Lift **Parking** 51 **Notes** LB

SCOTLAND

PITLOCHRY *continued*

Milton of Fonab Caravan Site *(NN945573)*

▶ ▶ ▶ ▶

Bridge Rd PH16 5NA
☎ 01796 472882 📠 01796 474363
e-mail: info@fonab.co.uk
dir: *0.5m S of town off A924*

PETS: Public areas disp bin **Exercise area on site Facilities**
food scoop/disp bags walks info vet info **Other** prior notice
required

Open Apr-Oct Last arrival 21.00hrs Last departure 13.00hrs

Set on the banks of the River Tummel, with extensive views
down the river valley to the mountains, this park is close to the
centre of Pitlochry, adjacent to the Pitlochry Festival Theatre. The
sanitary facilities are exceptionally good, with most contained in
combined shower/wash basin and toilet cubicles. 15 acre site.
154 touring pitches. Tent pitches. Motorhome pitches. 36 statics.

Notes Couples & families only, no motor cycles. 🐕

| ST FILLANS | Map 11 NN62 |

The Four Seasons Hotel

★ ★ ★ **83%** 🌸🌸 HOTEL

Loch Earn PH6 2NF
☎ 01764 685333 📠 01764 685444
e-mail: info@thefourseasonshotel.co.uk
web: www.thefourseasonshotel.co.uk
dir: *On A85, towards W of village*

PETS: Bedrooms unattended **Public areas** except main food
service area on leads **Grounds** disp bin **Exercise area** behind
hotel **Facilities** food (pre-bookable) food bowl water bowl
bedding dog chews feeding mat scoop/disp bags leads pet
sitting dog walking washing facs dog grooming cage storage
walks info vet info **On Request** fridge access torch towels
Other charge for damage pet concierge service **Resident Pets:**
Sham & Pagne (Münsterlanders)

Set on the edge of Loch Earn, this welcoming hotel and many
of its bedrooms benefit from fine views. There is a choice of
lounges, including a library, warmed by log fires during winter.
Local produce is used to good effect in both the Meall Reamhar
restaurant and the more informal Tarken Room.

The Four Seasons Hotel

Rooms 18 (6 annexe) (7 fmly) **S** £54-£108; **D** £108-£166 (incl.
bkfst) **Facilities** FTV Xmas New Year Wi-fi **Parking** 40 **Notes** LB
Closed 2 Jan-mid Feb RS Nov, Dec, Mar

| TUMMEL BRIDGE | Map 14 NN75 |

Tummel Valley Holiday Park *(NN764592)*

PH16 5SA
☎ 0844 335 3756 📠 01882 634302
e-mail: touringandcamping@parkdeanholidays.com
dir: *From Perth take A9 N to bypass Pitlochry. 3m after Pitlochry
take B8019 signed Tummel Bridge. Site 11m on left*

PETS: Charges varies (please phone) **Public areas** on leads
disp bin **Exercise area** 200yds **Facilities** food litter tray walks
info vet info **Other** prior notice required disposal bags available
Restrictions no dangerous dogs (see page 7)

Open Mar-Oct Last arrival 21.00hrs Last departure 10.00hrs

A well-developed site amongst mature forest in an attractive
valley, beside the famous bridge on the banks of the River
Tummel. Play areas and the bar are sited alongside the river,
and there is an indoor pool, children's clubs and live family
entertainment. This is an ideal base in which to relax. Please
note that this park does not accept tents or trailer tents. 55 acre
site. 34 touring pitches. 34 hardstandings. Motorhome pitches.
159 statics.

RENFREWSHIRE

LANGBANK
Map 10 NS37

Best Western Gleddoch House
★★★★ 73% HOTEL

PA14 6YE
☎ 01475 540711 📠 01475 540201
e-mail: reservations.gleddochhouse@ohiml.com
web: www.oxfordhotelsandinns.com
dir: *M8 to Greenock, onto A8, left at rdbt onto A789, follow for 0.5m, turn right, 2nd on left*

PETS: Bedrooms (17 GF) unattended **Charges** £5 per night £30 per week **Public areas** except restaurant & lounge on leads **Grounds** on leads **Exercise area** 10 mins **On Request** fridge access **Other** charge for damage

This hotel is set in spacious, landscaped grounds high above the River Clyde with fine views. The period house is appointed to a very high standard. The modern extension is impressive and offers spacious and very comfortable bedrooms. Warm hospitality and attentive service are noteworthy along with the hotel's parkland golf course and leisure club.

Rooms 70 (22 fmly) (17 GF) **Facilities** Spa FTV ⊛ ↨ 18 Putt green Gym Steam room Sauna Xmas New Year Wi-fi **Parking** 150

SCOTTISH BORDERS

BROUGHTON
Map 11 NT13

The Glenholm Centre
★★★ 🏠 GUEST ACCOMMODATION

ML12 6JF
☎ 01899 830408
e-mail: info@glenholm.co.uk
dir: *1m S of Broughton. Off A701 to Glenholm*

PETS: Bedrooms (2 GF) unattended **Grounds** disp bin **Exercise area** adjacent **Facilities** leads cage storage walks info vet info **On Request** fridge access torch **Resident Pets:** Minty & Sage (Bearded Collies)

Surrounded by peaceful farmland, this former schoolhouse has a distinct African theme. The home-cooked meals and baking have received much praise and are served in the spacious lounge-dining room. The bright airy bedrooms are thoughtfully equipped, and the service is friendly and attentive. Computer courses are available.

Rooms 3 en suite 1 annexe en suite (1 fmly) (2 GF) **S** £39-£42; **D** £64 **Facilities** TVL tea/coffee Dinner available Cen ht Licensed Wi-fi ↨ **Parking** 14 **Notes** LB Closed 20 Dec-1 Feb

GALASHIELS
Map 12 NT43

Kingsknowes
★★★ 77% HOTEL

Selkirk Rd TD1 3HY
☎ 01896 758375 📠 01896 750377
e-mail: enq@kingsknowes.co.uk
web: www.kingsknowes.co.uk
dir: *Off A7 at Galashiels/Selkirk rdbt*

PETS: Bedrooms Public areas except at meal times **Grounds Exercise area** nearby **Resident Pets:** Isla & Hector (Labradors)

An imposing turreted mansion, this hotel lies in attractive gardens on the outskirts of town close to the River Tweed. It boasts elegant public areas and many spacious bedrooms, some with excellent views. There is a choice of bars, one with a popular menu to supplement the restaurant.

Rooms 12 (2 fmly) **Facilities** Wi-fi **Parking** 65

Over Langshaw *(NT524400)*
★★★ FARMHOUSE

Langshaw TD1 2PE
☎ 01896 860244 📠 01896 860668 Mrs S Bergius
e-mail: overlangshaw@btconnect.com
dir: *3m N of Galashiels. A7 N from Galashiels, 1m right signed Langshaw, right at T-junct into Langshaw, left signed Earlston, Over Langshaw 1m, signed*

PETS: Bedrooms (1 GF) ground-floor, double bedroom only **Public areas** lounge only **Grounds** disp bin **Exercise area** Southern Upland Way (1m) **Facilities** feeding mat washing facs cage storage walks info vet info **On Request** fridge access torch towels **Restrictions** no Rottweilers **Resident Pets:** Tibbie, Jassie, Gyp & Flek (farm dogs)

There are fine panoramic views from this organic hillside farm which offers two comfortable and spacious bedrooms. Hearty breakfasts are provided at individual tables in the lounge and a friendly welcome is guaranteed.

Rooms 2 en suite (1 fmly) (1 GF); **D** £65-£75 **Facilities** TVL tea/coffee Cen ht Wi-fi **Parking** 4 **Notes** 🌐 500 acres dairy/sheep/organic

SCOTLAND

JEDBURGH — Map 12 NT62

Ferniehirst Mill Lodge
★★ GUEST HOUSE
TD8 6PQ
☎ 01835 863279
e-mail: ferniehirstmill@aol.com
web: www.ferniehirstmill.co.uk
dir: 2.5m S of Jedburgh on A68, onto private track to end

PETS: Bedrooms (1 GF) unattended Charges horse £6-£12 per night Grounds disp bin Exercise area adjacent Facilities washing facs cage storage walks info vet info On Request fridge access torch towels Stables Resident Pets: Maremma (Sheepdog), Flight & Mac (Whippets), 11 horses

Reached by a narrow farm track and a rustic wooden bridge, this chalet-style house has a secluded setting by the River Jed. Bedrooms are small and functional and there is a comfortable lounge in which to relax. Home-cooked dinners are available by arrangement, and hearty breakfasts are served in the cosy dining room.

Rooms 7 en suite (1 GF) S £30; D £60 Facilities TVL tea/coffee Dinner available Cen ht Fishing Riding Parking 10

KELSO — Map 12 NT73

The Roxburghe Hotel & Golf Course
★★★★ 77% COUNTRY HOUSE HOTEL
Heiton TD5 8JZ
☎ 01573 450331 ≣ 01573 450611
e-mail: hotel@roxburghe.net
web: www.roxburghe.net
dir: From A68 Jedburgh take A698 to Heiton, 3m SW of Kelso

PETS: Bedrooms (3 GF) unattended courtyard rooms only Sep accom 2 outdoor kennels Charges £10 per night Grounds Exercise area nearby Facilities food bowl water bowl washing facs cage storage walks info vet info On Request torch towels Other charge for damage cats must be caged

Outdoor sporting pursuits are popular at this impressive Jacobean mansion owned by the Duke of Roxburghe, and set in 500 acres of woods and parkland bordering the River Teviot. Gracious public areas are the perfect settings for afternoon teas and carefully prepared meals. The elegant bedrooms are individually designed, some by the Duchess herself, and include superior rooms, some with four posters and log fires.

Rooms 22 (6 annexe) (3 fmly) (3 GF) Facilities Spa STV 18 Putt green Fishing Clay shooting Health & beauty salon Mountain bike hire Falconry Archery Xmas New Year Wi-fi Parking 150

Ednam House
★★★ 80% HOTEL
Bridge St TD5 7HT
☎ 01573 224168 ≣ 01573 226319
e-mail: contact@ednamhouse.com
web: www.ednamhouse.com
dir: From S: A1 to Berwick, A698 or A7 to Hawick, A698 to Kelso. From N: A68 to Carfraemill, A6089 to Kelso

PETS: Bedrooms (3 GF) Public areas except dining room Grounds disp bin Exercise area nearby Facilities food bowl water bowl walks info vet info On Request fridge access torch Restrictions no Bernese Mountain Dogs or similar sized breeds

Overlooking a wide expanse of the River Tweed, this fine Georgian mansion has been under the Brooks family ownership for over 75 years. Accommodation styles range from standard to grand, plus The Orangerie, situated in the grounds, that has been converted into a gracious two-bedroom apartment. Public areas include a choice of lounges and an elegant dining room that has views over the gardens.

Rooms 32 (2 annexe) (4 fmly) (3 GF) Facilities FTV Free access to Abbey Fitness Centre Wi-fi Parking 60 Notes Closed 22 Dec-6 Jan

Springwood Caravan Park (NT720334)
▶▶▶▶
TD5 8LS
☎ 01573 224596 ≣ 01573 224033
e-mail: admin@springwood.biz
dir: 1m E of Kelso on A699, signed Newtown St Boswells

PETS: Public areas disp bin Exercise area many walks nearby Facilities food bowl water bowl walks info vet info Other prior notice required dogs must be on leads at all times

Open 25 Mar-17 Oct Last arrival 23.00hrs Last departure noon

Set in a secluded position on the banks of the tree-lined River Teviot, this well-maintained site enjoys a pleasant and spacious spot in which to relax. It offers a high standard of modern toilet facilities, which are mainly contained in cubicled units. Floors Castle and the historic town of Kelso are close by. 2 acre site. 20 touring pitches. 20 hardstandings. Motorhome pitches. 180 statics.

LAUDER — Map 12 NT54

Thirlestane Castle Caravan & Camping Site
(NT536473)

►►►

Thirlestane Castle TD2 6RU
☎ 01578 718884 & 07976 231032
e-mail: thirlestanepark@btconnect.com
dir: *Signed off A68 & A697, just S of Lauder*

PETS: Public areas on leads disp bin **Exercise area** 1 min **Facilities** walks info vet info **Other** prior notice required max 2 dogs per pitch; dogs must not be left unattended at any time **Restrictions** no dangerous dogs (see page 7)

Open Apr-1 Oct Last arrival 20.30hrs Last departure noon

Set in the grounds of the impressive Thirlestane Castle, with mainly level grassy pitches. The park and facilities are kept in sparkling condition. 5 acre site. 60 touring pitches. 17 hardstandings. Tent pitches. Motorhome pitches. 24 statics.

Notes ☺

PEEBLES — Map 11 NT24

Cringletie House
★★★★ ◉◉ COUNTRY HOUSE HOTEL
Edinburgh Rd EH45 8PL
☎ 01721 725750 📠 01721 725751
e-mail: enquiries@cringletie.com
web: www.cringletie.com
dir: *2m N on A703*

PETS: Bedrooms (2 GF) unattended **Charges Grounds Exercise area** nearby **Facilities** food bowl water bowl dog chews cage storage walks info vet info **On Request** fridge access torch **Other** all dogs welcomed with a dog biscuit! **Resident Pet:** Daisy (cat)

This romantic baronial mansion, built in 1861, is set in 28 acres of beautiful gardens and woodland; there is a walled garden with a 400-year-old yew hedge (perhaps the oldest in Scotland), a waterfall, sculptures and croquet lawn. In 1971 Scottish Heritage granted the property a Grade B listing, and in the same year the house became a hotel. The delightful public rooms, with welcoming fires, include a cocktail lounge with adjoining conservatory, and there are service bells in each room which still work. The award-winning, first-floor restaurant is graced by a magnificent hand-painted ceiling. The individually designed bedrooms have grace and charm, and for the ultimate luxury there's the Selkirk Suite.

Rooms 13 (2 GF) **S** £130-£230; **D** £160-£260 (incl. bkfst)* **Facilities** FTV Putt green ⛳ Petanque Giant chess & draughts In-room therapy treatments Xmas New Year Wi-fi **Services** Lift **Parking** 30 **Notes** LB

Macdonald Cardrona Hotel & Golf Course
★★★★ 77% ◉ HOTEL
Cardrona EH45 8NE
☎ 01896 833600 📠 01896 831166
e-mail: general.cardrona@macdonald-hotels.co.uk
web: www.macdonald-hotels.co.uk/cardrona
dir: *On A72 between Peebles & Innerleithen, 3m S of Peebles*

PETS: Bedrooms unattended sign 1st & 2nd floor bedrooms only **Charges** £10 per night **Public areas** except lounge & restaurant on leads **Grounds** on leads disp bin **Exercise area** 1m **Facilities** dog chews cage storage walks info vet info **On Request** towels **Stables** 2m

The rolling hills of the Scottish Borders are a stunning backdrop for this modern, purpose-built hotel. Spacious bedrooms are traditional in style, equipped with a range of extras, and most enjoy fantastic countryside. The hotel features some impressive leisure facilities, including an 18-hole golf course, 18-metre indoor pool and state-of-the-art gym.

Rooms 99 (24 fmly) (16 GF) **S** £95-£175; **D** £105-£185 (incl. bkfst)* **Facilities** Spa STV ⊛ ♨ 18 Putt green Fishing Gym Sauna Steam room Xmas New Year Wi-fi **Services** Lift **Parking** 200 **Notes** LB

Tontine
★★★ 82% HOTEL
High St EH45 8AJ
☎ 01721 720892 📠 01721 729732
e-mail: info@tontinehotel.com
web: www.tontinehotel.com
dir: *In town centre*

PETS: Bedrooms unattended certain bedrooms only **Public areas** assist dogs only disp bin **Exercise area** Tweed Green behind hotel **Facilities** walks info vet info **On Request** fridge access torch towels **Stables** 2m **Other** charge for damage **Restrictions** well behaved dogs only

Conveniently situated in the main street, this long-established hotel offers comfortable public rooms including the elegant Adam Restaurant and an inviting lounge and 'clubby' bar. Bedrooms, contained in the original house and the river-facing wing, offer a smart, classical style of accommodation. The lasting impression is of the excellent level of hospitality and guest care.

Rooms 36 (3 fmly) (10 smoking) **S** fr £55; **D** £85-£110 (incl. bkfst) **Facilities** STV FTV Xmas New Year Wi-fi **Parking** 24 **Notes** LB

SCOTLAND

PEEBLES *continued*

Crossburn Caravan Park *(NT248417)*

▶ ▶ ▶ ▶

Edinburgh Rd EH45 8ED
☎ 01721 720501   🖨 01721 720501
e-mail: enquiries@crossburncaravans.co.uk
dir: *0.5m N of Peebles on A703*

PETS: Public areas except shop disp bin **Exercise area on site**
dog walk **Facilities** walks info vet info **Other** max 2 dogs per
pitch **Resident Pets:** Zara (Rhodesian Ridgeback), Ginty (Jack
Russell)

Open Apr-Oct Last arrival 21.00hrs Last departure 14.00hrs

A peaceful site in a relatively quiet location, despite the proximity
of the main road which partly borders the site, as does the
Eddleston Water. There are lovely views, and the park is well
stocked with trees, flowers and shrubs. Facilities are maintained
to a high standard, and fully-serviced pitches are available. A
large caravan dealership is on the same site. 6 acre site. 45
touring pitches. 15 hardstandings. Tent pitches. Motorhome
pitches. 85 statics.

ST BOSWELLS   Map 12 NT53

Dryburgh Abbey Hotel

★ ★ ★ ★ 73% ◉◉ COUNTRY HOUSE HOTEL

TD6 0RQ
☎ 01835 822261   🖨 01835 823945
e-mail: enquiries@dryburgh.co.uk
web: www.dryburgh.co.uk
dir: *B6356 signed Scott's View & Earlston. Through Clintmains,
1.8m to hotel*

PETS: Bedrooms (8 GF) unattended **Sep accom Charges** £7
per night **Public areas** except restaurant & bistro **Grounds**
disp bin **Exercise area** surrounding countryside **Facilities** food
bowl water bowl washing facs cage storage walks info vet info
On Request fridge access torch towels **Stables** 0.5m **Other**
paddock for horses; max 2 dogs per bedroom **Resident Pets:**
Harry & Bracken (Cocker Spaniels)

Found in the heart of the Scottish Borders, and sitting beside
to the ancient ruins of Dryburgh Abbey and the majestic River
Tweed. This country house hotel, dating from the mid-19th
century, offers comfortable public areas and an array of
bedrooms and suites, each still displaying original features.
The award-winning Tweed Restaurant, overlooking the river,
showcases the chef's dedication to producing modern Scottish
cuisine, and The Abbey Bistro offers food from noon until 9pm.

Rooms 38 (31 fmly) (8 GF) **Facilities** FTV 🕑 Putt green Fishing
⊰ Sauna Xmas New Year Wi-fi **Services** Lift **Parking** 70

SOUTH AYRSHIRE

BALLANTRAE   Map 10 NX08

Glenapp Castle

★ ★ ★ ★ ★ ◉◉◉◉ COUNTRY HOUSE HOTEL

KA26 0NZ
☎ 01465 831212   🖨 01465 831000
e-mail: enquiries@glenappcastle.com
web: www.glenappcastle.com
dir: *S through Ballantrae, cross bridge over River Stinchar, 1st
right, hotel in 1m*

PETS: Bedrooms (7 GF) ground-floor bedrooms with direct
access to garden **Grounds Exercise area** adjacent **Facilities**
food bowl water bowl feeding mat scoop/disp bags leads pet
sitting dog walking washing facs cage storage walks info vet
info **On Request** fridge access torch towels **Other** charge for
damage **Resident Pets:** Midge & Mozzy (Springer Spaniels)

Friendly hospitality and attentive service prevail at this stunning
Victorian castle, set in extensive private grounds to the south
of the village. Impeccably furnished bedrooms are graced with
antiques and period pieces, and include two master rooms and
a ground-floor family suite. Breathtaking views of Arran and
Ailsa Craig can be enjoyed from the delightful, sumptuous day
rooms and from many of the bedrooms. Accomplished cooking,
using quality local ingredients is a feature of all meals; dinner is
offered on a well crafted and imaginative fixed six-course menu.
Much of the fruit, vegetables and herbs come from the hotel's
own garden. Guests should make a point of walking round the
wonderful 36-acre grounds, and take a look at the azalea pond,
walled vegetable gardens and restored Victorian greenhouses.

Rooms 17 (2 fmly) (7 GF) **S** £265-£450; **D** £415-£620 (incl. bkfst
& dinner)* **Facilities** STV FTV ⊰⊰ New Year Wi-fi **Services** Lift
Parking 20 **Notes** LB Closed Jan-mid Mar & Xmas week

BARRHILL   Map 10 NX28

Barrhill Holiday Park *(NX216835)*

▶ ▶ ▶ ▶

KA26 0PZ
☎ 01465 821355   🖨 01465 821355
e-mail: barrhill@surfree.co.uk
dir: *On A714 (Newton Stewart to Girvan road). 1m N of Barrhill*

PETS: Public areas on leads **Exercise area on site** adjacent to
park **Facilities** scoop/disp bags washing facs walks info vet
info **Resident Pet:** Mr Puss (cat)

Open Mar-Jan Last arrival 22.00hrs Last departure 10.00hrs

A small, friendly park in a tranquil rural location, screened from
the A714 by trees. The park is terraced and well landscaped,
and a high quality amenity block includes disabled facilities. 6
acre site. 30 touring pitches. 30 hardstandings. Tent pitches.
Motorhome pitches. 39 statics.

Notes No noise after 23.00hrs. ⌨

SOUTH LANARKSHIRE

ABINGTON
Map 11 NS92

Mount View Caravan Park *(NS935235)*
▶▶▶
ML12 6RW
☎ 01864 502808
e-mail: info@mountviewcaravanpark.co.uk
dir: *M74 junct 13, A702 S into Abington. Left into Station Rd, over river & railway. Site on right*

PETS: Public areas on leads **Exercise area** adjacent **Facilities** walks info vet info **Other** prior notice required pets to be kept on own pitch & walked off site **Restrictions** no Pit Bull Terriers **Resident Pet:** Hollie (Retriever)

Open Mar-Oct Last arrival 20.45hrs Last departure 11.30hrs

A delightfully maturing family park, surrounded by the Southern Uplands and handily located between Carlisle and Glasgow. It is an excellent stopover site for those travelling between Scotland and the south, and the West Coast Railway passes beside the park. 5.5 acre site. 51 touring pitches. 51 hardstandings. Tent pitches. Motorhome pitches. 20 statics.

Notes 5mph speed limit.

ABINGTON MOTORWAY SERVICE AREA (M74)
Map 11 NS92

Days Inn Abington - M74
BUDGET HOTEL
ML12 6RG
☎ 01864 502782   📄 01864 502759
e-mail: abington.hotel@welcomebreak.co.uk
web: www.welcomebreak.co.uk
dir: *M74 junct 13, accessible from N'bound and S'bound carriageways*

PETS: Bedrooms unattended **Charges** £5 per night
Public areas on leads **Grounds** **Exercise area** nearby **Facilities** walks info vet info **On Request** fridge access

This modern building offers accommodation in smart, spacious and well-equipped bedrooms, suitable for families and business travellers, and all with en suite bathrooms. Continental breakfast is available and other refreshments may be taken at the nearby family restaurant.

Rooms 52 (50 fmly) (8 smoking) **S** £39.95-£59.95;
D £49.95-£69.95

STIRLING

ABERFOYLE
Map 11 NN50

Trossachs Holiday Park *(NS544976)*
▶▶▶▶
FK8 3SA
☎ 01877 382614   📄 01877 382732
e-mail: info@trossachsholidays.co.uk
dir: *Access on E side of A81, 1m S of junct A821 & 3m S of Aberfoyle*

PETS: Public areas **Exercise area on site** enclosed dog field & woodland walk **Exercise area** footpath from park to Aberfoyle **Facilities** food food bowl water bowl dog chews cat treats walks info vet info **Other** prior notice required disposal bags available

Open Mar-Oct Last arrival 21.00hrs Last departure noon

An imaginatively designed terraced site offering a high degree of quality all round, with fine views across Flanders Moss. All touring pitches are fully serviced with water, waste, electricity and TV aerial, and customer care is a main priority. Set in grounds within the Queen Elizabeth Forest Park, with plenty of opportunities for cycling off-road on mountain bikes, which can be hired or purchased on site. There are self-catering units including lodges for rental. 40 acre site. 66 touring pitches. 46 hardstandings. Tent pitches. Motorhome pitches. 84 statics.

Notes Groups by prior arrangement only

BLAIRLOGIE · Map 11 NS89

Witches Craig Caravan & Camping Park
(NS821968)

▶▶▶▶

FK9 5PX
☎ 01786 474947
e-mail: info@witchescraig.co.uk
dir: *3m NE of Stirling on A91 (Hillfoots to St Andrews road)*

PETS: Public areas except amenity block & children's play area disp bin **Exercise area on site** woods **Facilities** vet info

Open Apr-Oct Last arrival 20.00hrs Last departure noon

In an attractive setting with direct access to the lower slopes of the dramatic Ochil Hills, this is a well-maintained family-run park. It is in the centre of 'Braveheart' country, with easy access to historical sites and many popular attractions. 5 acre site. 60 touring pitches. 53 hardstandings. 6 seasonal pitches. Tent pitches. Motorhome pitches.

CALLANDER · Map 11 NN60

Roman Camp Country House
★★★ ⊚⊚⊚ COUNTRY HOUSE HOTEL

FK17 8BG
☎ 01877 330003   ▤ 01877 331533
e-mail: mail@romancamphotel.co.uk
web: www.romancamphotel.co.uk
dir: *N on A84, left at east end of High Street. 300yds to hotel*

PETS: Bedrooms (7 GF) **Grounds** on leads disp bin **Exercise area** woods (10 mins' walk) **Facilities** cage storage walks info vet info **On Request** fridge access torch towels **Other** charge for damage paddock for horses

Originally a shooting lodge, this charming country house has a rich history. Twenty acres of gardens and grounds lead down to the River Teith, and the town centre and its attractions are only a short walk away. Food is a highlight of any stay and menus are dominated by high-quality Scottish produce that is sensitively treated by the talented kitchen team. Real fires warm the atmospheric public areas and service is friendly yet professional.

Rooms 15 (4 fmly) (7 GF) **S** £95-£100; **D** £150-£200 (incl. bkfst) **Facilities** STV FTV Fishing Xmas New Year Wi-fi **Parking** 80 **Notes** LB

Gart Caravan Park *(NN643070)*

▶▶▶▶

The Gart FK17 8LE
☎ 01877 330002   ▤ 01877 330002
e-mail: enquiries@theholidaypark.co.uk
dir: *1m E of Callander on A84*

PETS: Public areas except children's play area, toilet & shower block **Exercise area on site** 1-acre fenced woodland **Facilities** washing facs walks info vet info **Other** prior notice required max 2 pets per pitch **Resident Pets:** Jack & Bryn (dogs)

Open Etr or Apr-15 Oct Last arrival 22.00hrs Last departure 11.30hrs

A very well maintained spacious parkland site within easy walking distance of Callander. The on-site play area for children is excellent, whilst free fishing is available on a private stretch of the River Teith. A wide range of leisure activities is available within the locality. 26 acre site. 128 touring pitches. Motorhome pitches. 66 statics.

Notes No commercial vehicles.

CRIANLARICH · Map 10 NN32

The Crianlarich Hotel
★★★ 77% ⊚ HOTEL

FK20 8RW
☎ 01838 300272   ▤ 01838 300329
e-mail: info@crianlarich-hotel.co.uk
web: www.crianlarich-hotel.co.uk
dir: *At junct of A85 & A82*

PETS: Bedrooms Charges £10 per night **Public areas** except restaurant & public bar on leads **Exercise area** 2 mins **Facilities** water bowl cage storage walks info vet info **On Request** fridge access torch towels

Standing at what has been an important transport junction for many years, this hotel continues to cater to travellers' needs. The ground-floor areas are impressive, and the pleasant bedrooms are smartly appointed and offer all the usual amenities. Friendly relaxed service and high quality food makes this an enjoyable place to stay especially as it is close to Loch Lomond and the Trossachs National Park.

Rooms 36 (1 fmly) **Facilities** FTV ♫ Xmas New Year Wi-fi **Services** Lift **Parking** 30 **Notes** LB

LOCHEARNHEAD   Map 11 NN52

Tigh Na Crich
★★★★ BED AND BREAKFAST

FK19 8PR
☎ 01567 830235
e-mail: johntippett2@aol.com
web: www.tighnacrich.co.uk
dir: At junct of A84 & A85, adjacent to village shop

PETS: Bedrooms Charges £5 per night **Public areas** except in dining room on leads **Grounds** on leads **Exercise area** 100yds **Facilities** walks info vet info **On Request** fridge access torch towels **Other** charge for damage **Resident Pet:** Charlie (Poodle)

Tich Na Crich is located in the heart of the small village of Lochearnhead, surrounded by mountains on three sides and Loch Earn on the fourth. Inside is very well presented accommodation with many thoughtful extras provided. The generous breakfast is served in the comfortable dining room on individual tables looking out to the front of the property.

Rooms 3 en suite (1 fmly) **S** £40-£45; **D** £60-£65 **Facilities** FTV tea/coffee Cen ht **Parking** 3 **Notes** ⊛

STIRLING   Map 11 NS79

Barceló Stirling Highland Hotel
★★★★ 75% HOTEL

Spittal St FK8 1DU
☎ 01786 272727   📠 01786 272829
e-mail: stirling@barcelo-hotels.co.uk
web: www.barcelo-hotels.co.uk
dir: A84 into Stirling. Follow Stirling Castle signs to Albert Hall. Left, left again, follow Castle signs

PETS: Bedrooms unattended **Charges** £15 per stay **Public areas** assist dogs only on leads **Exercise area** 5 mins' walk **Facilities** walks info vet info **Other** charge for damage prior notice required

Enjoying a location close to the castle and historic town, this atmospheric hotel was previously a high school. Public rooms have been converted from the original classrooms and retain many interesting features. Bedrooms are more modern in style and comfortably equipped. Scholars Restaurant serves traditional and international dishes, and the Headmaster's Study is the ideal venue for enjoying a drink.

Rooms 96 (4 fmly) **Facilities** Spa STV ⊗ supervised Gym Squash Steam room Dance studio Beauty therapist Xmas New Year Wi-fi **Services** Lift **Parking** 96

STRATHYRE   Map 11 NN51

Creagan House
★★★★★ ◉◉ 🍴 RESTAURANT WITH ROOMS

FK18 8ND
☎ 01877 384638   📠 01877 384319
e-mail: eatandstay@creaganhouse.co.uk
web: www.creaganhouse.co.uk
dir: 0.25m N of Strathyre on A84

PETS: Bedrooms (1 GF) unattended **Public areas** except restaurant & lounge **Grounds** disp bin **Exercise area** National Park accessible from car park **Facilities** food bowl water bowl leads washing facs cage storage walks info vet info **On Request** fridge access torch towels

Originally a farmhouse dating from the 17th century, Creagan House has operated as a restaurant with rooms for many years. The baronial-style dining room provides a wonderful setting for the cuisine which is classic French with some Scottish influences. Warm hospitality and attentive service are the highlights of any stay.

Rooms 5 en suite (1 fmly) (1 GF) **S** £75-£95; **D** £130-£150 **Facilities** FTV tea/coffee Dinner available Cen ht Wi-fi **Parking** 16 **Notes** LB Closed 7-22 Nov, Xmas & 18 Jan-8 Mar RS Wed & Thu Closed

SCOTLAND

SCOTLAND

WEST DUNBARTONSHIRE

BALLOCH
Map 10 NS38

Sunnyside
★★★ BED AND BREAKFAST
35 Main St G83 9JX
☎ 01389 750282 & 07717 397548
e-mail: enquiries@sunnysidebb.co.uk
dir: From A82 take A811 then A813 for 1m, over mini-rdbt 150mtrs on left

PETS: Bedrooms (1 GF) unattended Charges £5 per week Public areas on leads Grounds disp bin Exercise area surrounding countryside Facilities food (pre-bookable) food bowl water bowl bedding dog chews scoop/disp bags leads washing facs cage storage walks info vet info On Request torch towels Other charge for damage

Set in its own grounds well back from the road by Loch Lomond, Sunnyside is an attractive, traditional detached house, parts of which date back to the 1830s. Bedrooms are attractively decorated and provide comfortable modern accommodation. Free Wi-fi is also available. The dining room is located on the ground floor, and is an appropriate setting for hearty Scottish breakfasts.

Rooms 6 en suite (2 fmly) (1 GF) S £32-£38; D £54-£65
Facilities FTV tea/coffee Dinner available Cen ht Wi-fi Parking 8

Lomond Woods Holiday Park (NS383816)
►►►►
Old Luss Rd G83 8QP
☎ 01389 755000 📠 01389 755563
e-mail: lomondwoods@holiday-parks.co.uk
dir: From A82, 17m N of Glasgow, take A811 (Stirling to Balloch road). Left at 1st rdbt, follow holiday park signs, 150yds on left

PETS: Charges dog 50p per night Public areas except children's play area on leads disp bin Exercise area on site perimeter walk Facilities walks info vet info Other prior notice required max 2 dogs per pitch Restrictions no dangerous dogs (see page 7)

Open all year Last arrival 20.00hrs Last departure noon

A mature park with well-laid out pitches and self-catering lodges screened by trees and shrubs, surrounded by woodland and hills. The park is within walking distance of Loch Lomond Shores, a leisure and retail complex, which is the main gateway to Scotland's first National Park. Amenities include the Loch Lomond Aquarium, an Interactive Exhibition, and loch cruises. Please note that this park does not accept tents. 13 acre site. 100 touring pitches. 100 hardstandings. Motorhome pitches. 35 statics.

Notes No jet skis

WEST LOTHIAN

EAST CALDER
Map 11 NT06

Linwater Caravan Park (NT104696)
►►►
West Clifton EH53 0HT
☎ 0131 333 3326 📠 0131 333 1952
e-mail: linwater@supanet.com
dir: M9 junct 1, signed to B7030 or from Wilkieston on A71

PETS: Public areas except toilet block disp bin Exercise area on site walks to parks & canal Facilities walks info vet info Other prior notice required Resident Pets: Mimi (Black Labrador), Minnow (Cocker Spaniel), Beth (Golden Retriever), Cobbles (cat), sheep, pigs, ducks, hens

Open late Mar-late Oct Last arrival 21.00hrs Last departure noon

A farmland park in a peaceful rural area within easy reach of Edinburgh. The very good facilities are housed in a Scandinavian-style building, and are well maintained by resident owners, who are genuinely caring hosts and nothing is too much trouble to ensure campers are enjoying themselves. There are three 'timber tents' for hire and nearby are plenty of pleasant woodland walks. 5 acre site. 60 touring pitches. 18 hardstandings. Tent pitches. Motorhome pitches. 4 wooden pods.

Notes No noise after 23.00hrs.

LINLITHGOW
Map 11 NS97

Bomains Farm
★★★★ GUEST HOUSE
Bo'ness EH49 7RQ
☎ 01506 822188 & 822861 📠 01506 824433
e-mail: bunty.kirk@onetel.net
web: www.bomains.co.uk
dir: A706, 1.5m N towards Bo'ness, left at golf course x-rds, 1st farm on right

PETS: Bedrooms unattended Charges £5 per night Grounds disp bin Exercise area adjacent Facilities walks info vet info Stables Other pets may be left unattended if proprietors have been made aware Resident Pets: Minnie (Bichon Frise), Penny (Mini Schnauzer)

From its elevated location this friendly farmhouse has stunning views of the Firth of Forth. The bedrooms which vary in size are beautifully decorated, well equipped and enhanced by quality fabrics, with many thoughtful extra touches. Delicious home-cooked fare featuring the best of local produce is served in a stylish lounge-dining room.

Rooms 6 rms (4 en suite) (1 pri facs) (1 fmly) Facilities STV FTV TVL tea/coffee Cen ht Wi-fi Golf 18 Fishing Parking 12

Beecraigs Caravan & Camping Site

(NT006746)

▶▶▶▶

Beecraigs Country Park, The Park Centre EH49 6PL
☎ 01506 844516 📠 01506 846256
e-mail: mail@beecraigs.com
dir: *From Linlithgow on A803 or from Bathgate on B792, follow signs to country park. Reception either at restaurant or visitor centre*

PETS: Public areas except buildings disp bin **Exercise area on site** main country park area **Exercise area** field & woodland adjacent **Facilities** walks info vet info **Other** dogs must be kept on leads at all times disposal bags available at visitor centre

Open all year rs 25-26 Dec, 1-2 Jan no new arrivals Xmas, New Year or BH Last arrival 21.00hrs Last departure noon

A wildlife enthusiast's paradise where even the timber facility buildings are in keeping with the environment. Beecraigs is situated peacefully in the open countryside of the Bathgate Hills. Small bays with natural shading offer intimate pitches, and there's a restaurant serving lunch and evening meals. The smart toilet block on the main park includes en suite facilities, and there is a luxury toilet block for tenters. 6 acre site. 36 touring pitches. 36 hardstandings. Tent pitches. Motorhome pitches.

Notes No ball games near caravans, no noise after 22.00hrs.

SCOTTISH ISLANDS

ISLE OF ARRAN

BLACKWATERFOOT
Map 10 NR92

Best Western Kinloch

★★★ **80%** HOTEL

KA27 8ET
☎ 01770 860444 📠 01770 860447
e-mail: reservations@kinlochhotel.eclipse.co.uk
web: www.bw-kinlochhotel.co.uk
dir: *Ferry from Ardrossan to Brodick, follow signs for Blackwaterfoot, hotel in village centre*

PETS: Bedrooms (7 GF) unattended **Charges** £10 per night
Public areas public bar only on leads **Grounds** on leads
Exercise area adjacent **On Request** fridge access **Stables** 5 mins' walk **Other** charge for damage

Well known for providing an authentic island experience, this long established stylish hotel is in an idyllic location. Smart public areas include a choice of lounges, popular bars and well-presented leisure facilities. Bedrooms vary in size and style but most enjoy panoramic sea views and several family suites offer excellent value. The spacious restaurant provides a wide ranging menu, and in winter when the restaurant is closed, the bar serves a choice of creative dishes.

Rooms 37 (7 fmly) (7 GF) **Facilities** STV ⓢ Gym Squash Beauty therapy ♫ New Year Wi-fi **Services** Lift **Parking** 2

BRODICK
Map 10 NS03

Kilmichael Country House

★★★ ◉◉ COUNTRY HOUSE HOTEL

Glen Cloy KA27 8BY
☎ 01770 302219 📠 01770 302068
e-mail: enquiries@kilmichael.com
web: www.kilmichael.com
dir: *From Brodick ferry terminal towards Lochranza for 1m. Left at golf course, follow signs*

PETS: Bedrooms (7 GF) **Grounds** on leads disp bin
Exercise area adjacent **Facilities** washing facs walks info
vet info **On Request** torch towels **Other** charge for damage
Resident Pets: Guiseppe (Dalmatian), 2 tortoises, chickens, ducks, turkeys, geese, peafowl & quail

Reputed to be the oldest on the island, this lovely house lies in attractive gardens in a quiet glen less than five minutes' drive from the ferry terminal. It has been lovingly restored to create a stylish, elegant country house, adorned with ornaments from around the world. There are two inviting drawing rooms and a bright dining room, serving award-winning contemporary cuisine. The delightful bedrooms are furnished in classical style; some are contained in a pretty courtyard conversion.

Rooms 8 (3 annexe) (7 GF) **S** £78-£98; **D** £130-£163 (incl. bkfst)*
Facilities Wi-fi **Parking** 14 **Notes** LB No children 12yrs Closed Nov-Feb (ex for prior bookings)

LOCHRANZA
Map 10 NR95

Lochranza Caravan & Camping Site

(NR942500)

▶▶▶

KA27 8HL
☎ 01770 830273 & 07733 611083
e-mail: info@arran-campsite.com
dir: *On A841 at N of island, beside Kintyre ferry & 14m N of Brodick for ferry to Ardrossan*

PETS: Public areas except indoor areas on leads **Exercise area** 0.5m

Open Mar-30 Oct Last arrival 22.00hrs Last departure 16.00hrs

A well-established park acquired by enthusiastic and knowledgeable owners who are steadily enhancing the park. There is an 18-hole golf course adjacent to the park and a restaurant near the park entrance whilst Arran Distillery and a hotel are close by. A wide variety of outdoor activities are easily accessible from the park. 2.2 acre site. 60 touring pitches. 10 hardstandings. Tent pitches. Motorhome pitches.

Notes No fires.

SCOTLAND

ISLE OF HARRIS

SCARISTA
Map 13 NG09

Scarista House
★★★★ ◎◎ 🍴 RESTAURANT WITH ROOMS

HS3 3HX
☎ 01859 550238 📠 01859 550277
e-mail: timandpatricia@scaristahouse.com
dir: On A859, 15m S of Tarbert

PETS: Bedrooms (2 GF) unattended **Public areas** library only **Grounds** on leads disp bin **Exercise area** 200yds **Facilities** food bowl water bowl pet sitting washing facs cage storage walks info vet info **On Request** fridge access torch towels **Resident Pets:** Molly (Cavalier King Charles Spaniel), Misty (cat)

A former manse, Scarista House is a haven for food lovers who seek to explore this magnificent island. It enjoys breathtaking views of the Atlantic and is just a short stroll from miles of golden sandy beaches. The house is run in a relaxed country-house manner by the friendly hosts. Expect wellies in the hall and masses of books and CDs in one of two lounges. Bedrooms are cosy, and delicious set dinners and memorable breakfasts are provided.

Rooms 3 en suite 2 annexe en suite (2 GF) **Facilities** tea/coffee Dinner available Direct Dial Cen ht **Parking** 12 **Notes** Closed Xmas, Jan & Feb No coaches

ISLE OF MULL

CRAIGNURE
Map 10 NM73

Shieling Holidays (NM724369)
▶ ▶ ▶ ▶

PA65 6AY
☎ 01680 812496
e-mail: sales@shielingholidays.co.uk
dir: From ferry left onto A849 to Iona. 400mtrs left at church, follow site signs towards sea

PETS: Charges Public areas except public buildings & toilets disp bin **Exercise area on site** 2m of coastal walks **Facilities** washing facs walks info vet info **Other** dogs must be kept on leads at all times

Open 12 Mar-1 Nov Last arrival 22.00hrs Last departure noon

A lovely site on the water's edge with spectacular views, and less than one mile from the ferry landing. Hardstandings and service points are provided for motorhomes, and there are astro-turf pitches for tents. The park also offers unique, en suite cottage tents for hire and bunkhouse accommodation for families. There is also a wildlife trail on site. 7 acre site. 90 touring pitches. 30 hardstandings. Tent pitches. Motorhome pitches. 15 statics.

TOBERMORY
Map 13 NM55

Highland Cottage
★★★ ◎◎ SMALL HOTEL

Breadalbane St PA75 6PD
☎ 01688 302030
e-mail: davidandjo@highlandcottage.co.uk
web: www.highlandcottage.co.uk
dir: A848 Craignure/Fishnish ferry terminal, pass Tobermory signs, straight on at mini rdbt across narrow bridge, turn right. Hotel on right opposite fire station

PETS: Bedrooms (1 GF) **Charges Public areas** except dining room & lounges **Grounds** on leads **Exercise area** 3 mins' walk **Facilities** washing facs cage storage walks info vet info **On Request** fridge access torch towels **Other** charge for damage **Restrictions** no large, hairy dogs (eg German Shepherds, St Bernards)

Providing the highest level of natural and unassuming hospitality, this delightful little gem lies high above the island's capital. Don't be fooled by its side street location, a stunning view over the bay is just a few metres away. 'A country house hotel in town' it is an Aladdin's Cave of collectables and treasures, as well as masses of books and magazines. There are two inviting lounges, one with an honesty bar. The cosy dining room offers memorable dinners and splendid breakfasts. Bedrooms are individual; some have four-posters and all are comprehensively equipped to include TVs and music centres.

Rooms 6 (1 GF) **S** £110-£150; **D** £150-£185 (incl. bkfst)* **Facilities** FTV Wi-fi **Parking** 6 **Notes** LB No children 10yrs Closed Nov-Mar

Tobermory
★★ 80% ◎ HOTEL

53 Main St PA75 6NT
☎ 01688 302091 📠 01688 302254
e-mail: tobhotel@tinyworld.co.uk
web: www.thetobermoryhotel.com
dir: On waterfront

PETS: Bedrooms (2 GF) **Public areas** only in reception on leads **Exercise area** 200yds **Facilities** cage storage walks info vet info **Other** charge for damage

This friendly hotel, with its pretty pink frontage, sits on the seafront amid other brightly coloured, picture-postcard buildings. There is a comfortable and relaxing lounge where drinks are served prior to dining in the stylish restaurant (there is no bar). Bedrooms come in a variety of sizes; all are bright and vibrant.

Rooms 16 (2 fmly) (2 GF) **S** £38-£65; **D** £76-£128 (incl. bkfst)* **Facilities** FTV New Year Wi-fi **Notes** Closed Xmas

ISLE OF SKYE

EDINBANE
Map 13 NG35

Skye Camping & Caravanning Club Site
(NG345527)

▶▶▶▶

Borve, Arnisort IV51 9PS
☎ 01470 582230 📠 01470 582230
e-mail: skye.site@thefriendlyclub.co.uk
dir: *Approx 12m from Portree on A850 (Dunvegan road). Site by loch shore*

PETS: Public areas except facility block (ex assist dogs) disp bin Exercise area lochside walk accessed from site Facilities food food bowl water bowl dog chews cat treats washing facs walks info vet info Other disposal bags available Resident Pets: Tara (dog), Smokey (cat), Highland cows, sheep, pigs, ducks & hens

Open Apr-Oct Last arrival 22.00hrs Last departure noon

The Club site on Skye stands out for its stunning waterside location and glorious views, the generous pitch density, the overall range of facilities, and the impressive ongoing improvements under enthusiastic franchisee owners. Layout maximises the beauty of the scenery and genuine customer care is very evident with an excellent tourist information room and campers' shelter being just two examples. The amenities block has a definite 'wow' factor with smart modern fittings, including excellent showers and the generously proportioned disabled room and family bathroom. 7.5 acre site. 105 touring pitches. 36 hardstandings. Tent pitches. Motorhome pitches. 2 wooden pods.

ISLEORNSAY
Map 13 NG71

Kinloch Lodge
★★★ ❀❀❀ COUNTRY HOUSE HOTEL
IV43 8QY
☎ 01471 833214 & 833333 📠 01471 833277
e-mail: reservations@kinloch-lodge.co.uk
web: www.kinloch-lodge.co.uk
dir: *6m S of Broadford on A851, 10m N of Armadale on A851*

PETS: Bedrooms (1 GF) Charges £20 per night Grounds on leads Exercise area 500mtrs Facilities vet info Other charge for damage

Owned and ran in a hands-on fashion by Lord and Lady MacDonald and their family, this hotel enjoys a picture postcard location surrounded by hills and a sea loch. Bedrooms and bathrooms are well appointed and comfortable, and public areas boast numerous open fires and relaxing areas to sit. There is a cookery school run by Claire MacDonald and a shop that sells her famous cookery books and produce.

Rooms 15 (8 annexe) (1 GF) S £240-£290; D £300-£420 (incl. bkfst & dinner)* Facilities STV FTV Fishing New Year Wi-fi Parking 40

PORTREE
Map 13 NG44

Cuillin Hills
★★★★ 77% ❀❀ HOTEL
IV51 9QU
☎ 01478 612003 📠 01478 613092
e-mail: info@cuillinhills-hotel-skye.co.uk
web: www.cuillinhills-hotel-skye.co.uk
dir: *Right 0.25m N of Portree off A855. Follow hotel signs*

PETS: Bedrooms (8 GF) annexe bedrooms only Grounds on leads disp bin Exercise area 100mtrs Other charge for damage

This imposing building enjoys a superb location overlooking Portree Bay and the Cuillin Hills. Accommodation is provided in smart, well-equipped rooms that are generally spacious; some rooms are found in an adjacent building. Public areas include a split-level restaurant that takes advantage of the views. Service is particularly attentive.

Rooms 26 (7 annexe) (3 fmly) (8 GF) Facilities STV Xmas New Year Wi-fi Parking 56

Rosedale
★★★ 73% ❀ HOTEL
Beaumont Crescent IV51 9DF
☎ 01478 613131 📠 01478 612531
e-mail: rosedalehotelsky@aol.com
web: www.rosedalehotelskye.co.uk
dir: *Follow directions to village centre & harbour*

PETS: Bedrooms (3 GF) bedrooms with easy external access Exercise area nearby Facilities walks info vet info On Request torch Other prior notice required

The atmosphere is wonderfully warm at this delightful family-run waterfront hotel. A labyrinth of stairs and corridors connects the comfortable lounges, bar and charming restaurant, which are set on different levels. The restaurant offers fine views of the bay. Modern bedrooms offer a good range of amenities.

Rooms 18 (1 fmly) (3 GF) S £40-£65; D £70-£150 (incl. bkfst)* Facilities Wi-fi Parking 2 Notes LB Closed Nov-mid Mar

Skeabost Country House

OXFORD
HOTELS & INNS

★★★ 75% ◉ COUNTRY HOUSE HOTEL

IV51 9NP

☎ 01470 532202 & 08444 146572 ▤ 01470 532761

e-mail: manager.skeabost@ohiml.com

web: www.oxfordhotelsandinns.com

dir: From Skye Bridge on A87, through Portree towards Uig. Left onto A850, hotel on right

PETS: Bedrooms (5 GF) unattended sign Charges £10 per night Public areas except food service areas Grounds on leads disp bin Exercise area 250yds Facilities water bowl scoop/disp bags washing facs cage storage walks info vet info On Request fridge access torch towels Other charge for damage

This delightful property stands in mature, landscaped grounds at the edge of Loch Snizort. Originally built as a hunting lodge by the MacDonalds and steeped in history, Skeabost offers a welcoming environment from the caring and helpful staff. The hotel provides award-winning food, charming day rooms and well appointed accommodation. The pretty grounds include a challenging 9-hole golf course, and there is salmon and trout fishing nearby. Wi-fi is available.

Rooms 14 (5 GF) Facilities STV FTV ₤ 9 Xmas New Year Wi-fi Parking 40 Notes LB

Flodigarry Country House

★★★ 78% ◉ COUNTRY HOUSE HOTEL

IV51 9HZ

☎ 01470 552203 ▤ 01470 552301

e-mail: info@flodigarry.co.uk

web: www.flodigarry.co.uk

dir: A855 from Portree, through Staffin to Flodigarry, hotel signed on right

PETS: Bedrooms (4 GF) unattended Flora Macdonald cottage only Grounds disp bin Facilities leads washing facs walks info vet info On Request torch towels Other charge for damage Resident Pet: Boo Boo (Boxer)

This hotel is located in woodlands on The Quiraing in north-east Skye overlooking the sea towards the Torridon Mountains. The dramatic scenery is a real inspiration here, and this charming house was once the home of the Scotland's heroine, Flora MacDonald. Guests are assured of real Highland hospitality and there is an easy going atmosphere throughout. A full range of activities is offered, with mountain walks, fishing and boat trips proving to be the most popular.

Rooms 18 (7 annexe) (3 fmly) (4 GF) S £80-£135; D £100-£210 (incl. bkfst)* Facilities FTV Xmas New Year Wi-fi Parking 40 Notes LB Closed Nov-15 Dec & Jan

Staffin Camping & Caravanning (NG492670)

▶▶▶

IV51 9JX

☎ 01470 562213 ▤ 01470 562213

e-mail: staffincampsite@btinternet.com

dir: On A855, 16m N of Portree. Turn right before 40mph signs

PETS: Public areas except toilet block area disp bin Exercise area adjacent Facilities walks info vet info

Open Apr-Oct Last arrival 22.00hrs Last departure 11.00hrs

A large sloping grassy site with level hardstandings for motor homes and caravans, close to the village of Staffin. The toilet block is appointed to a very good standard and the park now has a laundry. Mountain bikes are available for hire. 2.5 acre site. 50 touring pitches. 18 hardstandings. Tent pitches. Motorhome pitches.

Notes No music after 22.00hrs. 🛇

Wales

BEAUMARIS
Map 6 SH67

Best Western Bulkeley Hotel

Best Western

★★★ 78% HOTEL

Castle St LL58 8AW

☎ 01248 810415 📠 01248 810146

e-mail: reception@bulkeleyhotel.co.uk

web: www.bulkeleyhotel.co.uk

dir: A55 junct 8a to Beaumaris. Hotel in town centre

PETS: Bedrooms unattended **Charges** £7.50 per night
Public areas lounge & bar only on leads **Grounds** on leads
Exercise area 2 mins' walk **Facilities** food bowl water bowl
walks info vet info **On Request** torch towels **Other** charge for
damage please phone for further details of pet facilities

A Grade I listed hotel built in 1832, the Bulkeley is just 100 yards
from the 13th-century Beaumaris Castle in the centre of town; the
friendly staff create a relaxed atmosphere. Many rooms, including
18 of the bedrooms, have fine panoramic views across the
Menai Straits to the Snowdonia Mountains. The well-equipped
bedrooms and suites, some with four-posters, are generally
spacious, and have pretty furnishings. There is a choice of bars, a
coffee shop, a restaurant and bistro.

Rooms 43 (5 fmly) **Facilities** FTV Xmas New Year Wi-fi
Services Lift **Parking** 25

Bishopsgate House Hotel

★★ 85% 🏵 SMALL HOTEL

54 Castle St LL58 8BB

☎ 01248 810302 📠 01248 810166

e-mail: hazel@bishopsgatehotel.co.uk

dir: From Menai Bridge onto A545 to Beaumaris. Hotel on left in
main street

PETS: Bedrooms Charges £5 per night **Public areas** except
restaurant **Exercise area** beach & green opposite **Facilities**
food (pre-bookable) food bowl water bowl dog chews cat
treats scoop/disp bags leads pet sitting dog walking washing
facs cage storage walks info vet info **On Request** fridge access
torch towels **Other** charge for damage **Resident Pets:** Bonnie
(Jack Russell cross), Polly Anna (cat)

This immaculately maintained, privately owned and personally
run small hotel dates back to 1760. It features fine examples
of wood panelling and a Chinese Chippendale staircase.
Thoughtfully furnished bedrooms are attractively decorated
and two have four-poster beds. Quality cooking is served in the
elegant restaurant and guests have a comfortable lounge and
cosy bar to relax in.

Rooms 9 **S** £58-£68; **D** £95-£107 (incl. bkfst)* **Facilities** FTV
Xmas New Year Wi-fi **Parking** 8 **Notes** LB

DULAS
Map 6 SH48

Tyddyn Isaf Caravan Park *(SH486873)*

▶▶▶▶▶

Lligwy Bay LL70 9PQ

☎ 01248 410203 & 410667 📠 01248 410667

e-mail: mail@tyddynisaf.co.uk

dir: Take A5025 through Benllech to Moelfre rdbt, left towards
Amlwch to Brynrefail village. Turn right opposite craft shop. Site
0.5m down lane on right

PETS: Public areas except shop, bar & children's play area disp
bin **Exercise area** surrounding area **Facilities** food bowl water
bowl scoop/disp bags walks info vet info **Other** prior notice
required **Resident Pets:** 1 Labrador, cat, sheep, cattle

Open Mar-Oct rs Mar-Jul & Sep-Oct bar & shop opening limited
Last arrival 21.30hrs Last departure 11.00hrs

A beautifully situated, very spacious family park on rising ground
adjacent to a sandy beach, with magnificent views overlooking
Lligwy Bay. A private footpath leads direct to the beach and there
is an excellent nature trail around the park. There are very good
toilet facilities, including a new additional block with under-floor
heating and excellent unisex privacy cubicles, a well-stocked
shop, and café/bar serving meals, which are best enjoyed on the
terrace with its magnificent coast and sea views. 16 acre site.
30 touring pitches. 50 hardstandings. Tent pitches. Motorhome
pitches. 56 statics.

Notes No groups, maximum 3 units together. 🐾

WALES

MARIAN-GLAS	Map 6 SH58

Home Farm Caravan Park (SH498850)

▶▶▶▶▶

LL73 8PH
☎ 01248 410614 🖷 01248 410900
e-mail: enq@homefarm-anglesey.co.uk
dir: On A5025, 2m N of Benllech. Site 300mtrs beyond church

PETS: Charges £1-£2 per night Public areas except children's play area & sports field disp bin Exercise area on site dog walks Facilities food scoop/disp bags walks info vet info Stables 2m Other prior notice required

Open Apr-Oct Last arrival 21.00hrs Last departure noon

A first-class park, run with passion and enthusiasm, set in an elevated and secluded position sheltered by trees, with good planting and landscaping. The peaceful rural setting affords views of farmland, the sea, and the mountains of Snowdonia. The modern toilet blocks are spotlessly clean and well maintained, and there are excellent play facilities for children both indoors and out. There's a super visitors' parking area, a stunning water feature and a children's play area with top-notch equipment. The area is blessed with sandy beaches, and local pubs and shops cater for everyday needs. 6 acre site. 98 touring pitches. 21 hardstandings. Tent pitches. Motorhome pitches. 84 statics.

Notes No roller blades, skateboards or scooters.

PENTRAETH	Map 6 SH57

Rhos Caravan Park (SH517794)

▶▶▶

Rhos Farm LL75 8DZ
☎ 01248 450214 🖷 01248 450214
e-mail: rhosfarm@googlemail.com
dir: Site on A5025, 1m N of Pentraeth

PETS: Charges £1.50 per night Public areas except toilets & children's play area Exercise area on site 4-acre field Facilities walks info vet info Other prior notice required Resident Pets: Tess (Springer Spaniel), Jack (Chocolate Labrador)

Open Etr-Oct Last arrival 22.00hrs Last departure 16.00hrs

A warm welcome awaits families at this spacious park on level, grassy ground with easy access to the main road to Amlwch. A 200-acre working farm that has two play areas and farm animals to keep children amused, with good beaches, pubs, restaurants and shops nearby. The two toilet blocks are kept to a good standard by enthusiastic owners, who are constantly improving the facilities. 15 acre site. 98 touring pitches. Tent pitches. Motorhome pitches. 66 statics.

Notes ☺

WALES

RHOS LLIGWY
Map 6 SH48

Ty'n Rhos Caravan Park (SH495867)
► ► ►

Lligwy Bay, Moelfre LL72 8NL
☎ 01248 852417 📠 01248 853417
e-mail: robert@bodafonpark.co.uk
dir: *Take A5025 from Benllech to Moelfre rdbt, right to T-junct in Moelfre. Left, then approx 2m to site, pass x-roads leading to beach, site 50mtrs on right*

PETS: Public areas Exercise area nearby **Facilities** walks info vet info **Other** prior notice required

Open Mar-Oct Last arrival 21.00hrs Last departure noon

A family park close to the beautiful beach at Lligwy Bay, and cliff walks along the Heritage Coast. Historic Din Lligwy, and the shops at picturesque Moelfre are nearby. Please note that guests should register at Bodafon Caravan Park in Benllech where detailed directions will be given and pitches allocated. 10 acre site. 30 touring pitches. 4 hardstandings. 48 seasonal pitches. Tent pitches. Motorhome pitches. 80 statics.

Notes No campfires.

RHOSNEIGR
Map 6 SH37

Ty Hen (SH327738)
► ► ►

Station Rd LL64 5QZ
☎ 01407 810331 📠 01407 810331
e-mail: info@tyhen.com
dir: *From A55 junct 5 follow signs to Rhosneigr, at clock turn right. Entrance 50mtrs before Rhosneigr railway station*

PETS: Public areas except toilet block, swimming pool & children's play area disp bin **Exercise area on site** fields **Exercise area** beach (10 mins) **Facilities** walks info vet info **Resident Pets:** Scruff (Longhaired Terrier), Lunar (Black Labrador/Collie cross), Twix, Thomas & Meow (cats), Phebe & Maisey (Shetland ponies), Percy & Petal (donkeys)

Open mid Mar-Oct Last arrival 21.00hrs Last departure noon

Attractive seaside position near a large fishing lake and riding stables, in lovely countryside. A smart toilet block offers a welcome amenity at this popular family park, where friendly owners are always on hand. The park is close to RAF Valley, which is great for plane spotters, but expect some aircraft noise during the day. 7.5 acre site. 38 touring pitches. 5 hardstandings. Tent pitches. Motorhome pitches. 42 statics.

Notes 1 motor vehicle per pitch, children must not be out after 22.00hrs.

BRIDGEND

BRIDGEND
Map 3 SS97

Best Western Heronston
★ ★ ★ 75% HOTEL

Ewenny Rd CF35 5AW
☎ 01656 668811 & 666085 📠 01656 767391
e-mail: reservations@bestwesternheronstonhotel.co.uk
web: www.bw-heronstonhotel.co.uk
dir: *M4 junct 35, follow signs for Porthcawl, at 5th rdbt left towards Ogmore-by-Sea (B4265), hotel 200yds on left*

PETS: Bedrooms 4 ground-floor bedrooms only **Charges** £10 per night **Public areas** only for access to bedrooms on leads **Grounds** on leads disp bin **Exercise area** 1m **Facilities** walks info vet info **Other** charge for damage **Restrictions** no dangerous dogs (see page 7)

Situated within easy reach of the town centre and the M4, this large modern hotel offers spacious well-equipped accommodation, including ground floor rooms. Public areas include an open-plan lounge/bar, attractive restaurant and a smart leisure and fitness club. The hotel also has a choice of function and conference rooms, and ample parking is available.

Rooms 75 (4 fmly) (37 GF) (4 smoking) **S** £55-£110; **D** £65-£135 (incl. bkfst)* **Facilities** STV 🏊 Gym Steam room Sauna Spa pool New Year Wi-fi **Services** Lift **Parking** 160 **Notes** LB

PORTHCAWL
Map 3 SS87

Brodawel Camping & Caravan Park
(SS816789)
► ►

Moor Ln, Nottage CF36 3EJ
☎ 01656 783231
dir: *M4 junct 37, A4229 towards Porthcawl. Site on right off A4229*

PETS: Public areas except shop & toilets disp bin **Exercise area** nearby **Facilities** walks info vet info **Other** prior notice required disposal bags available

Open Apr-Sep Last arrival 19.00hrs Last departure 11.00hrs

A family run park catering mainly for families, on the edge of the village of Nottage. It is very convenient for Porthcawl and the Glamorgan Heritage Coast, each is within a five-minute drive. 4 acre site. 100 touring pitches. Tent pitches. Motorhome pitches.

Notes 🚭

WALES

SARN PARK MOTORWAY SERVICE AREA (M4) Map 3 SS98

Days Inn Bridgend Cardiff - M4
BUDGET HOTEL
Sarn Park Services, M4 Junct 36 CF32 9RW
☎ 01656 659218 📠 01656 768665
e-mail: sarn.hotel@welcomebreak.co.uk
web: www.welcomebreak.co.uk
dir: M4 junct 36

PETS: Bedrooms (20 GF) Charges £5 per stay Public areas on leads Grounds on leads disp bin Exercise area country walks nearby Facilities vet info Other charge for damage

This modern building offers accommodation in smart, spacious and well-equipped bedrooms, suitable for families and business travellers, and all with en suite bathrooms. Continental breakfast is available and other refreshments may be taken at the nearby family restaurant.

Rooms 40 (39 fmly) (20 GF) (5 smoking) S £39.95-£59.95; D £49.95-£69.95

CARDIFF

CARDIFF Map 3 ST17

Copthorne Hotel Cardiff-Caerdydd
★★★★ 75% ❀ HOTEL
Copthorne Way, Culverhouse Cross CF5 6DA
☎ 029 2059 9100 📠 029 2059 9080
e-mail: reservations.cardiff@millenniumhotels.co.uk
web: www.millenniumhotels.co.uk
dir: M4 junct 33, A4232 for 2.5m towards Cardiff West. Take A48 W to Cowbridge

PETS: Bedrooms lower ground-floor rooms only Public areas lounge & lobby only on leads Grounds on leads Exercise area lakeside walk in grounds (9.4 acres) Facilities cage storage walks info vet info On Request fridge access torch towels Other charge for damage

A comfortable, popular and modern hotel, conveniently located for the airport and city. Bedrooms are a good size and some have a private lounge. Public areas are smartly presented and include a gym, pool, meeting rooms and a comfortable restaurant with views of a lake.

Rooms 135 (7 fmly) (27 GF) S £42-£210; D £42-£210*
Facilities STV ⊕ Gym Sauna Steam room Treatment room ♫ Xmas New Year Wi-fi Services Lift Parking 225

Barceló Cardiff Angel Hotel
★★★★ 68% HOTEL
Castle St CF10 1SZ
☎ 029 2064 9200 📠 029 2039 6212
e-mail: angel@barcelo-hotels-co.uk
web: www.barcelo-hotels.co.uk/hotels/wales/barcelo-cardiff-angel-hotel
dir: Opposite Cardiff Castle

PETS: Bedrooms unattended Charges £15 per stay Public areas except dining room on leads Facilities vet info On Request fridge access torch Other charge for damage

This well-established hotel is in the heart of the city overlooking the famous castle and almost opposite the Millennium Stadium. All bedrooms offer air conditioning and are appointed to a good standard. Public areas include an impressive lobby, a modern restaurant and a selection of conference rooms. There is limited parking at the rear of the hotel.

Rooms 102 (3 fmly) Facilities STV Xmas New Year Wi-fi Services Lift Air con Parking 60

Best Western St Mellons Hotel & Country Club
★★★ 70% HOTEL
Castleton CF3 2XR
☎ 01633 680355 📠 01633 680399
e-mail: reservations.stmellons@ohiml.com
web: www.oxfordhotelsandinns.com
dir: M4 junct 28 follow A48 Castleton/St Mellons signs. Hotel on left after garage

PETS: Bedrooms (5 GF) Charges £10 per stay Public areas assist dogs only Grounds on leads disp bin Facilities cage storage walks info vet info On Request fridge access torch towels Other charge for damage Restrictions no large dogs: no Great Danes, Rottweilers or Bull Terriers

This Regency mansion has been tastefully converted into an elegant hotel with an adjoining leisure complex that attracts a strong local following. Bedrooms, some in purpose-built wings, are spacious and smart. The public areas retain pleasing architectural proportions and include relaxing lounges and a restaurant serving a varied choice of carefully prepared, enjoyable dishes.

Rooms 41 (20 annexe) (9 fmly) (5 GF) S £60-£150; D £70-£180*
Facilities Spa ⊕ Gym Squash Beauty salon Xmas Wi-fi Parking 100 Notes LB

WALES

CARDIFF *continued*

Campanile Cardiff

BUDGET HOTEL

Caxton Place, Pentwyn CF23 8HA
☎ 029 2054 9044 📠 029 2054 9900
e-mail: cardiff@campanile.com
dir: *Take Pentwyn exit from A48(M), follow signs for hotel*

PETS: Bedrooms Charges £5 per night **Grounds** on leads
Facilities water bowl walks info vet info **Other** charge for
damage

This modern building offers accommodation in smart, well-
equipped bedrooms, all with en suite bathrooms. Refreshments
may be taken at the informal bistro.

Rooms 47 (47 annexe)

Ibis Cardiff Gate

BUDGET HOTEL

Malthouse Av, Cardiff Gate Business Park, Pontprennau CF23 8RA
☎ 029 2073 3222 📠 029 2073 4222
e-mail: H3159@accor.com
web: www.ibishotel.com
dir: *M4 junct 30, follow Cardiff Service Station signs. Hotel on left*

PETS: Bedrooms (22 GF) unattended sign **Public areas** except
restaurant **Exercise area** 200mtrs **Facilities** cage storage
walks info **On Request** fridge access torch towels **Other** charge
for damage

Modern, budget hotel offering comfortable accommodation in
bright and practical bedrooms. Breakfast is self-service and
dinner is available in the restaurant.

Rooms 78 (19 fmly) (22 GF) (7 smoking)

CARMARTHENSHIRE

HARFORD Map 3 SN64

Springwater Lakes *(SN637430)*

▶ ▶ ▶

SA19 8DT
☎ 01558 650788
dir: *4m E of Lampeter on A482, entrance well signed on right*

PETS: Charges 1st dog free, £2 per extra dog per night
Public areas disp bin **Exercise area on site** 2 dog walks & exercise
areas **Facilities** walks info vet info **Other** prior notice required

Open Mar-Oct Last arrival 20.00hrs Last departure 11.00hrs

In a rural setting overlooked by the Cambrian Mountains, this
park is adjoined on each side by four spring-fed and well-stocked
fishing lakes. All pitches have hardstandings, electricity and TV
hook-ups, and there is a small and very clean toilet block and a
shop. 20 acre site. 30 touring pitches. 30 hardstandings. Tent
pitches. Motorhome pitches.

Notes Children must be supervised around lakes, no cycling on
site, no ball games.

LLANDOVERY Map 3 SN73

Erwlon Caravan & Camping Park *(SN776343)*

▶ ▶ ▶ ▶

Brecon Rd SA20 0RD
☎ 01550 721021 & 720332
e-mail: peter@erwlon.co.uk
dir: *0.5m E of Llandovery on A40*

PETS: Public areas on leads disp bin **Exercise area on site**
fenced area **Exercise area** 200mtrs **Facilities** washing facs
walks info vet info **Stables** 1m **Other** please phone for details
regarding horses

Open all year Last arrival anytime Last departure noon

A long-established, family-run site set beside a brook in the
Brecon Beacons foothills. The town of Llandovery and the hills
overlooking the Towy Valley are a short walk away. The superb,
Scandinavian-style facilities block has cubicled washrooms,
family and disabled rooms and is an impressive feature; ongoing
improvements include a campers' kitchen. 8 acre site. 75 touring
pitches. 15 hardstandings. Tent pitches. Motorhome pitches.

Notes Quiet after 22.30hrs

Llandovery Caravan Park *(SN762342)*

▶ ▶

Church Bank SA20 0DT
☎ 01550 721993 & 07970 650 606
e-mail: drovers.rfc@btinternet.com
dir: *A40 from Carmarthen, over rail crossing, past junct with
A483 (Builth Wells). Turn right for Llangadog, past church, 1st
right signed Rugby Club & Camping*

PETS: Public areas except sport pitches disp bin **Exercise area
on site** enclosed grassed area **Facilities** walks info vet info
Restrictions no dangerous dogs (see page 7)

Open all year Last arrival 20.00hrs Last departure 20.00hrs

A level, spacious and developing small site adjacent to the Rugby
Club on the outskirts of Llandovery. Toilets facilities are adequate
but there are plans to upgrade and improve the facilities. 8
acre site. 100 touring pitches. 32 hardstandings. Tent pitches.
Motorhome pitches.

Notes

WALES

LLANELLI   Map 2 SN50

Best Western Diplomat Hotel and Spa

★★★ 78% HOTEL

Felinfoel SA15 3PJ
☎ 01554 756156 📠 01554 751649
e-mail: reservations@diplomat-hotel-wales.com
web: www.diplomat-hotel-wales.com
dir: M4 junct 48, A4138 then B4303, hotel 0.75m on right

PETS: Bedrooms (4 GF) unattended Charges £10 per night Public areas except restaurant Grounds on leads disp bin Exercise area nearby Facilities cage storage walks info vet info On Request fridge access torch towels Other charge for damage Resident Pets: Heidi & Duke (Alsatian/Collie cross)

This Victorian mansion, set in mature grounds, has been extended over the years to provide a comfortable and relaxing hotel. The well-appointed bedrooms are located in the main house and there is also a wing of comfortable modern bedrooms. Public areas include Trubshaw's Restaurant, a large function suite and a modern leisure centre.

Rooms 50 (8 annexe) (2 fmly) (4 GF) S £85-£110; D £85-£110 (incl. bkfst) Facilities FTV ⓢ supervised Gym Sauna Steam room Sun beds Hairdresser ♫ Xmas New Year Wi-fi Services Lift Parking 250 Notes LB

NEWCASTLE EMLYN   Map 2 SN34

Cenarth Falls Holiday Park (SN265421)

►►►►►

Cenarth SA38 9JS
☎ 01239 710345 📠 01239 710344
e-mail: enquiries@cenarth-holipark.co.uk
dir: Off A484 on outskirts of Cenarth village towards Cardigan

PETS: Charges £2 per night Public areas except swimming pool areas & Coracles Health Country Club disp bin Facilities walks info vet info Other prior notice required

Open Mar-Nov Last arrival 20.00hrs Last departure 11.00hrs

A high quality park with excellent facilities, close to the village of Cenarth where the River Teifi (famous for its salmon and sea trout) cascades through the Cenarth Falls Gorge. A well-landscaped park with an indoor heated swimming pool and fitness suite, and a restaurant and bar. 2 acre site. 30 touring pitches. 30 hardstandings. Tent pitches. Motorhome pitches. 89 statics.

Notes No skateboards.

Argoed Meadow Caravan and Camping Site (SN268415)

►►►

Argoed Farm SA38 9JL
☎ 01239 710690
dir: From Newcastle Emlyn on A484 towards Cenarth, take B4332. Site 300yds on right

PETS: Public areas on leads disp bin Exercise area on site 3-acre field, walk by river Facilities washing facs walks info vet info Stables 2m

Open all year Last arrival anytime Last departure noon

Pleasant open meadowland on the banks of the River Teifi, very close to Cenarth Falls gorge, this site has a modern toilet block which adds to the general appeal of this mainly adults-only park. 3 acre site. 30 touring pitches. 5 hardstandings. Tent pitches. Motorhome pitches. 5 statics.

Notes No bikes or skateboards. 🔛

Moelfryn Caravan & Camping Park (SN321370)

►►►

Ty-Cefn, Pant-y-Bwlch SA38 9JE
☎ 01559 371231
e-mail: moelfryn@moelfryncaravanpark.co.uk
dir: A484 from Carmarthen towards Cynwyl Elfed. Pass Blue Bell Inn on right, 200yds take left fork onto B4333 towards Hermon. In 7m brown sign on left. Turn left, site on right

PETS: Public areas except shower block & play area on leads disp bin Facilities vet info Resident Pets: Kai (German Shepherd), Ginger, Patch & Kat (cats), Tara & Sultan (horses)

Open Mar-10 Jan Last arrival 22.00hrs Last departure noon

A small, beautifully maintained, family-run park in a glorious elevated location overlooking the valley of the River Teifi. Pitches are level and spacious, and well screened by hedging and mature trees. Facilities are spotlessly clean and tidy, and the playing field is well away from the touring area. Home-cooked meals can be ordered and Sunday breakfast delivered to the tent/caravan door. 3 acre site. 25 touring pitches. 16 hardstandings. 12 seasonal pitches. Tent pitches. Motorhome pitches.

Notes Games to be played in designated area only.

WALES

WALES

ABERAERON
Map 2 SN46

Aromatherapy Reflexology Centre
★★★ BED AND BREAKFAST

The Barn House, Pennant Rd SY23 5LZ
☎ 01974 202581
e-mail: aromareflex@googlemail.com
web: www.aromatherapy-breaks-wales.co.uk
dir: *S of Aberystwyth to Llanon. On leaving village left at 40mph sign. 2nd left to Barn House*

PETS: Bedrooms Sep accom 2 large kennels in open shed **Charges** £3.50 per night **Grounds** disp bin **Exercise area** 5 mins **Facilities** food bowl water bowl washing facs cage storage walks info vet info **On Request** fridge access **Resident Pets:** Celt (Welsh Terrier), Travis (Airedale Terrier)

Expect a warm welcome from this family-run bed and breakfast where Welsh is spoken. Set in its own ground, in a tranquil position with lovely views of Cardigan Bay. Bedrooms are comfortable and smartly presented. There is a choice of traditional, vegetarian or vegan breakfast available. Aromatherapy and Reflexology are available at the centre.

Rooms 3 rms (2 en suite) (1 pri facs) **S** £33-£45; **D** £60-£90 **Facilities** FTV tea/coffee Wi-fi **Parking** 7 **Notes** LB 🐾

ABERYSTWYTH
Map 6 SN58

Llety Ceiro Country House
★★★★ GUEST HOUSE

Peggy Ln, Bow St, Llandre SY24 5AB
☎ 01970 821900 ▤ 01970 820966
e-mail: marinehotel1@btconnect.com
dir: *4m NE of Aberystwyth. Off A487 onto B4353 for 300yds*

PETS: Bedrooms (3 GF) unattended **Charges** £5 per night £35 per week **Public areas** except restaurant on leads **Grounds** disp bin **Exercise area** 100yds **Facilities** food bowl water bowl cage storage walks info vet info **On Request** fridge access **Stables** nearby **Other** charge for damage

Located north of Aberystwyth, this house is well maintained throughout. Bedrooms are equipped with a range of thoughtful extras in addition to smart modern bathrooms. Morning coffees, afternoon teas and dinner are available in an attractive dining room, with a conservatory extension, and bicycle hire is also available.

Rooms 11 en suite (2 fmly) (3 GF) (1 smoking) **Facilities** FTV TVL tea/coffee Dinner available Direct Dial Cen ht Licensed Wi-fi **Parking** 21

Ocean View Caravan Park *(SN592842)*
▶▶▶

North Beach, Clarach Bay SY23 3DT
☎ 01970 828425 & 623361
e-mail: enquiries@oceanviewholidays.com
dir: *Exit A487 in Bow Street. Straight on at next x-roads. Site 2nd on right*

PETS: Charges £2 per night **Public areas** disp bin **Exercise area on site** large dog walking area **Facilities** walks info vet info **Restrictions** no Rottweilers, Pit Bulls or Doberman (see page 7)

Open Mar-Oct Last arrival 20.00hrs Last departure noon

In a sheltered valley on gently sloping ground, with wonderful views of both the sea and the countryside. The beach of Clarach Bay is just 200 yards away, and this welcoming park is ideal for all the family. 9 acre site. 24 touring pitches. 15 hardstandings. Tent pitches. Motorhome pitches. 56 statics.

DEVIL'S BRIDGE
Map 6 SN77

The Hafod Hotel
★★★ 68% HOTEL

SY23 3JL
☎ 01970 890232 ▤ 01970 890394
e-mail: hafodhotel@btconnect.com
dir: *Exit A44 in Ponterwyd signed Devil's Bridge/Pontarfynach onto A4120, 3m, over bridge. Hotel opposite*

PETS: Bedrooms Public areas by prior arrangement only on leads **Grounds Exercise area** adjacent **Facilities** washing facs walks info vet info **On Request** torch towels **Other** charge for damage prior notice required field available for horses (no liability accepted)

This former hunting lodge dates back to the 17th century and is situated in six acres of grounds. Now a family-owned and run hotel, it provides accommodation suitable for both business and leisure guests. Family rooms and a four-poster room are available. In addition to the dining area and lounge, there are tea rooms.

Rooms 17 (2 fmly) **S** £55; **D** £85-£100 (incl. bkfst)* **Facilities** Xmas New Year Wi-fi **Parking** 200

EGLWYS FACH Map 6 SN69

Ynyshir Hall
★★★ ◉◉◉ COUNTRY HOUSE HOTEL

SY20 8TA

☎ 01654 781209 & 781268 📠 01654 781366

e-mail: ynyshir@relaischateaux.com

web: www.ynyshir-hall.co.uk

dir: Off A487, 5.5m S of Machynlleth, signed from main road

PETS: Bedrooms unattended sign ground-floor bedrooms only Sep accom outside kennel Charges £10 per night Public areas except restaurant on leads Grounds disp bin Exercise area nearby Facilities food (pre-bookable) food bowl water bowl walks info vet info On Request torch towels Other charge for damage Resident Pets: Theo (Bernese Mountain Dog), Carreg Kelpie)

Set in beautifully landscaped grounds and surrounded by the RSPB Ynys-hir Nature Reserve, Ynyshir Hall is a haven of calm. The house was once owned by Queen Victoria and it is surrounded by mountain scenery. Lavishly styled bedrooms, each individually themed around a great painter, provide high standards of luxury and comfort. The lounge and bar, adorned with an abundance of fresh flowers, have different moods. The dining room offers highly accomplished cooking using the best, locally sourced ingredients including herbs, soft fruit and vegetables from the hotel's own kitchen garden and wild foods gathered nearby. Ynyshir Hall is an idyllic location for weddings.

Rooms 9 (2 annexe) S £245-£335; D £315-£405 (incl. bkfst)* Facilities ♨ Xmas New Year Parking 20 Notes LB No children 9yrs

GWBERT-ON-SEA Map 2 SN15

The Cliff Hotel
★★★ 75% HOTEL

SA43 1PP

☎ 01239 613241 📠 01239 615391

e-mail: reservations@cliffhotel.com

dir: From A487 into Cardigan, take B4548 towards Gwbert, 2m to hotel

PETS: Bedrooms (5 GF) unattended Charges £5 per night Public areas except restaurant & bars on leads Grounds on leads Exercise area adjacent Facilities cage storage walks info vet info On Request fridge access Other charge for damage prior notice required

Set in 30 acres of grounds with a 9-hole golf course, this hotel commands superb sea views from its cliff-top location overlooking Cardigan Bay. Bedrooms in the main building have excellent views and there is also a wing of modern rooms. Public areas are spacious and comprise a choice of bars, lounges and a fine dining restaurant. The spa offers a wide range of up-to-the-minute leisure facilities.

Rooms 70 (6 fmly) (5 GF) S £59-£85; D £75-£135 (incl. bkfst) Facilities Spa FTV ⊛ ♨ 9 Putt green Fishing Gym Xmas New Year Services Lift Parking 100 Notes LB

LAMPETER Map 2 SN54

The Falcondale Hotel & Restaurant
★★★★ 75% ◉◉ COUNTRY HOUSE HOTEL

SA48 7RX

☎ 01570 422910 📠 01570 423559

e-mail: info@fthefalcondale.co.uk

web: www.thefalcondale.co.uk

dir: 800yds W of High St (A475) or 1.5m NW of Lampeter (A482)

PETS: Bedrooms unattended sign Charges £10 per night Public areas except restaurants & with other guests' approval Grounds disp bin Exercise area hotel grounds Exercise area woods Facilities food (pre-bookable) food bowl water bowl bedding dog chews feeding mat scoop/disp bags leads washing facs cage storage walks info vet info On Request fridge access torch towels Stables nearby Other charge for damage Resident Pets: Pudgeley & Major (Cocker Spaniels)

Built in the Italianate style, this charming Victorian property is set in extensive grounds and beautiful parkland. The individually-styled bedrooms are generally spacious, well equipped and tastefully decorated. Bars and lounges are similarly well appointed with additional facilities including a conservatory and function room. Guests have a choice of either the Valley Restaurant for fine dining or the less formal Peterwells Brasserie.

Rooms 19 (2 fmly) S £99-£149; D £139-£189 (incl. bkfst)* Facilities FTV ♨ Xmas New Year Wi-fi Services Lift Parking 60 Notes LB

 WALES

CONWY

CONWY

BETWS-Y-COED
Map 6 SH75

Craig-y-Dderwen Riverside Hotel
★★★★ 75% ◉ COUNTRY HOUSE HOTEL
LL24 0AS
☎ 01690 710293 ▤ 01690 710362
e-mail: info@snowdoniahotel.com
web: www.snowdoniahotel.com
dir: A5 to Betws-y-Coed, cross Waterloo Bridge, take 1st left

PETS: Bedrooms (1 GF) unattended sign **Charges** £7.50 per night **Public areas** except restaurants on leads **Grounds** disp bin **Exercise area** 16 acres of fields **Facilities** food (pre-bookable) food bowl water bowl cat treats feeding mat litter tray scoop/disp bags washing facs cage storage walks info vet info **On Request** fridge access torch towels **Stables** 3m **Other** charge for damage please phone for information regarding horses

This Victorian country-house hotel is set in well-maintained grounds alongside the River Conwy, at the end of a tree-lined drive. Very pleasant views can be enjoyed from many rooms, and two of the bedrooms have four-poster beds. There are comfortable lounges and the atmosphere throughout is tranquil and relaxing.

Rooms 18 (2 fmly) (1 GF) (2 smoking) **S** £105-£115; **D** £120-£200 (incl. bkfst)* **Facilities** STV FTV Fishing ⌣ Badminton Volleyball New Year Wi-fi **Parking** 50 **Notes** LB Closed 23-26 Dec & 2 Jan-1 Feb

Best Western Waterloo

★★★ 78% HOTEL
LL24 0AR
☎ 01690 710411 ▤ 01690 710986
e-mail: reservations@waterloo-hotel.info
web: www.waterloo-hotel.info
dir: On A5, S of village centre

PETS: Bedrooms unattended lodge-style bedrooms only **Charges** £6.50 per night **Grounds** on leads **Facilities** cage storage walks info vet info **On Request** fridge access

This long-established hotel, named after the nearby Waterloo Bridge, is ideally located for visiting Snowdonia. Stylish accommodation is split between rooms in the main hotel and modern, cottage-style rooms located in buildings to the rear. The attractive Garden Room Restaurant serves traditional Welsh specialities, and the vibrant Bridge Inn provides a wide range of food and drink throughout the day and evening.

Rooms 45 (34 annexe) (12 fmly) (31 GF) **Facilities** ⓦ Gym Steam room Sauna Hair & beauty salon New Year Wi-fi **Parking** 100 **Notes** LB Closed 25-26 Dec

BETWS-YN-RHOS
Map 6 SH97

Plas Farm Caravan Park (SH897744)
►►►►
LL22 8AU
☎ 01492 680254 & 07831 482176
e-mail: info@plasfarmcaravanpark.co.uk
dir: A547 Abergele, right Rhyd y Foel Rd, 3m then left signed B5381, 1st farm on right

PETS: Sep accom large wooden pen **Charges** dog £1 per night £7 per week **Public areas** except children's play area disp bin **Exercise area on site** field & woodland **Facilities** washing facs walks info vet info **Other** max 2 dogs per pitch; dogs must be kept on short leads disposal bags available

Open Mar-Oct Last departure 11.00hrs

A small, quiet caravan park on a working farm, surrounded by rolling countryside and farmland. The park continues to improve, with plans in place for an additional 20 pitches. It is an ideal holiday location for both families and couples, with its modern facilities, fully-serviced pitches, and well-equipped children's play area, as well as spacious fields to roam through. Close to Bodnant Gardens and glorious beaches. 10 acre site. 40 touring pitches. 40 hardstandings. Tent pitches. Motorhome pitches.

CAPEL CURIG
Map 6 SH75

Cobdens
★★ 62% SMALL HOTEL
LL24 0EE
☎ 01690 720243 ▤ 01690 720354
e-mail: info@cobdens.co.uk
dir: On A5, 4m N of Betws-y-Coed

PETS: Bedrooms Charges £12.50 per stay **Public areas** bars only on leads **Grounds** on leads disp bin **Exercise area** adjacent **Facilities** food bowl water bowl cage storage walks info vet info **On Request** fridge access torch towels **Other** charge for damage

Situated in the heart of Snowdonia, this hotel has been a centre for mountaineering and other outdoor pursuits for many years. A wide range of meals using local produce is served in the restaurant. There are two bars including the aptly named Mountain Bar, built in the side of the mountain. A sauna room is also available.

Rooms 17 (4 fmly) **S** £30.50-£37.50; **D** £61-£75 (incl. bkfst)* **Facilities** STV FTV Fishing Sauna Pool table New Year Wi-fi **Parking** 40 **Notes** LB Closed Jan RS 24-25 & 31 Dec

WALES

COLWYN BAY
Map 6 SH87

The Northwood
★★★ GUEST HOUSE

7 Rhos Rd, Rhos-on-Sea LL28 4RS
☎ 01492 549931
e-mail: welcome@thenorthwood.co.uk
web: www.thenorthwood.co.uk
dir: Exit A55 junct 22 (Old Colwyn). At T-junct right, to next T-junct (facing sea). Left, pass pier, opposite harbour turn left into Rhos Rd. House on left adjacent to church

PETS: Bedrooms (2 GF) unattended Public areas except dining room & lounge on leads Grounds disp bin Exercise area adjacent Facilities food (pre-bookable) food bowl water bowl dog chews cat treats feeding mat litter tray scoop/disp bags leads pet sitting dog walking washing facs cage storage walks info vet info On Request fridge access torch towels Other charge for damage Resident Pets: Sam (cat), Sticky & Twiggy (lovebirds)

A short walk from the seafront and shops, this constantly improving guest house has a warm and friendly atmosphere and welcomes back many regular guests. Bedrooms are furnished in modern style, and freshly prepared meals utilising fresh produce (some home grown), can be enjoyed in the spacious dining room that overlooks the pretty patio.

Rooms 11 rms (10 en suite) (1 pri facs) (3 fmly) (2 GF)
Facilities TVL tea/coffee Dinner available Cen ht Licensed Wi-fi Parking 12 Notes LB

CONWY
Map 6 SH77

WELSH
RAREBITS
Hotels of
Distinction

Castle Hotel Conwy
★★★★ 79% @@ TOWN HOUSE HOTEL

High St LL32 8DB
☎ 01492 582800   📠 01492 582300
e-mail: mail@castlewales.co.uk
web: www.castlewales.co.uk
dir: A55 junct 18, follow town centre signs, cross estuary (castle on left). Right then left at mini-rdbts onto one-way system. Right at Town Wall Gate, right into Berry St then High St

PETS: Bedrooms Charges small dog £5, large dog £10 per night Public areas except restaurant & bar on leads Grounds on leads disp bin Exercise area 50mtrs Facilities bedding feeding mat leads pet sitting dog grooming cage storage walks info vet

info On Request fridge access torch towels Other charge for damage Resident Pet: Tizzy (Cocker Spaniel)

This family-run, 16th-century hotel is one of Conwy's most distinguished buildings and offers a relaxed and friendly atmosphere. Bedrooms are appointed to an impressive standard and include a stunning suite. Public areas include a popular modern bar and the award-winning Shakespeare's restaurant.

Rooms 28 (2 fmly) S £82-£92; D £130-£250 (incl. bkfst)
Facilities FTV Xmas New Year Wi-fi Parking 34 Notes LB

The Groes Inn
★★★★★ @ INN

Tyn-y-Groes LL32 8TN
☎ 01492 650545   📠 01492 650855
e-mail: enquiries@thegroes.com
web: www.groesinn.com
dir: A55, over Old Conwy Bridge, 1st left through Castle Walls on B5106 (Trefriw Road), 2m on right

PETS: Bedrooms (6 GF) unattended Charges £10 per night Public areas in hall area only on leads Grounds Exercise area adjacent Facilities dog chews feeding mat washing facs cage storage walks info vet info On Request torch Stables stabling can be arranged Other charge for damage Resident Pets: Buff (Wire Haired Fox Terrier), Hemi & Mica (Lurchers)

Located in the picturesque Conwy Valley, this historic inn dates from 1573 and was the first licensed house in Wales. The exterior and gardens have an abundance of shrubs and seasonal flowers and create an immediate welcome, which is matched by a friendly and professional staff. Public areas are decorated and furnished with flair to highlight the many period features, and a formal dining room is also available. Spacious bedrooms, in sympathetically renovated former outbuildings are equipped with a wealth of thoughtful extras, and many have balconies overlooking the surrounding countryside.

Rooms 14 en suite (1 fmly) (6 GF) S £91-£190; D £115-£220
Facilities FTV tea/coffee Dinner available Direct Dial Cen ht Wi-fi Golf 18 Squash Parking 100 Notes LB Closed 25 Dec

WALES

The Old Rectory Country House

★★★★★ 🏠 GUEST ACCOMMODATION
Llanrwst Rd, Llansanffraid Glan Conwy LL28 5LF
☎ 01492 580611
e-mail: info@oldrectorycountryhouse.co.uk
web: www.oldrectorycountryhouse.co.uk
dir: *0.5m S from A470/A55 junct on left, by 30mph sign*

PETS: Bedrooms (2 GF) unattended coach house bedrooms only **Charges Public areas Grounds** on leads disp bin **Exercise area** adjacent **Facilities** washing facs cage storage walks info vet info **On Request** fridge access torch towels **Other** charge for damage **Restrictions** no breed larger than a Labrador

This very welcoming accommodation has fine views over the Conwy estuary and towards Snowdonia. The elegant day rooms are luxurious and afternoon tea is available in the lounge. Bedrooms share the delightful views and are thoughtfully furnished, while the genuine hospitality creates a real home from home.

Rooms 3 en suite 2 annexe en suite (1 fmly) (2 GF) **S** £79-£119; **D** £99-£159 **Facilities** STV FTV tea/coffee Direct Dial Cen ht Wi-fi **Parking** 10 **Notes** LB No Children 3yrs Closed 14 Dec-15 Jan

Bron-Y-Wendon Caravan Park *(SH903785)*

▶▶▶▶▶
Wern Rd LL22 8HG
☎ 01492 512903 📠 01492 512903
e-mail: stay@northwales-holidays.co.uk
dir: *Take A55 W. Turn right at sign for Llanddulas A547 junct 23, then sharp right. 200yds, under A55 bridge. Park on left*

PETS: Charges £1 per night £7 per week **Public areas** except reception, shower block & games room; all pets must be kept under strict control disp bin **Exercise area** adjacent **Facilities** walks info vet info

Open all year Last arrival anytime Last departure 11.00hrs

A top quality site in a stunning location, with panoramic sea views from every pitch and excellent purpose-built toilet facilities. Pitch density is excellent, offering a high degree of privacy, and the grounds are beautifully landscaped and immaculately maintained. Staff are helpful and friendly, and everything from landscaping to maintenance has a stamp of excellence. An ideal seaside base for touring Snowdonia and visiting Colwyn Bay, Llandudno and Conwy. 8 acre site. 130 touring pitches. 85 hardstandings. Motorhome pitches.

St Tudno Hotel and Restaurant

★★★ ◉◉ HOTEL
The Promenade LL30 2LP
☎ 01492 874411 📠 01492 860407
e-mail: sttudnohotel@btinternet.com
web: www.st-tudno.co.uk
dir: *On Promenade towards pier, hotel opposite pier entrance*

PETS: Bedrooms Charges £10 per night **Public areas** coffee lounge only **Exercise area** beach adjacent **Facilities** food bowl water bowl walks info vet info **Other** charge for damage **Restrictions** small & medium dogs preferred; no boisterous or noisy dogs **Resident Pet:** Tarkwell (cat)

An excellent family-owned hotel with friendly and attentive staff, that enjoys fine sea views. The stylish bedrooms are well equipped with mini-bars, robes, satellite TVs and many other thoughtful extras. Public rooms include a lounge, a welcoming bar and a small indoor pool. The Terrace Restaurant, where seasonal and daily-changing menus are offered, has a delightful Mediterranean atmosphere. Afternoon tea is a real highlight.

Rooms 18 (4 fmly) **S** £67.50-£100; **D** £95-£215 (incl. bkfst) **Facilities** FTV 🏊 ♬ Xmas New Year Wi-fi **Services** Lift **Parking** 12 **Notes** LB

Dunoon

★★★ 82% HOTEL
Gloddaeth St LL30 2DW
☎ 01492 860787 📠 01492 860031
e-mail: reservations@dunoonhotel.co.uk
web: www.dunoonhotel.co.uk
dir: *Exit Promenade at war memorial by pier into Gladdaeth St. Hotel 200yds on right*

PETS: Bedrooms unattended sign **Charges** £9 per night £63 per week **Public areas** except restaurant (ex assist dogs) **Grounds** on leads **Exercise area** beach (500mtrs), park (1m) **Facilities** washing facs cage storage walks info vet info **On Request** fridge access torch towels **Other** charge for damage **Restrictions** small dogs & Labradors only

This impressive, privately owned hotel is centrally located and offers a variety of refurbished, well-equipped bedrooms. Elegant public areas include a tastefully appointed restaurant where competently prepared dishes are served together with a good choice of notable, reasonably priced wines. The caring and attentive service is noteworthy.

Rooms 49 (4 fmly) **S** £64-£98; **D** £108-£130 (incl. bkfst) **Facilities** FTV Pool table Wi-fi **Services** Lift **Parking** 24 **Notes** LB Closed 17 Dec-early Mar

Can-Y-Bae

★★★★ GUEST ACCOMMODATION

10 Mostyn Crescent, Central Promenade LL30 1AR
☎ 01492 874188 📠 01492 868376
e-mail: canybae@btconnect.com
web: www.can-y-baehotel.com
dir: A55 junct 10 onto A470, signed Llandudno/Promenade.
Can-Y-Bae on seafront promenade between Venue Cymru Theatre
& Band Stand

PETS: Bedrooms (2 GF) sign certain bedrooms only Charges 1st
night £5, extra nights £3 per night £23 per week Public areas
except restaurant (ex assist dogs) on leads Exercise area beach
adjacent (restrictions apply) Facilities food bowl water bowl
feeding mat walks info vet info Other charge for damage dog
grooming by appointment (charged) Resident Pet: Rolo (Airedale
Terrier)

A warm welcome is assured at this tastefully renovated house,
centrally located on the Promenade. Bedrooms are equipped with
both practical and homely extras and upper floors are serviced by
a modern lift. Day rooms include a panoramic lounge, cosy bar
and attractive basement dining room.

Rooms 16 en suite (2 GF) S £35-£45; D £80-£100 Facilities FTV
tea/coffee Dinner available Direct Dial Cen ht Lift Licensed Wi-fi
Notes LB No Children 12yrs

Epperstone

★★★★ GUEST ACCOMMODATION

15 Abbey Rd LL30 2EE
☎ 01492 878746 📠 01492 871223
e-mail: epperstonehotel@btconnect.com
dir: A550, A470 to Mostyn St. Left at rdbt, 4th right into York Rd,
Epperstone at junct of York Rd & Abbey Rd

PETS: Bedrooms sign bedroom 8 only (has private entrance)
Charges £5 per night Grounds Exercise area adjacent, &
beach (1km) Facilities washing facs cage storage vet info
On Request fridge access torch Stables 5m Other charge for
damage Restrictions small dogs only

This delightful property is located in wonderful gardens in a
residential part of town, within easy walking distance of the
seafront and shopping area. Bedrooms are attractively decorated
and thoughtfully equipped. Two lounges and a Victorian-style
conservatory are available. A daily-changing menu is offered in
the bright dining room.

Rooms 8 en suite (5 fmly) S £30-£35; D £60-£70 Facilities FTV
tea/coffee Direct Dial Wi-fi Parking 8

WALES

LLANRWST   Map 6 SH86

Maenan Abbey

★★★ 75% HOTEL

Maenan LL26 0UL
☎ 01492 660247 📠 01492 660734
e-mail: reservations@manab.co.uk
dir: 3m N on A470

PETS: Bedrooms unattended Charges £5 per night
Public areas except dining area & bar during food service
Grounds Exercise area surrounding area Facilities food
(pre-bookable) cage storage vet info On Request fridge
access towels Other charge for damage Resident Pets: Poppy
(Staffordshire cross), Harvey (Spaniel), Olliecat & Kittie (cats)

Set in its own spacious grounds, this privately owned hotel
was built as an abbey in 1850 on the site of a 13th-century
monastery. It is now a popular venue for weddings as the grounds
and magnificent galleried staircase make an ideal setting for
photographs. Bedrooms include a large suite and are equipped
with modern facilities. Meals are served in the bar and restaurant.

Rooms 14 (3 fmly) (4 smoking) Facilities Fishing Guided
mountain walks Xmas New Year Wi-fi Parking 60

See advert on page 419

LLANRWST *continued*

Bron Derw Touring Caravan Park *(SH798628)*

►►►►►

LL26 0YT

☎ 01492 640494   ▤ 01492 640494

e-mail: bronderw@aol.com

dir: *A55 onto A470 for Betwys-y-Coed & Llanwrwst. In Llanwrst left into Parry Rd signed Llanddoged. Left at T-junct, site signed at 1st farm entrance on right*

PETS: Public areas disp bin **Exercise area on site** a small paddock for exercising dogs **Facilities** washing facs vet info **Other** dog grooming available (approx 0.5m) **Resident Pets:** Meg (working Sheepdog), Caddy (cat)

Open Mar-Oct Last arrival 22.00hrs Last departure 11.00hrs

Surrounded by hills and beautifully landscaped from what was once a dairy farm, Bron Derw has been built to a very high standard and is now fully matured, with stunning flora and fauna displays. All pitches are fully serviced, and there is a heated, stone-built toilet block with excellent and immaculately maintained facilities. The tiled utility room, set in a modern conservatory alongside the facility block, houses a washing machine, tumble dryer and sinks for washing up and vegetable preparation. CCTV security cameras cover the whole park. 4.5 acre site. 43 touring pitches. 43 hardstandings. 15 seasonal pitches. Motorhome pitches.

Notes Children must be supervised, no bikes, scooters or skateboards.

Bodnant Caravan Park *(SH805609)*

►►►►

Nebo Rd LL26 0SD

☎ 01492 640248

e-mail: ermin@bodnant-caravan-park.co.uk

dir: *S in Llanrwst, exit A470 opposite Birmingham garage onto B5427 signed Nebo. Site 300yds on right, opposite leisure centre*

PETS: Charges dog 50p per night **Public areas** except children's play area disp bin **Exercise area on site** fenced area, short illuminated dog walk **Exercise area** Gwydyr Forest (1m) **Facilities** walks info vet info **Other** prior notice required pet store 0.5m, kennels nearby (day boarding); pets must not be left unattended at any time

Open Mar-end Oct Last arrival 21.00hrs Last departure 11.00hrs

This well maintained and stunningly attractive park is filled with flower beds, and the landscape includes shrubberies and trees. The statics are unobtrusively sited and the quality toilet blocks are spotlessly clean. All caravan pitches are multi-service, and the tent pitches serviced. There is a separate playing field and rally field. There are lots of farm animals on the park to keep children entertained, and Victorian farming implements are on display around the touring fields. 5 acre site. 54 touring pitches. 20 hardstandings. Tent pitches. Motorhome pitches. 2 statics.

Notes Main gates locked 23.00hrs-08.00hrs, no noise after 23.00hrs

Tynterfyn Touring Caravan Park *(SH768695)*

►

LL32 8YX

☎ 01492 660525

dir: *5m S of Conwy on B5106, signed Tal-y-Bont, 1st on left*

PETS: Charges £1 per night £7 per week **Public areas** disp bin **Exercise area on site** large field **Exercise area** 2m **Facilities** food bowl water bowl scoop/disp bags walks info vet info **Other** prior notice required **Resident Pets:** Nel & Suzie (Border Collies)

Open Mar-Oct rs 28 days in year tent pitches only Last arrival 22.00hrs Last departure noon

A quiet, secluded little park set in the beautiful Conwy Valley, and run by family owners. The grounds are tended with care, and the older-style toilet facilities sparkle. There is lots of room for children and dogs to run around. 2 acre site. 15 touring pitches. 4 hardstandings. Tent pitches. Motorhome pitches.

Notes 😊

Llawr-Betws Farm Caravan Park *(SJ016424)*

►►

LL21 0HD

☎ 01490 460224 & 460296

dir: *3m W of Corwen off A494 (Bala road)*

PETS: Public areas Facilities walks info vet info **Other** max 2 dogs per booking

Open Mar-Oct Last arrival 23.00hrs Last departure noon

A quiet grassy park with mature trees and gently sloping pitches. The friendly owners keep the facilities in good condition. 12.5 acre site. 35 touring pitches. Tent pitches. Motorhome pitches. 68 statics.

Notes 😊

WALES

DENBIGH
Map 6 SJ06

Cayo
★★★ GUEST HOUSE
74 Vale St LL16 3BW
☎ 01745 812686
e-mail: stay@cayo.co.uk
dir: Off A525 into town, at lights turn up hill, supermarket on right. Guest house up hill on left

PETS: Bedrooms Public areas Exercise area 5 mins Facilities walks info vet info On Request towels Restrictions small & medium size dogs only

A warm welcome is assured at this Victorian house, which is situated on the main street, just a short walk from the town centre. Bedrooms are comfortably and thoughtfully furnished with lots of homely extras. Good home cooking is provided in a Victorian-themed dining room, and a cosy basement lounge is also available.

Rooms 4 en suite S £28-£30; D £56-£60 Facilities FTV TVL tea/coffee Cen ht Wi-fi Notes Closed Xmas-New Year

LLANDRILLO
Map 6 SJ03

Hendwr Country Park (SJ042386)
▶▶▶
LL21 0SN
☎ 01490 440210
dir: From Corwen (A5) take B4401 for 4m. Right at Hendwr sign. Site 0.5m on right down wooded driveway. Or follow brown signs from A5 at Corwen

PETS: Charges dogs & cats free; charges for horses on application Public areas except shop & toilets disp bin Exercise area on site 6-acre wood adjacent (dogs must be on leads) Exercise area 1m Facilities food walks info vet info Stables Other prior notice required Restrictions no dangerous dogs (see page 7) Resident Pets: dogs, cats, horses, cattle, sheep

Open Apr-Oct Last arrival 22.00hrs Last departure 16.00hrs

Set in parkland at the end of a tree-lined lane, Hendwr (it means 'old tower') has a stream meandering through its grounds, and all around is the stunning Snowdonia mountain range. The toilet facilities are good. Self-catering holiday lodges are available. 11 acre site. 40 touring pitches. 3 hardstandings. 26 seasonal pitches. Tent pitches. Motorhome pitches. 80 statics.

LLANDYRNOG
Map 6 SJ16

Pentre Mawr Country House
★★★★★ ⬤ GUEST ACCOMMODATION
LL16 4LA
☎ 01824 790732 🖷 01824 790441
e-mail: info@pentremawrcountryhouse.co.uk
dir: From Denbigh follow signs to Bodfari/Llandyrnog. Left at rdbt to Bodfari, in 50yds left into country lane, Pentre Mawr on left

PETS: Bedrooms (7 GF) unattended Public areas except restaurant & pool areas Grounds disp bin Exercise area nearby Facilities food (pre-bookable) water bowl bedding dog chews cat treats scoop/disp bags leads pet sitting dog walking washing facs cage storage walks info vet info On Request fridge access torch towels Other charge for damage paddock available for horses (advance notice required) Resident Pets: Mollie, Maisie & Millie (Collies), Morris, Peter & Wellington (cats), 3 ponies

Expect a warm welcome from Graham and Bre at this superb family country house set in nearly 200 acres of meadows, park and woodland. The property has been in Graham's family for over 400 years. Bedrooms are individually decorated, very spacious and each is thoughtfully equipped. Breakfast is served in either the morning room or, on warmer mornings, on the Georgian terrace. Dinner is served in the formal dining room. There is a salt water swimming pool in the walled garden.

Rooms 3 en suite 8 annexe en suite (7 GF) D £130-£190 Facilities FTV tea/coffee Dinner available Cen ht Licensed Wi-fi ⚲ ☺⚓ Fishing Parking 14 Notes LB No Children 13yrs

WALES

LLANGOLLEN
Map 7 SJ24

Ty-Ucha Caravan Park (SJ232415)
►►

Maesmawr Rd LL20 7PP
☎ 01978 860677
dir: *1m E of Llangollen. Signed 250yds off A5*

PETS: Public areas except toilets & wash rooms disp bin
Exercise area 100yds **Facilities** walks info vet info **Other** dogs
must be kept on lead at all times **Resident Pet:** 1 cat

Open Etr-Oct Last arrival 22.00hrs Last departure 13.00hrs

A very spacious site in beautiful unspoilt surroundings, with a
small stream on site, and superb views. Ideal for country and
mountain walking, and handily placed near the A5. Pitch density
is excellent, facilities are clean and well maintained, and there
is a games room with table tennis. Please note that this site
does not accept tents. 4 acre site. 40 touring pitches. Motorhome
pitches.

Notes 🐾

RHUALLT
Map 6 SJ07

Penisar Mynydd Caravan Park (SJ093770)
►►►►

Caerwys Rd LL17 0TY
☎ 01745 582227 & 07831 408017   📠 01745 582227
e-mail: contact@penisarmynydd.co.uk
dir: *From Llandudno 1st left at top of Rhuallt Hill (junct 29). From
Chester take junct 29, follow Dyserth signs, site 500yds on right*

PETS: Charges dog £2 per night **Public areas** on leads disp bin
Exercise area on site dog walking area **Facilities** washing facs
walks info vet info **Resident Pets:** Meg (Jack Russell), George
(Border Terrier), Alfie (Shorkie)

Open Mar-15 Jan Last arrival 21.00hrs Last departure 21.00hrs

A very tranquil, attractively laid-out park set in three grassy
paddocks with superb facilities block including a disabled room
and dishwashing area. The majority of pitches are super pitches.
Everything is immaculately maintained, and the amenities of
the seaside resort of Rhyl are close by. 6.6 acre site. 75 touring
pitches. 75 hardstandings. Tent pitches. Motorhome pitches.

Notes No cycling. 🐾

RUABON
Map 7 SJ34

James' Caravan Park (SJ300434)
►►►

LL14 6DW
☎ 01978 820148   📠 01978 820148
e-mail: ray@carastay.demon.co.uk
dir: *Approach on A483 South, at rdbt with A539, turn right
(signed Llangollen) over dual carriageway bridge, site 500yds
on left*

PETS: Charges £2 per night **Public areas** on leads disp bin
Exercise area on site large field **Facilities** walks info vet info

Open all year Last arrival 21.00hrs Last departure 11.00hrs

A well-landscaped park on a former farm, with modern heated
toilet facilities. Old farm buildings house a collection of restored
original farm machinery, and the village shop, four pubs,
takeaway and launderette are a 10-minute walk away. 6 acre
site. 40 touring pitches. 4 hardstandings. Motorhome pitches.

Notes 🐾

RUTHIN
Map 6 SJ15

The Wynnstay Arms
★★★★ INN

Well St LL15 1AN
☎ 01824 703147   📠 01824 705428
e-mail: resevations@wynnstayarms.com
web: www.wynnstayarms.com
dir: *In town centre*

PETS: Bedrooms Charges £5 per night **Public areas** except
restaurant on leads **Exercise area** park nearby **Facilities**
washing facs cage storage walks info vet info **On Request**
fridge access torch **Other** charge for damage **Restrictions**
small dogs only

Established in 1549, this former coaching inn in the town centre
has been sympathetically renovated to provide good quality
accommodation and a smart café-bar. Imaginative food is served
in Fusions Brasserie, where the contemporary decor highlights the
many retained period features.

Rooms 7 en suite (1 fmly) **S** £45-£65; **D** £65-£105 **Facilities** FTV
tea/coffee Dinner available Cen ht Wi-fi **Parking** 14 **Notes** LB

ABERSOCH
Map 6 SH32

Porth Tocyn
★★★ 80% ®® COUNTRY HOUSE HOTEL

Bwlch Tocyn LL53 7BU
☎ 01758 713303 & 07789 994942 📄 01758 713538
e-mail: bookings@porthtocyn.fsnet.co.uk
web: www.porthtocynhotel.co.uk
dir: 2.5m S of Abersoch follow Porth Tocyn signs after Sarnbach

PETS: Bedrooms (3 GF) unattended Exercise area adjacent
Other charge for damage Restrictions certain dog breeds not
accepted, please phone to check

Located above Cardigan Bay with fine views over the area, Porth
Tocyn is set in attractive gardens. Several elegantly furnished
sitting rooms are provided and bedrooms are comfortably
furnished. Children are especially welcome and a playroom is
provided. Award-winning food is served in the restaurant.

Rooms 17 (1 fmly) (3 GF) S £72-£88; D £99-£176 (incl. bkfst)*
Facilities FTV ⚞ ⚞ Table tennis Wi-fi Parking 50 Notes LB
Closed mid Nov-week before Easter

Deucoch Touring & Camping Park (SH301269)
▶▶▶▶

Sarn Bach LL53 7LD
☎ 01758 713293 & 07740 281770 📄 01758 713293
e-mail: info@deucoch.com
dir: From Abersoch take Sarn Bach road, at x-rds turn right, site
on right in 800yds

PETS: Public areas except shower block disp bin Exercise area
1m Facilities walks info vet info Stables nearby Other prior
notice required Restrictions authorisation from site owners
required for large dogs & for more than 1 dog Resident Pets:
Chara (Samoyed) & Cassie (Staffordshire Bull Terrier cross)

Open Mar-Oct Last arrival 22.00hrs Last departure 11.00hrs

A sheltered site with sweeping views of Cardigan Bay and the
mountains, just a mile from Abersoch and a long sandy beach.
The facilities block is well maintained, and this site is of special
interest to watersports enthusiasts and those touring the Llyn
Peninsula. 5 acre site. 70 touring pitches. 10 hardstandings. Tent
pitches. Motorhome pitches.

Notes Families only. ☺

Rhydolion (SH283276)
▶▶▶

Rhydolion, Llangian LL53 7LR
☎ 01758 712342
e-mail: enquiries@rhydolion.co.uk
dir: From A499 take unclassified road to Llangian for 1m, turn
left, through Llangian. Site 1.5m after road fork towards Hell's
Mouth/Porth Neigwl

PETS: Charges dog £20, horse £20 per week Public areas on
leads disp bin Exercise area lane adjacent & 3m beach (0.5m)
Facilities vet info Other prior notice required field available for
horses Restrictions small dogs only; no German Shepherds or
Alsatians

Open Mar-Oct Last arrival 22.00hrs Last departure noon

A peaceful small site with good views, on a working farm close
to the long sandy surfers beach at Hell's Mouth. The simple,
revamped toilet facilities are kept to a high standard by the
friendly owners, and nearby Abersoch is a mecca for boat owners
and water sports enthusiasts. 1.5 acre site. 28 touring pitches.
Tent pitches.

Notes Families and couples only. ☺

BALA
Map 6 SH93

Pen-y-Bont Touring Park (SH932350)
▶▶▶▶

Llangynog Rd LL23 7PH
☎ 01678 520549 📄 01678 520006
e-mail: penybont-bala@btconnect.com
dir: From A494 take B4391. Site 0.75m on right

PETS: Charges contact for details Public areas disp bin
Exercise area on site woods & footpath Exercise area lake
(150yds) Facilities food food bowl water bowl dog chews leads
washing facs walks info vet info Other dogs are only permitted
at manager's discretion; disposal bags available

Open Mar-Oct Last arrival 21.00hrs Last departure noon

A family run attractively landscaped park in a woodland country
setting. Set close to Bala Lake and the River Dee, with plenty
of opportunities for water sports including kayaking and white
water rafting. The park offers good facilities including Wi-fi and
a motorhome service point, and many pitches have water and
electricity. Around the park are superb large wood carvings of
birds and mythical creatures depicting local legends. 7 acre site.
95 touring pitches. 59 hardstandings. Tent pitches. Motorhome
pitches. 1 bell tent/yurt.

Notes No camp fires, BBQs must be kept off ground, quiet after
22.30hrs.

WALES

Tyn Cornel Camping & Caravan Park
(SH895400)

▶▶▶▶

Frongoch LL23 7NU
☎ 01678 520759
e-mail: tyncornel@mail.com
dir: *From Bala take A4212 (Porthmadog road) for 4m. Site on left before National Whitewater Centre*

PETS: Charges £2 per night **Public areas** except shop & toilet blocks disp bin **Exercise area on site** 4-acre field **Exercise area** adjacent (2km walk) **Facilities** walks info vet info **Stables** 4m **Other** prior notice required **Resident Pet:** Mrs Cat (cat)

Open Etr-Oct Last arrival 20.00hrs Last departure 11.00hrs

A delightful riverside park with mountain views, popular with those seeking a base for river kayaks and canoes, with access to the nearby White Water Centre and riverside walk with tearoom. The helpful, resident owners keep the modern facilities, including a laundry and dishwashing room, very clean. 10 acre site. 67 touring pitches. 10 hardstandings. Tent pitches. Motorhome pitches.

Notes Quiet after 23.00hrs, no cycling, no camp fires or wood burning.

BANGOR Map 6 SH57

Treborth Hall Farm Caravan Park *(SH554707)*

▶▶▶

The Old Barn, Treborth Hall Farm LL57 2RX
☎ 01248 364399 🖹 01248 364333
e-mail: enquiries@treborthleisure.co.uk
dir: *A55 junct 9, 1st left at rdbt, straight over 2nd rdbt, site approx 800yds on left*

PETS: Charges £1.50 per night **Public areas** dogs must be kept on leads **Exercise area** numerous walks adjacent **Facilities** vet info **Other** prior notice required **Restrictions** no Bull Terriers, Rottweilers, Dobermans or Alsatians **Resident Pets:** cats

Open Etr-end Oct Last arrival 22.30hrs Last departure 10.30hrs

Set in eight acres of beautiful parkland with its own trout fishing lake and golf course, this park offers serviced pitches in a sheltered, walled orchard. Tents have a separate grass area, and there is a good clean toilet block. This is a useful base for families, with easy access for the Menai Straits, Anglesey beaches, Snowdon and the Lleyn peninsula. 8 acre site. 34 touring pitches. 34 hardstandings. Tent pitches. Motorhome pitches. 4 statics.

BARMOUTH Map 6 SH61

Llwyndu Farmhouse
★★★★ ⊜ GUEST ACCOMMODATION
Llanaber LL42 1RR
☎ 01341 280144
e-mail: intouch@llwyndu-farmhouse.co.uk
web: www.llwyndu-farmhouse.co.uk
dir: *A496 towards Harlech where street lights end, on outskirts of Barmouth, take next right*

PETS: Bedrooms certain bedrooms only **Public areas** except dining room on leads **Grounds** on leads disp bin **Exercise area** 0.25m **Facilities** washing facs cage storage walks info vet info **On Request** fridge access torch towels **Resident Pets:** Juke (Jack Russell), Khalilah & J.P.(horses)

This converted 16th-century farmhouse retains many original features including inglenook fireplaces, exposed beams and timbers. There is a cosy lounge and meals can be enjoyed in the licensed restaurant; two and three course dinners are offered. Bedrooms are modern and well equipped, and some have four-poster beds. Four rooms are in nearby buildings.

Rooms 3 en suite 4 annexe en suite (2 fmly) **S** fr £60; **D** £100-£120 **Facilities** FTV TVL tea/coffee Dinner available Cen ht Licensed Wi-fi **Parking** 10 **Notes** LB Closed 25-26 Dec RS Sun no dinner

WALES

Hendre Mynach Touring Caravan & Camping Park *(SH605170)*

▶▶▶▶▶

Llanaber Rd LL42 1YR
☎ 01341 280262 📠 01341 280586
e-mail: mynach@lineone.net
dir: *0.75m N of Barmouth on A496*

PETS: Charges 1st dog free, £1 per extra dog per night
Public areas disp bin **Exercise area** 50yds **Facilities** food food bowl water bowl dog chews leads walks info vet info **Other** toys & disposal bags available

Open Mar-9 Jan rs Nov-Jan shop closed Last arrival 22.00hrs Last departure noon

A lovely site with enthusiastic owners and immaculate facilities, just off the A496 and near the railway, with almost direct access to the promenade and beach. Caravanners should not be put off by the steep descent, as park staff are always on hand if needed. Spacious pitches have TV and satellite hook-up as well as water and electricity. A small café serves light meals and takeaways. 10 acre site. 240 touring pitches. 75 hardstandings. Tent pitches. Motorhome pitches. 1 static.

Trawsdir Touring Caravans & Camping Park *(SH596198)*

▶▶▶▶▶

Llanaber LL42 1RR
☎ 01341 280611 & 280999 📠 01341 280740
e-mail: enquiries@barmouthholidays.co.uk
dir: *3m N of Barmouth on A496, just past Wayside pub on right*

PETS: Charges £1 per night **Public areas** disp bin
Exercise area on site field for dog walking **Facilities** food food bowl water bowl leads washing facs vet info **Other** disposal bags available

Open Mar-Jan Last arrival 20.00hrs Last departure noon

Well run by enthusiastic wardens, this quality park enjoys spectacular views to the sea and hills, and is very accessible to motor traffic. The facilities are appointed to a very high standard, and include spacious cubicles containing showers and washbasins, individual showers, smart toilets with sensor-operated flush, and under-floor heating. Tents and caravans have their own designated areas divided by dry-stone walls, and the site is very convenient for large recreational vehicles. There is an excellent children's play area, plus glorious seasonal floral displays and an illuminated dog walk that leads directly to the nearby pub! There are also luxury holiday lodges for hire. 15 acre site. 70 touring pitches. 70 hardstandings. Tent pitches. Motorhome pitches.

Notes Families & couples only.

THE CIRCLE

The Royal Goat
★★★ 78% HOTEL

LL55 4YE
☎ 01766 890224 📠 01766 890422
e-mail: info@royalgoathotel.co.uk
web: www.royalgoathotel.co.uk
dir: *On A498 at Beddgelert*

PETS: Bedrooms certain bedrooms only **Charges** £10 per night **Exercise area** 100yds **Facilities** walks info vet info **Other** charge for damage **Restrictions** small dogs only

An impressive building steeped in history, the Royal Goat provides well-equipped accommodation, and carries out an annual programme of refurbishment. Attractively appointed, comfortable public areas include a choice of bars and restaurants, a residents' lounge and function rooms.

Rooms 32 (4 fmly) **S** £53-£60; **D** £70-£110 (incl. bkfst)*
Facilities FTV Fishing Xmas New Year Wi-fi **Services** Lift
Parking 100 **Notes** LB Closed Jan-1 Mar RS Nov-1 Jan

Bryn Gloch Caravan & Camping Park *(SH534574)*

▶▶▶▶

LL54 7YY
☎ 01286 650216
e-mail: eurig@bryngloch.co.uk
dir: *On A4085, 5m SE of Caernarfon*

PETS: Charges £1 per night **Public areas** disp bin
Exercise area on site long dog walk **Exercise area** footpaths leading from site **Facilities** washing facs walks info vet info **Other** disposal bags available

Open all year Last arrival 23.00hrs Last departure 17.00hrs

An excellent family-run site with immaculate modern facilities, and all level pitches in beautiful surroundings. The park offers the best of two worlds, with its bustling holiday atmosphere and the peaceful natural surroundings. The 28 acres of level fields are separated by mature hedges and trees, guaranteeing sufficient space for families wishing to spread themselves out. There are static holiday caravans for hire and plenty of walks in the area. 28 acre site. 160 touring pitches. 60 hardstandings. 50 seasonal pitches. Tent pitches. Motorhome pitches. 17 statics.

WALES

CAERNARFON

Map 6 SH46

Plas Dinas Country House

★★★★★ ◈ GUEST ACCOMMODATION

Bontnewydd LL54 7YF
☎ 01286 830214
e-mail: info@plasdinas.co.uk
dir: *3m S of Caernarfon, off A487, 0.5m down private drive*

PETS: Bedrooms (1 GF) unattended certain bedrooms only
Charges £10 per night **Public areas** except restaurant on leads
Grounds on leads disp bin **Exercise area** beach (10 mins' drive)
Facilities food bowl water bowl dog chews scoop/disp bags
cage storage walks info vet info **On Request** fridge access
torch towels **Other** charge for damage dogs may only be left
unattended for short periods if owner is in house **Restrictions**
no breed larger than a Labrador **Resident Pet:** Patsy (Miniature
Schnauzer)

Situated in 15 acres of beautiful grounds in Snowdonia, this
delightful Grade II listed building dates back to the mid-17th
century, but with many Victorian additions. Once the home of
the Armstrong-Jones family; there are many family portraits,
memorabilia and original pieces of furniture for guests to view.
The bedrooms are individually decorated and include four-poster
beds along with modern facilities.There is a stylish drawing
room where the fire burns in the winter, and fresh local produce
features on the dinner menu.

Rooms 10 en suite (1 GF) **S** £95-£110; **D** £140-£250
Facilities FTV tea/coffee Dinner available Direct Dial Cen ht
Licensed Wi-fi Golf 18 **Parking** 10 **Notes** LB No Children 13yrs
Closed Xmas & New Year

Riverside Camping *(SH505630)*

▶ ▶ ▶ ▶

Seiont Nurseries, Pont Rug LL55 2BB
☎ 01286 678781 & 673276 🖹 01286 677223
e-mail: brenda@riversidecamping.co.uk
dir: *2m from Caernarfon on right of A4086 towards Llanberis,
also signed Seiont Nurseries*

PETS: Charges £2 per night £14 per week **Public areas** except
restaurant, garden centre & shower blocks on leads disp bin
Exercise area on site walk by disused railway **Facilities** walks
info vet info **Other** prior notice required

Open Etr-end Oct Last arrival anytime Last departure noon

Set in the grounds of a large garden centre beside the small River
Seiont, this park is approached by an impressive tree-lined drive.
Immaculately maintained by the owners, there are good grassy
riverside tent pitches, clean and tidy toilet facilities and an
excellent café/restaurant. A haven of peace close to Caernarfon,
Snowdonia and some great walking opportunities. 4.5 acre site.
60 touring pitches. 8 hardstandings. 4 seasonal pitches. Tent
pitches. Motorhome pitches.

Notes No fires, no loud music. ⊛

Cwm Cadnant Valley *(SH487628)*

▶ ▶ ▶

Cwm Cadnant Valley, Llanberis Rd LL55 2DF
☎ 01286 673196 🖹 01286 675941
e-mail: aa@cwmcadnant.co.uk
dir: *On outskirts of Caernarfon on A4086 towards Llanberis, next
to fire station*

PETS: Public areas except toilets, wash up area & laundry disp
bin **Exercise area** woodland (200yds) **Facilities** walks info vet
info **Other** prior notice required

Open 14 Mar-3 Nov Last arrival 22.00hrs Last departure 11.00hrs

Set in an attractive wooded valley with a stream is this terraced
site with secluded pitches, a good camping area for backpackers
and clean, modernised toilet facilities. It is located on the
outskirts of Caernarfon in a rural location, close to the main
Caernarfon-Llanberis road and just a 10-minute walk from
the castle and town centre. 4.5 acre site. 60 touring pitches. 9
hardstandings. 5 seasonal pitches. Tent pitches. Motorhome
pitches.

Notes No noise after 23.00hrs, no wood fires.

Plas Gwyn Caravan & Camping Park
(SH520633)

▶▶▶

Llanrug LL55 2AQ
☎ 01286 672619
e-mail: info@plasgwyn.co.uk
dir: *A4086, 3m E of Caernarfon, site on right. Between River Seiont & Llanrug*

PETS: **Charges** 50p per night **Public areas** disp bin **Exercise area on site** field adjacent **Facilities** dog chews washing facs walks info vet info **Other** prior notice required dog scoop available **Resident Pets:** Kiri (Bichon Frisé), Millie (Springer Spaniel), Beth & Abbie (Cocker Spaniels), Amber (SpringerSpaniel/Cocker Spaniel cross)

Open Mar-Oct Last arrival 22.00hrs Last departure 11.30hrs

A secluded park in an ideal location for visiting the glorious nearby beaches, historic Caernarfon, the Snowdonia attractions, and for walking. The site is set within the grounds of Plas Gwyn House, a Georgian property with colonial additions, and the friendly owners are gradually upgrading the park. There are four fully serviced pitches, wooden camping pods and five static caravans for hire. 3 acre site. 42 touring pitches. 8 hardstandings. 8 seasonal pitches. Tent pitches. Motorhome pitches. 18 statics. 2 wooden pods.

Notes Minimal noise between 22.00-mdnt, total quiet between mdnt-08.00hrs.

CRICCIETH
Map 6 SH43

Min y Gaer
★★★★ GUEST HOUSE
Porthmadog Rd LL52 0HP
☎ 01766 522151
e-mail: info@minygaer.co.uk
dir: *On A497 200yds E of junct with B4411*

PETS: **Bedrooms Charges** £2.50 per night **Public areas** except dining room on leads **Grounds** on leads disp bin **Exercise area** 200mtrs **Facilities** feeding mat scoop/disp bags leads cage storage vet info **On Request** torch towels **Other** charge for damage **Restrictions** no breed larger than a Labrador **Resident Pet:** Daisy (Cocker Spaniel)

The friendly, family-run Min y Gaer has superb views from many of the rooms. The smart, modern bedrooms are furnished in pine, and the welcoming proprietors also provide a bar and a traditionally furnished lounge.

Rooms 10 en suite (1 fmly) S £35-£40; D £66-£75 Facilities FTV tea/coffee Cen ht Licensed Wi-fi Parking 12 Notes Closed Nov-14 Mar

Eisteddfa *(SH518394)*

▶▶▶▶

Eisteddfa Lodge, Pentrefelin LL52 0PT
☎ 01766 522696
e-mail: eisteddfa@criccieth.co.uk
dir: *From Porthmadog take A497 towards Criccieth. After approx 3.5m, through Pentrefelin, site signed 1st right after Plas Gwyn Nursing Home*

PETS: **Charges** 50p per night **Public areas** on leads disp bin **Exercise area on site** dog walks **Exercise area** 3m **Facilities** walks info vet info **Other** prior notice required dogs must be exercised on designated walks or off site

Open Mar-Oct Last arrival 22.30hrs Last departure 11.00hrs

A quiet, secluded park on elevated ground, sheltered by the Snowdonia Mountains and with lovely views of Cardigan Bay; Criccieth is nearby. The owners are carefully improving the park whilst preserving its unspoilt beauty, and are keen to welcome families, who will appreciate the cubicled facilities. There's a field and play area, woodland walks, tipis, six superb slate-based hardstandings, three static holiday caravans for hire, and a three-acre coarse fishing lake adjacent to the park. 24 acre site. 100 touring pitches. 17 hardstandings. Tent pitches. Motorhome pitches. 3 statics. 2 tipis. 1 wooden pod.

Notes No noise after 22.30hrs.

DOLGELLAU
Map 6 SH71

WELSH RAREBITS
Hotels of Distinction

Penmaenuchaf Hall
★★★ ⦿ COUNTRY HOUSE HOTEL
Penmaenpool LL40 1YB
☎ 01341 422129 📠 01341 422787
e-mail: relax@penhall.co.uk
web: www.penhall.co.uk
dir: *Off A470 onto A493 to Tywyn. Hotel approx 1m on left*

PETS: **Bedrooms** certain bedrooms only **Charges** £10 per night **Public areas** in hall lounge only **Grounds** on leads disp bin **Exercise area** 50yds **Facilities** food (pre-bookable) food bowl water bowl dog chews cat treats washing facs cage storage walks info vet info **On Request** fridge access torch towels **Other** charge for damage

Built in 1860, this impressive hall stands in 20 acres of formal gardens, grounds and woodland, and enjoys magnificent views across the River Mawddach. Sympathetic restoration has created a comfortable and welcoming hotel with spacious day rooms and thoughtfully furnished bedrooms, some with private balconies. Fresh produce cooked in modern British style is served in an elegant conservatory restaurant, overlooking the countryside.

Rooms 14 (2 fmly) S £100-£150; D £160-£250 (incl. bkfst)*
Facilities STV FTV ⛵ Complimentary salmon & trout fishing Coracling Xmas New Year Wi-fi Parking 30 Notes LB No children 6yrs

WALES

Ty Mawr

★★ **74%** SMALL HOTEL

LL45 2NH

☎ 01341 241440   🖹 01341 241440

e-mail: info@tymawrhotel.com

web: www.tymawrhotel.com

dir: *From Barmouth A496 (Harlech road). In Llanbedr turn right after bridge, hotel 50yds on left, follow brown tourist sigs*

PETS: Bedrooms unattended **Public areas** except restaurant **Grounds** disp bin **Exercise area** approx 200yds **Facilities** water bowl cage storage walks info vet info **On Request** fridge access **Stables** 0.5m **Resident Pets:** Carlo (Welsh Sheepdog), Chelly (Border Collie), Tara (Sheepdog)

Ty Mawr means 'Big House' in Welsh. Located in a picturesque village within Snowdonia National Park, this family-run hotel has a relaxed, friendly atmosphere. The attractive grounds opposite the River Artro provide a popular beer garden during fine weather. The attractive, rustically furnished bar offers a blackboard selection of food and a good choice of real ales; a more formal menu is available in the restaurant. Bedrooms are smart and brightly decorated.

Rooms 10 (2 fmly) **S** £50; **D** £80 (incl. bkfst)* **Facilities** STV **Parking** 30 **Notes** LB Closed 24-26 Dec

Legacy Royal Victoria

★★★ **68%** HOTEL

LL55 4TY

☎ 08444 119 003 & 0330 333 2803 🖹 08444 119 004

e-mail: res-royalvictoria@legacy-hotels.co.uk

web: www.legacy-hotels.co.uk

dir: *On A4086 (Caernarfon to Llanberis road), directly opposite Snowdon Mountain Railway*

PETS: Bedrooms standard & economy rooms only **Charges** £10 per night **Public areas** except restaurant & food service areas on leads **Grounds** on leads disp bin **Exercise area** nearby **Facilities** walks info **Other** charge for damage

This well-established hotel sits near the foot of Snowdon, between the Peris and Padarn lakes. Pretty gardens and grounds make an attractive setting for the many weddings held here. Bedrooms are well equipped. There are spacious lounges and bars, and a large dining room with a conservatory looking out over the lakes.

Rooms 106 (14 annexe) (7 fmly) **Facilities** FTV ♫ Xmas New Year **Services** Lift **Parking** 100

White Tower Caravan Park *(SH453582)*

▶ ▶ ▶ ▶

LL54 5UH

☎ 01286 830649 & 07802 562785 🖹 01286 830649

e-mail: whitetower@supanet.com

dir: *1.5m from village on Tai'r Eglwys road. From Caernarfon take A487 (Porthmadog road). Cross rdbt, 1st right. Site 3m on right*

PETS: Public areas except club house & swimming pool disp bin **Exercise area** 100mtrs **Facilities** walks info vet info **Stables** 1.5m

Open Mar-10 Jan rs Mar-mid May & Sep-Oct bar open wknds only Last arrival 23.00hrs Last departure noon

There are lovely views of Snowdonia from this park located just two miles from the nearest beach at Dinas Dinlle. A well-maintained toilet block has key access, and the hardstanding pitches have water and electricity. Popular amenities include an outdoor heated swimming pool, a lounge bar with family room, and a games and TV room. 6 acre site. 68 touring pitches. 68 hardstandings. 58 seasonal pitches. Tent pitches. Motorhome pitches. 68 statics.

LLANRUG
Map 6 SH56

Llys Derwen Caravan & Camping Site
(SH539629)

▶ ▶ ▶ ▶

Ffordd Bryngwyn LL55 4RD
☎ 01286 673322
e-mail: llysderwen@aol.com
dir: *A55 junct 13 (Caernarfon) onto A4086 to Llanberis, through Llanrug, turn right at pub, site 60yds on right*

PETS: Public areas caravan fields only on leads disp bin **Exercise area on site** separate field from caravans & tents **Facilities** walks info vet info **Resident Pets:** Lacey, Buffy, Brenna, Ria & Odin (Bernese Mountain Dogs)

Open Mar-Oct Last arrival 22.00hrs Last departure noon

A pleasant, beautifully maintained small site set in woodland within easy reach of Caernarfon, Snowdon, Anglesey and the Lleyn Peninsula. Visitors can expect a warm welcome from enthusiastic, hands-on owners, who keep the toilet facilities spotlessly clean. 5 acre site. 20 touring pitches. Tent pitches. Motorhome pitches. 2 statics.

Notes No open fires, no noise after 22.00hrs, no ball games.

PORTHMADOG
Map 6 SH53

Royal Sportsman
★★★ 80% ◎◎ HOTEL
131 High St LL49 9HB
☎ 01766 512015 📠 01766 512490
e-mail: enquiries@royalsportsman.co.uk
dir: *At rdbt junct of A497 & A487*

PETS: Bedrooms (9 GF) unattended ground-floor, courtyard bedrooms only **Charges** £5 per night **Public areas** except dining room & lounge **Grounds** disp bin **Exercise area** surrounding countryside **Facilities** food bowl water bowl pet sitting dog walking washing facs cage storage walks info vet info **On Request** fridge access torch towels **Stables** nearby **Other** charge for damage dog grooming available nearby **Resident Pet:** Gelert (Border Collie)

Ideally located in the centre of Porthmadog, this former coaching inn dates from the Victorian era and is a friendly, privately owned and personally run hotel. Rooms are tastefully decorated and well equipped, and some are in an annexe close to the hotel. There is a large comfortable lounge and a wide range of meals is served in the bar or restaurant.

Rooms 28 (9 annexe) (7 fmly) (9 GF) **S** £59-£83; **D** £85-£99 (incl. bkfst)* **Facilities** STV FTV Xmas New Year Wi-fi **Parking** 17 **Notes** LB

PWLLHELI
Map 6 SH33

Hafan Y Mor Holiday Park *(SH431368)*
LL53 6HJ
☎ 0871 231 0887 📠 01766 810379
dir: *From Caernarfon A499 to Pwllheli. A497 to Porthmadog. Park on right, approx 3m from Pwllheli. Or from Telford, A5, A494 to Bala. Right for Porthmadog. Left at rdbt in Porthmadog signed Criccieth & Pwllheli. Park on left 3m from Criccieth*

PETS: Charges £1 per night **Public areas** except restaurants, food servery & swimming pool disp bin **Exercise area on site** grassed areas & beaches **Facilities** food food bowl water bowl walks info vet info **Other** prior notice required max 2 dogs per pitch; essential to check pet policy when booking disposal bags available **Restrictions** no fighting or dangerous dogs (see page 7)

Open 20 Mar-2 Nov rs Mar-May & Sep-Oct reduced facilities Last arrival 21.00hrs Last departure 10.00hrs

Set between the seaside towns of Pwllheli and Criccieth on the sheltered Llyn Peninsula, this is an all action caravan park with direct beach access. Facilities include an indoor splash pool with flumes and bubble pools, wave rider, aqua jet racer and boating lake. 500 acre site. 73 touring pitches. Motorhome pitches. 800 statics.

TAL-Y-BONT
Map 6 SH76

Islawrffordd Caravan Park *(SH584215)*

▶ ▶ ▶ ▶ ▶

LL43 2AQ
☎ 01341 247269 📠 01341 242639
e-mail: jane@islawrffordd.co.uk
dir: *On sea side of main A496 coast road, 4m N of Barmouth, 6m S of Harlech*

PETS: Sep accom Charges £2 per night **Public areas** disp bin **Exercise area** adjacent to beach **Facilities** food food bowl water bowl dog chews scoop/disp bags leads washing facs walks info vet info **Other** prior notice required

Open Mar-1 Nov Last arrival 20.00hrs Last departure noon

Situated on the coast between Barmouth and Harlech, and within the Snowdonia National Park, with clear views of Cardigan Bay, the Lleyn Peninsula and the Snowdonia and Cader Idris mountain ranges, this excellent, family-run and family-friendly park has seen considerable investment since opening around five years ago. Fully matured, the touring area boasts fully serviced pitches, a superb toilet block with under-floor heating and top-quality fittings, and the park has private access to miles of sandy beach. Plans include refurbishing the restaurant, bar and games room. 25 acre site. 105 touring pitches. 75 hardstandings. Tent pitches. Motorhome pitches. 201 statics.

Notes Strictly families & couples only, no groups.

WALES

WALES

TYWYN — Map 6 SH50

Eisteddfa *(SH651055)*
★★★★ FARMHOUSE
Eisteddfa, Abergynolwyn LL36 9UP
☎ 01654 782385 📠 01654 782385 Mrs G Pugh
e-mail: hugh.pugh01@btinternet.com
dir: *5m NE of Tywyn on B4405 nr Dolgoch Falls*

PETS: Bedrooms (3 GF) Charges £5 per night £20 per week
Public areas Grounds disp bin Exercise area Facilities cage
storage walks info On Request torch Other charge for damage

Eisteddfa is a modern stone bungalow situated less than a mile
from Abergynolwyn, in a spot which is ideal for walking, and
for visiting the local historic railway. The bedrooms are well
equipped, and stunning views can be enjoyed from the attractive
dining room.

Rooms 3 rms (2 en suite) (3 GF) Facilities STV FTV TVL tea/coffee
Cen ht Parking 6 Notes LB Closed Dec-Feb 😺 1200 acres mixed

MONMOUTHSHIRE

ABERGAVENNY — Map 3 SO21

WELSH
RAREBITS
*Hotels of
Distinction*

Llansantffraed Court
★★★★ 78% @@ COUNTRY HOUSE HOTEL
Llanvihangel Gobion, Clytha NP7 9BA
☎ 01873 840678 📠 01873 840674
e-mail: reception@llch.co.uk
web: www.llch.co.uk
dir: *At A465 & A40 Abergavenny junct take B4598 signed Usk (NB
do not join A40). Towards Raglan, hotel on left in 4.5m*

PETS: Bedrooms unattended Charges dogs £10, cats £20
per night except restaurant, lounge (ex assist dogs) Grounds
disp bin Exercise area nearby Facilities food (pre-bookable)
food bowl water bowl bedding dog chews cat treats feeding
mat litter tray scoop/disp bags leads pet sitting dog walking
washing facs dog grooming cage storage walks info vet
info On Request fridge access torch towels Other charge for
damage prior notice required

In a commanding position and in its own extensive grounds, this
very impressive property, a privately owned country-house hotel,
has enviable views of the Brecon Beacons. Extensive public areas
include a relaxing lounge and a spacious restaurant offering
imaginative and enjoyable award-winning dishes. Bedrooms
vary in size and reflect the individuality of the building; all are
comfortably furnished and provide some thoughtful extras.
Extensive parking is available.

Rooms 21 (1 fmly) S £97-£105; D £125-£175 (incl. bkfst)*
Facilities STV FTV Putt green Fishing Clay pigeon shooting
school Wi-fi Child facilities Services Lift Parking 250 Notes LB

Angel Hotel
★★★ 79% @ HOTEL
15 Cross St NP7 5EN
☎ 01873 857121 📠 01873 858059
e-mail: mail@angelhotelabergavenny.com
web: www.angelhotelabergavenny.com
dir: *From A40 & A465 junct follow town centre signs, S of
Abergavenny, past rail & bus stations*

PETS: Bedrooms Charges £10 per night
Public areas except restaurant on leads Grounds on leads
Exercise area 50mtrs Facilities water bowl bedding pet sitting
dog walking cage storage walks info vet info On Request fridge
access towels

Once a coaching inn this has long been a popular venue for both
local people and visitors; the two traditional function rooms and a
ballroom are in regular use. In addition there is a comfortable
lounge, a relaxed bar and a smart restaurant. In warmer weather
there is a central courtyard that is ideal for alfresco eating. The
bedrooms include a four-poster room and some that are suitable
for families.

Rooms 35 (4 annexe) (2 fmly) S £74-£140; D £96-£190 (incl.
bkfst)* Facilities FTV New Year Wi-fi Services Lift Parking 30
Notes LB Closed 25 Dec RS 24 & 26-30 Dec

Pyscodlyn Farm Caravan & Camping Site
(SO266155)
▶▶▶
Llanwenarth Citra NP7 7ER
☎ 01873 853271 & 07816 447942
e-mail: pyscodlyn.farm@virgin.net
dir: *From Abergavenny take A40 (Brecon road), site 1.5m from
entrance of Nevill Hall Hospital, on left 50yds past phone box*

PETS: Sep accom Charges horse (negotiable) Public areas
disp bin Exercise area on site adjacent field Facilities washing
facs walks info Stables Other prior notice required Resident
Pets: 2 dogs, 2 cats, 2 horses

Open Apr-Oct

With its outstanding views of the mountains, this quiet park
in the Brecon Beacons National Park makes a pleasant venue
for country lovers. The Sugarloaf Mountain and the River Usk
are within easy walking distance and, despite being a working
farm, dogs are welcome. Please note that credit cards are not
taken on this site. 4.5 acre site. 60 touring pitches. Tent pitches.
Motorhome pitches. 6 statics.

Notes 😺

CHEPSTOW — Map 3 ST59

Castle View

★★★ 68% HOTEL

16 Bridge St NP16 5EZ

☎ 01291 620349   📠 01291 627397

e-mail: castleviewhotel@btconnect.com

dir: *M48 junct 2, A466 for Wye Valley, at 1st rdbt right onto A48 towards Gloucester. Follow 2nd sign to town centre, then to Chepstow Castle, hotel directly opposite*

PETS: Bedrooms unattended sign Charges Public areas except restaurant on leads Grounds on leads disp bin Exercise area castle green, park green & river banks (100mtrs) Facilities washing facs cage storage walks info vet info On Request fridge access torch towels Stables 1m Other charge for damage

This hotel was built around 300 years ago and offers unrivalled views of Chepstow Castle. Accommodation is comfortable - there are family rooms, double-bedded rooms, and some bedrooms that are situated in a separate building; a good range of guest extras is provided. There is a cosy bar area and a small restaurant where home-cooked food using fresh, local ingredients is offered.

Rooms 13 (4 annexe) (7 fmly) S £30-£60; D £68-£90 (incl. bkfst) Facilities Xmas New Year Wi-fi

DINGESTOW — Map 3 SO41

Bridge Caravan Park & Camping Site

(SO459104)

▶▶▶

Bridge Farm NP25 4DY

☎ 01600 740241   📠 01600 740241

e-mail: info@bridgecaravanpark.co.uk

dir: *Signed from Raglan. Off A449 (S Wales-Midlands road)*

PETS: Charges 50p per night Public areas except toilet block, shower block, launderette & reception Exercise area 100yds Facilities food food bowl water bowl dog chews scoop/disp bags washing facs walks info vet info Other prior notice required

Open Etr-Oct Last arrival 22.00hrs Last departure 16.00hrs

The River Trothy runs along the edge of this quiet village park, which has been owned by the same family for many years. Touring pitches are both grass and hardstanding, and there is a backdrop of woodland. The quality facilities are enhanced by good laundry equipment. 4 acre site. 94 touring pitches. 15 hardstandings. Tent pitches. Motorhome pitches.

Notes 🐾

MONMOUTH — Map 3 SO51

Church Farm

★★★ GUEST HOUSE

Mitchel Troy NP25 4HZ

☎ 01600 712176

e-mail: info@churchfarmguesthouse.eclipse.co.uk

dir: *From A40 S, left onto B4293 for Trelleck before tunnel, 150yds, left, follow signs to Mitchel Troy. Guest House on left 200yds beyond campsite*

PETS: Bedrooms Public areas except dining room Grounds disp bin Exercise area surrounding area Facilities cage storage walks info vet info On Request fridge access Resident Pet: Ollie (Labrador)

Located in the village of Mitchel Troy, this 16th-century former farmhouse retains many original features including exposed beams and open fireplaces. There is a range of bedrooms and a spacious lounge, and breakfast is served in the traditionally furnished dining room. Dinner is available by prior arrangement.

Rooms 9 rms (7 en suite) (2 pri facs) (3 fmly) S £33-£36; D £66-£72 Facilities TVL tea/coffee Dinner available Cen ht Parking 12 Notes LB Closed Xmas ⊗

SKENFRITH — Map 3 SO42

The Bell at Skenfrith

★★★★★ ◉◉ 🍴 RESTAURANT WITH ROOMS

NP7 8UH

☎ 01600 750235   📠 01600 750525

e-mail: enquiries@skenfrith.co.uk

web: www.skenfrith.co.uk

dir: *On B4521 in Skenfrith, opposite castle*

PETS: Bedrooms Charges £5 per night Public areas except restaurant Grounds Exercise area surrounding countryside Facilities water bowl walks info vet info On Request torch

The Bell is a beautifully restored, 17th-century former coaching inn which still retains much original charm and character. It is peacefully situated on the banks of the Monnow, a tributary of the River Wye, and is ideally placed for exploring the numerous delights of the area. Natural materials have been used to create a relaxing atmosphere, while the bedrooms, which include full suites and rooms with four-poster beds, are stylish, luxurious and equipped with DVD players. The garden produces many of the fresh ingredients used in the kitchen where award-winning quality food is produced for relaxed dining in the welcoming restaurant. The Bell at Skenfrith is the Overall Winner, and Winner for Wales, of the AA Wine Award 2011-12.

Rooms 11 en suite (2 fmly) S £75-£120; D £110-£220 Facilities tea/coffee Dinner available Direct Dial Cen ht Wi-fi Parking 36 Notes No Children 8yrs Closed last wk Jan-1st wk Feb RS Nov-Mar Closed Tue No coaches

WALES

TINTERN PARVA — Map 3 S050

Best Western Royal George

★★★ 78% HOTEL

Wye Valley Rd NP16 6SF
☎ 01291 689205 📄 01291 689448
e-mail: royalgeorgetintern@hotmail.com
web: www.bw-royalgeorgehotel.co.uk
dir: M48 junct 2, A466, 5m to Tintern, 2nd left

PETS: Bedrooms (10 GF) Charges £10 per night Public areas except restaurant & lounge at food service on leads Grounds on leads disp bin Exercise area 50yds Facilities water bowl cage storage walks info vet info On Request fridge access torch Other charge for damage

This privately owned and personally run hotel provides comfortable, spacious accommodation, including bedrooms with balconies overlooking the well-tended garden; there are a number of ground-floor bedrooms. The public areas include a lounge bar and a large function room, and a varied and popular menu is available in either the bar or restaurant. This hotel is an ideal base for exploring the counties of Monmouthshire and Herefordshire.

Rooms 15 (14 annexe) (6 fmly) (10 GF) S £65-£95; D £75-£120 (incl. bkfst)* Facilities FTV Xmas New Year Wi-fi Parking 50 Notes LB

Parva Farmhouse Riverside Guest House & Restaurant

★★★★ 🍴 GUEST HOUSE

Monmouth Rd NP16 6SQ
☎ 01291 689411 📄 01291 689941
e-mail: parvahoteltintern@fsmail.net
dir: On A466 at N edge of Tintern. Next to St Michael's Church on the riverside

PETS: Bedrooms Charges £3 per night Public areas except restaurant Grounds disp bin Exercise area Exercise area countryside adjacent Facilities water bowl vet info On Request fridge access torch Restrictions small & medium size dogs only Resident Pet: Frodo (Border Terrier cross)

This relaxed and friendly, family-run guest house is situated on a sweep of the River Wye with far-reaching views of the valley. Originally a farmhouse dating from the 17th century, many features have been retained, providing character and comfort in an informal atmosphere. The cosy Inglenook Restaurant is the place where quality ingredients are offered at breakfast and dinner. The individually designed bedrooms are tastefully decorated and enjoy pleasant views; one has a four-poster.

Rooms 8 en suite (2 fmly) S £45-£69; D £66-£99 Facilities FTV tea/coffee Dinner available Cen ht Licensed Parking 8 Notes No Children 12yrs

USK — Map 3 S030

Glen-yr-Afon House

★★★ 80% HOTEL

Pontypool Rd NP15 1SY
☎ 01291 672302 & 673202 📄 01291 672597
e-mail: enquiries@glen-yr-afon.co.uk
web: www.glen-yr-afon.co.uk
dir: A472 through High St, over river bridge, follow to right. Hotel 200yds on left

PETS: Bedrooms unattended Charges £10 per night Grounds on leads Exercise area river walk opposite Facilities walks info vet info Other charge for damage Resident Pet: 1 cat

On the edge of this delightful old market town, Glen-yr-Afon, a unique Victorian villa, offers all the facilities expected of a modern hotel combined with the warm atmosphere of a family home. Bedrooms are furnished to a high standard and several overlook the well-tended gardens. There is a choice of comfortable sitting areas and a stylish and spacious banqueting suite.

Rooms 28 (1 annexe) (2 fmly) S £99-£123; D £136-£159 (incl. bkfst)* Facilities STV FTV ⚓ Complimentary access to Usk Tennis Club New Year Wi-fi Services Lift Parking 151 Notes LB

The Three Salmons Hotel

★★★ 78% ◉◉ HOTEL

Bridge St NP15 1RY
☎ 01291 672133 📄 01291 673979
e-mail: general@threesalmons.co.uk
dir: M4 junct 24, A449, 1st exit signed Usk. On entering town, hotel on main road

PETS: Bedrooms (4 GF) unattended certain bedrooms only Charges £5 per night Grounds on leads disp bin Exercise area 500mtrs Facilities water bowl cage storage walks info vet info On Request fridge access torch towels Stables 2m

A 17th-century coaching inn located in the centre of a small market town with friendly, efficient staff who help create a welcoming atmosphere. Many changes have taken place these past years with quality and comfort the key to any guest stay. The food in the contemporary restaurant proves popular. Bedrooms are comfortable and a good range of extras are provided. There is a large function suite ideal for weddings and parties. Parking is secure.

Rooms 24 (14 annexe) (3 fmly) (4 GF) S £75-£105; D £85-£115 (incl. bkfst)* Facilities FTV Wi-fi Parking 25

NEATH PORT TALBOT

PORT TALBOT
Map 3 SS79

Best Western Aberavon Beach Hotel

★★★ **79%** HOTEL

Neath SA12 6QP
☎ 01639 884949 📄 01639 897885
e-mail: sales@aberavonbeach.com
web: www.aberavonbeachhotel.com
dir: M4 junct 41, A48 & follow signs for Aberavon Beach & Hollywood Park

PETS: Bedrooms Public areas except restaurant on leads **Grounds** on leads **Exercise area** beach 100yds (restricted access May-Sep) **Facilities** water bowl walks info vet info **On Request** fridge access **Other** charge for damage pets allowed unattended in bedrooms only if owners are on premises **Restrictions** no dangerous dogs (see page 7)

This friendly, purpose-built hotel enjoys a prominent position on the seafront overlooking Swansea Bay. Bedrooms, many with sea views, are comfortably appointed and thoughtfully equipped. Public areas include an all-weather leisure suite with swimming pool, open-plan bar and restaurant plus a choice of function rooms.

Rooms 52 (6 fmly) **Facilities** FTV ☜ Sauna 🎵 Xmas New Year Wi-fi **Services** Lift **Parking** 150 **Notes** LB

PEMBROKESHIRE

BROAD HAVEN
Map 2 SM81

Creampots Touring Caravan & Camping Park (SM882131)
▶▶▶

Broadway SA62 3TU
☎ 01437 781776
e-mail: creampots@btconnect.com
dir: From Haverfordwest take B4341 to Broadway. Turn left, follow brown tourist signs to site

PETS: Public areas except children's play area disp bin **Exercise area** beach (1.5m) **Facilities** walks info vet info **Other** prior notice required dogs must be kept on leads at all times

Open Mar-Jan Last arrival 21.00hrs Last departure noon

Set just outside the Pembrokeshire National Park, this quiet site is just one and a half miles from a safe sandy beach at Broad Haven, and the coastal footpath. The park is well laid out and carefully maintained, and the toilet block offers a good standard of facilities. The owners welcome families. 8 acre site. 71 touring pitches. 20 hardstandings. Tent pitches. Motorhome pitches. 1 static.

FISHGUARD
Map 2 SM93

The Cartref Hotel
★★ **65%** HOTEL

15-19 High St SA65 9AW
☎ 01348 872430 & 0781 330 5235 📄 01348 873664
e-mail: cartrefhotel@btconnect.com
web: www.cartrefhotel.co.uk
dir: On A40 in town centre

PETS: Bedrooms unattended **Charges** £5 per night £20 per week **Public areas** on leads **Exercise area** 100mtrs **Facilities** food bowl water bowl cage storage walks info vet info **On Request** fridge access torch towels **Stables** 4m **Resident Pet:** Toby (Jack Russell)

Personally run by the proprietor, this friendly hotel offers convenient access to the town centre and ferry terminal. Bedrooms are well maintained and include some family rooms. There is also a cosy lounge bar and a welcoming restaurant that looks out onto the high street.

Rooms 10 (2 fmly) **Facilities** FTV **Parking** 4

Gwaun Vale Touring Park (SM977356)
▶▶▶

Llanychaer SA65 9TA
☎ 01348 874698
e-mail: margaret.harries@talk21.com
dir: From Fishguard take B4313. Site 1.5m on right

PETS: Public areas except toilet block, laundry area, children's play area & other pitches disp bin **Exercise area on site** fenced area **Facilities** walks info vet info

Open Apr-Oct Last arrival anytime Last departure 11.00hrs

Located at the opening of the beautiful Gwaun Valley, this well-kept park is set on the hillside with pitches tiered on two levels. There are lovely views of the surrounding countryside, and good facilities. 1.6 acre site. 29 touring pitches. 5 hardstandings. Tent pitches. Motorhome pitches. 1 static.

Notes No skateboards. 🐾

WALES

Hasguard Cross Caravan Park *(SM850108)*

▶ ▶ ▶

SA62 3SL
☎ 01437 781443 🖹 01437 781443
e-mail: hasguard@aol.com
dir: *From Haverfordwest take B4327 towards Dale. In 7m right at x-rds. Site 1st right*

PETS: Public areas disp bin **Exercise area on site** dog walk **Facilities** washing facs walks info vet info **Other** prior notice required

Open all year rs Aug tent field for 28 days Last arrival 21.00hrs Last departure 10.00hrs

A very clean, efficient and well-run site in the Pembrokeshire National Park, just one and a half miles from the sea and beach at Little Haven, and with views of the surrounding hills. The toilet and shower facilities are immaculately clean, and there is a licensed bar (evenings only) serving a good choice of food. 4.5 acre site. 12 touring pitches. Tent pitches. Motorhome pitches. 42 statics.

Redlands Touring Caravan & Camping Park
(SM853109)

▶ ▶ ▶

SA62 3SJ
☎ 01437 781300
e-mail: info@redlandscamping.co.uk
dir: *From Haverfordwest take B4327 towards Dale. Site 7m on right*

PETS: Charges 1st dog free, 2nd dog £1 per night **Public areas** dogs must not roam free on leads disp bin **Exercise area on site** small fenced dog walk area **Facilities** food walks info vet info **Other** prior notice required max 2 dogs per pitch in high season **Restrictions** no Rottweilers or dangerous dogs (see page 7)

Open Mar-Dec Last arrival 21.00hrs Last departure 11.30hrs

Set in the Pembrokeshire National Park, close to sandy beaches and the famous coastal path, this family owned and run park is set in five acres of immaculately kept grassland and offers spacious, level pitches with glorious sea views for caravans, motorhomes and tents. Facilities are clean and well maintained, the park is well laid out with good hardstanding pitches, and the camping area offers two sizes of pitches, all with electric hook-up. Ideally situated for exploring the whole of Pembrokeshire. 6 acre site. 60 touring pitches. 32 hardstandings. Tent pitches. Motorhome pitches.

Notes No commercial vans or minibuses.

College Guest House

★★★★ GUEST HOUSE
93 Hill St, St Thomas Green SA61 1QL
☎ 01437 763710 🖹 01437 763710
e-mail: colinlarby@aol.com
dir: *In town centre, along High St, pass church, keep in left lane. 1st exit by Stonemason Arms pub, follow signs for St Thomas Green. 300mtrs on left by No Entry sign*

PETS: Bedrooms Charges Public areas except restaurant **Grounds** disp bin **Exercise area** 90mtrs **Facilities** food bowl water bowl feeding mat scoop/disp bags leads pet sitting washing facs cage storage walks info vet info **On Request** fridge access torch towels **Other** charge for damage **Resident Pets:** Bartie (Jack Russell/Collie cross), Alfie (Yorkshire Terrier)

Located in a mainly residential area within easy walking distance of the attractions, this impressive Georgian house has been upgraded to offer good levels of comfort and facilities. There is a range of practically equipped bedrooms, along with public areas that include a spacious lounge (with internet access) and an attractive pine-furnished dining room, the setting for comprehensive breakfasts.

Rooms 8 en suite (4 fmly) **S** £51-£57; **D** £70-£75 **Facilities** FTV TVL tea/coffee Cen ht Wi-fi

Nolton Cross Caravan Park *(SM879177)*

▶ ▶

Nolton SA62 3NP
☎ 01437 710701 🖹 01437 710329
e-mail: info@noltoncross-holidays.co.uk
dir: *1m off A487 (Haverfordwest to St David's road) at Simpson Cross, towards Nolton & Broadhaven*

PETS: Public areas disp bin **Exercise area** 200mtrs **Facilities** walks info vet info **Stables** 1.5m **Other** prior notice required

Open Mar-Dec Last arrival 22.00hrs Last departure noon

High grassy banks surround the touring area of this park next to the owners' working farm. It is located on open ground above the sea and St Bride's Bay (within one and a half miles), and there is a coarse fishing lake close by - equipment for hire and reduced permit rates for campers are available. 4 acre site. 15 touring pitches. Tent pitches. Motorhome pitches. 30 statics.

Notes No youth groups.

Castlemead
★★★★ RESTAURANT WITH ROOMS
SA70 7TA
☎ 01834 871358　📠 01834 871358
e-mail: castlemeadhotel@aol.com
web: www.castlemeadhotel.com
dir: *A4139 towards Pembroke, B4585 into village, follow signs to beach & castle, establishment on left*

PETS: Bedrooms (3 GF) Coach House bedrooms (with own access) only **Charges** £2 per night **Grounds Exercise area** dog-friendly beach **Other** well behaved dogs only

Benefiting from a superb location with spectacular views of the bay, the Norman church and Manorbier Castle, this family-run property is friendly and welcoming. Bedrooms, which include some in a converted former coach house at ground floor level, are generally quite spacious and have modern facilities. The public areas include a cosy bar, a sea-view residents' lounge and a restaurant which is also open to non-residents. There are extensive gardens to the rear.

Rooms 5 en suite 3 annexe en suite (2 fmly) (3 GF) **S** £43-£50; **D** fr £85 **Facilities** FTV tea/coffee Dinner available Direct Dial Cen ht Wi-fi **Parking** 20 **Notes** Closed Jan-Feb RS Nov maybe B&B only No coaches

Highland Grange Farm *(SN077154)*
★★★ FARMHOUSE
Robeston Wathen SA67 8EP
☎ 01834 860952　& 07855 359919　📠 01834 860952
Mrs N Jones
e-mail: highlandgrange@hotmail.co.uk
web: www.highlandgrange.co.uk
dir: *2m NW of Narberth at Robeston Wathen, 400mtrs off A40 at rdbt*

PETS: Bedrooms (3 GF) sign **Sep accom** kennels & pens **Charges Grounds** on leads disp bin **Exercise area** good walks **Facilities** food (pre-bookable) food bowl water bowl bedding dog chews cat treats feeding mat litter tray scoop/disp bags leads pet sitting dog walking washing facs dog grooming cage storage walks info vet info **On Request** fridge access torch towels **Stables** 200mtrs **Other** charge for damage prior booking essential for all pets; working farm - dogs must be under control; dog walk guide available **Restrictions** small dogs only **Resident Pets:** Joe Hamilton (Yorkshire Terrier), Spot (Jack Russell), cats

Awake to birdsong in comfortable accommodation at this peaceful farmhouse property, with spacious bedrooms that are all on the ground floor. The property is set in the small hilltop village of Robeston Wathen, 400 metres from the A40, between Whitland and Haverfordwest, and enjoys wonderful panoramic views. The dining room has separate tables where a good hearty breakfast is provided. There is also a spacious and comfortable lounge.

Rooms 3 rms (2 en suite) (1 pri facs) (1 fmly) (3 GF) **S** £35-£52; **D** £57-£68 **Facilities** FTV TVL tea/coffee Dinner available Cen ht Wi-fi Golf 0 **Parking** 6 **Notes** LB 🐾 150 acres mixed/sheep

WALES

NEWPORT
Map 2 SN03

Llysmeddyg
★★★★ @@ RESTAURANT WITH ROOMS
East St SA42 0SY
☎ 01239 820008
e-mail: contact@llysmeddyg.com
dir: On A487 in centre of town on Main St

PETS: Bedrooms (1 GF) unattended **Public areas** except restaurant **on leads Grounds** on leads **Exercise area** estuary walk (2 mins) **Facilities** pet sitting walks info vet info **On Request** fridge access torch **Stables** 5m **Other** charge for damage

Llysmeddyg is a Georgian townhouse offering a blend of old and new, with elegant furnishings, deep sofas and a welcoming fire. The owners of this property employed local craftsmen to create a lovely interior that has an eclectic style. The focus of the quality restaurant menu is the use of fresh, seasonal, locally sourced ingredients. The spacious bedrooms are comfortable and contemporary in design; bathrooms vary in style.

Rooms 5 en suite 3 annexe en suite (3 fmly) (1 GF) **S** £85-£165; **D** £100-£180 **Facilities** FTV tea/coffee Dinner available Cen ht Wi-fi ⌇ Golf 18 Riding **Parking** 8 **Notes** LB No coaches

ROSEBUSH
Map 2 SN02

Rosebush Caravan Park *(SN073293)*
►►
Rhoslwyn SA66 7QT
☎ 01437 532206 & 07831 223166 📠 01437 532206
dir: From A40, near Narberth, take B4313, between Haverfordwest & Cardigan take B4329, site 1m

PETS: Public areas disp bin **Exercise area** on site **Facilities** food walks info vet info **Other** prior notice required **Resident Pet:** Prince (Labrador)

Open 14 Mar-Oct Last arrival 23.00hrs Last departure noon

A most attractive park with a large ornamental lake at its centre and good landscaping. Set off the main tourist track, it offers lovely views of the Presely Hills which can be reached by a scenic walk. Rosebush is a quiet village with a handy pub, and the park owner also runs the village shop. Please note that due to the deep lake on site, children are not accepted. 12 acre site. 65 touring pitches. Tent pitches. Motorhome pitches. 15 statics.

Notes ⓦ

ST DAVID'S
Map 2 SM72

Warpool Court
★★★ 81% @@ COUNTRY HOUSE HOTEL
SA62 6BN
☎ 01437 720300 📠 01437 720676
e-mail: info@warpoolcourthotel.com
web: www.warpoolcourthotel.com
dir: At Cross Square left by The Bishops Restaurant (Goat St). Pass Farmers Arms pub, left in 400mtrs, follow hotel signs, entrance on right

PETS: Bedrooms unattended **Charges** £10 per night **Grounds** disp bin **Exercise area** 0.5m **Facilities** water bowl washing facs cage storage walks info vet info **On Request** fridge access torch towels

Originally the cathedral choir school, this hotel is set in landscaped gardens looking out to sea and is within easy walking distance of the Pembrokeshire Coastal Path. The lounges are spacious and comfortable, and the bedrooms are well furnished and equipped with modern facilities. The restaurant offers delightful cuisine.

Rooms 22 (3 fmly) **S** £165-£210; **D** £240-£480 (incl. bkfst & dinner)* **Facilities** ⓈⓈⓈ Table tennis Pool table Xmas New Year Wi-fi **Parking** 100 **Notes** LB Closed Nov & 1st half Dec

SAUNDERSFOOT
Map 2 SN10

St Brides Spa Hotel
★★★★ 82% HOTEL
St Brides Hill SA69 9NH
☎ 01834 812304 📠 01834 811766
e-mail: reservations@stbridesspahotel.com
web: www.stbridesspahotel.com
dir: A478 onto B4310 to Saundersfoot. Hotel above harbour

CLASSIC BRITISH HOTELS

PETS: Bedrooms apartments only (lounge area) **Charges** £15 per night **Public areas** except bar, restaurant & spa on leads **Exercise area** beach & woods (5 mins) **Facilities** food bowl water bowl bedding walks info vet info **On Request** fridge access **Other** charge for damage

Set overlooking Carmarthen Bay this contemporary hotel and spa takes prime position. Many of the stylish, modern bedrooms enjoy sea views and have balconies; there are also luxury apartments in the grounds. The hotel is open plan and has excellent views of the bay from the split-level lounge areas. Fresh local seafood

is a speciality in the modern airy restaurant which has a terrace for eating alfresco when the weather allows. The destination spa enjoys some of the very best views from the double treatment room and spa pool.

Rooms 46 (12 annexe) (6 fmly) (9 GF) **S** £125-£190; **D** £150-£280 (incl. bkfst) **Facilities** Spa FTV Gym Thermal suite Xmas New Year Wi-fi **Services** Lift **Parking** 65 **Notes** LB ⊗

Vine Cottage

★ ★ ★ ★ GUEST HOUSE

The Ridgeway SA69 9LA
☎ 01834 814422
e-mail: enquiries@vinecottageguesthouse.co.uk
web: www.vinecottageguesthouse.co.uk
dir: *A477 S onto A478, left onto B4316, after railway bridge right signed Saundersfoot, cottage 100yds beyond 30mph sign*

PETS: Bedrooms (1 GF) **Charges** £5 per stay **Public areas** except dining room **Grounds** disp bin **Exercise area** beach 0.5m **Facilities** dog chews feeding mat scoop/disp bags leads washing facs walks info vet info **On Request** fridge access torch towels **Other** charge for damage **Resident Pets:** Ruby & Megan (English Springer Spaniels)

A warm welcome awaits guests at this pleasant former farmhouse located on the outskirts of Saundersfoot, yet within easy walking distance of the village. Set in extensive, mature gardens which include some rare and exotic plants and a summer house where guests can sit and relax on warmer evenings. Bedrooms, including a ground-floor room, are modern and well equipped, and some are suitable for families. There is a comfortable, airy lounge. Breakfast is served in the cosy dining room.

Rooms 5 en suite (2 fmly) (1 GF) **S** £42-£48; **D** £70-£76 **Facilities** FTV tea/coffee Dinner available Cen ht **Parking** 10 **Notes** LB No Children 6yrs ⊛

Lochmeyler Farm Guest House *(SM855275)*

★ ★ ★ ★ ★ ⊜ FARMHOUSE

Llandeloy, Pen-y-Cwm SA62 6LL
☎ 01348 837724   📄 01348 837622   Mrs Margo Evans
e-mail: stay@lochmeyler.co.uk
web: www.lochmeyler.co.uk
dir: *From Haverfordwest A487 (St David's road) to Pen-y-Cwm, right to Llandeloy*

PETS: Bedrooms cottage suites only **Sep accom** outside kennel with secure run **Grounds** on leads disp bin **Exercise area** adjacent **Facilities** washing facs cage storage vet info **On Request** fridge access towels **Stables Other** charge for damage **Resident Pets:** George (Labrador), Patch (Collie), Sooty (Cocker Spaniel), Sweep (Springer Spaniel)

Located on a 220-acre dairy farm in a beautiful area, with easy access to the Pembrokeshire coast line, Lochmeyler provides high levels of comfort and excellent facilities. The spacious bedrooms, of which four are cottage style converted outbuildings, are equipped with a wealth of thoughtful extras and have private sitting rooms. Three are in the main house which has its own separate entrance. Comprehensive breakfasts are served in the dining room as well as dinner on request; a pleasant lounge is also available.

Rooms 7 en suite (5 GF) **S** £40-£50; **D** £70-£80 **Facilities** FTV tea/coffee Dinner available Direct Dial Cen ht Licensed Wi-fi **Parking** 7 **Notes** LB 220 acres dairy

TENBY
Map 2 SN10

Clarence House

★★ 64% HOTEL

Esplanade SA70 7DU

☎ 01834 844371 📄 01834 844372

e-mail: clarencehotel@freeuk.com

dir: *From South Parade (by town walls) into St Florence Parade & Esplanade*

PETS: Bedrooms unattended **Charges** £5 per night **Public areas** except restaurant on leads **Grounds** disp bin **Exercise area** beach (5 mins' walk) **Facilities** walks info vet info **On Request** fridge access torch towels

Owned by the same family for over 50 years, this hotel has superb views from its elevated position. Many of the bedrooms have sea views and all are comfortably furnished. The bar leads to a sheltered rose garden and a number of lounges. Entertainment is provided in high season, and this establishment is particularly popular with coach tour parties.

Rooms 76 (6 fmly) **Facilities** 🎵 **Services** Lift **Notes** Closed 18-28 Dec

Rosendale Guesthouse

★★★★ GUEST HOUSE

Lydstep SA70 7SQ

☎ 01834 870040

e-mail: rosendalewales@yahoo.com

web: www.rosendalepembrokeshire.co.uk

dir: *3m SW of Tenby. A4139 W towards Pembroke. Rosendale on right after Lydstep*

PETS: Bedrooms twin ground-floor bedrooms only **Charges** £2 per night **Grounds** on leads disp bin **Exercise area** Lydstep Headland (0.5m) **Facilities** food bowl water bowl feeding mat cage storage walks info vet info **On Request** fridge access torch towels **Other** charge for damage **Restrictions** no large dogs (eg Great Danes, St Bernards)

A warm welcome awaits all guests at this family-run establishment that is ideally located on the outskirts of the pretty village of Lydstep, not far from the seaside town of Tenby. Rosendale provides modern, well-equipped bedrooms; some with coast or country views, and three rooms that are on the ground floor of a separate building to the rear of the main house. The attractive welcoming dining room is the setting for breakfast served at well appointed tables.

Rooms 3 en suite 3 annexe en suite (3 GF) **Facilities** FTV tea/coffee Cen ht Wi-fi **Parking** 6 **Notes** LB No Children 16yrs

Esplanade

★★★★ GUEST ACCOMMODATION

The Esplanade SA70 7DU

☎ 01834 842760 & 843333 📄 01834 845633

e-mail: esplanadetenby@googlemail.com

web: www.esplanadetenby.co.uk

dir: *Follow signs to South Beach, exit South Parade into St Florence Parade. Premises on seafront adjacent to town walls*

PETS: Bedrooms town-view bedrooms only **Public areas** except restaurant at meal times on leads **Exercise area** beach adjacent **Facilities** washing facs walks info vet info **On Request** fridge access torch towels **Other** charge for damage

Located beside the historic town walls of Tenby and with stunning views over the sea to Caldey Island, the Esplanade provides a range of standard and luxury bedrooms, some ideal for families. Breakfast is offered in the elegant front-facing dining room, which contains a comfortable lounge-bar area.

Rooms 14 en suite (4 fmly) (1 GF) **S** £55-£120; **D** £70-£130 **Facilities** tea/coffee Direct Dial Cen ht Licensed Wi-fi **Notes** LB Closed 15-27 Dec

Trefalun Park (SN093027)

▶▶▶▶

Devonshire Dr, St Florence SA70 8RD

☎ 01646 651514 📄 01646 651746

e-mail: trefalun@aol.com

dir: *1.5m NW of St Florence & 0.5m N of B4318*

PETS: Charges £1 per night **Public areas** disp bin **Exercise area on site** field **Facilities** walks info vet info **Other** prior notice required **Resident Pets:** Rio (Great Dane), Buzz (Miniature Schnauzer), Ellar (German Shepherd), Sasha & Dasha (miniature Shetland ponies)

Open Etr-Oct Last arrival 19.00hrs Last departure noon

Set within 12 acres of sheltered, well-kept grounds, this quiet country park offers well-maintained level grass pitches separated by bushes and trees, with plenty of space to relax in. Children can feed the park's friendly pets. Plenty of activities are available at the nearby Heatherton Country Sports Park, including go-karting, indoor bowls, golf and bumper boating. 12 acre site. 90 touring pitches. 54 hardstandings. Tent pitches. Motorhome pitches. 10 statics.

Notes No motorised scooters

WOLF'S CASTLE
Map 2 SM92

Wolfcastle Country Hotel

WELSH
RAREBITS
*Hotels of
Distinction*

★★★ 78% ❀ COUNTRY HOUSE HOTEL

SA62 5LZ

☎ 01437 741688 & 741225 📠 01437 741383

e-mail: enquiries@wolfscastle.com

web: www.wolfscastle.com

dir: *On A40 in village at top of hill. 6m N of Haverfordwest*

PETS: Bedrooms unattended dogs not allowed in executive bedrooms **Charges** £5 per night **Public areas** except restaurant & bar **Grounds** on leads disp bin **Exercise area** 200mtrs **Facilities** food bowl water bowl dog chews feeding mat washing facs cage storage walks info vet info **On Request** fridge access torch towels

This large stone house, a former vicarage, dates back to the mid-19th century and is a friendly, privately owned and personally run hotel. It provides stylish, modern, well-maintained and well-equipped bedrooms. There is a pleasant bar and an attractive restaurant, which has a well deserved reputation for its food.

Rooms 20 (2 fmly) **Facilities** FTV New Year Wi-fi **Parking** 60 **Notes** LB Closed 24-26 Dec

---

POWYS

BRECON
Map 3 SO02

Canal Bank

★★★★★ BED AND BREAKFAST

Ty Gardd, Canal Bank LD3 7HG

☎ 01874 623464 & 07929 369149

e-mail: enquiries@accommodation-breconbeacons.co.uk

dir: *B4601 signed Brecon, left over bridge before petrol station, turn right, continue to end of lane*

PETS: Bedrooms Public areas except dining room on leads **Grounds** disp bin **Exercise area** 100yds **Facilities** washing facs walks info vet info **On Request** fridge access torch towels **Other** charge for damage **Resident Pet:** Chloe (Golden Retriever)

Expect a warm welcome at this delightful property, which was developed from a row of five 18th-century cottages. It provides very high quality, comfortable and well-equipped accommodation, and stands alongside the canal in a semi-rural area on the outskirts of Brecon, yet within walking distance of the town centre. Facilities here include a comfortable lounge, a very attractive breakfast room and a lovely garden.

Rooms 3 en suite; **D** £75-£98 **Facilities** FTV tea/coffee Cen ht Wi-fi **Parking** 5 **Notes** No Children 16yrs ❀

The Felin Fach Griffin

★★★★ ❀❀ INN

Felin Fach LD3 0UB

☎ 01874 620111

e-mail: enquiries@eatdrinksleep.ltd.uk

dir: *4m NE of Brecon on A470*

PETS: Bedrooms unattended **Public areas** except dining room **Grounds Exercise area** nearby **Facilities** food bowl water bowl dog chews scoop/disp bags walks info vet info **On Request** fridge access torch towels **Resident Pet:** Max (Kelpie Collie)

This delightful inn stands in an extensive garden at the northern end of the village of Felin Fach. The public areas have a wealth of rustic charm and provide the setting for the excellent food that is served. The bedrooms are carefully appointed and have modern equipment and facilities. The service and hospitality here are commendable.

Rooms 7 en suite (1 fmly) **S** £85-£100; **D** £110-£155 **Facilities** tea/coffee Dinner available Direct Dial Cen ht 🐾 **Parking** 61 **Notes** Closed 24-25 Dec No coaches

Borderers

★★★ GUEST ACCOMMODATION

47 The Watton LD3 7EG

☎ 01874 623559

e-mail: info@borderers.com

web: www.borderers.com

dir: *200yds SE of town centre on B4601, opp church*

PETS: Bedrooms (4 GF) unattended **Grounds** disp bin **Exercise area** 100mtrs **Facilities** food bowl water bowl bedding washing facs walks info vet info **On Request** fridge access torch towels **Resident Pets:** Ella (Black Labrador), Breagh (Chocolate Labrador)

This guest accommodation was originally a 17th-century drovers' inn. The courtyard, now a car park, is surrounded by many of the bedrooms, and pretty hanging baskets can be seen everywhere. The bedrooms are attractively decorated with rich floral fabrics, and there is one room that has easier access.

Rooms 4 rms (3 en suite) (1 pri facs) 5 annexe en suite (2 fmly) (4 GF) **S** £40-£50; **D** £56-£65 **Facilities** FTV tea/coffee Cen ht Wi-fi **Parking** 6

WALES

BRECON *continued*

The Lansdowne

★★★ GUEST ACCOMMODATION

The Watton LD3 7EG
☎ 01874 623321   📄 01874 610438
e-mail: reception@lansdownehotel.co.uk
dir: *A40/A470 onto B4601*

PETS: Bedrooms (1 GF) certain bedrooms only **Public areas** except restaurant on leads **Exercise area** 2 mins' walk **Facilities** washing facs walks info vet info **On Request** torch towels **Other** charge for damage

Privately-owned and personally-run, this Georgian house is conveniently located close to the town centre. The accommodation is well equipped and includes family rooms and a bedroom on ground-floor level. There is a comfortable lounge, a small bar and an attractive split-level dining room where dinner is available to residents.

Rooms 9 en suite (2 fmly) (1 GF) **S** £40-£45; **D** £60-£65 **Facilities** FTV tea/coffee Dinner available Direct Dial Cen ht Licensed **Notes** LB No Children 5yrs

Anchorage Caravan Park *(SO142351)*

▶ ▶ ▶

LD3 0LD
☎ 01874 711246 & 711230   📄 01874 711711
dir: *8m NE of Brecon in village centre*

PETS: Public areas disp bin **Exercise area** adjacent **Facilities** food washing facs vet info

Open all year rs Nov-Mar TV room closed Last arrival 23.00hrs Last departure 18.00hrs

A well-maintained site with a choice of south-facing, sloping grass pitches and superb views of the Black Mountains, or a more sheltered lower area with a number of excellent super pitches. The site is a short distance from the water sports centre at Llangorse Lake. 8 acre site. 110 touring pitches. 8 hardstandings. 60 seasonal pitches. Tent pitches. Motorhome pitches. 101 statics.

Notes 🐾

THE INDEPENDENTS

Caer Beris Manor

★★★ **77%** COUNTRY HOUSE HOTEL

LD2 3NP
☎ 01982 552601   📄 01982 552586
e-mail: caerberis@btconnect.com
web: www.caerberis.com
dir: *From town centre follow A483/Llandovery signs. Hotel on left*

PETS: Bedrooms (3 GF) unattended **Charges** £5 per night **Public areas** except main restaurant & conservatory **Grounds** disp bin **Exercise area Facilities** washing facs cage storage walks info vet info **On Request** torch towels **Stables** nearby **Other** charge for damage paddock available for horses

Guests can expect a relaxing stay at this friendly and privately owned hotel that has extensive landscaped grounds. Bedrooms are individually decorated and furnished to retain an atmosphere of a bygone era. The spacious and comfortable lounge and a lounge bar continue this theme, and there's an elegant restaurant, complete with 16th-century panelling.

Rooms 23 (2 fmly) (3 GF) **S** £73.95-£83.95; **D** £127.90-£147.90 (incl. bkfst)* **Facilities** FTV Fishing ⛵ Clay pigeon shooting Birdwatching Xmas New Year Wi-fi Child facilities **Parking** 100 **Notes** LB

Fforest Fields Caravan & Camping Park *(SO100535)*

▶ ▶ ▶

Hundred House LD1 5RT
☎ 01982 570406
e-mail: office@fforestfields.co.uk
dir: *From town follow New Radnor signs on A481. 4m to signed entrance on right, 0.5m before Hundred House village*

PETS: Public areas except toilets & showers disp bin **Exercise area on site** extensive woodland trails; fenced 'toilet' areas **Facilities** washing facs walks info vet info **Other** prior notice required **Restrictions** no noisy, aggressive or badly behaved dogs

Open Etr & Apr-Oct Last arrival 21.00hrs Last departure 18.00hrs

A sheltered park in a hidden valley with wonderful views and plenty of wildlife. Set in unspoilt countryside, this is a peaceful park with delightful hill walks beginning on site. The historic town of Builth Wells and the Royal Welsh Showground are only four miles away, and there are plenty of outdoor activities in the vicinity. 12 acre site. 60 touring pitches. 17 hardstandings. Tent pitches. Motorhome pitches.

Notes No loud music or revelry 🐾

CRICKHOWELL

Map 3 SO21

WELSH
RAREBITS
*Hotels of
Distinction*

Bear Hotel

★★★ 75% @ HOTEL

NP8 1BW
☎ 01873 810408 📠 01873 811696
e-mail: bearhotel@aol.com
dir: On A40 between Abergavenny & Brecon

PETS: Bedrooms (6 GF) unattended Public areas except restaurant on leads Grounds disp bin Exercise area 350yds Facilities food bowl water bowl dog chews scoop/disp bags walks info vet info On Request fridge access torch Other freshly cooked chicked offered to all visiting dogs

A favourite with locals as well as visitors, the character and friendliness of this 15th-century coaching inn are renowned. The bedrooms come in a variety of sizes and standards including some with four-posters. The bar and restaurant are furnished in keeping with the style of the building and provide comfortable areas in which to enjoy some of the very popular dishes that use the finest locally-sourced ingredients.

Rooms 34 (13 annexe) (6 fmly) (6 GF) Facilities STV FTV Wi-fi Parking 45 Notes RS 25 Dec

Manor

★★★ 75% @ HOTEL

Brecon Rd NP8 1SE
☎ 01873 810212 📠 01873 811938
e-mail: info@manorhotel.co.uk
web: www.manorhotel.co.uk
dir: On A40, 0.5m from Crickhowell

PETS: Bedrooms unattended certain bedrooms only Charges £5 per night Public areas except restaurant Grounds Exercise area adjoining footpaths Facilities walks info vet info Stables 7m to establishment's own farm Other charge for damage Resident Pets: Honey & Henry (Golden Retrievers), Cerys (Welsh Cob)

This impressive manor house, set in a stunning location, was the birthplace of Sir George Everest. The bedrooms and public areas are elegant, and there are extensive leisure facilities. The restaurant, with panoramic views, is the setting for exciting

modern cooking, and the family farm supplies meat and poultry to the hotel. This is a popular wedding venue.

Rooms 23 (2 fmly) S £60-£90; D £80-£160 (incl. bkfst)* Facilities STV FTV 🕙 Gym Fitness assessment Sunbed Xmas New Year Wi-fi Parking 200 Notes LB

CRIGGION

Map 7 SJ21

Brimford House (SJ310150)

★★★★ FARMHOUSE

Criggion SY5 9AU
☎ 01938 570235 Mrs Dawson
e-mail: info@brimford.co.uk
dir: Off B4393 after Crew Green turn left for Criggion, Brimford 1st on left after pub

PETS: Bedrooms Grounds disp bin Exercise area adjacent Facilities washing facs cage storage walks info vet info On Request fridge access torch towels Resident Pets: Emma (Black Labrador), 3 cats

This elegant Georgian house stands in lovely open countryside and is a good base for touring central Wales and the Marches. Bedrooms are spacious, and thoughtful extras enhance guest comfort. A cheery log fire burns in the lounge during colder weather and the hospitality is equally warm, providing a relaxing atmosphere throughout.

Rooms 3 en suite S £45-£60; D £60-£75 Facilities FTV TVL tea/coffee Cen ht Wi-fi Fishing Parking 4 Notes LB @ 250 acres arable/beef/sheep

ERWOOD

Map 3 SO04

Hafod-y-Garreg

★★★★ 🍽 BED AND BREAKFAST

LD2 3TQ
☎ 01982 560400
e-mail: john-annie@hafod-y.wanadoo.co.uk
web: www.hafodygarreg.co.uk
dir: 1m S of Erwood. Off A470 at Trericket Mill, sharp right, up track past cream farmhouse towards pine forest, through gate

PETS: Bedrooms Charges £5 per night Public areas except at dinner Grounds on leads Exercise area adjacent Facilities washing facs cage storage walks info vet info On Request fridge access torch Other charge for damage Restrictions no puppies Resident Pets: Ginger & Puss (cats), Rosie (goat), chickens

This remote Grade II listed farmhouse dates in part from 1401 and has been confirmed, by dendrochronology, as the 'oldest dwelling in Wales'. As you would expect the house has tremendous character, and is decorated and furnished to befit its age; the bedrooms have all the modern facilities. There is an impressive dining room and a lounge with an open fireplace. Warm hospitality from John Marchant and Annie McKay is a major strength here, and they were both finalists in the AA Friendliest Landlady of the Year award 2011-12.

Rooms 2 en suite; D £82 Facilities STV tea/coffee Dinner available Cen ht Wi-fi Parking 6 Notes No Children Closed Xmas 🐾

WALES

WALES

LLANDRINDOD WELLS — Map 3 SO06

The Metropole

CLASSIC BRITISH HOTELS

★★★★ 77% ⊛ HOTEL

Temple St LD1 5DY
☎ 01597 823700 📄 01597 824828
e-mail: info@metropole.co.uk
web: www.metropole.co.uk
dir: On A483 in town centre

PETS: Bedrooms unattended **Charges** £10 per night £70 per week **Public areas** except restaurants & food outlets on leads **Grounds** on leads disp bin **Exercise area** park adjacent to hotel **On Request** fridge access

The centre of this famous spa town is dominated by this large Victorian hotel, which has been personally run by the same family for well over 100 years. The lobby leads to Spencers Bar and Brasserie and to the comfortable and elegantly styled lounge. Bedrooms vary in style, but all are spacious and well equipped. Facilities include an extensive range of modern conference and function rooms, as well as the impressive leisure centre. Extensive parking is provided to the rear of the hotel.

Rooms 120 (11 fmly) **S** £82-£98; **D** £105-£125 (incl. bkfst) **Facilities** Spa FTV ⊛ Gym Beauty & holistic treatments Sauna Steam room Xmas New Year Wi-fi **Services** Lift **Parking** 150 **Notes** LB

Disserth Caravan & Camping Park (SO035583)

▶ ▶ ▶

Disserth, Howey LD1 6NL
☎ 01597 860277
e-mail: disserthcaravan@btconnect.com
dir: 1m off A483, between Howey & Newbridge-on-Wye, by church. Follow brown signs from A483 or A470

PETS: Public areas except reception & bar on leads disp bin **Exercise area** adjacent fields with footpaths **Facilities** food food bowl water bowl walks info vet info **Stables** 4m **Other** prior notice required dogs must be kept on short leads & must not be left unattended for lengthy periods on own pitch; max 2 dogs per pitch **Resident Pets:** Jake (dog), Jack & Oscar (cats)

Open Mar-Oct Last arrival 22.00hrs Last departure noon

A delightfully secluded and predominantly adult park nestling in a beautiful valley on the banks of the River Ithon, a tributary of the River Wye. This little park is next to a 13th-century church, and has a small bar open at weekends and busy periods. The chalet toilet block offers spacious, combined cubicles. 4 acre site. 30 touring pitches. 6 hardstandings. Tent pitches. Motorhome pitches. 25 statics.

Notes

LLANFYLLIN — Map 6 SJ11

Cain Valley

★★ 78% HOTEL

High St SY22 5AQ
☎ 01691 648366 📄 01691 648307
e-mail: info@cainvalleyhotel.co.uk
dir: At end of A490. Hotel in town centre, car park at rear

PETS: Bedrooms certain bedrooms only **Charges** £5 per night **Exercise area** 400yds **Facilities** vet info **On Request** torch

This Grade II listed coaching inn has a lot of charm and character including features such as exposed beams and a Jacobean staircase. The comfortable accommodation includes family rooms. A wide range of food is available in a choice of bars, or in the restaurant which has a well-deserved reputation for its locally sourced steaks.

Rooms 13 (2 fmly) (13 smoking) **Facilities** FTV Wi-fi **Parking** 10 **Notes** LB

LLANGAMMARCH WELLS — Map 3 SN94

The Lake Country House & Spa

★★★ ⊛⊛ COUNTRY HOUSE HOTEL

LD4 4BS
☎ 01591 620202 & 620474 📄 01591 620457
e-mail: info@lakecountryhouse.co.uk
web: www.lakecountryhouse.co.uk
dir: W from Builth Wells on A483 to Garth (approx 6m). Left for Llangammarch Wells, follow hotel signs

PETS: Bedrooms (7 GF) **Charges** £8 per night **Public areas** except lounge & restaurant areas **Grounds** disp bin **Exercise area Exercise area** 5 mins **Facilities** water bowl scoop/disp bags leads pet sitting dog walking walks info vet info **On Request** fridge access torch **Stables** 5m **Other** charge for damage owners to bring dog's own bedding & feeding bowls **Resident Pet:** Cassie (Collie/Labrador cross)

Expect good old-fashioned values and hospitality at this Victorian country house hotel. In fact, the service is so traditionally English, guests may believe they have a butler! The establishment offers a 9-hole, par 3 golf course, 50 acres of wooded grounds and a spa where the hot tub overlooks the lake. Bedrooms, some located in an annexe, and some at ground-floor level, are individually styled and have many extra comforts. Traditional afternoon teas are served in the lounge and award-winning cuisine is provided in the spacious and elegant restaurant.

Rooms 30 (7 GF) **Facilities** Spa FTV ⊛ ♨ 9 ⛳ Putt green Fishing ⛵ Gym Archery Horse riding Mountain biking Quad biking Xmas New Year Wi-fi **Parking** 70 **Notes** No children 8yrs

LLANGEDWYN — Map 7 SJ12

Plas Uchaf Country Guest House

★★★★ ⬤ GUEST HOUSE

SY10 9LD

☎ 01691 780588 & 07817 419747

e-mail: info@plasuchaf.com

dir: *Mile End services Oswestry A483/Welshpool, 2m White Lion right, 4.5m Llangedwyn, 150yds after school on right*

PETS: Bedrooms (1 GF) unattended ground-floor, garden bedroom only **Public areas** except lounge before 6pm on leads **Grounds** on leads disp bin **Exercise area** walled garden **Facilities** food bowl water bowl dog chews washing facs cage storage walks info vet info **On Request** fridge access torch towels **Other** paddock available for horses **Resident Pets:** Oscar, Horacio & Geri (cats), chickens

Located in a superb elevated position amongst extensive mature parkland, this elegant Queen Anne house has been sympathetically renovated to provide high standards of comfort and facilities. The interior flooring was created from recycled ship timbers from The Armada fleet of 1588, and furnishing styles highlight the many period features. Imaginative dinners are available, and a warm welcome is assured.

Rooms 6 en suite (1 fmly) (1 GF) **S** £52.50-£90; **D** £70-£90 **Facilities** FTV tea/coffee Dinner available Cen ht Licensed Wi-fi 🌊 🦮 **Parking** 30 **Notes** LB

LLANGURIG — Map 6 SN97

The Old Vicarage

★★★★ GUEST HOUSE

SY18 6RN

☎ 01686 440280 📠 01686 440280

e-mail: info@theoldvicaragellangurig.co.uk

dir: *A470 onto A44, signed*

PETS: Bedrooms Charges £2 per night **Public areas** except dining areas on leads **Grounds** on leads **Exercise area** 100yds **Facilities** water bowl washing facs walks info vet info **On Request** torch towels **Resident Pet:** Madge (Jack Russell)

Located on pretty mature grounds, which feature a magnificent holly tree, this elegant Victorian house provides a range of

thoughtfully furnished bedrooms, some with fine period items. Breakfast is served in a spacious dining room, and a comfortable guest lounge is also available. Afternoon teas are served in the garden during the warmer months.

Rooms 4 en suite (1 fmly) **S** £34-£40; **D** £56-£64 **Facilities** TVL tea/coffee Dinner available Cen ht Licensed Wi-fi **Parking** 6 **Notes** LB 🐾

LLANWRTYD WELLS — Map 3 SN84

Carlton Riverside

★★★★ ⬤⬤ RESTAURANT WITH ROOMS

Irfon Crescent LD5 4SP

☎ 01591 610248

e-mail: info@carltonriverside.com

dir: *In town centre beside bridge*

PETS: Bedrooms unattended **Exercise area** 0.25m **Facilities** walks info vet info **On Request** towels **Stables** 0.25m

Guests become part of the family at this character property, set beside the river in Wales's smallest town. Carlton Riverside offers award-winning cuisine for which Mary Ann Gilchrist relies on the very best of local ingredients. The set menu is complemented by a well-chosen wine list and dinner is served in the delightfully stylish restaurant which offers a memorable blend of traditional comfort, modern design and river views. Four comfortable bedrooms have tasteful combinations of antique and contemporary furniture, along with welcome personal touches.

Rooms 4 en suite **S** £50; **D** £75-£100 **Facilities** tea/coffee Dinner available Cen ht Wi-fi **Notes** LB Closed 20-30 Dec No coaches

Lasswade Country House

★★★★ ⬤⬤ RESTAURANT WITH ROOMS

Station Rd LD5 4RW

☎ 01591 610515 📠 01591 610611

e-mail: info@lasswadehotel.co.uk

dir: *Exit A483 onto Irfon Terrace, right onto Station Rd, 350yds on right*

PETS: Sep accom indoor kennels (no charge) **Charges** charge for horses only **Exercise area** walks & forest nearby **Facilities** walks info vet info **Stables** 400yds **Other** charge for damage owners must provide dog's own bedding grazing for horses & stabling can be arranged (contact for details) **Resident Pets:** Chaff (Border Collie), Steel (horse)

This friendly establishment on the edge of the town has impressive views over the countryside. Bedrooms are comfortably furnished and well equipped, while the public areas consist of a tastefully decorated lounge, an elegant restaurant with a bar, and an airy conservatory which looks towards the neighbouring hills. The kitchen utilises fresh, local produce to provide an enjoyable dining experience.

Rooms 8 en suite **S** £55-£70; **D** £70-£100 **Facilities** TVL Dinner available Cen ht Riding **Parking** 6 **Notes** LB No coaches

WALES

MIDDLETOWN   Map 7 SJ31

Bank Farm Caravan Park *(SJ293123)*

► ► ►

SY21 8EJ
☎ 01938 570526
e-mail: bankfarmcaravans@yahoo.co.uk
dir: *13m W of Shrewsbury, 5m E of Welshpool on A458*

PETS: Public areas dogs must be kept on leads **Exercise area on site** fields & woodland outside public area **Facilities** walks info vet info

Open Mar-Oct Last arrival 20.00hrs

An attractive park on a small farm, maintained to a high standard. There are two touring areas, one on either side of the A458, and each with its own amenity block, and immediate access to hills, mountains and woodland. A pub serving good food, and a large play area are nearby. 2 acre site. 40 touring pitches. Tent pitches. Motorhome pitches. 33 statics.

Notes

MONTGOMERY   Map 7 SO29

The Dragon

★★★★ ⊛ INN

SY15 6PA
☎ 01686 668359 📠 0870 011 8227
e-mail: reception@dragonhotel.com
dir: *Behind town hall*

PETS: Bedrooms unattended **Public areas** except dining areas on leads **Grounds** on leads **Exercise area** countryside nearby **Facilities** pet sitting dog walking vet info **On Request** torch towels **Stables** 0.5m **Other** charge for damage

This fine 17th-century coaching inn stands in the centre of Montgomery. Beams and timbers from the nearby castle, which was destroyed by Cromwell, are visible in the lounge and bar. A wide choice of soundly prepared, wholesome food is available in both the restaurant and bar. Bedrooms are well equipped and family rooms are available. There is a small indoor swimming pool in the grounds for guest use and ample parking to the rear of the property.

Rooms 20 en suite (6 fmly) **S** £57.20-£67.40; **D** £96.50-£106.80 **Facilities** FTV tea/coffee Direct Dial Wi-fi

RHAYADER   Map 6 SN96

Wyeside Caravan & Camping Park *(SO967690)*

► ► ►

Llangurig Rd LD6 5LB
☎ 01597 810183
e-mail: info@wyesidecamping.co.uk
dir: *400mtrs N of Rhayader town centre on A470*

PETS: Charges £1 per night £6 per week **Public areas** except facility blocks disp bin **Exercise area** 100yds **Facilities** walks info vet info

Open Feb-Nov Last arrival 22.30hrs Last departure noon

With direct access from the A470, the park sits on the banks of the River Wye. Situated just 400 metres from the centre of the market town of Rhayader, and next to a recreation park with tennis courts, bowling green and children's playground. There are good riverside walks from here, though the river is fast flowing and unfenced, and care is especially needed when walking with children. 6 acre site. 140 touring pitches. 22 hardstandings. Tent pitches. Motorhome pitches. 39 statics.

RHONDDA CYNON TAFF

MISKIN   Map 3 ST08

Miskin Manor Country Hotel

★★★★ 75% ⊛⊛ COUNTRY HOUSE HOTEL

Pendoylan Rd CF72 8ND
☎ 01443 224204 📠 01443 237606
e-mail: reservations@miskin-manor.co.uk
web: www.miskin-manor.co.uk
dir: *M4 junct 34, A4119, signed Llantrisant, hotel 300yds on left*

PETS: Bedrooms (7 GF) cottage bedrooms only **Charges** contact hotel for details **Public areas** except restaurant & dining areas on leads **Grounds** on leads disp bin **Facilities** washing facs walks info vet info **On Request** fridge access torch towels **Other** charge for damage **Resident Pets:** 2 cats

This historic manor house is peacefully located in 22-acre grounds, yet is only minutes away from the M4. Bedrooms are furnished to a high standard and include some located in converted stables and cottages. Public areas are spacious and comfortable and include a variety of function rooms. The relaxed atmosphere and the surroundings ensure this hotel remains popular for wedding functions as well as with business guests. There is a separate modern health and fitness centre which includes a gym, sauna, steam room and swimming pool.

Rooms 43 (9 annexe) (2 fmly) (7 GF) **Facilities** FTV ⓧ ⛴ Gym Wi-fi **Parking** 200

PONTYPRIDD
Map 3 ST08

Llechwen Hall

★★★ 74% ⊛ COUNTRY HOUSE HOTEL

llanfabon CF37 4HP

☎ 01443 742050 & 743020 📠 01443 742189

-mail: enquiries@llechwenhall.co.uk

dir: A470 N towards Merthyr Tydfil. At large rdbt take 3rd exit. At mini rdbt take 3rd exit, hotel signed 0.5m on left

PETS: Bedrooms (4 GF) unattended Public areas Grounds on leads disp bin Exercise area 300mtrs Facilities cage storage walks info vet info On Request fridge access torch towels Stables 2m

Set on top of a hill with a stunning approach, this country house hotel has served many purposes in its 200-year-old history including a private school and a magistrates' court. The spacious, individually decorated bedrooms are well equipped; some are situated in the separate coach house nearby. There are ground-floor, twin, double and family bedrooms on offer. The Victorian-style public areas are attractively appointed and the hotel is a popular venue for weddings.

Rooms 20 (8 annexe) (6 fmly) (4 GF) Facilities FTV Xmas New Year Wi-fi Parking 150

SWANSEA

LLANGENNITH
Map 2 SS49

Kings Head

★★★★ INN

own House SA3 1HX

☎ 01792 386212 📠 01792 386477

-mail: info@kingsheadgower.co.uk

PETS: Bedrooms (14 GF) sign ground-floor bedrooms only Charges dog £5 per night Public areas on leads Grounds n leads disp bin Exercise area beach 1m (access all year) Facilities walks info vet info Stables 150yds Other charge for damage stabling for horses can be arranged (contact for full details) Resident Pets: Skinny (Greyhound), Lucy (Alsatian), Sammy (cat), Frank (Connemara pony)

This establishment is made up from three 17th-century buildings set behind a splendid rough stone wall; it stands opposite the church in this coastal village. In two of the buildings comfortable, well-equipped bedrooms, including some on the ground floor, can be found. This is an ideal base for exploring the Gower Peninsula, whether for walking, cycling or surfing. Evening meals and breakfasts can be taken in the inn.

Rooms 27 en suite (3 fmly) (14 GF) Facilities FTV tea/coffee Dinner available Direct Dial Cen ht Pool table Parking 35

Notes LB Closed 25 Dec RS 24 Dec closed for check-in

PONTARDDULAIS
Map 2 SN50

River View Touring Park (SN578086)

►►►►

The Dingle, Llanedi SA4 0FH

☎ 01269 844876

e-mail: info@riverviewtouringpark.com

dir: From M4 junct 49 take A483 signed Llandeilo. 0.5m, 1st left after lay-by, follow lane to site

PETS: Charges 1st pet free, 2nd pet £1.50-£2 per night Public areas disp bin Exercise area on site dog walk in hay meadow Exercise area approx 3m Facilities food bowl water bowl walks info vet info Other prior notice required disposal bags available Resident Pet: Java (Labrador/Collie cross)

Open Mar-late Nov Last arrival 20.00hrs Last departure noon

This peaceful park is set on one lower and two upper levels in a sheltered valley with an abundance of wild flowers and wildlife. The River Gwli flows around the bottom of the park in which fishing for brown trout is possible. The excellent toilet facilities are an added bonus. This park is ideally situated for visiting the beaches of South Wales, The Black Mountains and the Brecon Beacons. 6 acre site. 60 touring pitches. 39 hardstandings. Tent pitches. Motorhome pitches.

PORT EINON
Map 2 SS48

Carreglwyd Camping & Caravan Park
(SS465863)

►►►

SA3 1NL

☎ 01792 390795 📠 01792 390796

dir: A4118 to Port Einon, site adjacent to beach

PETS: Public areas Exercise area on site dog walking area Exercise area walks accessible from site Facilities food vet info Other dogs must be under strict control at all times disposal bags available Resident Pets: Bruno (Black Labrador), Dare (German Shepherd), Emma (cat)

Open Mar-Dec Last arrival 18.00hrs Last departure 15.00hrs

Set in an unrivalled location alongside the safe sandy beach of Port Einon on the Gower Peninsula, this popular park is an ideal family holiday spot. Close to an attractive village with pubs and shops, most pitches offer sea views. The sloping ground has been partly terraced, and facilities are excellent. 12 acre site. 150 touring pitches. Tent pitches. Motorhome pitches.

WALES

RHOSSILI
Map 2 SS48

Pitton Cross Caravan & Camping Park
(SS434877)

►►►

SA3 1PH
☎ 01792 390593 📄 01792 391010
e-mail: admin@pittoncross.co.uk
dir: *2m W of Scurlage on B4247*

PETS: Charges £1 per night £7 per week **Public areas** except dog-free area disp bin **Facilities** food food bowl water bowl dog chews cat treats leads washing facs walks info vet info **Stables** 3m **Other** prior notice required disposal bags available **Resident Pets:** Buster & Dave (Sheepdogs), Tipsy & Amy (cats)

Open all year rs Nov-Mar no bread, milk or papers Last arrival 20.00hrs Last departure 11.00hrs

Surrounded by farmland close to sandy Menslade Bay, which is within walking distance across the fields, this grassy park is divided by hedging into paddocks. Nearby Rhossili Beach is popular with surfers. Performance kites are sold, and instruction in flying is given. 6 acre site. 100 touring pitches. 25 hardstandings. Tent pitches. Motorhome pitches.

Notes Quiet at all times, charcoal BBQs must be off ground.

See advert on this page

VALE OF GLAMORGAN

LLANTWIT MAJOR
Map 3 SS96

Acorn Camping & Caravan Site *(SS973678)*

►►►

Ham Lane South CF61 1RP
☎ 01446 794024
e-mail: info@acorncamping.co.uk
dir: *B4265 to Llantwit Major, follow camping signs. Approach site through Ham Manor residential park*

PETS: Charges 75p per night **Public areas** except shop, games room, shower block & children's play area disp bin **Exercise area** adjacent **Facilities** food food bowl water bowl dog chews cat treats walks info vet info **Other** prior notice required disposal bags available

Open Feb-8 Dec Last arrival 21.00hrs Last departure 11.00hrs

A peaceful country site in level meadowland, with some individual pitches divided by hedges and shrubs. It is about one mile from the beach, which can be reached via a cliff top walk, and the same distance from the historic town of Llantwit Major. An internet station and a full-size snooker table are useful amenities. 5.5 acre site. 90 touring pitches. 10 hardstandings. Tent pitches. Motorhome pitches. 25 statics.

Notes No noise 23.00hrs-07.00hrs.

WALES

WREXHAM

EYTON
Map 7 SJ34

The Plassey Leisure Park *(SJ353452)*

►►►►►

The Plassey LL13 0SP
☎ 01978 780277 📠 01978 780019
e-mail: enquiries@plassey.com
dir: *From A483 at Bangor-on-Dee exit onto B5426 for 2.5m. Site entrance signed on left*

PETS: Charges £2 per night £14 per week **Public areas** except bars, restaurants & shops disp bin **Exercise area on site** 1-acre grounds, 2m of walks **Facilities** food food bowl water bowl dog chews cat treats litter tray scoop/disp bags walks info vet info **Stables** 2m **Other** prior notice required **Restrictions** no dangerous dogs (see page 7)

Open Feb-Nov Last arrival 20.30hrs Last departure noon

A lovely park set in several hundred acres of quiet farm and meadowland in the Dee Valley. The superb toilet facilities include individual cubicles for total privacy and security, while the Edwardian farm buildings have been converted into a restaurant, coffee shop, beauty studio, and various craft outlets. There is plenty here to entertain the whole family, from scenic walks and swimming pool to free fishing, and use of the 9-hole golf course. 10 acre site. 90 touring pitches. 45 hardstandings. 60 seasonal pitches. Tent pitches. Motorhome pitches. 15 statics.

Notes No footballs, bikes or skateboards.

LLANARMON DYFFRYN CEIRIOG
Map 7 SJ13

The Hand at Llanarmon

★★★★ ⊛ INN

LL20 7LD
☎ 01691 600666 📠 01691 600262
e-mail: reception@thehandhotel.co.uk
dir: *Exit A5 at Chirk onto B4500 signed Ceiriog Valley, 11m to inn*

PETS: Bedrooms (4 GF) country bedrooms only **Charges** £5 per night **Public areas** except restaurant on leads **Grounds** on leads disp bin **Exercise area** country lane adjacent **Facilities** water bowl washing facs dog grooming walks info vet info **On Request** fridge access towels **Stables** 2m **Other** prior notice required

Refurbished to a high standard, this owner managed inn provides a range of thoughtfully furnished bedrooms, with smart modern bathrooms. Public areas retain many original features including exposed beams and open fires. Imaginative food utilises the finest of local produce. A warm welcome and attentive service ensure a memorable guest experience.

Rooms 13 en suite (4 GF) **Facilities** tea/coffee Dinner available Direct Dial Cen ht Wi-fi Pool table **Parking** 19

West Arms

★★★★ ⊛ INN

LL20 7LD
☎ 01691 600665 & 600612 📠 01691 600622
e-mail: gowestarms@aol.com
dir: *Off A483/A5 at Chirk, take B4500 to Ceiriog Valley*

PETS: Bedrooms (3 GF) ground-floor bedrooms only **Sep accom** kennels with hay **Charges** £6 per night **Public areas** except restaurant on leads **Grounds** disp bin **Exercise area** 300yds **Facilities** water bowl bedding washing facs cage storage walks info vet info **On Request** fridge access torch towels **Stables** 4m **Other** charge for damage

Set in the beautiful Ceiriog Valley, this delightful 17th-century inn has a wealth of charm and character. There is a comfortable lounge, a room for private dining and two bars, as well as an elegant, award-winning restaurant offering a set-price menu of imaginative dishes, utilising quality local produce. The attractive bedrooms have a mixture of modern and period furnishings.

Rooms 15 en suite (2 fmly) (3 GF) **S** £53-£125; **D** £87-£225 **Facilities** FTV tea/coffee Dinner available Direct Dial Cen ht Wi-fi Fishing **Parking** 22

Ireland

NORTHERN IRELAND

CO ANTRIM

ANTRIM
Map 1 D5

Six Mile Water Caravan Park (J137870)
►►►

Lough Rd BT41 4DG
☎ 028 9446 4963 & 9446 3113
e-mail: sixmilewater@antrim.gov.uk
dir: *1m from town centre, follow Antrim Forum/Loughshore Park signs. On Dublin road take Lough road (pass Antrim Forum on right). Site at end of road on right*

PETS: Public areas except toilets, showers, TV room & games room on leads disp bin **Facilities** walks info vet info **Other** prior notice required dogs must be on leads at all times

Open Mar-Oct Last arrival 21.45hrs Last departure noon

A pretty tree-lined site in a large municipal park, within walking distance of Antrim and the Antrim Forum leisure complex yet very much in the countryside. The modern toilet block is well equipped, and other facilities include a laundry and electric hook-ups. Plots are generously spaced. 9.61 acre site. 67 touring pitches. 37 hardstandings. Tent pitches. Motorhome pitches.

Notes Max stay 14 nights, no noise between 22.00hrs-08.00hrs.

BALLYMONEY
Map 1 C6

Drumaheglis Marina & Caravan Park
(C901254)

►►►►►

36 Glenstall Rd BT53 7QN
☎ 028 2766 0280 & 2766 0227 ▤ 028 2766 0222
e-mail: drumaheglis@ballymoney.gov.uk
dir: *Signed off A26, approx 1.5m from Ballymoney towards Coleraine. Also accessed from B66, S of Ballymoney*

PETS: Public areas except play area disp bin **Facilities** vet info

Open 17 Mar-Oct Last arrival 20.00hrs Last departure 13.00hrs

Exceptionally well-designed and laid out park beside the Lower Bann River, with very spacious pitches and two quality toilet blocks. Ideal base for touring Antrim and for watersports enthusiasts. 16 acre site. 55 touring pitches. 55 hardstandings. 20 seasonal pitches. Tent pitches. Motorhome pitches.

BUSHMILLS
Map 1 C6

Ballyness Caravan Park (C944393)
►►►►►

40 Castlecatt Rd BT57 8TN
☎ 028 2073 2393 ▤ 028 2073 2713
e-mail: info@ballynesscaravanpark.com
dir: *0.5m S of Bushmills on B66, follow signs*

PETS: Public areas except amenity building disp bin **Exercise area on site** pathway around ponds **Exercise area** 1m **Facilities** dog chews cat treats washing facs walks info vet info **Other** disposal bags & pet toys available **Resident Pet:** Gyp (German Shepherd)

Open 17 Mar-Oct Last arrival 21.00hrs Last departure noon

A quality park with superb toilet and other facilities, on farmland beside St Columb's Rill, the stream that supplies the famous nearby Bushmills distillery. The friendly owners built this park with the discerning camper in mind, and they continue to improve it to ever higher standards. There is a pleasant walk around several ponds, and the park is peacefully located close to the beautiful north Antrim coast. 16 acre site. 48 touring pitches. 48 hardstandings. Motorhome pitches. 65 statics.

Notes No skateboards or roller blades.

LARNE
Map 1 D5

Derrin House
★★★★ GUEST ACCOMMODATION

2 Princes Gardens BT40 1RQ
☎ 028 2827 3269 ▤ 028 2827 3269
e-mail: info@derrinhouse.co.uk
dir: *Off A8 Harbour Highway onto A2 (coast route), 1st left after lights at Main St*

PETS: Bedrooms (2 GF) **Exercise area** 5 mins' walk **Facilities** cage storage walks info vet info

Just a short walk from the town centre, and a short drive from the harbour, this comfortable Victorian house offers a very friendly welcome. The bedrooms are gradually being refurbished to offer smartly presented modern facilities. Public areas are light and inviting, hearty breakfasts are offered in the stylish dining room.

Rooms 7 en suite (2 fmly) (2 GF) **S** £35-£40; **D** £55-£57 **Facilities** TVL tea/coffee Cen ht Wi-fi **Parking** 3 **Notes** LB

IRELAND

BELFAST

BELFAST — Map 1 D5

Malmaison Belfast

★★★ 83% HOTEL

34 - 38 Victoria St BT1 3GH

☎ 028 9022 0200 📠 028 9022 0220

e-mail: lsteele@malmaison.com

web: www.malmaison.com

dir: M1 along Westlink to Grosvenor Rd. Follow city centre signs. Pass City Hall on right, left onto Victoria St. Hotel on right

PETS: Bedrooms Charges Public areas except bar or brasserie on leads **Facilities** food bowl water bowl bedding vet info **Other** please contact hotel for charges

Situated in a former seed warehouse, this luxurious, contemporary hotel is ideally located for the city centre. Comfortable bedrooms, boast a host of modern facilities, whilst the deeply comfortable, stylish public areas include a popular bar lounge. The 'Home Grown and Local' menu in the brasserie showcases local seasonal ingredients. The warm hospitality is notable.

Rooms 64 (8 fmly) **S** £85-£160; **D** £95-£200* **Facilities** STV Gym Wi-fi **Services** Lift **Notes** LB

DUNDONALD — Map 1 D5

Dundonald Touring Caravan Park (J410731)

▶ ▶ ▶

111 Old Dundonald Rd BT16 1XT

☎ 028 9080 9123 & 9080 9129 📠 028 9048 9604

e-mail: sales@castlereagh.gov.uk

dir: From Belfast city centre follow M3 & A20 to City Airport. Then A20 to Newtownards & follow signs to Dundonald & Ulster Hospital. At hospital right at sign for Dundonald Ice Bowl. Follow to end, turn right. (Ice Bowl on left)

PETS: Public areas except shower & toilet block on leads disp bin **Exercise area** park (5 mins' walk) **Facilities** walks info vet info **Other** dogs must be kept on leads & under control at all times

Open 16 Mar-Oct rs Nov-Mar Aire de Service restricted to motorhomes Last arrival 23.00hrs Last departure noon

A purpose-built park in a quiet corner of Dundonald Leisure Park on the outskirts of Belfast. This peaceful park is ideally located for touring County Down and exploring the capital. In the winter it offers an 'Aire de Service' for motorhomes. 1.5 acre site. 22 touring pitches. 22 hardstandings. Tent pitches. Motorhome pitches.

Notes No commercial vehicles.

CO LONDONDERRY

AGHADOWEY — Map 1 C6

IRISH COUNTRY HOTELS

Brown Trout Golf & Country Inn

★★★ 71% HOTEL

209 Agivey Rd BT51 4AD

☎ 028 7086 8209 📠 028 7086 8878

e-mail: jane@browntroutinn.com

dir: At junct of A54 & B66 junct on road to Coleraine

PETS: Bedrooms Public areas except upstairs restaurant on leads **Grounds** disp bin **Exercise area** 60 acres of woodland **Facilities** scoop/disp bags leads walks info vet info **On Request** fridge access torch towels **Other** charge for damage **Resident Pets:** Muffin & Lucy (Chocolate Labradors)

Set alongside the Agivey River and featuring its own 9-hole golf course, this welcoming inn offers a choice of spacious accommodation. Comfortably furnished bedrooms are situated around a courtyard area whilst the cottage suites also have lounge areas. Home-cooked meals are served in the restaurant and lighter fare is available in the charming lounge bar which has entertainment at weekends.

Rooms 15 (11 fmly) (4 smoking) **S** £60-£70; **D** £70-£110 (incl. bkfst)* **Facilities** STV FTV ♨ 9 Putt green Fishing Gym Game fishing ♫ Xmas New Year Wi-fi **Parking** 80 **Notes** LB

LONDONDERRY — Map 1 C5

MANOR HOUSE

Beech Hill Country House Hotel

★★★ 79% COUNTRY HOUSE HOTEL

32 Ardmore Rd BT47 3QP

☎ 028 7134 9279 📠 028 7134 5366

e-mail: info@beech-hill.com

web: www.beech-hill.com

dir: From A6 (Londonderry to Belfast road) exit at Faughan Bridge. Hotel signed. 1m to Ardmore Chapel. Hotel entrance opposite

PETS: Bedrooms (12 GF) unattended ground-floor, standard bedrooms only **Public areas** except restaurant & lounge on leads **Grounds** disp bin **Facilities** walks info vet info **On Request** fridge access **Stables** 0.5m **Other** charge for damage dogs accepted by prior arrangement only; local kennels by prior arrangement

Dating back to 1729, Beech Hill is an impressive mansion, standing in 32 acres of glorious woodlands and gardens. Traditionally styled day rooms provide much comfort, and meals are served in the attractively extended dining room. The splendid bedroom wing provides spacious, well-equipped rooms in addition to the more classically designed bedrooms in the main house.

Rooms 27 (10 annexe) (4 fmly) (12 GF) **Facilities** FTV New Year Wi-fi **Services** Lift **Parking** 75 **Notes** Closed 24-25 Dec

IRELAND

CO TYRONE

DUNGANNON
Map 1 C5

Cohannon Inn & Auto Lodge
★★ 72% HOTEL

212 Ballynakilly Rd BT71 6HJ
☎ 028 8772 4488 📠 028 8775 2217
e-mail: info@cohannon.com
dir: *400yds from M1 junct 14*

PETS: Bedrooms (21 GF) **Exercise area** 50mtrs **Facilities** walks info vet info **Other** charge for damage

Handy for the M1 and the nearby towns of Dungannon and Portadown, this hotel offers well-maintained bedrooms, located behind the inn complex in a smart purpose-built wing. Public areas are smartly furnished and wide-ranging menus are served throughout the day.

Rooms 42 (20 fmly) (21 GF) (5 smoking) **S** fr £39.95; **D** fr £49.95* **Facilities** New Year **Parking** 160 **Notes** RS 25 Dec

Dungannon Park *(H805612)*
▶▶▶

Moy Rd BT71 6DY
☎ 028 8772 8690 📠 028 8772 9169
e-mail: dpreception@dungannon.gov.uk
dir: *M1 junct 15, A29, left at 2nd lights*

PETS: Public areas except play area & amenity buildings on leads disp bin **Exercise area on site Facilities** walks info vet info **Other** prior notice required no pet fouling on site; dogs must be kept under control at all times

Open Mar-Oct Last arrival 20.30hrs Last departure 14.00hrs

Modern caravan park in a quiet area of a public park with fishing lake and excellent facilities, especially for disabled visitors. 2 acre site. 20 touring pitches. 12 hardstandings. Tent pitches. Motorhome pitches.

REPUBLIC OF IRELAND

CO CORK

BALLYLICKEY
Map 1 B2

Sea View House Hotel
★★★ ◉◉ HOTEL

☎ 027 50073 & 50462 📠 027 51555
e-mail: info@seaviewhousehotel.com
web: www.seaviewhousehotel.com
dir: *5km from Bantry, 11km from Glengarriff on N71*

PETS: Bedrooms (5 GF) **Charges Public areas** on leads **Grounds** on leads disp bin **Exercise area** walks nearby **Facilities** cage storage walks info vet info **Other** charge for damage **Restrictions** small dogs only

Colourful gardens and glimpses of Bantry Bay through the mature trees frame this delightful country house. Owner Kathleen O'Sullivan's team of staff are exceptionally pleasant and there is a relaxed atmosphere in the cosy lounges. Guest comfort and good cuisine are the top priorities. Bedrooms are spacious and individually styled; some on the ground floor are appointed to suit less able guests.

Rooms 25 (3 fmly) (5 GF) **S** €75-€95; **D** €150-€170 (incl. bkfst)* **Parking** 32 **Notes** LB Closed mid Nov-mid Mar

BANDON
Map 1 B2

Glebe Country House
★★★★ BED AND BREAKFAST

Ballinadee
☎ 021 4778294 📠 021 4778456
e-mail: glebehse@indigo.ie
dir: *Off N71 at Innishannon Bridge signed Ballinadee, 8km along river bank, left after village sign*

PETS: Bedrooms Public areas Grounds disp bin **Facilities** food (pre-bookable) food bowl water bowl bedding dog chews cat treats feeding mat leads washing facs cage storage walks info vet info **On Request** fridge access torch towels **Stables** nearby **Resident Pets:** Shadow (Miniature Schnauzer), Fluffy & Ginger (cats)

IRELAND

Glebe Country House

Situated in the charming village of Ballinadee this lovely bed and breakfast stands in well-kept gardens, and is run with great attention to detail. Antique furnishings predominate throughout this comfortable house, which has an elegant, lounge and dining room. Bedrooms are spacious and well appointed; the ground-floor room has access to the lovely garden. There is an interesting breakfast menu featuring local and garden produce. A country-house style dinner is available by arrangement.

Rooms 4 en suite (2 fmly) **S** €50-€60; **D** €90-€100 **Facilities** TVL tea/coffee Dinner available Direct Dial Cen ht Wi-fi **Parking** 10 **Notes** Closed 21 Dec-3 Jan

---

BLARNEY Map 1 B2

Ashlee Lodge

★★★★★ GUEST HOUSE

Tower

☎ 021 4385346 📠 021 4385726

e-mail: info@ashleelodge.com

dir: *4km from Blarney on R617*

PETS: Bedrooms (6 GF) 1 ground-floor bedroom only **Grounds** on leads disp bin **Exercise area** 500mtrs **Facilities** walks info vet info **On Request** towels **Resident Pet:** Tammy (cat)

Ashlee Lodge is a purpose-built guest house, situated in the village of Tower, close to Blarney and local pubs and restaurants. Bedrooms are decorated with comfort and elegance in mind, some with whirlpool baths; one room has its own entrance. The extensive breakfast menu is memorable and includes home baking and quality local produce. Guests can unwind in the sauna or the outdoor hot tub. Transfers to the nearest airport and railway station can be arranged, and tee times can be booked at many of the nearby golf courses.

Rooms 10 en suite (2 fmly) (6 GF) **S** €65-€95; **D** €80-€140 **Facilities** STV FTV TVL tea/coffee Dinner available Direct Dial Cen ht Licensed Wi-fi Sauna **Parking** 12 **Notes** LB

CASTLEMARTYR Map 1 C2

Castlemartyr Resort

★★★★★ 88% ⊛ HOTEL

☎ 021 4219000 📠 021 4623359

e-mail: reception@castlemartyrresort.ie

dir: *N25, 3rd exit signed Rosslare. Continue past Carrigtwohill & Midleton exits. Right at lights in village*

PETS: Bedrooms (30 GF) unattended ground-floor bedrooms only **Charges** €50 per stay **Grounds** on leads **Exercise area** 250mtrs **Facilities** food (pre-bookable) food bowl water bowl bedding washing facs walks info vet info **Stables** 10 mins' drive **Other** charge for damage **Restrictions** max weight 70lb **Resident Pets:** Earl & Countess (Irish Setters)

Castlemartyr Resort is an impressively restored 18th-century property, where old world grandeur and contemporary styles marry well. The individually decorated bedrooms in the Manor House make luxurious retreats, while the modern wing rooms are furnished in a more contemporary style. The hotel offers fine dining in the Bell Tower Restaurant and more casual eating in Knights Bar and the Clubhouse. The estate grounds offer a myriad of outdoor pursuits including golf on the Ron Kirby designed inland links style course, cycling, boating on the lake, and walking or jogging along the nature trails. There is also a stunning spa facility.

Rooms 109 (98 annexe) (6 fmly) (30 GF) **S** €205-€285; **D** €220-€295 (incl. bkfst)* **Facilities** Spa STV FTV ⊛ supervised ♨ 18 ⛳ Gym Bicycles Horse & carriage rides Target archery Clay pigeon shooting ♫ New Year Wi-fi **Services** Lift Air con **Parking** 200 **Notes** LB Closed 16-27 Dec

---

KINSALE Map 1 B2

Friar's Lodge

★★★★★ GUEST HOUSE

5 Friars St

☎ 086 2895075 & 021 4777384 📠 021 4774363

e-mail: mtierney@indigo.ie

dir: *In town centre next to parish church*

PETS: Bedrooms (4 GF) unattended **Exercise area** nearby **Facilities** walks info vet info **On Request** fridge access towels **Stables** nearby **Other** charge for damage

This new, purpose-built property near the Friary, has been developed with every comfort in mind. Bedrooms are particularly spacious. Located on a quiet street just a short walk from the town centre, with secure parking to the rear. A very good choice is offered from the breakfast menu.

Rooms 18 en suite (2 fmly) (4 GF) **Facilities** STV tea/coffee Direct Dial Cen ht Lift Wi-fi **Parking** 20 **Notes** Closed Xmas ⊛

IRELAND

SHANAGARRY   Map 1 C2

Ballymaloe House

★ ★ ★ ★ ★ ★ GUEST HOUSE
☎ 021 4652531 ▤ 021 4652021
e-mail: res@ballymaloe.ie
dir: *From N25 take R630 at Midleton rdbt. After 0.5m, left onto R631 to Cloyne. 2m beyond Cloyne on Ballycotton Rd*

PETS: Bedrooms (3 GF) bedrooms with porches only **Grounds** disp bin **Exercise area** nearby **Facilities** food bowl water bowl bedding dog walking cage storage walks info vet info **On Request** fridge access torch towels **Stables** 1m **Other** charge for damage **Restrictions** no dangerous dogs (see page 7) **Resident Pets:** Tommy & Flicker (dogs)

This charming country house is on a 400-acre farm, part of the Geraldine estate in east Cork. Bedrooms upstairs in the main house retain many original features, and the ground floor and courtyard rooms have garden patios. The relaxing drawing room and dining rooms have enchanting old-world charm. Ballymaloe is renowned for excellent meals, many of which are created using ingredients produced on the farm. There are a craft shop, café, tennis and small golf course on the estate.

Rooms 21 en suite 9 annexe en suite (2 fmly) (3 GF) **S** €85-€110; **D** €170-€250 **Facilities** TVL Dinner available Direct Dial Cen ht Licensed Wi-fi ⚄ ⚇ ⚈ Golf 9 ⚓ Fishing **Parking** 50 **Notes** LB Closed 23-26 Dec, 8-28 Jan

CO DONEGAL

DONEGAL   Map 1 B5

Harvey's Point Country Hotel

★ ★ ★ ★ 87% HOTEL
Lough Eske
☎ 074 9722208 ▤ 074 9722352
e-mail: sales@harveyspoint.com
web: www.harveyspoint.com
dir: *N56 from Donegal, then 1st right (Loch Eske/Harvey's Point)*

PETS: Bedrooms (34 GF) unattended courtyard bedrooms only **Public areas** except restaurant, bar & lounge on leads **Grounds** disp bin **Exercise area** private woods (100mtrs) **Facilities** pet sitting cage storage walks info vet info **On Request** fridge access torch **Stables Resident Pets:** Paddy (Labrador), geese, swans

Situated by the lake shore, this hotel is an oasis of relaxation; comfort and attentive guest care are the norm here. A range of particularly spacious suites and bedrooms is available, together with smaller rooms in the courtyard annexe. The kitchen brigade maintains consistently high standards in The Restaurant, with less formal dining in The Steakhouse at peak periods. A very popular Sunday buffet lunch is served weekly, with dinner entertainment on selected dates.

Rooms 70 (34 GF) **Facilities** Treatment rooms Pitch 'n' putt Bicycle hire Walking tours ♫ Xmas New Year Wi-fi **Services** Lift **Parking** 300 **Notes** LB Closed Mon & Tue Nov-Mar

Ard Na Breatha

★ ★ ★ ★ ▦ GUEST HOUSE
Drumrooske Middle
☎ 074 972 2288 & 086 842 1330 ▤ 074 974 0720
e-mail: info@ardnabreatha.com
web: www.ardnabreatha.com
dir: *From town centre onto Killybegs road, 2nd right continue to mini rdbt, sharp right at XL shop*

PETS: Bedrooms (3 GF) **Grounds** on leads disp bin **Exercise area** country road from house to forest **Facilities** walks info vet info **On Request** towels **Resident Pets:** 1 Labrador, 1 horse

This family-run guest house is just a short drive from the town centre. Bedrooms are all well-appointed and very comfortable, with a relaxing lounge for residents. Evening meals are served in the popular restaurant at weekends and during high season, but can be arranged for residents at other times. The menu features much of the produce from the family farm which surrounds the house.

Rooms 6 en suite (1 fmly) (3 GF) **S** €50-€69; **D** €70-€110 **Facilities** TVL tea/coffee Dinner available Direct Dial Cen ht Licensed Golf 0 **Parking** 16 **Notes** LB Closed Nov-Jan

DUNKINEELY   Map 1 B5

Castle Murray House and Restaurant

★ ★ ★ ★ RESTAURANT WITH ROOMS
St Johns Point
☎ 074 973 7022 ▤ 074 973 7330
e-mail: info@castlemurray.com
dir: *From Donegal take N56 towards Killybegs. Left to Dunkineely*

PETS: Bedrooms certain bedrooms only (check when booking) **Public areas** lounge area until 6pm on leads **Grounds** **Exercise area** small beach (1 min), large beach (6km) **Facilities** cage storage walks info vet info **On Request** fridge access torch **Other** charge for damage only 1 dog per bedroom; owners must provide dog's own basket or bed **Restrictions** small dogs only

Situated on the coast road of St Johns Point, this charming family-run restaurant with rooms overlooks McSwynes Bay and the castle. The bedrooms are individually decorated and appointed with guest comfort very much in mind, as is the cosy bar and sun lounge. There is a strong French influence in the cooking; locally landed fish, and prime lamb and beef are featured on the menus. Closed dates are subject to change, please telephone for details.

Rooms 10 en suite (2 fmly) **S** €50-€65; **D** €80-€110 **Facilities** FTV tea/coffee Dinner available Direct Dial Cen ht Wi-fi **Parking** 40 **Notes** LB RS Wknds Oct-Mar, 5 days May, Jun & Sep

PORTNOO
Map 1 B5

Boyle's Caravan Park *(G702990)*
►►

☎ 074 9545131 & 086 8523131 ▤ 074 9545130
e-mail: pboylecaravans@gmail.com
dir: *Exit N56 at Ardra onto R261 for 6m. Follow signs for Santa Anna Drive*

PETS: Public areas dogs must be kept on leads at all times; owners must clear up after their pets disp bin **Exercise area** nearby **Facilities** food bowl water bowl washing facs walks info vet info **Restrictions** no Dobermans, Alsatians, Bull Terriers or similar breeds

Open 18 Mar-Oct Last arrival 23.00hrs Last departure 11.00hrs

Set at Narin Beach and close to a huge selection of water activities on a magnificent stretch of the Atlantic. This open park nestles among the sand dunes, and offers well-maintained facilities. 1.5 acre site. 20 touring pitches. Tent pitches. Motorhome pitches. 80 statics.

Notes No skateboards. 🖾

RATHMULLAN
Map 1 C6

Rathmullan House
★★★★ 79% ◉◉ COUNTRY HOUSE HOTEL
☎ 074 9158188 ▤ 074 9158200
e-mail: info@rathmullanhouse.com
dir: *From Letterkenny, then Ramelton then Rathmullan, R243. Left at Mace shop, through village, hotel gates on right*

PETS: Bedrooms (9 GF) unattended 'doggie' room adjoining guests' own bedroom **Charges** contact hotel for details **Grounds** on leads disp bin **Exercise area** 500yds **Facilities** food (pre-bookable) food bowl water bowl bedding dog chews scoop/disp bags cage storage walks info vet info **On Request** fridge access torch towels **Stables** 500yds **Restrictions** max height 80cm; no Pit Bull Terriers **Resident Pets:** Suzy (Golden Retriever), Brushie & Odie (Jack Russells)

Dating from the 18th-century, this fine property has been operating as a country-house hotel for the last 40 years or so under the stewardship of the Wheeler family. Guests are welcome to wander around the well-planted grounds and the walled garden, from where much of the ingredients for the Weeping Elm Restaurant's menus are grown. The many lounges are relaxing and comfortable, while many of the bedrooms benefit from balconies and patio areas.

Rooms 34 (4 fmly) (9 GF) **S** €93.50-€148.50; **D** €187-€297 (incl. bkfst) **Facilities** Spa ◔ ◔ ◡ New Year Wi-fi Child facilities **Parking** 80 **Notes** LB Closed 11 Jan-5 Feb RS 15 Nov-12 Mar

DUBLIN
Map 1 D4

Glenshandan Lodge
★★★★ GUEST ACCOMMODATION
Dublin Rd, Swords
☎ 01 8408838 & 08765 92114 ▤ 01 8408838
e-mail: glenshandan@eircom.net
dir: *Beside Topaz on airport side of Swords Main St*

PETS: Bedrooms (5 GF) sign certain bedrooms only
Public areas Grounds disp bin **Exercise area** 100mtrs
Facilities food (pre-bookable) food bowl water bowl bedding
scoop/disp bags leads pet sitting dog walking washing facs
cage storage walks info vet info **On Request** fridge access
torch towels **Stables** 1m **Resident Pets:** Ali & Millie (Boxers)

Glenshandan Lodge is a family and dog-friendly house with hospitable owners and good facilities including e-mail access. Bedrooms are comfortable and one room has easier access. Secure parking available. Close to pubs, restaurants, golf, airport and the Kennel Club.

Rooms 9 en suite (5 fmly) (5 GF) **S** €25-€40; **D** €45-€60
Facilities FTV TVL tea/coffee Cen ht Wi-fi Golf 36 **Parking** 10
Notes LB Closed Xmas & New Year

LUCAN
Map 1 D4

Finnstown Country House Hotel
★★★ 79% ◉ HOTEL
Newcastle Rd
☎ 01 6010700 & 6010708 ▤ 01 6281088
e-mail: edwina@finnstown-hotel.ie
dir: *From M1 onto M50 S'bound. 1st exit for N4. Take slip road signed Newcastle/Adamstown. Straight on at rdbt, through lights, hotel on right*

PETS: Bedrooms (9 GF) unattended **Charges** €20 per stay
Grounds on leads disp bin **Exercise area** nearby **Facilities** washing facs cage storage walks info vet info **On Request** fridge access towels **Stables** 15 mins **Other** charge for damage **Resident Pets:** peacocks

Set in 45 acres of wooded grounds, Finnstown is a calm and peaceful country house in an urban setting. The elegant bar and drawing room is where informal meals are served throughout the day, with more formal dining at lunch and dinner in the restaurant. There is a wide choice of bedroom styles, situated both in the main house and in the annexes. All staff are very guest focussed.

Rooms 81 (54 annexe) (6 fmly) (9 GF) (17 smoking) **S** €60-€190; **D** €60-€250 (incl. bkfst) **Facilities** STV ◔ ◔ Gym Turkish bath 🎵 New Year Wi-fi **Services** Lift Air con **Parking** 300 **Notes** LB Closed 24-26 Dec

IRELAND

CO GALWAY

BARNA
Map 1 B3

The Twelve
★★★★ 79% ☺ HOTEL

Barna Village
☎ 091 597000 📄 091 597003
e-mail: enquire@thetwelvehotel.ie
dir: On outskirts of Barna

PETS: Bedrooms unattended sign two suites (with sitting rooms) only **Charges** £35 per night **Public areas** except restaurant & lounge on leads **Grounds** on leads disp bin **Exercise area** beaches & walks (200mtrs) **Facilities** food bowl water bowl dog chews cat treats feeding mat scoop/disp bags leads pet sitting dog walking washing facs dog grooming cage storage walks info vet info **On Request** fridge access torch towels **Other** charge for damage welcome gift; one dog per bedroom **Restrictions** max height 36"; no Boxers or Dobermans

Located just ten minutes west of Galway city, this hotel looks as if it has been on the site for decades. However, once inside the decor is striking and contemporary. The bedrooms come in a number of different sizes, but all are furnished with taste and with guest comfort in mind. The Pins is a vibrant and popular bar and bistro where food is served throughout the day. West Restaurant opens during the evening, and features fine dining from a well-compiled menu of local and seasonal produce. Le Petit Spa offers treatments based on seaweed products.

Rooms 47 (12 fmly) **S** €90-€145; **D** €100-€155 (incl. bkfst)*
Facilities Spa STV FTV Children's cookery programme ♫ Xmas New Year Wi-fi Child facilities **Services** Lift Air con **Parking** 140 **Notes** LB RS 22-27 Dec

CASHEL
Map 1 A4

Cashel House
★★★ ☺☺ COUNTRY HOUSE HOTEL

☎ 095 31001 📄 095 31077
e-mail: res@cashel-house-hotel.com
web: www.cashel-house-hotel.com
dir: S off N59, 1.5km W of Recess, well signed

PETS: Bedrooms (6 GF) unattended **Sep accom** 2 stables suitable for bigger dogs & gun dogs **Charges** horse €20 per night **Grounds** on leads disp bin **Exercise area** nearby **Facilities** food (pre-bookable) food bowl water bowl washing facs cage storage walks info vet info **On Request** fridge access torch towels **Stables Other** charge for damage **Resident Pets:** 1 Jack Russell, cats, horses

Cashel House is a mid-19th century property, standing at the head of Cashel Bay in the heart of Connemara, and set amidst secluded, award-winning gardens with woodland walks. Attentive service comes with the perfect balance of friendliness and professionalism from McEvilly family and their staff. The comfortable lounges have turf fires and antique furnishings. The restaurant offers local produce such as the famous Connemara lamb, and fish from the nearby coast.

Rooms 29 (4 fmly) (6 GF) (4 smoking) **Facilities** STV FTV Garden school Xmas New Year Wi-fi **Parking** 40

GALWAY
Map 1 B3

Ardilaun Hotel & Leisure Club
★★★★ 81% ☺ HOTEL

Taylor's Hill
☎ 091 521433 📄 091 521546
e-mail: info@theardilaunhotel.ie
web: www.theardilaunhotel.ie
dir: M6 to Galway City West, then follow signs for N59 Clifden, then N6 towards Salthill

PETS: Bedrooms (8 GF) ground-floor bedrooms adjoining garden only **Charges** €15 per night **Public areas** lobby only on leads **Grounds** on leads disp bin **Exercise area** nearby **Facilities** food bowl water bowl bedding dog chews walks info vet info **On Request** fridge access towels

This very smart country-house style hotel, appointed to a high standard, is located on the outskirts of the city near Salthill and has lovely landscaped gardens. The bedrooms have been thoughtfully appointed and the deluxe rooms and suites are particularly spacious. Public areas include a selection of comfortable lounges, the Camilaun Restaurant that overlooks the garden, Blazers bistro and bar, and extensive banqueting and leisure facilities.

Rooms 125 (17 fmly) (8 GF) (16 smoking) **Facilities** Spa STV ☺ supervised Gym Treatment & analysis rooms Beauty salon Spinning-cycle room ♫ New Year Wi-fi **Services** Lift **Parking** 380 **Notes** LB Closed 24-26 Dec RS Closed pm 23 Dec

RECESS
Map 1 A4

Lough Inagh Lodge
★★★ ◉ COUNTRY HOUSE HOTEL

Inagh Valley
☎ 095 34706 & 34694   📄 095 34708
e-mail: inagh@iol.ie
dir: *From Recess take R344 towards Kylemore*

PETS: Bedrooms (4 GF) unattended **Public areas** except at food service **Grounds** on leads **Exercise area** countryside walks nearby **Facilities** food bowl water bowl bedding dog chews walks info vet info **On Request** fridge access torch towels **Other** please phone for further details of pet facilities **Resident Pets:** Sophie (Mixed Terrier), Sasha (cat)

Dating from 1880, this former fishing lodge is akin to a family home, where guests are encouraged to relax and enjoy the peace. Overlooking Lough Inagh, and situated amid the mountains of Connemara, it is in an ideal location for those who enjoy walking and fishing. Bedrooms are individually decorated, some with spacious seating areas, and each is dedicated to an Irish literary figure. There are two cosy lounges where welcoming turf fires are often lit. Informal dining from a bar menu is available during the day. Dinner is a highlight of a visit to the lodge; the menus feature locally sourced produce cooked with care - seafood is a speciality.

Rooms 13 (1 fmly) (4 GF) **Facilities** Hill walking Fly fishing Cycling **Services** Air con **Parking** 16 **Notes** Closed mid Dec-mid Mar

CO KERRY

CASTLEGREGORY
Map 1 A2

Griffin's Palm Beach Country House *(Q525085)*
★★★ FARMHOUSE

Goulane, Conor Pass Rd
☎ 066 7139147 & 0872 111901   Mrs C Griffin
e-mail: griffinspalmbeach@eircom.net
dir: *1.5km from Stradbally*

PETS: Bedrooms (1 GF) unattended sign ground-floor bedroom only **Charges** €5 per night €35 per week **Public areas** except dining room & lounge **Grounds** on leads disp bin **Exercise area** beach 0.5m **Facilities** water bowl scoop/disp bags leads washing facs cage storage walks info **On Request** fridge access torch towels **Other** charge for damage **Resident Pets:** Daisy (Jack Russell), Scott (Sheepdog)

This farmhouse is a good base for exploring the Dingle Peninsula and unspoiled beaches. The comfortable bedrooms have fine views over Brandon Bay, and the delightful garden can be enjoyed from the dining room and sitting room. Mrs Griffin offers a warm welcome and her home baking is a feature on the breakfast menu.

Rooms 6 en suite (3 fmly) (1 GF) **S** €40-€45; **D** €70-€80 **Facilities** FTV TVL tea/coffee Cen ht Golf 9 **Parking** 10 **Notes** LB Closed Nov-Feb 150 acres mixed/arable/sheep

IRELAND

KENMARE — Map 1 B2

Sheen Falls Lodge

★★★★★ ◉◉ COUNTRY HOUSE HOTEL
☎ 06466 41600 🖹 06466 41386
e-mail: info@sheenfallslodge.ie
dir: *From Kenmare take N71 to Glengarriff over suspension bridge, take 1st left*

PETS: (14 GF) **Sep accom** 2 large pens barn & stables **Public areas** patio areas only on leads disp bin **Exercise area** beach (15km) **Facilities** food bowl water bowl bedding dog grooming cage storage walks info vet info **On Request** fridge access torch towels **Stables**

This former fishing lodge has been developed into a beautiful hotel with a friendly team of professional staff. The cascading Sheen Falls are floodlit at night, forming a romantic backdrop to the enjoyment of award-winning cuisine in La Cascade Restaurant. Less formal dining is available in Oscar's Bistro, and the Sun Lounge serves refreshments and light snacks throughout the day. The bedrooms are very comfortably appointed; many of the suites are particularly spacious. The leisure centre and beauty therapy facilities offer a number of exclusive treatments, and outdoor pursuits include walking, fishing, tennis, horse riding and clay pigeon shooting.

Rooms 66 (14 fmly) (14 GF) **S** €310-€455; **D** €310-€455* **Facilities** Spa STV ⊗ supervised ⌘ Fishing ⌘ Gym Table tennis Steam room Clay pigeon shooting Cycling Vintage car rides Library ♫ Xmas New Year Wi-fi **Services** Lift **Parking** 76 **Notes** LB ⊗ Closed 2 Jan-1 Feb RS Midwk in Feb, Mar, Nov & Dec

KILLARNEY — Map 1 B2

Fairview

★★★★★ 🛏 GUEST HOUSE
College St
☎ 064 6634164 🖹 064 6671777
e-mail: info@fairviewkillarney.com
dir: *In town centre off College St*

PETS: Bedrooms (1 GF) **Public areas** on leads disp bin **Exercise area** 1km **Facilities** bedding cage storage walks info vet info **On Request** fridge access towels **Stables** 3km **Other** charge for damage

This smart guest house is situated in the town centre and close to the bus/railway station. Great attention to detail has been taken in the furnishing and design of bedrooms to ensure guest comfort including some with air conditioning and jacuzzi baths. There is a lift to all floors and the impressive penthouse suite enjoys views of the mountains. There is a relaxing guest sitting room and the breakfast menu offers a selection of dishes cooked to order. Local activities include lake cruises, Killarney National Park and championship golf courses.

Rooms 29 en suite (1 GF) (2 smoking) **Facilities** STV TVL tea/coffee Dinner available Direct Dial Cen ht Lift Licensed Wi-fi **Parking** 11

CO KILDARE

ATHY — Map 1 C3

Coursetown Country House

★★★★★ BED AND BREAKFAST
Stradbally Rd
☎ 059 8631101 🖹 059 8632740
dir: *M7 onto M9, exit at Ballitore onto N78 to Athy, take R428*

PETS: Sep accom kennel suitable for large dog **Public areas** on leads **Grounds** on leads **Exercise area** nearby **Facilities** food bowl water bowl washing facs cage storage vet info **On Request** fridge access towels **Stables** 6m **Other** charge for damage **Restrictions** small dogs allowed in bedrooms; large dogs must stay in kennel **Resident Pets:** Leopold & Ophelia (cats)

This charming Victorian country house stands on a 100-hectare tillage farm and bird sanctuary. It has been extensively refurbished, and all bedrooms are furnished to the highest standards. Convalescent or disabled guests are especially welcome, and Iris and Jim Fox are happy to share their knowledge of the Irish countryside and its wildlife.

Rooms 5 en suite (1 GF) **S** €65-€85; **D** €90-€130 **Facilities** TVL tea/coffee Direct Dial Cen ht **Parking** 22 **Notes** No Children 12yrs Closed 15 Nov-15 Mar

CO MAYO

BALLINA — Map 1 B4

The Ice House

★★★★ 79% ◉◉ HOTEL
The Quay
☎ 096 23500 🖹 096 23598
e-mail: chill@theicehouse.ie
dir: *On Sligo road turn right at Judge's Garage into Riverside Estate. Right at T-junct into Quay Rd. Hotel on left*

PETS: Bedrooms (10 GF) unattended sign ground-floor bedrooms only **Public areas** except eating areas on leads **Exercise area** riverside walk **Facilities** food food bowl water bowl bedding dog chews cat treats feeding mat litter tray pet sitting dog walking cage storage walks info vet info **On Request** fridge access torch towels **Other** charge for damage **Restrictions** small dogs only

With a fascinating history, this property, a mile or so from the town centre, is a stunning mix of old and new. The contemporary decor features lots of wood, steel and glass creating a very light and airy interior, contrasted with a Victorian features and furnishing in the original house. The stylish bedrooms include suites that have river views from their balconies. An interesting menu is offered at dinner in the vaulted Pier Restaurant, once the ice store for the Moy fishery, with lighter fare offered during the day in the bright riverside bar.

Rooms 32 (7 fmly) (10 GF) **Facilities** Spa STV Laconium Steam room New Year Wi-fi **Services** Lift **Parking** 32 **Notes** Closed 25-26 Dec

IRELAND

KNOCK
Map 1 B4

Knock Caravan and Camping Park *(M408828)*

▶▶▶

Claremorris Rd
☎ 094 9388100   🖨 094 9388295
e-mail: caravanpark@knock-shrine.ie
dir: *From rdbt in Knock, through town. Site entrance on left 1km, opposite petrol station*

PETS: Public areas on leads **Exercise area** 200mtrs **Facilities** walks info vet info **Other** prior notice required **Restrictions** no Bull Terrier breeds, Bull Mastiffs, Dobermans, Alsatians, Rottweilers, Rhodesian Ridgebacks or any breed listed under Republic of Ireland's Control of Dogs Act (see page 7)

Open Mar-Nov Last arrival 22.00hrs Last departure noon

A pleasant, very well maintained caravan park within the grounds of Knock Shrine, offering spacious terraced pitches and excellent facilities. 10 acre site. 88 touring pitches. 88 hardstandings. Tent pitches. Motorhome pitches. 12 statics.

CO MONAGHAN

GLASLOUGH
Map 1 C5

The Lodge at Castle Leslie Estate
★★★★ 78% HOTEL
☎ 047 88100   🖨 047 88256
e-mail: info@castleleslie.com
dir: *M1 junct 14, N2 to Monaghan, N12 to N185 to Glaslough*

PETS: (10 GF) **Sep accom** stable in equestrian centre **Charges** horse/pony £30 per night horse/pony £110 per week **Grounds** on leads disp bin **Exercise area Facilities** food bowl water bowl washing facs cage storage walks info vet info **On Request** fridge access torch towels **Stables Other** charge for damage **Restrictions** no dogs listed under Republic of Ireland's Control of Dogs Regulations 1998 **Resident Pets:** 30 horses

Set in 1,000 acres of rolling countryside, the lodge is part of the Castle Leslie Estate which has been in the Leslie family since the 1660s. Bedrooms are in both the original hunting lodge and the converted stable block. Resident guests have two dining options including the fine dining restaurant in the castle. With a successful equestrian centre and a private fishing lake, this is an ideal location for those who enjoy country pursuits.

Rooms 29 (5 fmly) (10 GF) **S** €125-€150; **D** €180-€240 (incl. bkfst) **Facilities** Spa STV FTV Fishing Equestrian centre Wi-fi **Services** Lift **Parking** 100 **Notes** LB Closed 22-28 Dec RS Oct-1 Apr

CO ROSCOMMON

BOYLE
Map 1 B4

Lough Key Caravan & Camping Park
(G846039)

▶▶▶

Lough Key Forest Park
☎ 071 9662212   🖨 071 9673140
e-mail: info@loughkey.ie
dir: *Site 3km E of Boyle on N4. Follow Lough Key Forest Park signs, site within grounds. Approx 0.5km from entrance*

PETS: Public areas Exercise area on site **Exercise area** walks & trails in forest park **Facilities** walks info vet info **Other** prior notice required

Open Apr-20 Sep Last arrival 18.00hrs Last departure noon

Peaceful and very secluded site within the extensive grounds of a beautiful forest park. Lough Key offers boat trips and waterside walks, and there is a viewing tower. 15 acre site. 72 touring pitches. 92 hardstandings. Tent pitches. Motorhome pitches.

Notes 🐾

CO SLIGO

GRANGE
Map 1

Rowanville Lodge
★★★★ BED AND BREAKFAST
Moneygold
☎ 071 9163958   🖨 353 71 9163958
e-mail: rowanville@hotmail.com
dir: *On N15, 1km N of Grange village*

PETS: Sep accom kennels barn on leads **Grounds** disp bin **Exercise area Facilities** food (pre-bookable) food bowl water bowl bedding dog chews pet sitting dog walking washing facs cage storage walks info vet info **On Request** fridge access torch towels **Stables Resident Pets:** 1 Golden Retriever cross, 1 Cavalier King Charles Spaniel

This smart bed and breakfast is just five minutes from the town centre. It is part of Manor West retail park which has many shopping opportunities. Spacious well-appointed bedrooms are matched by comfortable public areas, including the Bar and Bistro where food is served throughout the day, with fine dining available in the Walnut Room. There is a high spec Leisure Club, and a variety of treatments are offered in the Harmony Wellness suites. A range of meeting and banqueting rooms are also available.

Rooms 4 en suite (4 fmly) (2 GF) **S** €40; **D** €60-€75 **Facilities** STV FTV TVL tea/coffee Dinner available Cen ht Wi-fi Golf 18 **Parking** 9 **Notes** LB Closed 20-27 Dec

IRELAND

CO TIPPERARY

NENAGH
Map 1 B3

Ashley Park House

★★★★ BED AND BREAKFAST

☎ 067 38223 & 38013 ▤ 067 38013
e-mail: margaret@ashleypark.com
web: www.ashleypark.com
dir: *6.5km N of Nenagh. Off N52 across lake, signed on left & left under arch*

PETS: Bedrooms unattended **Sep accom Charges** horse €20 per night horse €110 per week **Public areas Grounds** disp bin **Exercise area** adjacent **Facilities** food bowl water bowl pet sitting dog walking washing facs cage storage walks info vet info **On Request** fridge access torch towels **Stables** Resident Pets: horses, ducks, peacocks, hens, lambs in spring

This attractive, colonial style farmhouse was built in 1770. Set in gardens that run down to Lake Ourna, it has spacious bedrooms with quality antique furnishings. Breakfast is served in the dining room overlooking the lake, and dinner is available by prior arrangement. There is a delightful walled garden, and a boat for fishing on the lake is available.

Rooms 5 en suite (3 fmly) **Facilities** TVL tea/coffee Dinner available Cen ht Licensed Wi-fi Golf 18 Fishing **Parking** 30 **Notes** LB

CO WATERFORD

ARDMORE
Map 1 C2

Cliff House

★★★★ 82% ◉◉◉ HOTEL

☎ 024 87800 & 87801 ▤ 024 87820
e-mail: info@thecliffhousehotel.com
dir: *From Dungarvan: N25, signed Cork. Left onto R673. From Youghal: N25 signed Waterford. Right onto R673 signed Ardmore. In Ardmore take Middle Rd to hotel*

PETS: Sep accom kennel & dog run **Public areas** only on outdoor terrace on leads **Grounds** on leads disp bin **Exercise area** 100mtrs **Facilities** water bowl cage storage walks info vet info **On Request** fridge access torch towels **Stables** 5km

This is a unique property that is virtually sculpted into the cliff face overlooking Ardmore Bay, just a few minutes' walk from the village. Most of the individually designed bedroom suites and the public rooms enjoy the same great views, as do the relaxing leisure and spa facilities. Dinner in the award-winning House Restaurant is a particular highlight of any visit here; the menu features seasonal and local produce that are cooked with flair.

Rooms 39 (8 fmly) (7 GF) **Facilities** Spa STV FTV ☒ Fishing Gym Sauna Steam room Relaxation room Outdoor pursuits New Year Wi-fi **Services** Lift Air con **Parking** 52 **Notes** LB Closed 2 wks in Jan

CO WEXFORD

CAMPILE
Map 1 C2

Kilmokea Country Manor & Gardens

★★★★★ ▦ GUEST ACCOMMODATION

Great Island
☎ 051 388109 ▤ 051 388776
e-mail: stay@kilmokea.com
dir: *R733 from New Ross to Campile, right before village for Great Island & Kilmokea Gardens*

PETS: Bedrooms (2 GF) unattended sign ground-floor bedrooms in courtyard suite only **Sep accom** kennels in courtyard barns & stables **Public areas** except restaurant, lounge & conservatory on leads **Grounds** on leads disp bin **Exercise area** orchard & fields **Facilities** food (pre-bookable) food bowl water bowl bedding dog chews cat treats feeding mat litter tray scoop/disp bags leads pet sitting dog walking washing facs cage storage walks info vet info **On Request** fridge access torch towels **Stables Other** charge for damage small charges apply to some pet facilities Resident Pets: Jasmine (Labrador), Rosa (Springer Spaniel), Mojo (dwarf hamster), Jackie (horse), chickens, peacocks, ducks, goldfish

This fine property is an 18th-century former rectory, lovingly restored to its original glory by the hospitable Emma Hewlett

IRELAND

and her husband Mark. It is located in wooded and beautifully landscaped gardens that are in themselves a popular visitor attraction. The bedrooms are richly furnished in a mix of styles, but all have particularly comfortable beds. The drawing and reading rooms all retain the style and proportions of the era, with an honesty bar for those tempted to have a night-cap. Dinner is available by prior arrangement, served in what was the original dining room of the house, or in summer, in the conservatory. This is where a hearty and delicious breakfast is also served. Recent additions in the grounds include a swimming pool and an aromatherapy treatment service.

Rooms 4 en suite 2 annexe en suite (1 fmly) (2 GF) **S** fr €75; **D** €160-€300 **Facilities** STV TVL tea/coffee Dinner available Direct Dial Cen ht Licensed Wi-fi ⓣ ⓢ ⤸ Fishing Riding Sauna Gym **Parking** 23 **Notes** LB RS Nov-end Jan

CO WICKLOW

AUGHRIM
Map 1 D3

Clone House
★★★★ BED AND BREAKFAST
☎ 0402 36121 & 087 2517587
e-mail: stay@clonehouse.com
dir: *N11 from Dublin to Ashford, right at Texaco station signed Glenealy, right signed Rathdrum, to Aughrim, 2m S to house*

PETS: Public areas except dining room & lounge **Grounds** disp bin **Exercise area** 5km **Facilities** food bowl water bowl litter tray scoop/disp bags washing facs cage storage vet info **On Request** fridge access torch towels **Stables** 10km Resident **Pet:** Felix (cat)

Clone House dates from the 16th and 17th centuries, and is located between Arklow and Aughrim. The house has been refurbished with care and attention by Liam, who has created a truly comfortable retreat. There is a drawing room, library, parlour and dining room for guest use, each with open log fireplaces and a wonderful range of Irish art and literature to enjoy. The bedrooms have been beautifully decorated and furnished with guest comfort in mind; Aine is responsible for the home baking, and the delicious dinners which are available by prior arrangement.

Rooms 4 en suite **Facilities** TVL Dinner available Cen ht Wi-fi Golf 18 Fishing Riding **Parking** 10

ENNISKERRY
Map 1 D3

The Ritz Carlton Powerscourt
★★★★★ 86% ⚙⚙ HOTEL
Powerscourt Estate
☎ 01 2748888   📠 01 2749999
e-mail: powerscourtreservations@ritzcarlton.com
dir: *From Dublin take M50, M11, then N11, follow Enniskerry signs. In Enniskerry left up hill, hotel on right*

PETS: Bedrooms (39 GF) unattended sign **Charges** £50 per night **Grounds** on leads disp bin **Exercise area** nearby **Facilities** food (pre-bookable) food bowl water bowl bedding dog chews cat treats litter tray cage storage walks info vet info **On Request** torch towels **Restrictions** max weight 10kg

This very stylish hotel, built in the Palladian style, has a tranquil setting with stunning views over the gardens and woodlands to the Sugar Loaf. The bedrooms and suites are particularly spacious and well appointed with very impressive bathrooms that have TVs, deep tubs and walk-in showers. The luxuriously appointed public areas are airy and spacious with a variety of food options that includes the Gordon Ramsay at Powerscourt restaurant. The hotel also has a stunning spa, two golf courses, and includes fly fishing and equestrian pursuits among its many leisure facilities.

Rooms 200 (39 GF) **D** €255-€5,000* **Facilities** Spa STV ⓣ ⚡ 36 Putt green Fishing ⤸ Gym Cycling Mega chess Xmas New Year Wi-fi **Services** Lift Air con **Parking** 384 **Notes** LB

MACREDDIN
Map 1 D3

BrookLodge Hotel & Wells Spa
★★★★ 86% ⚙⚙ HOTEL
☎ 0402 36444   📠 0402 36580
e-mail: info@brooklodge.com
web: www.brooklodge.com
dir: *N11 to Rathnew, R752 to Rathdrum, R753 to Aughrim, follow signs to Macreddin Village*

PETS: Bedrooms (4 GF) sign **Sep accom** dogs can sleep in stables if unoccupied on leads **Grounds** disp bin **Exercise area** Exercise area nearby **On Request** towels **Stables Other** charge for damage

A luxury country-house hotel in a village-style setting which includes an 18-hole golf course, a pub, café and food shop. There is a choice of dining options - the award-winning Strawberry Tree Restaurant specialising in organic and wild foods and a more casual Italian restaurant. Bedrooms and lounges in the original house are very comfortable; there are also bedrooms in Brookhall, tailored for guests attending weddings and conferences. The Wells Spa offers extensive treatments and leisure facilities, and there are many outdoor activities including horse riding and off-road driving.

Rooms 90 (32 annexe) (27 fmly) (4 GF) **Facilities** Spa STV FTV ⓣ ⤸ ⚡ 18 Putt green Gym Archery Clay pigeon shooting Falconry Off road driving Xmas New Year Wi-fi **Services** Lift **Parking** 200

IRELAND

DOG-FRIENDLY PUBS

Below is a list of pubs that have told us that they allow dogs on the premises

ENGLAND

BEDFORDSHIRE
BEDFORD The Embankment
BEDFORD The Three Tuns
BOLNHURST
    The Plough at Bolnhurst
BROOM The Cock
HARROLD The Muntjac
LINSLADE The Globe Inn
ODELL The Bell
SALFORD The Swan
SOULDROP The Bedford Arms
SOUTHILL The White Horse
STANBRIDGE The Five Bells
SUTTON John O'Gaunt Inn
TILSWORTH The Anchor Inn
WOBURN The Black Horse

BERKSHIRE
ALDERMASTON Hinds Head
ALDWORTH The Bell Inn
ASCOT The Thatched Tavern
BOXFORD The Bell at Boxford
BRAY The Crown Inn
CHADDLEWORTH The Ibex
CRAZIES HILL The Horns
CURRIDGE The Bunk Inn
EAST GARSTON
    The Queen's Arms Country Inn
FRILSHAM The Pot Kiln
HERMITAGE
    The White Horse of Hermitage
HUNGERFORD The Pheasant Inn
HURLEY The Olde Bell Inn
KNOWL HILL
    Bird In Hand Country Inn
LECKHAMPSTEAD The Stag
MAIDENHEAD
    The George on the Green
MARSH BENHAM The Red House
MONEYROW GREEN The White Hart
NEWBURY The Yew Tree Inn
READING The Flowing Spring
RUSCOMBE
    Buratta's at the Royal Oak
SONNING The Bull Inn
STANFORD DINGLEY
    The Old Boot Inn

SWALLOWFIELD
    The George & Dragon
WALTHAM ST LAWRENCE The Bell
WHITE WALTHAM The Beehive
WINTERBOURNE
    The Winterbourne Arms
WOKINGHAM
    The Broad Street Tavern
YATTENDON The Royal Oak Hotel

BRISTOL
BRISTOL The Albion
BRISTOL Cornubia
BRISTOL The Kensington Arms

BUCKINGHAMSHIRE
AMERSHAM Hit or Miss Inn
BEACONSFIELD The Royal Standard
    of England
BLEDLOW The Lions of Bledlow
BOVINGDON GREEN The Royal Oak
BUCKINGHAM The Old Thatched Inn
CHALFONT ST GILES The Ivy House
CHALFONT ST PETER
    The Greyhound Inn
CHEDDINGTON The Old Swan
CHENIES The Red Lion
CHESHAM The Black Horse Inn
CHOLESBURY The Full Moon
CUBLINGTON The Unicorn
DENHAM The Falcon Inn
DENHAM The Swan Inn
DORNEY The Palmer Arms
FARNHAM COMMON The Foresters
FARNHAM ROYAL The Emperor
FORD The Dinton Hermit
FRIETH The Prince Albert
FULMER The Black Horse
GREAT HAMPDEN
    The Hampden Arms
GREAT MISSENDEN The Nags Head
HAMBLEDEN
    The Stag & Huntsman Inn
HEDGERLEY The White Horse
LACEY GREEN The Whip Inn
LOUDWATER The Derehams Inn
MENTMORE The Stag Inn
MILTON KEYNES The Swan Inn
OVING The Black Boy

PENN The Old Queens Head
PRESTON BISSETT The White Hart
RADNAGE
    The Three Horseshoes Inn
SEER GREEN The Jolly Cricketers
SKIRMETT The Frog
TURVILLE The Bull & Butcher
WEST WYCOMBE
    The George and Dragon Hotel
WHEELER END The Chequers Inn
WHITELEAF Red Lion

CAMBRIDGESHIRE
BABRAHAM
    The George Inn at Babraham
BARRINGTON The Royal Oak
BROUGHTON The Crown Inn
CAMBRIDGE Cambridge Blue
CAMBRIDGE Free Press
CAMBRIDGE The Punter
ELTON The Black Horse
ELTON The Crown Inn
FEN DITTON Ancient Shepherds
FENSTANTON King William IV
GRANTCHESTER The Rupert Brooke
GREAT CHISHILL The Pheasant
HEMINGFORD GREY
    The Cock Pub and Restaurant
HILDERSHAM The Pear Tree Inn
HINXTON The Red Lion Inn
KEYSTON Pheasant Inn
KIMBOLTON The New Sun Inn
LITTLE WILBRAHAM Hole in the Wall
MILTON Waggon & Horses
NEWTON The Queen's Head
OFFORD D'ARCY The Horseshoe
PETERBOROUGH The Brewery Tap
PETERBOROUGH Charters Bar &
    East Restaurant
REACH Dyke's End
STAPLEFORD
    The Rose at Stapleford
UFFORD The White Hart

DOG-FRIENDLY PUBS (continued)

CHESHIRE
ALDFORD The Grosvenor Arms
ASTON The Bhurtpore Inn
BUNBURY The Dysart Arms
BURLEYDAM
    The Combermere Arms
BURWARDSLEY The Pheasant Inn
CHESTER Albion Inn
CHESTER Old Harkers Arms
CHOLMONDELEY
    The Cholmondeley Arms
FARNDON The Farndon
GAWSWORTH Harrington Arms
HANDLEY The Calveley Arms
HAUGHTON MOSS The Nags Head
HUXLEY Stuart's Table at the
    Farmer's Arms
KETTLESHULME Swan Inn
KNUTSFORD The Dog Inn
LITTLE NESTON The Harp Inn
MACCLESFIELD The Windmill Inn
NORTHWICH The Red Lion
PARKGATE The Ship Hotel
PRESTBURY The Legh Arms
SHOCKLACH The Bull
STOAK The Bunbury Arms
SUTTON LANE ENDS
    The Hanging Gate Inn
SUTTON LAND ENDS Sutton Hall
SWETTENHAM
    The Swettenham Arms
TARPORLEY Alvanley Arms Inn
TUSHINGHAM CUM GRINDLEY
    Blue Bell Inn
WARMINGHAM The Bear's Paw
WINCLE The Ship Inn
WRENBURY The Dusty Miller
WYBUNBURY The Swan

CORNWALL
BLISLAND The Blisland Inn
BODINNICK Old Ferry Inn
BOLVENTOR Jamaica Inn
BOSCASTLE Cobweb Inn
BOSCASTLE The Wellington Hotel
CADGWITH Cadgwith Cove Inn
CALLINGTON
    The Coachmakers Arms
CALLINGTON Manor House Inn

CONSTANTINE Trengilly Wartha Inn
CRAFTHOLE The Finnygook Inn
CUBERT The Smugglers' Den Inn
DUNMERE The Borough Arms
FEOCK The Punchbowl & Ladle
FOWEY The Ship Inn
GOLDSITHNEY The Trevelyan Arms
GUNNISLAKE The Rising Sun Inn
GUNWALLOE The Halzephron Inn
HELSTON The Queens Arms
KINGSAND The Halfway House Inn
LAMORNA Lamorna Wink
LANLIVERY The Crown Inn
LOOE The Ship Inn
LUDGVAN White Hart
MANACCAN The New Inn
MARAZION Godolphin Arms
MEVAGISSEY The Ship Inn
MITCHELL The Plume of Feathers
MITHIAN The Miners Arms
MORWENSTOW The Bush Inn
MYLOR BRIDGE The Pandora Inn
NEWQUAY The Lewinnick Lodge
    Bar & Restaurant
PAR The Royal Inn
PENZANCE Dolphin Tavern
PENZANCE The Turks Head Inn
PERRANUTHNOE The Victoria Inn
PHILLEIGH Roseland Inn
POLKERRIS The Rashleigh Inn
POLPERRO Old Mill House Inn
PORT GAVERNE Port Gaverne Hotel
PORTHLEVEN The Ship Inn
PORTREATH Basset Arms
RUAN LANIHORNE The Kings Head
ST AGNES Driftwood Spars
ST AGNES Turks Head
ST BREWARD
    The Old Inn & Restaurant
ST EWE The Crown Inn
ST IVES The Sloop Inn
ST IVES The Watermill
ST JUST [NEAR LAND'S END]
    Star Inn
ST JUST [NEAR LAND'S END]
    The Wellington
ST MAWES The Victory Inn
ST MAWGAN The Falcon Inn
ST MERRYN The Cornish Arms

SALTASH The Crooked Inn
SENNEN The Old Success Inn
TINTAGEL The Port William
TORPOINT Edgcumbe Arms
TREBARWITH The Mill House Inn
TREBURLEY The Springer Spaniel
TREGADILLETT Eliot Arms
TRURO The Wig & Pen Inn
VERYAN The New Inn
WADEBRIDGE Swan
WADEBRIDGE The Quarryman Inn
WIDEMOUTH BAY Bay View Inn
ZENNOR The Gurnard's Head
ZENNOR The Tinners Arms

CUMBRIA
AMBLESIDE Wateredge Inn
APPLEBY-IN-WESTMORLAND
    The Royal Oak Appleby
APPLEBY-IN-WESTMORLAND
    Tufton Arms Hotel
ARMATHWAITE The Dukes Head Inn
BAMPTON Mardale Inn
BARBON The Barbon Inn
BASSENTHWAITE LAKE
    The Pheasant
BLENCOWE The Crown Inn
BOOT The Boot Inn
BOOT Brook House Inn
BORROWDALE
    The Langstrath Country Inn
BOUTH The White Hart Inn
BOWLAND BRIDGE
    Hare & Hounds Country Inn
BOWNESS-ON-WINDERMERE
    The Angel Inn
BRAITHWAITE Coledale Inn
BRAITHWAITE The Royal Oak
BROUGHTON-IN-FURNESS
    Blacksmiths Arms
CALDBECK Oddfellows Arms
CARTMEL The Cavendish Arms
CLIFTON George and Dragon
CONISTON
    The Black Bull Inn & Hotel
CONISTON The Sun, Coniston
CROOK The Sun Inn
CROSTHWAITE The Punch Bowl Inn
ELTERWATER The Britannia Inn

ENNERDALE BRIDGE
The Shepherd's Arms Hotel
ESKDALE GREEN Bower House Inn
GRASMERE The Travellers Rest Inn
GREAT LANGDALE
The New Dungeon Ghyll Hotel
GREAT SALKELD The Highland
Drove Inn and
Kyloes Restaurant
HAWKSHEAD Kings Arms
HAWKSHEAD The Sun Inn
HESKET NEWMARKET
The Old Crown
KESWICK Farmers Arms
KESWICK The George
KESWICK The Horse & Farrier Inn
KESWICK Keswick Lodge
KESWICK The Kings Head
KESWICK Pheasant Inn
KESWICK The Swinside Inn
KIRKBY LONSDALE The Sun Inn
KIRKBY LONSDALE The Whoop Hall
LITTLE LANGDALE Three Shires Inn
LOW LORTON The Wheatsheaf Inn
LOWESWATER Kirkstile Inn
LUPTON The Plough Inn
MILNTHORPE The Cross Keys
NEAR SAWREY Tower Bank Arms
OUTGATE Outgate Inn
PENRITH Cross Keys Inn
RAVENSTONEDALE The Black Swan
RAVENSTONEDALE The Fat Lamb
RAVENSTONEDALE Country Inn
SEATHWAITE Newfield Inn
SIZERGH The Strickland Arms
TEMPLE SOWERBY
The Kings Arms Hotel
TIRRIL Queen's Head Inn
TORVER Church House Inn
TROUTBECK Queen's Head
ULVERSTON The Stan Laurel Inn
WASDALE HEAD Wasdale Head Inn
WATERMILLOCK Brackenrigg Inn
WINDERMERE Eagle & Child Inn
YANWATH The Yanwath Gate Inn

DERBYSHIRE
ASHBOURNE Barley Mow Inn
ASHOVER Old Poets Corner
BAKEWELL The Bull's Head
BAKEWELL The Monsal Head Hotel
BARLOW The Trout at Barlow
BIRCHOVER Red Lion Inn
BRASSINGTON Ye Olde Gate Inne
CASTLETON The Peaks Inn
CASTLETON Ye Olde Nags Head
CHELMORTON The Church Inn
CHINLEY Old Hall Inn
DERBY The Alexandra Hotel
DERBY The Brunswick Inn
EYAM Miners Arms
FENNY BENTLEY Bentley Brook Inn
FOOLOW The Bulls Head Inn
GRINDLEFORD The Maynard
HATHERSAGE Millstone Inn
HATHERSAGE The Plough Inn
HAYFIELD The Royal Hotel
HOGNASTON The Red Lion Inn
HOPE Cheshire Cheese Inn
INGLEBY The John Thompson Inn
& Brewery
LITTON Red Lion Inn
MILLTOWN The Nettle Inn
SHARDLOW The Old Crown Inn
STANTON IN PEAK
The Flying Childers Inn
TIDESWELL The George Hotel
TIDESWELL Three Stags' Heads
WESSINGTON The Three Horseshoes

DEVON
ASHBURTON The Rising Sun
AVONWICK The Avon Inn
AVONWICK The Turtley Corn Mill
AXMOUTH The Harbour Inn
AXMOUTH The Ship Inn
BAMPTON The Quarrymans Rest
BEER Anchor Inn
BEESANDS The Cricket Inn
BICKLEIGH Fisherman's Cot
BIGBURY-ON-SEA Pilchard Inn
BLACKAWTON The Normandy Arms
BRAMPFORD SPEKE
The Lazy Toad Inn
BRANSCOMBE The Fountain Head

BRANSCOMBE The Masons Arms
BRENDON Rockford Inn
BROADHEMPSTON
The Monks Retreat Inn
BUCKLAND MONACHORUM
Drake Manor Inn
BUTTERLEIGH The Butterleigh Inn
CADELEIGH The Cadeleigh Arms
CHAGFORD Sandy Park Inn
CHARDSTOCK The George Inn
CHERITON BISHOP
The Old Thatch Inn
CLAYHIDON The Merry Harriers
CLEARBROOK The Skylark Inn
COCKWOOD The Anchor Inn
COLEFORD The New Inn
COLEFORD The Wheelwright Inn
DALWOOD The Tuckers Arms
DARTMOUTH Royal Castle Hotel
DENBURY The Union Inn
DITTISHAM The Ferry Boat
DODDISCOMBSLEIGH
The Nobody Inn
DOLTON Rams Head Inn
DREWSTEIGNTON The Drewe Arms
EAST ALLINGTON Fortescue Arms
EXETER The Hour Glass
EXETER Red Lion Inn
GEORGEHAM The Rock Inn
HARBERTON The Church House Inn
HONITON The Holt
HORSEBRIDGE The Royal Inn
ILFRACOMBE The George & Dragon
KINGS NYMPTON The Grove Inn
KINGSBRIDGE The Crabshell Inn
KINGSKERSWELL Barn Owl Inn
KINGSKERSWELL Bickley Mill Inn
KINGSTON The Dolphin Inn
LIFTON The Arundell Arms
LITTLEHEMPSTON Tally Ho Inn
LUSTLEIGH The Cleave Pub
LUTON (NEAR CHUDLEIGH)
The Elizabethan Inn
LYDFORD Dartmoor Inn
LYMPSTONE The Globe Inn
LYNMOUTH Rising Sun Hotel
MARLDON The Church House Inn
MEAVY The Royal Oak Inn
MODBURY California Country Inn

DOG-FRIENDLY PUBS (continued)

MORETONHAMPSTEAD
The White Hart Hotel
NEWTON ABBOT The Wild Goose Inn
NEWTON ST CYRES The Beer Engine
NORTH BOVEY The Ring of Bells Inn
NOSS MAYO The Ship Inn
OTTERY ST MARY The Talaton Inn
PARRACOMBE The Fox & Goose
PETER TAVY Peter Tavy Inn
PLYMOUTH The Fishermans Arms
PLYMTREE The Blacksmiths Arms
PORTGATE The Harris Arms
POSTBRIDGE Warren House Inn
RATTERY Church House Inn
SALCOMBE The Victoria Inn
SHEBBEAR The Devil's Stone Inn
SIDBURY The Hare & Hounds
SIDMOUTH Blue Ball Inn
SIDMOUTH Dukes
SLAPTON The Tower Inn
SOURTON The Highwayman Inn
SOUTH POOL The Millbrook Inn
SOUTH ZEAL Oxenham Arms
SPREYTON The Tom Cobley Tavern
STAVERTON Sea Trout Inn
STOKE FLEMING
The Green Dragon Inn
STRETE Kings Arms
THURLESTONE The Village Inn
TOPSHAM Bridge Inn
TORQUAY The Cary Arms
TOTNES The Durant Arms
TOTNES Royal Seven Stars Hotel
TOTNES Steam Packet Inn
TUCKENHAY The Maltsters Arms
UMBERLEIGH The Rising Sun Inn
WIDECOMBE IN THE MOOR
The Old Inn
WIDECOMBE IN THE MOOR
The Rugglestone Inn
WINKLEIGH The Kings Arms
WINKLEIGH The Duke of York
WOODBURY SALTERTON
The Digger's Rest
YEALMPTON Rose & Crown

DORSET
BISHOP'S CAUNDLE The White Hart
BLANDFORD FORUM Crown Hotel
BLANDFORD FORUM The Anvil Inn
BOURTON The White Lion Inn
BRIDPORT The George Hotel
BRIDPORT The Shave Cross Inn
BRIDPORT The West Bay
BUCKHORN WESTON
Stapleton Arms
BUCKLAND NEWTON
Gaggle of Geese
BURTON BRADSTOCK
The Anchor Inn
CATTISTOCK Fox & Hounds Inn
CHEDINGTON Winyards Gap Inn
CHIDEOCK The Anchor Inn
CHRISTCHURCH
The Ship In Distress
CORFE CASTLE The Greyhound Inn
CORFE MULLEN The Coventry Arms
EAST MORDEN The Cock & Bottle
EVERSHOT The Acorn Inn
FARNHAM The Museum Inn
GILLINGHAM The Kings Arms Inn
GUSSAGE ALL SAINTS
The Drovers Inn
KING'S STAG The Greenman
LODERS Loders Arms
LOWER ANSTY The Fox Inn
LYME REGIS Pilot Boat Inn
MOTCOMBE The Coppleridge Inn
NETTLECOMBE Marquis of Lorne
NORTH WOOTTON The Three Elms
OSMINGTON MILLS
The Smugglers Inn
PIDDLEHINTON The Thimble Inn
PIDDLETRENTHIDE
The European Inn
PIDDLETRENTHIDE The Piddle Inn
PIDDLETRENTHIDE
The Poachers Inn
PLUSH The Brace of Pheasants
POOLE The Cow
POOLE The Guildhall Tavern
POWERSTOCK
Three Horseshoes Inn
PUNCKNOWLE The Crown Inn
SHAPWICK The Anchor Inn

SHERBORNE The Kings Arms
SHERBORNE Queen's Head
STRATTON Saxon Arms
STUDLAND The Bankes Arms Hotel
SYDLING ST NICHOLAS
The Greyhound Inn
TARRANT MONKTON
The Langton Arms
TRENT Rose & Crown Trent
WEST BEXINGTON The Manor Hotel
WEST LULWORTH The Castle Inn
WEST LULWORTH Lulworth Cove Inn
WEST STOUR The Ship Inn
WEYMOUTH The Old Ship Inn
WIMBORNE ST GILES The Bull Inn
WINTERBORNE ZELSTON
Botany Bay Inne
WORTH MATRAVERS
The Square and Compass

CO DURHAM
BARNARD CASTLE
The Morritt Arms Hotel
DURHAM Victoria Inn
FIR TREE Duke of York Inn
HUTTON MAGNA The Oak Tree Inn
MIDDLESTONE Ship Inn
MIDDLETON-IN-TEESDALE
The Teesdale Hotel
NEWTON AYCLIFFE
Blacksmiths Arms
ROMALDKIRK Rose & Crown
SEAHAM The Seaton Lane Inn
STANLEY The Stables Pub
and Restaurant

ESSEX
AYTHORPE RODING
Axe & Compasses
BLACKMORE The Leather Bottle
BURNHAM-ON-CROUCH
Ye Olde White Harte Hotel
CASTLE HEDINGHAM The Bell Inn
CHAPPEL The Swan Inn
DEDHAM The Sun Inn
DEDHAM Marlborough Head Inn
FAIRSTEAD
The Square and Compasses
FEERING The Sun Inn

FELSTED The Swan at Felsted
FINGRINGHOE The Whalebone
GOLDHANGER The Chequers Inn
GOSFIELD The Green Man
GREAT BRAXTED The Ducane
HASTINGWOOD Rainbow & Dove
HORNDON ON THE HILL
    Bell Inn & Hill House
LANGHAM The Shepherd and Dog
LITTLE BRAXTED The Green Man
LITTLE DUNMOW Flitch of Bacon
LITTLEBURY The Queens Head Inn
MANNINGTREE The Mistley Thorn
MARGARETTING TYE
    The White Hart Inn
NORTH FAMBRIDGE
    The Ferry Boat Inn
PATTISWICK
    The Compasses at Pattiswick
PELDON The Peldon Rose
STOCK The Hoop

GLOUCESTERSHIRE
ALDERTON The Gardeners Arms
ANDOVERSFORD The Royal Oak Inn
ARLINGHAM The Old Passage Inn
BARNSLEY The Village Pub
BIBURY Catherine Wheel
BIRDLIP The Golden Heart
BLAISDON The Red Hart Inn
BLEDINGTON The Kings Head Inn
BROCKHAMPTON Craven Arms Inn
CHEDWORTH Hare & Hounds
CHEDWORTH Seven Tuns
CHELTENHAM
    The Gloucester Old Spot
CHIPPING CAMPDEN Eight Bells
CHIPPING CAMPDEN
    Noel Arms Hotel
CHIPPING CAMPDEN
    Seagrave Arms
CHIPPING CAMPDEN
    The Volunteer Inn
CIRENCESTER The Crown of Crucis
CLEARWELL The Wyndham Arms
CLEEVE HILL The Rising Sun
CLIFFORD'S MESNE The Yew Tree
COATES The Tunnel House Inn

COLESBOURNE
    The Colesbourne Inn
COLN ST ALDWYNS
    The New Inn At Coln
COWLEY The Green Dragon Inn
CRANHAM The Black Horse Inn
DURSLEY The Old Spot Inn
EBRINGTON The Ebrington Arms
EWEN The Wild Duck
FOSSEBRIDGE
    The Inn at Fossebridge
FRAMPTON MANSELL
    The Crown Inn
GREAT BARRINGTON The Fox
GUITING POWER The Hollow Bottom
HINTON The Bull Inn
LECHLADE ON THAMES
    The Trout Inn
LITTLE WASHBOURNE
    The Hobnails Inn
LITTLETON-ON-SEVERN White Hart
LOWER ODDINGTON The Fox
MARSHFIELD The Catherine Wheel
MARSHFIELD The Lord Nelson Inn
MEYSEY HAMPTON
    The Masons Arms
MINCHINHAMPTON
    The Weighbridge Inn
MORETON-IN-MARSH
    The Red Lion Inn
NAILSWORTH The Britannia
NAILSWORTH Tipputs Inn
NETHER WESTCOTE
    The Feathered Nest Inn
NEWLAND The Ostrich Inn
NORTH CERNEY Bathurst Arms
OLDBURY-ON-SEVERN
    The Anchor Inn
PAINSWICK The Falcon Inn
PAXFORD The Churchill Arms
POULTON The Falcon Inn
SAPPERTON The Bell at Sapperton
SHEEPSCOMBE The Butchers Arms
SOMERFORD KEYNES
    The Bakers Arms
SOUTH CERNEY The Old Boathouse
SOUTHROP The Swan at Southrop
STONEHOUSE The George Inn

STOW-ON-THE-WOLD
    The Eagle and Child
STOW-ON-THE-WOLD The Unicorn
STOW-ON-THE-WOLD
    White Hart Inn
STROUD Bear of Rodborough Hotel
STROUD The Ram Inn
STROUD Rose & Crown Inn
STROUD The Woolpack Inn
TETBURY The Priory Inn
TETBURY Snooty Fox Hotel
TETBURY The Trouble House
TODENHAM The Farriers Arms
TORMARTON
    Best Western Compass Inn
UPPER ODDINGTON
    The Horse and Groom Inn
WINCHCOMBE The White Hart Inn
    and Restaurant
WOODCHESTER The Old Fleece

GREATER MANCHESTER
DOBCROSS Swan Inn
MANCHESTER Marble Arch
MARPLE BRIDGE Hare & Hounds
OLDHAM The Roebuck Inn
OLDHAM The White Hart Inn
STALYBRIDGE
    Stalybridge Station Buffet Bar
STOCKPORT The Arden Arms
STOCKPORT The Nursery Inn
WALMERSLEY The Lord Raglan

HAMPSHIRE
ALTON The Anchor Inn
AMPFIELD White Horse at Ampfield
BALL HILL The Furze Bush Inn
BAUGHURST The Wellington Arms
BEAULIEU The Drift Inn
BEAUWORTH The Milburys
BENTLEY The Bull Inn
BENTWORTH The Sun Inn
BOLDRE The Red Lion
BRANSGORE
    The Three Tuns Country Inn
BUCKLERS HARD The Master
    Builders House Hotel
BURGHCLERE Carnarvon Arms
BURLEY The Burley Inn

DOG-FRIENDLY PUBS (continued)

CHALTON The Red Lion
CHARTER ALLEY The White Hart Inn
CHAWTON The Greyfriar
CHERITON The Flower Pots Inn
CROOKHAM VILLAGE The Exchequer
DOWNTON The Royal Oak
DROXFORD The Bakers Arms
DUMMER The Sun Inn
DUNBRIDGE The Mill Arms
EAST BOLDRE Turfcutters Arms
EAST END The East End Arms
EAST MEON Ye Olde George Inn
EAST STRATTON Northbrook Arms
EAST TYTHERLEY
   The Star Inn Tytherley
EASTON The Chestnut Horse
EASTON The Cricketers Inn
EMSWORTH The Sussex Brewery
EVERSLEY The Golden Pot
EXTON The Shoe Inn
FORDINGBRIDGE
   The Augustus John
FRITHAM The Royal Oak
HANNINGTON
   The Vine at Hannington
HAVANT The Royal Oak
HAWKLEY The Hawkley Inn
HERRIARD The Fur & Feathers
HOLYBOURNE The White Hart Hotel
HOOK Crooked Billet
HOOK The Hogget
HURSLEY The Dolphin Inn
HURSLEY The Kings Head
ITCHEN ABBAS The Trout
LEE-ON-THE-SOLENT
   The Bun Penny
LINWOOD The High Corner Inn
LITTLETON The Running Horse
LONGPARISH The Plough Inn
LOWER SWANWICK Old Ship
LOWER WIELD The Yew Tree
LYMINGTON Mayflower Inn
LYNDHURST New Forest Inn
LYNDHURST The Oak Inn
MAPLEDURWELL The Gamekeepers
MICHELDEVER The Dove Inn
MICHELDEVER
   Half Moon & Spread Eagle
MORTIMER WEST END The Red Lion

NEW ALRESFORD The Bell Inn
NORTH WALTHAM The Fox
NORTHINGTON The Woolpack Inn
OVINGTON The Bush
PETERSFIELD The Good Intent
PETERSFIELD The Trooper Inn
PETERSFIELD The White Horse Inn
PILLEY The Fleur de Lys
ROCKBOURNE The Rose & Thistle
ROCKFORD The Alice Lisle
ROMSEY The Cromwell Arms
ROMSEY The Dukes Head
ROMSEY The Three Tuns
SILCHESTER Calleva Arms
SPARSHOLT The Plough Inn
ST MARY BOURNE
   The Bourne Valley Inn
STEEP Harrow Inn
STOCKBRIDGE The Greyhound Inn
STOCKBRIDGE Mayfly
STOCKBRIDGE The Peat Spade
STOCKBRIDGE The Three Cups Inn
SWANMORE The Rising Sun
TANGLEY The Fox Inn
TICHBORNE The Tichborne Arms
UPPER FROYLE
   The Hen & Chicken Inn
WARNFORD The George & Falcon
WARSASH
   The Jolly Farmer Country Inn
WELL The Chequers Inn
WEST MEON The Thomas Lord
WHITCHURCH Watership Down Inn
WINCHESTER The Bell Inn
WINCHESTER The Golden Lion
WINCHESTER The Old Vine
WINCHESTER The Westgate Inn
WINCHESTER The Wykeham Arms

HEREFORDSHIRE
ASTON CREWS
   The Penny Farthing Inn
AYMESTREY The Riverside Inn
BODENHAM England's Gate Inn
BRINGSTY COMMON
   Live and Let Live
CAREY Cottage of Content
CRASWALL The Bulls Head
DORSTONE The Pandy Inn

HAMPTON BISHOP
   The Bunch of Carrots
HOARWITHY The New Harp Inn
KILPECK The Kilpeck Inn
KINGTON The Stagg Inn and
Restaurant
LEDBURY The Farmers Arms
LEDBURY Prince of Wales
LEDBURY The Trumpet Inn
LEOMINSTER The Grape Vaults
MUCH MARCLE The Slip Tavern
ORLETON The Boot Inn
ST OWENS CROSS The New Inn
SHOBDON The Bateman Arms
STAPLOW The Oak Inn
SYMONDS YAT [EAST]
   The Saracens Head Inn
TILLINGTON The Bell
WELLINGTON The Wellington
WEOBLEY Ye Olde Salutation Inn
WOOLHOPE The Butchers Arms

HERTFORDSHIRE
ALDBURY The Greyhound Inn
ALDBURY The Valiant Trooper
ASHWELL Three Tuns
AYOT GREEN The Waggoners
BARLEY The Fox & Hounds
BERKHAMSTED The Old Mill
BUNTINGFORD The Sword Inn Hand
FLAUNDEN The Bricklayers Arms
HEMEL HEMPSTEAD Alford Arms
HERONSGATE The Land of Liberty,
   Peace and Plenty
HITCHIN The Greyhound
HITCHIN The Radcliffe Arms
HUNSDON The Fox and Hounds
NORTHAW The Sun at Northaw
RICKMANSWORTH
   The Rose and Crown
ROYSTON The Cabinet Free House
   and Restaurant
ST ALBANS Rose & Crown
SARRATT The Cock Inn
SHENLEY The White Horse, Shenley
TRING The Cow Roast Inn
WELWYN GARDEN CITY
   The Brocket Arms
WILLIAN The Fox

DOG-FRIENDLY PUBS (continued)

N1 The Compton Arms
N1 The Crown
N1 The Drapers Arms
N1 The Duke of Cambridge
N1 The House
N6 The Flask
N19 The Landseer
NW1 The Chapel
NW1 The Engineer
NW1 The Lansdowne
NW1 The Prince Albert
NW1 The Queens
NW3 The Holly Bush
NW5 Dartmouth Arms
NW5 The Junction Tavern
NW5 The Lord Palmerston
NW6 The Salusbury
    Pub and Dining Room
NW8 The Salt House
NW10 William IV Bar & Restaurant
SE1 The Anchor & Hope
SE5 The Sun and Doves
SE10 The Cutty Sark Tavern
SE10 Greenwich Union Pub
SE10 North Pole Bar & Restaurant
SE21 The Crown & Greyhound
SE22 Franklins
SW1 The Buckingham Arms
SW1 Nags Head
SW1 The Orange
    Public House & Hotel
SW3 The Admiral Codrington
SW3 The Builders Arms
SW3 The Coopers of Flood Street
SW3 The Cross Keys
SW6 The White Horse
SW6 The Jam Tree
SW6 The Atlas
SW7 The Anglesea Arms
SW8 The Masons Arms
SW10 The Chelsea Ram
SW10 The Hollywood Arms
SW10 Lots Road Pub
    and Dining Room
SW11 The Bolingbroke Pub
    & Dining Room
SW11 The Fox & Hounds
SW13 The Bull's Head
SW13 The Idle Hour

SW14 The Victoria
SW15 The Spencer
SW15 The Telegraph
SW18 The Alma Tavern
SW18 The Cat's Back
SW18 The Earl Spencer
SW18 The Roundhouse
SW18 The Ship Inn
SW19 The Brewery Tap
W1 The Grazing Goat
W2 The Prince Bonaparte
W2 The Westbourne
W4 The Swan
W5 The Wheatsheaf
W6 Anglesea Arms
W6 The Dartmouth Castle
W8 The Scarsdale
W8 The Windsor Castle
W11 Portobello Gold
W14 The Cumberland Arms
W14 The Havelock Tavern
W14 The Jam Tree
WC1 Norfolk Arms
WC2 The George

GREATER LONDON
CHELSFIELD The Five Bells
HAM Hand & Flower

MERSEYSIDE
BARNSTON Fox and Hounds
GREASBY Irby Mill

NORFOLK
BAWBURGH Kings Head
BLAKENEY
    The Blakeney White Horse
BLAKENEY The Kings Arms
BRANCASTER The Ship Hotel
BRANCASTER STAITHE
    The Jolly Sailors
BRANCASTER STAITHE
    The White Horse
BRISLEY The Brisley Bell
    Inn & Restaurant
BURNHAM MARKET The Hoste Arms
BURNHAM THORPE The Lord Nelson
BURSTON The Crown

CLEY NEXT THE SEA
    The George Hotel
CROMER
    The Red Lion Food and Rooms
EAST RUDHAM The Crown Inn
EAST RUSTON The Butchers Arms
ERPINGHAM The Saracen's Head
GREAT RYBURGH The Blue Boar Inn
HEVINGHAM
    Marsham Arms Freehouse
HEYDON Earle Arms
HINGHAM The White Hart Hotel
HOLKHAM Victoria at Holkham
HOLT The Pigs
HORSTEAD Recruiting Sergeant
HUNSTANTON The King William IV
    Country Inn & Restaurant
HUNWORTH The Hunny Bell
ITTERINGHAM Walpole Arms
LETHERINGSETT The Kings Head
LITTLE FRANSHAM
    The Canary and Linnet
MUNDFORD Crown Hotel
NEWTON The George & Dragon
RINGSTEAD The Gin Trap Inn
SALTHOUSE The Dun Cow
SNETTISHAM The Rose & Crown
SWANTON MORLEY
    Darbys Freehouse
THOMPSON Chequers Inn
THORNHAM Lifeboat Inn
THORNHAM The Orange Tree
TITCHWELL Titchwell Manor Hotel
WARHAM ALL SAINTS
    Three Horseshoes
WELLS-NEXT-THE-SEA
    The Crown Hotel
WELLS-NEXT-THE-SEA
    The Globe Inn
WEST BECKHAM The Wheatsheaf
WESTON LONGVILLE
    The Parson Woodforde
WINTERTON-ON-SEA
    Fishermans Return
WIVETON Wiveton Bell

NORTHAMPTONSHIRE
ASHBY ST LEDGERS
   The Olde Coach House Inn
ASHTON The Old Crown
AYNHO The Great Western Arms
BULWICK The Queen's Head
CASTLE ASHBY The Falcon
CRICK The Red Lion Inn
FARTHINGSTONE The Kings Arms
FOTHERINGHAY The Falcon Inn
KILSBY The George
NASSINGTON The Queens Head Inn
NORTHAMPTON The Fox & Hounds
OUNDLE The Chequered Skipper
STOKE BRUERNE The Boat Inn
TITCHMARSH
   The Wheatsheaf at Titchmarsh
WADENHOE The King's Head
WESTON The Crown

NORTHUMBERLAND
BLANCHLAND The Lord Crewe Arms
CARTERWAY HEADS
   The Manor House Inn
FALSTONE The Pheasant Inn
HAYDON BRIDGE
   The General Havelock Inn
HEXHAM Battlesteads
   Hotel & Restaurant
HEXHAM Miners Arms Inn
LOW NEWTON BY THE SEA
   The Ship Inn
SEAHOUSES
   The Bamburgh Castle Inn
SLAGGYFORD The Kirkstyle Inn
WARDEN The Boatside Inn
WARENFORD The White Swan
NOTTINGHAMSHIRE
BEESTON Victoria Hotel
BLIDWORTH Fox & Hounds
CAUNTON Caunton Beck
CAYTHORPE Black Horse Inn
CAYTHORPE The Old Volunteer
EDWINSTOWE Forest Lodge
ELKESLEY Robin Hood Inn
HARBY Bottle & Glass
KIMBERLEY
   The Nelson & Railway Inn
MORTON The Full Moon Inn

TUXFORD The Mussel & Crab
UPTON The Cross Keys

OXFORDSHIRE
ARDINGTON The Boar's Head
BANBURY The Wykham Arms
BANBURY Ye Olde Reindeer Inn
BECKLEY The Abingdon Arms
BLOXHAM The Elephant & Castle
BRIGHTWELL BALDWIN
   The Lord Nelson Inn
BRIGHTWELL-CUM-SOTWELL
   The Red Lion
BURFORD The Inn for All Seasons
BURFORD The Lamb Inn
CASSINGTON The Chequers Inn
CHALGROVE The Red Lion Inn
CHECKENDON The Highwayman
CHINNOR The Sir Charles Napier
CHIPPING NORTON The Chequers
CHISELHAMPTON
   Coach & Horses Inn
CHRISTMAS COMMON
   The Fox and Hounds
CHURCH ENSTONE The Crown Inn
CLIFTON
   Duke of Cumberland's Head
CRAY'S POND The White Lion
CUMNOR Bear & Ragged Staff
CUMNOR The Vine Inn
DORCHESTER (ON THAMES)
   Fleur De Lys
FARINGDON The Lamb at Buckland
FARINGDON
   The Trout at Tadpole Bridge
FERNHAM The Woodman Inn
FRINGFORD The Butchers Arms
FULBROOK The Carpenters Arms
GORING Miller of Mansfield
GREAT TEW The Falkland Arms
HAILEY Bird in Hand
HAMPTON POYLE The Bell
HENLEY-ON-THAMES
   The Cherry Tree Inn
HENLEY-ON-THAMES
   The Five Horseshoes
HENLEY-ON-THAMES
   The Little Angel

HENLEY-ON-THAMES
   White Hart - Nettlebed
HIGHMOOR Rising Sun
HOOK NORTON
   The Gate Hangs High
KELMSCOTT The Plough Inn
KINGHAM The Kingham Plough
LANGFORD The Bell at Langford
LOWER SHIPLAKE The Baskerville
MURCOTT The Nut Tree Inn
OXFORD Turf Tavern
OXFORD The Anchor
PISHILL The Crown Inn
RAMSDEN The Royal Oak
SATWELL The Lamb at Satwell
SHILTON Rose & Crown
SHIPTON-UNDER-WYCHWOOD
   The Shaven Crown Hotel
SHUTFORD The George & Dragon
SOUTH STOKE The Perch and Pike
STEEPLE ASTON The Red Lion
SWINBROOK The Swan Inn
SYDENHAM The Crown Inn
TETSWORTH The Old Red Lion
THAME The James Figg
THAME The Thatch
WANTAGE The Hare
WEST HANNEY Plough Inn
WESTON-ON-THE-GREEN
   The Ben Jonson
WHEATLEY Bat & Ball Inn
WITNEY The Fleece
WITNEY The Three Horseshoes
WOODSTOCK The King's Head
WOOLSTONE The White Horse

RUTLAND
BARROWDEN Exeter Arms
CLIPSHAM The Olive Branch
EMPINGHAM The White Horse Inn
EXTON Fox & Hounds
LYDDINGTON
   The Marquess of Exeter
OAKHAM Barnsdale Lodge Hotel
OAKHAM The Grainstore Brewery
SOUTH LUFFENHAM
   The Coach House Inn
STRETTON
   The Jackson Stops Country Inn
WING Kings Arms

DOG-FRIENDLY PUBS (continued)

SHROPSHIRE
ADMASTON
    The Pheasant Inn at Admaston
BASCHURCH The New Inn
BISHOP'S CASTLE
    The Sun at Norbury
BISHOP'S CASTLE
    The Three Tuns Inn
BRIDGNORTH Halfway House Inn
CLEOBURY MORTIMER
    The Crown Inn
CLUN The White Horse Inn
CRAVEN ARMS The Sun Inn
CRESSAGE The Riverside Inn
HODNET The Bear at Hodnet
IRONBRIDGE The Malthouse
LITTLE STRETTON The Ragleth Inn
LUDLOW The Church Inn
LUDLOW The Unicorn
MADELEY All Nations Inn
MARTON The Lowfield Inn
MUCH WENLOCK
    The George & Dragon
MUCH WENLOCK Longville Arms
MUCH WENLOCK Wenlock Edge Inn
OSWESTRY The Bradford Arms
PAVE LANE The Fox
PICKLESCOTT Bottle & Glass Inn
SHREWSBURY The Armoury

SOMERSET
ASHCOTT Ring O'Bells
ASHILL Square & Compass
AXBRIDGE Lamb Inn
BABCARY Red Lion
BACKWELL The New Inn
BATH King William
BATH The Marlborough Tavern
BATH The Star Inn
BAWDRIP The Knowle Inn
BECKINGTON Woolpack Inn
BLUE ANCHOR The Smugglers
BRADFORD-ON-TONE
    White Horse Inn
CATCOTT The Crown Inn
CHEW MAGNA The Bear and Swan
CHEW MAGNA The Pony and Trap
CHISELBOROUGH The Cat Head Inn
CHURCHILL The Crown Inn

CLAPTON-IN-GORDANO
    The Black Horse
CLUTTON The Hunters Rest
COMBE HAY The Wheatsheaf Inn
COMPTON DANDO The Compton Inn
CONGRESBURY
    The Ship and Castle
CORTON DENHAM The Queens Arms
CRANMORE Strode Arms
CREWKERNE The Manor Arms
CROSCOMBE The Bull Terrier
CROSCOMBE The George Inn
DINNINGTON Dinnington Docks
DITCHEAT The Manor House Inn
DULVERTON
    Woods Bar & Dining Room
DUNSTER The Luttrell Arms
EAST COKER The Helyar Arms
EXFORD The Crown Hotel
FRESHFORD The Inn at Freshford
FROME The Horse & Groom
HINTON BLEWETT Ring O'Bells
HINTON ST GEORGE
    The Lord Poulett Arms
HOLCOMBE The Holcombe Inn
ILMINSTER New Inn
KILVE The Hood Arms
LANGPORT The Old Pound Inn
LANGPORT Rose & Crown
LONG SUTTON The Devonshire Arms
LOVINGTON The Pilgrims
LOWER LANGFORD
    The Langford Inn
MARTOCK The Nag's Head Inn
MONTACUTE The Kings Arms Inn
MONTACUTE The Phelips Arms
NORTH CURRY The Bird in Hand
NORTON ST PHILIP George Inn
NUNNEY The George at Nunney
OAKHILL The Oakhill Inn
OVER STRATTON The Royal Oak
PITNEY The Halfway House
PORLOCK The Ship Inn
PORLOCK The Bottom Ship
RUDGE The Full Moon at Rudge
SHEPTON BEAUCHAMP Duke of York

SHEPTON MALLET
    The Three Horseshoes Inn
SHEPTON MALLET
    The Waggon and Horses
SHEPTON MONTAGUE
    The Montague Inn
STOGUMBER The White Horse
TAUNTON Queens Arms
TAUNTON The Hatch Inn
TINTINHULL
    The Crown and Victoria Inn
TRISCOMBE The Blue Ball
WATERROW The Rock Inn
WELLS The City Arms
WEST BAGBOROUGH
    The Rising Sun Inn
WEST HUNTSPILL Crossways Inn
WHEDDON CROSS
    The Rest and Be Thankful Inn
WINSFORD Royal Oak Inn
WIVELISCOMBE White Hart
YARLINGTON The Stags Head Inn
YEOVIL The Masons Arms

STAFFORDSHIRE
ALSTONEFIELD The George
ANSLOW The Burnt Gate at Anslow
BURTON UPON TRENT
    Burton Bridge Inn
CAULDON Yew Tree Inn
COLTON The Yorkshireman
ECCLESHALL The George
HOPEDALE The Watts Russell Arms
SUMMERHILL
    Oddfellows in the Boat
WETTON Ye Olde Royal Oak
WOODSEAVES The Plough Inn
WRINEHILL The Hand & Trumpet

SUFFOLK
ALDEBURGH The Mill Inn
ALDRINGHAM The Parrot and
    Punchbowl Inn & Restaurant
BRANDESTON The Queens Head
BURY ST EDMUNDS The Linden Tree
BURY ST EDMUNDS The Nutshell
BUTLEY The Butley Oyster
CAVENDISH Bull Inn
CRATFIELD The Poacher

DUNWICH The Ship Inn
EARL SOHAM Victoria
FRAMLINGHAM The Station Hotel
GREAT BRICETT
   The Veggie Red Lion
GREAT GLEMHAM The Crown Inn
HALESWORTH The Queen's Head
MITCHAM The White Horse Inn
MOXNE The Swan
XWORTH Pykkerell Inn
LAVENHAM The Angel
LAXFIELD The Kings Head
   (The Low House)
LEVINGTON The Ship Inn
LIDGATE The Star Inn
LINDSEY TYE The Lindsey Rose
MELTON Wilford Bridge
ORFORD Jolly Sailor Inn
SIBTON Sibton White Horse Inn
SNAPE The Crown Inn
SNAPE The Golden Key
SNAPE Plough & Sail
SOUTHWOLD The Crown Hotel
STANTON The Rose & Crown
STOKE-BY-NAYLAND The Angel Inn
STOKE-BY-NAYLAND The Crown
STOWMARKET The Buxhall Crown
STRADBROKE The Ivy House
SWILLAND Moon & Mushroom Inn
THORPENESS The Dolphin Inn
WALBERSWICK The Anchor
WALBERSWICK Bell Inn
WESTLETON The Westleton Crown
WHEPSTEAD The White Horse

SURREY
ABINGER The Stephan Langton
ABINGER The Volunteer
ALBURY The Drummond at Albury
ALBURY William IV
BETCHWORTH The Red Lion
BRAMLEY Jolly Farmer Inn
CARSHALTON The Sun
CHIDDINGFOLD The Crown Inn
CHURT Pride of the Valley
CLAYGATE Swan Inn & Lodge
COBHAM The Cricketers
COLDHARBOUR The Plough Inn
COMPTON The Withies Inn

CRANLEIGH The Richard Onslow
DUNSFOLD The Sun Inn
EAST CLANDON The Queens Head
ELSTEAD The Golden Fleece
ELSTEAD The Woolpack
FARNHAM The Bat & Ball Freehouse
FARNHAM The Spotted Cow
   at Lower Bourne
FETCHAM The Bell
FOREST GREEN The Parrot Inn
HASCOMBE The White Horse
HASLEMERE The Wheatsheaf Inn
LEIGH The Plough
LEIGH The Seven Stars
LINGFIELD Hare and Hounds
LONG DITTON The Ditton
MICKLEHAM The Running Horses
NEWDIGATE The Surrey Oaks
OCKHAM The Black Swan
OCKLEY
   Bryce's at The Old School House
OCKLEY The Kings Arms Inn
RIPLEY The Talbot Inn
SOUTH GODSTONE Fox & Hounds
WEST END The Inn @ West End
WEST HORSLEY The King William IV
WITLEY The White Hart

SUSSEX, EAST
ALCISTON Rose Cottage Inn
ALFRISTON George Inn
ASHBURNHAM PLACE Ash Tree Inn
BERWICK The Cricketers Arms
BLACKBOYS The Blackboys Inn
BRIGHTON The Basketmakers Arms
BRIGHTON The Chimney House
BRIGHTON The Greys
BRIGHTON The Market Inn
BRIGHTON Preston Park Tavern
CHAILEY The Five Bells
   Restaurant and Bar
CHIDDINGLY The Six Bells
COOKSBRIDGE The Rainbow Inn
COWBEECH The Merrie Harriers
DANEHILL The Coach and Horses
DITCHLING The Bull
EAST CHILTINGTON
   The Jolly Sportsman
EAST DEAN The Tiger Inn

FLETCHING The Griffin Inn
GUN HILL The Gun
HARTFIELD Anchor Inn
HARTFIELD The Hatch Inn
ICKLESHAM The Queen's Head
MILTON STREET The Sussex Ox
RINGMER The Cock
RUSHLAKE GREEN Horse & Groom
RYE The George Tap
RYE The Globe Inn
SALEHURST Salehurst Halt
SHORTBRIDGE The Peacock Inn
THREE LEG CROSS The Bull
WADHURST The Best Beech Inn
WARTLING The Lamb Inn
WILMINGTON The Giants Rest
WINCHELSEA The New Inn
WITHYHAM The Dorset Arms

SUSSEX, WEST
AMBERLEY Black Horse
AMBERLEY The Bridge Inn
ASHURST The Fountain Inn
BALCOMBE The Cowdray
BOSHAM The Anchor Bleu
BURPHAM George & Dragon
CHARLTON The Fox Goes Free
CHICHESTER The Bull's Head
CHICHESTER The Earl of March
CHICHESTER Royal Oak Inn
COMPTON Coach & Horses
DIAL POST The Crown Inn
DUNCTON The Cricketers
EAST ASHLING Horse and Groom
EAST DEAN The Star & Garter
ELSTED The Three Horseshoes
FERNHURST The Red Lion
GRAFFHAM The Foresters Arms
HALNAKER
   The Anglesey Arms at Halnaker
HENLEY Duke of Cumberland Arms
HEYSHOTT Unicorn Inn
HORSHAM The Black Jug
KINGSFOLD The Dog and Duck
LAMBS GREEN The Lamb Inn
LODSWORTH
   The Halfway Bridge Inn
LODSWORTH The Hollist Arms
LURGASHALL The Noah's Ark

DOG-FRIENDLY PUBS (continued)

MAPLEHURST The White Horse
NUTHURST Black Horse Inn
OVING The Gribble Inn
PETWORTH The Black Horse
PETWORTH The Grove Inn
POYNINGS Royal Oak
ROWHOOK The Chequers Inn
SHIPLEY The Countryman Inn
SHIPLEY George & Dragon
SINGLETON The Partridge Inn
SLINDON The Spur
SOUTH HARTING The Ship Inn
STEDHAM Hamilton Arms/Nava
    Thai Restaurant
SUTTON The White Horse Inn
TILLINGTON The Horseguards Inn
TROTTON The Keepers Arms
WALDERTON The Barley Mow
WARNINGLID The Half Moon
WEST CHILTINGTON
    The Queens Head
WEST HOATHLY The Cat Inn
WINEHAM The Royal Oak
WISBOROUGH GREEN
    Cricketers Arms

WARWICKSHIRE
ALCESTER The Holly Bush
ALDERMINSTER The Bell
ALVESTON The Baraset Barn
BARFORD The Granville @ Barford
BROOM Broom Tavern
ETTINGTON The Chequers Inn
ETTINGTON The Houndshill
FARNBOROUGH
    The Inn at Farnborough
GAYDON The Malt Shovel
GREAT WOLFORD
    The Fox & Hounds Inn
HENLEY-IN-ARDEN The Bluebell
HUNNINGHAM
    The Red Lion, Hunningham
ILMINGTON The Howard Arms
KENILWORTH The Almanack
LAPWORTH The Boot Inn
LONG COMPTON The Red Lion
LONG ITCHINGTON
    The Duck on the Pond
OFFCHURCH The Stag at Offchurch

OXHILL The Peacock
PRESTON BAGOT The Crabmill
PRIORS MARSTON
    The Hollybush Inn
RATLEY The Rose and Crown
SALFORD PRIORS
    The Bell at Salford Priors
SHIPSTON ON STOUR
    White Bear Hotel
SHREWLEY The Durham Ox
    Restaurant and Country Pub
STRATFORD-UPON-AVON
    The Fox & Goose Inn
STRATFORD-UPON-AVON
    The One Elm
TEMPLE GRAFTON
    The Blue Boar Inn
WARWICK The Rose & Crown
WOOTTON WAWEN The Bulls Head

WEST MIDLANDS
BIRMINGHAM Penny Blacks
CHADWICK END The Orange Tree
HAMPTON IN ARDEN
    The White Lion Inn
SEDGLEY Beacon Hotel & Sarah
    Hughes Brewery

WIGHT, ISLE OF
ARRETON The White Lion
BEMBRIDGE
    The Crab & Lobster Inn
BEMBRIDGE The Windmill Inn
BONCHURCH The Bonchurch Inn
COWES The Fountain Inn
COWES Duke of York Inn
FRESHWATER The Red Lion
GODSHILL The Taverners
HULVERSTONE
    The Sun Inn at Hulverstone
NINGWOOD Horse & Groom
NITON Buddle Inn
NORTHWOOD Travellers Joy
ROOKLEY The Chequers
SEAVIEW The Seaview
    Hotel & Restaurant
SEAVIEW The Boathouse
SHALFLEET The New Inn
SHORWELL The Crown Inn

WHIPPINGHAM The Folly

WILTSHIRE
ALDBOURNE The Blue Boar
ALDBOURNE The Crown Inn
BERWICK ST JOHN The Talbot Inn
BOX The Quarrymans Arms
BRADFORD-ON-AVON
    The Dandy Lion
BRADFORD-ON-AVON
    The Kings Arms
BRINKWORTH The Three Crowns
BROAD CHALKE
    The Queens Head Inn
BROUGHTON GIFFORD The Fox
BURCOMBE The Ship Inn
BURTON The Old House at Home
COLLINGBOURNE DUCIS
    The Shears Inn
CORSHAM The Flemish Weaver
CORTON The Dove Inn
DEVIZES The Bear Hotel
DEVIZES The Raven Inn
DONHEAD ST ANDREW The Forester
EAST CHISENBURY Red Lion
EAST KNOYLE The Fox and Hounds
EBBESBOURNE WAKE
    The Horseshoe
FONTHILL GIFFORD
    The Beckford Arms
GREAT BEDWYN The Three Tuns
GREAT CHEVERELL The Bell Inn
HEYTESBURY
    The Angel Coaching Inn
HINDON Angel Inn
HINDON The Lamb at Hindon
HORNINGSHAM The Bath
    Arms at Longleat
HORTON The Bridge Inn
KILMINGTON The Red Lion Inn
LACOCK The George Inn
LACOCK Red Lion Inn
LIMPLEY STOKE The Hop Pole Inn
LOWER CHICKSGROVE
    Compasses Inn
MALMESBURY
    The Horse & Groom Inn
MALMESBURY The Smoking Dog
MALMESBURY The Vine Tree

MARLBOROUGH The Lamb Inn
MINETY Vale of the White Horse Inn
NEWTON TONEY The Malet Arms
NUNTON The Radnor Arms
OAKSEY The Wheatsheaf at Oaksey
PEWSEY The Seven Stars
PITTON The Silver Plough
ROWDE The George & Dragon
SALISBURY The Haunch of Venison
SALISBURY Old Mill
SALISBURY The Wig and Quill
SEEND Bell Inn
SEMINGTON
    The Lamb on the Strand
SEMINGTON The Somerset Arms
SHERSTON The Rattlebone Inn
STOFORD The Swan Inn
TOLLARD ROYAL King John Inn
UPPER CHUTE The Cross Keys Inn
UPPER WOODFORD The Bridge Inn
UPTON LOVELL Prince Leopold Inn
WARMINSTER The Angel Inn
WARMINSTER The Bath Arms
WHITLEY The Pear Tree Inn
WOOTTON RIVERS Royal Oak

WORCESTERSHIRE
BECKFORD The Beckford
BEWDLEY Little Pack Horse
BEWDLEY The Mug House Inn
    & Angry Chef Restaurant
BEWDLEY Woodcolliers Arms
BRANSFORD
    The Bear & Ragged Staff
CLENT The Bell & Cross
CLOWS TOP The Colliers Arms
DROITWICH The Chequers
DROITWICH The Old Cock Inn
FLYFORD FLAVELL The Boot Inn
GUARLFORD Plough and Harrow
KEMPSEY Walter de Cantelupe Inn
KINGTON The Red Hart
KNIGHTWICK The Talbot
MALVERN Nags Head
MALVERN The Wyche Inn
MARTLEY Admiral Rodney Inn
MARTLEY The Crown Inn
PERSHORE The Defford Arms
STONEHALL The Inn at Stonehall

UPTON SNODSBURY Bants

**YORKSHIRE,
EAST RIDING OF**
FLAMBOROUGH The Seabirds Inn
KILHAM The Old Star Inn
LOW CATTON The Gold Cup Inn
SOUTH CAVE The Fox and Coney Inn

YORKSHIRE, NORTH
APPLETON-LE-MOORS
    The Moors Inn
APPLETREEWICK The Craven Arms
AUSTWICK The Game Cock Inn
AYSGARTH
    The George & Dragon Inn
BAGBY The Bagby Inn
BEDALE The Castle Arms Inn
BOROUGHBRIDGE
    The Black Bull Inn
BOROUGHBRIDGE
    Crown Inn Roecliffe
BROMPTON-BY-SAWDON
    The Cayley Arms
BROUGHTON The Bull
BURNSALL The Red Lion
CHAPEL LE DALE The Old Hill Inn
CLAPHAM New Inn
CRAY The White Lion Inn
CRAYKE The Durham Ox
CROPTON The New Inn
EAST WITTON The Blue Lion
EAST WITTON The Cover Bridge Inn
EGTON The Wheatsheaf Inn
EGTON BRIDGE Horseshoe Hotel
GOATHLAND Birch Hall Inn
GREAT AYTON The Royal Oak
GREEN HAMMERTON
    The Bay Horse Inn
GRINTON The Bridge Inn
HAWES The Moorcock Inn
HOVINGHAM
    The Worsley Arms Hotel
KETTLEWELL The Kings Head
KILBURN The Forresters Arms Inn
KILNSEY The Tennant Arms
KIRKBY FLEETHAM
    The Black Horse Inn

KIRKBYMOORSIDE
    George & Dragon Hotel
KIRKHAM Stone Trough Inn
LEVISHAM Horseshoe Inn
LEYBURN The Old Horn Inn
LEYBURN Sandpiper Inn
LITTON Queens Arms
LONG PRESTON Maypole Inn
MALHAM The Lister Arms
MIDDLEHAM Black Swan Hotel
MIDDLEHAM The White Swan
MIDDLESMOOR Crown Hotel
MUKER The Farmers Arms
NUNNINGTON The Royal Oak Inn
OSMOTHERLEY The Golden Lion
PICKERING The Fox & Rabbit Inn
PICKERING The White Swan Inn
RIPON The George at Wath
ROBIN HOOD'S BAY Laurel Inn
SAWDON The Anvil Inn
SETTLE The Lion at Settle
SINNINGTON
    Fox & Hounds Country Inn
SKIPTON Devonshire Arms
TERRINGTON The Bay Horse Inn
    (The Storyteller Brewery)
THORNTON LE DALE The New Inn
WASS Wombwell Arms
WEST BURTON Fox & Hounds
WEST TANFIELD The Bruce Arms
WEST WITTON
    The Wensleydale Heifer
YORK Blue Bell
YORK Lamb & Lion Inn
YORK Lysander Arms

YORKSHIRE, SOUTH
BRADFIELD The Strines Inn
DONCASTER Waterfront Inn
PENISTONE The Fountain Inn Hotel
SHEFFIELD The Fat Cat
SHEFFIELD Kelham Island Tavern
TOTLEY The Cricket Inn

YORKSHIRE, WEST
ADDINGHAM The Fleece
BRADFORD New Beehive Inn
EMLEY The White Horse
HALIFAX The Old Bore

DOG-FRIENDLY PUBS (continued)

HALIFAX Shibden Mill Inn
HALIFAX The Three Pigeons
LEEDS The Cross Keys
LINTHWAITE The Sair Inn
LINTON The Windmill Inn
MARSDEN The Riverhead Brewery
   Tap & Dining Room
MYTHOLMROYD Shoulder of Mutton
OSSETT Ossett Brewery Tap
SOWERBY The Travellers Rest
SOWERBY BRIDGE The Alma Inn &
   Fresco Italian Restaurant
WIDDOP Pack Horse Inn

CHANNEL ISLANDS
GUERNSEY
CASTEL Fleur du Jardin
CASTEL Hotel Hougue du Pommier

JERSEY
ST AUBIN Old Court House Inn

ISLE OF MAN
PEEL The Creek Inn
PORT ERIN Falcon's Nest Hotel

SCOTLAND
ABERDEENSHIRE
BALMEDIE The Cock & Bull
   Bar & Restaurant
NETHERLEY The Lairhillock Inn

ARGYLL & BUTE
ARDUAINE Loch Melfort Hotel
CAIRNDOW
   Cairndow Stagecoach Inn
CLACHAN-SEIL Tigh an Truish Inn
CONNEL The Oyster Inn
CRINAN Crinan Hotel
DUNOON Coylet Inn
KILFINAN Kilfinan Hotel Bar
PORT APPIN The Pierhouse Hotel &
   Seafood Restaurant
PORT CHARLOTTE
   The Port Charlotte Hotel
STRACHUR Creggans Inn

CITY OF DUNDEE
BROUGHTY FERRY
   The Royal Arch Bar
DUNDEE Speedwell Bar

CITY OF EDINBURGH
EDINBURGH The Bow Bar
EDINBURGH
   The Shore Bar & Restaurant
RATHO The Bridge Inn

CITY OF GLASGOW
GLASGOW Stravaigin

CLACKMANNANSHIRE
DOLLAR Castle Campbell Hotel

DUMFRIES & GALLOWAY
ISLE OF WHITHORN
   The Steam Packet Inn
KIRKCUDBRIGHT Selkirk Arms Hotel
MOFFAT Annandale Arms
MOFFAT Black Bull Hotel
NEW GALLOWAY Cross Keys Hotel
NEWTON STEWART
   Creebridge House Hotel
NEWTON STEWART
   The Galloway Arms Hotel
SANDHEAD Tigh Na Mara Hotel

EAST AYRSHIRE
DALRYMPLE The Kirkton Inn
SORN The Sorn Inn

FIFE
ANSTRUTHER The Dreel Tavern
BURNTISLAND
   Burntisland Sands Hotel
ELIE The Ship Inn
ST ANDREWS The Inn at Lathones

HIGHLAND
ARDVASAR (Isle of Skye)
   Ardvasar Hotel
AVIEMORE The Old Bridge Inn
BADACHRO The Badachro Inn
CARBOST (Isle of Skye) The Old Inn
CARRBRIDGE The Cairn
CAWDOR Cawdor Tavern
FORT WILLIAM Moorings Hotel

FORTROSE The Anderson
GAIRLOCH The Old Inn
INVERIE The Old Forge
ISLEORNSAY (Isle of Skye)
   Hotel Eilean Iarmain
KYLESKU Kylesku Hotel
NORTH BALLACHULISH
   Loch Leven Hotel
PLOCKTON Plockton Inn
   & Seafood Restaurant
STEIN (Isle of Skye) Stein Inn
TORRIDON The Torridon Inn

MIDLOTHIAN
ROSLIN The Original Rosslyn Inn

MORAY
FOCHABERS Gordon Arms Hotel

PERTH & KINROSS
GLENDEVON An Lochan Tormaukin
   Country Inn and Restaurant
GUILDTOWN Anglers Inn
KILLIECRANKIE
   Killiecrankie House Hotel
KINNESSWOOD Lomond Country Inn
MEIKLEOUR Meikleour Hotel
PITLOCHRY Moulin Hotel

RENFREWSHIRE
HOUSTON Fox & Hounds

SCOTTISH BORDERS
ALLANTON Allanton Inn
ETTRICK Tushielaw Inn
GALASHIELS Kingsknowes Hotel
INNERLEITHEN Traquair Arms Hotel
KIRK YETHOLM The Border Hotel
LAUDER The Black Bull
LEITHOLM The Plough Hotel
MELROSE Burts Hotel
ST BOSWELLS
   Buccleuch Arms Hotel
TIBBIE SHIELS INN Tibbie Shiels Inn

STIRLING
CALLANDER The Lade Inn
DRYMEN The Clachan Inn
KIPPEN Cross Keys Hotel
KIPPEN The Inn at Kippen

WALES

BRIDGEND
KENFIG Prince of Wales Inn

CARDIFF
CREIGIAU Caesars Arms
GWAELOD-Y-GARTH
  Gwaelod-y-Garth Inn

CARMARTHENSHIRE
ABERGORLECH The Black Lion
LLANDEILO The Castle Hotel

CEREDIGION
LLWYNDAFYDD
  The Crown Inn & Restaurant

CONWY
BETWS-YN-RHOS
  The Wheatsheaf Inn
CAPEL CURIG Cobdens Hotel
CONWY The Groes Inn
DOLWYDDELAN Elen's Castle Hotel
LLANNEFYDD
  The Hawk & Buckle Inn

FLINTSHIRE
CILCAIN White Horse Inn
MOLD Glasfryn

GWYNEDD
ABERDYFI Penhelig Arms Hotel &
  Restaurant
BLAENAU FFESTINIOG
  The Miners Arms
LLANBEDR Victoria Inn
WAUNFAWR Snowdonia Parc
  Brewpub & Campsite

MONMOUTHSHIRE
ABERGAVENNY Clytha Arms
CHEPSTOW Castle View Hotel
LLANTRISANT The Greyhound Inn
LLANVAIR DISCOED The Woodlands
  Tavern Country Pub & Dining
PANTYGELLI The Crown
PENALLT The Boat Inn
PENALLT The Inn at Penallt
RHYD-Y-MEIRCH
  Goose and Cuckoo Inn
SHIRENEWTON
  The Carpenters Arms
SKENFRITH The Bell at Skenfrith
TINTERN PARVA Fountain Inn
TRELLECH The Lion Inn
USK Raglan Arms
USK The Nags Head Inn

PEMBROKESHIRE
ABERCYCH Nags Head Inn
AMROTH The New Inn
CAREW Carew Inn
LITTLE HAVEN St Brides Inn
LITTLE HAVEN The Swan Inn
NEWPORT Salutation Inn
ST DAVID'S Farmers Arms
ST DOGMAELS
  Webley Waterfront Inn & Hotel
STACKPOLE The Stackpole Inn

POWYS
BERRIEW The Lion Hotel
BRECON The Felin Fach Griffin
COEDWAY
  The Old Hand and Diamond Inn
CRICKHOWELL The Bear Hotel

CRICKHOWELL
  Nantyffin Cider Mill Inn
DYLIFE Star Inn
GLADESTRY The Royal Oak Inn
LLANDRINDOD WELLS
  The Laughing Dog
LLANFYLLIN Cain Valley Hotel
LLANGYNIDR The Coach & Horses
MACHYNLLETH Wynnstay Hotel
MONTGOMERY Dragon Hotel
NEW RADNOR Red Lion Inn
OLD RADNOR The Harp
TALYBONT-ON-USK Star Inn
TRECASTLE
  The Castle Coaching Inn

RHONDDA CYNON TAFF
PONTYPRIDD Bunch of Grapes

SWANSEA
LLANGENNITH Kings Head

VALE OF GLAMORGAN
COWBRIDGE The Cross Inn
COWBRIDGE Victoria Inn
EAST ABERTHAW Blue Anchor Inn

WREXHAM
ERBISTOCK Cross Foxes
GRESFORD Pant-yr-Ochain
LLANARMON DYFFRYN CEIRIOG
  West Arms

PLACES THAT ACCEPT HORSES

Establishments that have told us they accept horses (stables or paddock available)
S = stables P= paddock

ENGLAND

CHESHIRE

WYBUNBURY
Lea Farm — S

CORNWALL

CAMELFORD
Lakefield Caravan Park — S
CAWSAND
Wringford Down — P
ST AUSTELL
Court Farm Holidays — P
TRURO
Polsue Manor Farm — S

CUMBRIA

BRAMPTON
Farlam Hall — P
KESWICK
Low Nest Farm B&B — S
LOWESWATER
Grange Country House — P

DERBYSHIRE

ASHBOURNE
Mercaston Hall — S
HOPE
Round Meadow Barn — S
MATLOCK
Farley — S
RIPLEY
Golden Valley Caravan
    & Camping Park — S

DEVON

DARTMEET
Brimpts Farm — S
HONITON
Ridgeway Farm — S
PRINCETOWN
The Plume of Feathers Inn — P
STOWFORD
Townleigh Farm — S
TAVISTOCK
Sampford Manor — S

DORSET

MILTON ABBAS
Fishmore Hill Farm — P
MOTCOMBE
The Coppleridge Inn — P
TARRANT MONKTON
The Langton Arms — S

WAREHAM
Luckford Wood House — S

CO DURHAM

DARLINGTON
Headlam Hall — S

HAMPSHIRE

WARNFORD
George & Falcon — S

HEREFORDSHIRE

HEREFORD
Holly House Farm — S
STAPLOW
The Oak Inn — S
YARKHILL
Garford Farm — S

KENT

NEW ROMNEY
Honeychild Manor Farmhouse — S
STELLING MINNIS
Heathwood Lodge B&B — S

LINCOLNSHIRE

WINTERINGHAM
Winteringham Fields — S

NORFOLK

DOWNHAM MARKET
Crosskeys Riverside House — S
Lakeside Caravan Park & Fisheries — S
FAKENHAM
Caravan Club M.V.C. Site — S
THURSFORD
The Old Forge
Seafood Restaurant — S

NORTHUMBERLAND

OTTERBURN
The Otterburn Tower Hotel — S

OXFORDSHIRE

FARINGDON
Chowle Farmhouse
Bed & Breakfast — P
KINGHAM
Moat End — S
WANTAGE
Hill Barn — S

RUTLAND

OAKHAM
Barnsdale Lodge Hotel — P

SHROPSHIRE

BRIDGNORTH
The Halfway House Inn — S
CHURCH STRETTON
North Hill Farm — S
OSWESTRY
Pen-y-Dyffryn Country Hotel — S

SOMERSET

BURTLE
Orchard Camping — P
CLUTTON
The Hunters Rest — S
CREWKERNE
Manor Farm — S
EXFORD
Crown — S
HIGHBRIDGE
The Greenwood — P
LANGPORT
Thorney Lakes Caravan Park — S
OARE
Cloud Farm — S
WELLINGTON
Gamlins Farm Caravan Park — S

SUFFOLK

SAXMUNDHAM
Sandpit Farm — S
WORLINGWORTH
Pond Farm B&B — S

SUSSEX, EAST

BATTLE
Powder Mills — S
HEATHFIELD
Holly Grove — S
WADHURST
Little Tidebrook Farm — S

WILTSHIRE

BROMHAM
Wayside — S

WORCESTERSHIRE

BEWDLEY
Royal Forester Country Inn — S
WORCESTER
Oaklands B&B — S

PLACES THAT ACCEPT HORSES (continued)

YORKSHIRE, EAST RIDING OF
MARKET WEIGHTON
Robeanne House   S

YORKSHIRE, NORTH
HAWNBY
Laskill Grange   S
INGLETON
Gale Green Cottage   P
WEST KNAPTON
Wolds Way Caravan
and Camping   S

YORKSHIRE, SOUTH
WORSBROUGH
Greensprings Touring Park   S

SCOTLAND
SCOTTISH BORDERS
JEDBURGH
Ferniehirst Mill Lodge   S
ST BOSWELLS
Dryburgh Abbey Hotel   P

STIRLING
CALLANDER
Roman Camp Country House   P

WALES

DENBIGHSHIRE
LLANDRILLO
Hendwr Country Park   S
LLANDYRNOG
Pentre Mawr Country House   P

GWYNEDD
ABERSOCH
Rhydolion   P

MONMOUTHSHIRE
ABERGAVENNY
Pyscodlyn Farm Caravan
& Camping Site   S

POWYS
BUILTH WELLS
Caer Beris Manor   P
CRICKHOWELL
Manor   S
LLANGEDWYN
Plas Uchaf Country Guest House   P
LLANWRTYD WELLS
Lasswade Country House   P

REPUBLIC OF IRELAND
CO DONEGAL
DONEGAL
Harvey's Point Country Hotel   S

CO GALWAY
CASHEL
Cashel House   S

CO KERRY
KENMARE
Sheen Falls Lodge   S

CO MONAGHAN
GLASLOUGH
The Lodge at Castle Leslie Estate   S

CO SLIGO
GRANGE
Rowanville Lodge   S

CO TIPPERARY
NENAGH
Ashley Park House   S

CO WEXFORD
CAMPILE
Kilmokea Country
Manor & Gardens   S

CO WICKLOW
MACREDDIN
BrookLodge Hotel & Wells Spa   S

These establishments have told us that there are stables within 5 miles

ENGLAND

BEDFORDSHIRE
ASPLEY GUISE
Best Western Moore Place   nearby

BERKSHIRE
ASCOT
Macdonald Berystede
   Hotel & Spa   1m
HUNGERFORD
Three Swans Hotel   0.75m
RISELEY
Wellington Country Park   1m
WOKINGHAM
Best Western Reading
   Moat House   3m

BUCKINGHAMSHIRE
MARLOW
Macdonald Compleat Angler   3m

TAPLOW
Cliveden Country House Hotel   2m

CAMBRIDGESHIRE
HUNTINGDON
The Old Bridge Hotel   5m
UFFORD
The White Hart   5m
WISBECH
Crown Lodge   1m
Elme Hall   5m

CHESHIRE
CODDINGTON
Manor Wood Country CP   nearby
SANDIWAY
Nunsmere Hall Hotel   0.5m
STRETTON
The Park Royal   2m

CORNWALL
BUDE
The Cliff at Bude   2m
CAWSAND
Wringford Down   0.5m
FALMOUTH
Green Lawns   6m
FOWEY
Fowey Hall   3m
GOONHAVERN
Penrose HP   2m
GWITHIAN
Gwithian Farm Campsite   0.5m
HELSTON
Skyburriowe Farm   4m
KENNACK SANDS
Silver Sands HP   2m
LOOE
Fieldhead Hotel   nearby
Polborder House C&C Park   2m

OSTWITHIEL
den Valley HP — 100yds

MARAZION
Wheal Rodney HP — nearby
Godolphin Arms — 1m

MAWNAN SMITH
Budock Vean-
   The Hotel on the River — 5m

MULLION
Mullion Cove Hotel — 2m
Polurrian — 2m

NEWQUAY
Hotel California — 1m
Treloy Touring Park — 0.5m

PADSTOW
Dennis Cove Camping — 2m

PENZANCE
Bone Valley C&C Park — 100yds
Hotel Penzance — 5m

PERRANPORTH
Tollgate Farm C&C Park — 1m

POLPERRO
Penryn House — 5m

POLRUAN
Polruan Holidays-Camping
   & Caravanning — 5m

POLZEATH
Tristram C&C Park — nearby

REDRUTH
Lanyon HP — nearby

REJERRAH
Monkey Tree HP — 3m
Newperran HP — 2m

RUMFORD
Music Water Touring Park — nearby

ST AGNES
Driftwood Spars — 3m
Penkerris — 1m
Rose-in-Vale Country House — 3m

ST MERRYN
Trevean C&C Park — 1m

TRURO
Carnon Downs C&C Park — nearby
Truro C&C Park — 2m

VERYAN
The Nare Hotel — 0.5m

CUMBRIA

GRASMERE
BW Grasmere Red Lion — 1m

HAWKSHEAD
Kings Arms — 2m

PATTERDALE
Sykeside Camping Park — nearby

SILLOTH
Golf Hotel — nearby

TEBAY
Westmorland CP — 3m

ULVERSTON
Church Walk House — nearby

WATERMILLOCK
The Quiet Site — 5m

WINDERMERE
Beech Hill Hotel — 5m
Holbeck Ghyll Country
   House Hotel — 1.5m

DERBYSHIRE

BAKEWELL
Monsal Head Hotel — 2.5m

CROMFORD
Alison House — 2m

HARTINGTON
Charles Cotton — 3m

DEVON

ASHWATER
Blagdon Manor — 0.25m

AXMINSTER
Fairwater Head Hotel — 400mtrs

BIDEFORD
Pines at Eastleigh — 2m
Royal Hotel — 5m

BUDLEIGH SALTERTON
Pooh Cottage HP — 1m

BURRINGTON
Northcote Manor — 5m

DAWLISH
Peppermint Park — 2m

EGGESFORD
Fox & Hounds Country Hotel — 2m

EXETER
Barton Cross Hotel — 1m
BW Lord Haldon Country Hotel — 3m

HOLSWORTHY
Headon Farm Caravan Site — 2m
Noteworthy C&C — 4m

ILFRACOMBE
Strathmore — 1m

ILSINGTON
Ilsington Country House — 5m

LIFTON
Arundell Arms — 1m

LYNTON
Sunny Lyn HP — 2m

NEWTON ABBOT
Twelve Oaks Farm CP — 2m

SOURTON
Collaven Manor — 5m

SOUTH BRENT
Glazebrook House Hotel — 2m

SOUTH MOLTON
Riverside C&C Park — 1m

STOKENHAM
Old Cotmore Farm — nearby

THURLESTONE
Thurlestone Hotel — 5m

WOOLACOMBE
Woolacombe Sands HP — nearby

DORSET

ALDERHOLT
Hill Cottage Farm C&C Park — nearby

BRIDPORT
Bingham Grange
   Touring & CP — nearby

CHRISTCHURCH
Captain's Club Hotel — 5m

EVERSHOT
Summer Lodge
   Country House Hotel — 5m

MOTCOMBE
The Coppleridge Inn — 1m

ST LEONARDS
Forest Edge Touring Park — nearby

SWANAGE
Acton Field Camping Site — 5m
The Pines — 4m

TARRANT MONKTON
The Langton Arms — 1m

CO DURHAM

BARNARD CASTLE
The Morritt — 5m

ROMALDKIRK
Rose & Crown — 0.5m

GLOUCESTERSHIRE

ALVESTON
Alveston House Hotel — 5m

CHIPPING CAMPDEN
Noel Arms — 5m

CIRENCESTER
The Crown of Crucis — in village

EWEN
The Wild Duck — 5m

GLOUCESTER
Red Lion C&C Park — nearby

MARSHFIELD
Lord Nelson Inn — nearby

MORETON-IN-MARSH
Red Lion Inn — 1m

NEWENT
Pelerine C&C — 1m

SLIMBRIDGE
Tudor C&C — 2m

STABLES WITHIN 5 MILES (continued)

GREATER LONDON
HARROW WEALD
Grim's Dyke Hotel 5m

HAMPSHIRE
BROCKENHURST
Balmer Lawn 0.5m
Forest Park 10m
New Park Manor 2m
The Pig .... nearby
BURLEY
Moorhill House 2m
CADNAM
Bartley Lodge Hotel 5m
FARNBOROUGH
Holiday Inn Farnborough 5m
LINWOOD
Red Shoot Camping Park 2m
LYMINGTON
Passford House 0.5m
NORTHINGTON
The Woolpack Inn 1m
ROTHERWICK
Tylney Hall Hotel .... nearby
SOUTHAMPTON
HI Express Southampton
M27 Jct 7 .... 1.5m
SUTTON SCOTNEY
Norton Park 0.5m

HEREFORDSHIRE
ROSS-ON-WYE
Glewstone Court 3m
Pengethley Manor 5m
The Whitehouse Guest House 4.5m
SHOBDON
The Bateman Arms 1.5m

KENT
FOLKESTONE
Little Switzerland C&C Site 1m
KINGSGATE
The Fayreness 5m
ROYAL TUNBRIDGE WELLS
Hotel du Vin Tunbridge Wells 3m
SANDWICH
The Bell .... nearby
SITTINGBOURNE
Hempstead House Country Hotel 1.5m
WHITSTABLE
Seaview HP 5m

LANCASHIRE
GARSTANG
Claylands CP 5m

WHITEWELL
The Inn at Whitewell 1m

LEICESTERSHIRE
MARKET HARBOROUGH
Best Western Three Swans .... nearby
RAVENSTONE
Ravenstone Guesthouse .... in village

LINCOLNSHIRE
BOSTON
Orchard Park 1.5m
Pilgrims Way C&C Park 1m
MABLETHORPE
Park View Guest House 3m
MARTON
Black Swan Guest House 4m
WADDINGHAM
Brandy Wharf Leisure Park 5m

MERSEYSIDE
SOUTHPORT
Riverside HP 2m
Willowbank HH & Touring Park 5m

NORFOLK
BARNEY
The Old Brick Kilns 2m
FAKENHAM
Abbott Farm 3m
GORLESTON ON SEA
Jennis Lodge .... nearby
GREAT BIRCHAM
Kings Head .... nearby
GREAT YARMOUTH
The Grange Touring Park 2m
HUNSTANTON
Searles Leisure Resort 5m
KING'S LYNN
King's Lynn C&C Park 0.5m
SCRATBY
Scratby Hall CP 0.5m
SWAFFHAM
Breckland Meadows TP 5m
TITCHWELL
Titchwell Manor 2m
WATTON
Broom Hall Country Hotel 6m

NORTHUMBERLAND
BAMBURGH
Glororum CP 5m
BERWICK-UPON-TWEED
Lindisfarne Inn 3m
CORNHILL-ON-TWEED
Tillmouth Park Country House 4m

FALSTONE
The Blackcock Country Inn .... adjacent
OTTERBURN
The Otterburn Tower Hotel .... adjacent

OXFORDSHIRE
BLETCHINGDON
The Oxfordshire Inn .... adjacent
FARINGDON
Chowle Farmhouse B&B 0.5m
HENLEY-ON-THAMES
The Baskerville .... nearby
KINGHAM
The Kingham Plough 0.5m
KINGSTON BAGPUIZE
Fallowfields Country
House Hotel 800mtrs
WOODSTOCK
The Feathers Hotel 1m

SHROPSHIRE
LUDLOW
Haynall Villa 300yds
OSWESTRY
The Bradford Arms 2m

SOMERSET
BATH
Eagle House 2m
BURTLE
Orchard Camping 0.25m
CASTLE CARY
The George Hotel 3m
CLUTTON
The Hunters Rest 100yds
DULVERTON
Tarr Farm Inn 0.5m
HIGHBRIDGE
The Greenwood 2m
KILVE
Hood Arms Inn 0.25m
MINEHEAD
Alcombe House Hotel 2m
PORLOCK
Burrowhayes Farm C&C Site 2m
STON EASTON
Ston Easton Park 0.5m
WELLS
Coxley Vineyard 3m
WESTON-SUPER-MARE
Country View HP 1m
Lauriston Hotel 2m
WITHYPOOL
The Royal Oak Inn 1m
YEOVIL
The Helyar Arms 1m
The Masons Arms 0.5m

STAFFORDSHIRE
PENKRIDGE
Mercure Stafford
     South Hatherton   1.5m

SUFFOLK
BILDESTON
Bildeston Crown   1m
DARSHAM
Haw Wood Farm CP   3m
LOWESTOFT
Somerton House   2m
NEWMARKET
Best Western Heath Court   5m

SURREY
BAGSHOT
Pennyhill Park Hotel & The Spa   5m
STAINES
Mercure Thames Lodge   5m

SUSSEX, EAST
BATTLE
Brakes Coppice Park   3m
FOREST ROW
Ashdown Park Hotel   3m
HERSTMONCEUX
Cleavers Lyng Country House   1m
HOVE
Best Western Princes Marine   4m

SUSSEX, WEST
BARNS GREEN
Sumners Ponds Fishery
     & Campsite   2m
CHICHESTER
Ellscott Park   1m
Old Chapel Forge   0.25m
MIDHURST
Spread Eagle Hotel and Spa   3m
TILLINGTON
The Horse Guards Inn   0.5km
WEST MARDEN
Grandwood House   1m

WARWICKSHIRE
BAGINTON
The Oak   0.5m
RUGBY
Lodge Farm Campsite   3m
SHIPSTON ON STOUR
The Red Lion   nearby

WEST MIDLANDS
BALSALL COMMON
Haigs Hotel   1m

BIRMINGHAM
Holiday Inn Birmingham M6 Jct 7   2m
COVENTRY
Days Inn Corley - NEC - M6   2m
MERIDEN
Manor Hotel   3m
WOLVERHAMPTON
Novotel Wolverhampton   2m

WIGHT, ISLE OF
ARRETON
Blandings   nearby
COWES
Duke of York   2m
The Fountain Inn   3m
FRESHWATER
Heathfield Farm Camping   600mtrs

WILTSHIRE
CALNE
Blackland Lakes
H&L Centre   nearby
MALMESBURY
BW Mayfield House   0.25m
WARMINSTER
The Dove Inn   nearby
WESTBURY
The Cedar Hotel & Restaurant   2m

WORCESTERSHIRE
KEMPSEY
Walter de Cantelupe Inn   1.5m
MALVERN
The Cottage in the Wood Hotel   1.5m
STOURPORT-ON-SEVERN
Menzies Stourport Manor   0.5m
WORCESTER
The Dewdrop Inn   nearby

YORKSHIRE, EAST RIDING OF
SPROATLEY
Burton Constable HP   3m

YORKSHIRE, NORTH
ALNE
Alders CP   0.5m
BISHOP MONKTON
Church Farm CP   1m
HARROGATE
The Boar's Head   nearby
Rudding HP   1m
HELMSLEY
Feversham Arms Hotel   2m
Golden Square Touring CP   3m
HOVINGHAM
Worsley Arms   5m

MASHAM
Swinton Park   1.5m
PICKERING
Fox & Hounds Country Inn   nearby
The White Swan Inn   4m
RAVENSCAR
Raven Hall Country House   3m
RICHMOND
Brompton CP   100mtrs
Swale View CP   nearby
SCARBOROUGH
Jacobs Mount CP   1.5m
SKIPTON
The Coniston   2m
YORK
Holiday Inn York   adjacent

YORKSHIRE, SOUTH
DONCASTER
Campanile Doncaster   1m
SHEFFIELD
BW Plus Mosborough Hall Hotel   2m

YORKSHIRE, WEST
BINGLEY
Five Rise Locks Hotel   3m
GARFORTH
Best Western Milford Hotel   3m
ILKLEY
BW Rombalds Hotel   6m

SCOTLAND
ABERDEENSHIRE
BALLATER
Darroch Learg   1m
HUNTLY
Gordon Arms Hotel   2m

ARGYLL & BUTE
ARDUAINE
Loch Melfort   3m
BARCALDINE
Barcaldine House   5m

CITY OF ABERDEEN
ABERDEEN
Malmaison Aberdeen   2m

CITY OF EDINBURGH
EDINBURGH
Dalhousie Castle   5m
Novotel Edinburgh Park   3m

CITY OF GLASGOW
GLASGOW
Georgian House   7m

STABLES WITHIN 5 MILES (continued)

DUMFRIES & GALLOWAY
KIRKBEAN
Cavens — 1m
LOCKERBIE
Dryfesdale Country House — 100yds
NEWTON STEWART
Creebridge CP — 0.5m
SANDHEAD
Sands of Luce HP — 5m

HIGHLAND
ARISAIG
Cnoc-na-Faire — 1m
BEAULY
Lovat Arms — 3m
INVERNESS
Culloden House — 6m
MUIR OF ORD
Ord House — 1m
NAIRN
Boath House — 1m
SHIEL BRIDGE
Grants at Craigellachie — 1m
SHIELDAIG
Tigh an Eilean — 400yds

NORTH AYRSHIRE
BLACKWATERFOOT
Best Western Kinloch — nearby

PERTH & KINROSS
BLAIR ATHOLL
Atholl Arms Hotel — 1m
COMRIE
Royal — 3m
KENMORE
Kenmore Hotel — 1m
KINROSS
Green Hotel Golf & Leisure Resort — 4m

SCOTTISH BORDERS
PEEBLES
Macdonald Cardrona Hotel — 2m
Tontine — 2m
ST BOSWELLS
Dryburgh Abbey Hotel — 0.5m

WALES
ANGLESEY, ISLE OF
MARIAN-GLAS
Home Farm CP — 2m

CARMARTHENSHIRE
LLANDOVERY
Erwlon C&C Park — 1m

NEWCASTLE EMLYN
Argoed Meadow C&C Site — 2m

CEREDIGION
ABERYSTWYTH
Llety Ceiro Country House — nearby
LAMPETER
The Falcondale Hotel — nearby

CONWY
BETWS-Y-COED
Craig-y-Dderwen
   Riverside Hotel — 3m
The Groes Inn — nearby
LLANDUDNO
Epperstone — 5m

GWYNEDD
ABERSOCH
Deucoch Touring
   & Camping Park — nearby
BALA
Tyn Cornel C&C Park — 4m
LLANBEDR
Ty Mawr — 0.5m
LLANDWROG
White Tower CP — 1.5m
PORTHMADOG
Royal Sportsman — nearby

MONMOUTHSHIRE
CHEPSTOW
Castle View — 1m
USK
The Three Salmons Hotel — 2m

PEMBROKESHIRE
FISHGUARD
The Cartref Hotel 4m
HAVERFORDWEST
Nolton Cross CP — 1.5m
NARBERTH
Highland Grange Farm — 200mtrs
NEWPORT
Llysmeddyg — 5m

POWYS
BUILTH WELLS
Caer Beris Manor — nearby
CRICKHOWELL
Manor — own farm (7m)
LLANDRINDOD WELLS
Disserth C&C Park — 4m
LLANGAMMARCH WELLS
The Lake Country House — 5m

LLANWRTYD WELLS
Carlton Riverside — 0.25m
Lasswade Country House — 400yds
MONTGOMERY
The Dragon — 0.5m

RHONDDA CYNON TAFF
PONTYPRIDD
Llechwen Hall — 2m

SWANSEA
LLANGENNITH
Kings Head — 150yds
RHOSSILI
Pitton Cross C&C Park — 3m

WREXHAM
EYTON
The Plassey Leisure Park — 2m
LLANARMON DYFFRYN CEIRIOG
The Hand at Llanarmon — 2m
West Arms — 4m

NORTHERN IRELAND
LONDONDERRY
LONDONDERRY
Beech Hill Country
   House Hotel — 0.5m

REPUBLIC OF IRELAND
CO CORK
BANDON
Glebe Country House — nearby
KINSALE
Friar's Lodge — nearby
SHANAGARRY
Ballymaloe House — 1m

CO DONEGAL
RATHMULLAN
Rathmullan House — 500yds

DUBLIN
DUBLIN
Glenshandan Lodge — 1m

CO KERRY
KILLARNEY
Fairview — 3km

CO WATERFORD
ARDMORE
Cliff House — 5km

Maps

County Maps

The county map shown here will help you identify the counties within each country. You can look up each county in the guide using the county names at the top of each page. To find towns featured in the guide use the atlas and the index.

England

1 Bedfordshire
2 Berkshire
3 Bristol
4 Buckinghamshire
5 Cambridgeshire
6 Greater Manchester
7 Herefordshire
8 Hertfordshire
9 Leicestershire
10 Northamptonshire
11 Nottinghamshire
12 Rutland
13 Staffordshire
14 Warwickshire
15 West Midlands
16 Worcestershire

Scotland

17 City of Glasgow
18 Clackmannanshire
19 East Ayrshire
20 East Dunbartonshire
21 East Renfrewshire
22 Perth & Kinross
23 Renfrewshire
24 South Lanarkshire
25 West Dunbartonshire

Wales

26 Blaenau Gwent
27 Bridgend
28 Caerphilly
29 Denbighshire
30 Flintshire
31 Merthyr Tydfil
32 Monmouthshire
33 Neath Port Talbot
34 Newport
35 Rhondda Cynon Taff
36 Torfaen
37 Vale of Glamorgan
38 Wrexham

Orkney Islands

Shetland Islands

a h-Eileanan
an Iar

Highland

Moray

Aberdeenshire

City of
Aberdeen

SCOTLAND

Angus

Perth &
Kinross

City of
Dundee

Argyll
& Bute

Stirling

Fife

East
Lothian

North
Ayrshire

19   24

South
Ayrshire

Scottish
Borders

Dumfries &
Galloway

Northumberland

Tyne & Wear

Cumbria

Durham

Isle
of Man

North
Yorkshire

Lancashire

West
Yorkshire

East Riding
of Yorkshire

Isle of
Anglesey

Merseyside

6

South
Yorkshire

Conwy

30

Cheshire

Derbyshire

Lincolnshire

29

38

11

Gwynedd

ENGLAND

13

Shropshire

Norfolk

Ceredigion

15

9

12

WALES

Powys

16

14

10

5

Suffolk

Pembrokeshire

7

Carmarthenshire

Gloucestershire

1

Essex

Swansea

3

4

8

Oxfordshire

2

Greater
London

Wiltshire

Surrey

Kent

Somerset

Hampshire

West
Sussex

East
Sussex

Devon

Dorset

Cardiff

Isle of
Wight

Cornwall

Isles of
Scilly

Guernsey

Jersey

Argyll
& Bute

Stirling

18

22

Fife

Inverclyde

25

20

Falkirk

City of
Edinburgh

23

17

North
Lanarkshire

West
Lothian

Midlothian

North
Ayrshire

21

Scottish
Borders

19

South Lanarkshire

31   26   32

33

35   28   36

27   34

37

0   20   40   60   80   100 miles

0   20   40   60   80   100   120   140   160 kilometres

KEY TO ATLAS

Shetland Islands

16

Orkney Islands

- ● Establishment location
- ○ Town name
- ㊵ Motorway junction
- ㊲ Restricted motorway junction

13 14 15

○ Inverness

○ Aberdeen

○ Fort William

○ Perth

10 11 12

○ Glasgow ○ Edinburgh

○ Londonderry ○ Larne

○ Belfast

○ Stranraer

Newcastle upon Tyne

○ Carlisle

○ Kendal

○ Middlesbrough

1

○ York

○ Leeds ○ Kingston upon Hull

○ Galway ○ Dublin

○ Liverpool ○ Manchester 8 9

○ Holyhead 6 7 ○ Sheffield

○ Limerick ○ Lincoln

○ Rosslare ○ Nottingham

○ Aberystwyth ○ Norwich

○ Cork

○ Birmingham ○ Cambridge

○ Carmarthen ○ Gloucester ○ Colchester

○ Oxford

○ Cardiff ○ Bristol 4 LONDON 5

2 3 ○ Taunton ○ Guildford ○ Maidstone ○ Dover

○ Barnstaple ○ Southampton ○ Brighton

○ Exeter ○ Dorchester

○ Plymouth

○ Penzance

Isles of Scilly

Channel Islands 16

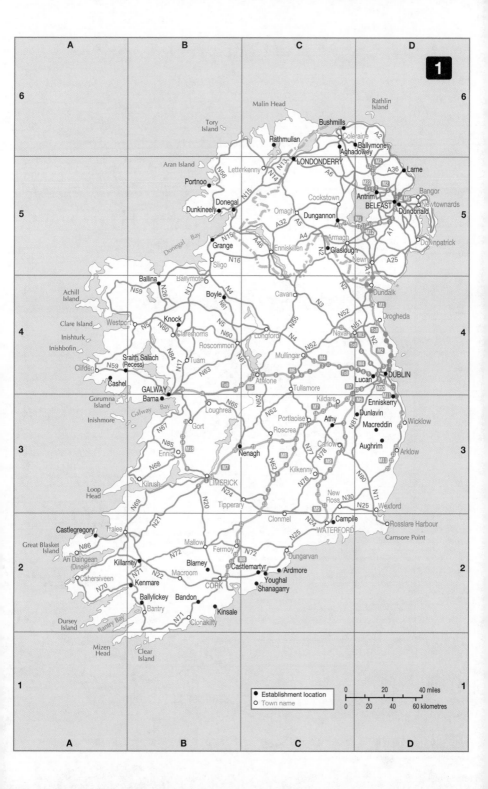

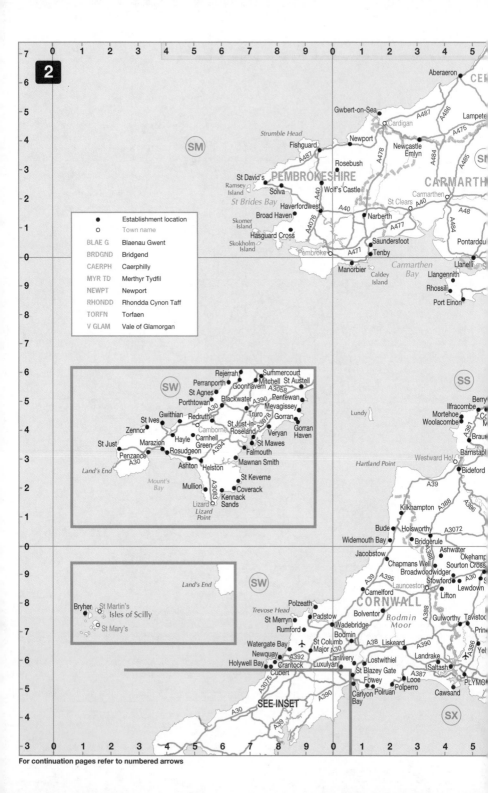

2

7
6 Aberaeron CE
5 Gwbert-on-Sea Lampete
Cardigan A487 A486
4 Strumble Head A475
Fishguard Newport Newcastle SM
3 A487 Rosebush Emlyn A484 A485
St David's PEMBROKESHIRE A478 CARMARTH
Ramsey Wolf's Castle A40
2 Island Solva St Clears Carmarthen
St Brides Bay Haverfordwest A40 A48
1 Skomer Broad Haven A4076 Narberth A484
Island A477
Hasguard Cross Saundersfoot Pontarddu
Skokholm A4139 Llanelli
Island Pembroke A477 Tenby Carmarthen
0 Manorbier Caldey Bay Llangennith
Island Rhossili
9 Port Einon

● Establishment location
○ Town name
BLAE G Blaenau Gwent
BRDGND Bridgend
CAERPH Caerphilly
MYR TD Merthyr Tydfil
NEWPT Newport
RHONDD Rhondda Cynon Taff
TORFN Torfaen
V GLAM Vale of Glamorgan

6 Rejerrah Summercourt SS
Perranporth Mitchell St Austell Berry
SW Goonhavern Ilfracombe
5 St Agnes A3058 Pentewan Mortehoe Co
Porthtowan Blackwater A390 Woolacombe M
Truro Mevagissey Lundy A361
4 St Ives Gwithian Redruth St Just-in- Gorran Braun
Zennor Camborne Roseland Veryan Gorran Barnstapl
Marazion Carnhell Haven Westward Ho!
3 St Just Hayle Green St Mawes Hartland Point Bideford
Penzance Rosudgeon Falmouth
A30 Ashton Mawnan Smith A39
2 Land's End Helston St Keverne
Mount's Mullion Coverack Kilkhampton A388 A386
1 Bay A3083 Kennack Bude Holsworthy A3072
Lizard Sands Widemouth Bay Bridgerule
Lizard Ashwater
Point Jacobstow Okehamp
0 Chapmans Well Sourton Cross
Broadwoodwidger A30
9 Camelford A39 A395 Stowford Lewdown
Land's End SW Launceston Lifton
8 Bryher St Martin's Polzeath CORNWALL Gulworthy Tavisto
Isles of Scilly Trevose Head Bolventor Bodmin
St Mary's St Merryn Padstow Moor Prin
7 Rumford Wadebridge A388
Watergate Bay St Columb Bodmin Landrake Yel
6 Newquay Major A30 Liskeard A390 Saltash A386
Holywell Bay Crantock A392 Lanlivery Lostwithiel A387 PLYMO
Cubert Luxulyan St Blazey Gate
5 Fowey Looe
Carlyon Polruan Polperro Cawsand
4 Bay SEE INSET A390 SX
A30
3 A39

For continuation pages refer to numbered arrows

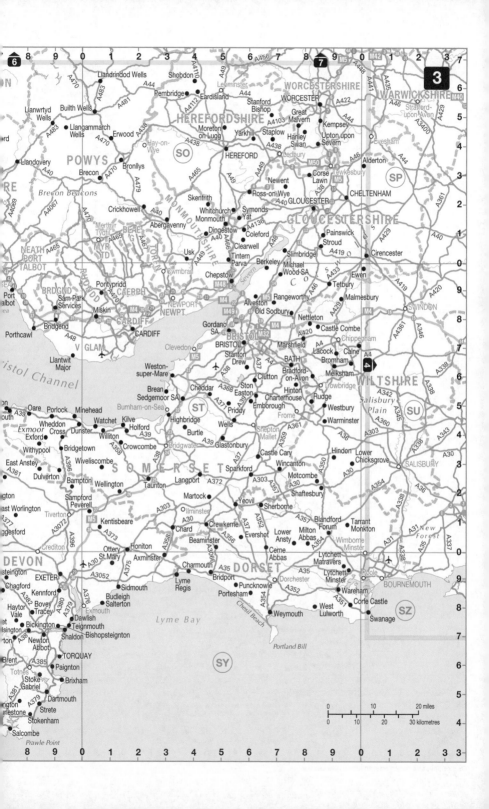

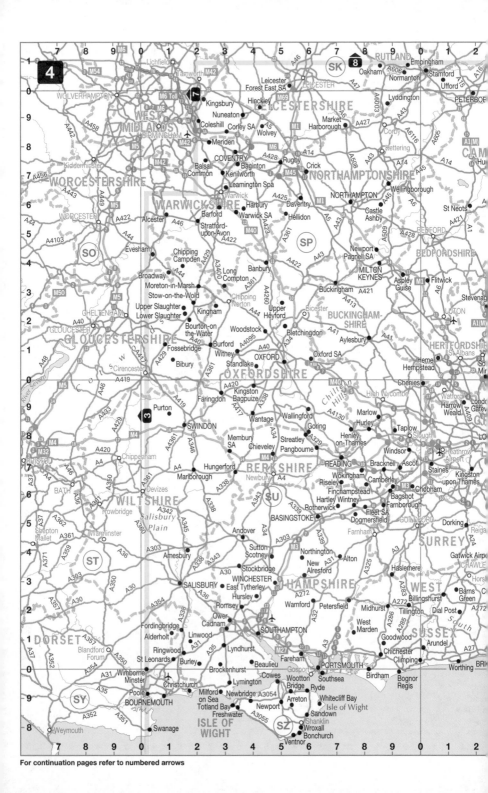

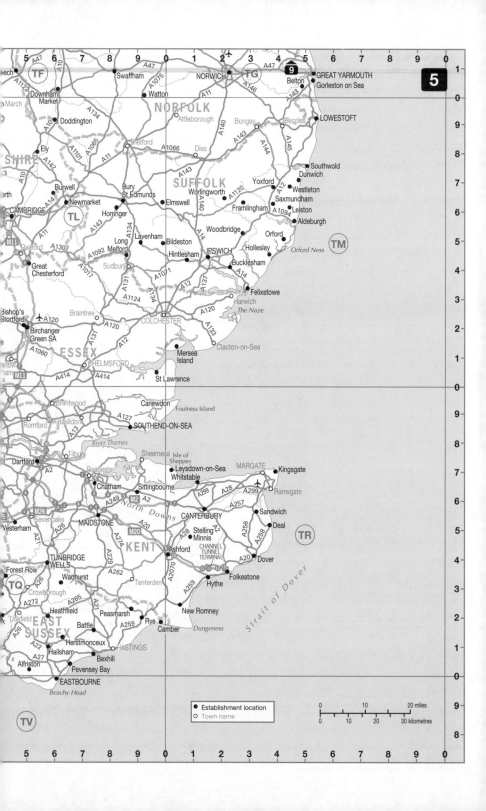

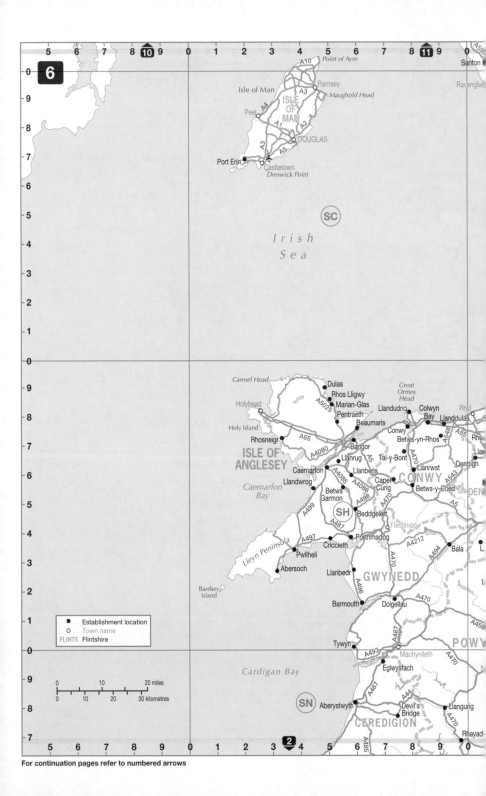

For continuation pages refer to numbered arrows

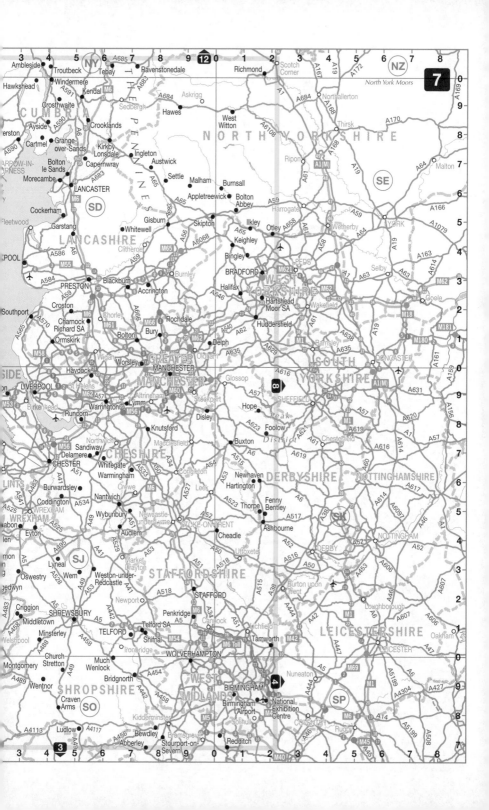

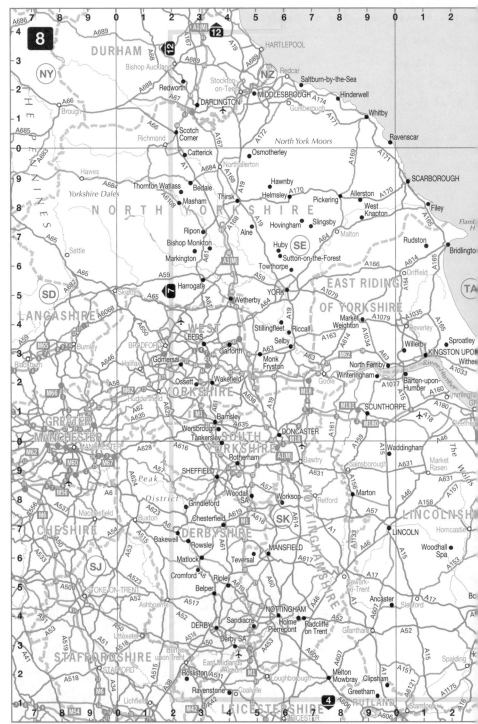

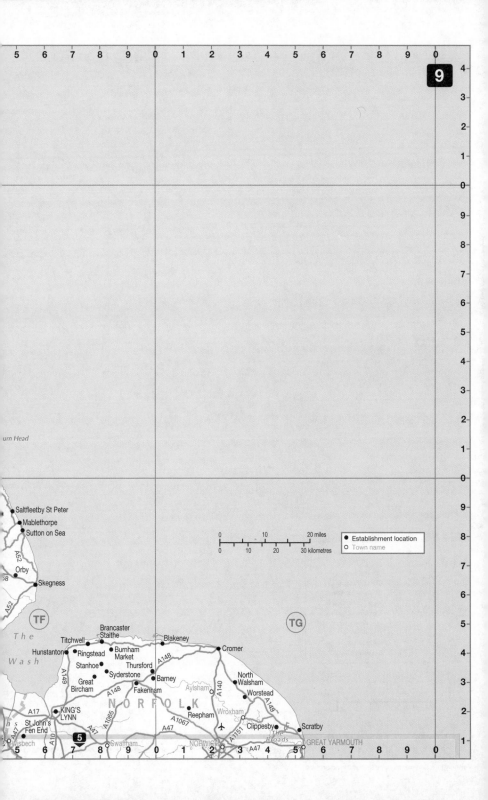

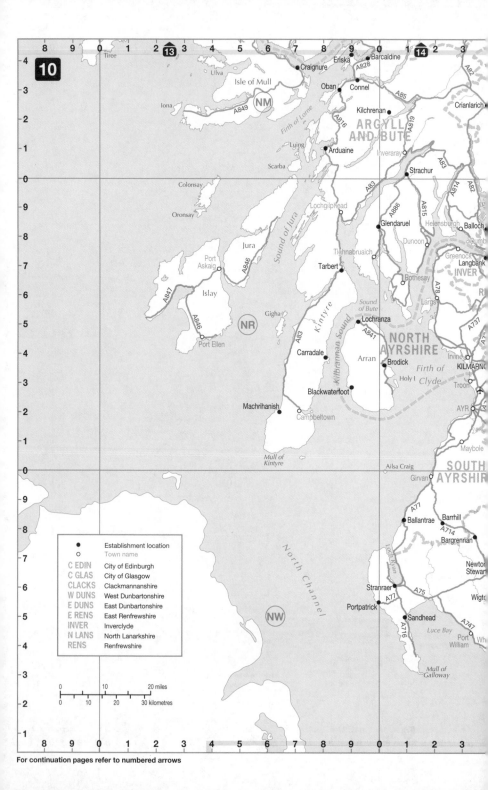

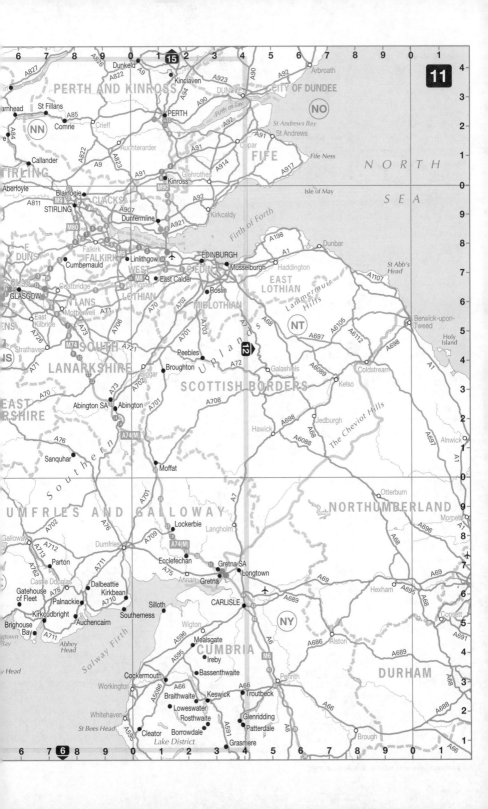

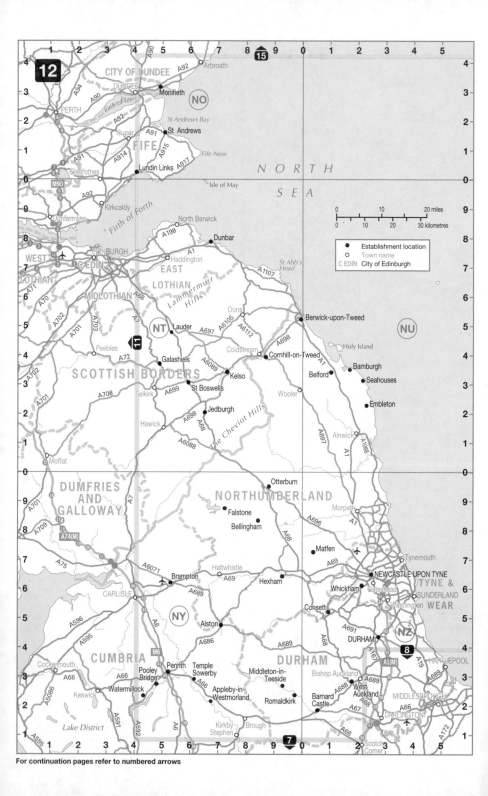

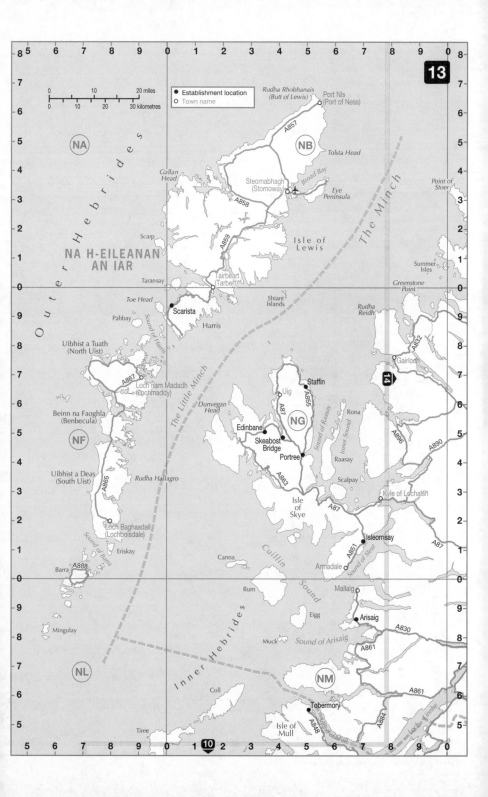

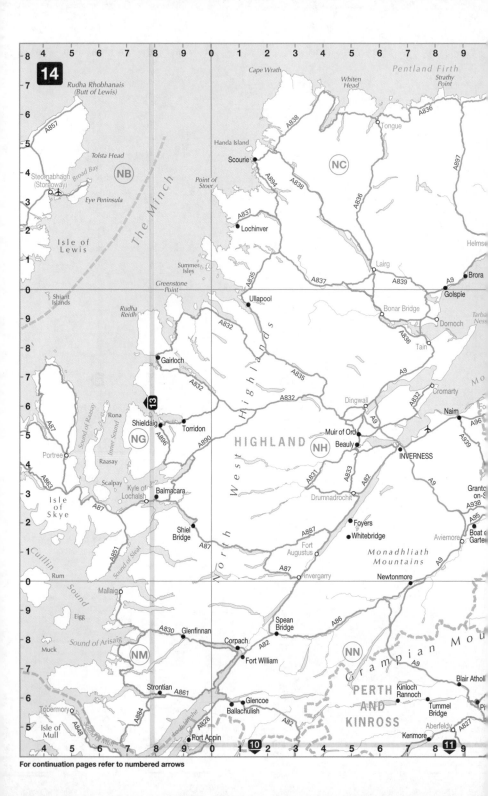

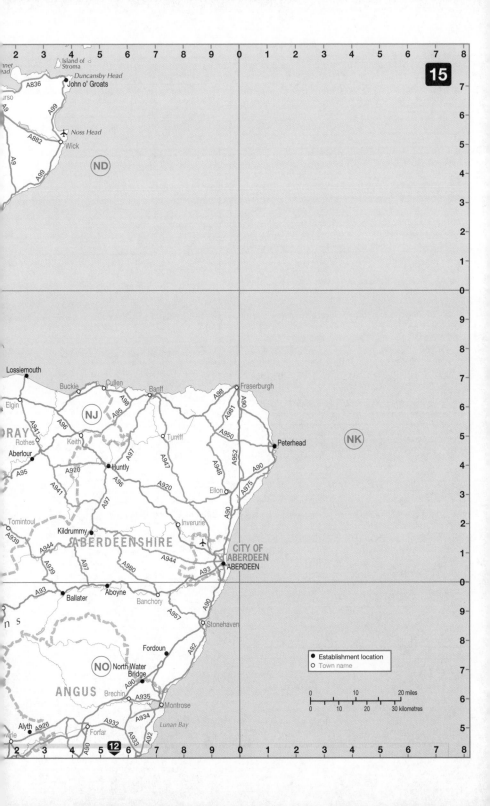

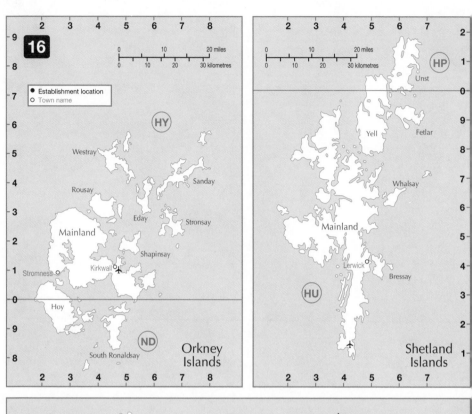

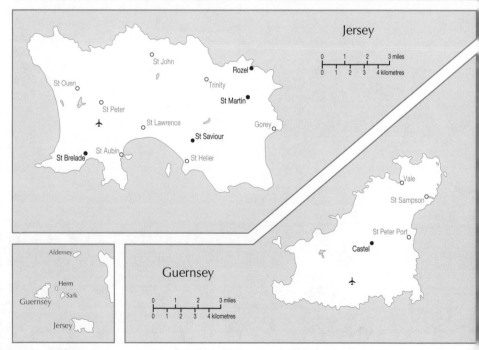

16

- ● Establishment location
- ○ Town name

Orkney Islands

HY

Westray

Sanday

Rousay

Eday

Stronsay

Mainland

Shapinsay

Stromness

Kirkwall

Hoy

ND

South Ronaldsay

Shetland Islands

HP

Unst

Yell

Fetlar

Whalsay

Mainland

Lerwick

Bressay

HU

Jersey

St John

Rozel

St Ouen

Trinity

St Peter

St Martin

St Lawrence

St Saviour

Gorey

St Brelade

St Aubin

St Helier

Vale

St Sampson

St Peter Port

Castel

Alderney

Herm

Sark

Guernsey

Jersey

Guernsey

Index

Index

INDEX

INDEX

H

INDEX

S

AA Media Ltd would like to thank the following photographers, companies and picture libraries for their assistance in the preparation of this book.

Abbreviations for the picture credits are as follows: - (t) top; (b) bottom; (l) left; (r) right; (AA) AA World Travel Library.

1 Sarah Garrett; 2t Lynda Clarke; 2ct Laura Wale; 2cb Ashley Gosling; 2b Ashley Gosling; 3t Kate Ainsworth; 3bl Chris Abbey; 3br Jon Bygate; 5t Kate Ainsworth; 5b Lesley Rutherford; 6tl Gavin Edwards; 7tr Kate Ainsworth; 8t Gavin Edwards; 8b Julie Brodie; 9t Kate Ainsworth; 9bl Beth Edwards; 9br Deborah Oakes; 10 Gavin Edwards; 11t Kate Ainsworth; 11bl Tristan Mills; 11br Ashley Gosling; 12t Gavin Edwards; 12c Jane Croft; 13t Kate Ainsworth; 13b Margaret Houston; 14t Gavin Edwards; 14cl Victoria Smith; 14cr Alan Purvis; 15t Kate Ainsworth; 15cl Jane Kennerley; 15cr Alex Collins; 17t Kate Ainsworth; 17c Damion Diplock/RSPCA Photolibrary; 18 clockwise edge ending with centre; 18tl Sean Dowson; 18tc Maureen Bartlett; 18tr Jackie Anderson; 18cr Rosalyn Wigg/Ursula Cross; 18br Karen Smith; 18bc Haydn Tomlinson; 18bl Michelle Clare; 18cl Vicky Cash; 18ct Audrey Tollett; 18cb Nicola White;19t Kate Ainsworth; 19c Lisa Knight; 42 AA/John Wood; 20-21 AA/Neil Setchfield; 48 AA/John Wood; 71 AA/Adam Burton; 97 AA/E A Bowness; 116 AA/Caroline Jones; 137 AA/N Hicks; 141 AA/Nigel Hicks; 149 AA/Wyn Voysey; 197 AA/Caroline Jones; 242 AA/Jeff Beazley; 366 © Peter Brogden/Alamy; 367 AA/Stewart Bates; 368-369 AA/Stephen Whitehorne; 395 AA/Stephen Whitehorne; 415 AA; 416-417 AA/Mari Sterling; 458-459 AA/Michael Short; 472 Wiveton Bell; 488 AA/Caroline Jones; 495 AA/Adam Burton; 511 AA/Wyn Voysey; 540 Ashley Gosling.

Every effort has been made to trace the copyright holders, and we apologise in advance for any unintentional omissions or errors. We would be pleased to apply any corrections in any following edition of this publication.

Please send this form to:
Editor, AA Pet Friendly Places to Stay,
Lifestyle Guides,
The Automobile Association,
13th Floor, Fanum House,
Basingstoke RG21 4EA

Readers' Report Form

or e-mail: lifestyleguides@theAA.com

Please use this form to tell us about any establishment you have visited, whether it is in the guide or not currently listed. Feedback from readers helps us to keep our guide accurate and up to date. However, if you have a complaint to make during a visit, we do recommend that you discuss the matter with the management there and then, so that they have a chance to put things right before your visit is spoilt.

Please note that the AA does not undertake to arbitrate between you and the establishment's management, or to obtain compensation or engage in protracted correspondence.

Date:

Your name (block capitals)

Your address (block capitals)

....

....

....

....

....

e-mail address:

Comments (Please include the name & address of the establishment) ....

....

....

....

....

....

....

....

(please attach a separate sheet if necessary)

Please tick here if you DO NOT wish to receive details of AA offers or products ☐

PTO

AA Pet Friendly Places to Stay 2012

Have you bought this guide before?   Yes   No

Do you regularly use any other accommodation, restaurant, pub or food guides?
If yes, which ones?

....

....

Why did you buy this guide? (circle all that apply)

holiday   short break   attending a show (eg Crufts)

other ....

How often do you stay in a Hotel, B&B or at a Campsite with your pets?
(circle one choice)

more than once a month   once a month   once in 2-3 months

once in six months   once a year   less than once a year

Please answer these questions to help us make improvements to the guide:

Which of these factors are most important when choosing pet-friendly
accommodation?

price   location   awards/rating   service

decor/surroundings   previous experience recommendation   proximity to exercise area

facilities for pets   extent of freedom for pets

other (please state) ....

Do you use the location atlas?   Yes   No

What elements of the guide do you find the most useful when choosing an
establishment?

description   photo   advertisement   star/pennant rating

information on pet facilities

What do you like best about the guide?

....

....

....

Can you suggest any improvements to the guide?

....

....

....

Thank you for returning this form

Please send this form to:
Editor, AA Pet Friendly Places to Stay,
Lifestyle Guides,
The Automobile Association,
13th Floor, Fanum House,
Basingstoke RG21 4EA

or e-mail: lifestyleguides@theAA.com

Readers' Report Form

Please use this form to tell us about any establishment you have visited, whether it is in the guide or not currently listed. Feedback from readers helps us to keep our guide accurate and up to date. However, if you have a complaint to make during a visit, we do recommend that you discuss the matter with the management there and then, so that they have a chance to put things right before your visit is spoilt.

Please note that the AA does not undertake to arbitrate between you and the establishment's management, or to obtain compensation or engage in protracted correspondence.

Date:

Your name (block capitals)

Your address (block capitals)

....
....
....
....
....

e-mail address:

Comments (Please include the name & address of the establishment) ....
....
....
....
....
....
....
....

(please attach a separate sheet if necessary)

Please tick here if you DO NOT wish to receive details of AA offers or products ☐

PTO

AA Pet Friendly Places to Stay 2012

Have you bought this guide before?   Yes   No

Do you regularly use any other accommodation, restaurant, pub or food guides? If yes, which ones?

....

....

Why did you buy this guide? (circle all that apply)

holiday   short break   attending a show (eg Crufts)

other ....

How often do you stay in a Hotel, B&B or at a Campsite with your pets? (circle one choice)

more than once a month   once a month   once in 2-3 months

once in six months   once a year   less than once a year

Please answer these questions to help us make improvements to the guide:

Which of these factors are most important when choosing pet-friendly accommodation?

price   location   awards/rating   service

decor/surroundings   previous experience   recommendation   proximity to exercise area

facilities for pets   extent of freedom for pets

other (please state) ....

Do you use the location atlas?   Yes   No

What elements of the guide do you find the most useful when choosing an establishment?

description   photo   advertisement   star/pennant rating

information on pet facilities

What do you like best about the guide?

....

....

....

Can you suggest any improvements to the guide?

....

....

....

Thank you for returning this form